Birken

THE
ALL ENGLAND
LAW REPORTS

1976
VOLUME 1

EDITOR
R N G Harrison BA
of Lincoln's Inn, Barrister

ASSISTANT EDITOR
R G C Flynn
of the Inner Temple, Barrister

LONDON
BUTTERWORTHS

ENGLAND: Butterworth & Co (Publishers) Ltd
                London: 88 Kingsway, WC2B 6AB

AUSTRALIA: Butterworths Pty Ltd
                Sydney: 586 Pacific Highway, Chatswood, NSW 2067
                Also at Melbourne, Brisbane, Adelaide and Perth

CANADA: Butterworth & Co (Canada) Ltd
                Toronto: 2265 Midland Avenue, Scarborough, M1P 4S1

NEW ZEALAND: Butterworths of New Zealand Ltd
                Wellington: 26-28 Waring Taylor Street 1

SOUTH AFRICA: Butterworth & Co (South Africa) (Pty) Ltd
                Durban: 152-154 Gale Street

USA: Butterworth & Co (Publishers) Inc
                Boston: 19 Cummings Park, Woburn, Mass 01801

©
Butterworth & Co (Publishers) Ltd
1976

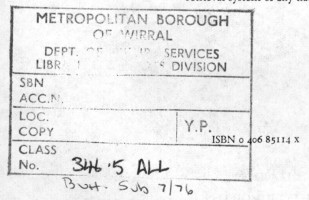
Printed in Great Britain by R J Acford Ltd, Industrial Estate, Chichester, Sussex

REPORTERS

House of Lords
Gordon H Scott Esq Barrister

Privy Council
Gordon H Scott Esq Barrister

Court of Appeal, Civil Division
Wendy Shockett Barrister
Gordon H Scott Esq Barrister
A S Virdi Esq Barrister

Mary Rose Plummer Barrister
Gavin Gore-Andrews Esq Barrister
L I Zysman Esq Barrister

Court of Appeal, Criminal Division
N P Metcalfe Esq Barrister

Sepala Munasinghe Esq Barrister

Courts-Martial Appeals
N P Metcalfe Esq Barrister

Chancery Division
Jacqueline Metcalfe Barrister
Diana Brahams Barrister

Evelyn Budd Barrister
F K Anklesaria Esq Barrister

Queen's Bench Division
Jacqueline Charles Barrister
M Denise Chorlton Barrister
J M Collins Esq Barrister
Janet Harding Barrister

Lea Josse Barrister
Gwynedd Lewis Barrister
Deirdre McKinney Barrister
Gerald Price Esq Barrister

Family Division
Phua Kai-Swan Esq Barrister

Revenue Cases
Rengan Krishnan Esq Barrister

Admiralty
N P Metcalfe Esq Barrister

MANAGER
John W Wilkes Esq

House of Lords

The Lord High Chancellor: Lord Elwyn-Jones

Lords of Appeal in Ordinary

Viscount Dilhorne
Lord Wilberforce
Lord Diplock
Lord Simon of Glaisdale

Lord Kilbrandon
Lord Salmon
Lord Edmund-Davies
Lord Fraser

Lord Russell of Killowen

Court of Appeal

The Lord High Chancellor

The Lord Chief Justice of England: Lord Widgery

The Master of The Rolls: Lord Denning

The President of the Family Division: Sir George Gillespie Baker

Lords Justices of Appeal

Sir John Megaw
Sir Denys Burton Buckley
Sir David Arnold Scott Cairns
Sir Edward Blanshard Stamp
Sir John Frederick Eustace Stephenson
Sir Alan Stewart Orr
Sir Eustace Wentworth Roskill
Sir Frederick Horace Lawton

Sir Leslie George Scarman
Sir Arthur Evan James
Sir Roger Fray Greenwood Ormrod
Sir Patrick Reginald Evelyn Browne
Sir Geoffrey Dawson Lane
Sir Reginald William Goff
Sir Nigel Cyprian Bridge
Sir Sebag Shaw

Chancery Division

The Lord High Chancellor

The Vice-Chancellor:
Sir John Anthony Plowman (retired 10th January 1976)
Sir Robert Edgar Megarry (appointed 12th January 1976)

Sir John Patrick Graham
Sir Peter Harry Batson Woodroffe Foster
Sir John Norman Keates Whitford
Sir John Anson Brightman
Sir Ernest Irvine Goulding

Sir Sydney William Templeman
Sir Raymond Henry Walton
Sir Peter Raymond Oliver
Sir Michael John Fox
Sir Christopher John Slade

Queen's Bench Division

The Lord Chief Justice of England

Sir Aubrey Melford Steed Stevenson
Sir Gerald Alfred Thesiger
Sir Basil Nield
Sir Bernard Joseph Maxwell MacKenna
Sir Alan Abraham Mocatta
Sir John Thompson
Sir Helenus Patrick Joseph Milmo
Sir Joseph Donaldson Cantley
Sir George Stanley Waller
Sir Hugh Eames Park
Sir Ralph Vincent Cusack
Sir Stephen Chapman
Sir John Ramsay Willis
Sir Graham Russell Swanwick
Sir Patrick McCarthy O'Connor
Sir John Francis Donaldson
Sir John Robertson Dunn Crichton
Sir Samuel Burgess Ridgway Cooke
Sir Bernard Caulfield
Sir Hilary Gwynne Talbot
Sir Edward Walter Eveleigh

Sir William Lloyd Mars-Jones
Sir Ralph Kilner Brown
Sir Philip Wien
Sir Peter Henry Rowley Bristow
Sir Hugh Harry Valentine Forbes
Sir Desmond James Conrad Ackner
Sir William Hugh Griffiths
Sir Robert Hugh Mais
Sir Neil Lawson
Sir David Powell Croom-Johnson
Sir Tasker Watkins VC
Sir John Raymond Phillips
Sir Leslie Kenneth Edward Boreham
Sir John Douglas May
Sir Michael Robert Emanuel Kerr
Sir Alfred William Michael Davies
Sir John Dexter Stocker
Sir Kenneth George Illtyd Jones
Sir Peter Richard Pain
Sir Kenneth Graham Jupp
Sir John Francis Scott Cobb

Sir Robert Lionel Archibald Goff

Family Division

The President of the Family Division

Sir Charles William Stanley Rees
Sir Reginald Withers Payne
Sir Neville Major Ginner Faulks
Sir James Roualeyn Hovell-Thurlow
    Cumming-Bruce
Sir John Brinsmead Latey
Dame Elizabeth Kathleen Lane
Sir Henry Vivian Brandon

Sir Robin Horace Walford Dunn
Sir William Arthur Bagnall
Sir Alfred Kenneth Hollings
Sir John Lewis Arnold
Sir Charles Trevor Reece
Sir Francis Brookes Purchas
Sir Haydn Tudor Evans
Dame Rose Heilbron

Sir Stephen Brown

CITATION

These Reports are cited thus:

[1976] 1 All ER

REFERENCES

These reports contain references, which follow after the headnotes, to the following major works of legal reference described in the manner indicated below.

Halsbury's Laws of England

The reference 35 Halsbury's Laws (3rd Edn) 366 para 524, refers to paragraph 524 on page 366 of volume 35 of the third edition, and the reference 2 Halsbury's Laws (4th Edn) para 1535, refers to paragraph 1535 on page 708 of volume 2 of the fourth edition of Halsbury's Laws of England.

Halsbury's Statutes of England

The reference 5 Halsbury's Statutes (3rd Edn) 302 refers to page 302 of volume 5 of the third edition of Halsbury's Statutes of England.

English and Empire Digest

References are to the replacement volumes (including reissue volumes) of the Digest, and to the continuation volumes of the replacement volumes.

The reference 31 Digest (Repl) 244, *3794*, refers to case number 3794 on page 244 of Digest Replacement Volume 31.

The reference Digest (Cont Vol B) 287, *7540b*, refers to case number 7540b on page 287 of Digest Continuation Volume B.

The reference 28(1) Digest (Reissue) 167, *507*, refers to case number 507 on page 167 of Digest Replacement Volume 28(1) Reissue.

Halsbury's Statutory Instruments

The reference 12 Halsbury's Statutory Instruments (Third Reissue) 125, refers to page 125 of the third reissue of volume 12 of Halsbury's Statutory Instruments; references to subsequent reissues are similar.

Encyclopaedia of Forms and Precedents

The reference 7 Ency Forms & Precedents (4th Edn) 247, Form 12, refers to Form 12 on page 247 of volume 7 of the fourth edition of the Encyclopaedia of Forms and Precedents.

Cases reported in Volume 1

Index

CURRENCY

Control – Foreign exchange control – Bretton Woods Agreements – Exchange contracts – Enforceability – Exchange contracts involving currency of member of International Monetary Fund and contrary to exchange control regulations of that member – Meaning of 'exchange contracts' – Contract for sale of goods – Plaintiffs English brokers dealing in metals – Defendant resident in Italy – Defendant buying and selling metals through agency of plaintiffs – Contracts involving currency of Italy and contrary to Italian exchange control regulations – Whether 'exchange contracts' and therefore unenforceable in England – Bretton Woods Agreements Order in Council 1946 (SR & O 1946 No 36), Sch, Part I, art VIII, s 2(*b*). **Wilson, Smithett & Cope Ltd v Terruzzi** 817

Foreign currency – Judgment. *See* **Judgment** (Payment of sum of money – Foreign currency).

DAMAGES

Breach of contract. *See* **Contract** (Breach – Damages).

Master and servant. *See* **Master and Servant** (Contract of service – Breach – Damages).

Sale of land. *See* **Sale of Land** (Contract – Breach – Damages)

Payment into court – Practice. *See* **Practice** (Payment into court).

Sale of land – Breach of contract. *See* **Sale of Land** (Contract – Breach – Damages).

DANGEROUS DRUGS

See **Drugs** (Dangerous drugs).

DEATH DUTY

Estate duty. *See* **Estate Duty.**

DEBENTURE

Priority – Company debenture. *See* **Company** (Debenture – Priority).

DECEPTION

Obtaining a pecuniary advantage by. *See* **Criminal Law** (Obtaining a pecuniary advantage by deception).

Obtaining property by deception. *See* **Criminal Law** (Obtaining property by deception).

DECREE

Foreign decree – Nullity. *See* **Nullity** (Foreign decree).

DECREE ABSOLUTE

See **Divorce** (Decree absolute).

DEDUCTIONS

Estate duty. *See* **Estate Duty** (Valuation – Allowances).

DEMURRAGE

See **Shipping.**

DEPORTATION

Immigrant. *See* **Immigration** (Deportation).

DETENTION

Children and young persons. *See* **Children and Young Persons** (Detention).

DEVELOPMENT

Land – Generally. *See* **Town and Country Planning.**

DISABILITY

Rating relief – Facilities for disabled person. *See* **Rates** (Relief – Facilities for disabled persons).

DISABLED PERSON

Rating – Relief. *See* **Rates** (Relief – Facilities for disabled persons).

DISABLEMENT BENEFIT

Industrial injury. *See* **Industrial Injury** (Disablement benefit)

DISCOVERY

Production of documents – Inspection – Objection to production for inspection – Professional lien – Inspection having effect of defeating lien – Inspection necessary for disposing fairly of action – Action by client against accountant for return of papers – Accountant claiming right of lien over papers in respect of unpaid fees – Accountant counter-claiming fees – Client wishing to obtain information in papers rather than papers themselves – Whether inspection should be ordered – RSC Ord 24, r 13(1). **Woodworth v Conroy** .. 107

DISCRETION

Care and control order – Appeal. *See* **Appeal** (Discretion – Review of exercise of discretion – Duty of appellate court – Infant – Care and control order).

DISMISSAL

Unfair dismissal. *See* **Unfair Dismissal.**

DISTRIBUTION

Settlement. *See* **Settlement** (Distribution).

DISUSED BURIAL GROUND

See **Burial** (Disused burial ground).

DIVERSION

Highway. *See* **Highway** (Diversion).

ELECTIONS

EMPLOYMENT

ENFORCEMENT NOTICE

ESTATE DUTY

ESTOPPEL

EVIDENCE

EX PARTE APPLICATION

EXCHANGE CONTROL

EXPENSES

EXPERT

EXTENDED TERM OF IMPRISONMENT

FACULTY

Cases Noted

Statutes, etc, noted

Words and Phrases

Corrigenda

[1971] 2 All ER
p 1253. **Lawrence v Commissioner of Police for the Metropolis.** Line *e* 4: for 's 5(1)(i)' read 's 1(1)'.

[1975] 3 All ER
p 651. **Baker v Foulkes.** Line *g* 5: for '[1975]' read '[1971]'.

[1976] 1 All ER
p 24. **Selvarajan v Race Relations Board.** Solicitors for the Race Relations Board: for *'Lawford & Co'* read *'Bindman & Partners'*.
p 224. **Ward v Tesco Stores Ltd.** Line *d* 2: for 'failed to show that the yoghourt was spilt' read 'failed to show that the yoghourt was not spilt'.
p 262. **R v Cato.** Counsel for Morris and Dudley: for *'Anthony Astell'* read *'Anthony Ansell'*.
p 343. **Harris v Birkenhead Corpn.** Counsel for the plaintiff: for *'G P Crowe'* read *'G P Crowe QC'*. Counsel for the second defendant: for *'M D Bryne'* read *'M D Byrne'*. Page 350, *h* 5: for 'the local authority were not possessed of information' read 'the local authority were not only possessed of information'.
p 809. **Re Whitfield's Estate.** Counsel for the executors: for *'Peter Oliver QC'* read *'Martin Nourse QC'*.

R v Greenstein   R v Green

COURT OF APPEAL, CRIMINAL DIVISION
STEPHENSON LJ, NIELD AND CHAPMAN JJ
10th, 11th, 29th JULY 1975

c

*Criminal law – Obtaining property by deception – Dishonesty – Belief of accused – Reckless-
ness – Cheque – Representation by defendant that there are or will be sufficient funds in
account to meet cheque on first presentation – Application for shares – Cheque drawn by
defendant for full amount of price of shares applied for – Defendant relying on fact that
issuing house would not allot full number of shares applied for – Defendant relying on return*
d *cheque from issuing house to provide sufficient funds to meet cheque drawn by him – Whether
jury entitled to conclude defendant had acted dishonestly – Theft Act 1968, s 15(1).*

*Criminal law – Obtaining property by deception – Deception – Cheque – Representation by
defendant that in ordinary course of business there would be sufficient funds to meet cheque on
presentation – Cheque in fact met on presentation – Funds to meet cheque only available in*
e *consequence of representation made by defendant – Application by defendant for shares –
Cheque drawn by defendant for initial payment – Defendant relying on fact that issuing
house would not allot full amount of shares applied for and would therefore send a return
cheque for difference in price – Defendant knowing that issuing house would not have allotted
shares if it had known defendant had insufficient funds to pay for shares applied for – Whether
defendant guilty of deception – Theft Act 1968, s 15(1).*

f

During the years 1971 and 1972 most public issues of shares were greatly over-subscribed. In order to improve their chances of obtaining the full number of shares they
wanted the appellants made a practice of applying for very large quantities of shares
which they did not have funds to pay for, in the knowledge that, when an issue was
over-subscribed, it was the practice of the issuing houses to allot shares to applicants in
g proportion to the quantity applied for. In most cases the appellants were required to
send a cheque for the full amount of the price of the shares applied for. In each case the
appellants drew cheques for the amount in question although at the time when the
cheques were drawn they did not have sufficient funds in their bank accounts to
meet the cheques on presentation. The appellants had no authority from their
banks to overdraw but relied on the fact that, when the shares were issued to
h them, they would receive a 'return cheque' from the issuing house for the
amount of the difference between the price of the shares applied for and the
price of those allotted. On most occasions, the cheques drawn by the appellants
were honoured on first presentation, the return cheques having previously been
cleared. On some occasions, however, the appellants' cheques were dishonoured
on first presentation. The appellants were charged on a number of counts with
j obtaining or attempting to obtain property by deception, contrary to s 15(1)[a] of
the Theft Act 1968. The charges alleged that the appellants had dishonestly

---

a Section 15(1) provides: 'A person who by any deception dishonestly obtains property belonging to another, with the intention of permanently depriving the other of it, shall on
conviction on indictment be liable to imprisonment for a term not exceeding ten years.'

A

obtained, or attempted to obtain, a letter of acceptance in respect of shares and
a return cheque belonging to an issuing house with the intention of permanently *a*
depriving the issuing house of the shares and cheque by deception. The deception alleged was that the original cheque delivered to the issuing house was then
a good and valid order for the payment of the amount on its face and that the appellants had authority to draw a cheque for that amount on the paying bank. All except
counts 4, 5 and 6 further alleged that the appellants had falsely represented that the
cheques would be paid (or honoured) on first presentation. In all those cases, the *b*
applications to the issuing houses included 'a binding undertaking [by the appellants]
that the cheque sent herewith will be paid on first presentation'. No such undertaking
was given so far as counts 4, 5 and 6 were concerned. Furthermore in the cases to
which counts 4, 5 and 6 related the cheques had in fact been met on first presentation.
The judge directed the jury, inter alia, that they should acquit the appellants if they
found that the appellants had honestly believed that the cheques would be met on *c*
first presentation or, in the case of counts 4, 5 and 6, that they had authority to draw
the cheques for the amounts in question. The appellants were convicted on all but
one of the counts, including counts 4, 5 and 6. On appeal, the appellants contended
that when they drew their cheques there had been no deception about the state of
their bank accounts on the date of first presentation and no dishonesty but a justifiable
confidence that the cheques would be honoured because the majority of cheques *d*
drawn by them had in fact been honoured over many months.

Held – The appeals would be dismissed for the following reasons—
    (i) The question whether the appellants had been guilty of dishonesty was a
question of fact for the jury. From the evidence the jury were entitled to conclude
that the appellants had made a dishonest representation to the issuing houses that *e*
there were, or would be, sufficient funds in their bank accounts to meet the cheques
on first presentation apart from the funds supplied by the issuing houses themselves
by means of the return cheques. Although in the case of the applications that were
the subject of counts 4, 5 and 6, the cheques had been met in full on first presentation,
the jury were entitled to conclude that the appellants had acted dishonestly in that
they had been reckless whether the issuing houses would present their return cheques *f*
first (see p 6 *f* and p 10 *e* to *j*, post).
    (ii) In relation to counts 4, 5 and 6 the jury were entitled to conclude that the
appellants had been guilty of deception by representing falsely that in the ordinary
course of business there would be sufficient funds in their accounts to meet the
cheques when in fact it was only as a result of the deception itself that sufficient funds
had been paid into the appellants' accounts in time for the cheques to be honoured on *g*
presentation (see p 11 *b* to *g*, post); dictum of Buckley J in *Re London & Globe Finance
Corpn* [1900-03] All ER Rep at 893 explained.

Notes
For obtaining property or a pecuniary advantage by deception, see Supplement to
10 Halsbury's Laws (3rd Edn) para 1586A.   *h*
    For the Theft Act 1968, s 15, see 8 Halsbury's Statutes (3rd Edn) 792.

Cases referred to in judgment
Director of Public Prosecutions v Ray [1973] 3 All ER 131, [1974] AC 370, [1973] 3 WLR
    359, HL; rvsg sub nom *Ray v Sempers* [1973] 1 All ER 860, [1973] 1 WLR 317, 57 Cr
    App Rep 324, DC.   *j*
Halstead v Patel [1972] 2 All ER 147, [1972] 1 WLR 661, 56 Cr App Rep 334, DC.
London & Globe Finance Corpn Ltd, Re [1903] 1 Ch 728, [1900-03] All ER Rep 891, 10
    Digest (Repl) 939, 6439.
R v Feely [1973] 1 All ER 341, [1973] 1 QB 530, [1973] 2 WLR 201, CA.
R v Page [1971] 2 All ER 870, [1971] 2 QB 330, [1971] 2 WLR 1308, CA.

Appeals

a These were appeals by Allan Greenstein and Monty Green against their convictions on 22nd May 1974 at the Central Criminal Court, before his Honour Judge King-Hamilton QC and a jury, of obtaining, and attempting to obtain, property by deception, contrary to s 15(1) of the Theft Act 1968. The facts are set out in the judgment of the court.

b *Brian Neill QC* and *A Hill* for the appellants.
David A Jeffreys and *J A Blair-Gould* for the Crown.

Cur adv vult

29th July. **STEPHENSON LJ** read the following judgment of the court: On 22nd
c May 1974 at the Central Criminal Court the appellants were convicted after an 11 day trial as follows: Allan Greenstein on two counts of obtaining property by deception, contrary to s 15(1) of the Theft Act 1968, and one count of attempting to obtain property by deception; Monty Green (his brother) on five counts of obtaining property by deception and two counts of attempting to obtain property by deception. Green was acquitted on one count (the first) of obtaining property by deception.
d Greenstein was sentenced to six months' imprisonment on each count concurrent, suspended for 12 months. Green was sentenced to 12 months' imprisonment on each count suspended for 18 months. Each appellant was ordered to pay £750 towards the legal aid costs of his defence. Both now appeal against their convictions by leave of the single judge.

The prosecution, the first of its kind, arose out of an operation known as 'stagging',
e i e applying to merchant banks or issuing houses for allotment of companies' shares, or local authorities' stock, being issued to the public for the first time with the intention not of keeping them but of selling them immediately at a profit. It was not suggested that stagging was itself illegal, but it is the method of stagging carried out by each appellant which is alleged to be illegal and an offence, or an attempt to commit an offence, against s 15 of the 1968 Act. Hence it was said by the judge to be
f an important case not only for the appellants but, as will appear when their method of stagging is explained, for merchant banks and issuing houses and for many individuals who apply for small amounts of stocks and shares which they want to hold as an investment and which they can pay for at once out of their own existing bank balances.

In 1971 and 1972 many private companies were 'going public' and seeking to raise
g capital by inviting applications for new shares. It was a time when the public, institutions and individuals, had money to spend on buying stocks and shares and such issues were frequently oversubscribed. The issuing houses had therefore far fewer shares to allot than were applied for. Those who applied for large quantities of shares received allocations of comparatively small quantities; those who applied for few shares got fewer still or had to ballot successfully to get any. In order to curb
h stagging applicants had generally to send with their applications payment, usually in the form of cheques, to pay the price of the shares they applied for in full. The issuing houses decided in their discretion how many shares to allot to each applicant and sent the applicant, with their letter allotting part of the shares applied for, a cheque for the difference between the amount of the applicant's cheque and the price of the shares actually allotted.

j In 1971 the appellants had banking accounts which were in credit but not to an extent which would enable them to apply for new shares on any large scale. They recognised that there were profits to be made by stagging, but that to be allotted shares in sufficient quantities to make worthwhile profits on sale it was necessary to apply for far more than they could expect to obtain or could pay for out of their existing credit balances. They also recognised that the return application money

cheques which would be sent to them by the issuing houses would put them in sufficient funds to pay for the reduced number of shares actually allotted to them and   *a*
even to honour their own cheques for the full amount, and that those return cheques
could and in many cases would be cleared in a short period which could further be
shortened by special arrangements. With this knowledge they embarked on large-
scale stagging operations initiated by applying for very large amounts of new issue
stocks and shares, accompanying their applications by cheques for very large sums
and receiving allocations of much smaller amounts accompanied by cheques for the   *b*
change in smaller but still substantial sums.

The basis of the scheme was the return cheque or 'change' cheque for the excess
application moneys. It was admitted that the appellants had made no arrangements
to overdraw with their different banks. If they had applied for shares in an issue
which was undersubscribed there would have been no return cheque and the appellants could not have paid for the shares allotted to them. Their cheques would have   *c*
'bounced'.

But in the years in which the appellants conducted their stagging operations new
issues were normally oversubscribed and allotments had to be scaled down and
return cheques for the unallotted balance of applications sent in repayment. To
distribute the new shares fairly the issuing houses wanted to know the total amount
applied for by any one applicant, though not necessarily his identity, and they dis-   *d*
couraged multiple applications, that is to say a single application by one bank on
behalf of several customers or more than one application by the same customer. To
improve their chances of obtaining a large number of new shares the appellants drew
cheques on more than one bank account; Greenstein used more than one address and
Green used different names and different addresses, applying sometimes in his own
name, at other times in the names of Monty Gibbs and Stuart Phillips, and for one   *e*
stock Greenstein submitted 21 applications in the same name and Green submitted
12 applications in the same pseudonym. Advised by a stockbroker named Turpin,
Green first worked his stagging scheme through a branch of the Midland Bank at 42
Cranbrook Road, Ilford, managed by a Mr Whittle.

For more than 18 months the scheme worked well for both appellants. The inflated
cheques went in with the applications. The return cheques were specially cleared for   *f*
a small charge before the inflated cheques were first presented. The scaled down
numbers of shares were paid for and the letters of allotment accompanying the return
cheques sold at a profit. But in some cases, 14 out of 136 we were told, the inflated
cheque could not be met on first presentation because the return cheque had not yet
been cleared; Mr Whittle marked the inflated cheque 'RD' (refer to drawer) or where
he had been informed by Green that they would be met on second presentation   *g*
'RDPR' (refer to drawer, please represent).

In July 1972 Mr Whittle told Green that his head office did not approve of this
method of stagging and it must stop. Greenstein had had similar warnings from Mr
Franklin, the manager of the Forest Gate branch of the National Westminster Bank,
first in November 1971 and again in May 1972. Other bank managers of branches
where the appellants operated accounts for these operations gave similar warnings in   *h*
November 1972. It was made plain to both that it was irregular banking practice and
the appellants then stopped their operations.

The Crown selected 11 transactions to charge as offences against s 15(1) of the Theft
Act 1968. What these specimen charges alleged was that the appellants had dishonestly obtained, or attempted to obtain, a letter of acceptance in respect of shares
and a return cheque belonging to an issuing house with the intention of permanently   *j*
depriving the issuing house of the same (that is the letter and cheque) by deception.
In all cases the deception charged was that the original cheque delivered to the
issuing house was then a good and valid order for the payment of the amount on its
face and that the appellant then had authority to draw a cheque for that amount on
the paying bank. All except counts 4, 5 and 6 (which concerned an issue of stock for

a the Dunbarton County Council) added 'and that the said cheque would be paid (or honoured) on first presentation.' Some of the counts against Green added the deception that the defendant was Monty Gibbs or Stuart Phillips.

Now the facts were substantially not in dispute and one of the matters which was not in dispute was that the issuing houses were in fact deceived by the appellants. The appellants had signed questionnaires recording the answers they had given to police questions, but, after an unsuccessful submission that they had no case to answer, they b did not give or call evidence beyond some documents which had been put in in cross-examination of witnesses for the prosecution. But those witnesses included representatives of several issuing houses who testified in effect that they believed that the appellants were making genuine applications for shares to the full amount of their cheques and were or would be able to pay the full amount on first presentation and that they would not have allotted to them any shares if they had known the true c position, namely that the appellants could only pay the full amount with the help of their own return cheque being cleared first.

It was also accepted that the drawing of a cheque on a bank for a given amount implies at least that the drawer has an account with that bank, that he has authority to draw on it for that amount, and that the cheque, as drawn, is a valid order for the payment of that amount in that in the ordinary course of events the cheque will be d duly honoured on presentation. It does not imply any representation that the drawer now has money in that bank to the amount drawn for, inasmuch as he may well have authority to overdraw, or may intend to pay in (before the cheque can be presented) sufficient money to meet it: see the passage in Kenny's Outlines of Criminal Law[1] which was approved in R v Page[2]. It was also conceded by the Crown at an early stage that the relevant date for considering the state of the bank account on which the cheque e was drawn was not the date when it was drawn but the date when it was first presented and that the law was correctly stated in Halstead v Patel[3] in the following terms:

'So far as dishonesty is concerned, it is quite clearly established on authority that a man who passes a cheque in respect of an account in which there are no immediate funds to meet the cheque does not necessarily act dishonestly if he f genuinely believes on reasonable grounds that when the cheque is presented to the paying bank there will be funds to meet it. For example the man who, overdrawn on Saturday, draws a cheque in favour of a third party in the honest and well-founded belief that funds will be put into his bank on a Monday, is a man whom many juries would undoubtedly acquit of dishonesty, because he has a genuine and honest belief that the cheque will be met in the ordinary course g of events.'

The issue of the Dunbarton County Council Stock by the Bank of Scotland requires separate consideration later. It was, however, clear from the forms of application and prospectuses sent out by other issuing houses or merchant banks that they were relying on the implication of law that the applicant's cheques would be honoured on h first presentation because they included a declaration—

'that due completion of this Application Form accompanied by a cheque will constitute a binding undertaking by me that the cheque sent herewith will be paid on first presentation and any allocation to me is strictly on this understanding'.

There was evidence from the issuing houses that their practice was to lend at in-j terest the moneys provided by applicants' cheques until used for the purchase of new shares or returned, and any breach of this understanding deprived them of the chance

---

1 19th Edn (1966), p 359, para 346
2 [1971] 2 All ER 870 at 874, [1971] 2 QB 330 at 333
3 [1972] 2 All ER 147 at 151, [1972] 1 WLR 661 at 665, per Lord Widgery CJ

of earning that interest as well as depriving other applicants of the chance of receiving
a larger issue of new shares.

The question for the jury therefore was not whether the appellants had obtained
the property of the issuing houses by deception but whether the deception by which
they had obtained it was criminal. Was it not merely irregular or a breach of contract
but a dishonest deception and in particular a dishonest deception in substantially the
respects alleged in the counts of the indictment? The jury by a majority answered
that question Yes on every count but the first.

Counsel for the appellants submitted to the trial judge, and submits to this court,
that there was no evidence, or no evidence on which a jury could safely convict, of the
dishonest deception by which the Crown alleged that the appellants obtained or
attempted to obtain these letters of acceptance and return cheques. Alternatively he
submits that the judge in his summing-up both before and after a question from the
jury misdirected them or failed to direct them adequately.

The learned judge ruled that the case was not difficult to understand nor one of real
complexity and that the question whether what the appellants were alleged to have
done was dishonest was essentially a question to be decided by a jury. 'There are
facts', he said, 'which can point in both directions in this case, and in the circumstances
I could not conscientiously say that there was no evidence fit to be left to the jury.'
We need only say, without enumerating the undisputed facts which point to dishonesty,
that we agree with him.

In summing up the case to the jury the judge laid down the law in a way which is
beyond criticism. He told the jury:

'. . . there is nothing illegal in stagging. The question you have to decide and
what this case is all about is whether these defendants, or either of them, carried
out their stagging operations in a dishonest way. To that question you apply
your own standards of dishonesty. It is no good, you see, applying the standards
of anyone accused of dishonesty otherwise everybody accused of dishonesty, if he
were to be tested by his own standards, would be acquitted automatically, you
may think. The question is essentially one for a jury to decide and it is essentially
one which the jury must decide by applying its own standards.'

That was correct: see R v Feely[1], and he repeated it more than once. He reminded
the jury that no one had apparently—

'lost a penny except in the rather far-fetched way that, I suppose, some applicants who might have got shares if the defendants had made more modest
applications, would have got them, but did not get them because there were not
enough to go round. They might have made a profit, either keeping them as an
investment, or selling them themselves, but that is far removed, you may think,
from any question of saying that if there was any dishonest deception here,
someone has been deprived, has been deceived of money.'

He reminded them that the profit the appellants made was some £2,000 only on the
transactions specified in the indictment; and that the appellants had sent cheques
'for very large sums of money when they had not got that amount of money, or
anything like it, in the bank'; but it was—

'important to bear in mind that the material time at which you have to consider the state of the applicant's respective bank accounts is not the date at which
the cheque is drawn, but the date at which the cheque is first presented for payment. A cheque, you see, is an order to the bank on which it is drawn to pay, on
demand, the sum mentioned on the face of the cheque. That is what "pay on
demand" means—when first presented. Therefore, any cheque which is not met

1 [1973] 1 All ER 341, [1973] 1 QB 530

a on first presentation is said to have bounced, or to be a dud cheque, or to be a bad cheque.'

He treated the allegation 'that the said cheque would be paid on first presentation' as 'the guts' of the charge and the shares allotted in the letter of acceptance and the money represented by the return cheque as the property obtained by the alleged deception. He read them part of the judgment from *R v Page*[1] and sub-ss (1) and (4) of
b s 15 of the Theft Act 1968. Then came this direction:

'Now, in considering whether Mr Green or Mr Greenstein had or may have had an honest belief in the truth of their representations, namely, the warranty that the cheque would be met on first presentation or, so far as counts four, five and six are concerned, where there was not a warranty, that they had authority to draw cheques for the amounts mentioned in those counts, the test is a subjective
c one. That is to say, it is not what you would have believed in similar circumstances. It is what you think they believed and if you think that they, or either of them, had an honest belief to that effect, well then, of course, there would not be any dishonesty. On the other hand, if there is an absence of reasonable grounds for so believing, you might think that that points to the conclusion that they or either of them, as the case may be, had no genuine belief in the truth of their represen-
d tations. In which case, applying your own standards, you may think that they acted dishonestly and it would be for you to say whether it has been established by the prosecution that they had no such honest belief because, as the burden of proof is on the prosecution—there is no burden on the defendants to prove to you that they did so believe.'

e He ended this part of his summing-up with a quotation from *Halstead v Patel*[2] and the general question: were they acting dishonestly?

After reviewing the evidence on the additional counts fully and fairly in a way which is also beyond criticism the learned judge told the jury to re-read the answers given by the appellants to the police, which were accepted as correct, and commented, again unexceptionally, on the fact that the appellants had not gone into the witness
f box. He concluded by reminding the jury of the main points made to them by counsel for the appellants.

The first point was that not one of the bank managers nor one of the representatives of the issuing houses nor the solicitors for one issuing house which complained of the appellants' conduct ever told them that what they were doing was illegal or criminal, or even warned them that it might be. On that the judge commented:

g 'As I have said before, this is the first prosecution. It has not yet been decided if what they did did amount to a dishonest criminal deception and it will be you who will decide the answer to that question. A breach of warranty? Well, you may think, undoubtedly. An irregular use of the bank accounts? Well, most managers eventually thought so. They did not like it. Unfair to other appli-
h cants? May be. But, whatever the answer to those questions it does not decide the question you have to answer. The last question. Dishonest? Criminal deception? Well, that is, to use a colloquial phrase, the 64,000 dollar question.'

Counsel for the appellants complains not of that but of the passage in which the judge proceeds to put what is stated to be his next point, that in relation to the register of cheques drawn on the account of Green and his wife at the Midland Bank
j of which the branch manager was Mr Whittle—

'it certainly looks as though the great majority of cheques were cleared, honoured, on second presentation, but he says, and this is right of course, that a

---

1 [1971] 2 All ER 870, [1971] 2 QB 330
2 [1972] 2 All ER 147, [1972] 1 WLR 661

lot of the evidence showed that in practice in a number of instances the excess applications were specially cleared and the credit telephoned through to the *a* branch bank at which the cheques were drawn with the result that the credit was there and, therefore, although, in fact, met on second presentation that is because the timing of the matter, late afternoon, perhaps, re-presented, but the credit was there because it had been telephoned through. He asked you to take the view that the reality of the situation is that, really, there is nothing in the point and that looking at the reality of the situation, except for possibly an hour *b* or two, there was money there to meet these cheques. But, of course, the schedule gives you the picture at a glance of what the situation was.'

Counsel for the appellants says that this appears to be a misunderstanding of his main point which the judge never put, that the great majority of cheques sent by Green with applications for shares in 1971 and 1972 were honoured on first presentation, *c* a point vital to the defence that there was no deception at the date of drawing the cheque about the state of the bank accounts on the date of first presentation and no dishonesty but a justifiable confidence that the cheques would be honoured because the majority were honoured over many months.

Counsel for the appellants' third point was that in the Dunbarton County Council issue, which was the subject of counts 4 and 5 against Green and count 6 against Green- *d* stein, the return cheques were in fact cleared and paid into these accounts before their own cheques were paid to the Bank of Scotland. This was admittedly true. It was one of the special features by which these transactions differed from the others. Other differences were that applicants for this stock had only to send cheques for ten per cent of the full price of the stock applied for and gave no express undertaking or warranty that their cheques would be met on first presentation. Hence the omission from these *e* three counts of the concluding words of the others. Yet another difference was that for this stock the two appellants made 33 separate applications which could not have been granted in full even if there had been no other applicants: one applied for over £2½ million worth of stock and the other for over £4 million, whereas the total offered was only £5 million. And if these applications had been combined into fewer applications accompanied by much larger cheques than accompanied the separate *f* applications they would have been specially cleared 'in the ordinary course of events' before the return cheques could have been paid to enable them to be met. All these differences had been pointed out to the jury by the judge, including the point made by counsel for the appellants that in fact the return cheques were paid first. His comment on this point to the jury was this:

g

'It so happened to work out in that way. Did the defendants know it would happen in that way when they drew their cheques? Or, were they just reckless about it, hoping it would happen in that way? Taking a chance? Did they hold themselves out as having authority to draw cheques for those quite enormous amounts without having made arrangements so to do or were they confident and justifiably confident that it would be alright because "we shan't get all we are *h* asking for or anything remotely like it and we shall get back a return cheque in time to pay our own cheques." Whatever the answer to those questions do they provide all the answers to the allegation against them that they obtained the allocation and that is the issue and they obtained the return excess cheques by deception in that they held themselves out as having authority to draw those to the amount specified in the counts?' *j*

Then he referred to counsel's last point that the schedule (Exhibit 231)—

'shows that with regard to each of the counts with which we are dealing there was always in the account enough money in credit—the account was always in credit enough sufficiently on the dates cheques were presented to cover the cost

a   of the shares actually allocated. Member of the jury, that is undoubtedly true
         so far as it goes and you will give to that what weight that merits.'

And he added a comment which we did not understand counsel for the appellants to
criticise. We shall have to consider further the points which counsel for the appellants
makes about the history of the scheme's working and about the Dunbarton transactions, because it is on these points only that, in our judgment, there can be any
b   serious criticism of the summing-up.
     The next day the judge completed his summing-up in a passage containing these
sentences:

         'The prosecution invite you to draw the inference that these two defendants
         were acting dishonestly in the way they conducted their operations. The defen-
c   dants, through their counsel, ask you to say that you would not be justified in
         drawing that inference.'

He then told the jury that the question with regard to the counts relating to transactions other than the Dunbarton transactions was: did the appellants obtain, or
attempt to obtain, the letters of allocation and the return cheques dishonestly by
d   deception as a result of either deliberately or recklessly representing that their own
cheques would be paid on their first presentation? Of counts 4, 5 and 6 relating to the
Dunbarton issue he said:

         'Finally, counts four, five and six, the Dunbarton issue. There is no doubt
         there that they obtained letters of allocation and returned cheques and the
e   question there was, were they obtained dishonestly and by deception—not by
         representing in an express warranty as was the case in all these other counts
         that the cheques would be met on express re-presentation—but by implying,
         representing, by the ordinary rules which apply to cheques, that they had authority
         to draw cheques specified in each case? If you think they were acting dishonestly,
         or made that implied representation, or did it deliberately, or recklessly, if it
f   was a misrepresentation, guilty. If you are not sure about it, not guilty. But if
         you are sure, then, of course, you must say guilty.'

After retiring for over four hours the jury returned with a request for a transcript
of Mr Whittle's evidence. The judge then read out (mostly for the second time) his
very full note of that evidence. The reading took 25 minutes. The jury then retired
g   for half an hour and returned their verdicts of not guilty on the first count and guilty
on counts 2 to 11 by a majority of 11 to one.
     Counsel for the appellants complains that the judge's summing-up was defective
in that he failed to bring out the vital fact that the appellants had so managed their
particular form of stagging from January 1971 until the latter part of 1972 that their
cheques had been met on first presentation and they were therefore entitled reason-
h   ably to expect that each of the transactions in which that expectation had in fact been
unjustified in the event would have resulted in their own cheques being met out of
the funds provided by the return cheques. It was incumbent on the judge, said
counsel for the appellants, to make that clear in relation to all the counts, in particular
to the majority which related to transactions in November 1972 when they were
about to call their operations off in deference to the protests of the banks and the
j   issuing houses. The jury's request for Mr Whittle's evidence showed that they were
seriously concerned about his acquiescence in Green's operations over this period
and the judge should have repaired his omission to mention counsel for the appellants'
main point in his summing-up by introducing it into his reading of Mr Whittle's
evidence. He should also have related his general directions on the law to the particular transactions to which the charges in the indictment referred and directed the

jury's mind to the state of each appellant's mind, and in relation to each transaction
when he might reasonably have expected the return cheque to be paid and what *a*
steps he took to have it specially cleared in time to anticipate the clearance of his own
cheque, so as to arrive at a conclusion about the honesty of the transactions.

We think that it might have been better if the judge had stressed counsel for the
appellants' point based on the higher proportion of cheques which were met on first
presentation, but we cannot believe that the point, made to them by counsel, escaped
the notice of the jury or was obliterated from their minds by the judge's reference *b*
to Exhibit 204. For they had already had read to them Mr Whittle's evidence in
cross-examination that 'in most cases the system worked all right because the money
was in the Midland Bank Head Office in time to meet his [Green's] outgoing cheques'
and the judge read that evidence to them. It was probably because Mr Whittle was
prepared to allow the system to go on working so long that the jury wanted his
evidence re-read and, having heard it again, acquitted Green on count 1. But that *c*
tolerance on his part was bound up with the successful working of the scheme and it
would have been an unusually dull jury which would not have had both in mind and
would not have appreciated the point based by the defence on its successful working.
Again we reject the criticism that the judge failed to relate his general directions to the
particular charges. This was, we agree with the judge and counsel for the Crown,
basically an uncomplicated case of passing 'dud' cheques which 'bounced'. Many did *d*
not, but those which were the subject of the indictment, except counts 4, 5 and 6, did.
And the only reason why those which did not bounce, including those which were the
subject of counts 4, 5 and 6, did not bounce was that they were met out of funds
belonging to and paid by the payees in whose favour the cheques were drawn in the
belief that they would be met out of funds which did not come from the payees
themselves. Once the jury realised that the only funds out of which the greater part *e*
of the appellants' cheques could be paid were funds not then in existence but funds
supplied by the issuing houses themselves because they thought, mistakenly, that
there were much larger funds in the appellants' bank accounts from other sources,
the jury were entitled, if not bound, to infer that the appellants' deception was
deliberately dishonest. Mr Eldred, a witness from one of the issuing houses, Singer &
Friedlander, stated that an application for new shares would not have been enter- *f*
tained had he known that their own return cheques were going to be used to fund
the application. But even without that evidence we think a jury might not have
agreed that the appellants' practice was, as Green said in answer to the police, 'not
really deception—just good business practice', or, as Greenstein said, 'perfectly legal',
but might by the light of common sense and common honesty have considered it a
swindle, and a swindle of the kind which s 15 of the Theft Act 1968 was intended to *g*
stop and punish.

There is at first sight a strong case for submitting that the convictions on counts 4,
5 and 6 are less securely based, and indeed that those counts should have been withdrawn from the jury. The three cheques to which they relate were in fact met in full
when first presented: why then were they not good and valid orders for the payment
of the amounts on their face, and did not the appellants have authority to draw them? *h*
The answer depends primarily on the consideration whether the state of affairs when
the cheques were drawn was such that in the ordinary course of events they would on
their future presentation be duly honoured; if they would be, it seems that they
would be valid and drawn with the authority of the appellants' bankers and no offence
against s 15 would be committed; if the cheques were drawn recklessly without regard
to whether there was any real prospect or chance of their being met, the offence *j*
against s 15 would be committed. The jury by their verdicts of guilty on those three
counts, after the judge's direction on them which we have read, must have found that
the appellants were reckless whether the Bank of Scotland would present their return
cheques first, and we find nothing in the evidence which prevented them from so
finding. Counsel for the appellants did, however, raise a new point, that on Buckley

J's well known definition of deception[1] approved by the House of Lords in *Director*
a *of Public Prosecutions v Ray*[2], there can be no deception unless a person is induced to
believe that a thing is true which is false in fact, and as in fact these cheques were honoured on first presentation they were all valid orders authorised by the appellants'
banks and there was therefore no actual deception, honest or dishonest.

If this point, not taken at the trial, were good in law, we should have to give effect
to it. But we think that Buckley J did not have in mind a case where the thing in
b which a person is induced to believe is a future state of affairs which comes about by a
lucky chance, or as here by the act of the very person who was induced by the deception to do it. The point might have been met by wording the deception alleged in
counts 4, 5 and 6 differently, but we think that in fact the deception there alleged is not
defeated nor were the cheques validated by the fact that the cheques were met out of
the return cheques of the deceived. After all, a cheque is not a valid order for payment,
c nor in the absence of permission by the paying bank to overdraw is it drawn with that
bank's authority, unless there are funds in the drawer's account to meet it or will be
in the ordinary course of events when it is first presented.

The appellant's cheques were not valid orders, nor drawn with the authority of
the paying banks, unless payment was made on the return cheques out of the funds
of those who drew them before the appellant's cheques were first presented for pay-
d ment. Even if it could be said that such drawing of return cheques to 'repay' money
which did not exist and could not have been paid was 'in the ordinary course of
events', that would not, in our opinion, make cheques drawn by the appellants for
amounts which they could never pay without such 'repayment' valid orders or drawn
with the authority of the paying banks. It may be no particular concern of a paying
bank where the funds in a customer's account come from; but had the appellants
e the authority, presumably to be implied from banking practice or the evidence given
to the jury, of any of their banks, to draw these inflated cheques, cheques which would
only be met if the payees were induced by the appellants to believe that they wanted to
buy the inflated amount of shares and could themselves pay for them? We think
that on the evidence the answer to that is, No, except that Green may have had from
Mr Whittle the temporary authority of his branch of the Midland Bank. And that
f was the answer which the jury gave by acquitting on the first count and convicting on
the others including counts 4, 5 and 6. If the appellants had no such authority, then
the deception alleged in counts 4, 5 and 6 (and common to all counts) was proved and
the distinguishing fact that the appellants' cheques referred to in those three counts
were met on first presentation goes only to dishonesty and not to the kind of deception
alleged. The judge's directions which we have read were correct on both deception
g and dishonesty. For these reasons we uphold all ten convictions and dismiss the
appeals.

Appeals dismissed.

Solicitors: *Bindman & Partners* (for the appellants); *Director of Public Prosecutions.*
h

Sepala Munasinghe Esq Barrister.

---

1 *Re London & Globe Finance Corpn* [1903] 1 Ch 728 at 732, [1900-3] All ER Rep 891 at 893
2 [1973] 3 All ER 131 at 133, 137, [1974] AC 370 at 379, 384

Selvarajan v Race Relations Board

COURT OF APPEAL, CIVIL DIVISION
LORD DENNING MR, LAWTON AND SCARMAN LJJ
15th, 16th, 30th JULY 1975

Race relations – Investigation of complaint – Race Relations Board – Duty to act fairly – Requirements of fairness – Parties entitled to be informed of substance of case against them – Duty of members of the board to consider all the evidence and papers in the case – Board delegating function of collecting information to officer of the board – Report of officer recommending board to form opinion that no discrimination had taken place – Three members of board only considering all the papers in case – Board concluding that no discrimination had taken place – Whether board having acted fairly.

Race relations – Investigation of complaint – Race Relations Board – Reinvestigation of complaint after investigation by conciliation committee – Report of conciliation committee – Whether board limited to considering report only – Whether board entitled to consider all the evidence before conciliation committee – Race Relations Act 1968, s 15(5).

Race relations – Investigation of complaint – Conciliation committee – Requirement to form an opinion whether 'any person' has been guilty of unlawful discrimination – Finding of committee – Finding that unlawful discrimination has taken place – Whether necessary to identify in finding person who has been guilty of discrimination – Race Relations Act 1968, s 15(3)(a).

The applicant was an Indian employed by the Inner London Education Authority ('the ILEA') as a lecturer grade I. He was employed in that post for 14 years. He applied for promotion to a lecturer grade II but another candidate, less well qualified academically and without such long service as the applicant, was appointed to the post. The applicant thought that the decision not to promote him had been made because of his colour or race and that there had been unlawful discrimination against him. He made a written complaint against the ILEA to the Race Relations Board ('the board'). The board referred the complaint to a conciliation committee under s 15(2)(a) of the Race Relations Act 1968. The conciliation committee investigated the complaint thoroughly over a period of nine months, receiving representations from all concerned. On 9th February 1972 the committee formed the opinion that unlawful discrimination against the applicant had occurred. The committee, having failed to secure a settlement between the parties or to obtain an assurance against any repetition of the discrimination, made a report to the board, as required by s 15(5) of the 1968 Act. The report simply stated the opinion formed by the committee and their failure to secure a settlement or an assurance against repetition of the discrimination. The report did not identify the ILEA as the person who had been guilty of the unlawful discrimination. The board, having considered that report and discussed the matter with the conciliation committee, took the view that the decision not to promote the applicant might have been due to his personality, and not to his colour or race. The board therefore decided to reinvestigate the complaint under s 15(5). For that purpose the board acted through one of their committees, the employment committee, which consisted of seven members. The collection of information for the reinvestigation was carried out by one of the board's conciliation officers; she wrote to the ILEA, on 16th August 1972, giving them a summary of the applicant's complaint and requesting their comments on it. The ILEA gave a detailed reply. Having received the ILEA's comments, the conciliation officer wrote to the applicant on 24th November, inviting him to reply by 8th December to certain points which might be adverse to him. Without waiting for the applicant's reply the

conciliation officer prepared a report, dated 4th December, for the members of the
a employment committee which was headed 'clearly predictable case' and which
contained a summary of the complaint and the answers to it, and a recommendation
that the employment committee should 'form an opinion of no unlawful discrimination'. The applicant did not reply by 8th December to the letter of 24th November.
On 13th December the employment committee met to consider the complaint.
Only the chairman of the committee and two other members had seen the full
b papers in the case; the other four members only had the record of the proceedings
before the conciliation committee and the conciliation officer's report of 4th December. The employment committee formed the opinion that the applicant's personality had been the cause of the decision not to promote him and that no unlawful
discrimination had occurred. The applicant applied for certiorari to quash the
employment committee's decision. He also applied for mandamus to compel the
c conciliation committee to form an opinion as to the 'person' who had discriminated
against him.

Held – (1) The application for certiorari would be refused for the following reasons—
   (i) An investigating body such as the board was under a duty to act fairly. In order
to comply with that duty it was not, however, necessary that every member of a
d non-judicial body making an investigation, or conducting an enquiry, should have
access to all the papers and evidence in the case. Where the body in question had a
large number of members it was usually sufficient if a quorum of three had done so.
In all the circumstances the board had acted fairly since (a) the employment committee had investigated the complaint as thoroughly as the conciliation committee
had done; (b) three members of the employment committee had considered all
e the papers in the case; (c) the board were entitled to delegate to their staff the function
of collecting information and the employment committee had not acted unfairly
in leaving the investigation of the complaint to the conciliation officer; (d) although
it had been a mistake for the conciliation officer in her report of 4th December to
prejudge the case by calling it 'clearly predictable' and to recommend to the employment committee the opinion which they should form, the report was merely a
f recommendation and had been so treated by the committee (see p 19 *a* to *c* and *f*,
p 20 *d* to *h*, p 21 *j* and p 22 *c d* and *g* to p 23 *b* and *g*, post); *Wiseman v Borneman* [1969]
3 All ER 275, *R v Gaming Board for Great Britain, ex parte Benaim* [1970] 2 All ER 528 and
Re Pergamon Press Ltd [1970] 3 All ER 535 applied.
   (ii) The board, in reinvestigating a complaint under s 15(5), were not limited to
considering the report of the conciliation committee but were entitled to have
g recourse to the evidence and papers which had been before that committee. The
reinvestigation was not an appeal, and the board were themselves entitled under
s 15(3) to enquire into everything which had influenced the conciliation committee.
Accordingly, the employment committee had not erred in law in taking into consideration the evidence which had been before the conciliation committee (see p 19 *j*
to p 20 *c*, p 23 *b* and p 24 *b* to *e*, post).
h (2) The application for mandamus also failed since the provision in s 15(3)(*a*) that
the conciliation committee should form an opinion whether 'any person' had been
guilty of unlawful discrimination did not require the committee to name the person
who in their opinion had been guilty of unlawful discrimination since it was clear
that the applicant's employers, the ILEA, were in the committee's opinion the
guilty person (see p 19 *h*, p 23 *b* and p 24 *g*, post).
j Per Lord Denning MR. What the duty to act fairly requires depends on the nature
of the investigation and the consequences which it may have on persons affected by it.
The fundamental rule is that, if a person may be adversely affected by the investigation and report, he should be informed of the substance of the case made against him
and be afforded a fair opportunity of answering it. The investigating body is, however,
the master of its own procedure (see p 19 *b* to *e*, post).

Notes

For consideration of complaints generally, and for the investigation of complaints *a* relating to employment, see 4 Halsbury's Laws (4th Edn) paras 1043, 1044.

For the Race Relations Act 1968, s 15, see 40 Halsbury's Statutes (3rd Edn) 114.

Cases referred to in judgments

Attorney-General (on the relation of McWhirter) v Independent Broadcasting Authority [1973] 1 All ER 689, [1973] QB 629, [1973] 2 WLR 344, CA.   *b*

Jeffs v New Zealand Dairy Production and Marketing Board [1966] 3 All ER 863, [1967] AC 551, [1967] 2 WLR 136, PC, Digest (Cont Vol B) 314, *186a*.

Maxwell v Department of Trade and Industry [1974] 2 All ER 122, [1974] QB 523, [1974] 2 WLR 338, CA.

Pergamon Press, Re [1970] 3 All ER 535, [1971] Ch 388, [1970] 3 WLR 792, CA, Digest (Cont Vol C) 107, 4188e.   *c*

R v Gaming Board of Great Britain, ex parte Benaim [1970] 2 All ER 528, [1970] 2 QB 417, [1970] 2 WLR 1009, 134 JP 513, CA, Digest (Cont Vol C) 397, 352Aa.

Wiseman v Borneman [1969] 3 All ER 275, [1971] AC 297, [1969] 3 WLR 706, 45 Tax Cas 540, [1969] TR 279, 48 ATC 278, HL, Digest (Cont Vol C) 536, 1613h.

Cases also cited   *d*

Anisminic Ltd v Foreign Compensation Commission [1969] 1 All ER 208, [1969] 2 AC 147, HL.

Ealing (London Borough) v Race Relations Board [1972] 1 All ER 105, [1972] AC 342, HL.

R v Deputy Industrial Injuries Comr, ex parte Moore [1965] 1 All ER 81, [1965] 1 QB 456, CA.

R v Registrar of Building Societies, ex parte a building society [1960] 2 All ER 549, [1960] 1 *e* WLR 669, CA.

Smith v East Elloe Rural District Council [1956] 1 All ER 855, [1956] AC 736, HL.

Spackman v Plumstead District Board of Works (1885) 10 App Cas 229, HL.

Ward v James [1965] 1 All ER 563, [1966] 1 QB 273, CA.

Appeal

The applicant, Govindaswamy Selvarajan, applied for (1) an order of certiorari to *f* quash a decision of the respondents, the Race Relations Board, given on 15th January 1972, that there had been no unlawful discrimination against the applicant, and (2) an order of mandamus directing the North Metropolitan Conciliation Committee to enter a complete finding of unlawful discrimination in accordance with s 15(3)(a) of the Race Relations Act 1968. The grounds on which the order of mandamus was sought were (i) that the conciliation committee had failed to enter a complete find- *g* ing with the result that the applicant's employer, the Inner London Education Authority ('the ILEA') had rejected the committee's finding on the ground that the ILEA was not mentioned as the person who had committed the unlawful discrimina- tion; and (ii) that that failure was the sole reason why a settlement had not been attempted with the result that the Race Relations Board were precluded from con- sidering the proceedings under s 19 of the 1968 Act. On 7th February 1974 the Divi- *h* sional Court of the Queen's Bench Division (Lord Widgery CJ, Boreham and May JJ) gave judgment dismissing the applications. The applicant appealed. By a respondent's notice, the Race Relations Board gave notice that on the hearing of the appeal they would contend that the Divisional Court's judgment should be affirmed on the additional ground that the board's duty in investigating complaints of discrimination pursuant to s 15 of the 1968 Act was to make only such enquiries as it bona fide con- *j* sidered necessary and was not to act judicially and/or fairly. The facts are set out in the judgment of Lord Denning MR.

The applicant appeared in person.
Michael Beloff for the Race Relations Board.

Cur adv vult

a   30th July. The following judgments were read.

LORD DENNING MR. This case raises questions about the procedure of the
Race Relations Board. The applicant, Govindaswamy Selvarajan, studied at the
University of Madras and got degrees in physics and law. In 1955 he came to England.
b   He was then aged 30. Two years later he entered the teaching profession here; and,
whilst teaching, he studied further so that he became a master of science in the
University of London; and he obtained the post-graduate certificate in education.
So he is well qualified academically. In September 1957 he was employed by the
Inner London Education Authority. In September 1961 he was appointed to the
City of Westminster College (now known as Walbrook College) as a lecturer in
c   mathematics and physics. He started as a lecturer grade I. He has been 14 years in
that post in the same grade. That is very unusual. In the ordinary way a lecturer is
promoted from grade I to grade II within a few years. He feels that he has not
been promoted because of his colour or race, and thus there has been unlawful
discrimination against him. He complained to the Race Relations Board. It was
referred to a conciliation committee and they formed the opinion that there had
d   been unlawful discrimination against him. But the Race Relations Board itself took
a different view. They refused to take proceedings on his behalf against his employers,
the Inner London Education Authority ('the ILEA'). He then applied to the Divisional Court for an order of certiorari to quash the board's determination. The
Divisional Court refused. He now appeals to this court.
The relevant section is s 3(1) of the Race Relations Act 1968. It says:

e
'It shall be unlawful for an employer or any person concerned with the
employment of others to discriminate against any other person . . . (b) . . . by
refusing or deliberately omitting to afford or offer him . . . the like opportunities for training and promotion as the employer makes available for persons
of the like qualifications employed in like circumstances . . .'

f   That section only came into force on 25th November 1968. Mr Selvarajan feels that,
even before that date, he had been less favourably treated than others; but his
actual complaint can, I think, only be made of matters arising after the Act was
passed.
In February 1971 the staff of the college were informed that ten posts were to be
upgraded to lecturer grade II, and that one of them had been allocated to the
g   science department. The successful candidate was to be responsible for 'careers
advice'. Lecturers grade I were invited to apply. There were three candidates.
They were interviewed by a selection board consisting of the principal, the vice-
principal, the head of the science department and an inspector of the ILEA. A Miss
Lancaster was appointed. She was not so well qualified academically as Mr
Selvarajan, nor had she anywhere near such long service. Mr Selvarajan was
h   aggrieved that she had been appointed instead of him. He made a written complaint to the Race Relations Board against the ILEA, fully documented with letters
of commendation for his work during his career.

The conciliation committee
On receiving that complaint the board, in accordance with their power under the
j   1968 Act, referred it to a conciliation committee; and it became the duty of the
conciliation committee to investigate it: see s 15(2)(a), (b). The committee was the
North Metropolitan Conciliation Committee. It had nine members of excellent
qualifications. All were unpaid, giving their services voluntarily except for travelling
expenses. The secretary was Miss Allport.
Section 15(3) of the 1968 Act says:

'In investigating any complaint the Board or a conciliation committee (a) shall make such inquiries as they think necessary with regard to the facts alleged in the complaint and form an opinion whether any person has done any act which is unlawful . . .'

In making their investigation, the board or the committee are entrusted with a task which has important consequences, both for the complainant and the accused. If they form an opinion that an accused has done an act which is unlawful, it means that civil proceedings may be brought against him for an injunction or damages (see s 19) and he will be put to all the worry and expense of contesting those proceedings. If they form an opinion that the accused has not done an act which is unlawful, it means that the complainant has no remedy at all.

The proceedings before the concilation committee

The procedure adopted by the conciliation committee was this. First, the secretary, Miss Valerie Allport, wrote to the principal of the college telling him of the complaint. She met him and the members of the staff and discussed it with him. She saw Mr Selvarajan and discussed it with him. She received a letter from him with his comments. She saw the representatives of the ILEA and discussed the case with them. She put their answer to Mr Selvarajan and invited him to make his representations in writing. He did so. She made reports of her interviews, and collected all the letters together, and prepared them in a file for a sub-committee.

Second, the sub-committee (Lady Seear and Mr Thomas) met on 14th July 1971 and saw Mr Salvarajan. They felt that there were several points which were adverse to the college. So their secretary put the points to the principal and got his answer. They considered them and decided to seek a further meeting. On 11th October the sub-committee (Dr Bayliss and Lady Seear) met the principal of the college and a representative of the ILEA. On 13th October the full sub-committee (Mr Thomas, Dr Bayliss, Mr Bery, Mr Keating, Mr T Robert and Lady Seear) met and considered the case. They agreed to recommend to the conciliation committee that unlawful discrimination had occurred and that this should be a 'starred case'.

Third, the secretary reported the result to Mr Selvarajan and the ILEA. Thereupon the ILEA asked for a further opportunity of being heard. This was granted. On 8th November the sub-committee heard them in full. Mr Selvarajan also made representations in writing and orally. He produced statements of several witnesses on his own behalf. The sub-committee considered the case on five days, 24th and 26th November, 8th and 22nd December 1971 and 26th January 1972. Finally the the case came back to the full conciliation committee on 9th February 1972, when ten members were present. They then formed the opinion that unlawful discrimination had occurred. The secretary notified this finding to all concerned.

Fourth, it then became the duty of the conciliation committee, under s 15(3)(b) of the 1968 Act, to—

'use their best endeavours by communication with the parties concerned or otherwise to secure a settlement of any difference between them and, where appropriate, a satisfactory written assurance against any repetition . . .'

The secretary made approaches to this end, but they were rejected by the ILEA outright. In a letter of 14th March 1972, the education officer wrote denying any discrimination. He said:

'They are not, therefore, able to accept this opinion or to enter into the discussions proposed in your letter about a settlement and assurances; and they require that the matter be reported to the Race Relations Board for further investigation.'

Fifth, having failed to secure a settlement and assurances, the conciliation committee on 22nd March 1972, as the 1968 Act requires, made a report to that effect

to the Race Relations Board: see s 15(5). This was a formal report stating simply
a that the conciliation committee had failed. But Dr Bayliss, the chairman, supplemented it by a confidential note setting out the matters which weighed with them:

> '. . . ten years at Grade I with Mr. Selvarajan's qualifications needed some
> explanation . . . We never had . . . any convincing explanation . . . There
> is a series of inconsistencies in the evidence presented by representatives of the
> *b* College and the ILEA which created the impression that they would use what-
> ever argument was convenient as a means of answering Mr. S[elvarajan]'s
> complaint . . . The ILEA have pushed our opinion aside and their letter makes
> it clear that they want the Board to ignore it. The Committee believe that a
> major public authority should not be allowed to get away with such cavalier
> treatment of one of the Board's regional committees . . .'

c
I must say that I sympathise with the conciliation committee. Here they were, a
group of able men and women, holding positions of responsibility, giving their time
and skill to the service of the community, without any remuneration. They had
investigated the complaint over a period of nine months, from May 1971 to February
1972. They had had representations in writing and orally from all concerned. They
d had given each side a full opportunity of meeting everything that was said on the
other side. They had heard oral evidence and received written statements. They
had discussed the case at length between themselves. It must have taken many hours.
They had formed the opinion that there had been unlawful discrimination against
Mr Selvarajan. Yet their opinion was rejected out of hand by the ILEA in terms,
as if to say: 'We don't care about your opinion. We are not going to discuss the
e matter with you. We are going straight to the Race Relations Board. We want them
to investigate it.'

The proceedings before the Race Relations Board
The Race Relations Board has a chairman and 11 members. It has authority to
act by a group of members selected by the chairman: see s 14(4) of the 1968 Act.
f In this matter they acted by the employment committee of the board. The chairman
of the employment committee is Sir Roy Wilson QC. The chairman of the board,
Sir Geoffrey Wilson, is a member of the employment committee. And there are
five others.

On 5th May 1972 Mrs Coussey, a conciliation officer, sent to each of the seven
members a file containing a record of all the proceedings before the conciliation
g committee. It was over 100 pages. She also sent the confidential note prepared by
the chairman of the conciliation committee; and, in addition, a summary made by
the secretary of the conciliation committee. The conciliation officer recommended
'that the Committee defer a decision pending discussions with the North Metropolitan
Conciliation Committee'.

On 10th May 1972 the full employment committee met. They decided to defer
h consideration until they had discussed the matter with members of the conciliation
committee. This meeting took place on 23rd May. It was attended by Sir Geoffrey
Wilson, the chairman of the board, and the principal conciliation officer, Mr Hills.
He made a report commenting that it was a question whether Mr Selvarajan's
failure was due to personality rather than race or colour. He recommended that
the committee should reinvestigate the case. The employment committee met on
j 7th June 1972. They decided that the board should reinvestigate the matter themselves. This was permissible under s 15(5) of the 1968 Act.

The reinvestigation was made in this way. On 16th August the conciliation officer,
Mrs Coussey, wrote to the ILEA with a summary of Mr Selvarajan's complaint.
On 17th November they replied in detail and attached a statement which covered
16 pages. On 24th November Mrs Coussey wrote to Mr Selvarajan setting out

several points which might be regarded as adversely affecting his case. The letter
concluded: *a*

'If you wish to dispute or comment on these points, or if you wish to put
forward any additional facts or arguments, you are invited to do so. You may
put your views forward in any of the following ways: by writing a letter for
the Committee's consideration; or to me personally and I will report them to
the Committee: or put them to the Committee yourself. In putting your views
to me or the Committee you may if you wish be assisted by a friend or an adviser. *b*
I should be very grateful if you would adopt one of these courses by 8 December
1972.'

Although Mr Selvarajan was invited to take one of those courses by 8th December,
he did not do so. On 13th December the employment committee met, but he had
not replied even by that date. Meanwhile Mrs Coussey had prepared a report for *c*
the board dated 4th December which needs careful consideration. It is headed:

'Clearly predictable case—Full papers to Mota Singh. [Then there followed a
short summary of the complaint and the answer in 1½ pages.] Comments. A
pre-opinion letter was sent to Mr. Selvarajan on 24 November. Representations
are due by 8 December. *Recommendation.* That the Committee form an opinion
of no unlawful discrimination.'   *d*

The employment committee was summoned for 13th December. The full papers in
Mr Selvarajan's case were sent to the chairman of the employment committee (Sir
Roy Wilson QC) and to one of the members, Mr Mota Singh, a barrister. The chairman of the board (Sir Geoffrey Wilson) also had them. At the meeting there were
present Sir Roy Wilson QC, Sir Geoffrey Wilson and four members of the committee,
together with five of the staff. Mr Mota Singh was unable to be present, but he sent *e*
his apologies, together with a message that he had read the papers and had formed
the view that there had been no unlawful discrimination, and asked that this view
be passed on to the other members of the committee. The other four members of
the committee had not had all the papers. They had the original set sent by Mrs
Coussey. Since then they only had the summary prepared by Mrs Coussey saying
it was 'Clearly predictable case' and recommending that there be a finding of 'no *f*
unlawful discrimination'.

At the meeting the chairman said that, having examined the papers, he agreed
with the view of Mr Mota Singh that there had been no unlawful discrimination.
The other members of the committee agreed. The committee then formed the
opinion that no unlawful discrimination had occurred. And that opinion was
recorded in the minutes.   *g*

On the next day the board received a letter from Mr Selvarajan, dated 13th
December. It did not give a reasoned reply. It contained much criticism of the
board. He said:

'The [Race Relations Board] in investigating the complaint from scratch is
acting outside reason . . . I cannot lend myself to be associated with the activi- *h*
ties of such an irrational body . . . I shall certainly endeavour to take the
whole matter to the High Court.'

On receipt of that letter, the chairman (Sir Roy Wilson QC) directed that the
matter should be reconsidered at their next meeting. It was so reconsidered at a
meeting on 10th January 1973. On this occasion Mr Mota Singh was present. The
employment committee confirmed its previous opinion.   *j*

On 31st July 1973 the Divisional Court gave leave to Mr Selvarajan to apply for
certiorari. He served a notice of motion covering five pages of reasons. On 7th
February 1974 the Divisional Court dismissed his application.

The position of the Race Relations Board

The board, in a respondent's notice, raised this contention: that the duty of the

board, in investigating complaints of discrimination, is only to make such enquiries
a as they bona fide consider necessary and not to act judicially and/or fairly.

That contention goes, I think, too far. In recent years we have had to consider the
procedure of many bodies who are required to make an investigation and form an
opinion. Notably the Gaming Board, who have to enquire whether an applicant
is fit to run a gaming club (see *R v Gaming Board for Great Britain, ex parte Benaim*[1]),
and inspectors under the Companies Acts, who have to investigate the affairs of a com-
b pany and make a report (see *Re Pergamon Press Ltd*[2]), and the tribunal appointed under
s 463 of the Income and Corporation Taxes Act 1970, who have to determine whether
there is a prima facie case (see *Wiseman v Borneman*[3]). In all these cases it has been held
that the investigating body is under a duty to act fairly; but that which fairness requires
depends on the nature of the investigation and the consequences which it may have on
persons affected by it. The fundamental rule is that, if a person may be subjected to
c pains or penalties, or be exposed to prosecution or proceedings, or deprived of remedies
or redress, or in some such way adversely affected by the investigation and report, then
he should be told the case made against him and be afforded a fair opportunity of
answering it. The investigating body is, however, the master of its own procedure. It
need not hold a hearing. It can do everything in writing. It need not allow lawyers. It
need not put every detail of the case against a man. Suffice it if the broad grounds are
d given. It need not name its informants. It can give the substance only. Moreover
it need not do everything itself. It can employ secretaries and assistants to do all the
preliminary work and leave much to them. But, in the end, the investigating body
itself must come to its own decision and make its own report.

Applying these principles in the present case to the two bodies concerned, it seems
to me that the conciliation committee conducted their investigations with the greatest
e care and the greatest fairness. They gave their services voluntarily without pay.
They spent many hours in hearing all concerned and considering all the reports.
They were impressed by Mr Selvarajan's high qualifications and long service. These
exceeded those of the other candidates. They thought they were such as to merit
his being promoted to lecturer grade II. On this account they inferred that there
was discrimination against him.

f Equally, however, the employment committee of the board conducted their
investigations with much care and fairness. They had before them all the papers
and information which was before the conciliation committee. But they thought
that the conciliation committee had made a mistake. There was no evidence to
show that Mr Selvarajan failed to get promotion because of his colour or his race.
Everything went to show that it was his personality which made him unsuitable.
g He was not the best person for the post. Nor, indeed, the right person. The successful
candidate, Miss Lancaster, was much more suitable. On this ground the board
formed the opinion that there was no unlawful discrimination.

Now for the particular points raised by Mr Selvarajan.

'Any person'
h Mr Selvarajan submitted that the conciliation committee—and the board—ought
to name 'any person' of whom they formed an opinion that he had been guilty of
unlawful discrimination. I do not think this is necessary. So long as it is reasonably
clear. In this case it must have been the appointments committee of the college and
also the ILEA.

j *'Investigate the complaint themselves'*
Mr Selvarajan submitted that under s 15(5) of the 1968 Act the board, if they
decided to investigate the complaint themselves, ought to have done so by making

1   [1970] 2 All ER 528, [1970] 2 QB 417
2   [1970] 3 All ER 535, [1971] 1 Ch 388
3   [1969] 3 All ER 275, [1971] AC 297

their own enquiries. They ought not to have had recourse to the evidence or papers
which were before the conciliation committee: but only to the report of that com-   *a*
mittee. Section 15(5) says: '. . . the Board shall consider the report.' Mr Selvarajan
submitted that the report itself was the thing. The board should not consider anything outside the report. A parallel might be made when the court considers the
award of the arbitrator or the report of an inspector under the planning legislation.
The court does not go outside it and consider the evidence. I do not think there is
any parallel. The reinvestigation by the board is not to be regarded as an appeal   *b*
from the conciliation committee. Section 15(3) says that, in investigating any complaint, the board 'shall make such inquiries as they think necessary'. That is quite
wide enough to enable them to enquire into all the things which influenced the
conciliation committee, and the evidence and reports before them.

The report by the conciliation officer   *c*
    It was, I think, unfortunate that the conciliation officer headed her report: 'Clearly
predictable case.' But there was a good reason underlying it. In preparing the papers,
it is very helpful for the staff to estimate the length of time needed to discuss the
case and the amount of work to be done by the members to make a summary.
But it was a mistake of the staff to prejudge the case by calling it 'clearly predictable'
and by recommending to the board the opinion which it should form. That is   *d*
undesirable because it might tempt the members of the board to take a short cut—
and not read the papers—and merely rubber stamp the recommendation. The
summary should outline the facts, the point in controversy and the issues. It should
not tell the committee what the result should be.

Delegation to some members only   *e*
    The most troublesome point is that several members of the board did not have
all the papers. Four of them had only the summary of a 'clearly predictable case'
of 1½ pages and a recommendation that the committee should form the opinion
of no unlawful discrimination. It may reasonably be inferred that these four were
not in a position to form an opinion of their own. They must have gone by the
opinion of the other three members who had received all the papers and had read   *f*
them.
    If this had been a judicial body, I do not think this would be right. Every member
of a judicial body must have access to all the evidence and papers in the case, he
must have heard all the arguments, and he must come to his own conclusion. The
maxim delegatus non potest delegare applies strictly to judicial functions. But it is
different with a body which is exercising administrative functions or which is making *g*
an investigation or conducting preliminary enquiries, especially when it is a numerous
body. The Race Relations Board has 12 members. The employment committee has
seven members. It is impossible to suppose that all of them need sit to determine a
matter. Nor that all of those who sit should have read all the papers or heard all the
evidence. But I do think that two or three, at any rate, must have done so. If there
is a quorum of, say, three, I should think a quorum must have done so. That is the   *h*
ordinary accepted method of carrying on business. It should be applied here also.
    We were referred to *Jeffs v New Zealand Dairy Production and Marketing Board*[1].
But in that case, on the construction of the statute, the board had no power to delegate its functions. It was necessary, therefore, for the board at least to have an
accurate summary of the evidence and of the submissions. But in the present case
the board undoubtedly had power to delegate its functions.   *j*

Conclusion
    In my opinion Mr Selvarajan's complaint has been fully investigated in accordance
with the 1968 Act. He has been most fairly treated. And the Race Relations Board

1 [1966] 3 All ER 863, [1967] AC 551

formed an opinion which was manifestly correct, namely, that there had been no
a unlawful discrimination against him. I would, therefore, dismiss this appeal.

LAWTON LJ. The broad question in this appeal is whether this court can, or
should, interfere with a decision of the Race Relations Board. It can within limits;
but, in my judgment, this is not a case in which it should.

b   The Race Relations Act 1968 gives some people rights and impinges on the rights
of others. Discrimination against persons on the ground of colour, race or ethnic or
national origins in relation to the provision of goods, facilities, services, employment
and accommodation (subject to certain exceptions) is declared unlawful. Parliament
appreciated, however, that exhorting people to love their neighbours is one thing,
getting them to do it is another. The Race Relations Board was set up to secure
c compliance with the provisions of the Act against discrimination and the resolution
of differences arising out of any of those provisions. The main function of the board
was to be conciliation and prevention. The Act did not enact that those who discriminate against others commit offences. The board has no power to initiate prosecutions. The most it can do is to start civil proceedings (a) for declarations that acts
were unlawful by virtue of the provisions against discrimination, (b) for damages
d to compensate those who have suffered loss by reason of discrimination, (c) for injunctions to restrain discrimination in specified circumstances and (d) for the revision of
contracts containing discriminatory terms: see ss 19, 21-23. The board has no jurisdiction to determine anything in a judicial sense. It has a duty to receive and investigate complaints (see s 15(1)); to use its best endeavours to secure a settlement of
differences (see s 15(3)); to form an opinion whether there has been any unlawful
e discrimination (see s 15(4)); and, if there has been and the board has been unable to
settle any difference, it can determine whether to bring civil proceedings of the
limited kind to which I have already referred. It investigates, conciliates, and
initiates. Forming an opinion that there has been no discrimination, as the board did
in this case, is not a definitive determination of an issue: it is a preliminary to a
decision whether proceedings should be initiated. In some respects its powers are
f like those of the Director of Public Prosecutions. He receives complaints from
public bodies and members of the public; he can start investigations; and if he is of
the opinion that there is sufficient evidence to justify a prosecution, he can initiate
one; but he does not decide guilt or innocence. As far as I know, the courts have
never interfered with the exercise of the director's discretion; but it does not follow
that they could not do so if he refused or failed to perform his public duties or acted
g corruptly or unfairly: see *Attorney-General (on the relation of McWhirter) v Independent
Broadcasting Authority*[1].
    In my judgment this court should be slow to interfere with any decisions the
Race Relations Board makes. It should only interfere in the following circumstances.
First, if the board has refused or failed to perform the functions which Parliament
has given it. It is inconceivable that it would ever refuse to perform these functions;
h but if its work became very heavy it might allow its staff to do that which it should
do itself. This is said by the applicant to have happened in this case. It might also
shy away from investigating complaints made against powerful bodies. The applicant
seems to have thought that his troubles have arisen from a reluctance on the part of
the board to investigate his complaint against the ILEA. Secondly, courts can and
should interfere if the board exceeds its powers. It has not been suggested in this
j case that it did, so nothing more needs to be said about that. Thirdly and finally,
this court can and should interfere if the board has acted unfairly or corruptly to the
prejudice of either a complainant or a person or body against whom complaint has
been made. There has been no suggestion of corruption in this case. I have used

---

1 [1973] 1 All ER 689 at 698, 705, [1973] 1 QB 629 at 649, 657

the adverb 'unfairly' in preference to the applicant's phrase 'contrary to the rules of
natural justice' for the reason I gave in *Maxwell v Department of Trade & Industry*[1]. *a*
The applicant's phrase is liable to lead courts into the trap of legalism. The common
sense of the British people has appreciated that there are circumstances in which
over strict attachment to legal forms can hinder the doing of what should be done.
This is shown by the widespread use of such expressions as 'barrack-room lawyer' or
'sea lawyer'.

Applying these principles to the facts of this case, the results are clear. At the *b*
meeting of the board's employment committee on 10th January 1973, those present
did form an opinion that what had been done by the ILEA was not unlawful discrimination. Whether they had sufficient material on which to do so is a matter which
I will consider in relation to alleged unfairness. The civil servant, Mrs Coussey,
had made a recommendation in the document dated 4th December 1972. It may
not have been as full as it should have been. The use of the heading 'clearly *c*
predictable case' was unfortunate, as was the fact that the recommendation was
made by her before she had seen the applicant's reply to the request for comments
which she had made to him on 24th November 1972. The fact remains that all she
did was to make a recommendation and the employment committee treated it as
such. The suspicion which the applicant has about the board's reluctance to investigate his complaint against the ILEA is swept away by the evidence. The board did *d*
investigate it. By letter dated 16th August 1972 Mrs Coussey, on behalf of the
board, reported to the authority what the applicant was alleging against them and
requested comments. By letter dated 19th November 1972 the authority gave their
answer, accompanied by no less than 15 foolscap pages of supporting statements.
The last of them is not without interest; it was a letter signed by 14 members of the
staff at Walbrook College, who had been the applicant's colleagues there. In it they *e*
protested at the suggestion that he had been subjected to discrimination.

I come now to the suggestion that the board acted unfairly. I found it difficult
to follow what the applicant was complaining about in this respect. As far as I could
make out his complaints came under the following heads: first, that the employment
committee of the board had not investigated his complaint as thoroughly as the
conciliation committee had done; secondly, that they had left the investigation to a *f*
civil servant, Mrs Coussey, instead of doing it themselves; thirdly, that they had
formed their opinion not to initiate proceedings without having adequate material
before them.

As to the first head of complaint, all the information which the conciliation committee had was passed on to the employment committee. As I have already
recounted, Mrs Coussey, on behalf of the board, did reopen with the ILEA the *g*
matter of the applicant's complaint and gave him an opportunity of commenting
on the material which that authority had put before the board. He acted tardily in
taking advantage of this opportunity and when he did he misused it in a way which
corroborated what the authority had said about his personality and why he had not
been promoted.

For my part I can see no reason at all why the board should not delegate to its *h*
staff the function of collecting information. It would be impractical for the members
of the board themselves to make investigations. How the board does what Parliament has entrusted it to do is not a matter for the courts to decide as long as it acts
fairly and in good faith. It is for the board, not the courts, to decide how much
information each of its members should have when considering a particular case.
As long as the board, or one of its constituent committees, has enough information *j*
to enable it to make a fair assessment of the case, the courts will not interfere. How
it gets the information is for the chairman and his advisers to decide. He may decide
in a particular case that each member of the board, or the committee, should have a

1   [1974] 2 All ER 122 at 131, 132, [1974] QB 523 at 539

copy of the whole file. In another case he may consider that the case can be adequately
a and fairly dealt with if one member has the file and reports to the others what is in it.
In this case three members of the employment committee had a copy of the complete file. This was enough to enable the committee to deal with the applicant's case
fairly.

In my judgment the applicant has failed to show cause for interfering in any way
with the employment committee's decision not to initiate proceedings. I would
b dismiss the appeal.

SCARMAN LJ. The North Metropolitan Conciliation Committee of the Race
Relations Board reported to the board that they had investigated a complaint by
Mr Selvarajan, a teacher, of unlawful discrimination against him by his employers,
c the ILEA; that they had formed the opinion that there was unlawful discrimination;
but that they had failed to secure a settlement of the difference or an assurance
from the ILEA that there would be no repetition of the act complained of. The
complaint was that he had been denied promotion because of his race. After receiving the report, the board decided to investigate the complaint themselves. They
formed a contrary opinion and reached a determination that they would take no
d further action.

Mr Selvarajan's case against the board is not what you might expect. He does not
rely on an allegation of lack of natural justice in the way the board handled his
complaint. He says no such question arises. He says that the board erred in law in
deciding themselves to investigate his complaint, when, as he submits, it was their
duty to send it back to the conciliation committee with an instruction to that
e committee to fulfil their statutory duty of making a report.

As I understand his argument, he takes the following points: (1) that there was no
report under the statute, because the conciliation committee failed to identify 'any
person' as having done the unlawful act: Race Relations Act 1968, s 15(3)(a); (2) that
the committee being seised of the complaint, the board had no jurisdiction themselves to investigate it; they were bound by the report; their purported investigation
f was, therefore, a nullity. This point is one of construction of s 15(5) of the 1968 Act.

Accordingly, he sought from the Divisional Court an order of certiorari to quash
the determination of the board and an order of mandamus to compel the conciliation
committee to form an opinion as to the person or persons who had discriminated
against him. The Divisional Court refused this relief, and he appeals to this court.

Inevitably, though Mr Selvarajan roundly asserted it was not his case, considerable
g discussion has arisen whether the board acted fairly in their handling of his complaint.
I agree with Lord Denning MR and Lawton LJ that the board was under an obligation
to act fairly, and did so. If it be any part of Mr Selvarajan's case that the board acted
unfairly, the contention fails, in my judgment, for the reasons that Lord Denning
MR and Lawton LJ have given. Whatever be the extent of their legal obligations,
the board dealt faithfully with Mr Selvarajan's complaint. They, and their officers,
h went to great trouble to get at the facts. The volume of documentary material
available to the board was prodigious: Sir Roy Wilson, Sir Geoffrey Wilson and Mr
Singh, all of them members of the board and its employment committee, studied
the papers in depth; the board had the complaint on its agenda at four meetings,
and deferred its final determination until it had considered Mr Selvarajan's written
observations in his letter of 13th December 1972. The complaint came for the first
j time to the attention of the board, as distinct from its conciliation committee, in
May 1972, when that committee's voluminous file (over 100 documents) together
with a note prepared by the committee's chairman, was sent to the board. There
ensued meetings between members of the conciliation committee, the chairman of
the Race Relations Board, and board officers. In June the board decided itself to
investigate the complaint. During the summer, an officer of the board sought to

make contact and to arrange a meeting with Mr Selvarajan: but he was not available. On 24th November Mr Selvarajan was invited by letter to make such further representations as he might wish either at a meeting or by letter. Finally, after receipt of his written reply, which was not sent until 13th December, the board made their final decision and duly informed Mr Selvarajan by letter of 15th January 1973. During those eight months Mr Selvarajan was given every opportunity to present and develop his complaint, while the board and its officers applied themselves conscientiously to its investigation.

The truth is that Mr Selvarajan's case, as he chose to present it, is based on a total misconception of the 1968 Act. He would have us believe that the Act has created a fixed hierarchy of institutions performing judicial functions, that at each level of the hierarchy the judicial duty must be done before the complaint under consideration can be passed on to the next level; and, if a conciliation committee reports that the complaint is justified but that it has not obtained a settlement or an assurance of no repetition, the board may not go beyond the report but must make their decision on the basis of the information contained in it; and on nothing else.

The Race Relations Board does not exercise judicial functions. Part II of the Act is absolutely clear. The board was created so that in the sensitive field of race relations compliance with the law and the resolution of differences could first be sought without recourse to the courts with their necessarily open and formalised judicial process. The board is an administrative agency charged with a number of critically important functions in the administration of the law; but it is not a judicial institution—nor is it the apex of a hierarchy of judicial institutions. The procedures are not adversarial but conciliatory: settlement, not litigation, is the business of the board, and it is left to the board to decide how best to perform the functions which the Act requires it to perform, namely, investigation, the formation of an opinion, conciliation, and, if all else fails, the taking of legal proceedings in the county court. I draw attention speciffcally to ss 14 and 15 of the Act.

The board is, of course, subject to the supervisory powers of the High Court. If it fails to perform a statutory function, mandamus will lie. If it fails to act fairly, the High Court can intervene by certiorari, prohibition, or mandamus to ensure that it does. Subject to such supervision (the limits of which in the case of an administrative agency charged with making decisions that directly affect private persons are by now well known) the Race Relations Board—not the courts—decides in its field how to go about the task of securing compliance with the law and resolving differences.

In the present case the conciliation committee undoubtedly made a report. I reject Mr Selvarajan's point that the committee failed to identify the person who in their opinion discriminated. The ILEA was his employer and took full responsibility. Under s 15(5) it then became the board's duty to consider the report, which has been done. The board then had to decide whether or not themselves to investigate the complaint. They decided to investigate. The board then had to form an opinion, which they did. They then had to decide what, if anything, to do, which they also did. After studying the immense amount of relevant material assembled and considered by the board, I wish to pay my tribute to them for the way they handled Mr Selvarajan's complaint.

I would dismiss the appeal.

Appeal dismissed.

Solicitors: *Lawford & Co* (for the Relations Board).

Wendy Shockett Barrister.

a
Bryanston Finance Ltd v de Vries (No 2)

COURT OF APPEAL, CIVIL DIVISION
BUCKLEY, STEPHENSON LJJ AND SIR JOHN PENNYCUICK
16th, 17th, 18th, 19th, 24th, 25th, 26th, 27th JUNE, 22nd JULY 1975

b
Injunction – Interlocutory – Principle governing grant – Prima facie case – Anticipated litigation – Abuse of process of court – Injunction to restrain anticipated litigation on ground it would constitute an abuse of process – Action for injunction restraining presentation of petition to wind up company on specified grounds – Motion for interlocutory injunction – Whether company having to establish prima facie case that petition abuse of process.

c
Injunction – Interlocutory – Principle governing grant – Injunction having effect of granting sole relief claimed in action – Petition to wind up company on just and equitable grounds – Injunction restraining petitioner moving court to wind up company – Whether interlocutory relief appropriate.

d
Company – Winding-up – Compulsory winding-up – Contributory's application – Locus standi – Minority shareholder – Petitioner holding 62 shares out of company's issued capital of 7½ million shares – Whether shareholder having sufficient interest in winding-up – Companies Act 1948, s 222(f).

e
Company – Winding-up – Compulsory winding-up – Just and equitable – Alternative remedy – Investigation of company's affairs by Department of Trade and Industry – Investigation in progress – Whether just and equitable that company be wound up before conclusion of investigation – Whether shareholder precluded from presenting petition to wind up company – Companies Act 1948, ss 164, 222(f).

The defendant held 62 shares in a company whose issued capital was 7,414,938 shares.
f The company was a holding company whose assets consisted mainly of shares in a number of subsidiary companies. S was the chairman and managing director of the company and the majority shareholder. The defendant objected to S's management of the company and its subsidiaries and, from 1969, engaged in substantial litigation with both S and the company. At the annual general meeting of the company held in 1974, the defendant raised various questions relating to an entry in the 1973 g accounts. He obtained little information and repeated those and other questions in a letter, to which he received no reply. In February 1975 he wrote again to S stating that if no reasonable reply or explanation were received within two days, he would petition the court to wind up the company under s 222(f)[a] of the Companies Act 1948 on the ground that it was just and equitable to do so. On the following day the company issued a writ claiming an injunction restraining the defendant from present-
h ing a petition to wind up the company on the ground of failure to answer any of the questions set out in his letter or on any ground connected therewith. On 18th March an ex parte injunction was granted in the same terms until trial or further order. In March a company wholly owned by S, ATSO, made an offer for the minority shares. The defendant served notice of motion to discharge the injunction on the ground that the ATSO offer constituted a relevant change in the circumstances of j the case. The motion was dismissed on 30th April. On 1st May the defendant attempted to file a petition under s 222(f) but it was dismissed as not being in the proper form. On 2nd May the company applied for an injunction restraining the defendant from

---

a   Section 222, so far as material, provides: 'A company may be wound up by the court if ...
    (f) the court is of opinion that it is just and equitable that the company should be wound up.'

presenting a petition under s 222(f) on any of the grounds asserted in affidavits
sworn by him or connected therewith. The defendant applied, with the support of **a**
other shareholders, under s 164[b] of the 1948 Act to the Department of Trade and
Industry for an investigation of the company's affairs and inspectors were appointed
on 6th May. At the hearing on 15th May the judge found that some at least of the
defendant's allegations, if substantiated, could lead to a winding-up order, and the
company conceded that the defendant might succeed in establishing that presentation
of a petition on the grounds asserted in his affidavits would not be an abuse of the pro- **b**
cess of the court. The judge held, however, that he should decide whether to grant the
injunction on the balance of convenience and that the defendant would suffer less
damage than the company. Accordingly he granted the injunction until judgment
or further order. The defendant appealed against both orders. The company contended that the judge's orders should be upheld on the further ground that the
defendant's shareholding was too small to give him a sufficient interest in a winding- **c**
up of the company; that the defendant was actuated by malice and therefore
any petition would be an abuse of process; that the defendant's petition could not
succeed; and that the investigation of the company's affairs made a winding-up
order unnecessary.

Held – (i) The injunction granted on 18th March was of a limited character and **d**
nothing had happened between that date and 30th April to justify its discharge.
The first appeal would therefore be dismissed (see p 33 c, p 36 j and p 38 b, post).

(ii) The appeal against the second injunction would however be allowed for the
following reasons—

(a) The second injunction was of a much broader nature than the first and in
effect prevented the defendant from presenting any petition to wind up the company **e**
under s 222(f) on the grounds of improper or oppressive conduct on the part of S.
The size of the defendant's shareholding and his motives in petitioning were irrelevant
so long as he had sufficient grounds. Furthermore, the investigation under s 164
was a different remedy from a winding-up; the investigation would not result in a
winding-up, nor inhibit the company from disposing of its assets, nor, if there were
a course of oppressive conduct, prevent its continuance (see p 33 d to p 34 d, p 36 j and **f**
p 38 a and b, post); Re a Company [1894] 2 Ch 349 distinguished.

(b) The company was only entitled to interlocutory relief to prevent anticipated
litigation if on the available evidence it could be said that presentation of a petition
would prima facie be an abuse of process. The court should not interfere with what
would otherwise be a legitimate petition unless there were sufficient prima facie
evidence. The judge's finding that some of the defendant's allegations might lead to **g**
a winding-up order, coupled with the company's concession, precluded the company
from contending that such a petition could not possibly succeed. It followed that
the company had failed to make out a sufficient prima facie case to justify the grant
of the injunction (see p 35 b to j, p 36 a to d and g to j, p 37 b to d and h and p 38 b and c,
post).

h

---

b Section 164 provides:
    '(1) The Board of Trade may appoint one or more competent inspectors to investigate
the affairs of a company and to report thereon in such manner as the Board direct—(a)
in the case of a company having a share capital, on the application either of not less than
two hundred members or of members holding not less than one tenth of the shares issued;
    (b) in the case of a company not having a share capital, on the application of not less than **j**
one fifth in number of the persons on the company's register of members.
    '(2) The application shall be supported by such evidence as the Board of Trade may
require for the purpose of showing that the applicants have good reason for requiring
the investigation, and the Board may, before appointing an inspector, require the applicants to give security, to an amount not exceeding one hundred pounds, for payment of
the costs of the investigation.'

Charles Forte Investments Ltd v Amanda [1963] 2 All ER 940 applied; *American Cyanamid Co v Ethicon Ltd* [1975] 1 All ER 504 distinguished.

Per Stephenson LJ and Sir John Pennycuick. The order sought would, if made, conclude once and for all the summary issue raised by the motion. There could be no question of the action itself being brought on for hearing at some later date on the same issue, and therefore the principles applicable were different from those applicable in the case of an injunction to restrain a defendant from doing acts alleged to be in violation of the plaintiff's legal right (see p 37 *f* and *g* and p 38 *d* to *f* and *h*, post).

Per Sir John Pennycuick. The procedure by way of writ claiming an injunction to restrain presentation of a winding-up petition, followed immediately by a motion claiming an interlocutory injunction in the same terms, is clumsy and inapposite (see p 38 *j* to p 39 *a*, post).

Notes

For the principles governing the grant of interlocutory injunctions, see 21 Halsbury's Laws (3rd Edn) 364-366, paras 763-766, and for cases on the subject, see 28(2) Digest (Reissue) 968-980, 67-161.

For injunctions to restrain a winding-up petition generally, see 7 Halsbury's Laws (4th Edn) para 1004, and for cases on the subject, see 10 Digest (Reissue) 934, 935, 5457-5463.

For the Companies Act 1948, ss 164, 222, see 5 Halsbury's Statutes (3rd Edn) 249, 289.

Cases referred to in judgment

American Cyanamid Co v Ethicon Ltd [1975] 1 All ER 504, [1975] AC 396, [1975] 2 WLR 316, HL.

Company, Re a [1894] 2 Ch 349, 63 LJCh 565, 71 LT 15, 10 Digest (Reissue) 929, 5411.

Forte (Charles) Investments Ltd v Amanda [1963] 2 All ER 940, [1964] 1 Ch 240, [1963] 3 WLR 662, CA; rvsg (1963) LT 330, 10 Digest (Reissue) 953, 5592.

Mann v Goldstein [1968] 2 All ER 769, [1968] 1 WLR 1091, 10 Digest (Reissue) 935, 5463.

Niger Merchants Co v Capper (1877) 18 Ch D 587 n, 25 WR 365, 10 Digest (Reissue) 935, 5459.

Rica Gold Washing Co, Re (1879) 11 Ch D 36, 40 LT 531, CA, 10 Digest (Reissue) 940, 5515.

Interlocutory appeals

By a writ issued on 19th February 1975 the plaintiff company, Bryanston Finance Co Ltd, sought an injunction against Juda de Vries restraining him from presenting a petition to wind up the company under s 222(*f*) of the Companies Act 1948 on the grounds of failure to answer any or all of certain questions or on any ground connected therewith. An ex parte injunction in those terms was granted on 19th February by Oliver J. On 18th March Megarry J continued the injunction until trial or further order. On 24th April Mr de Vries served notice of motion to discharge the injunction on the ground that there had been a relevant change in the circumstances of the case. On 30th April the motion was dismissed by Oliver J.

By a writ issued on 2nd May the plaintiff company sought an injunction restraining Mr de Vries from presenting a petition under s 222(*f*) of the 1948 Act to wind up the company on any of the grounds asserted and included in four affidavits sworn by Mr de Vries on 25th February, 17th March, 29th and 30th April. On 2nd May Oliver J granted an ex parte injunction in those terms and on 15th May Oliver J continued that injunction until trial or further order.

Mr de Vries appealed against the orders of Oliver J dated 30th April and 11th May. The facts are set out in the judgment of Buckley LJ.

Mr de Vries appeared in person.
Andrew J Bateson QC and *Ellis Meyer* for the plaintiff company.

Cur adv vult

22nd July. The following judgments were read.

BUCKLEY LJ. There are two appeals before this court. The first is from an order of Oliver J dated 30th April 1975 in an action of *Bryanston Finance Limited v de Vries* (which I will call 'the first action'). The other is from an order of the same learned judge dated 15th May 1975 in an action between the same parties (which I shall call 'the second action'). The defendant, Mr de Vries, is a small shareholder in the plaintiff company. He is indeed a small shareholder, for he holds 62 shares only of 25p each in a total issued capital of the plaintiff company amounting to 7,414,938 shares. He is, and has for some time been, engaged in a war with the chairman and managing director of the company, one Alfred Teddy Smith (whom I will call 'Mr Smith'), who holds about 57 per cent of the issued share capital of the company.

The plaintiff company is a holding company whose assets consist mainly of shares in a number of subsidiary companies, which are shown in the plaintiff company's accounts as divided into three divisions, namely a finance division consisting of five subsidiaries, including a banking company called National Union Bank Ltd, incorporated in the Bahamas, of which Mr Smith is the principal executive, a property dealing division consisting of a company called Bryston Property Group (London) Ltd, and an industrial division consisting of 11 subsidiary companies, including a company called Amalgamated Industrials Ltd. A company called English Precision Machines and Tools Ltd, of which Mr de Vries was a director and shareholder, was formerly a customer of National Union Bank Ltd (which I will call 'the bank'). In about 1969 a receiver of this company was appointed by the bank. It would seem that the feud between Mr de Vries and Mr Smith dates from this time.

In January 1969 Mr de Vries and others commenced an action against the bank and Mr Smith claiming damages for an alleged conspiracy by the defendants to injure the plaintiffs in their business. The plaintiffs in this action, other than Mr de Vries, came to terms with the defendants, but Mr de Vries fought the action and lost it. In February 1971 the plaintiff company, the bank and Mr Smith brought an action against Mr de Vries and another claiming remedies for defamation. The other defendant came to terms with the plaintiffs, but again Mr de Vries fought the action and lost it. However, on appeal Mr de Vries was successful in getting the decision reversed[1].

The consolidated accounts of the plaintiff company and its subsidiaries for the year ended 31st December 1972 contained a note in the following terms:

'11. Principal shareholder. The balances with the principal shareholder are made up as follows—

	1972 £000	1971 £000
Interest free advances from Mr A T Smith and Companies under his control	1712	1254
Advances to Mr A T Smith and companies under his control	1605	1097
	107	157

Interest Charges in 1972 in respect of advances to Mr A T Smith and companies under his control totalled £48,000 (1971—nil) including £32,000 relating to prior years.'

---

1 [1975] 2 All ER 609, [1975] 2 WLR 718

In the consolidated accounts for the following year the following note appeared:

'12. Principal shareholder. The balances with the principal shareholder which arise from the Group's banking business are made up as follows:

	1973 £000	1972 £000
Advances to companies under Mr A T Smith's control	2294	1605
Advances from Mr A T Smith and companies under this control	2067	1712
Net amount due by (to) principal shareholder	227	(107)

Since 31st December 1973 arrangements have been made under which all transactions between Bryanston Finance Limited and its subsidiaries and Mr A T Smith's companies under his control will be conducted through the account of one of Mr Smith's companies with the banking subsidiary and all balances have accordingly been transferred to this account. The net amount of interest receivable in 1973 in respect of balances with the principal shareholder amounted to £37,000 (1972 £48,000) of which £17,000 (1972 £32,000) related to prior years. Also included in the consolidated profit and loss account are charges made to companies under the control of the principal shareholder in respect of administration services provided by the group.'

It will be observed that the item which in the 1972 accounts is described as 'advances to Mr A T Smith and companies under his control' appears in the 1973 accounts as 'advances to companies under Mr Smith's control'. The note in 1972, however, still purports to deal with 'balances with the principal shareholder', which presumably means Mr Smith. In 1972 the net balance was adverse to the company, but in 1973 was in its favour, the difference amounting to £334,000.

At the annual general meeting in 1974 Mr de Vries asked a number of questions relating to this entry in the 1973 accounts. He obtained very little information by way of reply, and was thoroughly dissatisfied with the answers. By a letter dated 14th August 1974 Mr de Vries repeated these questions and asked a number of other questions, demanding a reply not later than 20th August 1974. Having received no reply, on 18th February 1975 Mr de Vries again wrote to Mr Smith referring to his earlier letter of 14th August 1974 raising the same questions again and other questions, and stating that if no reasonable reply or explantaion was received not later than 20th February 1975 he, Mr de Vries, would without further notice proceed to petition the court to wind up the company under s 222(f) of the Companies Act 1948.

On 19th February 1975 the company issued a writ against Mr de Vries claiming an injunction restraining him from presenting a petition for winding up the company on the ground of failure to answer any or all of the questions set out in or incorporated in Mr de Vries's letter of 18th February 1975 or on any ground connected therewith. On the same day the company obtained an ex parte injunction in the terms of the indorsement on the writ. The motion came before Megarry J on 25th February when he adjourned it to 17th March. In an affidavit sworn on 20th February Mr Fitzhugh, the secretary of the company, stated that the company was willing to answer such questions as after proper consultation with its professional advisers it was advised that it might and should lawfully answer. However, none of these questions has been answered. On 18th March 1975 Megarry J continued the injunction until trial or further order. No appeal has been made against that order, which was perfected and entered on 28th April 1975.

On 20th March 1975 a shareholder named Marcus Brown wrote to Mr de Vries offering to buy his shares at the original cost price, which was, I think, about 48p a share. Mr de Vries did not accept that offer. On 27th March it was announced in

the press that a company called A T Smith Organisation Ltd (which I will call
'ATSO') was to make an offer for the minority shares in the plaintiff company at
the price of 7p per share. This offer was made to the minority shareholders through
a company called Seton Trust Ltd by a circular dated 21st April 1975. The chairman
of Seton Trust Ltd was Mr Hegard, who is, or is alleged to be, an associate of long
standing of Mr Smith and was also a director of the plaintiff company. It appears
from the circular sent out by Seton Trust Ltd that ATSO was a private company
wholly owned by Mr Smith, and that its only directors were Mr Smith and a Mr
Morris. Mr Morris was not a shareholder in the plaintiff company, but was a director
of certain subsidiary companies in the group.

The directors of the plaintiff company at this time were Mr Smith (chairman
and managing director), Mr Green, Mr Hegard and Mr Joseph. The circular sent
out by Seton Trust Ltd containing the ATSO offer was accompanied by a circular
letter to the minority shareholders signed by Mr Green on behalf of himself, Mr
Hegard and Mr Joseph, who were therein described as 'the independent directors'.
The letter stated that the independent directors had appointed Rowe Rudd & Co
Ltd to advise them in compliance with the provisions of the City Code on Takeovers
and Mergers, who had been assisted by a firm of accountants, Goodman Jones &
Partners. Mr Hegard was a member of Rowe Rudd & Co Ltd. The offer was not
supported by any independent valuation of the assets of the company, nor was it
based on any recently audited accounts. The letter signed by Mr Green describes
the business of the group in very gloomy terms. It concludes by saying that the
independent directors were convinced that, should the offer not be accepted by
shareholders, it would probably not be possible for the plaintiff company to meet
its working capital commitments in the prevailing circumstances, that it might
become necessary to request the suspension of the company's quotation on the
Stock Exchange, and that some form of reconstruction of the company might have
to be effected. The independent directors unanimously recommended shareholders
to accept the offer.

On 24th April 1975 Mr de Vries served notice of a motion to discharge the injunction granted by Megarry J. This was on the basis that the ATSO offer constituted a
relevant change in the circumstances of the case. On 30th April 1975 Oliver J dismissed this motion with costs to be paid by Mr de Vries forthwith. This is the first
of the two orders now appealed against. Mr de Vries on this occasion declined to
give an undertaking not to petition for the winding-up of the plaintiff company
without first giving seven days' notice to the company.

On 1st May 1975 Mr de Vries attempted to file a petition for the winding-up of
the plaintiff company under s 222(f) of the 1948 Act. This attempt was abortive
because, as was pointed out to Mr de Vries by an official in the Registry of the Companies Court, the proposed petition did not contain any allegation that there was
likely to be a surplus of assets available for shareholders in a winding-up. It in fact
contained an allegation that the company was insolvent. On 2nd May 1975 the
company issued the writ in the second action, in which it claimed an injunction
restraining Mr de Vries from presenting a petition under s 222(f) on any of the
grounds asserted and included in four affidavits of his sworn in the first action or
on any ground connected with such grounds. On the same day Oliver J granted
an ex parte injunction in the terms of the indorsement on that writ. The motion
came on for hearing inter partes on 9th May 1975 and judgment was delivered by
the learned judge on 15th May when he continued the injunction until judgment
or further order. This is the second order now appealed against.

On the hearing of the motion counsel for the plaintiff company submitted that
the matter fell to be decided on the balance of convenience pending the trial of the
trial of the action (*American Cyanamid Co v Ethicon Ltd*[1]) and the learned judge adopted

_____

1   [1975] 1 All ER 504, [1975] AC 396

a this approach. For the plaintiff company, counsel contended that the evidence showed that a petition would clearly be an abuse of the process of the court, but he was content to concede for the purposes of the motion that there was a possibility that the defendant might succeed. The judge recognised that it was for the company to show that the proceedings sought to be restrained would be an abuse of process, but he thought that in this respect there was a genuine question to be tried. The learned judge stated the nature of the allegations on which Mr de Vries would rely

b in any such petition under eight heads, and said that some if not all of these, if they were to be substantiated, could lead to a winding-up order. He drew attention to the fact that Mr de Vries in his proposed petition had alleged that the company was insolvent and that this would clearly be fatal to the petition. He said that, although Mr de Vries now sought to withdraw that allegation, and was entitled to put in his petition what he liked, what he could not do was to delete a reference in

c one of his affidavits to the insolvency of the company.

It will, I think, be convenient to dispose of this point now. The learned judge was evidently referring to para 41 of an affidavit of Mr de Vries sworn on 6th May 1975. Mr de Vries was there dealing with the amount of certain reserves created by the company in respect of bad debts. He was at issue with Mr Joseph, who had sworn an affidavit on the company's behalf, as to the amount of these reserves.

d In an earlier affidavit he had asserted that these amounted to £4,000,000, but Mr Joseph had deposed to the fact that they were less than £3,000,000. In para 41 of his affidavit of 6th May Mr de Vries said that, having regard to the size of the business, even £3,000,000 would be insufferable. He asserted that at December 1973 the plaintiff company was financed as follows:

e

	£
Issued share capital	1,854,000
Share premium	725,000
Reserves	155,000

f

	2,734,000

Mr de Vries then added these words: 'So that, in any event, [the plaintiff company] has now lost more than its entire issued share capital and reserves and is therefore insolvent.' If the word 'insolvent' is here intended to mean that there could be no surplus of assets available for shareholders in a winding-up, I hope I may without offence

g to Mr de Vries say that this statement is a non sequitur and shows some confusion of thought. Whether there would be a surplus of assets in a winding-up would depend, amongst other things, on the values at which the assets of the company could be realised in comparison with the values at which they stood at December 1973 in the company's books, and on whether the debts which were treated as bad debts for the purpose of setting up the reserves were in fact to turn out to be bad

h debts. I would not myself be disposed, at this stage at any rate, to regard this passage in an affidavit of a litigant in person as an effective bar to his asserting in any future petition that there is likely to be a surplus of assets for the shareholders.

Oliver J referred in his judgment to the decision of this court in *Charles Forte Investments Ltd v Amanda*[1] where Willmer LJ expressed the view that a winding-up petition was not justified where a minority shareholder had other more satisfactory

j remedies available to him. The learned judge went on to consider what other remedies were available to Mr de Vries in the present case, and, as I understand his judgment, he was of the opinion that there was no alternative remedy of a kind to bring any such principle into play in the present case. He decided the case on what

1 [1963] 2 All ER 940, [1964] 1 Ch 240

he considered to be the balance of convenience, saying that the presentation of a
winding-up petition might cause irreparable damage to the company out of all   *a*
proportion to any damage which might be suffered by Mr de Vries in consequence
of the injunction. On this ground he continued the injunction.

In this court Mr de Vries has emphasised one subject which is not specifically
mentioned in the judge's eight heads and may not have been ventilated before him.
It relates to the acquisition by the company in July 1972 of the share capital of what
became and now is its property-owning and dealing subsidiary, Bryston Property   *b*
Group (London) Ltd (which I will call 'Bryston'). Bryston is a private company with
an issued share capital of 100 shares of £1 each. It was incorporated in October
1965 but did not commence business until January 1972. It then acquired a considerable number of residential properties in various parts of the country. In the period
from 24th January to 31st March 1972 it realised a net loss of £17,948, and at the
latter date its balance sheet showed an excess of liabilities over assets amounting to   *c*
£17,848. The annual return of Bryston made up to 31st December 1971 shows Mr
Smith as the registered holder of 99 of the issued shares of Bryston. It also shows
that he was one of the three directors of Bryston. By an agreement dated 26th May
1972 Mr Smith and a Mr O'Farrell, who were the holders of all the shares in Bryston,
agreed to sell the whole of the share capital of Bryston to the plaintiff company for a
consideration to be satisfied by the allotment to the vendors of fully paid ordinary   *d*
shares of the company of 25p each. The maximum number of shares to be so allotted
was to be 1,575,000. Of these 393,750 were to be issued on completion. If Bryston
achieved net profits in respect of the nine months' period ending 31st December
1972 of not less than £750,000, 393,750 further shares were to be allotted to the
vendors. Similarly, if Bryston's net profits for the financial year ending 31st December
1973 were to amount to £750,000, a further 393,750 shares were to be allotted to the   *e*
vendors. The remaining 393,750 shares were to be allotted to the vendors in the
event of the profits of Bryston for the year ending 31st December 1975 being not
less than £750,000. These figures were to be subject to certain adjustments in the
event of Bryston's profit falling short of or exceeding £750,000 in respect of any of
these years. In May 1972 Bryston sold one of its properties realising a profit of £35,585.
In about August 1972 Bryston entered into two contracts with Crestwood Property   *f*
Ltd for the sale to the latter company of two parcels of residential properties in
Hampstead. The profit on these transactions was such that the profits of Bryston
for the nine months ending 31st December 1972 exceeded £750,000. In the event,
the second of these two contracts was never completed and has been rescinded,
but the first was completed. Mr de Vries asserts that Crestwood Properties Ltd was
financed for the purpose of buying these properties by the bank, but of this there is,   *g*
I think, no satisfactory evidence before this court.

The published annual accounts of the plaintiff company for the year ended 31st
December 1972 contained a note to the effect that 393,750 ordinary shares of the
company were issued at a premium of £178,000 in part consideration of the acquisition of Bryston. They also state that a further 393,750 shares were issued in March
1973, also at a premium of £178,000. They also contain a note to the effect that Mr   *h*
Smith had a beneficial interest in the sale of Bryston and would in the next three
years receive 779,625 ordinary shares as consideration of the plaintiff company's
acquisition of Bryston. Counsel for the plaintiff company asserts that at the time of
the sale of the capital of Bryston to the plaintiff company, Mr Smith owned no more
than 34 per cent of the capital of Bryston, but this does not seem to accord with
the notes in the 1972 accounts of the plaintiff company.   *j*

The published accounts of the plaintiff company for the year ended 31st December
1972 show that Mr Smith's beneficial holding of ordinary shares of the company
had increased by nearly 1,000,000 shares. About 514,000 shares of this increase are
to be attributed to a conversion of 500,000 redeemable preference shares held by
Mr Smith into ordinary shares, but this leaves a large balance to be accounted for,

a some part of which must presumably have derived from Mr Smith's sale of his interest in Bryston.

These matters certainly suggest to me that there are questions relating to Mr Smith's management of the affairs of the plaintiff company, of the affairs of Bryston, and possibly of the affairs of the bank, which any minority shareholder might well consider to require investigation and which might well be held to justify the making of a compulsory winding-up order.

b At this point I ought to mention that on 6th May 1975 the Department of Trade and Industry appointed inspectors to investigate the affairs of the plaintiff company under s 164 of the Companies Act 1948 on the application of Mr de Vries with the support of an appropriate number of shareholders. That investigation is now proceeding.

I now turn to consideration of the two appeals before the court, and I can dispose c of the first shortly. Mr de Vries did not appeal against the order of Megarry J of 18th March 1975. The injunction then granted was of quite a limited character. In my judgment Oliver J was right in thinking that nothing had happened between 18th March 1975 and 30th April 1975 which would justify him in discharging the injunction granted by Megarry J. Accordingly, in my judgment, this appeal should be dismissed.

d The injunction granted by Oliver J on 15th May 1975 was of a much broader nature. The four affidavits of Mr de Vries referred to in it were of a wide-ranging character, and it seems to me that Mr de Vries would be in great difficulty in framing any petition for the winding-up of the company under s 222(f) of the 1948 Act founded on allegations of improper or oppressive conduct on the part of Mr Smith in the management of the company's affairs without running into conflict with the injunc- e tion, which, it will be remembered, restrains Mr de Vries from presenting a petition based on any of the grounds asserted or included in those affidavits or any ground connected with such grounds. The injunction consequently in effect prevents Mr de Vries from presenting any petition for the winding-up of the company under s 222(f).

Counsel for the plaintiff company has contended that a minority shareholder should not be permitted to petition for the winding-up of the company unless he f can satisfy the court that he will have a substantial financial interest as a result of the winding-up. He says that Mr de Vries's shareholding in the present case is so small that he cannot qualify as a petitioner. In my judgment, the smallness of a minority shareholder's holding is no bar to his petitioning for a winding-up order if what he may hope to recover in a liquidation of the company is likely to be appreciable in relation to the size of his shareholding. If it would be de minimis he might well be g treated as having no locus standi, but otherwise he should be treated as having as good a right to seek a winding-up order as any other contributor. He must have what Jessel MR called a 'tangible interest' in the winding-up (*Re Rica Gold Washing Co*[1]), but whether his interest has this character should be judged in relation to the size of his shareholding. Mr de Vries asserts that his shares in the company would in a winding-up be worth much more than the 7p a share offered by ATSO. If he can h frame a petition demonstrating a prima facie probability of this, the small number of shares which he holds should not, in my opinion, be any objection to his petition.

Counsel for the plaintiff company says that Mr de Vries's object is simply to wreck the plaintiff company, and that his only motive is enmity against Mr Smith. The learned judge, rightly in my opinion, thought that a petition could not be an abuse simply because the petitioner was actuated by malice. If a petitioner has a sufficient j ground for petitioning, the fact that his motive for presenting a petition, or one of his motives, may be antagonism to some person or persons cannot, it seems to me, render that ground less sufficient. If, on the other hand, he has no sufficient ground, his petition will be an abuse, whether he be actuated by malice or not. I personally

---

feel no doubt that Mr de Vries (whether rightly or wrongly) is genuinely of the
opinion that Mr Smith is conducting the affairs of the plaintiff company and of the   *a*
group for his own personal advantage and in a manner oppressive to the other
shareholders. If Mr de Vries were able to make this good, he would be very likely
to succeed in obtaining a winding-up order. The fact that his belief was coupled
with, or even fed or generated by, personal animosity against Mr Smith would not,
I think, disentitle him to such an order.

We were referred to Re a Company[1]. In that case the petitioner had not held   *b*
shares in the company for long enough to be entitled to petition for a winding-up
as a contributory. Nevertheless, he contended that advertisement of his petition
should not be restrained. Vaughan Williams J rather naturally took the view that
the petitioner was not acting in good faith for the legitimate purpose of obtaining
a winding-up order, but to embarrass the company. The case is clearly distinguishable
from the present one on the facts. In my opinion, it does not assist us.   *c*

Counsel for the plaintiff company says that if Mr de Vries is anxious to obtain a
winding-up order because the affairs of the company should be investigated, this is
unnecessary, because there is already an investigation on foot under s 164 of the
Companies Act 1948. I cannot accept this view. An investigation under this section
is a very different sort of remedy from a winding-up. It will not result in a winding-up
of the company or the realisation and distribution of its assets. It does not inhibit   *d*
the company from disposing of its assets. If there is a course of oppressive conduct
here, it will not prevent its being continued, at any rate while the investigation is
proceeding.

In the circumstances of this case, and assuming that there is substance in Mr de
Vries's complaints, it does not seem to me that either s 210 of the Companies Act
1948 or a minority shareholder's action would afford him a satisfactory form of   *e*
proceeding.

In this court, as below, counsel for the plaintiff company has mainly relied on
American Cyanamid Co v Ethicon Ltd[2]. In that case the House of Lords undoubtedly
stated principles which were intended to have a wide application. It is necessary,
however, to bear in mind the character of the case then before their Lordships'
House in order to appreciate the extent of that wide application. The case related   *f*
to an alleged threatened infringement of a patent. Lord Diplock, discussing the
principles to be applied and matters to be taken into consideration when an interlocutory injunction is sought, referred[3] to 'an application for an interlocutory injunction to restrain a defendant from doing acts alleged to be in violation of the plaintiff's
legal right . . .' Primarily, at any rate, it was that type of injunction which he had
in mind. Both his language and his reasoning indicate this. His attention was   *g*
addressed to the kind of action in which issues relating to the existence of a right
claimed by the plaintiff and the existence or threat of some infringement by the
defendant of that right are for the time being uncertain but will be investigated
and determined at the trial.

The action in the present case is of an exceptional and rather different character.
The only relief claimed in the writ in the second action is the injunction which I   *h*
have already mentioned. This is admittedly based on an assertion that the presentation of a petition of the kind sought to be restrained would be an abuse of the process
of the court. Whether this would be so would be the only issue to be determined
in the action. The issues which might arise for decision on the hearing of such a
petition, if Mr de Vries were permitted to present it, would not arise as substantive
issues, and might not arise at all, on the trial of the action. In relation to such a   *j*
petition the action as a whole is in the nature of an interlocutory proceeding.

1   [1894] 2 Ch 349
2   [1975] 1 All ER 504, [1975] AC 396
3   [1975] 1 All ER at 509, [1975] AC 406

If it be asked what legal right the plaintiff company relies on in the second action,
a from a violation of which the plaintiff company is seeking temporary protection
pending the trial of the action, the answer must be, it seems to me, the right not
to be involved in litigation which would constitute an abuse of the process of the
court; but the plaintiff company cannot assert such a right in respect of any particular
anticipated litigation without demonstrating that, at least prima facie, that litigation
would be an abuse.

b If it could now be said that on the available evidence the presentation by Mr de
Vries of such a petition as is described in the injunction would prima facie be an
abuse of process, the plaintiff company might claim to have established a right to
seek interlocutory relief. Otherwise I do not think it can. If it were demonstrated
that such a petition would be bound to fail, it could be said that to present it, or after
presentation to seek to prosecute it, would constitute an abuse: *Charles Forte Invest-*
c *ments Ltd v Amanda*[1]. Two difficulties face the plaintiff company here. First, the
learned judge, rightly in my opinion, said that it was clear that some, if not all,
of the allegations mentioned in his eight heads, if they were to be substantiated,
could lead to a winding-up order. Secondly, counsel for the plaintiff company conceded before the learned judge, as he told us, that Mr de Vries might succeed in
establishing that the presentation of a petition on grounds asserted in the four
d affidavits would not be an abuse of the process of the court. Counsel for the plaintiff
company says that this concession was made for the purposes of the hearing before
the judge only and should not bind him in this court. This is not, in my opinion,
a tenable position. On an interlocutory application a party can, of course, make a
concession limited to the purposes of that application. This is often done where
a party does not wish at an interlocutory stage to incur the expense and delay that
e might attend the investigation of some disputed issue. But such a concession must,
I think, be made for the purposes of that application in its entirety. If the interlocutory order be appealed, the party having made the concession below cannot resile
from it in the appellate court, at any rate without the leave of the court. The primary
function of the appellate court is to decide whether the judge at first instance has
reached the right conclusion on the material before him. This material must include
f any concession made before him. If the appellate court were to be satisfied that the
concession was made as the result of some misunderstanding, or that for some other
reason justice required that the party should be allowed to withdraw it, it might
allow the withdrawal of the concession. Otherwise the concession must hold.
It cannot be equated with the reservation of a point of law for argument in the
appellate court which is not open in the lower court. In the present case counsel
g for the plaintiff company has not asked us to permit him to withdraw his concession,
and, indeed, on the evidence as it stands it seems to me to be almost an inevitable
concession, from which I would in any event be slow to allow him to withdraw.
So we must, in my opinion, proceed on the footing that Mr de Vries might succeed
at the trial of the second action, if it were to come to trial, and that the learned
judge considered that a petition based on the allegations in the four affidavits might
h succeed. On this I agree with the judge, and I would add that, if the Bryston
transaction be also taken into consideration, the possibility of a petition succeeding
is, I think, considerably enhanced.

I consequently reach the conclusion that the supposed petition has not been
shown to be such as would be an abuse on the ground that it could not possibly
succeed.

j I have already dealt with the other suggested grounds for regarding such a petition
as a potential abuse of process, viz the very small size of Mr de Vries's stake in the
company, the antagonisms between himself and Mr Smith, and the possible availability of other more satisfactory remedies. I have also dealt with the possibility of

1 [1963] 2 All ER 940, [1964] 1 Ch 240

the petition being demurrable on the ground that no surplus may be available for
shareholders. No other ground has, I think, been suggested.

In these circumstances, I do not think that it has at present been established that
the plaintiff company is threatened with a petition which will constitute an abuse.
Moreover, until Mr de Vries presents his petition, no one can know precisely what
it will contain.

The learned judge thought that there was certainly a case to be tried in the second
action; that is to say, he thought that if that action was brought to trial the plaintiff
company might win it. Even if this be assumed, I do not think that the company
has, in the particular circumstances of this action and having regard to its particular
character, yet established prima facie that it has the legal right which it is attempting
to protect pending the trial. If the injunction is discharged, it is highly unlikely that
the second action will ever be tried. It would be too late. If the injunction is maintained, the plaintiff company has in effect already obtained the whole relief sought in
the action. In these circumstances, ought Mr de Vries to be restrained?

It has long been recognised that the jurisdiction of the court to stay an action in
limine as an abuse of process is a jurisdiction to be exercised with great circumspection, and exactly the same considerations must apply to a quia timet injunction
to restrain commencement of proceedings. These principles are, in my opinion,
just as applicable to a winding-up petition as to an action. The right to petition the
court for a winding-up order in appropriate circumstances is a right conferred by
statute. A would-be petitioner should not be restrained from exercising it except
on clear and persuasive grounds. I recognise that the presentation of a petition
may do great damage to a company's business and reputation, though I think that
the potential damage in the present case may have been rather exaggerated. The
restraint of a petition may also gravely affect the would-be petitioner, and not only
him, but also others, whether creditors or contributories. If the presentation of the
petition is prevented the commencement of the winding-up will be postponed until
such time as a petition is presented or a winding-up resolution is passed. This is
capable of far-reaching effects.

We have not been invited to substitute for the injunction granted by the learned
judge an injunction restraining advertisement without the leave of the court of any
petition which Mr de Vries may present, which might, it seems to me, have been a
possible via media.

In his speech in the *American Cyanamid* case[1] Lord Diplock recognised that there
might be special factors to be taken into consideration in the particular circumstances of individual cases. In my judgment, the fact that the second action is an
action designed to prevent the commencement of proceedings in limine is such a
special factor. In such a case the court should not, in my judgment, interfere with
what would otherwise be a legitimate approach to the seat of justice unless the
evidence is sufficient to establish prima facie that the plaintiff will succeed in establishing that the proceedings sought to be restrained will constitute an abuse of
process. In the present case, in my opinion, this has not been achieved. I would
consequently allow the appeal in the second action and discharge the injunction of
15th May.

STEPHENSON LJ. I agree with Buckley LJ's judgment, and add my own explanation why I think that the order in the second action was wrong.

There, in my opinion, the judge attempted to do an impossible thing: to decide
on the balance of convenience whether there is an abuse of the process of the court.
He was persuaded to confuse two distinct things: (1) the court's jurisdiction to prevent a would-be litigant from abusing its process; (2) the court's jurisdiction to help a

1   [1975] 1 All ER 504, [1975] AC 396

a would-be litigant by preventing another from taking some action which is alleged to be in violation of the litigant's legal right until the court has decided whether he has that right and whether it has been or will be violated. Completely different considerations apply to the two cases. In the first it is for the plaintiff to prove that the defendant's exercise of his right to bring legal proceedings is in fact an abuse of process; in the second it is for the plaintiff to prove that there is a serious issue to be tried in his action, not the defendant's, and that it is convenient that the court *b* should intervene to restrain the defendant before it is tried.

It is the practice for a company which objects to a shareholder improperly presenting a petition to wind it up to move for an injunction to restrain him. The court's jurisdiction to do so is a facet of its inherent jurisdiction to prevent an abuse of its process: *Charles Forte Investments Ltd v Amanda*[1] and *Mann v Goldstein*[2]. But the method of applying does not transform the substance of the proceeding or the nature *c* of what the applicant has to prove. If he applied to strike out the petition under the inherent jurisdiction, or under RSC Ord 18, r 9(1)(*d*) and (3), he would not be able to rely on anything said by the House of Lords in *American Cyanamid Co v Ethicon Ltd*[3] or on the balance of convenience; nor can he do so because considerations of the irretrievable damage to a company from advertising a baseless petition have led to the practice of applying for an injunction to restrain a would-be petitioner from *d* presenting it.

Counsel for the plaintiff company sought support for the judge's approach and order in the concluding sentence of the judgment of Jessel MR in *Niger Merchants Co v Capper*[4]. He claimed support there for his submission that the injunction he prayed was only interlocutory, that there was a serious issue to be tried after it had been granted or refused, and that at this stage the balance of convenience had there-*e* fore to be considered and the *American Cyanamid* case[1] applied. But the hearing to which the sentence refers was clearly a hearing of conflicting evidence on the question whether Mr Capper did threaten the company with winding-up, which he denied, and that case is no authority for the proposition that a plaintiff company, which moves for an injunction to restrain the presentation of a petition to wind it up as an abuse of the process of the court, can rely on a balance of convenience and reserve *f* its evidence to prove the abuse until the question whether it is an abuse is finally decided at the trial of the action. I agree with Sir John Pennycuick, whose judgment I have had the privilege of reading, that it is finally decided at this stage and there is nothing left to try.

This is not 'an application for an interlocutory injunction to restrain a defendant from doing acts alleged to be in violation of the plaintiff's legal right', but to restrain a *g* defendant from exercising his legal right to present a petition. So Lord Diplock's words in the *American Cyanamid* case[5] which Buckley LJ has quoted do not apply to such an application as this. Their Lordships do not seem to have had this sort of injunction in mind and they cannot have overruled *Forte's* case[1] by implication. *Forte's* case[1] still binds us to hold that unless the plaintiff company can prove that a petition is bound to fail—or perhaps that there is a suitable alternative remedy to a *h* petition—Mr de Vries cannot be restrained, even temporarily, from presenting it. Oliver J has found that it might succeed. Some of Mr de Vries's allegations, if substantiated, could lead the Companies Court to the conclusion that it is just and equitable to wind up the plaintiff company. He did not, and could not, find that there was no evidence to substantiate them. He was prevented from giving the proper effect to that finding by mistakenly applying the *American Cyanamid* case[3]. So he

j

1   [1963] 2 All ER 940, [1964] 1 Ch 240
2   [1968] 2 All ER 769, [1968] 1 WLR 1091
3   [1975] 1 All ER 504, [1975] AC 396
4   (1877) 18 Ch D 557 at 559
5   [1975] 1 All ER at 509, [1975] AC at 406

decided the case on the wrong basis. If he thought that investigation by the Department of Trade and Industry was a suitable alternative remedy, I respectfully disagree. *a*

I agree that the first appeal fails, but the second appeal must be allowed and Mr de Vries allowed to present his petition.

SIR JOHN PENNYCUICK. I agree, for the reasons given by Buckley LJ that the appeal in the first action should be dismissed and that the appeal in the second action *b* should be allowed. I should only like to add certain observations on the decision of the House of Lords in the *American Cyanamid* case[1]. It seems to me that that decision cannot be regarded as applicable to a motion for an injunction restraining the presentation of a threatened winding-up petition on the ground that presentation of the petition would be an abuse of the process of the court.

The issue between the intending petitioner and the company which would arise on *c* presentation of the petition is whether or not the company shall be compulsorily wound up. The motion seeks a summary order restraining the petitioner from starting the process which would raise this issue for litigation in the Companies Court. The order sought on the motion, if made, will from its very nature conclude once and for all, so far of course as concerns the ground on which the petition is based, the summary issue raised by the motion; that is to say, the petitioner is either *d* free to present his petition or he is prohibited from doing so. It is no doubt procedurally necessary under the present practice to bring the application for an injunction before the court by way of motion in an action commenced by writ seeking the same relief, the order sought on the motion being expressed in interlocutory form. But whether the application succeeds or fails, the order on it is the end of the action. The only issue in the action has been determined once and for all on the motion, *e* and there can be no question of the action itself being brought on for a hearing at some later date on the same issue. The motion of a full hearing with oral examination and cross-examination of an application to stop proceedings in limine is altogether at variance with the principles on which the court acts.

The decision in the *American Cyanamid* case[1] was, as I understand it, addressed to interlocutory motions in the sense of motions seeking interim relief pending *f* determination of the rights of the parties at the hearing of the action: cf per Lord Diplock[2]:

'The grant of an interlocutory injunction is a remedy that is both temporary and discretionary. When an application for an interlocutory injunction to restrain a defendant from doing acts alleged to be in violation of the plaintiff's legal right is made on contested facts, the decision whether or not to grant an *g* interlocutory injunction has to be taken at a time when ex hypothesi the existence of the right or the violation of it, or both, is uncertain and will remain uncertain until final judgment is given in the action.'

I do not think the decision should be read as applicable to motions which, though interlocutory in form, seek relief which will finally determine the issue in the action, *h* and more particularly motions seeking to stop proceedings in limine. I appreciate the wide words used by Lord Diplock[2]: 'In my view the grant of interlocutory injunctions in actions for infringement of patents is governed by the same principles as in other actions.' But these words must be read in their context, and I am sure Lord Diplock was not intending to say that the principles were applicable in a class of case not under consideration in which their application would be entirely *j* inappropriate.

I should like to add that where a company seeks relief of this kind the procedure

---

1 [1975] 1 All ER 504, [1975] AC 396
2 [1975] 1 All ER at 508, 509, [1975] AC at 406

a   by way of writ claiming an injunction to restrain presentation of a petition, followed immediately by a motion expressed to claim an interlocutory injunction in the same terms, appears clumsy and inapposite. It occurs to me that it should be possible to devise some more apt form of procedure, for instance, an originating motion in the Companies Court.

b   *Appeal against order dated 30th April dismissed; appeal against order dated 15th May allowed. Leave to appeal to the House of Lords refused.*

Solicitors: *Peter Mallack & Co* (for the plaintiff company).

A S Virdi Esq Barrister.

c

Daymond v South West Water Authority

d   HOUSE OF LORDS

LORD WILBERFORCE, VISCOUNT DILHORNE, LORD DIPLOCK, LORD KILBRANDON AND LORD EDMUND-DAVIES

20th, 21st, 22nd OCTOBER, 3rd DECEMBER 1975

e   *Water supply – Charges – Power of water authority to make charges – Charges for services performed – Liability of person who has not received services – Power of water authority to make such charges for services performed, facilities provided or rights made available by them as they think fit – Sewerage services – Occupier of house – House not connected to public sewers – Occupier not receiving sewerage services – Whether water authority having power to impose charge on occupier for sewerage services provided by the authority in their area – Water Act 1973, s 30(1).*

f   The plaintiff was the owner and occupier of a house situated in the areas of the first defendant, the local authority, and the second defendant, the water authority constituted under the Water Act 1973. The plaintiff's house was not connected to the public sewers. He received from the local authority rate demands payable on 26th April 1974 and 26th July 1974 each of which included demands for sewerage charges. *g*   Those demands were made in accordance with the Water Authorities (Collection of Charges) Order 1974[a], Part III. The plaintiff brought an action against the defendants seeking a declaration that the demands had been made without authority and were unlawful. The judge granted the declaration sought and the water authority appealed, contending (i) that s 30(1)[b] of the 1973 Act conferred on water authorities a general power to impose such charges for the services which they performed as *h*   they thought fit, and (ii) alternatively that the 1974 order had been validly made by the Secretary of State under the power conferred on him by s 254(1)[c] of the Local Government Act 1972, as applied and modified by s 34(1)[d] of, and para 5(2)(c)[e] of

---

  a SI 1974 No 448
  b Section 30, so far as material, is set out at p 43 *c* to *g*, post
j *c* Section 254(1), so far as material, is set out at p 52 *a* and *b*, post
  d Section 34(1), so far as material, provides: 'The following provisions of the [Local Government Act 1972], that is to say—section 254 (consequential orders, etc) . . . shall apply for the purposes of this Act as they apply for the purposes of that Act or, as the case may be, Part IV of that Act, but subject to the exceptions and modifications contained in Part I of Schedule 6 to this Act.'
  e Paragraph 5(2), so far as material, is set out at p 52 *c* and *d*, post

Sch 6 to, the 1973 Act, to make incidental, consequential, transitional or supplementary provisions for the calculation, collection and recovery on behalf of a water   *a*
authority by a local authority, during a transitional period, of charges in respect of
services provided by the water authority in the local authority's area.

Held (Lord Wilberforce and Lord Diplock dissenting) – In the absence of any express
provision as to who was liable to be charged, the natural inference to be drawn from
s 30(1) of the 1973 Act was that a water authority was empowered to charge only   *b*
those persons who actually availed themselves of the services, facilities and rights
provided by the authority. It followed that s 30(1) did not empower a water authority
to require payment of sewerage charges from persons whose premises were not
connected to public sewers. Furthermore para 5(2)(c) of Sch 6 to the 1973 Act did not
extend, or purport to extend, the categories of persons liable to be charged by a
water authority beyond those to whom s 30 applied and in any event, insofar as the   *c*
1974 order sought to impose such charges on such persons, it could not be said to be
incidental to, consequential on or supplementary to, the 1973 Act; nor did the 1974
order purport to be transitional. Consequently the 1974 order was ultra vires to the
extent that it authorised the recovery of sewerage charges from persons whose premises were not connected to public sewers. The appeal would therefore be dismissed
(see p 50 *a* to *j*, p 51 *g* to *j*, p 52 *j*, p 53 *b* to *j*, p 54 *b*, p 58 *a* and *b*, p 59 *j* to p 60 *a*, p 62 *g*   *d*
and p 64 *a* to *d*, post).
    Decision of Phillips J sub nom *Daymond v Plymouth City Council* [1975] 3 All ER
134 affirmed.

Notes

For the power of water authorities to make charges for services provided, see Supplement to 39 Halsbury's Laws (3rd Edn) para 918A, 6.   *e*
    For the Local Government Act 1972, s 254, see 42 Halsbury's Statutes (3rd Edn) 1078.
    For the Water Act 1973, ss 30, 34, Sch 6, para 5, see 43 Halsbury's Statutes (3rd
Edn) 1857, 1862, 1901.

Cases referred to in opinions

Black-Clawson International Ltd v Papierwerke Waldhof-Aschaffenburg AG [1975] 1 All   *f*
    ER 810, [1975] 2 WLR 513, HL.
Dockers' Labour Club and Institute Ltd v Race Relations Board [1974] 3 All ER 592, [1974]
    3 WLR 533, HL.
Dorling v The Local Board of Health for the District of Epsom (1855) 5 E & B 471.
Hammersmith Bridge Co v Hammersmith Overseers (1871) LR 6 QB 230, 40 LJMC 79, 24
    LT 267, 35 JP 518, 41 Digest (Repl) 65, 416.   *g*
Institute of Patent Agents v Lockwood [1894] AC 347, 63 LJPC 74, 71 LT 205, 6 R 219, HL.
Partington v Attorney-General (1869) LR 4 HL 100, 38 LJEx 205, 21 LT 370, HL; *affg* SC
    sub nom *Attorney-General v Partington* (1864) 3 H & C 193 Ex Ch, 44 Digest (Repl)
    333, 1675.
Soady v Wilson (1835) 3 Ad & El 248, 4 Nev & MKB 777, 111 ER 407, 41 Digest (Repl)
    65, 415.   *h*

Appeal

By a specially endorsed writ issued on 18th October 1974, as subsequently amended
and re-amended, the plaintiff, Philip Arthur John Daymond ('the ratepayer'), brought
an action against the defendants, Plymouth City Council ('the rating authority') and
the South West Water Authority ('the water authority'), alleging that the rating   *j*
authority had served on him rate demands payable on 26th April 1974 and 26th
July 1974 which in each case included, in addition to the amounts payable for the
general rate and water charges, a sum described in the demand as 'sewerage etc.
charge'. Those sums, amounting to £4·89, were demanded by the rating authority
from the ratepayer in pursuance of a notice issued to them by the water authority

a by virtue of art 7 of the Water Authorities (Collection of Charges) Order 1974[1], and in accordance with the order, in respect of services (other than the supply of water) provided by the water authority. The ratepayer claimed a declaration that the rating authority 'are not empowered lawfully to demand from him the sum of £4·89 or any sum on behalf of the [water authority] by way of a "sewerage etc. charge"'. By an order made on 5th May 1975, and dated and entered on 28th May, Phillips J[2] granted a declaration that the rating authority were not empowered b 'lawfully to demand from the [ratepayer] any sum in respect of sewerage or sewage disposal services on behalf of the [water authority]'. The water authority appealed to the House of Lords against that order pursuant to a certificate under s 12(2)(a) of the Administration of Justice Act 1969. The facts are set out in the opinion of Lord Wilberforce.

c *David Widdicombe QC, Michael Mann QC* and *Michael Harrison* for the water authority. *David Kemp QC* and *Anthony Guest* for the ratepayer.

Their Lordships took time for consideration.

d 3rd December. The following opinions were delivered.

LORD WILBERFORCE. My Lords, the question which we have to decide is whether an occupier of a hereditament not connected to a public sewer can be charged by a water authority for sewerage and sewage disposal services. The ratepayer is the owner and occupier of such a hereditament, namely a dwellinghouse at Plym-e stock, Devon, within the area of the South West Water Authority. His house is 400 yards from the nearest public sewer and is not connected to it. But the water authority has demanded from him as a 'general services charge' £2·45 payable on 26th April 1974 and £2·44 payable on 26th July 1974. It is accepted that about 95 per cent of these sums represents charges for sewerage and sewage disposal, the remainder for pollution prevention, fisheries and recreation.

f There are a great number of hereditaments in the country which are not connected to public sewers, so that this case is of general importance. We were informed that the amounts claimed add up to some £30 million in a year. And the consequence must be, if the ratepayer's contention is right, that this sum must be collected from other persons in each area, including occupiers of connected hereditaments, in addition to the charges which have already been demanded of them.

g The Act which now deals with sewerage and sewage disposal is the Water Act 1973. This is a comprehensive piece of legislation which brings together in one statute a number of subjects previously dealt with separately, and which sets up new water authorities with comprehensive powers in relation to all these subjects. Thus the Act deals with water supply, water resources, land drainage, prevention of pollution, fisheries, recreation and, of course, sewerage and sewage disposal. The new water h authorities took over powers previously vested in river authorities, and local authorities: as regards sewerage and sewage disposal, they took over powers previously vested in local authorities, and certain other bodies. Some of the previous legislation remains in force but it is not necessary to enter into greater detail.

Totally new powers of making charges were introduced. Under the pre-existing legislation there were various methods. Charges in respect of sewerage and sewage j disposal were made through the general rate, or in the case of trade effluents, through trade effluent charges. Charges in respect of the other matters were made either through a special rate, eg water rates for domestic supply, or by the use of water

---

1 SI 1974 No 448
2 [1975] 3 All ER 134

meters for commercial and industrial premises, or by direct charges or licence fees,
eg for abstraction, or fishing or recreation, or by precepts on local authorities which *a*
then recovered them through the rates.

In replacement of these complicated provisions the Water Act 1973 conferred on
the new water authorities a general power expressed in general words:

'30.—(1) Subject to the provisions of this Act, a water authority shall have
power to fix, and to demand, take and recover such charges for the services *b*
performed, facilities provided or rights made available by them (including
separate charges for separate services, facilities or rights or combined charges
for a number of services, facilities or rights) as they think fit . . .'

I shall deal with the rest of this section later, but it is necessary at once to appreciate
that this provision was clearly meant to be a flexible one capable of adaptation to the
various subjects dealt with by the Act, and of use in different ways. The first assump- *c*
tion one would make about its ambit was that it was intended to make permissible
all or any of the methods of charging previously used, and conversely that it was not
intended to prohibit well known and well tried methods of charging available in the
past, at least in the absence of some clear indication.

The actual charge on the ratepayer appears to have been made under a statutory
instrument, the Water Authorities (Collection of Charges) Order 1974[1], made on *d*
13th March 1974 and coming into operation on 27th March 1974 which purports to
have been made under a complicated chain of provisions adapted from the Local
Government Act 1972 (Local Government Act 1972, s 254(1)(*a*), as applied by the
Water Act 1973, s 34(1) and Sch 6, para 5(2)(*c*)). This order enabled the water authority
to issue a general services notice to the Plymouth City Council, as a rating authority
within the water authority's area, requiring the council to collect the amount of the *e*
general services on behalf of the water authority. The general services charge was
to cover all services provided other than the supply of water. It was to be collected
in the form of a poundage on the rateable value of each hereditament in the rating
area from every person liable to pay the general rate, ie from the occupier, and no
exemption or reduction was allowable on account of the fact that the hereditament
concerned might not be connected to a public sewer. This order only applied to the *f*
year commencing on 1st April 1974.

It is interesting to note that in a fresh statutory instrument made in respect of the
year beginning 1st April 1975[2], provision was made for a remission of 50 per cent
in favour of hereditaments not drained into a public sewer. This has, however, no
bearing on the present appeal.

The present proceedings took the form of an action by the ratepayer in the Queen's *g*
Bench Division for a declaration that there is no power lawfully to demand the sums
in question or any sums by way of a 'sewerage, etc charge'. This was tried by Phillips
J[3] who on 28th May 1975 granted the declaration asked. The parties then made use
of the Administration of Justice Act 1969, s 12, so as to bring the appeal directly to
this House. The rating authority, being merely agents for the water authority, have
not taken any part in the appeal. *h*

I must comment on one other matter which has caused some difficulty. When
the case was before Phillips J it seems to have been agreed between the parties that
the principal section in the Water Act 1973—s 30—under which charges may be made
for services performed, required that the person to be charged should be actually in
receipt of the services. The learned judge accepted this, and in his judgment expressed
the opinion that it was correct. From that it seemed to him to follow that the *j*
demands could not be justified under s 30, presumably on the ground that the ratepayer was not in receipt of the services. He then considered an alternative submission

---

1   SI 1974 No 448
2   Water Authorities (Collection of Charges) Order 1975 (SI 1975 No 396)
3   [1975] 3 All ER 134, [1975] 3 WLR 50

based on the 1974 order which on the face of it clearly authorises the demand. But
a in a careful and closely reasoned judgment he held that this statutory instrument
was ultra vires. The water authority in the first instance appealed against this decision,
but at a later stage they challenged the original assumption that the charge could
not be made under s 30, and indeed the main weight of their argument was based
on this section. This House, taking the view that it was the duty of the House to
state the true meaning of an Act of Parliament, especially one which affects many
b other people, whatever the parties may have agreed, allowed this course to be taken.
I have to draw attention to the difficulties which may be caused, especially in cases
intended to be handled under the Administration of Justice Act 1969, through
premature agreement as to points of law.

I now come to the substance of the appeal which, in the first instance, relates to the
question whether these charges may be made under the Water Act 1973, s 30. I set
c out the most material subsections ((1)-(6)):

> '(1) Subject to the provisions of this Act, a water authority shall have power to
> fix, and to demand, take and recover such charges for the services performed,
> facilities provided or rights made available by them (including separate charges
> for separate services, facilities or rights or combined charges for a number of
d> services, facilities or rights) as they think fit.
> '(2) A water authority may fix any of their charges by means of a scheme under
> section 31 below or by agreement with any person.
> '(3) Subject to subsections (4) to (6) below, a water authority may fix their
> charges by references to such criteria, and may adopt such system for the
> calculation of their amount, as appears to them to be appropriate.
e> '(4) In fixing charges for services, facilities or rights a water authority shall have
> regard to the cost of performing those services, providing those facilities or
> making available those rights.
> '(5) A water authority may make different charges for the same service, facility
> or right in different cases, but it shall be the duty of every water authority to
> take such steps as will ensure that, as from a date not later than 1st April 1981,
f> their charges are such as not to show undue preference to, or discriminate unduly
> against, any class of persons.
> '(6) The Secretary of State may, after consultation with the [National Water
> Council], give all or any of the water authorities directions as to the criteria to be
> applied or the system to be adopted by them under subsection (3) above and in
> giving a direction under this subsection the Secretary of State shall have regard to
g> the provisions of subsections (4) and (5) above.'

On the face of it this is a very wide section—there could hardly be a wider power
than that given by the words 'as they think fit'. The only apparent limitations are
(i) that contained in sub-s (4), by which regard must be had to the cost of performing
the services etc, (ii) the direction not, after 1st April 1981, to show any undue preference or discrimination, (iii) the power of the Secretary of State, after consultation
h with the National Water Council, to give directions as to criteria or system. But
broadly the power to fix charges is unlimited; it is certainly not defined. Although
I can understand the advantage of having a flexible power, for the reasons I have
explained, it remains, to me, surprising that Parliament could have passed so vague
a provision. It is indeed this extreme width of discretion which exposes the water
authorities to attack. Surely, it is claimed, it cannot have been intended that these
j new bodies—not directly elected, though containing persons elected to other bodies
—should have so wide a power as to impose what is in effect taxation, one committing
to these new bodies not only wide, and loosely controlled, powers to fix the amount
of the taxation, but the power to decide who is to be taxed.

My Lords, I think that if we can fairly find some limitation in the words used
which will bring them within the limits of constitutional propriety, we should do so,

and I do not think that there is much difficulty in this task. The words 'services performed, facilities provided or rights made available' themselves point the way *a* clearly enough so as to limit the persons liable to pay the charges to those for whom the services are performed, to whom the facilities are provided, for whom the rights are available. Such a limitation is consistent with other provisions in this part of the Act. Under s 30(2) charges may be fixed by a scheme under s 31 or by agreement with any person. Section 31 is drafted in similar language to that used in s 30 and in sub-s (2) uses the words 'the charges to be paid to an authority for any services, *b* facilities or rights' suggests that the persons to pay shall be those who benefit. Conversely there is nothing in s 30 which clearly points to a wider class of persons who may be liable—and I need not emphasise that in taxation matters clear words are needed to bring persons within taxation's reach. Subsection (3) refers to 'criteria' and 'system', but these references relate in terms to the fixing and calculation of charges and not to the selection of the persons who are to pay; sub-s (5) refers to undue *c* preference or undue discrimination, but this can be read with reference to the relative burdens to be imposed on chargeable persons; sub-s (6) gives powers to the Secretary of State to give directions to water authorities but again this refers to 'criteria' and 'system'. So I agree, so far, with the learned judge and with the ratepayer as to the necessity for limitation to be placed on s 30(1), and as to the nature of that limitation. *d*

The next question is to ask whether this leads to the conclusion which the learned judge accepted, and which is now urged by the ratepayer, that the ratepayer is not liable to the sewerage element in the general services charge. In my opinion it is at this point that the ratepayer's argument breaks down. For, in order to succeed in his claim for exemption, he must show that in respect of sewerage the water authority's services are performed for a class of persons in which he is not included. *e* But this contention, as I shall show, runs counter to over 100 years of practice and of authority. The clear fallacy in the argument lies in the supposition that the services performed by the water authority in respect of sewerage consist and consist only of draining individual premises through connection with a public sewer. In fact this is only one element in the matter. The main scope of the water authority's statutory responsibilities as regards sewerage and sewage disposal is stated in s 14. The relevant *f* part reads:

'(1) It shall be the duty of every water authority to provide, either inside or outside their area, such public sewers as may be necessary *for effectually draining their area* and to make such provision, whether inside or outside their area, by means of sewage disposal works or otherwise, as may be necessary for effectually *g* dealing with the contents of their sewers . . .'

Sewerage, and consequently sewage disposal, is clearly here regarded as something relating to, and benefiting, the area of the authority—the whole area. The right of an individual owner or occupier of premises to have his drains discharge into a public sewer is only a part, no doubt to him an important part, of the benefit which is derived from the performance of the services. The public sewers serve also for the *h* reception and drainage of surface water, so preventing flooding and possibly disease, and by reception and disposal of foul water serve to make the area as a whole more salubrious and pleasant to live in. Is it suggested that the ratepayer should be exempt from charges in respect of these services? A positive answer produces a reductio ad absurdum; and a negative answer, since it allows the ratepayer to be within the charge, reduces his claim to one based on criterion. But the water authority has *j* power to determine criteria.

It is for reasons such as these—briefly described and subject to numerous qualifications—that sewerage has for over 100 years been charged through the rates as a public health matter and as something of general, as well as a particular, benefit or, to use the words of the General Rate Act 1967, as a 'local purposes of a public nature' (s 1(2)).

This wording 'local purposes of a public nature' embraces of course a wide range
a of services, or facilities, performed or provided by local authorities as to which it is
thought right that the charge for them should be borne through the rating system by
ratepayers and as to which an objection by an individual ratepayer that he gets no
personal or specific benefit from it, though commonly made and understandable
enough, is not consistent with the system. You cannot object to pay rates because
you are childless or because your street is unlit or because your street gets flooded
b when it rains. The present case, and one can think of others, has the feature that,
side by side with benefits of a general character, which all hereditaments in the area
are presumed to enjoy, there are also particular benefits (i e discharge of private drains
into a public sewer) which are enjoyed by some and not others. This may be a ground
for a rebate or remission for those not so connected which the authority may grant
under its powers to fix charges by criteria (s 30(3)); it cannot take the service out of
c the section altogether. Nor can one sever the 'personal' from the 'general' element
so as to say that as no services are performed for the former, no charge can be made
for it. The service here is for sewerage: there is no warrant for splitting it into separate
elements.

My Lords, this view of the matter fits in with other provisions of this Act. There
is no difficulty as regards water supply since charges are inevitably made on con-
d sumers. But the water authorities also have power to spend money on pollution
prevention, fisheries and recreation. Some of this expenditure may admit of direct
charges on consumers, eg for fishing on reservoirs or use of other recreational facilities,
but the rest of it, and in the case of pollution the whole of it, can properly be regarded
as expenditure for the general benefit or for a purpose of a public nature. If the
ratepayer is right, there seems to be no basis on which charges for pollution preven-
e tion or in respect of fisheries and recreation can be made unless a direct 'benefit' to
the hereditament in question can be shown. But this is to reverse many years of
recognition of the public benefit derived from these matters and of the rightness of
charging for them through the rates. The percentage of the ratepayer's charge related
to these matters (five per cent or so) may be small but I have heard no answer to the
question why, if his contention as to sewerage is right, it does not involve exemption
f from this other element too.

The conception of 'public benefit' as a basis for a general charge is, of course, not
my own. It has been recognised by eminent judges, in well-known reported cases.
Soady v Wilson[1] was actually a case concerned with sewerage—the question being
whether the occupier of Somerset House, London, could be made to pay a sewerage
rate in respect of a sewer under the house, which he did not use, the house being
g effectively drained through another sewer into the Thames. But it was held that
direct benefit was not the test of liability for the rate. Lord Denman CJ[2] said that
the doctrine laid down in earlier cases was uniform and undisputed.

'It rests on the principle, that every one whose property derives benefit from
the works of the Commissioners may be assessed to the rates they impose. The
h benefit is not required to be immediate, nor do the cases . . . or the statutes,
say any thing of the nature or amount of the benefit. Possibly that benefit may
be so extremely small, that a jury would not have found the fact stated in the
case. But, on the other hand, the kind of benefit may be of high value, as if a
house were inaccessible, because surrounded by marshes, and the works of
sewage had made them hard and passable . . .'

j Just as well known is the case of the Grand Stand of Epson racecourse which had
no need of any sewerage service, having its own, and being much higher than the
town. But it was held liable to a rate for, inter alia, sewerage both on principle and

1   (1835) 3 Ad & El 248
2   3 Ad & El at 263

on the statutory words 'for the benefit of any district or part of a district'—a clear
parallel to which is s 14 in the Water Act 1973: *Dorling v Epsom Local Board of Health*[1]. *a*
I do not know on what basis these cases can be explained away.

So it is clear that if the words to be read into s 30(1) are 'for whose benefit the
services are performed' the proposed charge must be valid, unless we are to discard
the law and practice of 100 years. And, on the same principle, why should we read
into the section such words as 'for whose direct and immediate benefit the services
are performed' which would be necessary if the ratepayer is to succeed, when 'direct *b*
and immediate benefit' has never been the test of rateability? Finally if, rejecting
any qualification we read the section literally as it is, the charge is justified by the
words 'as they think fit'.

I am therefore of opinion that sewerage and sewage disposal services, having been
long recognised as services performed for the benefit of the area, generally, to which
they relate, may be recovered from all persons in the area deemed to benefit from *c*
them, and that a permissible system of recovery is to recover them through the
rating machinery from ratepayers generally.

There is one particular argument which I must mention. Section 16 of the Water
Act 1973 provides that owners or occupiers may in certain circumstances require the
water authority to provide a public sewer to be used for domestic purposes for the
drainage of their premises, subject to their paying certain charges specified in the *d*
section. It is said that this provision is inconsistent with an interpretation of s 30(1)
according to which such occupiers would have to pay sewerage charges while unconnected and indeed that s 16 cannot be operated at all, in respect of existing premises,
if that interpretation is applied.

My Lords, the relation between the two sections is not entirely easy to see, and
it may be that s 16, the conception of which seems to have been drawn from enact- *e*
ments relating to water supply, is not very aptly designed for its purpose. But in my
opinion, the section cannot be used to limit the meaning of s 30. In the first place
s 30 is a general provision, not limited to sewerage, but applying to all the matters
dealt with by the Act. I fail to see how a particular section related only to one of
these matters can affect—and limit—the meaning of a section of general application.
Secondly such inconsistency as there may be is not between s 16 and s 30(1), inter- *f*
preted as I would interpret it, but between s 16 and certain possible methods of
operating s 30(1). If that is correct, there may be a need for some adjustment in
certain cases of the charging system. The supposed inconsistency is not an argument
against the interpretation which I would favour of s 30(1) itself. If this brief argument
seems too simple, the fuller analysis of the section by my noble and learned friend,
Lord Diplock, supplies—to my mind—an unanswerable substitute. *g*

My Lords, on the view which I take of s 30(1)—that it authorises a general services
charge to be made on all rateable hereditaments, there is no ground for contending
that the 1974 order which lays down the detailed method of operating the charge is
invalid. In my opinion the 1974 charges were validly made.

I would allow the appeal.

h

VISCOUNT DILHORNE. My Lords, the amount involved in this appeal is
less than £4·89 but we were told that this is a test case and that the total sum involved
is of the order of £33,000,000 a year. The ratepayer contends that, as his house at
Plymstock is not connected with public sewers of the water authority, no payment
for sewerage can lawfully be demanded of him by them. If he is right, it will follow *j*
that no other householder in the country will, if his house is not connected to public
sewers, be liable to pay sewerage charges and £33,000,000 or so more will have to
be paid by those whose houses are so connected. If he is wrong, householders whose

1 (1855) 5 E & B 471

houses are not so connected will have to pay for sewerage, whether or not they
a already have an efficient sewerage and sewage disposal system installed at their own
expense, and for the year 1974-75 they will have to pay on the same basis as those
whose houses are so connected, though for the year 1975-76 and subsequent years the
Water Authorities (Collection of Charges) Order 1975[1], which does not affect this
case, makes it possible for those whose premises are not so connected to pay only half
the amount they would have to pay if their premises were connected.

b   On 29th January 1974 the Department of the Environment sent out a circular to
rating authorities telling them, inter alia, that to raise the sum demanded by water
authorities for sewerage and services other than the supply of water, they should
estimate the poundage of a charge which, levied on the whole rateable values
ascribed in the valuation list to *all* hereditaments in respect of which there was
liability to pay the general rate, would produce that amount. No account was to be
c taken of hereditaments exempt from general rate nor was any relief to be given on
account of charitable occupation or poverty, though the rating authority were told
that they could regard the sewerage charge as irrecoverable where they or the
justices had remitted the rate.

The department were thus directing rating authorities to treat hereditaments not
connected with public sewers in the same way as those which were and to make the
d occupiers of unconnected premises pay as if they were connected.

Pursuant to this circular, on 13th February 1974 the water authority notified the
Plymouth City Council that they required the payment of £751,578 for sewerage
and services other than water supply and consequently the council demanded
payment of £4·89 from the ratepayer.

On 27th March 1974 the Water Authorities (Collection of Charges) Order 1974
e made on 13th March came into operation. Article 8(1) provided that where a rating
authority received a general services notice from a water authority, they should be
under a duty to collect and recover, in accordance with the provision of the notice
and of the order, the general services charge. Article 8(2) provided that notice issued
before the coming into operation of the order in terms which complied with art 7(1)
to (3) thereof should be treated as a general services notice duly issued for the
f purposes of the order.

The notice given by the water authority complied with the terms of art 7 and has
therefore to be treated as having been duly issued under the order. Article 7(1)
provides that a water authority may issue a notice requiring a rating authority—

'to collect and recover on behalf of the water authority amounts payable to
the water authority in respect of services (other than the supply of water)
g   provided by the water authority . . .'

and art 7(2) provides that such a notice 'shall authorise the rating authority to demand
and collect the said amounts by means of a charge (in this order referred to as "a
general services charge")' which by art 9(2) is to be a charge at a uniform amount per
pound 'on the rateable value of each hereditament in the rating area of the rating
h authority . . .' Article 10(1), which is under the heading of 'Collection of General
Services Charge', states that 'the rating authority shall collect the general services
charge from every person who is liable to pay the general rate in respect of a
hereditament . . .'

So if the order is valid, the amount for sewerage which the ratepayer was asked to
pay must be paid by him. He, however, contends that the order was ultra vires and
j so of no effect. It is said that to charge every hereditament, whether or not connected
with a public sewer, is not sanctioned by the Water Act 1973 and that the Secretary
of State for the Environment and the Secretary of State for Wales had no power by
order to impose a charge for sewerage which the Act did not permit.

Before examining the statutory provisions under which this order was made, I

1 SI 1975 No 396

propose to consider the provisions of the Act which it is said do not permit such a
charge being made. Sewerage and sewage disposal prior to the enactment of the   *a*
Water Act 1973 had been for many, many years the responsibility of local authorities
and they recovered the cost by including charges for sewerage and sewage disposal
in the general rate demand so that for years the occupiers of premises not connected
with public sewers paid their share of the cost of sewerage in the local authority's
area.

The long title to that Act shows that it was intended to—   *b*

'make provision for a national policy for water, for the conferring and discharge
of functions as to water (including sewerage and sewage disposal, fisheries and
land drainage) and as to recreation and amenity in connection with water, for
the making of charges by water authorities and other statutory water
undertakers, and for connected purposes.'   *c*

It is convenient now to refer to an argument advanced on behalf of the ratepayer.
It was contended that the reference in the long title to the making of charges signified
that the method of charging was under the Act to be different from what it had been
before. In my opinion the long titles of other Acts dealing with other matters are
of no relevance to the question to be decided in this appeal and the reference in the
long title of the 1973 Act to the making of charges throws no light on what charges   *d*
a water authority can lawfully impose under that Act. It would have been surprising
to me if the long title had made no reference to the giving of power to these new
authorities to charge for their services.

The Act imposes many duties on the authorities. They have to take over the
functions of river authorities (s 9). It is their duty to take such action as may be
necessary or expedient, or as they may be directed, to conserve, redistribute or   *e*
augment water resources (s 10). They are also under a duty to supply water within
their respective areas and s 14(1) is in the following terms:

'It shall be the duty of every water authority to provide, either inside or
outside their area, such public sewers as may be necessary for effectually draining
their area and to make such provision, whether inside or outside their area, by   *f*
means of sewage disposal works or otherwise, as may be necessary for effectually
dealing with the contents of their sewers . . .'

They are also under the duty to maintain, improve and develop the salmon
fisheries, trout fisheries, freshwater fisheries and eel fisheries in their areas (s 18); to
exercise a general supervision over all matters relating to land drainage (s 19); and
to take such steps as are reasonably practicable for putting their rights as to the use   *g*
of water and of any land associated with it to the best use for the purposes of
recreation (s 20).

In the discharge of these duties they have very considerable freedom of action.
They must comply with such directions of a general character as may be given to
them with regard to fisheries and land drainage by the Minister of Agriculture,
Fisheries and Food and as to their other functions by the Secretary of State (s 5) and   *h*
they have to submit programmes of a general nature for the discharge of their
functions over a period of years for the approval of the appropriate Minister. They
must carry out any project involving substantial outlay on capital account in accordance with an approved programme (s 24). The majority of the members of each
authority are appointed by local authorities, the remainder being appointed by the
Secretary of State and the Minister. They are not directly responsible to any body   *j*
of electors and, subject to any such directions and conformity with an approved
programme, they decide how much should be spent in each year on the discharge
of their functions.

It is against this background that the financial provisions of the Water Act 1973
have to be considered. Each water authority must so discharge its functions as to

a secure that, taking one year with another, its revenue is not less than sufficient to meet its total outgoings properly chargeable to revenue account (s 29(1)).

Sections 30, 31 and 32 are the charging sections in Part III of the 1973 Act. Section 31 deals with charges under schemes and s 32 with charges made by reference to the volume of water supplied or effluent discharged, measured by meters.

Section 30 is a vital one in this appeal. It is in the following terms:

b '(1) Subject to the provisions of this Act, a water authority shall have power to fix, and to demand, take and recover such charges for the services performed, facilities provided or rights made available by them (including separate charges for separate services, facilities or rights or combined charges for a number of services, facilities or rights) as they think fit.

'(2) A water authority may fix any of their charges by means of a scheme c under section 31 below or by agreement with any person.

'(3) Subject to subsections (4) to (6) below, a water authority may fix their charges by reference to such criteria, and may adopt such system for the calculation of their amount, as appears to them to be appropriate.

'(4) In fixing charges for services, facilities or rights a water authority shall have regard to the cost of performing those services, providing those facilities or d making available those rights.

'(5) A water authority may make different charges for the same service, facility or right in different cases, but it shall be the duty of every water authority to take such steps as will ensure that, as from a date not later than 1st April 1981, their charges are such as not to show undue preference to, or discriminate unduly against, any class of persons.

e '(6) The Secretary of State may, after consultation with the [National Water Council], give all or any of the water authorities directions as to the criteria to be applied or the system to be adopted by them under subsection (3) above . . .

'(7) . . .
'(8) . . .
'(9) . . .
f '(10) . . .'

This section is silent as to the persons from whom water authorities can obtain payment of their charges. I find this most astonishing. The Act defines their duties and they have to secure that, taking one year with another, their revenue is sufficient to meet their outgoings chargeable to revenue account (s 29). Yet the section does g not either state who can be charged or who cannot be charged. Section 30(1) gives them power to fix their charges 'as they think fit' and sub-s (3) makes it clear that, subject to any directions they may be given by the Secretary of State, they may fix them by reference to such criteria and by the adoption of such a system of calculation of their amount as appears to them appropriate. Subsection (3) and this part of sub-s (1) clearly only relate to the determination of the amount of the charge and h not of the persons who can be required to pay. It is clear that a water authority can charge, if they wish, according to the use made of the services they perform, the facilities they provide and the rights made available. Sections 16 and 32 recognise this. They can also fix a charge according to the rateable value of premises.

Subsection (1) goes on to provide that they may 'demand, take and recover such charges . . . as they think fit'. Why it did not state from whom they could do so, j I do not know. The omission may have led to the question whether they could lawfully charge persons who did not avail themselves of the services, facilities or rights, escaping the attention of Parliament. I would not like to think that the omission was deliberate in order to avoid controversy during the passage of the bill through Parliament, though if Parliament had considered the question now to be determined, I would have expected the section to make its conclusion clear.

Our task is nevertheless to seek to ascertain from the language of the Act what was the intention of Parliament and to give effect to it. It is a difficult one and not *a* surprisingly has led to a difference of judicial opinion.

In the absence of any express provision, the determination of the question in issue must depend on what inferences can properly be drawn. Section 30 must have been intended to entitle water authorities to demand, take and recover their charges from some persons and classes of persons. Is it to be inferred that it was the intention of Parliament that they should be at liberty to charge anyone they thought fit in *b* Great Britain? That has only to be stated to be rejected for it is, to my mind, inconceivable that Parliament should have intended to entrust such an extensive power of taxation to a non-elected body. Is it then to be inferred that it was intended to give them only power to charge those living in their area and those who came into it and made use of their services, facilities and rights? I think that such a limitation must be implied.   *c*

If that is to be inferred, is it also to be inferred that they are completely at liberty to charge such of those persons as they think fit? In demanding, taking and recovering their charges, they are not subject to the Secretary of State's directions for sub-s (6) only applies in relation to the fixing of charges.

The natural inference to be drawn from a provision which only says that a statutory body can demand, take and recover such charges for the services it performs, the *d* facilities it provides and for the rights it makes available, as it thinks fit, is in my opinion that it can charge only those who avail themselves of its services, facilities and rights.

It was argued that if it had been the intention of Parliament that water authorities should not be entitled to do what local authorities had power to do and had done for many years, namely, to charge for sewerage as part of the general rate all occupiers liable to pay that rate, Parliament would have said so. In my opinion this is a wrong *e* approach for it is not to be assumed that in the absence of a contrary indication a new statutory body inherits the powers of its predecessors. Its powers are governed by and contained in the provisions of the Act under which it is established and it is to that Act that one must look to see what its powers are.

It was also argued that the ratepayer, despite the fact that his premises were not connected with the water authority's sewers, derived benefit from their sewerage *f* services. So he may. So may not only all the other inhabitants of the area but also those who come into it from outside and perhaps some who live outside. Parliament might have reached the conclusion, if it had considered it, that the charging of all occupiers in the area for sewerage was justified. But I can see nothing in s 30 or in the rest of the Act to support the view that that was Parliament's conclusion. The section does not say, as it could have done, that benefit was to be the test of chargeability *g* and so to interpret the section is to read into it something that is not and that could have been there. That I decline to do and I also decline to infer that a water authority can charge such of the inhabitants of its area as it thinks fit for that again means reading into the section something which is not there. If that was to be inferred, it would seem to follow that a water authority could, if it wished, impose a charge for water supplied based on rateable value on all occupiers in its area, whether or not supplied *h* with water, in the same way as it is now contended that they can charge for sewerage.

I see no grounds for rejecting what I think is the natural inference from the language of s 30(1) and I am accordingly of the opinion that its language does not give the water authority power to charge the ratepayer for sewerage services of which he does not avail himself.

Section 30 must not, however, be looked at in isolation. One must look at the other *j* sections of the 1973 Act to see whether they throw any light on the problem. I have already referred to ss 31 and 32, the only other charging sections in Part III of the Act. There are two other sections in Part II of the Act which is headed 'Functions of Water Authorites' to which I must refer.

The first is s 14. It does not, in my opinion, follow from the fact that that section *a* imposes on water authorities the duty of providing 'such public sewers as may be necessary for effectually draining their area' that they are entitled to charge all occupiers of hereditaments in their area for sewerage.

The second is s 16 which imposes a duty on a water authority to provide a public sewer to be used for domestic purposes for the drainage of premises if certain conditions are satisfied. The somewhat complicated provisions it contains are designed to secure for a water authority an adequate return for the expense incurred in providing

b a public sewer. In no case is it obliged to provide one unless it will receive what is called 'the qualifying amount', which is one-eighth of the cost of providing the necessary sewer or sewers. If the 'reckonable charges' are less than the qualifying amount, then a water authority need not provide a sewer or sewers unless a local authority undertakes to pay the difference or, in the case of sewers required for the drainage of new buildings, the owners of the premises undertake to pay the difference

c in addition to the reckonable charges. If a sewer is required for the drainage of buildings which are not new buildings, a water authority need not provide it unless, inter alia, the reckonable charges are not less than the qualifying amount.

'Reckonable charges' are defined in s 16(11) as follows:

d   ' "Reckonable charges", in relation to a sewer, means charges in respect of the drainage of premises attributable to its use and includes such proportion of any charge payable under Part III of this Act for services which include sewerage as is stated by the water authority to be so attributable'.

So the amount to be charged to an owner or occupier who wants a sewer provided is to depend on the use to be made of the sewer and is not simply related to the rateable value of his premises. But the charge is to include such proportion of any

e charge payable under Part III of the Act for services which include sewerage as is stated by the water authority to be attributable to its use. It is not easy to see what is the effect of these words. It may be argued that this part of the definition indicates that a general charge for sewerage not depending on the use of a sewer can be made on all owners or occupiers of hereditaments whether or not connected with a public sewer with the amount payable by each depending on the rateable value of the

f premises; but I do not think this will do, for the reckonable charges are to include that part of a charge payable for services which include sewerage which is thought by a water authority to be attributable to the use of the sewer, and a charge attributable to use is not a charge just based on a rateable value.

I do not think that this definition can therefore be said to give an indication that it was Parliament's intention to provide by s 30 that a charge could be made on all

g owners and occupiers of hereditaments based on rateable value and irrespective of whether use was made of public sewers. It may perhaps be that this part of the definition was inserted ex abundanti cautela to ensure that a person did not pay twice for sewerage. However this may be, this part of the definition cannot control or extend the meaning to be given to the words in s 30.

On the other hand, this section is, I think, significant in that it, like s 32, visualises a

h charge for sewerage being dependent on use and not on rateable value. Only if the payment to be made for the use of a sewer is of the right amount, is the water authority under a duty to provide one. This I think supports the conclusion I have reached as to the meaning of s 30, and in my opinion that part of the definition of reckonable charges which refers to services including sewerage is a wholly inadequate foundation for any inference that the powers of charging given by s 30 extend to,

j or were intended to extend to, charging persons who do not avail themselves of the services performed, the facilities provided or the rights made available.

The next question to be considered is: can the Secretary of State by an order made under the Act enlarge an authority's power of charging and enable it to charge for sewerage the owners or occupiers of premises not connected with the sewers of the authority. So the powers of the Secretary of State have to be looked at. Section 34(1)

of the Water Act 1973 applies s 254 of the Local Government Act 1972 with the
amendments contained in Part I of Sch 6 to the 1973 Act.   *a*
Section 254(1) so far as material reads as follows:

'The Secretary of State . . . may at any time by order make such incidental,
consequential, transitional or supplementary provision as may appear to him—
(a) to be necessary or proper for the general or any particular purposes of this
Act or in consequence of any of the provisions thereof or for giving full effect   *b*
thereto; or (b) . . . and nothing in any other provisions of this Act shall be
construed as prejudicing the generality of this section.'

Section 254(2) of the 1972 Act states that an order made under the section may in
particular include provision for certain matters. Paragraph 5(2) of Sch 6 to the 1973
Act adds to those matters and sub-para (c) thereof states that an order under s 254
may include provision—   *c*

'for the calculation, collection and recovery on behalf of a water authority by a
local authority during a transitional period of amounts payable in respect of
services provided in the local authority's area by the water authority and for
the apportionment during that period of any payment in whole or in part of
any demand by a local authority which includes any such amount as between   *d*
those services and the other purposes for which the demand is made.'

The Local Government Act 1974 amended this paragraph by the insertion of the
words 'in respect of which no provision is made by an agreement under section 32A
of this Act' after the words 'during a transitional period' and by the adding to it of
the following paragraph:

'(cc) without prejudice to the generality of paragraph (c) above, for the demand,   *e*
collection and recovery by a local authority of any such amount as is mentioned
in that paragraph in like manner as, and together with, any amount due to the
authority in respect of the general rate and for the extension of section 113 of,
and the modification of Schedule 12 to, the General Rate Act 1967 (power to
make rules, and forms of documents) to take account of any such provision made   *f*
by the order.'

It is against this background that the validity of the Water Authorities (Collection
of Charges) Order 1974 has to be judged. Part II of that order gave a water authority
power to require a rating authority to collect and recover amounts payable to a
water authority for the supply of water. This part of the order can in my opinion
properly be regarded as consequential since it did no more than provide machinery   *g*
for the collection of amounts due to a water authority and enabled water authorities
to require rating authorities to act as their agents.

Part III of the order is headed 'General Services Charge' and, as I have said, gives a
water authority power by a general services notice to require a rating authority to
collect and recover for it amounts payable to the water authority 'in respect of
services (other than the supply of water)'. No objection can be taken to this.   *h*

I have already referred to arts 7(2) and 9 and para 10(1). I do not think that an order
extending by art 10(1) a water authority's powers so as to enable it to charge for
sewerage non-users of the sewerage facilities provided is authorised by the additions
made by Sch 6 to the 1973 Act and by the Local Government Act 1974 to s 254 of the
Local Government Act 1972.

The new provision, sub-para (c), only relates to 'the amounts payable in respect of   *j*
services provided in the local authority's area'. It does not extend or purport to
extend the categories of persons liable to be charged by a water authority beyond
those to whom s 30 applies. The new para (cc) carries the matter no further for it
relates to the demand, collection and recovery 'of any such amount as is mentioned
in paragraph (c),' that is to say, amounts payable in respect of services provided.

These paragraphs do not assist the water authority. If they did, it would still be
a necessary to consider whether the provisions in the order as to the collection of
sewerage charges can be regarded as incidental, consequential, transitional or supplementary. If they do not, that has still to be considered, for the powers of the Secretary
of State are not confined to dealing with the matters referred to in s 254(2) as amended.

The power given to the Secretary of State is wide and his exercise of it cannot
successfully be challenged in the courts unless it is clear that the order he has made
b does not come under one or other of those headings.

The provision that art 10(1) of the order makes for the collection of sewerage
charges from every person liable to pay the general rate cannot be regarded as
incidental to or consequential on any purpose of the Water Act 1973. Can it be either
transitional or supplementary? The 1974 order was not stated to be transitional,
but it was only to apply for the year beginning on the 1st April 1974. It was amended
c by the Water Authorities (Collection of Charges) (Amendment) Order 1974[1] and was
followed by the Water Authorities (Collection of Charges) Order 1975[2]. The 1975
order by Part III thereof made similar provision to that contained in the 1974 order
for the collection of, inter alia, charges for sewerage from every person liable to pay
the general rate and was to apply in respect of services provided by water authorities
during the year 1975-76. I see no indication in the 1974 order or in the 1975 order
d that the imposition of the charge on all persons liable to pay the general rate was
intended to be transitional.

Was it supplementary? If, as the water authority contend, s 30 of the 1973 Act
gave them power to collect and recover sewerage charges from all persons liable to
pay the general rate then this paragraph really repeated what that section provided.
All the order need have done was to require rating authorities to act as agents for
e water authorities. If, on the other hand, it purported to add to the powers given by
s 30, it was in one sense supplementary but not, I think, in the sense in which that
word is used in s 254 of the Local Government Act 1972. In that section 'supplementary' means, in my opinion, something added to what is in the 1973 Act to fill in details
or machinery for which the 1973 Act itself does not provide; supplementary in the
sense that it is required to implement what was in the 1973 Act.

f A provision that all persons liable to pay the general rate should be liable for
sewerage is not necessary to give effect to s 30. It does not fill in any details omitted
in the Act. It is an extension of the section and the fact that the order makes provision,
inter alia, for the payment of sewerage charges by all those liable to pay the general
rate may be regarded as an indication that the Secretary of State did not regard s 30
as enabling that to be required.

g In this Act of 40 sections occupying 46 pages of print and with 10 closely printed
schedules filling 74 pages, I can find only one sentence which conceivably can be
interpreted as lending support to the water authority's contention and that is the
final sentence of the definition of reckonable charges in s 16. I cannot find anything
which I feel would justify me in coming to the conclusion that it was the intention
of Parliament by the words used in s 30 to do more than provide that water authorities
h should be able to charge those who avail themselves of the services performed,
facilities provided and rights made available.

It may be, I do not know, that in the discharge of their functions water authorities
will incur expense which they cannot properly debit to the users of their services,
facilities or rights. Under the Act persons can be charged for water supplied to them,
charges can be made for land drainage, those whose premises are connected with
j water authority sewers can be charged for sewerage and those who avail themselves
of the other services performed, facilities provided or rights made available can be
charged, for instance, those who avail themselves of facilities for fishing or of land

1   SI 1974 No 1081
2   SI 1975 No 396

made available for recreation; but if there are expenses which cannot properly be
debited to users, then there is a defect in the Act which should be remedied by an   *a*
amending Act and which cannot be put right by a statutory instrument made by the
Secretary of State. If there is such a defect, it is not for us sitting judicially to remedy
it by legislating to put into s 30 words which Parliament could, if it had wished, have
inserted.

Whether or not the Act contains sufficient provision for recoupment of the expenditure of a water authority, in my opinion it did not give power to such an authority   *b*
to require payment of sewerage charges from those whose premises are not connected
to public sewers and, for the reasons I have stated, the provisions in the order made
by the Secretary of State making them liable for sewerage charges were in my opinion
ultra vires.

I would therefore dismiss the appeal.

  c

LORD DIPLOCK. My Lords, I have read the speech of my noble and learned
friend, Lord Wilberforce. I agree so fully with his reasoning that I will not run the
risk of clouding its clarity by restating it in my own and less felicitous words. All
I intend to do is to mention some subsidiary considerations which, in my view, lend
support to the construction that he has given to s 30(1) of the Water Act 1973.   *d*

The question of construction that is in issue is not whether a water authority *could*,
if it thought fit, base its charges to occupiers of premises in its area for the sewage
services it provides on the value of the actual use made by the occupier of the
authority's sewers in draining his own premises. The question is whether the Act
prohibits the authority from charging for those services on a rating basis.

For more than a hundred years before that Act came into force, local authorities   *e*
responsible for public health had been invested by Parliament with the power and
duty of providing such public sewers as might be needed to dispose of foul effluent
and surface water from domestic and other premises in their districts. Throughout
that period Parliament thought it to be appropriate, and consistently legislated to
this effect, that the cost of doing so should be recoverable from the occupiers or
owners of all domestic hereditaments in their district by means of a charge included   *f*
in a general rate. The amount charged was fixed at a uniform poundage on the
annual value of each hereditament. It did not depend on the actual value to the
occupier or owner of the individual hereditament of the use which he made or was
able to make of the public sewers. Parliament had thus, for practical reasons that
are obvious, consistently rejected in favour of a 'rating' or local taxation basis the
alternative basis of charging for the actual value of user—a policy for which in a   *g*
free market economy an attractive theoretical justification could have been found
in the 19th century. Consequently, up until April 1974, occupiers of domestic premises that were not connected with a public sewer, whether by their own choice
or because there was no public sewer available with which connection could be
made, were rated for the cost of public sewers provided in the district at the same
poundage as the occupiers of other domestic premises in the district that were   *h*
connected to a public sewer.

The policy of dividing between the occupiers of hereditaments in a particular area
the cost of services provided for their common benefit in proportion to the annual
value of the hereditaments benefited instead of estimating the value of the actual
benefit each individual hereditament received, finds its historical origin in late
mediaeval times in the creation of Commissioners of Sewers to undertake land   *j*
drainage. As the law developed, liability to be rated by Commissioners of Sewers
was restricted to occupiers of hereditaments which lay within the geographical
boundaries of the area comprising land of which it could be shown that it derived
some benefit, albeit small, from the drainage works. So it is not surprising that when
a similar rating principle was first applied to the recovery of the cost of other services

provided by new kinds of local authorities for the inhabitants of their district, the
a judges in the first half of the 19th century should have had resort to the concept
of 'some benefit, albeit small' as the criterion by which to determine whether or not
individual hereditaments within the district were liable to be rated for those services.
Applying that criterion to sewerage the court in *Soady v Wilson*[1] and *Dorling v
Epsom Board of Health*[2] held that the occupiers of all premises within a district derived
sufficient benefit from the general improvement of sanitation in the district to make
b them liable to be rated even though the particular premises could not themselves
be connected to any of the public sewers.

My Lords, the words of s 30(1) 'as they think fit' are about as wide as they could be.
They were clearly intended to give to a water authority a discretion as to 'the methods
by which and the principles on which the charges are to be made' [scilicet] for any
'services performed, facilities provided or rights made available by' the authority
c (see s 31(1) and (4)), much wider than such limited discretions as to methods and
principles of charging as were, by the previous legislation, conferred on the various
local authorities by whom functions transferred by the Act to water authorities had
previously been discharged. Since power to compel a citizen to pay for services
rendered a sum in excess of their actual value to him is in the nature of taxation no
doubt some limit on the apparently unlimited charging powers of a water authority
d under s 30(1) and s 31(1) and (4) was intended to be imposed by necessary implication
despite the absence of any express words of limitation. In the absence of express
words, however, I can see no justification for imputing to Parliament an intention
to effect so radical a breach in continuity of legislative policy as to prohibit a water
authority from adopting the same method of charging for the self-same services as
that which previous Parliaments had consistently directed its predecessor authorities
e to adopt.

In the particular case of the provision of public sewers the continuity of legislative
policy is manifested by the provisions of s 14 and s 15 of the 1973 Act. The words of
s 14, which impose on a water authority duties in respect of public sewers and sewage
disposal works in relation to their area are identical with the words of s 14 of the
Public Health Act 1936, which imposed the like duties on local authorities in relation
f to their districts. Section 15 imposes a general duty on both water authorities and
local authorities to make arrangements whereby the functions of the water authority
to provide and maintain public sewers in each district in the water authority's area
shall be discharged by the local authority for that district in accordance with a
programme prepared and annually revised by it and approved by the water authority.
So in practice, so far as the provision and maintenance of public sewers is concerned,
g everything is to go on as it did before except that the water authority becomes
responsible for the strategic planning of the various sewerage systems within its
area and for determining the method by which and the principles on which the cost
of their provision and maintenance is to be met. It is not bound to continue to
recover the cost by the same method of rating all rateable hereditaments at a uniform
poundage as local authorities were obliged to use before, but I can see no reason for
h any implication that this time-honoured method alone was debarred to a water
authority.

I turn now to s 16. It does not seem to me, with great respect, that any inference
that is relevant to the instant appeal can be drawn from this complicated and
inadequately thought out section. Two things alone are tolerably plain.

1. The section is not concerned at all with the right of occupiers of domestic
j premises to have them connected at their own expense to an existing public sewer.
This right, formerly exercisable under s 34 of the Public Health Act 1936, is expressly
preserved to them as against the water authority by s 14(2)(a) of the Water Act 1973.

---

1   (1835) 3 Ad & El 248
2   (1855) 5 E & B 471

So s 16 can throw no light on the question whether or not an occupier of domestic premises who could have them connected to a public sewer but chooses not to, can *a* be rated for sewerage services at the same poundage on their annual value as occupiers of domestic premises that are so connected.

2. Section 16 lays down financial conditions on which water authorities can be compelled to construct *new* public sewers to be used for the drainage of existing or newly-erected domestic premises. The right of an occupier or owner of domestic premises to compel the construction of a public sewer to which his premises can be *b* connected is a novel right created for the first time by the section. The financial conditions are clearly drafted on the assumption that the water authority will, in one form or another, make an annual charge for the use of the new public sewer by the occupiers of premises for which it was requisitioned, and that such annual charge (*a*) will be proportionate to the expense incurred by the water authority in construct-ing the new sewer, and (*b*) will be additional to any rate or other form of charge to *c* which the occupiers of those premises would be liable in common with occupiers of other premises in the district for benefits derived by them from the existence of the remainder of the sewerage system.

There are two categories of domestic premises in respect of which a requisition for the construction of a new sewer may be made on a water authority. The first category comprises domestic premises, whether existing or proposed to be newly *d* built, whose owners or occupiers can obtain the financial backing of the local authority. For premises in this category it appears to be contemplated that the additional annual charge for the use of the new sewer will comprise two elements: (*a*) an annual charge ('the reckonable charges') payable by the occupiers of each of the premises in respect of which the requisition was made and not exceeding in the aggregate one-eighth of the cost of constructing the new sewer ('the qualifying *e* amount') and (*b*) an annual charge ('the relevant deficit') payable for a period of 12 years by the local authority and equal to the amount by which the reckonable charges fall short of one-eighth of the cost of constructing the new sewer. Although the section does not expressly so provide it would seem to be a reasonable inference that the draftsman contemplated that the reckonable charges, like the relevant deficit, would cease to be payable by the occupiers after the expiry of 12 years and *f* that thereafter sewerage charges in respect of the premises would be payable on the same basis as sewerage charges in respect of all other domestic premises in the district; but no inference can be drawn from this that any limitation was intended to be imposed on the discretion of the water authority under s 30(1) to determine what that basis should be.

The second category comprises domestic premises whose owners or occupiers are *g* unable to obtain the financial backing of the local authority. This can be sub-divided into two sub-categories. One consists of premises proposed to be newly built and in respect of which a requisition for the construction of a new sewer is made on a water authority by the owners of the premises. The only differences between the first category and this sub-category of the second are that, while the reckonable charges will be payable by the occupiers, any relevant deficit will be payable by the requisi- *h* tioning owners instead of by the local authority and that they may be required to deposit with the water authority as security for such payment a sum not exceeding the total cost of constructing the new sewer. It would seem a reasonable inference from this provision as to the sum exigible from the owners as security, that the draftsman contemplated that a water authority might so exercise its discretion as to eliminate any reckonable charges payable by the occupiers of the newly-built pre- *j* mises for the use of the new sewer, and to leave them liable only to pay sewerage charges on the same basis as sewerage charges are payable in respect of all other domestic premises in the district. But again no inference can be drawn from this that any limitation is imposed on the discretion of the water authority under s 30(1) to determine what that basis should be.

The other sub-category into which the second category can be sub-divided consists
a of existing domestic premises in respect of which a requisition for the construction
of a new sewer is made on a water authority by the owners or occupiers of the premises. In this case the financial condition to be satisfied is that the reckonable charges
payable annually by the occupiers of the premises for the use of the new sewer must
exceed the qualifying amount. The determination of what the reckonable charges
are to be, lies within the discretion of the water authority; and it seems to be a
b necessary implication from the section that the water authority must not exercise
that discretion in such a way as to deprive the requisitioners of their right to have
a new sewer constructed. This would involve that the reckonable charges payable
annually by the occupiers for the use of the new sewer must not be fixed by the
water authority at an amount which in the aggregate is less than one-eighth of the
cost of constructing the new sewer. Having regard to the cost of construction of
c new sewers in 1974, that aggregate amount will greatly exceed the total amount of
any rate or other form of charge for sewerage services which would have been payable in respect of those premises if they had been already connected to an existing
sewer. So there is no room for any inference that the reckonable charges for the use
of a new sewer are to be fixed at an amount which represents the difference between
a charge made by the water authority on occupiers of premises that are connected
d to an existing sewer and a charge made on occupiers of premises that are not connected to an existing sewer. There is thus no room for the only implication which
would assist the ratepayer in the instant appeal, viz that the Act requires a water
authority to adopt a method of charging for sewerage services provided in its area
which imposes on the occupiers of domestic premises which are not connected to an
existing public sewer a liability to pay a sum which represents a lesser proportion
e of the annual value of their premises than the liability imposed on the occupiers of
domestic premises which are connected to an existing public sewer.

I have ventured to deal in greater detail with some of the reasons already indicated
by my noble and learned friend, Lord Wilberforce, for differing from the construction
which the majority of your Lordships have placed on the Act. I have done so because
it seems not improbable that the decision of this House will be followed by further
f legislation. In this event, it seems desirable that the attention of the draftsman
should be directed to the defects in the present legislation so that the intention of
Parliament as to any limitations on the charging powers of water authorities in
respect of sewerage services may be made much clearer than it is in the Water Act
1973.

For my part, I would have allowed this appeal.

g

LORD KILBRANDON. My Lords, this case, which has received a good deal of
publicity, has been thought to raise the question: is it fair that a citizen whose premises
are not connected to a public sewer should be asked to contribute to the general cost
of the sewerage service? I open with that observation for the purpose of emphasising
h that that is not the question which is before your Lordships, although, as I shall try
to show, there are other matters of public importance which may be said to arise.
The question for decision is, whether the terms of the Water Act 1973 and the regulations made thereunder authorise the water authority, by means of a rate imposed
by the rating authority, to recover from the ratepayer, his premises not being connected to a public sewer, charges for the sewerage services performed by them, the
j sewerage facilities provided by them, or the rights in relation to sewerage made
available by them, based on the rateable value of those premises. The irrelevance of any
political consideration of right or wrong is underlined by the fact that, before the
Act was passed, sewerage charges were recovered by imposing a general rate, which
would have been exigible in respect of the ratepayer's hereditament, connection or
no connection.

My Lords, I have had the opportunity of examining the analysis of the Act and regulations which is contained in the speech of my noble and learned friend, Viscount *a* Dilhorne. I entirely agree with the conclusions to which that analysis has led him, and I do not think it would be profitable to state those conclusions in different terms. But I will add a few words on the interpretation of s 30, which must be at the heart of your Lordships' decision.

The Water Act 1973 makes entirely new arrangements as to the water, drainage, sewerage, sewage disposal and other environmental services. A new kind of authority *b* was set up; it might or might not consist of a majority of representatives of the local authorities operating in the given area, but it was not to be a democratically constituted body, in the sense of being answerable for its acts of administration to an elected council. This kind of functional authority, which in some functions but not others supplants older-established popular bodies (and the water authority is not, as a product of recent legislation, a unique specimen) was of course looked at a little *c* askance by some critics, though not by others. I only mention that fact in order to show that some controversy must attend the setting up of a body which is to take over local services, and necessarily to finance in some way the expenditure which it makes for the benefit of the inhabitants, or at least of some of them. One of the controversial questions obviously is going to be: who is to pay the charges which the body has to incur? The incidence of local taxation to meet local expenditure is *d* nowadays a very sensitive area of discussion. The part of the Act to which one must direct oneself in order to answer that question is the part which empowers the authority to fix, demand, take and recover such charges. That part is s 30, together with, so far as they throw light on s 30, ss 31 and 32.

In view of the controversial interest which was bound to be involved, it is a striking fact, to which your Lordships have already adverted, that s 30 gives no direct indica- *e* tion whatever as to the persons who are liable to contribute to the charges fixed by the authority. The authority may fix those charges by agreement with any person; that looks like a commercial bargain in respect of particular services performed, facilities provided or rights made available. In the alternative the charges, again for services, facilities and rights, may be fixed by a scheme (s 31(1)). In fixing their charges (s 30(4)), the authority must have regard to the cost of performing, providing and *f* making available. If this implies recovery by a substitute for the old general rate, the proviso seems tautological—because rates are levied only for the purpose of meeting a deficiency; it is not tautological if the cost of supplying individual 'customers' is in question. On the other hand, the powers, apparently discretionary, conferred on the authority, subject to the direction of the Secretary of State, are exceedingly wide. The authorities may fix, demand, take and recover charges as *g* they think fit, and by reference to such criteria as appears (sic) to them to be appropriate. For my part I do not consider such words adequate, if any other meaning is open, to empower an ad hoc non-representative body to impose what is in truth a tax, namely an impost under the head of charges for services, facilities and rights, on persons who do not directly receive such advantages. It would have been quite possible to impose such charges, if Parliament had thought fit, by putting all the *h* citizens under a liability to meet the cost of a general public improvement. But I am not prepared to spell, in the absence of clear words, such a power out of what Parliament actually said, in terms which are also capable of being interpreted in a different sense. I have never seen the word 'criteria' used in such a connection before, but I do not believe that it can possibly be intended to mean tests to be applied by a public body, at their discretion, in order to decide whether they are or are not justified *j* in levying a contribution on a person with whom they are in no commercial relationship.

It is a commonplace that the meaning of the provision is to be gathered from the Act as a whole, and your Lordships have analysed the Act for that purpose. I agree with those of your Lordships who find the provisions of, e g, s 16 much more appropriate to the ratepayer's than to the water authority's contention. I would also

suggest that it is unfortunate if liability to 'tax' can only be discovered by the
'taxpayer' after so prolonged an exercise of interpretative skills. And this leads me
to a second general point which I should like to make.
    This is a test case. It calls for a decision on the source from which a very large
sum of money is to be raised, and for the elucidation of a major aspect of policy.
It affects, directly, a substantial number of people, and indirectly, every ratepayer
in the country. If one may draw on the memory of one's own professional experience, it seems almost inevitable that the defence to the writ would be prepared in
collaboration with a body or person representative of all water authorities set up
by the new Act, that is, the whole of the authorities of England and Wales. These
representatives, in turn, although not to be identified with, certainly work in close
conjunction with, the ministries in which the bill was prepared, which conducted
the prior negotiations which serviced the responsible ministers, both in cabinet and
in Parliament, and which, in short, were responsible for the travaux préparatoires.
Since all this ought to have been so, I shall assume that it was so. In that state of
matters, the case was, by agreement of counsel, conducted before Phillips J[1] on the
footing that 'No charge can be made under s 30(1) for water supply, or for sewerage
or sewage disposal services, unless the person to be charged is actually in receipt of
them.' On 25th April 1975 the defence was formally amended accordingly, by leave
of the judge. I am not at all disposed to criticise counsel for making such a concession, because I should suppose that it was made on instructions. That is to say,
those who were in the best position to know were satisfied that Parliament did not
intend, by the terms of s 30(1), that, failing any other enactment or regulation,
the assessments complained of should be maintainable. Of course, if it were impossible to construe s 30(1) in any other sense than that they *were* maintainable, that
opinion would be quite valueless. But in my judgment that is not the case; the
construction which seems to have been put on it by the framers and promoters
of the legislation is perfectly open, and I am therefore led towards the belief that
that construction gives effect to the intention of Parliament.
    My last general point is this. The Water Act came into force on 18th July 1973.
By 30th April 1974, the date on which the ratepayer first refused to pay a 'sewerage,
etc., charge', a controversy had arisen as to what Parliament had intended, in relation to this very important policy question. My Lords, that must demonstrate that
this, of all cases, is one in which there could have been some source or sources on
which the courts could draw, in the exercise of their constitutional duties to interpret
legislation, over and above those to which custom, or yis inertiae, has arbitrarily
limited them. This matter has been raised again and again. I refer to the report[2]
by the Law Commission ordered by the House of Commons to be printed on 9th
June 1969. It is not merely a crude question whether Hansard should be quotable
in judicial proceedings: there are several other expedients which have been discussed
and recommended. Emphatic passages on this topic are to be found in the speech
of my noble and learned friend, Lord Simon of Glaisdale, in *Black-Clawson International Ltd v Papierwerke Waldhof-Aschaffenburg AG*[3]. I myself made a minor reference to it, as did my noble and learned friend, in *Dockers' Labour Club and Institute
Ltd v Race Relations Board*[4]. It is certain that there are other and more satisfying
ways of arriving at the meaning of an Act of Parliament, or any other document,
than by prolonged linguistic and semantic analysis. Until they are adopted,
interpretation may be a hit-or-miss affair, and often very expensive.
    On the view I have taken of the water authority's powers under s 30, the next
question is, whether the assessment complained of can be justified in virtue of the

1   [1975] 3 All ER 134 at 137, [1975] 3 WLR 50 at 53
2   Law Com 21 (Scot Law Com 11), The Interpretation of Statutes (HC 256)
3   [1975] 1 All ER 810 at 843-848, [1975] 2 WLR 513 at 549-554
4   [1974] 3 All ER at 600-602, [1974] 3 WLR at 542-544

provisions of the Water Authorities (Collection of Charges) Order 1974. In this matter also I am in entire agreement with the conclusions of my noble and learned friend, Viscount Dilhorne, and do not wish to add anything.

My Lords, I would dismiss this appeal.

LORD EDMUND-DAVIES. My Lords, s 30 of the Water Act 1973 is a deplorable piece of legislation. Those charged with the duty of applying it appear to have little inkling as to its import, for until recently they thought it had a meaning completely opposite to that for which they now contend. In this they have my sympathy, and I confess to envying those of your Lordships who find themselves able to indicate with apparent assurance the proper outcome of this appeal. For myself, the task has been so formidable that I lack confidence that I have arrived at the right result, and that is indeed an unfortunate condition to be left in when adjudicating on a matter of public importance. But in my judgment s 30 fails to provide a clear answer to the elementary question whether it empowers a water authority to oblige the occupier of a hereditament not connected with a main sewer to pay sewerage charges. And, lest it be thought that the obscurity has been merely dreamt up by the lawyers, it is worth pointing out that, whereas a year ago the water authority thought that the proper answer to the question was No, they now contend that it is Yes.

The appellants are one of nine regional water authorities, covering England and Wales, set up under the Water Act 1973 which is—

'An Act to make provision for a national policy for water, for the conferring and discharging of functions as to water (including sewerage and sewage disposal, fisheries and land drainage) and as to recreation and amenity in connection with water, for the making of charges by water authorities and other statutory water undertakers, and for connected purposes.'

Their area includes most of Devon and Cornwall and covers Plymstock where the ratepayer has a hereditament with no mains drainage and 400 yards away from the nearest sewer. In April and June 1974 the Plymouth City Council, as the rating authority acting on behalf of the water authority, served on the ratepayer demands for 'sewerage, etc., charge', the amount specified in the earlier charge being £2·45, in the later charge £2·44. The main question raised in this appeal is whether either of these sums is exigible from the ratepayer.

It is beyond doubt that before the 1973 Act the ratepayer would have been obliged to satsify both demands, the responsibility for providing sewerage and sewage disposal works being placed on the local authorities and their expenditure thereon being treated as part of their general expenditure recoverable from the whole body of ratepayers, regardless of whether their hereditaments were connected up. Among the functions transferred to the newly established water authorities was that relating to sewerage and sewage disposal.

Section 30(1)-(6) have already been set out by your Lordships. Subsection (7) provides:

'Where a water authority introduce a new system of charges, they may make such transitional charging arrangements as they think fit applying for a period not exceeding five years.'

Schedule 6 to the Act invokes s 254 of the Local Government Act 1972, which provides:

'(1) The Secretary of State or any appropriate Minister may at any time by order make such incidental, consequential, transitional or supplementary provisions as may appear to him—(a) to be necessary or proper for the general or any particular purposes of this Act or in consequence of any of the provisions thereof or for giving full effect thereto . . .'

Paragraph 5(2) of Sch 6 to the 1973 Act enacts that an order under s 254 of the 1972 Act may include provision—

'(c) for the calculation, collection and recovery on behalf of a water authority by a local authority during a transitional period of amounts payable in respect of services provided in the local authority's area by the water authority and for the apportionment during that period of any payment in whole or in part of any demand by a local authority which includes any such amount as between those services and the other purposes for which the demand is made.'

Pursuant to the foregoing provisions, the Secretary of State made the Water Authorities (Collection of Charges) Order 1974. Part III thereof, entitled 'General Services Charge', contains the following provisions:

'7.—(1) Subject to the provisions of this order, a water authority may issue a notice (in this order referred to as "general services notice") to any new rating authority whose rating area lies wholly or partly within the water authority's sewerage and sewage disposal area, requiring them to collect and recover on behalf of the water authority amounts payable to the water authority in respect of services (other than the supply of water) provided by the water authority in the area specified in the notice, being the rating area of the rating authority, or so much of that area as lies within the water authority's sewerage and sewage disposal area.

'(2) A general services notice shall be issued as soon as may be and shall authorise the rating authority to demand and collect the said amounts by means of a charge (in this order referred to as "a general services charge") which shall be expressed as a poundage to be determined by the rating authority in accordance with the provisions of article 9, and shall be charged by them on hereditaments in the area specified in the notice in accordance with the provisions of this part of this order . . .

'9.—(1) For the purposes of collecting the general services charge and of paying over to the water authority the general services payment specified in any general services notice, the rating authority to whom the notice has been issued shall calculate and determine the general services charge relating to the hereditaments within their rating area in accordance with the provisions of this article.

'(2) The general services charge shall be a charge at a uniform amount per pound on the rateable value of each hereditament in the rating area of the rating authority and that amount per pound is referred to in this part of this order as "the relevant poundage" . . .

'10.—(1) The rating authority shall collect the general services charge from every person who is liable to pay the general rate in respect of a hereditament in the area of the authority, or who is making a contribution in aid of rates under section 37 or 38 of the 1967 Act in respect of such an hereditament, and the amount payable by way of the charge in respect of any hereditament shall be the amount arrived at by multiplying the relevant poundage by the rateable value of that hereditament or, as the case may be, by the value entered in the valuation list as representing its rateable value.'

It was in purported pursuance of the foregoing provisions that the local authority made the aforesaid demands in respect of services to be provided by the water authority during the quarters beginning on 1st April and 1st July 1974.

The two subsidiary questions now arising for determination may be thus stated: 1. Does s 30(1) of the 1973 Act entitle a water authority to demand payment of sewerage and sewage disposal charges from a ratepayer whose hereditament is not connected with a sewer? 2. If the answer to 1. is No, does the 1974 order nevertheless entitle the water authority to make such a demand during the transitional period?

Question 1. As to this, when tried before Phillips J the case took an unfortunate
turn for, as the learned judge put it[1]:

'. . . the submissions of counsel for the plaintiff and of counsel for the defendants on this point came to agree with each other. There is, they say, an implied
limitation to the right to charge, derived from the words of s 30(1), confining
it to the persons *for whom* the services are performed, *for whom* the facilities are
provided, and *to whom* the rights are made available. According to this submission no charge can be made under s 30(1) for water supply, or for sewerage
or sewage disposal services, unless the person to be charged is actually in receipt
of them.'

The learned judge expressed himself as satisfied that *some* limitation had to be
placed on the apparently unrestricted language of s 30(1), and he concluded[1] that
'the demands for sewerage etc charges in question in this action, cannot be justified
under this section'. But the water authority now submit that this is wrong and that
they ought not to have agreed that the ambit of s 30(1) must be cut down in the
manner which found favour with the trial judge. Counsel for the water authority
recalled that under the pre-1973 law the ratepayer was, under the general rate,
charged in respect of the provision of sewerage and sewage disposal works and
submitted that, had it been intended that this liability was no longer to continue,
the Act would have made express provision for the purpose. And, by citing such
old cases as *Dorling v Epsom Board of Health*[2], *Soady v Wilson*[3] and *Hammersmith
Bridge Co v Hammersmith Overseers*[4] he urged that the ratepayer does in fact derive a
benefit, *albeit not in respect of his own hereditament*, from the provision of sewerage and
sewage disposal works in the area of the water authority. More to the point, in my
judgment, he drew our attention to s 14(1) of the 1973 Act, which provides:

'It shall be the duty of every water authority to provide, either inside or outside
their area, such public sewers as may be necessary for effectually draining their
area and to make such provision, whether inside o outside their area, by means
of sewage disposal works or otherwise, as may be necessary for effectually dealing
with the contents of their sewers . . .'

Basing himself on this provision, counsel for the water authority submitted that
the Act clearly contemplated that *all* hereditaments in the area of a water authority
must share in the cost of sewerage and sewage disposal works provided in its area,
and that exemption could not properly be claimed simply because a particular hereditament was not connected up. But I am in respectful agreement with my noble
and learned friend, Viscount Dilhorne, that it by no means follows from the nature
of the duty imposed by s 14 on water authorities that they are entitled to impose
sewerage charges on *all* occupiers of hereditaments in their area.

Having regard to the expansive language employed in the 1973 Act, there is great
force in the view expressed by Phillips J[5]:

'Section 30(1), read literally, seems to confer an unlimited power on the water
authority to charge whom they like, where they like, and how they like (subject
to the duty to avoid undue preference or discrimination, and to the overriding
power of the Secretary of State to prescribe criteria (sub-ss (5) and (6)).'

But the notion that wholly unrestricted powers of determining *who* is to be charged
have been vested in the new non-elected bodies constituting the water authorities

---

1 [1975] 3 All ER 134 at 137, [1975] 3 WLR 50 at 53
2 (1855) 5 E & B 471
3 (1835) 3 Ad & El 248
4 (1871) LR 6 QB 230
5 [1975] 3 All ER at 136, [1975] 3 WLR at 52

a will strike many as so unattractive that, on the face of it, any submission that such
was the express intention of Parliament would obviously lack cogency. Although
the learned trial judge did not indicate (and understandably so, in the circumstances)
the precise process which led him to concur in the restrictive interpretation of s 30(1)
which the water authority were themselves then accepting, it seems that Phillips J
was simply led to the conclusion that 'charges for the services performed' is
inappropriate language to justify the imposition of liability for sewerage charges on
b a ratepayer whose hereditament is served by no sewer.

The problem of interpretation involved is acute, but there is much to be said for
such an approach. What significance should be attached to s 16 of the 1973 Act is
also a difficult matter. For the ratepayer it can be said that if a ratepayer is liable to
pay sewerage charges even though his premises are not connected to a sewer, it is
difficult to see why he should be liable to pay additional sums to secure the full
c benefit of that for which he is already paying as much as any other ratepayer. On
the other hand, s 16 relates only to the provision of *new* sewers, and the law has
long been that a ratepayer proposing to have his drains connected up with an *existing*
public sewer can first be required to pay to the local authority the cost of the work
involved. Section 36 of the Public Health Act 1936 so provided, and s 14(2) of the
1973 Act makes that earlier provision applicable to the new water authorities. So
d it may properly be said by the water authority that, even if s 16 could be regarded
as operating unfairly on the ratepayer who desires to have a new sewer provided,
he is no worse off than occupiers of hereditaments have been for many years when
seeking to have them connected up with existing sewers.

Counsel for the water authority accepted that s 16 creates a difficulty for him in
relation to sewerage charges (though not to sewage disposal), but submitted that
e what he described as 'possibly a minor conflict' between s 16(1)(a) and s 30(1) was
due to inadvertent drafting of the Act. He referred us to the well-known words of
Lord Herschell LC in *Institute of Patent Agents v Lockwood*[1]:

'. . . there is a conflict sometimes between two sections to be found in the
same Act. You have to try and reconcile them as best you may. If you cannot,
f you have to determine which is the leading provision and which the subordinate
provision, and which must give way to the other.'

But those observations have in my judgment no application to such a case as the
present, for no 'conflict' arises unless one first determines that a water authority,
in charging for 'the services performed by them', *are* entitled to impose sewerage
charges on ratepayers whose hereditaments do not enjoy the benefit of sewerage
g services. Whether one may make such an assumption constitutes the problem at
the heart of this appeal, and in attempting to solve it one must have regard to such
other parts of the Act which appear to bear on the present case.

While I do not attach the same weighty significance to s 16 as my noble and learned
friend, Viscount Dilhorne, seemingly does, when one bears in mind that the basis of
h the water authority's case is that sewerage charges are due from the ratepayer by
reason of 'the services performed' by them, s 16 does seem to point away somewhat
from the chargeability of such hereditaments as that of the ratepayer. And so also
does s 32 of the 1973 Act, for the reasons given by my noble and learned friend,
Viscount Dilhorne. It is well established that all charges on the subject must be
imposed by clear and unambiguous language. So unbridled on the face of it is the
j remarkable language of s 30(1) that its literal application would render chargeable
almost anybody, on the basis that 'if the person sought to be taxed comes within the
letter of the law he must be taxed, however great the hardship may appear to the
judicial mind to be' (per Lord Cairns LC in *Partington v Attorney-General*[2]). But

1   [1894] AC at 360
2   (1869) 4 HL at 122

even the water authority do not contend that the subsection is to be literally and unrestrictedly interpreted and applied, and (even if they did) such an approach should *a* be adopted only if inescapable. Slight though the aforementioned indications against chargeability are, in the light of them I am not prepared to hold that the water authority has been clearly empowered by s 30 to impose and recover sewerage charges in respect of the ratepayer's hereditament. The breadth of the language used in s 30 is, in my judgment, its undoing. I would therefore answer question 1 in the negative.   *b*

Question 2. I can deal with this question briefly. If I am right in thinking that s 30(1) does not empower a 'sewerage, etc charge' to be made against the ratepayer, then in my judgment no order, whether 'transitional' or otherwise, can do so. Section 254 of the Local Government Act 1972, already quoted, confers on the Secretary of State power to make by order 'such incidental, consequential, transitional or supplementary provision' as appears to him necessary or proper 'for the general or any *c* particular purposes of this Act or in consequence of any of the provisions thereof or for giving full effect thereto'. If an Act confers *no* power on a charging authority to charge certain persons or class of persons, an order which declares that they *can* be charged is not 'incidental' or 'consequential' or 'supplementary' to the Act, and the mere fact that it may be 'transitional' cannot, of itself, make it, intra vires, if, were it intended to operate permanently, it would be ultra vires.   *d*

Such is, in my judgment, the case here. I respectfully adopt that part of the judgment below where the learned judge considered[1] the argument advanced on the water authority's behalf on the import of the word 'calculation' and the phrase 'amounts payable in respect of services provided in the local authority's area' appearing in Sch 6, para 5(2)(c). Counsel for the water authority also sought to attach significance to the phrase 'services *performed*' and contrasted it with the reference in s 30(1) *e* to 'facilities *provided*', submitting that the former is appropriate to the rendering of benefit to persons rather than to hereditaments and that the ratepayer *is* a beneficiary of the sewerage works provided generally by the water authority in their area. But in my judgment no such significance attaches, and it is noteworthy that in Sch 6, para 5(2)(c)—which is, of course, equally a part of the Act—there appears the phrase 'services *provided* in the local authority's area'. I would therefore answer question 2 *f* also in the negative.

In the result, I hold that the plaintiffs was entitled to the declaration made by Phillips J and I would dismiss this appeal.

Appeal dismissed.

Solicitors: *Sharpe, Pritchard & Co*, agents for *A G Conybeare Williams*, Exeter (for the *g* water authority); *Ward Bowie*, agents for *Whiteford, Bennett, Woolland & Bellingham*, Plymouth (for the ratepayer).

Gordon H Scott Esq   Barrister.

---

1   [1975] 3 All ER at 140, [1975] 3 WLR at 57

British Airways Board v Taylor

HOUSE OF LORDS

LORD WILBERFORCE, VISCOUNT DILHORNE, LORD SIMON OF GLAISDALE, LORD EDMUND-DAVIES AND LORD FRASER OF TULLYBELTON

3rd, 4th NOVEMBER, 10th DECEMBER 1975

Trade description – False or misleading statement – Provision of services – Promise in regard to future – Statement of fact distinguished from promise – Statement of existing intention – Booking and reservation of seat – Airline – Customer booking seat on particular flight – Airline writing letter confirming reservation for flight – Policy of airline to overbook flights – Seats available at time of customer's booking – Airline subsequently overbooking flight – Customer in consequence unable to travel on flight – Passenger travelling on following day – Whether letter from airline containing statement of fact as opposed to promise of future conduct – Trade Descriptions Act 1968, s 14(1).

By a letter dated 14th August 1973 British Overseas Airways Corporation ('BOAC') wrote to E, a customer, as follows: 'I have pleasure in confirming the following reservations for you:—London/Bermuda Flight B.A. 679—Economy Class—29 August Dep. 1525 hours Arr. 1750 hours.' It was BOAC's policy to operate an 'overbooking' system whereby they made reservations for more passengers than there were seats available on a particular flight. Although on 14th August there were sufficient seats available for E to travel on flight BA 679, BOAC subsequently overbooked that flight with the result that on 29th August there were more reservations than there were seats available. On 29th August E was informed at the airport that his flight was over-booked. In consequence he was obliged to travel by air the next day. On 1st April 1974, by virtue of the Air Corporations (Dissolution) Order 1973[a], the property, rights and liabilities of BOAC become those of the British Airways Board ('the Board'). On 26th June 1974 an information was laid against the Board alleging that the letter of 14th August to E contravened s 14(1)(b)[b] of the Trade Descriptions Act 1968 in that it had recklessly made a statement 'about the provision of services namely the transportation of a person by aeroplane which was false as to the time at which the service was to be provided'. The Board was convicted of the offence by a magistrates' court. The Divisional Court quashed the conviction on the ground that the letter from BOAC contained merely a promise as to future conduct as opposed to a statement of fact and that consequently the provisions of s 14(1) did not apply. The prosecutor appealed.

Held – (i) The justices were entitled on the evidence to find (a) that the letter of 14th August could be taken by E as a statement of fact that he had a definite and certain booking on the particular flight, and (b) that the statement was false within s 14(1) since, in view of the overbooking policy, E's booking was exposed to the risk that he might not obtain a seat on the aircraft (see p 69 e to h, p 72 a to c and f, p 74 f to h and p 77 e to g, post); dictum of MacKenna J in *R v Sunair Holidays Ltd* [1973] 2 All ER 1236, 1240 approved.

(ii) In the circumstances, however, the Board could not be held liable for the criminal acts of BOAC, for there had been no delegation of duty by the Board to BOAC and the 1973 order contained no provision that, on the dissolution of BOAC, offences by BOAC were to be treated as offences by the Board. Accordingly the appeal would be dismissed (see p 70 b to e and h to p 71 a, p 72 j, p 73 b and c, p 75 b and p 76 a and b, post).

Semble. The information should have alleged an offence under s 14(1)(a) of the 1968 Act (making a statement known to be false) and not an offence under s 14(1)(b)

---

a SI 1973 No 2175
b Section 14, so far as material, is set out at p 71 *b* to *d*, post   *c*

(recklessly making a false statement) (see p 68 *a* and *b*, p 71 *e* to *h*, p 72 *g* and *h*, p 74 *g* and *h*, p 75 *a* and *b* and p 78 *a* and *b*, post).

Decision of the Divisional Court of the Queen's Bench Division [1975] 3 All ER 307 affirmed on different grounds.

Notes

For false and misleading statements as to facilities and services under the Trade Descriptions Act 1968, see Supplement to 38 Halsbury's Laws (3rd Edn) para 820c, 3. For the Trade Descriptions Act 1968, s 14, see 37 Halsbury's Statutes (3rd Edn) 959.

Cases referred to in opinions

Beckett v Cohen [1973] 1 All ER 120, [1972] 1 WLR 1593, DC.

Linnett v Commissioner of Police for the Metropolis [1946] 1 All ER 380, [1946] KB 290, 115 LJKB 513, 174 LT 178, 110 JP 153, 44 LGR 95, DC, 30 Digest (Reissue) 112, 800.

R v Clarksons Holidays Ltd (1972) 57 Cr App Rep 38, CA.

R v Sunair Holidays Ltd [1973] 2 All ER 1233, [1973] 1 WLR 1105, 137 JP 687, 57 Cr App Rep 782, CA.

Tesco Supermarkets Ltd v Nattrass [1970] 3 All ER 357, [1971] 1 QB 133, [1970] 3 WLR 572, DC, Digest (Cont Vol C) 1024, 1142*a*.

Appeal

This was an appeal by the prosecutor, Kenneth Taylor, an inspector of trading standards for Manchester, against an order of the Divisional Court of the Queen's Bench Division[1] (Lord Widgery CJ, Waller and Kilner Brown JJ) dated 16th June 1975, quashing the decision of the Stockport justices, whereby, on 12th August 1974, on an information dated 26th June 1974 preferred by the prosecutor, the justices convicted the respondents, British Airways Board ('the Board'), of having on or about 15th August 1973 recklessly made a false statement concerning the provision of services, namely the transportation of a person by aeroplane, in a letter addressed to W J Edmunds, contrary to s 14(1)(*b*) of the Trade Descriptions Act 1968, and fined the Board £250. The Divisional Court refused leave to appeal to the House of Lords but certified under s 1(2) of the Administration of Justice Act 1960 that a point of law of general public importance was involved in their decision. On 10th July 1975 the appeal committee of the House of Lords granted the prosecutor leave to appeal. The facts are set out in the opinion of Lord Wilberforce.

Anthony Scrivener QC and *George Greenwood* for the prosecutor
Peter Webster QC and *David Prebble* for the Board.

Their Lordships took time for consideration.

10th December. The following opinions were delivered.

LORD WILBERFORCE. My Lords, the British Airways Board has been prosecuted by the Inspector of Trading Standards, Manchester, for an alleged offence under the Trade Descriptions Act 1968, s 14(1)(*b*). The information was in the following terms:

'On or about the 15th August 1973 at Marple in the Petty Sessional Division of Stockport in the course of a trade or business the accused recklessly made a statement namely "I have pleasure in confirming the following reservations for you:—London/Bermuda Flight B.A. 679—Economy Class—29 August Dep. 1525 hours Arr. 1750 hours" by means of a letter addressed to W. J. Edmunds about the provision of services namely the transportation of a person by aeroplane which was false as to the time at which the service was to be provided contrary to Section 14(1)(*b*) of the Trade Descriptions Act 1968.'

1   [1975] 3 All ER 307, [1975] 3 WLR 1197

The magistrates' court at Stockport found the offence proved and fined the Board
a £250. The Board appealed to the Divisional Court which allowed the appeal and
quashed the conviction, holding that the statement made was promissory in character,
and not a statement of an existing fact, so that it could neither be true or false.

At the request of the prosecutor the court certified the following point of law as of
general public importance under s 1(2) of the Administration of Justice Act 1960,
namely:
b
'Are magistrates entitled to find that a statement made by an airline to a
passenger confirming a reservation on a specific flight, on a specific date and at a
specific time was a false statement as to the time at which a service was to be
provided within s 14 of the Trade Descriptions Act 1968, in the following circumstances: (a) that at the date when the said statement was made to the passenger
c   the flight was not overbooked; (b) that the booking on the said flight had already
been made at the date; (c) that at all material times the airline had a general
policy of overbooking flights; (d) that the passenger was prevented from travelling
on the flight subsequently because of the operation of the policy.'

A number of findings of fact were made by the justices and recorded in the case
stated. I summarise the most relevant.
d   The passenger involved was Mr W J Edmunds, a resident of Bermuda, who
purchased a passenger ticket from British Overseas Airways Corporation for a flight
from Bermuda to London on 15th July 1973 and return. The ticket was bought on
what is known as an 'Earlybird Certificate' which, when properly completed, entitles
a passenger to a reduced fare, but obliges him to travel, both outward and on return,
on the specified flights and dates endorsed on the ticket. In Mr Edmunds's case the
e   return flight was specified as 29th August 1973 on Flight BA679.

On 14th August 1973 Mr Edmunds, then in London, telephoned BOAC Reservations to confirm, but was told that he was not booked on the specified flight. He
was advised to contact the Customer Relations Department. He did this, and was
orally assured that he was properly booked. He asked for confirmation in writing
and this was given by a letter dated 14th August 1973, the relevant terms of which
f   are set out in the information. This letter bore the heading on one side 'British
Overseas Airways Corporation', and on the other 'BOAC' superimposed on 'British
Airways' (sic). It contained a reference to 'assisting you next time you travel BOAC'.
I think that there is no doubt that this letter was written on behalf of BOAC and not
the British Airways Board. This has consequences which I shall mention later.

It will be seen that the question certified by the Divisional Court contains a refer-
g   ence to 'a general policy of overbooking flights', and there was evidence as to this
given before the justices. An officer of BOAC admitted that, in common with all
major international airlines, BOAC operated such a policy 'as a prudent business
exercise to counteract "no-shows", i e those passengers who make reservations on
flights but do not turn up'. This policy inevitably resulted in occasional off-loading
of passengers who had booked. Some statistics were given showing that, over a
h   12 month period, as regards BOAC's services from London, two passengers out
of 10,000 were off-loaded, whereas the number of 'no-shows' was considerably
greater.

My Lords, although a good deal was said in the course of argument by way of
explanation and justification for this policy, I must make it clear that we are not,
in this appeal, concerned with whether it is commercially sound or unsound, fair or
j   unfair to passengers generally, operated conscientiously or otherwise. Such questions
are, in any event, primarily within the control of administrative authorities, the
Civil Aviation Authority or the Secretary of State in this country and similar bodies
elsewhere. We are only concerned in this case with the letter addressed, after a
specific request, to Mr Edmunds on 14th August 1973. Was this a promise as to
what the airline intended to do, or was it a statement of fact as to the airline's service?

Before I attempt to deal with this issue I should remove from the discussion certain points which might arise on the form of the information. This contains two ingredients, namely, first, an allegation that the statement was made recklessly (s 14(1)(b) of the 1968 Act), secondly, that it was false as to the time at which the service was to be provided (s 14(1)(iii)). It might well be contended that these were inappropriate and that the charge should have been that the statement was known to be false (s 14(1)(a)) and that the matter, as to which it was false, was the provision of services (s 14(1)(i)). But counsel for British Airways Board disclaimed any such contention and both sides agreed that the appeal should be decided on the basis that, in both respects, the charge had been correctly framed.

My Lords, the distinction in law between a promise as to future action, which may be broken or kept, and a statement as to existing fact, which may be true or false, is clear enough. There may be inherent in a promise an implied statement as to a fact, and where this is really the case, the court can attach appropriate consequences to any falsity in, or recklessness in the making of, that statement. Everyone is familiar with the proposition that a statement of intention may itself be a statement of fact and so capable of being true or false. But this proposition should not be used as a general solvent to transform the one type of assurance with another: the distinction is a real one and requires to be respected particularly where the effect of treating an assurance as a statement is to attract criminal consequences, as in the present case. As Lord Widgery CJ said in *Beckett v Cohen*[1] it was never intended that the 1968 Act should be used so as to make a criminal statement out of what is really a breach of warranty.

Which character—promise or statement—should be attributed to the letter, seems on the face of it to be debatable. Lord Widgery CJ certainly thought the choice was nicely balanced, but in the end he concluded[2] that the essence of what was said was a promise 'we will not turn you out for anybody else'. I think that I would agree with this if our task was the normal one of the judicial construction of the letter. At the least I would not think it right to differ from Lord Widgery CJ's view. But there is a special feature about cases under the 1968 Act which alters the nature of the court's approach. In s 14, the section which describes the offence charged against the British Airways Board, it is provided, in sub-s (2), that for the purposes of the section 'anything (whether or not a statement as to any of the matters specified in the preceding subsection) likely to be taken for such a statement as to any of those matters as would be false shall be deemed to be a false statement as to that matter'. So the crucial question, in relation to the letter of 14th August 1973, is whether it was likely to be taken (sc by the addressee) for a statement as to the time at which the service was provided. Whether it was so likely is thus a question of fact to be found. That this is so was decided in a case on this section, *R v Clarksons Holidays Ltd*[3], one concerned with a brochure extolling the merits of a hotel at Benidorm, Spain. The language used was a hyperbolic type normally used in brochures, as to which Roskill LJ said[4]:

'The question of what this written representation meant was essentially a question of fact for the jury, subject only to this, that if the words . . . relied upon by the Crown were upon their true construction incapable of bearing the meaning which the Crown sought to attribute to them'

the case should be withdrawn from the jury. I respectfully agree with this: indeed it is an essential feature of the Act that, when it has to be considered whether descriptions or statements are misleading, it is the meaning which they are likely

---

1   [1973] 1 All ER 120 at 122, [1972] 1 WLR 1593 at 1596, 1597
2   [1975] 3 All ER at 312, [1975] 1 WLR at 1201
3   (1972) 57 Cr App Rep 38
4   57 Cr App Rep at 53

a to bear to the person or persons to whom they are addressed that matters, and not
the meaning which they might, on analysis, bear to a trained legal mind. A similar
approach was taken by MacKenna J (delivering the judgment of the Court of Appeal,
Criminal Division) in *R v Sunair Holidays Ltd*[1].

In the present case the justices made the following relevant findings:

b '(*a*) That the passenger ticket, the Earlybird Certificate and the letter of the
14th August 1973 separately and together contained an implied statement of an
existing fact. (*b*) That a passenger in possession of the passenger ticket would
believe that such a ticket stated a fact, namely a place had been reserved for
him or her on the flight specified *and at the time* so specified. Further, that the
Earlybird Certificate would only serve to reinforce in the mind of a passenger
that such a place was available on the flight so specified and at the time specified.

c The letter of the 14th August would similarly reinforce a passenger's view that a
certain fact existed (by implication) namely that he would fly in an aeroplane
from London to Bermuda on the 29th August 1973 on the flight and time specified. (*c*) The statement contained in the letter was false and made recklessly
since in view of the [Board's] admitted policy a reservation on the flight could
not be confirmed at the date of the letter as it was always possible that Mr.

d Edmunds would be off-loaded. It followed that no reservation had been made
in the sense that an ordinary person would take it to mean i.e. a certain booking.
This was especially so in view of the circumstances in which the letter was
written.'

In my opinion these were findings which the justices were entitled to make. And the
essence of them is that the letter, taken together with the ticket and the Earlybird

e Certificate, would be taken as a statement that Mr Edmunds had a certain booking,
which statement, in view of the overbooking policy, was untrue, since his booking
though very likely to be a firm one was exposed to a risk—small but, as events
proved, real—that it might not give him a seat on the aircraft. I think that the justices
were entitled to find that this would be taken as a statement of a fact, rather than as a
mere promise that Mr Edmunds would be flown on the day and at the time specified,

f and that they did so find.   It is on this finding so made, which perhaps was not
fully brought home to the Divisional Court, that I feel obliged to reach a different
conclusion.

Turning now to the questions certified, I would not answer these in the form in
which they are couched. The answer which I would suggest is that the justices
were entitled to find that the statement contained in the letter dated 14th August

g 1973 from British Overseas Airways Corpn to W J Edmunds, referred to in the
information, when read in the light of the ticket issued to W J Edmunds on 11th
July 1973 and the Earlybird Certificate, was a false statement within s 14(1) of the
Trade Descriptions Act 1968.

It remains, in the light of this answer, to decide the present appeal. It is well
established that this House is not confined to answering the question(s) certified for

h its opinion, but can and indeed should consider other material points bearing on
the substance of the appeal. Such a point concerns the identity of the defendant,
British Airways Board, a point taken before the justices, but in view of their decision
as to the statement, not decided by the Divisional Court. As I have stated, the letter
of 14th August 1973 was written on behalf of BOAC. It was not written on behalf of
British Airways Board. So the question inevitably arises whether there is any legal

j basis on which the Board can be liable in respect of an offence committed by BOAC
in making the statement contained in the letter. I am forced to the conclusion that
there is not. The relevant enactment under which British Airways Board was constituted is the Civil Aviation Act 1971, s 37. The Board was given (s 38) power to

1 [1973] 2 All ER 1233 at 1240, [1973] 1 WLR 1105 at 1113

'control all the activities' of the corporations which included BOAC. The corporations remained in existence but the Secretary of State was given power (s 57) to dissolve *a* them and to transfer to the Board all property, rights and liabilities of the corporations. In fact, BOAC continued to operate under its own name, but adding to it the name of British Airways as, in effect, a trade name paving the way for the eventual take-over by the British Airways Board. The offence in question was committed on 14th (or 15th) August 1973, and BOAC was not dissolved until 1st April 1974 when the Air Corporations (Dissolution) Order 1973 took effect. This provided that *b* all property, rights and liabilities which immediately before the order came into force were property, rights and liabilities of either of the corporations should be property, rights and liabilities of the Board.

My Lords, there is nothing here which can in any way support an argument that the British Airways Board could be prosecuted for BOAC's offences. The relationship between the two legal entities was that of facultative not mandatory control of one *c* by the other: there was no agency, no joint operation, no initiation or direction by British Airways Board of the act complained of, no delegation by British Airways Board of any statutory duty to BOAC so as to make the Board answerable for any failure to comply with such duty; no basis for a contention that BOAC's act could be attributable to the Board as having been done by the Board's directing mind (cf *Tesco Supermarkets Ltd v Nattrass*[1]). Finally, and the contrary was scarcely contended, *d* the dissolution order of 1st April 1974 was not, indeed, under the terms of s 57 of the Civil Aviation Act 1971, could not amount to, a provision making the offence of BOAC the offence of the Board. The fact is that BOAC could have been proceeded against at any time between 15th August 1973 and 1st April 1974 but that, after the latter date, no prosecution was possible.

The appeal must therefore be dismissed but I would not suggest that the prosecutor *e* should pay the Board's costs.

VISCOUNT DILHORNE. My Lords, in my opinion these proceedings were misconceived from the outset. The information laid on 26th June 1974 was against the British Airways Board and was based on a letter dated 14th August 1973 which *f* bore the heading 'British Overseas Airways Corporation and BOAC BRITISH AIRWAYS'. It was signed by a Miss Burford and underneath her signature were typed the words 'Passenger Reservations'. The justices found that the signatory of that letter 'had the necessary authority of the British Overseas Airways Corporation to deal with passenger reservations'.

If, as was contended, a statement in that letter amounted to the commission of an *g* offence against s 14(1)(*b*) of the Trade Descriptions Act 1968, BOAC should have been prosecuted, but on 26th June 1974 BOAC had ceased to exist. It was dissolved on 1st April 1974 by the Air Corporations (Dissolution) Order 1973.

The point was taken in the magistrates' court that the Board were not liable for the contents of the letter, but the justices came to the conclusion that they were as the notepaper had on it the words 'British Airways' and as the British Airways *h* Board had, by virtue of s 38 of the Civil Aviation Act 1971, power to control the activities of BOAC.

The fact that the Board had such powers clearly does not ipso facto make them responsible for any criminal acts committed by BOAC and the fact that the letter in question had the words 'British Airways' on it does not show them to be responsible criminally for a letter written by a person authorised by BOAC to deal with *j* passenger reservations.

The justices also held that the criminal liabilities of BOAC passed to the Board by virtue of art 2 of the Air Corporations (Dissolution) Order 1973. That article

---

1   [1970] 3 All ER 357, [1971] 1 QB 133

provides for the transfer of 'all property, rights and liabilities' of BOAC to the Board.
a That paragraph does not extend to criminal liabilities and in this House it was rightly
not contended that it did.

The information alleged that an offence contrary to s 14(1)(b) of the Trade
Descriptions Act 1968 had been committed. The material parts of that section read
as follows:

b   '(1) It shall be an offence for any person in the course of any trade or business—
(a) to make a statement which he knows to be false; or (b) recklessly to make a
statement which is false; as to any of the following matters, that is to say,—
(i) the provision in the course of any trade or business of any services, accommodation or facilities; (ii) . . . (iii) the time at which, manner in which or
persons by whom any services, accommodation or facilities are so provided . . .
c   '(2) For the purposes of this section—(a) anything (whether or not a statement
as to any of the matters specified in the preceding subsection) likely to be taken
for such a statement as to any of those matters as would be false shall be deemed
to be a false statement as to that matter; and (b) a statement made regardless
of whether it is true or false shall be deemed to be made recklessly, whether
or not the person making it had reasons for believing it might be false . . .
d   '(4) In this section "false" means false to a material degree . . .'

The information alleged that the following statement in the letter of the 14th
August 1973: 'I have pleasure in confirming the following reservations for you:—
London/Bermuda Flight B.A. 679—Economy Class—29 August Dep. 1525 hours
Arr. 1750 hours', was false as to the time at which the service was to be provided and
was made recklessly.
e I can see no ground for saying it was made recklessly or for saying that it was made
regardless of its truth or falsity. BOAC, in common with other international airlines,
followed an overbooking policy designed to ensure, if possible, a full passenger load
for their aircraft, it being their experience that a number of those who had made
reservations did not take them up. On occasions their policy led to passengers for
whom reservations had been made not getting on to an aircraft. This overbooking
f being a deliberate policy of BOAC, if the statement in the letter of 14th August
was false, it was false to their knowledge and not make recklessly regardless of its
truth or falsity.

Counsel for the Board did not take the point that the Board should have been
charged under s 14(1)(a) with making a statement known to be false. He did not
desire to do so no doubt wishing to obtain the views of the House as to the falsity
g or otherwise of the statement. Nevertheless, on the facts disclosed in the case stated,
if the Board had been responsible for that letter and the statement in it was false,
the conviction could not, in my opinion, have been upheld.

Mr Edmunds had bought a return ticket for a return journey from Bermuda to
London which was expressed to be valid only on the outward flight on the 15th July
at 23.10 hours and on the return flight on 29th August at 15.05 hours. His journeys
h were subject to the conditions on the 'Earlybird/Advance Purchase Excursion certificate, one of which was that he would be accepted 'for travel only on the flights and
dates endorsed on' his ticket. On the certificate there was printed in a box:

       'Once definite reservations have been made, refund if applicable will be
       limited to 75% of the fare(s). No refund can be made after commencement of
j   travel.'

On 14th August Mr Edmunds was informed that he was not booked on the flight
on 29th August scheduled to leave London Airport at 15.25 hours for Bermuda.
He was told to get in touch with the Customer Relations Department of BOAC.
He did so and was told that he was booked on that flight and that was confirmed by
the letter of 14th August from Passenger Reservations.

In these circumstances Mr Edmunds was clearly led to believe that he had a definite
and certain booking on the flight on 29th August as the justices found. There was *a*
no reason for him to ascribe a different meaning to the word 'reservation' when
used in the letter to that to be given to it in the Earlybird certificate.

The statement that his reservation was confirmed was made when BOAC, following
their policy of overbooking, knew that he might not get on the aircraft. It was, in
my opinion, clearly false, for it clearly implied that they had reserved a seat for him
and would keep one reserved for him when it was always their intention, should *b*
more passengers arrive for the flight than there was room for, not to carry one or
more of those for whom reservations had been made. It was false because it did
not state the qualification to which it was subject and it was false, in my view, to
their knowledge.

In expressing this opinion I do not wish to comment on BOAC's overbooking
policy or to be thought to criticise it for there may be very good reasons for it, but *c*
there can in my opinion be no justification for telling Mr Edmunds that his reservation
was confirmed and leaving him to suppose that he had a certain booking when that
was not the case and when it was not BOAC's intention that there should be on
14th August a certain booking for him.

In my opinion this appeal should be dismissed.

d

LORD SIMON OF GLAISDALE. My Lords, in my respectful view the principles of law applicable to the question certified for your Lordships' consideration
were stated cogently and accurately by MacKenna J giving the judgment of the
Court of Appeal in *R v Sunair Holidays Ltd*[1]. The certified question of law cannot
therefore be answered in the abstract. The issue in each case is what the relevant *e*
statement (in the instant case the letter of 14th August 1973) in all its circumstances
reasonably meant to its recipient.

The case stated by the justices has been subjected during argument to a close and
strict scrutiny. But in my view justices' findings must be read as a whole and (to
borrow an expression from parliamentary law) benevolently construed.

I have had the advantage of reading in draft the speeches prepared by my noble *f*
and learned friends, with which I agree. For the reasons they give I think that the
justices were entitled to find that the letter of 14th August 1973 was in its circumstances a false statement, within s 14(1) of the Trade Descriptions Act 1968.

It seems to me likely that the inspector laid the information under s 14(1)(*b*) (false
statement made recklessly) rather than under s 14(1)(*a*) (statement known to be
false) because the odds were that Mr Edmunds would not in the event be off-loaded
under the overbooking policy, although he might be. But this is based on a fallacy. *g*
It was the chance (not being so remote that it could be dismissed as being de minimis)
of Mr Edmunds being off-loaded that made the statement of 14th August in its
circumstances false *to the knowledge* of the maker of the statement. The Board,
though, disclaimed any reliance on this point, desiring a decision on the merits.

I agree with my noble and learned friend, Lord Fraser of Tullybelton, that the *h*
statement of 14th August in its circumstances was false as to the matters set out in
both s 14(1)(i) ('the provision in the course of . . . business of any services, accommodation or facilities') and s 14(1)(iii) ('the time at which . . . accommodation or
facilities are so provided').

However, since I agree that the Board are not to be held to be responsible for the
statement of 14th August 1973, I concur that the appeal should be dismissed. *j*

My noble and learned friend, Viscount Dilhorne, has emphasised that your Lordships
are not concerned with the merits of the overbooking policy. I do, however, feel
entitled to say that to an uninstructed outsider it would seem that the simple, fair
and economically sensible way of dealing with the 'no-show' mischief is for the airline

1   [1973] 2 All ER 1233 at 1236, [1973] 1 WLR 1105 at 1109

a to demand a forfeitable deposit with the reservation, and that if international agreement cannot be secured to some such arrangement it reflects little credit on the international organisation concerned.

LORD EDMUND-DAVIES. My Lords, two questions arise in this appeal: (1) did the letter dated 14th August 1973 sent to Mr Edmunds constitute a breach of s 14 of b the Trade Descriptions Act 1968? (2) if so, were the justices right in holding the Board liable for that breach?

For the reasons considered in detail by my noble and learned friend, Lord Wilberforce, I am in respectful agreement that, whatever be the proper answer to question (1), a negative answer must be given to question (2). In the result, this appeal from the decision of the Divisional Court in favour of the Board must be c dismissed, though on grounds which the Divisional Court did not find themselves called on to explore. It is, however, necessary to deal with question (1), which was argued at length below and again before this House. It expresses in a bald form what I believe to be the gist of the question certified by the Divisional Court, and is clearly of general public importance.

The facts giving rise to this appeal have been set out at length by my Lords and d need not now be repeated. The appeal itself raises in a neat form the difference between an assertion of existing fact and a promise as to future conduct. Section 14 of the 1968 Act relates only to the former, and Lord Widgery CJ was undoubtedly correct in saying in *Beckett v Cohen*[1]:

e '. . . s 14(1) . . . has no application to statements which amount to a promise with regard to the future, and which therefore at the time when they are made cannot have the character of being either true or false.'

But the facts of this case illustrate yet again that an assertion of existing fact and a promise of future conduct may both be found in one and the same statement. As MacKenna J said in the course of his admirable judgment in *R v Sunair Holidays Ltd*[2]:

f 'A promise or forecast may contain by implication a statement of present fact. The person who makes the promise may be implying that his present intention is to keep it or that he has at present the power to perform it. The person who makes the forecast may be implying that he now believes that his prediction will come true or that he has the means of bringing it to pass. Such implied statements of present intention, means or belief, when they are made, may well be within s 14 and therefore punishable if they were false and were made know-g ingly or recklessly. But if they are punishable, the offence is not the breaking of a promise or the failure to make a prediction come true. It is the making of a false statement of an existing fact, somebody's present state of mind or present means.'

This House is presently concerned with the legal character of the statement contained in the letter of 14th August 1973 sent to Mr Edmunds on the same day as h that on which he had been orally assured that the booking of his return flight to Bermuda had been effected and in response to his request for written confirmation of that assurance. The material words were: 'I have pleasure in confirming the following reservations for you:—London/Bermuda Flight B.A. 679—Economy Class— 29 August Dep. 15.25 hours Arr. 17.50 hours.' The Board assert that what in that letter Mr Edmunds claims was reasonably read by him as being a statement of j existing fact was in reality intended to be (and ought reasonably to have been) regarded as) nothing more than the expression of a sincerely entertained hope. Waller J[3] said:

1 [1973] 1 All ER 120 at 121, [1972] 1 WLR 1593 at 1596
2 [1973] 2 All ER 1233 at 1236, [1973] 1 WLR 1105 at 1109
3 [1975] 3 All ER 307 at 313, [1975] 1 WLR 1197 at 1201

'At that time, as the case finds, the flight was not overbooked. In other words, at that time there was space on that aircraft for Mr Edmunds. As I see it, the *a* fact was that the flight was arranged. The fact was that on that day there was space available for Mr Edmunds, and there was a promise for the future that that space would be kept for him. In my view that promise for the future was not an existing fact such as is required for a false statement under s 14 of the 1968 Act. It may well be that it was a warranty for the future, but it was not a statement of an existing fact.'   *b*

I respectfully disagree. Waller J appears to have accepted that there was an implied statement of fact in the letter, namely that the space was then available for Mr Edmunds, but he reads it as containing merely a *promise* that the space would continue to be available. He thus shared the view of Lord Widgery CJ[1] that the letter had moved 'out of the realm of fact into the realm of future promise'. I do not think *c* this was so. Bearing s 14(2)(*a*) in mind, the reasonable construction to be put on the letter was, surely, that the writer had taken steps to *secure* for Mr Edmunds a seat on the designated flight. In other words, it was both a statement of existing fact and a statement as to present intention, which was equally a statement of existing fact. The letter amounted to saying: 'Not only have we secured your seat for you, but we have the intention to ensure that it will remain reserved and available to you *d* on the designated flight.' In my judgment, such would be the interpretation reasonably placed on the letter by the recipient, and the justices were therefore entitled to find, as they did, that it 'contained an implied statement of an existing fact'. They further found: '. . . that the Earlybird Certificate would only serve to reinforce in the mind of a passenger that such a place was available on the flight so specified and at the time specified.' That, indeed, may well have been so, but I should make *e* it clear that my conclusion as to the proper answer to question (1) does not turn in any way on the special terms on which Mr Edmunds's Earlybird Certificate was issued. On the contrary, it is based solely on the circumstances leading up to the writing of the letter of 14th August and on the terms of the letter itself.

The falsity of the foregoing statements of existing fact which I hold were implied in the letter of 14th August is not, in my judgment, open to doubt. For, even though *f* when it was despatched to Mr Edmunds no overbooking on Flight BA 679 on 29th August had yet occurred, it was well known that overbooking might take place, with the consequence that (to put it at its lowest) there was a degree of risk that, even though the flight left on time, Mr Edmunds would not be one of its passengers. Fact was asserted when in reality only chance (albeit a good chance) existed. However commercially understandable overbooking may be in keenly competitive conditions, *g* to assure a would-be passenger that his seat had been secured for him when it was known that it had not and that it might eventuate that he would be turned away was to state that which was known to be false, and therefore came within sub-s (1)(*a*) of s 14 of the 1968 Act. The information charged the respondents with breaching sub-s (1)(*b*) by *recklessly* making a false statement, and the justices found that:

> 'The statement contained in the letter was *false and made recklessly* since in *h* view of the [Board's] admitted policy a reservation on the flight could not be confirmed at the date of the letter as it was always possible that Mr. Edmunds would be off-loaded.'

But the difference between the two states of mind is brought out by the provision in s 14(2)(*b*) that—   *j*

> 'a statement made regardless of whether it is true or false shall be deemed to be made recklessly, whether or not the person making it had reasons for believing that it *might* be false.'

---

1   [1975] 3 All ER at 312, [1975] 1 WLR at 1201

This indicates a state of mind different from that which, for the reasons stated,
a I hold must be imputed to those responsible for the letter of 14th August at the
time it was written and despatched. But, having made the point clear, it can be
left there as far as the present case is concerned, the Board understandably being
agreeable to regard the charge of recklessness as being correctly laid, even though,
as I have indicated, it seems to have been technically incorrect.

For these various reasons, I should have allowed this appeal had the proper party
b been prosecuted. But, the position being otherwise, I concur in holding that it
should be dismissed.

LORD FRASER OF TULLYBELTON. My Lords, British Airways Board ('the
Board'), which is the respondent in this appeal, was convicted of an offence under
s 14(1)(b) of the Trade Descriptions Act 1968 in respect that it had recklessly made
c a false statement as to the time at which a service was to be provided. The point of
law which was certified by the Divisional Court as being of general public importance
raises the question whether the statement was false and so constituted an offence
under the Act. But there is another, and logically prior, question whether, if any
offence was committed, the Board is the proper defendant to be charged with it.
This question arises because the statement alleged to be false was made in a letter
d signed by a person authorised not by the Board but by British Overseas Airways
Corporation. The justices held that the Board was responsible for the statement and
they expressed their opinion thus:

'We were of the opinion that: (a) the statement was made by the [Board]
since it was written on their headed writing paper and they had the power to
control all of the activities of the BOAC by virtue of section 38 of the Civil
e Aviation Act 1971 . . .'

They added a further reason but counsel who appeared for the prosecutor in this
House conceded, rightly in my opinion, that it could not be supported, and I need
not refer to it. The information in the present case was issued on 26th June 1974, by
which time BOAC had been dissolved and had ceased to exist, so that, unless the
f Board is responsible, nobody is. The Divisional Court did not find it necessary to
deal with the question of the Board's responsibility because they held that no false
statement had been made, but the question was raised again before this House and
I think it must be answered before the certified question.

The first reason given by the justices for holding the Board responsible was that
the letter was written on their headed writing paper. I have some doubt whether
g that conclusion can be reconciled with the finding of fact in the case stated that the
letter 'bore the heading British Overseas Airways Corporation, B.O.A.C., British
Airways'. 'British Airways *Board*', which is the name by which the Board was constituted under the Civil Aviation Act 1971, was not mentioned. But, assuming that
the conclusion is justified, it cannot go far towards fixing responsibility on the Board
in light of the finding that 'the signatory of the letter had the necessary authority
h of the British Overseas Airways Corporation to deal with passenger reservations,
but (by implication) did not have the authority of the Board'. That leads to the
justices' second, and I think more important, reason, which was that the Board
had power to control all of the activities of the BOAC by virtue of s 38 of the 1968 Act.
It was said that the Board must be treated as having delegated its powers to BOAC
and that it was therefore responsible for any offence committed by BOAC. In my
j opinion, that argument is not well founded. It was supported by reference to cases
such as *Linnett v Commissioner of Metropolitan Police*[1] where a duty expressly imposed
by statute on one party had been delegated by him to another. But s 38 did not
impose a duty; it only conferred a power to control the activities of BOAC. Moreover
BOAC had in August 1973 powers of its own, which it had possessed before the

1 [1946] 1 All ER 380, [1946] KB 290

Board was set up under the Civil Aviation Act 1971, and there is nothing to show that
BOAC sent the letter of 14th August 1973 under powers delegated to them by the **a**
Board rather than under their own independent powers.

If any offence was committed under the 1968 Act, it was not committed by the
Board and the Board is not, in my opinion, responsible for it. The result is that it
ought not to have been convicted. The conviction was quashed by the Divisional
Court, and the appeal from that court should, in my opinion, be dismissed.

If that is right, it is not strictly necessary to consider whether the alleged offence **b**
was committed at all, but as that was the point of law of general public importance
which was certified, and as we heard a full argument on it, I should state my opinion.
The circumstances in which the question arises were briefly these. Mr Edmunds
bought from BOAC a return ticket from Bermuda to London. It was called an
Earlybird Excursion Ticket, and the fare for it was lower than for an ordinary ticket.
It was subject to special conditions, one of which was that it was valid only for the **c**
flights and on the dates endorsed on the ticket. Mr Edmunds was given an Earlybird Certificate which set out the special conditions. His ticket was endorsed for the
outward journey by a flight on 15th July 1973 and for the return journey by Flight
BA 679 on 29th August 1973. He duly made the outward journey and, while in
London, he telephoned to BOAC to confirm that his return booking on 29th August
was in order. He received an oral assurance that it was, but he asked for written **d**
confirmation and in response to his request he received the letter of 14th August.
The material part of that letter stated: 'I have pleasure in confirming the following
reservations for you:—London/Bermuda B.A. 679—Economy Class—29 August Dep.
15.25 hours Arr. 17.50 hours.' Mr Edmunds naturally accepted the letter as confirmation that a seat had been definitely reserved for him on the flight and date
stated, which were the same as those endorsed on his ticket. But when he arrived **e**
at the airport on 29th August he was told that there was no room for him on the
flight because it had been overbooked, and he had to wait till the next day. That
situation arose because BOAC, like other airlines, had a policy of overbooking; that
is to say they would accept bookings for more passengers on a flight than there were
seats available on that flight. We were told, and I readily accept, that overbooking
was commercially necessary because of the large number of passengers who booked **f**
seats on particular flights and then did not appear. On some routes these 'no-shows'
formed a substantial proportion of the bookings, and as their tickets were available
for later flights, if their seats had all been left empty the result would have been a
serious loss of revenue to the airline, as well as unnecessary disappointment to other
would-be travellers. The overbooking was limited, and was calculated so that the
number of passengers overbooked would not exceed the number of 'no-shows' to be **g**
expected in the light of the airline's experience. On a few occasions it did exceed
that number and, unfortunately for Mr Edmunds, his return journey was one of
these occasions. We have, of course, no concern with the reasons for the overbooking
policy. The only question is whether, having regard to its existence in August 1973,
the statement in the letter of 14th August concerning Mr Edmunds's reservation
constituted an offence under s 14 of the 1968 Act. **h**

Earlier sections of the Act prohibit false descriptions of goods. Section 14(1) deals
with false or misleading statements as to services, and it provides as follows:

'It shall be an offence for any person in the course of any trade or business—
(a) to make a statement which he knows to be false; or (b) recklessly to make a
statement which is false; as to any of the following matters, that is to say,— **j**
(i) the provision in the course of any trade or business of any services, accommodation or facilities; (ii) the nature of any services, accommodation or facilities
provided in the course of any trade or business; (iii) the time at which, manner
in which or persons by whom any services, accommodation or facilities are so
provided . . .'

In this case the Board was charged under s 14(1)(b) with having 'recklessly' made a

false statement, as to (iii) 'the time at which' services were to be provided. Section 14
a has been considered by the courts in several cases. In *R v Sunair Holidays Ltd*[1]
MacKenna J, giving the judgment of the Court of Appeal, said this:

> 'The section deals with "statements" of which it can be said that they were, at
> the time when they were made, "false". That may be the case with a statement
> of fact, whether past or present. A statement that a fact exists now, or that it
b existed in the past, is either true or false at the time when the statement is made.
> But that is not the case with a promise or a prediction about the future. A pre-
> diction may come true or it may not. A promise to do something in the future
> may be kept or it may be broken. But neither the prediction nor the promise
> can be said to have been true or false at the time when it was made. We conclude
> that s 14 does not deal with forecasts or promises as such. We put in the qualify-
c ing words "as such" for this reason. A promise or forecast may contain by impli-
> cation a statement of present fact. The person who makes the promise may be
> implying that his present intention is to keep it or that he has at present the
> power to perform it. The person who makes the forecast may be implying that
> he now believes that his prediction will come true or that he has the means of
> bringing it to pass. Such implied statements of present intention, means or
> belief, when they are made, may well be within s 14 and therefore punishable
d if they were false and were made knowingly or recklessly. But if they are punish-
> able, the offence is not the breaking of a promise or the failure to make a predic-
> tion come true. It is the making of a false statement of an existing fact,
> somebody's present state of mind or present means.'

I respectfully agree with that explanation of the section. In the *Sunair* case[2], and
e in some of the earlier cases to which we were referred, the statements made by
travel agents and others were held to have been mere expressions of intention or
promises for the future, which, at the time they were made, were neither true nor
false. But in the present case I have reached the opinion that the statement in the
letter of 14th August concerning Mr Edmunds's reservation was false, because it
implied that BOAC then had an intention which they did not, in fact, have. The
f statement that they were 'confirming' the 'reservation' would, I think, convey to
Mr Edmunds that their intention on 14th August was to keep a seat on that flight
available for him against all comers. That would necessarily include the intention
to avoid booking so many other passengers on the flight as to create a risk that Mr
Edmunds might not get a seat. But as their real intention was to overbook, and thus
to create such a risk, the implication was false and the statement must be deemed,
g by virtue of s 14(2), to be false.

The point would be more obvious in a case where a particular seat or room is
reserved. If I ask for a particular room in an hotel and the manager replies that he
has reserved it for me for the dates that I want, there can be no doubt that he conveys
to me that it is his intention, at the time when he replies, to keep that room for me
and not to let it to anybody else on the specified dates. The same would be true of a
h numbered seat in a theatre. If I find when I arrive that someone else is occupying the
room, that might be for one of three reasons. It might be because of some mistake,
in which case the manager would probably have a defence to a charge under the
1968 Act by relying on s 24. Secondly, it might be because, although at the time
when he replied to me he intended to reserve the room for me, he later abandoned
that intention, perhaps because a more important guest wanted it. In that case he
j might escape liability under the Act because his letter had correctly expressed his
intention at the time when it was written. But, thirdly, it might be because he had
never intended to keep the room for me, if that would require him to refuse all
bookings that might possibly conflict with mine. In that case, his original statement

1 [1973] 2 All ER 1233 at 1236, [1973] 1 WLR 1105 at 1109
2 [1973] 2 All ER 1233, [1973] 1 WLR 1105

would be false because it implied that he had an intention that he did not in fact have. That seems to me to fit the present case exactly.   *a*

If the statement in the letter of 14th August was false, it remains to consider whether it was made 'recklessly' so as to constitute an offence under s 14(1)(*b*). In my opinion it was not made recklessly. The reason why it was false was that the intention which it implied was inconsistent with the actual intention of overbooking. That intention must, of course, have been known to the airline when the letter was written. It seems to me, therefore, that the airline made a statement which it knew *b* to be false and that the charge ought to have been made under para (*a*) of s 14(1).

There was some argument whether the statement fell within para (iii) of s 14(1) as a statement 'as to the time at which' a service was to be provided, or within para (i) as a statement 'as to the provision' of services. In my opinion, it falls within both these paragraphs. The statement was about the provision of services but the time including, of course, the date on which it was to be provided, was an essential part of *c* the statement.

It was faintly argued that the airline might escape liability by virtue of s 14(4) which provides: 'In this section "false" means false to a material degree . . .' The argument was that, as appears from the case stated, the number of passengers who were off-loaded because of the overbooking policy was very small in relation to the total number of passengers who booked seats, and therefore that the statement was *d* not false to any material degree. I cannot agree. The falsity of the statement was material to Mr Edmunds and that is enough for the present purpose.

I agree that the certified question should be answered in the way suggested by my noble and learned friend, Lord Wilberforce. I should add that I do not think there is any relevance in the circumstances mentioned in the question in para (a), namely, that at the date when the statement was made the flight was not overbooked or in *e* para (b) that the booking on the flight had already been made at that date.

I would dismiss the appeal.

Appeal dismissed.

Solicitors: *Turner Peacock* (for the prosecutor); *Richards, Butler & Co* (for the Board).

Gordon H Scott Esq   Barrister.   *f*

Owners of the ship Philippine Admiral v Wallem Shipping (Hong Kong) Ltd and others   *g*

PRIVY COUNCIL
LORD CROSS OF CHELSEA, LORD SIMON OF GLAISDALE, LORD SALMON, LORD FRASER OF TULLYBELTON AND SIR THADDEUS MCCARTHY
14th, 15th, 16th, 17th, 21st, 22nd, 23rd, 24th, 28th, 29th APRIL, 5th NOVEMBER 1975

Constitutional law – Foreign sovereign state – Immunity from suit – Exceptions – Commercial *h*
transaction – Admiralty – Action in rem – Ship owned by foreign state – Ship in possession
of third party – Ship used by third party for ordinary commercial purposes – Foreign state
having immediate right to possession of ship – Actions in rem against ship brought by charterers
and repairers in respect of alleged defaults by third party – Whether foreign state entitled to
claim immunity from suit.

By a treaty concluded in 1956 between Japan and the Republic of the Philippines *j*
('the republic') Japan made available to the republic the sum of US $550 million in respect of reparations for damage done to Filipino property during the second world war. In 1957 a Reparations Act was passed in the Philippines to govern the utilisation of goods acquired under the 1956 treaty. The 1957 Act provided, inter alia, (i) that

reparation payments should be utilised so as to ensure the maximum possible
a economic benefit to the Filipino people; (ii) that the republic's government should
not utilise reparations goods for the purpose of entering into competition with
private industries which served the public fairly and adequately; and (iii) that there
should be created a reparations commission ('the commission') to administer the
acquisition, utilisation and distribution of reparations goods and services. The commission was at all times the agent of the republic. Liberation Steamship Inc ('Libera-
b tion'), a privately-owned company incorporated in the republic, successfully applied
to the commission for the grant of an ocean-going ship, and in 1959 the commission
on behalf of the republic contracted with a Japanese ship-building company for the
construction of the ship. In 1960 the commission made a contract of conditional sale
of the ship to Liberation. Under the contract the commission retained the title and
ownership of the ship until the purchase price had been fully paid by Liberation. On
c 15th December 1960 the commission was registered as sole owner of the ship. Liberation took possession of the ship and operated her for commercial purposes in the
ordinary course of its shipping business until 1972. On 21st December 1972 Liberation
chartered the ship for a period of nine to 12 months at the charterers' option.
By that time Liberation was seriously in arrears with its payments under the sale
contract and accordingly the commission had an immediate right to recover possession
d of the ship. At the time of the charterparty and in the period immediately following
the ship was under repair at Hong Kong. Liberation was unable to settle the repairers'
account and on 8th May 1973 cancelled the charterparty. In May, June and July 1973
the repairers and the charterers brought separate actions in rem for the cost of goods
supplied and disbursements made for the ship and for breach of charterparty. The
ship was arrested at the instance of the charterers and, on 8th October, the Supreme
e Court of Hong Kong ordered that the ship be appraised and sold. On 29th October
the republic applied for an order that the order of 8th October and all subsequent
proceedings be set aside. On 14th and 17th December 1973 the Supreme Court
ordered that the writs and all subsequent proceedings be set aside on the ground that
the republic was entitled to claim sovereign immunity. On 26th April 1974 the Full
Court of Hong Kong reversed that judgment, holding that the doctrine of sovereign
f immunity did not apply since the ship was in the possession of Liberation which was
using her for its own commercial purposes. The republic appealed to the Privy Council,
contending (i) that ownership of a ship by a sovereign power coupled with an immediate right to possession was sufficient to found a claim for immunity whether or not
the sovereign power controlled or operated the ship, and (ii) that the use of the ship for
trading purposes was not inconsistent with its being either in or destined for public use.

g
Held – A foreign government was not entitled to claim sovereign immunity in cases
where an action in rem was brought against a vessel owned by that government if
the vessel was being used, either by the government itself or by a third party, for
trading purposes and not for the public service. In considering whether the ship was
at the relevant time a mere trading vessel, regard was to be had to the ship's past
h history which showed that the ship had always operated as an ordinary merchant
ship. The fact that Liberation's rights were subject to the Reparations Act and the
contract with the commission did not mean that the ship was to be treated as other
than an ordinary trading ship when considering the application of the doctrine of
sovereign immunity either at the commencement of the proceedings in rem or when
the claim to stay those proceedings was made. Moreover the ship had been used for
j commercial purposes while the republic was its owner and it could not be supposed
that such user would change after the republic had retaken possession of it.
Accordingly the appeal would be dismissed (see p 88 d and e, p 95 a to d and h to
p 96 c and g, post).
Dictum of Lord Maugham in *Compania Naviera Vascongada v SS Cristina* [1938] 1
All ER at 740 approved.

The Parlement Belge [1874-80] All ER Rep 104 distinguished.

The Porto Alexandre [1918-19] All ER Rep 615 and dicta of Lord Atkin and Lord **a**
Wright in *Compania Naviera Vascongada v SS Cristina* [1938] 1 All ER at 721, 735
disapproved.

Berizzi Bros Co v SS Pesaro (1925) 271 US 562 not followed.

Per Curiam. If the ship had not been an ordinary trading ship the republic would
have been entitled to immunity on the basis that it was not only the legal owner
but had an immediate right to possession (see p 96 *h* and *j* and p 97 *a* and *b*, post).   **b**

Notes

For sovereign immunity from suit, see 8 Halsbury's Laws (4th Edn) para 410, and for
cases on the subject, see 1 Digest (Repl) 54-61, *406-450*.

For sovereign immunity in Admiralty proceedings, see 1 Halsbury's Laws (4th Edn)   **c**
para 304, and for cases on the subject, see 1 Digest (Repl) 128-131, *143-166*.

Cases referred to in opinion

Baccus SRL v Servicio Nacional del Trigo [1956] 3 All ER 715, [1957] 1 QB 438, [1956] 3
    WLR 948, [1956] 2 Lloyd's Rep 448, CA, 1 Digest (Repl) 55, 412.

Berizzi Bros Co v SS Pesaro (1925) 271 US 562.   **d**

Charkieh, The (1873) LR 8 QB 197, 42 LJQB 75, 28 LT 190, 1 Asp MLC 533, 1 Digest
    (Repl) 130, 161.

Compania Espanola de Navegacion SA v The Navemar (1938) 303 US 68.

Compania Mercantil Argentina v United States Shipping Board (1924) 93 LJKB 816, 131 LT
    388, CA, 1 Digest (Repl) 57, 419.

Compania Naviera Vascongada v SS Cristina [1938] 1 All ER 719, [1938] AC 485, 107 LJP   **e**
    1, 159 LT 394, 19 Asp MLC 159, HL, 1 Digest (Repl) 129, 154.

Flota Maritima Browning de Cuba SA v SS Canadian Conqueror (1962) 34 DLR (2d) 628.

Gagara, The [1919] P 95, 88 LJP 101, 122 LT 498, 14 Asp MLC 547, CA, 1 Digest (Repl)
    130, 158.

Government of the Democratic Republic of the Congo v Velle (1971) 22 DLR (3d) 669.

Isbrandsten Tankers Inc v President of India (1971) 446 F 2d 1198.   **f**

Jassy, The [1906] P 270, 75 LJP 93, 95 LT 363, 10 Asp MLC 278, 1 Digest (Repl) 131, *164*.

Johore (Sultan of) v Ababakar Tunku Aris Bendahara [1952] 1 All ER 1261, [1952] AC 318,
    PC, 1 Digest (Repl) 57, 422.

Jupiter, The [1924] P 236, 93 LJP 156, 132 LT 624, 16 Asp MLC 447, 19 Ll R Rep 325,
    CA, 1 Digest (Repl) 130, 160.

Mighell v Johore (Sultan) [1894] 1 QB 149, [1891-4] All ER Rep 1019, 63 LJQB 593, 70 L T   **g**
    64, 58 JP 244, 9 R 447, CA, 1 Digest (Repl) 55, 409.

Parlement Belge, The (1880) 5 PD 197 [1874-80] All ER Rep 104, 42 LT 273, 4 Asp MLC
    234, CA, 1 Digest (Repl) 121, 70.

Porto Alexandre, The [1920] P 30, 89 LJP 97, 122 LT 661, 15 Asp MLC 1, 1 Ll L Rep 191,
    CA, 1 Digest (Repl) 129, 152.

Republic of Mexico v Hoffman (1945) 324 US 30.   **h**

Rich v Naviera Vacuba SA (1961) 197 F Supp 710.

Schooner Exchange, The v McFaddon (1812) 7 Cranch 116.

Swiss Israel Trade Bank v Government of Salta [1972] Lloyd's Rep 497.

Thai-Europe Tapioca Services Ltd v Government of Pakistan [1975] 3 All ER 961, [1975] 1
    WLR 1485, CA.

United States of America and Republic of France v Dollfus Mieg et Cie SA and Bank of   **j**
    England [1952] 1 All ER 572, [1952] AC 582, HL; *on appeal from Dollfus Mieg et*
    Compagnie SA v Bank of England [1950] 1 All ER 747, [1950] Ch 333, CA, 1 Digest
    (Repl) 58 *433*.

Young v The Scotia [1903] AC 501, 72 LJPC 115, 89 LT 374, 9 Asp MLC 485, PC, 1 Digest
    (Repl) 127, *136*.

Appeal

a By writs dated 23rd May and 7th September 1973 the first respondents, Wallem Shipping (Hong Kong) Ltd ('Wallem'), brought actions in rem in the Supreme Court of Hong Kong against the ship Philippine Admiral ('the ship') to recover sums of $75,207·57 and $90,160·41 together with interest and costs in respect of goods, materials and necessary disbursements supplied to the ship at Hong Kong and further claiming, if necessary, an order for the appraisement and sale of the ship. By a writ dated 2nd b June 1973 the second respondents, Telfair Shipping Corpn ('Telfair'), the charterers of the ship under a charterparty dated 21st December 1972, brought an action in rem against the ship for breach of the charterparty. On 2nd June 1973 a warrant of arrest was issued by the acting deputy registrar of the Supreme Court of Hong Kong at the instance of Telfair and on 12th July 1973 on the application of the chief bailiff of the Supreme Court an order was made to preserve the ship. On 8th c October 1973 Pickering J in the Supreme Court made an order that the ship be appraised and sold and the proceeds of sale paid into court. On 29th October 1973 the government of the Republic of the Philippines ('the republic') filed notice of motion in respect of the action by Telfair for an order that 'the writ of summons, the order for appraisement and sale dated 8th October 1973 and all subsequent proceedings herein be set aside'. On or about 29th October 1973 the republic made similar appli- d cations regarding the actions brought by Wallem. On 14th and 17th December 1973 Briggs CJ in the Supreme Court held that the doctrine of sovereign immunity applied to the ship and made orders setting aside the writs and all subsequent proceedings in respect of her. Wallem and Telfair appealed against the judgment of Briggs CJ and on 26th April 1974 the Full Court of the Supreme Court of Hong Kong (Huggins, McMullin and Leonard JJ) unanimously reversed that judgment and dismissed the e applications by the republic to have the writs set aside and the various actions stayed. On 16th May 1974 the Full Court granted the republic leave to appeal to the Privy Council. In order to secure the release of the ship pending the appeal to the Privy Council the republic filed a bail bond in the sum of $5,000,000 and on 27th May 1974 the Full Court released the ship from arrest and discharged the order of Pickering J made on 8th October 1973 for her appraisement and sale. The facts are set out in the f opinion of the Board.

T H Bingham QC and *David Sullivan QC* for the republic.
Anthony Evans QC and *Ian Hunter* for the respondents.

LORD CROSS OF CHELSEA. This is an appeal from the judgment of the g Full Court of the Supreme Court of Hong Kong (Huggins, McMullin and Leonard JJ) given on 26th April 1974. By it the court allowed appeals by the respondents, Wallem Shipping (Hong Kong) Ltd and Telfair Shipping Corpn, against orders made on the 14th and 17th December 1973 by Briggs CJ setting aside, on interlocutory applications made by the government of the Republic of the Philippines, the writs of summons and all subsequent proceedings in three actions in rem started in 1973 by the respon- h dents against a ship called 'Philippine Admiral'. Two of the actions (nos 103 and 139 of 1973) are actions brought by the first respondents (hereinafter called 'Wallem') for payment of goods supplied and disbursements made for the ship. The third (no 106 of 1973) is an action brought by the second respondents (hereinafter called 'Telfair') for damages for breach of a charterparty relating to the ship dated 21st December 1972. In actions 103 and 139 the writ is addressed to the owners and all others interested j in the ship and in no 106 to the owners of the ship. In each case the writ was served on the Liberation Steamship Company Inc (hereinafter called 'Liberation') a company incorporated in the Republic of the Philippines which had been operating the ship under the terms of an agreement for its conditional sale to it by the Reparations Commission an agency of the government of the republic which was at all material times the owner of the ship.

The facts of the case which were not in dispute in any material particular are set out at length in the judgment of Huggins J. They may be summarised as follows. By a a treaty made in 1956 between the Republic of the Philippines and Japan the latter country agreed to make available a total sum of $ US 550 million by way of reparations for damage done to Filipino property during the Second World War. Of this sum $ US 500 million was to be provided in the form of such capital goods and services as might be requested by the Philippine government and agreed by the Japanese government. In 1957 a Reparations Law (no 1789) was enacted in the Philippines which b laid down the mode in which reparations payments should be procured and used. It established (1) a mission in Japan as the sole and exclusive agent of the Philippine government to implement the treaty by procuring reparations goods and services and (2) a reparations commission whose function was to administer the acquisition, utilisation and distribution of reparations goods and services. The policy of the Act was stated to be that all reparations payments should be used in such a manner as to c assure the maximum possible economic benefit for the Filipino people in as equitable and widespread manner as possible. Capital goods were to be made available both for approved government projects and also to Filipino citizens and entities wholly owned by Filipino citizens whose applications had to be accompanied by a 'project study' in the prescribed form. It was laid down that the government should not use reparations goods for the purpose of entering into competition with private industries d where such industries had shown their capacity and readiness to serve the public fairly and adequately and that in general preference was to be given to private productive projects and that government projects were only to receive preference in a limited number of cases. No goods supplied to private enterprises were to be leased, sold or otherwise disposed of to anyone other than a Filipino citizen or to an equity wholly owned by Filipino citizens, which should continue to use the goods in the e projects for which they were originally intended or similar projects included in the development programme. The commission was directed to conduct so called 'end use' checks for the purpose of evaluating the actual utilisation of reparations goods and services and to make annual reports thereon to the authorities. Penalties were to be imposed on 'end users' who failed to use capital goods for the purposes for which they were intended. The proceeds from the sale of reparations goods disposed of f under the Act were to be placed to a special economic development fund to be used for the purposes therein specified.

Liberation applied to the reparations commission for the grant of an ocean going ship; its application was granted; and in 1959 the reparations mission entered into a contract on behalf of the government of the republic with a Japanese shipbuilding company for the construction of a vessel which—the contract stated—was being g procured under the reparations agreement for the Liberation Steamship Co of Manila. Payment was to be made by the Philippine government to the shipbuilders—presumably out of funds made available by Japan as part of the total reparations payment. On 16th November 1960 an agreement was made in Manila between the reparations commission and Liberation for the conditional purchase and sale of the vessel which was then called the 'Dagohoy' but was subsequently renamed the h 'Philippine Admiral' for a purchase price ($ US 3,434,288·89) to be paid by the instalments therein set out with interest on the unpaid balance. The contract provided so far as material (1) that in consideration of the payments to be made by Liberation the commission did 'conditionally cede, transfer and convey' to Liberation the utilisation of the vessel, (2) that the commission retained title to and ownership of the vessel until it was fully paid for and (3) that Liberation would take delivery and possession j of the vessel in Japan, and put the necessary officers and crew aboard in order to operate and use her in accordance with Philippine laws recognising that the contract was subject to the provisions of the Reparations Act, and to the terms and conditions in Annex A which were made an integral part of the contract. Annex A contained, inter alia, the following terms:

'1. It is herein covenanted and agreed upon that the title to and ownership of
the reparations goods subject to this contract shall remain with the Conditional
Vendor until the same shall have been fully paid for, and upon the full payment
of the purchase price as hereinbefore mentioned, this conditional deed of sale
shall become absolute, subject only to the limitations established by Republic
Act No. 1789 with respect to inspection, transfer and utilization of said reparations
goods . . .

'11. Should the Conditional Vendee fail to pay any of the yearly instalments
when due, or otherwise fail to comply with any of the terms and conditions
herein stipulated, as provided in R.A. No. 1789, or any of the rules and Regulations issued pursuant thereto, then this Deed of Conditional Sale shall automatically and without any further formality become ineffective and declared
rescinded, and all sums so paid by the Conditional Vendee before rescission by
reason thereof shall be considered as rentals and the Conditional Vendor and its
agents shall then and there be free to enter into the premises where such goods
are found, take possession of the same and dispose them according to law.

'12. It is hereby agreed, covenanted and stipulated by and between the parties
hereto that should the Conditional Vendor rescind this Deed of Conditional Sale
for any of the reasons stated in the preceding paragraphs, the Conditional Vendee,
by these presents, obligates itself to peacefully deliver the property subject of
this contract to the Conditional Vendor and in the event that the Conditional
Vendee refuses to peacefully deliver the possession of the property subject of
this contract to the Conditional Vendor and a suit is brought to court by the
Conditional Vendor to seek judicial declaration of rescission and to take possession
of the goods subject of this contract, the Conditional Vendee hereby obligates
itself to pay all the expenses to be incurred by reason of such suit and in addition,
obligates itself to pay as liquidated damages, penalty and attorney's fees, a sum
corresponding to ten percent (10%) of the value of the goods subject of this
contract.

'13. It is also agreed, covenanted and stipulated by and between the parties
hereto that in the event that the Conditional Vendor cancels or rescinds this
contract in accordance with Section 11 hereof, and the Conditional Vendor
decides to sell the said reparations goods in other parties at a price less than the
consideration herein stipulated, the Conditional Vendee hereby obligates itself
to pay the Conditional Vendor the difference in price in concept of penalty or
liquidated damages.'

On 15th December 1960 the reparations commission was registered as sole owner of
the vessel. Liberation took delivery and possession of the vessel in pursuance of the
contract and proceeded to operate her in the course of its shipping business. In 1963
the reparations commission took action to prevent a proposed charter of the ship to
an agency of the Indian government on the ground that such a charter would violate
the purpose for which the use of the ship had been entrusted to Liberation. Liberation
paid a number of instalments of the purchase price but there is no doubt that by 1973
it was seriously in arrear with its payments. By a charterparty dated 21st December
1972 the ship was chartered by Liberation to Telfair for a period of 'nine months to
about twelve months at charterers option'. At the time the ship was being repaired
at Hong Kong and remained in that port until after the judgment of the Full Court.
There was a dispute between Liberation and Telfair as to which was liable to pay for
the repairs. Liberation purported to cancel the charterparty and Telfair issued a writ
in rem (no 106) on 2nd June 1973 for damages for breach of the charterparty. Meanwhile Wallem had on 23rd May 1973 issued a writ in rem (no 103) in respect of goods
supplied and disbursements made for her between January and April 1973 and on
7th September 1973 Wallem issued another writ in rem (no 139) in respect of goods
supplied and disbursements made for her between May and July 1973. Liberation

entered appearances to all these writs as 'owners' of the Philippine Admiral. On 4th
June the ship had been arrested at the suit of Telfair in action 106. In the course of the *a*
next few months considerable expense was incurred by the bailiff in maintaining the
ship under arrest and as Liberation had taken no steps and seemed unlikely to be
going to take any steps to procure her release the acting deputy registrar of the
Supreme Court applied to the court for an order that the Philippine Admiral be
appraised and sold and the proceeds of sale paid into court. An order to that effect
was made by Pickering J on 8th October 1973. That order came to the notice of the *b*
reparations commission which on 10th October passed a resolution in the following
terms:

> 'RESOLVED, in view of the proposed sale in Hongkong, allegedly in pursuance of
> an order of the Hongkong Supreme Court, of the reparations vessel, M/S "Philip-
> pine Admiral" (formerly M/S "Dagohoy") procured for and delivered to the *c*
> Liberation Steamship Co., Inc. as an end-user of the same and which proposed
> sale was published in the Manila newspaper, "Bulletin Today" dated October 10,
> 1973, and considering that the aforesaid vessel remains the property of the
> Philippine Government, represented by the Reparations Commission, the same
> not having been fully paid for; considering further, that the published proposed
> sale could have been the result of the neglect and/or failure of the said enduser to *d*
> operate the vessel as a good father of a family and in a bonafide manner within
> the framework of pertinent laws and regulations; considering also, that the said
> enduser has been delinquent of the payments of its obligations to the Commission
> and which delinquency has aggregated in the amount of P$5,322,120·04 as of
> October 9, 1973; considering finally, that the said enduser, has continuously failed
> to make even a reply to the letters and telegrams of the Commission inquiring *e*
> about the status of the case against it in Hongkong and/or steps it had taken to
> bring the vessel to the Philippines, (1) to direct the immediate repossession of
> said vessel; and (2) to direct and authorise the Legal Department, in coordination
> with the DBP-Repacom Action Group to implement this resolution and to take
> such other steps and/or actions as may be necessary and warranted for the
> protection of the best interest of the Government.' *f*

On 29th October 1973 solicitors acting for the government of the Republic of the
Philippines filed notice of motion in the Telfair action (no 106) to apply for an order
'that the writ of summons, the order for appraisement and sale dated 8th October,
1973 and all subsequent proceedings herein be set aside'. On or about the same date
applications were filed by the same solicitors in four other actions (including no 103
and no 139) asking that the writs of summons and all subsequent proceedings be set *g*
aside. On 9th November 1973 by a presidential decree (no 332), which recited, inter
alia, that it had been shown that a majority of reparations endusers in the private
sector had failed properly to utilise the reparations goods or services received by them
and to pay the amortisations thereon as they fell due thus resulting in huge arrearages
to the detriment of the Philippine economy, various amendments were made to the
Reparations Act 1957. In particular the priority given to the private over the public *h*
sector was repealed and provision made for dealing with 'delinquent private endusers'.
This decree though made before the hearing before Briggs CJ was not in fact put in
evidence by the republic at that stage but only on the appeal to the Full Court.

On 14th December 1973 Briggs CJ made an order setting aside the writs and all
subsequent proceedings in the four actions (including no 103 and no 139) other than the
Telfair action and on 17th December he made a similar order in the Telfair action *j*
(no 106). The grounds of his judgment may be summarised as follows. (1) He rejected
a submission made on behalf of the republic that by reason of the terms on which
'endusers' were bound by the Reparations Law to use reparations goods the Philippine
Admiral was operating in the public service of the Philippines. She was—the judge
held—engaged in ordinary commercial transactions any profits from which went to

Liberation. The only direct benefits which the people of the Philippines derived from
a them came from the instalments of purchase price. But he held (2) following *The Porto
Alexandre*[1] that the fact that the ship in question was being used for ordinary commercial purposes did not exclude the application of the doctrine of sovereign immunity
and (3) that as the government was the owner of the ship and furthermore had an
immediate right to her possession by reason of Liberation's default under the contract
of conditional purchase the doctrine applied notwithstanding that the government
b was not in possession of the ship and had not been operating her itself for commercial
purposes.

The respondents appealed from this judgment to the Full Court, which on 26th
April 1974 unanimously reversed it and dismissed the applications by the republic
to have the writs set aside and the actions stayed.

The grounds for the decision as contained in the leading judgment given by Huggins
c J may be summarised as follows. (1) There was nothing in the presidential decree of
9th November 1973 to affect the conclusion reached by Briggs CJ, with which the full
court agreed, that the Philippine Admiral must be regarded as an ordinary trading
vessel and not a vessel employed in or destined for the public service of the Philippines.
(2) *The Porto Alexandre*[1] did not govern this case since there the Portuguese government
was in possession of and operating the ship whereas here Liberation was in possession
d of the ship and had been operating it for its own commercial purposes. (3) The case
was similar on its facts to *Republic of Mexico v Hoffman*[2] decided by the Supreme Court
of the United States in 1945, where the ship belonged to the Mexican state but was in
the possession of private charterers and the court held that the doctrine of sovereign
immunity did not apply. The fact, assuming it to be a fact, that the republic of the
Philippines had an immediate right to possession of the ship by reason of Liberation's
e breaches of the conditional sale contract did not affect the position.

After the decision of the Full Court the republic, in order to secure the release
of the ship pending an appeal to this Board, procured a bail bond to be filed in the
sum of 5,000,000 Hong Kong dollars and on 27th May 1974 the Full Court released
the Philippine Admiral from arrest and discharged the order of Pickering J made
on 8th October 1973 for her appraisement and sale.

f The argument before the Board fell under three heads. First and foremost whether
the Board should follow the decision in *The Porto Alexandre*[1]. Secondly whether, if the
Board should decide not to follow that decision, the Philippine Admiral ought nevertheless to enjoy immunity because it could not properly be regarded as a mere trading
ship. Thirdly whether, if the Board should consider that it ought to follow the decision
in *The Porto Alexandre*[1], that decision covered this case having regard to the fact that
g it was not alleged that the government of the republic was liable on any of the
contracts in respect of breach of which the actions had been brought and that although
it was the legal owner of the vessel it had not had possession or control of it at any
material time.

On the first question their Lordships were referred by counsel to a great number of
cases decided in the courts of this country and in various other jurisdictions, to several
h international conventions and to the views expressed by several academic writers on
international law. They will refer in this judgment to so much of this material as
appears to be particularly relevant. The story begins with the famous judgment of
Marshall CJ in *The Schooner Exchange*[3]. A trading vessel belonging to the plaintiffs had
been seized on the high seas by persons acting on the orders of the Emperor Napoleon,
taken to France, confiscated under the 'Rambouillet decrees' and fitted out as a French
j vessel of war. She had been driven by stress of weather into the port of Philadelphia
and the plaintiffs had issued a writ in rem claiming to have her restored to them.

---

1   [1920] P 30, [1918-19] All ER Rep 615
2   (1945) 324 US 30
3   (1812) 7 Cranch 116

Marshall CJ delivering the judgment of the Supreme Court held that a vessel of war
of a foreign state with which the United States was at peace and which the government   *a*
of the United States allowed to enter its harbours was exempt from the jurisdiction
of its courts. It was submitted in argument that if a sovereign engaged in trade he
would enjoy no immunity in respect of his trading operations; but the judgment left
that question open.

The case of a trading vessel was considered by Sir Robert Phillimore in *The Charkieh*[1].
The owners of the Batavier instituted Admiralty proceedings in rem against the   *b*
Charkieh and her freight for damages arising from a collision between the two ships
in the Thames. The Charkieh was one of a fleet of six or seven trading vessels, which
had previously belonged to a private company but had been bought by Ismail Pasha,
the Khedive of Egypt. She had been sent to England for repairs and to lessen expenses
she had brought a cargo with her. At the time of the collision she was under charter to
a British subject and advertised to carry cargo to Alexandria. Sir Robert held that the   *c*
Khedive was not entitled to the privileges of a sovereign prince; but that even if he
had been he would have lost such immunity by assuming the character of a trader.
By sending the ship to trade here he must be considered to have waived any privilege
which might otherwise attach to the vessel as property of a sovereign. It appears from
several passages in his judgment that Sir Robert distinguished proceedings in rem
from proceedings in personam and did not think that it followed that because no   *d*
suit could be brought against the sovereign personally no proceedings in rem could
be brought against property of his used by him in trade.

Next comes *The Parlement Belge*[2]. She was a packet owned by the King of the Belgians,
officered and manned by persons in his employ and flying the Belgian pennant,
which carried mails and also passengers and their luggage between Ostend and Dover.
Sir Robert Phillimore before whom the case came at first instance adhered to the   *e*
opinion which he had expressed in *The Charkieh*[1] that a vessel even though owned by a
sovereign and manned by his servants was not entitled to immunity if she was engaged
in commerce as in his view the Parlement Belge was. His decision was reversed on
appeal and the judgment of the Court of Appeal—delivered by Brett LJ—has sometimes been taken as saying that a sovereign can claim immunity for vessels owned by
him even if they are admittedly being used wholly or substantially for trading purposes.   *f*
In their Lordships' view the judgment does not lay down that wide proposition at
all and they agree with the analysis of it made recently by MacKenna J in the case of
Swiss Israel Trade Bank v Government of Salta[3]. The judgment certainly lays down two
propositions: (a) that a foreign sovereign cannot be sued in personam and (b) that an
action in rem cannot be brought against his ship if she is being used substantially for
public purposes—as the King of the Belgians said, and in the view of the court rightly   *g*
said, was the case of the Parlement Belge. But the question whether a state-owned
vessel admittedly used wholly or substantially for mere trading purposes would be
immune was left open.

The proposition that a sovereign cannot be sued in personam has been reaffirmed
in many subsequent cases. Thus in *Mighell v Sultan of Johore*[4]—a suit for breach of
promise of marriage alleged to have been made by a sovereign—Lord Esher MR said   *h*
that there was an absolute and unqualified rule which precluded the court from
exercising jurisdiction over the person of any sovereign. In *Compania Mercantil
Argentina v United States Shipping Board*[5], which was an action in personam brought to
recover freight overpaid to the shipping board which operated a merchant fleet for
ordinary commercial purposes, the action failed because the board was held to be a

j

---

1   (1873) LR 8 QB 197
2   (1880) 5 PD 197, [1874-80] All ER Rep 104
3   [1927] Lloyds Rep 497
4   [1894] 1 QB 149 at 159, [1891-4] All ER Rep 1019 at 1021, 1022
5   (1924) 93 LJKB 816

department of state. Again in *Baccus SRL v Servicio Nacional del Trigo*[1], where the
a defendants were a corporate body formed for the purpose of importing and exporting
grain for the Spanish government in accordance with the directions of the Spanish
Ministry of Agriculture and the policy from time to time laid down by the Spanish
government, though the Court of Appeal was divided on the question whether the
defendants were properly to be regarded as in substance a department of state none
doubted for a moment that if they were to be so regarded they were entitled to
b immunity. See also *Thai-Europe Tapioca Services Ltd v Government of Pakistan*[2], a case
decided by the Court of Appeal after the arguments in this appeal had been concluded.
The only possible exceptions to the generality of the rule that no proceedings in
personam can be brought against a sovereign or a sovereign state or a body which is a
department (or equivalent to a department) of a sovereign state of which there is any
trace in the English authorities brought to their Lordships' attention are (a) the case
c of an action relating to immovable property in the jurisdiction of the state in which
the action is brought, which was left open in *Sultan of Johore v Abubakar Tunku Aris
Bendahar*[3], and (b) the 'trust fund cases', in which the court has not been deterred
from administering a trust subject to its jurisdiction by the fact that a sovereign
claims an interest in it. If the sovereign does not choose to appear and argue its case
the court will decide on the conflicting claims as best it can in its absence.
d   Their Lordships will now revert to the question of sovereign immunity in actions
in rem against ships owned by or in possession or control of a sovereign and refer to
the English cases on that subject up to and including *The Porto Alexandre*[4] on which the
republic placed particular reliance. *The Scotia*[5] was an action in rem to recover
remuneration for salvage services. She was a ferry-boat built in this country for the
government of Canada and intended to be used to connect one part of a railway
e owned by the government with another. The services in question were rendered to
her while she was crossing the Atlantic from England to Canada. The Privy Council
rejected the submission of the plaintiff that the Scotia was at the time of the salvage
services still in the possession and control of her builders and held that the case fell
within the general rule that the Crown could not be impleaded in its own courts. That
case, which was, of course, decided before the Crown Proceedings Act 1947, does not in
f their Lordships' opinion throw any light on the question at issue in this case. *The
Jassy*[6] concerned a vessel which according to a statement made by the Roumanian
diplomatic representative in this country and communicated to the court via the
Foreign Office was the property of the King of Roumania and employed by him for
public purposes of the state, including the carriage of mail, passengers and cargo in
connection with the national railways. She had been involved in a collision with a
g Greek steamship in the Black Sea and was subsequently arrested in Liverpool at the
suit of the owners of that vessel. The case was indistinguishable from *The Parlement
Belge*[7], which was followed. *The Gagara*[8] was a merchant ship bought by the
plaintiffs in 1914 and registered in their names at Petrograd under the Russian merchant flag. In 1918 the Bolshevik government declared her to be national property,
loaded her with a cargo of wood and sent her on a voyage to Copenhagen. In the
h course of her voyage she put in at Reval where she was seized by the Estonians,
registered as of Estonian nationality and the property of the Estonian Republic and
sent to London under a new master with a cargo to be delivered to the Estonian
representative here. When she arrived here the plaintiffs issued a writ against her.

1   [1956] 3 All ER 715, [1957] 1 QB 438
j 2   [1975] 3 All ER 961, [1975] 1 WLR 1485
3   [1952] 1 All ER 1261, [1952] AC 318
4   [1920] P 30, [1918-19] All ER Rep 615
5   [1903] AC 501
6   [1906] P 270
7   (1880) 5 PD 197, [1874-80] All ER Rep 104
8   [1919] P 95

The argument both before Hill J and the Court of Appeal was directed entirely to the question whether or not having regard to the terms of the Foreign Office certificate *a* the Estonian National Council could properly be regarded as a sovereign state. The question whether the ship was being used for merely trading purposes and that immunity should be refused on that ground was not taken at all.

Next comes *The Porto Alexandre*[1], which is the sheet anchor of the republic's case. The ship, which was the property of the Portuguese government, was being employed by it in ordinary trading voyages earning freight. In September 1919 she loaded a *b* cargo of cork shavings for carriage to Liverpool under a bill of lading from which it appeared that the cargo was shipped by and consigned to the Portuguese Import and Export Co Ltd. She ran aground in the Mersey; salvage services were rendered to her by three Liverpool tugs; and a writ in rem was issued on behalf of the owners, masters and crews of the tugs against 'the owners of the Portuguese steamship Porto Alexandre her cargo and freight'. Unconditional appearance was entered for the cargo owners but *c* appearances under protest for the owners of the ship and the freight. Hill J[2] held with regret that although the Porto Alexandre was being used in ordinary commerce he was bound by the decision in *The Parlement Belge*[3] to set aside the writ so far as concerned the ship and the freight though the action could continue against the cargo owners. The Court of Appeal (Bankes, Warrington and Scrutton LJJ) affirmed his decision with a marked lack of enthusiasm on the same ground, namely that the *d* case was indistinguishable from *The Parlement Belge*[3], which was binding on them. For the reasons which they have already given their Lordships cannot agree that the decision in *The Parlement Belge*[3] obliged the Court of Appeal to decide *The Porto Alexandre*[1] as it did. In *The Parlement Belge*[3] the Court of Appeal said that the court could not exercise jurisdiction over 'the public property of any state which is destined for its public use'; but it did not say that a state-owned vessel engaged wholly or *e* substantially in ordinary commerce must be regarded as property 'destined to its public use'. It was careful to leave that point open.

In 1926 the point decided in *The Porto Alexandre*[1] came before the Supreme Court of the United States in *The Pesaro*[4]. That was a proceeding in rem against the Pesaro on a claim for damages arising out of the failure to deliver goods accepted by her at a port in Italy for carriage to New York. On the vessel being arrested the Italian govern- *f* ment asked that the suit be dismissed on the ground that the vessel was owned, possessed and controlled by it and was employed by it in the carriage of merchandise for hire in the service and interest of the whole Italian nation as distinguished from any individual member thereof. The court after referring to *The Schooner Exchange*[5] said[6]:

> 'We think the principles [there stated] are applicable alike to all ships held and *g* used by a government for a public purpose, and that when, for the purpose of advancing the trade of its people or providing revenue for its treasury, a govern- ment acquires, mans and operates ships in the carrying trade, they are public ships in the same sense that warships are. We know of no international usage which regards the maintenance and advancement of the economic welfare of a people in time of peace as any less a public purpose than the maintenance and *h* training of a naval force.'

In the course of its judgment the court referred to *The Parlement Belge*[3] and *The Porto Alexandre*[1] and a later case, *The Jupiter*[7], in which *The Porto Alexandre*[1] was followed, as showing the attitude of the English courts in the matter.

---

1   [1920] P 30, [1918-19] All ER Rep 615
2   [1920] P at 31, [1918-19] All ER Rep at 616
3   (1880) 5 PD 197, [1874-80] All ER Rep 104
4   (1925) 271 US 562
5   (1812) 7 Cranch 116
6   271 US at 574
7   [1924] P 236

On 10th April 1926 a convention was signed at Brussels between over 20 states,
a including the United Kingdom, for 'The Unification of certain Rules concerning the
Immunity of State-owned Ships'. Article 1 of that convention was in the following
terms:

'Sea-going ships owned or operated by States, cargoes owned by them, and
cargoes and passengers carried on State-owned ships, as well as the States which
b   own or operate such ships and own such cargoes shall be subject, as regards
claims in respect of the operation of such ships or in respect of the carriage of
such cargoes, to the same rules of liability and the same obligations as those
applicable in the case of privately-owned ships, cargoes and equipment.'

It will be observed that that article covers not only actions in rem but also actions
in personam. The convention, though ratified by a number of the signatories, has
c not yet been ratified by this country.
Their Lordships turn next to the well-known case of *The Cristina*[1]. She was a trading
ship registered at Bilbao and when that port was occupied by the insurgents in June
1937 the government of the Spanish Republic issued a decree requisitioning all vessels
registered there. The Christina was then on the high seas but when she reached
d Cardiff the Spanish consul there replaced the master and those of the officers and crew
who were thought to be in sympathy with the insurgents with persons well affected
to the government. The owners issued a writ in rem claiming to have possession of
the vessel as her owners, which the Spanish government moved to set aside as infringing its sovereign immunity. It is clear both from the arguments of counsel
before the appellate committee, which are fully reported in Lloyd's List Reports[2],
e and from the speeches of the Law Lords, that the question whether a sovereign state
can claim immunity in an action in rem against a ship employed by it solely for
trading purposes was never in issue at all. It was abundantly clear that the government
requisitioned the ship in order to assist it in putting down the rebellion and that in its
hands she was in the fullest sense 'publicis usibus destinata'. What the plaintiffs were
saying was that the English courts ought not to give effect to a decree which requisi-
f tioned a Spanish vessel when it was outside Spanish territorial waters and had been
implemented by high handed and probably tortious acts on the part of the Spanish
consul in the port of Cardiff. All five Law Lords agreed that as the vessel was in the
de facto possession and control of the Spanish government when the writ was issued
the writ impleaded a foreign sovereign state and must be set aside. The case is,
however, noteworthy in two respects. First for the statement of the doctrine of
g sovereign immunity by Lord Atkin[3] in the following words—so often repeated in
subsequent cases:

'The foundation for the application to set aside the writ and arrest of the ship
is to be found in two propositions of international law engrafted on to our domestic
law which seem to me to be well established and to be beyond dispute. The first
is that the courts of a country will not implead a foreign sovereign. That is, they
h   will not by their process make him against his will a party to legal proceedings,
whether the proceedings involve process against his person or seek to recover
from him specific property or damages. The second is that they will not by their
process, whether the sovereign is a party to the proceedings or not, seize or detain
property which is his, or of which he is in possession or control.'

j The second respect in which the case is noteworthy is for the division of opinion among
the Law Lords on the question, which did not arise for decision at all, whether the

---

1 *Companiera Naviera Vascongada v SS Cristina* [1938] 1 All ER 719, [1938] AC 485
2 (1938) 60 Ll L Rep 147-156
3 [1938] 1 All ER at 720, 721, [1938] AC at 490

decision in *The Porto Alexandre*[1] was right. Lord Atkin clearly thought that it was for he added to the passage quoted above the following words[2]:

'There has been some difference in the practice of nations as to possible limitations of this second principle, as to whether it extends to property used only for the commercial purposes of the sovereign or to personal private property. In this country, it is in my opinion well-settled that it applies to both.'

Lord Wright concurred in that view. He cited a number of the cases to which reference has already been made including *The Pesaro*[3] and *The Porto Alexandre*[1] and concluded[4]:

'In view of what I regard as the nature and purpose of the possession held by the respondent of the Cristina, it is not necessary to express a final opinion on the question, but as at present advised I am of opinion that these decisions of the United States Supreme Court and of the Court of Appeal correctly state the English law on this point.'

Lord Maugham, on the other hand, took a different view. He pointed out[5]—rightly as their Lordships think—that the Court of Appeal in *The Parlement Belge*[6] never said that ships belonging to a foreign government even if used for purely commercial purposes were entitled to immunity and he doubted whether the decision in *The Porto Alexandre*[1] was right. In support of his approach he referred to the Brussels convention of 1926 mentioned above. Lord Thankerton[7] agreed with Lord Maugham that *The Parlement Belge*[6] did not decide that a state-owned merchant ship engaged solely in ordinary trading was entitled to immunity and both he and Lord Macmillan reserved their opinions as to whether *The Porto Alexandre*[1] was rightly decided.

A case involving the effect of the same decree of the Spanish republican government as was relied on in *The Cristina*[8] came before the Supreme Court of the United States in the same year: see *The Navemar*[9]. There the court—though on the facts it was perhaps not necessary for it to do so—reaffirmed its earlier decision in *The Pesaro*[3] saying[10]:

'Admittedly a vessel of a friendly government in its possession and service is a public vessel, even though engaged in the carriage of merchandise for hire, and as such is immune from suit in the courts of admiralty of the United States.'

Their Lordships' attention was not called to any later English case in which the question on which there was a difference of opinion among the Law Lords in *The Cristina*[8] has been discussed. There have been several cases in which Lord Atkin's formulation of the doctrine of immunity has been applied to forms of property other than ships—notably *United States of America v Dollfus Mieg et Cie*[11], which related to some gold bars to which two foreign sovereign states had an immediate right to possession. But that case has relevance to the third head of the argument rather than to the question whether *The Porto Alexandre*[1] was rightly decided. The only other English authority to which their Lordships will refer at this point is *Sultan of Johore v Abubakar Tunku Aris Bendahar*[12]. The sultan, who was recognised by His Majesty's

 1 [1920] P 30, [1918-19] All ER Rep 615
 2 [1938] 1 All ER at 721, [1938] AC at 490
 3 (1925) 271 US 562
 4 [1938] 1 All ER at 735, [1938] AC at 512
 5 [1938] 1 All ER at 740, [1938] AC at 519, 520
 6 (1880) 5 PD 197, [1874-80] All ER Rep 104
 7 [1938] 1 All ER at 724, [1938] AC at 495, 496.
 8 [1938] 1 All ER 719, [1938] AC 485
 9 (1938) 303 US 68
10   303 US at 74
11 [1952] 1 All ER 572, [1952] AC 582
12 [1952] 1 All ER 1261, [1952] AC 318

Government as an independent sovereign, had obtained from a court set up in Singa-
a pore by the Japanese during the period of their occupation of Malaya a decree to
the effect that he was the owner of certain immovable property in Singapore. After
the war an ordinance was passed enabling any person aggrieved by such a decree to
apply to the appropriate court to have it set aside or to be given leave to appeal from
it. The sultan's son and other persons claiming that they were aggrieved by the
decree made an application under the ordinance to which they made the sultan
b respondent. He thereupon applied to have the proceedings stayed. The Board held
that the application under the ordinance should be treated as a continuation of the
proceedings started by the sultan himself before the Japanese court and that he must
be treated as having submitted to the jurisdiction. This made it unnecessary for their
Lordships to decide whether or not proceedings relating to the title to immovable
property in the jurisdiction of the court constituted an exception to the general rule
c that a foreign independent sovereign cannot be 'impleaded' in our courts. They did
however take occasion to say that in their opinion there had not been finally established in our law any absolute rule that a foreign independent sovereign cannot be
impleaded in our courts in any circumstances. In this connection they said that a
great deal of the reasoning in *The Parlement Belge*[1] would be inexplicable if there was
such an absolute rule and referred to the reservations made by the majority of the
d Law Lords in *The Cristina*[2] as to a sovereign's ships engaged in ordinary commerce.
  There is no doubt—as was indeed conceded by counsel for the republic—that since
the Second World War there has been both in the decisions of courts outside this
country and in the views expressed by writers on international law a movement away
from the absolute theory of sovereign immunity championed by Lord Atkin and Lord
Wright in *The Cristina*[2] towards a more restrictive theory. This restrictive theory
e seeks to draw a distinction between acts of a state which are done 'jure imperii' and acts
done by it 'jure gestionis' and accords the foreign state no immunity either in actions
in personam or in actions in rem in respect of transactions falling under the second
head.
  The first indication of this change of view to which their Lordships would refer is
f *Republic of Mexico v Hoffman*[3] decided by the United States Supreme Court in
1945. In that case the owner and master of the Lottie Carson, an American fishing
vessel, filed a suit in rem in the District Court for Southern California against the Baja
California for collision damage, and the Mexican ambassador claimed that proceedings
should be stayed on the ground that the Baja California was owned by and in the
possession of the Republic of Mexico. On examination of the facts it appeared that the
vessel was the property of the Republic of Mexico but that by a contract between the
g republic and a private Mexican corporation it was being operated by the corporation
for a term of five years in private freighting ventures. The officers and crew were
selected and paid by the corporation and for the use of the vessel the corporation
agreed to pay the government 50 per cent of the net profits earned by her but undertook to bear all losses. The Supreme Court rejected the claim to immunity on the
ground that the vessel was not in the possession or control of the Mexican government.
h The majority of the judges expressed no view as to the correctness of the decision in
The Pesaro[4], but Frankfurter J (in whose opinion Black J concurred) said[5] that it was
unsatisfactory to allow the decision in cases of this sort to turn on the presence or
absence of possession by the foreign government. He agreed[6] with the view expressed
by Lord Maugham in *The Cristina*[2] that there should be no immunity for ships owned

j
1 (1880) 5 PD 197, [1874-80] All ER Rep 104
2 [1938] 1 All ER 719, [1938] AC 485
3 (1945) 324 US 30
4 (1925) 271 US 562
5 324 US at 39, 40
6 324 US at 41

and operated by the foreign state for ordinary trading purposes and thought that *The Pesaro*[1] had been wrongly decided. It is to be noted that all the judges agreed that in cases in which immunity from suit is claimed on behalf of a foreign government it is the duty of an American court to ascertain, if it can, the view of the Department of State with regard to the particular claim or the policy adopted by the department to claims of that character and act in accordance with it. 'It is therefore not' said the Supreme Court[2] 'for the Courts to deny an immunity which our government has seen fit to allow, or to allow an immunity on new grounds which the government has not seen fit to recognise.' In that case the State Department had certified that it recognised that the Mexican government was the owner of the vessel but had refrained from certifying that it recognised ownership by a foreign government without possession as a ground for immunity. It did not appear from the cases that a claim of immunity in such circumstances had ever been allowed.

The next landmark in the shift of opinion abovementioned to which their Lordships would refer is a letter—the so-called 'Tate letter'—addressed on 19th May 1952 by J B Tate, the acting legal adviser of the State Department, to the then acting Attorney-General of the United States notifying him of a change in the policy of the Department of State with regard to the granting of sovereign immunity to foreign governments. The letter first refers to what it describes as two conflicting concepts of sovereign immunity. According to the classical or absolute theory a sovereign cannot without his consent be made a respondent in the courts of another sovereign, while according to the newer or restrictive theory immunity is only recognised with regard to acts done 'jure imperii' as opposed to acts done 'jure gestionis'. The letter goes on to list those countries whose courts accept the absolute or the restrictive theory respectively —including in the former class the United States itself and the British Commonwealth —pointing out that in many of the countries whose courts still applied the absolute theory academic writers tended to support the restrictive theory and that a number of those countries were in fact parties to and had ratified the Brussels Convention of 1926. It refers to the fact that the United States itself does not claim immunity from suit in foreign courts where it would not be entitled to do so according to the restrictive theory, and says that it will hereafter be the policy of the State Department to follow the restrictive theory of sovereign immunity when considering the claims of foreign governments for the grant of such immunity. It concludes as follows:

'It is realized that a shift in policy by the executive cannot control the courts but it is felt that the courts are less likely to allow a plea of sovereign immunity where the executive has declined to do so. There have been indications that at least some Justices of the Supreme Court feel that in this matter courts should follow the branch of the Government charged with responsibility for the conduct of foreign relations. In order that your Department, which is charged with representing the interests of the Government before the courts, may be adequately informed it will be the Department's practice to advise you of all requests by foreign governments for the grant of immunity from suit and of the Department's action thereon.'

It was not suggested by counsel on either side that their Lordships should seek the help of the Foreign and Commonwealth Office in deciding this appeal by ascertaining which theory of sovereign immunity it favours. But it is not perhaps wholly irrelevant to observe that the later American case of *Rich v Naviera Vacuba*[3] suggests that if the courts consult the executive on such questions what may begin by guidance as to the principles to be applied may end in cases being decided irrespective of any principle in accordance with the view of the executive as to what is politically expedient. In that

---

1   (1925) 271 US 562
2   (1945) 324 US at 35
3   (1961) 197 F Supp 710

case a merchant ship owned by the Republic of Cuba sailed from Cuba in August 1961
with a cargo of sugar. The master and some of the crew, wishing to seek political
asylum in the United States, sailed the ship into American territorial waters, where
she was taken into custody by the coast guard. Thereupon a number of persons issued
writs in rem against her to enforce various claims. The United Stated government
gave an assurance to the government of Cuba that if the latter declared the vessel to
be its property, requested her return and provided men to take the place of those
members of the crew who wished to stay in the United States, the ship would be
released. These conditions were fulfilled and a plea of sovereign immunity as a bar
to the various actions was made by the Attorney-General on behalf of the Republic
of Cuba. The plaintiffs submitted that the vessel was an ordinary trading vessel
engaged in commerce and that the executive was now going back on the policy of the
Tate letter. The court however allowed the plea of sovereign immunity saying that
'no policy with respect to international relations is so fixed that it cannot be varied in
the wisdom of the Executive. Flexibility, not uniformity, must be the controlling
factor in times of strained international relations'. See also in this connection *Isbrandsten
Tankers v President of India*[1].

According to the Tate letter the countries of the world were then fairly evenly
divided between those whose courts adhered to the absolute theory and those which
adopted the restrictive; but there is no doubt that in the last twenty years the restrictive theory has steadily gained ground. According to a list compiled by reference to
the various textbooks on international law and put before their Lordships by agreement between the parties there are now comparatively few countries outside the
Commonwealth which can be counted adherents of the absolute theory. It is not
altogether clear whether or not the Republic of the Philippines is one of them.

The only other cases to which their Lordships think it necessary to refer are two
recent Canadian cases: the first, *Flota Maritima Browning de Cuba SA v SS Canadian
Conqueror*[2]; the second, *Republic of Congo v Venne*[3].

The facts in *The Canadian Conqueror*[2] were that the vessel was one of seven ships
which in August 1958 were bought from a Canadian steamship company by a Cuban
bank. The bank on 19th August 1958 entered into a lease purchase agreement with
the plaintiff company ('Flota') providing for the operation of the ships by Flota under
a demise charter containing an option to Flota to purchase them. In October 1958
Flota alleged that the bank had broken the agreement in various respects and that it
was no longer binding on it. From that time it appears that Flota ceased to operate
the vessels. On 9th June 1959 the vessels were acquired by the Republic of Cuba from
the bank. At that time and ever since they had been anchored in the harbour of
Halifax, Nova Scotia, and were under the control of the Cuban government. On 4th
August 1960 Flota issued a writ in rem against the ships claiming damages for breach
of the agreement of 19th August 1958 and the Republic of Cuba applied by motion to
set the writ aside. The judge of first instance refused to accede to the application but
his judgment was reversed on appeal and on a further appeal to the Supreme Court
that court unanimously held that the claim to immunity should succeed. Ritchie J,
in whose judgment four other judges concurred, carefully refrained from accepting
the views expressed by Lord Atkin and Lord Wright in *The Cristina*[4] as to the immunity of state-owned trading ships. Indeed he made it clear that he preferred the
view expressed by Lord Maugham. But he decided in favour of the claim to immunity
because the plaintiffs had failed to show that the vessels which were owned by and in
the control of the Republic of Cuba were going to be used by it for ordinary trading
purposes. The republic had made no use of them since it acquired them; they were

---

1   (1971) 446 F 2d 1198
2   (1962) 34 DLR (2d) 628
3   (1971) 22 DLR (3d) 669
4   [1938] 1 All ER 719, [1938] AC 485

available to be used for any purpose which the government of Cuba might select; and they ought to be regarded as 'public ships of a sovereign state' at least until such *a* time as some decision was made by the sovereign state in question as to the use to which they were to be put. Locke J, who was the only other judge to deliver a judgment and with whose judgment one other judge agreed, based his judgment on the same grounds as those adopted by Ritchie J, namely that the ships were in the possession of the Republic of Cuba and that there was no evidence as to the use to which the republic intended to put them. He expressed no opinion on the question whether the *b* doctrine of immunity extended to property used purely for the commercial purposes of the sovereign.

In *Republic of Congo v Venne*[1] the respondent alleged that he had been employed by the government of the Congo acting through its duly accredited diplomatic representatives in Canada to prepare plans for the construction of the Congo National Pavilion for the 1967 exhibition in Montreal. The government eventually decided not to *c* construct the pavilion and refused to pay the respondent fees, for which he brought an action. The lower courts rejected the government's plea of sovereign immunity but the Supreme Court allowed the plea by a majority of seven to two. Ritchie J, delivering the majority judgment, declined—as he had declined in *The Canadian Conqueror*[2]—to express a concluded opinion whether or not the doctrine of sovereign immunity applied to commercial transactions. He held that the transaction in ques- *d* tion was not a commercial transaction but a contract made by the government in the performance of a public act of state. Laskin J on the other hand, delivering the minority judgment, expressed the view that the 'absolute' theory of sovereign immunity was 'spent' and that the transaction in question was not on the evidence covered by the restrictive theory.

Finally their Lordships must refer to the Convention on State Immunity signed at *e* Basle on 16th May 1972 by a number of member states of the Council of Europe. The United Kingdom was a signatory to the Convention itself—though not to the protocol added thereto—but has not yet ratified it. The preamble runs as follows[3]:

> 'The member States of the Council of Europe, signatory hereto, Considering that the aim of the Council of Europe is to achieve a greater unity between its *f* Members; Taking into account the fact that there is in international law a tendency to restrict the cases in which a State may claim immunity before foreign courts; Desiring to establish in their mutual relations common rules relating to the scope of the immunity of one State from the jurisdiction of the courts of another State, and designed to ensure compliance with judgments given against another State; Considering that the adoption of such rules will tend to advance *g* the work of harmonisation undertaken by the member States of the Council of Europe in the legal field,
> 'Have agreed as follows . . .'

The convention contains a number of provisions precluding contracting states from claiming immunity in various types of proceedings in personam brought against it in the courts of another contracting state but art 30 provides that it is not to apply to *h* proceedings in respect of claims relating to the operation of seagoing vessels owned or operated by a contracting state or to the carriage of cargoes and of passengers by such vessels or to the carriage of cargoes owned by a contracting state and carried on board merchant vessels. The explanatory report presented to Parliament with the convention explains that the purpose of art 30 is to exclude matters covered by the Brussels Convention of 1926 which is in force between a number of the member states *j* of the Council of Europe. The importance of the 1972 convention in relation to the question which their Lordships are called on to answer is that it shows that the fact

---

1   (1971) 22 DLR (3d) 669
2   (1962) 34 DLR (2d) 628
3   Council of Europe, European Series No 74

a that Her Majesty's Government in the United Kingdom has never ratified the 1926 convention cannot be taken to indicate that it has any doubt as to the wisdom of the provisions contained in it.

   Their Lordships turn now to consider what answer they should give to the main question raised by this appeal—whether or not they should follow the decision of the Court of Appeal in The Porto Alexandre[1]. There are clearly weighty reasons for not following it. In the first place, the court decided that case as it did because its members

b thought that they were bound so to decide by The Parlement Belge[2] whereas—as their Lordships think—the decision in The Parlement Belge[2] did not cover the case at all. Secondly, although Lord Atkin and Lord Wright approved the decision in The Porto Alexandre[1] the other three Law Lords who took part in The Cristina[3] thought that it was at least doubtful whether sovereign immunity should extend to state-owned vessels engaged in ordinary commerce. Moreover this Board in the Sultan of Johore

c case[4] made it clear that it considered that the question was an open one. Thirdly, the trend of opinion in the world outside the Commonwealth since the last war has been increasingly against the application of the doctrine of sovereign immunity to ordinary trading transactions. Lastly, their Lordships themselves think that it is wrong that it should be so applied. In this country—and no doubt in most countries in the western world—the state can be sued in its own courts on commercial contracts

d into which it has entered and there is no apparent reason why foreign states should not be equally liable to be sued there in respect of such transactions. There is of course no clear cut dividing line between acts done 'jure imperii' and acts done 'jure gestionis' and difficult borderline cases may arise. The Republic of Congo v Venne[5] is an example of such a case and others are given in the textbooks on international law (see e g Oppenheim[6]; Brownlie[7]; Greig[8]; O'Connell[9]). But similar difficulties arise

e under the 'absolute' theory, for there one has to decide whether the defendant—if not the foreign state itself—is or is not so closely connected with it as to make the action in substance one against the foreign state—a difficulty which caused a division of opinion in the Court of Appeal in Baccus SRL v Servicio Nacional del Trigo[10]. The only reason for following The Porto Alexandre[1] which appears to their Lordships to have much weight is that to apply the 'restrictive' theory to actions in rem while leaving

f actions in personam to be governed by the absolute theory would produce a very illogical result. The rule that no action in personam can be brought against a foreign sovereign state on a commercial contract has been regularly accepted by the Court of Appeal in England and was assumed to be the law even by Lord Maugham in The Cristina[11]. It is no doubt open to the House of Lords to decide otherwise but it may fairly be said to be at the least unlikely that it would do so, and counsel for the res-

g pondents did not suggest that the Board should cast any doubt on the rule. So counsel for the republic could and did argue with force that granted that the restrictive theory was to be preferred the courts should leave it to the government to ratify the 1926 and 1972 conventions and to introduce the legislation necessary to make them part of our law and should not tamper with the law as so far declared in England by applying the restrictive theory to actions in rem. But their Lordships—while recognising that

h there is force in that argument—are not prepared to accept it. Thinking as they do that

---

j

1 [1920] P 1
2 (1880) 5 PD 197
3 [1938] 1 All ER 719, [1938] AC 485
4 [1952] 1 All ER 1261, [1952] AC 318
5 (1971) 22 DLR (3d) 669
6 International Law (8th Edn, 1974), vol 1, p 274, n 2
7 Principles of Public International Law (2nd Edn, 1973), pp 323-325
8 International Law (1970), pp 217, 218
9 International Law (2nd Edn, 1970), vol 2, p 845
10 [1956] 3 All ER 715, [1957] 1 QB 438
11 [1938] 1 All ER at 737, [1938] AC at 515

the restrictive theory is more consonant with justice they do not think that they should be deterred from applying it so far as they can by the thought that the resulting position may be somewhat anomalous. For these reasons they propose not to follow *The Porto Alexandre*[1].

The question then arises whether the Philippine Admiral can properly be regarded as a mere trading vessel or was at the relevant time for one reason or another a ship 'publicis usibus destinata'. In order to answer that question one must consider both the past history of the vessel in question since she became the property of the foreign state and also the use to which she is likely to be put by that state in the future. Throughout her life the Philippine Admiral has been operated as an ordinary merchant ship earning freight by carrying cargoes and their Lordships agree with the judges in both courts below that the fact that Liberation was subject with regard to her to the provisions of the Reparations Law and the contract with the commission does not mean that she was not to be treated as an ordinary trading ship for the purposes of the doctrine of sovereign immunity when these proceedings started and also when the claim to stay them was made.

It is, of course, possible that a foreign sovereign might base a claim to immunity for a trading vessel on its alleged intention to use her in the future for some different, and undoubtedly public, purpose. If such a claim were made the court would be faced with several difficult questions, e g whether it would require any evidence of the intention over and above its mere assertion; whether the fact that it was formed in order to defeat the plaintiff's claim would be a relevant consideration; and at what time such a claim would have to be formulated to be listened to at all. It is, however, unnecessary for their Lordships to consider any such questions in this case for the republic does not even assert that the Philippine Admiral will not continue to be used as she has always been used—that is to say as a trading vessel—though the recent Presidential decree makes it perhaps likely that she will be so employed by the government rather than by private individuals. The republic naturally relied in this part of the case on the decision of the Supreme Court of Canada in *The Canadian Conqueror*[2]. Their Lordships do not find it necessary to express either agreement or disagreement with that decision; for it is clearly distinguishable from this case on its facts. The vessels in question in that case had not been put to any use by the Cuban government since it had acquired them; they were available for use by that government in any way it chose; and having regard to the political conditions obtaining in Cuba at that time it was by no means improbable that they would be used for other than purely commercial purposes. Here on the other hand one has use for commercial purposes for many years while the government was the owner and no reason whatever to suppose that such user is going to change after the government has retaken possession from Liberation. In the result therefore their Lordships are of the opinion that the appeal should be dismissed and that the republic should pay to the respondents their costs of it. They will humbly advise Her Majesty accordingly.

In the view that their Lordships have taken on the first two points the third point—namely whether if they had thought it right to follow *The Porto Alexandre*[1] the appeal should nevertheless be dismissed—does not arise; but as it was fully argued they think it right to say that had they thought that they should follow *The Porto Alexandre*[1] they would have advised that the appeal should be allowed. It is true that the republic was not in possession or control of the Philippine Admiral at any relevant time and that it was not liable on any of the contracts for the breach of which the actions were brought; but the republic was the legal owner of the vessel and what is more an owner with an immediate right to possession. In the *Dollfus Mieg* case[3], where the bars were in the possession of the bank and the arguments were conducted on the footing that the plaintiffs were their owners and that the foreign sovereigns had

1 [1920] P 30, [1918-19] All ER Rep 615
2 (1962) 34 DLR (2d) 628
3 [1952] 1 All ER 572, [1952] AC 582

no title to them, the foreign sovereigns succeeded in having the action against the bank
a for detinue or conversion of the bars stayed on the ground that an order in favour of the
plaintiffs would have interfered with the immediate right to possession of the bars
which they had under the contract of bailment to the bank. There can be no difference
for this purpose between gold bars and a ship and had their Lordships not thought
that the fact that the Philippine Admiral was an ordinary trading ship took her outside the scope of the doctrine of sovereign immunity they would have held as Briggs
b CJ held that the republic was entitled to have the actions stayed.

Appeal dismissed.

Solicitors: *Maxwell, Batley & Co*, agents for *Peter Mark & Co*, Hong Kong (for the
republic); *Holman, Fenwick & Willan*, agents for *Johnson, Stokes & Master*, Hong Kong
c (for the respondents).

Gordon H Scott Esq Barrister.

Rose v Plenty and another

d COURT OF APPEAL, CIVIL DIVISION
LORD DENNING MR, LAWTON AND SCARMAN LJJ
4th, 7th JULY 1975

*Vicarious liability – Master and servant – Act of servant in course of employment – Pro-
hibited act – Limitation on scope of employment – Act prohibited by master – Effect of
e prohibition – Prohibition affecting mode of conduct within scope of employment rather than
limiting scope of employment – Milkman – Employers expressly prohibiting milkmen from
carrying children on milk floats – Milkman carrying child on float for purpose of assisting
in delivery of milk – Child injured in consequence of milkman's negligent driving – Whether
employers liable for milkman's negligence.*

f A milkman was employed by his employers, a dairy company, to go round on a
milk float delivering milk to the employers' customers, collecting empty bottles and
obtaining payment for the milk. The employers exhibited notices at the milk depot
which expressly prohibited the milkman from employing children in the performance of his duties and from giving lifts on the milk float. Contrary to those prohibitions, the milkman invited the plaintiff, a boy aged thirteen, to assist him with the
milk round in return for payment. The plaintiff rode on the milk float and helped
g to deliver milk and return empty bottles to the float. Whilst riding on the milk
float, the plaintiff was injured when the milkman drove the float negligently. The
plaintiff brought an action for damages for negligence against the milkman and the
employers. He obtained judgment against the milkman, but his claim against the
employers was dismissed on the ground that the milkman had been acting outside
the scope of his employment in employing the plaintiff and carrying him on the
h float contrary to the employers' instructions. The plaintiff appealed against the
dismissal of his claim against the employers.

Held (Lawton LJ dissenting) – The employers' instructions only affected the milkman's mode of conduct within the scope of his employment and did not limit or
define the scope of the employment. It followed that, although the milkman's acts of
j employing the plaintiff and carrying him on the float were prohibited, they had been
performed by the milkman within the scope of his employment having been performed for the purpose of the employers' business. Accordingly the employers were
vicariously liable for the milkman's negligence and the appeal would therefore be
allowed (see p 100 *b c* and *h* to p 101 *d*, p 104 *c* to *f*, p 105 *e* to *g* and p 106 *c* and
d, post).

D

Limpus v London General Omnibus Co (1862) 1 H & C 526 and *Ilkiw v Samuels* [1963] 2 All ER 879 applied.   **a**
Twine v Bean's Express Ltd (1946) 175 LT 131 and *Conway v George Wimpey and Co Ltd* [1951] 1 All ER 363 distinguished.

Notes
For a master's liability for the tortious acts of his servant, see 25 Halsbury's Laws (3rd Edn) 538-543, paras 1025-1031, and for cases on the subject, see 34 Digest (Repl) **b**
160-165, 171-182, 1111-1140, 1199-1286.

Cases referred to in judgments
British Railways Board v Herrington [1972] 1 All ER 749, [1972] AC 877, [1972] 2 WLR 537, HL.
Canadian Pacific Railway Co v Lockhart [1942] 2 All ER 464, [1942] AC 591, 111 LJPC   **c**
    113, 167 LT 231, PC, 34 Digest (Repl) 172, 1217.
Conway v George Wimpey & Co Ltd [1951] 1 All ER 363, [1951] 2 KB 266, CA, 34 Digest (Repl) 181, 1283.
Duncan v Findlater (1839) 6 Cl & Fin 894, Macl & Rob 911, 7 ER 934, HL, 34 Digest (Repl) 155, 1075.
Harris v Birkenhead Corpn [1975] 1 All ER 1001, [1975] 1 WLR 379.   **d**
Hern v Nichols (1701) Holt KB 462, 1 Salk 289, 90 ER 1154, 1 Digest (Repl) 682, 2427.
Hilton v Thomas Burton (Rhodes) Ltd [1961] 1 All ER 74, [1961] 1 WLR 705, 34 Digest (Repl) 175, 1239.
Ilkiw v Samuels [1963] 2 All ER 879, [1963] 1 WLR 991, CA, Digest (Cont Vol A) 1131, 1261a.
Iqbal v London Transport Executive [1973] The Times 6th June, CA.
Limpus v London General Omnibus Co (1862) 1 H & C 526, 32 LJEx 34, 7 LT 641, 2 JP 147,   **e**
    158 ER 998; *affd* 9 Jur NS 333, [1861-73] All ER Rep 556, 34 Digest (Repl) 161, 1120.
Plumb v Cobden Flour Mills Co Ltd [1914] AC 62, 83 LJKB 197, 109 LT 759, HL, 34 Digest (Repl) 397, 2947.
Southern Portland Cement Ltd v Cooper [1974] 1 All ER 87, [1974] AC 623, [1974] 2 WLR 152, PC.
Staveley Iron & Chemical Co Ltd v Jones [1956] 1 All ER 403, [1956] AC 627, [1956] 2   **f**
    WLR 479, HL; *affg* sub nom *Jones v Staveley Iron & Chemical Co Ltd* [1955] 1 All ER 6, [1955] 1 QB 474, [1955] 2 WLR 69, CA, 34 Digest (Repl) 246, 1791.
Twine v Bean's Express Ltd (1946) 175 LT 131, CA; *affg* [1946] 1 All ER 202, 34 Digest (Repl) 181, 1282.
Young v Edward Box & Co Ltd [1951] 1 TLR 789, CA, 34 Digest (Repl) 181, 1284.
                                                           g

Cases also cited
Houghton v Pilkington [1912] 3 KB 308, [1911-13] All ER Rep 1135, DC.
Joel v Morison (1834) 6 C & P 501.
Lloyd v Grace Smith & Co [1912] AC 716, [1911-13] All ER Rep 51, HL.
Stone v Taffe [1974] 3 All ER 1016, [1974] WLR 1575, CA.
                                                           h

Appeal
The plaintiff, Leslie Francis Rose, suing by his father and next friend, Leslie George Rose, brought an action against the first defendant, Christopher Plenty, and the second defendants, Co-operative Retail Services Ltd, the first defendant's employers, claiming damages for personal injuries resulting from the first defendant's negligence in driving a milk float on which the plaintiff was riding as a passenger. On 16th July   **j**
1974 his Honour Judge Russell, sitting as a deputy judge of the Queen's Bench Division at Bristol gave judgment for the plaintiff against the first defendant for damages of £620 and interest, but dismissed the plaintiff's claim against the second defendants. The plaintiff appealed against that part of the judgment dismissing his claim against the second defendants on the following grounds: (1) that the judge should have held

a that in obtaining the plaintiff's assistance to deliver milk to the second defendants' customers and requiring the plaintiff to ride on the second defendants' milk float for that purpose, the first defendant was doing work which he was authorised to do in an unauthorised manner and was therefore acting within the course of his employment and the second defendants were vicariously liable for the first defendant's negligent driving; (2) that the judge should have held that the instructions given by the second defendants to the first defendant and other milkmen employed by the second

b defendants, prohibiting them from carrying anyone on their milk floats, could not in law have affected the second defendants' vicarious liability for the first defendant's negligence because (a) the first defendant was acting within the scope of his employment in driving the milk float and delivering milk to the second defendants' customers, (b) the plaintiff had no knowledge of those instructions, and (c) the plaintiff was travelling on the milk float by arrangement with the first defendant to help

c him to do the very work which he was employed to do. The facts are set out in the judgment of Lord Denning MR.

C S Rawlins for the plaintiff.
William Barrett for the second defendants.
The first defendant did not appear and was not represented.

d

LORD DENNING MR. The first defendant, Mr Christopher Plenty, was a milk roundsman employed at Bristol by the second defendants, Co-operative Retail Services Ltd ('Co-operative Services'). He started working for them at Easter 1970. There were notices up at the depot making it quite clear that the roundsmen were not allowed to take children on the vehicles. One notice said: 'Children and young

e persons *must not in any circumstances be employed by you* in the performance of your duties.' Both employers and trade union did their utmost to stop it. No doubt Mr Plenty knew it was not allowed. But in spite of all these warnings, the practice still persisted. Boys used to hang about the depot waiting to be taken on: and some of the roundsmen used to take them.

Soon after Mr Plenty started work as a milk roundsman a boy, the plaintiff, Leslie

f Rose, who was just over 13, went up to Mr Plenty and asked if he could help him. Mr Plenty agreed to let him do it. The boy described his part in these words: 'I would jump out of the milk float, grab the milk, whatever had to go into the house, collect the money if there was any there and bring the bottles back.' That is what he did. Mr Plenty paid the boy 6s for the weekends and 4s for the weekdays.

Whilst young Leslie Rose was going round some houses, Mr Plenty would go to

g others. On 21st June 1970, unfortunately, there was an accident. After going to one house, Leslie Rose jumped on the milk float. He sat there with one foot dangling down so as to be able to jump off quickly. But at that time Mr Plenty, I am afraid, drove carelessly and negligently. He went too close to the kerb. As the milk float went round the corner, the wheel caught Leslie's leg. He tried to get his leg away, but he was dragged out of the milk float. His foot was broken with a compound

h fracture; but it has mended. So it was not very serious. Afterwards, by his father as his next friend, he brought an action for damages against Mr Plenty and against his employers, Co-operative Services. The judge found that Mr Plenty was negligent, but he felt that young Leslie was old enough to bear some part of the blame himself. He assessed the responsibility for the accident at 75 per cent to Mr Plenty and 25 per cent to the boy. He assessed the total damages at £800. He gave judgment against

j Mr Plenty for three-quarters of it, £600. But he exempted the employers from any liability. He held that Mr Plenty was acting outside the scope of his employment and that the boy was a trespasser on the float. The boy, through his father, now appeals to this court. He says the employers, Co-operative Services, are liable for the acts of their milk roundsman.

This raises a nice point on the liability of a master for his servant. I will first take the notices to the roundsmen saying they must not take the boys on. Those do not necessarily exempt the employers from liability. The leading case is *Limpus v London* *a* *General Omnibus Co*[1]. The drivers of omnibuses were furnished with a card saying they 'must not on any account race with or obstruct another omnibus . . .' Nevertheless the driver of one of the defendants' omnibuses did obstruct a rival omnibus and caused an accident in which the plaintiff's horses were injured. Martin B[2] directed the jury that, if the defendants' driver did it for the purposes of his employer, the defendants were liable; but if it was an act of his own, and in order to effect a *b* purpose of his own, the defendants were not responsible. The jury found for the plaintiff. The Court of Exchequer Chamber[3] held that the direction was correct. It was a very strong court which included Willes and Blackburn JJ. Despite the prohibition, the employer was held liable because the injury resulted from an act done by the driver in the course of his service and for his master's purposes. The decisive point was that it was *not* done by the servant for his own purposes, but for *c* his master's purposes.

I will next take the point about a trespasser. The boy was a trespasser on the milk float so far as Co-operative Services were concerned. They had not given him any permission to be on the float and had expressly prohibited the milk roundsman from taking him on. There are two early cases where it was suggested that the employer of a driver is not liable to a person who is a trespasser on the vehicle. *d* They are *Twine v Bean's Express Ltd*[4] and *Conway v George Wimpey & Co Ltd*[5]. But these cases are to be explained on other grounds; and the statements about a trespasser are no longer correct. Those statements were made at a time when it was commonly supposed that occupiers of premises were under no duty to use care in regard to a trespasser. But that stern rule has now been abandoned, especially when the trespasser is a child: see *British Railways Board v Herrington*[6], *Southern Portland* *e* *Cement Ltd v Cooper*[7] and *Harris v Birkenhead Corporation*[8]. So far as vehicles are concerned, I venture to go back to my own judgment in *Young v Edward Box & Co Ltd*[9], when I said:

'In every case where it is sought to make the master liable for the conduct of his servant the first question is to see whether the servant was liable. If the *f* answer is Yes, the second question is to see whether the employer must shoulder the servant's liability.'

That way of putting it is, I think, to be preferred to the way I put it later in *Staveley Iron & Chemical Co Ltd v Jones*[10].

Applying the first question in *Young v Box*[11], it is quite clear that the driver, Mr Plenty, was liable to the boy, Leslie Rose, for his negligent driving of the milk float. *g* He actually invited the boy to ride on it. So the second question arises, whether his employers, Co-operative Services, are liable for the driver's negligence. That does not depend on whether the boy was a trespasser. It depends, as I said in *Young v Box*[11], on whether the driver, in taking the boy on the milk float, was acting in the course of his employment.

In considering whether a prohibited act was within the course of the employment, *h*

1 (1862) 1 H & C 526
2 1 H & C at 529, 530
3 (1863) 9 Jur NS 333, [1861-73] All ER Rep 556
4 (1946) 175 LT 131
5 [1951] 1 All ER 363, [1951] 2 KB 266
6 [1972] 1 All ER 749, [1972] AC 877
7 [1974] 1 All ER 87, [1974] AC 623
8 [1975] 1 All ER 1001, [1975] 1 WLR 379
9 [1951] 1 TLR 789 at 793
10 [1955] 1 All ER 6 at 8, [1955] 1 QB 474 at 480
11 [1951] 1 TLR 789

a it depends very much on the purpose for which it is done. If it is done for his employers' business, it is usually done in the course of his employment, even though it is a prohibited act. That is clear from *Limpus v London General Omnibus Co*[1], *Young v Box*[2] and *Ilkiw v Samuels*[3]. But if it is done for some purpose other than his master's business, as, for instance, giving a lift to a hitchhiker, such an act, if prohibited, may not be within the course of his employment. Both *Twine v Bean's Express Ltd*[4] and *Conway v George Wimpey & Co Ltd*[5] are to be explained on their **b** own facts as cases where a driver had given a lift to someone else contrary to a prohibition and not for the purposes of the employers. *Iqbal v London Transport Executive*[6] seems to be out of line and should be regarded as decided on its own special circumstances. In the present case it seems to me that the course of Mr Plenty's employment was to distribute the milk, collect the money and to bring back the bottles to the van. He got or allowed this young boy, Leslie Rose, to do part **c** of that business which was the employers' business. It seems to me that although prohibited, it was conduct which was within the course of the employment; and on this ground I think the judge was in error. I agree it is a nice point in these cases on which side of the line the case falls; but, as I understand the authorities, this case falls within those in which the prohibition affects only the conduct within the sphere of the employment and did not take the conduct outside the sphere altogether. **d** I would hold this conduct of Christopher Plenty to be within the course of his employment and the master is liable accordingly, and I would allow the appeal.

In parting with the case, it may be interesting to notice that this type of case is unlikely to arise so much in the future, since a vehicle is not to be used on a road unless there is in force an insurance policy covering, inter alia, injury to passengers.

e

LAWTON LJ. Ever since 1946 employers of drivers have been entitled to arrange their affairs on the assumption that if they gave clear and express instructions to their drivers that they were not to carry passengers on the employers' vehicles, the employers would not be liable in law for any injury sustained by such passengers. They were entitled to make that assumption because of the decision of this court in **f** *Twine v Bean's Express Ltd*[4]. No doubt since 1946 employers when negotiating with their insurers have sought to get reductions in premiums and have done so because of the assumption which, so it seems to me, they were entitled to make about freedom from liability to unauthorised passengers. It may well be that the judgment of Lord Greene MR, as reported, is not as clear as the judgments of that great judge normally were; but it was the judgment of the Master of the Rolls and it was accepted **g** by the other two members of the court, both judges of very great distinction who were later to go to the House of Lords: Morton and Tucker LJJ. If between 1946 and 1951 any employers had the kind of doubts about *Twine's* case[4] which in more recent years have been expressed by academic writers, their minds would have been put at rest by another decision of this court in 1951, namely *Conway v George Wimpey & Co Ltd*[5]. That was a case in which a lorry driver employed by a firm of contractors **h** on a site where many other contractors were working, contrary to his express instructions, gave an employee of another firm of contractors a lift in his lorry. This man was injured whilst a passenger. The problem for the court was whether the injured man could claim against the employers of the lorry driver who had given him a lift. This court, in a unanimous decision, adjudged that the injured man could not claim. The leading judgment was given by Asquith LJ; he gave his

j

---

1 (1862) 1 H & C 526
2 [1951] 1 TLR 789
3 [1963] 2 All ER 879, [1963] 1 WLR 991
4 (1946) 175 LT 131
5 [1951] 1 All ER 363, [1951] 2 KB 266
6 [1973] The Times, 6th June

reason for saying that what the lorry driver had done had not been done in the
course of his employment. He said[1]:   *a*

'. . . I should hold that taking men other than the defendants' employees on
the vehicle was not merely a wrongful mode of performing an act of the class
which the driver . . . was employed to perform, but was the performance of
an act of a class which he was not employed to perform at all.'

These two cases have not been overruled by the House of Lords. Insurers have *b*
proceeded ever since on the assumption that these cases are properly decided. It
would I think be most unfortunate if this court departed from clear decisions save
on good and clear grounds. What has been submitted is that those two judgments
should not be followed; because when the first defendant, the driver of the milk
float, employed the plaintiff to carry bottles for him, he was employing him to do
acts which furthered the second defendants' business interests. In my judgment he *c*
was doing nothing of the sort. The first defendant had been employed to drive the
milk float and deliver the milk. He had not been authorised to sub-contract his work.
What he was doing was setting the plaintiff to do the job for which he had been
employed and for which he was getting paid. In my judgment in so doing he was
acting outside the scope of his employment—just as in the same way as was the driver
in *Conway v George Wimpey & Co Ltd*[2].   *d*
    If a general principle should be needed to support my opinion in this case, I would
adopt the same approach as Lord Greene MR in *Twine's* case[3]. What duty did the
second defendants owe to the plaintiff? Counsel for the plaintiff says: 'Oh well, they
put the driver with the milk float on the road; they put him into a position to take
passengers if he were minded to disobey his instructions and therefore it is socially
just that they should be responsible.' I do not agree. When they put the first defen- *e*
dant with his float on the road they put him into a position where he had to take
care not to injure those with whom he was reasonably likely to have dealings or to
meet, that is all other road users and his customers. They expressly excluded anyone
travelling as a passenger on his milk float. He was instructed expressly that he was
not to carry passengers. Had he obeyed his instructions, he would not have had a
passenger to whom he owed a duty of care. It was his disobedience which brought *f*
the injured plaintiff into the class of persons to whom the second defendants vicariously owed a duty of care. He had not been employed to do anything of the kind.
In my judgment, the plaintiff has failed to establish that the second defendants owed
him any duty of care.
    I appreciate that in *Ilkiw v Samuels*[4], to which Lord Denning MR has already referred,
Diplock LJ, did say that a broad approach must be made to this problem. But the *g*
broad approach must not be so broad that it obscures the principles of law which are
applicable. Therein lies the danger of too broad an approach. That can be illustrated
by examining Diplock LJ's suggested general question[5], namely, what was the job
on which he, the employee, was engaged for his employer? If that general question
is asked without reference to the particular circumstances, the answer in *Twine v
Bean's Express Ltd*[3] would have been to make Bean's Express liable for his injuries. *h*
The van driver in that case had been employed to drive carefully. He had not been
employed to drive negligently. When Twine was injured the driver was doing the
job he had been employed to do, namely to drive. Unless this court is prepared to
say that *Twine v Bean's Express Ltd*[3] was wrongly decided, for my part I cannot see
how that case can be distinguished from this. In the course of the argument an
illustrative example was put to counsel for the plaintiff. He was asked whether if in *j*
Twine's case[3] the driver had asked the passenger to do some map reading for him

1   [1951] 1 All ER at 367, [1951] 2 KB at 276
2   [1951] 1 All ER 363, [1951] 2 KB 266
3   (1946) 175 LT 131
4   [1963] 2 All ER 879 at 889, [1963] 1 WLR 991 at 1004
5   [1963] 2 All ER at 889, [1963] 1 WLR at 1004

a in order that he could get more quickly to the place where in the course of his
   employment he wanted to go, whether that fact would have made the employers
   liable. Counsel for the plaintiff said it would. In my judgment fine distinctions of
   that kind should have no place in our law, particularly in a branch of it which affects
   so many employers and their insurers. Having regard to what has been decided in
   the past, in my judgment it would be wrong now, without the authority either of
   the House of Lords or of Parliament, not to follow the 1946 and 1951 cases.
b   I would dismiss the appeal.

   SCARMAN LJ. Should there be an attentive visitor from Mars sitting in court at
   this moment, he might be forgiven for thinking that he was witnessing the exposure
   of an irreconcilable breach between two lines of authority in the English common
c law. But in my judgment no such breach has in fact been opened and the two lines
   of authority that have led Lawton LJ to differ from the judgment of Lord Denning
   MR are perfectly well capable, when properly analysed, of being reconciled with
   the principles of the law as asserted, not for the first time, by Lord Denning MR in
   his judgment in this case.
       Let me begin with a statement of the general principle of vicarious liability, as I
d understand it in its application to compensation for accidental damage. In words
   which have frequently been quoted both in the courts and in the universities, Salmond
   on Torts[1] refers to the basis of vicarious liability for accidental damage as being one
   of public policy. That view is supported by quotations (dated no doubt, but still full
   of life) of a dictum of Lord Brougham[2] and of another, one hundred years or more
   earlier, of Sir John Holt[3]. That it is 'socially convenient and rough justice'[4] to
e make an employer liable for the torts of his servant in the cases to which the principle
   applies, was recognised in *Limpus v London General Omnibus Co*[5]; see the judgment
   of Willes J[6]. I think it important to realise that the principle of vicarious liability
   is one of public policy. It is not a principle which derives from a critical or refined
   consideration of other concepts in the common law, e g the concept of trespass or
   indeed the concept of agency. No doubt in particular cases it may be relevant to
f consider whether a particular plaintiff was or was not a trespasser. Similarly, when,
   as I shall indicate, it is important that one should determine the course of employment
   of the servant, the law of agency may have some marginal relevance. But basically,
   as I understand it, the employer is made vicariously liable for the tort of his employee
   not because the plaintiff is an invitee, nor because of the authority possessed by the
   servant, but because it is a case in which the employer, having put matters into
g motion, should be liable if the motion that he has originated leads to damage to
   another. What is the approach which the cases identify as the correct approach in
   order to determine this question of public policy? First, as Lord Denning MR has
   already said, one looks to see whether the servant has committed a tort on the
   plaintiff. In the present case it is clear that the first defendant, the servant of the
   dairy company, who are the second defendants, by the negligent driving of the
h milk float, caused injury to the plaintiff, a boy 13½ years old, who was on the float
   at his invitation. There was therefore a tort committed by the servant. The next
   question, as Lord Denning MR has said, is whether the employer should shoulder
   the liability for compensating the person injured by the tort. With all respect to
   the points developed by Lawton LJ, it does appear to me to be clear, since the decision
   of *Limpus v London General Omnibus Co*[5], that that question has to be answered by

j ───
   1   16th Edn (1973), p 462
   2   *Duncan v Findlater* (1839) 6 Cl & Fin 894 at 910
   3   *Hern v Nicholls* (1701) 1 Salk 289
   4   *ICI Ltd v Shatwell* [1964] 2 All ER 999 at 1012, [1965] AC 656 at 685, per Lord Pearce
   5   (1862) 1 H & C 526
   6   1 H & C at 539

directing attention to what the first defendant was employed to do when he committed the tort that has caused damage to the plaintiff. The first defendant was, of *a* course, employed at the time of the accident to do a whole number of operations. He was certainly not employed to give the plaintiff a lift, and if one confines one's analysis of the facts to the incident of injury to the plaintiff, then no doubt one would say that carrying the plaintiff on the float—giving him a lift—was not in the course of the first defendant's employment. But in *Ilkiw v Samuels*[1] Diplock LJ indicated that the proper approach to the nature of the servant's employment is a broad one. *b* He said:

'As each of these nouns implies [he is referring to the nouns used to describe course of employment, sphere, scope and so forth] the matter must be looked at broadly, not dissecting the servant's task into its component activities—such as driving, loading, sheeting and the like—by asking: What was the job on which *c* he was engaged for his employer? and answering that question as a jury would.'

Applying those words to the employment of the first defendant, I think it is clear from the evidence that he was employed as a roundsman to drive his float round his round and to deliver milk, to collect empties and to obtain payment. That was his job. He was under an express prohibition—a matter to which I shall refer later— not to enlist the help of anyone doing that work. And he was also under an express *d* prohibition not to give lifts on the float to anyone. How did he choose to carry out the task which I have analysed? He chose to disregard the prohibition and to enlist the assistance of the plaintiff. As a matter of common sense, that does seem to me to be a mode, albeit a prohibited mode, of doing the job with which he was entrusted. Why was the plaintiff being carried on the float when the accident occurred? Because it was necessary to take him from point to point so that he could assist in *e* delivering milk, collecting empties and, on occasions, obtaining payment. The plaintiff was there because it was necessary that he should be there in order that he could assist, albeit in a way prohibited by the employers, in the job entrusted to the first defendant by his employers.

We have taken a brief look at the historical origins of the doctrine of vicarious liability. One finds in the analysis of the facts which I have just given an echo of *f* words used by Sir John Holt as long ago as 1700. In *Hern v Nichols*[2] he was enunciating, with I think a good deal of prophetic wisdom, the principle of vicarious liability as he saw it. He said, and one notes the factor of public policy in his thinking: '. . . seeing somebody must be a loser by this deceit, it is more reason that he that employs and puts a trust and confidence in the deceiver should be a loser, than a stranger.' His words have no direct application to the facts of this case, but there is a family *g* relationship. The 'deceiver' is the first defendant in whom the second defendants had placed their trust and confidence. It is he who has encouraged the plaintiff (who acted, of course, in ignorance of the prohibition and perfectly reasonably), to accompany him on his float and assist him in doing the second defendants' business. The plaintiff was a stranger to the second defendants. When in the course of such assistance, the 'stranger' was injured by the servant's negligence, the question which, *h* according to Sir John Holt, one should ask is: should the stranger be without remedy against the employer who put trust and confidence in the servant merely because he disobeyed instructions not known to the stranger?

It does seem to me that the principle that I have been attempting to describe is to be found in the case law, notably in *Limpus v London General Omnibus Co*[3], *Hilton v Thomas Burton (Rhodes) Ltd*[4] and *Ilkiw v Samuels*[5]. Yet it is said that the flow of this *j*

---

1   [1963] 2 All ER at 889, [1963] 1 WLR at 1004
2   (1701) 1 Salk 289
3   (1862) 1 H & C 526
4   [1961] 1 All ER 74, [1961] 1 WLR 705
5   [1963] 2 All ER 879, [1963] 1 WLR 991

current of authority must be dammed and the stream of the law diverted because
a of the two decisions to which Lawton LJ has referred: *Twine v Bean's Express Ltd*[1]
and *Conway v George Wimpey & Co Ltd*[2]. Both of those decisions seem to me distinguishable on their facts. In *Twine's case*[3], at the very end of the judgment, Lord
Greene MR said: 'The other thing that he [i e the servant] was doing simultaneously
was something totally outside the scope of his employment, namely, giving a lift to a
person who had no right whatsoever to be there.' In that case the conclusion of fact
b was that the express prohibition on giving lifts was not only a prohibition but was
also a limiting factor on the scope of the employment; and, of course, once a prohibition is properly to be treated as a defining or limiting factor on the scope of employment certain results follow. In *Twine's case*[1] the driver was engaged to drive his
employers' van, his employers having a contract with the Post Office. When so
doing, he gave Mr Twine a lift from A to B. True A and B happened to be, both of
c them, offices of the Post Office. Yet I can well understand why the court reached
the conclusion that in the circumstances of that case it was not possible to say that
the driver in giving Mr Twine a lift was acting within the scope of his employment
or doing improperly that which he was employed to do. Similarly when one looks
at *Conway's case*[2], one again sees that on the facts of that case the court considered
it right so to define the scope of employment that what was done, namely giving
d somebody a lift, was outside it and was not a mode of doing that which the servant
was employed to do. That also was a case of a lift: the person lifted was not in any
way engaged, in the course of the lift or indeed otherwise, in doing the master's
business or in assisting the servant to do the master's business; and no doubt it was
for that reason that Asquith LJ was able to say[4] that what was done—that is giving
somebody else's employee a lift from the airport home—was not a mode of per-
e forming an act which the driver was employed to do, but was the performance
of an act which he was not employed to perform. In the present case the first
defendant, the servant, was employed to deliver milk, to collect empties, to obtain
payment from customers. The plaintiff was there on the float in order to assist the
first defendant to do those jobs. I would have thought therefore that whereas
Conway v George Wimpey & Co Ltd[2] was absolutely correctly decided on its facts,
f the facts of the present case lead to a very different conclusion. The dividing factor
between, for instance, the present case and the decisions in *Twine v Bean's Express
Ltd*[1] and *Conway v George Wimpey & Co Ltd*[2] is the category into which the court,
on the study of the facts of the case, puts the express prohibition issued by the
employers to their servant. In *Ilkiw v Samuels*[5] Diplock LJ, in a judgment to which
I have already referred, dealt with this problem of the prohibition, and quoted a
g dictum of Lord Dunedin in *Plumb v Cobden Flour Mills Co Ltd*[6], which itself has
been approved in the Privy Council case of *Canadian Pacific Railway Co v Lockhart*[7].
Lord Dunedin said[8]: '. . . there are prohibitions which limit the sphere of
employment, and prohibitions which only deal with conduct within the sphere of
employment.' Now those words are in fact an echo of what has long been the law.
Much the same thing but in a different social context was said by Lord Blackburn
h in *Limpus v London General Omnibus Co*[9] and I will quote just one sentence:

---

1 (1946) 175 LT 131
2 [1951] 1 All ER 363, [1951] 2 KB 266
3 175 LT at 132
4 [1951] 1 All ER at 367, [1951] 2 KB at 276
5 [1963] 2 All ER at 889, [1963] 1 WLR at 1004
6 [1914] AC 62 at 67
7 [1942] 2 All ER 464, [1942] AC 591
8 [1914] AC at 67
9 (1862) 1 H & C at 542

'A footman might think it for the interest of his master to drive the coach,
but no one could say that it was within the scope of the footman's employment,
and that the master would be liable for damage resulting from the wilful act
of the footman in taking charge of the horses.'

And, coming right down to today, one finds the same idea being followed and
developed by this court in *Iqbal v London Transport Executive*[1]. In that case the Court
of Appeal had to consider whether London Transport Executive was liable for the
action of a bus conductor in driving, contrary to his express instructions, a motor bus a
short distance in a garage. Of course, the court had no difficulty at all in distinguishing between the spheres of employment of a driver and a conductor in London
Transport. Accordingly, it treated the prohibition on conductors acting as drivers of
motor buses as a prohibition which defined his sphere of employment. Now there was
nothing of that sort in the prohibition in this case. The prohibition is twofold:
(1) that the first defendant was not to give lifts on his float; and (2) that he was not to
employ others to help him in delivering the milk and so forth. There was nothing
in those prohibitions which defined or limited the sphere of his employment. The
sphere of his employment remained precisely the same after as before the prohibitions were brought to his notice. The sphere was as a roundsman to go round the
rounds delivering milk, collecting empties and obtaining payment. Contrary to
instructions, this roundsman chose to do what he was employed to do in an improper
way. But the sphere of his employment was in no way affected by his express
instructions.

Finally, I think one can see how careful one must be not to introduce into a study
of this sort of problem ideas of trespass and agency. It is perfectly possible, on the
principle that I am now considering, that an employer may authorise his servant, if
the servant chooses to do it—'permit' is perhaps a better word—to give lifts. But
the effect of that permission does not make the employer liable if in the course of
recreational or off duty but permitted activity the servant drives the vehicle negligently and injures the passenger. *Hilton v Thomas Burton (Rhodes) Ltd*[2] is a case in
which the plaintiff failed although the journey was a permitted journey, because
he was not able to show that the journey on which he was being carried was a journey
which occurred in the course of the servant's employment. Conversely one has the
classic case of *Limpus v London General Omnibus Co*[3] when what the servant was doing
was a defiance and disregard of the bus company's instructions. Nevertheless the
plaintiff who was injured by the defiant and disobedient acts was entitled to recover
against the employer.

It is for those reasons that I agree with Lord Denning MR, and if that visitor from
Mars is still in court after this long judgment, he will return to his planet conscious
that one member of the court sees no irreconcilable difference opening up in the
common law.

*Appeal allowed; judgment for the plaintiff against the second defendants for £620 damages
plus £63·90 interest. Leave to appeal to the House of Lords granted.*

Solicitors: *Riders* agents for *Bobbetts, Harvey & Grove*, Clifton, Bristol (for the plaintiff);
Barlow, Lyde & Gilbert, agents for *Sansbury Hill & Co*, Bristol (for the second defendants).

Wendy Shockett   Barrister.

1   [1973] The Times, 6th June
2   [1961] 1 All ER 74, [1961] 1 WLR 705
3   (1862) 1 H & C 526

Woodworth and another v Conroy and others
Conroy v Woodworth and another

COURT OF APPEAL, CIVIL DIVISION
BUCKLEY, LAWTON LJJ AND SIR JOHN PENNYCUICK
8th, 9th OCTOBER, 5th NOVEMBER 1975

Accountant – Lien – Unpaid fees – Particular lien – Books and papers of client coming into possession of accountant during course of ordinary professional work – Whether accountant entitled to exercise lien over books and papers for unpaid fees.

Discovery – Production of documents – Inspection – Objection to production for inspection – Professional lien – Inspection having effect of defeating lien – Inspection necessary for disposing fairly of action – Action by client against accountant for return of papers – Accountant claiming right of lien over papers in respect of unpaid fees – Accountant counterclaiming fees – Client wishing to obtain information in papers rather than papers themselves – Whether inspection should be ordered – RSC Ord 24, r 13(1).

The defendants were a firm of accountants who had acted on behalf of the plaintiffs. During the period of their professional relationship with the plaintiffs the defendants came into possession of a number of documents, including certain tax files ('the files'), belonging to the plaintiffs. Eventually the relationship was terminated and the plaintiffs asked for the return of the files. The defendants refused and sent fee notes to the plaintiffs claiming that substantial sums for fees were due to them. The plaintiffs brought an action claiming from the defendants the return of the files. By their defence and counterclaim the defendants alleged that they had a lien over the files for unpaid fees and they counterclaimed the fees. By their reply and defence to counterclaim the plaintiffs alleged that they had paid the defendants all that was due to them. Further they did not admit that the defendants had done the work for which they were charging or that the charges for it were reasonable. After the close of pleadings the defendants delivered a list of documents which included the files over which they claimed a lien, but they objected to producing the files, taking the view that the plaintiffs were not concerned to recover the files themselves but to obtain the information in the files, and that, since that object would be achieved by inspection, the defendants' lien would in effect be defeated. The plaintiffs applied for an order for inspection of the files.

Held – (i) Accountants were entitled to a particular lien for unpaid fees over any books of account, files and papers which had been delivered to them in the course of their ordinary professional work by their clients and also over any documents which had come into their possession whilst acting as their clients' agents in the course of their ordinary professional work (see p 110 h and j and p 112 h, post).

(ii) Such a lien was a valid ground for objecting to inspection of the documents in question for the purpose of an action between the accountants and their clients and where such an objection was taken it was for the court to determine, under RSC Ord 24, r 13(1)ᵃ, whether inspection was necessary for disposing fairly of the action. Since the defendants had not been content to rest their defence on their lien but had counterclaimed their fees and the plaintiffs had exercised their right to put the defendants to proof that the work had been done as alleged and that the fees charged were reasonable, issues had been raised which could not be disposed of fairly without the contents of the documents being put in evidence. Accordingly an order for inspection would be made (see p 111 c d and g to j and p 112 d e and h, post).

---

a   Rule 13(1) is set out at p 111 b, post

Notes

For examples of particular liens, see 24 Halsbury's Laws (3rd Edn) 154, para 284, and for *a* cases on particular liens, see 32 Digest (Repl) 286-293, *315-389*.

For the grounds for resisting the production of documents, see 12 Halsbury's Laws (3rd Edn) 50-60, paras 71-79, and for cases on the subject, see 18 Digest (Reissue) 134-162, *1041-1302*.

Cases referred to in judgments   *b*

Bevan and Whitting, Re (1864) 33 Beav 439, 55 ER 438.

Hawkes, Re, Ackerman & Lockhart [1898] 2 Ch 1, [1895-9] All ER Rep 964, 67 LJCh 284, 78 LT 336, CA, 18 Digest (Reissue) 93, *695*.

Hill, Re, ex parte Southall (1848) 17 LJ Bcy 21, 32 Digest (Repl) 290, *341*.

Lord v Wormleighton (1822) Jac 580, 37 ER 969.

                                                                                 c

Cases also cited

Chantrey Martin & Co v Martin [1953] 2 All ER 691, [1953] 2 QB 286, CA.

Crompton (Alfred) Amusement Machines Ltd v Comrs of Customs and Excise [1972] 2 All ER 353, [1972] 2 QB 102, CA.

Faithfull, Re, Re London, Brighton & South Coast Railway Co (1868) LR 6 Eq 325, 18 LT 502.   *d*

Furlong v Howard (1804) 2 Sch & Lef 115.

Hope v Liddell (1855) 7 De GM & G 331, 44 ER 129.

Kemp v Kemp (1842) 2 Mood & R 43.

Rapid Road Transit Co, Re [1909] 1 Ch 96, 78 LJ Ch 132.

Interlocutory appeals   *e*

By a writ issued on 28th October 1971 the plaintiffs, John Rollo Woodworth and R Wood Commercial Investigators Ltd, brought an action ('the first action') against the defendants, Arnold Conroy, Raymond Harris and Bernard Dollar, practising as Raymond, Harris and Bernard Dollar, claiming the return by the defendants to the plaintiffs of all the plaintiffs' papers, documents and correspondence relating to the plaintiffs' affairs in the defendants' possession and arising during the period from *f* 1st December 1967 to 17th September 1971. By their defence the defendants alleged that they were entitled to exercise a lien over the documents for unpaid fees and the defendants conterclaimed the amount of the fees alleged to be unpaid. By a summons dated 3rd December 1974 the defendants applied under RSC Ord 24, r 2(5), for an order dispensing with discovery of such documents as the defendants were entitled to retain by way of lien as claimed in their defence and counterclaim. *g* On 6th February 1975 Master Waldman ordered that discovery by the defendants be limited to lists of documents until further order. On 19th May 1975 Griffiths J allowed an appeal by the plaintiffs against that order, and ordered that there be inspection of documents within 28 days.

By a writ issued on 25th January 1975 the plaintiff, Josephine Yvonne Conroy, brought an action ('the second action') against the defendants, the plaintiffs in the *h* the first action, claiming sums amounting to £4,308 alleged to be due to her under certain agreements made in May 1968 and May 1970. On 19th May 1975 Griffiths J made an order in favour of the defendants, the plaintiffs in the first action, for inspection of documents over which the defendants in the first action claimed the right to exercise a lien.

The defendants in the first action and the plaintiff in the second action appealed *j* against the orders of Griffiths J.

Roger Henderson for the defendants in the first action and the plaintiff in the second action.

C Hookway for the plaintiffs in the first action and the defendants in the second action.

Cur adv vult

a

5th November. **LAWTON LJ** delivered the first judgment at the invitation of Buckley LJ. The appeals in these actions are from orders of Griffiths J, whereby he adjudged in favour of the plaintiffs in the first action and of the defendants in the second action that they should have inspection of certain documents which the other side in both actions had claimed should not be inspected because they were covered *b* by a lien to which the defendants in the first action were entitled. In making these orders the learned judge reversed the orders of Master Waldman.

The following questions were discussed in argument but, in my judgment, it is not necessary to reach a decision on all of them. First, have accountants any lien for unpaid fees over books, correspondence and papers which have been delivered to them by their clients or which have come into their possession in the course of acting for *c* their clients? Secondly, if they have, is it a general lien or a particular lien? If the latter, to what documents does it extend? Thirdly, if a client sues for the return of his books and any correspondence or papers which may have come into existence, can inspection be refused on the ground that the accountants have a lien for unpaid fees? Fourthly, if inspection can be refused for this reason, does it make any difference if the accountants counterclaim for their fees and by way of defence the client alleges *d* that he has paid them all he is bound to do, that the fees claimed are excessive and unreasonable and that the accountants acted negligently in respect of the matters for which they are claiming fees?

The questions which were under discussion in argument arise more clearly in the first action than in the second. If the claim to resist inspection fails in the first action, it must fail in the second; but the converse would not follow.

e

In the first action, by specially endorsed writ issued on the 18th October 1971, the two plaintiffs claimed from the defendants, a firm of accountants, the return of all their papers, documents and correspondence relating to their affairs which were 'in the Defendants' possession and arising during the period the 1st December, 1967 and ending on the 27th September, 1971'. By an amendment of the statement of claim endorsed on the writ which was made on the 7th December 1971, the plaintiffs *f* specifically referred to tax files as having been detained by the defendants and added a claim for damages for the detention of the papers, documents, tax files and correspondence. I do not find it necessary to go into much detail about the circumstances out of which the claim arose. It suffices to record that between the 1st December 1967 and the 17th September 1971 the defendants as accountants had been in a professional relationship with the plaintiffs. What they had been retained to do as account- *g* ants is in issue in the action. On the 17th September 1971 the relationship came to an end. On the 1st October 1971 the plaintiffs' solicitors wrote to the defendants asking for the return of their clients' papers. The defendants refused and on the 8th October they sent fee notes to both plaintiffs claiming that substantial sums for fees were due to them. The details of what was claimed depends on the arrangements alleged to have been made for the payment of fees and whether the first plaintiff's *h* liability for fees was accepted by the second named plaintiffs. The details do not matter. If anything was due, it has not been paid.

By their defence and counterclaim the defendants alleged that they had a lien over the papers and files for unpaid fees. They counterclaimed for these fees. By their reply and defence to counterclaim the plaintiffs alleged that they had paid the defendants all they had ever agreed to pay and that there were no fees outstanding *j* so that the defendants had no lien. Further they did not admit that the defendants had done the work for which they were charging or that their charges for it were reasonable. As a parting shot they alleged that the defendants had been negligent in the preparation of books and accounts whereby they had suffered loss which they wanted to set off against the defendants' claim for fees. They gave no particulars of either negligence or loss.

The plaintiffs allege that the defendants' refusal to hand over papers and tax files has put them into difficulties. The defendants accept that this is probably so. Both **a** plaintiffs want the papers for the purpose of making tax returns and agreeing assessments with the Inland Revenue. Further, the second named plaintiffs have a statutory obligation to produce and file accounts; they want their papers for this purpose too. The papers and files which the defendants hold have no intrinsic value for the plaintiffs. What they want is the information in them. It they could get inspection in the action, and take the copies which RSC Ord 24, r 9, would allow them to do, **b** they would probably get the information they wanted. The defendants suspect that they might then discontinue the action. This would leave the defendants with the prospect of getting a judgment for their fees on their counterclaim, which they might not be able to enforce, and a useless lien on pieces of paper. By issuing a writ and getting inspection in the action the plaintiffs would have defeated the lien, which, if the plaintiffs, or either of them, got into financial difficulties, might be of greater **c** value to the defendants against a receiver or liquidator than an unsatisfied judgment.

After the close of the pleadings, the defendants delivered a long list of documents. They objected to producing the documents identified in part 2 of the first schedule to this list. These documents included four files as well as the usual ones covered by professional privilege. The ground stated in the list of documents for the objection was that they were all privileged. This was not an accurate use of language. What **d** the defendants wanted to do was to object to the plaintiffs having inspection of the four files because they were the subject of the defendants' alleged lien for unpaid fees. They now accept that their lien could only apply to the contents of files numbered 2, 3 and 4. Master Waldman decided that there should be no inspection of these files without further order. Griffiths J ordered inspection.

The first matter to be decided is whether in law the defendants as accountants **e** could have any kind of lien over the plaintiffs' papers and tax files. Surprisingly, the researches of counsel, which have been extensive, have revealed no case in which any court has adjudged that accountants have a lien. As long ago as 1848, Knight-Bruce V-C expressed a firm opinion that they had in a case which raised the question; but no judgment was given, an order being made by consent for the return of the books in dispute to the accountants 'without prejudice to any question': see *Re Hill,* **f** *ex parte Southall*[1]. I can see no reason whatsoever why accountants should not have a lien of some kind. Books of account and other documents are entrusted to them by their clients for work to be done on and in connection with them, often by entering up ledgers and almost always by analysis. Work in connection with books of account often involves corresponding with third parties and making compilations of various kinds. The kind of work they do may be very different from that of a craftsman who **g** is making or repairing a chattel (the kind of work which gave rise to the common law concept of particular liens); but since the beginning of the 19th century arbitrators, architects, conveyancers and parliamentary agents have been adjudged capable of having particular liens: see Halsbury's Laws[2]. Solicitors, bankers, factors, stockbrokers and insurance brokers have long enjoyed the right to general liens[3]. I would adjudge that accountants in the course of doing their ordinary professional **h** work of producing and auditing accounts, advising on financial problems, and carrying on negotiations with the Inland Revenue in relation to both taxation and rating have at least a particular lien over any books of account, files and papers which their clients delivered to them and also over any documents which have come into their possession in the course of acting as their clients' agents in the course of their ordinary professional work. Accountants may enjoy a wider lien than this; but I find it **j** unnecessary for the purposes of this appeal to say more than I have.

---

1   (1848) 17 LJBcy 21
2   24 Halsbury's Laws (3rd Edn) 154, para 284
3   Ibid 148, para 271

Before turning to the remaining questions in this appeal, it is necessary to examine
a the powers of the court in relation to inspection. Once a party has disclosed documents in his possession, custody or power relating to the matters in question in an
action he 'must allow the other party to inspect the documents referred to in the list
(other than any which he objects to produce) and to take copies thereof . . .': see
RSC Ord 24, r 9. Rule 10 deals with the inspection of documents referred to in the pleadings and any affidavits. Rule 11 empowers the court to order inspection when ob-
b jection has been made; but the exercise of this power is subject to r 13(1) which
provides as follows:

> 'No order for the production of any documents for inspection or to the Court
> shall be made under any of the foregoing rules, unless the Court is of the opinion
> that the order is necessary either for disposing fairly of the cause or matter or
> for saving costs.'
c

A valid claim for privilege is, of course, a proper ground of objection. The rules do
not identify any other grounds. Rule 13(2) envisages, however, that objection can be
made on grounds other than privilege; but in such cases the test for the validity of
the objection is that set out in r 13(1). It follows, in my judgment, that any objection
to inspection based on a lien must be judged by the test in r 13(1).
d   Now the claim in the first action is in detinue. The plaintiffs are alleging that the
defendants have wrongly detained their chattels. The defendants claim they have
not because the law has given them a right to possession adverse to that of the plaintiffs. This is derived from their lien for unpaid fees. Had there been no other issues on
the pleadings, at the trial this one could have been disposed of fairly without any
inspection of the subject-matter of the lien. The defendants would have had to satisfy
e the court that they had a lien, that they had done work on or in connection with the
books, papers and files and that they had not been paid their reasonable charges
for what they had done. Once they had proved their lien they would have been
entitled to judgment.
      RSC Ord 24, r 13(1), gives the court a discretion but judges no doubt would be guided
by what has been decided in the past in relation to similar kinds of lien. The right
f of a solicitor to withhold papers from inspection by his client, even in litigation
between them, was recognised as long ago as 1822: see *Lord v Wormleighton*[1]. In later
cases the limitations on this right have been discussed (for an example, see *Re Hawkes,
Ackerman v Lockhart*[2]) but the basic right has not been queried.
      The defendants, however, in the first action were not content to rest their defence
on their lien; they counterclaimed for their fees and, as already stated, the plaintiffs
g by way of defence put forward a number of pleas. The first was that there had been
an agreement about fees, that they had paid what was due under this agreement
and that there were no other fees due to the defendants. This issue could be tried
without inspection of the files in question since the court would have to decide what,
if anything, had been agreed and what, if anything, had been paid under the agreement. The plaintiffs, however, have gone further. They have exercised their right
h to put the defendants to proof that work has been done as alleged and that the fees
charged are reasonable. In addition they have alleged negligence in the doing of the
work. If these defences are put forward in good faith, it would be impossible to try
the issues raised without evidence being led as to what work had been done and how
it was done. The best evidence of what had been done would be in the files and the
court would have to assess their contents in order to decide whether the fees charged
j were reasonable and whether the work had been done negligently. Unless there is
some other element in the case, inspection of the files would be necessary in order to
dispose fairly of these issues.
      The defendants contended that there was another element. They submitted that

1   (1822) Jac 580
2   [1898] 2 Ch 1, [1895-9] All ER Rep 964

these defences were nothing more than tactical moves to raise issues on the pleadings
which would justify an order for inspection. They invited attention to the precipitate
way in which the action had been started after the defendants had claimed their fees
and to the absence of any correspondence before the writ was issued making allegations
against the defendants of the kind now to be found in the pleadings. They also
pointed to the way these defences had been pleaded; bare denials that the work had
been done and that the charges were reasonable, coupled with an allegation of
negligence unsupported by any particulars and without identification of the damage
alleged to have resulted. All this gives cause for suspicion; and in the case of the negligence plea its inherent defects and the way it has been put forward lead me to conclude
that it has no substance. I do not feel justified, however, in coming to the same
conclusion about the other pleas.

I have considered two other possible courses which might be effective to protect
what the defendants claim to be their lien pending the decision whether they are
entitled to it. The first would be to order the defendants to produce the files to the
master so that he could decide whether there were triable issues on the defences
put forward. The objection to this is that the master would have to carry out a
preliminary enquiry covering much the same ground as the court will have to go
over at the trial. It would take a long time and would be expensive in costs. The
second course would be to order the plaintiffs to bring the amount of the fees claimed,
or part thereof, into court as a condition of getting an order for inspection. There
is a precedent for such an order: see *Re Bevan and Whitting*[1]. This might be unfair to
the plaintiffs if they were able to establish their defence that there had been an
agreement about fees and that they had paid the defendants all they were entitled
to receive. In my judgment, there should be an inspection of the three files.

The parties and issues in the second action are different. The plaintiff, Josephine
Yvonne Conroy, is claiming against the defendants sums which she alleges are due
under agreements with one or other or both of them; they are the plaintiffs in the
first action. They deny liability and counterclaim against the plaintiff and her husband
for money alleged to have been had and received by them and for a declaration that
the plaintiff and her husband are responsible for making certain payments under a
hire-purchase contract. The only relevant connection between the two actions for
the purpose of these appeals is that the plaintiff's husband is a partner in the firm
who are the defendants in the first action. It is said that he has in his power for the
purposes of RSC Ord 24 documents which are in the possession of the defendants
in the first action in their capacity as the accountants of the plaintiffs in that action
and that he should produce them for inspection. If the appeal in the first action is
dismissed and inspection is given of the files, the plaintiffs in that action (being the
defendants in the second action) will have got what they want so there will be no
point in the plaintiff and her husband resisting inspection in the second action.

I would dismiss the appeals in both cases.

BUCKLEY LJ. I have the authority of Sir John Pennycuick, who cannot be here
this morning, to say that he agrees with the judgment which has just been delivered.
I also agree with it and do not wish to add anything.

Appeals dismissed.

Solicitors: *Hobson and Arditti* (for the defendants in the first action and the plaintiff
in the second action); *G Lebor & Co* (for the plaintiffs in the first action and the
defendants in the second action).

Jill Watkins Barrister.

1　(1864) 33 Beav 439

a   # Law v Gustin (formerly Law)

FAMILY DIVISION
BAGNALL J
21st, 24th MARCH 1975

b   *Nullity – Foreign decree – Recognition – Basis of recognition – Real and substantial connection between petitioner and foreign country – Wife leaving husband to go and live in foreign country with intention of marrying national of that country – Wife obtaining decree of nullity in competent court of foreign country after 12 months' residence there – Whether decree should be recognised by English court.*

c   The husband and wife were married in England in 1966 and had their only matrimonial home in Lancashire. While living there they met G, a United States serviceman who was a native of Kansas. In due course G returned to Kansas and on 15th December 1967 the wife left home without giving any indication of where she was going. Subsequently the husband received a number of letters from the wife which showed that she had followed G to Kansas, that she intended to stay there and in due
d   course to marry G should she become free to do so. On 18th November 1968 the wife filed a nullity petition in the appropriate Kansas court. The husband was given notice of the proceedings. On 2nd January 1969 a decree of nullity was pronounced by that court based on an allegation that at the time of the marriage the husband had had no intention of consummating it. After the decree the wife married G and they set up home together in Kansas. The husband sought an order declaring that the decree
e   was valid.

Held – The court would recognise a decree of nullity granted by the competent court of a foreign country or territory in cases where a real and substantial connection was shown between that country or territory and the party who had obtained the decree. Although at the time of the decree the wife had been resident in the state of Kansas
f   for barely 12 months, taking into account all the circumstances both before and after the pronouncement of the decree, in particular the wife's relationship with G, the proper conclusion was that a real and substantial connection had been shown to exist between the wife and the state of Kansas at the time when the decree was pronounced. A declaration would be granted accordingly (see p 116 *a* to *d* and *f* to *j*, post).

g   *Merker v Merker* [1962] 3 All ER 928, dictum of Lord Wilberforce in *Indyka v Indyka* [1967] 2 All ER at 727, *Blair v Blair and Barlie* [1968] 3 All ER 639 and *Mayfield v Mayfield* [1969] 2 All ER 219 applied.

Notes
For recognition of foreign decrees of nullity, see 8 Halsbury's Laws (4th Edn) paras 500-502, and for cases on the subject, see 11 Digest (Reissue) 557-560, 1232-1246.

h   **Cases referred to in judgment**
Alexander v Alexander (1969) 113 Sol Jo 344, 11 Digest (Reissue) 549, *1215*.
Blair v Blair and Barlie [1968] 3 All ER 639, [1969] 1 WLR 221, 11 Digest (Reissue) 550, *1221*.
Indyka v Indyka [1967] 2 All ER 689, [1969] 1 AC 33, [1967] 3 WLR 510, HL, 11 Digest (Reissue) 551, *1224*.
j   *Mayfield v Mayfield* [1969] 2 All ER 219, [1969] P 119, [1969] 2 WLR 1002, 11 Digest (Reissue) 550, *1219*.
Merker v Merker [1962] 3 All ER 928, [1963] P 283, [1962] 3 WLR 1389, 11 Digest (Reissue) 516, *1048*.
Salvesen (or Von Lorang) v Austrian Property Administrator [1927] AC 641, [1927] All ER Rep 78, 96 LJPC 105, 137 LT 571, HL, 11 Digest (Reissue) 541, *1180*.

Petition

By a petition dated 12th March 1973 the husband, Albert Webster Law, sought a **a**
declaration that a decree of nullity granted to the wife, Joan Gustin, formerly Joan
Law, by the District Court of Wyandotte County, Kansas, in the United States of
America, was valid. On 23rd November 1973 the hearing of the petition came before
Bagnall J who adjourned the proceedings and invited the Queen's Proctor to instruct
counsel as amicus curiae to argue the question of the validity of the decree obtained
by the wife. The facts are set out in the judgment.   **b**

Nigel Fricker and *William Norris* for the husband.
Gilbert Rodway for the Queen's Proctor as amicus curiae.
The wife did not appear and was not represented.

c

BAGNALL J. By his petition in this case the husband seeks an order declaring
to be valid a decree pronounced on 2nd January 1969 by the District Court of Wyandotte County, Kansas, in the United States of America. The effect of that decree was
to declare null and void the marriage contracted in this country on 4th April 1966
between the husband and the wife, now known as Joan Gustin, formerly, of course,
Joan Law.   **d**

I have had expert evidence from two separate deponents to affidavits that under
the law applicable in the state of Kansas the decree to which I have referred was effective as a decree of nullity of marriage. The question I have to determine is whether
that decree ought to be recognised and be declared to be valid by this court.

When the matter first came before me some considerable time ago counsel for the
husband frankly admitted that the case might not be straightforward and that doubts **e**
existed as to the principles of law which I ought to apply. In those circumstances I
took steps to obtain the assistance of the Queen's Proctor and he instructed counsel to
make submissions to me as amicus curiae. I am indebted to him for that service, as
I am equally indebted to counsel for the husband for the interesting arguments that
have been placed before me. In the end, however, the Queen's Proctor, through
counsel, intimated that he did not feel justified in opposing the relief sought by the **f**
husband either on grounds of law or on grounds of fact.

The parties were married, as I have said, on 4th April 1966 in Cheshire and had their
only matrimonial home at Newton-le-Willows in Lancashire. While they were there
they met a Mr Gustin who was in this country doing what we would call his national
service in the United States Air Force. During the same period the wife had employment with that air force and in due course Mr Gustin returned to his native state, that **g**
is to say the state of Kansas in the United States of America, and subsequently on 15th
December 1967 the wife left home leaving a very short note which gave no indication
either of her intended destination or of when she would return. Later it was discovered that she had gone to Kansas, of which Mr Gustin is a native, and in due course
she initiated the process which led to the decree pronounced in that state with which
I am concerned.   **h**

During the intervening period the wife sent a number of letters to the husband
from which it was plain, first, that she was staying in Kansas, and secondly that she
had no intention of returning either to him or to this country. In September 1968 a
draft of the petition to be presented to the court in Kansas was sent to the husband
and on 18th November the relevant petition was filed in Kansas supported by an
affidavit sworn by the wife. Steps were taken in two ways to bring those proceedings **j**
to the notice of the husband. First, a notice was published once a week for three consecutive weeks in a local newspaper circulated in the relevant district in the state of
Kansas said to be a newspaper authorised by law to publish legal notices. It is of course
wholly unreasonable to suppose that any of those publications came to the actual
notice of the husband, but in addition it appears from secondary evidence, though I

a   have not seen the original document, that a letter giving notice of process was sent by attorneys representing the wife. The relevant letter was dated 15th November 1968, but was only received by the husband on 22nd December. The time limit for him to take the procedural steps open to him to defend the proceedings in Kansas expired on 27th December. In due course, as I have said, the decree was pronounced on 2nd January 1969. The basis on which the decree of nullity was founded was an allegation that the marriage ceremony was entered into through fraudulent conduct on the

b   part of the husband, he having no intention to consummate the marriage. I think that is all I need say by way of recital of the relevant facts and documents.

It is clear from the authority of *Merker v Merker*[1] that this court assumes jurisdiction to recognise and declare the validity of a decree of nullity, just as it does in the case of a decree of divorce. That case was a nullity case and in the course of his judgment Sir Jocelyn Simon P said[2]:

c

'A decree of nullity of marriage pronounced by a foreign court of competent jurisdiction will, in the absence of fraud or unless contrary to natural justice, be recognised as binding and conclusive by the courts of this country [and having cited authority[3] for that proposition Sir Jocelyn Simon P went on:] The first question to determine is, therefore, whether the decree of the [foreign] court is in the

d   international sense the judgment of a court of competent jurisdiction in the matter.'

At that stage the concept of domicile as understood in this country lay at the foundation of the decision whether the foreign court in question was indeed a court of competent jurisdiction, and that authority seems to me to establish the proposition that, as one would expect, the same test was applied, whether the decree of the

e   foreign court was a decree of divorce or a decree of nullity.

Recently the whole of this admittedly difficult field of jurisprudence has been considered in the House of Lords in the well-known case of *Indyka v Indyka*[4] in relation, at any rate, to recognition of decrees of divorce. In the course of his opinion Lord Wilberforce, after asking himself how far the courts in this country should go in relaxing the long-standing dependence of this jurisdiction on the concept of domicile,

f   went on[5]:

'In my opinion, it would be in accordance with the developments that I have mentioned and with the trend of legislation—mainly our own but also that of other countries with similar social systems—to recognise divorces given to wives by the courts of their residence wherever a real and substantial connexion

g   is shown between the petitioner and the country, or territory, exercising jurisdiction.'

The facts in *Indyka v Indyka*[4] were such that other connections, for example that of nationality, could be invoked in order to found the jurisdiction of the foreign court whose decree was there in issue. Speaking for myself I have some doubt whether the principle thus enunciated by Lord Wilberforce could be said to constitute the ratio

h   decidendi of all or even the majority of their Lordships who were concerned in that decision, but so far at any rate as a court of first instance is concerned, the doubts that I should otherwise have expressed and related to an analysis of the opinions in *Indyka v Indyka*[4] have been resolved for me.

There are three decisions at first instance, *Blair v Blair*[6], *Mayfield v Mayfield*[7] and

---

j   1   [1962] 3 All ER 928, [1963] P 283
2   [1962] 3 All ER at 934, [1963] P at 296
3   *Salvesen (or von Lorang) v Austrian Property Administrator* [1927] AC 641, [1927] All ER Rep 78
4   [1967] 2 All ER 689, [1969] 1 AC 33
5   [1967] 2 All ER at 727, [1969] 1 AC at 105
6   [1968] 3 All ER 639, [1969] 1 WLR 221
7   [1969] 2 All ER 219, [1969] P 119

Alexander v Alexander[1]. Each of those cases proceeded on the footing that, since the decision in *Indyka v Indyka*[2], there was a new ground governing the recognition of *a* foreign decrees, at any rate in relation to divorce, described as a real and substantial connection with the country whose jurisdiction was sought. Those cases are, of course, not binding on me, but I have no doubt that I ought to follow them.

The questions therefore which I have to decide are first, is it now established that when the wife obtained the relevant decree in Kansas she had a real and substantial connection with that state? And secondly, if so, was the relevant decree obtained by a *b* process which recognised those rules of natural justice which are to be found in any civilised system of jurisprudence? Dealing first with the second of those questions I have given anxious consideration to the question whether the relevant rule of such a system of jurisprudence, namely, that the husband had adequate notice of and opportunity to defend the proceedings in Kansas, had been satisfied. With some hesitation I have reached the conclusion that I ought to find that sufficient notice was given *c* and that the decree cannot be criticised on the basis of natural justice.

The question whether there was established a real and substantial connection between the wife and the state of Kansas must be a question of fact, to be decided, as a jury would decide such a question, on a consideration of all the relevant circumstances. The principal difficulty in the way of the husband, to which my attention was properly drawn by both counsel, was the comparatively short period of residence, *d* amounting to perhaps rather less than 12 months, before the Kansas decree was pronounced. But it is plain that Kansas was at all material times the home state of Mr Gustin; it is also clear that no other reason was given for the wife to leave this country and her husband and go to Kansas than that she wished to follow Mr Gustin and in due course, if she was free to do so, to marry him.

As I have said such letters as she wrote all emanating from Kansas showed no in- *e* tention either of returning to this country or of going anywhere else, either in or outside the United States of America. In due course, the decree having been pronounced, the wife and Mr Gustin did in fact marry and have remained settled in the state of Kansas.

I am, I have no doubt, entitled to consider what has happened subsequently to the pronouncing of the decree in that state in order to guide me to the right answer to *f* the question of fact that I have posed. I understand that the same question has been considered in a number of cases when various characteristics of the relevant parties and of their residence abroad has been weighed in the balance in order to see whether or not they establish real and substantial connection. I have not been referred to the cases and it seems to me that that was a proper course to take. In a question of this nature every case must depend on its own facts and its own circumstances, and to my *g* mind the process of decision in not assisted by a consideration of the conclusions which have been reached in other cases dealing with different people and different circumstances.

Answering the question purely as a question of fact, I have no doubt that the proper conclusion is that the wife had established a real and substantial connection with the state of Kansas at the time the decree was pronounced by the appropriate court in *h* that state.

Accordingly, I am satisfied that I ought to accede to the prayer in the petition and declare that the decree of annulment is valid. That disposes of the whole matter and I simply make that declaration.

Declaration accordingly.   *j*

Solicitors: *Louis Berkson & Globe*, Liverpool.

Phua Kai-Swan Esq Barrister.

1   (1969) 113 Sol Jo 344
2   [1967] 2 All ER 689, [1969] 1 AC 33

Esso Petroleum Ltd v Commissioners of Customs and Excise

HOUSE OF LORDS
LORD WILBERFORCE, VISCOUNT DILHORNE, LORD SIMON OF GLAISDALE, LORD FRASER OF
TULLYBELTON AND LORD RUSSELL OF KILLOWEN
10th, 11th NOVEMBER, 10th DECEMBER 1975

Purchase tax – Chargeable goods – Pictures, prints, engravings etc – Goods produced in quantity for general sale – Sale – Consideration for supply of goods – Goods produced for distribution to customers purchasing specified other goods – Coins bearing likenesses of members of English World Cup soccer team – Coins produced by petrol suppliers for distribution by petrol stations to motorists purchasing specified quantity of suppliers' petrol – Whether coins supplied in consideration of money payments by motorists – Whether coins produced for 'sale' to motorists – Purchase Tax Act 1963, Sch 1, Group 25.

Contract – Intention to create legal relationship – Inference or intention from circumstances – Business operation – Sales promotion scheme – Offer by suppliers to give coins to purchasers of suppliers' goods – Coins bearing likenesses of members of English World Cup soccer team – Coins produced by petrol suppliers for distribution by proprietors of petrol stations to motorists buying suppliers' petrol – Posters advertising gift of one coin for every four gallons of petrol purchased – Whether intention of suppliers, proprietors or customers that proprietors should enter into contractual obligation to supply coins to customers.

In 1970 the taxpayers ('Esso') devised a petrol sales promotion scheme. The scheme involved the distribution of millions of coins to petrol stations which sold Esso petrol. Each of the coins bore the likeness of one of the members of the English soccer team which went to Mexico in 1970 to play in the World Cup competition. The object of the scheme was that petrol station proprietors should encourage motorists to buy Esso petrol by offering to give away a coin for every four gallons of Esso petrol which the motorist bought. The coins were of little intrinsic value but it was hoped that motorists would persist in buying Esso petrol in order to collect the full set of 30 coins. The scheme was extensively advertised by Esso in the press and on television with phrases such as: 'Going free, at your Esso Action Station now', and: 'We are giving you a coin with every four gallons of Esso petrol you buy.' Folders were also circulated by Esso to petrol stations which stated, inter alia: 'One coin should be given to every motorist who buys four gallons of petrol—two coins for eight gallons and so on.' 4,900 petrol stations joined the scheme. Large posters were delivered by Esso to those stations, the most prominent lettering on the posters stating: 'The World Cup coins', 'One coin given with every four gallons of petrol'. The Customs and Excise Commissioners claimed that the coins were chargeable to purchase tax under s 2(1)^a of the Puchase Tax Act 1963 on the ground that they had been 'produced in quantity for general sale' and therefore fell within Group 25^b of Sch 1 to the 1963 Act.

Held (Lord Fraser of Tullybelton dissenting) – The coins had not been 'produced . . . for . . . sale', within Group 25 of Sch 1, and were not therefore chargeable for the following reasons—

---

a   Section 2(1), so far as material, provides: 'Subject to the provisions of this section, the goods which are chargeable goods are those comprised in the Groups listed in Part I of Schedule 1 to this Act . . .'

b   Schedule 1, so far as material, provides: '. . . GROUP 25 *comprising* Pictures, prints, engravings, photographs, figures, busts, reliefs and similar articles of a kind produced in quantity for general sale . . .'

(i) On the basis that the posters and other advertising material constituted an offer by the garage proprietors to enter into a contract with each customer to supply a *a* coin with every four gallons of petrol sold, the contract envisaged was not a contract of 'sale', since the consideration for the transfer of the coins was not a money payment but the undertaking by the customer to enter into a collateral contract to purchase the appropriate quantity of Esso petrol (see p 119 *d*, p 121 *e* and *f*, p 122 *f* to p 123 *d* and p 126 *h* and *j*, post); *Taylor v Smetten* (1883) 11 QBD 207, *Scott & Co Ltd v W Solomon* (1905) 69 JP 137 and *Bulpitt & Sons Ltd v S Bellman & Sons Ltd* (1962) LR 3 RP 62 *b* distinguished.

(ii) (per Viscount Dilhorne and Lord Russell of Killowen, Lord Wilberforce and Lord Simon of Glaisdale dissenting) Furthermore, in the circumstances, and in particular in view of the fact that the coins were of little intrinsic value to customers, it could not be inferred that either Esso or the petrol station proprietors on the one hand, or the customers on the other, intended that there should be a legally binding *c* contract to supply the coins to customers who bought the appropriate quantity of petrol. It followed that the coins had been produced for distribution by way of gift and not by way of sale (see p 120 *g* and *h*, p 121 *a* to *e* and p 126 *a* to *d*, post); dicta of Scrutton and Atkin LJJ in *Rose and Frank Co v J R Crompton Bros Ltd* [1924] All ER Rep at 249, 252 and of Megaw LJ in *Edwards v Skyways Ltd* [1964] 1 All ER at 500 considered.   *d*

Notes

For goods chargeable to purchase tax, see 33 Halsbury's Laws (3rd Edn) 223-225, paras 382, 383.

For the intention to create legal relations as a requisite of an enforceable contract, see 9 Halsbury's Laws (4th Edn) paras 300-308, and for cases on the subject, see 12 *e* Digest (Reissue) 21-26, 2-21.

For the nature of the transaction of sale, see 34 Halsbury's Laws (3rd Edn) 5-7, paras 1-4, and for cases on the subject, see 39 Digest (Repl) 443-445, 1-15.

For the Purchase Tax Act 1963, s 2, Sch 1, Group 25, see 26 Halsbury's Statutes (3rd Edn) 625, 687.

Section 2(1) of, and Sch 1 to, the 1963 Act are repealed by the Finance Act 1972, s 134(7), *f* Sch 28, Part II, as from a date to be appointed under s 54(8) of the 1972 Act following the abolition of purchase tax with effect from 1st April 1973 by s 54(1) of the 1972 Act.

Cases referred to in opinions

Balfour v Balfour [1919] 2 KB 571, [1918-19] All ER Rep 860, CA, 12 Digest (Reissue) 21, 3.
Bulpitt & Sons Ltd v S Bellman & Sons Ltd (1962) LR 3 RP 62, 45 Digest (Repl) 404, 153.
Carlill v Carbolic Smoke Ball Co [1893] 1 QB 256, [1891-4] All ER Rep 127, 62 LJQB 257, *g* 67 LT 837, 57 JP 325, 4 R 176, CA, 12 Digest (Reissue) 66, 342.
Chappell & Co Ltd v Nestlé Co Ltd [1959] 2 All ER 701, [1960] AC 87, [1959] 3 WLR 168, HL, Digest (Cont Vol A) 312, 569a.
Edwards v Skyways Ltd [1964] 1 All ER 494, [1964] 1 WLR 349, Digest (Cont Vol B) 138, 12b.
Heilbut, Symons & Co v Buckleton [1913] AC 30, [1911-13] All ER Rep 83, HL, 39 Digest *h* (Repl) 513, 565.
Rose and Frank Co v J R Crompton & Bros Ltd [1923] 2 KB 261, [1924] All ER Rep 245, CA, 12 Digest (Reissue) 22, 4.
Scott & Co v Solomon [1905] 1 KB 577, 69 JP 137, DC.
Taylor v Smetten (1883) 11 QBD 207, 52 LJMC 101, 48 JP 36, DC, 25 Digest (Repl) 494, *j* 521.

Appeal

By an originating summons dated 25th October 1972 the respondents, Esso Petroleum Co Ltd ('Esso'), claimed against the appellants, the Customs and Excise Commissioners ('the commissioners'), a declaration that the 'World Cup Coins' manufactured to the

order of Esso and supplied by them to petrol service station proprietors were not
a chargeable goods under the Purchase Tax Act 1963, s 2(1) and Sch 1. On 20th June
1973 Pennycuick V-C dismissed the summons, holding that the coins had been distributed to petrol stations for sale to customers and were therefore chargeable under
Group 25 of Sch 1 to the 1963 Act being goods of the kind described in Group 25 which
had been produced in quantity for general sale. Esso appealed and on 31st January
1975 the Court of Appeal (Lord Denning MR, Stephenson and Geoffrey Lane LJJ)
b allowed the appeal, holding that the coins had not been produced for general sale
but for distribution as gifts to customers who purchased Esso petrol. The
commissioners appealed. The facts are set out in the opinion of Lord Russell of
Killowen.

Christopher Staughton QC and *Peter Gibson* for the commissioners.
c *D C Potter QC, Peter Scott* and *Peter G Whiteman* for Esso.

Their Lordships took time for consideration.

10th December. The following opinions were delivered.

d **LORD WILBERFORCE.** My Lords, I have had the benefit of reading in advance
the opinion prepared by my noble and learned friend, Lord Simon of Glaisdale. I
agree with his analysis of the transaction. The case being one of impression, as to an
essentially simple situation, I do not consider it useful to add any fresh arguments of
my own.
       I would dismiss the appeal.

e

VISCOUNT DILHORNE. My Lords, the only question for decision in this
appeal is whether the coins distributed by Esso to garage proprietors, for them to give
to customers who bought four gallons or more of petrol, were coins 'produced in
quantity for general sale'. If they were, then they came within Group 25 in Sch 1 to
the Purchase Tax Act 1963, and the respondents are liable to pay purchase tax on them
f to the amount of some £200,000.
       That the coins were produced in quantity and for general distribution is clear and
not disputed. Were they produced for sale? They were sold by Esso to some 4,900
retailers of petrol for £3 per thousand, but that does not determine the tax liability.
The question to be decided is, were they sold or intended to be sold by the garage
proprietors to purchasers of petrol?
g   Each coin bore the head of one of the 30 members of the English squad for the
World Cup and was wrapped in an opaque covering. The intention of Esso was to
promote the sale of their petrol by tempting persons to buy petrol from their dealers
in the hope of securing a complete set of coins, and they advertised their 'World Cup
Coin Collection' extensively in the press and on television.
       They distributed to garages posters for exhibition on the forecourts. One series of
h posters had on it 'Collect the complete set. One coin given with every four gallons of
petrol.' Another series had the words: 'Collect the full set of thirty coins. One coin
given when you buy four gallons of petrol.' They sent each of their dealers who
participated in the campaign a pamphlet telling him to give one coin to each customer buying four gallons; two coins if eight gallons were bought and so on, and that
if he did so and gave a free collection card in which the coins could be placed he would
j 'then ensure the success of this promotion by increasing gallonage sales on your
station'. The dealers were also supplied with 'luxury collector' cards which they
were told to sell for 2s 6d each.
       If the coins were a free gift to every customer who purchased four gallons of petrol
or multiples of that quantity, then the appeal must be dismissed. If, on the other
hand, a legal contract was entered into between the customer and the dealer which,

in addition to the supply of petrol, involved the dealer in a legally binding obligation
to transfer a coin or coins to the customer, and if that legal contract amounted to a   *a*
sale, then the appeal must be allowed.

Was there any intention on the part of the garage proprietor and also on the part
of the customer who bought four gallons, or multiples of that quantity, of petrol to
enter into a legally binding contract in relation to a coin or coins? In *Rose and Frank Co
v J R Crompton & Bros Ltd*[1], Scrutton LJ said[2]:
                                                                                          b
> 'Now it is quite possible for parties to come to an agreement by accepting a
> proposal with the result that the agreement does not give rise to legal relations.
> The reason of this is that the parties do not intend that their agreement shall give
> rise to legal relations. This intention may be implied from the subject matter of
> the agreement, but it may also be expressed by the parties. In social and family
> relations such an intention is readily implied, while in business matters the   *c*
> opposite result would ordinarily follow.'

And Atkin LJ said[3]:

> 'To create a contract there must be a common intention of the parties to enter
> into legal obligations, mutually communicated expressly or impliedly.'
                                                                                          d
The facts of that case were very different from those of this. In that case there was
an agreement dealing with business matters. In this case the question has to be
considered whether there was any agreement as to a coin or coins between the garage
proprietor and the customers and also, if there was, was it intended on both sides to
be one having legal relations? If a coin was just to be given to the motorist, it would
not be necessary for there to have been any agreement between him and the garage   *e*
proprietor with regard to it

In *Edwards v Skyways Ltd*[4], where the facts were also very different from those in
this case and where the plaintiff was seeking to recover the amount of an ex gratia
payment, Megaw J referred to these passages in *Rose and Frank v J R Crompton & Bros
Ltd*[5] and said[6]:

> 'In the present case, the subject-matter of the agreement is business relations'   *f*
> not social or domestic matters. There was a meeting of minds—an intention to
> agree. There was, admittedly, consideration for the company's promise. I accept
> the propositions of counsel for the plaintiff that in a case of this nature the onus is
> on the party who asserts that no legal effect was intended, and the onus is a heavy
> one.'
                                                                                          g
I do not wish in any way to criticise or qualify these statements, but I do not feel
that they provide a sound foundation for the decision of this appeal.

True it is that Esso are engaged in business. True it is that they hope to promote
the sale of their petrol, but it does not seem to me necessarily to follow or to be
inferred that there was any intention on their part that their dealers should enter
into legally binding contracts with regard to the coins; or any intention on the part   *h*
of the dealers to enter into any such contract or any intention on the part of the
purchaser of four gallons of petrol to do so.

If on the facts of this case the conclusion is reached that there was any such
intention on the part of the customer, of the dealer and of Esso, it would seem to

                                                                                          j
1   [1923] 2 KB 261, [1924] All ER Rep 245
2   [1923] 2 KB at 288, [1924] All ER Rep at 249
3   [1923] 2 KB at 293, [1924] All ER Rep at 252
4   [1964] 1 All ER 494, [1964] 1 WLR 349
5   [1923] 2 KB 261 at 288, 293, [1924] All ER Rep 245 at 249, 252
6   [1964] 1 All ER at 500, [1964] 1 WLR at 355

exclude the possibility of any dealer ever making a free gift to any of his customers,
a however negligible its value, to promote his sales.

If what was described as being a gift which would be given if something was purchased was something of value to the purchaser, then it could readily be inferred that
there was a common intention to enter into legal relations. But here, whatever the
cost of production, it is clear that the coins were of little intrinsic value.

I do not consider that the offer of a gift of a free coin is properly to be regarded as
b a business matter in the sense in which that word was used by Scrutton LJ[1] in the
passage cited above. Nor do I think that such an offer can be comprehended within
the 'business relations' which were in the Skyways case[2], as Megaw LJ said, 'the subject-
matter of the agreement'. I see no reason to imply any intention to enter into contractual relations from the statements on the posters that a coin would be given if four
gallons of petrol were bought.

c Nor do I see any reason to impute to every motorist who went to a garage where the
posters were displayed to buy four gallons of petrol any intention to enter into a
legally binding contract for the supply to him of a coin. On the acceptance of his
offer to purchase four gallons there was no doubt a legally binding contract for the
supply to him of that quantity of petrol, but I see again no reason to conclude that
because such an offer was made by him, it must be held that, as the posters were
d displayed, his offer included an offer to take a coin. The gift of a coin might lead to a
motorist returning to the garage to obtain another one, but I think the facts in this
case negative any contractual intention on his part and on the part of the dealer as to
the coin and suffice to rebut any presumption there may be to the contrary.

If, however, there was any contract relating to the coin or coins, the consideration
for the entry into that contract was not the payment of any money but the entry into
e a contract to purchase four gallons or multiples of that quantity of petrol, in which
case the contract relating to the coin or coins cannot be regarded as a contract of sale.

I therefore, while of opinion that there was no legally binding contract as to the
coins and so that it has not been established that they were produced for sale, am
also of opinion that if there was any such contract it was not one for sale.

In my opinion this appeal should be dismissed.

f

LORD SIMON OF GLAISDALE. My Lords, I have had the advantage
of reading in draft the speech prepared by my noble and learned friend, Lord Russell
of Killowen. I beg to take advantage of his explanation of the facts that have led to
the appeal and the statutory provisions by which they are to be judged.

g I am, however, my Lords, not prepared to accept that the promotion material
put out by Esso was not envisaged by them as creating legal relations between the
garage proprietors who adopted it and the motorists who yielded to its blandish-
ments. In the first place, Esso and the garage proprietors put the material out for
their commercial advantage, and designed it to attract the custom of motorists. The
whole transaction took place in a setting of business relations. In the second place, it
h seems to me in general undesirable to allow a commercial promoter to claim that
what he has done is a mere puff, not intended to create legal relations (cf Carlill v
Carbolic Smoke Ball Co[3]). The coins may have been themselves of little intrinsic value;
but all the evidence suggests that Esso contemplated that they would be attractive
to motorists and that there would be a large commercial advantage to themselves
from the scheme, an advantage in which the garage proprietors also would share.
j Thirdly, I think that authority supports the view that legal relations were envisaged.
In Rose and Frank Co v J R Crompton & Bros Ltd Scrutton LJ said[4]:

---

1   [1923] 2 KB at 288, [1924] All ER Rep at 249
2   [1964] 1 All ER at 500, [1964] 1 WLR at 355
3   [1893] 1 QB 256, [1891-4] All ER Rep 127
4   [1923] 2 KB 261 at 288, [1924] All ER Rep 245 at 249

'Now it is quite possible for parties to come to an agreement by accepting a proposal with the result that the agreement concluded does not give rise to legal relations. The reason of this is that the parties do not intend that their agreement shall give rise to legal relations. This intention may be implied from the subject matter of the agreement, but it may also be expressed by the parties. In social and family relations such an intention is readily implied, while in business matters the opposite result would ordinarily follow.'

In the same case Atkin LJ said[1]:

'To create a contract there must be a common intention of the parties to enter into legal obligations, mutually communicated expressly or impliedly. Such an intention ordinarily will be inferred when parties enter into an agreement which in other respects conforms to the rules of law as to the formation of contracts. It may be negatived impliedly by the nature of the agreed promise or promises, as in the case of offer and acceptance of hospitality, or of some agreements made in the course of family life between members of a family as in *Balfour v Balfour*[2].'

In *Edwards v Skyways Ltd*[3] Megaw J quoted these passages, and added:

'In the present case, the subject-matter of the agreement is business relations, not social or domestic matters . . . I accept the proposition . . . that in a case of this nature the onus is on the party who asserts that no legal effect was intended, and the onus is a heavy one.'

I respectfully agree. And I would venture to add that it begs the question to assert that no motorist who bought petrol in consequence of seeing the promotion material prominently displayed in the garage forecourt would be likely to bring an action in the county court if he were refused a coin. He might be a suburb Hampden who was not prepared to forego what he conceived to be his rights or to allow a tradesman to go back on his word.

Believing as I do that Esso envisaged a bargain of some sort between the garage proprietor and the motorist, I must try to analyse the transaction. The analysis that most appeals to me is one of the ways in which Lord Denning MR considered the case[4], namely a collateral contract of the sort decribed by Lord Moulton in *Heilbut, Symons & Co v Buckleton*[5]:

'. . . there may be a contract the consideration for which is the making of some other contract. "If you will make such and such a contract I will give you one hundred pounds", is in every sense of the word a complete legal contract. It is collateral to the main contract . . .'

So here. The law happily matches the reality. The garage proprietor is saying, 'If you will buy four gallons of my petrol, I will give you one of these coins'. None of the reasons which have caused the law to consider advertising or display material as an invitation to treat, rather than an offer, applies here. What the garage proprietor says by his placards is in fact and in law an offer of consideration to the motorist to enter into a contract of sale of petrol. Of course, not every motorist will notice the placard, but nor will every potential offeree of many offers be necessarily conscious that they have been made. However, the motorist who does notice the placard, and in reliance thereon drives in and orders the petrol, is in law doing two things at the same time. First, he is accepting the offer of a coin if he buys four gallons

1   [1923] 2 KB at 293, [1924] All ER Rep at 252
2   [1919] 2 KB 571, [1918-19] All ER Rep 860
3   [1964] 1 All ER 494 at 500, [1964 1 WLR 349 at 355
4   [1975] 1 WLR 406 at 409
5   [1913] AC 30 at 47, [1911-13] All ER Rep 83 at 90

of petrol. Secondly, he is himself offering to buy four gallons of petrol: this offer
a is accepted by the filling of his tank.

Has there then been a sale of the coins, so that they can be said to have been 'produced in quantity for general sale' within Group 25 of Sch 1 to the Purchase Tax Act
1963? I think that the main emphasis here is on 'quantity' and 'general'. But it would
be contrary to all principles of sound statutory construction not to give each word its
full significance. I agree with my noble and learned friend, Lord Russell of Killowen,
b for the reasons which he gives, that the definition of 'purchase' in s 40(1) throws no
light on the meaning of 'sale' in the schedule. 'Sale' must therefore be interpreted in the
primary sense demanded by the context of a taxing statute (unless some secondary
meaning must be preferred in order to avoid injustice, absurdity, anomaly or stulti-
fication of the statutory objective). The primary sense of 'sale' in this context is its
primary meaning in ordinary legal usage. This is expressed in s 1 of the Sale of Goods
c Act 1893 (which codified the common law), namely 'a contract whereby the seller
transfers or agrees to transfer the property in goods to the buyer for a money
consideration, called the price'. Here the coins were not transferred for a money consideration. They were transferred in consideration of the motorist entering into a
contract for the sale of petrol. The coins were therefore not produced for sale, and do
not fall within the schedule. They are exempt from purchase tax.
d   I would therefore dismiss the appeal.

LORD FRASER OF TULLYBELTON. My Lords, the facts in this case have been
fully set out in the speech which is about to be delivered by my noble and learned
friend, Lord Russell of Killowen, and which I have had the advantage of reading in
e print. I need not therefore rehearse them. The only question for decision is whether
these coins were 'produced . . . for . . . sale'. In my opinion they were, and I would
therefore hold that they fell within the Group 25 of Sch I to the Purchase Tax Act 1963.

The matter that is in my view of decisive importance is the wording on the posters
which were displayed in the forecourts of Esso petrol retailers during the promotion
scheme.   The originals of these posters were large, 60 by 40 inches, and each poster
f was headed in large letters 'Free World Cup Coins'. Below that was a picture either
of one of the coins or of a group of the coins and below the picture on one poster were
the words: 'Collect the complete set. One coin given with every four gallons of petrol',
and on the other poster: 'Collect the full set of thirty coins. One coin given when
you buy four gallons of petrol.' The feature of that wording, which is of special
significance, is the correlation of one coin to every four gallons; a definite scale of
g issue, or ration, was thus promised, and the plain inference is that any motorist who
bought four gallons of petrol would have a right also to receive a coin. It is as if a
baker had a poster in his shop window promising that any person who bought a
dozen buns would be given one extra bun free of charge to make up a 'bakers' dozen'.
Standing that promise by the retailer, it is in my opinion impossible to avoid the
inference that when a motorist ordered some petrol he was offering to enter into a
h contract on the terms advertised by the retailer, and therefore that when his offer
was accepted he had a contractual right to one coin with every four gallons of petrol.
The analysis by Pennycuick V-C[1] of what would happen when a motorist ordered
petrol is in my opinion the correct one.

Various reasons have been suggested for taking the contrary view, and the one that
appears to me to be the strongest is also the simplest, namely that the poster and
j advertisements repeatedly use the words 'gift' 'given' and 'free'. It is said that the use of
these words, together with the small value of the coins and the fact that the price of
petrol was not increased during the promotion period shows that the coins were truly
given away. But the purpose of the promotion scheme was to attract motorists, and
perhaps their children, and to persuade them to buy Esso rather than some other

1 [1973] 1 WLR 1240 at 1245

brand of petrol, and it cannot be right that a motorist who had been persuaded to buy four gallons of Esso should be liable to be met at the end of the transaction with *a* a refusal to give him a coin. No doubt it was unlikely that any Esso retailer who was taking part in the promotion would fail to deliver a coin with four gallons of petrol, because he would lose goodwill if he did. But the same is true in greater or less degree of every retailer who may be tempted to give short weight or inferior quality in breach of his contract, and the unlikeliness of such an event cannot in my opinion affect the legal quality of the transaction. It was even more unlikely that any motorist *b* would sue to enforce his right to the coin or to recover damages for failure to deliver one. But the same is true of many small retail transactions which are undoubtedly contracts capable of being enforced by legal prodeedings, but not worth enforcing. Accordingly I regard that also as irrelevant. The fact that the inclusive price could not be apportioned so as to attribute any particular part of it to the coin is also irrelevant, and does not by itself indicate that the coin was not bought along with the petrol for *c* one inclusive price: see *Taylor v Smetton*[1], *Scott & Co Ltd v Solomon*[2]. It was argued that these cases, where coupons carrying valuable rights were included in packets of tea, were distinguishable because the coupons were either physically inside the packet or were part of the wrapper, so that it was impossible to buy the tea without the coupons. But I cannot see that that makes any difference, because here the delivery of the coin would be, for all practical purposes, contemporaneous with delivery of the petrol, *d* so that both would form part of the one transaction just as the tea and the coupon did.

I recognise that the reason why an advertisement or display of goods for sale at a stated price is only an invitation to treat and not an offer for sale (as explained by my noble and learned friend, Lord Russell of Killowen, in his speech) has no application to the advertisement of the coins, because the petrol retailer could always remove the advertisement if the supply of coins threatened to run out. But while that is so, I *e* do not regard it as a sufficient reason for declining to recognise what seems to me a simple operation of acquiring four gallons of petrol and a coin as a sale of both articles in one transaction, nor as a reason for breaking it up into two separate operations, a sale of the petrol and a collateral contract for acquiring the coin.

For these reason I would allow the appeal.

f

LORD RUSSELL OF KILLOWEN. My Lords, the question in this appeal is whether certain goods were chargeable for the purposes of the now defunct purchase tax; and that depends on whether, being goods of a type within the description contained in Group 25 of Sch 1 to the Purchase Tax Act 1963, they were 'produced in quantity for general sale'. As will be seen the goods were undoubtedly produced in quantity *g* and, if produced for sale, it is not disputed that the sale envisaged in the production was 'general' sale. Thus the argument has centred on the question whether the goods were 'produced . . . for sale'. Pennycuick V-C concluded that they were; the Court of Appeal (Lord Denning MR and Stephenson and Lane LJJ) concluded that they were not. The amount of purchase tax involved is the substantial sum of some £200,000.

The goods in question were medals bearing the likenesses of the 30 members of *h* the England soccer squad which went to Mexico in 1970 for the World Cup, together with reproductions of their signatures and their names, one player to each medal, the other side bearing the word 'Esso' and the words 'England World Cup Squad, Mexico 1970'.

The respondents ('Esso') conceived in 1970 a petrol sales promotion scheme. Esso had some 6,000 petrol outlets in this country, some owned by Esso subsidiaries but *j* most by other proprietors. The scheme involved the production of millions of these medals, the intention being that these medals should be distributed, to use a neutral phrase, by petrol pump proprietors to motorists buying Esso petrol on the basis of

1 (1883) 11 QBD 207
2 [1905] 1 KB 557, 69 JP 137

one medal to each motorist buying four gallons of petrol, two if eight, and so on.
a The medals were to be in opaque wrappers, and it was hoped that a motorist would
persist in buying Esso petrol in the hope of collecting the full set of 30. It was to be,
according to Esso, the biggest promotion scheme ever promoted by Esso.

The promotion scheme was extensively advertised by Esso in the press and on
television, the public being urged to start collecting the set of 30 medals. Typical
extracts from such advertisements were the phrases: 'Free from Esso'; 'Going free,
b at your Esso Action Station now'; 'We are giving you a coin with every four gallons
of Esso petrol you buy'; 'We are also giving you a free collector card to mount them
in. (For only 2/6, you can buy the handsome permanent mounting board . . .)'; 'One
free coin with every 4 gallons.'

Esso circularised the 6,000 outlets, of which some 4,900 adopted the scheme. The
medals were made available to outlet proprietors at 30s for 500—slightly under three
c farthings each, the temporary collector cards without charge, permanent mounting
cards at 2s each. A folder circulated by Esso to the outlets to encourage their promotion scheme contained these phrases: 'One coin should be given to every motorist
who buys four gallons of petol—two coins for eight gallons and so on'; 'Free collector
cards should be offered to all motorists at the start of the promotion'. Large posters
(60 by 40 inches) were supplied by Esso to the forecourts of proprietors joining the
d scheme. The most prominent lettering in the posters is 'Free World Cup coins'; one
also says: 'One coin given with every four gallons of petrol'; the other example says:
'One coin given when you buy four gallons of petrol.' A further pamphlet of instructions to outlets said: 'Give one coin to each customer buying four gallons of
petrol . . .'; 'Give free collector cards to every customer you serve'; 'Try to sell luxury
collector card at 2/6 each'; 'You will then ensure the success of this promotion by
e increasing gallonage sales on your station.' The last document to which reference
should be made is the free collector's card, which includes the phrase 'You will be
given a coin each time you buy four gallons of petrol from an Esso station . . . This
temporary collector card is free . . .'

My Lords, it is not in dispute that unless the medals were produced at the instance
of Esso for the purpose of, i e with a view to, their being sold by garage proprietors to
f motorists there cannot be the suggested charge of purchase tax. The first question
accordingly is whether, notwithstanding the liberal references in the documents
attending the promotion scheme to 'giving', 'gifts', and 'free', that which would and
did take place gave rise to a contract, enforceable by a motorist who bought four
gallons from a participating proprietor, that he should receive one of these medals.
It is to be borne in mind in this connection that the mere fact that Esso and the garage
g proprietors undoubtedly had a commercial aim in promoting the scheme does not
deprive the delivery of a medal of the quality of a gift as distinct from a sale; for
benevolence is not a necessary feature of a gift which may well be motivated by self
interest. On the other hand it is trite law that if on analysis a transaction has in law
one character, the fact that the parties either accidentally or deliberately frame the
transaction in language appropriate to a transaction of a different character will not
h deny to it its true character.

We have here, my Lords, a promotion scheme initiated by Esso, who procured the
production of the medals. Each medal was of negligible intrinsic value, though the
incentive to soccer enthusiasts to collect all 30 may have been strong. Plainly it was
never in Esso's mind that this negligible intrinsic value should be reflected in an
increase in the pump price of petrol, and it never was; indeed the price of a gallon
j could not be increased by $\frac{3}{16}$ of a penny. In my opinion it would have been thought by
Esso, and rightly, that there could have been no occasion, in order to ensure success
of the scheme, for an outlet proprietor to subject himself to a contractual liability to
deliver a coin to a motorist who had bought four gallons. The subject-matter was
trivial: the proprietor was directly interested in the success of the scheme and would
be in the highest degree unlikely to renege on the free gift offer, and indeed there is

no suggestion that a motorist who qualified and wanted a medal ever failed to get one; from the motorist's viewpoint, if this had ever happened, I cannot think that he would have considered that he had a legal grievance, though he might have said that he would not patronise that outlet again; similarly in my opinion if a garage advertised 'Free Air' and after buying petrol or oil the motorist was told that the machine was out of order that day. In my opinion, the incentive for the garage proprietor to carry out the scheme was such as to make it quite unnecessary to invest, or for Esso to intend to invest, the transaction with the additional compulsion of a contractual obligation, and in all the circumstances of the case I am unable to regard that which under the scheme was intended by Esso to take place in relation to the medals, and did take place, as something which would be intended to or regarded as creating a legal contractual relationship. In forming that opinion I regard the minimal intrinsic value of a medal as important. I would not wish it to be thought that my opinion, if correct, would, in other cases in which a sales promotion scheme involves substantial benefits, give carte blanche to participants to renege on 'free' offers. I am simply of opinion, in agreement with the Court of Appeal, though not I fear with the majority of your Lordships, that in the instant case, because of the absence of any contractual element, it should not be said that any medal was produced for general sale.

Suppose however that there was a contractual obligation on the proprietor to deliver a medal to the motorist who had bought four gallons of petrol, the further question arises whether there was a contract of sale of the medal for a price in money, which (subject to a point taken by the respondents under s 40 of the Purchase Tax Act 1963) is involved in the reference in Group 25 to 'sale'. Pennycuick V-C analysed the transaction as being, by a combination of the medal posters and the price marked on the petrol pump, one invitation to treat by the proprietor: the motorist by ordering four gallons made an offer to pay the pump price on the terms of that invitation to treat; the proprietor accepted that offer by supplying the petrol; consequently an unascertained part of the price paid was for the right to receive the medal; therefore it was a sale of the medal for a price in money. (My Lords, when I embark on a consideration of these niceties, I confess to being fortified in some measure in my view on the first point.) Now it is of course clear that a mere statement of the price of petrol on the pumps is not itself an order to sell petrol at that price; this follows the ordinary situation that the display of goods in a window, or advertisement of goods for sale, even at a stated price, is not to be treated as itself an offer capable of acceptance, but is only an invitation to treat. The reason for this is the eminently sound one that the vendor might otherwise find himself bound to a series of contracts that he would be quite unable to fulfil: since it is a mere invitation to treat he reserves to himself the ability to refuse an offer from a would-be purchaser. But, my Lords, those considerations have no relevance to the matter of these medals. The question of liability to hand over medals remains at all times under the control of the proprietor: knowing his gallonage of saleable petrol he knows at all times whether he has his maximum liability of one-quarter in number of medals; further if he has no medals available he retains the ability, before accepting a motorist's order of four gallons, to cancel or withdraw the offer of a medal. There are no reasons why the posters, assuming them to be capable of being the foundation of a contract, should not be regarded as in themselves an offer to the motorist that if he buys four gallons of petrol the proprietor will hand him one medal. This, if the matter lies in contract, appears to me to be the simple and straightforward approach. That is what, ignoring words such as 'gift' and 'free' the posters say: 'If you buy four gallons of petrol I will hand you one medal'. The motorist *entitles himself* (if he wishes one) to receive a medal by carrying out a contract for the purchase of petrol. This is not, my Lords, sale of the medal at a price in money.

An alternative argument was advanced on behalf of the respondents, supposing that there was not a sale at a price in money. Section 40(1) of the Purchase Tax Act 1963 defines 'purchase' in the following terms:

a
' "purchase" means any contract which is a contract of sale within the meaning of the Sale of Goods Act 1893 and also a contract similar to such a contract in other respects but made for a consideration wholly or partly in . . . money, and includes any transaction, in whatsoever form expressed, in so far as its effect is in substance the same as the effect of such a contract as aforesaid; and references to goods being bought include, in relation to a purchase made for a consideration not, or not only, in money, and in relation to any such transaction as aforesaid,

b
references to goods being acquired in any manner . . .'

In the instant case, on the above analysis, it is said that the contract for the delivery of the medal was 'a contract similar to such a contract in other respects but made for a consideration wholly or partly in money's worth and not, or not only, in money'. If, it was argued, that is what 'purchase' means, 'sale' in Group 25 must have the com-

c
plementary meaning. I leave aside, my Lords, the question whether the carrying out of a contract to purchase four gallons is properly to be described as money's worth. I do not derive any guidance from this definition on the meaning of 'sale' in Group 25. It would indeed be odd if the prima facie meaning in Group 25 was designed to be extended merely by a definition of purchase and not by a definition of sale. But the truth of the matter is that 'purchase' is so defined for the purpose of recognising the

d
circumstances which constitute a tax point, when tax is charged in respect of a purchase by a retailer from a wholesaler: see s 9. It is true that s 9(4) refers to a 'seller' and in that instance he is a seller notwithstanding that the goods in question may not have been disposed of solely for a price in money; but that is because he is 'the seller under the purchase' which necessarily imports into the transaction the definition of 'purchase'. I find no justification for importing from the definition of 'purchase', inserted for

e
quite other and particular reasons, a construction of 'sale' in Group 25 other than its prima facie meaning.

I refer, my Lords, to certain authorities to which your Lordships' attention was called.

Bulpitt & Sons Ltd v S Bellman & Sons Ltd[1] (Ungoed-Thomas J) was a case in which a trader sought to avoid an injunction against selling below a minimum fixed retail

f
selling price by the device of 'giving', with goods sold, coupons worth a considerable amount in terms of entitlement to other goods. He rightly failed. But this does not assist in the present appeal; it was a mere and barefaced device to avoid an obligation; moreover if what had been done had been a distribution of medals of minimal in-trinsic value the decision might well have been otherwise. In *Taylor v Smetten*[2] a man sold pound packets of tea for 2s 6d each, each purchaser acquiring at the same time a

g
right to a 'prize', the prizes being of varying nature and value, and the purchaser of the tea not knowing what his prize was to be until he had bought the tea and found the prize described on a coupon within the packet. The man was convicted of running a lottery. The pound of tea was worth the money paid, but as was said in the judg-ment of the court it was 'impossible to suppose that the aggregate prices charged and obtained for the packages did not include the aggregate prices of the tea and the prizes'.

h
It appears from the report that this was the man's constant method of trading. The purchaser was held to be buying the tea and a chance. I do not doubt the correctness of the decision, but I do not find it persuasive on either of the main points in the present appeal.

In *Scott & Co Ltd v W Solomon*[3] the appellants were convicted of dealing in plate without a licence. They sold tea and with each packet were coupons which in sufficient

j
numbers would entitle the presenter of the coupons to claim from the tea vendor valuable articles of various sorts, depending on the number of the coupons, some of

---

1   (1962) LR 3 RP 62
2   (1883) 11 QB 207
3   [1905] 1 KB 577, 69 JP 137

which were articles of plate such as watches. The argument for conviction was that there was a binding contract with the tea purchasers as soon as sufficient coupons were presented, to transfer the ownership of the watch, the consideration being the payment of money for tea and coupons. There was no evidence of any increse in the price of the tea on the introduction of the coupons. Lord Alverstone CJ said[1]:

'[This evidence] seems to me to point to one view of the facts, namely, that it was all one transaction. In respect of the payment for the tea, the various purchasers each of them got what has been called this "coupon". Mr. *Danckwerts* does not dispute, and I do not think he could dispute, that that was a sale of coupons. The suggestion that there is full value given for the tea, meaning that there is nothing charged for these coupons, is simply absurd. This very large business, to the extent of thousands of pounds, of Scott and Company, the appellants, could not possibly be carried on if there were no charge for the coupons. The coupons having been delivered out with the tea, the person who received them either having purchased them themselves, or having obtained them from other purchasers, on presenting them become entitled to receive certain articles, and, amongst others, became entitled in certain events, according to the number of coupons they presented, to receive a very considerable number of articles of plate, watches, and other things of the kind. It seems to me that, looked at in its real essence, this transaction is a trading in watches by means of receiving payment for them by instalments when the money is paid for the tea, and by afterwards recognising the value of those various instalments as evidenced by the coupons by giving back various articles—in this particular case, watches.'

Again, I do not doubt the correctness of that decision, but I do not find it persuasive on either of the two points in the present appeal.

Finally the decision in this House in *Chappell & Co Ltd v Nestlé Co Ltd*[2] affords in my opinion no assistance; it merely decided that there was no 'ordinary retail selling price' of the records in question, having regard to the fact that Nestlé would not have sold them at the price of 1ˢ 6d had the purchaser not produced evidence of the consumption of a required amount of Nestlé's chocolate.

For the reasons that I have stated, I am of opinion that the decision of the Court of Appeal was correct and that this appeal should be dismissed.

Appeal dismissed.

Solicitors: *Solicitor, Customs & Excise; Durrant Piesse* (for Esso).

Gordon H Scott Esq　Barrister.

1　(1905) 69 JP at 139
2　[1959] 2 All ER 701, [1960] AC 87

Farrell and another v Alexander

COURT OF APPEAL, CIVIL DIVISION
LORD DENNING MR, LAWTON AND SCARMAN LJJ
3rd, 4th, 30th JULY 1975

Rent restriction – Premium – Illegal premium – Requirement of payment as condition of grant of tenancy – Requirement by 'any person' – Meaning of 'any person' – Person other than landlord – Outgoing tenant – Premium required by outgoing tenant as condition of procuring landlord to grant new lease to incoming tenant – Whether premium required by outgoing tenant illegal – Whether illegal on ground landlord had delegated to outgoing tenant function of finding new tenant and granting lease – Rent Act 1968, s 85(1).

Rent restriction – Premium – Illegal premium – Requirement of premium as condition of assignment of tenancy – Proposed assignment – Agreement to assign tenancy in consideration of payment of premium – Landlord requiring surrender of tenancy in exercise of power contained in lease – Landlord agreeing to grant new lease to proposed assignee – Premium paid to outgoing tenant following grant of new tenancy – Whether premium recoverable as having been paid as a condition of or in connection with assignment of tenancy – Rent Act 1968, s 86(1)(2).

Judgment – Judicial decision as authority – Court of Appeal – Decision per incuriam – Court in previous case having construed statute in sense which words cannot bear – Words of statute capable of only one meaning – Whether Court of Appeal bound to follow previous decision even though plainly wrong.

The defendant was the tenant of an unfurnished flat under a protected tenancy. Her lease, which was for a term of 7½ years, provided that if she desired to assign the premises she first had to offer to surrender the lease without consideration to the landlords. In January 1973 the plaintiffs offered to purchase from the defendant, subject to contract, the remaining 4½ years of the lease for the sum of £4,000 which sum was to include certain fixture and fittings in the premises. On 22nd January one of the plaintiffs paid a deposit of £400 to the defendant's estate agents. At that stage of the transaction the plaintiffs and the defendant contemplated that the transaction would be carried out by an assignment of the lease by the defendant to the plaintiffs. When the defendant approached the landlords about the assignment to the plaintiffs, the landlords decided to exercise their right to call for a surrender of the lease. The landlords were, however, willing to grant a new lease of the premises to the plaintiffs at a regulated rent if satisfactory references were provided and the plaintiffs were found to be suitable when interviewed. The plaintiffs provided satisfactory references and when interviewed were found to be suitable. The defendant wished to ensure that she got the agreed sum of £4,000 for the lease. Accordingly, by a contract dated 30th March 1973 between the plaintiffs and the defendant, it was agreed that the transaction should be effected by a surrender of the lease by the defendant to the landlords and the simultaneous grant by the landlords to the plaintiffs of a new lease and that on the grant of the new lease the plaintiffs would pay to the defendant £4,000 for the carpets, curtains, chattels and fittings in the premises. The agreement also provided for payment of ten per cent of the £4,000 to the estate agents as stakeholders. On the same date, 30th March, completion of the transaction took place at the landlords' offices. After the landlords' solicitors had completed their part of the transaction and withdrawn from the office, the plaintiffs' solicitor handed to the defendant's solicitor a cheque for £3,600, being the balance of the agreed sum of £4,000 less the deposit of £400; a few days later the defendant sent the plaintiffs a receipt for the £4,000 as consideration for the purchase of the fixtures, fittings, chattels

E

and other equipment in the premises. On a subsequent valuation, the fixtures and fittings etc were found to be worth only £1,002. The plaintiffs brought an action *a* claiming that the balance of the £4,000, i e £2,998, was repayable by the defendant under s 90(1)*ᵃ* of the Rent Act 1968 as being an illegal premium under s 86*ᵇ* or s 85*ᶜ* of the 1968 Act. The county court judge dismissed the claim on the grounds that the completed transaction was not an 'assignment' of the protected tenancy and was not therefore caught by s 86, and that since the premium had not been required by the landlords, it was not illegal under s 85 because the decision of the Court of Appeal in *b* *Zimmerman v Grossmanᵈ* bound him to hold that the words 'any person' in s 85 were limited to the landlord and did not include an outgoing tenant. The plaintiffs appealed.

Held (Lord Denning MR dissenting) – The appeal would be dismissed for the following reasons—   *c*

(i) The premium had not been required or received 'as a condition of' or 'in connection with' the assignment of a protected tenancy, within s 86(1) or (2) of the 1968 Act. The real nature of the completed transaction was a surrender of a lease by the defendant and the grant of a new lease to the plaintiffs and the transaction was not an assignment in the guise of a surrender and grant. It followed that the whole of the £4,000, including the deposit of £400, had been paid under an agreement providing *d* for the surrender and grant of the new lease and had not been paid as a condition of or in connection with an assignment of the defendant's protected tenancy (see p 140 *b* and *e* and p 144 *a* to *c* and *g* to *j*, post).

(ii) Since the premium had not been required by the landlords as a condition of the grant of the protected tenancy to the plaintiffs, the premium was not illegal under s 85(1) of the 1968 Act. The words 'any person' in s 85(1) were limited to landlords *e* and therefore s 85(1) did not extend to an outgoing tenant who had required a premium as a condition of the grant of a protected tenancy. The Court of Appeal was bound so to hold by its previous decision in *Zimmerman v Grossmanᵈ*, for that decision had not been given in ignorance of the relevant terms of the 1968 Act and therefore could not be treated as having been given per incuriam. In that case the court had considered all the relevant statutory provisions; even though it had been open to the court to *f* attribute a wider meaning to the words 'any person' in s 85(1) than had been attributed by a previous decision of the court to the wording 'a person' in the enactment which s 85(1) had replaced, the court had been justified in taking the view that the change of wording in s 85(1) of the 1968 Act had not altered the existing law; the 1968 Act was a consolidating enactment and the presumption in such an enactment was that Parliament did not intend to alter the law (see p 141 *e* to *h*, p 142 *e* and *f*, p 143 *g*

---

a   Section 90 provides: 'Where under any agreement (whether made before or after the commencement of this Act) any premium is paid after the commencement of this Act and the whole or any part of that premium could not lawfully be required or received under the preceding provisions of this Part of this Act, the amount of the premium or, as the case may be, so much of it as could not lawfully be required or received, shall be recoverable by the person by whom it was paid'   *h*

b   Section 86, so far as material, provides:
'(1) Subject to the following provisions of this section any person who, as a condition of the assignment of a protected tenancy, requires the payment of any premium or the making of any loan (whether secured or unsecured) shall be guilty of an offence under this section.

'(2) Subject to the following provisions of this section, any person who, in connection with the assignment of a protected tenancy, receives any premium shall be guilty of an *j* offence under this section . . .'

c   Section 85(1) provides: 'Any person who, as a condition of the grant, renewal or continuance of a protected tenancy, requires, in addition to the rent, the payment of any premium or the making of any loan (whether secured or unsecured) shall be guilty of an offence under this section.'

d   [1971] 1 All ER 363, [1972] 1 QB 167

d and p 146 *d* to p 147 *b*, post); *Remmington v Larchin* [1921] 3 KB 404 and *Zimmerman v*
a *Grossman* [1971] 1 All ER 363 followed; *Young v Bristol Aeroplane Co Ltd* [1944] 2 All
ER 293 applied.

(iii) Furthermore, in the circumstances, it could not be contended that the landlords
had delegated to the defendant their functions of finding a new tenant and granting
a new lease so as to bring him within the words 'any person' in s 85(1) even if there was
such an exception to the principle that those words referred only to landlords (see
b p 140 *f* and *g* and p 145 *b* and *c*, post); dictum of Widgery LJ in *Zimmerman v Grossman*
[1971] 3 All ER at 372 considered.

Per Lord Denning MR and Scarman LJ. The per incuriam exception to the binding
force of a previous decision extends to a case where the plain words of a statute are
capable of only one meaning and the meaning attributed to them by the previous
decision is an impossibility (see p 137 *d* and p 145 *g* to *j*, post).

c **Notes**
For premiums on the grant or assignment of a protected tenancy, see 23 Halsbury's
Laws (3rd Edn) 798-802, paras 1576-1578, and for cases on the subject, see 31(2) Digest
(Reissue) 1062-1068, *8351-8375*.

For the binding force of decisions of the Court of Appeal, see 22 Halsbury's Laws
d (3rd Edn) 799, 802, para 1687, and for cases on the subject, see 30 Digest (Reissue)
269-274, *763-804*.

For the Rent Act 1968, ss 85, 86, 90, see 18 Halsbury's Statutes (3rd Edn) 867, 868, 872.

Cases referred to in judgments
Bank of England v Vagliano Brothers [1891] AC 107, [1891-4] All ER Rep 93, 60 LJQB 145,
  64 LT 353, sub nom *Vagliano v Bank of England* 55 JP 676, HL, 3 Digest (Repl) 273, *799*.
e *Bowers v Gloucester Corpn* [1963] 1 All ER 437, [1963] 1 QB 881, [1963] 2 WLR 386, 61
  LGR 209, DC, 45 Digest (Repl) 155, *614*.
Campbell College, Belfast (Governors) v Valuation Comr for Northern Ireland [1964] 2 All ER
  705, [1964] 1 WLR 912, [1964] RVR 325, [1964] NI 107, HL, 30 Digest (Reissue) 262,
  688.
Conqueror Property Trust Ltd v Barnes Corpn [1944] 1 All ER 34, [1944] KB 96, 113 LJKB
f 30, 170 LT 54, 108 JP 28, 42 LGR 57, DC, 31(2) Digest (Reissue) 1032, *8181*.
Director of Public Prosecutions v Ottewell [1968] 3 All ER 153, [1970] AC 642, [1968]
  3 WLR 621, 132 JP 499, 52 Cr App Rep 679, HL, Digest (Cont Vol C) 224, *5364l*.
Dun v Dun [1959] 2 All ER 134, [1959] AC 272, [1959] 2 WLR 554, PC, Digest (Cont Vol
  A) 573, *2628b*.
Elmdene Estates Ltd v White [1960] 1 All ER 306, [1960] AC 528, [1960] 2 WLR 359,
g HL, 31(2) Digest (Reissue) 1062, *8354*.
Gilbert v Gilbert and Boucher [1928] P 1, 96 LJP 137, 137 LT 619, CA, 27(2) Digest (Reissue)
  874, *6972*.
Greene v Church Comrs for England [1974] 3 All ER 609, [1974] Ch 467, [1974] 2 WLR 349,
  CA.
Grey v Inland Revenue Comrs [1959] 3 All ER 603, [1960] AC 1, [1959] 3 WLR 759, [1959]
h TR 311, 38 ATC 313, HL, 39 Digest (Repl) 333, *723*.
Mason, Herring and Brooks v Harris [1921] 1 KB 653, [1921] All ER Rep 741, 90 LJKB
  993, 125 LT 180, 31(2) Digest (Reissue) 1063, *8357*.
R v Blane (1849) 13 QB 769, [1843-60] All ER Rep 397, 3 New Mag Cas 168, 3 New Sess
  Cas 597, 18 LJMC 216, 13 LTOS 257, 13 JP 825, 13 Jur 854, 116 ER 1458, 3 Digest
  (Repl) 442, *337*.
j *R v Bow Road Domestic Proceedings Court, ex parte Adedigba* [1968] 2 All ER 89, [1968]
  2 QB 572, [1968] 2 WLR 1143, 132 JP 310, CA, 30 Digest (Reissue) 260, *666*.
Remmington (or Remington) v Larchin [1921] 3 KB 404, [1921] All ER Rep 298, 90 LJKB
  1248, 125 LT 749, 85 JP 221, 19 LGR 528, CA, 31(2) Digest (Reissue) 1062, *8352*.
Royal Crown Derby Porcelain Co Ltd v Russell [1949] 1 All ER 749, [1949] 2 KB 417, CA,
  31(2) Digest (Reissue) 1107, *8593*.

Tiverton Estates Ltd v Wearwell Ltd [1974] 1 All ER 209, [1975] Ch 146, [1974] 2 WLR 176, CA.

Yeovil Glove Co Ltd, Re [1964] 2 All ER 849, [1965] Ch 148, [1964] 3 WLR 406, CA, Digest (Cont Vol B) 45, 372*a*.

Young v Bristol Aeroplane Co Ltd [1944] 2 All ER 293, [1944] KB 718, 113 LJKB 513, 171 LT 113, CA; *affd* [1946] 1 All ER 98, [1946] AC 163, 115 LJKB 63, HL, 30 Digest (Reissue) 269, 765.

Zimmerman v Grossman [1971] 1 All ER 363, [1972] 1 QB 167, [1971] 2 WLR 199, 22 P & CR 195, CA, 31(2) Digest (Reissue) 1067, 8375.

Cases also cited

British Eagle International Airlines Ltd v Compagnie Nationale Air France [1975] 2 All ER 390, [1975] 1 WLR 758, HL.

Cumbes v Robinson [1951] 1 All ER 661, [1951] 2 KB 83, CA.

Inland Revenue Comrs v Duke of Westminster [1936] AC 1, [1935] All ER Rep 259, HL.

Maclay v Dixon [1944] 1 All ER 22, 170 LT 49, CA.

Appeal

The plaintiffs, Colette Denise Gina Farrell and her daughter, Suzanne Deidre O'Farrell, brought an action in Wandsworth County Court claiming that they were entitled to recover from the defendant, Jacintha Marian Alexander, the sum of £2,998 being an illegal premium contrary to ss 85 and 86 of the Rent Act 1968 which was recoverable from the defendant under s 90(1) of the 1968 Act. In their particulars of claim the plaintiffs alleged that in or about January 1973 the defendant, who was then the tenant under a protected tenancy of a flat known as Flat F, 20 Randolph Crescent, London, W9. agreed to assign her tenancy to the plaintiffs provided that they paid to her the sum of £4,000 for the carpets, curtains and certain other fixtures and fittings which condition the plaintiffs accepted; that that transaction was effected by means of a device recorded in an agreement in writing dated 30th March 1973 between the defendant and the plaintiffs whereby the defendant agreed to surrender to her landlords the unexpired term of her protected tenancy subject to the simultaneous grant by the landlords of a new tenancy to the plaintiffs and the plaintiffs agreed on the grant of the new tenancy to pay to the defendant the sum of £4,000; that completion of that transaction had taken place on 30th March and the plaintiffs had paid the sum of £4,000 to the defendant; that the reasonable price of the carpets, curtains, fixtures and fittings was £1,002 and no more; that in the premises the defendant by the transaction described had required payment of and/or received a premium as a condition of and/or in connection with, the assignment of her protected tenancy, alternatively as a condition of, and/or in connection with, the grant, renewal or continuance of a protected tenancy, contrary to ss 86 and 85 of the 1968 Act, the amount of the premium being the sum by which £4,000 exceeded £1,002, namely £2,998. In a reserved judgment given on 11th June 1974, his Honour Judge Ifor Lloyd QC held that the £2,998 was a lawful premium and therefore was irrecoverable by the plaintiffs because, with regard to s 85 of the 1968 Act, which prohibited premiums on or in connection with the grant of a protected tenancy, *Zimmerman v Grossman*[1] bound him to hold that the words 'any person' in s 85 were limited to the landlord and did not include a third person such as an outgoing tenant; and that s 86, which prohibited premiums on the assignment of a protected tenancy, did not apply because the true nature of the transaction in connection with which the premium was paid by the plaintiffs was a transaction of surrender and determination of the old lease followed by the grant of a fresh lease by the defendant's landlords to the plaintiffs, and was not an assignment of the defendant's lease. The plaintiffs appealed. The facts are set out in the judgment of Lawton LJ.

Walter Blum for the plaintiffs.
Michael Barnes for the defendant.

1   [1971] 1 All ER 363, [1972] 1 QB 167

Cur adv vult

30th July. The following judgments were read.

LORD DENNING MR.

1 *The facts*

There is an attractive part of London called Little Venice. It is so called because of Regent's Canal. This case is about a flat there. By a lease dated 4th February 1970, the Church Commissioners let a flat, F, 20 Randolph Crescent, to the defendant, Mrs Alexander. The term was 7½ years from 29th September 1969. The rent was £650 a year for the first three years and £800 for the next 4½ years. It was a protected tenancy. That is, a contractual tenancy with a regulated rent. The lease contained a provision for the rent to be varied so as to be equal to the registered rent.

After being there three years, Mrs Alexander determined to sell the flat. She put it into the hands of estate agents. They issued particulars in these words:

'LEASE	4¼ years.
RENT	£800 p.a.
RATES PAYABLE:	£198·77 (Rateable Value: £286)
PRICE	£4,500 (to include the fitted carpets, curtains and kitchen equipment and certain other items such as the many spotlights).'

That asking price of £4,500 was in reality the price which Mrs Alexander was demanding for the *assignment* of the lease. The furniture and fittings, etc were only worth £1,002. The balance was payable for the assignment of the tenancy. Mrs Alexander had paid no premium herself for the lease: but here she was, after three years, asking £4,500. She was advised to ask this sum, because the estate agent thought she could get it. Any incoming tenant would be glad to get a protected tenancy; for he or she would get security of tenure after the 4¼ years had expired and would only have to pay the registered rent.

Mrs Farrell was just such an incoming tenant. She lived in Worcestershire and wanted to find a flat for her daughter who had obtained a post in the Victoria and Albert Museum. Mrs Farrell offered to pay £4,000 and Mrs Alexander accepted it. Mrs Farrell paid a deposit of £400 to the estate agents. The agents wrote to the solicitor for Mrs Alexander on 25th January 1973:

'We write to inform you that our mutual client, Mrs. D. Alexander . . . has accepted an offer of £4,000 made subject to contract for the fixtures and fittings etc. to be included in the sale at the time of the Assignment of her leasehold interest in the above property. The proposed Assignee is Mrs. C. D. Farrell . . . and [her] solicitors . . . are Messrs. Braby Waller & Co. . . . We are in possession of a 10% deposit . . .'

They wrote a similar letter to Mrs Farrell's solicitors.

Those letters show clearly that the estate agents regarded the proposed transaction to be an assignment of the tenancy, together with the furniture and fittings. There is a letter, too, from Mrs Alexander showing that she also regarded it as an assignment. The estate agents put the furniture and fittings at £4,000, but their real value was only £1,002.

If the transaction had been completed in that form, it would clearly have been illegal. It would be prohibited by s 89 of the Rent Act 1968; and Mrs Farrell could have recovered the excess £2,998 from Mrs Alexander under s 88.

But it was not completed in that form. When the estate agents approached the landlords (the Church Commissioners) for their consent, they suggested that, instead of an assignment, there should be a surrender by the outgoing tenant, Mrs Alexander, of her lease to the landlords, and then a grant by the landlords of a new lease to the

incoming tenant, Mrs Farrelll. This was in accordance with a clause in the lease to
Mrs Alexander which the Church Commissioners often insert in their leases. We   *a*
considered it in *Greene v Church Comrs for England*[1] and expressed some doubt as to
its validity.

The solicitors for Mrs Farrell were agreeable for the transaction to go through in
this way. So on 6th March 1973, her solicitors wrote to the Church Commissioners,
saying: '. . . although initially it was the intention to assign the existing lease to our
Client it is now proposed that Mrs. Alexander's lease be surrendered and a new lease   *b*
. . . granted . . .' In the result, the solicitors, instead of preparing an assignment,
prepared a memorandum of agreement in these words:

> '1. SUBJECT as hereinafter mentioned the present Lessee shall immediately
> prior to completion of the new Lease hereinafter mentioned surrender to the
> Church Commissioners for England (hereinafter referred to as "the Landlords")   *c*
> with vacant possession ALL THAT her estate and interest in the premises known as
> Flat F 20 Randolph Crescent . . . being a Lease for seven and one half years
> from the twenty-ninth day of September [1969] . . .
> '2. THE completion of the said Surrender shall be subject to acceptance of the
> same by the Landlords and to the simultaneous grant by the Landlords to the
> new Lessees of a new Lease . . . with vacant possession for the term of NINE YEARS   *d*
> from the twenty-fifth day of December [1972] at [£850] per annum exclusive . . .
> '4. UPON Completion the new Lessee shall pay to the present Lessee the sum of
> [£4,000] for the carpets curtains chattels fixtures and fittings in the said premises
> in accordance with the Inventory agreed between the parties . . . and ten per
> centum (10%) of the said sum of [£4,000] shall be paid to [the agents] as
> Stakeholders . . .'   *e*

That memorandum was signed on 30th March 1973, and on the same day Mrs Farrell
paid the balance of the £4,000. Mrs Alexander gave this receipt:

> 'I . . . HEREBY ACKNOWLEDGE to have received the sum of Four Thousand Pounds
> (£4,000) from MRS. . . . FARRELL and MISS. . . . O'FARRELL being the consideration   *f*
> for the purchase of the fixtures, fittings, chattels and other equipment in and
> about the above property as at the 30th March 1973 . . .'

It is plain, therefore, that to outward appearances nothing was paid for the new tenancy; but £4,000 was paid for the furniture and fittings. Seeing that they were only
worth £1,002, the balance of £2,998 must have been paid for the grant of the new
tenancy. But it was not paid to the landlords, the Church Commissioners. If it had   *g*
been paid to them, it would have been plainly illegal, being prohibited by s 85 of
the 1968 Act, and the excess sum of £2,998 could have been recovered under s 88.
But £2,998 was not paid to the landlords. It was paid to the outgoing tenant, Mrs
Alexander.

It is said that, because the £2,998 was not paid to the landlords, but to the outgoing
tenant, the transaction was perfectly lawful. This would be a most remarkable result.   *h*
If it is correct, it opens up a great gap in the Rent Acts. It means that sitting tenants
can exploit the housing shortage—to their own great advantage—but the landlords
cannot. Nor can statutory tenants. But contractual tenants can do so, provided they
get the co-operation of the landlords. And who can say what the tenants will pay to
the landlords—'under the counter'—for this co-operation? The Church Commissioners are willing to co-operate without being paid. But other landlords might   *j*
want a share in the money, so long as nobody knew about it. I turn, therefore, to
the statutes to see if they permit this great gap to be driven through them.

---

1   [1974] 3 All ER 609, [1974] Ch 467

2 The statutes

a   In times of housing shortage, Parliament has had to step in to help those in need. It has passed legislation so as to prevent landlords from evicting tenants and to restrain landlords from increasing rents. At the same time it has sought to stop people from exploiting the shortage. It has enacted provisions which make these acts unlawful: (1) If a landlord, on granting a new tenancy, requires or receives any sum from the tenant in addition to the rent, he is guilty of an offence and is liable to

b   repay the amount. This was done by s 1(2) of the Increase of Rent and Mortgage Interest (War Restrictions) Act 1915, s 8(1) of the Increase of Rent and Mortgage Interest (Restrictions) Act 1920 and s 85(1) of the 1968 Act. (2) If a contractual tenant, assigning his tenancy to an incoming tenant, requires or receives any sum from the incoming tenant as the price of the assignment, he is guilty of an offence and liable to repay the amount. Likewise, if on assigning his tenancy, he sells the furniture and

c   fittings to the incoming tenant and required an excessive price for them which is more than their real value, he is guilty of an offence and liable to repay the excess. These provisions were first introduced in ss 2 and 3 of the Landlord and Tenant (Rent Control) Act 1949, and appear now in ss 86, 88 and 89 of the 1968 Act. (3) If a statutory tenant (who could not, of course, assign his tenancy) takes any money from an incoming tenant as the price of giving up possession to him he is guilty of an offence and lia-

d   ble to repay the amount. This was introduced in s 15(2) of the 1920 Act and appears in s 13 of the 1968 Act. And, if a statutory tenant makes an arrangement with his landlord by which a new tenant is allowed into the house, the statutory tenant cannot require or receive any sum from the incoming tenant as the price of letting him in. This provision was introduced by s 17(4) of the Rent Act 1957, and is now in s 14 of the 1968 Act.

e   You might think that those provisions would be effective to prevent people exploiting the housing shortage for their own advantage. But the lawyers have devised a scheme by which, it is said, a contractual tenant can exploit the shortage to his own advantage. It is this. Instead of assigning his tenancy to an incoming tenant, he can make an arrangement with the landlord by which the outgoing tenant surrenders his existing tenancy to the landlord, and the landlord at the same time grants a new

f   tenancy to the incoming tenant. The landlord cannot charge any premium to the incoming tenant. But the outgoing tenant can do so, and retain the money for his own benefit. As a camouflage, the outgoing tenant calls it payment for the furniture and fittings. But it is in reality a payment for the new tenancy.

I must say that this device of the lawyers seems to me to be plainly in contravention of the statutes. I will take the 1968 Act. If you should read through ss 85, 86, 87 and 89,

g   you will see the words 'any person' used in each of those sections. To my mind they mean the same thing in each section. They mean what they say—'any person'. They include the landlord. That is obvious from s 85(1) which speaks of the 'grant' of a tenancy. They include a tenant. That is obvious from s 86(1) which speaks of the 'assignment' of a tenancy. They include a landlord as well as a tenant. That is obvious from ss 87(2) and 89(1), both of which speak of the 'grant, renewal, continuance or

h   assignment' of a tenancy, all in one breath.

So the meaning of 'any person' is obvious. It includes a landlord or a tenant. To my mind this device of the lawyers is contrary to s 85(1), which says:

'Any person who, as a condition of the grant, renewal or continuance of a protected tenancy, requires, in addition to the rent, the payment of any premium

j   [which includes any fine or other like sum and any other pecuniary consideration] ... shall be guilty of an offence ...'

'Any person' includes an outgoing tenant. By this device he requires the payment of money as a condition of his surrender and the grant of a new tenancy by the landlord. The device is contrary to s 89(1) also. It says:

'Any person who, in connection with the proposed grant, renewal, continuance
or assignment, on terms which require the purchase of furniture, of a protected   a
tenancy—(a) offers the furniture at a price which he knows or ought to know
is unreasonably high, or otherwise seeks to obtain such a price for the furniture
. . . shall be liable to a fine . . .'

Take this very case. There was a grant of a protected tenancy by the Church Commissioners to Mrs Farrell. In connection with that proposed grant, Mrs Alexander,   b
or her agents, offered the furniture at a price which they knew, or ought to have known,
was unresonably high. The words 'in connection with the proposed grant' clearly
cover this case.

To my mind, when the outgoing tenant or her agents obtain money by this device,
it is plainly illegal as being contrary to ss 85 and 89 of the 1968 Act; and the excess
sum (over and above the real value of the furniture and the fittings) can be recovered   c
by the incoming tenant under ss 88 and 90(1) of the 1968 Act.

3 *The cases*
There are only two cases in the books on a surrender and new lease. The first is
Remmington (or Remington) v Larchin[1]. That was decided on s 8 of the 1920 Act. The
judges held that 'a person' in that section meant 'a landlord' and not 'a tenant'.   d
But at that time there was nothing to prevent a tenant from taking a premium on
the assignment of his lease. It had recently been so held in *Mason, Herring and Brooks v
Harris*[2]. If there was nothing to prevent it on an assignment, there was no reason to
prevent it on a surrender and new grant. Atkin LJ[3] expressly mentioned that point.
Afterwards, in 1949, the rule about assignment was altered. 'A person' was forbidden
to take a premium on an assignment of tenancy: see s 2(2) of the 1949 Act. Clearly   e
'a person' there included a tenant. The 1949 Act thus gave a different meaning to
'a person' to that which had been given in *Remmington v Larchin*[1], and it rendered that
case no longer of authority on the meaning of the statute.

Furthermore, the judges in *Remmington v Larchin*[1] found the case one of much difficulty. The one argument which turned the scale was that s 8 was a penal provision
and, on that account, ought to be given a narrow construction limiting a 'person'   f
to a 'landlord'. Nowadays that rule of interpretation is much discredited. It is not
to be applied simply because the penal provision is difficult to construe, but only
when it is truly ambiguous so as to be capable of two meanings: see *Bowers v Gloucester
Corpn*[4] and *Director of Public Prosecutions v Ottewell*[5]. It has to give way to the much
better rule that the courts should look to the mischief and interpret the statute so as
to effect a remedy, even though it is a penal provision, especially when it carries a   g
civil remedy too. We do that every day in cases under the Factories Acts. In my
opinion, *Remmington v Larchin*[1] is no authority on the interpretaion of s 85 of the 1968
Act.

The second case is *Zimmerman v Grossman*[6], where this court does seem to have held
that a tenant could lawfully demand a premium on a surrender and new lease. But
the court there regarded the earlier case of *Remmington v Larchin*[1] as binding on them.   h
I think they were wrong in so doing. *Remmington v Larchin*[1] was decided in the early
days on the old Act of 1920. The statute had been altered afterwards beyond measure
expressly in 1949 when it prohibited a premium on 'assignments'. Moreover, the
court seems to have thought that Parliament in the later satutes impliedly approved

j

1   [1921] 3 KB 404, [1921] All ER Rep 298
2   [1921] 1 KB 653, [1921] All ER Rep 741
3   [1921] 3 KB at 411, [1921] All ER Rep at 301
4   [1963] 1 All ER 437, [1963] 1 QB 881
5   [1968] 3 All ER 153 at 157, [1970] AC 642 at 649
6   [1971] 1 All ER 363, [1972] 1 QB 167

Remmington v Larchin[1] and, by re-enacting s 2(1) of the 1949 Act in substantially
a the same terms as s 8 of the 1920 Act, intended to make that decision applicable to
the 1968 Act. Indeed, Widgery LJ said[2] that it was as if Parliament had added in
parenthesis: 'It is the intention of Parliament that these words be given the meaning
given to them in *Remmington v Larchin*[1].'

   I am afraid that I take a different view. The court was not referred to the stream of
recent authority in which it has been said emphatically that, by re-enacting a statute
b in the same words, Parliament does not thereby approve every wrong decision that
the courts had given to those words: see *Royal Crown Derby Porcelain Co v Russell*,[3]
Dun v Dun[4], *Re Yeovil Glove Co Ltd*[5], and *R v Blane*[6], referred to in *R v Bow Road
Domestic Proceedings Court, ex parte Adedigba*[7].

   As I read the judgment in *Zimmerman v Grossman*[8] this court left to themselves
would have held that 'any person' in s 85 of the 1968 Act meant any person. They
c only decided differently because they thought they were bound by *Remmington v
Larchin*[1]. *Zimmerman v Grossman*[8] is thus not an authority on the meaning of the
Act. It is only an authority on the doctrine of judicial precedent. And, as such, it
is erroneous. Sufficient to say, however, that it is no authority on the meaning of the
words 'any person'.

   Finally, I would say this. The words of the 1968 Act are plain. They admit of no
d doubt. They cover this case. No court is entitled to throw over the plain words of a
statute by referring to a previous judicial decision. When there is a conflict between
a plain statute and a previous decision, the statute must prevail. That appears from
the decision of the House of Lords in *Governors of Campbell College, Belfast v Valuation
Comr for Northern Ireland*[9].

e *4 Conclusion*
   In my opinion, therefore, *Remmington v Larchin*[1] is no authority on the 1968 Act;
and *Zimmerman v Grossman*[8] was wrongly decided. So much so that I do not think it
is binding on us. I have often said that I do not think this court should be absolutely
bound by its previous decisions, any more than the House of Lords. I know it is said
that when this court is satisfied that a previous decision of its own was wrong, it should
f not overrule it but should apply it in this court and leave it to the House of Lords
to overrule it. Just think what this means in this case. These ladies do not qualify
for legal aid. They must go to the expense themselves of an appeal to the House of
Lords to get the decision revoked. The expense may deter them and thus an injustice
will be perpetrated. In any case I do not think it right to compel them to do this
when the result is a foregone conclusion. I would let them save their money and reverse
g it here and now.
   I would allow the appeal, accordingly.

LAWTON LJ. The trial judge dismissed the plaintiffs' claim because he thought
that the decision of this court in *Zimmerman v Grossman*[8] (Davies, Widgery and
h Karminsky LJJ) bound him. Three questions arise. First, did that case apply? Secondly,
if it did, would this court be justified in not following it? Thirdly, if it did not, how
should the relevant provisions of the Rent Act 1968 be construed and applied?

1   [1921] 3 KB 404, [1921] All ER Rep 298
2   [1971] 1 All ER at 369, [1972] 1 QB at 177
j 3   [1949] 1 All ER 749, [1949] 2 KB 417
4   [1959] 2 All ER 134, [1959] AC 272
5   [1964] 2 All ER 849 at 860, [1965] Ch 148 at 183
6   (1849) 3 QB 769, [1843-60] All ER Rep 397
7   [1968] 2 All ER 89 at 95, [1968] 2 QB 572 at 583
8   [1971] 1 All ER 363, [1972] 1 QB 167
9   [1964] 2 All ER 705, [1964] 1 WLR 912

Lord Denning MR has summarised the facts. I am going to take the unusual course of making my own summary so that I can deal in my own way with the plaintiffs' *a* main submission which was that the transaction under consideration was not what it purported to be.

The facts

In January 1973, young Miss O'Farrell, one of the plaintiffs, wanted to rent an unfurnished flat in West London. She went to a firm of estate agents. They had one *b* to offer but at a price. It was Flat F, 20 Randolph Crecsent, W9. She was told that she could have the remainder of a lease which had 4½ years to run for £4,500. With her mother, who is a doctor practising in the country, the other plaintiff, she inspected the flat. She met the tenant, Mrs Alexander, the defendant, who in February 1970 had been granted a 7½ year lease by the Church Commissioners. The defendant pointed out various fittings such as a cooker and a refrigerator which were to go with the flat *c* on transfer. The plaintiffs liked what they saw. Mrs Farrell was prepared to finance the acquisition. On January 22 1973 Mrs Farrell went back to the agents. She told them that she liked the flat. They asked her to make an offer. She did: £4,000. The agents, who were in fact sub-agents, telephoned the main agents who were willing to accept the offer. Miss O'Farrell was told. She handed over a cheque for £400 as a deposit. In her evidence Miss O'Farrell said nothing about her acceptance and pay- *d* ment of the deposit being 'subject to contract', but the estate agents treated it as such and claimed to hold the £400 as stakeholders. In her dealings with the estate agents nothing seems to have been said about the legal form which the transaction was to take, but at the trial the defendant's counsel accepted that what was contemplated by the plaintiffs and the defendant at this stage of the transaction was an assignment. Solicitors were instructed by both parties. By letter dated 25th January 1973, the *e* main agents told the defendant's solicitors that they had accepted 'an offer of £4,000, made subject to contract for the fixtures and fittings, etc. to be included in the sale at the time of the Assignment of her leasehold interest . . .' With this letter they enclosed sale particulars, which set out the rateable value of the flat—£286. The solicitors could not have been told in plainer terms, if they knew any landlord and tenant law, that they were being asked to help the defendant to obtain an illegal premium on *f* the assignment of a protected tenancy: see ss 1(1)(a) and 86 of the Rent Act 1968. Undeterred by any knowledge they may have had, they started discussions with the plaintiffs' solicitors to complete the transaction. The latter did know the legal position and advised Miss O'Farrell that, if she and her mother paid the £4,000, they might get back the greater part of it.

When preparing the completion documents the defendant's solicitors ran into a *g* snag. The defendant's lease provided that if at any time she wanted to assign her interest in the flat she had first to offer to make an absolute surrender to her landlords, the Church Commissioners. If they did not accept the offer within 28 days they were to be deemed to have rejected it. Then the defendant would be free to assign in accordance with the terms of the lease. When the defendant approached the Church Commissioners about giving up possession of her flat they told her that they would *h* exercise their rights under the lease to accept a surrender. A new way of transferring the tenancy to the plaintiffs had to be found. The Church Commissioners stated that they would consider accepting the plaintiffs as tenants subject to their having satisfactory references and being found suitable when interviewed. They were interviewed; their references were found to be satisfactory. The Church Commissioners were willing to grant them a lease for a term of nine years from 25th December 1972, *j* at a yearly rent of £850, renewable at three yearly intervals. They were to get a longer term than the defendant had had and at a slightly higher rent.

This was all very well for the plaintiffs: they were not required to pay any premium to the Church Commissioners. The defendant, however, wanted the agreed sum of £4,000 and she was not prepared to surrender her lease until she was sure of getting

it. The solicitors on both sides discussed ways and means. They decided that the
a transaction should be effected by a contract between the plaintiffs and the defendant
whereby the defendant was to surrender her lease to the Church Commissioners
immediately before they granted a new lease to the plaintiffs, and on such grant the
plaintiffs were to pay the defendant the sum of £4,000 'for the carpets, curtains,
chattels and fittings in the said premises'. A contract giving effect to these terms was
signed on 30th March 1973. On the same day completion took place at the offices
b of the Church Commissioners. Each of the three parties was represented by a solicitor.
The plainitffs' solicitor handed to the Church Commissioners' solicitor, and he accepted
a letter dated 29th March 1973, approving the draft lease and enclosing a cheque for
£212·50 in payment of a quarter's rent from 25th March 1973. The defendant's
solicitor then handed over her lease to the Church Commissioners.

After the Church Commissioners' solicitor had left the room the plaintiffs' solici-
c tor handed to the defendant's solicitor a banker's draft for £3,600, being the sum
of £4,000 less the deposit of £400 paid on 22nd January 1973. A few days later
the defendant's solicitor sent the plaintiffs' solicitor a receipt dated 30th March
1973 for the £4,000. It purported to be a receipt for the purchase of 'fixtures, fittings,
chattels and other equipment in and about the above property as at the 30th March
1973'. It was nothing of the kind. The plaintiffs admit that £1,002 represented a
d reasonable price for what passed with the tenancy, but they allege that even if this
be an under-estimate, a considerable part of the so-called purchase price should be
treated 'as if it were a premium required to be paid as a condition of the grant,
renewal, continuance or assignment of the protected tenancy': see s 88 of the Rent Act
1968. At the trial the defendant accepted that this was so if the plaintiffs' claim did
come within ss 85 to 90 of the 1968 Act. A few days later the Church Commissioners
e executed a new lease in the terms agreed with the plaintiffs' solicitors. There was no
evidence that the Church Commissioners knew anything about the payment of £4,000.

As soon as the transaction had been completed the plaintiffs had valued the chattels
and fittings which had been transferred. The valuation they were given was £1,002.
By letter dated 23rd July 1973, the plaintiffs' solicitors claimed from the defendant
repayment of £2,998 on the ground that this sum was an illegal premium. By letter
f dated 30th July 1973 the defendant's solicitors rejected the claim. They put their
client's case succinctly as follows: 'The old Lease was surrendered to the Landlords
and the new Lease granted by the Landlords without payment of consideration and
the agreed price for the furniture fixtures and fittings passed between different
parties'.

On these facts the trial judge adjudged first, that the transaction which was com-
g pleted was not an assignment, even if the defendant thought it was, but a surrender
of a lease by the defendant and the grant of a new lease by the Church Commissioners
to the plaintiffs; secondly, that the facts of this case could not be distinguished in
any material way from those in *Zimmerman v Grossman*[1] with the consequence
that that case applied and required him to dismiss the claim.

h Submissions

Counsel for the plaintiffs made three submissions. First, that the transaction should
be regarded by this court as an assignment. The parties had intended that there should
be an assignment. As late as 13th March 1973, the defendant, as is shown by one of
her letters, thought that she was going to assign her lease to the plaintiffs. The
surrender and grant of a new lease, it was said, was nothing more than a legal cloak
j to hide the real nature of what was being done. Secondly, that the Church Commissioners had delegated to the defendant the landlord's functions of finding a tenant and
granting a new lease with the consequence that she stood in their shoes and that any
requirement was made by a landlord for the purposes of s 85 of the Rent Act 1968.

1 [1971] 1 All ER 363, [1972] 1 QB 167

Thirdly, that *Zimmerman v Grossman*[1] was a decision of this court given per incuriam; that it was wrongly decided and should not be followed.   *a*

Counsel for the defendant sought to refute all of these submissions. His contentions were first, that the transaction took effect in law as a surrender and a grant of a new tenancy and as nothing else. Secondly, that on the evidence it was impossible to say that the Church Commissioners had put the defendant in their place for finding a new tenant. Thirdly, that *Zimmerman v Grossman*[1] had not been decided per incuriam. It was a unanimous decision of this court and was binding. Only the House of Lords   *b* could say that it had been wrongly decided.

In my judgment, on the evidence, counsel for the plaintiffs' contention that the transaction was an assignment got up in legal garb to look like a surrender and a grant of a new lease is untenable. A sham transaction can only come about if those interested want it to be a sham: for an example, see *Conqueror Property Trust Ltd v Barnes Corpn*[2]. There were three parties to the transaction under consideration in this appeal.   *c* The Chuch Commissioners were not taking part in a sham; they wanted to exercise their rights under the lease granted to the defendant in February 1970, which was nearly two years before the plaintiffs and the defendant started negotiations. They had reserved their rights for the protection of their own interests; and the strong inference is that they wanted them in order to exercise more effective control over who was to be in possession of their property than was possible under the usual form   *d* of covenant against assigning or under-letting without consent. When they came to exercise their rights in March 1973, they acted with deliberation. They took up the plaintiffs' references and interviewed them in order to assess their suitability as tenants. They did not accept them merely because the defendant had put their names before them. They cannot be said to have left the choice of tenants to the defendant. When the transaction took on its legal garb, its clothes were real and suitable for the occasion.   *e* The defendant was released from the covenants in her lease. The plaintiffs entered into covenants with the Church Commissioners and in return got a substantial term of years and a protected tenancy. There was no assignment. It follows that the defendant had not received any part of the £4,000 in connection with an assignment of a protected tenancy. That disposes of counsel for the plaintiffs' first submission. It also disposes of his second. The Church Commissioners had not delegated to the   *f* defendant their functions as landlords of finding a tenant and granting a new lease. Counsel for the plaintiffs contended that they had in order to bring this case within a possible exception to the principle enunciated in *Zimmerman v Grossman*[1]. In his judgment in that case Widgery LJ[3] had envisaged the possibility of such an exception; he made no finding as to its existence because the evidence in that case would not have supported a finding that the landlord had delegated his functions to the outgoing   *g* tenant. Similarly on the evidence in this case there could be no such finding.

Once the evidence about an intention to assign is assessed for what it is, namely the background history, in my judgment the facts of this case are indistinguishable from those in *Zimmerman v Grossman*[1]. In that case the plaintiff, the tenant for a term of three years of a flat within the Rent Act 1968, wished to move elsewhere. His landlords agreed to accept a surrender from him and grant a new lease to a suitable   *h* tenant if he introduced one to them. The plaintiff met the defendant, who wished to take the flat. She orally agreed with the plaintiff to buy the fixtures and fittings in the flat for £300 provided the landlords agreed to accept her as a tenant. They did and granted her a new lease. The defendant paid the plaintiff £100 and refused to pay the balance on the ground that the £300 was far in excess of the true value of the fixtures and fittings (the county court judge found this to be so) and was in conse-   *j* quence an illegal premium by virtue of s 85(1) of the Rent Act 1968. The plaintiff's

---

1   [1971] 1 All ER 363, [1972] 1 QB 167
2   [1944] 1 All ER 34, [1944] KB 96
3   [1971] 1 All ER at 372, [1972] 1 QB at 181

claim for the balance of £200 succeeded. The facts in *Zimmerman v Grossman*[1] in
a turn were indistinguishable from those in *Remmington v Larchin*[2] which was another
decision of this court (Bankes, Scrutton and Atkin LJJ) on a similar provision in the
Increase of Rent and Mortgage Interest (Restrictions) Act 1920, and to the same effect
as *Zimmerman v Grossman*[1].

Per incuriam
b   Since this case on its facts cannot be distinguished from the two earlier cases, why
should they not be followed? The only ground put forward on behalf of the plaintiffs
was that the law had developed between 1921 and 1972 and that the 1972 decision had
been made per incuriam. It was pointed out by counsel for the plaintiffs that nowhere in the report of the arguments and of Widgery LJ's judgment is there any
c reference to ss 13 to 15 of the Rent Act 1968. This is so. These sections relate to the
statutory tenancies. Section 13 forbids statutory tenants to demand payment as a condition of giving up possession. Section 15 makes any person requiring such a payment
guilty of a criminal offence. The submission was that if the court had been referred
to these sections and had considered them it would have appreciated that Parliament
had intended to stop people making money out of the transfer of protected tenancies,
whatever the circumstances and the legal garb in which the transaction was dressed.
d I do not accept that ss 13 to 15 affect the construction of ss 85 to 90 to anything like the
extent suggested. It matters not, however, because the court now knows that counsel
for the plaintiff in *Zimmerman v Grossman*[1] did refer the court to s 13. We have
learned this from the law reporter, Mrs E M Wellwood, who reported this case for
the Law Reports. She has let us have her notebook. She made a note of counsel's
reference to s 13 and of the argument which he based on it. It follows that *Zimmerman
e v Grossman*[1] was not a case where this court had construed a statute in ignorance of
another relevant statutory provision: see *Young v Bristol Aeroplane Co Ltd*[3]. The reason
counsel for the plaintiffs put forward for submitting that Widgery LJ's judgment (with
which the other members of the court agreed[4]) had been made per incuriam is
unsound.
f   In the course of argument Widgery LJ's judgment was closely examined as was the
decision in *Remmington v Larchin*[2]. It became clear that we would have to consider
once again the circumstances in which this court can disregard its own earlier decision.
For me *Young v Bristol Aeroplane Co Ltd*[5] provides the authoritative decision. It has
stood without criticism from the House of Lords for 31 years. It has been followed
time and time again. I regard it as a part of the law which it is my judicial duty to
apply. The only ground for not following *Zimmerman v Grossman*[1] which could
g possibly apply is that Widgery LJ's judgment was per incuriam. As I have already stated,
the reason submitted by counsel for the plaintiffs for saying it was has no factual
foundation.
     Before I wrote this part of this judgment I had the advantage of reading that which
Lord Denning MR has just delivered. I decided that it was necessary for me to make
a detailed analysis of Widgery LJ's judgment. The report of the case sets out in detail
h the arguments put forward by counsel on behalf of the unsuccessful defendant. He
invited[6] the court's attention to the legislative history of s 85 of the 1968 Act. He
submitted[7] that the Landlord and Tenant (Rent Control) Act 1949 was of 'considerable
importance because it defined "premium" for the purposes of the Act as a payment

---

j 1 [1971] 1 All ER 363, [1972] 1 QB 167
   2 [1921] 3 KB 404, [1921] All ER Rep 298
   3 [1944] 2 All ER 293 at 300, [1944] KB 718 at 729
   4 [1971] 1 All ER at 372, 373, [1972] 1 QB at 181
   5 [1944] 2 All ER 293, [1944] KB 718
   6 [1972] 1 QB at 169, 170
   7 [1972] 1 QB at 170

"in addition to the rent" and it prohibited the requiring of a premium on the assignment of a tenancy'. It was the absence in the 1920 Act of any reference to an assign-   *a*
ment which had inclined Atkin LJ in *Remmington v Larchin*[1] to the opinion that under
that Act 'a person' meant 'a landlord' and not 'a tenant'. Counsel went on to point
out[2] that the Rent Act 1965 had amended s 2 of the 1949 Act and that these amendments had been re-enacted in s 85 of the 1968 Act but with the significant change that
'a person' had become 'any person'. He is reported as saying[2]:

> 'The words "any person" are very wide words. They can include a person,
> other than the landlord, who is in a position to impose a condition on a tenant in
> connection with the grant, renewal or continuance of a tenancy.'

It follows that the court had had before it all the relevant statutory provisions
and had been alerted to the arguments which could be founded on those provisions.   *c*
Widgery LJ reviewed the whole of the legislative history. He examined the judgment
in *Remmington v Larchin*[1] in detail and went on to consider the argument that the
statutory changes made after 1920 had rendered that decision irrelevant. He dealt
with it in these terms[3]:

> 'I have considered this argument and I recognise the weight attached to it but,   *d*
> standing by itself, it ignores another argument which I find of greater force, and
> that is the well-known principle of construction that, where Parliament has
> re-enacted specific words which have already been the subject of judicial inter-
> pretation, it is presumed that Parliament when re-enacting those words, intends
> them to have the meaning which the courts have put on them in their earlier
> use.'

He construed s 2(1) of the 1949 Act[3] 'as though it had added, in parenthesis, "(it is
the intention of Parliament that these words be given the meaning given to them in
Remmington v Larchin[1])".'   Whether Widgery LJ was right or wrong in the way he
dealt with this argument (and I am of the opinion he was right) there was nothing
per incuriam about what he said.

He next examined the decision of the House of Lords in *Elmdene Estates Ltd v White*[4].   *f*
It was not directly in point but *Remmington v Larchin*[1] had been discussed. Nothing
had been said to throw doubt on its correctness.

The Rent Act 1965 changes were scrutinised in detail. Widgery LJ decided[5] that
there was nothing in the 1965 Act to prevent *Remmington's* case[1] remaining good
law. He went on as follows[5]:

> 'The 1965 Act has been repealed. It is replaced by the provisions of the Rent
> Act 1968 . . . The 1968 Act is a consolidating Act. It may be true that there are,
> here and there, amendments of consequence, but it is in the main a consoli-
> dating Act and, although the lay-out of the provisions of s 85 differ significantly
> from the lay-out of the corresponding provisions in the 1965 Act, I can find nothing
> either in the language used or in the format of the legislation, to cause me to   *h*
> depart from the well-known principle that consolidating Acts presumably are
> not intended to change the law.'

It was the 1968 Act which had changed 'a person' to 'any person'. The passage in
Widgery LJ's judgment which I have just quoted shows that this change, to which

1 [1921] 3 KB 404, [1921] All ER Rep 298
2 [1972] 1 QB at 170
3 [1971] 1 All ER at 369, [1972] 1 QB at 177
4 [1960] 1 All ER 306, [1960] AC 528
5 [1971] 1 All ER at 372, [1972] 1 QB at 180

Lord Denning MR has attached so much importance, was considered. It was not
a overlooked per incuriam. Being of the opinion that *Zimmerman v Grossman*[1] is
binding on this court, I have not thought it appropriate to consider whether that
case and *Remmington v Larchin*[2] were rightly decided. Nevertheless because of the
importance which Lord Denning MR has attached to the change in wording to 'any
person', I feel justified in inviting attention to the Consolidation of Enactments
(Procedure) Act 1949 which enables 'corrections and minor improvements' to be
b made in bills consolidating enactments. A stringent procedure is laid down for
identifying such 'corrections and minor improvements' and for affording opportunities
for discussion: see s 1. 'Corrections and minor improvements' are defined in s 2 as
follows:

c ' "corrections and minor improvements" means amendments of which the
effect is confined to resolving ambiguities, removing doubts, bringing obsolete
provisions into conformity with modern practice or removing unnecessary
provisions or anomalies which are not of substantial importance, and amendments designed to facilitate improvement in the form or manner in which the
law is stated, and includes any transitional provisions which may be necessary
in consequence of such amendments . . .'

d
If a change from 'a person' in the 1965 Act to 'any person' in s 85 of the 1968 Act has
the effect which Lord Denning MR is of the opnion it has, one consequence would
be that tenants who were not persons under the 1965 Act and therefore immune from
criminal prosecution would have become liable to prosecution under the 1968 Act.
I would not consider this change in the law either a correction or a minor improvement.

e
Conclusion
As did *Zimmerman v Grossman*[1], this appeal has revealed a gap which Parliament
has left (whether wittingly or unwittingly I know not) in its attempts to prevent
the exploitation of those in need of houses or flats. Many would think that this gap
should be closed as quickly as possible. I certainly do. I would close it at once if I
f could; but, in my opinion, I could only do so by stretching the law. Adapting
Shakespeare's words, I might be doing a great right but I would be doing a little
wrong and as Portia said[3]: 'Twill be recorded for a precedent, And many an error
by the same example will rush into the state. It cannot be.'
I would dismiss the appeal.

g

SCARMAN LJ. The plaintiffs, who are appellants in this court, sought by action
in the Wandsworth County Court to recover a premium of £2,998 which they said
was unlawfully required of them as a condition of the grant of a tenancy of an unfurnished flat. They in fact paid a sum of £4,000 as 'key money', but it was admitted
h that £1,002 of the sum was referable to funiture and fittings. It was the outgoing
tenant, the defendant in the action, who required and was eventually paid the
premium as a condition of making the flat available to them. The claim was put in
two alternative ways: first, reliance was placed on s 86 of the Rent Act 1968, and it
was said that the premium was required as a condition of, or received in connection
with, the assignment of a protected tenancy; alternatively, reliance was placed on
j s 85 and it was said that the premium was required as a condition of the grant of a
protected tenancy. The county court judge negatived both ways of putting the claim.

---

1   [1971] 1 All ER 363, [1972] 1 QB 167
2   [1921] 3 KB 404, [1921] All ER Rep 298
3   Merchant of Venice, IV. i. 220

He held that the plaintiffs failed to make a case under s 86 because there was no assignment; and they failed under s 85 because the defendant was not their landlord *a* and the judge held that he was bound by a decision of this court, *Zimmerman v Grossman*[1], to construe the prohibition contained in the section as limited to a landlord.

I agree with Lawton LJ and the county court judge in their analysis and assessment of the facts. The transaction, when completed, was not an assignment but a surrender of a lease by the defendant and the grant of a new lease by the landlords, the Church Commissioners, to the plaintiffs. True, the negotiations when they *b* began were for an assignment of the lease of the outgoing tenant—the defendant; and the original bargain, subject to contract, was certainly for an assignment. The change in the character of the transaction—from an assignment by the defendant of her lease to a grant of a new tenancy by the landlords—occurred because the Church Commissioners, as landlords, wanted it done that way. There was nothing sham or bogus about the change; the solicitors to all concerned understood and accepted *c* it; and completion was on the new basis.

Is the absence of an assignment fatal to a claim based on s 86? Subsection (1) provides that any person who requires a premium as a condition of the assignment of a protected tenancy is guilty of an offence. The defendant was, without doubt, requiring a premium as a condition of assignment right up to the time when, on the insistence of the Chuch Commissioners, the nature of the transaction was changed. *d*

To recover the premium the plaintiff has to show not only the commission of a criminal offence under s 86, but a case for recovery under s 90. Section 90(1) provides the remedy for one who has paid an illegal premium. The relevant words of the subsection are: 'Where under any agreement . . . any premium is paid . . . and . . . could not lawfully be required or received under . . . this Part of this Act [it] shall be recoverable by the person by whom it was paid'. Two preliminary points. First, *e* it was not suggested in argument, and I do not accept, that there can be any recovery other than under the subsection. Secondly, the subsection refers (as do ss 85 and 86) to premiums required or received. This is a distinction which in the present case I think we may disregard. I agree with the view, tentatively expressed by Widgery LJ in *Zimmerman v Grossman*[2], that receiving is an alternative to requiring. If a premium is paid because one who has it in his power to grant or withhold possession requires *f* it as a condition of a protected tenancy, there is a requirement; if a premium is paid because the desperately eager applicant volunteers it as an inducement to him who can make the tenancy available, the premium, though not required as a condition, is received in connection with the grant or the assignment, as the case may be. We are considering a case in which the premium was required. The question is: under what agreement was the premium paid? It was paid in two instalments: £400 on *g* 22nd January 1973, when both parties were proceeding on the basis of assignment, and £3,600 on completion, when the agreement being completed was for the surrender of one tenancy and the grant of a new one. On completion, the earlier payment was treated, and brought into account, as an advance on account of the £4,000 then due.

In my judgment, it follows that the whole of the £4,000, including the advance of *h* £400, was paid under the 'surrender' agreement; and it is not possible, therefore, to treat it as a payment on condition of, or in connection with, an assignment. In my judgment, therefore, the absence of an assignment is fatal to a claim based on s 86.

Thus analysed, the premium was paid under an agreement which provided for the grant of a protected tenancy. It would appear, therefore, at first sight that it could be recovered as being illegal under s 85(1) which, so far as relevant, provides: 'Any *j* person who, as a condition of the grant...of a protected tenancy, requires, in addition to the rent, the payment of any premium...shall be guilty of an offence...' But no,

---

1 [1971] 1 All ER 363, [1972] 1 QB 167
2 [1971] 1 All ER at 371, [1972] 1 QB at 180

a the defendant who required it was not the landlord and the Court of Appeal in *Zimmerman v Grossman*[1] has held that the prohibition imposed by the subsection is limited to a landlord. In so holding, the court purported to follow *Remmington v Larchin*[2]—a decision of this court on the earlier legislation. Counsel for the plaintiffs sought to overcome the seemingly insuperable difficulty in two ways. He submitted that, on the facts, the defendant was the agent of the landlords to obtain a tenant so that the premium she required could be treated as a premium required by her as

b their agent. The purpose of his submission was to take advantage of a possible way round the section suggested by Widgery LJ in *Zimmerman's* case[3]. I very much doubt whether any such way exists. But, if it does, the facts of this case do not enable it to be taken. Unable, as I think he is, to distinguish *Zimmerman v Grossman*[1], counsel for the plaintiffs was left with only one challenge, which he manfully accepted. He submitted that the decision of the court was 'per incuriam'. He relied on a passage

c in *Young v Bristol Aeroplane Co Ltd*[4] which, in justice to his argument, I shall quote. Lord Greene MR said in that passage:

> 'Where the court has construed a statute or a rule having the force of a statute, its decision stands on the same footing as any other decision on a question of law. But where the court is satisfied that an earlier decision was given in ignorance

d of the terms of a statute or a rule having the force of a statute the position is very different. It cannot, in our opinion, be right to say that in such a case the court is entitled to disregard the statutory provision and is bound to follow a decision of its own given when that provision was not present to its mind. Cases of this description are examples of decisions given per incuriam.'

e Counsel for the plaintiffs commented that Widgery LJ's judgment (with which, be it noted, the other members of the court agreed[5]) contains no reference to ss 13, 14 and 15 of the 1968 Act. And in an argument, to which I think he was led by comments from the court, he stressed the apparent omission of Widgery LJ to have regard to ss 86 to 89 when construing s 85. Let me admit at once that, unembarrassed by authority, I would not read s 85 as limited to a landlord: 'any person', the phrase

f used by the subsection, I would expect to mean 'any person'. But *Zimmerman v Grossman*[1] is authority binding on this court, unless we can truly say that the judgment was 'per incuriam'. But was it 'per incuriam'? To say that the careful judgment of Widgery LJ, reviewing as it did the history of the relevant legislation, was 'per incuriam'—a phrase in a foreign tongue which I translate as 'Homer nodded'—smacks of absurdity. I do not know, and would not dream of enquiring, whether ss 13 to 15

g were present to his mind; they could not have been decisive in any event. Equally, ss 86 to 89, whether or not he had them in mind, were relevant only as part of the context, and could not have been decisive. Can one, however, extend the 'per incuriam' exception so as to include a case where the only indication that 'Homer nodded' is that one thinks the court put on the words of the statute a meaning which they cannot bear, and one which leads to a result that appears to be contrary to the purpose of

h the statute? For myself I would agree with Lord Denning MR that one can—in a proper case. But to do so we must be prepared to say not merely that we prefer another construction to that favoured by the court whose decision is under challenge; we must be able to demonstrate that the words of the statute are capable of only one meaning and that the meaning attributed to them by the previous decision is an impossibility. Mistake, not a difference of opinion, is the criterion.

j

1   [1971] 1 All ER 363, [1972] 1 QB 167
2   [1921] 3 KB 404, [1921] All ER Rep 298
3   [1971] 1 All ER at 372, [1972] 1 QB at 181
4   [1944] 2 All ER 293 at 300, [1944] KB 718 at 729
5   [1971] 1 All ER at 372, 373, [1972] 1 QB at 181

Though I doubt whether the court in *Zimmerman v Grossman*[1] was under any
necessity to follow *Remmington v Larchin*[2], their reasons for doing so are entitled to   **a**
respect, and may well be sound. They may have been wrong, but they did not fail
to face the problem; and their answer, though I think another was open to them, is
not to be treated as given 'per incuriam'. Let me explain why.

Remmington v Larchin[2] was certainly a binding precedent until 1949, when for the
first time Parliament made illegal the requirement of a premium on the assignment
of a tenancy. Section 2(1) of the Landlord and Tenant (Rent Control) Act 1949,   **b**
re-enacting the earlier legislation, provided that 'a person' shall not, as a condition of
the grant of a tenancy, require the payment of a premium. But s 2(2) introduced new
law: it enacted, for the first time, that 'a person' shall not, as a condition of the assignment of a tenancy, require the payment of a premium. 'A person' in the subsection
clearly included an outgoing tenant. Did this new subsection modify the meaning
previously attributed by this court in *Remmington v Larchin*[2] to the words re-enacted   **c**
in sub-s (1) so that they also included a person other than the landlord? In *Zimmerman
v Grossman*[3] Widgery LJ posed the question and gave reasons for his conclusion that
it was still necessary to follow *Remmington v Larchin*[2] and to limit sub-s (1) to a landlord, even though the case could have no application to sub-s (2). This was a reasoned
conclusion, and Widgery LJ himself commented on the weight of the argument
he was rejecting. There can be two opinions, of course, on the point. But it is not   **d**
possible to dismiss the conclusion of Widgery LJ as being per incuriam; indeed,
he may well have been right, even though some disagree with him.

In 1968 the law was consolidated into the Rent Act 1968. There was, however, a
change of wording. For the first time the relevant section, now s 85(1), spoke
of 'any' person requiring the premium. Did the substitution of 'any' for 'a' make
all the difference, and enable the court in *Zimmerman v Grossman*[1] to reject the   **e**
authority of *Remmington v Larchin*[2]?

This was a question which, in my judgment, could have been answered either way.
Had the Rent Act 1968 been a codifying statute, as counsel for the plaintiff in
Zimmerman v Grossman[1] erroneously submitted it was, the court could have applied
its mind to the interpretation of the section unembarrassed by the case law on the
earlier legislation: see *Bank of England v Vagliano*[4]. But it is not a codifying statute: **f**
it is a consolidating statute, i e one which purports without change of the law to reduce
into one comprehensive enactment a number of previous separate enactments. In
such a statute only 'corrections and minor improvements' may be embodied:
Consolidation of Enactments (Procedure) Act 1949, s 1.

Section 2 of the 1949 Act defines corrections and minor amendments in terms which
Lawton LJ has already quoted. Reform of the law, alterations of substance, are not   **g**
to be expected in a consolidating statute. The object of such an Act is 'to reproduce
the law as it stood before': per Lord Hanworth MR in *Gilbert v Gilbert and Boucher*[5].
Accordingly, it is well settled that there is a presumption that Parliament does not
intend to alter the existing law when it enacts a consolidating statute: Maxwell,
Interpretation of Statutes, and cases there cited[6].

Of course, the presumption can be rebutted, it must yield 'to plain words to the   **h**
contrary': *Grey v Inland Revenue Comrs*, per Viscount Simonds[7]. Faced with this
issue, the court in *Zimmerman v Grossman*[1] felt itself unable to find that the change
of wording effected by s 85 of the 1968 Act was such as to rebut the presumption and to

---

1   [1971] 1 All ER 363, [1972] 1 QB 167
2   [1921] 3 KB 404, [1921] All ER Rep 298
3   [1971] 1 All ER at 369, [1972] 1 QB at 177
4   [1891] AC 107 at 145, [1891-4] All ER Rep 93 at 113
5   [1928] P 1 at 7
6   12th Edn (1969), p 21
7   [1959] 3 All ER 603 at 606, [1960] AC 1 at 13

introduce a reform of substance into the law. Bearing in mind the tenor of the
a Consolidation of Enactments (Procedure) Act 1949, I think the court was abundantly
justified in refusing to attribute to the new wording a meaning different from that
attributed to the earlier wording of the provision. It was a perfectly reasonable view
that the change of words would have to be much more drastic in character than those
in the section to enable the court to have said that Parliament had intended, in the
wrong sort of statute, to change the existing law.

b   For these reasons I am not prepared to say that *Zimmerman v Grossman*[1] was a
decision reached per incuriam and I would dismiss the appeal.

Nevertheless, I have immense sympathy with the approach of Lord Denning MR.
I decline to accept his lead only because I think it damaging to the law in the long term
—though it would undoubtedly do justice in the present case. To some it will appear
that justice is being denied by a timid, conservative adherence to judicial precedent.
c They would be wrong. Consistency is necessary to certainty—one of the great objectives of law. The Court of Appeal—at the very centre of our legal system—is responsible
for its stability, its consistency, and its predictability: see my comments in *Tiverton
Estates Ltd v Wearwell*[2]. The task of law reform, which calls for wide-ranging techniques
of consultation and discussion that cannot be compressed into the forensic medium,
is for others. The courts are not to be blamed in a case such as this. If there be blame,
d it rests elsewhere. Parliament has had since 1922 the opportunity to change the law,
but has not taken it, and cannot be thought to have taken the opportunity in the
Rent Act 1968, since to do so in that Act would involve a neglect by Parliament
itself of its own enactment (the Consolidation of Enactments (Procedure) Act 1949).
Parliament must use very plain words indeed to justify such a view of its intentions
being accepted by the courts. I happen to think that a wrong turning was taken by
e the Court of Appeal in 1921. But only the legislature, or the House of Lords in its
judicial capacity, can put the courts on what I believe to be the right road.

Appeal dismissed. Leave to appeal to the House of Lords granted.

f Solicitors: *Hutchings, Hutchings & Plum*, Torquay (for the plaintiffs); *Theodore Goddard
& Co* (for the defendant).

Wendy Shockett Barrister.

---

1   [1971] 1 All ER 363, [1972] 1 QB 167
2   [1974] 1 All ER 209 at 228, [1975] Ch 146 at 172

Re St Mary's, Broadwater

CHICHESTER CONSISTORY COURT
CHANCELLOR BUCKLE
8th NOVEMBER 1972, 4th FEBRUARY 1974

Ecclesiastical law – Faculty – Jurisdiction – Sale of chattel – Monument – Funeral accoutre-ment associated with tomb – Jousting helmet – Helmet dissociated from tomb – Jurisdiction to grant faculty – Factors governing exercise of discretion.

The rector and churchwardens of a parish, with the approval of the parochial church council, petitioned for a faculty authorising them to sell a jousting helmet said to be of late 15th or early 16th century origin which was one of the funeral accoutrements associated with the tomb of the late Thomas West, eighth Lord De La Warr, situated in the north side of the chancel in the church. Until 1969 the helmet was kept in the vestry but, when its potential value was appreciated, it was removed to a bank vault. The proposed sale was opposed by the Diocesan Art Council and indirectly by the Keeper of the Tower of London. The descendant of the eighth Lord De La Warr raised no objection to the sale. There were 2,400 people resident in the parish and attendances at the church were quite good. Apart from services, meetings of one kind or another were held every day of the week. The staff consisted of a vicar and two curates (one attached to a daughter church). The petitioners wished to extend their pastoral work within the parish and to draw more people into church activities but they were hampered partly by insufficient parochial income and partly by lack of staff. The sale of the helmet would enable them to employ another assistant curate. The cost of insuring the helmet while it was in the bank was £3. If the helmet were to be returned to the church the premiums would be between £20 and £25 and it would be a condition of the insurance policy that the helmet be suspended 15 feet from the ground and securely chained. Before its removal to the bank only one request to view the helmet had been made.

Held – (i) The ownership of the helmet was in the churchwardens who, in addition to the actual faculty, required the consent of the parochial church council to a sale (see p 149 h and p 152 j to p 153 a, post).

(ii) In the circumstances, and having regard in particular to the comparative dis-interest shown in the helmet and the fact that there had already been a dissociation of the helmet from the tomb, a faculty for its sale would be granted, such sale to take place in the open market (see p 152 a and b and p 153 c to e, post).

Notes

This case should be read in conjunction with *Re St Andrew's, Thornhaugh* p 154, post.

For faculties relating to monuments, see 14 Halsbury's Laws (4th Edn) para 1316, and for faculties relating to the contents of churches, see ibid, para 1318.

Cases referred to in judgment

St Gregory's, Tredington, Re [1971] 3 All ER 269, [1972] Fam 236, [1971] 2 WLR 796.
St Helen's, Brant Broughton, Re [1973] 3 All ER 386, [1974] Fam 16, [1973] 3 WLR 228.

Petition for faculty

By a petition dated 19th July 1969 the Rev Peter Marrow, the rector of the parish of Broadwater in the diocese of Chichester, John Dalton Symonds and Ralph Julius Vigar, the churchwardens of the parish, sought a faculty authorising the sale of a jousting helmet described as:

a
'Late XV or early XVI Century fighting helm, with reinforced escalloped edge skull-piece, rear portion fluted and pierced with four holes each side at rear of ear position. A full visor escalloped reinforcing above single viewing split. The visor's dexter side has an opening with protecting flange. The visor is secured with a latch and bolt below this aperture. The base of the backplate has been repaired at some ancient time with a bar, secured on the inside.'

b
The petition was supported by the parochial church council. The facts are set out in the judgment of the chancellor.

Robert Wakefield for the petitioners.

Cur adv vult

c
4th February 1974. **THE CHANCELLOR** read the following judgment: Application has been made by the rector, the Rev Peter Marrow, and the churchwardens of the parish of Broadwater for this court's authority to sell a jousting helmet stated in the schedule to the petition, and in a formal valuation made in 1969, to be of late 15th or early 16th century origin. The schedule and valuation gave an accurate description of the helmet but nothing, I think, turns on that as it is not a point in issue in this case.

d
The petition was unanimously supported by the parochial church council at the time the application was submitted as appears from a certificate of the rector and the then secretary, Mr R A P Mountifield, given on 18th July 1969. Before citation issued the matter was raised at a meeting of the Diocesan Art Council at the end of October 1969 when Mr Francis Steer, the council's and indeed probably the county's most distinguished antiquary, reported on the application, stating that he had made careful investigation and discovered that the helmet was almost certainly one of the

e
funeral achievements (described at the hearing as an accoutrement) of the late Thomas West, eighth Lord De La Warr[1] and one of the great historical treasures of Sussex. In the reported opinion of the Keeper of the Queen's Armoury in the Tower of London it should not be moved without the consent of the heirs of Lord De La Warr; the Keeper would oppose the faculty and, if sold, he would forbid export. After discussion the council passed the following resolution unanimously:

f
'That in the opinion of the Council the helmet should be placed on reclaimable loan at the Queen's Armoury in the Tower of London and that adequate photographs and description of the helmet should be provided and displayed at some convenient place near the tomb of the 8th Lord De La Warr',

g
which is situate on the north side of the chancel of the church.

This resolution obviously made it certain that the faculty sought would have to be moved for in open court (as would probably have been the case in any event) but first the petitioners were informed of the report and of the terms of the resolution, together with questions of my own as to ownership, valuation, reasons for sale and the proposed use of the proceeds should a sale be permitted. As to my first question I was satisfied

h
that the ownership was in the churchwardens who are 'taken, in favour of the church, to be for some purposes a kind of corporation at the common law for the conservation of the goods of the parish': see *Re St Gregory's, Tredington*[2], where this passage is cited as authority for the proposition taken from Blackstone's Commentaries[3] by the Deputy Dean of the Arches, G H Newsom QC. The answers to my other questions appear at later stages of this judgment.

j
Correspondence passed through the registry throughout 1970 between the petitioners and Mr Steer, who justifiably, particularly in view of his strong opposition to the sale, did not think it his duty to give gratuitous advice to the parish on whom rested, as

---

1 Died 11th October 1525
2 [1971] 3 All ER 269 at 272, [1972] Fam 236 at 240
3 Blackstone's Commentaries (8th Edn, 1778), vol 1, p 394

he rightly said, the onus of proof of their right through lawful means to dispose of the helmet. All that really transpired was that the present Lord De La Warr would raise *a* no objection to the sale and that the petitioners were determined to bring their application before the court notwithstanding the Art Council's opposition. Accordingly I ordered that citation issue on 7th December 1970 and asked whether the Art Council would wish to be heard in court and if so through whom. The answers were, predictably, Yes, and that they would wish to be heard through Mr Steer. This being so I saw no point in asking the archdeacon to intervene (c f *Re St Gregory's, Tredington*[1]) or, *b* in view of the strong opposition to be expressed by Mr Steer and, indirectly, by the Keeper of the Tower, to refer the matter for further advice to the Central Council for the Care of Churches (the name of the council at the time, now the Council for Places of Worship). At the time of this invitation I also asked whether in view of its expressed importance in Sussex history the council knew whether any museum, body of trustees or the like within the county was known to be interested in purchasing the helmet to *c* which the reply, the answer of the council's secretary, Canon M C Langton, was that only the Keeper of Armour in the Tower was known to be interested if any question of purchase were to arise: no other interested person etc was known. For a variety of reasons it was not convenient to all concerned to bring on the hearing, which took place at Broadwater, until November 1972. At the hearing the applicants were represented by counsel and Mr Steer kindly gave me every assistance as judge's *d* witness pursuant to r 6 of the Faculty Jurisdiction Rules 1967[2]. Under r 6(3) I had put the following questions to him: (i) Do you approve of the proposed sale or not? (ii) If Yes, do you think there is any likely recipient within the county who would be interested in acquiring it (i e the helmet) in view of its local importance? (iii) If not, please give your reasons against its disposal? It will be seen that there is some duplication in these questions with those raised in the correspondence but the rules require *e* the chancellor to ask them so that the witness may be cross-examined on his answers.

Beyond a brief reference to *Re St Gregory's, Tredington*[3] by counsel for the petitioners (see now also *Re St Helen's, Brant Broughton*[4]) the question of jurisdiction was not argued, nor could it be in a court of first instance. But counsel for the petitioners did deduce from the *Tredington* case[3] three possible types of application with which the court could find itself confronted: (a) The disposal of an item given or acquired for use as in *f* church plate cases where the court would properly feel severely restricted in the exercise of its jurisdiction; my note of his argument does not state whether this 'severe restriction' applied only where the object was still being used for its original purpose and the point was not elaborated, but for myself I would have thought that in certain circumstances the severity could properly be relaxed as the law stands at present. However this was not an example within case (a). (b) The disposal of a paint- *g* ing or antique furnishing especially given for use in a church; in such a case the court would be circumscribed by the donor's wishes. I would have taken issue with counsel for the petitioners on many of such cases but again he was not faced with such a case as on any view this helmet, whatever its intrinsic worth 500 years ago or now, could not be put forward as anything other than a personal memorial, albeit of great histori-cal and, as Mr Steer would argue, artisitic merit. (c) The disposal of an item not given *h* for use and with no expressed wish or where the wish is not known; in these cases the court has a freer hand in exercising its discretion and it was not necessary to find that a financial or other emergency for disposal exists in the parish. This, submitted counsel for the petitioners, was such a case. As will appear however, he submitted that there was such a crisis 'in the sense that despite enjoying, or rather in the main having earned, a fairly substantial income, the extension of pastoral work within the *j*

---

1 [1971] 3 All ER 269 at 271, [1972] Fam 236 at 239, 240
2 SI 1967 No 1002
3 [1971] 3 All ER 269, [1972] Fam 236
4 [1973] 3 All ER 386, [1974] Fam 16

parish was hampered for lack of staff and the proceeds of sale of this helmet would
a make the employment of such a person possible or possible without subsidy.

Whether or not the first two of these propositions were entirely acceptable to Mr
Steer, or acceptable with qualifications, were not matters to which it was necessary
for him to advert as they did not affect his case against the sale. One may infer,
however, that he did not find proposition (c) acceptable. His answers to my three
questions were broadly speaking as follows: (i) I disapprove of the disposal of the
b helmet. (ii) and (iii) One should not dissociate associated objects, whether they are
commemorative of persons or events or not. This helmet formed part of the funeral
accoutrements which would be associated with his tomb. In a case such as that of a
De La Warr, the funeral would be modelled on that of a state funeral. The helmet
would have been suspended above the tomb as in the case of the Black Prince in
Canterbury; the helmet was nevertheless, or perhaps therefore, an integral part of
c the tomb and should not be dissociated from it, least of all in the case of the Broadwater tomb. There are other examples in Sussex but this is of a different type. For a
deal of his research Mr Steer relied on the careful historical research of the late William
Burgess (1827-81) which he clearly trusted as authentic (as I do) and an article of his
'The Tomb and Helm of Thomas La Warre, in the Church of Broadwater, Sussex':
see the Archaeological Journal, Vol 36 (1879). All in all, security apart, there was no
d distinction between an object given for use and an object associated with the memorial
itself.

All this evidence, from Mr Steer's standpoint, I accept and nothing in his cross-
examination threw doubt on its credibility. He said he did not want the helmet to go
to the Tower and objected to a sale to the Tower. He would, however, prefer to see
it go on loan (as distinct from a sale) rather than that it should be sold. So far as
e security was concerned the helmet could be covered in a glass case and an alarm system installed. He did not deal with details of cost but such precaution might well
reduce the cost of insurance. I have taken Mr Steer's evidence out of the order in
which the case proceeded before me but it seemed to me more convenient to compare
his approach at the outset with the submissions of counsel for the petitioners. In so
doing, however, I do not think I have done his case any injustice.

f I now turn to the evidence called in support of the application. First counsel for
the petitioners called the rector, Mr Marrow, Mr Henry John Millidge, the treasurer for
18 years, and, very briefly, Mr Ralph Julius Vigar, a churchwarden and co-petitioner.
I must deal with these now in their turn.

First Mr Marrow, who is the rector of Broadwater, which also contains the daughter
church of St Stephen, informed me that there were approximately 24,000 persons
g residing in the parish. Five services were held every Sunday at the parish church
when the attendances were 'quite good'. There were also four services at St Stephen's.
In addition there were many occasional services and church activities for persons of
all ages in connection with the church. Meetings of one kind or the other were held
every day of the week. The staff consisted, besides himself, of two curates (one attached to St Stephen's) and a parish worker. For a parish with such a population there
h was a definite need for more people to help and the present staff just could not visit
properly. It was partly a matter of money and his main need now was the help of
another assistant curate but the difficulty was lack of sufficient parochial income. I
pause to note that in the accounts for the year ended on 31st December 1971 the
assistant clergy fund received diocesan grants of over £1,300.

As to the helmet itself, this had been in the church, kept in the vestry, until 1969 as
j its potential value had not been realised. In that year as I recall from personal attendance at a visitation in each archdeaconry, the question of theft of armour was specifically dealt with at the request of the Ecclesiastical Insurance Office which was
alarmed at the amount of theft and the quite inadequate cover and protection hitherto
adopted. The office specifically suggested to Mr Marrow that the helmet be formally
valued by a firm in Lewes. I do not think it is desirable to state in a public document

the sum mentioned then to be involved, but Mr Marrow and his parochial church
council thought, as a result, that it would be irresponsible (his word) to keep the **a**
helmet at risk. Up to the recent past it has, therefore, been kept in the vaults of a
bank at a modest premium. The rector only recalled one request to view the helmet
by the Victoria and Albert Museum prior to the deposit and there had been none
since. This comparative disinterest in no way invalidates Mr Steer's point but it does
weigh in the balance when one views the practicalities of the matter. The rector,
therefore, wanted a sale even at 1969 prices, and as his and Mr Steer's views were **b**
poles apart, nothing worthwhile could be expected to emerge from the opportunity
I afforded Mr Steer to cross-examine this witness.

I next heard Mr Millidge who is responsible for the accounts of both churches. He
produced the latest set of duly audited accounts. These were set out in extremely
clear form, differentiating between the two churches and the various sub-accounts
connected with each, some funds being handled by sub-treasurers to whom credit **c**
is also due. It is clearly a most time-consuming task and I have found the accountancy
generally, and the summary, of the greatest assistance in understanding the economics
of this case.

Mr Millidge told me that over the years there had been a small decrease in church
attendances but that giving was generous. Dealing specifically with the assistant clergy
account he told me that the relevant figures of payment to this account (which the **d**
proceeds of this sale are intended to benefit) over recent years were as follows:
1970, £3,664; 1971 (produced), £3,839; 1972, £3,900; 1973 (then estimated and probably
still not certain), £4,500. (Collections on the first Sunday in each month are allocated
to this fund.) I learnt a good deal also on matters not really relevant to recount but
they all filled in the picture of a parish which really tries, but the crux of the matter
is that to draw more people into the fold and interests of the church some staff are **e**
needed even if this consists basically of one more curate. Mr Millidge assured me that
this was the view of the parochial church council. He supported the application as
perhaps, with respect, one expects an honorary treasurer to do.

Last of the witnesses was Mr Vigar. He produced a letter from the Ecclesiastical
Insurance Office which I think has been mistakenly withdrawn from my papers. It
was a quotation as to comparative costs of insurance and for the present purpose I accept **f**
the figures given to me by counsel for the petitioners. As I have said, insurance in the bank
costs just £3. The premium to restore the helmet to the church would be about
£20-£25. Apart from the further risk of casual vandalism in regard to other articles
in the church if the helmet were restored, the Ecclesiastical Insurance Office also
require as a condition of insurance that the helmet be suspended 15 feet from the
ground and securely chained so that the helmet is at some distance from the naked **g**
eye.

That then is the petitioners' case and I have already stated Mr Steer's. One now
reaches the dilemma as to which view should prevail in the individual circumstances
of this case. In my experience there are rarely any rights or wrongs in the views held
by those who apply for faculties of this kind and those who, having a different
approach, think it is their duty to record their opposition, whether strictly as parties **h**
opponent or as statutory advisers from whom the judge seeks advice. If I refuse this
faculty I cannot order the petitioners to restore the helmet: they are only bound to
do so if they have been convinced by the opposing evidence that they ought to do so.
They also require in addition to the actual faculty the consent of the parochial church
council as successors to the vestry so that dual authority for disposal is required: see
the passages from Sir Robert Phillimore's work[1], The Ecclesiastical Law of the Church **j**
of England, cited for easier reference in the Tredington case[2]. With the necessary
faculty and consent (the latter no doubt being forthcoming still), a sale would be

---

1   (1873), vol II, p 1797
2   [1971] 3 All ER 269 at 272, [1972] Fam 236 at 240

possible and it would not matter in which order the necessary authorities were given:
a c f *Re St Helen's, Brant Broughton*[1] when first heard by the late Dean of the Arches,
Dr W S Wigglesworth (and I think binding). If they accept the opposition case they
would have to re-associate the helmet with the tomb at the cost and risk I have
mentioned. I would not like to say they would be wrong to do so, and no blame could
attach to them if things turned out against them: c f *Re St Helen's, Brant Broughton*[2]
at first instance in the Consistory Court of Lincoln, cited with approval on appeal.
b However what I am saying is that I cannot force the petitioners to do as Mr Steer
would wish. It is for them, with the parochial church council, to decide whether to
accept Mr Steer's point of view or not. This acceptance as I say carries an element of
risk which, with all the conditions involved, the petitioners may not be willing to
take.

I have stated Mr Steer's case and on the other side of the coin I cannot force his view
c on the petitioners either. The weakness of his case, I thought, was that in the most
honest manner he had to admit that dissociation had already taken place. On the
whole I think I ought to grant the faculty sought as prayed and it will be for the
petitioners, with the parochial church council's consent, to act on its authority or not.

I may say that the price likely to be obtained now on the open market is likely to
be considerably higher than that previously envisaged and I have ascertained that the
d Tower of London is unlikely to be able to meet it. I had thought that that would at
least have been a reasonable compromise but it is unlikely to come about.

For the reasons I have tried to express, I propose to authorise a sale on the open
market by auction by Messrs Sotheby & Co with a reserve price agreed by that firm
with the registrar or, in the unlikely event of their disagreement, by reference to
myself. The registrar will fix any other arrangements he thinks necessary to facilitate
e the sale at the best price in the short time available. The petitioners will pay all due
court costs of and incidental to the hearing and the final resolution of the matter,
these being recouped to them out of the net proceeds of sale in due course.

The proceeds of sale will be applied first in recouping to the petitioners such court
costs and also the taxed costs of the petitioners of the hearing and of the costs and
expenses of Mr Steer.
f Subject as aforesaid the proceeds of sale are to be paid to the registrar of the diocese
for investment pending the transfer of such proceeds to Chichester Diocesan Board of
Finance which is to invest the money, with power from time to time to vary investments, and to pay the income to the Broadwater parochial church council for or
towards the stipend of the new assistant curate whom the parochial church council
must undertake to secure as aforesaid. Subject as aforesaid any surplus income shall
g be paid to the parochial church council for its general purposes or, in priority thereto,
for any purpose within the parish of Broadwater which the board may think to be
more useful in pastoral work within the parish. For this purpose I think the board of
finance ought to be joined as a party (without cost to the board) both as proposed
recipient of the purchase money and as an acknowledgement that it accepts the trusts
proposed. The Archdeacon of Chichester may also apply to be joined to enable him
h to intervene if necessary to secure the due execution of this order if its authority is
acted on. Further as managing trustees of the fund the parochial church council
should be joined and not merely consent.

Finally all parties are to have liberty to apply for further directions as they may
severally be advised. In particular I have in mind that a moderate sum of capital may
be required to find a home for any new curate and his family. I give this as an example
j which I would be willing to entertain should application be made for the purpose by
the persons involved.

I want to say just a short word as to the Art Council's part in this affair. There is no

---

1 [1973] 3 All ER 386 at 388, [1974] Fam 16 at 17
2 [1973] 3 All ER 386 at 389, [1974] Fam 16 at 19, 20

question of their being brought into disrepute because I have not followed their
advice simpliciter. The council's functions are laid down by statute and I seek their   *a*
advice which is nearly always followed or an accommodation reached through their
efforts. I have the same functions and others and occasionally the priorities compete.
In such cases I must judge which should prevail; one side or the other cannot attain
the end it would in all sincerity seek to achieve.

Faculty granted.   *b*

Solicitors: *Lee, Bolton & Lee* (for the petitioners).

Mary Rose Plummer Barrister.

c

Re St Andrew's, Thornhaugh

PETERBOROUGH CONSISTORY COURT
CHANCELLOR FITZWALTER BUTLER   *d*
29th APRIL, 4th JUNE 1975

*Ecclesiastical law – Faculty – Jurisdiction – Sale of chattel – Monument – Funeral accoutre-
ment associated with tomb – Ownership – Consent of owner to sale – Owner not traced –
Whether court having jurisdiction to grant faculty authorising sale – Faculty Jurisdiction*   *e*
Measure 1964, s 3.

*Ecclesiastical law – Faculty – Sale of chattel – Factors governing exercise of discretion –
Article in nature of national treasure and of high intrinsic quality – Financial needs of
church – Absence of any urgent and expensive requirement of funds for repair of church –
Article forming part of funeral accoutrements associated with tomb in church – Whether*   *f*
faculty should be granted.

The petitioners, the rector and churchwardens of a small village church, petitioned
for a faculty to authorise them to sell a helmet dating from 1520-30 which for many
years had hung some 12 feet above the tomb of Sir William Russell, the first Duke of
Bedford, in the south transept of the church. Sir William was a distinguished soldier
of the Elizabethan age and his tomb dated from a period soon after his death in 1613.   *g*
It appeared that the helmet had been preserved by Sir William to form part of
the accoutrements of his tomb. It was complete and a very good specimen. The
church itself was of considerable architectural and historical interest. An extensive
restoration of the church had been effected between 1884 and 1889 and it was in a
very good state of repair. The outstanding object of interest in the church was the
Russell tomb which had recently been cleaned and restored at the expense of the   *h*
Bedford family. The motive of the petitioners in wishing to sell the helmet was
to husband all the resources committed to their charge. They pointed out that
in 1974 for the first time the parish had failed to find its diocesan quota and the budget
forecast for 1975 indicated a substantial deficit. It was expected that a sale of the
helmet would realise from £700 to £1,000 and the petitioners suggested that a
replica could be provided out of the proceeds of sale and that the balance of the   *j*
money should be used to create a fabric fund, the capital of which would not be
used, and that the interested parties should be notified of the proposed sale and
given the opportunity of taking steps for the helmet to be preserved for the national
heritage. They also emphasised the danger to which an object such as the helmet
must always be exposed when left in a church which was normally unlocked.

Held – (i) The court had no jurisdiction to grant the faculty sought for the following
a reasons—
(a) The ownership of the monument and its accoutrements remained in the heir-at-
law to Sir William. Accordingly at common law the court had no jurisdiction to
grant a faculty for the sale of the helmet (see p 160 *a* and *b*, post).
(b) Since no evidence had been adduced as to who was the heir-at-law of Sir
William the court had no material on which to exercise its jurisdiction under s 3
b of the Faculty Jurisdiction Measure 1964 to grant the faculty sought (see p 160 *f*, post).
Re St Mary's, Broadwater p 148, ante, considered.
(ii) Assuming however that the court had jurisdiction to grant the faculty sought,
it should be extremely cautious in directing the sale of anything in the nature of a
national treasure, particularly if the article (as in the present case) was of high intrinsic
quality and perhaps almost unique in its design, although that factor could never
c be a conclusive basis for a decision of a court. If a parish were suddenly faced with an
urgent and expensive requirement for the repair of its church it might be proper
to order the sale of a valued artistic or historical treasure, but no need for serious,
urgent or expensive repairs had arisen in the instant case and the church was in good
general condition. The helmet had for centuries occupied the same place in the
church and Sir William's intention had clearly been that it should form part of the
d accoutrements of his tomb. As a matter of principle a monument and its accoutrements should be regarded as one entity and a case in which justification could be
found for the separation by an order for sale of an accoutrement would be exceptional.
security posed no problem and in the circumstances a faculty for the sale of the
helmet should in any event be refused (see p 161 *b* to *j*, post).
Re St Mary's, Westwell [1968] 1 All ER 631 and *Re St Gregory's, Tredington* [1971] 3
e All ER 269 distinguished.

Notes

Section 3 of the Faculty Jurisdiction Measure 1964 applies only to faculties for the
'moving, demolition, alteration or execution of other work' to monuments (see
s 3(1)) and it would seem therefore that the court has no jurisdiction under s 3 to
f grant a faculty authorising the sale of a monument or its accoutrements in a case
where the owner withholds his consent or cannot be found.
For property in monuments, see 14 Halsbury's Laws (4th Edn) para 1085, and for
cases on the subject, see 19 Digest (Repl) 494, 3234-3236.
For faculties relating to monuments, see 14 Halsbury's Laws (4th Edn) para 1316,
and for faculties relating to the contents of churches, see ibid para 1318.
g For the Faculty Jurisdiction Measure 1964, s 3, see 10 Halsbury's Statutes (3rd Edn)
307.

Cases referred to in judgment

Corven's Case (1612) 12 Co Rep 105, 77 ER 1380, sub nom *Garven & Pym's Case*, Godb
199, sub nom *Pym v Gorwyn*, Moore KB 878, 19 Digest (Repl) 496, 3279.
h *St Gregory's, Tredington, Re* [1971] 3 All ER 269, [1972] Fam 236, [1971] 2 WLR 796.
St Helen's, Brant Broughton, Re [1973] 3 All ER 386, [1974] Fam 16, [1973] 3 WLR 228.
St Mary's, Broadwater, Re, p 148, ante.
St Mary's, Westwell [1968] 1 All ER 631, [1968] 1 WLR 513, Digest (Cont Vol C) 308,
3717*b*.
Wyche's (Lady) Case (1469) YB 9 Edw IV, fo 14, pl 8, sub nom *Gray's (Lady) Case*,
j cited in Moore KB at 878, 7 Digest (Repl) 564, 158.

Petition for faculty

The Rev G H Bradshaw, rector of the parish of Thornhaugh, in the diocese of Peterborough, Mr A Walker and Mr G White, the churchwardens of the parish, petitioned
for a faculty authorising the sale of a helmet which for many years had hung above

the tomb of Baron Russell of Thornhaugh, first Duke of Bedford, in the south transept
of the church. The petition was opposed by the Ven the Archdeacon of Oakham on   *a*
behalf of the Diocesan Advisory Committee, Mr A R Dufty, CBE, FSA, Master of
the Armouries in Her Majesty's Tower of London, Mrs Dorothy Ellison, a parishioner
resident in the parish of Thornhaugh, and the Very Rev the Dean of Peterborough
on behalf of the Church of England Council for Places of Worship. The facts are set
out in the judgment of the chancellor.

b

The petitioners and the objectors appeared in person.

Cur adv vult

4th June. **THE CHANCELLOR** read the following judgment: The petitioners
are the rector and churchwardens of the parish of St Andrew, Thornhaugh in the
diocese of Peterborough and they seek by their petition a faculty for the sale of a   *c*
helmet which for many years has hung above the tomb of Sir William Russell
(described in the petition as Baron Russell of Thornhaugh, first Duke of Bedford)
in the south transept of the church. The objectors are the Ven the Archdeacon of
Oakham (on behalf of the Diocesan Advisory Committee), Mr A R Dufty, CBE,
FSA, Master of the Armouries in Her Majesty's Tower of London, Mrs Dorothy
Ellison, a parishioner resident in the parish of Thornhaugh, and the Very Rev the   *d*
Dean of Peterborough (on behalf of the Church of England Council for Places of
Worship). The case for the petitioners was presented by Mr D O Powell, a parishioner
of Thornhaugh, who gave evidence himself and called in support of the petition the
rector, the Rev G H Bradshaw. All the objectors gave evidence in support of their
objections.
   Thornhaugh is a small village situated about eight miles from Peterborough and   *e*
about half a mile from the Great North Road. It has a small church of considerable
architectural merit and historical interest. The church consists of a small but broad
chancel, a high nave, a north aisle and vestry, a south transept, south porch and
western tower. Both the nave and the chancel (though the latter was much altered
in the 15th century) contain interesting features of transitional or early English work.
It seems probable that at some time about the 15th century the tower fell and crushed   *f*
the south arcade of the nave, with the result that the present south wall (which contains a fine perpendicular window) and the present transept and porch were built.
An extensive restoration of the church took place between 1884 and 1889. The church
at the time of the last quinquennial survey and today is in very good condition and
when I visited it I was impressed by the care that is obviously bestowed on its maintenance and appearance, and this I venture to hope will always be continued. The   *g*
outstanding object of interest is the Russell tomb in the south transept.
   Sir William Russell's recumbent effigy in armour lies on the tomb between four
obelisks at the corners. At his foot kneels his page and behind his head is a cartouche
bearing his coats of arms. The kneeling figures of his three sons and three daughters
are on opposite sides of the tomb. Until recently removed the helmet hung some
twelve feet above the tomb. Sir William was a distinguished soldier of the Elizabethan   *h*
age. When the Duke of Alençon came to this country as a suitor for the hand of the
Queen, he challenged a number of English knights to combat in a tourney with
French knights. Sir William was one of the first pair of knights chosen to uphold the
English honour. On that occasion the helmet which is the subject of the present
proceedings was displayed before his pavilion. It almost certainly is of earlier date
than the time of Sir William, and it seems tolerably certain that it was preserved by   *j*
him to form part of the accoutrements of his tomb. He died in 1613 and the tomb
dates from a period soon after his death. Not very much is known about his character
and personality, except that he was a comrade-in-arms and close friend of Sir Philip
Sidney, who left him a valuable suit of gilt armour which did not include the helmet
which is the subject of these proceedings. The poet Shelley has well described Sir

Philip Sidney as 'sublimely mild, a spirit without spot' and it is fair to assume, there-
a fore, that his close friend Sir William Russell, too, must have been a noble and
upright man, whom posterity should delight to honour. The tomb fortunately
escaped the ravages of the Civil War and, despite some slight damage to some of the
effigies, remains today in good condition. It was cleaned and restored at the expense
of the Bedford family comparatively recently. Early in 1974 the helmet was taken
down from its place without any legal authority, placed in a carrying box and con-
b veyed to Messrs Sotheby's in London for the purpose of an estimate of its value
being obtained. A little time before the hearing it was brought back to Peterborough
and was displayed in court during the hearing. For the time being it is in a secure
place of custody.

Mr Powell, in presenting the case for the petitioners, emphasised that their motives
were not wanton nor based on thoughtless fund raising, but on a determination
c carefully to husband all the resources committed to the charge of the rector and
churchwardens of Thornhaugh Church. I entirely accept their bona fides and am of
opinion that forethought and care were devoted to the preparation of their case and
that the presentation of it displayed lucidity, moderation and fairness. Mr Powell
called my attention to the fact that in 1974 for the first time the parish of Thornhaugh
(the benefice of which is united to that of Wansford) failed to find its diocesan quota
d and that the budget forecast for 1975 indicated a substantial deficit. He estimated
that the sale of the helmet through the medium of Messrs Sotheby might be expected
to realise from £700 to £1,000. He quite rightly, in my view, emphasised the danger
to which an object of this kind must always be exposed when left in a church which
is normally kept unlocked—as one would wish that all churches should be during
the day. He himself suggested that, if I saw fit to grant this application, the petitioners
e would be willing that the following conditions should be attached to the faculty:
(i) that a worthy replica of the helmet should be provided out of the proceeds of
the sale; (ii) that the balance should be used to create a fabric fund, the capital of
which would not be used; (iii) that before disposal of the helmet took place, a parish
meeting should be called at which the intention of the petitioners would be explained;
and (iv) that interested parties should be informed of the proposed sale and given
f the opportunity of taking steps for the helmet to be preserved for the national
heritage.

The Ven the Archdeacon of Oakham, in presenting the objection of the Diocesan
Advisory Committee, called my attention to the committee's general policy with
regard to the sale of 'national treasures' and contended that the church should be
considered as the custodian rather than the owner of such. While agreeing that in
g an extreme case when a poor parish was suddenly faced with a serious, urgent and
expensive problem of repair for its church, it might be necessary to support the sale
of a treasure such as this helmet, he contended that the facts of the present case are
very different in that Thornhaugh Church was in a good state of repair and was not
threatened with any emergency. He stressed the aesthetic and historical considerations which arose in this case, that the helmet was part of the whole memorial, form-
h ing a kind of crown to the setting; and that there was a real danger that the helmet
might easily, if sold, disappear into some private collection and its place as part of
the national heritage be lost for ever. While appreciating the security risk, he thought
that the helmet if secured by a chain and sited 12-15 feet above ground, would not
be easy to steal.

Mr Dufty stated that his views were supported by the Society of Antiquaries of
j London and the Victoria and Albert Museum. He said that no application for assistance in the maintenance of the tomb had been received by the Armouries of the
Tower. In his view, the tomb and its accoutrements should be regarded as belonging
together, as both must have been together accepted by the church. The helmet
which was the subject of these proceedings dated from about 1520-30, was complete
and a very fine specimen. It was quite normal for helmets to be of earlier date than

the monument of which they formed part. The security of the helmet in question did not present any unusually difficult problems. He knew only of three applications *a* for the sale of helmets, only one of which, *Re St Mary's, Broadwater*[1], to which I shall refer later in this judgment, was successful.

Mrs Dorothy Ellison said that at the meeting of the parochial church council when the question of the sale of the helmet was discussed she had voted against the proposal. She emphasised the fact that there were no immediate structural requirements of the church and that the helmet should be regarded as part of the heritage of the *b* community of Thornhaugh.

The Very Rev the Dean of Peterborough also dealt with the question of security. His council would resist the suggestion of replacing the helmet, where it hung in the church, with a fibreglass or other replica. Even if the difference would be difficult to detect from ground level, there would be something fraudulent in the deliberate action of replacing the genuine by a substitute; and, only if the genuine article were *c* lost through theft, should a substitute replace it. In the view of his committee, articles placed in the church constituted a trust. Whoever erected the monument and placed the helmet above it did so in the confident expectation that both would remain there undisturbed. The helmet and the monument below it now formed part of our national cultural heritage.

Having summarised the evidence and the arguments presented to me, I must now *d* indicate the issues which I have to decide. They appear to me to be twofold. The first is whether I have jurisdiction to grant the faculty sought by the petitioners. The second is whether, if I have jurisdiction, I ought on the merits of the case to make an order in favour of the petitioners. In order to decide the first question, it is necessary that I should come to a firm conclusion on the ownership of the helmet. There appears to be no modern authority relating to church monuments and their *e* accoutrements and my researches into the law have carried me back many centuries. I do derive valuable assistance from Coke's observations in his Institutes[2]. The relevant observations are set out also in Phillimore's Ecclesiastical Law[3]. Coke says[2]:

> 'Concerning the building or erecting of tombs, sepulchres or monuments for *f* the deceased in church, chancell, common chapell, or churchyard in convenient manner, it is lawfull, for it is the last work of charity that can be done for the deceased, who while he lived was a lively temple of the Holy Ghost, with a reverend regard, and Christian hope of a joyfull resurrection [words which, I trust, may appropriately be related to Sir William Russell]. And the defacing of them is punishable by the common law, as it appeareth in the book of 9 E. 4.14 *g* (the *Lady Wiche's* case[4], wife of Sir Hugh Wiche). And so it was agreed by the whole court, Mich 10 Jac 1, in the common [pleas] between Corven and Pym[5] . . . And for the defacing thereof, they that build or erect the same shall have the action during their lives, (as the Lady Wiche had in the case of 9 E. 4[4]) and after their deceases, the heir of the deceased shall have the action.'

The report of *Lady Wyche's* case[4] in the Year Book tells us:

> '. . . the lady brought a bill in the King's Bench against a parson, quare unam *h* tunicam vocatam, a coat armour, and pennons with the arms of the late Sir Hugh Wyche her husband, and a sword, in a chapel where he was buried. And the parson claimed them as oblations, and that therefore they did belong to him;

---

1 Page 148, ante
2 3 Co Inst 202
3 2nd Edn (1895), vol 1, p 691
4 *Lady Wyche's Case* (1469) YB 9 Edw 4, fo 14, pl 8
5 *Corven's Case* (1612) 12 Co Rep 105

and there it is holden . . . the parson cannot claim them as oblations, neither ought
he to have said things, for that they were hanged there in honour of the deceased
and therefore for the same reason, although a gravestone, coat of armour, tomb
etc. are annexed to the freehold of the parson, yet in regard the church is free
to all the inhabitants for burying the parson cannot take them. And the Chief
Justice said that the lady might have a good action during her life because she
herself caused the said things to be set up there and after her death the heir to
the deceased shall also have his action because that (as the book says) they were
hanged there for the honour of his ancestor. Therefore they are in the nature
of heirlooms, which by the common law belong to the heir, as being the
principal of the family.'

To Coke's report of *Corven's Case*[1] and also in Phillimore's Ecclesiastical Law[2], there
is appended a useful note indicating the opinion of Dr Gibson, a luminary of former
days in matters of ecclesiastical law, which is to the same effect. He states[3]:

'Monuments, Coart-Armour and other Ensigns of Honour, set up in memory
of the Deceased, may not be removed at the pleasure of the Ordinary or Incumbent. On the contrary, if either they, or any other Person, shall take away or
deface them, the Person who set them up, shall have an Action against them
during his life, and after his death, the Heir of the deceased shall have the same,
who (as they say) is inheritable to Arms, etc. as to Heir-looms; and it avails not,
that they are annext to the Freehold, tho' that is in the Parson.'

In my view the legal position with regard to rights in a monument is concisely and
correctly summarised in Halsbury's Laws of England[4]: 'Under modern law rights
in a monument presumably pass to the person entitled under the will or intestacy
of the person who set it up.' During the hearing the Dean of Peterborough called
my attention to a recent opinion of the Legal Advisory Commission of the General
Synod that a monument in a church is the property of the person erecting it and
thereafter of the heir or heirs-at-law of the person commemorated and cited
Elphinstone, Parish Property[5], and the definition of 'owner' in s 3(4) of the Faculty
Jurisdiction Measure 1964, to which I must further refer in a moment, which provides:
' "Owner" means the person who erected the monument in question and, after his
death, the heir or heirs at law of the person or persons in whose memory the monument was erected.' The only indication which I have been able to find of a contrary
view with regard to the ownership of a church monument or its accoutrements is in
the judgment of Chancellor Buckle in *Re St Mary's, Broadwater*[6] decided by him
in 1974.

In that case the heir-at-law appears to have been identified and consulted and it
was generally accepted that he was completely disinterested in the helmet of his
ancestor. I have had the advantage of seeing a transcript of Chancellor Buckle's
judgment, in which he granted the petition for a faculty for the sale of the helmet
in the open market. He does not appear to have based his decision on an 'implied
consent' to the sale having been given by the heir-at-law, but rather on the basis
that, as the heir-at-law had abjured all interest in the helmet, the ownership of it
had devolved on the churchwardens as customary owners of the movable goods and
ornaments in a church. I find the assimilation of the accoutrements of a monument
to an article such as church plate a little difficult to follow, but I hesitate to criticise

1   (1612) 12 Co Rep 105
2   2nd Edn (1895), vol 1, pp 691, 692
3   Gibson's Codex Juris Ecclasiastici Anglicani (2nd Edn, 1761), vol 1, pp 453, 454
4   13 Halsbury's Laws (3rd Edn) 389, para 872; cf 14 Halsbury's Laws (4th Edn) para 1085,
    footnote 4
5   Handbook of Parish Property (1973), p 6
6   Page 148, ante

any expression of opinion by the very experienced chancellor in the absence of a full
report of the case. I have, however, no hesitation in holding as a matter of law that *a*
the ownership of the monument in Thornhaugh Church to Sir William Russell
and of all its accoutrements remains in the heir-at-law to Sir William. I am satisfied that at common law I accordingly would have no jurisdiction to grant the petition
by the rector and churchwardens for the sale of the helmet but I must now turn my
attention to my powers under the Faculty Jurisdiction Measure 1964. Section 3
provides: *b*

'(2) . . . a court may grant a faculty to which this section applies:—although
the owner of the monument withholds his consent thereto or cannot be found
after reasonable efforts to find him have been made . . .
'(3) No faculty to which this section applies shall be granted if the owner of
the monument in question withholds his consent thereto but satisfies the court *c*
that he is, within a reasonable time, willing and able to remove the monument
. . . and to execute such works as the court may require to repair any damage
to the fabric.'

Before I could exercise jurisdiction under this section, the petitioners would have to
satisfy me either that the owner of the monument could not be found after reasonable
efforts to find him had been made—a burden I feel could not, in any event, have *d*
been discharged by them—or in the alternative that the owner of the monument
had withheld his consent to the removal. No evidence was adduced before me as to
who is the heir-at-law to Sir William Russell. I have seen a letter addressed to the
rector suggesting that the present Duke of Bedford claims to be the heir-at-law.
This may well be the case, but I cannot assume this without any kind of evidence
having been adduced at the hearing. If the present duke is the heir-at-law, it may *e*
well be that he would oust my jurisdiction to order a sale of the helmet in the open
market by evidence that he was prepared to move it to his collection at Woburn
Abbey. These are, however, matters of conjecture; and as no evidence has been
given at the hearing on which I could exercise jurisdiction under s 3 of the 1964
measure, I hold that on that ground also I have no jurisdiction in the present case *f*
to grant the faculty which is sought.

I do not think, however, that I ought to leave the matter there and it would, in
my opinion, be more satisfactory if I were to state the principles that I would apply
in deciding the petition on the merits and on the assumption (contrary to what I have
already held) that I have jurisdiction to deal with it. I accept the general submission
made on behalf of the Diocesan Advisory Committee that a court should be extremely
cautious in directing the sale of anything in the nature of a national treasure, particu- *g*
larly if the article (as in this case) is of high intrinsic quality and perhaps almost
unique in its design. I bear in mind the submission made by Mr Powell on behalf of
petitioners in his final speech that regard must be had to the worship, mission and
ministerial needs of the church from which it is desired to remove the treasure.
Indeed the Archdeacon of Oakham on behalf of the Diocesan Advisory Committee *h*
conceded that the high artistic or historical value of the object concerned can never
be a conclusive basis for the decision of a court and that there may be cases where a
parish which was paying its way but has very little to spare is suddenly faced with an
urgent and expensive requirement for the repair of its church and where it would be
proper in those circumstances to order the sale of a valued artistic or historical
treasure. That principle I hold to be right and one properly to be applied in deciding
an application of this kind. In Re St Mary's, Westwell[1] Lord Dunboyne, Commissary- *j*
General, in granting a faculty for the sale of two livery pots formerly used as communion vessels, said[2]: 'I am persuaded that nothing but the sale of the flagons will

1   [1968] 1 All ER 631, [1968] 1 WLR 513
2   [1968] 1 All ER at 634, [1968] 1 WLR at 517

save the church from deteriorating beyond repair.' In *Re St Gregory's, Tredington*[1],
a where the Deputy Dean of Arches overruled the decision of Chancellor Gage and
allowed the sale of two silver flagons formerly used as communion vessels, the
evidence was that the church was in a serious state of disrepair and was faced with a
financial emergency caused by the condition of the fabric. I believe that nothing in
this present judgment conflicts with any general principle laid down by the learned
deputy dean in giving the decision of the Court of Arches, but I distinguish on their
b facts both of the cases which I have just mentioned from the present case in which
the undisputed evidence is that no need for serious, urgent or expensive repairs has
arisen and that the church is in good general condition.

Further, in both cases to which I have just referred stress was laid on the fact that
the objects which it was desired to sell, though in the distant past they had been
used as communion vessels, had long ceased to be used as such and had for many
c years been removed from the church and placed in a bank or other surroundings for
safe deposit and that there was no proposal that they should be brought back to the
church or restored to their original use. In the present case the helmet has for centuries until very recently occupied the same place in the church and will be returned
to that place if I refuse to grant a faculty for its sale. This consideration too
distinguishes the present case from the cases I have cited.

d As I have already indicated, apart from *Re St Mary's, Broadwater*[2], I can discover
no case in which the sale of a monument or an accoutrement of a monument has
been ordered. I hold that as a matter of principle a monument and its accoutrements
should be regarded as one entity and that a case in which justification could be found
for their separation by an order for the sale of an accoutrement would be exceptional
indeed. In the present application I can find no consideration which would justify
e so unusual a course.

My attention has rightly been directed from several quarters to the question of
security. I realise that to allow an artistic or historical treasure to be on display in a
church always involves an element of risk. I do not regard the element in the present
case as particularly high—certainly no higher than in *Re St Helen's, Brant Broughton*[3]
where the Dean of Arches upheld the decision of Chancellor Goodman refusing a faculty
f for the sale of a 15th century German painting of the Ascension which had been
installed in the church in 1887 above the altar in the centre of the reredos. The dean
also emphasised the fact that the donor's intention was that the picture should be the
centre of an architectural scheme which was still being fulfilled. These considerations,
in my view, apply mutatis mutandis to Sir William Russell's helmet. It appears to
me that in the present case reasonable measures have already been taken to secure
g the safety of the helmet and that without any substantial expense being incurred
these safety precautions can be strengthened. I reject the suggestion that the helmet
might properly be replaced by a replica in fibreglass or other similar material.
The Dean of Peterborough in his evidence regarded such a substitution as savouring
of fraud. I will confine myself to saying that, in my view, it would not be proper in
the circumstances of the present case.

h For these reasons, I have come to the conclusion that, despite the care and fairness
with which the case for the petitioners has been presented, they have failed to
establish a case which would justify an order for the sale of so valuable a treasure
which has so long been associated with Thornhaugh Church. I am of opinion that,
assuming that I have jurisdiction, I ought to refuse this application on the merits.

j *Faculty refused. Order for the return of the helmet to the position in Thornhaugh Church
from which it had been taken.*

Mary Rose Plummer Barrister.

1 [1971] 3 All ER 269, [1972] Fam 236
2 Page 148, ante
3 [1973] 3 All ER 386, [1974] Fam 16   F

Metropolitan Police Commissioner v Curran   *a*

HOUSE OF LORDS

LORD DIPLOCK, LORD HAILSHAM OF ST MARYLEBONE, LORD KILBRANDON, LORD SALMON
AND LORD EDMUND-DAVIES

10th, 11th NOVEMBER, 17th DECEMBER 1975

Road traffic – Driving with blood-alcohol proportion above prescribed limit – Evidence – *b*
Failure to supply specimen – Specimen for laboratory test – Person driving, attempting to
drive or in charge of vehicle while unfit through drink – Accused lawfully arrested and required
to provide specimen – Accused refusing – Accused charged with being in charge while unfit
and with failing to provide specimen – Accused acquitted of being in charge – No provision
for punishment by way of fine or imprisonment for failing to provide specimen where accused
not in charge at relevant time – Whether open to court to convict accused of failing to provide   *c*
specimen – Road Traffic Act 1972, ss 5(2)(3)(5), 9(3), Sch 4, Part 1.

The appellant was found by a police constable sitting in a stationary car. He had the
ignition key with him and was very drunk. The constable arrested him under s 5(5)*a*
of the Road Traffic Act 1972 on the ground that he was committing an offence under
s 5 in that he was in charge of a motor vehicle on a road when unfit to drive through   *d*
drink or drugs. Having been given an opportunity of providing a specimen of breath
for a breath test at the police station, the appellant was required to provide a specimen
of blood or urine. He refused to do so. He was charged on an indictment containing
two counts: (1) being unfit to drive through drink when in charge of a motor vehicle
on a road, contrary to s 5(2) of the 1972 Act; and (2) failing without reasonable excuse
to provide a specimen of blood or urine for a laboratory test, contrary to s 9(3)*b* of the   *e*
1972 Act. At the trial the appellant pleaded not guilty to both counts and, in reliance
on the defence available to him under s 5(3) of the 1972 Act, claimed that at the time
when he was found by the constable the circumstances were such that there was no
likelihood of his driving the car so long as he remained unfit to drive. The jury
acquitted the appellant on count 1 but convicted him on count 2. The appellant was
fined £10, disqualified from driving for 12 months, and had his driving licence   *f*
endorsed. He appealed against conviction only, contending that he could not be guilty
of an offence under s 9(3) since an acquittal of the offence under s 5(2), on the ground
that he had not, or was deemed not to have, been in charge of the vehicle at the
relevant time, entitled him to be acquitted of the offence under s 9(3) having regard in
particular to the fact that Part 1 of Sch 4*c* to the 1972 Act provided no punishment in
respect of an offence under s 9(3) in cases where an accused was found not to have been   *g*
in charge of a motor vehicle.

Held – The appellant's conviction on count 2 was not inconsistent with his acquittal
on count 1, for the offence under s 9(3) was not in any way connected with the appellant's guilt or innocence of the offence which he was suspected of committing when
he was arrested. The defence under s 5(3) was expressly limited to a charge under   *h*
s 5(2) and the provisions of Part 1 of Sch 4 had no relevance to the definition of the
offence under s 9(3) but dealt only with the mode of prosecution and punishment.
Accordingly the appeal would be dismissed (see p 165 h to p 166 a and e f and h, p 167 e,
p 169 g to j, p 170 b and c, p 172 c, p 174 c and e to g, p 176 c and p 177 c, post).

Per Curiam. Where an accused who relies on the defence under s 5(3) of the 1972
Act is acquitted of an offence under s 5(2) but is convicted of an offence under s 9(3),   *j*
it is open to the court, for the purpose of sentence, to determine that the accused was
in fact in charge of the vehicle at the relevant time, and is therefore liable to a fine or

---

a   Section 5, so far as material, is set out at p 175 *a* to *c*, post
b   Section 9(3) is set out at p 164 *c*, post
c   Schedule 4, so far as material, is set out at p 166 *c* to *e*, post

imprisonment under Sch 4, Part 1, col 4; such a determination is not inconsistent with
a the accused's acquittal under s 5(2) if the acquittal was based merely on the fact that,
although the accused was in actual charge of the vehicle, he was deemed not to have
been in charge by virtue of s 5(3). Where, however, a person is acquitted under s 5(2)
and the court does not make a finding that he was in actual charge of the vehicle at
the relevant time, the court has no power under Sch 4, Part 1, col 4, to impose a fine or
imprisonment on him for an offence under s 9(3), but, under col 5, does have the power
b to disqualify him from holding a licence and, under col 6, is obliged to endorse his
licence (see p 166 g and h, p 167 c d and f, p 168 f to j, p 170 d and e, p 172 e to g and j
to p 173 a and c, p 174 d and g, p 176 g and h and p 177 d to f, post).

R v Richardson (John) [1975] 1 All ER 905 overruled.

Decision of the Court of Appeal, Criminal Division, sub nom R v Curran [1975] 2
All ER 1045 affirmed.

c
Notes
For failure to provide a specimen of blood or urine for a laboratory test without
reasonable excuse, see Supplement to 33 Halsbury's Laws (3rd Edn) para 1061A, 8.

For the Road Traffic Act 1972, ss 5, 9 and Sch 4, Part I, see 42 Halsbury's Statutes
(3rd Edn) 1646, 1655, 1849.

d
Cases referred to in opinions
Baker v Foulkes [1975] 3 All ER 651, [1975] 1 WLR 1551, HL.
Inland Revenue Comrs v Joiner [1975] 3 All ER 1050, [1975] 1 WLR 1701, HL.
R v John [1974] 2 All ER 561, [1974] 1 WLR 624, [1974] RTR 332, CA.
R v Lennard [1973] 2 All ER 831, [1973] 1 WLR 483, 137 JP 585, 57 Cr App Rep 542,
[1973] RTR 252, CA.
e R v Richardson (John) [1975] 1 All ER 905, [1975] 1 WLR 321, 60 Cr App Rep 136, [1975]
RTR 173, CA.
Williams v Osborne [1975] RTR 181, 61 Cr App Rep 1, DC.
Wiltshire v Barrett [1965] 2 All ER 271, [1966] 1 QB 312, [1965] 2 WLR 1195, 129 JP 348,
CA, Digest (Cont Vol B) 160, 1691a.

f ## Appeal
On 25th October 1974 in the Crown Court sitting at 4 St James's Square, SW1, before his
Honour Judge Everett QC and a jury, the appellant, John Curran, was convicted of
failing without reasonable excuse to provide a specimen of blood or urine for a
laboratory test, contrary to s 9(3) of the Road Traffic Act 1972. The appellant was fined
£10 with an order that he be disqualified from driving for 12 months and that his
g driving licence be endorsed. The appellant appealed against conviction. The appeal
was dismissed by the Court of Appeal, Criminal Division[1] (Lord Widgery CJ, James
LJ and Ashworth J) on 8th May 1975, but leave to appeal to the House of Lords was
granted, the court having certified that the decision involved a point of law of general
public importance. The facts are set out in the opinion of Lord Diplock.

h Neil Taylor QC and David Mills for the appellant.
Donald Farquharson QC and Ann Goddard for the Crown.

Their Lordships took time for consideration.

17th December   The following opinions were delivered.

j **LORD DIPLOCK.** My Lords, the appellant was found by a police constable
sitting in a stationary car in a street. The ignition key was in the car with him and he
was very drunk. In the reasonable belief that the appellant had committed an
offence under s 5(2) of the Road Traffic Act 1972 of being a person in charge of a
motor vehicle, which was on a road, when he was unfit to drive through drink, the

1   [1975] 2 All ER 1045, [1975] 1 WLR 876

constable arrested him and took him to a police station. After being given an opportunity to provide a specimen of breath for a breath test while at the police station, *a*
the appellant was required to provide a specimen of blood or urine. He refused to
do so.

It should be said at the outset that there are three matters that are not in dispute:
(1) that since the constable had reasonable grounds for his belief that the appellant
had committed an offence under s 5(2), the arrest was lawful under s 5(5) (see *Wiltshire v Barrett*[1]); (2) that the requirement to provide a specimen of blood or urine *b*
for a laboratory test was lawfully made under s 9(1); and (3) that the appellant's
failure to provide it was 'without reasonable excuse' within the meaning of that
expression in s 9(3), since he was neither physically nor mentally unable to provide a
specimen nor would the provision of the specimen have entailed a substantial risk
to his health (see *R v Leonard*[2], *R v John*[3], *Williams v Osborne*[4]).

So there would appear to be an undefended case of an offence under s 9(3) of the *c*
1972 Act which provides:

'A person who, without reasonable excuse, fails to provide a specimen for a
laboratory test in pursuance of a requirement imposed under this section shall
be guilty of an offence.'

The appellant was duly charged at Middlesex Crown Court on an indictment *d*
which contained two counts. The first was for an offence under s 5(2); the second for
an offence under s 9(3). On his arraignment and in the absence of the jury a submission was made on his behalf to the judge. It was indicated that the appellant
did not dispute that at the material time he was unfit to drive through drink and that
in substance his defence to the charge under s 5(2) would be based on s 5(3) of the
1972 Act which provides: *e*

'For the purposes of subsection (2) above a person shall be deemed not to have
been in charge of a motor vehicle if he proves that at the material time the
circumstances were such that there was no likelihood of his driving it so long as
he remained unfit to drive through drink or drugs.'

It was submitted that, on the true construction of the Act, if the appellant were to be *f*
acquitted of the offence under s 5(2) on the ground that at the material time he was
not in charge or was to be deemed not to have been in charge of the motor vehicle,
he was in law entitled also to be acquitted of the offence under s 9(3) of failing to
provide a specimen for a laboratory test.

The judge rejected this submission. The trial proceeded on both counts. The jury
brought in a verdict of not guilty of the offence charged under s 5(2) and, in accordance *g*
with the ruling that he had previously given, the judge directed the jury to find the
appellant guilty of the offence charged under s 9(3). For this offence the appellant
was sentenced to be fined £10, to be disqualified from driving for 12 months
and to have his driving licence endorsed.

Against his conviction, though not against his sentence, the appellant appealed to
the Court of Appeal[5] on a point of law raised by the judge's ruling. The Court of *h*
Appeal dismissed the appeal but granted the appellant leave to appeal to your
Lordships' House. The point of law involved was certified as being:

'Whether the offence of failing without reasonable excuse to provide a specimen
for a laboratory test contrary to s 9(3) of the Road Traffic Act 1972 can be established without establishing that the defendant was a peron in charge of, or
driving, or attempting to drive, a motor vehicle on a road or other public place.' *j*

1 [1965] 2 All ER 271, [1966] 1 QB 312
2 [1973] 2 All ER 831, [1973] 1 WLR 483
3 [1974] 2 All ER 561, [1974] 1 WLR 624
4 [1975] RTR 181
5 [1975] 2 All ER 1045, [1975] 1 WLR 876

My Lords, the answer to this question depends on the true construction of the
a Road Traffic Act 1972. It is primarily a consolidation Act, and, while it incorporates
certain amendments to give effect to recommendations of the Law Commission
and the Scottish Law Commission, none of these amendments relates to any of the
provisions of the Act that are relevant to the question of construction which is involved in the instant case. As has been recently emphasised by this House in *Inland
Revenue Comrs v Joiner*[1], it is the consolidation Act that your Lordships have to construe
b and if you find, as I do in the instant case, that the actual words are clear and unambiguous in their meaning it is not permissible to have recourse to the corresponding provisions in the earlier Act repealed by the consolidation Act and to treat
any difference in their wording as capable of casting doubt on what is clear and
unambiguous language in the consolidation Act itself.

I start with a general observation about the content and structure of the Road
c Traffic Act 1972. It creates more than a hundred different statutory offences. The
ingredients of each offence are stated in the particular section of the Act by which
the offence is created. The mode of prosecution of each offence (viz summarily or on
indictment or both) is not dealt with in the particular section by which it is created,
nor is the type of punishment that may be imposed on conviction for that offence.
These matters are left to be dealt with by Part I of Sch 4 to the Act, which by s 177 is
d made applicable to each of the offences created by those provisions of the Act that are
specified in col 1 of that Part of the Schedule. That Part of the Schedule is in convenient tabular form. It sets out against the number of the particular section or subsection by which the offence is created, the mode of trial and the punishment that
may be imposed on a person convicted of that offence. It provides for four different
types of punishment for offences with which it deals, viz imprisonment, fine, dis-
e qualification from holding or obtaining a driving licence, and endorsement of the
conviction on the offender's driving licence. Column 4 shows the maximum punishment by way of fine or imprisonment. Column 5 shows whether or not the court
is obliged, or empowered at its discretion, to order disqualification from holding or
obtaining a driving licence; and col 6 shows whether or not the court is obliged to
order endorsement of the offender's driving licence. The reference in s 177(1) to
f 'prosecution and punishment' as being the subject-matter of Part I of Sch 4 makes it
clear that disqualification and endorsement as well as fine and imprisonment are to
be classified as 'punishment' for the purposes of the Act—as indeed they are as a
matter of common sense, and always have been for the purposes of the right of appeal
against sentence under the Criminal Appeal Act 1907.

My second observation is that ss 8 and 9 of the 1972 Act create obligations on
g citizens of an unusual kind which had no precedent in English penal law when they
were first introduced by the Road Safety Act 1967. What these sections provide is a
procedure by which a person who is reasonably suspected by a policeman of having
committed an offence under s 5 or s 6 can be required to provide material evidence
in the form of a specimen of his blood or urine which may be used against him at his
trial for an offence under either section, and without which, in case the of an offence
h under s 6, no prosecution could ever be brought against him. So the procedure
under ss 8 and 9 applies to persons when they are suspects only. They may not in
fact have committed the offence under s 5 or s 6 of which they are suspected; but if
they have, their refusal to provide a specimen of blood or urine would prevent their
being prosecuted for any offence under s 6 and would enhance their prospects of
escaping conviction for an offence under s 5. If the procedure is to achieve its evident
j purpose it is essential that a refusal without reasonable excuse to provide a specimen
of blood or urine should attract penal sanctions irrespective of whether or not it
ultimately proved that the person refusing to provide the specimen had been guilty
of the offence of which he was suspected.

In my opinion this is what s 9(3) quite plainly does. The language of the subsection

1   [1975] 3 All ER 1050 at 1057, 1059, 1060, 1062, 1063, [1975] 1 WLR 1701 at 1708, 1711, 1712,
    1714, 1715, 1716

is simple, clear and unambiguous and in my view not fairly capable of any other meaning. There is nothing in that language to suggest that the offence thereby *a* created is in any way connected with the suspect's guilt or innocence of the offence which he was suspected of having committed when he was arrested.

The argument for placing a strained construction on the words of s 9(3) is based on the wording of the entry in col 4 of Part I of Sch 4 relating to the offence created by that subsection. As already mentioned this entry shows 'the maximum punishment by way of fine or imprisonment which may be imposed on a person convicted *b* of the offence'. It is convenient to set out the relevant part of that entry alongside the corresponding entries relating to disqualification and endorsement. I omit words relating only to second offences.

4 Punishment	5 Disqualification	6 Endorse- ment
(i) Where it is shown that at the relevant time . . . the offender was driving or attempting to drive a motor vehicle on a road or other public place, 4 months or £100 or both; . . . (ii) Where in any other case it is shown that at that time the offender was in charge of a motor vehicle on a road or other public place, 4 months or £100 or both.	(a) Obligatory if it is shown as mentioned in paragraph (i) of Column 4. (b) Discretionary if it is not so shown.	Obligatory.

My Lords, cols 4, 5 and 6 do not deal with whether a defendant is guilty or innocent of the offence referred to in col 1. They deal with punishment alone and do not come into operation unless and until there has been a finding of guilt, i e in a case tried on indictment, after the jury has returned a verdict of guilty. The instructions which these columns contain are addressed to those responsible for determining what sentence should be imposed and not to those responsible for determining guilt. The *f* instructions to the latter are contained in the section of the Act which is referred to in col 1.

It is true that, in the case of an offence under s 9(3), col 4 contains no provision for a maximum punishment *by way of fine or imprisonment* which may be imposed on a first offender guilty of an offence under s 9(3) of whom it is not shown, to the satisfaction of the sentencer, that he was a person who was either driving or attempting *g* to drive a motor vehicle on a road or other public place or was a person who was in actual charge of such a vehicle. It is to be observed that being shown to have been in *actual* charge of a motor vehicle is sufficient to attract the punishment by way of fine or imprisonment prescribed in col 4; despite the absence of any likelihood that the person in actual charge would drive it while he remained unfit to drive through drink or drugs. The 'deeming' provision in s 5(3) applies only where the charge is *h* of an offence under s 5(2). It has no application to an offence under s 9(3).

If fine and imprisonment were the only kinds of punishment available for an offence under s 9(3) there would be some force in the argument that the existence of a punitive sanction is an essential characteristic of every criminal offence; and that the absence of any specific provision for the punishment of that offence where neither of the matters referred to in col 4 was shown, gave rise to an implied limita- *j* tion on the definition of the offence to be found in s 9(3). The alternative conclusion would be that Parliament, though it had fixed relatively low maximum penalties for the offence when aggravating circumstances were shown, had nevertheless intended that in the absence of any of those aggravating circumstances the offence should attract the penalties appropriate to a misdemeanour at common law, viz

fine or imprisonment unlimited by any maxima. This is an inference that, for my
a part, I should be hesitant to draw in construing modern statutes.
    Fine and inprisonment, however, are not the only punishments available for an
offence under s 9(3). In addition to col 4 of Part I of Sch 4 there are cols 5 and 6.
The entry in col 5 relating to disqualification from holding or obtaining a driving
licence is couched in terms that are significantly different from those of col 4. It
divides offences under s 9(3) into two categories, dealt within paras (*a*) and (*b*) respec-
b tively, according to whether disqualification is obligatory or discretionary. Paragraph (*a*), which makes it obligatory, applies only where it is shown that at the
relevant time the offender was driving or attempting to drive a motor vehicle on a
road or other public place. It deals with offences committed in the circumstances
referred to in the first part of para (i) in col 4. Paragraph (*b*) on the other hand which
makes disqualification discretionary deals with offences committed in *any* other
c circumstances. The change in language in para (*b*) of col 5 is in significant contrast
not only to the language of para (*a*) but also to the language of para (ii) of col 4. If
the draftsman had intended to restrict the discretionary punishment of disqualification
to cases where it was shown that the offender had been in charge of a motor vehicle
at the relevant time, the appropriate words in which to do so would have been
before his very eyes as he was laying out the table in Part I of Sch 4. Column 6 in its
d turn makes the punishment of endorsement of the offender's driving licence obligatory without any such qualification as is to be found in relation to fine and
imprisonment in col 4.
    The existence of these other punishments which may be imposed for offences
under s 9(3), where it is not shown that the offender at the relevant time was driving
or attempting to drive or was in actual charge of a motor vehicle on a road or other
e public place, destroys the foundation for the implication sought to be drawn by
counsel for the appellant from the absence of any provision in col 4 for a maximum
fine or period of imprisonment for offenders where this is not shown. It also negatives
any inference that Parliament intended such offences to attract the penalties of a
misdemeanour at common law.
    I would accordingly answer the certified question in the affirmative; but would
f add that where it is not shown that the defendant was a person in *actual* charge of,
or driving or attempting to drive, a motor vehicle on a road or other public place,
the only punishments which may be imposed are disqualification, which lies within
the discretion of the court, and endorsement, which is obligatory.
    The result, as is so often the case with these ill-drafted statutory provisions dealing
with drink offences in connection with motor vehicles, can hardly be regarded as
g satisfactory. A fine would in many cases appear to be the most appropriate penalty
for a refusal to provide a specimen of blood or urine by a person who was not in actual
charge of, or driving or attempting to drive, a motor vehicle though he was reasonably suspected of it. It seems likely that the omission to provide for a power to
impose a fine in such cases was due to inadvertence of the draftsman of the provision
in s 3(3) of the Road Safety Act 1967 part of which is reproduced in s 9(3) and part
h reflected in the entry in col 4 of Part I of Sch 4 to the 1972 consolidation Act. He
appears to have overlooked the possibility that a person who was lawfully required
to provide a specimen of blood or urine because he was reasonably suspected of
having committed a drink offence in connection with a motor vehicle might turn
out later not to have been in charge of, or driving or attempting to drive, the vehicle.
There was little excuse for this lacuna since *Wiltshire v Barrett*[1], from which the
j possibility arises, had been decided in 1965; and there was no corresponding lacuna
in the language used in s 5(2) of the Road Safety Act 1967 which is reflected in the
entry in col 5 of Part I of Sch 4 to the 1972 consolidation Act.
    Shortly before the decision of the Court of Appeal in the instant case there had
been two decisions of that court that were in conflict on the same point of law as is

1   [1965] 2 All ER 271, [1966] 1 QB 312

involved in the instant case. They were *Williams v Osborne*[1] and *R v Richardson*[2].
In *Williams v Osborne*[1], which the Court of Appeal preferred and followed in the   a
instant case, the court had not been referred to Part I of Sch 4 to the Road Traffic
Act 1972 at all. In *R v Richardson*[2], so far as can be gathered from the judgment,
the court was referred to the entry in col 4 of Part I of Sch 4, but not to the entries in
cols 5 and 6. The court did not give any further consideration to the construction
of the 1972 Act, which was the only statute governing the offence, but concentrated
its attention on the construction of s 3(3) of the Road Safety Act 1967. It found the   b
wording of this subsection of the repealed statute to be ambiguous and the court's
attention was never drawn to s 5(2) of the same Act as an aid in resolving the
ambiguity.

The judgment of the Court of Appeal in *R v Richardson*[2] illustrates the danger of
going behind the actual language used in a consolidation Act when its meaning read
in the context of that Act itself is clear and unambiguous. The presumption that a   c
consolidation Act was not intended to alter the previous statute law which it repeals
and replaces is a legitimate aid to its interpretation where its language is fairly and
equally capable of bearing more than one meaning; but one of the purposes of a
consolidation Act is to resolve possible ambiguities in the language of the statutes
which it repeals—not to perpetuate them or to add to the obscurity of the law. The
language of those provisions of the Road Safety Act 1967 which dealt with the offence   d
of refusing to provide a specimen of blood or urine for a laboratory test, may not
have been so clear as the language of those provisions which replaced them in the
Road Traffic Act 1972; but this is the worst possible reason for resorting to the repealed
statute in order to discover some ambiguity which is not apparent in the language
of the provisions of the consolidation Act itself.

There remains to be considered the actual disposition of the instant appeal. It is an   e
appeal against conviction only on the point of law raised in the certified question.
Since that question is to be answered in the affirmative the appeal against conviction
must be dismissed. There was no appeal against sentence and in the light of the
answer given to the certified question, the sentence of disqualification and endorsement was a sentence that the judge was in any event empowered to pass on the
appellant's conviction of the offence under s 9(3). Whether the judge was empowered   f
to impose a fine as well depends on whether he was satisfied that the appellant was
in actual charge of the motor vehicle in which he was found at the time of his arrest.
The verdict of the jury on the first count of the indictment for the offence under
s 5(2) throws no light on this for, of itself, it is consistent with their having found
either that the Crown had not established that the appellant was in actual charge
of the vehicle or that notwithstanding that the Crown had established this, the   g
appellant had established the defence available to him under s 5(3) under which he
was to be *deemed* not to have been in charge of the vehicle for the purposes of that
offence—a defence that was not available to him on the charge in the second count
of an offence under s 9(3). Nevertheless it is a reasonable inference from the way in
which the appellant's case was adumbrated in the original submission of law made
to the judge and from the judge's summation of the evidence to the jury that the   h
defence under s 5(3) was the real issue of fact determined by the verdict of the jury;
and there is no sufficient ground for doubting that the judge was satisfied that the
appellant was in actual charge of the motor vehicle at the time of his arrest, although
there may have been no likelihood of his driving it before he sobered up.

I would dismiss the appeal.

i

LORD HAILSHAM OF ST MARYLEBONE. My Lords, for the reasons which
follow I am of the opinion that this appeal should be dismissed.

On 24th October 1974 the appellant was arraigned at the Middlesex Crown Court

1 [1975] RTR 181
2 [1975] 1 All ER 905, [1975] 1 WLR 321

in St James's Square on an indictment containing two counts, each relating to events
which had taken place on 8th May 1974. The two counts were: (1) a count charging
the appellant under s 5(2) of the Road Traffic Act 1972 (being unfit to drive through
drink when in charge of a motor vehicle on a road); (2) a count charging the appellant
under s 9(3) of the 1972 Act with failing without reasonable excuse to provide the
required specimen of blood or urine for the prescribed laboratory test.

In the event, the appellant was acquitted of the first and convicted on the second
count. He was fined £10, and disqualified for 12 months (discretionary for this
offence when not driving or attempting to drive) and his licence endorsed (obligatory
for this offence).

He appealed without leave on a pure point of law to the Court of Appeal, Criminal
Division[1], and his appeal was dismissed. The court certified a question of general
public importance (of which more later) and gave leave to appeal to your Lordships'
House. There was, and is, no appeal against sentence, and no leave to appeal against
the summing-up was sought.

The appellant's contention has been throughout that the two verdicts are inconsistent and, in particular, that the verdict of conviction on the second count is inconsistent
with the verdict of acquittal on the first.

He has maintained this position throughout. It was raised first before his actual
arraignment by agreement between counsel, when it was argued in advance of the
trial that the two counts stood or fell together. When the decision went against him
his counsel expressly admitted that, if the appellant were convicted on the first
count, he could have no separate argument on the second, and when he was acquitted
on the first count he immediately appealed on the ground, to quote Lord Widgery
CJ[2], that 'a conviction of the "sample" offence [s 9(3)] . . . is inconsistent with acquittal
of the offence of being in charge of the car when unfit through drink [s 5(2)].'

One ground of the appellant's argument was the same throughout, though it is not
identical with the reasons given by the Court of Appeal, nor with the question certified
to your Lordships as of general public importance.

The appellant argued that he was entitled on both charges to avail himself of the
special defence available to him under s 5(3) of the 1972 Act, of which the burden,
on the balance of probabilities, rests on the defendant, to the effect that a person
accused under s 5(2) of the Road Traffic Act 1972 shall be deemed not to have been
in charge of a motor vehicle if he proves that at the material time the circumstances
were such that there was no likelihood of his driving the vehicle so long as he remained
unfit to drive. The defence was clearly available to him on the first count, but the
appellant's contention was that this special defence was available to him on the second
count as well. That this was his contention of law appears manifestly from the
transcript of the preliminary argument before the trial, and, on the second count,
and on a fair reading of the transcript, it was, I believe, his main and perhaps his only
contention in the event of a conviction on the first count.

Insofar as this was the appellant's only contention it was, in my opinion, plainly
wrong. The deeming provision of s 5(3) is expressly limited in application to s 5(2),
and even in s 5(2), to which it is admittedly applicable, the expression 'in charge' is
clearly used in the first sentence in a sense free from the application of the deeming
provision, since the burden of proof that a defendant was in physical charge of the
car under the section must clearly rest on the prosecution throughout, whereas,
in order to invoke and apply the deeming provision under s 5(3), the burden of
proof expressly rests on the defence. When the court has to apply punishment after
conviction in accordance with the provisions of s 177 and Sch 4 to the 1972 Act the
expression 'in charge', where it occurs, is manifestly free of any application of the
deeming provision of s 5(3), both on the words and on the sense of the statute.

---

1   [1975] 2 All ER 1045, [1975] 1 WLR 876
2   [1975] 2 All ER at 1047, [1975] 1 WLR at 878

When the case came to be left to the jury, in addition to the special defence under
s 5(3), the circuit judge made reference to evidence given by the accused to the   *a*
effect that he was, in any event, not in physical charge of the relevant vehicle at all.
I need not summarise this evidence, because I believe that a fair reading of the transcript supports the view that Lord Widgery CJ[1] was right in describing the s 5(3)
defence as 'really the only live point on the first count', and that in bringing in the
verdict they did, there can be little doubt that 'it was on this subsection [s 5(3)] that
the jury acquitted the appellant of the offence of being in charge when unfit.'   *b*

If this is right, and I think it is, it is clear that the two verdicts are not incompatible.
As I understand it, where it is alleged that general verdicts of the same jury on successive counts are incompatible with one another, since, in the nature of the case,
no reasons are given by the jury, an appellate court can only upset the verdict of
conviction, in the absence of any complaint about the summing-up (of which none is
made here), if there is no logical path by which they can be reconciled. Here there   *c*
is a path by which the two verdicts can be reconciled, and that one which almost certainly
reflects the view actually taken by the jury, and it follows that they are not inconsistent
with one another and the appeal fails.

Unfortunately, this is not by any means the end of the matters in dispute. But
before I proceed to these, and whatever the merits of the foregoing, I am quite clear
from what had passed that the circuit judge then proceeded to pass sentence on the   *d*
footing that it had been shown to his satisfaction that the appellant was in actual
physical charge of the vehicle at the time of the offence. Subject to one serious question
of law (to which I will return), this is quite enough to justify the imposition of a
sentence, as was imposed, of a fine of £10 under col 4 of para 5 of Sch 4 to the 1972
Act, and a sentence of disqualification, discretionary but not obligatory, under col 5
of the same paragraph. As there was no appeal against sentence, my view, therefore,   *e*
is that, subject to the point of law, which I will discuss in a moment, the sentence
must stand, though I add with whatever emphasis I can command that I would not
myself have thought that, in the light of the relative mildness of the fine, disqualification was appropriate to the case. I add, however, further, that I say this only on the
short transcript available to your Lordships, and that there may have been factors
unknown to me which would change my assessment of the matter.   *f*

I now turn to the substantive points which occupied most of the attention of the
appellate committee, and to which, as I shall endeavour to show, no wholly satisfactory solution presents itself. The question certified by the Court of Appeal as of
general public importance was in the following terms:

'Whether the offence of failing without reasonable excuse to provide a specimen
for a laboratory test contrary to s 9(3) of the Road Traffic Act 1972 can be estab-   *g*
lished without establishing that the defendant was a person in charge of, or
driving, or attempting to drive, a motor vehicle on a road or other public place.'

To this question so formulated a qualified affirmative answer can now be given on
the limited and narrow ground that, where a defendant escapes conviction under
s 5(2) by availing himself of the defence afforded by s 5(3) of the 1972 Act but was
physically in charge at the time of his arrest, it is not necessary to prove more than   *h*
that he was physically in charge of the vehicle.

But is it necessary to prove as much? The Court of Appeal thought not, and in
doing so in effect decided that the decision in *R v Richardson*[2] was wrong and should
not be followed. The decision of the Court of Appeal was based on the general
proposition that, contrary to this decision, a person may be found guilty under s 9(3)
notwithstanding the fact that he was never at the relevant time in charge of the   *j*
relevant or indeed any motor vehicle at all. The court came to this conclusion because

---

1   [1975] 2 All ER at 1048, [1975] 1 WLR at 879
2   [1975] 1 All ER 905, [1975] 1 WLR 321

they found *R v Richardson*[1] to be inconsistent with the decision in *Williams v Osborne*[2],

a in which it was held by the Divisional Court that for a suspect to refuse to give the required sample on the grounds that the suspect had not at the relevant time been actually in charge of the vehicle was not a 'reasonable excuse' for declining to give a sample so as to be a defence to a charge under s 9(3). Whether or not the Court of Appeal was entitled to follow *Williams v Osborne*[2] in the face of *R v Richardson*[1] is a question I will not canvass further. *Williams v Osborne*[2] was decided on 22nd January

b 1975. *R v Richardson*[1], which was not brought to the attention of the Divisional Court, had been decided on 10th December 1974. *Williams v Osborne*[2] was a 'reasonable excuse' case and based on the line of authority of which *R v Leonard*[3] is an example. *R v Richardson*[1] was a case about the essential ingredients of an offence under s 9(3) and it would follow that, if *Richardson*[1] were right, no question of 'reasonable excuse' would arise, as the offence under s 9(3) would not be proved because of the

c failure of an essential ingredient. I am not, at present, prepared to say more about *Williams v Osborne*[2] than that the Court of Appeal were clearly right in thinking that the approach to the Act of each of the two cases is inconsistent with the other and requires to be reconciled.

In order to decide the matter it is, however, necessary to go rather deeper into the construction of the 1972 Act. In the instant appeal, the appellant was arrested under

d s 5(5) of the 1972 consolidation Act, and was offered, and accepted, an opportunity to take a breath test under s 9 of the Act. The breath test, when taken, proved positive, and that was what entitled the police officer to require, as he did, the appellant to provide the prescribed blood or urine specimen which he refused to do, thus giving rise to the second count in the indictment.

If one looks at the words of s 5(5), the arrest is authorised, on the grammatical

e construction of the words, only on the ground that an offence has, in fact, been committed. But it has long been established, at least since *Wiltshire v Barrett*[4] and, in truth, long before that, that when such words are used in connection with one of these offences requiring in the interests of safety the removal of a suspected driver from the road, the effect is to enable the officer to arrest him, when, on reasonable grounds, he forms the view that the suspect has been committing the offence even

f though it may subsequently turn out that he was not guilty. In view of the verdict on the first count, the arrest in this case must be justified on the basis of the doctrine in *Wiltshire v Barrett*[4] and not on the basis that an offence under s 5 had actually been committed. The requirement of a blood specimen is, accordingly on this view, to be justified on the basis of an arrest effected not because an offence had actually been committed, but because it had apparently been committed. We must now,

g therefore, consider whether a refusal to provide the required laboratory specimen, made in such circumstances without reasonable excuse, gives rise of itself to an offence under s 9(3) of the 1972 Act. If it does, it is because it is not necessary for the prosecution to establish, if the fact be challenged, to the satisfaction of the jury that the suspect was at the time of the alleged offence in actual physical charge of the vehicle in question. The question of reasonable excuse hardly arises in this connec-

h tion. If being in charge is an essential ingredient of the offence, no reasonable excuse is required. The prosecution fails because it has failed to prove what is necessary. If it succeeds, it is because the essential ingredients do not include that the accused should actually have been in charge.

The words of s 9(3) do not include any reference to a necessity that the accused should actually have been driving or attempting to drive the relevant vehicle or

j actually in charge of it. Viewed grammatically the only tests of the offence are the failure to comply with the requirement, and the absence of reasonable excuse.

1 [1975] 1 All ER 905, [1975] 1 WLR 321
2 [1975] RTR 181
3 [1973] 2 All ER 831, [1973] 1 WLR 483
4 [1965] 2 All ER 271, [1966] 1 QB 312

Nevertheless, *R v Richardson*[1] is authority for the proposition that it is an essential ingredient of an offence under s 9(3) that the accused should have been either driving or attempting to drive or else in actual charge of the relevant vehicle at the relevant time. *a*

The decision in *R v Richardson*[1] is based on the proposition that a distinction is to be drawn between what must be proved in order to establish that a requirement under s 9 is lawful (for which only a valid arrest is required) and what must be proved in order to prove that an offence under s 9(3) has been committed. In the latter case, where the fact is challenged, *R v Richardson*[1] is authority for the proposition *b* that, in addition to the lawfulness of the requirement, and the fact of the unreasonable refusal, it must be proved that the accused was either (a) driving or attempting to drive, or (b) in charge of the relevant vehicle at the relevant time.

This conclusion is arrived at by looking at s 177 and Sch 4 to the Act, in addition to s 9(3) and in conjunction with it. At first sight this would seem to be impermissible, since it is s 9(3) which defines and constitutes the offence, whereas s 177 and the *c* Schedule only deal with the method of prosecution (summary trial or indictment) and the maximum punishments available.

Nevertheless, it must be said that a refusal to read the Act in the way proposed by James LJ in *R v Richardson*[2] leads to some bizarre, inappropriate, and even to some unjust consequences. Column 4 of Sch 4 is headed 'punishment' and provides for a 'punishment' under that column only 'where it is shown' that the offender *d* was either driving or attempting to drive (in which case the maxima are higher) or when he was in charge (in which case lower maxima are provided), and this is so whether the case is triable summarily or on indictment, though the particular penalties appropriate for the former method of trial were altered in 1974. The result is that, at any rate so far as regards s 177 and the Schedule, where a man is lawfully arrested solely under the doctrine of *Wiltshire v Barrett*[3], and lawfully *e* required to produce a specimen, no penalty appears to be available by way of fine and imprisonment since in such a case the defendant will not have been driving, attempting to drive or in charge. This means, for instance, that in a case where a defendant was not proved to be in charge, though guilty of an offence, he may not be fined or imprisoned, unless a common law penalty is available. This result is so unacceptable that James LJ[2] felt constrained, notwithstanding the absence of any *f* cross-reference between the section constituting the offence and s 177 and the Schedule, to draw the inference that no offence was committed at all in these circumstances. The words of s 177 are sufficiently plain to exclude the possibility of treating the case as one of common law misdemeanour with undefined penalties of fine and imprisonment attached, and, if the grammatical meaning of s 9(3) is to be accepted, it will therefore follow inexorably that a road traffic offence is intended in which *g* neither fine nor imprisonment is available, as a penalty. If so, the offence is unique, and the result undesirable, so undesirable, in fact, that James LJ[2] felt constrained to hold that such could not have been the intention of the legislature.

Even odder consequences follow if one next looks on to col 5, which deals with disqualification. This presents no difficulty so far as regards drivers driving or attempting to drive. Reasonably enough, the draftsman prescribes by express *h* reference to col 4 that in such a case disqualification is obligatory, as it does in the corresponding case where there is an offence under s 5. But, instead of following the language of col 4(ii), which one would have thought was staring him in the face when he drafted col 5, the draftsman provides that disqualification is available but discretionary 'if it is not shown' that the driver was driving or attempting to drive instead of prescribing that the driver should have been 'in charge'. In other words, *j* and simply pursuing grammatical meanings, if s 9(3) means what it says and no more, the man who was not in charge but was rightly arrested under *Wiltshire v Barrett*[3],

1   [1975] 1 All ER 905, [1975] 1 WLR 321
2   [1975] 1 All ER at 909, [1975] 1 WLR at 327
3   [1965] 2 All ER 271, [1966] 1 QB 312

and lawfully required thereafter under s 9(1) to provide a specimen but fails to do
a so without reasonable excuse (a) has committed an offence, but (b) can even on
indictment neither be fined nor imprisoned, yet (c) may be disqualified under col (5)
and must have his licence endorsed under col (6) even though he had nothing to
do with the car in question and many never have held a driving licence. This seems
a fantastic result. The particular combination of penalties available would be not
only unique, but uniquely inappropriate and unjust, uniquely inappropriate because
b a person who was neither in charge nor driving or attempting to drive, but who
nevertheless was misguided enough to withhold a specimen when lawfully required
could most appropriately be dealt with by fine and not disqualification, and unjust
because disqualification is a penalty to which, if he holds a licence, such an offender
should not usually be subjected in the circumstances, and, if he does not hold a
licence, disqualification is ineffective as well as inappropriate, and ridiculous because
c the offence could properly and far better be dealt with by a fine.

There are, however, also solid grounds for preferring the contrary view, namely
that we must take this ill-drafted Act exactly as we find it where we can, and apply
the results no matter what odd consequences appear to follow. Since many of the
other consequences of the Act appear equally strange, it may be that this is the
greater wisdom. The reasons of policy which make it less unacceptable to do so in
d the present case were well presented to us by counsel for the respondent. These
were that s 9 is not primarily concerned with driving or motoring offences at all,
but with the provision of evidence in the form of specimens by certain categories of
persons appropriately to be described as suspects, namely those who have been
lawfully arrested under s 5 or s 8 of the 1972 Act and provided with an opportunity
to undergo a breath test. The result of the test of the laboratory specimen is the
e only method of proving an offence under s 6, and a most useful piece of evidence
in support either of the prosecution or the defence in charges under s 5 by reason
of the provisions of s 7. According to this argument, there is not sufficient reason
for disregarding the apparently unambiguous language of s 9(3) as to definition and
the apparently unambiguous consequences as to penalty provided by cols 4, 5 and 6
of Sch 4, however inappropriate these may seem in the rare casus omissus postulated
f above. This view implies that *R v Richardson*[1] was wrongly decided and, since it
has commended itself to a majority of my noble and learned friends as the least
unattractive of a number of unattractive options, I am prepared to accept it as such
with great reluctance and even greater misgivings. Where the balance of absurdity
is so nicely adjusted it may be that the grammatical meaning of the statutory words
is to be preferred.

g But, lest anyone should think that I am being unreasonable in constantly pillorying
the drafting of this part of this Act, in addition to the consequences I have set out in
discussing *R v Richardson*[1], let me briefly add the following reflection based on
considerations of textual criticism rather than the legal canons of construction which
hitherto I have conscientiously sought to apply.

I regard it as wholly incredible that either Parliament or the draftsman should
h have seriously and subjectively intended the legal consequences I have now
hesitantly and reluctantly decided to be the law.

The fact appears to be that when the draftsman was considering what are now
ss 9(3), 177 and the relevant parts of Sch 4 in the 1972 Act, he had wholly forgotten,
at least until he came to the entry in col 5, and probably even then, that he should
provide an express penalty to fit the case of a man who had been lawfully arrested
j under s 5 by reason of the doctrine of *Wiltshire v Barrett*[2], lawfully required to provide
a specimen of blood or urine, but who unreasonably failed to supply that specimen,
and who, nonetheless, had neither been driving, attempting to drive, nor been in
charge of the relevant motor vehicle at the relevant time. This, no doubt, was
because the decision in *Wiltshire v Barrett*[2] represents so-called judge-made law

1   [1975] 1 All ER 905, [1975] 1 WLR 321
2   [1965] 2 All ER 271, [1966] 1 QB 312

putting a gloss on the defective draftsmanship of what is now s 5(5) which does not in terms incorporate the doctrine. When he went on to draft col 5, the draftsman *a* was using as his model the comparable s 3(3) of the Road Safety Act 1967 (where the penalties were in the section and not in a schedule), and was not concerned to draft it in conformity with comparable entry in col 4, which stems from a different source (s 1(2) ff in the Road Safety Act 1967). In construing a consolidation Act which itself is unambiguous, we are, of course, bound to consider its terms rather than the terms of any antecedent statutes. If this were not so, the whole benefit of consolidation *b* might be lost and, as I have said, I am prepared to accept that the terms of the 1972 Act are unambiguous even if the consequences are absurd. But it is to be hoped that Parliament may take an early opportunity of revising this group of sections which have provided so much litigation, with so little merit, at so much public expense. In their present state they do little credit to British law, cost an immensity of money, and occupy a great deal of time in argument about the meaning of clauses *c* which an amending statute could easily frame in a form free from doubt.

In the meantime, and for the reasons described in the earlier part of this speech, I would dismiss this appeal on the narrow ground that the two verdicts are not incompatible and that that is the only question which strictly we are bound to decide. It follows, moreover, from what I have said about *R v Richardson*[1], that I agree with the opinion expressed by my noble and learned friends to the effect that, on a charge *d* under s 9(3), the matters of fact on which the decision as to penalty under cols 4 and 5 of Sch 4 depend are matters of fact for the court after verdict and not matters of fact for the jury at the trial. With the reluctance and the misgivings already expressed I give an affirmative answer to the question certified.

LORD KILBRANDON. My Lords, I have had the advantage of reading the *e* speech prepared by my noble and learned friend, Lord Diplock. For the reasons given by him, I would dismiss this appeal.

LORD SALMON. My Lords, I need not repeat the relevant facts which are so lucidly set out in the judgments of my noble and learned friends, Lord Diplock and Lord Hailsham of St Marylebone. I have no doubt at all that on the strict literal and *f* grammatical meaning of s 9(1) and (3) of the Road Traffic Act 1972, looked at in isolation, any person arrested under s 5(5) of that Act and required by a constable whilst at a police station to provide a specimen of his blood or urine for a laboratory test is guilty of an offence if he fails to provide such a specimen, even if he has in fact never driven, or attempted to drive, or been in charge of any car at any time.

There is, however, no power under the Act to punish such a person by fine or *g* imprisonment; but there is a power to punish him by disqualifying him from driving and an obligation to punish him by endorsing his licence. I entirely agree with my noble and learned friend, Lord Hailsham of St Marylebone, that, for the reasons which he gives, the literal and grammatical meaning of s 9(1) and (3) together with Part I of Sch 4, to which I shall presently refer, produces unique, bizarre, inappropriate, absurd and unjust results which I am sure that Parliament can never have intended. *h* In my view, it is reasonably plain that the real purpose of the legislation relating to breath tests and laboratory specimens first introduced by the Road Safety Act 1967 was designed to obtain evidence about the alcohol intake only of persons driving or attempting to drive a motor vehicle or in charge of a motor vehicle when the police had grounds for thinking that they had drunk too much.

I am sure that the legislation was not designed to give the police the right to require a specimen in order to measure the alcoholic intake of any individual save in relation to his driving or being in charge of a motor vehicle. Accordingly I do not believe that Parliament can ever have realised that any person could be found guilty of an offence under s 3(1) and (3) of the 1967 Act supposedly reproduced by s 9(1) and (3) of and

1 [1975] 1 All ER 905, [1975] 1 WLR 321

Sch 4 to the 1972 Act unless he was shown to have been driving or in charge of a motor vehicle at the relevant time.

It is necessary for me to set out, so far as relevant, s 5 of the 1972 Act:

'(1) A person who when driving or attempting to drive a motor vehicle on a road . . . is unfit to drive through drink . . . shall be guilty of an offence.

'(2) . . . a person who, when in charge of a motor vehicle which is on a road . . . is unfit to drive through drink . . . shall be guilty of an offence.

'(3) For the purposes of subsection (2) above a person shall be deemed not to have been in charge of a motor vehicle if he proves that at the material time . . . there was no likelihood of his driving it so long as he remained unfit to drive through drink . . .

'(5) A constable may arrest without warrant a person committing an offence under this section.'

Any ordinary legislator reading that section in the bill before it became an Act would have naturally concluded that, unless anyone was driving, attempting to drive or in charge of a motor vehicle, he could not properly be arrested under s 5(5) and therefore could not be guilty of an offence under s 9. And on the literal and natural and ordinary meaning of s 5(5), the legislator would have been right.

Section 5(1) and (5) of the 1972 Act, however, derive from and are in virtually the same words as s 6(1) and (4) of the Road Traffic Act 1960 when the obligation of motorists, in certain circumstances, to submit to breath tests and furnish specimens of blood or urine were unknown in our law.

In *Wiltshire v Barrett*[1] the Court of Appeal decided that s 6(4) of the 1960 Act could not be given its literal meaning but should be construed as if it read: 'a constable may arrest a person *apparently* committing an offence under this section.' This was because if any person driving or in charge of a motor car who appears to a policeman to be unfit to drive through drink is not immediately stopped from driving there is an obviously grave risk that innocent members of the public may be maimed or killed. The only practical way for the policeman to stop a person from driving would be to arrest him; and it should be his duty to do so. If, however, a policeman were liable to pay damages for arresting a driver whom he had reason to suspect is incapable of driving through drink but who in the end is acquitted of being so incapacitated, even the most conscientious policeman might hesitate to do his duty. I ventured to say[2]:

'It is a pity that the draftsman of s. 6(4) of the 1960 Act did not state expressly the intention of Parliament in plain and unambiguous language . . . I can only respectfully express the hope that in any further statute in which a power of arrest on reasonable suspicion without warrant may be given, the intention of Parliament will be expressed in plain terms.'

These words seem to have fallen on stony ground for a year later when the 1967 Act (which certainly was not a consolidating Act) was passed, the misleading language of s 6(4) of the 1960 Act was re-introduced verbatim into the new Act giving a police constable power to arrest without warrant.

Section 3(3) of the 1967 Act was in the same terms as s 9(3) of the 1972 Act but had the following most important words added to it:

'. . . and (a) if it is shown that at the relevant time he was driving or attempting to drive a motor vehicle on a road. . . he shall be liable to be proceeded against and punished as if the offence charged were an offence under section 1(1) of this Act; and (b) in any other case, if it is shown that at that time he was in charge of a motor vehicle on a road . . . he shall be liable to be proceeded against and punished as if the offence charged were an offence under section 1(2) of this Act.'

I agree with the view expressed in the judgment of the Court of Appeal delivered

1   [1965] 2 All ER 271, [1966] 1 QB 312
2   [1965] 2 All ER at 281, [1966] 1 QB at 333

by James LJ in *R v Richardson*[1] that these words in the 1967 Act, although not free
from ambiguity, mean that the person referred to in s 3(3) must be a person who   *a*
falls within either (*a*) or (*b*) and that therefore no one can be convicted under that
subsection who is not shown to have been driving or attempting to drive or to have
been in charge of a motor vehicle at the relevant time. This construction at least
makes sense, is manifestly just, and is almost certainly what the legislators intended.
Accordingly, if the present prosecution had been brought under the 1967 Act, I
should have decided the appeal in favour of the appellant. This prosecution, however,   *b*
is brought under the 1972 Act—a consolidation Act which, amongst other things, is
supposed to clear up any ambiguities in the preceding legislation. However ridiculous
and unjust the results of the consolidation Act may be, and this one produces
peculiarly ridiculous and unjust results, it has been enacted by Parliament and it is
our duty to enforce it. And I fear there is no doubt what it says, although there is
equally little doubt that it says it inadvertently.   *c*

Section 9 of the 1972 Act (as I have already pointed out) looked at in isolation, is
unambiguous. It makes it an absolute offence for a person to refuse a specimen
when a specimen is duly required after having been arrested under s 5(5). Section 177 of
and Part I of Sch 4 to the Act do not in my view mitigate; they only reinforce the
plain meaning of s 9. Column 1 is headed 'Provision creating offence'. In this column
we find at the relevant place '9(3)'. Column 2 is headed 'General nature of offence'   *d*
which is 'Failing to provide a specimen of blood or urine for a laboratory test'.
Column 3 is headed 'Mode of prosecution' which is described '(*a*) Summarily (*b*) On
indictment'. Then come the three important columns headed respectively
'Punishment', 'Disqualification' and 'Endorsement'. Column 4 deals with maximum
fines and imprisonment and cols 5 and 6 deal respectively with disqualification and   *e*
endorsement which are also generally recognised as punishment. Indeed, disqualification is often regarded as a much more severe punishment than a fine:

'Column 4 (1) Where it is shown that at the relevant time (as defined in
Part V of this Schedule) the offender was driving or attempting to drive a motor
vehicle on a road or other public place, 4 months or £100 or both; . . . (ii) Where
in any other case it is shown that at that time the offender was in charge of a   *f*
motor vehicle on a road or other public place, 4 months or £100 or both.
'Column 5 (*a*) Obligatory if it is shown as mentioned in paragraph (i) of column 4.
(*b*) Discretionary if it is not so shown.
'Column 6 Obligatory.'

It is clear that, even if a defendant has not been shown to be driving or in charge of a
motor vehicle, he commits an offence if he fails to give a specimen of his blood or   *g*
urine when duly required to do so after arrest because it is clearly stated in cols 5
and 6 of the Schedule that when he is not shown to have done either of these things
he may nevertheless be disqualified and his licence must be endorsed. He cannot,
however, be fined or imprisoned. There is no other possible construction to put on
the Schedule. In my view, the words 'in charge' in para (ii) of col 4 of the Schedule
bear the same meaning as they bear in the section under which the accused is arrested.   *h*

I reach these conclusions on the questions posed by this appeal with the greatest
reluctance because I feel that they make the law enacted by Parliament look absurd.
This is the only statute creating a motoring offence for which you cannot be fined.
It is made all the more incongruous by the fact that you may nevertheless be disqualified and must have your licence endorsed if found guilty of such an offence.
I find no consolation in the fact that if a man who has not been driving or in charge   *j*
of a motor vehicle refuses to provide a specimen of his blood or urine, he cannot
be convicted under s 6 and it may not be so easy to convict him under s 5. He could
not in any event be convicted under either s 5 or s 6 if he was not driving or in
charge at the relevant time. If a man could be convicted under s 9 only when he was
driving or in charge of a motor vehicle he would be liable to exactly the same

penalties as he would have been if convicted under s 5 or s 6. Surely s 9 cannot be
a   designed to punish the person who has neither been driving nor in charge of a motor
vehicle for being difficult enough to stand on what some may regard as his ordinary
rights.

My Lords, this appeal is against conviction only and for the reasons stated I have
reluctantly come to the conclusion that the appeal should be dismissed. I am
normally chary of venturing to suggest any alteration by the legislature in this branch
b   of the law. I fear as I indicated in *Baker v Foulkes*[1] that its last state may be even
worse than its first. The alteration to which I have referred of the Road Safety Act
1967 by the Road Traffic Act 1972 is a vivid illustration of how this sometimes
happens. Nevertheless, the 1972 Act produces such exceptionally grotesque results
that I certainly hope that s 9 and the references to it in the Schedule will be radically
redrafted so as to remove the glaring anomalies which they now contain.
c

LORD EDMUND-DAVIES. My Lords, I am in entire agreement that, for the
reasons appearing in the speech of my noble and learned friend, Lord Diplock, the
question raised by the point of law of general public importance certified by the
Court of Appeal, Criminal Division, calls for an affirmative answer. It follows that
the appeal must be dismissed, and I desire to add only a few observations.

d   It should be said that, though concurring in holding that *R v Richardson*[2] was
wrongly decided, I have great sympathy with James LJ in his grappling with a
problem of construction of the Road Traffic Act 1972 which ought never to have
arisen and which may still give rise to injustice. I say that for this reason: in the
instant case I think that this House is entitled to take it that the learned trial judge
formed the view that the defendant was in reality in charge of the vehicle at the
e   relevant time and, that being his view, the conclusion of the jury that the defendant
must be acquitted on the first count by reason of the 'deeming' provision contained
in s 5(3) left unimpaired his power to impose a term of imprisonment not exceeding
four months, or a fine up to £100, or both. On the other hand, had the trial judge
considered that the defendant had in reality not been in charge of the vehicle, his
powers of punishment would be limited to imposing a period of disqualification
f   and to ordering the endorsement of the defendant's licence. This illogical and
irrational restriction on the court's powers could well lead to the imposition of
disqualification in circumstances not warranting it, for the simple reason that no
other course seemed open to the court.

The effect would be to destroy, for practical purposes, the discretionary nature of
the power to disqualify in all cases not falling within para (i) of col 4 of Sch 4 to the
g   1972 Act. Nothing could be more calculated to arouse a rankling feeling of injustice
than to impose the severe punishment of disqualification in circumstances which
do not warrant it.

Accordingly, despite the fears expressed by my noble and learned friend, Lord
Salmon, in *Baker v Foulkes*[1] that legislation to amend the 1972 Act might well not
improve the present situation, I take the view that Sch 4 is one of the several parts of
h   the Act which cry out for the speedy attention of the legislature.

However that may be, as far as the instant case is concerned, I concur with my
Lords in holding that the Court of Appeal, Criminal Division, arrived at the right
conclusion. The appeal therefore must accordingly be dismissed.

Appeal dismissed.

j   Solicitors: *Anthony & Co* (for the appellant); *Solicitor, Metropolitan Police.*

Gordon H Scott Esq Barrister.

---

1   [1975] 3 All ER 651 at 658, [1975] 1 WLR 1551 at 1558
2   [1975] 1 All ER 905, [1975] 1 WLR 321

G

Sovmots Investments Ltd v Secretary of   a
State for the Environment and another
Brompton Securities Ltd v Secretary of
State for the Environment and another   b

QUEEN'S BENCH DIVISION
FORBES J
9th, 10th, 11th, 12th, 13th, 16th, 17th, 18th, 19th JUNE, 16th JULY 1975

Housing – Compulsory purchase – Property to be acquired – House – Part of building – c
Acquisition of property for purpose of providing housing accommodation – 'House' including
part of building which is occupied or intended to be occupied as a separate dwelling – Part of
building not standing directly on land underneath it – Whether local authority having
power to acquire compulsorily part only of building – Housing Act 1957, ss 96(b), 97(1),
189(1).

d

Housing – Compulsory purchase – Property to be acquired – House – Appurtenances belong-
ing thereto or normally enjoyed therewith – Ancillary rights – Easements and quasi-ease-
ments – Easements and rights necessary or desirable for enjoyment of property acquired –
Easements and rights not in existence at date of acquisition – Whether possible to create
easements and rights by virtue of compulsory acquisition – Housing Act 1957, s 189(1).

e

Housing – Compulsory purchase – Property to be acquired – Land – Description of land –
Scope of description – Ancillary rights – Quasi-easements either necessary or desirable for
reasonable enjoyment of land acquired – Whether such rights to be expressly included in
description of land in compulsory purchase order.

Housing – Compulsory purchase – Confirmation of order by Secretary of State – Factors to f
be taken into account – Cost – Whether cost a relevant factor to be taken into consideration
by Secretary of State in deciding whether to confirm order.

The first applicants were the owners of a complex of buildings ('the complex'),
including a tower block, designed primarily for use as offices and showrooms and
situated in central London. From the roof of one wing of the complex ('the podium') g
rose legs which supported six floors of residential maisonettes, each maisonette
occupying two floors, there being 36 maisonettes in all. The building of the complex
was completed in the winter of 1966-67 but thereafter the complex remained
unoccupied. In September 1972 the local authority made a compulsory purchase
order in respect of the 36 residential maisonettes under the Acquisition of Land
(Authorisation Procedure) Act 1946 and the Housing Act 1957, s 97(1)[a] and Sch 7. h
The first applicants objected to the order and the Secretary of State appointed an
inspector to hold a local inquiry. Before the inquiry the first applicants granted a
lease of the 36 maisonettes to the second applicant for a term of 45 years. The
description of the land in the compulsory purchase order, as amended at the inquiry,
was as follows: '36 residential maisonettes on the 3rd, 4th, 5th, 6th, 7th and 8th
floors forming part of and adjacent to the east side of the [complex], together with j
1) the corridors giving access to the said maisonettes; 2) the entrance hall, staircase
and lifts at the south end; and 3) the staircase above podium level at the north end'.
In order to allow the property to be used for residential purposes it was accepted

a Section 97(1) is set out at p 189 b, post

that it would be necessary for the local authority to acquire certain additional ancillary
a rights. Those rights included: (1) a right for the tenants of the maisonettes to use
the northern staircase below podium level as a fire escape; (2) a right to use the
goods lift (in common with the occupiers of the part not acquired) for the purpose
of removing rubbish from the maisonettes; (3) a right of support for the maisonettes
from the building below them; (4) a right of free passage for water, soil, electricity,
gas and other services through the pipes which served the maisonettes; and (5) a right
b of access to the outside of the building for the purposes of window cleaning, maintenance and repair. The local authority claimed that those rights would pass to
them on the conveyance of the maisonettes under the first rule in *Wheeldon v Burrows*[b]
or under s 62 of the Law of Property Act 1925. Following the inspector's report the
Secretary of State confirmed the compulsory purchase order. The applicants moved
to quash the order contending, inter alia, that the local authority had no power under
c ss 96[c] and 97(1) of the 1957 Act to acquire compulsorily a part of a building as housing
accommodation.

Held – (i) By virtue of the extended definition of 'house' in s 189(1)[d], a local authority
had power to acquire a part of a building under ss 96(b) and 97(1) even though that
part did not stand directly on the land underneath it; ss 96 and 97 were among the
d provisions of the 1957 Act 'relating to the provision of housing accommodation'
within para (b) of the definition of 'house' in s 189(1) for, although s 92[e] was the only
section in Part V of the 1957 Act which was expressly concerned with the provision
of accommodation, ss 96 and 97 were part of the code contained in ss 92 to 97 which
governed the powers and duties of local authorities in relation to the provision of
accommodation (see p 190 *h* to p 191 *a*, p 192 *g* and *h* and p 202 *f*, post).
e   (ii) The order would however be quashed for the following reasons—
   (a) A local authority had no power to acquire any ancillary rights, whether easements or quasi-easements and whether necessary or merely desirable, which were
not in existence when the compulsory purchase order was made, since such rights
could not be described as 'appurtenances belonging [to the building] or usually
enjoyed therewith', within the definition of 'house' in s 189(1) of the 1957 Act, for
f those words clearly imported a pre-existing state of affairs. It followed that, since the
ancillary rights in question were not in existence when the compulsory purchase
order was made, they could not be included in the order (see p 194 *a b* and *e* to *g*,
p 196 *g* and p 202 *f*, post).
   (b) Since the land which was the subject-matter of a compulsory purchase order
was not being transferred by mutual agreement, there was no scope in law or equity
g for imputing any agreement by the landowner as to the description of the land
which was to be acquired by the local authority. It followed that if the local authority
wished to acquire ancillary rights already in existence (other than the strictly legal
easements (or profits) which were appurtenant to the land described), i e quasi-easements either necessary to the reasonable enjoyment of the land or mere quasi-
easements of convenience, words adequate to cover them should have been included
h in the description of the land in the compulsory purchase order (see p 201 *f* to p 202 *c*
and *g h*, post); *Re Peck and the London School Board* [1893] 2 Ch 315 applied.
   (c) It followed that, since the ancillary rights which were claimed by the local
authority, but which either could not be, or had not been, included in the compulsory

b (1879) 12 Ch D 31, [1874-80] All ER Rep 669
j c Section 96 is set out at p 188 *h* to p 189 *b*, post
d Section 189(1), so far as material, provides: '. . . "house" includes—(a) any yard, garden
   outhouses, and appurtenances belonging thereto or usually enjoyed therewith, and (b)
   for the purposes of any provisions of this Act relating to the provision of housing accommodation, any part of a building which is occupied or intended to be occupied as a separate
   dwelling . . .'
e Section 92 is set out at p 189 *g* to *j*, post

purchase order, were necessary to the enjoyment of the maisonettes as housing accommodation, the Secretary of State had no power to confirm the order since *a* the land could not be used for the purpose for which it was sought to be acquired (see p 196 *h* and *j* and p 197 *d*, post).

Per Forbes J. In considering whether to confirm a compulsory purchase order under Part V of the 1957 Act the Secretary of State is under a duty to take into account the question of cost (see p 186 *c* to *f*, post); dictum of Ackner J in *J Murphy & Sons Ltd v Secretary of State for the Enviroment* [1973] 2 All ER at 32 doubted.   *b*

Notes

For powers to acquire land by compulsory purchase, see 8 Halsbury's Laws (4th Edn) 6-41, paras 1-57, and for cases on the subject, see 11 Digest (Reissue) 103-264, 5-1129.

For the Housing Act 1957, ss 92, 96, 97, 189, Sch 7, see 16 Halsbury's Statutes (3rd   *c* Edn) 187, 190, 242, 263.

For the Law of Property Act 1925, s 62, see 27 Halsbury's Laws (3rd Edn) 438.

Cases referred to in judgment

Ayr Harbour Trustees v Oswald (1883) 8 App Cas 623, HL, 11 Digest (Reissue) 103, *5*.
Beswick v Beswick [1967] 2 All ER 1197, [1968] AC 58, [1967] 3 WLR 932, HL, 12   *d* Digest (Reissue) 49, *256*.
Borman v Griffith [1930] 1 Ch 493, 99 LJCh 295, 142 LT 645, 19 Digest (Repl) 39, *204*.
Bryan v Wetherhead (1625) Cro Car 17, 79 ER 620, 17 Digest (Reissue) 430, *1918*.
Dowty Boulton Paul Ltd v Wolverhampton Corpn [1971] 2 All ER 277, [1971] 1 WLR 204, 135 JP 333, 69 LGR 192, 11 Digest (Reissue) 126, *153*.
Great Western Railway Co v Swindon and Cheltenham Extension Railway (1884) 9 App   *e* Cas 787, 53 LJCh 1075, 51 LT 798, 48 JP 821, HL, 11 Digest (Reissue) 108, *36*.
James v Plant (1836) 4 Ad & El 749, 6 Nev & MKB 282, 6 LJEx 260, 111 ER 967, 19 Digest (Repl) 17, *50*.
London and Westcliff Properties v Ministry of Housing and Local Government [1961] 1 All ER 610, [1961] 1 WLR 519, 125 JP 229, 59 LGR 244, 12 P & CR 154, Digest (Cont Vol A) 654, *108a*.
Murphy (J) & Sons Ltd v Secretary of State for the Environment [1973] 2 All ER 26, [1973] 1 WLR 560, 137 JP 401, 71 LGR 273, 25 P & CR 268.
Peck and the London School Board, Re [1893] 2 Ch 315, 62 LJCh 598, 68 LT 847, 3 R 511, 11 Digest (Reissue) 264, *1129*.
Phillips v Low [1892] 1 Ch 47, 61 LJCh 44, 65 LT 552, 19 Digest (Repl) 56, *309*.
Pinchin v London and Blackwall Railway Co (1854) 5 De GM & G 851, 3 Eq Rep 433, *f* 24 LJCh 417, 24 LTOS 196, 18 JP 822, 1 Jur NS 241, 43 ER 1101, 11 Digest (Reissue) 216, *661*.
Stourcliffe Estates Co Ltd v Bournemouth Corpn [1910] 2 Ch 12, [1908-10] All ER Rep 785, 79 LJCh 455, 102 LT 629, 74 JP 289, 8 LGR 595, CA, 11 Digest (Reissue) 123, *136*.
Trim v Sturminster Rural District Council [1938] 2 All ER 168, [1938] 2 KB 508, 107 LJKB *g* 687, 159 LT 7, 102 JP 249, 36 LGR 319, CA, 26 Digest (Repl) 687, *46*.
Wheeldon v Burrows (1879) 12 Ch D 31, [1874-80] All ER Rep 669, 48 LJCh 853, 41 LT 327, CA, 19 Digest (Repl) 48, *269*.

Motions

By notices of motion dated 30th October and 1st November 1974, the applicants,   *h* Sovmots Investments Ltd ('Sovmots') and Brompton Securities Ltd ('Brompton'), applied (i) for an order that the London Borough of Camden (Centre Point Residential Accommodation) Compulsory Purchase Order 1972 made by the second respondent, the London Borough of Camden ('Camden'), and confirmed on 12th September 1972 by the first respondent, the Secretary of State for the Environment ('the Minister'),

on 30th August 1974, be suspended until the final determination of the proceedings
a and (ii) for an order quashing the compulsory purchase order. The facts are set out
in the judgment.

Keith Goodfellow QC and Brian Knight for Sovmots.
Alistair Dawson for Brompton.
Gordon Slynn QC and Andrew Morritt for the Minister.
b David Widdicombe QC and Guy Roots for Camden.

Cur adv vult

16th July.   **FORBES J** read the folowing judgment: In this case the applicants,
Sovmots Investments Ltd ('Sovmots') and Brompton Securities Ltd ('Brompton'),
c move to quash an order known as the London Borough of Camden (Centre Point
Residential Accommodation) Compulsory Purchase Order 1972, made by the London
Borough of Camden ('Camden') under the Acquisition of Land (Authorisation
Procedure) Act 1946 and the Housing Act 1957, s 97(1) and Sch 7, and confirmed by
the Secretary of State for the Environment.   The order is concerned with a complex
of buildings situate on the south-east corner of St Giles's Circus, that is the intersection
d of Oxford Street and New Oxford Street with Tottenham Court Road and Charing
Cross Road. So far as is material to this matter the complex consists of three important
parts: to the west is a tower block of 34 storeys intended for use as offices; to the
east is a block known as the Earnshaw wing by reason of the fact that it fronts on to
Earnshaw Street.   This wing contains a basement car park, a ground and upper
ground floor which are intended for shops or showrooms, above that a first floor open
e floor space intended for showroom or offices, and above that what is described as the
mezzanine office floor intended for offices.   The roof of the mezzanine office floor
has been referred to as the podium and in counting floors counts as the second floor.
From the podium, which is merely the flat roof of the mezzanine offices, rise legs
which support six floors of maisonettes, each maisonette occupying two floors and
there being 36 maisonettes in all.   The remaining portion of the building is known as
f the bridge block; it runs across between the office tower and the Earnshaw wing
and contains two storeys of showrooms or offices—two storeys only because a new
road runs underneath it, hence the term the bridge block. The tower block is one
of the most prominent and tallest buildings in London.   The freeholder of the site
is the Greater London Council ('the GLC').   The first applicants, Sovmots, are the
owners of a 150 year lease of the site which began on 29th September 1960. The second
g applicants, Brompton, own a lease of the 36 maisonettes for 45 years from 29th
September 1973.   The complex itself was completed in the winter of 1966-67.   Up
to the last day of the inquiry which followed the compulsory purchase order no
part of the complex had ever been occupied.
On 12th September 1972 Camden made the compulsory puchase order which is
challenged in this case. They made it in respect solely of the 36 residential maisonettes
h on the 3rd, 4th, 5th, 6th, 7th and 8th floors of the complex.   It would be foolish to
shut one's eyes to the fact that there had been for some time before the making of
that order considerable comment in the press and in Parliament about the fact that
these residential units had been left unoccupied for so many years, and indeed one
of the reasons given by Camden for making the order was that, in their submission,
it was 'intolerable to right thinking people and contrary to the best interests of the
j community at large that the residential accommodation at Centre Point should
remain unoccupied'.   Sovmots objected to the making of the order and the Secretary
of State, as he was bound to do in the circumstances, held a local inquiry by a person
appointed by him for that purpose, Mr Peter Boydell QC, who sat with an assessor
and heard objections for very many days in January and February 1974.   The appointed
person reported to the Secretary of State on 28th March 1974, and on 30th August

the Secretary of State wrote a letter giving his decision that he had confirmed the
compulsory purchase order with certain amendments. It was found convenient by *a*
counsel in this case to refer to the appointed person as 'the inspector' and to the Secretary
of State as 'the Minister' and I shall follow that practice. At the time of the making
of the order Brompton held no interest in the land but by the time of the inquiry
they were leaseholders and they were therefore permitted to appear and make
objection at the inquiry.

The two main contentions for the applicants are: (1) A local authority has no power *b*
under the Housing Act 1957 to acquire compulsorily part of a building, and (2) if
such a power does exist then there must be specified in the compulsory purchase
order all the ancillary rights which may be desired in order that such part may be
effectively used for the purpose for which it is being acquired. There were several
subsidiary contentions. (3) A local authority has no power to acquire compulsorily
rights which do not exist at the time of making the compulsory purchase order. *c*
I think it is more convenient to regard this as one of the arguments which may be
used in support of the two main contentions. (4) The compulsory purchase order
as made is void for uncertainty and the Minister has no power to amend it. The
determination of this question depends on the determination of the second main
point above and I shall defer consideration of it until then. (5) Camden has been
guilty of an illegality and therefore the Minister should not have confirmed the *d*
order. (6) The inspector and/or the Minister took into account irrelevant factors or
failed to take into account relevant factors in the following respects: (a) in directing
himself that the fact that the maisonettes were unoccupied until the end of the
inquiry was a relevant consideration; (b) in directing himself that the cost of acquisition was not a relevant consideration or not a primary consideration; (c) in failing to
take into account a suggestion of the objectors that 35 maisonettes only should be *e*
acquired and not the 36 set out in the compulsory purchase order.

Points 3 and 4 above fall to be considered with the two main contentions and it
might be more convenient if I were to deal with points 5 and 6 before turning to
those main topics.

Point 5, the illegality point. The illegality or alleged illegality of which counsel
for Brompton complains arose in this way. After the making of the order and before *f*
the holding of the public inquiry there was correspondence between Camden and
the GLC the upshot of which in summary was this. Camden undertook not to serve
a notice to treat in respect of the GLC's freehold interest unless called on to do so
by the GLC; they also undertook to abide by the terms of the GLC's lease to Sovmots
and to obtain the GLC's consent to any arrangement about the use of the common
parts. In return the GLC undertook not to oppose the confirmation of the compul- *g*
sory purchase order. Counsel for Brompton contends that this was an illegal bargain
in that it fettered the hands of Camden, because not only did it preclude them from
acquiring the freehold, it also fettered the powers of sale given by s 94 of the Housing
Act 1957 and bound them to certain covenants in the lease, in particular those relating
to assignments and underlettings of the property, the acquisition of rights over
adjoining premises to the benefit of the land acquired, and the carrying out of altera- *h*
tions and additions to the premises. He relied on *Ayr Harbour Trustees v Oswald*[1],
Stourcliffe Estates Co Ltd v Bournemouth Corpn[2], *Dowty Bolton Paul Ltd v Wolverhampton
Corpn*[3], and in particular *London and Westcliff Properties v Minister of Housing and
Local Government*[4]. I am unable to accept this argument. Here the local authority
is not failing to exercise in full powers which they had persuaded Parliament were
necessary in full as in the case of *Ayr Harbour Trustees v Oswald*[1]. Nor have they *j*

1 (1883) 8 App Cas 623
2 [1910] 2 Ch 12, [1908-10] All ER Rep 785
3 [1971] 2 All ER 277, [1971] 1 WLR 204
4 [1961] 1 All ER 610, [1961] 1 WLR 519

entered into a bargain expressly forbidden by the Act which gave them the statutory
a powers as was the position in the *London and Westcliff Properties* case[1]. Rather have
they decided, as I think I must presume, that they can adequately exercise their statutory powers by acquiring a lease for 150 years instead of the whole freehold interest
in the maisonettes. As will be seen when I come to deal with the main contentions
there seems no doubt that a statutory authority cannot compulsorily acquire an
easement over land in the absence of express statutory authority even though the
b acquisition of an easement would be sufficient for their purposes; the whole land must
be acquired. This is not to say that they have no power to acquire an easement if the
owner of land agrees to sell them one. All the cases indicate that this course is open
to a statutory authority. If there is nothing wrong with a statutory authority saying
to an owner: 'Rather than pay for your freehold I will buy from you an easement if
you agree', I can see nothing wrong either with such an authority saying: 'Rather
c than pay for your freehold I am content to take a lease'. And if a local authority can
do that there seems to be nothing which could be called illegal in the action of
Camden here in agreeing to be satisfied with the acquisition of Sovmots' leasehold
interest without disturbing the freehold of the GLC. Accordingly I reject the contention
of counsel for Brompton on this point.

Point 6 is concerned with matters in which it is said the inspector at the inquiry
d failed to direct himself aright and consequently the Minister failed likewise when
he accepted the inspector's report and confirmed the compulsory purchase order on
the basis of it. For the purpose of considering the three matters complained of under
this heading it was necessary to look at some of the passages in the transcript of
the proceedings before the inspector and of course the text of his report and of the
Minister's letter. There is no dispute on the facts relevant to the first matter. It is
e a fact that up to the last day of the inquiry, as the inspector reported, the maisonettes
were unoccupied. It is also a fact that they were the subject of a lease to Brompton
which required Brompton to use their best endeavours to let them. It is also a fact
that as designed it was felt that they were unsuitable for letting separately from the
rest of the complex and that Brompton had found it necessary to carry out considerable
internal work in order to make them so suitable, and that the work was still proceed-
f ing at the time of the inquiry. During the course of the inquiry it is clear that much
time was spent on considering whether or not the lease to Brompton was likely to
produce occupation of these maisonettes, and as much time on the type of tenant
likely to use them as a result of Brompton's operations. Clearly too there were many
suggestions made at the inquiry on Camden's behalf that it was disgraceful that these
maisonettes should be left unoccupied for so long, and personal attacks were made on
g Sovmots and those interested in that company for leaving the complex empty. It
was in fact suggested, as it had been suggested before the inquiry began, that it was
deliberate policy on behalf of Sovmots to leave the property unoccupied because of
the rapid capital appreciation of property of this kind. The inspector deals with these
points quite clearly in his report. He acquits Sovmots of any deliberate policy of keeping the property unoccupied. He deals with the question of the type of tenant that
h Brompton was likely to attract and contrasts that type of tenant with the type of
tenant who would occupy the property if the compulsory purchase order were confirmed. But he never makes a specific finding on the question of whether or not in
his view there was a likelihood in the immediate future of the property being put to
residential use if the compulsory purchase order were not confirmed. Much
ingenuity has been displayed by both counsel for Sovmots and counsel for Camden
j in seeking to extract inferences from certain passages in the inspector's report about
conclusions he may have come to on this topic. But then at the end of the report
comes a passage to which in particular counsel for Sovmots takes exception. In part D
of his report the inspector turns to what he calls 'remaining matters'. He starts with

1 [1961] 1 All ER 610, [1961] 1 WLR 519

the objection of a Mr Somers and then turns to the representation of Mr David Gee
who appeared on behalf of Shelter. He spends two short paragraphs, some six lines,   *a*
in dealing with Mr Gee's representation. He then passes to part E entitled 'Summary
and Recommendation'. This part starts off in this way:

> '1) Two of the most important and impressive witnesses were Mr John Toomey,
> the Vice-Chairman of the Covent Garden Community Association and Mr
> David Gee who spoke on behalf of Shelter. 2) Mr Toomey described the character   *b*
> of the dwellings and the shops and other buildings which until 1959 occupied
> the site where Centre Point now stands and he described the small and closely
> knit community who lived and worked there.'

The inspector then went on to report Mr Toomey's contention that it was important
that community life should be restored to this area and, in para 3, the inspector   *c*
recommends that the Secretary of State should take account of this. And then para 4
reads as follows:

> 'Mr Gee emphasised what I regard as the two most important features of this
> case. First that these maisonettes have been empty ever since they were built;
> and secondly that tens of thousands of Londoners have no home whatever of their
> own. The emptiness of these maisonettes and the emptiness of the lives of   *d*
> these homeless Londoners provide a stark contrast. The case for making the
> maisonettes available for 36 of these homeless families is, in my view, powerful.
> There is, as I have concluded in the earlier parts of this report, no compelling
> reason in fact or law to withhold confirmation of the order.'

He then goes on to make his recommendation for confirmation of the order.   *e*
   Now counsel for Sovmots concedes that the fact that the maisonettes were empty
was capable of being a relevant consideration at the time when Camden made the
the compulsory purchase order but, he says, on a proper reading of the report, there
was no basis for suggesting that the sublease was not genuine or would not result in
letting and in those circumstances the fact that the maisonettes had been vacant
since they were built had ceased to have any legal relevance. The only possible   *f*
antithesis, he suggests, was occupation if Camden acquired the property as against
occupation if private arrangements were left undisturbed, a matter which as I have
already indicated the inspector fully dealt with. But I think he is reading far too much
into those words of the inspector. It is noteworthy that the representation of Mr
David Gee is noted at the bottom of p 100 of the report, that the 'Summary and
Recommendation' begins on p 101, and the passage to which I have referred (para 4)   *g*
is on p 102. The hundred pages which precede those three are taken up with a detailed
consideration of the facts, the main and subsidiary arguments, and the conclusions to
which the inspector came on them. Counsel for Sovmots attaches importance to the
fact that para 4, to which I have already referred, occurs in that part of the report
marked 'Summary and Recommendation'. But when one looks at it, it cannot be
said that it is a summary either of the report itself or of the matters which transpired   *h*
at the inquiry. Rather is it a summary of the evidence of Mr Toomey and Mr Gee,
the two witnesses with whom the inspector was last concerned; when in para 4 the
inspector refers to the two most important features of the case he is in my view dealing
with the two most important features emphasised by Mr Gee and Mr Toomey,
and in describing them as features cannot I think be said to be intending this to be a
conclusion. The real nub of this paragraph seems to me to be the sentence which   *j*
starts in the middle of it: 'The case for making the maisonettes available for 36 of
these homeless families is in my view powerful.'
   That seems to me to be a conclusion to which the inspector was perfectly entitled
to come and certainly not one with which any court should feel itself entitled to
interfere. I do not think that in dealing with the emptiness of the property in this

way the inspector misdirected himself and I find myself therefore unable to accept
a the submissions of counsel for Sovmots on this point.

The second point on which he maintains the inspector misdirected himself is the
question of the cost of acquisition. At the inquiry Camden argued that cost was a
wholly irrelevant consideration, or at least not a primary consideration, but nevertheless prudently armed itself with figures concerned with cost, and cost was very
much an argument at the inquiry. I can deal with the position briefly I think in this
b way. Originally Centre Point was conceived as a complex unit for letting to a single
tenant. The maisonettes were expected to be occupied by the directors and executives
of the concern, necessarily a very large one, which would become tenants of the
complex. As such they originally consisted of a single room on the ground floor
(a living room with kitchen) and two bedrooms and a bathroom upstairs. When
Brompton took over the lease they considered that they could not reasonably let
c them in this way and work was necessary to erect partitions so as to provide a separate
kitchen and living room on the ground floor. It seems slightly ironical that although
Brompton by their lease were bound to let the maisonettes at rents of not less than
£2,000 per annum exclusive of outgoings, it was conceded on all sides that the
maisonettes, even as altered by Brompton, were well below the standards required
of local authority housing, and there was much argument as to the precise amount
d which would be required to bring them up to that standard if acquired by Camden. It
is further to be noted that the figures produced showed, as I understand the matter,
that on the calculations of Camden the annual loss for each maisonette would be
either £2,740 or £3,520 depending on whether one took an interest rate of 10 per
cent or 12½ per cent. The figure put forward by the objectors was very much higher,
ranging between just under £7,000 to nearly £9,000 per annum per maisonette.
e Even these figures made no allowance for any works required to bring the maisonettes
up to the standard of local authority housing, nor did they take into account any
possible compensation for injurious affection. It can be seen, therefore, that cost was
taken as a serious issue at the inquiry. Camden's argument that cost was not a relevant
consideration was based on *J Murphy & Sons Ltd v Secretary of State for the Environment*[1].
This was a case involving a compulsory purchase order made by Camden for land
f for housing, and a simultaneous planning inquiry, because the land which they wished
to acquire had no planning permission for residential development. In that case,
as in this, it is clear that considerable evidence was brought at the inquiry as to the
cost of developing the site, and indeed the inspector in that case considered that the
above average cost was 'yet another factor demonstrating the unsuitability of the site
for housing'. Nevertheless the Secretary of State confirmed the compulsory purchase
g order and granted planning permission saying in the course of his decision letter[2]:
'The cost of developing a site for a particular purpose is not thought to be a relevant
consideration in determining whether planning permission should be granted.'

Ackner J took the view that cost was an irrelevant consideration in determining
whether planning permission should be granted under s 29 of the Town and Country
Planning Act 1971. He also appears to have said[3] that it was similarly irrelevant
h when considering a compulsory purchase order. If Ackner J was intending to say
that cost can never be a relevant consideration either in a planning appeal or on a
compulsory purchase order (and that I am told is how this decision is interpreted in
Whitehall) then I find myself unable to agree with him. Of course planning is concerned with land use, but the Minister charged with the overall duty of considering
applications for planning permission and the confirmation of planning proposals for
j particular areas must, it seems to me, be entitled to bear in mind the likelihood of
the proposed development being carried into effect. If the Minister is faced with rival
proposals for the development of a particular piece of land, and on land use grounds

1   [1973] 2 All ER 26, [1973] 1 WLR 560
2   [1973] 2 All ER at 30, [1973] 1 WLR at 564
3   [1973] 2 All ER at 32, [1973] 1 WLR at 566

either rival solution is equally attractive but one of them could only be carried out by
an eccentric millionaire while the other would be regarded as a wise commercial   *a*
venture by any sensible commercial undertaking, it seems to me that the Minister
would be perfectly entitled to take this matter into account when deciding on the
planning use of that particular piece of ground. One cannot shut one's eyes to the
fact that at any rate a few years ago the practice of what was known as cost-benefit
analysis was regarded as a useful tool in arriving at a proper decision on land use
problems. Before the Minister's interpretation of Ackner J's decision became current,   *b*
the economic viability of a projected scheme was frequently the subject of attack or
justification at planning inquiries. Perhaps the longest inquiry ever held in the
planning field was the special inquiry into proposals for the third London Airport
by the commission presided over by Sir Eustace Roskill. The economic factors were
not only there canvassed at great length; they were regarded by the commission as
of such importance as to override the environmental objections and to determine the   *c*
commission's recommendations.

I think the position is a fortiori with compulsory purchase orders made by local
authorities under Part V of the Housing Act 1957. It seems to me that the Minister
has a duty to consider cost in these cases, or at any rate in suitable cases may well
have such a duty. The provision of housing accommodation after all involves the
proper deployment not only of the ratepayers' but also the taxpayers' money and it   *d*
seems to me that the Secretary of State is entitled to take these matters into account
in suitable cases and that therefore cost can be relevant. That I think is the extent
to which the court can give a ruling: cost may or may not be a relevant consideration
depending on the circumstances of the case; all that the court can do is to say that
cost can be a relevant consideration and leave it to the Minister to decide whether
in any circumstances it is or is not. Of course it follows that the weight to be given to   *e*
cost, if it is a relevant factor, is also a matter for the Minister and not one in respect of
which any court is entitled to substitute its opinion. Questions therefore whether in
any particular case cost is relevant, is a primary, or only a secondary consideration,
are not for the courts but entirely for the Minister. I would conclude that it is impossible to say that cost can never be a relevant consideration either in a planning matter
or in a compulsory purchase matter. It can be in both or either and it will depend in   *f*
every case on the circumstances of the case. It is then a matter for the Minister to
decide whether or not in any particular instance cost is in fact a relevant consideration.
In the instant case I think the inspector was put in some difficulty because no attempt
was made to differentiate between relevance and weight, and the inspector was to
some extent left with the submission that whether cost was a relevant consideration
or a primary consideration was one and the same argument. What in fact he con-   *g*
cluded is to be found in para 186, p 70. He said this: 'Cost of acquisition is not a primary
factor at this stage but it cannot be totally ignored.' And in his conclusion at para 190:
'The likely cost of these maisonettes is not unacceptably high. It is likely to be
commensurate with the benefits which would be secured.'

Perhaps that is not the end of counsel for Sovmots' submission because he puts it
alternatively in this way, that the inspector erroneously considered that cost was in   *h*
law not a relevant consideration and therefore did not report fully on the financial argument; had he realised that cost was not irrelevant he would have reported more fully.
I think the answer to this point is to be found in the passage I earlier read from the
Inspector's report: 'Cost of acquisition is not a primary factor at this stage but it
cannot be totally ignored.'

The only way to construe that passage is that the inspector clearly considered that   *j*
cost was relevant but he also considered that it was not a primary factor at that stage.
I do not see how a court can interfere with that conclusion. He was certainly entitled
to consider that cost was not a primary factor and if in doing so he paid less attention
to the argument on cost than he might have done if he had considered it to be otherwise does not seem to me to be a matter with which the court can possibly be concerned.

In the event I hold that cost can certainly be a relevant factor, that the inspector
a clearly accepted that it was, but that, not being a primary factor, it did not require
as much detailed consideration as it would otherwise have done. I therefore cannot
accept this submission of counsel for Sovmots either.

The last of the subsidiary points taken by counsel for Sovmots is that the inspector
failed to take into account one of the objections of Sovmots, namely that the order
should be varied by substituting for the 36 maisonettes sought to be acquired, 35
b maisonettes only. The basis of this objection was a suggestion made by counsel for
Sovmots at the inquiry, Sir Derek Walker-Smith QC, that one of the 36 maisonettes
should be left for occupation by a caretaker who might well be required by Sovmots
for the efficient supervision of the remainder of the complex which would be left
in their ownership. This suggestion arose in this way. During the course of the
inquiry a Mr Barnes was called as a witness for Camden and on the second day Sir
c Derek cross-examined him with questions about caretaking in relation to the
premises, apparently intending to canvass this suggestion. On the third day he returned to this matter and the witness said that he had not understood that to be the
purport of the previous day's questions. There then occurs this passage in the
transcript:

d   'The inspector: I do not think I did either, Sir Derek. Your suggestion is that one
should be extracted as it were.
        'Sir Derek: Yes.
        'The inspector: For the use of the occupiers of the main office block and the
bridge block.
        'Sir Derek: That is so, sir, on the basis that you may say in your wisdom at
e   the end of the day, though we are seeking to contend to the contrary, that the
35 would go but we would all say that one of those should be reserved for this
administrative purpose.
        'The inspector: And the order could therefore be modified to that extent.
        'Sir Derek: Indeed.'

f On the basis of this passage in the transcript counsel for Sovmots maintains that it
was made plain to the inspector that one of the proposals for the amendment of
the order which the objectors were making was that 35 and not 36 maisonettes should
in fact be acquired, and that the inspector so understood the matter. At a later stage
of the inquiry counsel for Camden asked certain questions of one of Sovmots' witnesses
in relation to the caretaking matter, and he also made some reference to it in his
g final speech. The inspector nowhere made reference in his report to this aspect of
the matter and no mention is made of the possibility of an amendment to extract
one maisonette from the ambit of the compulsory purchase order. Counsel for
Sovmots says that that means that the report is imperfect and that the Minister in
confirming the order had not been made aware of one of the objections which he
should have taken into account. But the reason for this omission by the inspector
h of any reference to this point may well be the manner in which it was dealt with by
Sovmots' counsel at the inquiry in his final speech. The only part of that speech which
could be construed as a reference to this matter occurs on p 31 of the transcript of
the 11th day of the inquiry at a point where Sir Derek is dealing in his final speech
with the onus which he suggested lay on Camden to prove that this particular accommodation was suitable for an identified need. He refers to a question which the
j inspector put to him on the third day. The question from the inspector finished: 'I
do not suppose you would go so far would you as to say that Camden would find it
impossible to find 36 suitable applicants for these maisonettes.' Having quoted
this Sir Derek goes on:

      'Sir, it may be that the answer to that question is: yes, they would, but in my
submission it would not prove Camden's case. What they would have to show is

that 36 households, or it may only be 35, could and would be suitably
accommodated in the maisonettes at suitable cost.'   a

Now those words 'or it may only be 35' amount to the only reference in the whole of
that speech, which occupied some 78 pages of the transcript, to this particular question.
It frequently happens in inquiries, as in litigation, that matters are put in the course
of a long case to witnesses and then abandoned at a subsequent stage by counsel for
the party, and I do not think that it could be said that the inspector was not entitled   b
to take the view that this point had been abandoned in that sort of fashion. He was
surely entitled to believe that so experienced and painstaking an advocate as Sir
Derek would, if this matter was still a matter of any substance, have devoted more to
it in his final speech than a passing and oblique reference in six words only in the
course of a long and careful analysis of all the submissions which Sovmots wished
to make to the inspector. In the circumstances I am satisfied that the inspector was   c
entitled to regard this as a point which was no longer alive and in those circumstances
it seems to me the whole basis of counsel for Sovmots' argument fails.

I now turn to the two main contentions for the applicants, and the first of them is
that a local authority has no power under the Housing Act 1957 to acquire compulsorily a part of a building divorced from the land on which it stands. Counsel for
Sovmots advances two principal arguments in support of this contention. The first   d
is that on the proper construction of the Act itself this conclusion is seen to emerge;
the second, that this Act is a consolidating Act and the history of its provisions also
supports this conclusion.

There is a line of authorities which starts with the judgment of Lord Cranworth LC in
Pinchin v London and Blackwall Railway Co[1], as explained by Lord Watson in *Great Western
Railway v Swindon and Cheltenham Extension Railway Co*[2]. The effect of these cases can,   e
I think, be summarised in this way. In the absence of any peculiar powers conferred
by the special Act, the Lands Clauses Consolidation Act 1845 does not empower a
statutory authority to acquire compulsorily either strata of land or a mere easement
over land: the whole land in solido must be acquired. The definition of 'lands'
in s 3 of the 1845 Act, on which this principle is based, has now been replaced by the
definition in s 1(3) of the Compulsory Purchase Act 1965, which is as follows: '..."land"   f
includes anything falling within any definition of that expression in the enactment
under which the purchase is authorised . . .' Section 1(2) of that Act provides: 'In
construing this Part of this Act the enactment under which the purchase is authorised
and the compulsory purchase order under the Act of 1946 shall be deemed to be the
special Act.' The 1946 Act is the Acquisition of Land (Authorisation Procedure) Act
1946, and the definition of land in that Act is similar in import to that in the 1965 Act.   g
The governing definition is therefore that in s 189(1) of the Housing Act 1957 which
is in the following terms: '..."land" includes any right over land . . .'

There is nothing in this definition which appears to me to require a departure from
the general rule which I have mentioned, and indeed I understand that this is accepted
by all parties to this dispute.

The relevant powers of acquisition conferred on local authorities under the 1957   h
Act are to be found in ss 96 and 97 which are in the following terms:

'96.—A local authority shall have power under this Part of this Act—(a) to
acquire any land, including any houses or buildings thereon, as a site for the
erection of houses, (b) to acquire houses, or buildings which may be made suitable
as houses, together with any lands occupied with the houses or buildings, or any   j
estate or interest in houses or in buildings which may be made suitable as houses,
(c) to acquire land (including houses or other buildings) proposed to be used for

1   (1854) 5 De GM & G 851 at 862
2   (1884) 9 App Cas 787 at 803

any purpose authorised by sections ninety-three or ninety-five of this Act, whether
or not the land forms part of a site for the erection of houses, (d) to acquire land
for the purpose of the carrying out thereon by them of works for the purpose
of, or connected with, the alteration, enlarging, repair or improvement of an
adjoining house. (e) to acquire land for the purpose of the sale or lease of the land
under the powers conferred by paragraph (a) of subsection (1) and by subsection
(2) of section one hundred and five of this Act.

'97.—(1) Land for the purposes of this Part of this Act may be acquired by a
local authority by agreement, or they may be authorised to purchase land compulsorily for those purposes by the Minister; and the Seventh Schedule to this Act
shall apply in relation to a compulsory purchase under this section . . .'

Then s 97(2) deals with the power to acquire land even though it is not immediately
required for those purposes.

Now it seems to me that one must read these sections together and when so read I
have no doubt at all that when s 97 speaks of land and its acquisition by agreement or
compulsorily it is referring to all the matters set out in s 96. It is apparent when one
looks at s 96 that paras (a)(c)(d) and (e) all begin with the words 'to acquire land'
or 'any land' whereas (b) begins with the words 'to acquire houses or buildings', etc.
It seems to me impossible to contend that the legislature intended that local
authorities should have power to acquire 'land' as set out in s 96 (a) (c) (d) and (e) by
the methods referred to in s 97 and not to acquire 'houses' as set out in para (b). I
therefore conclude that Parliament in passing these two sections intended 'land'
to be a word apt to include houses or buildings.

Then one turns to s 189(1) for the definition of house. That definition is as follows:

'. . . "house" includes—(a) any yard, garden, outhouses, and appurtenances
belonging thereto or usually enjoyed therewith, and (b) for the purposes of any
provisions of this Act relating to the provision of housing accommodation, any
part of a building which is occupied or intended to be occupied as a separate
dwelling . . .'

Leaving aside that part of the definition which falls under para (a) that part under
para (b) (which I shall refer to as 'the extended definition') is expressed to be relevant only 'for the purposes of any provisions of this Act relating to the provision of
housing accommodation'. Now what are the provisions of this Act relating to the
provision of housing accommodation? Counsel for Sovmots urges me to take the
view that the only sections dealing with the provision of housing accommodation are
those provisions contained in s 92:

'92.—(1) A local authority may provide housing accommodation—(a) by the
erection of houses on any land acquired or appropriated by them, (b) by the
conversion of any buildings into houses, (c) by acquiring houses, (d) by altering,
enlarging, repairing or improving any houses or buildings which have, or an
estate or interest in which has, been acquired by the local authority. Any such
powers as aforesaid may, for supplying the needs of the district, be exercised
outside the district of the local authority.'

Then there are three further subsections, and I do not think I need read anything
except perhaps sub-s (4):

'For the purposes of this Part of this Act "provision of housing accommodation"
include the provision of lodging-houses, and separate houses or cottages containing one or several tenements, and, in the case of a cottage, a cottage with a
garden of not more than one acre.'

Counsel for Sovmots points out, although it cannot strictly be taken to assist in the
construction of the Act, that the marginal note to this section is 'mode of provision

of accommodation', but he goes on to make the point that when one examines this
section it is clear that it is the only section in Part V which is concerned actually with *a*
the provision of accommodation itself. Sections 93, 94 and 95 are concerned with the
provision of facilities of one kind or another ancillary to housing accommodation
and ss 96 and 97 are concerned with the acquisition of land in order that accommodation might be provided. So, he argues, while s 92, by incorporating the
extended definition of house, entitles a local authority to provide houses in parts
of buildings, it does not entitle a local authority to acquire a part of a building under *b*
s 96(*b*). Now the first difficulty consequent on this construction seems to me to be
this: that it necessarily follows that if that construction is right then a local authority
has no power to acquire a part of a building even by agreement, for s 97 deals with the
procedure for acquisition whether compulsorily or by agreement. However, there is
another and, it seems to me, more formidable difficulty in counsel for Sovmots' way.
The draftsman of the Act clearly intended that the extended definition of house should *c*
not be a definition which was applicable to the word house wherever it appeared in
the Act. The draftsman was intent on limiting its application to those provisions
relating to the provision of housing accommodation. The Act itself is divided into
several parts. These parts are given sub-headings. While it is not permissible to look
at marginal notes as an aid to construction of a statute it seems to be well settled that
sub-headings are in a different category and one may look at them at any rate to *d*
resolve any ambiguities (see Craies on Statute Law[1]). Part I of the Act is sub-headed
'General Provisions as respects Local Authorities'. Part II is sub-headed 'Provisions
for securing the repair, maintenance and sanitary condition of houses'. This is the
Part which deals by way of demolition and closing orders with unfit premises beyond
repair at reasonable cost and what the local authority may do with unfit premises
which are capable of repair at reasonable cost. Part III is sub-headed 'Clearance and *e*
Re-development', and there are provisions dealing with clearance areas and re-
development areas. Part IV is sub-headed 'Abatement of Overcrowding'. Parts II,
III and IV of the Act are all thus dealing with various aspects of housing accommodation and the words 'house' or 'houses' appear scattered thickly through these
provisions. The draftsman of the Act was thus at pains to say that this extended
definition of house in s 189(1) was not intended to apply to that word where it appeared *f*
in those Parts of the Act. But when one comes to Part V (that is a Part sub-headed
'Provision of Housing Accommodation') the sections contained in that Part are
concerned either directly or indirectly with actually providing houses for people to
live in. Thus s 92 contains the method by which a local authority may actually provide
housing accommodation either by building new houses, by converting buildings which
are not dwelling-houses into houses, by acquiring houses as they stand or by altering *g*
or improving any existing houses. There are supplementary provisions in ss 93 to 95
to which I have already referred. Then in s 96 the local authority is given power to
acquire land for the specific purpose of providing houses by the methods outlined in
s 92. Now all these sections must be read together, and so read they provide a code
governing the powers and duties of local authorities in relation to providing housing
accommodation. They are, read in this way, responsive to the description given in *h*
the sub-heading to this Part of the Act; but even without the assistance of that sub-
heading I think it is clear that they are sections 'relating to the provision of housing
accommodation'. An additional difficulty is this, that, if counsel for Sovmots' argument is right, the power of a local authority under s 92(1)(*c*) to provide housing accommodation 'by acquiring houses' permits them to do so by acquiring a part of a building,
but when one comes to precisely the same words in s 96(*b*) it does not. It seems to me *j*
consistent with authority and good sense that the proper construction of the definition section to which I have referred is that the extended definition of house applies
to that term wherever it is used in Part V.

---

1 7th Edn (1971), pp 210-212

Thus counsel for Sovmots' first point, that the ordinary construction of the Housing
a Act 1957 does not allow one to conclude that a local authority is empowered to take
part of a building, in my view fails.

His second argument in support of his main proposition is that one arrives at the
same conclusion by following a process of reasoning based on the fact that the 1957
Act was a consolidation Act. The argument goes like this. In a consolidation Act
one presumes that Parliament has not intended to change the law. The reason for
b this is put, with his customary clarity, by Lord Reid in *Beswick v Beswick*[1]:

> '. . . it is the invariable practice of Parliament to require from those who have
> prepared a consolidation Bill an assurance that it will make no substantial change
> in the law and to have that checked by a committee. On this assurance the Bill
> is then passed into law, no amendment being permissible.'

c One is therefore justified in coming to the conclusion that Parliament in passing a
consolidation Act passed it in reliance on an assurance that it did in fact make no substantial change. Not only was the Housing Act 1957 a consolidation Act but so was its
predecessor, the Housing Act 1936, and the predecessor of that Act in its turn, the
Housing Act 1925. The provisions of the 1925 Act which correspond to ss 92, 96 and 97
of the 1957 Act are to be found respectively in ss 58, 63 and 64 of the earlier Act. The
d question one has to ask oneself is this: under those provisions of the 1925 Act was a
local authority empowered to acquire a part only of a building? If the answer to that
question is Yes, then of course the whole of counsel for Sovmots' argument falls
to the ground. If the answer is No, then, says counsel for Sovmots, if one traces the
history of the manner in which the extended definition of 'house' appeared in the 1957
Act, it is plain that Parliament thought that it was making no change to the law set
e out in the 1925 Act and that therefore these words in the 1957 Act must be construed
in such a way as not to give the local authority a power to acquire part of a building
which it did not have, ex concessis, under the 1925 Act.

Section 58(1) of the 1925 Act is in these terms:

> 'A local authority shall have power under this part of this Act . . . (*b*) to acquire
f > any estate or interest in any houses which may be made suitable as dwelling-
> houses for the working classes together with any land occupied with such
> houses . . .''

The definition of 'dwelling-house' in s 135 of the 1925 Act contains only the equivalent of the first part of the definition of house contained in s 189 of the 1957 Act. It is
conceded that the only provision which would entitle a local authority to acquire a
g part of a building is that contained in the second part of the definition in that section.
This extended definition does not appear in the 1925 Act and so it must follow that
there was no power in 1925 to do what the local authority wishes to do in the instant
case. In s 62(2) of the Housing Act 1930 appears for the first time the extended definition
of 'house' (in this case, 'or dwelling-house') included in the second part of the definition
in the 1957 Act. That subsection is in these terms:
h
> 'For the purpose of any provisions of this Act relating to the provision of
> housing accommodation, the expressions "house" or "dwelling-house" include,
> unless the context otherwise requires, any part of a building which is occupied,
> or intended to be occupied, as a separate dwelling.'

j Counsel for Sovmots then invites attention to those sections of the 1930 Act which
relate to the provision of housing accommodation. These are to be found, effectively,
in Part III, for Part IV confers no powers relating to the provision of accommodation
at all. Part III is subheaded: 'Provisions with respect to the Provision of Housing
Accomodation and Government Assistance towards Cost of Re-housing Operations.'

---

1   [1967] 2 All ER 1197 at 1202, [1968] AC 58 at 73

Counsel for Sovmots argument can really be summarised in this way. If one looks
at that part of the Act it is principally concerned with government assistance towards *a*
the cost of providing housing accommodation and therefore the extended definition
of 'house' applies really only in the context of computing the number of 'houses'
which would qualify for government assistance. He goes on, of course, to say that
when the 1936 Act was passed that was in its turn a consolidating Act, consolidating the
provisions of the 1925 and 1930 Acts and the extended definition of 'house' to which I
have already referred is there to be found in s 188(3). The provisions relating to *b*
government assistance have been transferred to Part VI. In its turn, therefore, the
1936 Act must be construed as meaning that the extended definition once again
applies only in those parts of the 1936 Act which are concerned with computing
government grant or assistance. The equivalent argument applies when one comes
to construe the 1957 Act.

Counsel for the Minister counters this with a somewhat complicated argument *c*
based on s 65(1) and (2) of the Housing Act 1930 and the undoubted fact that the
two acts must be construed as one. He will forgive me, I am sure, if I do not follow
him into the intricacies of this argument because in my view there are two short
answers to counsel for Sovmots' argument on this point. The first is that there seem to
me to be no provisions in the 1957 Act which relate to government grant or assistance
towards the cost of providing housing accommodation. If that is so then it is difficult *d*
to see, if one were to accept the proposition for which counsel for Sovmots contends,
that there is anything to which the extended definition of 'house' in the 1957 Act
could apply; but Parliament must have intended it to apply to something and so
must have intended to change the law. The other answer seems to me to be this:
the presumption that Parliament intended to make no substantial change in the law
in passing a consolidation Act is only a presumption, and one useful in solving any *e*
ambiguity. Once again Lord Reid in *Beswick v Beswick*[1] gives the answer:

'In construing any Act of Parliament we are seeking the intention of Parliament,
and it is quite true that we must deduce that intention from the words of the Act.
If the words of the Act are only capable of one meaning we must give them that
meaning no matter how they got there. If, however, they are capable of having *f*
more than one meaning we are, in my view, well entitled to see how they got
there.'

I cannot really think, despite counsel for Sovmots' arguments, that there is any
ambiguity in the expression 'the provisions of this Act relating to the provision of
housing accommodation' as used in the 1957 Act. They seem to me to apply clearly
to the whole of Part V of that Act and therefore equally to ss 96 and 97. There is no *g*
room for applying the presumption because there is no ambiguity. It follows therefore
that, on this argument too, counsel for Sovmots first contention fails and that there
is power in a local authority under the Housing Act 1957 to acquire a part of a building
for the purpose of providing housing accommodation.

To decide that a local authority has power under the Housing Act 1957 to acquire
part of a building is not however an end of the matter. It is here that one must examine *h*
counsel for Brompton's argument that a statutory authority has no power to acquire
rights which did not exist at the time of the making of the compulsory purchase order.
It is important to differentiate this argument from the argument that any rights
which are required must be specified in the compulsory purchase order which is the
second main contention of counsel for Sovmots. Counsel for Brompton's argument
is directed to the question whether there exists any power to acquire non-existent *j*
rights at all.

The start of this argument is once again the judgment of Lord Cranworth LC in
Pinchin's case[2]:

1   [1967] 2 All ER at 1202, [1968] AC at 73
2   (1854) 5 De GM & G 851 at 862

'. . . the Legislature did not mean that if I have a field free from a right of way,
a   I shall be bound upon any compensation to substitute for that a field subject
to a right of way; if it is to be taken from me, it must be taken from me *in
solido.*'

The basis of this dictum is that in the absence of peculiar powers in the special Act
there is no general power given to a statutory authority to create and take an interest
b   which did not previously exist. The principle is put succinctly in Halsbury's Laws[1]:

'There is no power to create and take an interest in land such as a lease without
acquiring the freehold or other interests unless specific power to do so is given in
the special Act; nor is there power to create and purchase an easement without
purchasing the land unless special provision is made or in either case the owner
agrees.'
c

Examples of a special power to create and take rights in the nature of leases are to
be found in the Agriculture Act 1947, s 93, and to create and take easements in the
Water Act 1948, s 1.

It may help to clarify the position if I take an example. Suppose a local authority
desires to acquire Blackacre for the purpose of exercising some of its own powers.
d   Suppose an easement of way exists in favour of Blackacre over Whiteacre, an
adjacent piece of land. There is no doubt that under the general rule the local
authority has the power to acquire compulsorily the existing easement over Whiteacre. On the other hand, if no such easement exists, the local authority cannot acquire
one compulsorily however convenient or even necessary it might be for the purpose
for which they wish to acquire Blackacre. They have the power to acquire it, in the
e   sense that it is permissible for them to do so by agreement with the owner of Whiteacre,
but if that owner will not agree they must either acquire the whole of his land or do
without the easement.

Is there anything in the Special Act (ie the Housing Act 1957) which adds to or
subtracts from this general position? It is important at this juncture to consider that
part of the definition of 'house' in s 189(1) which has not so far figured in the argument.
f   This is in these terms: ' "house" includes—(*a*) any yard, garden, outhouses and appurtenances belonging thereto or usually enjoyed therewith...' Assume that Blackacre in
the example above is a 'house' without having to pray in aid the extended definition,
i e that it does not form part of a building. It seems clear that para (*a*) neither adds
to nor detracts from the general rule to which I have referred. In *Trim v Sturminster
RDC*[2], a case on the definition of 'house' in the Housing Act 1936, which is in precisely
g   the same terms as para (*a*), Slesser LJ in referring to the term appurtenances as there
used said this[3]:

'The word "appurtenances" has had applied to it, through a long series of cases
mostly dealing with the question of the meaning of the word in demises, a certain
limited meaning, and it is now beyond question that, broadly speaking, nothing
will pass, in the case of a demise, under the word "appurtenances" which would
h   not equally pass under a conveyance of the principal subject-matter without the
word "appurtenances". That is to say, as pointed out in the early case of *Bryan
v. Wetherhead*[4] in 1623, the word "appurtenances" will pass with the house, the
orchard, yard, curtilage and gardens, but not the land, and that view, as far as I
have understood the authorities, has never been departed from, except that in
certain cases it has been held, on the material in those cases, that the word
j   "appurtenances" may be competent to pass incorporeal hereditaments . . .'

1   8 Halsbury's Laws (4th Edn) para 56
2   [1938] 2 All ER 168, [1938] 2 KB 508
3   [1938] 2 All ER at 170, [1938] 2 KB at 515
4   (1625) Cro Car 17

The term 'appurtenances' therefore is apt to include easements.

But the qualifying phrase attached to the term 'appurtenances' is 'belonging   *a*
thereto or usually enjoyed therewith', words which clearly import a pre-existing
state of affairs. The existing easement of way in my example is an appurtenance which
'belongs' to a 'house'; the local authority therefore has the power to acquire it compulsorily under s 97. If no such easement exists it is not an appurtenance belonging
to the house so there is no power to acquire it.

So far the situation has been considered where Blackacre and Whiteacre are in   *b*
different ownerships. Does it make any difference if they are in the same ownership?
I think not. Of course on this hypothesis the way across Whiteacre to Blackacre is
not strictly an easement at all; it can only at most be a quasi-easement as the term is
normally employed. But the addition of the words 'or usually enjoyed therewith'
in the definition is apt to cover such quasi-easements: see per Tindal CJ in the old
case of *James v Plant*[1]:   *c*

> 'We all agree that, where there is a unity of seisin of the land, and of the way
> over the land, in one and the same person, the right of way is either extinguished
> or suspended, according to the duration of the respective estates in the land and
> the way; and that, after such extinguishment, or during such suspension of the
> right, the way cannot pass as an appurtenant under the ordinary legal sense of   *d*
> that word. We agree also in the principle laid down by the Court of King's
> Bench, that, in the case of an unity of seisin, in order to pass a way existing in
> point of user, but extinguished or suspended in point of law, the grantor must
> either employ words of express grant, or must describe the way in question as
> one."used and enjoyed with the land" which forms the subject matter of the
> conveyance.'   *e*

So long as the way, while not being an easement, was one usually enjoyed with Blackacre, the local authority again has power to acquire such a way compulsorily, but if
there was no such way in existence even as a quasi-easement before the compulsory
purchase order then the local authority has no power to create and take it
compulsorily.

Lastly, these two examples have been of acquisition of a house which is not part   *f*
of a building. Is any difference introduced if a house is only a house by reason of the
extended definition? Now although a part of a building on this hypothesis is brought
within the definition of 'house' by reason of the extended definition in para (*b*) it
must also be defined by reference to para (*a*). The same considerations must therefore
apply as in the case of a 'house' which is not part of a building. I find myself driven to
the conclusion therefore that there is no power in Camden or indeed in any local   *g*
authority to make, or in the Minister to confirm, a compulsory purchase order in
respect of easements or quasi-easements which did not exist at the time of the making
of that order.

What then is the situation in the present case? It was part of Camden's case for making the compulsory purchase order that the maisonettes had been empty for so long;
there is no doubt, and it is not only conceded but asserted by Camden, that they were   *h*
empty at the time of making the compulsory purchase order. During the course of
the inquiry there was considerable argument about the description of the land in the
compulsory purchase order, a subject to which I shall have to return, and a suggested
amendment was put forward by Camden. It is here necessary to explain something
of the geography of the maisonettes and of the remainder of the Earnshaw wing
which was to be left in the hands of Sovmots. The maisonettes themselves are disposed   *j*
each on two floors, 12 at a time on either side of a central corridor. The ground
floors of the maisonettes run north and south, the upper floors, consisting of two bedrooms and a bathroom, lie transversely and run east and west; thus one bedroom of

1 (1836) 4 Ad & El 749 at 761

a one mainsonette is over its own ground floor, the other bedroom is over the ground
floor of the other maisonette on the same floor but on the opposite side of the corridor.
The corridors giving access to the maisonettes run inside the residential building
on the 3rd, 5th and 7th floors only. The Earnshaw wing contains two staircases, one
at the southern and the other at the northern end. At the southern end there is also
a passenger lift which serves only the maisonettes. In addition there is a goods lift
which serves the upper part of the ground floor shops and then proceeds to podium
b level. There is no access to either lift from the showroom and office levels. At the
northern end of the building the staircase above podium level was clearly intended
by the architects as an emergency staircase only, i e as a fire escape for the maisonettes,
but below podium level it is or can be a means of access to the showrooms and office
floors. On the other hand the southern staircase is, above podium level, a means of access
to the maisonettes, and below that could be used as a fire escape for those on the
c showroom and office floors.   The method of removing refuse from the maisonettes
which was anticipated would be used was by means of a refuse chute which debouched
at podium level at the northern end, and from thence refuse could be carried to
the goods lift at the southern end of the podium and from there to ground floor level.
    During the inquiry there was much argument about the extent of the rights,
if any, which the local authority were entitled to acquire having regard to the des-
d cription of the land set out in the schedule to the compulsory purchase order. The
description was as follows:

'36 residential maisonettes on the 3rd, 4th, 5th, 6th, 7th and 8th floors forming
part of and adjacent to the east side of the property known as Centre Point,
London, WC1, together with such parts of the building which are necessary for
access thereto and the maintenance therof.'
e
The map which accompanied the compulsory purchase order as made showed, as
the subject of compulsory purchase, not only the plan of the residential accommodation itself but also half the width of the adjoining streets. As a result of these arguments the local authority thought it prudent at the inquiry to ask the Minister to
amend the order by substituting for the description of the land to which I have just
f referred the following:

'36 residential maisonettes on the 3rd, 4th, 5th, 6th, 7th and 8th floors
forming part of and adjacent to the east side of the property known as Centre
Point, London, WC1, together with 1) the corridors giving access to the said
maisonettes; 2) the entrance hall, staircase and lifts at the south end, and 3)
the staircase above podium level at the north end.'
g
They also asked the Minister to amend the map annexed to the order by substituting for the original a new map which showed merely the outline of the residential
building and no more. The Minister confirmed the order with these amendments.
    On the amended description Camden were thus seeking to acquire from Sovmots
the entrance hall and the passenger lifts at the south end of the Earnshaw wing and
h the whole of the staircase from ground floor level to the top of the maisonettes at
that end; they were also taking the northern staircase but there only above podium
level. There would thus be left in the exclusive ownership of Sovmots the staircase
below podium level at the northern end and the goods lift at the southern end of the
Earnshaw wing, but in order to allow the property to be used for residential purposes
certain additional ancillary rights were conceived to be necessary. For instance it
j will be apparent that although the staircase above podium level at the northern
end was intended to be acquired as a means of escape in case of fire, the staircase
below that level was not to be acquired so that some right of passage over this staircase
as a fire escape would be necessary. Similarly there is no right to use the goods lift
for the purpose of removing refuse specified in the description of the land; nor is
there any right to go to the place at which the goods lift reaches ground floor level.

There is nothing specified for the passage of the usual services, gas, electricity, water, sewage and the like; and there is no right of access to the outside of the building for the purpose of cleaning, maintenance and repair. In addition therefore to amending the description of the land in the schedule to the compulsory purchase order Camden caused a list to be drawn up called a 'Note of Ancillary Rights and Obligations for inclusion in the Conveyance'. It contained two sections setting out first certain rights which Camden maintained would pass on the conveyance under the first rule in *Wheeldon v Burrows*[1] or under s 62 of the Law of Property Act 1925, and secondly rights which they said they would reserve in the conveyance in favour of the tenants or occupiers of the remainder of the building, i e that part which Camden was not disposed to acquire. The rights which Camden maintained they would acquire pursuant to s 62 of the Law of Property Act or *Wheeldon v Burrows*[1] were these, put briefly: (1) a right for the tenants of the maisonettes to use the northern staircase below podium level as a fire escape; (2) a right to use the goods lift (in common with the occupiers of the part not acquired) for the purpose of removing rubbish from the maisonettes; (3) a right of support for the maisonettes from the building below them; (4) a right of free passage for water, soil, electricity, gas and other services through the pipes which served the maisonettes; and (5) a right of access to the outside of the building for purposes of window cleaning, maintenance and repair.

The rights which Camden said they would reserve in the conveyance in favour of Sovmots were a right for Sovmots tenants to use the staircase at the south end of the building below podium level as a fire escape, and secondly, a right of shelter from the acquired premises. It was conceded that none of the rights to which I have just referred which were included in the note of ancillary rights were legal rights existing at any stage, but it was said that they were those quasi-easements or rights which would pass on a conveyance under the rule in *Wheeldon v Burrows*[1] or under s 62 of the Law of Property Act 1925 as I have indicated.

At the time of the making of the compulsory purchase order there were no tenants in the building. There was indeed no lease of the building made to Brompton at that stage. There was therefore nobody to use the northern staircase below podium level as a fire escape, no rubbish to be removed down the goods lift, no water, electricity or gas passing through the pipes or wires, and no soil to run through the drains. It can of course truly be said that the maisonettes received support from the building below them and it might even be said that, as the pipes and drains existed at the time of the making of the order, the right to use them must be presumed to be one enjoyed with the building. Those matters apart it appears that none of the other rights set out in the list were 'appurtenances usually enjoyed' with the maisonettes and that as they did not exist at the time of the compulsory purchase order, Camden have no power to acquire them compulsorily.

As part of their case in answer to counsel for Sovmots second main contention Camden and the Minister argue that the ancillary rights set out in the first section of the list are 'necessary for the reasonable enjoyment of the building for the purposes for which it is acquired', and there was certainly evidence at the inquiry which indicated that rights of that kind would be necessary in order to allow the building to be used for housing purposes. Counsel for Sovmots and counsel for Brompton argue that if these ancillary rights are necessary to the enjoyment of the maisonettes as housing accommodation and that Camden have no power to acquire such rights, it must follow that the maisonettes cannot be used as a result of this compulsory purchase order for the provision of housing accommodation. It follows, they say, that the Minister cannot confirm the order because the land cannot be used for the purpose for which it is sought to be acquired. It seems to me that this is right. Counsel for the Minister at one time I think maintained that this could be cured by the making

1   (1879) 12 Ch D 31, [1874-80] All ER Rep 669

of a fresh compulsory purchase order by Camden for the rights in question; the
a reasoning behind this being that these rights are now actually being enjoyed by
Brompton as a result of the lease which they have taken since the making of the
original compulsory purchase order, but this is to take far too cynical a view of the
efficacy of the public inquiry procedure. It is to assume that any local inquiry held by
the Minister into any objections by Sovmots and Brompton to the new compulsory
purchase order would be a mere matter of form and that the Minister was bound
b to confirm the new order however cogent any arguments by the objectors might be.
I do not consider the matter can be cured by a proleptic argument of this character.

It should be noted that the second part of the list, which sets out the rights which
Camden said they would reserve in the conveyance in favour of Sovmots has no relevance in this argument at all. The compulsory purchase order, confirmed as modified,
would have the effect of preventing the exercise by Sovmots of any of these rights
c (if any existed) leaving Sovmots only to their remedy in claiming compensation for
injurious affection. Perhaps Camden might be able to reduce the burden of compensation which would otherwise fall on them by granting rights of this kind to
Sovmots and if they did interesting questions might arise under the doctrine enunciated
in the *Ayr Harbour Trustees* case[1], but it does not seem to me that any of these matters
is relevant at this stage to the issues which I have to determine.

d If I am right about the first main point, it may be that there is no need to pursue
counsel for Sovmots' second main submission which is concerned with the necessity
to specify rights of this character in the compulsory purchase order. Insofar as there
may be quasi-easements here which do exist and, in any event in case I am wrong,
I think that I should now turn to consider this submission.

The second main argument is concerned with the question to what extent does a
e local authority acquiring 'land' have to specify the ancillary rights, if any, which it also
wishes to acquire. These ancillary rights are those rights or quasi-rights which would
pass on a conveyance either under s 62 of the Law of Property Act 1925 or under
what has been called the first rule in *Wheeldon v Burrows*[2].

The Minister and the acquiring authority in this case make two submissions in
relation to this matter. First they say the compulsory purchase order impliedly
f authorises acquisition of rights and quasi-rights under s 62 of the 1925 Act and
Wheeldon v Burrows[2] without express reference to them in the compulsory purchase
order, and secondly, that although there may be reasons which make it desirable to
refer to s 62 rights in the notice to treat there is no reason in law why that notice
should refer to those rights and quasi-rights. The argument in support of these submissions goes in this way. A compulsory purchase order authorises acquisition of the
g land of another under a statutory power and there may be acquired with that land
anything which may be required as ancillary thereto. The compulsory purchase order
will be followed by a conveyance transferring the land or by a deed poll under s 9 of
the Compulsory Purchase Act 1965. Section 62 and *Wheeldon v Burrows*[2] operate on
the basis of non-derogation from grant and the grant is the actual conveyance or deed
poll. The rights to be transferred are those necessary to the enjoyment of the property.
h The implications in s 62 and *Wheeldon v Burrows*[2] only arise where the conveyance is
silent; if these rights can arise when the conveyance is silent, equally they can arise
when a compulsory purchase order is silent, and counsel for the Minister quoted
in support of this argument *Phillips v Low*[3], *Borman v Griffith*[4], and Megarry and Wade
on the law of Real Property[5], as well as Emmet on Title[6]. Counsel for the Minister
put his argument shortly in this way: (a) The first question is: What goes with the

j ───────────────────────────────
1 (1883) 8 App Cas 623
2 (1879) 12 Ch D 31, [1874-80] All ER Rep 669
3 [1892] 1 Ch 47
4 [1930] 1 Ch 493
5 3rd Edn (1966), p 829
6 16th Edn (1974), p 513

conveyance? The answer—all s 62 and *Wheeldon v Burrows*[1] rights. (b) Then if the purchaser's contract is otherwise silent he will get, on specific performance, the *a* *Wheeldon v Burrows*[1] and s 62 rights. (c) This is not a situation in contract but a situation in compulsory purchase, but it follows that if the compulsory purchase order is otherwise silent the s 62 and *Wheeldon v Burrows*[1] rights pass.

Counsel for Sovmots criticises this argument: he says it is arguing backwards and I confess I sympathise with him. It seems that on a vendor and purchaser summons the question which the court asks itself is not: what will the conveyance contain? and *b* from that one can deduce what the parties intended in the contract which they have made; the question is, what is the contract which the parties have made and from that one can deduce the conveyance to which they are entitled? Counsel for Sovmots adds that it is one thing to deduce an intention between contractual parties who are free to make what bargain they wish and quite another thing to deduce the intention when an acquiring authority is acquiring land ex hypothesi without the consent of *c* the owner of that land. There are other objections to the argument of counsel for the Minister which counsel for Sovmots puts forward which seem to me to be formidable. They derive from contrasting the position of purchase by agreement with the position of purchase by compulsion. It would therefore be as well to start by shortly considering the steps which are normally necessary in either situation.

Where there is a sale by private treaty there is normally nothing more than first *d* a contract and then a conveyance. With compulsory purchase the position is more complicated. First the acquiring authority must make the compulsory purchase order; then the compulsory purchase order must be confirmed by the confirming authority. The next step is service of the notice to treat. Following this there would be assessment of compensation and then either a conveyance or a deed poll under s 9 of the Compulsory Purchase Act 1965, vesting the land in the authority. *e*

Turning back to private treaty, the contract will be the determining factor. Equity will, normally, decree specific performance of a contract for the purchase of land, and once the contract is made the vendor is in the position of, or at any rate analogous to, a constructive trustee. The conveyance to which the purchaser is entitled will be a conveyance of that which the vendor contracted to sell. In compulsory purchase the position is again more complicated. First, the confirming authority has no power to *f* increase or add to the lands described in the schedule to the compulsory purchase order as made: see para 5 of Sch 1 to the Acquisiton of Land (Authorisation Procedure) Act 1946. Secondly, the notice to treat cannot extend to lands not authorised to be purchased or in other words cannot extend beyond limits of the compulsory purchase order as confirmed. When one comes to consider what conveyance must be made to the acquiring authority the determining factor will thus be the com- *g* pulsory purchase order as made, because nothing that happens after that can extend the scope of the order.

However, the dissimilarities do not end there. After the contract the private vendor cannot deal with the land in any way which runs counter to the contract he has made. He cannot in general sell or create any new interest in the land and he must manage and preserve it with the same care as would be necessary in the case of any ordinary *h* trustee. Further, because in equity land passes to the purchaser at the contract stage, the risk also passes, and so if fire destroys the property or flood overwhelms it the loss falls not on the vendor but on the purchaser. The position is quite different in the case of land the subject of a compulsory purchase order. The making of the order does not effect any change in the ownership of the land whether in law or in equity, or in the owner's ability to dispose of the land as he pleases; nor is any risk transferred to the *j* acquiring authority. Indeed, even after service of the notice to treat, the owner continues as owner and may deal as he likes with the land so long as he does not thereby increase the burden of compensation falling on the acquiring authority. It is only when

---

1 (1879) 12 Ch D 31, [1874-80] All ER Rep 669

the price has been ascertained that a relationship of vendor and purchaser arises and
from that moment the parties' status, rights and duties become the same as on a
private contract for sale.

I think there is one other and more fundamental difference between the situation
where land is contracted to be sold and where it is compulsorily acquired. One of
the basic principles both of law and of equity is that a man shall be held to his bargain.
In interpreting what is the bargain it is permissible to look at the intention of the
parties. A purchaser of land is always entitled to ask a court to look at the purpose
for which, to the knowledge of both parties, the land was to be used by him if this
will assist in determining what was the contract. Thus in *Borman v Griffith*[1], a case
much relied on by counsel for the Minister, the relevant facts were that the
original landowner let to the plaintiff a property which had two means of access,
one by a driveway which led to another property but also gave access to the front of
the plaintiff's land, and one by an unmetalled road which gave access to the back of
the plaintiff's land. Both parties knew that the plaintiff was proposing to use the land
for the purpose of a poultry dealer and rabbit farmer. A dispute arose whether the
lease, which was silent on the subject, included a right for the plaintiff to use the drive.
Maugham J starts his judgment in this way[2]:

> 'Evidence as to surrounding circumstances is admissible to enable the agreement
> to be understood: and among the surrounding circumstances of which evidence
> might so be given would be the intention of both the parties as to the way in
> which the premises were to be used by the tenant. But I hardly need the evidence
> which I have that the plaintiff was entering into a lease in order to carry on the
> trade of a poultry dealer and rabbit farmer, as the agreement states that he is
> taking the premises for that purpose.'

At the end of the next paragraph, referring to the alternative way to the rear of the
plaintiff's premises, he says[2]:

> 'It has been established that at many times of the year it would be quite
> impossible for heavy vehicles to get to the premises along that way. It never had
> been used as a way before the date of the contract, and it was quite impracticable
> for many of the purposes of a poultry dealer.'

The learned judge then went on to deal with the principles which govern the grant of
a decree of specific performance, but I think it is clear that the real ratio decidendi of
that case is that a purchaser is entitled to such rights as were intended to pass under
the contract; and that since the drive was the only way which could suitably be used
for the purposes for which the lessor knew the lessee intended to use the land, the
parties must have intended that a right of way over that drive should be included in
the lease. I am content, respectfully and thankfully, to adopt, as setting out accurately
the law on this subject, two passages from the Law of Real Property by Megarry and
Wade[3]:

> 'A purchaser of land is ordinarily entitled by the contract to existing easements
> or profits which are appendant or appurtenant to the land sold. As regards
> quasi-easements, he is entitled to such rights as may fairly be implied into the
> contract. [and:] It therefore seems that there is no general rule that a contract
> entitles the purchaser to all the rights which an unrestricted conveyance would
> pass to him. He is rather entitled only to existing easements, and such quasi-
> easements as are necessary or intended.'

What may be 'intended' or 'fairly implied into the contract' may be determined from

1   [1930] 1 Ch 493
2   [1930] 1 Ch at 496
3   3rd Edn (1966), p 835

the surrounding circumstances including, and most important, the way in which
both parties knew the premises were to be used.

I do not understand that either law or equity has the same tender concern for the
intention of the parties in a case of compulsory purchase. Indeed until assessment of
compensation there is no bargain. Certainly it could not be said that at the time of
making the compulsory purchase order any intention of the parties could be ascertained which would throw any light on the extent of the rights eventually to be
acquired by the acquiring authority. Both counsel for the Minister and counsel for
Sovmots relied on *Re Peck and the London School Board*[1]. That was a case in which the
board had served a notice to treat in respect of certain land 'with the appurtenances'.
The land in question included three houses and was part of a larger holding and
there was a way of convenience used by the tenants of the houses over part of the land
not being acquired. The question at issue was whether the board was entitled to a
form of conveyance which would have the effect of passing to them this way of convenience. Now both counsel for the Minister and counsel for Sovmots displayed their
customary ingenuity in arguing for interpretations of the judgment of Chitty J in
that case which supported their general propositions. For myself I cannot see that any
such ingenuity is necessary. It seems to me quite a simple case in which Chitty J
decided that a notice to treat describing the land 'with the appurtenances' meant just
what it said. The way of convenience was not an 'appurtenance'; it would properly
be described as a way 'enjoyed with' the land. Since the notice to treat was confined
to appurtenances and did not include these additional words it did not extend to
embracing that particular way of convenience. This case is therefore authority for
the proposition that unless mention is made of them in the notice to treat quasi-
rights of mere convenience are not covered by descriptions such as 'Blackacre' or
'Blackacre with the appurtenances'. Of course on the facts of that case the matter
fell to be determined on the description of the land contained in the notice to treat,
but as already concluded above, the governing description is that contained in the
compulsory purchase order as made because the notice to treat cannot extend
further than that.

I return to the two passages from Megarry and Wade[2]: 'A purchaser of land is
ordinarily entitled by the contract to existing easements or profits which are appendant
to or appurtenant to the land sold. As regards quasi-easements, he is entitled to such
rights as may fairly be implied into the contract'. Now what 'may fairly be implied
into the contract'? The answer is 'such quasi-easements as are necessary or intended'.
But how does it come about that such quasi-easements are to be implied? The answer
is, I think, because there is in contract a rule almost exactly parallel to the rule in
Wheeldon v Burrows[3]. It will be remembered that that rule was said to derive from
the maxim that a grantor shall not derogate from his grant; and that the quasi-
easements which it was said would pass to the grantee were such as were not only in
existence at the time of the grant but were 'necessary to the reasonable enjoyment
of the property granted'. I apprehend that this is not a rule peculiar to conveyancing
but one applicable in essence at any rate in contract. I cannot believe that a man can
contract to sell a property and then do something on his adjoining land which renders
nugatory to some degree the purpose for which both parties intended the contract land to be used. It is this principle which enabled Maugham J to decide *Borman
v Griffith*[4] in the way he did. I apprehend that had the access to the back of the
plaintiff's land in that case been usable for the purposes of a poultry dealer,
Maugham J would have considered that the access by the drive was a mere convenience
and would have rejected the plaintiff's claim, not because such a way of convenience
would not pass under the rule in *Wheeldon v Burrows*[3] (as it would not) but because

1   [1893] 2 Ch 315
2   3rd Edn (1966), p 835
3   [1879] 12 Ch D 31, [1874-80] All ER Rep 669
4   [1930] 1 Ch 493

the parties by their contract would not have intended a mere way of convenience
a to pass.

The true position is therefore this. In a contract for the sale of land the intention
of the parties as to the future use of the land is either ascertainable from the contract
or, if not, evidence of the surrounding circumstances is admissible so that that intention may be determined. In a contract for the sale of Blackacre the rights which
the vendor impliedly contracts to sell with Blackacre to the purchaser are the appur-
b tenant easements and all those rights in the nature of quasi-easements which are
necessary for the reasonable enjoyment of the property for the use intended by the
parties; provided of course that such rights were actually used for the benefit of the
property contracted to be sold at the time of the contract. But the vendor does not
contract to sell quasi-easements of mere convenience unless specifically included in the
contract.

c   Now counsel for the Minister's argument was in essence that a contract to sell
Blackacre with no additional words would include all those rights which would pass
on a conveyance of Blackacre with nothing more, i e the rights which would pass under
Wheeldon v Burrows[1] or s 62 of the Law of Property Act 1925. I cannot accept this
argument. First, it is the contract to which one turns to determine the extent of the
conveyance and not vice versa. Secondly, the authorities do not support the contention
d insofar as it relates to s 62 of the Law of Property Act 1925. The cases show that a
contract to sell Blackacre with no additional words entitles the vendor to exclude
the appropriate parts of s 62. Thirdly, though it may be said that a contract to sell
Blackacre is effectively a contract to sell Blackacre plus the *Wheeldon v Burrows*[1]
rights this is not because the grant determines what the parties intended in the contract. *Borman v Griffith*[2], as I have indicated, depends on the intention of the parties
e to be deduced from the contract, particularly as regards the use to which the parties
intended the property should be put. The fact that this produces the same result
as would the operation of *Wheeldon v Burrows*[1] on the subsequent grant is not
because the grant determines what must be presumed to be the contract; it is due to
a direct coincidence of the rules which in these circumstances govern both contract
and conveyance.

f   I accept that a contract to sell Blackacre without additional words will suffice to
pass the ancillary rights to which I have referred, but it does not follow from this that
the same position can thereby be taken to obtain when land is compulsorily acquired.
The principle to which I have referred operates by deducing from the contract
itself or from the surrounding circumstances the intention of the parties in making
the contract. A contract to sell Blackacre may well be construed as a contract to pass
g quasi-easements which are necessary for the reasonable enjoyment of the property
for the purpose for which both parties intended it should be used. It does not seem
to me that an analogous situation inevitably arises when a compulsory purchase order
is made. As already indicated the governing description is that to be found in the
compulsory purchase order as made. At that stage it is impossible to say that the
landowner intends to sell the land for any particular purpose or even that he intends
h to sell at all. It may well be that his intention is to take every legitimate step in his
power to prevent the confirmation of the compulsory purchase order and to frustrate
the intention of the acquiring authority. The essence of the contractual situation is
that there is consensus between the parties as to the intended use of the land and hence
as to the ancillary rights necessary for the enjoyment of the land for that purpose.
The parties are taken mutually to agree that the description of the land in the contract
j includes those rights. How it can be said that where there is a compulsory purchase
order either law or equity can impute some agreement by the landowner as to the
description of the land contained in the order I do not know. That description is not

1   (1879) 12 Ch D 31, [1874-80] All ER Rep 669
2   [1930] 1 Ch 493

a matter of mutual agreement. It is a unilateral statement made by the acquiring authority of what they desire to take from the landowner not with his consent but willy nilly. As such it should specify precisely what is required beyond the strictly legal easements (or profits) which are appurtenant to the land described; and if it does not do so the acquiring authority will be authorised to acquire nothing beyond the land itself and such appurtenant rights. Any notice to treat which subsequently attempted to include either such quasi-easements as are implied under *Wheeldon v Burrows*[1] or the wider words of s 62 of the 1925 Act would go beyond the authorisation. Of course the power to acquire such rights is given at any rate in the case of a 'house' by para (*a*) of the definition of that term in s 189(1) of the 1957 Act; but if that power is to be exercised then the compulsory purchase order must include words apt to cover them. There is no difficulty about this; the words 'Blackacre, and the appurtenances belonging thereto or usually enjoyed therewith' would appear on the authority of *Peck's* case[2] to suffice.

In the view I have taken of this point I do not need to deal in detail with counsel for Brompton's submission that the compulsory purchase order as made was void for uncertainty. I have no difficulty in construing it as it stands as limited to the property and the easements which I have specified. I take a similar view about the compulsory purchase order as confirmed. I do not accept the argument that the Minister cannot amend the description. If the original compulsory purchase order had been uncertain I think the Minister has power to amend it to make its operation clear. Counsel for Brompton's argument is that if the original compulsory purchase order was uncertain one cannot be sure that the Minister is not extending it by making it certain, and that he is not allowed to do by para 5 of Sch 1 to the Acquisition of Land (Authorisation Procedure) Act 1946. I think this argument is more ingenious than sound. If the original meaning was ambiguous and the Minister by amendment resolves the ambiguity I do not think that it can be said that he was thereby authorising the acquiring authority 'to purchase compulsorily any land which the order would not have authorised that authority so to purchase if it had been confirmed without modification'. To arrive at this result would not only require a ruling from the court that the ambiguity should be resolved in the opposite sense but also that in practice the land under the court's ruling was less extensive than under the Minister's.

I therefore hold: (1) that a local authority has the power under Part V of the Housing Act 1957 to acquire a part of a building even though that part does not stand directly on the land underneath it; (2) that such an authority has, however, no power to acquire any ancillary rights whether easements or quasi-easements and whether necessary or merely desirable unless those rights are in existence at the time of the making of the compulsory purchase order; (3) that where such rights are in existence and the local authority desires to acquire them, there is no necessity in the case of true easements appurtenant to the land in question to specify them in the compulsory purchase order; but where such rights are quasi-easements either necessary to the reasonable enjoyment of the land or mere quasi-easements of convenience, words adequate to cover them must be included in the compulsory purchase order.

I confess that I am not sorry to come to this conclusion. The power to acquire compulsorily what has been called in this case a 'flying freehold'—that is a part of a building divorced from the land on which the building stands—appears to me to be undoubted. It is clearly a very useful power for a housing authority to have available in these days 'high-rise' residential development. But exercise of that power may well be attended by considerable difficulties for all concerned. If a local authority wishes to acquire for housing purposes one flat on one of the upper floors of a block of flats there will be no particular difficulty so long as the property either is or has recently

1 (1879) 12 Ch D 31, [1874-80] All ER Rep 669
2 [1893] 2 Ch 315

been occupied. Whether it has been sold freehold or was the subject of a lease there
a will be some document or some agreement defining the rights of the occupier in
relation to the remainder of the property. The owner of the remainder will then
know exactly where he stands; the identification of the rights acquired and of the
rights extinguished will be easy and the assessment of appropriate compensation
attended by not more than the usual difficulties. But where you have an unoccupied
building and the local authority seeks to acquire only part of it, neither those rights
b acquired nor those extinguished may be easy of identification and protracted and
expensive proceedings both to determine those questions and to assess the consequent
compensation may well be necessary.

For the reasons I have given I do not think that this compulsory purchase order
can stand.

c *Motions granted.*

Solicitors: *Goodman, Derrick & Co* (for Sovmots); *Cowan, Lipson & Rumney* (for
Brompton); *Treasury Solicitor; Solicitor, London Borough of Camden.*

Janet Harding Barrister.

d

Keen v Parker

QUEEN'S BENCH DIVISION
e LORD WIDGERY CJ, O'CONNOR AND LAWSON JJ
29th, 30th OCTOBER 1975

*Road traffic – Licence – Driving licence – Provisional licence – Conditions attached to pro-
visional licences – Motor bicycle not having sidecar attached – Sidecar – Structure attached
to motor bicycle for purpose of carrying goods – Whether sidecar limited to structure for
f safe carriage of passenger – Motor Vehicles (Driving Licences) Regulations 1971 (SI 1971
No 451), reg 6(1)(d)(2)(e).*

A roadworthy attachment to a motor bicycle is a 'side-car' for the purposes of the
Motor Vehicles (Driving Licences) Regulations 1971, reg 6(1)(d)(2)(e)[a] even though it
is only designed for the carriage of goods; there is no requirement that, to constitute
a 'side-car', an attachment must be constructed and fit for the safe carriage of a pas-
g senger. Accordingly, the driver of a motor bicycle with an attachment designed to
carry goods, who possesses only a provisional licence is exempted, under reg 6(1)(d) and
(2)(e) of the 1971 regulations, from the prohibitions on carrying a pillion passenger
who is not a qualified driver (see p 207 d to h, post).

Dicta of Ashworth J in *Cox v Harrison* [1968] 3 All ER at 813 disapproved.

h **Notes**
For the construction of motor-cycles and attachments thereto, see 33 Halsbury's
Laws 430, 431, para 726; for restrictions on provisional licences, see Supplement to
ibid para 775.

For the Motor Vehicles (Driving Licences) Regulations 1971, reg 6, see 22 Halsbury's
j Statutory Instruments (3rd Reissue) 183.

Case referred to in judgments
Cox v Harrison [1968] 3 All ER 811, [1968] 1 WLR 1907, 133 JP 75, DC, Digest (Cont Vol
C) 924, *259c.*

a Regulation 6, so far as material, is set out at p 205 *f* and *g*, post

Case stated

On 18th July 1974 an information was preferred by the respondent, Gerald David Parker, **a**
chief superintendent of police, against the appellant, Wilfred Donald Keen, that he
being the holder of a provisional licence to drive a motor vehicle failed to comply
with the conditions subject to which it was granted in that on a certain road called
Outer Circle Drive, Lincoln, he rode a motor bicycle, not having thereto a sidecar,
while carrying on it a person who was not the holder of a licence authorising him to
drive a vehicle of that class or description, contrary to s 88 of the Road Traffic Act **b**
1972.

On 31st December 1974 justices for the county of Lincoln acting in and for the petty
sessional division of the city of Lincoln found the appellant guilty of the offence
charged and ordered that his driving licence be endorsed with the particulars of the
offence. The appellant indicated his dissatisfaction with the adjudication and required
the justices to state a case for the opinion of the High Court.   **c**

The question for the opinion of the High Court was whether the justices were
correct in law in their decision that, for the purposes of reg 6 of the Motor Vehicles
(Driving Licences) Regulations 1971 and s 88(2) of the Road Traffic Act 1972, 'side-car'
meant a structure attached to a motor bicycle and capable of carrying persons in
safety, or whether they should have found that 'side-car' also included a structure
attached to a motor bicycle and constructed or adapted solely for the carriage of **d**
goods.

The appellant appeared in person.
Anthony Hidden for the respondent.

Cur adv vult

e

30th October. **O'CONNOR J** delivered the first judgment at the invitation of
Lord Widgery CJ: This is an appeal by way of case stated from an adjudication of the
Lincoln justices whereby they convicted the appellant of an offence on 31st December
1974. He was summonsed that, being the holder of a provisional licence to drive a
motor vehicle, he failed to comply with the conditions subject to which it was granted
in that on a certain road called Outer Circle Drive, Lincoln, he rode a motor bicycle, **f**
not having attached thereto a sidecar, while carrying on it a person who was not the
holder of a licence authorising him to drive a vehicle of that class or description,
contrary to s 88 of the Road Traffic Act 1972.

That rather complicated wording to describe what in truth was a very simple offence
results from the statutory legislation made in that behalf.

The facts found by the justices are again in a very short compass. The appellant **g**
was the holder of a provisional driving licence, that is he was a learner driver. He
was riding a 500 cc motor-cycle in Lincoln and carrying a pillion passenger. Attached
to the motor-cycle was a construction consisting of four planks of wood seven feet
long mounted on a steel framework supported by a wheel properly constructed.
The platform was about two feet wide. Attached to the framework was a small
platform 30 inches square which was hung underneath it, and sitting on it there was a **h**
tool-box. This was used by the appellant to carry his ladders and buckets because
he was a window cleaner.

The question in this case is whether he was riding a motor bicycle with a sidecar or
not. Was the platform on which he carried his ladders and buckets properly to be
described as a sidecar? If it was a sidecar, then he committed no offence. If it was not
a sidecar, he was properly convicted. At the end of the hearing yesterday we held **j**
that it was a sidecar and allowed the appeal, and I am now giving the reasons for that
decision.

Before I look at the statutory provisions, it is perhaps as well to state in simple
English what the scheme of things is. Everybody knows that in the ordinary course of
events a learner driver (that is a person who holds a provisional driving licence)

is not allowed to drive a vehicle unless he is accompanied by an authorised driver,
a namely somebody who does hold a full licence. But for motor-cycles there is an exception, and it works in this way. First of all, the holder of a provisional licence is not
allowed to ride a solo motor-cycle of more than 250 cc. This is to prevent young
people arming themselves with great big motor-cycles before they have passed the
test. The learner driver is permitted to ride that kind of solo motor-cycle without an
authorised driver, but not allowed to carry as a pillion passenger somebody who is
b not himself or herself an authorised driver. But where a motor-cycle, however
powerful, is fitted with a sidecar, then the learner driver is permitted to carry on the
motor-cycle a passenger who is not an authorised driver. Why that should be so
does not matter; that is what the provisions amount to.

I will look shortly at the relevant sections which create this offence. I start with
s 88(2) of the Road Traffic Act 1972 which provides that a provisional driving licence
c shall be granted subject to conditions, and then, in sub-s (2)(c), 'shall not authorise a
person to drive a motor cycle whereof the cylinder capacity of the engine exceeds
250 cubic centimetres, not being a vehicle having three wheels, unless he has passed
the test of competence . . .'

The only definition of 'motor cycle' in the 1972 Act itself is to be found in s 190(4)
where a motor-cycle is defined as meaning 'a mechanically propelled vehicle, not
d being an invalid carriage, with less than four wheels and the weight of which unladen
does not exceed eight hundredweight'. No doubt the reason for that definition is
because a great deal of the Act is concerned with the taxation of different classes of
motor vehicles, and for tax purposes what the ordinary citizen would call a three-
wheeler is classified as a motor-cycle. There is no definition in the Act of motor
bicycle and there is no definition of sidecar. In the nature of things, as soon as a regula-
e tion uses the words 'motor bicycle' ordinary English requires the construction that
it is a two-wheeled vehicle because 'bicycle' by definition means two wheels.

I pass next to the Motor Vehicles (Driving Licences) Regulations 1971[1], and reg 6
lays down the conditions to be attached to provisional licences. Regulation 6(1)(a)
requires the supervision of a qualified driver and reg 6(1)(d) lays it down that 'in
the case of a motor bicycle not having attached thereto a side-car, while carrying on it
f a person who is not a qualified driver' a person shall not drive or ride such a motor
vehicle. That is a use of the vehicle which is prohibited. The terms of the conditional
licence do not allow a rider of a motor bicycle not having attached thereto a sidecar
to carry an unqualified driver as a passenger.

The requirement of an authorised driver is exempted by reg 6(2), which reads: 'The
condition specified in paragraph (1)(a) of this Regulation shall not apply when the
g holder of the provisional licence . . . (e) is riding a motor bicycle, whether or not having
attached thereto a side-car'. Thus, as I have said, the actual working out of this
legislation is quite simple. Let me repeat it.

The rider of a motor bicycle need not have an authorised supervisor. He must not
carry a passenger unless that passenger is a duly authorised driver with a full licence,
but if his motor bicycle has a sidecar, then he may carry a passenger who is not an
h authorised driver.

In the present case, faced with the question whether the attachment to the appellant's motor bicycle was a sidecar, the justices were referred to the decision of this
court in *Cox v Harrison*[2]. Again to state the problem before I look at the authority,
it arose in this way. The suggestion is that for an attachment to be classified as a
sidecar it must be constructed for the carriage of passengers or a passenger, and for
j the safe carriage of a passenger; if it is an attachment which is only useful for
carrying goods, then it is not a sidecar.

In *Cox v Harrison*[2], which was decided under the 1963 regulations[3] which for this

1   SI 1971 No 451
2   [1968] 3 All ER 811, [1968] 1 WLR 1907
3   Motor Vehicles (Driving Licences) Regulations (SI 1963 No 1026)

purpose were the same, what had happened was this. The appellant there sought to
overcome the difficulty of not being allowed to ride a 500 cc motor-cycle; he thought   *a*
that by just attaching a third wheel with a tubular frame without any platform or
carriage it would enable him to say that that was a sidecar or a three-wheeled vehicle,
and therefore to carry a pillion passenger who was not an authorised driver. That
was the purpose of the case which was being tried there. Ashworth J, who gave
the judgment of the court, had this to say about it. He said[1]:

b

'. . . a motor cycle ridden by a learner driver and carrying a pillion passenger
is prima facie a dangerous vehicle, partly due to its nature and partly due to the
fact that in a given case the driver is inexperienced, and in order to meet that
difficulty Parliament has in effect done two things, first it has provided that if
the pillion passenger is a qualified driver he may be carried, and secondly,
whether he is qualified or not, if the vehicle has got a sidecar then a passenger may   *c*
be carried, as I read it in that sidecar. [I pause there to say that there is nothing in
the regulation which requires that construction.] That was the intention, although
the wording does not expressly say so, because it was thought no doubt that if
the learner driver on the motor cycle had the additional safeguard of a passenger
in a sidecar, there was less risk of an accident happening. Although it is not
necessary to decide the point, I agree with counsel for the appellant that on the   *d*
wording if in fact the motor cycle is provided with something which is properly
called a sidecar, then a passenger may be carried either in the sidecar or as a
pillion passenger on the machine itself, but of course it must be a sidecar.'

I pause there for a moment. To my mind, the wording of the regulation is clear, and
once there is a sidecar attached to the motor bicycle the passenger can be carried
either as a pillion rider on the motor bicycle itself or in the sidecar if it is one fitted   *e*
for passengers. Ashworth J continued[2]:

'No decision of this court has been found by counsel for the appellant in which
the question: "What is a sidecar?", has come up for decision, but his industry
has enabled him to unearth a decision which is referred to in 115 JUSTICE OF THE
PEACE AND LOCAL GOVERNMENT REVIEW; at p 611, under "Notes of the Week",   *f*
a decision of the Bristol justices is cited. In that case a contraption was fitted by
the side of a motor cycle in the shape of a box which was used to carry building
materials. The prosecution contended that as the attachment was not able to
take passengers, it was not a sidecar within the meaning of the regulations. The
defence argued that it was a sidecar properly attached, and that it was not necessary that it should be for the conveyance of passengers, and the justices accepted   *g*
the submission of the defence and dismissed the summons. It may be that the
issue raised in that case will come up for decision before this court in the same or
slightly different form in some future case, and, therefore, I feel for my part that
it would be unwise to express a positive decision whether that decision of the
Bristol justices was right or wrong. I say that with all the more reason because it
is not necessary for the purposes of the present case to decide whether the side-   *h*
car must be one that is constructed or adapted for the carriage of passengers and
nothing else, or whether a sidecar can properly be constructed by means of a
chassis and some box or basket on it which would carry materials rather than
passengers.'

I pause there to say that in giving the decision of the court Ashworth J was deliberately leaving open the question whether an attachment constructed for the carriage   *j*
of goods and not passengers could qualify as a sidecar. It was unnecessary to the
decision. The learned judge, however, did go on to express his own opinion about the

1   [1968] 3 All ER at 813, [1968] 1 WLR at 1911
2   [1968] 3 All ER at 813, [1968] 1 WLR at 1912

matter, and in my judgment that opinion, while of great weight, is nevertheless
a   obiter and we are not bound to follow it. The learned judge said[1]:

> 'For my part, I would prefer to leave that issue to be decided when it is raised,
> but I am quite certain that to constitute an attachment a sidecar, it must be
> capable of carrying persons, and the facts found in this case show to my mind
> that there was no form of structure on this attachment.'

b   Thus, he came down firmly on the view that a sidecar is an attachment constructed
and fit for the safe carriage of a passenger. It was on those dicta that the justices in
the present case, having directed themselves admirably as appears from the case,
came to the conclusion that they should follow that view of the true construction
of the 1971 regulations and the 1972 Act and convicted the appellant.

The problem adumbrated by Ashworth J has arisen in the present case because
c   here we are dealing with an attachment to a motor bicycle which was properly designed and constructed for the carriage of goods, namely the ladders of a window
cleaner and his buckets and sponges and so forth, and the question therefore falls to
be decided: is that a sidecar within the meaning of the regulations?

It seems to me that it is a sidecar. There is no requirement in any of the statutory
provisions to which I have referred laying it down that the sidecar must be one con-
d   structed for and fit for the safe carriage of a passenger. It simply is not so defined.
Some slight help is to be gained by the fact that in the 1950 regulations[2] there is a
provision (reg 16(3)(a)) 'that for the purposes of this sub-paragraph a motor bicycle
shall not be deemed to be constructed or adapted to carry more than one person
unless it has a sidecar constructed for the carriage of a passenger attached.'

That is a completely different piece of legislation, and it is to be noted that it has
e   disappeared from the present regulations, and indeed had done so by 1963. Thus,
Parliament has had ample opportunity, if it so wished, to limit the interpretation of
the word 'sidecar' to an 'attachment constructed for and fit for the safe carriage of a
passenger' and has not seen fit to do so. In those circumstances it seems to me that a
roadworthy attachment to a motor bicycle which is designed for the carriage of goods
is just as much a sidecar as a roadworthy attachment constructed for the carriage of
f   a passenger.

For my part I would like to compliment the justices on the great care with which
they went into this case and the way in which they stated the case for the decision of
this court, but for those reasons I am satisfied that they came to a wrong conclusion
in law, and the question which they asked whether they were correct is to be answered,
No, 'sidecar' does not necessarily mean a structure attached to a motor bicycle capable
g   of carrying passengers in safety.

For those reasons the appeal should be allowed.

LAWSON J. I agree.

h   **LORD WIDGERY CJ.** I also agree and I agree with all the reasons so clearly given
in the judgment of O'Connor J.

I add a few words of my own partly because the view which we take of the meaning
of 'sidecar' is, I think, different from the view generally held up to now, and also in
deference to the justices who have given this case a great deal of careful attention and
stated it quite admirably.

j   The factual situation with which we are dealing is one of a driver who has a provisional licence only, who wishes to take a passenger on his motor bicycle and wishes
to take a passenger who is not himself a fully qualified driver. The requirements
make it perfectly clear that to meet that situation there must be a sidecar attached

---

1   [1968] 3 All ER at 813, [1968] 1 WLR at 1912
2   Motor Vehicles (Driving Licences) Regulations (SI 1950 No 333)

to the motor bicycle, and I find it of some help in deciding on the true meaning of
'side-car', and in particular in deciding whether a sidecar must be adapted for the car- **a**
riage of passengers, to look at that situation and ask oneself why the legislature thought
it proper and appropriate to insist on the presence of a sidecar before a provisionally
licensed driver could take an unqualified passenger.

Ashworth J in *Cox v Harrison*[1] obviously thought that a sidecar was intended to
carry a passenger. He resiled from it, as the extract already read indicates, and
accepted later in his judgment that there was no need for the passenger to be travel- **b**
ling in the sidecar. The moment one concedes that, which I think is an entirely
proper concession, it is very difficult, I think, to justify the conclusion that the
legislature was insisting on the sidecar being adapted for the carriage of passengers.

I take the other view, namely that the reason why the legislature thought it
necessary to insist on the presence of a sidecar in this situation was because the third
wheel gives additional stability. It does so equally whether the intended burden is a **c**
body or goods. The fact that Parliament has had concern for the third wheel in this
connection is, I think, reinforced by s 88 of the 1972 Act to which O'Connor J has
already referred under which a driver with a provisional licence only cannot be
authorised to drive a motor-bicycle whereof the cylinder capacity of the engine exceeds
250 cc, not being a vehicle having three wheels. The reference there to three wheels
must, I think, be a reference to the additional stability which comes from the third **d**
wheel.

I entirely agree that the appeal should be allowed and the conviction quashed.

I am reminded that there is an endorsement on the appellant's driving licence
in respect of this offence, and that endorsement must of course be removed with
the quashing of the conviction.

Appeal allowed. Conviction quashed.   **e**

Solicitors: *Sharpe, Pritchard & Co*, agents for *R A Crabb*, Lincoln.

Jill Watkins Barrister.

f

Gaskins v The British Aluminium Co Ltd

COURT OF APPEAL, CIVIL DIVISION
LORD DENNING MR, ORR AND BROWNE LJJ
22nd, 23rd OCTOBER, 6th NOVEMBER 1975

g

*Practice – Payment into court – Non-disclosure of payment in – Application at trial for
payment out – Application by plaintiff opposed by defendant – Application having effect of
disclosing payment in – Application made by plaintiff after seeing prospects of success
diminishing – Jurisdiction of judge to continue hearing following disclosure of payment in – Whether plaintiff entitled to make application at trial – Whether judge should
order new trial following disclosure of payment in and refusal of plaintiff's application –
RSC Ord 22, rr 5, 7.*

h

The plaintiff suffered an eye injury as a result of an accident at work. On 6th December 1973 he issued a writ against the defendants, his employers, claiming damages
for negligence. The defendants disputed liability alleging that the accident had
occurred as a result of the plaintiff's own negligence and breach of statutory duty. **j**
On 23rd January 1975 the defendants paid £5,500 into court in satisfaction of the
claim. The plaintiff did not accept the payment in and on 24th March 1975 the
action came to trial. On the first day of the hearing, after the plaintiff had given

1   [1968] 3 All ER 811, [1968] 1 WLR 1907

evidence and been cross-examined, it became apparent that his prospects of succeed-
a ing had considerably diminished. The plaintiff, therefore, applied to the trial judge
under RSC Ord 22, r 5[a], for an order that the money in court be paid out to him.
The application was opposed by the defendants. The judge refused to make the
order sought but ordered a new trial before a fresh judge on the ground that there
had been a breach of RSC Ord 22, r 7[b], in that the fact that money had been paid into
court had been revealed to him. The plaintiff appealed against the judge's refusal
b to order payment out.

Held – The appeal would be dismissed for the following reasons—
    (i) (Browne LJ dissenting) As a general rule no application should be made by the
plaintiff to a judge during the course of a trial for the payment out of money in
court without the defendant's consent. Accordingly the judge was entitled to dis-
c miss the plaintiff's application on the ground that it was opposed by the defendants
(see p 212 c and d and p 213 h to p 214 a, post).
    (ii) In any event the judge was entitled to dismiss the application on the ground
that, since the beginning of the trial, the risks had altered in that the plaintiff's
prospects of success had considerably diminished (see p 212 d, p 213 j to p 214 a and
p 218 f and g, post).
d   Per Curiam. Since RSC Ord 22, r 7, is directory and not mandatory, where a
plaintiff, seeing that the trial had taken a course which diminishes his prospects of
success, applies for the payment out of money in court, the judge, having refused
the application, should consider whether to exercise his discretion to continue the
hearing himself in order to see that the plaintiff gains no advantage by his premature
disclosure of the payment in (see p 212 e and h, p 213 h and j and p 217 b and c, post);
e Millensted v Grosvenor House (Park Lane) Ltd [1937] 1 All ER 736 applied.

Notes
For payment into and out of court, see 30 Halsbury's Laws (3rd Edn) 381-386, paras
709-720, and for cases on the subject, see 51 Digest (Repl) 576-599, 2091-2255.

f **Cases referred to in judgments**
Cumper v Pothecary [1941] 2 All ER 516, [1941] 2 KB 58, 110 LJKB 577, 165 LT 243, CA,
    51 Digest (Repl) 577, 2100.
Dawson v Spaul (1935) 152 LT 444, 51 Digest (Repl) 594, 2235.
Frazer and Haws Ltd v Burns (1934) 49 Ll R Rep 216, CA.
Griggs v Petts [1939] 4 All ER 39, [1940] 1 KB 198, 109 LJKB 13, 161 LT 317, CA, 51
g   Digest (Repl) 596, 2248.
Millar v Building Contractors (Luton) Ltd [1953] 2 All ER 339, sub nom Practice Note
    [1953] 1 WLR 780, 51 Digest (Repl) 589, 2197.
Millensted v Grosvenor House (Park Lane) Ltd [1937] 1 All ER 736, [1937] 1 KB 717, 106
    LJKB 221, 156 LT 383, 51 Digest (Repl) 584, 2146.
Williams v Boag [1940] 4 All ER 246, [1941] 1 KB 1, 109 LJKB 913, 165 LT 56, CA, 51
h   Digest (Repl) 580, 2118.

Case also cited
French (A Martin) v Kingswood Hill Ltd [1960] 2 All ER 251, [1961] 1 QB 96, CA.

Interlocutory appeal
j This was an appeal by the plaintiff, Philip Leslie Gaskins, against the order made
by Croom-Johnson J sitting at Birmingham on 25th March 1975 at the trial of the
plaintiff's action against the defendants, The British Aluminium Co Ltd, whereby

---

a Rule 5, so far as material, is set out at p 211 c, post
b Rule 7, so far as material, is set out at p 211 h, post

H

he refused the plaintiff's application made after the commencement of the trial for
leave to take out moneys paid into court by the defendants. The facts are set out in *a*
the judgment of Lord Denning MR.

Richard Rougier QC and *Peter Andrews* for the plaintiff.
M Stuart-Smith QC and *J F M Maxwell* for the defendants.

Cur adv vult
b

6th November. The following judgments were read.

LORD DENNING MR. Nearly three years ago the plaintiff, Philip Leslie Gaskins,
lost an eye in an accident. He was working at a foundry at Redditch. His job was to cast
ingots of aluminium. The boiling aluminium was poured into moulds which were
cooled by water. By some mischance some of the boiling aluminium went into the *c*
water, and there was an explosion. Hot bits flew up into the plaintiff's face and burnt
it. One bit went into his right eye and he lost the sight of it. He was disfigured and
skin was grafted on. He was off work for six months. On 6th December 1973 he
issued a writ against the defendants, his employers, claiming damages for an unsafe
system of work. The defence was that he failed to use the goggles which were *d*
provided for him.
     On 23rd January 1975 the defendants paid £5,500 into court in satisfaction of the
claim. The plaintiff had 21 days in which to accept it. If he had done so, he would
have got the money and all his costs. But he decided not to take it out. The case
went for trial. It came before Croom-Johnson J at Birmingham on Monday, 24th
March 1975.
     On the first day the plaintiff himself gave evidence; he was cross-examined to *e*
some effect, especially because he had given contradictory accounts of the accident.
Immediately after it, he had said that he was wearing goggles and a hot piece of
metal had penetrated the goggles from the outside. But the goggles, when examined,
showed that the hot piece had penetrated from the inside. So he gave a second
explanation by saying that there were two explosions. After the first, he had dis- *f*
placed the goggles so that they slipped down round his neck. Then the second
explosion threw up a hot piece into his eye, and it fell back into the displaced goggle
and made a hole from the inside. His answers were not very convincing. Then an
expert was called on his behalf. The expert was supposed to prove that the system
was unsafe. But cross-examined, he admitted that, so long as the defendants provided suitable goggles and took steps to see that they were worn, they had achieved
reasonable safety. The only suggestion he made of any fault was that there comes *g*
a point when the man in charge should stop the process; but he admitted the plaintiff
was in a position to stop it himself.
     At the end of the first day, therefore, the plaintiff's case was going very badly for
him. His advisers appreciated this. So they decided to accept, if they could, the £5,500
in court. The defendants would not agree. So the plaintiff's counsel asked the judge *h*
to order it. (I may say that the plaintiff's counsel there is not the counsel who appeared
before us.) This interchange (abbreviated) took place:

> '*Plaintiff's counsel:* . . . the case has not gone as well as one predicted. [But]
> it is far from lost, and it nevertheless seems prudent to make this application at
> this stage . . .
>   '*Croom-Johnson J:* At the moment I have only heard part of the evidence, but *j*
> I think I have got to decide it on some other principle than that . . . [Are you
> not saying:] I think if I go on, I am probably going to get less than there is in
> court so I want to grab what I can now?
>   '*Plaintiff's counsel:* . . . that is a little overstating it. If I go on, I might [get
> less.] I might equally get a lot more . . .

a
'*Croom-Johnson J* [to defendants' counsel]: Do you maintain your opposition?
'*Defendants' counsel:* Yes, I do.
'*Croom-Johnson J:* If you maintain your opposition, I think . . . I should not give . . . leave to take the money out.'

The plaintiff appeals to this court.

b
The case raises questions of practice of some importance. Under the Rules of the Supreme Court, if the defendant makes a payment into court more than 21 days before the trial, the plaintiff has a *right* to accept it within those 21 days and get his costs. If the payment is made *less* than 21 days before the the trial, the plaintiff has a *right* to accept it so long as he does it *before* the trial starts. If the plaintiff lets those times pass, he no longer has a right to accept it, but has to obtain an order of the court[1]: RSC Ord 22, r 5, says: '. . . the money remaining in court shall not be paid

c
out except in pursuance of an order of the Court which may be made at any time before, at or after the trial or hearing of the action . . .' If the parties agree on a settlement, the court will, of course, make an order for payment out in order to effect the settlement. But what if they do not agree? Can the plaintiff be allowed to take the money out in the face of the defendant's opposition?

d
I think a distinction must be drawn between an application made *before* the trial, and one made at or after it. When the application is made *before* the trial, it will usually be made to the master. He *can* make an order allowing it. If the chances of success or failure—or of greater or less damages—are substantially the same as they were at the time of the payment into court, the master may allow the payment out to the plaintiff, but he will usually allow it only on the terms that the plaintiff pays all the costs from the date of the payment into court. If the chances have sub-

e
stantially altered, then the master should not allow the plaintiff to take the payment out: for the simple reason that it would be unfair to hold the defendant to a sum which he offered in different circumstances. He can say: 'Non haec in foedera veni.' I think the defendant should indicate to the master the circumstances which have altered the position, such as a decision of the courts which has changed the way in which damages are to be assessed, or the discovery of further evidence or information

f
affecting the chances: see *Dawson v Spaul*[2], *Frazer v Burns*[3], *Williams v Boag*[4], *Cumper v Pothecary*[5]. But I do not think the defendant should be required to state circumstances which, if disclosed to the plaintiff at this stage, would affect the conduct of the case at the trial, as, for instance, by making the plaintiff aware of the questions which he might be asked in cross-examination.

g
When the application is made *at* the trial, it will necessarily be made to the judge who tries the case. (It is not practicable to ask him to adjourn the case for it to be heard by another judge.) But then there arises RSC Ord 22, r 7, which forbids any mention to the judge of the fact of payment in or the amount of it. It says:

h
'. . . the fact that money has been paid into court under the foregoing provisions of this Order shall not be pleaded and no communication of that fact shall be made to the Court at the trial or hearing of the action or counter-claim or of any question or issue as to the debt or damages until all questions of liability and of the amount of debt or damages have been decided.'

That rule is clear and specific. There must be no disclosure of the fact of payment in —nor of the amount—except, of course, when the case is settled by agreement. But this rule does not say what is to happen if it is broken. It is sometimes supposed that, if the payment in is disclosed, the judge should order a new trial. But I do not

j
think this is correct. The judge has a discretion in the matter. Suppose, for instance,

1   RSC Ord 22, r 3
2   (1935) 152 LT 444
3   (1934) 49 Ll L Rep 216
4   [1940] 4 All ER 246, [1941] 1 KB 1
5   [1941] 2 All ER 516, [1941] 2 KB 58

that by inadvertence the papers contain a reference to the payment into court and
the judge reads it. Or a witness blurts out that he refused the payment into court. *a*
The judge need not order a new trial. He can go on and try the case: see *Millensted v
Grosvernor House (Park Lane) Ltd*[1]. Suppose next that the plaintiff realises that he is
likely to lose—or get less—and applies to accept the money in court—the judge
should not order a new trial. He should go on and try the case himself, just as Slade J
did in *Millar v Building Contractors (Luton)*[2]. Were it otherwise, you would find that
counsel, as soon as he felt the case was going against him, would apply to take the *b*
money out. He would say to himself: 'I will either get the money out or I will get a
new trial before a different judge. And at that trial I may do better. Heads I win.
Tails I cannot lose.' Again, if the judge were to order a new trial, it would inflict on
the defendant a grave injustice, especially when the plaintiff was impecunious or
legally aided. After coming to fight one trial, the defendant would be forced to
incur all the expenses of a second trial—to which the plaintiff would come forewarned *c*
and forearmed—all owing to the plaintiff breaking RSC Ord 22, r 7. It is, indeed,
obvious that if the plaintiff were allowed at the trial to apply to take money out of
court—without the consent of the defendant—a door would be opened to abuses
of the worst description. So much so that we should lay down a positive rule that no
such application should be made at the trial without the consent of the defendant.

In the present case I think the judge was right to refuse the application for payment *d*
out. He was right on the ground given by him—that it was not to be done in the
face of opposition by the defendant. He would also be right on the further ground
that, on the facts, the plaintiff's prospects were considerably diminished—so much
so that he ought not to be allowed to take the money out.

There is only one thing I regret. After the judge had refused the application,
counsel for the defendants said: 'The trial will have to be adjourned and heard before *e*
another judge'; and the judge acceded to that suggestion. It might have been better
if counsel had asked the judge to continue with the hearing himself, and the judge
had done so. He would see to it that the plaintiff gained no advantage by his
premature disclosure of the payment in.

I would dismiss the appeal accordingly.

f

ORR LJ. I agree, and as to the facts of the case as outlined by Lord Denning MR
would only add, since it has some bearing on the amount paid into court, that the
plaintiff was alleging a loss of future earnings which was ultimately agreed in the
sum of £3,120. Two issues arise on this appeal: the first, whether the judge was
entitled to reject the plaintiff's application without considering it on the merits, *g*
and the second, whether on the merits the application should have been granted.

The first of these issues depends on the true construction of RSC Ord 22, rr 5 and 7,
to the terms of which Lord Denning MR has referred, and the only authority which
I have found of any real assistance on this point is *Millensted v Grosvenor House (Park
Lane) Ltd*[1], in which it was held by this court that what was then r 6 and is now
r 7 of RSC Ord 22 is directory and not compulsory and that if the fact of payment *h*
into court is disclosed to the judge before he delivers judgment the rule does not
compel him to refuse to continue to hear the case and he has a discretion to do so if he
considers that no miscarriage of justice will be caused thereby. In *Williams v Boag*[3]
this court held that the rule does not, as is clear from its language, prevent a judge
or master being informed of a payment into court on an interlocutory application
before trial, but neither in that case nor in *Cumper v Pothecary*[4] was the court concerned with an application by a plaintiff during the trial to take out money in court. *j*

---

1 [1937] 1 All ER 736, [1937] 1 KB 717
2 [1953] 2 All ER 339, [1953] 1 WLR 780
3 [1940] 4 All ER 246, [1941] 1 KB 1
4 [1941] 2 All ER 516, [1941] 2 KB 58

In *Millar v Building Contractors (Luton) Ltd*[1] Slade J was concerned with such an
application made after final speeches but before judgment, which he rejected in the
exercise of his discretion, but it had not been argued before him that by reason of
r 7 he should not entertain the application.

On the issue as to the construction of rr 5 and 7 counsel for the plaintiff submitted
that it would be surprising if the provision in r 5 that an order for payment out may
be made 'at any time before at or after the trial or hearing of the action' were to be
cut down by r 7 to the extent that an application for such an order could not be
made during almost the whole of the trial. In my judgment, however, it would
be much more surprising that r 7, if counsel for the plaintiff is right as to its intention,
does not specifically except from its effect the disclosure of a payment into court made
in the course of an application for payment out, and with great respect to the contrary view, I cannot find any assistance for the plaintiff's argument in RSC Ord 22,
r 4(3), which in my judgment is dealing only with the acceptance, as of right under
RSC Ord 22, r 3(2), of money paid into court in the course of the hearing, and is
merely providing that in such an event there is to be an order of the court dealing
with the costs of the action.

In my judgment r 7, on its true construction, applies to any disclosure of a payment
into court whether or not made in the course of an application to take money out
of court. So construed, r 7, inasmuch as it has been held to be directory only, presents
no practical difficulty in the case of an application made by consent to take money
out of court, although it is true that its language does not aptly fit a case in which
the approval of the court is required for the acceptance of the money, since all
questions 'of the amount of—the damages' have not been decided until approval is
given, but where approval is refused, and no higher offer is made, the case will
normally go for trial before another judge.

Where, however, an application for payment out is made during the trial and
without the consent of the defendant, different considerations arise, because such an
application may well be made on behalf of a plaintiff whose case has gone badly,
and with a view to obtaining, if leave to take out the money is refused, a new trial
before another judge in which the plaintiff will have an opportunity of repairing
to some extent what has gone wrong in his case at the first trial and to which he
will in all probability come forearmed with knowledge as to the defendant's case.
It has been argued that there would be a hardship to a plaintiff if such an application
could not be made merely because it is opposed, considering that the defendant is
allowed by the rules to make a further payment into court during the trial; but
where the only reason for the application is that the case is going on for longer than
was anticipated, and where the risks have not substantially changed during the
trial, it is unlikely that the application would be opposed, and in any event it seems
to me that the hardship, if there be any, caused to the plaintiff by not allowing such
an application if it is opposed is minimal compared with the very serious injustice
that could be caused to a defendant by allowing the plaintiff, in circumstances where
the risk has changed, to obtain a second trial.

In these circumstances I agree with Lord Denning MR that there is no good reason
why the direction contained in r 7 should not be enforced as respects a contested
application to take money out of court during the hearing. I think that as a rule
such an application ought not to be entertained, and if there are special circumstances
which lead the judge to entertain the application and he refuses it I think he should
consider very carefully whether there is any sufficient reason why he should not
continue to hear the case.

In the present case, the transcript has left me in some doubt whether the judge
rejected the application on the ground that it was opposed or on the ground that the
risk had substantially changed during the hearing, but, in my judgment, he would

1 [1953] 2 All ER 339, [1953] 1 WLR 780

have been right to reject it on the first of those grounds, and as to the second, the
only possible conclusion was that the risks had substantially changed to such an   *a*
extent that it would be wrong to allow the money to be taken out, and for those
reasons I too would dismiss the appeal.

BROWNE LJ. I agree that this appeal should be dismissed, though I have the
misfortune to differ from Lord Denning MR and Orr LJ on one point.

On 25th January 1973 the plaintiff suffered an accident while working for the   *b*
defendants as a caster. I do not think I need describe the process on which he was
working in their foundry at Redditch in Worcestershire. He suffered various burns
from molten metal. His most serious injuries were the complete loss of the sight of
his right eye, and considerable cosmetic damage on the eye and eyelids.

By his statement of claim delivered on 31st January 1974 the plaintiff alleged an
unsafe system of work, or alternatively, if there was a proper system, a failure by a   *c*
Mr Hutchings, who was working with the plaintiff, to carry out the system. There
was also an allegation of defective equipment. The defendants denied negligence
and alleged contributory negligence, one of the allegations being that the plaintiff
had failed to wear goggles provided for him.

On 23rd January 1975 the defendants paid into court £5,500. Counsel for the plaintiff told us that the special damages were agreed at £215, and the future loss of   *d*
earnings at £3,120. The amount paid into court was, I think, clearly a good deal
less than the damages the plaintiff would have been likely to recover if he succeeded
in his action and was not guilty of any contributory negligence; but of course I
express no opinion whatever about figures.

The case came on for hearing before Croom-Johnson J at Birmingham on 24th
March 1975. The plaintiff was called and his evidence finished. His expert witness,   *e*
Mr Cubitt-Smith, was called, examined in chief and cross-examined. His cross-
examination seems not to have been quite finished at the end of the day, though
nearly so. He would then have been re-examined. Counsel for the plaintiff (who
did not appear for the plaintiff at the trial) told us that Mr Hutchings was in court
on subpoena from the plaintiff, but he did not know whether he would have been
called or not. Whether the defendants would have called evidence or not we do
not know.

I am not going through the evidence, but it is clear that the case had not gone well
for the plaintiff; at the lowest, as counsel for the plaintiff said to the judge next
morning, 'the case has not gone as well as one predicted'. At the sitting of the court
on 25th March, counsel for the plaintiff applied for payment out of the money in
court. The application was opposed by counsel for the defendants. The judge refused   *g*
the application and ordered a new trial. The plaintiff appeals and asks for an order
for payment out.

The appeal raises three questions: (1) Is a plaintiff entitled to make an application
for payment out after the trial has started and before judgment is given? (2) If a
plaintiff makes an application for payment out more than 21 days after the payment in, but before the trial has started, or (if he is entitled to do so) during the   *h*
trial before judgment, on what principles should the discretion of the judge or
master to order or refuse payment out be exercised? (3) Did Croom-Johnson J exercise
his discretion wrongly in the present case?

As to (1) counsel for the defendants submits that the effect of RSC Ord 22, r 7, is
that once the trial has started no application for payment out can be made until after
judgment has been given, unless the defendant consents. He says that 'at' the trial
in r 5 refers only to the period after judgment has been given, between then and the
end of the hearing when questions of costs and so on are being discussed. He says
that if a plaintiff can apply during the trial before that stage it could lead to serious
abuses. If a plaintiff's case is going badly, he could apply for payment out. He will
then either get the money out of court or be able to get a new trial, at which he

would hope to do better, perhaps with the help of additional or improved evidence.
a Costs would not be an adequate sanction or safeguard. He refers to what Slade J
said in *Millar v Building Contractors (Luton) Ltd*[1]:

> 'It is obvious that the plaintiff thinks that, if I were to accede to the applica-
> tion, she is likely to recover more by accepting the amount in court than she is
> likely to recover as a result of my judgment. It is not only a question of costs;
> *b* it is also one of the amount to be recovered, and I think it would be unfair to
> the defendants to allow the plaintiff to adopt an attitude which really, in collo-
> quial parlance, amounts to: "Heads I win; tails I do not lose". If I were to accede
> to an application of this kind, it might encourage a plaintiff not to take the
> money out of court under R.S.C., Ord. 22, r. 2, not to make an application for
> leave to take it out at the commencement of the trial, or even in the course of
> *c* the evidence, but to wait until the closing speeches, and then, if the judge should
> indicate that he was not impressed by the plaintiff's evidence, to say, at the
> eleventh hour and fifty-ninth minute: "Now is the time to make my applica-
> tion." I have no doubt whatever that in the exercise of my judicial discretion
> I ought to refuse this application.'

d Counsel for the plaintiff says in substance that RSC Ord 22, r 5, means what it says,
and that r 7 does not derogate from it.

On this point I agree with counsel for the plaintiff. The words of r 5 are wide
and general: '. . . the money remaining in court shall not be paid out except in
pursuance of an order of the Court which may be made at any time, at or after
the trial or hearing of the action . . .' In their natural meaning these words are
clearly wide enough to include an application made *during* the trial. In *Cumper v
e Pothecary*[2] this court thought that was the meaning of the words. Goddard LJ
said in delivering the judgment of the court[3]:

> 'If the plaintiff can accept as of right up to the eve of trial, why might he not
> do so during the trial? The note in THE ANNUAL PRACTICE to which counsel for
> for the respondent referred clearly has reference to the concluding words of
> *f* r. 3 [now r 5], which says that an order may be made at any time before, at or
> after the trial. In other words, the plaintiff may ask for an order at any time,
> but it does not mean that he is necessarily entitled to it.'

I appreciate that this was obiter and that no point was raised about r 7, but it seems
to me to support my view of the natural meaning of the words. I find it impossible
g to limit them in the way suggested by counsel for the defendants.

In *Millar v Building Contractors (Luton) Ltd*[1] Slade J said:

> 'My jurisdiction is contained in R.S.C., Ord. 22, r. 3. It is clear that I have
> jurisdiction to accede to the application of counsel for the plaintiff, and it is
> equally clear from the wording of the rule and from the judgment of GODDARD,
> L.J. in *Cumper v. Pothecary*[4], that I have complete discretion to grant or to refuse
> *h* the application.'

But apparently no point was taken about r 7 in that case. In *Griggs v Petts*[5],
the defendant made no objection.

I think some support for the view that an application for payment out can be
made during the trial is given by RSC Ord 22, r 4(3); that sub-rule might be intended
j

1 [1953] 2 All ER at 339, [1953] 1 WLR 780 at 781
2 [1941] 2 All ER 516, [1941] 2 KB 58
3 [1941] 2 All ER at 520, [1941] 2 KB at 67
4 [1941] 2 All ER at 520-523, [1941] 2 KB at 63-71
5 [1939] 4 All ER 39 at 42, [1940] 1 KB 198 at 202

to apply only to a payment, or further payment, into court under r 3(2) after the
trial has begun, but it is expressed in general terms.

As to r 7, this court held in *Millensted v Grosvenor House (Park Lane) Ltd*[1] (a) that
the rule then corresponding to r 7 was 'directory and not compulsive'; (b) that the
fact that the payment into court had been disclosed did not prevent the trial judge
from going on with the further hearing of the case if he thought it right in his
discretion to do so. Slesser LJ said[2]:

> 'To test this matter, I will assume that the mention of the payment into court
> had been made to a judge or jury, before he delivered judgment, in a case
> where the oral judgment and the written order agreed in all respects. In my
> opinion, in such a case, a departure from rule would not, of itself, compel the
> judge to refuse to continue to hear the case, nor, if he did continue to hear it,
> in his discretion, would it be a ground for this court to order a new trial. The
> part of the rule, in my opinion, dealing with this matter, like the earlier limb,
> which says no mention of payment into court shall appear in the pleadings, is
> directory, and not compulsive; that is to say, a judge, in his discretion, when
> such matter was mentioned to him or the jury, if he were of opinion that the
> statement as to payment in could not reasonably be calculated to cause any
> miscarriage, would be entitled to allow the case to proceed.'

Scott LJ said[3]:

> 'But I do not think any such sanction can be read into the rule by implication
> As the words stand, they constitute a direction to counsel, parties, and wit-
> nesses, the observation of which the framers of the rule thought was generally
> in the interest of the administration of justice; and I think that a dereliction
> from the duty so indicated is an incident which the judge trying the case is
> left free to deal with, in his complete discretion, acting under the inherent
> jurisdiction of the court, according to the actual circumstances of the case in
> which the incident happens. I think that that is so whether the trial be before a
> judge and jury, or a judge alone.'

Farwell J said[4]:

> 'The purpose of the order is obvious. It was made to prevent the premature
> disclosure of a fact which was not relevant to the issues to be tried, but the
> disclosure of which might prejudice one or more of the parties to the proceedings.
> It is to be noticed that the order makes no express provision for the event of an
> infringement of the rule. It is, of course, the duty of both judge and counsel
> to observe the rule, but what is to be done if the rule, by inadvertence or other-
> wise, is broken? In my judgment, this is in every case a matter for the trial
> judge to determine, having due regard to the object for which the rule was
> made. If he thinks it proper or necessary for the due administration of justice,
> he may refuse to hear the action any further and direct it to be tried before
> another tribunal. On the other hand, if he is satisfied that no injustice will be
> done, he may allow the matter to proceed, and, if he adopts the latter course,
> that, in itself, affords no ground for an appeal from the order which is ultimately
> made.'

As r 7 is only directory and not compulsive, it cannot in my judgment override what
I think is the clear meaning of r 5, and in my view a plaintiff is entitled to make

1 [1937] 1 All ER 736, [1937] 1 KB 717
2 [1937] 1 All ER at 739, [1937] 1 KB at 722, 723
3 [1937] 1 All ER at 740, [1937] 1 KB at 725
4 [1937] 1 All ER at 741, [1957] 1 KB at 727

application during the trial for payment out, whether or not the defendant consents.
a Further, I find difficulty in reconciling counsel for the defendants' suggestion that
r 7 does not prohibit an application if the defendant does consent (as is quite often
done in practice) with the last line and a half of r 7, since in those circumstances no
question of liability or amount has been decided.

What was said by Goddard and Du Parcq LJJ in *Williams v Boag*[1] related to the
disclosure of a payment into court on an application before trial to amend the
b defence, and I do not think it throws any light on the relationship between rr 5 and 7.

I see the danger of abuses on which counsel for the defendants relies, but I think
this could be reduced if it is realised that the judge has discretion to go on with the
hearing, though of course he would almost certainly not do so if the defendant
objected. A plaintiff would not usually apply during the trial for payment out unless
his case was doing badly, and he would therefore be likely to do worse if the case
c goes on before the same judge than if there was a new trial. But if this danger is
felt to be serious, I think the right solution is to amend the rules, not to give what
I regard as a wrong construction to the existing rules.

As to (2), counsel for the plaintiff submitted that when an application is made after
the end of the period during which the plaintiff can take the money out as of right,
whether before or at the trial, the master or judge should generally exercise his
d discretion in favour of allowing payment out, unless he is satisfied that payment out
will cause injustice to the defendant which cannot be compensated by costs. He
suggested that payment out should usually be ordered unless on the material then
before the master or judge he can decide with certainty that the degree of risk of
which the payment into court was an estimate has changed substantially, so that
the plaintiff will not succeed in the action or will not get as much as the money in
e court. Counsel for the defendants submitted that objection to payment out by the
defendant should be conclusive and that an order for payment out should never be
made if the defendant objects. Alternatively, I think he said that if the defendant
tells the master or the judge that in his view there has been a change of circumstances since the payment in which makes the payment in too generous, this should
be accepted as conclusive and the application refused.

f I think that both counsel for the plaintiff and counsel for the defendants are wrong.
I have no doubt that counsel for the defendants' first submission is wrong. It would
take away all discretion from the court, and substitute the discretion of the defendant.
As appears below, I think his second submission goes too far, as do counsel for the
plaintiff's submissions.

The authorities give little guidance. In *Cumper v Pothecary*, Goddard LJ, delivering
g the judgment of the court, said[2]:

> 'Indeed, we think it is desirable to say that it must not be thought that a
> defendant who has paid a sum into court is entitled as of right to resile from that
> step. He must, in our opinion, show that there are good reasons for his applica-
> tion—for instance, the discovery of further evidence, which puts a wholly different
> **h** complexion on the case, as in *Frazer & Haws Ltd.* v. *Burns*[3] and *Williams* v.
> *Boag*[4], or a change in the legal outlook brought about by a new judicial
> decision, as in the present case, and there may be others. Having once put a
> valuation on the plaintiff's case, the defendant ought not to be allowed to alter
> it without good reason. We think the same considerations apply if the matter
> comes before the court on an application by the plaintiff to have the money
> **j** paid out to him. The court is not to consider merely whether the amount paid

---

1 [1940] 4 All ER 246 at 248, 249, [1941] 1 KB 1 at 3, 4
2 [1941] 2 All ER 516 at 522, 523, [1941] 2 KB 58 at 70
3 (1934) 49 Ll R Rep 216
4 [1940] 4 All ER 246, [1941] 1 KB 1

in is large or small, nor is it called on to take into account the sort of circumstances which would be proper if, for instance, it were asked to approve a settlement on behalf of an infant, apart from matters such as fraud or mistake affecting the original payment. It should consider whether there is a sufficient change of circumstance since the money was paid in to make it just that the defendant should have an opportunity of withdrawing or reducing his payment.'

Both that case and *Frazer and Haws Ltd v Burns*[1], treat a change of circumstances since payment in as at least a very important factor. Slade J said in *Millar's* case[2] that it would be 'unfair' to allow the plaintiff to take the money out of court.

It would obviously be impossible and undesirable to try to lay down hard and fast rules about how the discretion of the master or the judge should be exercised; the most which can be done is to suggest general guidance. I think the right approach is for the master or the judge to ask himself whether there is a real possiblity that there has been a substantial change of risk, either as to liability or amount, since the payment in was made. In my view, he should not accept as decisive the defendant's statement that there has been such a change, though it would be a powerful factor if the defendant cannot reasonably be expected to go further. Of course a defendant cannot always be expected to show his hand by disclosing what fresh evidence he has. But in some cases he can do so without any difficulty as in *Dawson v Spaul*[3] and *Cumper v Pothecary*[4]. In *Frazer and Haws Ltd v Burns*[1] and *Williams v Boag*[5], the defendants seem to have felt no embarrassment in disclosing their fresh evidence to show that there had been an alteration in the situation. Usually I think that the defendant can reasonably be expected to go beyond a mere assertion.

As to (3), I do not find it clear from the transcript on what grounds Croom-Johnson J exercised his discretion in refusing the application. The passage which Lord Denning MR has quoted suggests that he refused simply because the defendant objected; if so, I think he was wrong for the reason already given. But I am not satisfied that he did refuse the application solely on this ground. He said that 'in the circumstances of a case like this' he would refuse the application. He said: 'I have got to decide it on some other principle than that' ('that' being apparently that the plaintiff had already lost his case, although the judge had only heard part of the evidence) and 'it seems to me that I am in the position of being asked to make a decision without having heard a great deal of the evidence in the case.' In spite of my doubt as to the judge's reasons, his decision to refuse the application for payment out was in my view right. By the end of the first day, there was a real possibility that there had been a substantial change in the risk since the payment in was made, and it would have been unjust to the defendants to order payment out.

I would, therefore, dismiss the appeal.

Appeal dismissed. Leave granted to apply to the judge to continue the hearing. Leave to appeal to the House of Lords refused.

Solicitors: *Pattinson & Brewer*, agents for *Stanley A Coleman & Hill*, Birmingham (for the plaintiff); *Rowleys & Blewitts*, Birmingham (for the defendants).

Gavin Gore-Andrews Esq   Barrister.

---

1   (1934) 49 Ll L Rep 216
2   [1953] 2 All ER 339, [1957] 1 WLR 780
3   (1935) 152 LT 444
4   [1941] 2 All ER 516, [1941] 2 KB 58
5   [1940] 4 All ER 246, [1941] 1 KB 1

a

Ward v Tesco Stores Ltd

COURT OF APPEAL, CIVIL DIVISION
MEGAW, LAWTON AND ORMROD LJJ
13th NOVEMBER 1975

b Negligence – Duty to take care – Breach of duty – Burden of proof – Evidential burden – Accident not one that would ordinarily have occurred if defendants had complied with duty – Absence of explanation by defendants showing that they had complied with duty – Defendants owners and managers of supermarket – Duty to keep floors clean and clear of spillage – Customer slipping on yoghourt spilt on floor – No evidence how long yoghourt had been on floor or whether defendants had had reasonable opportunity to clear it up – Whether judge *c* entitled to infer that defendants in breach of duty in absence of explanation by them.

The defendants owned and managed a supermarket store. While shopping in the store, the plaintiff slipped on some yoghourt which had been spilt on the floor and was injured. She brought an action against the defendants claiming damages for personal injuries allegedly caused by the defendants' negligence in the maintenance *d* of the floor. It was not suggested that the plaintiff had in any way been negligent in failing to notice the spillage on the floor as she walked along doing her shopping. At the trial the defendants gave evidence that spillages occurred about ten times a week and that staff had been instructed that if they saw any spillages on the floor they were to stay where the spill had taken place and call somebody to clear it up. Apart from general cleaning, the floor of the supermarket was brushed five or six *e* times every day on which it was open. There was, however, no evidence before the court as to when the floor had last been brushed before the plaintiff's accident. The plaintiff gave evidence that three weeks after the accident, when shopping in the same store, she had noticed that some orange squash had been spilt on the floor; she kept her eye on the spillage for about a quarter of an hour and during that time nobody had come to clear it up. The trial judge held that the plaintiff had proved a *f* prima facie case and that the defendants were liable for the accident. The defendants appealed, contending that the onus was on the plaintiff to show that the spillage had been on the floor an unduly long time and that there had been opportunities for the management to clear it up which had not been taken, and that unless there was some evidence when the yoghourt had been spilt on to the floor no prima facie case could be made against the defendants.

g

Held (Ormrod LJ dissenting) – It was the duty of the defendants and their servants to see that the floors were kept clean and free from spillages so that accidents did not occur. Since the plaintiff's accident was not one which, in the ordinary course of things, would have happened if the floor had been kept clean and spillages dealt with as soon as they occurred, it was for the defendants to give some explanation to *h* show that the accident had not arisen from any want of care on their part. Since the probabilites were that, by the time of the accident, the spillage had been on the floor long enough for it to have been cleared up by a member of the defendant's staff, the judge was, in the absence of any explanation by the defendants, entitled to conclude that the accident had occurred because the defendants had failed to take reasonable care. Accordingly the appeal would be dismissed (see p 222 *b* to *j*, p 223 *g* *j* and p 224 *a* to *e*, post).

Dictum of Erle CJ in *Scott v The London and St Katherine Docks Co* (1865) 3 H & C at 601 applied.

Turner v Arding & Hobbs Ltd [1949] 2 All ER 911 approved.

Dictum of Devlin J in *Richards v W F White & Co* [1957] 1 Lloyd's Rep at 369, 370 explained.

Notes
For the burden of proof in actions for negligence, see 28 Halsbury's Laws (3rd Edn) *a*
73-75, paras 75, 76, and for cases on the subject, see 36 Digest (Repl) 140, 141, 735-746.

Cases referred to in judgments
Richards v W F White & Co [1957] 1 Lloyd's Rep 367.
Scott v The London and St Katherine Docks Co (1865) 3 H & C 596, 5 New Rep 420, 34
  LJEx 220, 13 LT 148, 11 Jur NS 204, 159 ER 665, Ex Ch, 36 Digest (Repl) 145, 772. *b*
Turner v Arding & Hobbs Ltd [1949] 2 All ER 911, 36 Digest (Repl) 57, 310.

Cases also cited
Byrne v Boadle (1863) 2 H & C 722.
Dollman v A & S Hillman Ltd [1941] 1 All ER 355, CA.
Stowell v Railway Executive [1949] 2 All ER 193, [1949] 2 KB 519. *c*

Appeal
This was an appeal by the defendants, Tesco Stores Ltd, against the judgment of his
Honour Judge Nance given in the Liverpool County Court on 21st February 1975
whereby he ordered that the plaintiff, May Ward, should recover against the defendants damages of £178·50 for personal injuries received when she slipped and fell *d*
while shopping in the defendants' supermarket at Smithdown Road, Liverpool, on
29th June 1974. By consent the sum awarded was reduced to £137·10. The facts
are set out in the judgment of Lawton LJ.

David Owen for the defendants.
N Dugdale for the plaintiff. *e*

LAWTON LJ delivered the first judgment at the invitation of Megaw LJ. This
is an appeal by the defendants from a judgment of his Honour Judge Nance given
in the Liverpool County Court on 21st February 1975, whereby he adjudged that the
plaintiff should recover against the defendants £178·50 damages and her costs on
scale 2, for personal injuries said to have been caused by the negligence of the defen- *f*
dants in the maintenance of the floor in their supermarket at Smithdown Road,
Liverpool. By consent the sum awarded has been reduced to £137·10. The higher
figure was due to an arithmetical error.

On 29th June 1974, at about midday, the plaintiff went to the defendants' supermarket. It is a large one and is carried on in premises which used to be a cinema.
Inside, the premises were laid out in the way which is usual nowadays in supermarkets. *g*
On duty there was a total of about 30 to 35 staff; but in the middle of the day that
number was reduced because staff had to be relieved in order to enable them to
get their midday meals.

The plaintiff went round the store, carrying a wire basket, as shoppers are expected
to do in supermarkets. She was doing her shopping at the back of the store when
she felt herself slipping. She appreciated that she was slipping on something which *h*
was sticky. She fell to the ground, and sustained minor injuries. She had not seen
what had caused her to slip. It was not suggested, either at the trial or in this court,
that she had in any way been negligent in failing to notice what was on the floor as
she walked along doing her shopping. When she was picking herself up she appreciated that she had slipped on some pink substance which looked to her like yoghourt.
It was yoghourt. Later, somebody on the defendants' staff found a carton of yog- *i*
hourt in the vicinity which was two-thirds empty.

A member of the staff helped to pick the plaintiff up. The manager was called.
The plaintiff was taken to his office. She was dealt with there in a kindly and con-
siderate way. The defendants offered to, and did, arrange for such of her clothes as
had been soiled by the fall to be cleaned.

That is all the plaintiff was able to prove, save for one additional fact. About
a three weeks later when she was shopping in the same store she noticed that some
orange squash had been spilt on the floor. She kept an eye on the spillage for about
a quarter of an hour. During that time nobody came to clear it up.
The trial judge was of the opinion that the facts which I have related constituted a
prima facie case against the defendants. I infer that this case, which involves only a
small amount of damages, has been brought to this court because the defendants are
b disturbed that any judge should find that a prima facie case is established merely
by a shopper proving that she slipped on a supermarket floor.
At the trial the defendants called some evidence. Their manager spoke about the
store and how many staff were employed. He went on to say that the staff had the
following instruction about spillages: 'Stay where the spill has taken place and call
someone else.' He said that usually in a store of this kind and size there was to be
c found some member of the staff near where the spillage had occurred. He went on
to say that the store had a system for keeping the floor clean. Contractors came in
every night to give it a general clean-up. Twice a week those contractors carried out
'buffing', which in the south of England would be called 'polishing'. The manager
said that every day whilst the store was open the floor was brushed five or six times.
The defendants did not call any evidence as to when the store floor had last been
d brushed before the plaintiff's accident. It follows that there was no evidence before
the court as to whether the floor had been brushed a few moments before the
accident, or an hour, or possibly an hour and a half. The court was left without any
information on what may have been an important matter.
The manager in cross-examination said that spillages did occur from time to time;
he thought there were about ten breakages a week, but most of them came from
e the breaking of squash bottles
It follows that those in charge of the store knew that during the course of a working
week there was a likelihood of spillages occurring from time to time. It was accepted
at the trial that shoppers, intent on looking to see what is on offer, cannot be expected
to look where they are putting their feet. The management should have appreciated
that if there are patches of slippery substances on the floor people are liable to step
f into them and that, if they do, they may slip. It follows too that if those are the
conditions to be expected in the store there must be some reasonably effective system
for getting rid of the dangers which may from time to time exist. The only precautions which were taken were, first, the system of having the floor brushed five or six
times during the working day and, secondly, giving instructions to the staff that if
they saw any spillage on the floor they were to stay where the spill had taken place
g and call somebody to clean it up.
The main complaint of the defendants in this case has been that the trial judge
should never have taken the view that the plaintiff had proved a prima facie case.
It was submitted before this court that it was for the plaintiff to show that the spillage
had been on the floor an unduly long time and that there had been opportunities
for the management to clean it up which they had not taken. In support of that
h proposition, counsel for the defendants invited our attention to _Richards v W F
White & Co_[1]. It is necessary to say something about the facts of that case because,
as in all cases of negligence, the facts are important. A dock labourer who was
working on a ship in dock which was being unloaded slipped on a patch of oil and
injured himself. At the material time between 300 and 400 men in various trades
were working on the ship. In the course of his judgment Devlin J said[2]:

j
'If there had been evidence which showed that there was some danger, not
perhaps of oil but some other danger, which was being left on the ship for two or
three days, or anything of that sort, which the shipowners were doing nothing

1 [1957] 1 Lloyd's Rep 367
2 [1957] 1 Lloyd's Rep at 369, 370

about, a *prima facie* case of negligence would be made out; but to make out a
prima facie case of negligence in a case of this sort, there must, I think, be some
evidence to show how long the oil had been there, some evidence from which it
can be inferred that a prudent shipowner, who had a reasonable system of
inspection for the purpose of seeing that dangers of this sort were not created,
ought to have noticed it.'

That case was decided on its own facts. I doubt whether Devlin J intended to
make any general statement of principle. If he did, I would not agree with what he
said. This case, too, has to be decided on its own facts, to which established principles
must be applied. The relevant principles were enunciated in the classical judgment
of Erle CJ in *Scott v The London and St Katherine Docks Co*[1]:

'But where the thing is shewn to be under the management of the defendant
or his servants, and the accident is such as in the ordinary course of things does
not happen if those who have the management use proper care, it affords
reasonable evidence, in the absence of explanation by the defendants that the
accident arose from want of care.'

In this case the floor of this supermarket was under the management of the
defendants and their servants. The accident was such as in the ordinary course of
things does not happen if floors are kept clean and spillages are dealt with as soon
as they occur. If an accident does happen because the floors are covered with spillage,
then in my judgment some explanation should be forthcoming from the defendants
to show that the accident did not arise from any want of care on their part; and in
the absence of any explanation the judge may give judgment for the plaintiff. Such
burden of proof as there is on defendants in such circumstances is evidential, not
probative. The trial judge thought that prima facie this accident would not have
happened had the defendants taken reasonable care. In my judgment he was justified in taking that view because the probabilities were that the spillage had been on
the floor long enough for it to have been cleaned up by a member of the staff.

The next question is whether the defendants by their evidence gave any explanation to show that they had taken all reasonable care. The only explanation which
they gave was that to which I have already referred. The judge weighed the evidence
and decided as a matter of fact from which in this case there can be no appeal that
the precautions taken were not enough, and that the plaintiff in consequence had
proved her case. In coming to that conclusion he followed the judgment of Lord
Goddard CJ in *Turner v Arding & Hobbs Ltd*[2]:

'The duty of the shopkeeper in this class of case is well established. It may be
said to be a duty to use reasonable care to see that the shop floor, on which
people are invited, is kept reasonably safe, and if an unusual danger is present
of which the injured person is unaware, and the danger is one which would not
be expected and ought not to be present, the onus of proof is on the defendants
to explain how it was that the accident happened.'

It is clear from a later passage in his judgment that Lord Goddard CJ, in referring
to the burden of proof, was not saying that the defendant had to disprove negligence.
What he had intended to say is apparent from what he said later[2]:

'Here, however, I think that there is a burden thrown on the defendants
either of explaining how this thing got on the floor or giving me far more evidence
than they have as to the state of the floor and the watch that was kept on it
immediately before the accident.'

The learned judge had that passage in mind when he decided as he did. In my
judgment he was right; and accordingly I would dismiss this appeal.

1 (1865) 3 H & C 596 at 601
2 [1949] 2 All ER 911 at 912

ORMROD LJ.   I have the misfortune to disagree with the judgment of Lawton LJ.
a Starting from the beginning, I do not think that it was established that this accident
was caused by any want of care on the part of the defendants.   The accident described
by the plaintiff—and she did no more than describe the accident, namely that she
slipped in some yoghourt which was on the floor of the supermarket—could clearly
have happened no matter what degree of care these defendants had taken.   The
crucial question is how long before the accident the yoghourt had been on the floor.
b Had some customer knocked it off the shelf a few moments before, then no reasonable system which the defendants could be expected to operate would have prevented
this accident.   So I think that the plaintiff fails at the outset.

So far as the proposition which Lawton LJ has cited from Erle CJ[1] is concerned, all
I would say is that, since this accident could quite easily have happened without any
want of care on the part of the defendants, I do not think that that broad proposition
c is applicable.

I for my part am unable to distinguish this case in any material respect from the
judgment of Devlin J in *Richards v W F White & Co*[2], to which Lawton LJ referred.
The learned judge put the matter in the clearest possible terms[3] in the passage
which Lawton LJ has read.   I cannot improve on that statement of the law, and
would not attempt to.   It seems to me quite clear that unless there is some evidence
d as to when the yoghourt got on to this floor no prima facie case can be made against
these defendants.   I would only add that to hold otherwise would seem to me to
put on the defendants a wholly unreasonable burden, not only of care, but also of
proof.   I ask myself what evidence could they have called?   It would have been
fortunate, perhaps, if they had been able to show that their sweeper had passed over
this bit of the floor five minutes before the accident.   But it would not have shown
e that their system was either better or worse than if the sweeper had gone by that
bit of the floor an hour earlier.   And I cannot think that the case would have been
carried any further by calling evidence from such employees as may or may not
have been about.   This is a supermarket, not a place with counters and assistants
behind the counters.   I cannot imagine what evidence they could give except to say
that they had not noticed the spill; and the matter would have been taken no
f further.

For those reasons, in my judgment counsel for the defendants' submission is right,
and I would allow the appeal.

MEGAW LJ.   I agree with the conclusion expressed by Lawton LJ, and with the
g reasons given by him for that conclusion.   But as unfortunately the court is not
unanimous I feel that it is desirable that I should add a few words of my own, not,
I believe, in any way departing from the reasons given by Lawton LJ.

It seems to me that the essence of the argument put forward on behalf of the
defendants in this appeal is this.   Never mind whether the defendants had any system
of any sort to protect their customers against the risk of slipping on the floor of the
supermarket as a result of breakages or spillages, which on their own evidence
h happened about ten times a week.   Even if they had no system of any sort to guard
against such a risk to their customers, nevertheless, when an accident happens such
as the accident in this case, a lady customer who undoubtedly slips, through no fault
of her own, on such a spillage on the floor, she cannot recover against the defendants.
And why can she not recover?   Because she is unable to prove that the spillage did
j not take place within a matter of a few seconds before she slipped and fell on it:
so that, however perfect a system the defendants had had, it would not have enabled
them to prevent this particular accident.

---

1   *Scott v The London and St Katherine Docks Co* (1865) 3 H & C 596 at 601
2   [1957] 1 Lloyd's Rep 367
3   [1957] 1 Lloyd's Rep at 369, 370

With great respect to those who support that proposition, it appears to me to be contrary to the law as I understand it to be. It is for the plaintiff to show that there has occurred an event which is unusual and which, in the absence of explanation, is more consistent with fault on the part of the defendants than the absence of fault; and to my mind the learned judge was wholly right in taking that view of the presence of this slippery liquid on the floor of the supermarket in the circumstances of this case: that is that the defendants knew or should have known that it was a not uncommon occurrence; and that if it should happen, and should not be promptly attended to, it created a serious risk that customers would fall and injure themselves. When the plaintiff has established that, the defendants can still escape from liability. They could escape from liability if they could show that the accident must have happened, or even on balance of probability would have been likely to have happened, irrespective of the existence of a proper and adequate system, in relation to the circumstances, to provide for the safety of customers. But, if the defendants wish to put forward such a case, it is for them to show that, on balance of probability, either by evidence or by inference from the evidence that is given or is not given, this accident would have been at least equally likely to have happened despite a proper system designed to give reasonable protection to customers. That, in this case, they wholly failed to do. Really the essence of counsel for the defendants' argument—and he did not shrink from it—was: 'Never mind whether we had no system at all: still, as the plaintiff has failed to show that the yoghourt was spilt within a few seconds before the accident, she must fail.' As I have said, in the circumstances of this case, I do not think that the plaintiff, to succeed, had to prove how long it was since the defendants' floor had become slippery.

I take the view that the decision of the learned judge in this case is fully in line with the decision of Lord Goddard CJ in *Turner v Arding & Hobbs Ltd*[1], which has been cited by Lawton LJ. Indeed, I am unable to see how, consistently with that decision, on the facts and the evidence here the learned judge could have reached any other conclusion.

As regards the decision of Devlin J in *Richards v W F White & Co*[2], to which Lawton LJ and Ormrod LJ have referred, I agree with Lawton LJ that that case has to be looked at in relation to its very special facts. When the learned judge said: 'but to make out a *prima facie* case of negligence in a case of this sort, there must, I think, be some evidence to show how long the oil had been there', I am confident that he did not intend to lay down any general principle. It is, to my mind, not a part of the law, as I have said, that in this case the plaintiff must fail merely because she is unable to disprove that the yoghourt fell on the floor within a few seconds of the time that she trod on it.

I agree that the appeal should be dismissed.

Appeal dismissed.

Solicitors: *A W Mawer & Co*, Liverpool (for the defendants); *Sharpe Pritchard & Co*, agents for *E Rex Makin & Co*, Liverpool (for the plaintiff).

Mary Rose Plummer   Barrister.

1   [1949] 2 All ER 911 at 912
2   [1957] 1 Lloyd's Rep 367

Portland Managements Ltd v Harte and others

COURT OF APPEAL, CIVIL DIVISION
MEGAW, SCARMAN AND BRIDGE LJJ
27th, 28th OCTOBER 1975

Trespass to land – Defence – Burden of proof – Lawful possession – Defendant in possession – Owner proving title to land and intention to recover possession – Burden on defendant to set up title or right consistent with fact of ownership vested in plaintiff.

Court of Appeal – New trial – Election to call no evidence – Respondent at trial having elected to call no evidence – Appellant's appeal allowed – Circumstances in which new trial will be ordered despite respondent's election – Election influenced by erroneous view of law expressed by trial judge at early stage of argument – Action by appellant for possession of land – Respondent's defence raising claim to protection under Rent Acts.

The plaintiffs were the owners of a house with a registered absolute title since 21st March 1973. Although they claimed to be entitled to immediate possession, they had never been able to obtain vacant possession. In July 1974 they brought proceedings for possession of the house against a number of persons who were in occupation as squatters. Evidence was given on behalf of the defendants that D had an interest in the house and was in possession. By consent D was joined as a defendant. In their particulars of claim the plaintiffs alleged against D that she had never been in occupation of the house at all; alternatively that if she was in occupation, she was a trespasser, and they relied on their registered title as giving them a right to immediate possession. By her defence D asserted that she was in occupation of the premises as the tenant of P who at the time of the granting of the tenancy was the lawful owner of the freehold of the premises. At the hearing before the county court judge the plaintiffs opened their case by putting in the land certificate as conclusive evidence of their title. At an early stage of the argument the judge indicated to counsel for the plaintiffs his strongly-held opinion that proof of absolute title of ownership in the plaintiffs was not by itself sufficient to establish a cause of action against a person in possession. During the course of the hearing he expressed that view strongly and emphatically more than once. Counsel for the plaintiffs nevertheless stood firm on his title as against D. He did however call evidence to deal with the squatters. A number of witnesses on behalf of the plaintiffs stated that they had visited the premises in July and August 1974 to execute a warrant for possession obtained by the plaintiffs against unsuccessful defendants in other proceedings and had seen no evidence or signs that D was in occupation. Counsel for D elected to call no evidence. The judge did not believe the plaintiffs' witnesses and he nonsuited the plaintiffs holding that the onus was on the plaintiffs to prove that D was a trespasser and not for D to refute it. The plaintiffs appealed.

Held – (i) Where an absolute owner of land brought an action for trespass against a person alleged to be in possession, all that the owner had to prove was his title and an intention to regain possession. If the defendant either admitted the plaintiff's ownership or was faced with evidence, which the court accepted, that the plaintiff was in fact the owner, the burden was on the defendant to confess and avoid by setting up a title or right to possession consistent with the fact of ownership vested in the plaintiff. It followed therefore that the ground of the judge's decision was wrong in law and the appeal would be allowed (see p 229 g to j, p 230 f and g, p 231 c and d, p 234 e and p 235 b and c, post): dicta of Lord Blackburn in *Danford v McAnulty* (1883) 8 App Cas at 462 and of Lord Tucker and Wynn Parry J in *Delaney v T P Smith Ltd* [1946] 2 All ER at 24, 25, 26 applied.

(ii) Although as a general rule where a defendant had elected to call no evidence

I

a new trial would not be ordered by the Court of Appeal, that rule was not a rule
of law but was discretionary and the court had to consider whether justice required   a
that there should be a rehearing. The court would however require very exceptional
circumstances to be established before departing from its ordinary rule. Since the
election by D's counsel to call no evidence had been influenced by the erroneous
view of the law strongly and prematurely expressed by the judge, the trial thereafter merited the description 'mistrial'. Another factor which had to be taken into
account was that if D were right she could claim the protection of the Rent Acts.   b
Having regard to those factors a new trial would be ordered subject to D complying
with conditions requiring the repayment of costs paid to her by the plaintiffs and
the giving of security for costs of the appeal and further hearing (see p 232 c g and h,
p 233 a to c and e f, p 234 e and p 235 f to h, post); *Alexander v Rayson* [1935] All ER Rep
185 and *Laurie v Raglan Building Co* [1941] 3 All ER 332 distinguished; dictum of
Ormerod LJ in *Storey v Storey* [1960] 3 All ER at 282 explained.   c

Notes
For proof of the plaintiff's title in proceedings for the recovery of land, see 32 Halsbury's Laws (3rd Edn) 375, para 602, and for cases on the subject, see 38 Digest (Repl)
926, 927, 1177-1193.

Cases referred to in judgments   d
Alexander v Rayson [1936] 1 KB 169, [1935] All ER Rep 185, 105 LJKB 148, 154 LT 205,
     CA, 51 Digest (Repl) 725, 3161.
Danford v McAnulty (1883) 8 App Cas 456, 52 LJQB 652, 49 LT 207, HL, 38 Digest
     (Repl) 923, 1171.
Delaney v T P Smith Ltd [1946] 2 All ER 23, [1946] KB 393, 115 LJKB 406, 175 LT 187,
     CA, 46 Digest (Repl) 388, 310.   e
Doe d Humphrey v Martin (1841) 1 Car & M 32, 174 ER 395, NP.
Laurie v Raglan Building Co Ltd [1941] 3 All ER 332, [1942] 1 KB 152, 111 LJKB 292,
     166 LT 63, CA, 51 Digest (Repl) 725, 3164.
Mount v Childs (1948) 64 TLR 559, CA, 31(2) Digest (Reissue) 996, 7960.
Ocean Estates Ltd v Pinder [1969] 2 AC 19, [1969] 2 WLR 1359, PC, Digest (Cont Vol C)
     1033, 98a.   f
Ryan v Clark (1849) 14 QB 65, 18 LJQB 267, 13 LTOS 300, 13 Jur 1000, 117 ER 26, 46
     Digest (Repl) 388, 309.
Storey v Storey [1960] 3 All ER 279, [1961] P 63, [1960] 3 WLR 653, 124 JP 485, CA, 51
     Digest (Repl) 725, 3165.

Cases also cited   g
Brassington v Brassington [1961] 3 All ER 988, [1962] P 276, CA.
Doyle v Olby (Ironmongers) Ltd [1969] 2 All ER 119, [1969] 2 QB 158, CA.

Appeal
The plaintiffs, Portland Managements Ltd, brought proceedings against David
Harte and six other named persons and other persons unknown for possession of a   h
house known as 72 Coningham Road, W12. Bridget Devereux and Joseph Nolan
were subsequently added as defendants to the proceedings. On 16th October 1974 his
Honour Judge McIntyre QC sitting in the West London County Court made an order
for immediate possession against the first six defendants who had admitted through
their counsel that they had no right to remain in possession of the property. Mr
Nolan did not appear and was not represented, an order for possession with respect
to the same property having been made against him in other proceedings. The   j
judge, however, dismissed the plaintiffs' claim for possession against Miss Devereux.
The plaintiffs appealed. The facts are set out in the judgment of Scarman LJ.

Romie Tager for the plaintiffs.
Ralph Gibson QC and *Richard Brock* for Miss Devereux.

SCARMAN LJ delivered the first judgment at the invitation of Megaw LJ. 72
Coningham Road, Shepherds Bush, is a house of some three storeys and a basement
and has been the subject of heavy, and no doubt expensive, litigation since 1973.
The plaintiffs in this action, who are the appellants in this court, are the owners of
the house. They have had a registered absolute title to the house since 21st March
1973. It would appear from such of the history of the house since then as we have
learnt in the course of the appeal that they have never succeeded in obtaining vacant
possession. They have, however, ever since March 1973 maintained that they are
the owners of the house and entitled to immediate possession.

The history of litigation that has beset this house since 1973 need not be investigated in detail by us. Suffice it to say that on 12th July 1974 the plaintiffs sought,
under RSC Ord 113, an order for possession against some seven named persons and
other persons unknown. Their originating summons issued under the order was
served on seven named defendants; an affidavit was sworn by the solicitor to the
plaintiffs; and the application was heard by Kerr J in chambers on 26th July. When
they reached the judge in chambers, the plaintiffs were given two affidavits, one
sworn by a Miss Devereux and the other sworn by a Mr Nolan. The effect of these
affidavits was that the deponents were setting up a claim on behalf of Miss Devereux
to an interest in the whole of the house, and Miss Devereux was asserting that she was
in possession. By consent, Miss Devereux and Mr Nolan were then added as parties
to the proceedings before Kerr J. Kerr J ordered that the summons should be transferred to the county court and that thereafter the claim of the plaintiffs against the
seven named defendants in their summons and against Miss Devereux and against
Mr Nolan should proceed as an ordinary possession case in the county court. It is
common ground that thereafter the action has continued in the county court as an
action for possession in which the cause of action alleged against the defendants is
trespass. It is to be noted in passing that Kerr J ordered that the costs of the proceedings
before him should be costs in cause.

Contemporaneously with the proceedings before Kerr J, there were occurring the
final stages of a county court action brought by these plaintiffs against Mr Nolan
himself. The plaintiffs had sued Mr Nolan in the county court for possession and had
won their action. Mr Nolan in the course of that action had given evidence and had
called Miss Devereux, who gave evidence in which she indicated that she was lawfully
a tenant in possession of the house. All this evidence of Mr Nolan and Miss Devereux,
it must be assumed, was disbelieved by the county court judge, since he made an
order for possession at the suit of the plaintiffs. Mr Nolan appealed, and his appeal
was pending when Kerr J dealt with the plaintiffs' originating summons against the
squatters. The appeal was in fact heard three days after Kerr J had transferred the
proceedings before him to the county court; and the appeal was dismissed.

The next event was that on 27th August 1974 the plaintiffs delivered particulars of
claim in their county court action, that is the action which had been brought into
being by the order of Kerr J. The particulars of claim were described by the county
court judge when the matter ultimately came on for trial as a 'curious' document.
I do not think that is a fair description of the document. It appears to me to be a
perfectly properly and appropriately drafted statement of the plaintiffs' case.

The plaintiffs by now were suing the so-called squatters, all seven of whom were
described as the 'first defendants'; Miss Devereux, brought in by order of Kerr J,
as the second defendant; and Mr Nolan, brought in by order of Kerr J, as the third
defendant. The plaintiffs, very naturally, had to plead somewhat elaborately so as to
take care that the various contingencies, any one of which might arise when the
evidence was given, were considered by the county court judge. Suffice it to say,
for the purposes of this appeal, that the plaintiffs alleged against Miss Devereux,
who is the respondent to the present appeal, that she was never in occupation, or not
at any material time in occupation, of the house at all. Alternatively, they claimed
against Miss Devereux that, if she was, she was a trespasser; and they relied on their

registered title as giving them the right to immediate possession of—or, as was said
in the old cases, the right of entry to—this house. There were other allegations against *a*
the other defendants.

Mr Nolan, no doubt somewhat bruised by his forensic defeat in the county court
and in the Court of Appeal, which had ended as recently as the end of the preceding
July, took no part in these county court proceedings at all. Miss Devereux in due
course filed a defence. The terms of the defence are of some importance to the issue
which has been argued in the appeal. In para 3 of her defence, after denying the plain- *b*
tiffs' title—a denial which, of course, soon evaporated at the trial when the registered
certificate of title was produced: nevertheless in her pleading she denied it—she
alleged as follows:

'It is admitted and averred that [Miss Devereux] is in occupation of the premises
as the lawful tenant of one Prendergast who at the time of the granting of the *c*
tenancy was the lawful owner of the freehold of the premises.'

In other words, she is confessing and avoiding. If, contrary to her contention, the
plaintiffs prove their title, she seeks to avoid their claim for possession by setting up a
lawful tenancy vested in her.

The action came on for trial before his Honour Judge McIntyre. Both the plaintiffs
and Miss Devereux were represented by counsel at the trial. The plaintiffs opened *d*
their case by putting in the land certificate and describing to the court the various
steps in their title, all of which can be seen in the land certificate. Counsel for the
plaintiffs submitted that the land certificate was conclusive evidence of the title of
the plaintiffs, and so far as one can see the judge accepted that submission—as indeed
he had to do, since it was a correct submission in point of law. The judge, however,
at a very early stage in the argument, indicated to counsel for the plaintiffs his very *e*
strongly-held opinion that proof of an absolute title of ownership in the plaintiffs
was not by itself sufficient to establish a cause of action in trespass against someone
who was in possession. One sees from the notes of judgment how he put it; and I
cannot do better than quote the words of the judge. He said in the course of his
judgment:

'During the submissions made to me by [counsel for the plaintiffs] when open- *f*
ing his case, [counsel] suggested that where the title to a property is proved or
admitted, if a defendant says in [her] Defence that she is a tenant of that property,
then the onus is cast on the tenant to prove her alleged tenancy. I find this submission to be contrary to all the rules of procedure in the civil courts and goes
against all that I have experience in 47 years at the Bar and on the Bench.' *g*

The learned trial judge is there expressing a very strong view as to the law; and
this view he expressed strongly and emphatically, and more than once, to counsel
for the plaintiffs when he was opening the plaintiffs' case. Counsel for the plaintiffs
nevertheless stood firm on his title as against Miss Devereux. But he did call evidence
to deal with the squatters who were the first defendants. That evidence is of some
importance. He first of all called a Mr Barker, who visited the premises on four days *h*
in July 1974 and found them occupied; but never saw Miss Devereux there. He called a
Mr St Leger Moore, an official of the plaintiffs, who went to the premises either at the
end of August or in early September 1974 to execute the warrant of possession that the
plaintiffs had obtained against the unsuccessful defendants; and he again described
the premises as he saw them; but found no Miss Devereux there. Counsel for the plaintiffs also called Mr I M Torrance, a solicitor who is a partner in the firm of solicitors *j*
acting for the plaintiffs. Mr Torrance went there with Mr Moore to see that the warrant
of possession was executed against Mr Nolan. Mr Torrance also described the premises
as he saw them, and he said that he found no ladies' apparel there; also, he saw no
evidence or signs of Miss Devereux. This evidence was of some importance to the
plaintiffs' case against Miss Devereux, although, of course, it was called to deal with

a the other limb of the case, because the primary submission on behalf of the plaintiffs was that Miss Devereux was never in occupation, or not at any material time in occupation.

That evidence having been called, counsel for Miss Devereux elected to call no evidence. He elected to call neither his own client, Miss Devereux, nor any witnesses, although we have been told that he was armed with the presence of Miss Devereux and a number of possible witnesses at the trial.

b At the conclusion of the evidence, therefore, the judge had in front of him the land certificate, which was evidence of the ownership of these premises vested in the plaintiffs; he had no evidence at all to indicate that there was any interest in being contrary to the plaintiffs' interest, which, if there were no other such interest, carried with it the right of immediate possession; and he had absolutely no evidence to suggest that Miss Devereux was at any material time in possession or occupation of the *c* premises.

That being the state of the evidence, I am bound to say that I find the judgment of Judge McIntyre a very surprising judgment indeed. He apparently did not believe the evidence of the witnesses called for the plaintiffs. What the grounds for his incredulity are, I am not aware. But he stated that they were unsatisfactory witnesses and he did not believe them. He appears to have thought that because he did not *d* believe them he could infer that Miss Devereux was in fact in occupation or possession.

No doubt the judge's mind on this issue was influenced by the fact that he had seen, with the consent of counsel, the affidavits of Miss Devereux and Mr Nolan that had been put before Kerr J in chambers in July 1974 and which, it will be recalled, had been served on the plaintiffs when they attended the judge in his chambers.

e It has been common ground, however, in the appeal as between counsel for the plaintiffs and counsel for Miss Devereux, that those affidavits were not in evidence in the county court proceedings (which in fact his Honour Judge McIntyre heard on 16th October 1974). Nevertheless the judge appears to have been influenced by what he had read in those affidavits so as to draw an inference—which was not open to him on the evidence in fact before the court—that Miss Devereux was in possession.

f The judge nonsuited the plaintiffs, and he did so because he held to the point of law which he had so strongly expressed to counsel for the plaintiffs in the course of his opening. He said:

> 'If in a civil case a landlord says "You are not in possession as a tenant; you are a trespasser" then in my opinion the onus is on the plaintiff (landlord) to prove
g > that allegation, not on the defendant to refute it. The plaintiff must adduce prima facie evidence supporting his allegation of trespass.'

In so holding, the judge was, as is now conceded by Miss Devereux on this appeal, in error. Possession is, of course, a very important matter to be considered in the action of ejectment, or the action for trespass. But the law is perfectly clear. If a stranger to the title is seeking, by reliance on some lesser or derivative interest, to *h* obtain possession from someone who is in possession, then the defendant can rely on his possession to defeat that sort of claim. But if the absolute owner is suing, and if the absolute owner has shown by his conduct an intention to recover possession, then it is not enough for the defendant merely to assert or give evidence that he is in possession; he has got to show that he is there on the basis of some title which is consistent with the ownership of the premises being vested in the plaintiff.

j We were referred to a number of authorities. The law is old, and I can refer to it very shortly. In *Danford v McAnulty*[1] Lord Blackburn, in the course of his speech, used these words:

> 'For a long time an action for the recovery of land at law was brought by ejectment, and it was so established as to be trite law—a commonplace expression

1   (1883) 8 App Cas 456 at 462

of law—that in ejectment, where a person was in possession those who sought to turn him out were to recover upon the strength of their own title; and consequently *a* possession was at law a good defence against any one, and those who sought to turn the man in possession out must shew a superior legal title to his. If, however, they did shew that, still if the person who was in possession could shew that although they had shewn a superior legal title to the possession, yet he had an equitable ground for saying that they should not turn him out, he as the law stood was obliged to go to a Court of Equity, and as the plaintiff there, as the "actor" *b* (to use a civil law expression), to make out that there was a sufficient reason for a Court of Equity to interfere, and to prevent his being turned out of possession, on this equitable ground.'

The position as between an owner and another in possession of the land of the owner has been considered in fairly recent times by the Court of Appeal in *Delaney v T P* *c* *Smith Ltd*[1]. I need not refer to the facts of that case, but there are two passages from the judgments which indicate the law as I understand it to be. Tucker LJ said[2]:

'It is clear that the plaintiff was in fact founding his claim on the tenancy agreement pleaded by him. It is no doubt true that a plaintiff in an action of trespass to land need only in the first instance allege possession. This is sufficient to support his action against a wrongdoer, but is not sufficient as against the lawful *d* owner, and in an action against the freeholder the plaintiff must at some stage of the pleadings set up a title derived from the defendant . . . It is sufficient, I think, to refer to the judgment of PATTESON, J., in *Ryan* v. *Clark*[3], where he explained the nature of this plea as follows: ". . . it admits such a possession as would maintain the action against a wrongdoer, but asserts a freehold in the defendant with a right to the immediate possession".' *e*

Wynn-Parry J took the same view. He said[4]:

'So where a plaintiff by his reply admits the title of the defendant, but pleads a demise from him, there is a true confession and avoidance. The plaintiff is concluded by his confession and must fail in his action unless he proves the case *f* set up by his reply, namely, a demise from the defendants.'

Now, it is true that the parties are the other way round in the present case; but the principle of the law is plain. If the case of the person in possession is, or has to be, that the other side is the owner and that his title derives from a tenancy which the other side has to recognise, then this is confession and avoidance, and the burden of proof is on the party setting up the tenancy. *g*

I would give only one further reference to authority on this part of the case. That is a passage in the speech of Lord Diplock in the Privy Council case, *Ocean Estates Ltd v Pinder*[5]. That was an appeal from the Court of Appeal for the Bahama Islands; but the law on the point is the same in the Bahamas as it is in England. Lord Diplock recognises that mere ownership does require a scintilla of further evidence in order to establish a cause of action in trespass; but that scintilla is no more than *h* the evincing of an intention to regain possession. He puts it in this way[6]:

'This contention is based upon a relic of the ancient law of seisin under which actual entry upon land was required to perfect title and to enable the owner to bring a personal action founded on possession such as ejectment or trespass . . .

1 [1946] 2 All ER 23, [1946] KB 393
2 [1946] 2 All ER at 24, 25, [1946] KB at 397
3 (1849) 14 QB 65 at 71
4 [1946] 2 All ER at 26, [1946] KB at 400
5 [1969] 2 AC 19
6 [1969] 2 AC at 25

a   It is in their Lordships' view unnecessary to consider to what extent at the present
day, more than a century after the abolition of forms of action, actual entry by
the person having title to the land is necessary to found a cause of action in trespass as distinct from ejectment or recovery of possession. Put at its highest against
the plaintiffs it is clear law that the slightest acts by the person having title to
the land or by his predecessors in title, indicating his intention to take possession, are sufficient to enable him to bring an action for trespass against a defendant
b   entering upon the land without any title unless there can be shown a subsequent
intention on the part of the person having the title to abandon the constructive
possession so acquired.'

I cite those cases in support of the proposition, which appears to me to be clear law,
that when an owner of land is making a case of trespass against a person alleged to
c   be in possession, all that the owner has to prove is his title and an intention to regain
possession. If the defendant to the action either admits his ownership or is faced with
evidence, which the court accepts, that the plaintiff is in fact the owner, then the
burden is on the defendant to confess and avoid; that is to say, to set up a title or
right to possession consistent with the fact of ownership vested in the plaintiff.
The judge wholly misconceived the law, and in consequence his judgment in favour
d   of Miss Devereux dismissing the suit for possession against her was a judgment based
on an error of law. In dismissing the action against Miss Devereux, he made an order
for costs in these terms: he ordered, so far as concerns Miss Devereux, that the plaintiffs were not entitled to possession of the land as against her; that judgment should
be entered for her; and that she recover her costs to be taxed on scale 4, to include
the High Court affidavit and appearance; and he ordered that the costs should be
e   paid by a named date. We know from the notes of evidence that the matter was
brought back to the county court judge on 6th December, when he ordered that £596
should be brought into court on account of costs, to await further order. In fact since
that date the plaintiffs, having failed to get any stay of execution in regard to those
costs, have paid them.
The plaintiffs now appeal to this court. They submit that, the judge having erred
f   in law, they are entitled to have their appeal allowed, judgment for possession against
Miss Devereux and, of course, a judgment for costs. Counsel who has conducted the
case for Miss Devereux on this appeal (neither he nor his junior were in the case before
the county judge), has not really sought to dispute that the judge was in error or that
the appeal must be allowed. He has submitted that there should be a retrial. As he
frankly conceded at the beginning of his argument, he faces the difficulty that Miss
g   Devereux, by her counsel, elected to call no evidence. He says, however, that, in the
exceptional circumstances of this case, there should be a retrial. He submits that Miss
Devereux has, or may well have, a credible case of the existence of a tenancy to put
before the court. He submits that her counsel's election to call no evidence must
have been to some extent influenced by the strongly-held error of the judge expressed
at the very opening of the case to counsel for the plaintiffs; and he reminds the court
h   that, if Miss Devereux be right in her case, she is entitled to the benefit of the Rent
Acts, and that this court would be slow to exclude from the judgment seat someone
who is saying that she is entitled to the protection of the Rent Acts, whatever errors
may have occured in the trial, or in the conduct of her case at the trial.
This is a difficult submission to make good. Ever since *Alexander v Rayson*[1] it has
been recognised that one who elects to call no evidence at trial is not going to succeed
j   in obtaining a new trial from the Court of Appeal. The position was succinctly put
by Lord Greene MR in *Laurie v Raglan Building Co*[2]. That was a running-down case.
Defence counsel at the trial took the view that, on the face value of the evidence

---

1   [1936] 1 KB 169, [1935] All ER Rep 185
2   [1941] 3 All ER 332, [1942] 1 KB 152

called for the plaintiff, there was no cause of action. Dealing with the possibility of a new trial, Lord Greene MR said[1]:

> 'At the trial in the present case, the counsel who appeared at the trial for the plaintiff said that he assumed that counsel for the defendants was not going to call any evidence. Counsel for the defendants [who was, of course, a very experienced counsel in that class of work] was silent with regard to that challenge and proceeded with his argument. Before us, he admitted that, if the judge had put to him the question which he ought to have put, he would have said that he did not intend to call any evidence. That being so, it is clear to my mind that there can be no question of a new trial . . .'

There is no doubt that that is the practice of the Court of Appeal. It is, however, not a rule of law; it is a discretionary rule; and it is a rule from which, if the circumstances be sufficiently unusual, the court can authorise a departure.

We were referred to an appeal in a family case, *Storey v Storey*[2]. Again, the facts of the case are of no assistance to us, but Ormerod LJ, giving the judgment of the court, said[3]:

> 'There are, however, two sets of circumstances under which a defendant may submit that he has no case to answer. In the one case there may be a submission that, accepting the plaintiff's evidence at its face value, no case has been established in law, and in the other that the evidence led for the plaintiff is so unsatisfactory or unreliable that the court should find that the burden of proof has not been discharged . . . There can, we think, be no doubt that in the former type of submission a defendant is bound by his election, and there can be no new trial. This rule, in our opinion, however, does not of necessity apply to the second type of case where the judge is invited to dismiss the case because of the unsatisfactory or unreliable nature of the evidence. In some cases it may well be that the appellate court will be able to decide the case without sending it back, but in others, and this in our judgment is certainly one, justice could not be done without a re-hearing.'

Counsel for the plaintiffs has forcefully argued that the present case falls clearly into the first class of cases, namely one in which it was submitted that there was no case to answer even on the face of the plaintiff's case, and that that was really the point which was being taken. And so it was. But also, of course, there are indications of the second type of situation mentioned by Ormerod LJ being present in this case, because the judge saw fit to pass some very critical remarks about the evidence called by the plaintiffs which he said he was not prepared to accept. I do not think that this discretionary rule can or ought to be fitted into any sort of pattern of categories. Is this a Category 1 case? or, Is this a Category 2 case? are not questions which should be asked or answered. I think the court has to look and see whether justice requires that there should be a rehearing. The court will require very exceptional circumstances to be established before departing from its ordinary rule. But, as I read the judgment of Ormerod LJ, if those circumstances do arise, then it is appropriate for this court to order a retrial notwithstanding the election below to call no evidence.

If that be so, then this case resolves into this question: are the facts such that, notwithstanding the election, there should be a retrial? Counsel for Miss Devereux has first sought to show us that Miss Devereux may well have a credible case to put before the court. He is, of course, confronted immediately with very real difficulty on that submission. Miss Devereux gave evidence in the Nolan action. One must assume that she was disbelieved. Nevertheless, she was not a party to that action; and I will say no more than that we have been shown a good deal of material, the

1   [1941] 3 All ER at 337, [1942] 1 KB at 155, 156
2   [1960] 3 All ER 279, [1961] P 63
3   [1960] 3 All ER at 282, [1961] P at 68

evidential value of which it is quite impossible for this court to assess, which indicates
a that Miss Devereux may have a case to put before the court. By itself, therefore, the
nature of Miss Devereux's case would not suffice, I think, to enable this court to
depart from its ordinary rule. But Miss Devereux failed to present this evidential
case to the court after an error by the judge which was expressed prematurely and
over-emphatically and in a way which could well have led her counsel to think that it
would only irritate the judge if he were to develop a complicated factual case based
b on the evidence of his client and a number of supporting witnesses. The judge ought
not to have intervened as early as he did, expressing, before he had heard full argument,
a strong view which, by consent of both counsel and in my judgment at any rate,
is a totally erroneous view of the law. He did it, and I am bound to say I think that
the trial thereafter merits the description 'a mistrial'. This is a factor of great
importance in determining whether there should be a new trial, notwithstanding
c the election not to call evidence.

There is a further factor, nothing like so serious as that to which I have just referred,
namely that, if Miss Devereux is right, she can claim the protection of the Rent Acts.

Counsel for Miss Devereux, in the course of his submissions, referred us to *Mount v
Childs*[1] in the Court of Appeal. In the course of his judgment in that case, Tucker LJ
said[2]:
d
'A number of matters have been raised before us, some of which appear to have
been raised before the judge, but all of which, at any rate, are open to the tenant
on this appeal because they arise out of the evidence given in the County Court.
It is the duty of this court in cases where premises may be affected by the Rent
Restriction Acts to be satisfied that all the necessary requirements have been
fulfilled before an order for possession is allowed to stand.'
e
Those are cautionary words relevant to this case which the court must heed. For
myself, I doubt whether that factor alone would suffice, in a case of this sort, to go
behind an election not to call evidence, and to order a new trial. But when that factor
is combined with the element of error that vitiated this trial and the possibility of a
credible defence, it appears to me that, notwithstanding the forceful arguments
f of counsel for the plaintiffs, this court must in justice order a new trial.

Let me say, before I come to consider the terms on which a new trial should be
ordered, that I have no doubt that the appeal must be allowed, and that, should there
be no new trial, judgment will have to be entered for possession in favour of the
plaintiffs. This is a matter of some importance, because if Miss Devereux does not
comply with whatever terms this court thinks appropriate for the granting of a new
g trial, she will be faced with an order for possession. Thus, at the end of the day the
plaintiffs' appeal has succeeded; but Miss Devereux has achieved this degree of
success: that she has persuaded me that there should be a new trial; but I take the
view that a new trial can be allowed only on very stringent terms. In the particulars
of the claim the plaintiffs have sought damages limited to £1,000; and they submit
that there should be a term that a sum on account of damages or mesne profits
h should be brought into court as a condition of a new trial. The position is odd. If the
plaintiffs' primary case should succeed, namely that Miss Devereux is not in possession, there can be no claim for mesne profits. If, on the other hand, Miss Devereux
succeeds in her case, which is that she has been in occupation since February 1973,
she is liable, on her view of the matter, to pay arrears of rent over that period at £8 a
week, which comes to over £1,000. I think that some account should be taken of
j this claim for damages or mesne profits in imposing terms for a new trial; and I
will indicate in a few minutes how that can, in my judgment, be dealt with.

When one comes to costs, first of all the costs already paid by the plaintiffs to Miss

1   (1948) 64 TLR 559
2   64 TLR at 560

Devereux will have to be repaid. That is the sum of £596, a sum which includes all the taxed costs in the county court, and, of course, the costs in the proceedings *a* before Kerr J. Then Miss Devereux will have to pay the plaintiffs' taxed costs since the reference by Kerr J to the county court. Kerr J dealt with the costs before him as 'costs in cause'; and that order can stand. But since his reference—that is since the inception of the county court action—the plaintiffs are entitled to the costs of the county court action; and they are entitled to the costs of the appeal to this court. Those costs will include the costs of the various applications for stays of execution, *b* applications which in the end proved unsuccessful.

There remains the problem of security for the plaintiffs' costs to be incurred in the retrial. I would suggest for consideration that Miss Devereux should be put on terms to bring into court a substantial sum of money, not to be paid out without the order of the judge, that sum of money to be available, according to the event, either for paying the plaintiffs' costs in the retrial or, if there be a balance over and above, to *c* go towards such damages or mesne profits as the plaintiffs may recover, if they do recover them.

The sum, therefore, of the conditions and terms that I have in mind is as follows. The £596 has to be repaid. The plaintiffs are to have their costs in the county court and in this court. A sum of money, which I think should be £1,500, must be brought into court as security for costs, or damages, as the case may be. And finally, I think *d* that the new trial should be brought on just as soon as possible. Exactly when that can be done may have to be determined by how soon Miss Devereux can comply with the financial terms to which I have already referred. If for any reason she does not comply with those terms, or if for any reason there is not a new trial, then the appeal must be allowed and the order will then become: judgment in favour of the plaintiffs for possession, with costs here and below. *e*

BRIDGE LJ. Subject to one minor matter of detail, I entirely agree in the order proposed. The minor matter of detail is this. My understanding is that the total amount which has been paid by the plaintiffs already to Miss Devereux pursuant to orders for costs made in her favour, may include some costs relating to one or more *f* unsuccessful applications for stays of execution, and may by a small sum exceed the figure of £596 mentioned by Scarman LJ. As I understand it—and this is what I would agree—it is to be a condition of the grant of a new trial that the total amount, whatever it may be—no doubt the figure can be agreed—already paid by the plaintiffs to Miss Devereux is repaid within a time to be determined; and in addition the sum of £1,500 mentioned by Scarman LJ be bought into court to be available to meet *g* the various financial contingencies envisaged. On all other matters I find myself so entirely in agreement with the judgment of Scarman LJ that, although we are reversing the learned county court judge, I do not find it necessary to add any observations of my own; nor do I wish to do so.

MEGAW LJ. I agree. Counsel for the plaintiffs put his appeal on two grounds. The *h* first ground is that the learned judge was wrong in law as to the burden of proof.

It is apparent from the terms of the notes of judgment, approved by the learned judge, that he took the view strongly, and expressed it strongly, and at an early stage, that the plaintiffs had taken on themselves to prove not only their ownership of the property, but also 'that Miss Devereux has no such right of occupation, licence, tenancy, estate or interest'. 'This', says the judge, 'they have not done'. The judge *j* expresses the same view again, even more strongly, in a passage part of which Scarman LJ has already read. That passage reads in this way:

'If in a civil case a landlord says "You are not in possession as a tenant; you are a trespasser", then in my opinion the onus is on the plaintiff (landlord) to prove

that allegation, not on the defendant to refute it. The plaintiff must adduce prima
facie evidence supporting his allegation of trespass. This submission was made
by counsel, quite forcibly and repeatedly. I say that he is wrong. If I am wrong in
this, then the Court of Appeal will put me right.'

I am afraid that the learned judge is wrong. Counsel who has represented Miss
Devereux in this court has fairly and frankly said that he has been unable to find any
authority, nor has he been able to think of any argument which he could properly
present to the court, in support of that view. If it be necessary to refer to authorities,
the authorities to which Scarman LJ has referred, and also I think the older decision
of *Doe d Humphrey v Martin*[1], leave no doubt. Counsel for the plaintiffs did not, I
think, cite to the learned judge those, or any, authorities. But I do not think that
counsel can be blamed, since he would not have had any reason to anticipate, when
he prepared himself for the hearing, that he would be faced with this point.

In these circumstances, I do not find it necessary to consider the second of the
grounds put forward by counsel for the plaintiffs, which related to the judge's treatment of the evidence, or lack of evidence, regarding the issue whether or not Miss
Devereux was in occupation of, or lived in, the premises, or any part of them, at any
relevant time. I would say no more about that ground than that in my view it raises,
in relation to the hearing, serious issues which it is not, in the circumstances, necessary
to decide and on which it is undesirable to express any view. I say 'undesirable'
because I agree that this is an appropriate case in which a new trial should be ordered;
and the less said by this court in expressing any view on matters that may there be
in contention the better. Nor is it necessary, and for the same reason it is not desirable,
to express any view as to the fresh evidence which has, on the motion of the plaintiffs
and without objection on the part of counsel for Miss Devereux, been adduced in
this court.

There remains, however, what I regard as a difficult question, as to the proper
order which should be made in these circumstances by this court. Counsel who
appeared for Miss Devereux in the county court—not, be it stressed again, being either
of the counsel who have represented her in this court—at the end of the case for the
plaintiffs elected to call no evidence. In the ordinary way, that would prevent an order
for a new trial. If counsel elects, his client is bound; and if the election is made on the
basis of a mistaken view of the law—for example, of the burden of proof—then the
defendant, when on appeal the error of law emerges and is corrected, cannot expect
to be allowed to go back and try again by adducing evidence which was, by deliberate
decision, not adduced at the hearing. Ever since *Alexander v Rayson*[2] this has been a
generally accepted principle and the reasons for it are obvious. It is usually wholly
unfair to a plaintiff that litigation should be conducted on the basis of the defendant
eating his cake because of a point of law and then, when the point of law turns out to
be wrong, still having the cake to eat again. But this court is not bound to apply that
principle as the law of the Medes and Persians. This court is entitled to look at the
particular facts and to make such order as will best do justice to both parties. In the
present case, it appears to be clear that it was the judge himself who promoted and
strongly maintained the supposed proposition of law. True, it was adopted by counsel
who then appeared for Miss Devereux. It would have been hard for him in the circumstances to do otherwise. Yet the result has been that the plaintiffs have been forced
to come to this court, and have been required to pay to Miss Devereux or her solicitors
no less a sum than £596, being the taxed costs of the High Court proceedings and the
county court proceedings—a stay of execution regarding costs having been refused.
Indeed, as has been pointed out, further costs have been paid by the plaintiffs to Miss
Devereux in respect of further unsuccessful applications for a stay in respect of costs.

---

1   (1841) 1 Car & M 32
2   [1936] 1 KB 169, [1935] All ER Rep 185

Moreover it would seem that on the case as pleaded on behalf of Miss Devereux, if it were true and were to prevail, she has been occupying this house, or part of it, *a* rent-free and, I gather, asserts that she continues to do so. On her own case, I apprehend, and counsel for Miss Devereux I think agrees, she could not deny that she owes by now a substantial, and continually increasing debt to the plaintiffs, as freehold owners, in respect of her claimed occupation as a tenant. What the sum is will have to be decided, if the question should arise.

With hesitation, I agree that in the present case the appropriate order for the court *b* to make in allowing the appeal is, not to make an order forthwith for possession, but to make an order for a new trial, subject to the due fulfilment by Miss Devereux of certain conditions. If those conditions should not be fulfilled, then the order of this court ought to be that the appeal should be allowed and the order for possession would be made, with costs to be paid by Miss Devereux to the plaintiffs in respect of the proceedings here and below. I agree with the conditions as indicated in his judg- *c* ment by Scarman LJ, subject to the minor correction which has been mentioned by Bridge LJ. I would add that in my judgment it is appropriate that the fresh trial should take place before a different judge. I fully agree that this court should direct that, so far as possible, the hearing of the fresh trial in the county court should be brought on with expedition.

The costs that will be payable in the event of the conditions being complied with *d* are that Miss Devereux will have to pay the plaintiffs' taxed costs since the date of the reference by Kerr J to the county court, and Miss Devereux will have to pay to the plaintiffs their taxed costs of this appeal. The amount of those costs, of course, will not be known until taxation has taken place. The conditions of the fresh trial should be that the costs already paid by the plaintiffs to Miss Devereux, both the sum of £596 and such further sums as represent moneys that have in fact been paid by way *e* of costs under orders made in these proceedings, should be repaid to the plaintiffs' solicitors (I leave out for the moment the time within which such payment is to be made); and, in addition, by way of security for the costs that will now have to be taxed as a result of these proceedings and by way of security for such costs, if any, as may hereafter, as a result of the further hearing, become payable by Miss Devereux to the plaintiffs, and by way of having a sum available for payment out of what I may *f* call broadly mesne profits, should the further trial so result, the sum of £1,500 is to be paid into court by Miss Devereux.

The court would wish to hear counsel for Miss Devereux as to anything that he desires to say, and also counsel for the plaintiffs, with regard to any queries that arise on the order as indicated by the court, and as to the time within which the payments are to be made if the conditions are to be met.   *g*

Appeal allowed. Order for new trial (before a different county court judge and brought on with expedition), subject to Miss Devereux complying with the following conditions: repayment by her of £596 costs paid to her by plaintiffs, and of all other sums of costs so paid by the plaintiffs; payment of £1,500 as security, to cover costs of appeal and of any further hearing, and against mesne profits due if the further trial should so result; all payments h and repayments to be made within 28 days. On non-fulfilment by Miss Devereux of the conditions, appeal allowed; order for possession. Liberty to either party to apply. Leave to appeal to the House of Lords refused.

Solicitors: *Bailey & Peltz* (for the plaintiffs); *Lissner & Co* (for Miss Devereux).

j

Mary Rose Plummer Barrister.

Barnes and another v BPC (Business Forms) Ltd

QUEEN'S BENCH DIVISION
PHILLIPS J
22nd MAY 1975

Industrial tribunal – Procedure – Advocate – Witnesses – Right of advocate to call witnesses in order chosen by him – Tribunal interfering with right – Duty of appellate court – Advocate instructed by tribunal to interpose witnesses – Likelihood of prejudice to advocate's client – Duty of appellate court to determine whether likelihood of prejudice before setting aside tribunal's decision.

The appellants were dismissed by the respondents, their employers. The appellants brought proceedings against the respondents claiming compensation for unfair dismissal. The hearing took place before an industrial tribunal on 27th March 1974 and was adjourned. It was resumed on 28th and 29th May. On 29th May, when there was about one hour left, one of the appellants, T, had completed his evidence-in-chief and was about to be cross-examined when the chairman of the tribunal requested the appellants' solicitor to interpose four other witnesses who had attended on that day by virtue of a witness order issued by the tribunal. The purpose of the request was to avoid the necessity of requiring those witnesses to attend on a subsequent date. The appellants' solicitor was unwilling to comply with the request but the chairman in effect instructed him to do so. Accordingly the witnesses were called and examined and the proceedings were then adjourned to 8th July 1974 when T completed his evidence and the hearing was concluded. The tribunal held that although the dismissals were unfair they were 'principally for redundancy reasons' and compensation should be assessed accordingly. The appellants appealed on the grounds, inter alia, (i) that the protracted hearing spread over 3½ months had undermined the reliability of the tribunal's recollection of the evidence and (ii) that the instruction to the appellants' solicitor to call the four witnesses on 29th May had deprived the appellants of their fundamental right to call witnesses in the order they thought best and was a breach of natural justice.

Held – The appeal would be dismissed for the following reasons—
  (i) Although prolonged delays between the dates of hearing should be avoided when possible, such delays were sometimes unavoidable and could not be a ground for interfering with a tribunal's decision (see p 238 *g* to *j*, post).
  (ii) The action of the chairman in instructing the appellants' solicitors to interpose witnesses was an irregularity. Where such an irregularity had occurred the appellate court was bound to consider what effect it had had and whether there had been any real possibility of prejudice to the person who had been wrongly compelled to call witnesses in a different order from that which he had intended. In the circumstances, however, it had not been shown that there was any likelihood of prejudice to the appellants (see p 239 *e f* and *j* to p 240 *a* and *e f*, post); *Briscoe v Briscoe* [1966] 1 All ER 465 distinguished.

Note
For the procedure before industrial tribunals, see Supplement to 38 Halsbury's Laws (3rd Edn) para 808J, 3.

Case referred to in judgment
Briscoe v Briscoe [1966] 1 All ER 465, [1968] P 501, [1966] 2 WLR 205, 130 JP 124, DC, Digest (Cont Vol B) 50, 421a.

Appeal

This was an appeal by Barry William Barnes and Denis William Taylor against a *a* decision of an industrial tribunal (chairman H C Easton Esq) sitting at Manchester dated 22nd August 1974 whereby it was held that the appellants had been dismissed from their employment by the respondents, BPC (Business Forms) Ltd, 'principally for redundancy reasons', but that 'in all the circumstances of the case their dismissal was unfair within the meaning of the Industrial Relations Act 1971'. The appellants sought an order that their dismissals had not been for redundancy reasons and that *b* the compensation to which they were entitled should be assessed on the basis that they would not have been dismissed for redundancy reasons within a period of six months from the date of the dismissals. The grounds of appeal were: (i) that the decision insofar as it found that the principal reason for the dismissals was redundancy was wrong in law; (ii) that the protracted hearing before the tribunal, spread over four days, i e 27th March, 28th May, 29th May and 8th July 1974, had forced unnatural *c* reliance on the chairman's notes of evidence, nullified the recollection of the demeanour of witnesses and generally militated against a fair and just hearing of the matter; (iii) that the chairman had erred in compelling the appellants' solicitor to interpose four witnesses between the evidence-in-chief of the appellant Taylor given on 29th May 1974 and his further evidence given on 8th July; that the chairman's decision was a wrongful interference with the discretion of an advocate or legal *d* representative to call witnesses in what order he wished and decided proper and was unfair and contrary to the interests of justice; and (iv) that there was fresh evidence in the matter.

Christopher Rose QC and *J L Hand* for the appellants.
Richard Yorke QC and *Caroline Alton* for the respondents.   *e*

PHILLIPS J. Two preliminary points are taken by counsel for the appellants, arising out of what he says are procedural defects in the conduct of the proceedings before the industrial tribunal.

The first is that the hearing took place on four separate days over a period of 3½ *f* months, 27th March, 28th and 29th May and 8th July 1974, the decision being given on 22nd August 1974. My attention has been drawn to two passages where it is said, and in my view rightly said for present purposes, that the decision reveals, or submissions of counsel reveal, that evidence given on an earlier occasion had been forgotten by a later occasion, so long had elapsed between them. This course was adopted despite repeated applications and requests on behalf of the appellants for consecutive *g* days of hearing. I do not think that there is anything in this point. Unfortunately, all courts and tribunals have from time to time to adjourn, and not infrequently, but too frequently, the adjourned dates are often far apart. The real answer is that it cannot be helped, particularly in the case of tribunals such as this which include amongst its members part-time members.

Having said that, I think it regrettable that it should happen and I am sure that as *h* many steps as are possible ought to be taken so that consecutive hearings may be obtained. But I am satisfied that it is no ground to interfere with these proceedings, in the circumstances of this case.

However, when the case goes on to the last of the matters that are going to be brought before me—that is, as I understand it, to consider whether the evidence justifies the decision—it may be a relevant matter to bear in mind that the hearing was *j* spread over this number of days separated by so wide an interval.

The second matter of complaint is that the solicitor appearing for the appellants was compelled against his wishes to interpose and call out of order certain witnesses. The circumstances were that on 29th May 1974, when there was about one hour's hearing left, the evidence of Mr Taylor, one of the appellants, had been completed

in chief, and in the ordinary course the next thing to happen would have been the
a cross-examination of that witness. An application was then made by counsel on
behalf of the respondents that the chairman should order the solicitor for the appellants to interpose certain witnesses. On the face of it that sounds a very strange
procedure, but on examination it is not as strange as it sounds. What had happened
was this. The four witnesses were senior employees of the respondents. They attended
by virtue of a witness order issued by the chairman on behalf of the tribunal.
b Their absence from work was causing inconvenience to the respondents and, if they
did not give their evidence that day, they would have to come back at a later date
when the hearing was resumed and that would cause inconvenience. And so it was
sensible enough on the part of counsel for the respondents to make this suggestion.
However, rightly or wrongly—it does not really matter for present purposes, and I
I will assume rightly—the solicitor for the appellants was unwilling to call them.
c But the chairman in effect instructed him to do so. Of course, he could not have
compelled him to do so, but I suppose the sanction is this, that if he did not there
might have been some difficulty in getting a witness order for their attendance on a
later occasion. At all events he bowed to the wishes of the chairman and called
them. And so there were interposed, at the end of the evidence-in-chief of Mr Taylor,
those witnesses. They gave evidence that day, were examined, cross-examined and
d re-examined and the whole proceedings were then adjourned until 8th July on which
day the hearing was completed.

I will say at once that I think that the action taken by the chairman, although
understandable and done in order to achieve as much convenience as possible, was
unfortunate. Plainly, solicitors and counsel are entitled to conduct, within the rules
of court or of procedure, the proceedings as they think fit and, in particular, to call
e witnesses in the order they wish, subject to any particular rules which may apply,
as in the case of criminal proceedings. And so I think it was an unwise decision for the
chairman to have made and one which I hope will not be repeated by other chair-
men on other occasions. The parties and their advisers must be left to conduct the
case as they think fit, subject to the rules.

What counsel submits on behalf of the appellants, however, is that the appellants
f have been deprived of a fundamental right which belonged to their legal representative, that is to say the right to call witnesses in the order that he thought best. There
has, therefore, he says, been a breach of natural justice. He relies on *Briscoe v Briscoe*[1],
a decision of the Divisional Court of the Probate, Divorce and Admiralty Division, in
which judgments were given by Karminski and Lane JJ. I will not take time to read
that case, but a similar situation had arisen there and, an appeal having come before
g that court, the appeal was allowed and the case remitted to the justices for a further
hearing. What happened there was that, it being a matrimonial case, counsel for the
husband wished to call a witness before calling the husband, but he was told that he
could not and that he must call the husband first, and did. So that was a case where the
effect of the action taken by the learned magistrate was to oblige counsel to call a
witness, that is to say the husband, whom he might, but equally might not, have
h called, because he was put into the situation that, if he did not call the husband,
he was not going to be allowed to call a witness whom he certainly did wish to call.
So one can see at once that there was a substantial practical impairment of his right
to conduct the case as he thought fit. I do not read that decision as laying down as a
proposition of law that wherever counsel has been prevented from calling witnesses
in the order in which he thinks fit, ipso facto the decision subsequently arrived at is
j vitiated. I read the decision in this sense, that once that has happened the appellate
court will not readily find that what was wrongly done was done without ill effect.
But I do not think it goes so far as to say that it is irrelevant for the appellate court to
consider what were the effects of the departure from the proper procedure. I think

---

1 [1966] 1 All ER 465, [1968] P 501

the position therefore is that, when there has been such an irregularity, the appellate court must look at the situation to see whether there is any prejudice or, more importantly, any real possibility of prejudice to the person who has been wrongly compelled to call witnesses in a different order from that which he intended and wanted.

I think that this applies especially to a tribunal such as this industrial tribunal, the members of which are enjoined to avoid undue legalism, to make the procedure as flexible and as informal as possible—although, having said that, I hasten to add that I do not go back on what I said earlier, that I think it is unwise, and not to be repeated, for a chairman to dictate to solicitor or counsel the way in which he conducts the case. So I do think it is necessary to look here to see whether there is any possibility of prejudice having been suffered.

The whole of this evidence which was interposed at the end of the day was completed in about an hour. There were four witnesses, senior employees of the respondents. I have not been taken in detail through the notes of their evidence, but I have been told, and for present purposes accept, that their evidence, insofar as it was favourable to the appellants, was accepted by the tribunal. The only possibility of prejudice, apart from the nominal prejudice which is always suffered to some extent when solicitors or counsel are prevented from calling witnesses in the order they wish, is this: it is said that had they been called in their proper turn, it might be the case that they would have been able to give some additional evidence on some other points. For example, it is said that, the appellants having completed their evidence, some points might have come out which could have been usefully amplified or elucidated by the evidence of the interposed witnesses. That is a possibility, of course, but it is only a possibility in the sense that most things are a possibility, and I have not been shown any chapter and verse to show that it was a very likely possibility in this particular case.

Lastly it is said, and one understands this, that it is a distressing position for an advocate to be in, to have to call in effect supporting witnesses before he has had an opportunity to complete the calling of the witnesses whose evidence they may support. But interpreting *Briscoe v Briscoe*[1] in the way in which I do, and bearing in mind that one is dealing here with industrial tribunals, I do not think that the justice of the case requires that I should on this ground alone declare that these proceedings were defective and that I ought therefore to set the decision aside and remit it. And so on these preliminary points I find against the appellants.

Appeal dismissed by consent following adjournment.

Solicitors: *Gregory, Rowcliffe & Co*, agents for *Towns, Needham & Co*, Manchester (for the appellants); *Ward Bowie*, agents for *Booth & Co*, Manchester (for the respondents).

Janet Harding Barrister.

---

1 [1966] 1 All ER 465, [1968] P 501

Wetherall v Harrison

QUEEN'S BENCH DIVISION
LORD WIDGERY CJ, O'CONNOR AND LAWSON JJ
31st OCTOBER 1975

Magistrates – Evidence – Specialised knowledge of magistrate – Specialised knowledge of circumstances forming background of particular case – Advice to other justices after retirement to consider verdict – Propriety – Medical evidence given at hearing – Member of bench a medical practitioner – Extent to which medical practitioner may draw on specialised knowledge to advise himself and other justices in considering evidence.

The respondent, a motorist, was taken to a police station having undergone a breath test which had proved positive. At the police station the appropriate procedure was followed. Having been asked to provide a specimen for a laboratory test, the respondent elected to give specimens of urine but failed to produce the second specimen within an hour. He then agreed to give a specimen of blood, as being the only alternative. From that moment, however, his behaviour changed and he appeared to be having a fit. In view of the respondent's behaviour, the police surgeon was unable to obtain a specimen of blood from him. The police surgeon could not, however, find any medical abnormalities. An information was preferred against the respondent charging him with failing, without reasonable excuse, to provide a specimen for a laboratory test, contrary to s 9(3) of the Road Traffic Act 1972. In his evidence before the justices the police surgeon ruled out all medical reasons for the respondent's behaviour, and was of the opinion that the respondent had been simulating a fit. One member of the justices' bench was a medical practitioner and, in the retiring room, gave his opinion on the medical evidence of the police surgeon relating to the issue whether the fit was simulated or genuine. The bench had also had wartime experience of inoculations and the fear that they could create in certain individuals. In the event the bench acquitted the respondent, taking the view that his fit had not been simulated, and therefore that he had had a reasonable excuse for failing to provide a specimen. On appeal,

Held – It was not improper for a justice with specialised knowledge of the circumstances forming the background of a particular case to draw on that specialised knowledge for the purpose of interpreting the evidence which he had heard. Although he was not entitled in effect to give evidence to himself or to the other justices, he could employ his basic knowledge in considering, weighing up and assessing the evidence given before the court and, on request, tell his fellow justices how his specialised knowledge had caused him to look at the evidence. The justices had not therefore acted improperly and the appeal would be dismissed (see p 244 b to p 245 c, post).

Notes

For judicial notice of facts within the tribunal's knowledge, see 15 Halsbury's Laws (3rd Edn) 338, para 615.

For the Road Traffic Act 1972, s 9, see 42 Halsbury's Statutes (3rd Edn) 1655.

Case referred to in judgments

Reynolds v Llanelly Associated Tinplate Co Ltd [1948] 1 All ER 140, 40 BWCC 240, CA, 34 Digest (Repl) 552, *3783*.

Cases also cited

R v Field (Justices), ex parte White (1895) 64 LJMC 158.
R v Rosser (1836) 7 C & P 648.

K

Case stated

On 11th February 1975 an information was preferred by the appellant, Malcolm   **a**
Wetherall, a police constable, against the respondent, Alan David Harrison, that he,
being a person who had driven a motor vehicle on a road, did on 1st February 1975,
at Mere Way police station, without reasonable excuse fail to provide a specimen for a
laboratory test, contrary to s 9(3) of the Road Traffic Act 1972. The justices for the
county of Northampton acting in and for the petty sessional division of Northampton
heard the information sitting as magistrates' court at Northampton on 24th April 1975.   **b**
The justices concluded that the respondent had not refused without reasonable excuse
to provide a specimen and therefore dismissed the information. At the request of the
appellant the justices stated a case for the opinion of the High Court. The facts are
set out in the judgment of Lord Widgery CJ.

David Barker for the appellant.   **c**
The respondent did not appear and was not represented.

LORD WIDGERY CJ. This is an appeal by case stated by justices for the petty
sessional division of Northampton in respect of their adjudication as a magistrates'
court at Northampton on 24th April 1975. On that occasion they were dealing with   **d**
an information preferred by the appellant against the respondent, alleging that the
respondent, without reasonable excuse, had failed to provide a specimen for a laboratory test, contrary to s 9(3) of the Road Traffic Act 1972.

It is unnecessary to dwell on the early history of the matter because the facts
followed a familiar pattern. The respondent was driving and attracted the appellant's
attention because along London Road he was driving without red rear lights. The   **e**
car was stopped; a conversation with the police officer ensued. The police officer
suspected alcohol in the respondent's body. He was invited to take a breath test
which was positive, and he was arrested. At the police station, a second breath test
was also positive. Then came the request for blood or urine. The initial requests
were properly made. When asked for blood at the police station, he said that he
would rather give urine. He was then asked for two specimens of urine within an   **f**
hour, but failed to produce the second specimen within that time. He was again
asked for a specimen of blood, which is wholly consistent with the procedure laid
down, and it is from that point onwards that the facts become important.

At 4.08 a m the appellant requested the respondent to provide a specimen of blood.
The respondent said 'What do you think? Is this the only way out for me?' A police
sergeant said 'I cannot make any form of decision for you. You have been asked to   **g**
supply a sample of blood, are you prepared to do so, yes or no?' The respondent
said, 'Well if that is the case, yes I will'. He then sat with his head in his hands and to
the appellant's question whether he was all right he made no reply. The appellant
police officer asked the respondent to stand up and he did so, but he did not speak
and he began to stare at the wall. When asked if he was all right, the respondent
said 'I am floating. I feel as though I am on a cloud', and he continued to stare at the   **h**
wall. The sergeant passed his hand in front of the respondent's face but there was no
reaction. Then the respondent began to breathe slowly, then quicker and he started
to gasp for air. When his clothing was loosened he slumped back against the wall
and tilted sideways and moaned. When the police officers tried to lift him upright
the respondent resisted, rolled about and had to be restrained to prevent him injuring himself. He then breathed normally but each time the police officers at-   **j**
tempted to raise the respondent he threw his arms and legs about. Also he had
apparently urinated in his trousers.

A doctor, Dr Price, had been called to take the blood specimen, and at this stage he
arrived at the police station, and the respondent was struggling but soon relaxed in
the presence of the doctor. The doctor examined him and found no abnormalities.

When asked for a specimen of blood, the respondent started to struggle again and the
a doctor could not take a specimen. The respondent accepted a drink of water which
he drank normally. The doctor made another approach but the respondent struggled
and was taken to the detention room where he relaxed and apparently slept. Dr Price
made a further approach and the respondent struggled again. The doctor requested
a blood specimen but received no reply and decided that he could not take blood.
Dr Price ruled out in his evidence before the court all medical reasons for the
b respondent's behaviour and was of the opinion that the respondent was simulating
a fit.

The respondent gave evidence dealing with the reason why he had not given a
specimen of blood, but did not call any medical evidence to rebut that given by
Dr Price. The explanation given by the respondent in evidence was of having been
apprehensive in the past whenever he had been required to have an injection and
c that on this occasion he felt hot and faint. He expressed apprehension to the appellant who tried to reassure him. He also had difficulty in breathing, he was struggling
for air and his stomach felt tight. He had genuinely tried to give a urine sample and
agreed to give a blood sample. His manner of driving had not been erratic, and then
he goes on to deal with the circumstances of the alleged offence.

Pausing there for a moment, it will be appreciated that the whole issue in this
d case was whether there was reasonable excuse for the failure to give a blood sample.
The stage had been reached when the respondent was bound to give a blood sample
and if he did not give one then either his excuse was a reasonable excuse or not. The
respondent was saying 'I could not give a blood sample because I was ill. I had a sort
of fit', and the appellant through the mouth of Dr Price was saying 'Not at all, he
was simulating a fit. There was no earthly reason why he should not give a sample of
e blood.' That was the issue.

Here comes the unusual twist, if I may so describe it, in the case. On the bench
was a practising registered medical practitioner, Dr Robertson, and the bench 'had
regard to his professional opinion of the respondent's reactions and behaviour according to the evidence, and Dr. Robertson's own reasons are separately attached'. Now I
take that to mean that in the retiring room Dr Robertson, possibly at the invitation of
f the other members of the bench, gave his views on the matters traversed by Dr Price,
in other words, gave his view whether it was a simulated fit or a genuine fit. The
justices said not only did they listen to Dr Robertson's reasons, but they also had
a layman's experience and viewpoint of wartime inoculations and the fear that they
could create in certain individuals.

The matter comes before us really in this form, that we are invited to say whether
g the justices acted with propriety in having regard to information given to them by
Dr Robertson and drawing on their own wartime experiences so far as they did. In
the event, they acquitted the respondent, obviously not being satisfied that his fit was
simulated and therefore not being satisfied that he acted without reasonable excuse.

Counsel for the appellant put the matter before us really inviting us to say, for the
advantage of justices hereafter, what should happen when a magistrate has specialised
h knowledge of this kind; should he use it or should he not?

In argument we were referred to three authorities. The only one I need refer to,
and the most recent, is *Reynolds v Llanelly Tinplate Co Ltd*[1]. That was concerned with
arbitrators and judges and the extent to which they could have regard to their own
personal knowledge. For my part, I do not think that the position of a justice of the
peace is the same, in this regard, as the position of a trained judge. If you have a
j judge sitting alone, trying a civil case it is perfectly feasible and sensible that he should
be instructed and trained to exclude certain factors from his consideration of the
problem. Justices are not so trained. They are much more like jurymen in this
respect. I think it would be wrong to start with the proposition that justices use of

---

1 [1948] 1 All ER 140

their own local or personal knowledge is governed by exactly the same rule as is laid down in the case of trained judges. I do not believe that a serious restriction on a *a* magistrate's use of his own knowledge or the knowledge of his colleagues can really be enforced. Laymen (by which I mean non-lawyers) sitting as justices considering a case which has just been heard before them lack the ability to put out of their minds certain features of the case. In particular, if the magistrate is a specialist, be he a doctor or an engineer or an accountant, or what you will, it is not possible for him to approach the decision in the case as though he had not got that training, and indeed I *b* think it would be a very bad thing if he had to. In a sense, the bench of justices is like a jury, it is a cross-section of people, and one of the advantages which they have is that they bring a lot of varied experience into the courtroom and use it.

So I start with the proposition that it is not improper for a magistrate who has special knowledge of the circumstances forming the background to a particular case to draw on that special knowledge in interpretation of the evidence which he has *c* heard. I stress that last sentence, because it would be quite wrong if the magistrate went on, as it were, to give evidence to himself in contradiction of that which has been heard in court. He is not there to give evidence to himself, still more is he not there to give evidence to other justices; but he can employ his basic knowledge in considering, weighing up and assessing the evidence given before the court is I think beyond doubt.   *d*

Furthermore, I do not see why he should not, certainly if requested by his fellow justices to, tell his fellow justices the way in which his specialised knowledge has caused him to look at the evidence. On no bench of justices should there be a leader who is so aggressive that he tries to assume responsibility for the decision and excludes the others, whether he is proceeding on the basis of a specialised subject or not, and that certainly goes for justices with specialised knowledge, because it would *e* be quite wrong for the doctor in the present case to have gone into the justices' retiring room and immediately proceeded to persuade all the justices because of his specialised knowledge. He ought really to have waited until asked to make a contribution on his specialist subject. Whether he is asked or not, he should not press his views unduly on the rest of the bench. He should tell them in a temperate and orderly way what he thinks about the case, if they want to know, and then leave them *f* to form their own conclusion if they wish so to do. Here again it is most important that the justice with specialised knowledge should not proceed to give evidence himself to his fellow justices contradictory to that which they have heard in the court below. He can explain the evidence they have heard; he can give his own view as to how the case should go and how it should be decided; but he should not be giving evidence behind closed doors which is not available to the parties.   *g*

Applying those principles to the instant case, there was certainly no reason why Dr Robertson should not, when forming his own conclusion about this case, have referred to his own knowledge, and his own knowledge and experience was that this kind of fit was genuine, and knowing that it would be right that in reviewing and considering the evidence in this case he should have that knowledge in the background and use it if he thought fit. Since his fellow justices obviously knew he was a doctor *h* and I think asked him for the benefit of his views, I see no reason at all why he should not tell them what his views were. That does not seem to me to be contrary to any principle to be applied here, and I do not believe in this case either that the doctor went beyond the scope of the authority which I am trying to apply.

For my part therefore I would say that this is a case in which there is no reason to suppose that the procedure employed was wrong and therefore there is no error of *j* law disclosed in the papers.

Under these circumstances the appeal has to be dismissed.

O'CONNOR J. I agree. I would only add a few words on the topic of the way in which justices with specialised knowledge should approach their duties in using *a* it. I endorse fully what Lord Widgery CJ has said, but they must not, so to speak, start giving evidence in the case because it offends a number of our rules; above all, it is not in the presence of the parties and is not open to cross-examination. But if that is borne in mind, that the person with specialised knowledge must not give evidence, then it seems to me that it is entirely legitimate for him to express his views that he himself has been helped to form on the evidence in the case and on the issues in the case as a result of his own specialised knowledge and to communicate them to his fellow

b justices, if he so wishes, always bearing in mind that he must not start substituting what he might have said in evidence, as opposed to using his knowledge to assess the evidence which is available.

LAWSON J. I agree with both judgments that have been delivered.

c *Appeal dismissed.*

Solicitors: *Sharpe, Pritchard & Co,* agents for *R C Beadon,* prosecuting solicitor, Northamptonshire County Council.

Lea Josse   Barrister.

d

Hanson v London Rent Assessment Committee and others
e # R v London Rent Assessment Committee, ex parte Hanson

QUEEN'S BENCH DIVISION
LORD WIDGERY CJ, PARK AND MAY JJ
f 10th, 11th NOVEMBER 1975

Rent restriction – Rent – Determination of fair rent – Objection – Objection to rent determined by rent officer – Reference to rent assessment committee – Withdrawal of objection – Withdrawal after reference to committee and before hearing – Effect – Jurisdiction of committee to proceed with hearing and to determine fair rent – Rent Act 1968, Sch 6, paras 5, 6(1), 9(1).

g The applicant was the tenant of certain premises. On an application by the landlords a rent officer determined that the fair rent for the premises was £800 a year. The tenant objected to the determination and the matter was referred to a rent assessment committee under Sch 6, paras 5[a] and 6(1)[b], to the Rent Act 1968 for review. Notice was given that an oral hearing was required and a date was fixed for the hearing. A few days before that date, however, the applicant wrote a letter to the rent assessment

h committee whereby he purported to withdraw his objection. The committee, however, decided to proceed with the hearing and, in exercise of their powers under para 9(1) of Sch 6[c], determined a fair rent of £900 a year. The applicant appealed against the committee's decision, and sought an order of certiorari to quash it, contending that, once he had withdrawn his objection, the rent assessment committee had no jurisdiction to proceed with the hearing and to fix a rent.

j

Held – Once a written objection to a determination of a fair rent by a rent officer had

---

a Paragraph 5, so far as material, is set out at p 247 *d,* post
b Paragraph 6(1), so far as material, is set out at p 247 *e,* post
c Paragraph 9(1) is set out at p 247 *h,* post

been referred to a rent assessment committee, the committee were bound to consider
the matter and to confirm the rent determined by the rent officer or to determine a
fair rent itself. No attempted withdrawal on the part of any of the parties could avoid
the obligation on the rent assessment committee to determine the fair rent on the
basis of their own assessment, for, once the matter was before the committee, such a
withdrawal would be liable to prejudice other parties (see p 249 f to p 250 e and h,
post).

Notes
For the determination of a fair rent by a rent assessment committee, see Supplement to 23 Halsbury's Laws (3rd Edn) para 1571B, 7.
    For the Rent Act 1968, Sch 6, paras 5, 6, 9, see 18 Halsbury's Statutes (3rd Edn) 915,
916, 917.

Cases referred to in judgments
Boal Quay Wharfingers Ltd v King's Lynn Conservancy Board [1971] 3 All ER 597, [1971]
    1 WLR 1558 [1971] 2 Lloyd's Rep 114, CA.
R v Hampstead and St Pancras Rent Tribunal, ex parte Goodman [1951] 1 All ER 170,
    [1951] 1 KB 541, 115 JP 77, 49 LGR 263, DC, 31(2) Digest (Reissue) 1045, 8241.

Case also cited
R v Kensington and Chelsea Rent Tribunal, ex parte MacFarlane [1974] 3 All ER 390, [1974]
    1 WLR 1486, DC.

Appeal and motion for certiorari
The applicant, John Hanson, appealed against a decision of the first respondent, the
London Rent Assessment Committee, dated 7th September 1974 whereby the committee determined that the fair rent for premises known as 21 Bramerton Street,
London, SW1, of which the applicant was the tenant and the second respondents, the
Church Commissioners for England, were the landlords, was £900 per annum
exclusive of rates. The applicant also moved for an order of certiorari to remove the
committee's decision into the High Court for the purpose of its being quashed. The
facts are set out in the judgment of Lord Widgery CJ.

George Hastings for the applicant.
Harry Woolf for the committee.
Richard Moshi for the Church Commissioners.

LORD WIDGERY CJ. In these proceedings the applicant moves for an order of
certiorari to bring up into this court with a view to its being quashed a decision made
by the London Rent Assessment Committee on the 7th September 1974 whereby it
fixed as a fair rent for premises known as 21 Bramerton Street, Chelsea, a rent of £900
per annum exclusive of rates.
    The applicant today is the tenant of 21 Bramerton Street. The landlords of the
premises are the Church Commissioners, and they of course are concerned with the
proceedings as the recipients of whatever rent is in due course determined as the
fair rent.
    The facts of this case so far as relevant are extremely limited in scope and quantity.
The Rent Act 1968, amongst other activities, provides for the fixing of a fair rent for
residential property in certain circumstances, and the method which is adopted in the
relevant part of the 1968 Act is the appointment of officials known as rent officers
who, on application from landlords or tenants, or now the local authority, fix what
they regard as a fair rent for the premises in question. If either the landlord or the
tenant, or any other interested party, is dissatisfied with the rent so fixed, the Act
provides for the issue to be referred to a body called a rent assessment committee
whose duty it is officially to determine the fair rent.

a
All that had happened in this case. The premises, as I have said, were let to the applicant by the Church Commissioners. The Church Commissioners approached the rent officer asking him to determine the fair rent for the premises and the rent officer determined a fair rent of £800 a year. The applicant, being dissatisfied with that determination, objected to it and as a result required the matter to be determined by a rent assessment committee, as I have endeavoured to explain.

b
It is appropriate at this point to look a little more closely at the provisions of the 1968 Act which bring about that consequence. They are conveniently collected in Sch 6 to the 1968 Act, where one has a simple and clear code of conduct which is laid down for persons concerned with the provisions to which I have referred. I do not take time by looking at the procedure of applications to a rent officer which occupy the first four paragraphs of Sch 6. One comes to the action which has to be taken by persons dissatisfied with the rent officer's conclusion when para 5 of Sch 6 is reached.

c
That provides:

d
'After considering, in accordance with paragraph 4 above, what rent ought to be registered or, as the case may be, whether a different rent ought to be registered . . . [and then there is an important provision:] he shall notify the landlord and the tenant accordingly by a notice stating that if, within twenty-eight days of the service of the notice or such longer period as he or a rent assessment committee may allow, an objection in writing is received by the rent officer from the landlord or the tenant the matter will be referred to a rent assessment committee.'

So, following the decision of the rent officer, both parties are told what that decision is and told that unless objection is made within 28 days that rent will be confirmed.

e
Schedule 6 goes on in para 6 to describe what happens if objection is taken. It is laid down in para 6(1) that:

f
'If such an objection as is mentioned in paragraph 5 above is received, then—
(a) if it is received within the period of twenty-eight days specified in that paragraph or a rent assessment committee so direct, the rent officer shall refer the matter to a rent assessment committee . . .'

That is an important sentence in my view because it is clearly mandatory and it says in the plainest terms that if either of the parties to the contract makes objection within 28 days, the rent officer *shall* refer the matter to the rent assessment committee.

g
When we get on to para 7 of the schedule we are told what happens when the matter is so referred. Paragraph 7 requires the rent assessment committee to give the sort of notice which one would expect in cases of this kind, and if either of the parties wants an oral hearing, it is provided in para 8 that the rent assessment committee shall set up an oral hearing accordingly.

When all that has been done, and when the rent assessment committee has made such enquiries as they think fit, their duty is to be found in para 9(1) of the schedule in these terms:

h
'The committee shall make such inquiry, if any, as they think fit and consider any information supplied or representation made to them in pursuance of paragraph 7 or paragraph 8 above and—(a) if it appears to them that the rent registered or confirmed by the rent officer is a fair rent, they shall confirm that rent; (b) if it does not appear to them that that rent is a fair rent, they shall determine a fair rent for the dwelling-house.'

j
Again there is no room for choice, options or doubt. The duties of the committee are clearly laid down once the matter has been referred to them. They must conduct such enquiries as the schedule provides for and then come up with a fair rent either by confirmation of the rent fixed by the rent officer or by the exercise of their own judgment.

As I have already indicated, in this case the landlords approached the rent officer
and obtained an assessment of the fair rent from him. The parties, including the pre- *a*
sent applicant who was the tenant, were notified of what had happened, and within
28 days an objection was raised by the applicant to the rent assessed by the rent officer,
which I remind myself again was £800 per year.

Notice was given to the rent assessment committee that an oral hearing was required. A date was fixed for the oral hearing, 15th August 1974. Everything was
prepared for the committee to hear the parties and then proceed in accordance with *b*
its duty to fix a fair rent.

But a few days before 15th August the applicant evidently began to doubt the
wisdom of the course which he had adopted. He was advised by well-known surveyors in this matter and, reading between the lines, one is driven to the conclusion
that, if one may use the vernacular, he was getting cold feet and was not at all sure
that it was in his interest to go on with this matter. So eventually he told his surveyors *c*
on 8th August to make arrangements to withdraw his objection.

On 8th August a letter was written by the advisers to the tenant to the rent assessment committee in these terms:

'Dear Sirs, No. 21 Bramerton Street; Objection to Rent Assessment We write following our telephone conversation of this morning. Acting on behalf of the [applicant] *d*
of the above address, we confirm that we shall not be placing our objection before
the London Rent Assessment Panel on Thursday 15th August.'

There is evidence which indicates how that letter came to be written. The evidence
which I think we should accept at this stage, because it is not contradicted, is to the
effect that the surveyors acting for the applicant telephoned to the rent assessment
committee to ask what the procedure would be if the applicant wished to withdraw *e*
his objection to the rent officer's figure. The evidence is that they were told that a
letter of withdrawal would be sufficient and in some way the phraseology similar
to that in the letter which I have read seems to have been mentioned and approved.
I say 'in some way' because I am far from satisfied that this letter was actually composed in the office of the rent assessment committee. But that a clerical officer
employed in that office gave some assistance to the compilation of the letter is not *f*
seriously in dispute, and so the letter went off.

It will be remembered that 15th August was the date fixed for the hearing of this
matter before the committee. The 15th August duly arrived and the committee were
informed that the office had received the letter of 8th August which I have read. The
panel took the view that the phraseology was ambiguous; it was not altogether clear
whether the applicant was abandoning all interest in the matter or whether he was *g*
merely saying he would not come in person and hoped that the committee would
look after his interests in his absence, or something like that.

To cut a long story short, the committee decided that they should not act on the
letter of 8th August but should hear the matter. Since the tenant was not present,
hearing the matter on his side did not include hearing any evidence from him. After
the hearing stage in the morning of 15th August, the committee moved on, as is *h*
their practice, to look at the house and inspect it. When they got to the house they
could not get in because they were told that the applicant's objection had been withdrawn and there was no further matter which concerned them about this house.
Some confusion followed as a result of that, and eventually the committee went away.

They, however, fixed a fair rent and they fixed a fair rent at £900 a year, and it is the
fact that that exceeded what the rent officer himself fixed, and which rent the app- *j*
licant reluctantly might have been prepared to pay, which is the cause of our being
here today dealing with this particular dispute.

The way in which it is put is twofold. It is submitted by counsel for the applicant
that there is power for someone who has objected and set the wheels of Sch 6 in
motion to withdraw his objection and thus resile from the battle, as it were, leaving

the matter as though he had never objected at all. If that is the law, as counsel for
a the applicant submits it is, then it would follow, he says, that on the writing of the
letter of 8th August 1974 the applicant's objection was withdrawn, his liability to
have his rent increased if the committee so thought was also nullified and he was left
in a position as though he had never made any objection at all. That is the argument
on the applicant's side, and it is said that if that is right, there are two consequences
which follow. The first is that the committee lacked jurisdiction when it eventually
b proceeded to fix the rent as it did. Alternatively, I think it is said that there was a
denial of natural justice in that the applicant did not in the event have an opportunity
of making oral representations to the committee.

The central and vital fact in this dispute is whether there is a right for an objector
to withdraw his objection, and, if so, what the consequences of that withdrawal may
be.

c I approach this problem on the footing that in general where you have a statutory
procedure of this kind which involves the making of objections or applications, in
general a person who makes an objection or an application should have the right to
withdraw if he can do so without prejudicing other interested parties.

I think that considerable support for that general proposition is to be found in
Boal Quay Wharfingers Ltd v King's Lynn Conservancy Board[1]. The passage which illus-
d trates the point that I am now seeking to make is to be found in the judgment of
Salmon LJ[2] where he referred to the Rent Act 1968, although to a different part of it
than that with which we are concerned, and said this: '[The Rent Act 1968] contains
an example of such a statutory provision', that is to say a provision for actual withdrawal. He continued:

e 'The Landlord and Tenant (Rent Control) Act of 1949, however, contained no
such provision; and in *R v Hampstead and St Pancras Rent Tribunal, ex parte
Goodman*[3] the court held that since there was nothing in that Act to prevent an
application being withdrawn, it could be withdrawn at any time. That I think
is an authority for the view I have expressed.'

f I respectfully agree with Salmon LJ, and I start with the assumption that if the
existence of a right of withdrawal can march in double harness with the protection
of other parties concerned, then the right of withdrawal ought to be there. But I do
not think in this case that it is possible to say that a withdrawal, at all events once the
matter is before the committee, can be made without a possible prejudice to other
parties.

I am impressed by the fact that other parts of the 1968 Act, such as those referred to
g by Salmon LJ do specifically contemplate withdrawal of an application in certain
circumstances. The part we are concerned with contains no such provision at all.

Furthermore, the issue which arises when application is made to a rent officer to
fix a fair rent is not a matter which is simply inter partes and simply concerns the
landlord and tenant at the moment when the issue arises. The effect of the fixing
of a fair rent is that the rent is fixed in rem, as Lord Parker put it in one of his judg-
h ments, for others who come as landlord or tenant thereafter. It is not, I think, consistent with the general policy of the 1968 Act, or indeed with the purpose enshrined
in Sch 6 which I have read, that there should be any kind of unlimited right for a
person, who has by objection set the machinery in motion, to decide to withdraw his
objection and thus as it were reverse the machinery to a position which it formerly
occupied.

j I think it is just possible that there may be a right of withdrawal for an objector if
he withdraws before the matter has been referred to the rent assessment committee.

---

1 [1971] 3 All ER 597, [1971] 1 WLR 1558
2 [1971] 3 All ER at 605, [1971] 1 WLR at 1569
3 [1951] 1 All ER 170, [1951] 1 KB 541

He has to be very quick if he is going to withdraw before that happens. I would not decide it today because the point does not arise directly here, but it may very well be that there is an unlimited right of withdrawal of objection up to the point when the matter is actually referred to the rent assessment committee, but thereafter in my judgment there is no general right of withdrawal at all; that is to say there is no means whereby on a so-called withdrawal the party can extricate himself and put himself in the position as though he had never lodged an objection at all.

Again, as this branch of the law develops, it may be that other consequences may be found to flow from a purported withdrawal. It may be that it will be right to say—and here again another day will be the day to say it—that a purported withdrawal excuses the rent assessment committee from providing an oral hearing for which the withdrawer had previously opted, and there may be many requirements of that kind whereby following a purported withdrawal the procedure can be somewhat streamlined and made the more effective, and a decision obtained more quickly. But what I am quite satisfied about, speaking for myself, is that once the matter has been referred to the rent assessment committee the rent assessment committee must produce an answer in the terms of a fair rent, and no attempted withdrawal or any other manoeuvres on the part of the parties can avoid the obligation on the rent assessment committee to come up with a fair rent doing their own assessment of what is a fair rent for the premises.

It is in my view therefore on the facts of this case, that, whatever construction one puts on the letter of 8th August 1974, insofar as it was intended to be or purported to be a withdrawal of the objection, it was ineffective for that purpose. It was was much too late for any such withdrawal to be of effect at all, and therefore the committee were entirely within their jurisdiction in hearing the application on the morning of 15th August, as in fact they did.

Furthermore, the fact that they had jurisdiction, and the fact that the withdrawal was ineffectual, as I have described, means that no error of law can be found in the committee's findings, and that is relevant because, although I am not sure whether I have mentioned it in the course of this judgment heretofore, apart from the application for certiorari, there is an appeal against the rent assessment committee's decision brought under the Tribunals and Inquiries Act 1958. That appeal in my judgment must be dismissed because, for the reasons which I hope I have made clear, there is in my view no error of judgment discernible in the decision of the committee.

There remains of course the application for certiorari, and all I find it necessary to say about that is that it was in this case brought far too late to justify consideration in this case at all. The decision of the rent assessment committee was 7th September 1974, and the motion for leave to quash it by certiorari is dated 25th July 1975, something like nine months later, which, as the Court of Appeal emphasised only last week, is much too long for any ordinary certiorari application and would be fatal in this case in my judgment to the application of the prerogative order.

For those reasons I would refuse this application.

PARK J. I agree.

MAY J. I also agree.

Appeal dismissed; motion refused.

Solicitors: *Lorenz & Jones* (for the applicant); *Treasury Solicitor; Radcliffes* (for the Church Commissioners).

Lea Josse   Barrister.

Central Electricity Generating Board v Clwyd County Council

CHANCERY DIVISION
GOFF J
11th APRIL, 21st, 22nd MAY 1975

Commons – Registration – Common land – Land subject to rights of common – Rights of common – Non-registration – Effect – Rights not exercisable – No rights of common over land registered within statutory period – Land registered by authority as common land shortly before expiry of statutory period – Objection to registration by owner of land – Hearing by commissioner – Whether open to commissioner to consider whether rights of common existed at date of registration – Whether rights extinguished in consequence of failure to register them within statutory period – Whether commissioner precluded from finding that land common land as being land subject to rights of common – Commons Registration Act 1965, ss 1(2)(b), 22(1).

An electricity board owned certain land on which they proposed to build a power station. The land was completely unenclosed. It had at one time been manorial land but had been taken out of the manor by various conveyances. It was alleged that the land was subject to rights of common but no application was made for the registration of such rights under the Commons Registration Act 1965 by any individual before the statutory period[a] for making such applications expired on 2nd January 1970. The local authority were however entitled to make the appropriate registrations at any time up to 31st July 1970. Thereafter, in the event of non-registration, any rights of common would, under s 1(2)(b)[b] of the 1965 Act, cease to be exercisable over the land. On 17th July, however, the local authority registered the electricity board's land as common land. The electricity board objected to the registration and accordingly the matter was referred to a commons commissioner under s 5(6) of the 1965 Act. The hearing before the commissioner took place in December 1973 and he gave his decision in March 1974. The commissioner took the view that for the purpose of deciding whether or not to confirm the registration he had to consider whether the land was subject to rights of common immediately before the registration on 17th July 1970. He held that the fact that no rights of common had been registered at that date, or the fact that no commoner could have applied for registration of any right of common after 2nd January 1970, was irrelevant and that the 'rights of common, if any, over the land had not been extinguished for want of registration on 17th July 1970'. He then proceeded to hear the evidence and found that there was sufficient evidence to establish the fact that the land was subject to rights of common on 17th July 1970 and was therefore 'common land' within s 22(1)[c] of the 1965 Act. Accordingly he confirmed the registration. The electricity board appealed.

Held – The provision of s 1(2)(b) that no rights of common should be exercisable unless they had been registered meant that such rights would be extinguished in the event of failure to register them within the prescribed period. It followed therefore that, since any rights of common which might have existed over the electricity board's land had been extinguished under s 1(2)(b) for want of registration before the date of the hearing before the commissioner, it was not open to him as a matter of law

---

a   See the Commons Registration (Time Limits) Order 1966 (SI 1966 No 1470), as amended by the Commons Registration (Time Limits) (Amendment) Order 1970 (SI 1970 No 383)
b   Section 1(2), so far as material, is set out at p 253 g, post
c   Section 22(1), so far as material, is set out at p 254 d and e, post

to confirm the registration, for the land was neither 'land subject to rights of common' nor 'waste land of a manor', within s 22(1) of the 1965 Act, and was not therefore 'common land' for the purposes of the 1965 Act. The appeal would therefore be allowed (see p 254 f to h, p 255 b and d to f and p 256 b and c, post).

Notes

For time limits and procedure for registration of common land, see 6 Halsbury's Laws (4th Edn) paras 673, 674, and for appeals from commons commissioners, see ibid para 699.

For the Commons Registration Act 1965, ss 1, 5, 22, see 3 Halsbury's Statutes (3rd Edn) 920, 923, 933.

Cases referred to in judgment

Behrens v Richards [1905] 2 Ch 614, 74 LJCh 615, 93 LT 623, 69 JP 381, 3 LGR 1228, 46 Digest (Repl) 385, 282.

Blount v Layard (1888) [1891] 2 Ch 681, CA, 25 Digest (Repl) 10, 66.

Brinckman v Matley [1904] 2 Ch 313, [1904-7] All ER Rep 941, 73 LJCh 642, 91 LT 429, 2 LGR 1057, CA, 26 Digest (Repl) 272, 21.

Chinnock v Hartley Wintney RDC, Phillips v Hartley Wintney RDC (1899) 63 JP 327, 26 Digest (Repl) 294, 167.

Edwards v Bairstow [1955] 3 All ER 48, [1956] AC 14, [1955] 3 WLR 410, 36 Tax Cas 220, [1955] TR 209, 34 ATC 198, 48 R & IT 534, HL, 28(1) Digest (Reissue) 567, 2089.

Poole v Huskinson (1843) 11 M & W 827, 152 ER 1039, 26 Digest (Repl) 294, 166.

Symes & Jaywick Associated Properties Ltd v Essex Rivers Catchment Board [1936] 3 All ER 908, [1937] 1 KB 548, 106 LJKB 279, 156 LT 116, 101 JP 179, 35 LGR 163, CA, 47 Digest (Repl) 719, 646.

White v Taylor (No 2) [1968] 1 All ER 1015, [1969] 1 Ch 160, [1968] 2 WLR 1402, 19 P & CR 412, Digest (Reissue) 37, 525.

Cases also cited

Cooke v Amey Gravel Co Ltd [1972] 3 All ER 579, [1972] 1 WLR 1310.

Dalton v Angus (1881) 6 AC 740, [1881-5] All ER Rep 1, HL.

New Windsor Corpn v Mellor [1974] 2 All ER 510, [1974] 1 WLR 1504.

Wilkes v Gee [1973] 1 All ER 226, [1973] 1 WLR 111.

Case stated

On 17th July 1970 the respondents, Clwyd County Council (formerly Flintshire County Council), caused certain land known as Dee Marsh Saltings ('the land') belonging to the appellants, the Central Generating Electricity Board, to be registered as common land under s 3 of the Commons Registration Act 1965. The appellants objected to the registration. On 14th March 1974 Mr Commissioner Francis QC, after an inquiry held on 11th and 12th December 1973, confirmed the registration. At the request of the appellants the commissioner stated a case for the decision of the High Court pursuant to s 18(1) of the 1965 Act. By an originating motion dated 10th February 1975 the appellants sought the determination of, inter alia, the following questions of law set out in the case stated: (i) whether, for the purpose of the determination by the commissioner under s 6 of the 1965 Act whether to confirm the provisional registration of the land as common land, the relevant date for deciding whether the land was subject to rights of common was the date of the provisional registration of the land under the 1965 Act or the date of hearing by the commissioner; (ii) whether, if on the appropriate date for determining the position no rights of common had been provisionally registered over the land, the commissioner could properly confirm the registration on the ground that the land was common land within s 22(1) of the 1965 Act, being land subject to rights of common; (iii) whether there was any or any sufficient evidence to justify the finding of the commissioner that the

land was on 17th July 1970 land subject to rights of common within the statutory
definition; (iv) whether on the facts found by the commissioner the land was on 17th
July 1970 land subject to rights of common within the meaning of the statutory
definition. The facts are set out in the judgment.

Charles Sparrow QC and *Gavin Lightman* for the appellants.
The respondents did not appear and were not represented.

GOFF J. This is an appeal by way of case stated from a decision dated the 14th
March 1974 of Mr H E Francis QC, sitting as a special commissioner under the
Commons Registration Act 1965, and it lies only on a matter of law.

The subject-matter of the proceedings is an area of the saltings in the estuary of
the river Dee. The nature and character of saltings are well described by Scott LJ
in *Symes and Jaywick Associated Properties v Essex Rivers Catchment Board*[1]. It is land
which by its nature is not fit for agriculture and one would think not very suitable for
grazing sheep and cattle. All the relevant parts of the area were completely unenclosed. It had at one time been manorial land but, as the commissioner found, it
had been taken out of the manor by certain conveyances, and it was not manorial
land at any relevant time.

The appellants desire to use part of it for the erection of a power station, a proposal
which aroused considerable local opposition; and in consequence a local farmer,
Mr John Winston Thomas, the owner of Pentre Farm, wished to register rights of
common over the appellants' land in the Saltings; but the statutory date at which
the right for anyone to apply to register rights of common expired was 2nd January
1970. Unhappily for him, Mr Thomas failed to make any application until 14th
May 1970. He was therefore out of time and his application failed.

The respondents, who were then the Flintshire County Council, were, however, in a
position to register the land as common land after 2nd January 1970, since under the
relevant statutory orders that could be done down to 31st July 1970. Whether to
assist Mr Thomas, or for their own purposes in defeating the appellants' plans, or
for other reasons, the respondents did in fact register the appellants' land as common
land on 17th July 1970 so that they were just in time. Nobody else applied either in
time or at all to register rights of common, and none were ever registered. Section
1(2) of the Commons Registration Act 1965 provides:

> 'After the end of such period, not being less than three years from the com-
> mencement of this Act, as the Minister may by order determine . . . (b) no
> rights of common shall be exercisable over any such land unless they are regis-
> tered either under this Act or under the Land Registration Acts 1925 and 1936.'

I should observe that no rights of common were registered under the Land
Registration Acts. The period prescribed for s 1(2) expired on 31st July 1970.

The appellants objected to the registration and the matter was referred to the
commissioner under s 5(6) of the 1965 Act. The relevant words of s 5(6) are: '. . . shall
refer the matter to a Commons Commissioner'.

It will be seen that when the respondents registered the land as common land the
rights of common over it, if any, were bound within a short time to become non-
exercisable by virtue of s 1(2)(b) of the 1965 Act, and nothing could save them, although
at that time that statutory provision was not yet operative. By the time, however, that
the commissioner came to deal with the matter the section had taken full force and
effect and no rights of common having been registered, none could thereafter be
exercised.

The commissioner held an inquiry on 11th and 12th December 1973 and, as I have
said, gave his decision on 14th March 1974. He took the view that for the purpose of

---

1   [1936] 3 All ER 908 at 916, 917, [1937] 1 KB 548 at 563

deciding whether to confirm or to refuse to confirm the registration he must consider whether the land in question was subject to rights of common immediately before the registration, that is on 17th July 1970 He said:

'The fact that no rights of common had been registered at that date, or the fact that no commoner could after 2nd January 1970 apply for the registration of any right of common appears to me to be irrelevant. The rights of common (if any) over the land had not been extinguished for want of registration on 17th July 1970.'

He then proceeded to hear evidence, as a result of which he found that there was sufficient to establish the fact that the land in question was on 17th July 1970 land subject to rights of common within the meaning of the statutory definition, and he therefore confirmed the registration. The effect of that decision, subject to this appeal, is that the registration has, by virtue of s 6(1) of the 1965 Act, become final; and by s 10 it is to be conclusive evidence of the matters registered as at the date of registration.

The appellants say that that was wrong and that the commissioner, finding that when he had to deal with the matter even if there were rights of common they could no longer be exercised, ought on that short ground to have refused to confirm the registration. I should refer to the definition in s 22(1) of the 1965 Act which provides:

'In this Act, unless the context otherwise requires,—"common land" means—
(a) land subject to rights of common (as defined in this Act) whether those rights are exercisable at all times or only during limited periods; (b) waste land of a manor not subject to rights of common; but does not include a town or village green or any land which forms part of a highway . . .
'"Rights of common" includes cattlegates or beastgates (by whatever name known) and rights of sole or several vesture or herbage or of sole or several pasture, but does not include rights held for a term of years or from year to year . . .'

It will be observed that s 1(2)(b) provides that no rights of common shall be exercisable over any such land unless duly registered, whereas the interpretation of the section says that common land means land subject to rights of common. In order to mount his objection counsel for the appellants must show that the effect of s 1(2)(b) is to extinguish unregistered rights so that thereafter the land is no longer subject to rights of common.

In my judgment, he has discharged that burden. He relies first on the words 'whether those rights are exercisable at all times or only during limited periods'. Those words are all-embracing, and when one finds that description of the words 'subject to rights of common', and then finds under s 1(2)(b) that no rights of common in the circumstances in the events which have happened are exercisable, it seems clearly to follow that the rights must have been extinguished and the land is no longer subject to rights of common.

The matter does not, however, rest there because there is a savings clause in s 21(1) which provides:

'Section 1(2) of this Act shall not affect the application to any land registered under this Act of section 193 or section 194 of the Law of Property Act 1925 . . .'

That subsection clearly notes, therefore, that but for the savings clause something in the Act would affect those sections. Section 193(1)(d) provides: '. . . the rights of access shall cease to apply—(i) to any land over which the commonable rights are extinguished under any statutory provision . . .' And s 194(3) has a proviso as follows: '. . . Provided that this section shall cease to apply—(a) to any land over which the rights of common are extinguished under any statutory provision . . .'

It is to those two provisions that the saving in s 21 is clearly directed, and the signifi-
a cance is that whilst s 1(2)(*b*) of the 1965 Act refers only to the rights not being exercisable, it is saved from operating under the provisions in ss 193 and 194 which refer to
the rights being extinguished; and therefore clearly the legislature was contemplating
s 1(2)(*b*) as working an extinguishment. That is emphasised by the parenthesis in
s 21(1) of the 1965 Act which reads as a definition of the relevant parts of s 193 and
s 194 as follows: 'rights of access to, and restriction on inclosure of, land over which
b rights of common are exercisable'. In my judgment it is plain that in the 1965 Act
the legislature was using the expression 'cease to be exercisable' as synonymous with
'extinguished'.

The matter was heard before me a little while ago, and I had reached that conclusion. But shortly afterwards it came to the notice of counsel for the appellants that the
respondents, the Clwyd County Council as successors to the Flintshire County Council,
c had in their hands a letter from the Department of the Environment in which arguments to the contrary were propounded. Counsel very properly drew that to my
attention and I therefore restored the matter for further hearing, and he has dealt
with those arguments, although the respondents themselves have not appeared to
support them.

It appears to be suggested that it was right for the commissioner to look only at
d the date of registration, because if he confirmed the registration it could stand, notwithstanding the failure to register any rights of common, and could not be amended
under s 13 of the 1965 Act because that could only be applied if there was some change
of circumstance or something outside the failure to register rights of common. I
cannot accept that view. It seems to me that if the commissioner were right in
looking at that date and therefore confirming the registration, it would become
e conclusive evidence that the land was common land at the time of registration but
nothing more. And accordingly, when the rights ceased to be exercisable, it would
cease to be common land and therefore it would lead inevitably to an application,
an unanswerable application, to amend the register. Of course, land may be registered as common land though there are no rights of common over it, because the
definition includes 'waste land of a manor not subject to rights of common', but
f that is not this case.

In support of that argument the letter in question drew attention to the provisions
of ss 6(3) and 12(*b*), and it was said that if the argument were not correct one would
expect some similar automatic provision in the Act applying to the case of land
ceasing to be common land through the failure to register any rights of common
over it.

g I am satisfied that there is nothing in that argument. Section 6(3) is dealing with the
registration of land as common land being cancelled, and it provides that the registration authority shall also cancel the registration of any person as the owner thereof.
But the cancellation of the registration of the land as common land does not of
itself affect any question of ownership, and therefore, the provisions of s 6(3) are
required to deal with that situation. So in s 12(*b*), where it is provided that on notifica-
h tion that the land has been registered under the Land Registration Acts, the registration of the ownership under the 1965 Act shall be deleted. That is of the same
character because the registration under the Land Registration Act does not of itself
affect the registration under the 1965 Act, and so an express provision is required.

The letter takes a further point in support of the argument in which reference is
made to s 5(7) of the 1965 Act which provides:

j   'An objection to the registration of any land as common land or as a town or
        village green shall be treated for the purposes of this Act as being also an
        objection to any registration (whenever made) under section 4 of this Act of any
        rights over the land',

and it is pointed out that there is no converse provision. However, that in my

judgment has no weight. An objection to the registration of any land as common
land is a complete attack on its status and must involve objecting to any rights of *a*
common registered over it, but the converse is not true; an attack on a right of
common registered over land does not necessarily involve attacking the whole status
of the land as common land, which it may continue to be because of other rights or as
manorial land over which there are no rights.

In my judgment, therefore, at the time when the commissioner heard the matter
the land was not subject to rights of common, and on that short ground he ought *b*
to have refused to confirm the registration. What is referred to him under s 5(6) is
'the matter', and the matter in my view is whether or not the land is common land.
To confirm registration because at that time it might have been right, when you know
at the hearing that it is wrong, leaving the objector to apply to amend the register,
seems to me to be a wrong course to pursue. On that short ground, therefore, this
appeal succeeds and I refuse to confirm the registration. *c*

Counsel for the appellants dealt with other points also. He submitted that the
registration was in any event inherently bad because one cannot register land as
common land on the ground that it is subject to rights of common unless there is on
the register a registration of rights of common or the local authority, when register-
ing it as common land, itself registers such rights. It is not necessary for me to determine that question in this case. It is I think a difficult one. There is no respondent *d*
here to argue the contrary, and it may be important in other cases, and I therefore
decline to express a view on that one way or the other.

Counsel for the appellants also attacked the decision on the assumption that he
was wrong on the first point, on the ground that the decision was wrong in law, and I
ought to deal with that line of argument. At the hearing only one person claimed
a right of common, and that was Mr Thomas. But the appellants proved that he had *e*
bought part of the common and it is clear from *White v Taylor*[1] that that had the
effect of destroying his right, if it was a right appurtenant.

The commissioner found that the land purchased by Mr Thomas was not part of
the common. He said:

'Finally, it appears to me that the rule relied on by [counsel for the appellants] *f*
only operates where the land was part of the common at the date of purchase by
the commoner. In this case, as I see it, the 23 acres purchased by Mr. David
Thomas in 1956 had long since ceased to be part of the common. It could have
ceased to be part of the common by approvement, or under statutory authority.
Presumably, it was conveyed by the Crown to one or other of the British Transport Commission's predecessors in title—e.g. the Chester and Holyhead Railway *g*
Company—although it is not clear to me whether the Conveyance dated 15th
September 1856 by the Crown in favour of that Company included the 23 acres.'

It may be that the commissioner was there confusing the position with the fact that,
as he had found, this part of the land had ceased to be part of the waste of the manor,
and approvement is a manorial term. If that is what he had in his mind at that
stage in his decision it was, in my respectful view, irrelevant. But if he was in truth *h*
saying that that land had ceased to be part of the common, there was no evidence of
that at all. Therefore for Mr Thomas to have any right it would have to be shown
that his right was appendant.

Counsel for the respondents, however, put his whole case on the ground that
whatever rights there were were appurtenant and, although the commissioner was
not satisfied of the origin of the rights which he found, there was no evidence of any *i*
right appendant. All the evidence was evidence of user which, if it supports anything,
shows an appurtenant and not an appendant right.

In my judgment, therefore, it was clear on the facts found that Mr Thomas had

1   [1968] 1 All ER 1015, [1969] 1 Ch 160

not and could not have had any rights of common over the property in question.
a But, as the commissioner found, other persons had enjoyed the land, and he said:

'In my view, the premise is not well founded, because the evidence satisfied
me that not only the owner of Pentre Farm [i e Mr Thomas], but the owners of
other neighbouring farms, had common rights of grazing over the land.'

b And he found, in addition to what I have stated earlier, that the land was on 17th
July 1970 subject to rights of common within the meaning of the statutory definition.
   In my judgment, with all respect to the commissioner, his decision was wrong on
one or other or both of two overlapping grounds: first, that it was too general; and
secondly, that the evidence was such that in reaching that conclusion the commissioner must be taken to have misdirected himself within the meaning of the cases
explained by Lord Radcliffe in Edwards v Bairstow[1]. The relevant passage is well
c known and I need not read it fully; Lord Radcliffe summed up as follows:

'I do not think that it much matters whether this state of affairs is described
as one in which there is no evidence to support the determination, or as one in
which the evidence is inconsistent with, and contradictory of, the determination,
or as one in which the true and only reasonable conclusion contradicts the
d determination. Rightly understood, each phrase propounds the same test. For
my part, I prefer the last of the three, since I think that it is rather misleading
to speak of there being no evidence to support a conclusion when, in cases such
as these, many of the facts are likely to be neutral in themselves and only to take
their colour from the combination of circumstances in which they are found
to occur.'

e Speaking of generality, in my judgment the onus lay on the respondents when the
registration was challenged to allege and prove at least one right of common exercisable over the property. No specific right was formulated, none was registered, and
none was adduced or adumbrated at the hearing, and the decision fails to specify
the nature of the common rights which were found to exist beyond saying that they
f were rights of grazing; it fails to quantify the extent of the rights; it fails to show
the land to which it was appendant or appurtenant; and it fails to show who claimed
to own the right.
   In my judgment it is not sufficient to support a registration to say 'Well, there has
been a lot of user, therefore one must assume that somebody has got a right'. It
must be much more definite than that. Of course, where one is dealing with a village
g green, general evidence of user is all that one requires or can expect. But where it is a
question of a particular right, though evidence of user is the way of proving it, the
right in my judgment ought to be properly formulated and properly found.
   So far as the other objection which I have mentioned is concerned, there was of
course evidence of user of the land in question for pasturage of cattle. But there was
very considerable evidence showing that there was no right. And before I mention
that in detail I shall refer to two authorities on which counsel for the appellants
h relied. The first was Chinnock v Hartley Wintney Rural District Council[2]. He relied
on this passage:

'"In order to constitute a valid dedication to the public of a highway by the
owner of the soil it is clearly settled that there must be an intention to dedicate—
there must be an animus dedicandi of which the user by the public is evidence
j and no more, and a single act of interruption by the owner is of much more
weight upon a question of intention than many acts of enjoyment."[3] To this I

1 [1955] 3 All ER 48 at 57, 58, [1956] AC 14 at 35, 36
2 (1899) 63 JP 327 at 328
3 Poole v Huskinson (1843) 11 M & W 827, per Parke B

may add that in my judgment, user by the public over land belonging to a non-resident owner is less cogent evidence of dedication than where the user is *a* necessarily brought to his personal notice; and, further, that the weight to be attached to user must depend somewhat upon the nature of the land itself, whether it is cultivated land or rough and unproductive land.'

That is a case of dedication of a highway, but the principles there stated are applicable to the type of case with which the commissioner was concerned.   *b*

The other authority is *Behrens v Richards*[1] in which the court refused to grant an injunction to restrain persons from trespassing because the landowner was not injured thereby and Buckley J made some pertinent observations about the distinction between matters being done as of right and matters being done by the indulgence of the owner when dealing with this kind of property. He said[2]:

'To those who are conversant with the Cornish coast or with many other parts *c* of the coast in this country it will be familiar that there are frequently to be found rough tracks or paths which have in fact been used without objection made by the landowner for very many years. From this fact alone it is difficult in surroundings such as there are in this case to infer an intention to dedicate. I cite again, as I did in *Brinckman* v. *Matley*[3], Bowen L.J.'s words in *Blount* v. *Layard*[4], "that nothing worse can happen in a free country than to force people *d* to be churlish about their rights for fear that their indulgence may be abused, and to drive them to prevent the enjoyment of things which, although they are matters of private property, naturally give pleasure to many others besides the owners, under the fear that their good nature may be misunderstood," and "that, however continuous, however lengthy, the indulgence may have been, a jury ought to be warned against extracting out of it an inference unfavourable *e* to the person who has granted the indulgence." In permitting persons to stray along the cliff edge or wander down the cliff face or stroll along the foreshore the owner of the land was permitting that which was no injury to him and whose refusal would have been a churlish and unreasonable act on his part. From such a user nothing, I think, is to be inferred.'

f

Whilst I appreciate that the question is not what I myself would have decided were I dealing with it at first instance, but whether the case falls within the principles stated by Lord Radcliffe, nevertheless in looking to see what evidence there was I think one ought to bear in mind the principles stated in the last two cited cases.

It is clear, and the commissioner found, that a number of facts existed which told heavily against there being any rights of common over the property in question. *g* Part of it had been enclosed without objection; not the part which is the subject-matter of this application, nor Mr Thomas's land, but part of these Saltings. Fishermen, in the days when they had horsecarts to take their catch away, grazed their horses on it. And most cogently of all, there were cases in which the owners of neighbouring farms, who were enjoying the Saltings, took licences for the purpose.

If the matter stopped there, it might be a case in which one would say, 'Well, *h* I would have reached a different conclusion', but still there was evidence on which the commissioner could find as he did, but it does not stop there. In addition to those facts there is the most cogent fact to which I have adverted more than once, that nobody registered any claims, and nobody appeared at the hearing to assert any claims other than the respondents; and the respondent council did not particularise or formulate the claims which they said they were asserting, or state on whose behalf *j*

1 [1905] 2 Ch 614
2 [1905] 2 Ch at 619, 620
3 [1904] 2 Ch 313, [1904-7] All ER Rep 941
4 (1888) [1891] 2 Ch 681

a
they were asserted. At all events the commissioner found nothing more specific than that the owners of other neighbouring farms had rights, not specifying which farms.

More important still, there was clearly no evidence at all to support any rights appendant. The case had to be and was presented on the basis that there were rights appurtenant. But the commissioner was not satisfied that it had been shown that the rights were appurtenant. He said this:

b
> 'True, it was referred to by [counsel for the respondents] as an appurtenant right, but there was no evidence before me to show whether it was in origin an appurtenant or appendant right. Presumably, no such evidence is now obtainable. But it seems to me that this somewhat technical and arbitrary rule of law ought not to be applied in the absence of clear evidence that the right of common in question was in fact an appurtenant right.'

c
There he was dealing with the purchase of part of the land by Mr Thomas, but it is quite clear that the other persons were in no different or better position. And the commissioner there reaches the conclusion that there was no evidence before him to show whether it was in origin an appurtenant or appendant right, and that there was no clear evidence that the right in question was in fact an appurtenant right. There being no evidence that it was an appendant right, and the commissioner's view of the evidence whether it was an appurtenant right being as I have stated, it seems to me that the case falls very clearly within the last part of the citation from Lord Radcliffe[1]. Many of the facts were neutral in themselves; they might have been enjoyment as of right; they might have been indulgence by a more or less or actual absent landowner; but they take their colour from the combination of circumstances in which they are found to occur, and taking that colour in my judgment there was no sufficient evidence to support the commissioner's finding that the land was subject to rights of common within the meaning of the statutory definition, even if it was not defective for want of particularity.

d

e

If therefore I am wrong, and I do not think I am, on the premise that the registration should not have been confirmed because the rights had all ceased to exist at the time of the hearing, and that was the relevant time at which to look, still in my judgment for the reasons I have given it ought not to be confirmed. I therefore, with respect, reverse the decision of the commissioner and, in the words of s 6, refuse to confirm the registration.

f

Appeal allowed.

g

Solicitors: *A L Wright*, Central Electricity Generating Board.

F K Anklesaria Esq Barrister.

1 *Edwards v Bairstow* [1955] 3 All ER at 58, [1956] AC at 36

R v Cato and others

COURT OF APPEAL, CRIMINAL DIVISION
LORD WIDGERY CJ, O'CONNOR AND JUPP JJ
13th, 14th, 15th OCTOBER 1975

Criminal law – Manslaughter – Recklessness or gross negligence – Consent of victim – Consent no defence – Relevance of victim's consent to accused's act – Whether consent should be taken into account for the purpose of determining whether accused guilty of recklessness or gross negligence.

Criminal law – Manslaughter – Causing death by unlawful act – Unlawful act – Injection of heroin – Unlawful act constituted by injecting into victim heroin which at the time and for the purposes of the injection accused had unlawfully taken into his possession.

Criminal law – Administering poison or other destructive or noxious thing – Noxious thing – Substance likely to cause danger in common use – Heroin – Whether heroin a 'noxious thing' – Offences against the Person Act 1861, s 23.

Criminal law – Administering poison or other destructive or noxious thing – Maliciously administering poison etc – Meaning of 'maliciously' – Foresight – Absence of foresight – Direct act causing death – Injection of heroin into victim's body – Accused deliberately inserting syringe into victim's body knowing it contained noxious substance – Accused unaware that substance likely to cause death or serious bodily harm – Whether accused having acted 'maliciously' – Offences against the Person Act 1861, s 23.

After drinking at a public house, the appellant returned with a friend, F, to the house that they shared. F produced a bag of white powder, which he said was heroin, and some syringes. He invited the appellant to have a 'fix' with him. They injected each other a number of times, following a procedure whereby each man prepared a mixture of heroin and water in the syringe to his own liking and for his own consumption and then gave it to the other to administer by injection. They continued to give each other injections right through the night. By the following morning they were both very ill. The appellant's life was saved but F died. The appellant was charged with the manslaughter of F and with unlawfully and maliciously administering a noxious thing to F, contrary to s 23[a] of the Offences against the Person Act 1861. At his trial the appellant gave evidence that, although he knew that the injection of heroin might result in addiction, he had no idea that it could give rise to death or serious bodily harm. The judge directed the jury, inter alia, that they could convict the appellant of manslaughter if they found that he had caused F's death by recklessness or gross negligence or by an unlawful and dangerous act, and that F's consent was no defence to the charge. The appellant was convicted on both counts and appealed against convictions, contending, inter alia, (i) that the effect of the judge's direction was to indicate to the jury that they could not take F's consent into account for the purpose of determining whether the appellant had been guilty of recklessness or gross negligence; (ii) that, on the basis that the appellant had not committed an offence under s 23 of the 1861 Act, the administration of heroin was not an offence and therefore there was no unlawful act on which a charge of manslaughter could be based; (iii) that heroin was not a 'noxious thing' within s 23 of the 1861 Act; and (iv) that it had not been

---

a Section 23, so far as material, is set out at p 268 *d*, post

administered 'maliciously' within s 23 since the appellant had not foreseen that his
a acts might result in death or serious harm for F.

Held – The appeal would be dismissed for the following reasons—
(i) Although F's consent to the injection of heroin was no defence to a charge of manslaughter, it was something which had to be taken into account when the jury came to
consider whether the appellant had acted with recklessness or gross negligence.
b The failure of the judge to point out that consent was relevant to the question of
recklessness or gross negligence could not, however, lead to the conclusion that the
verdict was unsafe or unsatisfactory (see p 226 g and h and p 267 a to c, post).
(ii) On the assumption that the administration of heroin did not constitute an offence
under s 23 of the 1861 Act, there was nevertheless an unlawful act on the part of the
appellant which could found a conviction for manslaughter; the unlawful act could
c be described as injecting F with a mixture of heroin and water which at the time of the
injection and for the purposes of the injection the appellant had unlawfully taken
into his possession (see p 267 g, post).
(iii) Although an article could not be considered 'noxious' within s 23 merely because
it was potentially harmful if taken in an overdose, an article could properly be described as 'noxious' if it was liable to cause injury in common use. In view of the harm
d which could result from the use of heroin which was not limited to harm from an
overdose in the sense of an accidental excess, the drug constituted a 'noxious thing'
for the purposes of s 23 (see p 268 e to h, post).
(iv) The appellant's act of injecting the heroin into F had been carried out
'maliciously' within s 23 since the act was a direct one and the appellant had deliberately inserted the syringe into F's body knowing that it contained a noxious substance
e (see p 269 f and g, post); R v Cunningham [1957] 2 All ER 412 distinguished.

Notes
For the crime of administering a noxious thing, see 10 Halsbury's Laws (3rd Edn)
737, 738, para 1415, and for cases on the subject, see 15 Digest (Repl) 1002, 1003,
9866-9875.
f For the Offences against the Person Act 1861, s 23, see 8 Halsbury's Statutes (3rd
Edn) 155.

Case referred to in judgment
R v Cunningham [1957] 2 All ER 412, [1957] 1 QB 396, [1957] 3 WLR 76, 121 JP 451, 41
Cr App Rep 155, CCA, Digest (Cont Vol A) 434, 9858a.

g **Cases also cited**
R v Blaue [1975] 3 All ER 446, [1975] 1 WLR 1141, CA.
R v Coney (1882) 8 QBD 534, CCR.
R v Dyson [1908] 2 KB 454, CCA.
R v Harris [1968] 2 All ER 49 n, [1968] 1 WLR 769, CA.
R v Hennah (1877) 13 Cox CC 547.
h R v Instan [1893] 1 QB 450, CCR.
R v Lamb [1967] 2 All ER 1282, [1967] 2 QB 981, CA.

Appeal and applications
On 26th June 1975 in the Crown Court at St Albans before Thesiger J the appellant,
Ronald Philip Cato, and the applicants, Neil Adrian Morris and Melvin Dudley, were
j convicted on indictment as follows: Cato of manslaughter (count 1) and administering
a noxious thing, contrary to s 23 of the Offences against the Person Act 1861 (count 2);
and Morris and Dudley each of assisting an offender (Cato) by giving information
(count 3) and by destroying possible evidence (count 4). On 4th July 1975 Cato was
sentenced to four years' imprisonment concurrent on counts 1 and 2; Morris to concurrent terms of borstal training and Dudley to two years' imprisonment concurrent.

Cato appealed against his convictions, Morris and Dudley applied for leave to appeal against their convictions, and all three sought leave to appeal against their sentences. *a* The facts are set out in the judgment of the court.

Louis Blom-Cooper QC and *G R Robertson* for Cato.
Anthony Astell for Morris and Dudley.
David Jeffreys for the Crown.

b

LORD WIDGERY CJ delivered the following judgment of the court: Following a trial at St Albans Crown Court in June of this year the following sentences were imposed on the appellant Cato and the applicants Morris and Dudley in respect of counts in the indictment. First of all, Cato was sentenced to four years' imprisonment on count 1 for manslaughter of Anthony Farmer. He was also sentenced to four years *c* concurrent on a charge under s 23 of the Offences against the Person Act 1861 of administering a noxious thing. The other two applicants, Morris and Dudley, were not concerned with the manslaughter charge directly. Their offences were of assisting Cato in what might be described as a 'cover-up' of the death of Farmer. In respect of those offences Morris was sentenced to borstal training and Dudley to two years' imprisonment, but in respect of each of them a condition precedent to it was the *d* conviction of Cato on the manslaughter charge or the charge under s 23. Unless that could be established, then the offences charged against Morris and Dudley did not arise.

Equally, it is accepted by their counsel that if the conviction of Cato for manslaughter or administering a noxious thing is upheld, then Dudley and Morris have nothing further to say in regard to their conviction in this case. Thus, nearly everything in *e* regard to guilt or innocence revolves around the conviction of Cato of manslaughter.

The victim, as I have said, was a young man called Anthony Farmer. The events leading up to his death occurred on 25th July 1974. On that day Cato and Farmer had been in each other's company for most of the day. The evidence suggests certain intervals when they were apart, but by and large they seem to have been together all that day, and they spent much of the day with Morris and Dudley as well. All *f* four of them at that time were living at a house called 34 Russell Street, and on 25th July their activities brought them to the Crown public house where they were until closing time, and after closing time they went back to 34 Russell Street.

There were others living in the house. They went to bed, and the four (that is to say, Cato, Morris, Dudley and the deceased Farmer) remained downstairs for a time. The moment came when Farmer produced a bag of white powder and some syringes *g* and invited the others to have a 'fix' with him; and so they did. The white powder was put in its bag on the mantelpiece, the syringes were distributed amongst the four who were to participate, and the procedure which they adopted (which may or may not be a common one) was to pair off so that each could do the actual act of injection into the other half of his pair. Following this procedure Morris and Dudley paired off together and so did Cato and Farmer (the deceased). All four had a number of in- *h* jections following this procedure, but the time came when Dudley and Morris went to bed, leaving Cato and Farmer downstairs in the sitting room. Cato and Farmer continued to give each other these injections from time to time right through the night.

The actual method, which I have probably described sufficiently already, may deserve a moment's repetition because so much hinges on it. The method, as I have *j* already indicated, was that each would take his own syringe. He would fill it to his own taste with whatever mixture of powder and water he thought proper. He would then give his syringe to the other half of his pair—in this case Farmer would give his syringe to Cato—and the other half of the pair would conduct the actual act of injection. It is important to notice that the strength of the mixture to be used was a entirely dictated by the person who was to receive it because he prepared his own syringe; but it is also to be noticed that the actual act of injection was done by the other half of the pair, which of course has a very important influence on this case when one comes to causation.

When the following morning came Farmer and Cato were still downstairs. They were apparently fast asleep, although everybody thought they were well enough at 8 a m when they were seen. But as the next hour or two passed it became apparent b that they were both in difficulties. Cato indeed was having difficulty in breathing, and probably his life was saved only because somebody gave him some rudimentary first aid. No one was able to do the same for Farmer, and by 11 a m Farmer was dead. The cause of death was that his respiratory system ceased to function consequent on intoxication from drugs.

When it was discovered Farmer was dead steps were taken to try and cover up by c Morris and Dudley, and I need not deal with them in detail at this stage. But in the end the full story came out and the charges to which I have already referred were brought against these three men in consequence of those actions.

At the trial there was quite a volume of expert evidence. First, there was a pathologist who conducted the elementary, if I may say so, and preliminary examination of the body and discovered there was insufficient evidence of natural disease to account d for death and that an autopsy would be necessary. Then there was other further detailed investigation of specimens of various parts of the body which showed (I am concentrating this quite a lot) a quantity of morphine in the body consistent with the injections of heroin which had been taken, according to their confessions, through the night. But it was noteworthy, so the expert said, that there was no morphine in the blood—a pointer, as we understand it, to a longer interval between the injection and e the death than would have appeared to have occurred having regard to the recital of the facts that I have given. Furthermore, a Dr Robinson, who was called on behalf of the defence, strongly made the point that there was not enough morphine visibly present in the samples to account for death because it was not a fatal dose. She had not seen the samples or worked on them herself because she had come into the case f later than that, but she clearly took the view that although there was morphine in the body, and although the morphine may have contributed to the death, it was not exclusively responsible for it because there was, as she said, a missing factor; and she concluded that there was a missing factor because in her view the size of the dose received by the deceased Farmer was insufficient to cause death.

The trial judge left the manslaughter charge to the jury on the two alternative bases which the Crown had suggested, and it will be appreciated at once what they g were. The first alternative was that the death was caused by the injection and the consequent intrusion of morphine into the body, and that was an unlawful act so that the killing was the result of an unlawful act and manslaughter on that footing. Alternatively, it was said that a verdict of guilty would be justified on the footing that there had been no unlawful act, but that the injection of heroin had been done with h recklessness or gross negligence, which of course would be sufficient to sustain the conviction of manslaughter.

The judge put it this way:

> 'Now, manslaughter in law is causing or contributing to the causing or accelerating (that is the hastening on) the death of a human being quite inadvertently by j doing an unlawful and dangerous act, or, alternatively, by doing a lawful act with gross negligence, that is to say, recklessly.'

He gets the alternatives there perfectly well.
He went on to say:

> 'The consent of the victim is quite immaterial, quite irrelevant, just as it is in

the not uncommon case of manslaughter, such as in the next case I have to try . . .
The prosecution say here that this was manslaughter in either of two ways, that is *a*
to say, either death was caused, although quite inadvertently, by an unlawful and
dangerous act, or, alternatively, by doing an act with gross negligence, recklessly'.

In amplification of that direction, which is repeated more than once, the judge quite
early in the course of his summing-up handed to the jury six questions which he had
written out for their consideration, and he told the jury that they should ask them- *b*
selves these six questions, and that if they answered 'yes' to all of them, then the
verdict should be guilty. These were the questions in their original version:

'(1) Did Cato take possession of some heroin in a syringe and then inject the
contents of the syringe into Anthony Farmer? (2) Did such injection by Cato
endanger the life of Anthony Farmer? (3) Did the injection of heroin by Cato *c*
contribute to or accelerate the death of Anthony Farmer? (4) Was the heroin so
injected likely to do harm to Anthony Farmer, although not necessarily serious
harm? (5) Did Cato realise (a) that it was unlawful for him or Farmer to be in
possession of heroin; (b) that heroin was likely, if injected, to do some harm to the
deceased Anthony Farmer?'

The sixth question was introduced by a statement of the judge that this was a slightly *d*
fresh question because it dealt with the other approach to the case suggested by the
Crown: 'Was the conduct of Cato, in respect of the injection, grossly negligent or, in
other words, reckless?'
    Consequent on some argument later in the course of the hearing the judge made two
amendments to those questions. For question (1) he substituted these words: *e*

'Did he [i e Cato] take into his hand, so as to control and carry out the injection,
a syringe which contained heroin and also water which was mixed and then
supplied the dose by injection to Tony Farmer?'

In question (3) he amended the phraseology in this way. He inserted the word 'cause'
so that the question read: 'Did such injection of heroin by Cato cause, contribute to *f*
or accelerate the death of Anthony Farmer?' The previous version, it will be
remembered, did not contain the word 'cause'.
    So those six questions were delivered to the jury for them to consider, not, as it
turned out, to produce a special verdict, but for them to consider with an instruction
from the judge that if they could answer them all, Yes, they must convict of manslaughter, and that if they could not answer them all, Yes, they should come back and *g*
ask for further guidance.
    Of course that last direction of the judge is obviously important. The jury did not
come back and ask for further guidance, and if they were following the letter of his
instruction, and there is really no reason to suggest that they did not on this point,
the fact that they did not come back must mean that they were able to answer all
the six questions in the affirmative. So much for the broad outline of the circumstances *h*
in which these charges were brought and the developments at the trial.
    We can now turn to look more precisely at counsel's submissions in supporting
Cato's appeal against conviction. We have had a long and very helpful argument
from counsel for Cato in which all the features of this difficult, and in some respects
intriguing, case have been considered. It seems to us that the first and most important
single factor to which he directed our attention was concerned with causation, that is *j*
to say with the link alleged to exist between the injection of heroin and the death of
Farmer.
    First of all, he invited us to look at the evidence of causation, and he pointed out
that the medical evidence did not at any point say 'This morphine killed Farmer';
the actual link of that kind was not present. The witnesses were hesitant to express

a such a view and often recoiled from it, saying it was not for them to state the cause of death.

It is perfectly true, as counsel for Cato says, that the expert evidence did not in positive terms provide a link, but it was never intended to. The expert witnesses here spoke to factual situations, and the conclusions and deductions therefrom were for the jury. The first question was: was there sufficient evidence on which the jury could conclude, as they must have concluded, that adequate causation was present?

b When one looks at the evidence it is important to realise that no other cause of Farmer's death was supplied. Dr Robinson thought that there might have been another drug, and she said at one stage it might have been cocaine, but there was never any cocaine found in the body. The only cause of death actually supplied by the evidence was morphine. No natural disease was present and no other drug was identified. Furthermore, the symptoms of the external appearance of the body, and

c the nature of the final terminal cause, were consistent with poison by the administration of heroin in the way which was described.

Further, when the people who lived in the house were giving their evidence about the death of Farmer, it was, as the judge pointed out, quite clear that they thought there was no doubt about what the cause had been. It may be of course that young people living in those circumstances know a great deal about the symptoms of

d heroin poisoning; I know not.

The judge said:

'Members of the jury, it seems to me that that evidence about the condition of Cato when he was senseless on the floor and was put to bed, what he looked like and so forth is quite material in regard to the cause of Tony Farmer's death because Cato and he had both been dosing themselves with the same sort of

e thing, in the same sort of way, in the same sort of number of times, and that is clear evidence in this particular case. The opinions of the people in the house is of course not medical opinion but everybody there seemed to draw the conclusion that probably the heroin injections had caused both of them to be in the condition they were in.'

f That is an important and proper conclusion, if the jury thought fit to adopt it, because the fact that Cato very nearly suffered the same fate as Farmer, and showed the same kind of symptoms following the same kind of injections, is a pointer to indicate that the cause of Farmer's condition was the heroin which he had taken; and, furthermore, the jury were entitled, if they thought fit, to be influenced by the fact that the non-medical evidence from the residents was of the kind which the judge related.

g Of course behind this whole question of the sufficiency of evidence of causation is the fact that it was not necessary for the prosecution to prove that the heroin was the only cause. As a matter of law, it was sufficient if the prosecution could establish that it was a cause, provided it was a cause outside the de minimis range, and effectively bearing on the acceleration of the moment of the victim's death.

When one has that in mind it is, we think, really possible to say that if the jury had

h been directed to look for heroin as a cause, not de minimis but a cause of substance, and they came back with a verdict of not guilty, the verdict could really be described as a perverse one. The whole background of the evidence was the other way and there certainly was ample evidence, given a proper direction, on which a charge of manslaughter could be supported.

But what about the proper direction? It will be noted that in none of the versions

j which I have quoted of the judge's direction on this point, nor in any of those which I have not quoted which appear in the summing-up, is there any reference to it being necessary for the cause to be a substantial one. It is said in clear terms in one of the six questions that the jury can consider whether the administration of the heroin was a cause or contributed to or accelerated the death, and in precise terms the word 'contributed' is not qualified to show that a substantial contribution is required.

Counsel for Cato, whose eagle eye misses nothing, sees here, and seeks to exploit here, what is a misdirection on the part of the trial judge. In other words, taking the a
judge's words literally, it would be possible for the jury to bring in a verdict of guilty of manslaughter even though the contribution was not of substance.

Before pursuing that, it is worth reminding oneself that some of the more recent dicta in the textbooks about this point do not support as strongly as was once the case the theory that the contribution must be substantial.

In Smith and Hogan[1] there is this rather interesting extract: b

'It is commonly said by judges and writers that, while the accused's act need not be the sole cause of the death, it must be a substantial cause. This appears to mean only that a minute contribution to the cause of death will not entail responsibility. It may therefore be misleading to direct a jury that D is not liable unless his conduct was a "substantial" cause. Killing is merely an acceleration of c
death and factors which produce a very trivial acceleration will be ignored.'

Whether that be so or not, and we do not propose to give that passage the court's blessing today at all events, if one looks at the circumstances of the present case with any real sense of reality, we think there can be no doubt that when the judge was talking about contribution the jury knew perfectly well that he was talking about d
something more than the mere de minimis contribution. We have given this point particular care in our consideration of the case because it worried us to some extent originally, but we do feel in the end, having looked at all the circumstances, that there could not have been any question in this case of the jury making the mistake of thinking that the contribution would suffice if it were de minimis. Therefore in our judgment there is no substance in the attack of counsel for Cato on the basis of causation, e
whether it be an attack on the available evidence or on the trial judge's treatment of that evidence.

The next main point which I think the court would wish to deal with is the fact that the trial judge on more than one occasion, as the extracts which I have read show, told the jury that the consent of Farmer (the victim) was quite irrelevant. Occasionally he says the consent of Farmer is no defence to the charge, but more often he says the f
consent of Farmer is quite irrelevant. Counsel for Cato says that that was a misdirection because he says there are two factors, two aspects of this case, which have to be considered separately. It may be that if one asks oneself whether the consent of the victim could provide a defence to a charge of manslaughter, the answer should be a vivid No. In general, as a simple proposition, where this kind of injury is done by one person to another the consent of the person injured is not a defence. On the other g
hand, one of the matters which the jury at some stage had to consider in the instant case was whether Cato had acted with recklessness or gross negligence, and counsel says, and we think rightly, that when considering that aspect of the case the consent of Farmer is something which could not be wholly excluded.

In those circumstances we have tried to look at these two aspects of the matter separately. We think that the judge, when saying so positively that the consent of h
Farmer was irrelevant or was no defence, was anticipating a question in the jury's mind that they might have been uncertain whether it would be a defence or not. One has to realise that laymen will often think that a person who dies in Farmer's circumstances will not produce a charge of manslaughter against his friend if in fact he consented to what was being done to him and the friend did not attempt to do more than that. We think it could very well have been the case that the jury might have asked the judge directly: is consent a defence? and if they had, he would have i
had to say No, and his saying No in the course of his summing-up appears to be an anticipation of that kind of question in the jury's mind.

---

1   Criminal Law (3rd Edn, 1973), p 217

But of course in a perfect world the judge, when faced with this question, would have dealt with both aspects of the matter in contrast. He would have said: 'It is not a defence in the sense that merely by proving Farmer's permission the matter is at an end; but when you come to consider the questions of gross negligence or recklessness of course you must take it into account.' Whether he would have gone further we very much doubt. If a persistent juror had said: 'Well, what do you mean by "take into account"? What have we got to do?' it may very well be that the judge would be stumped at that point and really could not do any more than say 'You must take it into account'. Lawyers understand what it means, but jurors very often do not, and although I have taken more time to discuss this point than perhaps it really requires, we have come to the conclusion that there is not here any matter which gives us cause to think that the conviction may be unsafe or unsatisfactory. We support the judge in dealing head on with the question of whether consent was a defence or not, and we do not think that he could usefully have said much more in regard to gross negligence or recklessness in order to avoid any possible confusion at that end of the scale.

The next matter, I think, is the unlawful act. Of course on the first approach to manslaughter in this case it was necessary for the prosecution to prove that Farmer had been killed in the course of an unlawful act. Strangely enough, or it may seem strange to most of us, although the possession or supply of heroin is an offence, it is not an offence to take it, and although supplying it is an offence, it is not an offence to administer it. At least it is not made to be an offence, and so counsel for Cato says there was no unlawful act here. That which Cato did—taking Farmer's syringe already charged and injecting the mixture into Farmer as directed—is not an unlawful act, says counsel for Cato because there is nothing there which is an offence against the Misuse of Drugs Act 1971, and when he shows us the terms of the section it seems that that is absolutely right.

Of course if the conviction on count 2 remains (that is the charge under s 23 of the Offences against the Person Act 1861, of administering a noxious thing), then that in itself would be an unlawful act. The prohibition in that Act would be enough in itself, and it is probably right to say that as we are going to uphold the conviction on count 2, as will appear presently, that really answers the problem and destroys the basis of counsel for Cato's argument.

But since he went to such trouble with the argument, and in respect for it, we think we ought to say that had it not been possible to rely on the charge under s 23 of the 1861 Act, we think there would have been an unlawful act here, and we think the unlawful act would be described as injecting the deceased Farmer with a mixture of heroin and water which at the time of the injection and for the purposes of the injection Cato had unlawfully taken into his possession. As I say, it is not really necessary to rely on that because of our views on the other count, but we would not wish it to be thought that we had felt counsel for Cato's argument on this point would have succeeded had it been effectively open to him. So much then for the unlawful act.

Lastly, on the first count is the question of recklessness. Of course if the jury convicted on the second approach, the reckless approach, they must have considered whether there was recklessness. They were indeed instructed so to do.

Counsel for Cato makes the complaint that the judge has not dealt sufficiently with this aspect of the case to give the jury a proper, fair and adequate direction about it. Of course he recognises—he is far too experienced, if I may say so, not to recognise—that he cannot expect every judge in the hurly-burly of every case to sum up with the polished perfection which counsel can produce in this court some months later. But even so, making all allowances for that, the complaint is made that the judge did not do anything to help the jury as to the meaning of recklessness, and in particular that the trial judge did not refer to one aspect of Cato's evidence which might have proved of some importance.

Cato, when pressed as to his knowledge of the potentiality of heroin when injected, said that he knew that it might give rise to addiction, but he had no idea that it could give rise to death or serious bodily harm. Of course in deciding whether Cato had himself acted recklessly one would have to have regard to the fact, if it was accepted, that he did not know about the potentiality of the drug. It is said that this was not really sufficiently provided for in the summing-up.

We think it was. After all, recklessness is a perfectly simple English word. Its meaning is well known and it is in common use. There is a limit to the extent to which the judge in the summing-up is expected to teach the jury the use of ordinary English words. Although we have listened to counsel for Cato on this point, with respect, we do not find that criticism justifies our concluding the manslaughter verdict was in any measure unsafe or unsatisfactory, so we shall dismiss the appeal so far as that conviction is concerned.

I have already given away the fact that a similar consequence will follow in respect of the offence under s 23 of the 1861 Act, but I must just go back and look at the reasons for it.

The offence under s 23 is in these terms:

'Whosoever shall unlawfully and maliciously administer to or cause to be administered to or taken by any other person any poison or other destructive or noxious thing, so as thereby to endanger the life of such person, or so as thereby to inflict upon such person any grievous bodily harm, shall be guilty of [an offence].'

Thus, a number of things have to be proved in order to establish the offence, and the two which are relevant to the argument of counsel for Cato are 'maliciously' and 'noxious'. The thing must be a 'noxious thing' and it must be administered 'maliciously'.

What is a noxious thing, and in particular is heroin a noxious thing? The authorities show that an article is not to be described as noxious for present purposes merely because it has a potentiality for harm if taken in an overdose. There are many articles of value in common use which may be harmful in overdose, and it is clear on the authorities when looking at them that one cannot describe an article as noxious merely because it has that aptitude. On the other hand, if an article is liable to injure in common use, not when an overdose in the sense of an accidental excess is used but is liable to cause injury in common use, should it then not be regarded as a noxious thing for present purposes?

When one has regard to the potentiality of heroin in the circumstances which we read about and hear about in our courts today we have no hesitation in saying that heroin is a noxious thing and we do not think that arguments are open to an accused person in a case such as the present, whereby he may say: 'Well the deceased was experienced in taking heroin; his tolerance was high', and generally to indicate that the heroin was unlikely to do any particular harm in a particular circumstance. We think there can be no doubt, and it should be said clearly, that heroin is a noxious thing for the purposes of s 23.

What about 'maliciously'? Counsel for Cato says that 'maliciously' requires some foresight into the consequences, and he has referred us to *R v Cunningham*[1], which is put before us as authority for that proposition. It was a rather unusual case. The prisoner had stolen a gas meter and its contents from the cellar of a house, the contents no doubt having been money in a slot machine. He did it in a rough and unskilled way and left an escape of gas from the position which the meter had occupied. The gas percolated up into the higher reaches of the house, and eventually got into the bedroom of an elderly lady who was subjected to considerable exposure to coal gas as a result of what had happened. When the prisoner was charged with an

---

offence under s 23 the question arose whether the requirment of malice had been
satisfied. Byrne J, giving the reserved judgment of the Court of Criminal Appeal,
said[1]:

> 'Counsel argued, first, that mens rea of some kind is necessary. Secondly, that
> the nature of the mens rea required is that the appellant must intend to do the
> particular kind of harm that was done, or, alternatively, that he must foresee
> that that harm may occur yet nevertheless continue recklessly to do the act.
> Thirdly, that the judge misdirected the jury as to the meaning of the word
> "maliciously".'

Then Byrne J, after referring to four cases[2], continued[3]:

> 'We have considered those cases, and we have also considered, in the light of
> those cases, the following principle which was propounded by the late Professor
> C. S. Kelly in the first edition of his Outlines of Criminal Law published in 1902
> and repeated in the sixteenth edition, edited by Mr. J. W. Cecil Turner and
> published in 1952, ibid at p. 186 " . . . in any statutory definition of a crime, malice
> must be taken not in the old vague sense of 'wickedness' in general, but as re-
> quiring either (i) An actual intention to do the particular *kind* of harm that in
> fact was done; or (ii) recklessness as to whether such harm should occur or not
> (i e the accused has foreseen that the particular kind of harm might be done and
> yet has gone on to take the risk of it). It is neither limited to nor does it indeed
> require any ill will towards the person injured" . . .'

We think that this is an accurate statement of the law.

No doubt this is correct in the R v Cunningham[4] type of case where the injury to the
victim was done indirectly; done, as it was in that case, by the escape of gas making
itself felt in the wholly different part of the house. No doubt if the injury to the
victim is indirect, then the element of foresight arises and the element of foresight
will be taken from the words of Byrne J in R v Cunningham[4]. But these problems do
not arise when the act complained of is done directly to the person of the victim, as it
was in this case. We think in this case where the act was entirely a direct one that the
requirement of malice is satisfied if the syringe was deliberately inserted into the body
of Farmer, as it undoubtedly was, and if Cato at a time when he so inserted the
syringe knew that the syringe contained a noxious substance. That is enough, we
think, in this type of direct injury case to satisfy the requirement of maliciousness.

I am conscious of the fact that I have not done justice to counsel for Cato's argument, but those are the reasons why we conclude that the convictions against Cato
must stand and as a consequence, for the reasons I have described, so must the
conviction against Morris and Dudley.

[Counsel addressed the court on the applications for leave to appeal against sentence.]

LORD WIDGERY CJ. Having listened to counsel's argument, we are of the opinion
that all these sentences are what one might describe as on the high side. On the
other hand, we do not find it possible to deal with any one of these three otherwise
than in terms of custodial sentence.

---

1   [1957] 2 All ER at 413, [1957] 1 QB at 399
2   R v Faulkner (1877) 13 Cox CC 550, R v Latimer (1886) 17 QBD 359, R v Martin (1881) 8 QBD
    54, R v Pembliton (1874) LR 2 CCR 119.
3   [1957] 2 All ER at 414, [1957] 1 QB at 399, 400
4   [1957] 2 All ER 412, [1957] 1 QB 396

Having decided those two matters of principle, we have then had to try and produce the most sensible answer we can out of the powers available to this court and having particular regard to the limitation on the sentences which are available for those under 21.

Doing our best in those circumstances, we shall allow the appeals and substitute sentences as follows: first of all, in the case of Cato we think that had we a free hand we should have sentenced him to prison for something of the order of 18 months to two years. We cannot do that because of his age. We substitute the only possible alternative having regard to his age, which is borstal training on both counts concurrent.

So far as Morris and Dudley are concerned, Morris is subject to the same type of limitation as Cato, being under 21 at the relevant time: Dudley is not. We think that Morris and Dudley should be treated alike and that in place of the sentences imposed on them they will each serve a sentence of six months' imprisonment concurrent on each count.

Appeal against convictions dismissed; applications for leave to appeal against sentence allowed; sentences varied.

7th November. The court refused leave to appeal but certified under s 33 of the Criminal Appeal Act 1968 that the following points of law of general importance were involved in dismissing the appeals against conviction: 'Where the defendant has injected another person by syringe with an unmeasured quantity of heroin with the other's consent (the quantity being selected and prepared by that other person) (i) in relation to a charge of manslaughter (where death results) (a) is that other person's consent a defence? (b) is the injection an unlawful act? (ii) in relation to a charge under s 23 of the Offences against the Person Act 1861 (a) is that person's consent a defence? (b) is heroin a noxious thing? (c) is proof of foresight of the consequences of the injection required to show that the heroin was administered maliciously?'

Solicitors: *Simons, Muirhead & Allan* (for Cato); *Ian Sherratte & Co* (for Morris and Dudley); *Director of Public Prosecutions.*

N P Metcalfe Esq Barrister.

Practice Note

COURT OF APPEAL, CRIMINAL DIVISION
LORD WIDGERY CJ AND MAY J
19th DECEMBER 1975

Prison – Release on licence – Conviction of further offence – Duty of Crown Court – Revocation of licence – Duty to consider whether any sentence of imprisonment for further offence should be concurrent or consecutive to sentence for offence in respect of which licence revoked – Criminal Justice Act 1967, ss 60, 62(1)(2)(7).

Notes

For release of prisoners on licence and revocation of such licence, see Supplement to 30 Halsbury's Laws (3rd Edn) para 1188A.

For the Criminal Justice Act 1967, ss 60, 62, see 25 Halsbury's Statutes (3rd Edn) 888, 891.

At the sitting of the court **LORD WIDGERY CJ** stated that he had to give the following practice direction on the subject of revocation of parole licences.

1. When a prisoner who has been released on licence on the recommendation of r .e Parole Board under s 60 of the Criminal Justice Act 1967 is convicted of a further offence during the currency of the licence the conviction does not automatically revoke his licence.

2. Section 62(7) of the 1967 Act, however, provides that if such a person appears before the Crown Court that court may revoke his licence in the circumstances there set out.

3. In such cases the Crown Court should consider all the facts and decide whether the offender should be returned to custody for a term of not less than the remaining effective period of his licence. If so, the court should revoke his licence. The court should then consider whether any sentence of imprisonment passed in respect of the offence committed during the currency of his licence should be concurrent or consecutive to the sentence for the offence in respect of which the court has revoked the licence.

4. The effect of revoking a licence is ordinarily that the offender will be required to serve the time remaining from the date of revocation to the end of the sentence (with remission) or 30 days whichever is the greater. If the offender was on licence in respect of an extended sentence, or was a young prisoner, the effect of revocation is that he will again be required to serve the remainder of the original sentence, with remission not exceeding one-third of that part of his sentence unexpired at the time of recall.

5. If the Crown Court passes a sentence of imprisonment for an offence committed whilst on licence but does not revoke that licence, any subsequent revocation under s 62(1) or s 62(2) of the 1967 Act cannot make the new sentence consecutive to the original sentence. For this reason it is important that the Crown Court should consider in each case what is the appropriate action to take.

N P Metcalfe Esq Barrister.

Practice Direction   *a*

FAMILY DIVISION

Divorce – Consent applications – Divorce Registry – Procedure.

The attention of solicitors is drawn to two minor adjustments of procedure made to   *b*
the current Divorce Registry practice which permits consent applications being made
to a registrar without attendance (registrar's direction of 10th April 1974[1]):
 1.   Attendance will be required in respect of an application to a registrar for a
consent order for custody of, or access to, a child under r 92(2) of the Matrimonial
Causes Rules 1973[2] as amended by the Matrimonial Causes (Amendment) Rules 1975[3].
On any such application, the Registry will fix a date and time for the hearing. It   *c*
would assist the registrar considering the application, and avoid possible adjournment,
if the solicitor attending the hearing is familiar with the circumstances relating to
the children and is able to advise the registrar accordingly.
 2.   On the issue of a consent summons or filing a notice of application seeking
an order which includes an agreed term for payments *direct to* a child in excess of
the amounts qualifying for the time being as 'small maintenance payments' under   *d*
s 65 of the Income and Corporation Taxes Act 1970, the solicitor should certify either
on the summons or the notice whether the child is, or is not, living with the party
who will be making the payments under the proposed terms.

                                                                    D NEWTON   *e*
22nd December 1975   Senior Registrar.

---

1   [1974] 2 All ER 1120, [1974] 1 WLR 937
2   SI 1973 No 2016
3   SI 1975 No 1359

a R v Herrod, ex parte Leeds City District Council
R v Inner London Crown Court, ex parte London Borough of Greenwich
b # R v Inner London Crown Court, ex parte London Borough of Lewisham

COURT OF APPEAL, CIVIL DIVISION
LORD DENNING MR, JAMES AND SHAW LJJ
8th, 9th, 10th OCTOBER, 7th NOVEMBER 1975

c

Gaming – Amusements with prizes – Permit for provision of amusements with prizes – Resolution by local authority not to grant or renew permits – Statutory exception – Resolution not applicable to premises used or to be used wholly or mainly for the purposes of a pleasure fair consisting wholly or mainly of amusements – 'Pleasure fair' – Local authority resolving not to grant or renew permits – Local authority refusing applicant permit for premises to be **d** *used for prize bingo – Whether premises to be used for that purpose to be used for purposes of 'pleasure fair consisting wholly or mainly of amusements' – Betting, Gaming and Lotteries Act 1963, Sch 6, para 4 (as substituted by the Gaming Act 1968, s 53, Sch 11, Part II).*

Certiorari – Delay – Discretion – Refusal of order – Unreasonable delay by applicant – Application made within prescribed time limit – Jurisdiction of court to refuse order on **e** *ground of delay – Burden on applicant of showing that despite delay in all circumstances order should be granted – Prescribed time limit not an entitlement but a maximum rarely to be exceeded – RSC Ord 53, r 2(2).*

In June 1970 Leeds City Council ('Leeds') granted W a permit under s 49 of the Betting, Gaming and Lotteries Act 1963 for a period of three years, permitting the provision **f** of amusements with prizes at certain premises which he occupied and used for the purposes of prize bingo. Shortly after, on 10th July 1970, Leeds passed a resolution, pursuant to Sch 6, para 3*ª*, to the 1963 Act, as amended, that 'permits shall be neither granted nor renewed on or after 1st July, 1970, for the provision of amusements with prizes on any premises other than' premises used for the purpose of a pleasure fair. When his permit expired W applied for its renewal. Leeds refused the application **g** on the ground that W came within the resolution of 10th July 1970. W appealed to the Crown Court, which in October 1973 allowed the appeal on the ground that the premises came within the exempting provisions of para 4(2)*ᵇ* of Sch 6 to the 1963 Act, as amended, being 'premises used or to be used wholly or mainly for the purposes of a pleasure fair consisting wholly or mainly of amusements'. In July 1974, on an application by Leeds, the Divisional Court*ᵉ* quashed the court's decision, holding **h** that the words 'pleasure fair' in para 4(2) were limited to the type of fair traditionally provided by travelling showmen, i e fairs at which there were roundabouts, dodgems, hoop-la etc, and did not extend to premises used wholly or mainly for the playing of prize bingo.

On 29th July 1970 the London Borough of Greenwich ('Greenwich') passed a resolution under Sch 6, para 3, to the 1963 Act, that permits for amusements with prizes **j** would not be granted in respect of 'premises which are not purpose built for the provision of public entertainment'. In 1973 H and S planned to acquire certain shop

---

a Paragraph 3, as amended and so far as material, is set out at p 283 *c*, post
b Paragraph 4, as amended and so far as material, is set out at p 283 *d*, post
c [1974] 3 All ER 362   L

premises and convert them into a place for the playing of prize bingo. They applied
for a permit under s 49 of the 1963 Act. Greenwich refused the application pursuant   *a*
to their resolution of 29th July 1970. On 22nd October 1973 the Crown Court allowed
an appeal by H and S, holding that the premises were within the exempting provision
in para 4(2) of Sch 6 to the 1963 Act, and granted the permit. In reliance on that decision,
and in anticipation that they would be granted planning permission, H and S exchanged
contracts for the purchase of the premises and incurred substantial expenditure in
connection with the purchase. In March 1974 H and S obtained the necessary planning   *b*
permission. On 5th April Greenwich applied to the Divisional Court for an order of
certiorari to quash the Crown Court's decision. At the hearing, in November 1974,
it was common ground that, according to the decision in the *Leeds* case*d*, the Crown
Court's decision was wrong in law, but H and S contended that the court should, as a
matter of discretion, refuse the application in view of the delay of 5½ months between
the decision of the Crown Court and the making of the application. The Divisional   *c*
Court*e*, however, granted an order, holding that only in very exceptional circumstances
would the court refuse certiorari on the ground of delay in a case where the application
had been made within the six months' time limit prescribed by RSC Ord 53, r 2(2)*f*.
    Both W and H and S appealed against the decisions of the Divisional Court.

Held – The appeals would be allowed for the following reasons—   *d*
    (i) The expression 'pleasure fair' in para 4(2) of Sch 6 to the 1963 Act was to be
construed in accordance with the wide definition contained in s 75*g* of the Public
Health Act 1961, and in other private local Acts whereby Parliament had entrusted
the control of pleasure fairs to local authorities, and was not to be confined to the type
of pleasure fair provided by travelling showmen. So construed, the expression included
premises which were wholly or mainly used for prize bingo. It followed that, by   *e*
virtue of para 4(2), the local authorities were not entitled to pass a 'blanket' resolution
under para 3 not to grant or renew permits for premises which were to be used for
prize bingo; each application for such a permit had to be considered on its merits (see
p 281 *j* to p 282 *c* and *g h*, p 286 *d* to *g*, p 287 *e* and *j* to p 288 *b*, p 290 *g* to *j* and p 291 *b c*
and *g h*, post).
    (ii) An application for the remedy of certiorari was not an appeal but a request to   *f*
the High Court to exercise its power of supervision over inferior tribunals. The
relief was subject to the overriding rule that it was discretionary and consequently
the question of delay in making the application was a material and relevant consideration. Once the issue of delay had been raised it was incumbent on the applicant to
discharge the burden of showing that in all the circumstances he should in the exercise
of that discretion be granted the relief sought. The time limit of six months prescribed   *g*
by RSC Ord 53, r 2(2), was not an entitlement but a maximum rarely to be exceeded.
It followed (James LJ dissenting) that, in any event, Greenwich had left it far too late
to apply for certiorari and their application should have been refused on that ground
(see p 278 *c* to *g*, p 288 *c* to *g* and p 292 *e* to p 293 *b*, post).
    Per Shaw LJ. Pleasure fairs are places of public resort for entertainment and
amusement of a traditional character, the attributes shared by the different forms of   *h*
entertainment being that they are of a rudimentary and sometimes a crude kind,
demanding neither intellectual skill nor aesthetic appreciation; if the entertainment
involves any skill, it is at a minimal level and of a simple sort (see p 291 *e* and *f*, post).
    Decisions of the Divisional Court of the Queen's Bench Division [1974] 3 All ER
362 and [1975] 1 All ER 114 reversed.

d [1974] 3 All ER 362   *j*
e [1975] 1 All ER 114
f Rule 2(2), so far as material, provides: 'Leave shall not be granted to apply for an order of
    certiorari to remove any judgment, order, conviction or other proceeding for the purpose
    of its being quashed, unless the application for leave is made within 6 months ... or ... the
    delay is accounted for to the satisfaction of the Court ...'
g Section 75, so far as material, is set out at p 281 *e* to *g*, post

Notes

a For permits for the provision of amusements with prizes, see Supplement to 18 Halsbury's Laws (3rd Edn) para 469B, 3, and for cases on the subject, see Digest (Cont Vol C) 395, 396, 316aa-316e.

For the discretionary nature of certiorari, see 1 Halsbury's Laws (4th Edn) paras 161-167, and for cases on the subject, see 16 Digest (Repl) 450, 451, 2580-2590.

For the Betting, Gaming and Lotteries Act 1963, s 49, Sch 6, paras 3, 4, see 14

b Halsbury's Statutes (3rd Edn) 593, 800.

For the Public Health Act 1961, s 75, see 26 Halsbury's Statutes (3rd Edn) 563.

Cases referred to in judgments

Bowman, Re, South Shields (Thames Street) Clearance Order 1931 [1932] 2 KB 621, [1932]

c   All ER Rep 257, 101 LJKB 798, 147 LT 150, 96 JP 207, 30 LGR 245, 26 Digest (Repl) 694, 88.

Capper v Baldwin [1965] 1 All ER 787, [1965] 2 QB 53, [1965] 2 WLR 610, 129 JP 202, 63 LGR 163, DC, Digest (Cont Vol B) 320, 316c.

Hewison v Skegness Urban District Council [1963] 1 All ER 205, [1963] 1 QB 584, [1963] 2 WLR 141, 127 JP 118, 61 LGR 105, DC, Digest (Cont Vol A) 623, 316a.

d *R v Glamorgan Appeal Tribunal, ex parte Fricker* (1917) 115 LT 930, 81 JP 85, 15 LGR 142, DC, 16 Digest (Repl) 478, 2972.

R v Northumberland Compensation Appeal Tribunal, ex parte Shaw [1952] 1 All ER 122, [1952] 1 KB 338, 116 JP 54, 50 LGR 193, 2 P & CR 361, CA, 16 Digest (Repl) 479, 2978.

R v Sheward (1880) 9 QBD 741, 49 LJQB 716, CA, 16 Digest (Repl) 516, 3487.

e *R v Stafford Justices, ex parte Stafford Corpn* [1940] 2 KB 33, 109 LJKB 584, 162 LT 393, 104 JP 266, 38 LGR 255, CA, 16 Digest (Repl) 451, 2590.

Sagnata Investments Ltd v Norwich Corpn [1971] 2 All ER 1441, [1971] 2 QB 614, [1971] 3 WLR 133, 69 LGR 471, CA.

f **Cases also cited**

Attorney-General v Till [1910] AC 50, HL.

Cooper v Wandsworth Board of Works (1863) 14 CNBS 180.

Holmes v Bradfield Rural District Council [1949] 1 All ER 381, [1949] 2 KB 1, DC.

Lennon v Gibson Howes Ltd [1919] AC 709, PC.

Mersey Docks & Harbour Board v Henderson Bros (1888) 13 App Cas 595, CA.

g *R v City and County of Exeter Justices, ex parte Fowler* [1966] 3 All ER 49, [1966] 1 WLR 1121, DC.

Wyld v Silver [1962] 3 All ER 309, [1963] Ch 243, CA.

Appeals

h   *R v Herrod, ex parte Leeds City District Council*

Leeds City District Council applied to the Divisional Court of the Queen's Bench Division for an order of certiorari to remove into the High Court for the purpose of its being quashed an order of Mr Recorder Herrod QC dated 10th October 1973 granting to Charles Henry Walker a permit for the provision of amusement with prizes at premises situate at and known as The Fraternity Bridge and Social Club,

j 568 Meanwood Road, Leeds 6. On 9th July 1974 the Divisional Court[1] (Lord Widgery CJ, Thompson and Talbot JJ) granted the order sought. Mr Walker appealed. The facts are set out in the judgment of Lord Denning MR.

---

1 [1974] 3 All ER 362, [1974] 1 WLR 1275

R v Inner London Crown Court, ex parte London Borough of Greenwich
The London Borough of Greenwich applied to the Divisional Court of the Queen's   *a*
Bench Division for an order of certiorari to remove into the High Court for the purpose
of its being quashed an order of Judge Layton dated 22nd October 1973 in the Crown
Court sitting at Inner London Sessions House, Newington Causeway, SE1, granting
to Alan Michael Hunt and Graham Smith a permit for the provision of amusement
with prizes at premises situate at and known as 2a, 2b Woolwich New Road, SE18.
On 7th November 1974 the Divisional Court[1] (Lord Widgery CJ, Bridge and Kilner   *b*
Brown JJ) granted the order sought. Mr Hunt and Mr Smith appealed. The facts
are set out in the judgment of Lord Denning MR.

R v Inner London Crown Court, ex parte London Borough of Lewisham
The London Borough of Lewisham applied to the Divisional Court of the Queen's
Bench Division for an order of certiorari to remove into the High Court for the purpose   *c*
of its being quashed a decision made by Judge Macleay sitting with a lay justice in
the Crown Court at Inner London Sessions House, Newington Causeway, SE1, dated
15th February 1974 granting to Alan Michael Hunt and Graham Smith a permit
for the provision of amusement with prizes at premises situate at and known as 155
Lewisham High Street, London, SE13. On 17th February 1975 the Divisional Court
(Lord Widgery CJ, Ashworth and Bridge JJ) granted the order sought. Mr Hunt and   *d*
Mr Smith appealed. The facts are set out in the judgment of Lord Denning MR.

R J Harvey QC, David Tudor Price and *Roger Shawcross* for the appellants.
Raymond Sears QC and *David Lamming* for the Leeds City District Council.
Robin Simpson QC and *Victoria Gilbert* for the London Borough of Greenwich.
Andrew Leggatt QC and *Colin Smith* for the London Borough of Lewisham.   *e*

Cur adv vult

7th November 1975. The following judgments were read.

LORD DENNING MR. The question in these cases is whether premises used for   *f*
playing 'prize bingo' are a pleasure fair within the meaning of the Betting, Gaming
and Lotteries Act 1963. If the premises are *not* a pleasure fair, a local authority can
pass a resolution giving a 'blanket refusal' prohibiting prize bingo to be played there,
or anywhere else in the town. But if it is a pleasure fair, they cannot give a 'blanket'
refusal. They must hear the application separately and decide on its merits.

1 *The Leeds case*   *g*
Some years ago the Leeds City Council granted a permit for prize bingo to be played
at premises called the Fraternity Bridge and Social Club, 568 Meanwood Road, Leeds.
On 10th April 1970 Leeds City Council passed a 'blanket' resolution saying:

'. . . permits shall be neither granted nor renewed on or after 1st July, 1970,
for the provision of amusements with prizes on any premises other than premises   *h*
used, or to be used, wholly or mainly for the purpose of a "pleasure fair"
consisting wholly or mainly of amusements.'

On 7th June 1970 (shortly before that blanket resolution came into operation)
the occupier, Mr Walker, was granted a permit for prize bingo on the premises.
This permit was for three years. In consequence he equipped the premises at much
expense for prize bingo and employed staff to run it. On 1st July, as I have said, the   *j*
'blanket' resolution came into effect. On 2nd February 1973 Mr Walker applied for a
renewal of the permit. He said that the premises 'are established and conducted
for the purpose of amusements with prizes in the nature of prize bingo'.

---

1   [1975] 1 All ER 114, [1975] 2 WLR 310

On 20th June 1973 the council refused to renew the permit on the ground that it
a came within the 'blanket' resolution of 10th April 1970. They said that his premises
(used for prize bingo) were not a 'pleasure fair'.

Mr Walker appealed to the Crown Court. On 10th October 1973 the recorder,
Mr Herrod QC, allowed the appeal. He held that premises used for prize bingo
were a 'pleasure fair'. He granted Mr Walker a permit. Two months later, on 14th
December 1973, the council applied to the Divisional Court for certiorari to quash the
b recorder's decision. On 9th July 1974 the Divisional Court[1] quashed his decision.
They held that the user for prize bingo was not a pleasure fair and that Mr Walker
was caught by the 'blanket' resolution. So Mr Walker would have to shut down the
place and dismiss his staff. He had carried it on quite well and lawfully for four years,
but he would have to shut it down. He appeals to this court.

c **2 *The Greenwich case***

We are here concerned with 2a and 2b New Road, Greenwich. For many years they
were used by Tesco as a self-service grocery store. Then in 1973 two partners, calling
themselves Carousel, planned to acquire the premises and convert them into a place
for prize bingo. For this purpose they would need to get planning permission from
the Greenwich council (who were the planning authority); and also need to get
d permission for amusements with prizes. This permission would also have to be
obtained from the Greenwich council (who were the licensing authority for
amusements with prizes).

The council refused planning permission; but Carousel lodged an appeal to the
Minister. They were quite confident that their appeal would be granted; because
there had been similar cases where a local council had refused planning permission
e but the Minister, on appeal, had granted it. Their confidence was not misplaced.
The Minister, in due course, did grant planning permission.

In 1973 the council also refused permission for amusements with prizes. They
refused it because three years before, on 29th July 1970, the council had passed a
resolution that they would not grant any permits for amusements with prizes in
respect of 'premises which are not purpose built for the provision of public entertain-
f ment'. These premises fell within that embargo; because they were purpose built
for a retail shop, and not for public entertainment. Carousel appealed to the Crown
Court. On 22nd October 1973 the Crown Court allowed the appeal and granted
Carousel a permit for amusements with prizes, together with £100 costs. That
decision of the Crown Court was 'final'. The Act said so in terms. So Carousel were
entitled to treat it as 'final'. And they did so. Carousel asked for the £100 awarded
g them for costs; and the council did not dispute it. Carousel also went on with their
plans to purchase the premises. In December 1973 they exchanged contracts to buy
them for £80,050. They paid the deposit and many other outgoings. Everything
went forward on the basis of 'finality' until, on 19th February 1974, the council wrote
saying they were asking counsel whether they could appeal against the decision of
the Crown Court. The answer of counsel must have been No, because there was, of
h course, no appeal. On 28th March 1974 Carousel were granted planning permission,
as they had expected. After all this had happened, eventually on 5th April 1974, the
Greenwich council applied for certiorari to quash the decision of the Crown Court.
That was 5½ months after the Crown Court gave its decision.

Carousel submitted that there was unreasonable delay in making the application
and that, on that account, the Divisional Court should refuse the remedy. But the
j Divisional Court[2] granted it. They said that a person who applies for certiorari is
given six months; and is prima facie entitled to take the whole of it. Lord Widgery CJ
said[3]:

1 [1974] 3 All ER 362, [1974] 1 WLR 1275
2 [1975] 1 All ER 114, [1975] 2 WLR 310
3 [1975] 1 All ER at 118, [1975] 2 WLR at 314

'. . . that six months' time limit, which has been in the rules for nearly 100 years, is generally regarded throughout the country as being a limit within which an *a* applicant can safely act . . . anyone who seeks to resist certiorari on the basis of lapse of time when less than six months had elapsed has got to make out his case and make out a strong case . . .'

I am afraid that I cannot agree. It seems to put the remedy by certiorari on the same level as an appeal; and not only as an appeal, but as an appeal in which the appellant *b* has virtually six months in which to give notice of appeal. This would be an extra-ordinary favour to grant. We all know that in appeals from a judge of the High Court, the time limit is six weeks. In appeals from a decision of magistrates (whether by case stated or otherwise) the time limit is 14 days. These time limits are deliberately made short so that people can know where they stand. Can it really be supposed that a person—who has an order of the Crown Court in his favour—has to wait for six *c* months before he can safely act on it? And, what is more, when the order is by statute expressly made 'final', that is without appeal to any higher court?

The truth is, of course, that certiorari is not an appeal at all. It is an exercise by the High Court of its power to supervise inferior tribunals: see *R v Northumberland Compensation Appeal Tribunal, ex parte Shaw*[1]. The time limit of six months is not an entitlement. It is a maximum rarely to be exceeded. Short of six months, there is *d* the overriding rule that the remedy by certiorari is discretionary. If a person comes to the High Court seeking certiorari to quash the decision of the Crown Court—or any other inferior tribunal for that matter—he should act promptly and before the other party has taken any step on the faith of the decision. Else he may find that the High Court will refuse him a remedy. If he has been guilty of any delay at all, it is for him to get over it and not for the other side. In support, I would refer to *R v* *e* *Sheward*[2] where five months elapsed. And in *R v Glamorgan Appeal Tribunal, ex parte Fricker*[3] Lord Reading CJ said:

'. . . the applicant could not succeed, for two months and a half had elapsed before he came to this court. If it is desired to take such an objection an application must be made at once . . .'
f

So also *R v Stafford Justices*[4] by Greene MR.

In the present case the Greenwich council left it far too late to apply for certiorari to quash the decision of the Crown Court. On that ground alone I think the application of the Greenwich council should have been refused.

3 *The Lewisham case*   *g*
For some years now the premises at 155 Lewisham High Street have been used for prize bingo. The Lewisham council granted a permit for the purpose.

On 18th April 1973 the Lewisham council passed a resolution that the council do not grant or renew permits under s 49 of the 1963 Act (for the provision of amusements with prizes) in respect of 'premises built, converted, adapted or designed for use as a place where persons may participate in prize bingo'.
h
On 3rd October 1973 the leaseholders of no 155 applied for a permit saying that they intended to conduct gaming by way of amusements with prizes in the form of prize bingo on the premises. The council refused the application on the ground of the 'blanket' resolution. The leaseholders appealed to the Crown Court. The Crown Court allowed the appeal and granted the permit. This was on 15th February 1974. The chairman said: 'We are willing to state a case if anyone wants one stated.'
j

1 [1952] 1 All ER 122 at 127, 128, [1952] 1 KB 338 at 346, 347
2 (1880) 9 QBD 741
3 (1917) 115 LT 930 at 932
4 [1940] 2 KB 33 at 45

The Lewisham council did not ask for a case to be stated. They had 14 days to do so.
a But they did not do it. The leaseholders treated the order of the Crown Court as final (as they were entitled to do). They spent about £2,000 in converting and improving the premises, and took on staff.

Five months later, on 15th July 1974, the Lewisham council sought leave to move for certiorari to quash the decision of the Crown Court. On 2nd October 1974 notice of motion was served on the leaseholders. On 17th February 1975 the Divisional
b Court heard the application. They granted certiorari without argument, seeing that their case was covered by the combined effect of *R v Herrod, ex parte Leeds City District Council*[1] and *R v Inner London Crown Court, ex parte London Borough of Greenwich*[2].

4 *The general question*

In all three cases the question depends on the nature of prize bingo. To decide it,
c I must try to explain it. I expect that everybody knows ordinary bingo. It is played at bazaars, places of work, and so forth, for small prizes, and is perfectly lawful. Now prize bingo is like ordinary bingo, but played with a sophisticated apparatus. Instead of cards with numbers on them, there are dials facing the players. A player puts in a coin (5p for two cards). Thereupon two dials light up showing numbers corresponding to two cards. When the game starts, instead of someone drawing a number
d out of a hat, a machine throws a ball into the air. A gaily dressed lady plucks one of them and calls out the number. If it is one of the numbers on the dial, the player crosses it out by pulling a cover over it. If he gets all his numbers crossed out correctly before the other players, he gets a prize. This is obviously a lottery or a game of chance, but it is not a 'gaming machine' because the element of chance is not provided by means of the machine but by means of the gay lady: see s 26(2) of the Gaming Act
e 1968.

In some of these premises there are also some 'one-armed bandits'. These are gaming machines. The player puts in a coin. This enables him to pull a handle to forecast a result. Cylinders revolve and give an answer. If he succeeds, he gets the winnings. If he fails, he loses his money. This is undoubtedly a 'gaming machine' because the element of chance is provided by means of a machine: see s 26(1) of the 1968 Act and
f *Capper v Baldwin*[3].

There is yet another form of bingo called cash bingo. This takes place on several premises simultaneously. It needs complicated apparatus and many players. The winnings may be very large. This form of bingo comes under the Gaming Board and needs a licence from them: see s 20 of the 1968 Act.

Finally there are halls called bingo halls. These are licensed premises where people
g can buy intoxicating liquor and also play prize bingo.

Now there are a series of authorities who have control of those various premises.

(i) *The local planning authority*—When it is proposed to use premises for prize bingo, the promoters have to get planning permission. When they apply to the local planning authority, it is often refused—not because the place itself is unsuitable but because that authority regards prize bingo as socially undesirable. If that happens, the pro-
h moters appeal to the Minister; and he allows the appeal. He does so on the ground that planning permission is only concerned with planning matters, and not with the social desirability of the activities carried on. So the promoters get permission from the Minister.

(ii) *Justices' on-licence*—If the premises are licensed for the sale of intoxicating liquor on the premises—and the promoters wish to install a prize bingo apparatus on those
j premises—the promoters must obtain the permission of the licensing justices: see Sch 11 to the 1968 Act bringing in para 1 of Sch 9: but he does not have to obtain any

1 [1974] 3 All ER 362, [1974] 1 WLR 1275
2 [1975] 1 All ER 114, [1975] 2 WLR 310
3 [1965] 1 All ER 787, [1965] 2 QB 53

permit from the local authority. The licensing justices must hear each application on its merits. They cannot give a 'blanket' refusal.

(iii) *Local authority permits*—When premises are not licensed for intoxicating liquor, the promoters of prize bingo have to obtain a permit from the local authority, i e the town council: see s 49 of the Betting, Gaming and Lotteries Act 1963. If it is refused, they can appeal to the Crown Court, formerly to Quarter Sessions: see Sch 6 to that Act.

Before 1968 a local authority which had to consider numerous applications for permits was entitled to lay down a general policy which it proposed to follow in coming to its individual decisions. Once laid down, the local authority was entitled to apply the policy in the individual cases which came before it. But it was not to apply it so rigidly as to reject an applicant without hearing what he had to say. After hearing what he had to say, the local authority could decide against him. But if they refused a permit, he was entitled to appeal to Quarter Sessions. And on the appeal there was a complete rehearing. The recorder was entitled to disregard the policy and to substitute his own views on the case: see the authorities collected in *Sagnata Investments v Norwich Corpn*[1]. I am afraid that the recorders at Quarter Sessions often did reverse the decisions of the local authorities. They granted permits which the local authorities had refused. In consequence, the local authorities complained to the government department. These complaints had this effect; in the Gaming Act 1968 a provision was inserted enabling the local authorities in some circumstances to pass policy resolutions declaring that they would issue no more permits in respect of premises of a specified class. Such resolutions can be passed by the local authority without hearing the persons affected and without giving them any right of appeal. In short, the local authorities are authorised to pass resolutions by which they can give a 'blanket' refusal to grant or renew a permit without hearing the applicant and without any appeal from their decision. This would seem to be contrary to natural justice, even in the case of an application for the 'grant' of a permit. All the more so where it is the refusal to 'renew' an existing licence. Once having been granted a permit, the applicant may have invested much money in his venture. A refusal to 'renew' his permit may cause him serious economic loss. Yet Parliament has authorised the local authorities to gave a 'blanket' refusal. This may be so unfair in its result that the courts should confine this power within strict limits. They should confine it to those circumstances which are clearly covered by the statute, and not extend it one whit beyond.

Take first gaming machines. The power to make 'blanket refusal' is given by para 3 of Sch 9 to the 1968 Act. It authorises the local authority to pass a policy resolution saying they will not grant or renew any permits in respect of premises 'of a class specified in the resolution'. They might resolve, for instance, that they would not allow any gaming machines in any retail premises except cafés or restaurants; or that they would limit machines to one or two. But there is an exception in para 4. It says that no such resolution (giving a blanket refusal) can be made in respect of 'any premises to be used wholly or mainly for the provision of amusements by means of' gaming machines. This exception is clearly designed to include an 'amusement arcade' which is, of course, full of gaming machines, fruit machines, and so forth. The local authority cannot pass a blanket resolution refusing to grant or renew a permit for an amusement arcade. It must consider each application on its merits, giving the applicant a hearing, with a right of appeal to the Crown Court: see Sch 9, para 13.

Take next amusements with prizes. These include prize bingo. A blanket power is given by the substitute para 3 of Sch 6 to the 1963 Act. It authorises the local authority to pass a policy resolution saying that they will not grant or renew any permit for 'any premises of a class specified in the resolution'. They might, for instance, resolve

---

1   [1971] 2 All ER 1441, [1971] 2 QB 614

that they would not grant a permit for prize bingo in any retail premises except a café or restaurant. But there is an exception in para 4. It says that no such resolution (giving a 'blanket' refusal) can be made in respect of 'any premises used or to be used wholly or mainly for the purposes of a pleasure fair consisting wholly or mainly of amusements'.

What then is a 'pleasure fair'? It is not defined in the 1968 Act. But a 'travelling-showmen's pleasure fair' is defined in s 52. It means 'a pleasure fair consisting wholly or mainly of amusements provided by travelling showmen' which is held on less than 28 days in a year, i e which has planning permission under the General Development Order[1]. At such a travelling showmen's pleasure fair, it is lawful to have amusements with small prizes for small stakes, provided that it is not the principal attraction: see s 49(1)(2)(3)(e). But none of that tells us what a 'pleasure fair' is when taken by itself without any amusements provided by travelling showmen.

Other statutes

In order to find out the meaning of 'pleasure fair', we were invited to look at several statutes in which those words had been defined by Parliament. These were statutes in which Parliament had entrusted local authorities with the control of 'pleasure fairs' and had authorised those authorities to make byelaws for the purpose. They were mostly private Acts for towns and cities. The committees of both Houses actually issued 'model clauses' to be inserted in private Acts defining the expression 'pleasure fair'. The statutes always used these model clauses. Finally all local authorities were empowered in a public Act to make byelaws for the good order and public safety at any 'pleasure fair'. It is s 75(2)(3) of the Public Health Act 1961. In all these statutes there is this one definition of 'pleasure fair':

'. . ."pleasure fair" means any place—(i) which is for the time being used wholly or mainly for providing, whether or not in combination with any other entertainment, any entertainment to which this section applies, and (ii) for admission to which, or for the use of the contrivances in which, a charge is made . . .'

'. . . the entertainments to which this section applies are the following:—(a) circuses; (b) exhibitions of human beings or of performing animals; (c) merry-go-rounds, roundabouts, swings, switchback railways; (d) coco-nut shies, hoop-las, shooting galleries, bowling alleys; (e) dodgems or other mechanical riding or driving contrivances; (f) automatic or other machines intended for entertainment or amusement; (g) anything similar to any of the foregoing.'

It is apparent that that definition applies not only to a 'fun-fair' where there are many entertainments of all kinds, but also to a small plot or place where there is only one merry-go-round or one bowling alley, or one set of dodgems. So also to a place where there is one set of coconut shies or one hoop-la stall or one shooting gallery, whether or not prizes are awarded. Likewise where there is one set of prize bingo. I should have thought it plain that the local authority could make byelaws for all those places on the ground that each was a 'pleasure fair'. Each of them should be under the control of the local authority, as to the times of opening and closing, the provision of exits and gangways, fire appliances, and so forth.

Are those statutes relevant?

Lord Widgery CJ[2], thought that those statutes were not in pari materia with the Gaming Acts. He thought that no attention should be paid to the definition in them of 'pleasure fair'. I am afraid that I do not agree. Both sets of Acts deal with the control of pleasure fairs. Both entrust the control of them to the local authorities. One set deals with byelaws for maintaining good order at 'pleasure fairs'. The other set

---

1   See the Town and Country Planning General Development Order 1973 (SI 1973 No 31), Sch 1, Class IV

2   [1974] 3 All ER at 365, [1974] 1 WLR at 1279

deals with permits for amusements with prizes at 'pleasure fairs'. I should think that the subject-matter is so similar in both sets that the words 'pleasure fair' mean the same in both. Apart from this, I think it pretty plain that the sections in each set of Acts were drafted by the same set of lawyers, whether in the ministry or in the offices of the local authorities; or, at any rate, that they were consulted on them. They would all be aware of the definition of 'pleasure fair' for the purpose of making byelaws; and may fairly be assumed to use it in the same sense in the Gaming Acts. I would hazard a guess that it was only by an oversight in drafting that they did not include it in the Gaming Act 1968.

At any rate, I am of opinion that the definition is very relevant to the interpretation of the Acts; and that we should apply it just as if it was incorporated in them. After all, there is no other guidance to be found anywhere. So we might as well go by it. Applying that definition, a 'pleasure fair' includes premises which are used wholly or mainly for prize bingo.

The 1964 Act

A short word about the Betting, Gaming and Lotteries Act 1964. It was passed so as to do away with *Hewison v Skegness Urban District Council*[1]: see *Sagnata Investments v Norwich Corpn*[2]. It gave the local authorities power to limit the number of gaming machines in public houses, cafés and restaurants, and so forth, but it did not apply to an 'amusement place'. In the case of an 'amusement place', the local authority can grant or refuse a permit but *not* limit the number of machines. The 1964 Act defines an 'amusement place' as—

'premises used, or to be used, wholly or mainly—(a) for the provision of amusements by way of machines; or (b) for the purposes of a pleasure fair consisting wholly or mainly of amusements'.

It seems to me that in the 1964 Act, 'pleasure fair' had the same meaning as in the other Acts. If a permit is given for a pleasure fair, e g a bowling alley or a shooting gallery, or prize bingo (that being the main purpose), the promoters can install one or two one-armed bandits without needing a special permit in that behalf. Similarly, if a permit is given for an amusement arcade (gaming machines being the main purpose) the promoters can install prize bingo as a minor attraction.

Conclusion

In my opinion, premises which are used wholly or mainly for prize bingo are a 'pleasure fair' within the meaning of the Gaming Acts. The local authorities are not at liberty to pass a resolution giving a 'blanket refusal' to grant or renew a permit for prize bingo. They must consider each application on its merits. They can, if they please, adopt a general policy on the matter, but they must consider each case separately and hear the parties concerned. If they refuse it, there is an appeal to the Crown Court.

I would, therefore, allow the appeals in all three cases. The 'blanket' resolutions were invalid. In each case the applicant is entitled to have his case heard separately; and a permit granted or refused on its merits.

JAMES LJ. These three appeals involve the determination of a question which is common to them all. It is: were the premises used, or to be used, wholly or mainly for the purposes of playing 'prize bingo' used, or to be used, for the purposes of a 'pleasure fair' within the meaning of those words in sub-para 2 of para 4 of Sch 6 to the Betting, Gaming and Lotteries Act 1963, as amended by the Gaming Act 1968?

---

1   [1963] 1 All ER 205, [1963] 1 QB 584
2   [1971] 2 All ER 1441 at 1445, [1971] 2 QB 614 at 623, 624

The appeal in *R v Inner London Crown Court, ex parte London Borough of Greenwich* involves a further question concerning the exercise of discretion by the Divisional Court in ordering that certiorari should go. If the appellants succeed on the question common to all the appeals, this question need not be decided. In view of the basis on which the Divisional Court decided this question it is, however, necessary to refer to it.

This judgment is to be read as if there were set out in it the relevant statutory provisions of the Betting, Gaming and Lotteries Act 1963 and the Gaming Act 1968. To recite all the provisions would be tedious and unhelpful. The relevant parts are s 49(1)(2) and (3) of the 1963 Act, Sch 6 to that Act, as amended by the Gaming Act 1968, in particular, paras 1 to 9 inclusive of that schedule, and those parts of Sch 9 to the 1968 Act which are made applicable to applications for the purposes of s 49 of the 1963 Act by Sch 6 to that Act. It is however convenient to set out the provisions of paras 3 and 4 of Sch 6 to the 1963 Act.

'3. Any local authority may pass either of the following resolutions, that is to say—(a) that (subject to paragraph 4 of this Schedule) the authority will not grant any permits in respect of premises of a class specified in the resolution; (b) that (subject to paragraph 4 of this Schedule) the authority will neither grant nor renew any permit in respect of premises of a class specified in the resolution.
'4.—(1) No resolution under paragraph 3 of this Schedule shall have effect in relation to the grant or renewal of permits in respect of premises to which this paragraph applies.
'(2) This paragraph applies to any premises used or to be used wholly or mainly for the purposes of a pleasure fair consisting wholly or mainly of amusements.'

At this stage I make these general observations on the statutory provisions. The blanket form of resolution authorised by para 3 of Sch 6 is available only to the local authority and not to licensing justices as the 'appropriate authority'. When a blanket resolution passed under the power given by para 3 is in force in relation to premises the subject-matter of an application for a permit for the purposes of s 49, the local authority is bound by the resolution and cannot consider the merits of the particular case or whether injustice will result from a refusal to grant or renew an existing permit. Where no such resolution is in force the local authority have a discretion to grant or refuse the application for a permit, but the exercise of that discretion must be on consideration of the merits of the application and there is a statutory restriction as to the circumstances in which renewal may be refused. On appeal to the Crown Court from a refusal to grant or renew a permit for the purpose of s 49 the Crown Court must dismiss the appeal if satisfied that it was the duty of the local authority to refuse the application on the ground that there was in force in respect of the premises a resolution pursuant to Sch 6, para 3.

In each of these three cases there was in force a resolution of the local authority and the application was refused by the local authority on the ground that they were under a duty to refuse it because the resolution applied to the premises in question. In the *Leeds* case the city council resolved on 10th April 1970 that—

'permits shall be neither granted nor renewed on or after 1st July 1970 for the provision of amusements with prizes on any premises other than premises used or to be used wholly or mainly for the purpose of a "pleasure fair" consisting wholly or mainly of amusements.'

In the *Greenwich* case the borough council resolved on 28th July 1970 to accept the recommendation of its Finance and General Purposes Committee—

'that the Council resolves not to grant any permits under s 49 of the Betting

Gaming and Lotteries Act 1963 in respect of premises of the class specified hereunder: Class of premises   Premises which are not purpose built for the
provision of entertainment.'

In the *Lewisham* case on 18th April 1973 the borough council resolved to adopt the
recommendation of the Finance and General Purposes Committee—

'that the Council forthwith do not grant or renew permits under s 49 of the
Betting, Gaming and Lotteries Act 1963, as amended by Sch 11 of the Gaming
Act 1968, for the provision of amusements with prizes in respect of the following
classes of premises.'

The recommendation then specified eight classes of premises and in addition
'Premises built converted adapted or designed for use as a place where persons may
participate in prize bingo'.

In each case the applicant or applicants appealed to the Crown Court.   In each case
the Crown Court has held that the resolution could not take effect in relation to the
application because the application was one in respect of premises used or to be used
wholly or mainly for the purposes of a pleasure fair consisting wholly or mainly of
amusements.   In each case the local authority moved in the Divisional Court for an
order of certiorari.   The *Leeds* case was heard first in point of time and on 9th July 1974
the Divisional Court[1] quashed the order of the recorder.   On 7th November 1974 the
Divisional Court[2] granted the application of the borough of Greenwich for certiorari
and quashed the order of Judge Layton at the Inner London Crown Court.   The application was subject to the court holding that the council were not disentitled to relief by
reason of delay, bound to succeed on the basis of the earlier decision in the *Leeds*
case[1].   On 17th February 1975 the *Lewisham* case came before the Divisional Court.
Certiorari was granted without argument, the case being covered by the two earlier
decisions.   The order of the Inner London Crown Court was quashed.

I must say a little more about the facts.   On 7th June 1970 Mr Walker was granted
a three year permit under s 49 for prize bingo on club premises at 568 Meanwood
Road, Leeds.   He equipped the premises and used them for prize bingo.   Nobody
suggested that Mr Walker conducted the use of the premises otherwise than in an
orderly and proper way.   In February 1973 he applied for the renewal of the permit and
on 20th June the local authority refused to renew the permit.   They decided that the
premises were not a pleasure fair and gave effect to the council's resolution which had
been in force since 1st July 1970.   By reason of the 'blanket resolution', as it has been
called, Mr Walker was refused the opportunity of carrying on the business he had
been conducting for three years without criticism or objection.

The premises involved in the *Greenwich* appeal were at one time a grocery stores
at 2a and 2b New Road, Woolwich.   Mr Hunt and Mr Smith made plans to purchase
the premises and made application for a permit for the use of the premises for the
purposes of prize bingo.   They also applied for planning permission to cover the change
of use.   After refusal by the local authority of planning permission they eventually
obtained it on 28th March 1974 by order of the Minister.   On 13th August 1973 the
same authority refused to grant a permit.   There was no dispute that the premises
were not purpose built for the provision of public entertainment.   The issue was
whether the premises were to be used as a pleasure fair.   If they were the resolution
did not bite.   The Crown Court, on 22nd October 1973, held that the premises were to
be used as a pleasure fair and granted a permit.   As this stage Mr Hunt and Mr Smith
had the permit under s 49 but had been refused planning permission to develop the
premises.   But such was their optimism in respect of their appeal to the Minister
against that refusal that they went ahead with their plans to use the premises for

---

1   [1974] 3 All ER 362, [1974] 1 WLR 1275
2   [1975] 1 All ER 114, [1975] 2 WLR 310

prize bingo. Contracts for the purchase of the premises were exchanged and a substantial deposit paid. Other expenditure was incurred. They sought and received payment of the £100 costs awarded by the Crown Court. Four months after the decision of the Crown Court they were informed by the council that an appeal was being considered. The 1963 Act provides that the decision of the Crown Court shall be 'final'. So there was no right of 'appeal'. Then, a week after planning permission had been granted by the Minister, the local authority moved the Divisional Court for the grant of an order of certiorari. That was on 5th April 1974, five months and two weeks after the decision they sought to challenge.

The application to the Lewisham borough council related to premises at 155 Lewisham High Street. The premises had been used for prize bingo under the local authority's permit prior to an application in October 1973 by Mr Hunt and Mr Smith for a permit to continue that use. They were informed on 19th October that the application was refused because there was a resolution in force prohibiting the granting or renewing of permits in respect of classes of premises including the premises in question. So here, as in the *Leeds* case, the effect of the blanket resolution, if it bites on the premises, is to bring to an end an existing business activity without regard to the merits of an application to continue the business or the justice of the individual case.

Prior to the coming into force of the Gaming Act 1968, a local authority was bound to consider applications for permits under s 49 of the 1963 Act on their merits. An application might be granted or refused as being within or contrary to the general policy of the local authority within its area. If refused on that ground, the unsuccessful applicant might have his appeal to the court allowed if the court took a different view from that dictated by the policy of the local authority. The Gaming Act 1968 for the first time enabled a local authority to resolve not to grant or renew permits under s 49 in a blanket form. Holders of permits and would-be applicants for permits have no opportunity of challenging the resolution. The Crown Court can enquire on an appeal as to the existence of a resolution applicable to the premises and, if satisfied that there was such a resolution, cannot go behind it. Parliament has placed in the hands of local authorities, as defined in the Act, powers the exercise of which may prevent a person from commencing a business, even from continuing in an existing business, without his objection being heard on its merits. It seems to me that in these circumstances it is the duty of the court to be vigilant to ensure that the fetter imposed on the individual is not used in circumstances for which it was not provided. Paragraph 4(2) of Sch 6, if capable of bearing a narrow or a wide construction, should in my judgment be given the wide construction, thus limiting the premises to which resolutions passed under para 3 can apply.

The meaning given to the words 'pleasure fair' by the Divisional Court in relation to all three appeals is that expressed in the judgment of Lord Widgery CJ in the *Leeds* case[1]. Lord Widgery CJ pointed out that the 1963 Act, as amended, uses the words 'pleasure fair' in two places and that the presumption is that the words are intended to bear the same meaning in both places. He continued[2]:

'Here, in the earlier use of the phrase "pleasure fair", the circumstances in my judgment are clear enough as to its meaning, because it will be remembered that the first reference to "pleasure fair" within s 49 were the words "at any pleasure fair consisting wholly or mainly of amusements provided by travelling showmen". The moment one talks about a "pleasure fair provided by travelling showmen" a blaze of light is thrown on the problem because we all know what is meant by that phrase. They may vary a little in individual constituents, but

---

1   [1974] 3 All ER 362, [1974] 1 WLR 1275
2   [1974] 3 All ER at 365, [1974] 1 WLR at 1278, 1279

everybody knows what you are talking about when you use that phrase. You have
at such fairs roundabouts, dodgems, hoop-la, cheap-jacks selling various articles   *a*
and fortune tellers—"all the fun of the fair". People use the phrase and it is
well known. It seems to me that a tribunal of fact required to construe the expression "pleasure fair consisting wholly or mainly of amusements provided
by travelling showmen" would be in no difficulty as to how an individual case
should be decided. When we come on to Sch 6 and we get "premises used or
to be used wholly or mainly for the purposes of a pleasure fair consisting wholly   *b*
or mainly of amusements", we have exactly the same phrase except that the
reference to travelling showmen is omitted. It seems to me that the proper way
to construe the difference is to regard the reference to "pleasure fair" in Sch 6
as having the same sort of meaning that it has in the travelling showmen pleasure
fair but, not being operated by travelling showmen, it can remain permanently
in one place.'   *c*

   With great respect to Lord Widgery CJ, I think he fell into error. Section 49(1)(c)
creates an exception to the requirement of a permit in respect of the premises. The
reason for creating the exception is apparent from the concluding words: '. . . which is
held on any day of a year on premises not previously used in that year on more than
twenty-seven days for the holding of such a pleasure fair.' The exception coincides   *d*
with the user of premises for a period for which planning permission for the use would
not have to be obtained. Both in that provision and in s 49(3)(e) the words 'such a
pleasure fair' appear. The plain indication, in my judgment, is that a pleasure fair
provided by travelling showmen is one type of pleasure fair but that the words
'pleasure fair' are not confined to that one type. It is not right in my judgment to
import the limitation imposed by the words 'provided by travelling showmen' in   *e*
the exception at s 49(1)(c) into the unqualified words 'pleasure fair' in para 4(2) of
Sch 6. The words 'pleasure fair' are to be given the same meaning in both places, but
in s 49(1)(c) and (2)(e) the Act is dealing with one particular form of pleasure fair.
For these reasons I am unable to agree with the construction placed on 'pleasure
fair' by the Divisional Court.
   But what is the meaning to be given to those words? 'Pleasure' and 'fair' are both   *f*
ordinary words in common usage. In combination 'pleasure fair' is not a phrase
used in common parlance. There is nothing in the ordinary use of language which I
find to be of assistance in defining what a 'pleasure fair' is. On the other hand I find
nothing in the description of 'prize bingo', as explained to the court, which in my
judgment would make it inappropriate to describe as a 'pleasure fair' premises used
for the purpose of prize bingo.   *g*
   The 1963 Act does not define 'pleasure fair'. In Part III of the Gaming Act 1968,
which provides for the use of gaming machines, s 34 contains provisions comparable
to those contained in s 49 of the 1963 Act. In s 34(1) premises used wholly or mainly
for the purpose of a pleasure fair in respect of which a s 49 permit is in force are referred
to at (c), and 'a travelling showmen's pleasure fair' is separately included at (d).
By s 52 of the 1968 Act 'travelling showmen's pleasure fair' is defined, but there is no   *h*
definition of 'pleasure fair'. The terms in which the travelling showmen's type of
pleasure fair is defined equate the activity with one for which an application for
planning permission for the user of land would not be required. I find in ss 34 and 52
of the 1968 Act support for the view that the use of premises as a pleasure fair is wider
than the use for a travelling showmen's pleasure fair but, apart from that measure
of support, the sections do not assist in defining 'pleasure fair'.   *j*
   The argument of counsel for the appellants is that 'pleasure fair' in the 1963 Act
has a statutory precedent, if not strictly a statutory origin, in the provisions of a number
of private Acts of Parliament, of standard clauses and model clauses drafted for the
purpose of incorporation in private Acts by committees of the House of Lords and the
House of Commons, and, finally, in the provisions of the Public Health Act 1961, s 75.

Examples of local private Acts are the Rochdale Corporation Act 1948[1], the Huddersfield Corporation Act 1949[2] and the West Bromwich Corporation Act 1949[3]. In each of those Acts it is provided 'the expression "pleasure fair" means any place . . . and anything similar to any of the foregoing'. That wording follows the wording of cl 146(2) of the Standard Clauses Revised Edition 1937. The Model Clauses (Revised Edition 1950), cl 111(2) and (3) reads:

'(2) In this section—(a) the expression "pleasure fair" means any place—(i) which is for the time being used wholly or mainly for providing (whether or not in combination with any other entertainment) any entertainment to which this section applies; and (ii) for admission to which or for the use of the contrivances in which a charge is made . . .

'(3) Subject to the provisions of the next following sub-section the entertainments to which this section applies are the following:—(a) circuses; (b) exhibitions of human beings or of performing animals; (c) merry-go-rounds, roundabouts, swings, switchback railways; (d) coco-nut shies, hoop-la, shooting galleries; (e) dodgems or other mechanical riding or driving contrivances; (f) automatic or other machines intended for entertainment or amusement; (g) anything similar to any of the foregoing.'

Section 75(1) of the Public Health Act 1961 empowers local authorities to make byelaws for regulating the hours during which pleasure fairs may be open to the public, for securing safe and adequate ingress to and egress from pleasure fairs and for the prevention and suppression of nuisances and the preservation of sanitary conditions, cleanliness, order and public safety at any pleasure fair. Section 75(2) and (3) defines 'pleasure fair' in the same terms as cl 111 of the model clauses which I have cited. Thus, there is a consistent definition of 'pleasure fair' in this sphere of local government. It seems to me beyond doubt that a local authority could make byelaws under s 75 regulating and controlling premises used wholly or mainly for prize bingo on the basis that the premises were used for a 'pleasure fair' within the meaning of the section. Is some other meaning to be given to 'pleasure fair' in the Betting, Gaming and Lotteries Act 1963? The Divisional Court in the *Leeds* case[4] found it impossible to say that the two pieces of legislation are so similar in purpose that Parliament can be taken as having intended in passing the 1963 Act to carry into it the detailed definition of 'pleasure fair' in the Public Health Act 1961. Counsel for the appellants argues that the Acts are in pari materia or so similar in purpose that it is permissible for the court to derive help in the construction of the 1963 Act from the provisions of the Public Health Act 1961 and the history of the use of the words 'pleasure fair' in earlier legislation. I have doubts whether the legislation can properly be said to be in pari materia. But the purpose of both s 75 of the Public Health Act 1961 and s 49 of the Betting, Gaming and Lotteries Act 1963 is to vest control in the local authority over premises used by the public for forms of entertainment. In the Public Health Act 1961 the provision is intended to give control over good order, discipline, safety and health hazards. In the 1963 Act it is intended to give control over the suitability of the premises and the person carrying on the activity on the premises by the method of granting and renewing permits. Non-compliance with byelaws applicable to the premises would be relevant to the grant or refusal of a permit. In my judgment the purpose behind the legislation is sufficiently similar to enable the court to be assisted in the way counsel for the appellants contends. Further, where there is no definition in the 1963 Act, but there is a definition, having a respectable history in statutory form, which must be applied by the same local

---

1 11 & 12 Geo 6 c xlvii
2 12 & 13 Geo 6 c xxxvii
3 12 & 13 Geo 6 c lii
4 [1974] 3 All ER 362, [1974] 1 WLR 1275

authorities as exercise the powers under s 49 of and Sch 6 to the 1963 Act, it would be contrary to good sense to give a different meaning to 'pleasure fair' where the words are used in that Act.

I would construe 'pleasure fair' in s 49 and in the Sch 6 to the 1963 Act in the sense defined in the Public Health Act 1961. On that basis, in my judgment, the premises involved in each of these appeals were a 'pleasure fair', the resolution of the local authority in each case could not apply to the premises and the decisions of the Crown Court were correct. It follows that the orders of the Divisional Court quashing those decisions were wrong and the appeals should be allowed in each case.

I turn to consider briefly the point taken by counsel for the appellants in his argument in the *Greenwich* case. It is that the borough council applied to the Divisional Court[1] at a time so long after the date of the order of the Crown Court that in the circumstances the court should, in the exercise of its discretion, refuse to make the order. The circumstances are those to which I have referred earlier in the judgment in which the appellants went ahead with their plans for the user of the premises and thereby incurred considerable expense. The facts are fully set out in the judgment of Lord Widgery CJ[2]. On the facts I would arrive at the same conclusion as the Divisional Court on this point. I agree with the statement of Lord Widgery CJ that the authorities support the proposition that since the remedy of certiorari is discretionary, the court can and sometimes should impose a tighter limitation than six months. As it is a question of the exercise of discretion, the conclusion in each case must depend on its own facts. As RSC Ord 53, r 2, expressly refers to six months, not a variable period such as 'a reasonable time', as the period beyond which leave shall not be granted, it may well be that the circumstances in which a shorter period of limitation should be applied will be rare. I find myself, however, differing from Lord Widgery CJ in the approach evidenced in his words[3]: 'I think that anyone who seeks to resist certiorari on the basis of lapse of time when less than six months had elapsed has to make out his case, and make out a strong case . . .' With great respect, I think that that is putting the burden on the wrong party. An applicant for certiorari seeks a discretionary remedy in his favour. Once an issue is raised as to delay in making the application it is, in my judgment, for the applicant to discharge the burden of showing that in all the circumstances he should, in the exercise of that discretion, be granted the relief sought. It is for the party resisting the application to establish those facts which he asserts as circumstances relevant to the exercise of discretion but, in my judgment, it is not for him to discharge the burden implicit in the words which I have quoted.

SHAW LJ. I agree that these appeals should be allowed, and as this court is differing from the decision of the Divisional Court, I briefly add my own reasons.

The crucial question common to all three appeals is whether premises where the game of bingo is played for prizes fall within the concept of what is referred to in Sch 6 to the Betting, Gaming and Lotteries Act 1963 as 'a pleasure fair consisting wholly or mainly of amusements'. The importance of the answer to this question arises from the provisions of that schedule in regard to the grant or renewal by a local authority of permits required by s 49 of the 1963 Act to enable premises to be used for affording amusements with prizes.

In general, the grant or renewal of such a permit is at the discretion of the local authority (Sch 6, para 7(2)); but there is an appeal to the Crown Court against refusal (para 8, adopting para 11 of Sch 9 to the Gaming Act 1968). Such an appeal is determined on the merits of the individual case and the decision of the Crown Court is final (para 10) so long as the appeal is competent.

1   [1975] 1 All ER 114, [1975] 2 WLR 310
2   [1975] 1 All ER at 117, [1975] 2 WLR at 313
3   [1975] 1 All ER at 118, [1975] 2 WLR at 314

a   There is, however, a situation in which merits do not count and an appeal against refusal does not lie. By Sch 6, para 3, a local authority is empowered to pass a resolution that it will not grant or renew any permit required by s 49 in respect of premises of a class specified in the resolution. So long as such a resolution is in force, an application for the grant or renewal of any permit for premises falling within the specified classes must be refused (para 6) regardless of merits. If an appeal to the Crown Court is instituted, that court is required to dismiss the appeal when it appears that b the premises fall within a class prescribed by a resolution of the local authority (para 9).

    Thus the exercise of the power of a local authority to pass such a resolution and the extent of the application of the resolution when passed are subject to no external control or review. It is manifest that a power so peremptory and untrammelled may be drastic in its consequences and arbitrary in its application. It derogates from the right of an owner or an occupier of premises to use them for purposes which are c not intrinsically unlawful and which might be considered innocuous or even beneficial so far as the public interest is concerned. It is equally plain that when a statute confers a power with such characteristics and potential consequences to the subject the limits of that power must be closely scrutinised and strictly drawn (see, e g, Re Bowman[1]). As a necessary corollary, any qualification of, or exemption from, the exercise of the power should be given as liberal a construction as is consonant with d the language used in the statute concerned.

    Schedule 6 makes a solitary exception to the operation of a resolution whereby a class of premises may be disqualified from being used for the provision of amusements with prizes. Paragraph 4 states that no resolution under Sch 6, para 3, shall have effect in relation to the grant or renewal of permits in respect of premises used or to be used wholly or mainly for the purposes of a pleasure fair consisting wholly or mainly of e amusements. In regard to such premises it is provided by para 7 that the grant of a permit shall be at the discretion of the appropriate authority and that the renewal of a permit shall not be refused save on certain specified grounds. Moreoover, where there is a refusal to grant or to renew a permit in respect of premises used for the purposes of a pleasure fair consisting wholly or mainly of amusements, an appeal lies on the merits to the Crown Court notwithstanding any resolution under para 3.

f   Hence the importance and significance of what is connoted by the phrase 'pleasure fair'. It is nowhere defined in the Gaming Acts. In the report of the hearing of the Leeds case in the Divisional Court[2], there is a passage where in the course of his judgment Lord Widgery CJ quotes the reference in s 49(1)(c) of the 1963 Act to 'any pleasure fair consisting wholly or mainly of amusements provided by travelling showmen'. He goes on to say:

g

    'The moment one talks about a "pleasure fair provided by travelling showmen" a blaze of light is thrown on the problem because we all know what is meant by that phrase. They vary a little in individual constituents, but everybody knows what you are talking about when you use that phrase.'

    The proposition thus stated is an attractive one but, with respect, it can hardly h claim a logical foundation. Section 49(1)(c) confers a special privilege on a particular species of pleasure fair which is there described. To argue from the particular to the general in order to arrive at a concept of the genus 'pleasure fair' is to follow a road which has no end. A later passage[3] in the same judgment quotes s 34(1) of the Gaming Act 1968, which ends thus:

j

    '. . . (c) on any premises used wholly or mainly for the purpose of a pleasure fair consisting wholly or mainly of amusements. . . and (d) a travelling showmen's pleasure fair.'

---

1   [1932] 2 KB 621 at 633, [1932] All ER Rep 257 at 261
2   [1974] 3 All ER 362 at 365, [1974] 1 WLR 1275 at 1278
3   [1974] 3 All ER at 365, [1974] 1 WLR at 1279

Lord Widgery CJ concluded[1] that the conjunction of those two passages in sequence
reinforced the view that 'pleasure fair' had the same broad sense in both those provisions. *a*
But this does not touch the question what *is* the broad sense in which the expression
'pleasure fair' is to be understood in the context of the Gaming Acts? When proprietary rights are either imperilled or protected according to the answer one gives
to that question, it does not seem to me acceptable to employ the logic of the man
in the street who says that he has no need of a precise definition of a horse since he
knows one when he sees it.   *b*

The attention of this court was called, as the attention of the Divisional Court was
also, to a number of Acts in which the expression 'pleasure fair' occurs and where it is
given a statutory definition in the respective Acts of Parliament. Most of them are
private or local Acts and their terms are based on model clauses formulated by
Parliamentary committees. The definition of 'pleasure fair' common to all the
statutes concerned is contained in a section which reads thus: *c*

'. . . the expression "pleasure fair" means any place—(i) which is for the time
being used wholly or mainly for providing (whether or not in combination with
any other entertainment) any entertainment to which this section applies; and
(ii) for admission to which or for the use of the contrivances in which a charge
is made . . .'   *d*

It may here be observed parenthetically that this last element corresponds exactly
to the incidence of the provisions of s 49 of the Betting, Gaming and Lotteries Act
1963, the sidenote to which is 'Provision of amusements etc. at certain commercial
entertainments'. The definition continues by setting out the entertainments to which
the section applies. They are—

'. . . (a) circuses; (b) exhibitions of human beings or of performing animals; *e*
(c) merry-go-rounds, roundabouts, swings, switchback railways; (d) coco-nut
shies, hoop-las, shooting galleries, bowling alleys; (e) dodgems or other mechanical
riding or driving contrivances; (f) automatic or other machines intended for
entertainment or amusement; (g) anything similar to any of the foregoing.'

This definition is found also in s 75 of the Public Health Act 1961. Two features of *f*
it call for particular notice. The first is that it invariably appears in the context of the
functions of a local authority to supervise and control places of entertainment in the
area which it administers. Thus, by way of example, in relation to pleasure fairs
as defined in the terms which have been stated, the West Riding County Council
(General Powers) Act 1951 gives power to the local authority to make byelaws for
regulating the hours during which they may be open, for securing public safety, for
the prevention and suppression of nuisances and for the preservation of public order *g*
and of cleanliness.

The second feature is the reference to automatic or other machines intended for
entertainment or amusement. This is a comparatively modern addition to the list
of entertainments any of which may (whether or not in combination with any other)
make any place a pleasure fair. It demonstrates that in considering the nature of a
pleasure fair one is not restricted to traditional ideas of 'the fun of the fair' such as *h*
coconut shies or bearded ladies. Contemporary trends are not to be ignored in seeking
to identify a pleasure fair in concrete terms.

It appears to me to be evident that the Public Health Act 1961 and the numerous
private Acts incorporating this definition are designed in this regard to serve one and
the same function in relation to pleasure fairs, namely control in the public interest.
This is, as I see it, exactly what the Betting, Gaming and Lotteries Act 1963 is designed *j*
to do in relation to pleasure fairs though from a different standpoint of public interest.
It is all in the same field.

It would be odd indeed if in two aspects of this same function different definitions

1 [1974] 3 All ER at 365, [1974] 1 WLR at 1279

of the same subject-matter should obtain, and that the same official in the same local
a authority should have to ascribe to the same phrase different meanings according to
whether he is dealing with the premises at which a game is permitted to be played,
on the one hand, or with the hours during which it may be played, on the other.
Good sense as well as consistency in the application and administration of the law are
a solid enough foundation for the view that the same idea is to be understood when the
same words are used in contexts which are so closely related one to another.

b   I therefore come to the conclusion that the definition of 'pleasure fair' in s 75 of the
Public Health Act 1961, and in other statutes relating to matters of local government,
is properly to be adopted in the construction of the Gaming Acts wherever the same
expression is used.

This is sufficient to dispose of the main question raised by these appeals, but in my
view there is another approach which would lead to the same conclusion. I revert to
c the passage[1] in Lord Widgery CJ's judgment in the *Leeds* case when he spoke of the
expression 'pleasure fair' as having the same broad sense wherever it was used in the
Gaming Acts. As I have said, the problem of construction is to ascertain what that
broad sense is. This cannot be done by conjuring up some diffuse picture or impression. It is necessary to begin with fundamentals. If the phrase 'pleasure fair' is
not to be regarded as a term of art but as a noun qualified by an adjective, each word
d being understood in its ordinary sense, it can only mean a fair principally devoted to
providing entertainment and amusement in contradistinction to a trade or market
fair which has the promotion of commerce as its object. How is the definition of a
pleasure fair in this sense to be attempted? All fairs are places of public resort, and
it is a simple step to decide that pleasure fairs are places of public resort for entertainment and amusement of a traditional character. What then is the common
e denominator of such diversions as coconut shies, hoop-la, exhibitions of freaks,
dodgem cars and so on? The attribute shared by these and other forms of the fun of
the fair is that the entertainment afforded is of a rudimentary and sometimes a crude
kind. It demands neither intellectual judgment nor aesthetic appreciation; and if it
involves any skill at all, it is at a minimal level and of a simple sort. The game of
prize bingo which has been described fully in the judgment of Lord Denning MR
f conforms in all respects to these common characteristics of the fun of the fair. What
particular form the entertainment or amusement provided takes must depend on
the mood of the time. Traditional forms become outmoded or cease to entertain
and fresh ones take their place. Roll-a-penny gives way to bingo and so on. Variety
cannot be an essential so long as a popular form of amusement is provided. If a
particular amusement has for the time being caught the imagination or interest of a
g substantial part of the public, why should it not be purveyed by itself for general
enjoyment at a fair? Bearing in mind the considerations earlier adverted to, which
demand a liberal construction of an exemption from a statutory provision which
may operate harshly, I would hold on first principles that the expression 'pleasure
fair' is apt to include premises where facilities are provided for playing prize bingo
whether or not any form of amusement or entertainment is available. On these
h grounds I would allow all three appeals and make the orders proposed. There
remains a further question which arose in the *Greenwich* case where the appellants
resisted the application by the borough council for an order of certiorari on the ground
that there had been unreasonable delay in applying for leave. The circumstances
out of which that assertion developed are fully set out in the judgment of Lord
Widgery CJ[2], and I need not now recount them. In the result, the contention that
j delay might serve to defeat an application for leave was recognised as having substance
and validity, but on the facts of the case the court held that the order for certiorari
should go.

---

1 [1974] 3 All ER at 365, [1974] 1 WLR at 1279
2 [1975] 1 All ER 114 at 117, [1975] 2 WLR 310 at 313

RSC Ord 53, r 2(2), provides:

'Leave shall not be granted to apply for an order of certiorari . . . unless the application for leave is made within 6 months after the date of the proceedings . . . or . . . the delay is accounted for to the satisfaction of the Court or judge to whom the application is made . . .'

Lord Widgery CJ said[1]:

'I think that the circumstances in which a shorter period of limitation should be applied will be rare. I think that anyone who seeks to resist certiorari on the basis of lapse of time when less than six months had elapsed has got to make out his case and make out a strong case, but I am prepared for the purposes of this judgment to assert that, given a sufficiently strong case, the court can and should impose stricter limits on the application for certiorari.'

The question is whether that passage accurately states where the onus lies in a case where application for leave is made after substantial delay but within the period of six months. Lord Widgery CJ, with whom the other members of the court agreed, was of the view that in such a situation the party seeking to resist the application would be required to show some exceptional circumstance of hardship or injustice as a result of the delay if the court were to be persuaded to reject the application. 'For my part', said Lord Widgery CJ[1]:

'I have no doubt that that six months' time limit, which has been in the rules for nearly 100 years, is generally regarded throughout the country as being a limit within which an applicant can safely act.'

It seems to me, as to the other members of this court, that if the view adverted to by Lord Widgery CJ has developed, it has done so because of an erroneous understanding of RSC Ord 53, r 2, and its predecessors.

An applicant for a prerogative order (or in earlier history a prerogative writ) is not in the position of a litigant who seeks to assert some right to which he claims he is entitled. He is rather a suppliant who seeks to invoke those remedial measures on the ground that the High Court would wish to correct some irregularity in the administration of justice which has caused him to be aggrieved so that justice may be done. Whether the order sought will be granted or refused is a matter wholly within the court's discretion; prerogative orders are not to be claimed as of right.

Accordingly it is for an applicant to show that in all the circumstances justice will be better served if the order goes than if it does not. If there has been unreasonable delay, then even though the application for leave is made within the six months, resulting hardship to an opposing party may well be a reason for refusing the order sought. It is true that the six months can be extended, but only if the delay is accounted for to the satisfaction of the court; and, if it is so accounted for, the question whether the case is a proper one for granting relief will only be answered in the affirmative if the applicant shows that in all the circumstances the demands of justice are best served by that answer. It is for him to show that on balance it is right to make the order and not for an opposing party to show it would be wrong to do so.

As I read RSC Ord 53, r 2(2), its object is to impose a limit in time on the jurisdiction of the court to grant an order. It is not its intention to enlarge the opportunity of an applicant to seek it.

The history of the matter set out in the leading judgment in the Divisional Court[2] reveals, in my view, that the Greenwich council were guilty of unreasonable and unwarrantable delay in applying for an order of certiorari; and also that the then respondents were thereby caused severe hardship. I see no ground for attributing

1   [1975] 1 All ER at 118, [1975] 2 WLR at 314
2   [1975] 1 All ER at 117, [1975] 2 WLR at 313

a that hardship to their having incurred heavy expense in anticipation of planning consent. In the first place, they did get that consent; and in the second place, businessmen cannot be expected to enter on a fallow period in regard to their business interests while someone in the offices of a local authority ponders for months what, if anything, is to be done next. Bureaucratic delays may sometimes be difficult to avoid, but private interests ought not to suffer because of them. On this ground, if it stood alone, I would allow the appeal in the *Greenwich* case.

b

Appeals allowed. Leave to appeal to the House of Lords granted to Leeds City District Council and the London Borough of Lewisham.

Solicitors: *Mincoff, Science & Gold*, Newcastle (for Mr Walker); *Philip Ross, Elliston & Bieber* (for Mr Hunt and Mr Smith); *Sharpe, Pritchard & Co* (for the Leeds City District

c Council); *Town Clerk* (for the London Borough of Greenwich); *Borough Solicitor* (for the London Borough of Lewisham).

Gavin Gore-Andrews Esq Barrister.

d

Federal Commerce and Navigation Co Ltd v Tradax Export SA

The Maratha Envoy

e

QUEEN'S BENCH DIVISION
DONALDSON J
14th, 15th, 23rd MAY 1975

f *Shipping – Demurrage – Time lost waiting for berth – Port charterparty – Arrived ship – Time at which ship becomes an arrived ship – Time at which ship begins waiting for berth within area of port – Ship required to wait at anchorage outside port because of congestion – Ship sailing to port and returning immediately to anchorage – Whether ship having arrived on entering area of port before returning to anchorage.*

g The charterers chartered a ship from the owners on the Baltimore Form C charterparty. Her destination was 'One port out of Amsterdam or Rotterdam or Antwerp or Ghent or one safe port German North Sea all in Charterers' option' where she was to deliver her cargo. On 1st December 1970 the charterers ordered the master to proceed to the River Weser and, on 4th or 5th December, gave a further order to discharge at Bremen. It was common ground, however, that that was a bad nomination since the ship's draft exceeded the limits for discharge at that port. The

h ship arrived at the Weser light vessel on 7th December and anchored. Berths in the available ports in the River Weser, i e Nordenham, Brake and Bremen, were allocated by a committee. In the event of congestion vessels were required to wait at the light vessel or up-stream in the Weser and to take their turn, there being no waiting areas within the limits of those ports. On 7th December a second nomina-

j tion was made requiring the vessel to proceed to Bremen after lightening at Brake. That nomination also was bad, since it involved two ports of discharge. On 8th December the vessel set course for the Weser, although there was no available berth, and proceeded up-stream to Brake. She then returned to the light vessel. On 10th December the charterers specified Brake as the port of discharge. No berth was available, however, but on 12th December the ship repeated the excursion up the River Weser to Brake. There she turned, using her anchor to accomplish the manoeuvre, and again returned to the light vessel. On 29th December a berth was **a** allocated to the ship and she sailed for Brake, berthing there on 30th December. A dispute arose between the parties, the owners claiming that the ship had become an arrived ship when she entered the legal or commercial area of the port of Brake on one or other of her excursions up the River Weser.

Held – Under a port charterparty a vessel became an 'arrived ship' when the voyage **b** had ended at the port named and she was waiting for a berth. Accordingly, even if she had passed within the area of the port of Brake on either of her two trips up the river, the ship had not become an arrived ship for on neither trip had she anchored, except for the purpose of the turning manoeuvre, or come to rest or, in any real sense, waited. It followed, therefore, that the ship had not become an arrived ship before 30th December and the owners' claim failed (see p 298 f to p 299 c, post).   **c**
The Johanna Oldendorff [1973] 3 All ER 148 applied.

Notes
For the meaning of arrived ship, see 35 Halsbury's Laws (3rd Edn) 366-368, paras 524, 525, and for cases on the commencement of laytime, see 41 Digest (Repl) 477-482, 2514-2557.   **d**

Cases referred to in judgment
Cantiere Navale Triestina v Russian Soviet Naphtha Export Agency [1925] 2 KB 172, [1925] All ER Rep 530, 94 LJKB 579, 133 LT 162, 16 Asp MLC 501, CA, 41 Digest (Repl) 475, 2501.
Delian Spirit, The, Shipping Developments Corpn v V/O Sojuzneftexport [1971] 2 All ER **e** 1060, [1972] 1 QB 103, [1971] 2 WLR 1434, [1971] 1 Lloyd's Rep 506, CA.
Johanna Oldendorff, The, E L Oldendorff & Co GmbH v Tradax Export SA [1973] 3 All ER 148, [1974] AC 479, [1973] 3 WLR 382, [1973] 2 Lloyd's Rep 285, HL.
Leonis Steamship Co Ltd v Rank Ltd [1908] 1 KB 499, 77 LJKB 224, 13 Com Cas 136, CA, 41 Digest (Repl) 478, 2530.
Roland-Linie Schiffahrt GmbH v Spillers Ltd [1956] 3 All ER 383, [1957] 1 QB 109, [1956] **f** 3 WLR 620, [1956] 2 Lloyd's Rep 211, 41 Digest (Repl) 467, 2443.
Sociedad Financiera de Bienes Raices SA v Agrimpex Hungarian Trading Co for Agricultural Products, The Aello [1960] 2 All ER 578, [1961] AC 135, [1960] 3 WLR 145, [1960] 1 Lloyd's Rep 623, HL; affg [1958] 2 All ER 695, [1958] 2 QB 385, [1958] 3 WLR 152, [1958] 2 Lloyd's Rep 65, CA; affg [1957] 3 All ER 626, [1957] 1 WLR 1228, [1957] 2 Lloyd's Rep 423, 41 Digest (Repl) 333, 1304.   **g**

Cases also cited
Armement Adolf Deppe v John Robinson & Co Ltd [1917] 2 KB 204, [1916-17] All ER Rep 1084, CA.
Carga del Sur Compania Naviera SA v Ross T Smyth & Co Ltd [1962] 2 Lloyd's Rep 147.
Zim Israel Navigation Co Ltd v Tradax Export SA, The Timna [1970] 2 Lloyd's Rep 409; **h** affd [1971] 2 Lloyd's Rep 91, CA.

Action
By a writ issued on 21st March 1973 Federal Commerce and Navigation Co Ltd ('the owners') brought an action against Tradax Export SA ('the charterers') claiming damages for breach of a charterparty dated 8th January 1970 and/or demurrage thereunder **j** amounting to £16,124·13 and interest thereon. By their points of claim the owners alleged that the charterers had chartered from the owners vessels to be nominated to perform eight consecutive voyages from Great Lakes/St Lawrence ports 'to one port out of Amsterdam or Rotterdam or Antwerp or Ghent or one safe port German North Sea all in Charterers' option', the vessels to deliver the cargo 'always afloat,

a agreeable to Bills of Lading'; that on the eighth voyage, for which the charterers had nominated the ship Maratha Envoy, the charterers had been in breach of the charterparty in failing to nominate a discharging port at any time prior to 11th December 1970 or alternatively 10th December; and that the owners were entitled to demurrage on the basis that the Maratha Envoy had arrived at Brake, the port nominated by the charterers, on 12th December; alternatively that, if a purported nomination made by the charterers on 7th December was valid, the ship

b had arrived at Brake on 8th December. By their defence the charterers admitted that they had failed to nominate a discharging port prior to 7th December or alternatively 10th December, but they denied that they were liable to pay any damages on that account, because that breach had not caused the owners any loss since the ship had not arrived at Brake until 30th December. The facts are set out in the judgment of Donaldson J.

c

Anthony Colman for the owners.
Christopher Staughton QC and *Nicholas Legh-Jones* for the charterers.

Cur adv vult

d 23rd May. **DONALDSON J** read the following judgment: This case involves a claim by shipowners for demurrage. It also involves the problem of how and when a vessel becomes an arrived ship in the context of the port of Brake on the River Weser.

On 28th November 1970 the Maratha Envoy completed loading a cargo of soya bean meal and yellow corn at Chicago. She had been chartered from her owners on the Baltimore Form C charterparty. Her destination was 'One port out of

e Amsterdam or Rotterdam or Antwerp or Ghent or one safe port German North Sea all in Charterers' option' where she was to deliver the cargo 'always afloat, agreeable to Bills of Lading'.

The charter provided that the master was to apply to the charterers' agents for discharging port orders 96 hours before the vessel was due off Lands End and the charterers' agents were to give such orders within 48 hours of the master's application.

f On 1st December 1970 the charterers ordered the master to proceed to the River Weser. This was followed on 4th or 5th December by the more specific order to discharge at Bremen. Unfortunately, the vessel drew 32-33 feet and there was a draught limitation of 31 feet for discharge at Bremen. It follows, as is now admitted, that this was a bad nomination. At 22.10 hours on 7th December 1970 the vessel arrived at the Weser light vessel and anchored. There she remained, apart from two brief

g excursions up the River Weser, until late on 29th December 1970, when she sailed for Brake, berthing at 04.00 hours on 30th December. But it is the excursions which matter, for the owners claim that one or other made the Martha Envoy an 'arrived ship'. If they are right, the charterers owe them something of the order of £30,000 as demurrage. If they are wrong, the whole cost of waiting falls on the owners.

The River Weser contains four ports. Coming from the sea, they are Bremerhaven,

h Nordenham, Brake and Bremen. Bremerhaven is not a grain port. Berths in the other three ports are allocated by a committee, known as the Kleine Allocation, which is composed of representatives of the silo owners at the three grain ports. The chairman of the committee is always the chairman of the Bremer Warehousing Co. When a grain vessel is bound for Weser ports, the agents of both owners and charterers telephone to the Kleine Allocation giving details of its cargo and the

j estimated time of arrival. If there is no congestion, a berth is allocated in time for the vessel to go straight there, subject only, on occasion, to a brief wait to catch the tide. But if there is congestion, vessels must wait for a berth to become available. This they do at Blexen Reede, which is immediately up-stream of Bremerhaven, at Hohe Weg, which is at the mouth of the river just beyond the junction with the River Jade, or at the Weser light vessel which is to seaward of the island of

Wangerooge. There are no waiting areas for large grain vessels within the limits
of the ports of Nordenham, Brake or Bremen.   *a*
    Vessels take their turn for a berth from the time of arrival at the light vessel,
irrespective of whether they wait there or at one of the other two waiting areas.
The only occasion when vessels are taken out of turn is when doing so will reduce
the overall congestion. This can happen if the vessel first on turn cannot give over-
side discharge, whereas a later arrival can do so, or if a berth becomes available but
the draught is insufficient for the first vessel. But turn is never affected by a con-   *b*
sideration of the identity of the charterer or of his liability to pay the shipowner
demurrage if the vessel is delayed. No grain ship may berth other than at a berth
allocated to it by the Kleine Allocation.
    As I have said, the first nomination of a discharging port was a nullity, because,
on the vessel's draught, she could not lie always afloat at Bremen. The second
nomination was made sometime on 7th December 1970, and required the vessel to   *c*
proceed to Bremen after lightening at Brake. It was not passed directly to the master
by radio as required by the charterparty, but seems to have been sent to the owners'
agents. It was also given long after the proper time. This second nomination sparked
off a flurry of telex messages between the owners, the charterers and their respective
agents. The terms of these exchanges do not matter. What does matter is that the
vessel weighed anchor at 03.00 hours on 8th December 1970, only five hours after   *d*
her arrival at the light vessel, and set course for the Weser. This manoeuvre was
unique. Grain vessels cannot berth in the Weser unless a berth has been allocated
by the Kleine Allocation. None had been allotted. There are no waiting places in
any of the three grain ports and anchoring in the river in or near the area of the ports
is forbidden. The river is a compulsory pilotage area and on no previous occasion
had the pilots ever been asked, or if asked had ever agreed, to take a vessel up river   *e*
when there was no berth for her. However, on this occasion the pilots had agreed
to take the vessel up river to Brake on the flood tide on the strict condition that
she was then turned round and went back to the light vessel, whilst there was still
sufficient water to enable her to do so. With the aid of three tugs and two pilots,
the vessel completed her excursion up river at position no 1. This, it is agreed, is at
the (t) in the word 'Solltiefe' (or dredged channel) where it appears on German   *f*
chart no 5 a little south of km 42. When the manoeuvre had been completed, or
at all events when she began her return journey to the sea, the vessel had drifted
downstream to position no 2. This, it is agreed, is on the leading line in the middle
of the dredged channel to the east of the word 'Klippkanne' on the same chart. The
time at which the vessel turned was about 07.20 hours and she was back at
Bremerhaven before it was possible to tender notice of readiness at 09.00 hours.   *g*
Needless to say, the notice was rejected. The vessel never obtained clearance from
either the health or customs authorities. After this excusion, happily described by
counsel for the charterers as a 'voyage of convenience', all concerned discussed by
telex whether the vessel had become an arrived ship at Brake. No conclusion was
reached and each party took up irreconcilable positions. In the middle of this discussion the charterers seem to have become afraid that the vessel might try to dis-   *h*
charge at some port other than in the Weser and warned the owners that, if they
did so, they would be liable to the receivers, who held bills of lading calling for discharge partly in Bremen and partly in the River Weser. They also seemed to have
come to the conclusion that the nomination of Bremen after lightening at Brake
was no better than that of Bremen simpliciter.
    In my judgment, they were right. The first nomination was bad because the   *j*
vessel on her draught could not lie safely afloat at Bremen, if indeed she could have
got there at all. The second nomination was bad, either for the same reason or
because, there being no lightening clause, the order involved two ports of discharge.
On 10th December 1970 the charterers therefore made their third, and only effective,
nomination of a discharging port when they specified Brake.

In the light of the threat that some of the receivers were entitled to require de-
a livery at Bremen, the owners naturally and reasonably sought and obtained the
receivers' agreement to discharge at Brake before taking any further action. However, this having been done, the vessel weighed anchor at 07.30 hours on Saturday, 12th
December 1970, and set off on her second excursion up the River Weser. This, like
the first, was a pure 'voyage of convenience', because once again there was no available berth and the pilots were only prepared to take her up river if she returned
b to the light vessel on the same tide. The second voyage was in fact a carbon copy
of the first, including the turning point and the drift down river to position no 2.
But on this occasion she obtained special health clearance at or whilst passing
Bremerhaven. No customs clearance was ever obtained, since this is only given
when a vessel has berthed. As the vessel turned during office hours at about
11.45 hours, it was possible to give notice of readiness whilst the vessel was within
c a stone's throw of the berths at Brake, but this notice too was rejected.

Commercially, these two trips up the river were a complete nonsense. As Sellers J
said in *Roland-Linie Schiffahrt v Spillers*[1], of a similar, but hypothetical, trip from the
Spurn Head anchorage to Hull and back: 'It would have been an idle and wasteful
formality...' But the two trips were undertaken and it is necessary to consider
whether they had any, and if so what, legal effect. The claims by the owners are
d complicated in form, but in substance counsel on their behalf says that (a) the vessel
became an arrived ship at Brake on 8th or 12th December 1970; (b) the cost of waiting
at the light vessel until she weighed anchor on whichever trip led to the vessel becoming an arrived ship is recoverable as damages for failure to give discharging port
orders timeously; and (c) once the vessel became an arrived ship, lay-time began
to run and, as soon as the remaining lay-time was exhausted, the vessel came on
e demurrage. Counsel for the charterers replied that the vessel never became an
arrived ship before 30th December 1970 and that, although the discharging port
orders were given late, the owners suffered no damage. Even if they had been given
sooner, the vessel could not have 'arrived' earlier than that date. Although he was
inclined to argue, in the alternative, that if the vessel became an arrived ship on
12th December, the charterers were not responsible for the delay between the
f moment on 10th December when the third (and good) nomination was given and
the moment when the vessel weighed anchor on 12th December, this refinement
can be ignored because this delay was the inevitable consequence of the charterers'
suggestion that the bill of lading holders had been given independent rights. If the
owners are right and the vessel became an arrived ship on 8th or 12th December,
they clearly succeed in their demurrage claim. It is also reasonable to assume that
if a valid nomination had been made at an earlier time, the vessel would have proceeded past the Weser light vessel on a trip similar to those which she undertook
on 8th and 12th December and there would have been no delay at the light vessel.
Accordingly, on this hypothesis, the owners would also succeed in that part of their
claim which depends on the charterers' failure to give a timeous nomination. The
only real issue is thus whether the ship became an arrived ship on either 8th or
12th December.

Counsel for the owners submits that the ship, whether at the light vessel or in
the river, was commercially at the immediate and effective disposition of the charterers. At the light vessel she was at a place where waiting ships usually lie. Whilst
on passage between there and Brake, she was even more immediately at their disposition. Although she had no health or customs clearance on 8th December and
no customs clearance on 12th December, the obtaining of these clearances was a
formality which would have caused no delay. Accordingly, their absence is immaterial
to a decision on whether the vessel was an arrived ship: see *The Delian Spirit*[2]. Thus
far I am with him.

1   [1956] 3 All ER 383 at 386, [1957] 1 QB 109 at 120
2   [1971] 2 All ER 1060, [1972] 1 QB 103

Counsel for the owners goes on to submit that when the vessel turned in the river she was within the legal limits of the port of Brake. The fact that she could not remain there he dismisses on the footing that once a ship has arrived, lay-time runs even if she leaves the port, provided only that the departure does not constitute a breach of charterparty on the part of the owners: see *Cantiere Navale Triestina v Russian Soviet Naphtha Export Agency*[1].

Most ports have defined limits, even if there are sometimes different limits for different purposes. Brake is an exception. The town itself, the Binnenhafen, the Kielholhafen and the Holzhafen all lie on the west bank of the river. On this bank the port extends to the north to a point which is just to seaward of the place where the vessel turned. She therefore either crossed or passed by the northern boundary of the port. But which was it?

The dredged channel which passes the entrance to the Binnenhafen and goes on to Bremen is controlled by the Federal and not by the Brake port authorities. Counsel for the owners sought to persuade me that this did not matter, because the port of Brake extended to an area on the east bank of the river opposite the town. The port was, in his submission, 'a port with a hole' and it was sufficient that the vessel was in the hole. Unfortunately, the evidence did not bear this out. There was evidence that the port authority had built a jetty on the east bank of the river with the permission of the Federal authorities. But Herr Naumann, the manager of the Bremen branch of the charterers' agents, told me that it was not used for commercial purposes, and photographs suggest that the bank behind it is used for recreation. In any event, one jetty extending into the river does not make a port or part of a port. Futhermore, the jetty was built in 1973 and I am concerned with the position in 1970.

I have therefore to find an eastern boundary in, or at all events at the edge of, the river itself. This boundary is the subject of a long-standing dispute between the Federal government and the government of Lower Saxony. The former denies that the port of Brake includes any part of the river, whereas the latter claims that the port extends into the river for about 40 metres from the west bank. Part of the vessel may in fact have crossed this line during the turning manoeuvre. I do not think that I have to decide this German constitutional dispute, even for the limited purpose of determining the rights of the parties to this action, and I would not presume to go further. If the Federal government is right, a grain ship lying alongside the quay and discharging at Brake never enters the port. If the government of Lower Saxony is right, she is just inside the limits of the port at this moment. But we are talking about a relatively narrow river and, in a commercial legal sense, vessels must in my judgment be taken to be within the port of Brake when they are off the quay, and I think that in that sense a vessel enters the port when she passes the northern boundary where it meets the river near the refinery.

Counsel for the owners submits that this finding is enough for the owners. But I am afraid that it is not. There was a time when *Leonis v Rank*[2], was the last word on what was an arrived ship. Then it was *The Aello*[3]. Currently, thanks to the determination of Tradax Export SA, the charterers in the present action, it is *The Johanna Oldendorff*[4]. Perhaps it will one day be the Maratha Envoy. Meanwhile, I have to apply the law as laid down in *The Johanna Oldendorff*[4]. Of course, the speeches of their Lordships are not to be construed as if they were a statute, but the sense is clear. A ship is arrived when she has come to rest within the port[5], and either is at a place where waiting ships usually lie or is waiting at some other place in the port[6].

1   [1925] 2 KB 172, [1925] All ER Rep 530
2   [1908] 1 KB 499
3   *Sociedad Financiera de Bienes Raices SA v Agrimpex Hungarian Trading Co for Agricultural Products* [1960] 2 All ER 578, [1961] AC 135
4   [1973] 3 All ER 148, [1974] AC 479
5   [1973] 3 All ER at 157, [1974] AC at 535, per Lord Reid
6   [1973] 3 All ER at 157, [1974] AC at 535, 536, per Lord Reid

A ship is arrived when she has ended her voyage at the port named[1]. A ship is arrived
a and the voyage stage ends when she is moored at a convenient place from which
she can get to a berth as soon as one is vacant[2].

Personally, I doubt whether it matters whether the vessel is moored or anchored
or indeed whether she has come to rest. If the owner prefers to let his vessel lie in
the appropriate place and hold her there by engine power, or even to circulate gently
around the appropriate area, that is his privilege. But the essential feature is that
b the voyage shall have ended and the vessel be waiting. This never happened in the
case of the Maratha Envoy. On the second trip she dropped an anchor to assist in
the turning manoeuvre, but on neither trip did she ever anchor in any other sense
or moor or come to rest or, in any real sense, wait. She was on a trip to Brake and
back to the light vessel, with no pause other than such as was inherent in the
manoeuvre of turning on to a reciprocal course in a very narrow fairway. This,
c in my judgment, does not constitute arrival in a commercial or in a legal sense. It
follows that the vessel was never an arrived ship before 30th December 1970.

On this conclusion, the failure to give orders timeously caused the owners no loss
and such demurrage as was due if lay-time began to run only on 30th December 1970
has already been paid. The owners' claims therefore fail and must be dismissed.
I would only add that if my decision is correct, no ship in the history of commercial
d law has been, or is ever likely to be, nearer to arriving without actually doing so.

The solution to this problem is to hand in the 'Weser lightship clause', which,
I am told, provides for vessels waiting at the lightship for a berth to become available
to be treated as being arrived at their port of destination, subject to the owners'
bearing the cost of shifting to the berth when it is available. Owners can press for
the inclusion of such a clause in their charterparties, but, if they do so, it will probably
e be reflected in the freight rate.

*Judgment for the charterers on claim for demurrage; judgment for owners on admitted claim
for expenses of shifting vessel from Brake to Bremen.*

f Solicitors: *Holman, Fenwick & Willan* (for the owners); *Richards, Butler & Co* (for
the charterers).

E H Hunter Esq   Barrister.

---

1 [1973] 3 All ER at 171, 172, [1974] AC at 552, per Viscount Dilhorne
2 [1973] 3 All ER at 176, [1974] AC at 557, 558, per Lord Diplock

Heywood v Wellers (a firm)

COURT OF APPEAL, CIVIL DIVISION

LORD DENNING MR, JAMES AND BRIDGE LJJ

15th OCTOBER, 13th NOVEMBER 1975

Contract – Breach – Damages – Mental distress – Solicitor – Circumstances in which damages for mental distress may be recovered against solicitor – Within solicitor's contemplation that mental distress likely to result from failure to perform contract with client – Solicitor employed by client to apply for injunction to protect her from molestation by man – Interim injunction obtained – Solicitor failing to enforce injunction after further breaches – Client suffering mental distress in consequence of continued molestation – Whether client entitled to recover damages for mental distress.

On 5th February 1973 the plaintiff instructed a firm of solicitors to apply for an injunction to restrain a man called M from molesting her. The solicitors were negligent in the conduct of the litigation. In particular, they obtained an interim injunction on 27th February restraining M from molesting the plaintiff, but when M again molested the plaintiff on 20th April in breach of the injunction, they failed to enforce the injunction by bringing M before the court. It was probable that if M had been brought before the court and had been warned, no further molestation would have occurred. As a result of the failure to enforce the injunction, the plaintiff was again molested by M on 25th May and on 8th November. She suffered mental distress in consequence of the molestation committed on those dates. In the course of the litigation the plaintiff had paid £168 on account of costs but, in view of the solicitors' conduct of the litigation, she refused to pay any further costs and asked the solicitors to discontinue it. They served notice of discontinuance. Acting in person the plaintiff brought an action in the county court against the solicitors claiming the return of the £168 paid in costs, and damages of £150 for negligence and as compensation for her time and effort spent in conducting the action against the solicitors. The judge held that the solicitors had been negligent. He expressed the view that the solicitors could set off such costs as were recoverable by them in the injunction litigation against the damages recoverable by the plaintiff for negligence; in the end, however, he held that the solicitors were not entitled to any costs in the injunction litigation, but that if they repaid the £168 paid for costs by the plaintiff she should not be entitled to recover any further sum in respect of damages for negligence. The plaintiff appealed, conducting the appeal in person.

Held – (i) The plaintiff was entitled to recover damages for the mental distress which she had suffered as a result of the molestation consequent on the solicitors' negligent failure to enforce the injunction. The services for which the parties had contracted were that the solicitors should take action to protect the plaintiff from molestation. At the time of the contract it was, therefore, within the solicitors' contemplation, and was reasonably foreseeable, that if they negligently failed to enforce any remedy which was obtained to stop the molestation, it was likely to continue and distress to the plaintiff was likely to result. The damages for the mental distress should be assessed at £150, whether it was assumed that damages ran from the date of the first breach of the injunction, 20th April, or only (per James LJ) from the date of the second breach; there should be deducted from that sum £25 for the costs which the plaintiff would have incurred if the solicitors had performed their duty and enforced the injunction. Accordingly, the plaintiff was entitled to recover damages for negligence of £125, in addition to the return of the £168 paid for costs (see p 306 g to p 307 d, p 308 h and j, p 309 e to g and p 310 a to c and g to p 311 b, post); *Jarvis v Swan's Tours Ltd* [1973] 1 All ER 71 applied; *Cook v S* [1967] 1 All ER 299 distinguished.

(ii) As the law stood[a], the plaintiff could not be compensated in damages for her
a time, effort and strain in conducting the action and appeal in person; work done
and time spent in conducting an action were the subject of costs in the action
and not damages, and a litigant in person was only entitled to recover as costs her
out-of-pocket expenses (see p 307 d to f, p 308 g and p 310 f, post); *Buckland v Watts*
[1969] 2 All ER 985 applied.

Per Lord Denning MR. The solicitors were not entitled to recover any costs in
b the injunction litigation. Their contract with the plaintiff was an entire contract
which they were bound to carry on to the end and, not having done so, they were
not entitled to any costs. Furthermore, since the work which they had done was
useless, because it did nothing to forward the object which the client had in view,
to protect her from molestation, they could recover nothing for it (see p 306 b to e,
post); *Underwood, Son & Piper v Lewis* [1894] 2 QB 306 and dictum of Tindal CJ in
c *Hill v Featherstonhaugh* (1831) 7 Bing at 571, 572 applied.

Notes
For a solicitor's liability for negligence, see 36 Halsbury's Laws (3rd Edn) 99-102, paras
135-137, and for cases on the subject, see 43 Digest (Repl) 103, 104, 343-345, 910-922,
3572-3602.
d For damages for breach of contract affecting convenience, see 12 Halsbury's Laws
(4th Edn) para 1188.

For the principles on which costs are awarded to a successful litigant, see 30
Halsbury's Laws (3rd Edn) 421, 422, para 796.

Cases referred to in judgments
Addis v Gramophone Co Ltd [1909] AC 488, [1908-10] All ER Rep 1, 78 LJKB 1122, 101
e   LT 466, HL, 17 Digest (Reissue) 79, 1.
Buckland v Watts [1969] 2 All ER 985, [1970] 1 QB 27, [1969] 3 WLR 92, CA, Digest
(Cont Vol C) 1100, 4760a.
Coldman v Hill [1919] 1 KB 443, [1918-19] All ER Rep 434, 88 LJKB 491, 120 LT 412,
CA, 22 Digest (Reissue) 197, 1657.
Cook v S [1967] 1 All ER 299, sub nom *Cook v Swinfen* [1967] 1 WLR 457, CA,
f   Digest (Cont Vol C) 898, 894a.
Cox v Phillips Industries Ltd [1975] The Times, 21st October.
Groom v Crocker [1938] 2 All ER 394, [1939] 1 KB 194, 108 LJKB 296, 158 LT 477, CA,
43 Digest (Repl) 117, 1058.
Hadley v Baxendale (1854) 9 Ex 341, [1843-60] All ER Rep 461, 23 LJ Ex 179, 23 LTOS 69,
17 Digest (Reissue) 101, 109.
g *Hall and Barker, Re* (1878) 9 Ch D 538, 47 LJCh 621, 43 Digest (Repl) 53, 417.
Hill v Featherstonhaugh (1831) 7 Bing 569, 5 Moo & P 541, 131 ER 220, 43 Digest (Repl)
343, 3573.
Jackson v Horizon Holidays Ltd [1975] 3 All ER 92, [1975] 1 WLR 1468, CA.
Jarvis v Swan's Tours Ltd [1973] 1 All ER 71, [1973] QB 233, [1972] 3 WLR 954, CA, 17
Digest (Reissue) 111, 166.
h *King v Phillips* [1953] 1 All ER 617, [1953] 1 QB 429, [1953] 2 WLR 526, 17 Digest (Reissue)
147, 389.
Scottish Co-operative Wholesale Society Ltd v Meyer [1958] 3 All ER 66, [1959] AC 324,
[1958] 3 WLR 404, AC, 10 Digest (Reissue) 943, 5526.
Underwood, Son & Piper v Lewis [1894] 2 QB 306, [1891-4] All ER Rep 1203, 64 LJQB
60, 70 LT 833, CA, 43 Digest (Repl) 54, 418.
j
Appeal
The plaintiff, Sheila Ann Heywood, appealed against so much of the judgment of
his Honour Judge McDonnell, sitting at Croydon County Court, given on

---

a   See the Litigants in Person (Costs and Expenses) Act 1975 which is to come into force on
a date to be appointed

20th December 1974 on the trial of the plaintiff's action against the defendants, Wellers, a firm of solicitors, in which she claimed the return of moneys paid to the *a* defendants in respect of costs and damages for negligence, as held that the plaintiff was entitled to recover the moneys paid in respect of costs but was not entitled to recover any further sum in respect of damages. The facts are set out in the judgment of Lord Denning MR.

The plaintiff appeared in person.   *b*
Keith Simpson for the defendants.

Cur adv vult

13th November. The following judgments were read.

LORD DENNING MR. It all started in a public house. The plaintiff, Sheila Heywood, met there Reginald Marrion. He was a police officer with 18 years' service, *c* a married man with two sons. She was on her own with one son, living in a house at Penge, where she took in sub-tenants. They became friendly and associated much together. She lent him £50 and he said he would pay her back at £10 a month. He paid the first month £10, but nothing afterwards. She tried to break off the association. He was upset about it. He forced his attentions on her against her will. He actually struck her; so severely that he dislocated her shoulder. She complained *d* to the police inspector. On 4th July 1972 Marrion was suspended from duty. The police authorities took disciplinary proceedings against him. Rather than face them, he resigned from the force. That was on 23rd October 1972. He still pestered her, going to her house against her wishes. So she thought she would sue him for the £40 he owed her. She went to solicitors for that purpose.

The firm were Wellers of Bromley, the defendants. They had a branch office *e* at 37A Widmore Road, Bromley. On 18th January 1973 Mrs Heywood called there. She was taken in to see Mr John Price. He was quite a young man, only 22 years of age. She thought he was a solicitor. In point of fact he was only a clerk. He was not qualified, but was hoping to become a legal executive. He had passed some of the examinations leading to it. She never saw any of the partners in the firm, nor any qualified person.   *f*

She told Mr Price that she had lent Mr Marrion £50, of which £40 was still outstanding. She said she wanted a solicitor's letter sent to him claiming repayment. Mr Price asked how she came to make the loan. She then told Mr Price of her past relationship with Mr Marrion, and said that she wanted to get rid of him. Mr Price suggested that she should apply for an injunction. He explained what this meant, namely that the court would order Mr Marrion to refrain from pestering her and *g* not to resort to her house. He said that proceedings could be taken in the county court. She asked how long it would take and how much it would cost. He said three weeks, and it could cost £25. She told Mr Price, however, only to claim the £40 at that stage.

On 23rd January 1973 Mr Price wrote to Mr Marrion claiming the £40. On 28th January he replied, saying he had no money and would not pay. The letter *h* was very abusive of Mrs Heywood. He said that she was a wicked woman and mentally deranged. On that same evening he went to her house, insisted on her letting him in, and threatened her with violence.

That incident was the last straw. On 5th February 1973 she went to Mr Price and asked him to apply for an injunction. He suggested that she should apply for legal aid, but her means were too great. On 12th February 1973 she wrote to him saying *j* that she did not wish to 'impose upon national charity'. She reminded him in her letter that 'your estimated cost of this injunction was £25 and the cost of the debt action was £3 (to me)', and enclosed her cheque for £25. The judge found that she thought that £30 would be sufficient to cover the cost; and that, had she known the cost which would be involved, she would never have started proceedings.

So, believing that it would only cost £25 for an injunction and take three weeks, she instructed Mr Price to take proceedings. The rest of the story is one long tale of the mistakes that Mr Price made.

On 21st February 1973 he instructed counsel to settle proceedings for an injunction. Counsel advised that, as there was no claim for damages, they could not be taken in the county court but had to be taken in the High Court. So Mr Price started them in the High Court without telling Mrs Heywood or warning her of the extra cost which this would involve.

On 27th February 1973 he issued a writ in the High Court and on that very day instructed counsel to apply ex parte for an interim injunction, supported by an affidavit sworn that day by Mrs Heywood. It was a mistake to do this, because it would mean extra costs and there was no great urgency to justify it. After much hesitation, the judge granted it. Mr Price never told Mrs Heywood that the ex parte injunction would double the cost.

On 27th February 1973 he got process servers to serve the writ and papers on Mr Marrion. They found him in a public house and handed them to him; but he let them fall on to the floor, saying he did not want them and was not interested in them. It was undoubtedly good service.

On 2nd March 1973 Mr Price instructed counsel to apply to continue the injunction until trial. This application was made on notice to Mr Marrion and was undoubtedly good. The judge made this order:

'(a) restraining the Defendant from touching molesting or otherwise seeking physical contact with the Plaintiff; (b) restraining the Defendant from visiting entering or otherwise approaching the dwelling-house at 4 Avington Grove, Penge, London, S.E.20 owned and partially occupied by the Plaintiff; (c) restraining the Defendant from telephoning, speaking to or otherwise accosting the Plaintiff; (d) restraining the Defendant from threatening, abusing or in any way seeking to intimidate the Plaintiff either by word or by deed until after the hearing of the trial or further order. Plaintiff's costs, including ex parte application, in any event.'

On 15th March 1973 the order for an injunction was served personally on Mr Marrion. Mr Marrion never entered an appearance. He should have done it within 14 days from service of the writ, that is by 13th March. But he never entered it. Seeing that there was no appearance, Mr Price was in a position to obtain final judgment. All that he had to do was to serve a statement of claim on Mr Marrion. Then, if Mr Marrion did not serve a defence (as he probably would not), Mrs Heywood could move for judgment in default: see RSC Ord 13, r 6, and RSC Ord 19, r 7. In that way Mrs Heywood would have obtained a final injunction by the middle of April 1973, together with a final order for costs against Mr Marrion. That failure of Mr Price (to take proper steps in default of appearance) was the most serious fault he made.

On 30th March 1973 Mr Marrion broke the injunction, by telephoning her late at night. On 20th April he broke it again. Mr Marrion telephoned to Mrs Heywood, called at her house and pestered her exceedingly. On 25th May Mr Marrion again broke it seriously. He called on her at her house and put her in great fear. She was very distressed. On every occasion Mrs Heywood gave a full report in writing to Mr Price, but he took no steps to bring the breaches before the court. On the contrary, he advised Mrs Heywood that she could do nothing about these visits unless she got in touch with the police and refused to let Mr Marrion in. The judge found that the effect on her was this: 'Mr Price said that I had to let the police find Marrion on the premises. What was the good of an injunction if I had to have a policeman watching?' Instead of bringing the breaches before the court, on 2nd June Mr Price took out a summons for directions; and then spent six or seven months in trying to serve it, in getting it heard, and in getting an order for a speedy trial. That was quite wrong.

Seeing that there was no appearance, there was no need for any summons for directions; and, in any case, a summons for directions should not be taken out until after close of pleadings: see RSC Ord 25, r 1. Here the pleadings were never closed. On 9th August 1973 (very belatedly) Mr Price served a statement of claim, but the defence was never put in. He should have served the statement of claim as long ago as March 1973; and got judgment then. In May the solicitor did issue a summons for £50 for money lent. Mr Marrion paid £40. That ended that item.

On 8th November 1973 Mr Marrion again broke the injunction. Mrs Heywood wrote to Mr Price telling it all. She said that Mr Marrion had called at her house and left her feeling like a nervous wreck.

On several occasions Mr Price advised Mrs Heywood that it was no use bringing Mr Marrion before the court because—

'Mr Marrion would only be committed if by his conduct he tried to get Mrs Heywood to stop proceedings, used or threatened violence, or by his conduct forced Mrs Heywood out of her house and from living there.'

That advice was much mistaken. The one thing that Mrs Heywood wanted was to have Mr Marrion brought before the court. She did not want to have him committed to prison. If he had been brought before the court for those plain breaches of the injunction, the court would have given him a severe warning; and that would, in all probability, have been sufficient to stop him.

On 17th January 1974, whilst Mr Price was away, a partner in Wellers wrote to Mrs Heywood asking her to send another £100 on account of costs. (She had already paid £175.) This snapped her patience. She replied saying that this demand for a further £100 was extortion and asked them to drop the case immediately. So they served notice of discontinuance. They got out their bill of costs showing £446·39 owing to them. But Mrs Heywood got her complaint in first.

On 18th March 1974 Mrs Heywood issued a plaint in the Bromley County Court against Wellers claiming (as amended):

£170·00 Paid
£150·00 Damages and Expenses

£320·00 Plus Legal Costs.

She conducted her own case. She told us that she did not go to other solicitors because she felt they would not put her case properly against fellow solicitors. She explained to us that she had great difficulty in getting the papers from Wellers. They wanted their costs first. She only got them by giving a cheque which she stopped as soon as she got the papers. Her case was heard by the county court judge for three days. He decided in her favour. He found that the solicitors had been negligent. He awarded her the money she had paid to the solicitors (for the injunction): £175 less £7 (for the £40 loan). That is £168. But he gave her no damages in addition. She appeals to this court. The solicitors gave notice of cross-appeal but at the last minute withdrew it. They no longer challenged the judge's finding that they were negligent.

I am afraid that the solicitors were much at fault. They ought not to have left this matter to a young junior clerk with no qualifications—with no supervision by any partner. In his hands mistakes were made from beginning to end. He gave wrong advice as to the cost and length of proceedings. He took proceedings in the High Court when he ought, I should have thought, to have gone to the magistrates next door. He made an unnecessary application ex parte for an injunction. He failed to appreciate the significance of 'no appearance' by the defendant. Instead of getting judgment by default quickly, he spent months and months on a summons for directions, and so forth. When the injunction was broken, he failed to bring Mr Marrion

before the judge, as he should have done; but instead gave wrong advice to Mrs
Heywood, saying that there was not enough evidence to commit. The upshot of it
all was that the proceedings were absolutely useless to her. She got no protection
against molestation: and she was, in fact, molested on three or four occasions. She
paid the solicitors all the money they asked—£175—and got nothing for it. No
wonder she refused their latest demand for another £100, and told them to stop.
She was quite justified in doing this. The judge himself said so in these words: 'She
was led to believe by this erroneous advice that the injunction was quite useless to
her in that it afforded her no protection against the attentions of Mr. Marrion; and
when faced with a further demand for £100 on account of costs, reasonably concluded
that the money she had already spent had been utterly wasted.'

This brings me to the law. Mrs Heywood conducted her case herself in person,
both before the judge and before us. I wish that she had been legally represented.
Counsel for Wellers was very fair and helped us all he could. But still we could have
wished for argument on her side.

The judge approached the case on this footing: Mrs Heywood was entitled to
damages for negligence, but the solicitors were entitled to their costs which they
could set off against her damages. He said that Wellers 'are not . . . precluded from
setting off what is properly due to them for their costs'. He then calculated the set-off
in this way. On the one hand Mrs Heywood was entitled to damages for negligence
which he set out under items which he numbered (i) to (vii)[1]. He disallowed the
defendants any costs under item (ii) altogether. He awarded the plaintiff damages
under items (i), (iii), (iv) and (v). He did not quantify those damages, but said that
as against them the defendants could set off all the costs recoverable by them save
for 'the costs properly incurred in obtaining the interim injunction, and in advising
the plaintiff as to the breaches of the injunction up to the end of May 1973'. He also
awarded Mrs Heywood damages under item (vi) (the November incident) which
was, he said, 'the most serious breach of duty on the part of the defendants'. He
did not quantify those damages but set off against them all those costs save as
aforesaid.

So the judge held that they could set off their costs against her damages, with the
result that she was not entitled to any damages and they were not entitled to their
costs (which they had calculated at £446·39). But as she had already paid them £175

---

1 The items were as follows: (i) The plaintiff, having been told proceedings could be taken in
the county court or the High Court, was not told that counsel advised that they could only
be instituted in the High Court until she was already committed to High Court proceedings.
(ii) Where there is no evidence that an injunction is urgently needed to prevent real
injury, most judges are reluctant to grant injunctions of the kind in question on an ex parte
application, and so the application ex parte should not have been made without explaining
to the plaintiff that it might well be refused, would add to the expense and would only
expedite the grant of an injunction by a week or two. (iii) After Mr Marrion had failed to
appear before the judge in chambers on 2nd March, the defendants should have considered
what steps should be taken to obtain judgment in default of appearance, and should then
have set about having a statement of claim settled and served upon him. (iv) It was a
tactical error not to follow counsel's advice in June, to write to Mr Marrion threatening that
the consequences of any further breach of the injunction would be committal to prison.
(v) The failure to follow up Mr Marrion's letter of 2nd July, by inviting him to submit to
judgment, and if he failed to do so immediately applying for judgment in default of
appearance or defence. (vi) Failure to instruct counsel properly with respect to the incident
on 18th November, and seriously mis-stating the effect of counsel's advice when communicating it to the plaintiff. (vii) Minor matters which resulted in additional costs and delay,
such as the delay in proceeding with the action which resulted in the employment of
enquiry agents to serve or attempt to serve the summons for directions, and the un-
explained failure to mention the November incident in the application for legal aid on 6th
December.

on account of those costs, she was entitled to have the money repaid to her. He said: 'If the whole of the money which the plaintiff has paid on account of costs is returned a to her, she should not in my judgment, recover any further sum in respect of damages.'

Now, I think the judge was in error in thinking that the solicitors were entitled to recover any costs at all. There are two reasons: in the first place, the contract of the solicitors was an *entire* contract which they were bound to carry on to the end; and, not having done so, they were not entitled to any costs: see *Underwood, Son & b Piper v Lewis*[1]. The law as to *entire* contract was put vividly by Jessel MR in *Re Hall & Barker*[2]:

> 'If a man engages to carry a box of cigars from London to Birmingham, it is an entire contract, and he cannot throw the cigars out of the carriage half-way there, and ask for half the money; or if a shoemaker agrees to make a pair of c shoes, he cannot offer you one shoe and ask you to pay one half the price.'

In the second place, the work which they did do was useless. It did nothing to forward the object which the client had in view. It did nothing to protect her from molestation. Being thus useless, they can recover nothing for it: see *Hill v Featherstonhaugh*[3], where Tindal CJ said:

> '... If an attorney, through inadvertence or inexperience,—for I impute no improper motive to the Plaintiff,—incurs trouble which is useless to his client, he cannot make it a subject of remuneration ... could a bricklayer, who had placed a wall in such a position as to be liable to fall, charge his employer for such an erection?'

Clearly not.

So the solicitors were entitled to nothing for costs; and Mrs Heywood could recover the £175 as money paid on a consideration which had wholly failed. She was, therefore, entitled to recover it as of right. And she is entitled to recover as well damages for negligence. Take this instance. If you engage a driver to take you to the station to catch a train for a day trip to the sea, you pay him £2—and then the car breaks down owing to his negligence. So that you miss your holiday. In that case you can recover, not only your £2, but also damages for the disappointment, upset and mental distress which you suffered: see *Jarvis v Swan's Tours Ltd*[4]; *Jackson v Horizon Holidays Ltd*[5].

So here, Mrs Heywood employed the solicitors to take proceedings at law to protect her from molestation by Mr Marrion. They were under a duty by contract to use reasonable care. Owing to their want of care she was molested by this man on three or four occasions. This molestation caused her much mental distress and upset. It must have been in their contemplation that, if they failed in their duty, she might be further molested and suffer much upset and distress. This damage she suffered was within their contemplation within the rule in *Hadley v Baxendale*[6]. That was the test applied by Lawson J in the recent case of *Cox v Phillips Industries Ltd*[7]. Counsel for the solicitors urged that damages for mental distress were not recoverable. He relied on *Groom v Crocker*[8] and *Cook v S*[9]. But those cases may have to be reconsidered.

1   [1894] 2 QB 306, [1891-4] All ER Rep 1203
2   (1878) 9 Ch D 538 at 545
3   (1831) 7 Bing 569 at 571, 572
4   [1973] 1 All ER 71, [1973] QB 233
5   [1975] 3 All ER 92, [1975] 1 WLR 1468
6   (1854) 9 Ex 341, [1843-60] All ER Rep 461
7   [1975] The Times, 21st October
8   [1938] 2 All ER 394, [1939] 1 KB 194
9   [1967] 1 All ER 299 at 302, 303, [1967] 1 WLR 457 at 461

In any case they were different from this. Here Wellers were employed to protect
a her from molestation causing mental distress—and should be responsible in damages
for their failure.

It was suggested that, even if Wellers had done their duty and taken the man to
court, he might still have molested her. But I do not think they can excuse themselves on that ground. After all, it was not put to the test; and it was their fault
it was not put to the test. If they had taken him to court as she wished—and as they
b ought to have done—it might well have been effective to stop him from molesting
her any more. We should assume that it would have been effective to protect her,
unless they prove that it would not: see *Coldman v Hill*[1] by Scrutton LJ; *Scottish
Co-operative Wholesale Society Ltd v Meyer*[2].

So the remaining question is: what damages should be awarded to Mrs Heywood
for the molestation she suffered on three or four occasions, and the mental distress
c and upset she suffered? The judge, unfortunately, did not quantify the damages.
In her claim as amended she put them at £150. I would allow her that sum. Some
reduction should be made for the fact that, if Wellers had done their duty (and
saved her from the molestation), it would have cost her something. I should put that
at the figure which Mr Price gave in the beginning, £25.

There remains the item on which Mrs Heywood felt most keenly. That was her
d own costs and effort in conducting this litigation in person against the solicitors.
She has suffered much in toil and tears. She has had sleepless nights over it. I wish
that we could have given her compensation on this account. If she had lost the case,
Wellers (although acting in person) could have charged their full costs against her,
including their profit costs. If she had lost this appeal, they would have charged her
a very large sum. But she, acting in person, gets only her out-of-pocket expenses
e both in the county court and here: and no more. It was so held by this court in
Buckland v Watts[3]. This position will soon be remedied by the recent Act on the
costs of litigants in person: Litigants in Person (Costs and Expenses) Act 1975. It
was passed on 1st August 1975, but it only comes into operation 'on such day as the
Lord Chancellor may appoint'. And we understand that he has not yet appointed
a day. So, whilst we can and do award her costs, they cannot recompense her for her
f own personal work and strain.

I would allow the appeal with costs and give judgment for her for £168 plus £125,
that is £293.

JAMES LJ. I take the facts as stated in the judgment of Lord Denning MR.
g After a careful and detailed review of the evidence in the course of which he made
his findings of fact, the learned circuit judge set out seven criticisms[4] of the defendants' handling of the High Court action. Those criticisms he described as 'well
founded'. In respect of the first, third, fourth and fifth criticisms he found that conduct
of the defendants amounted to absence of proper care and skill entitling the plaintiff
to damages. He did not seek to quantify the damages under each of these heads
h separately, but, as he was entitled to do on the material available to him, assessed
the damages for these breaches of duty on the broad basis of being the equivalent of
the costs recoverable by the defendants from the plaintiff, save for those costs properly incurred in obtaining the interim injunction and in advising the plaintiff on
breaches up to the end of May 1973. In respect of the second criticism the learned
judge held that the costs of obtaining the ex parte injunction should be disallowed.
j The sixth criticism the learned judge found to involve the most serious breach of

---

1 [1919] 1 KB 443 at 457, [1918-19] All ER Rep 434 at 442
2 [1958] 3 All ER 66 at 88, [1959] AC 324 at 367
3 [1969] 2 All ER 985, [1970] 1 QB 27
4 See p 305, footnote 1, ante

duty by the defendants. He ordered that the consequence of this breach, superimposed on the others involved in the seven criticisms, should be that the defendants   *a*
were disentitled to all costs in respect of the High Court action and that they should
pay back to the plaintiff the whole of the £175 she had paid on account of costs. An
adjustment of £7 was later provided for but that is of no present relevance. After
stating his conclusion the judge added: 'If the whole of the money which the plaintiff has paid on account of costs is returned to her, she should not, in my judgment,
recover any further sum in respect of damages.'   *b*

The defendants argue that that sentence indicates that the learned judge had
applied his mind to all the heads of damage under which the plaintiff had submitted
she should recover damages and concluded that his order satisfied all her claims
insofar as they were valid. I cannot accept that argument. I do not think it right to
construe the passage cited from the judgment as applicable to damages under a
head of damage to which the judge had not referred.   *c*

The plaintiff's dissatisfaction with the order of the learned judge (to whom she
paid generous tribute for his patience and helpfulness, and rightly so) falls under
two main heads. (i) The order did not award her damages for the fact that she was
forced to bring proceedings against solicitors (the defendants) in the local county
court and to bring this appeal. Because her claim was against solicitors for failure
in their duty to their client, she felt compelled to conduct the action in person. That   *d*
placed on her shoulders the work, the strains and the responsibility normally carried
by a litigant's legal adviser. The costs to which she is entitled as a litigant in person
are not sufficient to compensate for the actual work done and time spent and do
not reflect at all the mental strain. (ii) The order did not award her any damages for
the vexation, distress and anxiety caused by the defendants' failure to enforce the
injunction obtained. As a direct and foreseeable consequence she was subjected to   *e*
the repeated intrusions and molestations of Marrion.

She does not make serious complaint of the fact that the judge satisfied her claim
for damages under the seven criticisms he enumerated by depriving the defendants
of their costs and ordering them to repay £168 and I do not think we should disturb
that part of the judge's order. But she does complain that she should have an
additional sum under each of the two headings.   *f*

I fully understand the plaintiff's sense of grievance on the first point. I accept
that she is genuine in her statement that she felt forced to act on her own behalf.
But the position in law and in reality is that she could have instructed other solicitors.
Quite apart from that, the law provides that the work done in preparing for and conducting such an action as the plaintiff brought shall be the subject of costs in the action
and not damages. There is no way in which Mrs Heywood can recover damages   *g*
under this heading.

In my opinion the position is very different under her second heading. It is well
known and settled law that an action by a client against a solicitor alleging negligence
in the conduct of the client's affairs is an action for breach of contract: *Groom v
Crocker*[1]. It is also the law that where, at the time of making a contract, it is within
the contemplation of the contracting parties that a foreseeable result of a breach   *h*
of the contract will be to cause vexation, frustration or distress, then if a breach occurs
which does bring about that result, damages are recoverable under that heading
(*Jarvis v Swan's Tours Ltd*[2]). Not in every case of breach of contract on the part of
a solicitor towards his client will damages be recoverable under this head. It is only
when the service or services contracted for are such that both solicitor and client
contemplate that a failure by the solicitor to perform the contract will foreseeably   *j*
occasion vexation, frustration or distress. An example of where damages were not
recoverable is *Cook v S*[3]. In that case Lord Denning said:

1   [1938] 2 All ER 394, [1939] 1 KB 194
2   [1973] 1 All ER 71, [1973] QB 233
3   [1967] 1 All ER 299 at 303, [1967] 1 WLR 457 at 461, 462

a 'In these circumstances I think that, just as in the law of tort, so also in the law of contract, damages can be recovered for nervous shock or anxiety state if it is a reasonably foreseeable consequence. So the question became this: when a client goes to a solicitor, is it a reasonably foreseeable consequence that, if anything goes wrong with the litigation owing to the solicitor's negligence, there will be a breakdown in health? It can be foreseen that there will be injured feelings; mental distress; anger, and annoyance. But for none of these can damage

b be recovered. It was so held in *Groom* v. *Crocker*[1] on the same lines as *Addis* v. *Gramophone Co., Ltd.*[2] Is it reasonably foreseeable that there may be an actual breakdown in health? I do not think so. It was suggested in this case that there were special circumstances in that the plaintiff was peculiarly liable to nervous shock. I am afraid that she was. The history of her life shows one nervous break-down after another. If this special circumstance was brought home to the defen-

c dant, it might enlarge the area of foreseeability so as to make him liable; but it was not pleaded. Moreover when counsel for the plaintiff put questions to the defendant, he did not succeed in showing that special circumstances were brought home to him. All the defendant knew was that she was a woman obviously highly strung and worried as any woman would be in the circumstances. That does not mean, however, that he should foresee that, if he was negligent, she

d would suffer injury to health. In all these cases of nervous shock and breakdown in mental health, it is very difficult to draw the line. In *King* v. *Phillips*[3] I asked: "Where is the line to be drawn?" I found the answer given by Lord Wright: "Only where 'in the particular case the good sense of the . . . judge, decides'."'

That case is very different on its facts from the present. In the present case the
e application of 'good sense' makes it abundantly clear that the client wanted action taken which would rid her of molestation and annoyance. It is in relation to that action that her contract with the solicitors required the exercise of proper skill and care on their part. Good sense indicates that it was foreseeable at the time of the con-tract that failure to enforce any remedy obtained to stop the molestation and annoyance would result in its continuance or the risk of repetition. Vexation,
f frustration and distress were therefore likely to result from a breach of contract in this case. Further, the feelings of the plaintiff are not merely the feelings of an unsuccessful litigant who is disappointed or annoyed at the outcome of the case which would not sound in damages. In my judgment the plaintiff brings herself within those circumstances in which damages under this head are recoverable. The learned circuit judge did not award her all the damages to which she was entitled
g in respect of the defendants' failure to enforce the injunction.

The injunction was obtained on 27th February 1973 and, on 2nd March, was con-tinued until trial. After that date Marrion called at the plaintiff's house in breach of the injunction on 20th April and again on 25th May. On the finding of the judge these visits did not result from the defendants' negligent failure to enforce the in-junction. The defendants took the view that because the plaintiff had invited Marrion
h into the house on the first occasion in order to avoid a scene there was no purpose in seeking to commit him. Counsel on 29th May advised against action based on the second visit alone. It would appear likely that he was not informed of the first breach and so the judge found it to be. If he had been fully briefed as to the facts his advice may or may not have been different. However that may be, the advice that the defendants received was not followed. It is from this date that in my judgment
j damages flow. During the following months the plaintiff was subject to the ever present threat of molestation and, on 8th November, the threat materialised and she was left feeling, as she described it, 'a nervous wreck'.

1   [1938] 2 All ER 394, [1939] 1 KB 194
2   [1909] AC 488, [1908-10] All ER Rep 1
3   [1953] 1 All ER 617 at 624, [1953] 1 QB 429 at 442

In my judgment the plaintiff is entitled to damages in addition to the relief given
her by the trial judge and, doing the best I can, I would assess the damages, against *a*
which must be set off the costs which would be likely to have been borne by her in
obtaining the enforcement of an injunction, at £150. If the defendants had enforced
the injunction with skill and care in carrying out the plaintiff's instructions it is
probable that some of the costs involved would not have been taxed as recoverable
from Marrion. Also, it may well be that the plaintiff would have failed to recover
from Marrion the costs or part of the costs which he was ordered to pay. It must be *b*
assumed however that the plaintiff would not have been advised to proceed in an
action likely to cost her more than the value of the benefit or relief sought. It does
not lie in the defendants' mouth to say the contrary.

In my judgment, justice will be done in this case if one estimates—and it can only
be an estimate—that the plaintiff would have had to bear £25 in costs herself had
the defendants fulfilled their contractual obligation. This sum must be set off against *c*
the £150 damages.

I would allow the appeal and order that the plaintiff recover £125 damages in addition to the benefit of the order of the circuit judge which did in effect order that
the defendants repay to her £150. .

d

BRIDGE LJ. The learned judge obviously tried this case most carefully and conscientiously. It was no easy task because he had not the advantage of professional
presentation of the plaintiff's case; though, no doubt, counsel for the defendants
helped the judge as he helped us. As I read his judgment, the judge reached his
final conclusion on the basis that, since the High Court litigation had in the end, *e*
through the defendants' negligent conduct of it, proved abortive, justice would be
done if the plaintiff recovered all the costs she had paid.

I suspect that the question of awarding damages to the plaintiff to reflect the value
of the relief she would have obtained from the unwelcome attentions of Mr Marrion
if the litigation had been properly conducted by the defendants, was never expressly
canvassed in the court below. At all events I am not surprised that matter got over- *f*
looked. The plaintiff's main theme before us, and I have no doubt also before the
judge, was that she ought to be compensated for all her time and trouble in preparing
and conducting her case in these proceedings as a litigant in person. That was never,
in law, an arguable head of damage. Although the evidence was all there, other
possible heads of damage only emerged from the careful analysis of this case by
Lord Denning MR and James LJ in the course of the argument in this court. *g*

To the extent that the defendants' breach of their duty to the plaintiff resulted
in further molestation of the plaintiff by Mr Marrion which would probably have
been avoided if they had not been negligent, I agree that in principle the plaintiff
is entitled to recover damages. The fact that what the plaintiff suffered from such
molestation took the form of nothing worse than vexation, anxiety and distress of
mind does not bar her. There is, I think, a clear distinction to be drawn between *h*
mental distress which is an incidental consequence to the client of the misconduct of
litigation by his solicitor, on the one hand, and mental distress on the other hand
which is the direct and inevitable consequence of the solicitor's negligent failure to
obtain the very relief which it was the sole purpose of the litigation to secure. The
first does not sound in damages; the second does.

If Mr Marrion had been brought before the court when he should have been and *j*
warned of the consequences of any future breach of the injunction, it is probable that he
would then have left the plaintiff in peace. It is also probable that the plaintiff would
then properly have incurred some liability in costs. I agree with Lord Denning MR
and James LJ in assessing this latter figure at £25. There is some doubt, I think,
whether the defendants can be held guilty of negligence for their failure to act after

a Marrion's first breach of the injunction on 20th April 1973, or only following the further breach of 24th May and the defendants' failure to follow the advice of counsel then received, as I think the judge has found. But perhaps it is not of great importance since there is obviously no scientific yardstick for measuring the quantum of damages appropriate to this head of claim.

Assuming in the plaintiff's favour that damages run from the earlier date, I would put no higher figure on them than the figure of £150 proposed by Lord Denning MR *b* and James LJ, subject to deduction of the sum of £25 already referred to.

I agree that the appeal should be allowed and the plaintiff should recover £125 damages in addition to the benefit of the order in her favour in the county court.

Appeal allowed; judgment for the plaintiff for £293.

c Solicitors: *Wellers*, Bromley.

Wendy Shockett Barrister.

d # LTSS Print and Supply Services Ltd v London Borough of Hackney and another

COURT OF APPEAL, CIVIL DIVISION
CAIRNS, LAWTON AND GOFF LJJ
e 6th, 7th, 29th OCTOBER 1975

Town and country planning – Enforcement notice – Effect – Reversion to earlier lawful use – Purpose for which land may be used without planning permission – Purpose for which land could lawfully have been used if development enforced against had not been carried out – Established use – Use unlawful at its inception but no longer liable to enforcement action *f* *by reason of lapse of time – Whether permission required for a resumption of that use after service of enforcement notice – Town and Country Planning Act 1971, s 23(9).*

Town and country planning – Development – Use classes – Warehouse – Use as a wholesale warehouse or repository for any purpose – Meaning of wholesale warehouse – Meaning a question of fact – Open to Secretary of State to conclude that warehouse a building used *g* *primarily for storage – Cash and carry establishment used primarily for sale of goods not a warehouse – Town and Country Planning (Use Classes) Order 1972 (SI 1972 No 1385), Sch, Class X.*

A company ('LTSS') owned the freehold of certain land on part of which there was a building. There was no evidence as to what use the building had been put before *h* 1961; in particular there was no evidence that the building had ever been used as a wholesale warehouse. From 1961, however, the building was used for dealing in veneers and plywood, the trade being mainly wholesale. Some years later it was being used for a timber importing business, there being no evidence to indicate that that included retail sales. By 1971 the timber importers had left and thereafter the building was used for the retail sale of furniture to the public. On no occasion was planning *j* permission obtained for any of those uses. In December 1972 the local authority served on the occupiers of the building and LTSS an enforcement notice under s 87 of the Town and Country Planning Act 1971 which required the use of the building for the sale of furniture to be discontinued. The occupiers appealed to the Secretary of State under s 88 of the 1971 Act, contending, inter alia, that, if the enforcement notice stood, the building could revert to its former use as a wholesale warehouse,

under s 23(9)[a] of the 1971 Act, and that it was, therefore, open to them to set up a
'cash and carry wholesale grocery warehouse' since such an establishment was a
'wholesale warehouse' within Class X of the Schedule to the Town and Country
Planning (Use Classes) Order 1972[b]. An inquiry was held. The inspector concluded
that the enforcement notice was valid and recommended that planning permission
for use for the sale of furniture should be refused. The Secretary of State accepted a
finding by the inspector that the established use of the building, within s 94 of the 1971
Act, was as a wholesale warehouse or repository, but he dismissed the appeal and
affirmed the enforcement notice subject to amending it to refer to retail sales. The
Secretary of State further held that a cash and carry establishment was not a wholesale
warehouse and also pointed out that an established use was not a lawful use of land
for the purposes of s 23(9) of the 1971 Act, but was merely a use which had 'become
immune from enforcement action', and therefore that the occupiers had no
right to revert to the previous use as a wholesale warehouse. LTSS appealed to the
Divisional Court[c] which allowed the appeal and remitted the case to the Secretary
of State on the ground that he had been wrong in law in holding that an established
use was not a lawful use for the purposes of s 23(9). The Secretary of State appealed
and by a respondent's notice LTSS contended that the decision of the Divisional
Court should be affirmed on the additional ground that the Secretary of State had
been wrong in holding that use of the building as a cash and carry wholesale warehouse
did not constitute use as a 'wholesale warehouse' within Class X of the Use Classes Order.

Held – The appeal would be allowed for the following reasons—
　(i) If a change of use for which planning permission was required was made without
planning permission, the change of use was unlawful and, unless something supervened to make it lawful, the continuance of that use remained unlawful even though,
in consequence of the lapse of time, it became immune from enforcement proceedings.
Accordingly the Secretary of State had been correct in holding that the occupiers were
not entitled to revert to the use as a wholesale warehouse (see p 316 g to j, p 317 j,
p 320 d e and h, p 321 f, p 322 g and h, p 323 a and p 324 a and b, post); dictum of Lord
Denning MR in R v Governor of Pentonville Prison, ex parte Azam [1973] 2 All ER at 749
applied; W T Lamb & Sons Ltd v Secretary of State for the Environment [1975] 2 All ER
117 overruled.
　(ii) The word 'warehouse' was an ordinary English word and it was for the Secretary
of State to determine as a question of fact and degree whether a cash and carry wholesale warehouse constituted a 'wholesale warehouse' within Class X of the Use Classes
Order. Accordingly it was open to the Secretary of State to conclude that a warehouse
was a building used primarily for the storage of goods whereas, in a cash and carry
establishment, the main activity carried out was the sale of goods for cash, the storage
of goods being merely ancillary to that activity (see p 318 h, p 319 j to p 320 b, p 321
f to h and p 325 d and g, post); dictum of Lord Reid in Brutus v Cozens [1972] 2 All ER
at 1299 applied.
　Decision of the Divisional Court of the Queen's Bench Division [1975] 1 All ER 374
reversed.

Notes
For development for which planning permission is required, see 37 Halsbury's Laws
(3rd Edn) 269-272, para 370, and for cases on the subject, see 45 Digest (Repl) 335-
340, 33-55.
　For the Town and Country Planning Act 1971, ss 23, 87, 88, 94, see 41 Halsbury's
Statutes (3rd Edn) 1608, 1690, 1692, 1702.
　For the Town and Country Planning (Use Classes) Order 1972, Sch, Class X, see 21
Halsbury's Statutory Instruments (3rd Reissue) 141.

a　Section 23(9) is set out at p 314 j, post
b　SI 1972 No 1385
c　[1975] 1 All ER 374

Cases referred to in judgments

a *Azam v Secretary of State for the Home Department* [1973] 2 All ER 765, [1974] AC 18, [1973] 2 WLR 1058, HL; *affg* sub nom *R v Governor of Pentonville Prison,ex parte Azam* [1973] 2 All ER 741, [1973] 2 WLR 949, CA.

Brutus v Cozens [1972] 2 All ER 1297, [1973] AC 854, [1972] 3 WLR 521.

Calcaria Construction Co (York) Ltd v Secretary of State for the Environment (1974) 27 P & CR 435, 72 LGR 398.

b *Campbell (AG) (Properties) Ltd v Parramatta City Council* [1961] NSWR 542.

Decorative and Caravan Paints Ltd v Nottingham Corpn (17th April 1974) unreported; noted in 214 EG 1355.

Lamb (W T) and Sons Ltd v Secretary of State for the Enviroment [1975] 2 All ER 1117, DC.

R v Borley (1844) 8 JP 263, 15 Digest (Repl) 1213, 12347.

Webber v Minister of Housing and Local Government (1967) 18 P & CR 491, 65 LGR 332.

c Case also cited

John Howard's Case (1751) Fost 77, 168 ER 39.

Appeal

This was an appeal by the Secretary of State for the Enviroment against a decision of the Divisional Court of the Queen's Bench Division[1] (Lord Widgery CJ, Bridge and
d Shaw JJ) given on 5th November 1974 allowing an appeal by LTSS Print and Supply Services Ltd ('LTSS') against a decision of the Secretary of State dated 10th April 1974 upholding an enforcement notice, dated 6th December 1972, served on LTSS and others by the London Borough of Hackney ('the local authority') whereby the local authority, pursuant to s 87 of the Town and Country Planning Act 1971, required that the use of certain premises, owned by LTSS and occupied by Frederick A Jones
e (Wholesale)Ltd, for the sale of furniture should be discontinued. The Divisional Court ordered that the Secretary of State's decision be remitted to him for consideration in the light of the judgment of the court. By a respondent's notice dated 2nd January 1975 LTSS gave notice that, at the hearing of the appeal against the order of the Divisional Court, they would contend that it should be affirmed on, inter alia, the
f following additional grounds: (i) that the Secretary of State had misdirected himself as to the meaning of the expression 'wholesale warehouse' in the Town and Country Planning (Use Classes) Order 1972, and (ii) that he was bound (a) to consider whether, on the facts, if the enforcement notice took effect, the occupiers of the premises would be lawfully entitled to use the premises as a wholesale cash and carry warehouse as they intended and (b) to conclude that they were so entitled, that matter being a consideration relevant to the excercise of his discretion whether to uphold the
g enforcement notice or whether to grant planning permission for the development to which that notice related. The facts are set out in the judgment of Cairns LJ.

Harry Woolf for the Secretary of State.
Alistair Dawson for LTSS.
The local authority was not represented.

h   *Cur adv vult*

29th October. The following judgments were read.

CAIRNS LJ. This is an appeal from the decision of the Divisional Court of the Queen's Bench Division[1] in a case under the Town and Country Planning Act 1971. The appeal
j is brought by leave of the Divisional Court. The appellant is the Secretary of State for the Enviroment and the respondent is a company, LTSS Print and Supply Services Ltd, to which I shall refer as 'LTSS'. The appeal relates to a building which consti-tutes the southern part of 138 Kingsland Road, Shoreditch, and of which LTSS is the freeholder.

1 [1975] 1 All ER 374, [1975] 1 WLR 138

In December 1972 the London Borough of Hackney ('the local authority') served
on LTSS and on the occupiers of the premises (among others) an enforcement   *a*
notice under s 87 of the 1971 Act. The notice recited that the premises were being used
for the sale of furniture without planning permission and required such sale to be
discontinued.

The occupiers appealed under s 88 of the 1971 Act to the Secretary of State and he
directed an inquiry. Section 88(7) provides that when such an appeal is brought the
appellant is deemed to have applied for planning permission for the development   *b*
to which the notice relates. The inquiry was held and the inspector reported on 20th
December 1973 concluding that the notice was not invalid on the basis that the use
that was being made of the premises was for retail sale of furniture and that this
was in breach of planning control. He recommended that planning permission should
not be granted for such use.

By a decision letter dated 10th April 1974 the Secretary of State dismissed the appeal,   *c*
upholding the enforcement notice and refusing planning permission for the current
use, but he amended the notice to make it refer specifically to retail sales.

The occupiers had not been effectively represented at the inquiry and took no
further step (being in fact a company in liquidation). LTSS, having been served with
the enforcement notice, was entitled under s 246 of the 1971 Act to appeal to the High
Court on points of law and exercised that right. The local authority took no further   *d*
part in the proceedings.

On the hearing of that appeal the Divisional Court held that the Secretary of State
had misconstrued one of the provisions of the 1971 Act and that this *might* have
affected his decision to refuse planning permission for retail sales. The court accordingly remitted the matter to him for reconsideration in the light of the judgments
that were delivered.   *e*

The Secretary of State appeals to this court contending: (1) that the Secretary of
State was right in the construction of the provision in question and the Divisional
Court was wrong; and (2) that if the Secretary of State was wrong on this point it
could not be shown to have influenced his ultimate decision. By respondent's notice
LTSS contended that the decision in the Divisional Court should be affirmed on   *f*
additional grounds.

The history of these premises as found by the inspector was as follows. From at
least 1961 they were used for some years for dealing in veneers and plywood, the trade
being mainly wholesale. This was followed by a timber importing business, and
there was nothing to indicate that this included any retail sales. By 1971 the timber
importers had left and furniture was being displayed for retail sale. From October
1972 the use was for retail sale of furniture to the public. There was no evidence of   *g*
planning permission having been obtained for any of these uses.

When the enforcement notice was served it was desired to have it set aside and to
have planning permission granted for the retail business in furniture. But, failing
that, it was desired to set up a 'cash and carry wholesale grocery warehouse'.

Now use as a wholesale warehouse is within Class X of the Town and Country
Planning (Use Classes) Order 1972[1]. Under s 22(2)(*f*) of the 1971 Act, when premises   *h*
are used for a purpose within a class the use for another purpose within that class
does not constitute development. Section 23(9) provides:

> 'Where an enforcement notice has been served in respect of any development of
> land, planning permission is not required for the use of that land for the purpose
> for which (in accordance with the provisions of this Part of this Act) it could law-   *j*
> fully have been used if that development had not been carried out.'

The case of the occupiers presented to the Secretary of State, and of LTSS on appeal
from him, was as follows: If the enforcement notice stood, the premises could again

be used as a wholesale warehouse, this being the purpose which was authorised by
s 23(9). A 'cash and carry wholesale warehouse' was a 'wholesale warehouse' within
Class X. The ground on which the inspector found that use for the retail sale of furniture was objectionable was that the site, on a principal traffic route out of and into
London, with no adequate parking space, was not suitable for a business involving a
lot of vehicular movement to and from the site. But, it was said, a cash and carry
grocery business would involve just as much vehicular movement. Therefore, there
was no good reason for withholding planning permission for the current use.

Now s 94 of the 1971 Act provides, inter alia, that a use of land is 'established' if it
was begun before the beginning of 1964 without planning permission and has continued
since the end of 1963. A use which is an established use is immune from enforcement action (s 87(1)). The inspector found that the established use of the appeal site
was as a wholesale warehouse or repository within Class X and the Secretary of State
accepted this finding.

The inspector at the end of para 72 of his report said:

'There is also bound to be a good deal of vehicular movement to and from the
site from its established use, though it is arguable at the least whether this includes
a use of the whole premises as a wholesale cash and carry.'

The Secretary of State held in para 8 of his decision letter that a cash and carry
establishment was not a wholesale warehouse, and in para 11 he expressed himself
as follows:

'It is pointed out that an established use is not a lawful use of land for the purposes of s 23(9) of the 1971 Act, it is merely a use which at a certain time becomes
immune from enforcement action. Once an established use has been materially
changed to another use involving development, it is considered that the established use has been abandoned and there is no right to revert to the established
use, which in this case was use as a wholesale warehouse. For the reasons given in
para 8 above it is not considered that the previous use as a wholesale warehouse
carries the right to be used as a "wholesale grocers cash and carry warehouse"
and it is considered therefore that there is no right to revert to this use as was
said to be your client's intention if the notice was upheld.'

In para 13 the Secretary of State accepted the conclusions and recommendations
of the inspector except as to established use—which I take to mean that whereas the
inspector was in doubt whether the established use would cover a cash and carry
warehouse the Secretary of State was satisfied that it would not.

The Divisional Court[1] (Lord Widgery CJ, Bridge and Shaw JJ) allowed LTSS's appeal
from the decision of the Secretary of State because they held that he was wrong in
law in holding that there was no right under s 23(9) to revert to a use for which no
planning permission had been obtained, but which was immune from enforcement
because it had become an established use. They considered it very unlikely that the
Secretary of State would have decided to give planning permission for the current
use if he had taken a different view of s 23(9), but thought it possible that he might
have been influenced by the error of law which they held him to have made and
accordingly remitted the case to him for reconsideration in the light of the judgments.

Now the primary question on this appeal is as to the meaning of the word' lawfully'
in s 23(9), taken in conjunction with the words 'in accordance with the provisions
of this Part of this Act'. Lord Widgery CJ said[2]:

'I think that that subsection permits the return to any use which could be
carried on at the time of the development enforced against without breach of

---

1   [1975] 1 All ER 374, [1975] 1 WLR 138
2   [1975] 1 All ER at 376, [1975] 1 WLR at 141

the terms of the planning Acts and without there being any risk of enforcement action being taken against him.'

Bridge J agreed with the judgment of Lord Widgery CJ, subject to reserving his opinion whether there would be a right to revert to the earlier use if that use had begun after the end of 1963. In the later case of *W T Lamb & Sons Ltd v Secretary of State for the Environment*[1] Bridge J held that there would be such a right because the continuance of a use begun in breach of planning control was not unlawful unless and until an enforcement notice had been served in respect of it. In that judgment the other members of the Divisional Court (Eveleigh and Wien JJ) concurred.

In the present case the Divisional Court found strong support for their construction of s 23(9) in the contrast between its wording and the wording of sub-ss (5) and (6) of the same section, which read as follows:

'(5) Where planning permission to develop land has been granted for a limited period, planning permission is not required for the resumption, at the end of that period, of the use of the land for the purpose for which it was normally used before the permission was granted.

'(6) In determining, for the purposes of subsection (5) of this section, what were the purposes for which land was normally used before the grant of planning permission, no account shall be taken of any use of the land begun in contravention of . . . previous planning control.'

The view of the Secretary of State means in effect that a use which was begun in contravention of Part III of the 1971 Act is one which could not lawfully have been carried on in accordance with that Part of the Act. And if that is right, the question arises why Parliament used different language in sub-s (9) from that in sub-ss (5) and (6).

Before this court, stress was laid by counsel for the Secretary of State on the words 'In accordance with the provisions of this Part of this Act'. Enforcement is not dealt with in Part III, but in Part V. Section 89, which is in Part V, contains provisions as to penalties for non-compliance with an enforcement notice. This makes it difficult to see how 'lawfulness' for the purpose of s 23(9) can depend, as the Divisional Court held in *W T Lamb & Sons Ltd v Secretary of State for the Enviroment*[1], on whether or not an enforcement notice has been served. Similarly, I do not, with great respect, think it can depend, as Lord Widgery CJ put it, on the use being one which could be carried on without there being any risk of enforcement action. The other condition mentioned by Lord Widgery CJ was 'without breach of the planning Acts'. This again would not give effect to the words 'in accordance with the provisions of this Part of this Act'.

There is nothing in Part II of the 1971 Act which in terms prohibits the continuance of a use. What is provided by ss 22 and 23, which are the first two sections of Part III, is that, in general, planning permission is required for a *change* of use. So if a change of use for which planning permission is required is made without planning permission it is an unlawful change of use. Is continuance of a use so unlawfully begun nevertheless lawful in accordance with the provisions of Part III? In my judgment, it is not.

If a state of affairs or an activity has been initiated by infringing statutory provisions, then I do not consider that it can ever be said to be lawful in accordance with the provisions unless something has supervened to make it lawful. And mere immunity from process does not make it lawful. This view accords with the decision of the Court of Appeal and the House of Lords in a case in a very different field from planning, *Azam v Secretary of State for Home Affairs*[2], where it was held that an illegal immigrant into the United Kingdom was still an illegal entrant, although owing to the lapse of time he could no longer be prosecuted for his illegal entry. A passage in the judgment of Lord Denning MR expresses the principle very clearly[3]:

1   [1975] 2 All ER 1117
2   [1973] 2 All ER 741, [1974] AC 18
3   [1973] 2 All ER at 749, [1974] AC at 29

'. . . between 1968 and 1973, if a Commonwealth immigrant landed clandestinely, he was after six months virtually untouchable. He could not be prosecuted for the unlawful landing. He could not be removed. He could not be deported, unless he committed a fresh criminal offence and was recommended for deportation. But this does not mean that after six months he was here as of right; or that his presence here was lawful. His presence here was unlawful in its inception. It continued to be unlawful during the six months that he could be prosecuted for it. After the six months, it continued to be unlawful. It is a general rule of law that the expiry of a time limit does not make that lawful which was previously unlawful. It only bars the remedy in respect of it.'

That Lord Widgery CJ himself at one time was of the opinion that this doctrine applied to a situation similar to that in the present case appears form his judgment in *Webber v Minister of Housing*[1]. There the immunity was under a different section, which in certain cases prohibited the serving of an enforcement notice after four years' user. Widgery J said[2]:

'The second fallacy which seems to me to be embedded in [counsel's] argument is that it makes the mistake, which I suppose is common to us all from time to time, of thinking that four years' user creates a right to use the land for the purpose for which it was used during those four years. In fact, as will be remembered, the Acts make it perfectly clear that the only result of four years' user is that you are immune, or the owner is immune, from enforcement action so long as he continues that use. If he chooses of his own accord to discontinue the use and substitue another, it is clearly wrong to suppose that he has any kind of right to revert to and resume the original use.'

Counsel for the Secretary of State recognised that the most powerful argument against him was that based on the difference in language between sub-ss (5) and (6) of s 23, on the one hand, and sub-s (9) on the other. He pointed out, however, that the 1971 Act is mainly a consolidating Act, and that this difference of language has existed ever since the Town and Country Planning Act 1947 in which the corresponding subsections were s 18(5) and s 24(4). The situation was then very different, because up to the appointed day under the 1947 Act there had been no general requirement of planning permission for development. Since in 1947 the provisions were in the context of two different sections, one dealing with 'supplementary provisions as to the grant of permission' and the other with 'supplementary provisions as to enforcement', it is not very surprising if the draftsman's mind was not directed to a comparison of the language of the two provisions. Further, it may be said that both in 1947 and in 1971 Parliament intended that when use for a limited period came to an end the occupier should be entitled to revert to the last lawful use (any intervening unlawful use being disregarded), whereas when an enforcement notice had been served reverter should be allowed only to the use which was current immediately before the development the subject of the enforcement notice, and if that use was not lawful in accordance with that part of the Act, then planning permission would be required for any use it was proposed to adopt. In my opinion, that is indeed the effect of the different wording.

In the end, I am not satisfied that the difference in wording is a sufficiently strong indication of the meaning of s 23(9) to outweigh the considerations which lead me to interpret it as allowing reverter to a previous use only if that use was lawfully begun under Part III of the 1971 Act or its predecessors. If that is right, then the Secretary of State does not need to rely on his second ground of appeal and, as I will explain later, the grounds set up by LTSS in the respondent's notice cannot avail them.

1   (1967) 18 P & CR 491
2   18 P & CR at 495

As, however, the issues arising on the second ground of appeal and on the respondent's notice have been fully argued, and as counsel have expressed a wish to have the *a* decision of this court on them, I will express my opinion about them. It is convenient to take first the respondent's notice, because counsel for LTSS concedes that he could not resist the appeal on the second ground without establishing at least one of the grounds in the respondent's notice.

The grounds advanced in the respondent's notice may be summarised as follows: (1) the Secretary of State should have concluded that the use as a wholesale warehouse *b* began otherwise than in breach of planning control and/or began before the 1st July 1948; (2) the Secretary of State misdirected himself as to the meaning of 'wholesale warehouse' in Class X of the Use Classes Order; (3) the Secretary of State should have considered whether, if the enforcement notice took effect, the occupiers would be entitled to use the premises as a cash and carry wholesale warehouse and should have concluded that they would; (4) the Secretary of State ought not to have amended *c* the enforcement notice. The fourth ground was not pursued at the hearing of the appeal.

As to ground (1), counsel for LTSS accepted that the onus was on them. There was no evidence as to how the premises were used before 1961. There was no indiction that it was contended at the inquiry that the use as a wholesale warehouse began before 1948 or with planning control. Paragraph 11 of the decision letter is only con- *d* sistent with the finding that it was not. There is no substance in this contention of LTSS.

Grounds (2) and (3) can be taken together, because the only misdirection alleged under (2) is that it is contended that a 'cash and carry wholesale warehouse' is a 'wholesale warehouse' within the meaning of the relevant paragraph of the Use Classes Order. The Use Classes Order 1972 contains no definition of a wholesale warehouse *e* or of a warehouse. The Town and Country Planning (Use Classes) Order 1948[1], art 2(2), defined a wholesale warehouse as 'a building where business, principally of a wholesale nature, is transacted and goods are stored or displayed, but only incidentally to the transaction of that business'. It may be that the definition was given in order to distinguish a wholesale warehouse from a repository which in that order was in a different class. I do not consider that a definition which has been dropped can be *f* used to govern the meaning of 'wholesale warehouse' in the new order. Counsel for LTSS relied on dictionary definitions, some 19th century cases and one Australian case. The Shorter Oxford Dictionary gives as one definition of a warehouse, 'the building in which a wholesale dealer keeps his stock of goods for sale'. In *R v Borley* Patteson J defined a warehouse[2] as 'a place used for the showing and sale of goods and wares by factors and traders'. In *A G Campbell (Properties) Ltd v Parramatta City* *g* *Council*[3], a projected building where goods sufficient for a fortnight's trade were to be held and displayed to buyers who were to serve themselves and arrange transport to their retail stores was held by the New South Wales Land and Valuation Court to be 'for the purpose of a warehouse' within the meaning of a planning scheme. The word 'warehouse' is, however, an ordinary English word, and I do not consider that its meaning is a matter of law (see *Brutus v Cozens* per Lord Reid[4]). Its meaning *h* may not have been the same in 1972 as in 1844 and may not be the same in England as it is in Australia. Unless the Secretary of State put some clearly untenable meaning on the words I do not consider that his interpretation of them could be challenged. In *Decorative Paints Ltd v Nottingham Corpn*[5] a building where furniture etc was stored and customers came in, selected goods and took them away, retail sales

1 SI 1948 No 955
2 (1844) 8 JP 263 at 264
3 [1961] NSWR 542
4 [1972] 2 All ER 1297 at 1299, [1973] AC 854 at 861
5 (1970) 214 EG 1355

exceeding wholesale sales by a ration of 3 to 1, was held by the Secretary of State not
a to be a warehouse for the purpose of the Town and Country Planning (Use Classes)
Order 1963[1] (in which Class X was the same as in the 1972 order). The Divisional
Court upheld his decision, and Lord Parker CJ said in his judgment:

> 'The appeal here, as I understand it, is based on the well-known fact that it is
> common today for sales, not merely wholesale sales but also retail sales of
> goods stored in a warehouse to take place therein. As [counsel] puts it, a ware-
b > house shades off into a shop. That may well be true, and indeed as I see it that
> was the view of the Minister, who as a matter of fact and degree held that in the
> circumstances of the present case the use had become use as a shop. That being so
> as it seems to me the appellants here must fail unless it can be said that use as a
> warehouse includes use as a shop, or that there was no evidence to support the
c > finding.'

The grounds on which the Secretary of State in the present case decided that a cash
and carry establishment was not a wholesale warehouse were expressed in para 8
of his decision letter as follows:

> 'There is no definition of the word 'warehouse' either for general purposes of
> the 1971 Act or for the purposes of the Town and Country Planning General
d > Development Order 1963-1973. The view is taken that a building can properly
> be described as a wholesale warehouse where it is used primarily for storage of
> goods prior to their distribution elsewhere and where any other activities carried
> on in the building, such as offices, are entirely ancillary to the storage of goods
> in the building. Your client argued that in a wholesale warehouse ancillary sales
> may take place in any quantity provided the goods are for resale and not for
e > consumption and may be collected by customers on a cash and carry basis. It is
> accepted that the business of warehousing may contain a wholesale sales element,
> but for the use of the building for such sales to be permitted, these sales must be
> ancillary to the use of the building as a warehouse as described above. In this
> context "wholesale" is taken to mean selling, generally in bulk, to retailers in
> the trade for resale elsewhere or to manufacturers, professional builders and the
f > like. The selling of goods to the general public in larger quantities than are usual
> in a retail shop or at a discount and on a cash and carry basis would not bring
> such sales within the term "wholesale". In a cash and carry establishment, the
> main activity carried on in the building is the retail sale of goods for cash, and any
> storage of goods in such premises is normally ancillary to the sale of goods carried
> on in the building. Whether the customers attending at the premises are retailers,
g > manufacturers, builders etc, purchasing for business purposes or whether they
> are members of the public buying the goods for their own use or consumption,
> the use of the building is not a use as a wholesale warehouse but use for the sale of
> goods. It follows that if such a method of business was adopted it could as a matter
> of fact and degree involve a material change of use of the wholesale warehouse
> constituting development.'

h The problem for the court in the present case was not the same as in *Decorative
Paints Ltd v Nottingham Corpn*[2], because in that case the question was of the nature
of the actual user, whereas in this case the question is what would be the proper
description of a suggested user. The suggested user is, however, one where it is
contemplated that the sale of goods to be carried away would be conducted on a
j scale where the vehicular traffic involved would be comparable to that involved in
the retail sale of furniture. It is a question of fact and degree whether a business so
conducted would be a wholesale warehouse and, in my opinion, the conclusion of
the Secretary of State that it would not should be accepted by the courts.

1   SI 1963 No 708
2   (1970) 214 EG 1355

It was not suggested on behalf of LTSS that any other use they might wish to make
of these premises could properly be described as use as a wholesale warehouse. *a*
So, whether I am right or wrong in my construction of s 23(9), I would hold that the
decision of the Divisional Court cannot be upheld on the grounds put forward in the
respondent's notice, and that the appeal would succeed on the Secretary of State's
second ground.

It is with very great diffidence that I express conclusions on a planning matter different
from those arrived at by a court constituted as the Divisional Court was on this *b*
occasion. All the points were, however, much more fully argued before us than they
were before that court, and for the reasons I have given, I would allow the appeal,
leaving the decision of the Secretary of State to stand.

LAWTON LJ.　The main question which requires answering in this appeal can be *c*
stated, so it seems to me, as follows: if the occupier of premises uses them in a way
which requires planning permission, but he has not got it, and does so long enough to
acquire immunity from enforcement proceedings, can such use be deemed a lawful
use for the purposes of s 23(9) of the Town and Country Planning Act 1971?

No planning permission had ever been granted for the use as a wholesale warehouse
of the premises under consideration in this appeal. The evidence did not justify an *d*
inference that such use had been going on before the Town and Country Planning
Act 1947 came into operation. When such use began, some time between 1st July
1948 (the appointed day under the 1947 Act) and 1961, it was an unlawful development (see s 12(1) of the 1947 Act). Under s 23(1) of the 1947 Act, if the local planning
authority had thought expedient to do so, it could, within four years of such development beginning, have served on both the owner and occupier an enforcement notice. *e*
This would have been the first step to starting enforcement proceedings. This provision granted immunity from proceedings after the end of four years. It did not
make lawful that which had started as an unlawful development. This was the
opinion of Widgery J, with which Lord Parker CJ agreed, in *Webber v Minister of
Housing and Local Government*[1]. This, in my judgment, was right in principle. The
Limitation Acts confer immunity from proceedings; they do not confer rights without *f*
specific provisions, such as are to be found in ss 3 and 16 of the Limitation Act 1939.
In *R v Governor of Pentonville Prison, ex parte Azam* Lord Denning MR in the Court
of Appeal stated the principle as follows[2]:

'It is a general rule of law that the expiry of a time limit does not make that
lawful which was previously unlawful. It only bars the remedy in respect of it.'

The House of Lords did not disapprove or qualify this statement of principle. The *g*
majority of their Lordships appear to have followed it: see the speech of Lord
Wilberforce[3] and that of Lord Pearson[4]. The immunity from enforcement proceedings given by s 23(1) of the 1947 Act reappeared with a change of wording, but
not of meaning, in s 87(3) of the 1971 Act. It follows, in my judgment, that the phrase
'lawfully used' in s 23(9) of the 1971 Act means a use for which planning permission *h*
had been granted or was not required under sub-ss (2), (3), (4) and (7) of the same
section. A use for which there was no planning permission, or statutory exemption
from planning permission, would be one arising out of an unlawful development.
If it came within s 87(3) of the 1971 Act, although unlawful, it would be one which
was immune from enforcement proceedings.

For my part, I find no difficulty in the difference in wording between sub-ss (9) *j*
and (6) of s 23. The latter is derived by statutory descent from s 18(5) of the 1947 Act.

1　(1967) 18 P & CR 491 at 495
2　[1973] 2 All ER 741 at 749, [1974] AC 18 at 29
3　[1973] 2 All ER at 772, [1974] AC at 63
4　[1973] 2 All ER at 775, 776, [1974] AC at 68

a It is pertinent to remember that this Act was forward-looking; it had to graft the new concept of planning permission on to the lawful existing uses. For some time after the appointed day, in cases where permission was granted to develop land for a limited period only, it would be likely that the previous use would not, for historical reasons, have required planning permission at all. The use in s 18(5) of the words 'no account shall be taken of any use of the land begun in contravention of previous planning control . . .' was a convenient way of indicating that the resumed use had to *b* be one for which planning permission was not required. Section 18(5) envisages the resumption of a use which had been lawful when it began, not one which had been unlawful but which had become immune from enforcement proceedings. Subsection (6) of the 1971 Act does the same.

I am fortified in this view by the presence in sub-s (9) of the words in parenthesis 'in accordance with the provisions of this Part of this Act'. The purpose for which land, *c* under the subsection, could have been used lawfully if the illegal development had not begun, had to be such as complied with the provisions of Part III of the Act; in other words, the purpose for which planning permission had been granted or was not required. A use which had begun unlawfully but which was immune from enforcement proceedings under s 87(3) was not one which was in accordance with Part II of the Act.

d A query does arise, however, about the derivation of the reference in s 23(9) to Part III. The enforcement provisions in the 1947 Act were in the same Part of that Act as s 24(4), which was the precursor of s 23(9) of the 1971 Act. Nearly the whole of the 1947 Act was repealed by the Town and Country Planning Act 1962, which was a consolidating Act. Section 24(4) became, with some change of wording, s 13(9) of the 1962 Act and was in Part III of that Act. The enforcement provisions are in Part *e* IV. Section 23(9) of the 1971 Act is in the same terms as s 13(9) of the 1962 Act; but the enforcement provisions in the 1971 Act are in Part V. There is nothing in the 1962 Act to indicate why this change was made; but made it was, and in language which was clear. It follows, in my judgment, that the Secretary of State was right in deciding that there could be no resumption of use of the premises as a wholesale warehouse.

Even if there could have been, in my judgment, the Secretary of State was entitled *f* to decide that the proposed use as a cash and carry wholesale warehouse, after compliance with the enforcement notice, would not have been a resumption of use as a wholesale warehouse. By 1972 the description 'cash and carry wholesale warehouse' was in common usage. What the description implied was an issue of fact for the Secretary of State to decide (see *Brutus v Cozens* per Lord Reid[1]). Unless he attributed to the description a meaning which was perverse, this court ought not to say that *g* he was wrong in giving it the meaning he did. It is a tenable opinion that by 1972 the public generally had come to see a 'cash and carry wholesale warehouse' as premises to which anyone could go who was prepared to buy for cash the goods on offer in quantities not smaller than those specified by those running the premises. In common usage it is the willingness to sell to anyone which distinguishes a cash and carry wholesale warehouse from the traditional wholesale warehouse which will *h* normally only deal with the retailers. Far from holding that the Secretary of State was wrong, I would adjudge that he had given the description its correct meaning.

I would allow the appeal.

GOFF LJ. The change of use of the premises when in 1971 they began to be used *j* for displaying furniture for sale to the public was undoubtedly a development for which permission was required under ss 22(1) and 23(1) of the Town and Country Planning Act 1971.

Subject, therefore, to the amendment which the Secretary of State made, and which it was agreed before us he had power to make, limiting the effect of the enforcement

---

1   [1972] 2 All ER 1297 at 1299, [1973] AC 854 at 861

notice to retail sales, that notice was clearly valid and properly upheld by the Secretary
of State.   *a*

Then, he correctly proceeded to treat the appeal as an application for planning
permission for that use, and decided to refuse permission. In his letter of decision he
disclosed that he had directed himself that the notice did not entitle LTSS to revert
without planning permission to the former established use as a wholesale warehouse,
and his understanding of the meaning of that expression.

On appeal by LTSS to the Divisional Court that court held that the Secretary of *b*
State had misdirected himself in that, as they held, LTSS were entitled so to revert by
virtue of s 23(9) of the 1971 Act. The court thought it very unlikely that his decision
on the planning application could have been affected by that misdirection of himself,
but since there was some possibility they allowed the appeal on that ground, described
by Lord Widgery CJ as a very narrow one, and ordered that the matter should go
back to the Secretary of State for reconsideration in the light of their judgments.   *c*

On this appeal by the Secretary of State it is submitted that the Secretary of State
did not misdirect himself, but took a correct view of s 23(9), and, in any case, that the
decision should not have been remitted as it was very unlikely that the Secretary of
State had been influenced by his interpretation of s 23(9), and that LTSS had not
discharged the onus which was on them to establish that if the Secretary of State had
made an error of law that error of law had influenced his decision.   *d*

The point of law in issue is whether, it being at all material times too late to serve
an enforcement notice because of the provisions of s 87(1) of the 1971 Act, the wholesale warehouse user was 'lawful' within the meaning of s 23(9), as LTSS contend
and the Divisional Court has held, or whether, though immune from attack, it
remained, was and is unlawful.

Under a respondent's notice LTSS sought to argue that it was in any event lawful, *e*
since in the evidence the warehouse user commenced otherwise than in breach of
planning control and, further or alternatively, commenced before 1st July 1948. In my
judgment, the evidence was wholly insufficient to establish any such conclusion of
fact, and the point of law remains as I have just stated it. By their respondent's notice
LTSS further contend that the Secretary of State misdirected himself as to the meaning
of 'wholesale warehouse', a point to which I will return later.   *f*

In my judgment, with the greatest respect to the very strong Divisional Court,
its decision was wrong and the Secretary of State was right on the interpretation and
effect of s 23(9) for two reasons, although, as Cairns LJ said, the case was not fully
argued before the Divisional Court as it has been before us.

First, in my judgment, the warehouse user was not in any case a purpose for which
the land could lawfully have been used within the meaning of s 23(9). As it was not *g*
shown to have commenced before the appointed day under the 1947 Act, i e 1st July
1948, it was a use the adoption of which required planning permission which was not
obtained. Not only, therefore, as it seems to me, was it unlawful to start it, but it
was also unlawful to carry it on, because that was in defiance of the Act and initially
liable to be stopped by enforcement procedure. With all respect, I find myself quite
unable to accept the view of the Divisional Court in *W T Lamb & Sons Ltd v Secretary of* *h*
State for the Environment[1] that a user begun in contravention of planning control is,
within s 23(9), lawful during the time that it is still liable to be attacked by an
enforcement notice. Bridge J said:

'Non constat that the continuance of that use beyond July 1969 would have
involved a breach of law. It would only have involved a breach of law if subse- *j*
quently an enforcement notice relating to that use had been served, had taken
effect, and had been contravened.'

It is true that then only could criminal proceedings be taken, but that does not in

[1] [1975] 2 All ER 1117 at 1122

a my view mean that what was being done was lawful. Surely, indeed, the whole basis of the enforcement procedure is that it is not.

Once one gets that far, then, in my judgment, s 87(1) is merely a time bar creating a state of immunity but not altering the legal quality of what was being done. In my judgment, this is so on the principle enunciated by Lord Denning MR in *R v Governor of Pentonville Prison, ex parte Azam*[1]:

b   'So, in practice it meant that, between 1968 and 1973, if a Commonwealth immigrant landed clandestinely, he was after six months virtually untouchable. He could not be prosecuted for the unlawful landing. He could not be removed. He could not be deported, unless he committed a fresh criminal offence and was recommended for deportation. But this does not mean that after six months he was here as of right: or that his presence here was lawful. His presence here c   was unlawful in its inception. It continued to be unlawful during the six months that he could be prosecuted for it. After the six months, it continued to be unlawful. It is a general rule of law that the expiry of a time limit does not make that lawful which was previously unlawful. It only bars the remedy in respect of it.'

The last two sentences are perfectly general and, in my view, apply directly to this case.

d   I am fortified in this conclusion by what Lord Widgery CJ himself said in *Webber v Minister of Housing and Local Government*[2]:

      'The second fallacy which seems to me to be embedded in [counsel's] argument is that it makes the mistake, which I suppose is common to us all from time to time, of thinking that four years' user creates a right to use the land for the pur- e   pose for which it was used during those four years. In fact, as will be remembered, the Acts makes it perfectly clear that the only result of four years' user is that you are immune, or the owner is immune, from enforcement action so long as he continues that use. If he chooses of his own accord to discontinue the use and substitute another, it is clearly wrong to suppose that he has any kind of right to revert to and resume the original use.'

f It is true that Lord Widgery CJ was there not considering s 23(9), and he was con- cerned only with the effect of voluntary discontinuance, but nevertheless it is entirely in line with the conclusion I have reached and the reasons for it which I have endeavoured to express. I am not overlooking the fact that the instant case is one of an established use and not a four year time ban. There is, however, nothing in the Town and Country Planning Act 1971 which in terms makes an established use an g answer to an enforcement notice, or which expressly gives it any effect at all, save s 94(7), which in certain circumstances makes a certificate of established use conclusive against the Secretary of State.

It seems to me, therefore, that, apart from the value of a certificate in satisfying a prospective purchaser, or mortgagee or as conclusive evidence on an appeal against h an enforcement notice, an established use under s 94(1) operates not as a legalisation of the use to which it refers or as in any way removing the requirements of planning control, but is showing, save in a case to which s 94(1)(c) applies, where no planning permission was in any event required which is not relevant, that the breach occurred before the end of 1963 (see s 94(1)(a) and (b)), so precluding the service of an enforce- ment notice under s 87(1) and affording correlative grounds for appeal within s 88(1)(d).

j There is, however, as I have said, a second reason why I disagree with the decision below, and that is as follows. Even if the conclusion I have reached would otherwise be wrong, still s 23(9) only allows one to return to a purpose for which (in accordance

---

1   [1973] 2 All ER 741 at 749, [1974] AC 18 at 29
2   (1967) 18 P & CR 495

with the provisions of 'this Part of this Act', that is to say, Part III) it could lawfully
have been used. Now the provisions requiring planning permission to be obtained   *a*
are in that Part of the Act, but the provisions for enforcement are not. They are in
Part V. In determining, therefore, whether the proposed use is lawful within the meaning of s 23(9) one is not, in my judgment, entitled to crave in aid the time bar in s 87 at
all. Thus one is left simply with the carrying on of a use which ought not to have been
commenced, because planning permission was required and had not been obtained.

It is true that the genesis of s 23(9) is to be found in s 24(4) of the Town and Country   *b*
Planning Act 1947 where the provisions requiring planning control and the sections
dealing with enforcement were in the same Part of the Act. In my judgment, however,
that does not entitle one to read s 23(9) of the 1971 Act as if the words 'in accordance
with the provisions of this Part of this Act' were not there, or to read in a gloss or
clause such as 'but subject to the provisions as to enforcement contained in Part V'.

The Divisional Court in this case founded itself very strongly on the difference in   *c*
language between sub-s (9) of s 23 and sub-ss (5) and (6), and clearly a cogent argument
can be mounted on it, but, in my judgment, having considered it most carefully,
that consideration does not lead me to alter or doubt the conclusion I have reached
as already stated. It is to be observed that the contrasting provisions approach the
matter from different angles, and so may readily have the same meaning though
expressed very differently. Subsection (6) is negative. It directs one to ignore any use   *d*
of the land begun in contravention of the provisions of Part III of the Act or in contravention of previous planning control. Subsection (9) is positive. It allows what is
lawful. The question remains what is lawful. And that is, in my judgment, to be
answered in the way I have indicated.

Counsel for the Secretary of State sought to escape the difficulty of the language
of s 23(6) by an historical review of the planning legislation from the 1947 Act onwards.   *e*
I confess I found it extremely difficult to follow his argument, and in the end I have
not derived much assistance from it one way or the other. It does, however, support
the Secretary of State's case, I think, to this extent: it shows that the situation envisaged in what was s 18(5) of the 1947 Act and is now s 23(5) of the 1971 Act, on the
one hand, and that in s 24(4) of the 1947 Act, now s 23(9), on the other, were, when
the respective forms of language were first conceived, treated differently in this res-   *f*
pect, that the proviso to s 18(5) of the 1947 Act disallowed a normal use, not only if
begun in contravention of that Act, but also if in contravention of previous planning
control, whereas s 24(4), in conjuction with s 12(1), in no way struck at uses contrary
to previous planning control. There was, therefore, in any event a reason for using a
different approach to a different language, so that the express reference in sub-s (6)
to a use begun in contravention of planning control does not necessarily import   *g*
that 'lawfully' in sub-s (9) includes uses begun even after the 1947 Act in contravention
of planning control.

For these reasons, I would allow this appeal, and it becomes unnecessary to consider the Secretary of State's second point which was based on the RSC Ord 94, r 12(4)
and (5), and particularly r 12(5), but I would have thought that if the Secretary of
State had misdirected himself on the point of law, then, although the risk of this   *h*
having influenced his decision might have been very slight, unless it was a mere
scintilla, which I do not think it was, it was right to remit the decision under r 12(5).
However, I need not say more about that.

The conclusion I have reached also defeats the points taken in the respondent's
notice, but in case the matter should be taken higher, I think it desirable to say a few
words on paras 2 and 3 which fall to be taken together.   *j*

The point is that on the footing that LTSS could revert to the established use as a
wholesale warehouse, then it was submitted that the Secretary of State took too
narrow a view of what that allowed and, therefore, did not properly weigh the
extent of the traffic difficulties which would be caused by that user as compared with
that likely to be occasioned by the furniture business which was the subject of the

enforcement notice. In particular, objection was taken to this passage in his decision
a letter:

> 'In this context "wholesale" is taken to mean selling, generally in bulk, to
> retailers in the trade for resale elsewhere or to manufacturers, professional
> builders and the like. The selling of goods to the general public in larger quanti-
> ties than are usual in a retail shop or at a discount and on a cash and carry basis
b > would not bring such sales within the term "wholesale". In a cash and carry
> estblishment, the main activity carried on in the building is the retail sale of
> goods for cash, and any storage of goods in such premises is normally ancillary
> to the sale of goods carried on in the building.'

The Town and Country Planning (Use Classes) Order 1948, art 2(2), did contain a
definition of wholesale warehouse as meaning 'a building where business, princi-
c pally of a wholesale nature, is transacted and goods are stored or displayed, but
only incidentally to the transaction of that business', but the latest order, that of 1972,
does not, nor did that of 1963, although they maintain the alternatives 'wholesale
warehouse or repository'.

In these circumstances, in my judgment, the 1972 order does not raise any question
of construction which would, of course, be a question of law, but simply a pure question
d of fact: what is the meaning in the ordinary use of English language of the words
'wholesale warehouse'? (See per Lord Reid in *Cozens v Brutus*[1].)

As was pointed by Lord Parker CJ in *Decorative and Caravan Paints Ltd v Nottingham
Corpn*[2] that although the expression 'warehouse' shades off into a shop, still it is a
matter of fact and degree.

In *Calcaria Construction Co Ltd v Secretary of State*[3] the application for detailed plan-
e ning permission for a large supermarket with parking space for no less than 992 cars
manifestly went outside the outline planning permission which had been obtained
for 'erection of warehouse for wholesale and retail distribution of foodstuffs and
household goods'. However, it is to be noted that O'Connor J said[4]:

> 'The ordinary meaning of "warehouse" which I quoted from the dictionary
f > is supported in cases, at which I need not look, under the Workmen's Compen-
> sation Acts; these all tend to show that where the word "warehouse" is used
> the main function of the building is intended to be for storage, and, of course,
> distribution from the building.'

That being so, I am clearly of opinion that the Secretary of State was fully entitled
to take the view he did, that the uses authorised within the limits of the words
g 'wholesale warehouse' would not be comparable with regard to the traffic they would
attract with that of the proposed user. On this aspect of the matter I fully agree with
what Lord Widgery CJ said in the court below[5]: 'His [the Secretary of State's]
general description of activities implicit in the phrase "warehouse" and indeed
"wholesale warehouse" I find quite unobjectionable.' I also would allow the appeal.

h *Appeal allowed. Cross-appeal dismissed. Leave to appeal to the House of Lords granted.*

Solicitors: *Kingsley Napley & Co* (for LTSS); *Treasury Solicitor*.

A S Virdi Esq Barrister.

j
1 [1972] 2 All ER at 1299, [1973] AC 854 at 861
2 (1970) 214 EG 1355
3 (1974) 27 P & CR 435
4 27 P & CR at 439
5 [1975] 1 All ER 374 at 375, [1975] 1 WLR 138 at 140

Re D (a minor) (wardship: sterilisation)   *a*

FAMILY DIVISION
HEILBRON J
29th, 30th, 31st JULY, 17th SEPTEMBER 1975

Ward of court – Jurisdiction – Protection of ward – Fundamental rights of ward – Right of   *b*
woman to reproduce – Sterilisation operation – Non-therapeutic reasons for operation –
Ward a mentally retarded girl – Proposal to perform operation to sterilise girl – Operation
irreversible – Fear that girl might be seduced and give birth to mentally abnormal child –
Operation advised by consulting paediatrician in charge of girl's case – Girl's parent con-
senting to operation – Girl incapable of giving informed consent to operation – Girl having
sufficient intellectual capacity to enable her to marry in due course and to make her own   *c*
choice whether to be sterilised – Whether court should exercise wardship jurisdiction to
prevent operation.

Official Solicitor – Guardian ad litem – Wardship proceedings – Institution of proceedings –
No duty on Official Solicitor to institute proceedings.

                                                                   d

D, a girl, was born in November 1963 with a condition which was subsequently
diagnosed as Sotos Syndrome, the symptoms of which included accelerated growth
during infancy, epilepsy, generalised clumsiness, an unusual facial appearance and
behaviour problems including emotional instability, certain aggressive tendencies
and some impairment of mental function which could result in dull intelligence or
possibly more serious mental retardation. Although D suffered from those signs and   *e*
symptoms she was not considered to be as seriously retarded as some children suffering from mental handicaps. In due course D was sent to an appropriate school but she
did not do well, partly because she exhibited a number of serious behaviour problems,
including hostility and a certain amount of violence towards other children. Accordingly, in October 1973 D was sent to a school specialising in children who had
learning difficulties and associated behaviour problems. The move was a success. *f*
D showed a marked improvement in her academic skills, in her soical competence and
in her behaviour problems. She had an intelligence quotient of about 80, indicating a
dull normal intelligence, and she had the understanding of a child of about nine or 9½
years of age. A consultant paediatrician confirmed that her clumsiness was likely to
lessen and her behaviour to continue to improve. D's mother however was convinced
that D was seriously retarded mentally and she did not accept that there had been any   *g*
improvement in D's behaviour or ability to care for herself. Dr G, a consultant paediatrician who, from an early stage, had taken an interest in D's case, thought that D's
behaviour had deteriorated, that she would always remain substantially handicapped
and that she would therefore be unable either to care for or maintain herself or to
look after any children she might have. It was common ground, however, that D
had sufficient intellectual capacity to enable her to marry in due course. When D was   *h*
a young child her parents had decided that they should apply to have her sterilised
when she was about 18 years of age to prevent her from having children who might be
abnormal and over the years they discussed the matter several times with Dr G.
When D reached puberty at the age of ten, the mother's concern increased; she was
worried that D might be seduced and possibly give birth to an abnormal child. She
consulted Dr G who took the view that there was a real risk that D might give birth to   *j*
an abnormal foetus. Accordingly he agreed that D should be sterilised without waiting
for her to grow any older. Arrangements were made for the operation to be carried
out in May 1975. Other professional people concerned with D's welfare challenged the
social and behavioural reasons for performing such an operation on a girl of 11 which
would be irreversible and permanent. Dr G however refused to defer the operation.

a Mrs H, who was an educational psychologist attached to the educational department of D's local authority, thereupon applied to the court to make D a ward of court and sought an order continuing the wardship in order to delay or prevent the proposed operation from being carried out.

Held – (i) The operation proposed was one which involved the deprivation of a basic
b human right, i e the right of a woman to reproduce, and therefore, if performed on a woman for non-therapeutic reasons and without her consent, would be a violation of that right. Since D could not give an informed consent, but there was a strong likelihood would understand the implications of the operation when she reached the age of 18, the case was one in which the courts should exercise its protective powers. Her wardship would accordingly be continued (see p 332 *g* and *h* and p 333 *c*, post).

c (ii) A decision to carry out a sterilisation operation on a minor for non-therapeutic purposes was not solely within a doctor's clinical judgment. In the circumstances the operation was neither medically indicated nor necessary, and it would not be in D's best interests for it to be performed since the evidence showed that D's mental and physical condition and attainments had already improved, that her future prospects were unpredictable, and that she was as yet unable to understand or appreciate the implications of the operation, whereas it was likely that in later years she would
d be able to make her own choice (see p 335 *b* to *d*, post).

Per Heilbron J. The Official Solicitor is an officer of the court and it is not his duty or function to institute wardship proceedings (see p 336 *f* and *g*, post).

Notes
e For the court's jurisdiction over wards of court, see 21 Halsbury's Laws (3rd Edn) 216-217, paras 478, 479, and for cases on the subject, see 28(2) Digest (Reissue) 911-916, 2220-2248.

For the duties of the Official Solicitor, see 10 Halsbury's Laws (4th Edn) para 950.

Cases referred to in judgment
f *Caton, Re, Vincent v Vatcher* (1911) 55 Sol Jo 313, 43 Digest (Repl) 459, 4926.

J v C [1969] 1 All ER 788, [1970] AC 668, [1969] 2 WLR 540, HL, 28(2) Digest (Reissue) 800, 1230.

R (P M) (an infant), Re [1968] 1 All ER 691, [1968] 1 WLR 385, 28(2) Digest (Reissue) 921, 2296.

Rhodes v Swithenbank (1889) 22 QBD 577, 58 LJQB 287, 60 LT 856, CA, 28(2) Digest
g (Reissue) 906, 2179.

Taylor's Application, Re [1972] 2 All ER 873, [1972] 2 QB 369, [1972] 2 WLR 1337, CA.

Wellesley v Duke of Beaufort (1827) 2 Russ 1, 5 LJOSCh 85, 38 ER 236, LC; *affd* sub nom *Wellesley v Wellesley* (1828) 2 Bli NS 124, HL, 28(2) Digest (Reissue) 924, 2330.

X (a minor), Re [1975] 1 All ER 697, [1975] 2 WLR 335, CA.

h **Originating summons**
This was a summons in wardship proceedings instituted by the plaintiff, Mrs Hamidi, on 12th June 1975, whereby Mrs Hamidi sought an order that an infant girl, D, should continue to be a ward of court. The first defendant was D's mother. The infant was added as second defendant to the proceedings and the Official Solicitor was appointed her guardian ad litem. The summons was heard in chambers and judgment was
j delivered in open court. The facts are set out in the judgment of Heilbron J.

Barbara Calvert QC and *Robert Hazell* for Mrs Hamidi.
F H Potts QC and *Peter Fox* for the mother.
Joseph Jackson QC and *Margaret Booth* for the Official Solicitor as guardian ad litem.

Cur adv vult

17th September. **HEILBRON J** read the following judgment.

The nature of this application

This is an application to invoke the wardship jurisdiction of this court in entirely novel circumstances. The case is primarily of great importance to the child concerned. As it also raises a matter of principle of considerable public importance I have decided to give this judgment in open court. The hearing itself took place over a number of days in chambers. As I have already just mentioned as this case concerns an infant I have taken care to cloak the identities of those witnesses, and of those matters which I feel are necessary, to conceal and so protect the infant from any possibility that her identity might be disclosed. I shall, therefore, hereafter refer to her as D and to her mother as Mrs B.

This child is a girl of 11 years of age, and the hearing before me was concerned with two issues: (1) whether it was appropriate to continue wardship proceedings which were initiated on 12th June 1975, and (2) whether a proposed operation to sterilise this child should be prevented. It is important, therefore, in the first place, to refer in some detail to the child on whom it was proposed to perform this serious operation.

The child

D is a girl who was born in Sheffield on 29th November 1963. Sadly soon after her birth she was found to be handicapped, in that she was mentally backward, she suffered from epilepsy and her physical development began to advance at an exceptional rate. D was, and still is, under the care of her general practitioner and of the consultant paediatrician attached to the Sheffield Northern General Hospital, Dr Gordon. Dr Gordon has always taken a most compassionate and concerned interest in his patient, her serious condition and the consequent problems which beset the child, the mother and the rest of her family.

D was born into a family consisting of father, mother and two other daughters. Her father died on 15th October 1971 leaving a mother who has, therefore, over the past four years had to bring up this family alone in extraordinarily difficult circumstances, described by one doctor as appalling, living as they do in grossly overcrowded conditions in a house with only two bedrooms and no inside bathroom or toilet. Mrs B and D sleep together in one bed. Mrs B, who is now 51 years of age, works part-time as a cleaner, and she is, in my judgment, an excellent, caring and devoted mother, whose life has been, and still is, beset with tremendous difficulties, many of which cannot readily be appreciated by those who have not had to deal with the problems which she has so courageously faced. She is not only a very hard-working woman, whose home was described as spotless, but she impressed everyone with her qualities of sincerity and commonsense.

Eventually a firm diagnosis of D's condition was made. She was found to be suffering from a syndrome which comprised a somewhat unusual group of congenital abnormalities. Dr Sotos was the Argentinian doctor whose name was attached to this syndrome, and it is now known as Sotos Syndrome. Its cause is obscure, but it may include some or all of the following signs and symptoms, namely, accelerated growth during infancy, epilepsy, generalised clumsiness, an unusual facial appearance, behaviour problems including emotional instability, certain aggressive tendencies, some impairment of mental function which could result in dull intelligence or possibly more serious mental retardation. D suffered from these signs and symptoms but she was not considered to be as seriously retarded as some children suffering from mental handicaps.

When she was about 4½ years of age, Dr Gordon wrote to the school's medical officer drawing his attention to D's disabilities and asking him to see her, as she would require special education. I refer to this letter because it is an example of the normal and

advantageous co-operation between the various professions, persons and agencies
a concerned with the welfare of children which now exists in this country.

D was in due course sent to a school which was thought to be appropriate. She did
not, however, do very well, partly because she exhibited a number of serious behaviour problems, including hostility and a certain amount of violence towards some
other children. She was accordingly referred by the school's medical officer to a
consultant child psychiatrist, Dr T, to consider her transfer to a more suitable school,
b and when, in August 1973, D was examined by this psychiatrist, it is important to
point out that he concluded that she was quite capable of discussing with him her
difficulties and unhappiness at school, but Dr T considered that Mrs B did not fully
appreciate the true nature of D's handicap, and as a result somewhat over-protected
her. There was other evidence to the same effect and I accept that conclusion; I do
not, however, feel it is in any way a ground for criticising Mrs B. To be over-zealous
c in looking after a handicapped child is a very understandable attitude from a very
devoted mother.

D was duly transferred in October 1973 to a school which specialises in work with
children who have learning difficulties and associated behavioural problems. The
move was a success. I pause to pay my tribute to the dedication and devotion to his
pupils of Mr Y, the present headmaster. I entirely agree with counsel for the Official
d Solicitor that Mr Y was wise, understanding, outstanding in his sphere and completely
detached. I unreservedly accept his evidence, which was an entirely objective appraisal
of D's progress.

Mrs Hamidi, the plaintiff, who is an experienced, trained and qualified educational
psychologist, attached to the local authority educational department, also gave
evidence. As an educational psychologist she observes, tests and assesses the social,
e behavioural and academic skills of various children in order to assist them to fulfil
their potential at school, and in general, and to that end she not only had case con-
ferences with D's teachers in regard to her behaviour problems, her emotional and
general development, so as to help her to avoid her clumsiness and to improve her
general academic performance, but she developed a personal relationship with her,
and observed, interviewed and assessed her on the results of standard psychological
f tests.

From the evidence of Mr Y and Mrs Hamidi it appears that D has an intelligence
quotient of about 80—an indication of a dull normal intelligence range. I am satisfied
on their evidence that she has a fair academic standard, and her reading, language
and conversational skills are reasonably good. She can write but with some difficulty
and not very well. She has the understanding of a child of about nine to 9½ years of age.
g Mr Y and Mrs Hamidi asserted that her clumsiness has lessened and that she was
now able to ride a bicycle, swim and dress herself—albeit slowly. Her interests,
which included worship of a well-known 'pop star', were those of a normal girl of her
age, and although even at school there were still instances of bad behaviour, she was
not a severe management problem, and her behaviour was, and still is, improving.

The evidence of Dr Snodgrass, a consultant paediatrician and senior lecturer in
h child health called on behalf of the plaintiff, Mrs Hamidi, confirmed that her clumsiness is likely to lessen, and her behaviour to continue to improve. Mrs B was convinced, however, that D was seriously mentally retarded, and she maintained that
there was no real improvement in D's behaviour or ability to care for herself, and
although in her affidavit, she stated: 'At home D behaves reasonably well', in
evidence she gave a number of instances of D's difficulties and behaviour problems.
j I can appreciate Mrs B's reluctance to accept the school's assessment. I am sure,
like many children, D tends to behave better at school than at home or when out
with her mother and sisters, when she can be a very real problem and sometimes a
very serious embarrassment.

Dr Gordon, relying to some extent on what Mrs B told him, but also on his own
assessment of his patient, thought her behaviour had deteriorated, and that she was

and would always remain so substantially handicapped, as to be unable either to care for, or maintain herself, or to look after any children she might have.   **a**

I am satisfied, and I find, that this young girl has shown marked improvement in her academic skills, in her social competence and in her behaviour problems, which improvement unfortunately neither the mother nor Dr Gordon could accept.

Mr Y, contrary to Dr Gordon's view, maintained that it was unrealistic to be dogmatic about D's future chances of employment, whether or not she would be capable of looking after a family, or her future role in society. The effect of the other medical **b** evidence also supports Mr Y's views on this aspect of D's future and I am satisfied that it would indeed be premature to make such predictions in the case of this 11 year old girl.

I have referred to D's present and future behaviour, social attitudes and academic attainments in some detail, in deference to the substantial body of evidence presented to me, although in the context of this case they are only one aspect of a considerably **c** larger problem, namely whether this child should undergo an operation for sterilisation.

The background to the decision to operate

When Mrs B first realised that she had given birth to a handicapped child, she recalled with deep concern that, many years before, she had lived near a family **d** who had the misfortune to have three mentally retarded children, and their plight and their troubled lives had deeply affected her. She and her husband not unnaturally were extremely worried about D's future, as at that time they thought D could never improve, and so even when D was a very young child they decided that when she reached the age of about 18 they would take the necessary steps to prevent her from having any children, and would apply to have her sterilised. From the decision **e** made in those early days Mrs B has never resiled, and she has in consequence, over the years, had several discussions about this operation with Dr Gordon.

When D reached puberty by the age of ten Mrs B's concern increased, and so she discussed the operation once again with Dr Gordon on 7th January 1975. Mrs B said, and I accept, that when she reiterated to Dr Gordon that she would like D sterilised when she was older, the doctor said: 'We can do it now.' This is indeed confirmed by the **f** doctor in his affidavit when he says that rather than wait any longer the decision should be taken then. Mrs B agreed that the operation should be performed. She was very worried lest D might be seduced and possibly give birth to a baby, which might also be abnormal. She had always believed that D would not, or should not, marry and in any event would be incapable of bringing up a child. Her anxieties are genuine and understandable.   **g**

Dr Gordon took the view that there was a real risk that D might give birth to an abnormal foetus. I have already referred to some of his other anxieties. As to the possibility of producing an abnormal child, the evidence of Dr Snodgrass and Dr Newton, the well-known consultant psychiatrist called on behalf of the Official Solicitor, confirmed that there was, as Dr Gordon stated, an increased risk of such an eventuality. On the other hand, they pointed out that no one with this particular **h** syndrome had ever been known to have a baby, and it is not therefore possible to make any precise predictions whether or not they are able to do so.

At that consultation in January Dr Gordon, with Mrs B's agreement, came to a decision provided that Miss Duncan, the consultant gynaecologist, who is a senior lecturer and gynaecologist to the Sheffield and Northern General Hospital, to whom he referred, concurred in his recommendation the operation should be performed. **j** Miss Duncan saw and interviewed both D and Mrs B on 17th February 1975, but she did not examine the child, and I think there is little doubt that Miss Duncan did not give very much independent consideration to the wider implications of this operation, but was content in large measure to rely on Dr Gordon's recommendation and assessment of the situation. She did, however, agree to perform the sterilisation,

namely a hysterectomy, and I am satified that D was booked to enter hospital on
4th May for that operation to be carried out on 6th May. No one else was consulted
prior to that decision. It is surprising that Dr T, the child psychiatrist, was not,
for, prior to the date of the recommendation, he had on a number of occasions
interviewed and examined the child, and his views, as Dr Gordon later agreed in
evidence, must have been of considerable importance in evaluating the numerous
problems, medical, social, educational and psychiatric, which such a vital decision
involved.

Dr Gordon maintains, however, that his recommendation was one which was based
on clinical judgment as a doctor, and that he and the gynaecologist should be the sole
judges whether or not it should be performed, provided of course that they had the
parent's consent.

Despite Dr Gordon's assertion that his decision should be upheld because it was
based on his clinical judgment, he nevertheless, in putting forward his grounds for
recommending this operation, stated that such reasons or such grounds were of a
twofold character, i e that they were both medical and social. The medical reasons
included the possibility that she might give birth to an abnormal child, that her
epilepsy might cause her to harm a child, and that the only satisfactory method of
birth control was this operation. The social reasons included his opinion that D would
be unable in the future to maintain herself save in a sheltered environment, her
inability due to epilepsy and other handicaps to cope with a family if she were to
marry, without substantial support, the deterioration in her behaviour for which he
said there was no known method of improvement and the possibility that she might
have to enter an institution as he alleged for social or criminal reasons in the future.

Certain persons concerned with D's welfare, however, took a different view. They
were the former and present headmaster of her school, Mrs Hamidi and the social
worker involved with the family. They believed that an operation for sterilisation
in the case of a minor, particularly a girl of 11, being irreversible and permanent, was
a matter of grave concern, and so on 26th March Mrs Hamidi wrote on their behalf
and on her own to the senior school medical officer, pointing out in detail the conflict
between Mrs B and the school and the welfare services in regard to D's attainments
and their concern in regard to the proposed operation, which they pointed out could
affect the whole of her future.

On 21st April there was a meeting between Dr Gordon and those professionals
working with the child and her family, at which Dr Gordon's social and behavioural
reasons for performing this operation were seriously challenged. Dr Gordon, however, refused to acknowledge that these views could possibly be wrong or exaggerated
or premature. I think Dr Gordon, whose sincerity cannot be challenged, was persuaded by his emotional involvement with Mrs B's considerable problems and
anxieties, and his strong personal views in favour of sterilisation—as he stated in his
affidavit, 'Sterilisation is now an emotive word, and we must try to change its image'—
to form a less than detached opinion in regard to a number of matters which were
not in my view in reality matters of clinical judgment, but which were concerned, to
a large extent, with grounds which were other than medical. I feel it is a pity that he
was not prepared to accept that others, whose duties, training and skills were directed
to the assessment and amelioration of many of these problems, had much to
contribute in the formulation of a decision of this gravity.

In my judgment Dr Gordon's views as to D's present and future social and behavioural problems were somewhat exaggerated and mistaken. I think in this area
his views were clouded by his resentment at what he considered unjustified
interference.

In the event Dr Gordon did not accept the alternative views, and he and Miss
Duncan refused to defer the operation despite the grave implications for the child.
Mrs Hamidi and the others, therefore, wrote to the area administrator of the health
authority requesting an urgent and independent review of this decision. The area

administrator consulted the local authority's specialist in community medicine (child health) and he later replied saying that she had made a very careful appraisal of the case, but could not interfere. Mrs Hamidi and her colleagues, however, were not daunted and they thereupon consulted solicitors, and in due course these proceedings got under way. It is only right that I should pay tribute to their courage, persistence and humane concern for this young girl.

These proceedings

In due course an application was made to this court and, although Mrs Hamidi asked that D's care and control be transferred from Mrs B, the first defendant, that has not been pursued, and it is common ground that there can be no question of depriving Mrs B of continuing to care for D, which she has done so splendidly. Mrs Hamidi further requested the appointment of the Official Solicitor as guardian ad litem to the infant. He consented so to act and D became respondent to these proceedings.

Is wardship appropriate?

I have first of all to decide whether this is an appropriate case in which to exercise the court's wardship jurisdiction. Wardship is a very special and ancient jurisdiction. Its origin was the sovereign's feudal obligation as parens patriae to protect the person and property of his subjects, and particularly those unable to look after themselves, including infants. This obligation, delegated to the chancellor, passed to the Chancery Court, and in 1970 to this division of the High Court.

The jurisdiction in wardship is very wide, but there are limitations. It is not in every case that it is appropriate to make a child a ward, and counsel for Mrs B has argued with his usual skill and powers of persuasion that, as this case raises a matter of principle of wide public importance, and is a matter which affects many people, continuation of wardship would be inappropriate.

In his powerful argument, counsel for the Official Solicitor, on the other hand, submitted that the court in wardship had a wide jurisdiction which should be extended to encompass this novel situation, because it is just the type of problem which this court is best suited to determine when exercising its protective functions in regard to minors. As Lord Eldon LC said many years ago in *Wellesley v Duke of Beaufort*[1]:

'This jurisdiction is founded on the obvious necessity that the law should place somewhere the care of individuals who cannot take care of themselves, particularly in cases where it is clear that some care should be thrown around them.'

It is apparent from the recent decision of the Court of Appeal in *Re X (a minor)*[2] that the jurisdiction to do what is considered necessary for the protection of an infant is to be exercised carefully and within limits, but the court has, from time to time over the years, extended the sphere in the exercise of this jurisdiction.

The type of operation proposed is one which involves the deprivation of a basic human right, namely the right of a woman to reproduce, and therefore it would, if performed on a woman for non-therapeutic reasons and without her consent, be a violation of such right. Both Dr Gordon and Miss Duncan seem to have had in mind the possibility of seeking the child's views and her consent, for they asked that this handicapped child of 11 should be consulted in the matter. One would have thought that they must have known that any answer she might have given, or any purported consent, would have been valueless. Nevertheless Dr Gordon did ask Mrs B to discuss the proposed operation with D, and Miss Duncan did intend, she said, to seek the child's consent prior to the operation.

---

1 (1827) 2 Russ 1 at 20
2 [1975] 1 All ER 697, [1975] 2 WLR 335

Mrs B therefore discussed the proposed operation with the child, and asked her if she would like to have babies when she was old enough to have them. I do not think any useful purpose would be served by referring to this unfortunate episode in any further detail, but I express surprise that such a request should have been made, or such a discussion thought fitting. As the evidence showed, and I accept it, D could not possibly have given an informed consent. What the evidence did, however, make clear was that she would almost certainly understand the implications of such an operation by the time she reached 18.

This operation could, if necessary, be delayed or prevented if the child were to remain a ward of court, and as Lord Eldon LC, so vividly expressed it in *Wellesley's* case[1]: 'It has always been the principle of this Court, not to risk the incurring of damage to children which it cannot repair, but rather to prevent the damage being done.'

I think that is the very type of case where this court should 'throw some care around this child', and I propose to continue her wardship which, in my judgment, is appropriate in this case.

The operation—should it be performed?

In considering this vital matter, I want to make it quite clear that I have well in mind the natural feelings of a parent's heart, and though in wardship proceedings parents' rights can be superseded, the court will not do so lightly, and only in pursuance of well-known principles laid down over the years. The exercise of the court's jurisdiction is paternal, and it must be exercised judicially, and the judge must act, as far as humanly possible, on the evidence, as a wise parent would act. As Lord Upjohn pointed out in *J v C*[2], the law and practice in relation to infants—

'have developed, are developing and must, and no doubt will, continue to develop by reflecting and adopting the changing views, as the years go by, of reasonable men and women, the parents of children, on the proper treatment and methods of bringing up children; for after all that is the model which the judge must emulate for ... he must act as the judicial reasonable parent.'

It is of course beyond dispute that the welfare of this child is the paramount consideration, and the court must act in her best interests.

The proposed sterilisation operation

The question of the sterilisation of a minor is one aspect of a sensitive and delicate area of controversy into which I do not propose to enter. I am dealing here with the case of this particular young girl, but the evidence, including that which disclosed that Dr Gordon has recommended and Miss Duncan has performed two prior operations of this nature on handicapped children in Sheffield, indicates the possibility that further consideration may need to be given to this topic, consideration which would involve extensive consultation and debate elsewhere.

Dr Gordon's reason for wishing this operation to be performed was, of course, to prevent D ever having a child. He recognised, as did Mrs B, that there are other methods of achieving that objective, but his view was that D could not satisfactorily manage any form of contraception. Mrs B was concerned lest D might be seduced and become pregnant. She too was against all forms of contraception.

A good deal of evidence was directed to ascertaining whether Mrs B's fears were soundly based or not. The answer is in the nature of things somewhat speculative, but it was common ground that D had as yet shown no interest in the opposite sex, and that her opportunities for promiscuity, if she became so minded, were virtually non-existent, as her mother never leaves her side and she is never allowed out alone. Much of the evidence, which I found convincing, was to the effect that it

1 (1827) 2 Russ 1 at 18
2 [1969] 1 All ER 788 at 831, [1970] AC 668 at 722, 723

was premature even to consider contraception, except possibly to allay the mother's fears.

Mrs B's genuine concern, however, cannot be disregarded. A body of evidence was produced, therefore, to indicate the advantages and disadvantages of various forms of contraception. I shall not, however, burden this judgment with any detailed examination of it, save to say that I do not accept on the evidence Dr Gordon's contention that this young girl, if and when the time arrived, would not be a suitable subject for one of the various methods described by the doctors. I think it is only necessary to refer to the fact that Miss Duncan herself stated in evidence that if Mrs B had been willing to accept one of the methods of contraception, she would have advised one before sterilisation, and I entirely accept Professor Huntingford's evidence that there were certainly two methods, either one of which could be safely and satisfactorily used. I think it was a pity that both Dr Gordon and Mrs B were so reluctant to accept this possibility, or even the alternative of abortion, if, unhappily, it ever proved necessary, rather than the proposed use of such an irrevocable procdure.

It was common ground that D had sufficient intellectual capacity to marry, in the future of course, and that many people of a like kind are capable of, and do so. Dr Gordon agreed that this being so, she and her future husband would then be the persons most concerned in any question of sterilisation, and such an operation might have a serious and material bearing on a future marriage and its consequences.

The purpose of performing this operation is permanently to prevent the possibility of reproduction. The evidence of Professor Huntingford, consultant and professor of obstetrics and gynaecology at the University of London and at St Bartholomew's Hospital and the London Hospital Medical Colleges, was that in his view such an operation was normally only appropriate for a woman who consented to it, possibly at the conclusion of child-bearing, and then only after careful and anxious consideration by her and her husband of many factors and, what is most important, with full knowledge of all its implications.

Professor Huntingford, Dr Snodgrass and Dr Newton were all agreed that such an operation was not medically indicated in this case, and should not be performed. Dr Snodgrass said he was firmly of the view that it was wrong to perform this operation on an 11 year old, on the pretext that it would benefit her in the future. Dr Newton said:

'In my opinion sterilisation of a child before the age of consent can only be justified if it is the treatment for some present or inevitable disease. In this case, sterilization is not a treatment for any of the signs or symptoms of Sotos Syndrome, from which she suffers. I am totally against this operation being performed on D.'

Professor Huntingford stated: 'In my considered opinion it will not be in the best interests of the ward to be sterilized having regard to her age and all other relevant factors.' He had never ever heard of a child of this age being sterilised. Dr Snodgrass, with his great experience of handicapped children of all types, had never known anyone suffering from epilepsy to be sterilised for that reason, nor would he consider recommending such an operation, even if a child was mentally retarded. D was only one of at least a hundred thousand people of a similar degree of dull normal intelligence. If it ever became necessary he would, he said, be prepared to recommend abortion, not sterilisation. Dr Gordon, however, maintained that, provided the parent or parents consented, the decision was one made pursuant to the exercise of his clinical judgment, and that no interference could be tolerated in his clinical freedom.

The other consultants did not agree. Their opinion was that a decision to sterilise a child was not entirely within a doctor's clinical judgment, save only when sterilisation was the treatment of choice for some disease, as, for instance, when in order to treat a child and to ensure her direct physical well-being, it might be necessary to perform

a hysterectomy to remove a malignant uterus. Whilst the side effect of such an opera-
a tion would be to sterilise, the operation would be performed solely for therapeutic
purposes. I entirely accept their opinions. I cannot believe, and the evidence does not
warrant the view, that a decision to carry out an operation of this nature performed
for non-therapeutic purpòses on a minor, can be held to be within the doctor's sole
clinical judgment.

It is quite clear that once a child is a ward of court, no important step in the life of
b that child, can be taken without the consent of the court, and I cannot conceive of a
more important step than that which was proposed in this case.

A review of the whole of the evidence leads me to the conclusion that in a case of a
child of 11 years of age, where the evidence shows that her mental and physical
condition and attainments have already improved, and where her future prospects
are as yet unpredictable, where the evidence also shows that she is unable as yet to
c understand and appreciate the implications of this operation and could not give a
valid or informed consent, but the likelihood is that in later years she will be able to
make her own choice, where, I believe, the frustration and resentment of realising (as
she would one day) what had happened, could be devastating, an operation of this
nature is, in my view, contra-indicated.

d For these, and for the other reasons to which I have adverted, I have come to the
conclusion that this operation is neither medically indicated nor necessary, and that
it would not be in D's best interests for it to be performed.

The Official Solicitor

Counsel for the Official Solicitor has asked me to deal with one important aspect in
regard to the position of the Official Solicitor, which has arisen in these proceedings.
e As a single judge I am somewhat reluctant to do so, but in deference to the arguments
put before me, and because I think it may be of some assistance, I will, though quite
briefly in this already rather long judgment, accede to that request.

The Official Solicitor has functions which are wide and varied, including assisting the
court in matters where the court considers the services of a solicitor are desirable or
f necessary, as for instance acting in certain High Court bail applications for persons
without adequate means, or in appropriate cases acting on behalf of persons committed for contempt of court and applying for their release, and of course acting on
behalf of persons under disability, including infants, in regard to whom he has a
number of important functions and duties. This function occurs for instance in wardship proceedings where it is possible that the interests of the infant may take second
g place to the evidence and arguments of the adult adversaries, unless the court has the
assistance of an experienced and impartial person, whose only interest is the child's
welfare.

He is appointed, therefore, by order of the court to represent the interests of, and
act as guardian ad litem to, the infant, who is made a party to the ensuing litigation,
but only provided the Official Solicitor consents, his consent being a prerequisite to
h acting.

Counsel for Mrs Hamidi most persuasively submitted that the Official Solicitor's
duties were not limited to his appointment by order of the court. She submitted that
the Official Solicitor could initiate and then prosecute wardship proceedings, acting
on his own account as the infant's next friend.

She conceded, however, that the Official Solicitor could not act in any case unless
j first invited, and she agreed that his consent was a condition precedent. She further
conceded that there was no evidence of any such invitation in this case. There was no
authority to suggest that the Official Solicitor had ever initiated proceedings in this
way, nor that it had ever been his practice so to do. In *Re R (P M) (an infant)*[1] it was

---

1   [1968] 1 All ER 691 at 692, [1968] 1 WLR 385 at 387

stated: '[The Official Solicitor] is not only an officer of the court and the ward's guardian, but he is a solicitor and the ward is his client.'

The Official Solicitor, in my judgment, though a solicitor, does not seek clients. He only acts on behalf of minors who are the subject of existing procedures. This practice has always been followed by him on the basis that he has neither the authority nor the jurisdiction to institute proceedings concerning the welfare of children, though when he does act, as was pointed out in *Rhodes v Swithenbank*[1] (approved in *Re Taylor's Application*[2]), he always does so as 'the officer of the Court to take all measures for the benefit of the infant in the litigation in which he appears as next friend'.

Re Caton, Vincent v Vatcher[3], which was decided in 1911 and is only reported in the Solicitor's Journal, concerned a person under disability, a woman of unsound mind. The then Official Solicitor was actually criticised for instituting and pursuing legal proceedings on her behalf, when the court had directed him to take such steps as he thought proper for her better maintenance and comfort, Eve J saying[3]: 'The Official Solicitor took up a mistaken attitude and mistook his functions.'

It was submitted on behalf of Mrs Hamidi that r 112 of the Matrimonial Causes Rules 1973[4], which states that a person under disability may sue by a next friend or defend by guardian ad litem in matrimonial proceedings, who can be the Official Solicitor if he consents, supported her contention that the Official Solicitor could, if invited, likewise institute wardship proceedings. I do not find it possible to draw such an analogy,

Apart from the fact that there is no evidence that the Official Solicitor was so invited, one has only to envisage the intolerable situation, and the practical difficulties, that would arise if the Official Solicitor's jurisdiction were to be enlarged as suggested.

That alone, of course, would not be a conclusive argument in favour of the present practice, nor is the fact that there is no authority which has been produced to suggest that the present practice is wrong, but where there is a long established usage, as there is in this matter, and no authority or compelling reason to the contrary, I would deem it wrong to interfere. I am satisfied that her submission is based on a misconception of the Official Solicitor's functions.

It was also argued that, as this case came before the court quite fortuitously, if the Official Solicitor is not the person or authority to initiate the proceedings, then who is? That is a question which has not yet been investigated, and I make no further comment other than to say that if there is a gap, it is not for the Official Solicitor to fill it, and in my view it is not the duty or function of the Official Solicitor to institute wardship proceedings.

Order accordingly.

Solicitors: *Marian F Norrie & Bowler*, Sheffield (for Mrs Hamidi); *Ashton, Hewitt, Barlow & Wise*, Sheffield (for Mrs B); *Official Solicitor*.

Mary Rose Plummer Barrister.

1   (1889) 22 QBD 577 at 579
2   [1972] 2 All ER 873 at 878, [1972] 2 QB 369 at 381
3   (1911) 55 Sol Jo 313
4   SI 1973 No 2016

Haggard v Mason

QUEEN'S BENCH DIVISION
LORD WIDGERY CJ, O'CONNOR AND LAWSON JJ
29th OCTOBER 1975

Drugs – Dangerous drugs – Supply – Offer to supply controlled drug – Mens rea – Belief of defendant and person to whom offer made that substance a controlled drug – Belief erroneous – Offer by defendant to third party to supply him with lysergide – Third party purchasing substance believing it to be lysergide – Substance not lysergide or any other controlled drug – Whether defendant guilty of offering to supply a controlled drug – Misuse of Drugs Act 1971, s 4(1)(3)(a).

The defendant purchased, in the form of impregnated blotting paper, 1,000 'tabs' of a substance which at the time he believed to be lysergide (LSD), a controlled drug of class A in Sch 2, Part I, to the Misuse of Drugs Act 1971. The defendant intended to resell the drug. For that purpose he was introduced to H. The defendant offered to sell a quantity of lysergide to H. H accepted that offer, and bought from the defendant some of the substance which the defendant had earlier purchased. At the time of the sale both parties believed that the substance was lysergide. It subsequently transpired that it was a quite different substance which was not a controlled drug. The defendant was convicted by justices of offering to supply a controlled drug to H in contravention of s 4(1)[a] of the 1971 Act, contrary to s 4(3)(a) thereof, and an order was made under s 27(1)[b] of the 1971 Act for the destruction of the substance supplied to H and the forfeiture of a sum of £146 which had been found in the defendant's possession. The defendant appealed, contending that, since what he had offered to supply was not a controlled drug, he was not guilty of an offence under s 4(3)(a).

Held – (i) The offence was complete at the moment when the defendant met H and offered to supply him with lysergide. It was immaterial that what was in fact supplied was not a controlled drug. Accordingly the appeal would be dismissed (see p 340 *d e* and *j*, post).

(ii) The justices had no power, however, under s 27 to order the forfeiture of the £146 found in the defendant's possession and the forfeiture order should be varied accordingly (see p 340 *h* and *j*, post).

Notes
For controlled drugs, see Supplement to 26 Halsbury's Laws (3rd Edn) para 491B, and for restrictions on the supply or offer to supply of controlled drugs, see ibid para 491C, 2.

For the Misuse of Drugs Act 1971, ss 4, 27, see 41 Halsbury's Statutes (3rd Edn) 883, 905.

---

a Section 4, so far as material, provides:
  '(1) Subject to any regulations . . . it shall not be lawful for a person—(a) to produce a controlled drug; or (b) to supply or offer to supply a controlled drug to another . . .
  '(3) . . . it is an offence for a person—(a) to supply or offer to supply a controlled drug to another in contravention of subsection (1) above; or (b) to be concerned in the supplying of such a drug to another in contravention of the subsection; or (c) to be concerned in the making to another in contravention of that subsection of an offer to supply such a drug.'
b Section 27(1), so far as material, provides: '. . . the court by or before which a person is convicted of an offence under this Act may order anything shown to the satisfaction of the court to relate to the offence, to be forfeited and either destroyed or dealt with in such other manner as the court may order.'

N

Case stated

This was an appeal by way of a case stated by the justices for the city of Newcastle *a* upon Tyne in respect of their adjudication as a magistrates' court, sitting at Market Street, Newcastle on 27th August 1974.

On 17th July 1974 an information was preferred by the respondent, Sidney Mason, against the appellant, David Antony Haggard, that he between 1st May 1974 and 1st June 1974 in the city of Newcastle upon Tyne offered to supply lysergide, a controlled drug of class A to Anthony Gerald Heward in contravention of *b* s 4(1) of the Misuse of Drugs Act 1971, contrary to s 4(3) of the 1971 Act. The justices found the following facts: (a) On 17th or 24th May 1974 the appellant travelled to Leeds University, and for £250 purchased in the form of impregnated blotting paper one thousand 'tabs' of a substance which he, at the time, believed to be lysergide (LSD). Lysergide was a class 'A' controlled drug within the provisions of the 1971 Act. (b) The appellant's intention was to purchase lysergide *c* or cannabis, and resell it for profit. (c) The appellant approached various acquaintances who were in a position to introduce him to 'acid heads' (regular users of lysergide), with a view to the sale to such persons of the substance he had purchased as lysergide. (d) As a result of one of those approaches the appellant was introduced to Anthony Gerald Heward at a meeting which had been arranged for the purpose of the sale of lysergide by one Eddy Husband. (e) At this meeting the appellant *d* offered to sell to Heward a quantity of lysergide, and a sale took place of some of the substances which the appellant had purchased in Leeds. (f) At the time of this transaction both the appellant and Heward believed that the substance sold was lysergide, a controlled drug. (g) The substance purchased as lysergide in Leeds and later sold by the appellant to Heward as lysergide, was in fact 2,5 Dimethoxy 4 Bromoamphetamine (Bromo STP). Bromo STP was an hallucinogenic drug, similar *e* in appearance and effect to lysergide, but not controlled under the 1971 Act or regulations made thereunder.

It was contended by the appellant that the offence 'to offer to supply a controlled drug to another' under s 4(3)(a) of the 1971 Act required that any substance proffered as a controlled drug must in fact be a controlled drug, and that if the substance actually proffered and subsequently supplied was not a controlled drug, there could *f* be no unlawful offer to supply within the section. Analogy was sought to be drawn with the decision of the House of Lords in *Haughton v Smith*[1] in which it was held that an offence of attempted handling of stolen goods required that the goods to be handled must in fact be in existence and stolen at the time of the attempt. Thus it was argued that a controlled drug could only be offered for supply if the substance proffered was in fact a controlled drug. It was conceded that the appellant had *g* the necessary intent to commit the offence but, although fortuitous under the circumstances, he was not in a position to supply the controlled drug.

It was contended by the respondent that the words 'offer to supply a controlled drug to another' must be given their ordinary and apparent meaning. Thus, it was argued that once an offer had been made unlawfully to supply a controlled drug the offence under s 4(3)(a) was complete. It was the making of the offer which was *h* forbidden by the section, and the existence of the specific controlled drug or the nature of any drug actually supplied in pursuance of the offer was immaterial. Analogy was drawn with *R v McDonough*[2] in which the Court of Criminal Appeal held that an incitement to receive stolen goods was complete on the making of the incitement even though the goods might not yet have been stolen, or might not in fact have been stolen at all or even in existence. Thus the offence of incitement was committed whether or not the act incited was ever carried out, and the offence of offering to supply controlled drugs under s 4(3) of the 1971 Act was committed when the offer

1　[1973] 3 All ER 1109, [1975] AC 476
2　(1962) 47 Cr App Rep 37

was made, and whether or not the supply of the controlled drug in question ever
took place. *R v McDonough*[1] was cited as an example of such an alternative charge
as was alluded to by Lord Hailsham of St Marylebone LC in *Haughton v Smith*[2].

The justices were of opinion that the appellant had offered to supply lysergide
to Heward both through the agency of Eddy Husband, and, more specifically, when
he visited Heward and the sale took place. The justices were also of opinion that
when the offer was made to Heward the appellant genuinely believed that the substance he would supply should his offer be accepted was lysergide. They were not
referred to any case law directly affecting the penal provision, and in its absence
they 'interpreted the section within what we took to be the spirit and intent of the
Misuse of Drugs Act, 1971'. It was the justices' opinion that s 4 of the 1971 Act created a
wide-reaching offence prohibiting offers to supply controlled drugs, and that the
offence was complete once the offer was made to *supply* a substance which was a
controlled drug, even if that substance was not yet in the possession of the offeror,
or if it was later discovered not to be the drug offered, or indeed if it was not a
controlled drug at all. Accordingly they convicted the appellant of the offence charged,
and imposed a fine of £400, to be paid at £10 per week, and a sentence of 12 months'
imprisonment suspended for two years, no other method of dealing with him other
than imprisonment being appropriate owing to the gravity of the offence under s 20
of the Powers of Criminal Courts Act 1973. The justices made an order under s 27
of the 1971 Act that seven drops of Bromo STP be forfeited and destroyed; and an
order under s 27 of the 1971 Act that £146, being the remaining proceeds of the
appellant's illegal dealings, be forfeited and dealt with as a fine.

The question for the opinion of the High Court was whether an offence was committed contrary to s 4(3)(*a*) of the 1971 Act where an offer was made, either directly
or through an agent, to supply a controlled drug and the substance which the offeror
intended to supply and which he in fact supplied transpired not to be a controlled
drug.

Michael Lewis QC for the appellant.
Anthony Hidden for the respondent.

LAWSON J delivered the first judgment at the invitation of Lord Widgery CJ.
This is an appeal by way of case stated from a decision of the justices for the city of
Newcastle upon Tyne sitting at Market Street in Newcastle on 27th August 1974.
On that day they were hearing an information preferred on the 17th July 1974 by
the respondent against the appellant charging that he, between 1st May 1974 and
1st June 1974 in Newcastle upon Tyne, offered to supply lysergide, a controlled
drug of class A, to Anthony Gerald Heward, in contravention of s 4(1) of the Misuse
of Drugs Act 1971, contrary to s 4(3) of that Act.

Section 4(1) of the Misuse of Drugs Act, 1971 provides: 'Subject to any regulations
under section 7 of this Act for the time being in force, it shall not be lawful for a
person . . . (*b*) to supply or offer to supply a controlled drug to another.' Section 4(3)(*a*)
provides that it is an offence for a person to supply or offer to supply a controlled
drug to another in contravention of s 4(1). Lysergide, the subject of the information,
was in fact a controlled drug of the class A set out in Sch 2 to the 1971 Act.

The facts found by the justices are as follows. On a date in May 1974 before 24th May
the appellant travelled to Leeds University and for £250 purchased in the form of
impregnated blotting paper 1,000 'tabs' of a substance which he at the time believed
to be lysergide (LSD), which is a class A drug. The appellant's intention was to
purchase lysergide or cannabis and resell it for profit.

The appellant approached various acquaintances who were in a position to introduce

---

1   (1962) 47 Cr App Rep 37
2   [1973] 3 All ER 1109, [1975] AC 476

him to 'acid heads' (that is regular users of lysergide) with a view to the sale to such persons of the substance he purchased as lysergide.

As a result of one of these approaches the appellant was introduced to Anthony Gerald Heward at a meeting which had been arranged for the purpose of the sale of lysergide by one Eddy Husband. At this meeting the appellant offered to sell to Heward a quantity of lysergide and the sale took place of some of the substance which the appellant had purchased in Leeds. At the time of this transaction both the appellant and Heward believed that the substance sold was lysergide, a controlled drug.

The substance which in fact the appellant had brought in Leeds as lysergide, and which he sold to Heward as lysergide, was another different drug which is known by a short name 'Bromo STP'. At the material time Bromo STP was not a drug which was controlled under the 1971 Act.

The short point therefore is this: bearing in mind that the appellant was charged and convicted of the offence of offering to supply a controlled drug, it is the fact that what he in fact did supply, and that which was intended to be the physical subject of his offer to supply, turned out to be something which was not a controlled drug.

In my judgment the offence was completed at the time when, to follow the findings of the justices, the appellant met Heward and offered to sell him a quantity of lysergide. To my mind that was a clear situation in which the justices were right to find that there was an offer to supply a controlled drug, an offer made by the appellant to Heward, the person to whom the offer was made.

It matters not in relation to the offence of offering to supply that what is in fact supplied pursuant to that offer, the offer having been accepted, is not in fact a controlled drug. Of course if the charge had been supplying a controlled drug, it is clear that the fact that a controlled drug was not in fact supplied would mean that that offence could not have been established.

Having listened to the arguments and contentions made on behalf of the parties before them, the justices concluded that the appellant had offered to supply lysergide to Heward and therefore convicted him of the offence of offering to supply. They sentenced him to a fine. They imposed a sentence of imprisonment which they suspended for two years in the exercise of their powers under s 20 of the Criminal Courts Act 1973. They made an order for the destruction of seven drops of Bromo STP, which were the subject of the transaction between the appellant and Heward (the matter to which the information related), and they finally ordered the forfeiture of a sum of money which was apparently in the appellant's possession. In making that order of forfeiture the justices purported to act under s 27 of the Misuse of Drugs Act 1971, which provides that the court by or before which a person is convicted of an offence under the Act may order anything shown to the satisfaction of the court to relate to that offence to be forfeited or dealt with in such other manner as the court may order.

In my judgment the justices had no power to make an order such as they purported to make in this case, and subject to that point, in my judgment this appeal brought by way of case stated should be dismissed, but the justices' order should be varied by deletion of that part of the order which relates to the forfeiture in the sum of £146.

O'CONNOR J. I agree.

LORD WIDGERY CJ. I agree also.

Appeal against conviction dismissed. Forfeiture order varied.

Solicitors: *Bindman & Partners*, agents for *Allan, Henderson, Beecham & Lee*, Newcastle upon Tyne (for the appellant); *Collyer Bristow & Co*, agents for *D E Brown*, Newcastle upon Tyne (for the respondent).

N P Metcalfe Esq Barrister.

Harris v Birkenhead Corporation and another (Pascoe and another third party, Alliance Assurance Co Ltd fourth party)

COURT OF APPEAL, CIVIL DIVISION

MEGAW, LAWTON AND ORMROD LJJ

10th, 11th, 12th NOVEMBER 1975

Occupier – Negligence – Occupation or control – Local authority – House unoccupied in consequence of compulsory purchase order – Notice of entry served on owner and tenant of house following compulsory purchase order – Notice stating local authority would enter and take possession of house on expiry of 14 days – House subsequently vacated by tenant and left unoccupied – House not secured or bricked up by local authority – House made ruinous in consequence of activities of vandals – Child trespasser entering house – Child injured in consequence of ruinous condition – Whether local authority occupiers – Whether liable to child for breach of duty.

G owned a house which was near a children's playground. In August 1966 the local authority, in furtherance of a slum clearance and redevelopment programme, made a compulsory purchase order which covered buildings in a substantial area, including G's house. The order was confirmed by the Minister in May 1967. Unlike other houses in the street, G's house was in good condition and at the time was let through her agents to R. On 3rd July 1967 the local authority served on G a notice to treat and also a notice of entry under the Housing Act 1957. A notice of entry in the same terms was served on R. The notice of entry stated that the local authority would on the expiration of 14 days from the service of the notice enter on and take possession of the property. A letter which accompanied the notices stated that the local authority needed to secure vacant possession of the property. It added that officers of the local authority would call on the occupiers to make arrangements for vacant possession to be given and to offer accommodation to those qualified for rehousing. R continued to live in the house for a further six months. In due course R went to see the appropriate officer of the local authority and informed him that she would not require rehousing as she was making her own arrangements. She did not inform the local authority of the precise date of her departure. On 13th December 1967 R gave G's agents a week's notice that she was leaving. On her departure she left the keys, at the agents' request, at a place where the agents could collect them. She did not inform the local authority of her departure, following which the house remained vacant. The local authority were aware that property left vacant in the area was promptly attacked by vandals, broken into and made desolate and ruinous, and they employed staff to inspect such properties and to record that they required bricking up. By the end of January 1968 G's house had fallen into a derelict condition as a result of the activities of vandals. The local authority did not brick it up although they attended to four such properties in adjacent streets. On 6th March 1968 the infant plaintiff, who was aged 4½, wandered from the playground into the derelict house through an open and unsecured door. Having climbed to the second floor, she fell out of a window to the street below and was seriously injured. She brought an action against the local authority and G claiming damages for personal injuries under the Occupiers' Liability Act 1957. The defendants denied liability. The trial judge held that at the relevant time the local authority were the occupiers of the premises and that they were liable to the plaintiff. He dismissed the action against G. The local authority appealed.

Held – The appeal would be dismissed for the following reasons—

(i) The local authority were the legal occupiers of the house at the time of the accident, for the effect of the notice of entry and the statutory authority on which it was based was that the local authority were asserting their right to control the pro- *a* perty after the expiry of 14 days and it was in consequence of the assertion of that right that the property had become empty. The assertion of such a right, even though it had not been followed by an actual or symbolic, or a 'deemed', taking of possession, was sufficient, as soon as the property became vacant, to make the local authority, as the persons having the immediate right of control, the occupiers for the purposes of liability to the infant plaintiff (see p 348 *f* to *j*, p 349 *e* and p 352 *b* and *j* to p 353 *a*, *b* post).

(ii) As occupiers the local authority were liable for breach of duty to the infant plaintiff since they knew that where such property was left unoccupied it was liable to be vandalised and put in a dangerous condition and, having been put on notice that the house was likely to be empty in the near future, they were in a position to take the steps which a reasonable and humane occupier would have taken, to secure *c* the house in order to prevent the risk of a child trespasser going into it (see p 350 *e to g*, p 351 *c* and *f* to *h* and p 352 *g* to p 353 *a*, post); *British Railways Board v Herrington* [1972] 1 All ER 749 applied.

Decision of Kilner Brown J [1975] 1 All ER 1001 affirmed.

Notes   *d*
For the duty owed by occupiers of premises to trespassers, see 28 Halsbury's Laws (3rd Edn) 53, 54, para 49, and for cases on the subject, see 36 Digest (Repl) 70, 71, *376-382*.

For the standard of care in relation to trespassing children, see 28 Halsbury's Laws (3rd Edn) 17, 18, para 15, and for cases on the subject, see 36 Digest (Repl) 120, 121, *600-611*.   *e*

Cases referred to in judgments
British Railways Board v Herrington [1972] 1 All ER 749, [1972] AC 877, [1972] 2 WLR 537, HL.
Hartwell v Grayson Rollo & Clover Docks Ltd [1947] KB 901, [1947] LJR 1038, CA, 24 Digest (Repl) 1089, 401.   *f*
Wheat v E Lacon & Co Ltd [1966] 1 All ER 582, [1966] AC 552, [1966] 2 WLR 581, HL; *affg* [1965] 2 All ER 700, [1966] 1 QB 335, [1965] 3 WLR 142, CA, Digest (Cont Vol B) 451, *135a*.

Cases also cited
Birmingham City Corpn v West Midland Baptist (Trust) Association (Inc) [1969] 3 All ER 172, [1970] AC 874, HL.   *g*
Dawson v Great Northern and City Railway Co [1905] 1 KB 260, [1904-7] All ER Rep 913, CA.
Hiberian Property Co Ltd v Liverpool Corpn [1973] 2 All ER 1117, [1973] 1 WLR 751.
Lewisham Borough Council v Roberts [1949] 1 All ER 815, [1949] 2 KB 608, CA.
Macara (James) Ltd v Barclay [1944] 2 All ER 589, [1945] 1 KB 148, CA.
Penny v Northampton Borough Council (19th July 1974) unreported; [1974] Bar Library *h* transcript 260, CA.
Phipps v Rochester Corpn [1955] 1 All ER 129, [1955] 1 QB 450.
Stone v Taffe [1974] 3 All ER 1016, [1974] 1 WLR 1575, CA.
Telfer v Glasgow Corpn 1974 SLT (Notes) 51.

Appeal and cross-appeal   *j*
The plaintiff, Julie Harris, a minor suing by her next friend, Christina Westcott, brought an action against the first defendants, Birkenhead Corporation ('the corporation'), and the second defendant, Jessie Kathleen Gledhill, claiming damages under the Occupiers' Liability Act 1957 in respect of the injuries which she received on 6th March 1968 when she fell from the second floor window of an empty and derelict

house, 239 Price Street, Birkenhead, and was seriously injured. The second defen-
a dant joined Eric Matthew Pascoe and Douglas McNeil Carson, partners in a firm of
estate agents known as Bailey & Neep, who managed the property on her behalf,
as third party. She also issued a third party notice on her insurance company, the
Royal Insurance Co Ltd, but she did not pursue her claim against them and they took no
part in the action. Mr Pascoe and Mr Carson joined their insurance company, the Allied
Assurance Co Ltd, as fourth party. On 16th December 1974 Kilner Brown J[1] sitting
b at Liverpool held the corporation liable for the accident on the ground that they were
the occupiers of the premises at the relevant time and he held that the second
defendant was not the occupier at the relevant time and was accordingly not liable
for the accident. He awarded the plaintiff £20,000 damages against the corporation.
The corporation appealed. The proceedings by Mr Pascoe and Mr Carson against the
Alliance Assurance Co Ltd were stayed by the judge pending the outcome of the appeal.
c The plaintiff cross-appealed, contending that in the event of the corporation's appeal
being allowed and the judgment against the corporation being set aside, the judgment in favour of the second defendant against the plaintiff should be set aside and
judgment should be entered for the plaintiff against the second defendant for £20,000.
The facts are set out in the judgment of Megaw LJ.

d *Michael Morland QC* and *Charles James* for the corporation.
G P Crowe and *David Clarke* for the plaintiff.
Gerard Wright QC and *M D Bryne* for the second defendant.
The third and fourth parties did not appear and were not represented.

e **MEGAW LJ.** The infant plaintiff was 4½ years old when, on 6th March 1968, she fell
from a second storey window of a derelict house, 239 Price Street, Birkenhead. She
was very seriously injured. She, through her next friend, brought an action against
Birkenhead Corporation as first defendants; and against Mrs Jessie Kathleen Gledhill
as second defendant. Two third parties and a fourth party were added to the
proceedings.
f   The action was tried before Kilner Brown J[1] at Liverpool. On 16th December 1974
he gave judgment for the plaintiff against the first defendants for £20,000. That was
the amount which had been agreed by all parties concerned to be the proper sum of
damages on the assumption that any party was held to be liable. The learned judge
gave judgment for the second defendant against the plaintiff with costs, but he
directed that those costs should be paid by the first defendants. The learned judge's
g formal judgment also contained provisions as to the third party and fourth party
proceedings with which we are not concerned.
The first defendants appeal. They contend that the judge was wrong to hold them
liable. There is a cross-appeal by the plaintiff, contending that, if the first defendants'
appeal should succeed, then the plaintiff, contrary to the learned judge's decision,
should have judgment for £20,000 against the second defendant. There is also an
h amended notice of cross-appeal on behalf of the second defendant to which in the
circumstances it is unnecessary to refer.
The facts relating to this tragic accident are set out in the learned judge's judgment[1].
On one matter of evidence, counsel for the first defendants criticises the judge's
finding. I shall refer to that point later. In other respects, no criticism is made of the
judge's findings; and the facts are substantially undisputed. I shall, however,
j summarise what appear to me to be the facts which are relevant for the purpose of
this appeal.
The plaintiff lived with her mother at 157 Beckworth Street, Birkenhead. Almost
opposite the house was a children's playground, Vittoria Court. On the afternoon of

1 [1975] 1 All ER 1001, [1975] 1 WLR 379

6th March 1968 the plaintiff's mother took her to the playground. The plaintiff and
another small girl wandered away from the playground. They made their way along   *a*
Moreton Street, which is a designated children's play street. At the end of Moreton
Street they entered the house, 239 Price Street, the front door of which is in fact in
Moreton Street at the corner with Price Street. The door was open or broken down.
The whole house was in a derelict condition, with broken windows. The two little
girls made their way up the stairs to a room on the second floor. The plaintiff must
have climbed on to the window-sill, which was only about two feet above the floor   *b*
of the room. The window was open, or the glass broken, or both. The plaintiff fell
from the window-sill to the street below, some 30 feet. These facts are by way of
reasonable reconstruction of what must have happened. No one, so far as I know,
noticed the children entering the house. But the fall from the window was seen by a
passer-by.

It is accepted on all sides that the plaintiff must, in law, be regarded as a trespasser   *c*
in the house at the time of her accident. On her behalf it was sought to establish that
either the first defendants, whom I shall call 'the corporation', or the second defendant,
or both, was or were in law to be treated as the occupier or occupiers of 239 Price
Street at the time of the accident; and that, being an occupier, the corporation or
the second defendant, or both, was or were in breach of a duty owed to the trespassing
infant plaintiff.   *d*

How had the house come to be in this ruinous condition, unsecured? What was the
basis on which it was sought to make the corporation, or the second defendant,
liable? What was the connection of each of them, respectively, with the ruinous
239 Price Street, which might involve the status of occupier at the time of the accident?

The second defendant had become the owner of the house in 1956. She had employed a firm of estate agents, Messrs Bailey & Neep, to manage the property on her   *e*
behalf. They were responsible to her, presumably for finding tenants, and for
collecting the rents, and having necessary repairs carried out.

For some time—I do not think it matters how long—before July 1969, the second
defendant's tenant in 239 Price Street had been a Mrs Redmond. She was a good
and careful tenant. Until the end of 1967, when Mrs Redmond left and the house
became empty, 239 Price Street had been kept in very good condition, despite what   *f*
had been happening to property round about.

Much of the property in Price Street and neighbouring streets had fallen into decay.
In 1966 the corporation decided to make a compulsory purchase order under s 43 of
the Housing Act 1957. Section 43 is in Part III of the Act, which is concerned with
clearance and redevelopment. The order, made on 26th August 1966, and confirmed
by the Minister on 15th May 1967, was known as the 'County Borough of Birkenhead   *g*
(Cottage Street Clearance Area) Compulsory Purchase Order, 1966'. It covered
buildings in a substantial area, including Cottage Street, at least a part of Price Street,
and some neighbouring streets and alleys. The Minister's confirmation of the order
involved an amendment which took 239 Price Street outside the clearance area. That
house was still covered by the order, and was subject to compulsory purchase, but
that was not on the basis that it itself was unfit for habitation. As I have said, it had   *h*
been kept in good condition. Nevertheless, with the rest of the neighbourhood, it
was to be compulsorily purchased so that the whole area might be used for building
blocks of flats.

On 3rd July 1967 the corporation served on the second defendant a notice to treat
and, at the same time, a notice of entry in respect of 239 Price Street. On the same
date a notice of entry in the same terms was served on Mrs Redmond, the tenant.   *j*
A covering letter, in substantially similar terms, was sent to each of these ladies by
the corporation. Nothing turns on the terms of the notice to treat. It was a necessary
preliminary step towards the assessment of compensation for the compulsory purchase. The terms of the notice of entry are important. It is headed: 'The Housing
Act 1957'. It is further headed: 'Notice of Intention to Enter'. It is addressed to the

second defendant. A corresponding notice, of the same date, was sent to the tenant:
a it was addressed to: 'The Occupier'. There are two recitals, the first of which recites
the order made on 26th August 1966, and confirmed by the Minister of Housing.
(It would seem that the wrong date was given for that confirmation; but nothing
turns on that.) The second recital says: 'Notice to Treat for the said property was
served upon the owners of the said property on the Third day of July 1967'. It then
said:

b
'Now THEREFORE the Council in exercise of the power conferred upon them
by paragraph 9 of Part 2 of the Third Schedule to the Housing Act, 1957, HEREBY
GIVE YOU NOTICE that they will upon the expiration of fourteen days from the service
of this Notice upon you enter on and take possession of the said property described in the Schedule hereto.'

c   As I have said, that notice was dated and served on 3rd July 1967. The schedule
referred to 239 Price Street.
So there was, in the clearest terms, an averment that the corporation would, on
the expiration of 14 days from the service of that notice, which is to be taken as having
been served on 3rd July, enter on and take possession of 239 Price Street, which, of
course, involved an assertion by implication of a legal right in the corporation so to
d do. The purported statutory authority for this notification, peremptory and unambiguous in its terms, was para 9 of Part II of Sch 3 to the Housing Act 1957. Paragraph 9
had in fact been repealed by s 39(4) of and Sch 8 to the Compulsory Purchase Act 1965,
the commencement date of which, by s 40 thereof, was 1st January 1966. The purported
statutory authority no longer existed. But it has, as I understand it, been agreed
between the parties that that misstatement in the notice of entry of the purported
e statutory authority does not matter. It is not suggested that the misdescription by the
corporation of the statutory power matters, since statutory power did exist, for para 9
had, in effect, been replaced by s 11(1) of the Compulsory Purchase Act 1965. The
relevant part of s 11(1) of that Act is:

f
'If the acquiring authority have served notice to treat in respect of any of the
land and have served on the owner, lessee and occupier of that land not less
than fourteen days notice, the acquiring authority may enter on and take
possession of that land, or of such part of that land as is specified in the
notice; and then any compensation agreed or awarded for the land of which
possession is taken shall carry interest . . .'

g   There, then, is the statutory authority which, if the conditions as to notices are
fulfilled, gives the acquiring authority the right to enter on the land and take
possession of it, even though compensation has not yet been assessed.
It will be observed that in the present case the corporation's notice of entry prescribed the minimum period of 14 days and affirmatively and unequivocally asserted
that it would enter and take posession on the expiration of the 14 days.
h   The covering letter, also dated 3rd July 1967, to which I have referred, was not
consistent with the terms of the notice of entry. It begins by saying: 'You will find
enclosed a Notice to Treat, Claim Form in triplicate, and Notice of Entry.' The
letter continues:

j
'The Council need to secure vacant possession of the property and one of their
officers will call on the occupiers to make arrangements for vacant possession to
be given and to offer such other accommodation as there is available to those who
qualify for rehousing. While the property remains occupied the Notice of Entry
does not affect present liabilities for rent etc., and rent should be paid by the occupiers and lessees, and collected by landlords in the usual way. The Housing
Manager will arrange for suitable housing accommodation to be offered to those
occupiers who were resident in the area at the time of the official count and a

member of his department will call upon all occupiers in the course of the next
few months to ascertain the needs of the various occupiers. I should perhaps *a*
mention that the Council have power to enforce the Notices when vacant possession cannot be arranged by agreement, or offers of other accommodation are
refused. The Council are usually able to avoid this final recourse to their compulsory powers and I hope that, with your co-operation, this will be possible in
your case.'

So the one document was saying that the corporation was going to exercise its *b*
statutory authority to take posession at the end of 14 days, and the other document
appears to say that it was not minded to do so until some unspecified, substantially
later, date. The documents can, I think, only be reconciled (if they have to be reconciled) by the assumption that the corporation is asserting that it will, indeed, be deemed
to have taken possession on the expiry of the 14 days, but that, having thus notionally *c*
entered and taken possession, as it asserts in the notice of entry, it will continue to
allow the occupier to reside there for as long as the corporation sees fit so to allow.

In other circumstances, the apparent discrepancy between the notice of entry and
the covering letter might give rise to difficulties. In the circumstances of the present
case, I do not think that we need take time in contemplating those potential difficulties or in considering whether the possible reconciliation which I have suggested *d*
is correct. I say that because it is conceded, or, it may be, asserted, on behalf
of the corporation that, from the expiry of 14 days after the service of that notice of
3rd July 1967, the corporation, despite the terms of the covering letter, had the unqualified right to enter on and take possession of 239 Price Street at any time. The
corporation was not, it is said, obliged to take possession at the end of the 14 days;
it was entitled to refrain from actually entering into possession for as long as it chose, *e*
stretching into infinity, despite the specific terms of the notice. But it could lawfully
enter into possession on 17th July 1967, or on any day thereafter, as of right and without
a fresh notice or any amendment of the existing notice. The corporation did not enter
on or take possession of 239 Price Street until some days after the accident in March
1968.

I continue with the history. I shall have to return to the question of the effect of *f*
that notice.

Mrs Redmond, the tenant, continued to live in 239 Price Street for a further five
or six months after July 1967. She did not, in the end, wish to be rehoused by the
corporation. She found a new place of abode for herself. She left the house 239 Price
Street on 20th or perhaps 23rd December 1967. She did not specifically inform the
corporation or any official of it of, at any rate, the precise prospective date of her *g*
departure; nor, after she had left, of the fact that she had left. She did tell a Mr
Harrison, who was a rent-collector employed by Messrs Bailey & Neep, the second
defendant's agents who managed the property. On 13th December 1967 she gave
him a week's notice. He asked her to leave the keys at another house, in Vittoria
Street, where Mr Harrison also collected rents on behalf of Messrs Bailey & Neep.
Mrs Redmond left the keys in the Vittoria Street house. There is no evidence that *h*
Mr Harrison informed anyone that Mrs Redmond had left; nor, so far as we have
been told, was there any evidence what happened to the keys.

I referred earlier to a criticism which has been made on behalf of the corporation
of a finding of fact by Kilner Brown J. That arises on the evidence of Mrs Redmond;
and I can conveniently deal with it at this point in the history. Mrs Redmond's
evidence was given by way of a written statement admitted under the Civil Evidence
Act 1968. Having told of her dealings with Mr Harrison, which I have already
summarised, she continued, as follows:

'Some weeks before I left 239 Price Street, I went to see Mr Rhodes in the Legal
Department of the Birkenhead Corporation to tell him that [the second defen-
dant] was the owner of the house and I would be giving notice to leave to the rent

collector, Mr Harrison. The point of my going to see this gentleman before I left 239 Price Street was to make it quite clear to him that I did not wish to be rehoused by the Corporation as my husband and myself were purchasing our own house.'

In his judgment the learned judge said[1]:

'[Mrs Redmond] called on Mr Rhodes. She informed him and she also informed Mr Harrison, who was employed by Mr Pascoe of [Bailey & Neep] to collect rents, that she did not wish to be rehoused, she preferred to make her own arrangements. She would leave just before Christmas 1967, and would leave the keys at a house in nearby Vittoria Street.'

Again, the judge said[2]:

'Now although Mrs Redmond was not a tenant of the local authority she was seen by the appropriate officer. She notified the appropriate officer that she was making private arrangements and would be leaving before Christmas.'

The criticism is that the learned judge was inaccurate because these passages in his judgment suggest that Mrs Redmond had said that she had told Mr Rhodes, an official of the corporation, that she would leave before Christmas 1967, and that she would leave the keys at the house in Vittoria Street; whereas in fact Mrs Redmond's evidence was that she had said those things to Mr Harrison, but not to Mr Rhodes or to any other representative of the corporation. True, she had indicated to Mr Rhodes that she did not require to be rehoused, and that she was going to move out; but she did not specify to him, so it is said, 'before Christmas', or any specific date, nor did she claim to have said anything to him regarding the keys. There might—I say no more than that—be some substance in this criticism, if this had been the sole evidence of the corporation's knowledge before the date of the accident that 239 Price Street had been vacated. But, as will appear, and as is indeed indicated in the learned judge's judgment itself, the knowledge of the corporation was shown, apart altogether from any inference which might properly be drawn as to what Mrs Redmond said in her conversation, or conversations, with Mr Rhodes.

So, to resume the narrative, Mrs Redmond moved out shortly before Christmas 1967. The house was left empty. The corporation, who on the evidence were well aware that property left vacant in this area was promptly attacked by vandals, broken into and made desolate and ruinous, did nothing. It is said on their behalf that they did not know—or perhaps rather that there was no evidence that they did know—that the house was vacant. It was thus that the plaintiff, on 6th March 1968, with her small companion, was able to enter 239 Price Street through an open and unsecured door and, having gone up the stairs and climbed on to the window-sill of a smashed or open second floor window, to fall to the street below.

So far as concerns the corporation's appeal, two questions arise. First, was the corporation the occupier of 239 Price Street at the relevant time, so as to give rise to the possible existence of a duty towards persons who might be in the house, including trespassing children? Secondly, if the corporation was the occupier in that sense, did it, on the facts which appeared on the evidence and the inferences to be drawn therefrom, owe, and fail in the discharge of, a duty owed to the infant plaintiff, by reason of the corporation's failure to take any steps to make the house secure against entry by trespassing children? I turn to the first question. Was the corporation the occupier?

It is well-established law that there may be more than one occupier of property, at the same time, for the purposes of occupier's liability: *Wheat v E Lacon & Co Ltd*[3].

1   [1975] 1 All ER at 1004, [1975] 1 WLR at 382
2   [1975] 1 All ER at 1006, [1975] 1 WLR at 384
3   [1966] 1 All ER 582, [1966] AC 552

Therefore this is not a case where it is necessarily 'either or' as between the corporation and the second defendant. Nevertheless, the corporation's submission *a* does include the contention that the second defendant at all relevant times continued to be the occupier for the purpose of the existence of a duty towards persons entering the house.

The corporation says that it was not the occupier, so that no question of a breach of occupier's duty can arise. The occupier, if any, was the second defendant. In law, it is contended, she remained the owner, and the occupier. In law, she could have *b* entered into physical possession after Mrs Redmond left, or could have put a new tenant into possession. There was nothing in the notice to treat or the notice of entry to prevent her lawfully so doing. By the conduct of the second defendant's agent, Mr Harrison, in asking the tenant, Mrs Redmond, to hand over the keys, not to the corporation, but so as to be collected by him (Mr Harrison), the second defendant has shown, notionally, her intent, or the intent of her agent on her behalf, to retain *c* control of the house, and thus to exclude the corporation from control. The corporation, it is said, on the other hand, though it was entitled to take possession at any time, following on the expiry of the 14 days after the notice of entry, had not done so, and it is contended on behalf of the corporation that unless and until it did so, either by sending some representative there to enter on the premises with the intention of taking possession, or by carrying out some symbolic ceremony such as accepting the *d* proffered keys, if they had been proffered, it (the corporation) was not an occupier. The mere immediate right which it had by virtue of the statutory authority created by the steps that it had taken to serve the notices, to enter and to take possession and to use the house for any purpose—repair or demolition or anything else—is not enough, it is said, to make it an occupier for this purpose. It is put as a matter of law, and it must be dealt with as such. The proposition is that the actual taking of *e* possession or some symbolic taking of possession is necessary before one can become an occupier of property for this purpose.

I do not propose to deal with this as a general proposition of law to a greater extent than is necessary for the decision of this particular case on the facts as they appear before us. It may be, though I certainly would not like to be taken as suggesting that it would be, that there might be cases in which one who had the immediate right *f* to enter on premises would be held not to have become the occupier of those premises for purposes of liability to someone who came on the premises, unless and until he had actually and physically entered into possession. But, whatever principle might operate in such cases, it could not, in my judgment, extend so far as to apply on the facts of this case; the facts being that the corporation has lawfully asserted an immediate right to enter and control, involving the right at any moment of time to *g* dispossess the owner and the person occupying the house when the assertion is made; and when, as a result of that assertion of legal right, the pre-existing occupier has moved out and the house is empty.

I say that by reference to the terms of the notice of entry and the statutory authority on which it is based. By that notice of entry the corporation was asserting its right to control this property after the expiry of the 14 days. And it was asserting the right *h* to exercise that control at any time thereafter when it saw fit. In my judgment, such an assertion of a right of control, even though it has not been followed by an actual or symbolic, or a 'deemed', taking of possession, is sufficient, at any rate when, as here happened before Christmas 1967, the property ceases to be physically occupied by any other person, to make the person who has that immediate right of control the occupier for these purposes. I do not see why it should be suggested that as *i* between the corporation and the second defendant or her tenant there should be any duty owed by either of these ladies to the corporation, after the notice of entry in the terms which I have cited had been served on them, to give the corporation notice that they were leaving the house—leaving it to the corporation who had, and had asserted, the right to enter and control it. But if there was no such duty as between

the second defendant and the corporation, how can the corporation's liability to a
a third party—the infant plaintiff—be affected or abrogated by the fact that the second
defendant had not told the corporation that she was no longer physically in
possession of the house, by herself or any tenant?

No authority was cited to us by counsel for the corporation to support his proposition that one who had complete legal right of control could not be an occupier
unless and until he, by himself or his servants or agents, had actually moved into the
b occupation of the property. It is, therefore, something which has to be put as a matter
of general principle. As a matter of general principle, I do not think that it can stand,
at least with the width of operation suggested. I would refer to the speech of Lord
Denning in *Wheat v Lacon & Co Ltd*[1], where he says this:

'In SALMOND ON TORTS (14th Edn., 1965) p. 372, it is said that an "occupier" is
c "he who has the immediate supervision and control and the power of permitting
or prohibiting the entry of other persons". This definition was adopted by
ROXBURGH, J., in *Hartwell v. Grayson Rollo and Clover Docks, Ltd.*[2], and by DIPLOCK,
L.J., in the present case[3]. There is no doubt that a person who fulfils that test is an
"occupier". He is the person who says "come in"; but I think that test is too
narrow by far. There are other people who are "occupiers", even though they do
d not say "come in". If a person has any degree of control over the state of the
premises it is enough.'

Then Lord Denning goes on to consider what he describes as four groups of cases.
Without going through them, it appears to me that when one looks at the cases referred
to in those four groups it makes it clear that in law the quality of being in physical
possession, or having been in actual physical possession, is not in all cases—and is
e not in this case—a necessary ingredient of the legal status of occupier for the purposes
with which we are concerned.

Accordingly, on the facts of this case, applied to the law as I understand it to be,
I take the view that the learned judge was entirely right in his conclusion that the
corporation was to be treated as occupier for the purpose of consideration of liability
towards this trespassing child.

f And so I go on to the second question: the corporation being the occupier for that
purpose, was the judge right in holding that it was liable for a breach of duty towards
the infant plaintiff?

It is here, and not in connection with the first question of 'occupier or not', that the
question of knowledge of the corporation becomes relevant. Our task in this appeal
on this second question has, in my view, been rendered substantially simpler by a
g concession which was made, and as I think rightly and necessarily made on the
evidence, by counsel for the corporation. In calling our attention to the leading authority
on the question of duty to infant trespassers, *British Railways Board v Herrington*[4],
counsel very properly read us, amongst other passages, a passage from the speech
of Lord Morris of Borth-y-Gest. It is unnecessary for me to restate the well-known facts
of *Herrington's* case[4], in which a small child had been killed by coming into contact
h with an electric rail. What Lord Morris[5] said in relation to the facts of that case was:

'The duty that lay on the appellants was a limited one. There was no duty to
ensure that no trespasser could enter on the land. And certainly an occupier owes
no duty to make his land fit for trespassers to trespass in. Nor need he make
surveys of his land in order to decide whether dangers exist of which he is unaware.

j

1   [1966] 1 All ER at 594, [1966] AC at 578, 579
2   [1947] KB 901 at 907
3   [1965] 2 All ER 700 at 711, [1966] 1 QB 335 at 368
4   [1972] 1 All ER 749, [1972] AC 877
5   [1972] 1 All ER at 767, [1972] AC at 909

The general law remains that one who trespasses does so at his peril. But in the present case there were a number of special circumstances: (a) the place where the fence was faulty was near to a public path and public ground; (b) a child might easily pass through the fence; (c) if a child did pass through and go on to the track he would be in grave danger of death or serious bodily harm; (d) a child might not realise the risk involved in touching the live rail or being in a place where a train might pass at speed. Because of these circumstances (all of them well known and obvious) there was, in my view, a duty which, while not amounting to the duty of care which an occupier owes to a visitor, would be a duty to take such steps as common sense or common humanity would dictate; they would be steps calculated to exclude or to warn or otherwise within reasonable and practicable limits to reduce or avert danger.'

Now, counsel for the corporation accepted that, mutatis mutandis, the four special circumstances referred to in that passage under the letters (a) to (d) were present as special circumstances on the evidence in the present case, subject to this (from his point of view) vital qualification: that, as he asserted, the corporation had no knowledge, and had no reason to have knowledge, that this particular house had been vacated and had fallen into a derelict condition. But, subject to that reservation, counsel assented to the proposition that these special circumstances were shown on the evidence in this case. So I translate those special circumstances into the words applicable in the present case: (a) the place where the door of 239 Price Street was, was near to a public street; (b) a child might easily pass through the door; (c) if a child did pass through and go into the house he or she would be in grave danger of death or serious bodily harm; (d) a child might not realise the risk involved in going into that house.

On the facts of this case, all those matters were duly established on the evidence. On those facts being duly established, subject to the question of knowledge by the corporation of the emptiness and state of the house, there could, in my judgment, be no doubt that the test as laid down in *Herrington's* case[1] for liability of the occupier would be fulfilled. Would a humane person, knowing of those facts, have regarded it as something that ought to be done, to take reasonable steps to prevent children from trespassing into that area of danger? It is not suggested that, if it had been known that the house was unoccupied and in this vandalised condition, there would have been any practical difficulty in steps being taken to secure this house against infant trespassers between the date when it fell into this ruinous condition by the end of January 1968, and six weeks later on 6th March 1968, when the accident happened.

So I turn to the question whether or not the corporation had knowledge of the fact that the house was empty and of the fact that the house, being so empty, had been treated by vandals in such a way that it had fallen into a ruinous condition. The question, of course, is whether they had knowledge by such a time that, acting reasonably, they would have been in a position before the accident happened to take steps to secure the house.

In my judgment, the learned judge was right in the conclusion which, as I understand it, he reached on the evidence, that the corporation did have knowledge of those facts. After he had referred, in a passage which I have already cited, to the evidence of Mrs Redmond, a passage which is criticised on behalf of the corporation, the judge continued in this way[2]:

'In my view, the local authority were not possessed of information that it would be available for demolition, but their officer who recorded the necessity for bricking up must through his subordinates have noticed, if they had kept their eyes open as they toured the area, that there was yet another house ready for treatment.'

---

1 [1972] 1 All ER 749, [1972] AC 877
2 [1975] 1 All ER at 1006, [1975] 1 WLR at 384

The reference in that passage is to documentary evidence which was produced at
a the trial (because no oral evidence was called on behalf of the corporation) coming
from the corporation's records and no doubt fairly and accurately produced by the
corporation as being relevant in this case, showing the steps taken to secure various
houses in this Cottage Street Clearance Area. The record runs from 6th February
1967 to 29th November 1968; that is the part, at any rate, with which we are concerned. It shows that between 29th December 1967 and 6th February 1968 four proper-
b ties in streets adjacent to Price Street had in fact been attended to in various ways,
with the intention of securing them, they having ceased to be occupied by reason of
things that had happened under this clearance scheme. It is to that that the learned
judge is referring. It is apparent that there were officials of the corporation who were
taking steps to see that houses were thus secured as and when they became vacant.
The judge is saying, as I understand it, that it is a reasonable inference, on a balance
c of probability, that those persons who had that responsibility and who would have had
a responsibility to report back to their superiors any other house which they saw
in need of the same treatment, must, in the course of their work in this area for that
purpose, have observed in the weeks before 6th March 1968, that this house, 239 Price
Street, being unoccupied, had fallen into this ruinous condition as a result of the
operation of vandals.
d   Counsel for the plaintiff referred us to evidence that had been given by a lady
who lived in a house next door to 239 Price Street, a Mrs Cameron, which at any rate
on one view of it might be treated as having been affirmative evidence that officials
of the corporation had come to her house during this period between the end of
January and the beginning of March 1968. But, for myself, I think that, on the examination of that evidence made in reply by counsel for the corporation, it would have
e been unwise for the judge to have placed any substantial reliance on that evidence—
not because Mrs Cameron was seeking to say anything untruthful, but because it
was apparent that her state of memory (not surprisingly) was defective.   Nevertheless, there is the inference to be drawn from the known facts as to what officials
of the corporation were doing in that area; and, as I see it, there was a further inference on which the learned judge was entitled to act from the evidence which had
f been given by Mrs Redmond, to which I have already referred. When that evidence
is taken in its literal terms, it does show (and there was no contradiction of this)
that Mrs Redmond had, some weeks before Christmas 1967, gone to see an official
of the corporation and had told him that she did not require corporation rehousing
but that she was going to move out herself. The corporation were therefore put on
notice that this was something that was likely to happen; and I do not think that it
g is an unfair inference that what must have been said by Mrs Redmond was that it was
going to happen somewhere in the very near future. In those circumstances, again,
it would seem that the corporation must have been put on the alert with regard
to this house.
     Taking the whole of the material, I would find it impossible to say that the learned
judge was wrong in the conclusion to which he came that the corporation did know.
h But even if that were wrong, I should take the view that the circumstances show that
the corporation ought to have known; and, as I understand the law, in a case of this
sort that is sufficient to create the existence of liability.
     So I would reject the contention on behalf of the corporation that they did not know
of the facts which would give rise to the existence of this danger. As I say, knowing
those facts, there is nothing that has been put forward that would have prevented
j the taking of precautions which, if they had been taken, would in all human probability have prevented this accident; and the circumstances were such that if the facts
were known, as they either were known or ought to have been known, common
humanity required that such measures should have been taken.
     The only remaining point, as I understand it, put forward by counsel for the cor-
poration is that a young child, unsupervised, may always fall out of a window into a

street and therefore there is, as it were, no real causative connection here between
any failure to board up this particular house and the fact of this child's accident. It   *a*
is not an argument which I regard, with all respect to counsel, as being a possible
argument. I think that causation here was plainly shown.
I would dismiss this appeal.

LAWTON LJ. I agree with the judgment which has just been delivered by Megaw   *b*
LJ and have only one short comment to add.

In the course of his submissions, counsel for the corporation invited the court's
attention to a passage in the speech of Lord Diplock in *British Railways Board v
Herrington*[1]. The passage was to this effect:

> 'The duty [to child trespassers] does not arise until the occupier has actual   *c*
> knowledge either of the presence of the trespasser on his land or of facts which
> make it likely that the trespasser will come on to his land; and has also actual
> knowledge of facts as to the condition of his land or of activities carried out
> on it which are likely to cause personal injury to a trespasser who is unaware
> of the danger.'

In his submissions, counsel for the corporation construed the words 'actual know-   *d*
ledge' as meaning positive knowledge. For my part, I doubt whether Lord Diplock
did intend 'actual knowledge' to mean what counsel submitted it did mean; and for
this reason. In many branches of the law, plaintiffs and prosecutors have to prove
knowledge. It has long been accepted that a man cannot claim he has no knowledge
when he has shut his eyes to the obvious. Nor can he claim that he has no knowledge   *e*
when he has knowledge of what are sometimes called primary facts and has not drawn
the inferences which can reasonably be drawn from those primary facts.

If my understanding of Lord Diplock's words 'actual knowledge' is right, then the
corporation was in this situation. 239 Price Street, Birkenhead, was in a clearance
area. No less than 27 houses in that street and many more houses in adjoining streets
were covered by the County Borough of Birkenhead (Cottage Street Clearance Area)   *f*
Compulsory Purchase Order 1966. Magistrates and judges all over the United Kingdom know that once houses in clearances area are left unoccupied, vandals, vagrants
and other socially difficult persons move in and put those premises into a dangerous
condition. It was accepted by counsel for the corporation that the corporation knew
what tends to happen in clearance areas. The only point made was that it had no
positive knowledge that 239 Price Street had been vacated. But, as Megaw LJ has pointed   *g*
out, the evidence established that its officials, charged with safeguarding derelict
premises, were moving about this area during the period between the time when it
was left unoccupied by Mrs Redmond and when the infant plaintiff sustained her
injuries. Had they looked at all, they would have seen that these premises were empty
and derelict and that they required some attention to safeguard children from
entering and possibly injuring themselves. It seems to me, therefore, that the know-   *h*
ledge which the corporation was proved to have was the kind of 'actual knowledge'
which Lord Diplock envisaged in *British Railways Board v Herrington*[2].

ORMROD LJ. I agree; and would wish to add very little indeed. The only
question on the first part of this case is whether the corporation is properly regarded
in law as a person occupying or in control of the premises in which the accident
happened. For the reasons which have been given by Megaw and Lawton LJJ, there

---

1 [1972] 1 All ER 749 at 796, [1972] AC 877 at 941
2 [1972] 1 All ER at 796, [1972] AC at 941

is, in my judgment, only one possible answer to that question. They were at all
a material times the persons with the right to control that property. It would have been
almost absurd to suggest that, in the circumstances of this case, the second defendant
could have been expected by the law to go to expense in securing these premises
against the damage which was inevitable and was bound to happen to them immediately or very soon after the tenant had vacated them. In those circumstances it
would be a disastrous injustice to her to hold her liable for this appalling accident;
b and I am glad to be able to agree with the judgments which have just been given that
this appeal would be dismissed.

Appeal and cross-appeal dismissed. Leave to appeal to the House of Lords refused.

Solicitors: Berrymans, agents for Weighmans, Liverpool (for the corporation); Percy
c Hughes & Roberts, Birkenhead (for the plaintiff); Byrne Frodsham & Co, Widnes,
Cheshire (for the second defendant).

Mary Rose Plummer Barrister.

d

Hinds and others v The Queen
Director of Public Prosecutions v Jackson
e # Attorney General of Jamaica (intervener)

PRIVY COUNCIL
LORD DIPLOCK, VISCOUNT DILHORNE, LORD SIMON OF GLAISDALE, LORD EDMUND-DAVIES
AND LORD FRASER OF TULLYBELTON
f 25th, 26th, 30th JUNE, 1st, 2nd, 3rd, 28th JULY, 1st DECEMBER 1975

*Jamaica – Constitutional law – Judicature – Higher judiciary – Jurisdiction – Constitution
impliedly prohibiting transfer of jurisdiction to courts consisting of members of lower judiciary
– Constitution containing special provisions for appointment and tenure of office of members
of higher judiciary – Statute establishing special court to deal with firearm offences – Division
of court consisting of members of lower judiciary – Division having jurisdiction over offences
previously cognisable only by higher judiciary – Whether statutory provisions establishing
g provision void as being inconsistent with Constitution – Jamaica (Constitution) Order 1962
(SI 1962 No 1550), Sch 2, ss 2, 97(1) – Gun Court Act 1974 (Jamaica), ss 4(b), 5(2).*

*Jamaica – Constitutional law – Separation of powers – Judicature – Punishment of offences –
Transfer of power to executive body – Validity – Firearms offences – Statute establishing
h mandatory sentence – Detention at hard labour during Governor-General's pleasure –
Convicted person only to be discharged at direction of Governor-General acting in accordance
with recommendation of review board – Majority of members of review board not members
of judiciary – Whether provision for mandatory sentence void – Jamaica (Constitution) Order
1962 (SI 1962 No 1550), Sch 2, s 2 – Gun Court Act 1974 (Jamaica), ss 8(2), 22(1).*

*Jamaica – Constitutional law – Fundamental rights and freedoms – Criminal proceedings to
j be in public – Presumption that proceedings in camera reasonably required in interests of
public safety, public order or protection of private lives of persons concerned in
proceedings – Special court established to deal with firearms offences – Provision that court
should sit in camera – Whether provision unconstitutional – Jamaica (Constitution) Order
1962 (SI 1962 No 1550), Sch 2, s 20(3)(4) – Gun Court Act 1974 (Jamaica), s 13(1).*

On 1st April 1974 the Jamaican Parliament passed the Gun Court Act 1974, being
'an Act to provide for the establishment of a court to deal particularly with firearms   **a**
offences and for purposes incidental thereto or connected therewith'. There had been
no preceding legislation to enable the 1974 Act to alter any of the provisions of the
Constitution of Jamaica[a]. Section 3 of the 1974 Act established a court of record to be
called 'the Gun Court'. Under s 4, the Gun Court was empowered to sit in three
divisions: (a) the 'Resident Magistrate's Division' consisting of one resident magistrate;
(b) the 'Full Court Division' consisting of three resident magistrates; and (c) the   **b**
'Circuit Court Division' consisting of a judge of the Supreme Court exercising the
jurisdiction of a circuit court. By virtue of ss 3(2), 4(c) and 5(3), a Circuit Court Division
presided over by a judge of the Supreme Court had the status of a superior court
of record with jurisdiction to try firearms offences in all the parishes of Jamaica.
Sections 10(1) and 17(1) empowered the Chief Justice to assign any judge of the Supreme
Court to sit as the judge of a Circuit Court Division and to designate any circuit   **c**
court to be a Circuit Court Division. Section 5(1) gave the Resident Magistrate's
Division jurisdiction to hear and determine all offences triable summarily under s 20
of the Firearms Act 1967 (Jamaica) and any other offences triable summarily under
the 1974 Act committed in any parish of Jamaica. Under s 17(2) the Chief Justice was
empowered to designate any resident magistrate's court to be a division of the Gun
Court and, for the purpose of constituting a Full Court Division, to assign any resident   **d**
magistrates to a court so designated. Section 6(1) provided that any court before
which any case involving a firearm offence was brought other than a division of the
Gun Court should forthwith transfer that case for trial by the Gun Court. Sections
4(b) and 5(2) gave the Full Court Division jurisdiction to hear and determine either
summarily or an indictment (a) any firearm offence and (b) any offence other than a
capital offence alleged to have been committed by a person who at the time of the   **e**
hearing was detained under the provisions of s 8(2), i e a person guilty of an offence under
s 20 of the Firearms Act 1967 (Jamaica) or of an offence specified in the Schedule to the
1967 Act. Section 13(1) provided, inter alia, that 'In the interest of public safety,
public order or the protection of the private lives of persons concerned in the proceedings', proceedings before the Gun Court should be in camera. By virtue of s 8(2)
and s 22(1) and (2) a person convicted of an offence under s 20 of the Firearms Act 1967   **f**
was subject to a mandatory sentence of hard labour at the Governor-General's
pleasure and was not to be discharged except at the direction of the Governor-General
acting in accordance with the advice of a review board consisting of five persons
appointed by the Governor-General. Only one member of the review board, the
chairman, was to be a judge either of the Court of Appeal or the Supreme Court
so that the majority of the board consisted of persons not appointed in accordance   **g**
with the provisions of Chapter VII of the Constitution which related to the appointment of persons exercising judicial powers. The five appellants were each convicted
by a Resident Magistrate's Division of the Gun Court of being in unlawful possession of firearms and ammunition contrary to s 20 of the 1967 Act. In accordance
with s 8(2) of the 1974 Act they were sentenced to detention at hard labour during
the Governor-General's pleasure. They appealed, contending, inter alia, (i) that the   **h**
establishment of the Gun Court sitting in the three divisions was unconstitutional
in that the 1974 Act purported to confer on resident magistrates a jurisdiction which,
under Chapter VII of the Jamaican Constitution, was exercisable only by a judge of
the Supreme Court; (ii) that s 13(1) of the 1974 Act relating to proceedings in camera
was contrary to s 20(3) of Chapter III of the Constitution which provided that all
proceedings of every court should be in public; and (iii) that the provisions of the 1974
Act relating to mandatory sentences of hard labour during the Governor-General's
pleasure, acting with the advice of the review board, were unconstitutional in that
they interfered with the right of a convicted person to have his sentence determined
by a court.

a   Jamaica (Constitution) Order 1962 (SI 1962 No 1550), Sch 2

Held – (i) The establishment of a Circuit Court Division of the Gun Court was not
a inconsistent with the Constitution of Jamaica since the effect of the 1974 Act was
merely to enlarge the existing criminal jurisdiction of a properly appointed Supreme
Court judge of a circuit court so as to enable him to try firearms offences committed
outside the parish for which the circuit court was held. Similarly, the establishment of
a Resident Magistrate's Division was not inconsistent with the Constitution since its
original jurisdiction to hear and determine offences summarily was the same as that
b of a Resident Magistrate's Court except that its jurisdiction extended to cover offences
committed in any parish of Jamaica, being offences under or ancillary to the 1967
Act and triable summarily (see p 362 d to p 363 b and p 374 h, post).

(ii) However (Viscount Dilhorne and Lord Fraser of Tullybelton dissenting), the
provisions of the 1974 Act establishing a Full Court Division consisting of three
resident magistrates were in conflict with Chapter VII of the Constitution since it was
c the manifest intention of the Constitution that, where Parliament established a new
court to exercise part of the jurisdiction which was being exercised by members of
the higher judiciary at the time when the Constitution came into force, the persons
appointed to be members of that court were to be appointed in the same manner
and entitled to the same security of tenure as members of the higher judiciary.
Accordingly s 97(1)[b] of the Constitution did not entitle the Jamaican Parliament to
d set up a new court composed of members of the lower judiciary with a jurisdiction
characteristic of the Supreme Court extending to the trial not only of firearms offences
but of all criminal offences, however serious, with the exception of capital offences.
Accordingly those provisions were void under s 2[c] of the Constitution (see p 363 c d
and g to j, p 367 c d and h j and p 368 c, post).

(iii) Section 13(1) of the 1974 Act was not unconstitutional since, by virtue of
e s 20(4)(c)(ii)[d] of Chapter III and the introductory words of s 13(1), there was a rebuttable
presumption that court proceedings in camera were reasonably required in the interests of 'public safety, public order or the protection of the private lives of persons
concerned in the proceedings' and no evidence had been adduced by the appellants
to rebut that presumption (see p 368 g to p 369 b and f, post).

(iv) Sections 8(2) and 22(1) of the 1974 Act purported to transfer from the judiciary
f to an executive body not appointed under Chapter VII of the Constitution a complete discretion to determine the severity of the punishment to be inflicted on a certain class of offender. The combined effect of those sections was to give the review
body the power to fix the duration of a sentence not previously fixed by anyone
else. Those sections had been enacted after the coming into force of the Constitution
and were inconsistent with those provisions of the Constitution which related to the
g separation of powers. It followed that ss 8(2) and 22(1) were void under s 2 of the
Constitution (see p 369 j to p 370 a and g h, p 372 a and b and p 374 h, post).

(v) Although the provisions of the 1974 Act relating to the establishment of a Full
Court Division of the Gun Court and a mandatory sentence of hard labour during the
Governor-General's pleasure were void, it did not follow that the remainder of the
Act was so inextricably bound up with its invalid provisions that it could not inde-
h pendently survive. Even with the elimination of the Full Court Division the whole
range of firearms offences would still be cognisable by the Circuit Court Division and
the Resident Magistrate's Division. Offences against s 20 of the Firearms Act 1967
would still be tried speedily in camera by those two divisions subject to the limitations
(a) that the maximum sentence which could be imposed on offenders would be that

j ───

b Section 97, so far as material, is set out at p 365 j, post
c Section 2 of the Constitution, so far as material, provides: '... if any other law is inconsistent
   with this Constitution, this Constitution shall prevail and the other law shall, to the extent
   of the inconsistency, be void.'
d Section 20(4), so far as material, is set out at p 368 f, post

prescribed by the 1967 Act, and (b) that the jurisdiction of the two divisions, while
extending to firearms offences committed in any parish in Jamaica, would not extend   *a*
to offences other than firearms offences committed outside the parish within which
the division sat by persons already convicted under s 20 of the 1967 Act. It followed
that the void provisions of the 1974 Act were severable from the remaining provisions
which would still provide a sensible legislative scheme for dealing with firearms
offences (see p 373 *d* to *f* and *h* to p 374 *b* and *j*, post); dictum of Viscount Simon in
Attorney-General for Alberta v Attorney-General for Canada [1947] AC at 518 applied.   *b*

(vi) Accordingly, since the appellants had been convicted by a Resident Magistrate's
Division, the appeals against conviction would be dismissed but each appeal would
be remitted to the Court of Appeal of Jamaica for that court to pass appropriate
sentences in substitution for the mandatory sentences passed on the appellants by
the Resident Magistrate's Division (see p 374 *c* to *f*, post).

c

Notes
For the judicature of Jamaica, see 6 Halsbury's Laws (4th Edn) para 971.
For the separation of executive, legislative and judicial powers, see 8 ibid para 813.

d

Cases referred to in opinions
Attorney General v Antigua Times Ltd [1975] 3 All ER 81, [1975] 3 WLR 232, PC.
Attorney-General for Alberta v Attorney-General for Canada [1947] AC 503, [1947] LJR
1392, PC, 8(2) Digest (Reissue) 719, *301*.
*Attorney-General of the Commonwealth of Australia v R and Boilermakers' Society of Australia,
Kirby v R and Boilermakers' Society of Australia* [1957] 2 All ER 45, [1957] AC 288, [1957]   *e*
2 WLR 607, PC, 8(2) Digest (Reissue) 742, *320*.
Attorney-General for Ontario v Attorney-General for Canada [1925] AC 750, 94 LJPC
132, (1924) 4 DLR 529, PC, 8(2) Digest 738, *307*.
Deaton v Attorney-General and Revenue Comrs [1963] IR 170, Digest (Cont Vol A) 1304,
132a.
Ladore v Bennett [1939] 3 All ER 98, [1939] AC 468, 108 LJPC 69, PC, 8(2) Digest (Reissue)   *f*
706, *219*.
Liyange v R [1966] 1 All ER 650, [1967] AC 259, [1966] 2 WLR 682, PC, 8(2) Digest
(Reissue) 759, *349*.
State v O'Brien [1973] IR 50.

g

Appeals
On various dates in April 1974 Moses Hinds, Elkanah Hutchinson, Henry Martin
and Samuel Thomas, the appellants in the first appeal, were separately and summarily
convicted by a Resident Magistrate's Division of the Gun Court, a court established under s 3 of the Gun Court Act 1974 (Jamaica), of being in unlawful possession
of firearms and ammunition contrary to s 20(4)(*c*)(i) of the Firearms Act 1967 (Jamaica)   *h*
and sentenced under s 8(2) of the 1974 Act to be detained at hard labour during the
Governor-General's pleasure. The appellants each appealed against conviction and
sentence to the Court of Appeal of Jamaica and, by consent, their appeals were heard
together by the Court of Appeal in July and August 1974. On 22nd October 1974
the Court of Appeal (Luckhoo P(Ag), Zacca JA(Ag), Swaby JA dissenting) dismissed the
appeals. In April 1974 Trevor Jackson, the respondent in the second appeal, was   *j*
similarly convicted and sentenced by a Resident Magistrate's Division in respect of the
same offence as the appellants in the first appeal. On 5th December 1974 the Court of
Appeal of Jamaica (Graham-Parkins and Swaby JJA, Zacca JA (Ag) dissenting) allowed
the respondent's appeal and set aside his conviction. By orders dated 15th November
and 9th December 1974 the Court of Appeal of Jamaica respectively granted the

appellants in the first appeal and the respondent, the Director of Public Prosecutions
a for Jamaica, in the second appeal leave to appeal to the Privy Council. In granting
leave the Court of Appeal certified that both appeals involved final decisions on a
number of questions regarding the interpretation of the Constitution of Jamaica.
The first and second appeals were consolidated and all five persons sentenced to be
detained at hard labour treated as appellants for the purposes of the appeal to the
Privy Council. The facts are set out in the majority opinion of the Board.
b

Richard Mahfood QC, Lloyd Barnett and *Ronald Henriques* (all of the Jamaican Bar) for
the appellants.
James Kerr QC (Director of Public Prosecutions for Jamaica), *Stuart McKinnon* and
Henderson Downer (of the Jamaican Bar) for the Crown.
Hon Leacroft Robinson QC (Attorney General of Jamaica), *Gerald Davies* and *Austin Davis*
c (of the Jamaican Bar) for the Attorney General of Jamaica as intervener.

LORD DIPLOCK. In 1974 the Parliament of Jamaica passed the Gun Court Act
1974 as an ordinary Act of Parliament. It had not been preceded by legislation passed
under the special procedure prescribed by s 49 of the Constitution for an Act of
d Parliament to alter provisions of the Constitution, nor does the Gun Court Act
itself contain any express amendment of those provisions. All that it purports to do
is to establish a new court called the Gun Court with power to sit in three different
kinds of divisions: a Resident Magistrate's Division, a Full Court Division and a Circuit
Court Division, and to confer on one or other of these divisions jurisdiction to try
certain categories of offenders for criminal offences of every kind. Prior to the
e passing of the Act and at the date of the coming into force of the Constitution these
offences would have been cognisable only in a resident magistrate's court or in a
circuit court of the Supreme Court of Jamaica. The Act also lays down the procedure
to be followed in each kind of division and, in particular, provides that all trials should
be held in camera, and that for certain specified offences relating to the unauthorised
possession, acquisition or disposal of firearms or ammunition, the Gun Court should
f impose a mandatory sentence of detention at hard labour from which the detainee
can only be discharged at the direction of the Governor-General acting in accordance
with the advice of the Review Board, a non-judicial body established by the Act.
The five named individuals who are parties to the consolidated appeals to Her
Majesty in Council, four as appellants in the first appeal and one as respondent in the
second appeal, were each convicted by a Resident Magistrate's Division of the Gun
g Court of an offence which carried with it under the Act the mandatory sentence of.
detention at hard labour.
Each of them appealed to the Court of Appeal against his conviction and also against
his sentence, on the grounds that the Gun Court Act 1974, or alternatively those provisions of the Act under which he had been tried and sentenced, were inconsistent with
the Constitution of Jamaica and were therefore void under s 2 of the Constitution. The
h appeals of the first four detainees were heard together and earlier than that of the
fifth detainee. They came on before a court composed of Swaby JA and Zacca JA(Ag)
prescribed over by Luckhoo P(Ag). Separate judgments were delivered by all three
members of the court. Luckhoo P(Ag) and Zacca JA(Ag) concurred in the result that
the appeals should be dismissed although their reasons for doing so were not identical.
Swaby JA dissented. He would have allowed the appeals. The appeal of the fifth
j detainee was heard a few months later by a court that was differently constituted,
insomuch as Graham-Perkins JA presided in place of Luckhoo P(Ag). This was enough
to tip the balance. Graham-Perkins JA and Swaby JA delivered a joint judgment
allowing the appeal although on a ground different from those relied on in the latter's
earlier dissenting judgment. Zacca JA(Ag) adhered to his previous opinion and was in
favour of dismissing the appeal.

The unsuccessful parties to these appeals have now appealed to Her Majesty in
Council under s 110(1)(c) of the Constitution. It is common ground that the constitu- *a*
tional issues raised by the appeal that was the subject of the later judgments in the
Court of Appeal are indistinguishable from those raised by the four appeals that were
the subject of the earlier judgments. Before their Lordships' Board all the appeals
have been consolidated and all five detainees have been treated as appellants in
the consolidated appeal.

The questions raised as to the true interpretation of Chapter VII of the Consti- *b*
tution which relates to 'The Judicature' are of outstanding public importance. The
attack on the constitutional validity, of those provisions of the 1974 Act under which
the appellants were tried and sentenced by a Resident Magistrate's Division of the
Gun Court can most conveniently be dealt with under four heads: jurisdiction,
procedure, sentence and severability.

The arguments have been wide ranging—and necessarily so, for when the consti- *c*
tutional validity of an Act passed by the Parliament of Jamaica is in issue, the problem
cannot be solved by the court's confining its attention to those specific provisions of
the Act that are directly applicable to the particular case. Looked at in isolation from
the legislative scheme embodied in the Act when taken as a whole, it may be that
those specific provisions, if separately enacted, would not have been inconsistent with
the Constitution; but if other provisions of the Act are invalid a question of severa- *d*
bility arises. The court accordingly cannot avoid the task of examining the constitutional validity of the other provisions of the Act in order to see whether those which
must be struck down as invalid form part of a single legislative scheme of which the
specific provisions applicable to the particular case are also an integral and inseparable
part.

The inseverability of the provisions of the 1974 Act, which create the three divisions *e*
of the court, was the main thrust of the appellants' challenge under the head of
jurisdiction. This does not involve a direct attack on the specific provisions of the Act
under which the appellants were tried and convicted by a resident magistrate, when
looked at in isolation. What is attacked directly is the constitutional validity of those
provisions of the Act which purport to confer jurisdiction to try offences on the other
two divisions of the Gun Court: a Circuit Court Division and a Full Court Division. *f*
The next steps in the argument are: (1) The 1974 Act embodies a comprehensive
legislative scheme for the establishment of a single court, the Gun Court, with power
to sit in separate divisions; and to confer on the Gun Court jurisdiction to try certain
categories of offenders for criminal offences of all kinds. (2) The jurisdiction exercisable by the Gun Court when sitting in a Resident Magistrate's Division is an integral
and inseparable part of the jurisdiction intended to be conferred on the court. It *g*
cannot consistently with the legislative scheme of the Act survive the striking down
of the jurisdiction exercisable by the other two divisions. (3) A Gun Court consisting
only of a Resident Magistrate's Division would be a different kind of court from that
which Parliament intended to create.

This was the argument on which the fifth detainee succeeded in his appeal to the
Court of Appeal. It is, indeed, the only ground on which there is a majority judg- *h*
ment in the appellants' favour. In order to deal with it their Lordships cannot shirk
the task of ruling on the constitutional validity of those provisions of the Act which
purport to confer jurisdiction to try offences on the Circuit Court Division and on
the Full Court Division of the Gun Court. Such rulings, in their Lordships' view,
cannot be characterised as obiter dicta. They form necessary steps in any reasoning
disposing of the appellants' case insofar as it is based on inseverability. *j*

That the appellants' contentions under each of the four heads, jurisdiction, procedure, sentence and severability, raise questions of constitutional law of considerable
difficulty is evident from the conflicts of opinion, particularly under the first head,
that are disclosed in the four closely reasoned judgments of those judges of the Court
of Appeal who sat in one or both of the appeals. Their Lordships desire to express

their indebtedness to those judgments and to the arguments addressed to them
a by counsel for the parties at the hearing by this Board.

A written constitution, like any other written instrument affecting legal rights or
obligations, falls to be construed in the light of its subject-matter and of the surrounding circumstances with reference to which it was made. Their Lordships have been
quite properly referred to a number of previous authorities dealing with the exercise
of judicial power under other written constitutions, established either by Act of the
b Imperial Parliament or by Order in Council made by Her Majesty in right of the
Imperial Crown, whereby internal sovereignty or full independence has been granted
to what were formerly colonial or protected territories of the Crown. These other
constitutions differ in their express provisions from the Constitution of Jamaica,
sometimes widely where, as in the case of Canada and Australia, they provide for a
federal structure, but much less significantly in the case of the unitary constitutions
c of those states which have attained full independence in the course of the last two
decades. In seeking to apply to the interpretation of the Constitution of Jamaica
what has been said in particular cases about other constitutions, care must be taken
to distinguish between judicial reasoning which depended on the express words used
in the particular constitution under consideration and reasoning which depended on
what, though not expressed, is nonetheless a necessary implication from the subject-
d matter and structure of the constitution and the circumstances in which it had been
made. Such caution is particularly necessary in cases dealing with a federal constitution in which the question immediately in issue may have depended in part on
the separation of the judicial power from the legislative or executive power of the
federation or of one of its component states and in part on the division of judicial
power between the federation and a component state.

e Nevertheless all these constitutions have two things in common which have an
important bearing on their interpretation. They differ fundamentally in their nature
from ordinary legislation passed by the parliament of a sovereign state. They embody
what is in substance an agreement reached between representatives of the various
shades of political opinion in the state as to the structure of the organs of government
through which the plenitude of the sovereign power of the state is to be exercised
f in future. All of them were negotiated as well as drafted by persons nurtured in the
tradition of that branch of the common law of England that is concerned with public
law and familiar in particular with the basic concept of separation of legislative,
executive and judicial power as it had been developed in the unwritten constitution
of the United Kingdom. As to their subject-matter, the peoples for whom new constitutions were being provided were already living under a system of public law in
g which the local institutions through which governments was carried on, the legislature,
the executive and the courts, reflected the same basic concept. The new constitutions,
particularly in the case of unitary states, were evolutionary not revolutionary. They
provided for continuity of government through successor institutions, legislative,
executive and judicial, of which the members were to be selected in a different way,
but each institution was to exercise powers which, although enlarged, remained of a
h similar character to those that had been exercised by the corresponding institution
that it had replaced.

Because of this a great deal can be, and in drafting practice often is, left to necessary
implication from the adoption in the new constitution of a governmental structure
which makes provision for a legislature, an executive and a judicature. It is taken for
granted that the basic principle of separation of powers will apply to the exercise
j of their respective functions by these three organs of government. Thus the constitution does not normally contain any express prohibition on the exercise of legislative
powers by the executive or of judicial powers by either the executive or the legislature.
As respects the judicature, particularly if it is intended that the previously existing
courts shall continue to function, the constitution itself may even omit any express
provision conferring judicial power on the judicature. Nevertheless it is well

established as a rule of construction applicable to constitutional instruments under which this governmental structure is adopted that the absence of express words to that *a* effect does not prevent the legislative, the executive and the judicial powers of the new state being exercisable exclusively by the legislature, by the executive and by the judicature respectively. To seek to apply to constitutional instruments the canons of construction applicable to ordinary legislation in the fields of substantive criminal or civil law would, in their Lordships' view, be misleading—particularly those applicable to taxing statutes as to which it is a well-established principle that express words *b* are needed to impose a charge on the subject.

In the result there can be discerned in all those constitutions which have their origin in an Act of the Imperial Parliament at Westminster or in an Order in Council, a common pattern and style of draftsmanship which may conveniently be described as 'the Westminster model'.

Before turning to those express provisions of the Constitution of Jamaica on which *c* the appellants rely in these appeals, their Lordships will make some general observations about the interpretation of constitutions which follow the Westminister model.

All constitutions on the Westminster model deal under separate chapter headings with the legislature, the executive and the judicature. The chapter dealing with the judicature invariably contains provisions dealing with the method of appointment *d* and security of tenure of the members of the judiciary which are designed to assure to them a degree of independence from the other two branches of government. It may, as in the case of the Constitution of Ceylon, contain nothing more. To the extent to which the constitution itself is silent as to the distribution of the plenitude of judicial power between various courts it is implicit that it shall continue to be distributed between and exercised by the courts that were already in existence when *e* the new constitution came into force; but the legislature, in the exercise of its power to make laws for the 'peace, order and good government' of the state, may provide for the establishment of new courts and for the transfer to them of the whole or part of the jurisdiction previously exercisable by an existing court. What, however, is implicit in the very structure of a constitution on the Westminster model is that judicial power, however it be distributed from time to time between various courts, *f* is to continue to be vested in persons appointed to hold judicial office in the manner and on the terms laid down in the chapter dealing with the judicature, even though this is not expressly stated in the constitution (*Liyanage v R*[1]).

The more recent constitutions on the Westminster model, unlike their earlier prototypes, include a chapter dealing with fundamental rights and freedoms. The provisions of this chapter form part of the substantive law of the state and until *g* amended by whatever special procedure is laid down in the constitution for this purpose, impose a fetter on the exercise by the legislature, the executive and the judiciary of the plentitude of their respective powers. The remaining chapters of the constitutions are primarily concerned not with the legislature, the executive and the judicature as abstractions, but with the persons who shall be entitled collectively or individually to exercise the plenitude of legislative, executive or judicial powers— *h* their qualifications for legislative, executive or judicial office, the methods of selecting them, their tenure of office, the procedure to be followed where powers are conferred on a class of persons acting collectively and the majorities required for the exercise of those powers. Thus, where a constitution on the Westminster model speaks of a particular 'court' already in existence when the constitution comes into force, it uses this expression as a collective description of all those individual judges who, *j* whether sitting alone or with other judges or with a jury, are entitled to exercise the jurisdiction exercised by that court before the constitution came into force. Any

---

1 [1966] 1 All ER 650 at 658, [1967] AC 259 at 287, 288

express provision in the constitution for the appointment or security of tenure of
judges of that court will apply to all individual judges subsequently appointed to
exercise an analogous jurisdiction, whatever other name may be given to the 'court'
in which they sit (*Attorney-General for Ontario v Attorney-General for Canada*[1]).

Where, under a constitution on the Westminster model, a law is made by the
parliament which purports to confer jurisdiction on a court described by a new name,
the question whether the law conflicts with the provisions of the constitution dealing
with the exercise of the judicial power does not depend on the label (in the instant
case 'The Gun Court') which the parliament attaches to the judges when exercising
the jurisdiction conferred on them by the law whose constitutionality is impugned.
It is the substance of the law that must be regarded, not the form. What is the nature
of the jurisdiction to be exercised by the judges who are to compose the court to
which the new label is attached? Does the method of their appointment and the
security of their tenure conform to the requirements of the constitution applicable
to judges who, at the time the constitution came into force, exercised jurisdiction of
that nature? (*Attorney-General for Australia v R and Boilermakers' Society of Australia*[2]).

One final general observation: where, as in the instant case, a constitution on the
Westminster model represents the final step in the attainment of full independence
by the peoples of a former colony or protectorate, the constitution provides machinery
whereby any of its provisions, whether relating to fundamental rights and freedoms
or to the structure of government and the allocation to its various organs of legislative, executive or judicial powers, may be altered by those peoples through their
elected representatives in the parliament acting by specified majorities, which is
generally all that is required, though exceptionally as respects some provisions the
alteration may be subject also to confirmation by a direct vote of the majority of the
people themselves. The purpose served by this machinery for 'entrenchment' is to
ensure that those provisions which were regarded as important safeguards by the
political parties in Jamaica, minority and majority alike, who took part in the
negotiations which led up to the constitution, should not be altered without mature
consideration by the parliament and the consent of a larger proportion of its members
than the bare majority required for ordinary laws. So in deciding whether any provisions of a law passed by the Parliament of Jamaica as an ordinary law are inconsistent
with the Constitution of Jamaica, neither the courts of Jamaica nor their Lordships'
Board are concerned with the propriety or expediency of the law impugned. They
are concerned solely with whether those provisions, however reasonable and expedient, are of such a character that they conflict with an entrenched provision of the
Constitution and so can be validly passed only after the Constitution has been amended
by the method laid down by it for altering that entrenched provision.

Turning now to the Gun Court Act 1974, the purpose of the Act as described in its
long title is 'to provide for the establishment of a Court to deal particularly with
firearms offences and for purposes incidental thereto or connected therewith'.
Their Lordships will deal first with the jurisdiction of the court established by the Act,
secondly with procedure, thirdly with the mandatory sentence for offences against s 20
of the Firearms Act 1967 of which the appellants were convicted, and finally with the
question of severability.

Jurisdiction

Although the institution established by the Act is given a single name 'The Gun
Court' (s 3(1)) and provided with a single seal (s 3(3)), in substance it comprises three
different courts called 'divisions' with differing status, differing composition,
differing jurisdiction and differing powers. These divisions, in their Lordships' view,
call for separate consideration.

1 [1925] AC 750
2 [1957] 2 All ER 45, [1957] AC 288

(1) *The Circuit Court Division*

The division exercising the widest jurisdiction is called the 'Circuit Court Division'. It is constituted by a 'Supreme Court judge exercising the jurisdiction of a Circuit Court' (s 4(c)); it is a superior court of record (s 3(2)), and its jurisdiction is the same as that of a circuit court established under the Judicature (Supreme Court) Law, except that the geographical limits of its jurisdiction in respect of a 'firearm offence' extend to all parishes of Jamaica (s 5(3)). The Chief Justice may designate any circuit court to be a Circuit Court Division of the Gun Court (s 17(1)) and may assign any Supreme Court judge to sit as the judge of a Circuit Court Division (s 10(1)). Nothing in the Act, however, is to be construed as divesting of any jurisdiction a circuit court not designated as a Circuit Court Division of the Gun Court (s 21(1)).

A 'firearm offence' is defined by s 2 of the 1974 Act as meaning—

'(a) any offence contrary to section 20 of the Firearms Act, 1967; (b) any other offence whatsoever involving a firearm and in which the offender's possession of the firearm is contrary to section 20 of the Firearms Act, 1967.'

Section 20 of the Firearms Act 1967 deals with the unauthorised possession of fire-arms or ammunition and creates offences all of which are triable summarily before a resident magistrate or on indictment by a circuit court.

In substance, therefore, all that is done by those provisions of the Act to which reference has been made is to enlarge the previously existing criminal jurisdiction of a Supreme Court judge holding a circuit court so as to confer on him jurisdiction to try 'firearm offences' committed outside the parish for which the circuit court is held, if that circuit court has been given the designation of a 'Circuit Court Division' of the Gun Court. In their Lordships' view there is nothing in the Constitution of Jamaica that prohibits Parliament from extending the geographical limits of the criminal jurisdiction exercisable by a properly appointed Supreme Court judge in the exercise of the jurisdiction of a circuit court under the Judicature (Supreme Court) Law, whatever label may be attached by Parliament to the Supreme Court judge when exercising the extended jurisdiction.

(2) *The Resident Magistrate's Division*

Their Lordships will deal next with the division of the Gun Court which exercises the most restricted jurisdiction. It is called a 'Resident Magistrate's Division' and similar considerations apply to it. It is constituted by one resident magistrate (s 4(a)) and is a court of record; but unlike a Circuit Court Division, it is not a superior court of record (s 3(2)). Its original jurisdiction to hear and determine criminal offences summarily is the same as that of a resident magistrate's court established under the Judicature (Resident Magistrates) Act, except that the geographical limits of its jurisdiction are extended to all offences committed in any parish of Jamaica in respect of (i) offences triable summarily under s 20 of the Firearms Act 1967 and offences ancillary thereto created by s 18 of the 1974 Act and (ii) all other summary offences committed by a specified category of offenders ('detainees') to which further reference will be made hereafter (s 5(1)(a) and (c); s 9(a); s 10(2)). The Chief Justice may designate any resident magistrate's court to be a Resident Magistrate's Division of the Gun Court (s 17(2)) and may assign any resident magistrate to sit as a Resident Magistrate's Division.

In addition to this limited extension of the geographical limits of the original criminal jurisdiction previously exercisable by a properly appointed resident magis-trate under the Judicature (Resident Magistrates) Act, the 1974 Act also makes a similar extension of the geographical limits of his jurisdiction to conduct the pre-liminary examination into any firearm offence which is a capital offence and any other capital offence alleged to have been committed by a detainee (s 5(1)(b)).

So here too the 1974 Act does no more than extend in respect of certain specified
offences the geographical limits of the criminal jurisdiction exercisable by a properly
appointed resident magistrate under the Judicature (Resident Magistrates) Act,
and to attach to him the label a 'Resident Magistrate's Division' of the Gun Court
when exercising his jurisdiction over these offences.

(3) The Full Court Division

Different considerations, however, apply to a 'Full Court Division' of the Gun Court
which exercises a jurisdiction intermediate between that of a Circuit Court Division
and a Resident Magistrate's Division. This is composed of three resident magistrates
sitting together (s 4(b)) and acting by a majority (the Interpretation Act 1968, s 54).
The Chief Justice may designate any resident magistrate's court to be a Full Court
Division of the Gun Court and may assign any resident magistrate to be a member of
that division (s 17(2)).

A Full Court Division is thus a new court in substance as well as form. Unlike
a Circuit Court Division and a Resident Magistrate's Division, it is of different composition from any previously existing court in Jamaica. Its jurisdiction too is different
from that of any previously existing court. It does not extend to any capital offence,
but with this exception it extends to all 'firearm offences' and to all other offences
of whatever kind committed by detainees whether a firearm was involved in the
offence or not, and its sentencing powers for such offences are co-extensive with
those of a circuit court.

To appreciate how wide this jurisdiction is, it is necessary to examine those provisions
of the Act which create the category of offenders whom their Lordships have hitherto
referred to as 'detainees'. The Act provides that any court other than a division of the
Gun Court before which a case involving a firearm offence is brought shall forthwith
transfer the case for trial by the Gun Court (s 6(1)) and shall remand the accused
in custody to appear before the Gun Court (s 6(3)). On his appearing before the Gun
Court, the Act provides that the hearing of any charge against him of an offence of
unauthorised possession of firearms or ammunition under s 20 of the Firearms Act
1967 shall ordinarily be commenced within seven days of his first appearance (s 8(1)).
The practical consequence of this provision is that the charge of unlawful possession
will be heard and determined before any other offence that he may be charged with.
On conviction of the offence of unlawful possession, the Act prescribes the mandatory
sentence of detention at hard labour during the Governor-General's pleasure. Their
Lordships will have occasion to consider the constitutionality of this sentence later.
Its relevance for the purpose of considering the extent of the jurisdiction exercisable
by a Full Court Division of the Gun Court is that the practical consequence of these
provisions is to confer on a Full Court Division jurisdiction to try all other crimes,
however serious, short of capital offences, committed by any person who has also
committed an offence under s 20 of the Firearms Act 1967, even though those other
crimes have nothing to do with firearms. The jurisdiction conferred on a court consisting of three resident magistrates thus extends to all non-capital offences which
were previously triable only on indictment before a Supreme Court judge exercising
the jurisdiction of a circuit court of the Supreme Court, if the offender is a person who
has been in unlawful possession of a firearm. Since committal for trial in a circuit
court of the Supreme Court is preceded by a preliminary examination before a
resident magistrate's court, the practical consequence of the provision for mandatory
transfer for trial by the Gun Court of cases involving a firearm offence is to ensure
that all offences falling within the jurisdiction conferred on a Full Court Division of
the Gun Court shall be tried by that division to the exclusion of a circuit court of the
Supreme Court.

The attack on the constitutionality of the Full Court Division of the Gun Court
may be based on two grounds. The first is that the 1974 Act purports to confer on a

court consisting of persons qualified and appointed as resident magistrates a jurisdiction which under the provisions of Chapter VII of the Constitution is exercisable only by a person qualified and appointed as a judge of the Supreme Court. The second ground is much less fundamental. It need only be mentioned briefly, for it arises only if the first ground fails. It is that even if the conferment of jurisdiction on a Full Court Division consisting of three resident magistrates is valid, s 112 of the Constitution requires that any assignment of a resident magistrate to sit in that division should be made by the Governor-General acting on the recommendation of the Judicial Service Commission and not by the Chief Justice as the 1974 Act provides.

Chapter VII of the Constitution, 'The Judicature', was in their Lordships' view intended to deal with the appointment and security of tenure of all persons holding any salaried office by virtue of which they are entitled to exercise civil or criminal jurisdiction in Jamaica. For this purpose they are divided into two categories: (i) a higher judiciary, consisting of judges of the Supreme Court and judges of the Court of Appeal, and (ii) a lower judiciary, consisting of those described in s 112(2), viz:

> 'Resident Magistrate, Judge of the Traffic Court, Registrar of the Supreme Court, Registrar of the Court of Appeal and such other offices connected with the courts of Jamaica as, subject to the provisions of the Constitution, may be prescribed by Parliament.'

Apart from the offices of judge and registrar of the Court of Appeal which were new, these two categories embraced all salaried members of the judiciary who exercised civil or criminal jurisdiction in Jamaica at the date when the Constitution came into force. A minor jurisdiction, particularly in relation to juveniles, was exercised by justices of the peace but, as in England, they sat part-time only, were unpaid and were not required to possess any professional qualification.

Common to both categories, with the exception of the Chief Justice of the Supreme Court and the President of the Court of Appeal, is the requirement under the Constitution that they should be appointed by the Governor-General on the recommendation of the Judicial Service Commission—a body established under s 111 whose composition is different from that of the Public Service Commission and consists of persons likely to be qualified to assess the fitness of a candidate for judicial office.

The distinction between the higher judiciary and the lower judiciary is that the former are given a greater degree of security of tenure than the latter. There is nothing in the Constitution to protect the lower judiciary against Parliament passing ordinary laws (a) abolishing their office (b) reducing their salaries while they are in office or (c) providing that their appointments to judicial office shall be only for a short fixed term of years. Their independence of the good-will of the political party which commands a bare majority in the Parliament is thus not fully assured. The only protection that is assured to them by s 112 is that they cannot be removed or disciplined except on the recommendation of the Judicial Service Commission with a right of appeal to the Privy Council. This last is a local body established under s 82 of the Constitution whose members are appointed by the Governor-General after consultation with the Prime Minister and hold office for a period not exceeding three years.

In contrast to this, judges of the Supreme Court and of the Court of Appeal are given a more firmly rooted security of tenure. They are protected by entrenched provisions of the Constitution against Parliament passing ordinary laws (a) abolishing their office, (b) reducing their salaries while in office or (c) providing that their tenure of office shall end before they attain the age of 65 years. They are not subject to any disciplinary control while in office. They can only be removed from office on the advice of the Judicial Committee of Her Majesty's Privy Council in the United Kingdom given on a reference made on the recommendation of a tribunal of enquiry consisting of persons who hold or have held high judicial office in some part of the Commonwealth.

The manifest intention of these provisions is that all those who hold any salaried judicial office in Jamaica shall be appointed on the recommendation of the Judicial Service Commission and that their independence from political pressure by Parliament or by the Executive in the exercise of their judicial functions shall be assured by granting to them such degree of security of tenure in their office as is justified by the importance of the jurisdiction that they exercise. A clear distinction is drawn between the security of tenure appropriate to those judges who exercise the jurisdiction of the higher judiciary and that appropriate to those judges who exercise the jurisdiction of the lower judiciary.

Their Lordships accept that there is nothing in the Constitution to prohibit Parliament from establishing by an ordinary law a court under a new name, such as the 'Revenue Court', to exercise part of the jurisdiction that was being exercised by members of the higher judiciary or by members of the lower judiciary at the time when the Constitution came into force. To do so is merely to change the label to be attached to the capacity in which the persons appointed to be members of the new court exercise a jurisdiction previously exercised by the holders of one or other of the judicial offices named in Chapter VII of the Constitution. In their Lordships' view, however, it is the manifest intention of the Constitution that any person appointed to be a member of such a court should be appointed in the same manner and entitled to the same security of tenure as the holder of the judicial office named in Chapter VII of the Constitution which entitled him to exercise the corresponding jurisdiction at the time when the Constitution came into force.

Their Lordships understand the Attorney General to concede that salaried judges of any new court that Parliament may establish by an ordinary law must be appointed in the manner and entitled to the security of tenure provided for members of the lower judiciary by s 112 of the Constitution. In their Lordships' view this concession was rightly made. To adopt the familiar words used by Viscount Simonds in *Attorney-General of Australia v R and Boilermakers' Society of Australia*[1], it would make a mockery of the Constitution if Parliament could transfer the jurisdiction previously exercisable by holders of the judicial offices named in Chapter VII of the Constitution to holders of new judicial offices to which some different name was attached and to provide that persons holding the new judicial offices should not be appointed in the manner and on the terms prescribed in Chapter VII for the appointment of members of the judicature. If this were the case there would be nothing to prevent Parliament from transferring the whole of the judicial power of Jamaica (with two minor exceptions referred to below) to bodies composed of persons who, not being members of 'the Judicature', would not be entitled to the protection of Chapter VII at all.

What the Attorney General does not concede is that Parliament is prohibited by Chapter VII from transferring to a court composed of duly appointed members of the lower judiciary jurisdiction which, at the time the Constitution came into force, was exercisable only by a court composed of duly appointed members of the higher judiciary.

In support of his contention that Parliament is entitled by an ordinary law to downgrade any part of the jurisdiction previously exercisable by the Supreme Court, he relies on s 97 of the Constitution which provides as follows:

'(1) There shall be a Supreme Court for Jamaica *which shall have such jurisdiction and powers as may be conferred upon it by this Constitution or any other law.*
'(2) ...
'(3) ...
'(4) The Supreme Court shall be a superior court of record and, save as otherwise provided by Parliament, shall have all the powers of such a court.'

---

1   [1957] 2 All ER at 52, [1957] AC at 313

It is, in their Lordships' view, significant that s 103(1) and (5) which provide for the establishment of the Court of Appeal are in identical terms with the substitution of the words 'Court of Appeal' for 'Supreme Court'.

The only other provisions of the Constitution which expressly confer jurisdiction on the Supreme Court or the Court of Appeal are (i) s 25(2) and (3) which give them original and appellate jurisdiction respectively to hear and determine claims for redress for any contravention of the provisions of Chapter III relating to fundamental rights and freedoms, and (ii) s 44(1) which gives to them original and appellate jurisdiction respectively in disputes about membership of either House of Parliament.

The jurisdiction that was characteristic of judges of a court to which the description of 'a Supreme Court' was appropriate in a hierarchy of courts which included, in addition, inferior courts and 'a Court of Appeal', was well known to the makers of the Constitution in 1962. So was the jurisdiction that was characteristic of judges of a court to which the description of 'a Court of Appeal' was appropriate.

In their Lordships' view s 110 of the Constitution makes it apparent that in providing in s 103(1) that: 'There shall be a Court of Appeal for Jamaica . . .' the draftsman treated this form of words as carrying with it by necessary implication that the judges of the court required to be established under s 103 should exercise an appellate jurisdiction in all substantial civil cases and in all serious criminal cases; and that the words that follow, viz 'which shall have such jurisdiction and powers as may be conferred upon it by this Constitution or any other law', do not entitle Parliament by an ordinary law to deprive the Court of Appeal of a significant part of such appellate jurisdiction or to confer it on judges who do not enjoy the security of tenure which the Constitution guarantees to judges of the Court of Appeal. Section 110(1) of the Constitution which grants to litigants wide rights of appeal to Her Majesty in Council but only from 'decisions of the Court of Appeal', clearly proceeds on this assumption as to the effect of s 103. Section 110 would be rendered nugatory if its wide appellate jurisdiction could be removed from the Court of Appeal by an ordinary law without amendment of the Constitution.

Their Lordships see no reason why a similar implication should not be drawn from the corresponding words of s 97. The Court of Appeal of Jamaica was a new court established under the Judicature (Appellate Jurisdiction) Law 1962, which came into force one day before the Constitution, viz on 5th August 1962. The Supreme Court of Jamaica had existed under that title since 1880. In the judges of that court there had been vested all that jurisdiction in Jamaica which in their Lordships' view was characteristic of a court to which in 1962 the description 'a Supreme Court' was appropriate in a hierarchy of courts which was to include a separate 'Court of Appeal'. The three kinds of jurisdiction that are characteristic of a Supreme Court where appellate jurisdiction is vested in a separate court are: (1) unlimited original jurisdiction in all substantial civil cases; (2) unlimited original jurisdiction in all serious criminal offences; (3) supervisory jurisdiction over the proceedings of inferior courts (viz of the kind which owes its origin to the prerogative writs of certiorari, mandamus and prohibition).

That s 97(1) of the Constitution was intended to reserve in Jamaica a Supreme Court exercising this characteristic jurisdiction is, in their Lordship's view, supported by the provision in s 13(1) of the Jamaica (Constitution) Order in Council 1962, that 'The Supreme Court in existence immediately before the commencement of this Order shall be the Supreme Court for the purposes of the Constitution'. This is made an entrenched provision of the Constitution itself by s 21(1) of the Order in Council, and confirms that the kind of court referred to in the words 'There shall be a Supreme Court for Jamaica' was a court which would exercise in Jamaica the three kinds of jurisdiction characteristic of a Supreme Court that have been indicated above.

If, as contended by the Attorney General, the words italicised above in s 97(1) entitled Parliament by an ordinary law to strip the Supreme Court of all jurisdiction in civil and criminal cases other than that expressly conferred on it by s 25 and

s 44, what would be left would be a court of such limited jurisdiction that the label
'Supreme Court' would be a false description; so too if all its jurisdiction (with those
two exceptions) were exercisable concurrently by other courts composed of members
of the lower judiciary. But more important, for this is the substance of the matter,
the individual citizen could be deprived of the safeguard, which the makers of the
Constitution regarded as necessary, of having important questions affecting his civil
or criminal responsibilities determined by a court, however named, composed of judges
whose independence from all local pressure by Parliament or by the executive was
guaranteed by a security of tenure more absolute than that provided by the
Constitution for judges of inferior courts.

Their Lordships therefore are unable to accept that the words in s 97(1), on which
the Attorney General relies, entitle Parliament by an ordinary law to vest in a new
court composed of members of the lower judiciary a jurisdiction that forms a significant part of the unlimited civil, criminal or supervisory jurisdiction that is characteristic
of a 'Supreme Court' and was exercised by the Supreme Court of Jamaica at the
time when the Constitution came into force, at any rate where such vesting is
accompanied by ancillary provisions, such as those contained in s 6(1) of the Gun Court
Act 1974, which would have the consequence that all cases falling within the jurisdiction of the new court would in practice be heard and determined by it instead
of by a court composed of judges of the Supreme Court.

As with so many questions arising under constitutions on the Westminster model,
the question whether the jurisdiction vested in the new court is wide enough to constitute so significant a part of the jurisdiction that is characteristic of a Supreme Court
as to fall within the constitutional prohibition is one of degree. The instant case is
concerned only with criminal jurisdiction. It is not incompatible with the criminal
jurisdiction of a 'Supreme Court', as this expression would have been understood
by the makers of the Constitution in 1962, that jurisdiction to try summarily specific
minor offences which attracted only minor penalties should be conferred on inferior
criminal courts to the exclusion of the criminal as distinct from the supervisory jurisdiction of a Supreme Court. Nor is it incompatible that a jurisdiction concurrent with
that of a Supreme Court should be conferred on inferior criminal courts to try a
wide variety of offences if in the particular case the circumstances in which the offence
was committed makes it one that does not call for a severer punishment than the
maximum that the inferior court is empowered to inflict. In this class of offences
the answer to the question whether the concurrent jurisdiction conferred on the
inferior court is appropriate only to a 'Supreme Court' depends on the maximum
punishment that the inferior court is empowered to inflict.

At the time of the coming into force of the Constitution the maximum sentence
that a resident magistrate was empowered to inflict for any of the numerous offences
which he had jurisdiction to try was one year's imprisonment and a fine of $100. It
is not necessary for the purposes of the instant appeals to consider to what extent
this maximum might be raised, either generally or in respect of particular offences,
without trespassing on the jurisdiction reserved by the Constitution to judges of the
Supreme Court. The limit has in fact been raised to two years in respect of some
offences including those under s 20 of the Firearms Act 1967. Their Lordships would
not hold this to be unconstitutional; but to remove all limits in respect of all criminal
offences, however serious, other than murder and treason, would in their Lordships'
view destroy the protection for the individual citizen of Jamaica intended to be
preserved to him by the establishment of a Supreme Court composed of judges
whose independence from political pressure by Parliament or the Executive was
more firmly guaranteed than that of the inferior judiciary.

It is this that, in respect of a particular category of offenders, is sought to be achieved
by the provisions of the Gun Court Act 1974 relating to the jurisdiction and powers of
a Full Court Division of the Gun Court. As has been pointed out, the practical consequence of these provisions as they stand would be to give to a court composed of

members of the lower judiciary, jurisdiction to try and to punish by penalties, extending in the case of some offences to imprisonment for life, all criminal offences however grave, apart from murder or treason, committed by any person who has also committed an offence under s 20 of the Firearms Act 1967. Even if, by reason of the invalidity of s 8(2) of the 1974 Act, the jurisdiction of the Full Court Division over that category of offender does not extend to crimes in which no firearm is involved this would not, in their Lordships' view, affect the principle. It would not reduce the gravity of the class of offences which the Full Court Division had jurisdiction to try or the severity of the sentences which it had power to impose. Its only effect would be a reduction, which would probably be only slight, in the number of cases to be tried by a Full Court Division.

In their Lordships' view the provisions of the 1974 Act, insofar as they provide for the establishment of a Full Court Division of the Gun Court consisting of three resident magistrates, conflict with Chapter VII of the Constitution and are accordingly void by virtue of s 2.

Procedure

It is provided by s 13(1) of the 1974 Act, which starts with the introductory words 'In the interest of public safety, public order or the protection of the private lives of persons concerned in the proceedings', that all three divisions of the Gun Court shall sit in camera. The court is also empowered to direct that no particulars of the trial other than the name of the accused, the offence charged and the verdict and sentence shall be published without the prior approval of the court.

The appellants contend that this is contrary to s 20(3) in Chapter III of the Constitution, which provides that all proceedings of every court shall be held in public. This general rule that trials shall be in public entrenches in the Constitution of Jamaica a previously existing common law rule. It is, however, subject to a number of exceptions which are laid down in s 20(4). The exception relevant to the instant case is to be found in para (c)(ii) and permits persons other than the parties and their legal representatives to be excluded from the proceedings—

'to such extent as the court . . . may be empowered or required by law to do so in the interests of defence, public safety, public order, public morality, the welfare of persons under the age of twenty-one years or the protection of the private lives of persons concerned in the proceedings.'

The introductory words of s 13(1) of the 1974 Act amount to a declaration by Parliament that the hearing in camera of the kinds of cases which fall within the jurisdiction of the Gun Court is reasonably required for the protection of the interests referred to, which include public safety and public order. By s 48(1) of the Constitution the power to make laws for the peace, order and good government of Jamaica is vested in Parliament; and prima facie it is for Parliament to decide what is or is not reasonably required in the interests of public safety or public order. Such a decision involves considerations of public policy which lie outside the field of the judicial power and may have to be made in the light of information available to a government of a kind that cannot effectively be adduced in evidence by means of the judicial process.

In considering the constitutionality of the provisions of s 13(1) of the 1974 Act, a court should start with the presumption that the circumstances existing in Jamaica are such that hearings in camera are reasonably required in the interests of 'public safety, public order or the protection of the private lives of persons concerned in the proceedings'. The presumption is rebuttable. Parliament cannot evade a constitutional restriction by a colourable device (*Ladore v Bennett*[1]). But in order to rebut

---

1   [1939] 3 All ER 98 at 105, [1939] AC 468 at 482

a the presumption, their Lordships would have to be satisfied that no reasonable member of Parliament who understood correctly the meaning of the relevant provisions of the Constitution could have supposed that hearings in camera were reasonably required for the protection of any of the interests referred to; or, in other words, that Parliament in so declaring was either acting in bad faith or had misinterpreted the provisions of s 20(4) of the Constitution under which it purported to act.

b No evidence has been adduced by the appellants in the instant case to rebut the resumption as respects the interests of public safety and public order. Unlike the judges of the Court of Appeal, their Lordships have no personal knowledge of public safety and public order. Unlike the judges of the Court of Appeal, their Lordships have no personal knowlege of the circumstances in Jamaica which gave rise to the passing of the 1974 Act. They have noted, however, the account contained in the judgment of Luckhoo P in the Court of Appeal of matters of common knowledge

c of which he felt able to take judicial notice. These plainly negative any suggestion that Parliament was acting in bad faith in declaring that s 13 was in the interests of public safety and public order.

The reference to the protection of the private lives of persons concerned in the proceedings as well as to 'public safety' and 'public order' would appear to be based

d on a misinterpretation of this phrase where it is used in s 20(4) of the Constitution. The phrase, which also appears in s 22(2)(a)(ii) as a limitation on freedom of expression, is not directed to the physical safety of individuals but to their right to privacy, i e to protection from disclosure to the public at large of matters of purely personal or domestic concern which are of no legitimate public interest. Its use in s 13(1) of the 1974 Act in collocation with public safety and public order suggests that the draftsman was treating it as if it meant 'the protection of the lives of private persons con-

e cerned in the proceedings' and was intended to refer to the intimidation of witnesses in cases involving firearms which Luckhoo P referred to as being a matter of common knowledge. However that may be, this particular interest is relied on in s 13(1) only as an alternative to the interests of public safety and public order. Even if the words referring to it are struck out of the subsection, that which remains suffices to bring

f the provision for hearings in camera within the exception laid down by s 20(4)(c)(ii) of the Constitution.

In their Lordships' view s 13 of the 1974 Act is not in conflict with any of the provisions of the Constitution.

Sentence

g Their Lordships have already had occasion to refer to the mandatory sentence of detention 'at hard labour during the Governor-General's pleasure' which is prescribed by s 8(2) of the 1974 Act for an offence under s 20 of the Firearms Act 1967. To ascertain what is the real effect of such a sentence it is necessary to turn to s 22 of the 1974 Act. Subsection (1) provides:

h   'Save as otherwise provided by section 90 of the Constitution of Jamaica, no person who is detained pursuant to subsection (2) of section 8 shall be discharged except at the direction of the Governor-General, who shall act in that behalf on and in accordance with the advice of the Review Board established under the following provisions.'

j The Review Board is to consist of five persons of whom the chairman is to be a judge or former judge of the Supreme Court or the Court of Appeal; but none of the others is a member of the judiciary. They are the Director of Prisons and the Chief Medical Officer or their respective nominees, a nominee of the Jamaica Council of Churches and a person qualified in psychiatry nominated by the Prime Minister after consultation with the Leader of the Opposition. Thus, the majority of the Review Board

does not consist of persons appointed in the manner laid down in Chapter VII of the
Constitution for persons entitled to exercise judicial powers.

In substance, therefore, the power to determine the length of any custodial sentence imposed for an offence under s 20 of the Firearms Act 1967 is removed from the
judicature and vested in a body of persons not qualified under the Constitution to
exercise judicial powers. The only function left to the Gun Court itself in relation to
the length of the custodial sentence is the right, reserved to it by s 8(3)(b) of the 1974
Act, to make recommendations for the consideration of the Review Board in any case
which in the court's opinion so warrants; but the Review Board, though it must take
the recommendation into consideration, is not obliged to follow it. The power of
decision rests with the Review Board alone.

In the field of punishment for criminal offences, the application of the basic principle
of separation of legislative, executive and judicial powers that is implicit in a constitution on the Westminster model makes it necessary to consider how the power
to determine the length and character of a sentence which imposes restrictions
on the personal liberty of the offender is distributed under these three heads of
power.

The power conferred on Parliament to make laws for the peace, order and good
government of Jamaica enables it not only to define what conduct shall constitute a
criminal offence but also to prescribe the punishment to be inflicted on those persons
who have been found guilty of that conduct by an independent and impartial court
established by law (see Constitution, Chapter III, s 20(1)). The carrying out of the
punishment where it involves a deprivation of personal liberty is a function of the
executive power; and, subject to any restrictions imposed by a law, it lies within the
power of the executive to regulate the conditions under which the punishment is
carried out.

In the exercise of its legislative power, Parliament may, if it thinks fit, prescribe a
fixed punishment to be inflicted on all offenders found guilty of the defined offence,
as, for example, capital punishment for the crime of murder. Or it may prescribe a
range of punishments up to a maximum in severity, either with or, as is more common,
without a minimum, leaving it to the court by which the individual is tried to
determine what punishment falling within the range prescribed by Parliament is
appropriate in the particular circumstances of his case.

Thus Parliament, in the exercise of its legislative power, may make a law imposing
limits on the discretion of the judges who preside over the courts by whom offences
against that law are tried to inflict on an individual offender a custodial sentence the
length of which reflects the judge's own assessment of the gravity of the offender's
conduct in the particular circumstance of his case. What Parliament cannot do,
consistently with the separation of powers, is to transfer from the judiciary to any
executive body whose members are not appointed under Chapter VII of the Constitution, a discretion to determine the severity of the punishment to be inflicted on
an individual member of a class of offenders. Whilst none would suggest that a Review
Board composed as is provided in s 22 of the 1974 Act, would not perform its duties
responsibly and impartially, the fact remains that the majority of its members
are not persons qualified by the Constitution to exercise judicial powers. A breach
of a constitutional restriction is not excused by the good intentions with which the
legislative power has been exceeded by the particular law. If, consistently with the
Constitution, it is permissible for Parliament to confer the discretion to determine
the length of custodial sentences for criminal offences on a body composed as the Review Board is, it would be equally permissible to a less well-intentioned Parliament
to confer the same discretion on any other person or body of persons not qualified to
exercise judicial powers, and in this way, without any amendment of the Constitution, to open the door to the exercise of arbitrary power by the Executive in the
whole field of criminal law.

In this connection their Lordships would not seek to improve on what was said by

the Supreme Court of Ireland in *Deaton v Attorney-General and Revenue Comrs*[1], a
a case which concerned a law in which the choice of alternative penalties was left to
the executive:

'There is a clear distinction between the prescription of a fixed penalty and the
selection of a penalty for a particular case. The prescription of a fixed penalty is
the statement of a general rule, which is one of the characteristics of legislation;
b this is wholly different from the selection of a penalty to be imposed in a particular case . . . The Legislature does not prescribe the penalty to be imposed in an
individual citizen's case; it states the general rule, and the application of that rule
is for the Courts . . . the selection of punishment is an integral part of the administration of justice and, as such, cannot be committed to the hands of the
Executive . . .'

c   This was said in relation to the Constitution of the Irish Republic, which is also based
on the separation of powers. In their Lordships' view it applies with even greater
force to constitutions on the Westminster model. They would only add that under
such constitutions the legislature not only does not, but it *can* not, prescribe the
penalty to be imposed in an individual citizen's case (*Liyanage v R*[2]).
d   It is contended by the respondents in the instant appeal that the sentence 'to be
detained at hard labour during the Governor-General's pleasure' prescribed by s 8(2)
of the 1974 Act is a fixed penalty applicable to all offenders against s 20 of the Firearms
Act 1967 and that, as such, it does not fall within the constitutional restrictions on the
exercise of legislative power. In support of this contention reliance is placed on the
fact that at the time when the Constitution came into force a similar form of sentence was prescribed for persons under the age of 18 years convicted of a capital offence
e (the Juveniles Law, s 29(1)) and for habitual criminals (the Criminal Justice (Administration) Law, s 49), and that in the case of both these categories of offenders the length
of the period of detention of the individual was left to be determined by the Executive.
Reliance is also placed on the preservation by s 90 of the Constitution of Her Majesty's
prerogative of mercy, as amounting to a recognition that the length of all custodial
f sentences is a matter which may lawfully be determined by a body exercising
executive and not judicial powers.
As their Lordships have already emphasised, Parliament cannot evade a constitutional restriction by a colourable device. It is the substance of the sentencing provisions of ss 8(2) and 22 of the 1974 Act that matters, not their form. To adapt the
words used in the judgments of the Supreme Court of Ireland in *State v O'Brien*[3]
g where a sentencing provision in similar terms to s 8(2) of the 1974 Act was held to be
unconstitutional[4]:

'. . . from the very moment of sentence the convicted person is undergoing
punishment for a term which the judge was not to determine but which was
to be determined by [the Review Board]';

h   and[5]:

'The section . . . placed it in the hands of [the Review Board] to determine
actively and positively the duration of the prisoner's sentence, and not just to
affect an act of remission. The determination of the length of sentence for a
criminal offence is essentially a judicial function.'

j
_____

1 [1963] IR 170 at 182, 183
2 [1966] 1 All ER 650, [1966] 2 WLR 682
3 [1973] IR 50
4 [1973] IR at 64, per Walsh J
5 [1973] IR at 59, 60, per O'Dalaigh CJ

Their Lordships would hold that the provisions of s 8 of the 1974 Act relating to the mandatory sentence of detention during the Governor-General's pleasure and the *a* provisions of s 22 relating to the Review Board are a law made after the coming into force of the Constitution which is inconsistent with the provisions of the Constitution relating to the separation of powers. They are accordingly void by virtue of s 2 of the Constitution.

Section 29(1) of the Juveniles Law and s 49 of the Criminal Justice (Administration) Law are of no assistance to the respondents' argument. They were passed before the *b* law-making powers exercisable by members of the legislature of Jamaica by an ordinary majority of votes were subject to the restrictions imposed on them by the Constitution—though they were subject to other restrictions imposed by the Colonial Laws Validity Act 1865. The validity of these two laws is preserved by s 4 of the Jamaica (Constitution) Order in Council[1]. No law in force immediately before 6th August 1962 can be held to be inconsistent with the Constitution; and under s 26(8) of the *c* Constitution nothing done in execution of a sentence authorised by such a law can be held to be inconsistent with any of the provisions of Chapter III of the Constitution. The constitutional restrictions on the exercise of legislative powers apply only to new laws made by the new Parliament established under Chapter V of the Constitution. They are not retrospective.

The royal prerogative of mercy, which has been exercised in Jamaica since it first *d* became a territory of the British Crown, is expressly preserved by s 90 of the Constitution, which provides that it shall be exercised on Her Majesty's behalf by the Governor-General acting on the recommendation of the Privy Council. It is, as is recognised by its inclusion in Chapter VI of the Constitution, an executive power; but, as an executive power, it is exceptional and is confined, as it always has been since the Bill of Rights, to a power to remit in the case of a particular individual a punish- *e* ment which has already been lawfully imposed on him by a court—whether it be a punishment fixed by law for the offence of which he was found guilty or one determined by a judge in exercise of his judicial functions. In contrast to this the function of the Review Board under s 22(1) of the 1974 Act is not to remit in the case of a particular individual a custodial sentence whose duration has already been fixed by law or by a judge in the exercise of his judicial functions, but itself to fix the duration of a *f* sentence which has not previously been fixed by anyone else. This, in their Lordships' view, is a power of a wholly different character from that of the prerogative of mercy. Even if it were an exercise of that exceptional executive power, the respondents would be faced by the dilemma that under s 90 of the Constitution it is exercisable only on the recommendation of a different body, the Privy Council, and not on the recommendation of a body constituted in the same manner as the Review Board. *g*

Severance

For the reasons that have been given under the previous headings 'Jurisdiction' and 'Sentence', their Lordships have held the 1974 Act to be inconsistent with the Constitution to the extent that: (1) it provides for the establishment of a Full Court Division of the Gun Court and confers on that Division jurisdiction to try offences *h* which lie outside the jurisdiction of the lower judiciary of Jamaica; and (2) it confers on a Resident Magistrate's Division and Circuit Court Division of the Gun Court a power and obligation to impose a sentence of detention at hard labour during the Governor-General's pleasure and provides for the establishment of a Review Board with power to determine the duration of such sentence in the individual case.

Under s 2 of the Constitution the provisions of the 1974 Act dealing with these *j* two matters are therefore void. The final question for their Lordships is whether they are severable from the remaining provisions of the Act so that the latter still remain enforceable as part of the law of Jamaica.

1 SI 1962 No 1550

Regarded purely as a matter of drafting they are readily severable. All references
a to the Full Court Division, the Review Board and to the mandatory sentence of detention could be struck out, and what was left would be a grammatical piece of legislation requiring no addition or amendment. But this, though it may point strongly to
severability, is not enough. The test of severability has been laid down authoritatively
by this Board in *Attorney-General for Alberta v Attorney-General for Canada*[1]:

b 'The real question is whether what remains is so inextricably bound up with
the part declared invalid that what remains cannot independently survive or,
as it has sometimes been put, whether on a fair review of the whole matter it
can be assumed that the legislature would have enacted what survives with out
enacting the part that is ultra vires at all.'

c As regards the establishment of the Full Court Division, its jurisdiction coincides, and
is exercisable concurrently, with that of the Circuit Court Division, except that it
does not extend to capital offences. If the Full Court Division were eliminated the
whole range of firearms offences would still be cognisable by the two remaining
divisions of the Gun Court. The practical consequence would be that firearms offences
which lie outside the jurisdiction of a resident magistrate under the Judicature
d (Resident Magistrates) Act, would be tried in camera by jury in the Circuit Court
Division instead of being tried in camera without a jury in the Full Court Division.
In their Lordships' view what remains after the elimination of the Full Court Division
still constitutes a practical and comprehensive scheme for dealing with firearms
offences which it can be assumed that Parliament would have enacted if it had realised
that it could not confer on a Full Court Division the jurisdiction which it purported
e to confer on that division by s 5(2). Their Lordships are confirmed in their view as to the
severability of these provisions by the fact, of which they have been informed by the
Attorney General, that although a Resident Magistrate's Division of the Gun Court
has been established and is operating satisfactorily it has not been found necessary
up to the present to set up any Full Court Division.

Their Lordships would observe that the question of severance with which they
f are dealing is different from that which is dealt with in the judgment of Graham-
Perkins and Swaby JJA. They had held the establishment of the Circuit Court Division as
well as that of the Full Court Division to be invalid. The elimination of both of these
divisions would transform the Gun Court from a court with comprehensive jurisdiction to try all 'firearm offences' whatever their gravity into a court with jurisdiction
confined to the trial of a limited number of comparatively minor offences. It is un-
g necessary for their Lordships to express any view whether on this assumption the
provisions relating to the establishment of the Resident Magistrate's Division would
have been severable from the invalid provisions of the Act.

As regards the power of the Gun Court to impose a sentence of detention at hard
labour during the Governor-General's pleasure, the length of which is to be determined by the Review Board, the practical consequence of the elimination of this power
h would be that (*a*) offences against s 20 of the Firearms Act 1967 would still be tried
speedily and in camera in a Resident Magistrate's Division or Circuit Court Division
of the Gun Court but the maximum stentence to be imposed would be that prescribed by the relevant provisions of the Firearms Act 1967 which, it is to be noted,
are not repealed expressly by the 1974 Act; and (*b*) the geographical limits of the
jurisdiction of a Resident Magistrate's Division and a Circuit Court Division of the
j Gun Court would still extend to firearms offences committed in any parish in Jamaica,
but would not extend to offences other than firearms offences committed outside
the parish within which the division sat by persons who had already been convicted
of an offence under s 20 of the Firearms Act 1967.

1 [1947] AC 503 at 518, per Viscount Simon

What remains after all those provisions of the Act that are invalid have been eliminated still represents a sensible legislative scheme for dealing with persons charged *a* with any firearm offence by providing (1) for the trial in camera of all such offences, wherever they have been committed in Jamaica, by a centralised court composed of members of the judiciary used to dealing with such offences; and (2) for the trial for an offence of unlawful possession of a firearm to take place speedily and to precede the trial of the same offender for any other firearm offence he may have committed.

This may be only half the loaf that Parliament believed that it was getting when it *b* passed the 1974 Act but their Lordships do not doubt that Parliament would have preferred it to no bread. They would accordingly hold the invalid provisions of the Act to be severable.

Disposition of these appeals   *c*

It follows that the appellants, whose trials for offences under s 20 of the Firearms Act 1967 took place before a Resident Magistrate's Division of the Gun Court, were convicted by a court of competent jurisdiction; but that the sentences imposed on them 'that they be detained at hard labour during the Governor-General's pleasure' were unlawful sentences which the resident magistrate had no power to award. The appellants' appeals to the Court of Appeal included appeals against these sen- *d* tences. By s 13(3) and s 21 of the Judicature (Appellate Jurisdiction) Law 1962 the Court of Appeal, if they think that a different sentence ought to have been passed, 'shall quash the sentence passed at the trial, and pass such other sentence warranted in law by the verdict (whether more or less severe) . . . as they think ought to have been passed'.

The sentence warranted by law in the instant appeals was such a sentence as a *e* resident magistrate had power to pass under s 20 of the Firearms Act 1967 on the summary trial on information of an offence under that section.

Their Lordships have therefore humbly advised Her Majesty that (1) the appeal of Moses Hinds, Elkanah Hutchinson, Henry Martin and Samuel Thomas against their convictions be dismissed; (2) the appeal of the Director of Public Prosecutions against the order of the Court of Appeal quashing the conviction of Trevor Jackson *f* be allowed and his conviction restored; and (3) the cases in both appeals be remitted to the Court of Appeal to pass such other sentences as they think ought to have been passed in substitution for the sentences passed by the resident magistrate.

Dissenting opinion by **VISCOUNT DILHORNE** and **LORD FRASER OF** *g* **TULLYBELTON.** We do not agree with our noble and learned friends that the provisions of the Gun Court Act 1974 as to the Full Court Division of the Gun Court, its jurisdiction and powers conflict with Chapter VII of the Constitution of Jamaica. In our opinion those provisions were validly enacted by an Act passed in the normal way by the Parliament of Jamaica.

We agree that the provisions of that Act as to the Resident Magistrate's Division *h* and the Circuit Court Division of the Gun Court did not contravene the Constitution. We agree also that the requirement that persons convicted of firearms offences must be sentenced to be detained at hard labour during the Governor-General's pleasure, the detention being terminable only on the advice of a non-judicial body, the Review Board established under the Act, was in conflict with the Constitution. We agree in holding that the provisions of the Act making such sentences mandatory and as to *j* the Full Court, its jurisdiction and powers are severable from the rest of the Act.

The appellants in the first appeal and the respondent in the second were convicted in a Resident Magistrate's Division of the Gun Court and sentenced, as the Act requires, to detention at hard labour. Only if the provisions of the Act as to the Full Court Division and the mandatory sentences are not severable will their invalidity affect their a convictions in the Resident Magistrate's Division. As we all agree that they are severable, it is not in our opinion necessary for the disposal of these appeals or as part of the reasoning leading to the conclusions reached to decide whether the provisions establishing the Full Court are invalid.

That court has, we were informed, never sat. When considering particular provisions of an Act, it is, of course, right to have regard to its other provisions but it does not follow that the Board should pronounce on the validity of provisions when

b their validity does not affect the result of the case under consideration and it is not in our experience the normal practice of the Board to decide questions not directly relevant to the determination of an appeal. An instance where the Board refrained from deciding such a question is to be found in the recent decision of the Board in *Attorney General v Antigua Times*[1].

In the circumstances we consider that anything said as to the validity of the pro-

c visions of the Act relating to the Full Court Division cannot be anything but obiter. Reluctant though we are to add to obiter dicta, nevertheless as it is said that the case raises questions of outstanding public importance, we feel that it is incumbent on us to do so.

The creation of the Full Court Division with its jurisdiction and powers did not involve any transfer of judicial power to the executive. That division, consisting of

d three resident magistrates sitting together, was given in relation to firearms offences and offences, other than capital, committed by persons detained at hard labour following conviction for firearms offences, jurisdiction and powers previously only exercisable by a circuit court presided over by a Supreme Court judge. The jurisdiction and powers of a circuit court were not reduced. After the enactment of the 1974 Act, a circuit court which is part of the Supreme Court can still deal with firearms

e offences and other offences committed by persons convicted of firearms offences but we recognise that the machinery provisions of the 1974 Act would lead to all such cases being dealt with in one or other of the divisions of the Gun Court unless transferred by that court to another court. They would be tried either by the Circuit Court Division of the Gun Court presided over by a Supreme Court judge or, if not capital offences, by the Full Court Division.

f Luckhoo P, in the course of his judgment, said.

> 'It is a matter of general public knowledge that in recent years crimes of violence in which firearms, unlicensed or illegally obtained, were used gave cause for grave public concern and indeed alarm. The several measures taken over the past six or seven years to control the rising incidence of crimes of this
>
> g nature have proved unsuccessful. Persons were shot and killed by day and by night in the course of robbing, rape and other offences or for no apparent reason. Witnesses for the Crown at trial or persons accused of such crimes were often intimidated. Victims of the crimes themselves were not infrequently killed or shot at, most probably with a view to their elimination as eye witnesses who could testify against the perpetrators of these crimes.'

h

It is not therefore surprising that the government and Parliament of Jamaica should have decided that special measures to deal with such offences were necessary and the reason why Parliament made provision for the establishment of a Full Court Division with its wide powers and jurisdiction may have been that it was considered necessary to provide more facilities for the trial of such offences than were available in the

j circuit courts. It may have been thought that the case load of the circuit courts was such that the establishment of the Full Court Division was necessary to secure trials without undue delay. In this country for a long period of time quarter sessions had jurisdiction to try and to sentence offenders for a large number of crimes which

---

1 [1975] 3 All ER 81, [1975] 3 WLR 232

were also triable at assizes before a High Court judge and it was only comparatively recently that a chairman of quarter sessions had to have legal qualifications. Crown *a* courts and circuit courts in this country have each jurisdiction to try a wide range of offences and their powers as to sentence are the same. For the Parliament of Jamaica to create an intermediate court between a resident magistrate's court and a circuit court cannot be regarded as very revolutionary. We do not doubt that before Jamaica became an independent territory and the Constitution came into force, there would have been no difficulty about the creation of a court with the powers and jurisdiction *b* of the Full Court, consisting of three resident magistrates, and that no special procedure would have to be followed to bring that about. Now it is said that, since the Constitution came into force, to create such a court by ordinary enactment conflicts not with any express provisions in the Constitution but with something that is implied so that before such a court is validly established, the Constitution requires to be amended to such an extent as will make provisions as to the Full Court Division no *c* longer inconsistent with the Constitution.

The many constitutions that have been drawn up in recent years and accepted by territories on their becoming independent were, it cannot be doubted, the product of prolonged and detailed consideration. Though they differ in some respects, in the main they follow what our noble and learned friend, Lord Diplock, has felicitously called 'the Westminster model'. They are more sophisticated than many written *d* constitutions of greater antiquity and none of them, which are not federal constitutions, we believe, limit the legislative capacity of the parliament of the territory to which they apply. The Constitution of Jamaica certainly does not. Its Parliament can alter, modify, replace, suspend, repeal or add to any provision of the Constitution, of the Jamaica (Constitution) Order in Council 1962[1] and of the Jamaica Independence Act 1962, a United Kingdom Act. Certain provisions of the Constitution are entrenched, that is to *e* say, they can only be altered or repealed or amended by Parliament if special procedures laid down in s 49 of the Constitution are followed. A Bill to alter any of the provisions of the Constitution is not to be deemed to have passed in either House unless it was supported in each House by the votes of the majority of all the members of each House and in some cases by the votes of not less than two-thirds of all the members. If a Bill is to alter certain provisions of the Constitution, the Jamaica (Constitution) Order in Council or the Jamaica Independence Act, there must be a delay of *f* three months between the introduction of the Bill into the House of Representatives and the commencement of the first debate on it and a further three months' delay between the conclusion of the debate and the passage of the Act. An amendment of the Jamaica Independence Act or of the Jamaica (Constitution) Order in Council[1] also requires a referendum to the electors. *g*

That the Parliament of Jamaica has power to create a court such as the Full Court Division, and give to three resident magistrates sitting together the jurisdiction and powers given to the Full Court Division by the 1974 Act is not open to doubt, but if any of the provisions doing so conflict with the Constitution in its present form, then it could only do so effectively if the Constitution was first amended so as to secure that there ceased to be any inconsistency between the provisions and the Constitution. *h* The Constitution does not prescribe that any special procedure has to be laid down for the valid enactment of a Bill to which s 50 (see below) does not apply which conflicts with the Constitution. It requires that a special procedure shall be followed for the amendment of the Constitution.

If the need for the 1974 Act and for the establishment of the Full Court Division was urgent, as it may well have been, the passage of that Act and the establishment of that *j* court would inevitably have been delayed for a considerable time if the Constitution had first to be amended before such an Act could have validity.

---

1   SI 1962 No 1550

a While one of the objects of a written constitution on the Westminster model is to secure that changes in 'entrenched' provisions are only made if strongly supported in the legislature, another important object is to make it easy to discern in advance whether or not a particular legislative proposal conflicts with the Constitution. Section 2 of the Constitution provides that any law inconsistent with the Constitution is to the extent of the inconsistency void. This is subject to the exception contained in s 50 which provides that an Act containing provisions inconsistent with ss 13 to 26
b inclusive of the Constitution shall, if passed on a final vote in each House by the votes of not less than two-thirds of all its members, take effect despite the inconsistency. It is not suggested that the 1974 Act is inconsistent with these sections but the sections with which it is said to be inconsistent are not identified.

Chapter VII of the Constitution headed 'The Judicature' deals in Part 1 with the Supreme Court, in Part 2 with the Court of Appeal, in Part 3 with appeals to the Privy
c Council and in Part 4 with the Judicial Service Commission. It does not deal with any other courts and it does not provide that the creation by Parliament of any other court is inconsistent with the Constitution.

Section 97(1), the first section in that Chapter, is clear, precise and unambiguous. It is in the following terms:

d 'There shall be a Supreme Court for Jamaica which shall have such jurisdiction and powers as may be conferred upon it by this Constitution or any other law.'

The Supreme Court cannot be altered or abolished without prior amendment of the Constitution. Its existence is entrenched. This section clearly distinguishes between the Supreme Court on the one hand and its jursidiction and powers on the other. To
e find out what are its jurisdiction and powers one must look at the Constitution and the 'other law'. Those given by the Constitution can only be altered or amended by amendment of the Constitution. 'Law' for the purpose of the Constitution is defined by s 1 thereof as including any instrument having the force of law and any unwritten rule of law.

The Jamaica (Constitution) Order in Council 1962[1] contained transitional provisions.
f By s 13(1) it provided that the Supreme Court in existence at the commencement of the Order was to be the Supreme Court for the purposes of the Constitution and that the Chief Justice and other judges of that court should continue in office. It was silent as to the jurisdiction and powers of the court but it provided by s 4(1) for the continuance in force of laws existing at the date of the commencement of the Order. It is to those laws and to the Constitution itself that one must look to ascertain the juris-
g diction and powers of the Supreme Court when the Constitution came into force.

One of the main functions of the legislature of Jamaica is to make laws. By such laws passed in the ordinary way it can add to the jurisdiction and to the powers of the Supreme Court. There is nothing in the Constitution to indicate that it cannot by a Bill passed in that way reduce or alter the jurisdiction and powers (other than those given by the Constitution) which by virtue of the Jamaica (Constitution) Order
h in Council[1] the Supreme Court had when the Constitution came into force. There is also nothing in the Constitution to suggest that unless the Constitution was amended, the Supreme Court was to continue to possess all the powers and jurisdiction it had at that time. In fact there is nothing in the 1974 Act which purports to alter the Supreme Court, its jurisdiction or powers (see s 21(1)), though, as we have said, the machinery provisions of that Act are designed to ensure that firearms offences
i and offences committed by those guilty of firearms offences are tried in one of the divisions of the Gun Court, it may be in the Circuit Court Division of that court or in the Full Court Division.

1   SI 1962 No 1550

We agree that the constitutions on the Westminster model were evolutionary and not revolutionary but it does not follow from that that the Parliament of a territory cannot by ordinary enactment alter the jurisdiction and powers of any court named in the Constitution. It is not necessary to express an opinion on whether, when a constitution is silent as to the distribution of judicial power between various courts, it is implicit that they retain the jurisdiction and powers they had on the coming into force of the constitution for it is expressly provided by s 4 of the Jamaica (Constitution) Order in Council[1] that all laws in existence when the Constitution came into force are, until amended or repealed, to continue in force. So apart from the jurisdiction and powers given by the Constitution itself, provision was expressly made for the distribution of judicial power between the courts of Jamaica by the existing laws and not changed on the Constitution coming into operation.

We agree that when a constitution on the Westminster model speaks of a particular court in existence when the constitution comes into force, it uses the word 'court' as a collective description of the individual judges entitled to sit and exercise its jurisdiction but we see no valid ground for assuming that it is contrary to the constitution for another court to be given power to try persons for offences previously only triable in the Circuit Court of the Supreme Court.

If s 97(1) had read: 'There shall be a Supreme Court which shall have such jurisdiction and powers as it had when this Constitution came into operation and such additional powers as are conferred on it by the Constitution or any other law', then we would not dissent from our noble and learned friends but s 97(1) does not say that and should not be interpreted as if it did.

Section 97(1) is the only section of the Constitution which refers to the jurisdiction of the Supreme Court. If the creation of the Full Court Division with its powers and jurisdiction contravenes the Constitution, it is presumably this section which would require to be amended. Presumably it would have to state that Parliament could by ordinary enactment give to another court powers and jurisdiction exercised by the Supreme Court. But the Constitution by s 97(1) already makes it clear that apart from that conferred by the Constitution itself, the Supreme court is to have such powers and jurisdiction as are given to it by Parliament and in our view if Parliament can give jurisdiction to that court by a law passed in the ordinary fashion, it can alter that which has been given by such a law also by an ordinary enactment. If it can do this, it follows that it can validly enact without conflict with the Constitution that a new court is to be established and give that court powers and jurisdiction which are also exercisable by the Supreme Court.

In our opinion the Attorney General's contention that any transfer of the Supreme Court's jurisdiction, other than that conferred by the Constitution, made by Parliament by ordinary enactment is not inconsistent with the Constitution, is well founded provided that the character of the Supreme Court as a superior court of record is not destroyed. It is not suggested that the creation of the Full Court Division deprived the Supreme Court of that character. Section 97(4) provides that the Supreme Court 'save as otherwise provided by Parliament, shall have all the powers of such a court'. It is thus manifest that it is within the power of Parliament without contravening the Constitution to reduce the powers of the Supreme Court as a superior court of record below those normally possessed by such a court so long as its character as a superior court of record is not destroyed. This being so, it appears to us odd that it should be said that without any reduction of the powers of the Supreme Court, to make some of its jurisdiction exercisable by another court is contrary to the Constitution.

The remaining sections of the Part of Chapter VII headed 'The Supreme Court' deal with the appointment of judges and acting judges of that court, their tenure of

1 SI 1962 No 1550

office, remuneration and oaths. Parliament can without amendment of the Constitution prescribe the qualifications for appointment as a Supreme Court judge (s 98(3)). It can also, without doing anything conflicting with the Constitution, fix their remuneration and terms and conditions of service so long as they are not altered to the disadvantage of an existing judge. So Parliament could if it wished—it is inconceivable that it would—reduce the qualifications, salary and conditions of service for a new Supreme Court judge to those of a resident magistrate. But it is said that without amendment of the Constitution, it cannot give three resident magistrates power to try some offences triable by the Supreme Court.

It is also said that any express provision in a constitution for the appointment or security of judges of a particular court will apply to all individual judges subsequently appointed to exercise an analogous jurisdiction whatever other name may be given to the 'court' in which they sit. For this proposition *Attorney-General for Ontario v Attorney-General for Canada*[1] is cited. We cannot see that that case supports any such proposition. All that that case decided appears to us to be that a provincial legislature had exceeded its powers and contravened the British North America Act. If that proposition is right, it means that jurisdiction in relation to firearms offences and other offences committed by persons guilty of such offences can only be exercised by a Supreme Court judge though the jurisdiction and powers of the Supreme Court are far more extensive than that. And it appears to us that this proposition is inconsistent with the clear terms of s 97(1).

In reaching their conclusion the majority attach significance to Part 2 of Chapter VII headed 'The Court of Appeal'. Section 103(1) and (5) of the Part are precisely similar to s 97(1) and (4) apart from the substitution of the Court of Appeal for the Supreme Court. The other sections of this Part follow the same pattern as the other sections of Part 1. They deal with the appointment of judges, their tenure of office, remuneration, etc. Again Parliament can prescribe the qualifications for their appointment (s 104(3)) and their emoluments and conditions of service (s 107).

We see no reason to construe s 103(1) and (5) differently from s 97(1) and (4) and we do not think that the terms of s 103 provide any ground for not giving effect to the language of s 97(1). It is said that the words 'There shall be a Court of Appeal' import that the judges of that court should exercise an appellate jurisdiction in all substantial civil cases and all serious criminal cases and that the words 'which shall have such jurisdiction and powers as may be conferred on it by this Constitution or any other law' do not entitle Parliament to deprive the Court of Appeal of a significant part of its appellate jurisdiction which it had when the Constitution came into force or to confer it on any other judges who do not enjoy the same security of tenure as judges of the Court of Appeal. Such a construction involves a limitation of the meaning of the words that it is to have the jurisdiction given by the Constitution and any other law and is to imply such a restriction on the same words in s 97(4).

Nor can we agree that s 110(1) of the Constitution which deals with appeals from the Court of Appeal to the Privy Council clearly proceeds on the assumption made by the majority with regard to the Court of Appeal. The contrast between s 110(1) and s 103(1) we think significant. Section 110 states when an appeal lies from the Court of Appeal. Section 103 does not say when an appeal lies to the Court of Appeal. To find out when an appeal does lie, one has to look at the other provisions of the Constitution and any other law and, save as provided by the Constitution, it is left to Parliament to decide by passing an ordinary Act when an appeal shall or shall not lie.

Importance is attached by our noble and learned friends to the Judicial Service Commission established by Part 4 of Chapter VII. Puisne judges are appointed by the Governor-General on the advice of that Commission (s 112(1)) and by s 112(2) appointment to the offices of resident magistrate, judge of the Traffic Court, registrar of the Supreme Court and registrar of the Court of Appeal and appointment 'to such other offices connected with the courts of Jamaica as, subject to the provisions of this Constitution, may be prescribed by Parliament' is similarly made. We are not satisfied that a resident magistrate sitting in a Full Court Division of the Gun Court holds a new office. If he does it is not one so prescribed and s 112 does not apply to it. He is still a resident magistrate and his salary, terms and conditions of employment remain, so far as we are aware, unaltered.

There is no question of anyone sitting in any Division of the Gun Court who has not been appointed on the advice of the Judicial Service Commission either as a judge of the Supreme Court or as a resident magistrate. For the purpose of constituting a Full Court Division the Chief Justice may assign any resident magistrate to the division (Gun Court Act 1974, s 17(2)). As one would expect, the security of tenure, remuneration and conditions of employment of a resident magistrate differ from those of a Supreme Court judge but just as it is possible for Parliament by ordinary enact-ment to increase the powers and jurisdiction of a resident magistrate sitting alone, so in our view is it possible for Parliament without resort to any special procedure to give increased jurisdiction and powers to three resident magistrates sitting together in excess of those possessed by a single magistrate without contravening the Constitution.

So far we have considered the provisions of the Constitution which bear on the question of the validity of the provisions of the 1974 Act relating to the Full Court Division. In our opinion not only do they give no support to the view that those provisions of the 1974 Act are inconsistent with the Constitution but they clearly show the contrary to be the case. They clearly distinguish between the Supreme Court and the Court of Appeal and the jurisdiction and powers of those Courts and there is in our view no basis for implying from the use of the words 'Supreme Court' and 'Court of Appeal' a limitation on the meaning of the words which follow in ss 97(4) and 103(1).

A written constitution must be construed like any other written document. It must be construed to give effect to the intentions of those who made and agreed to it and those intentions are expressed in or to be deduced from the terms of the consti-tution itself and not from any preconceived ideas as to what such a constitution should or should not contain. It must not be construed as if it was partly written and partly not. We agree that such constitutions differ from ordinary legislation and this fact should lead to even greater reluctance to imply something not expressed. While we recognise that an inference may be drawn from the express provisions of a consti-tution (see *Attorney-General for Australia v R and Boilermakers' Society of Australia* per Viscount Simonds[1]) we do not agree that on the adoption of a constitution a great deal is left to necessary implication. If this were so, a written constitution would largely fail to achieve its object. If it does not define clearly what parliament can do and cannot do by ordinary enactment, then the government and parliament of a territory may find that as a result of judicial decision after a considerable lapse of time all the time spent in legislating has been wasted and that laws urgently required have not been validly enacted.

No doubt the Constitution of Jamaica was drafted by persons nurtured in the com-mon law. That is apparent from the Constitution itself. The principle that there should be a separation of powers between the three organs of government is not just taken for granted. Effect is given to that principle by the written terms of the Constitution and consequently there is no room for the assumption.

No question arises in connection with the Full Court Division of any transfer of judicial power to the executive. The question to be decided is as to the division of judicial power and there is in our opinion not only no valid ground for implying that

---

1   [1957] 2 All ER 45 at 51, [1957] AC 288 at 312

Parliament cannot by ordinary legislation validly alter the jurisdiction the Supreme Court had when the Constitution came into force under any law other then the Constitution, but also the terms of ss 97(4) and 103(1) negative any such implication.

It is for the reasons we have stated that we have come to the conclusion that the provisions of the Gun Court Act 1974 as to the Full Court Division and its jurisdiction are not void as inconsistent with the terms of the Constitution.

Appeals against conviction dismissed. Appeals against sentence remitted to the Court of Appeal of Jamaica.

Solicitors: *Druces & Attlee* (for the appellants); *Charles Russell & Co* (for the Crown and the Attorney General as intervener).

Gordon H Scott Esq Barrister.

Security Trust Co v The Royal Bank of Canada

PRIVY COUNCIL
LORD CROSS OF CHELSEA, LORD SIMON OF GLAISDALE AND LORD EDMUND-DAVIES
3rd, 4th, 9th, 10th JUNE, 1ST DECEMBER 1975

Company – Debenture – Priority – Competing charges – Order of registration – Floating charge on property of company – Company acquiring right to purchase land subject to mortgage for part of purchase money – Debenture registered – Receiver appointed under debenture – Debenture creating first charge on company's property – Company subsequently completing purchase of land subject to mortgage for outstanding purchase price – Mortgage registered – Whether mortgage and debenture competing charges – Whether mortgage entitled to priority over debenture – Registration of Records Act (c 193) (Bahama Islands), s 10.

By a contract dated 20th September 1968 the trustee of a will agreed to sell to a limited company ('Fisher') approximately 450 acres of real estate in the Bahama Islands at a purchase price of $2,000 per acre (aggregating $900,000). Under the terms of the contract it was agreed, inter alia, (i) that $200,000 should be paid in cash or by certified cheque by Fisher to the trustee on completion of the contract; (ii) that the balance of the purchase price be paid by Fisher executing and delivering to the trustee a purchase money mortgage in the sum of $700,000; (iii) that on receipt of those payments the trustee would deliver to Fisher on 20th December 1968 the deed of purchase relating to the property; (iv) that Fisher might, however, defer the completion of the contract for a period not to exceed 12 months from the date of the contract. In the event Fisher exercised its option under the contract so that the completion date was extended to 19th February 1970. By a further agreement dated 19th February 1970 between the trustee and Fisher it was agreed, inter alia, (i) that the trustee would execute on that date a conveyance to Fisher of 461·537 acres of the property, the subject of the first contract; (ii) that Fisher would execute on that date a purchase money mortgage respecting the unpaid balance of the purchase price; (iii) that the conveyance and the mortgage would be held by the trustee as escrow agent until Fisher paid the trustee the sum of $200,000, Fisher agreeing to make that payment on or before 90 days from 19th February 1970; (iv) that time should be of the essence of the contract. On 19th February, in accordance with the second agreement, the trustee executed a conveyance of the property to Fisher for

$923,074 and Fisher executed a mortgage whereby it reconveyed the property to the trustee by way of security for the sum of $723,000, part of the purchase price, with interest until payment. Both the conveyance by the trustee and the mortgage by Fisher were delivered as escrows. Fisher failed to pay to the trustee the $200,000 within 90 days of 19th February as required by the agreement. Subsequently, on 4th June, Fisher created a debenture in favour of a bank. Under the debenture Fisher charged all its undertaking, goodwill and property both present and future with payment of all moneys and liabilities intended to be thereby secured. Clause 4(d) of the debenture provided that the charge thereby treated should be 'a fixed first charge on all other the present freehold and leasehold property of [Fisher]'. Under the debenture all of Fisher's property which was not the subject of the fixed charge was to be treated as a floating security but so that Fisher could not create any mortgage, charge or lien in priority to or pari passu with the charge created in favour of the bank. The debenture was registered pursuant to s 10ᵃ of the Registration of Records Act (c 193) of the Bahama Islands on 30th July. On 30th November the bank appointed a receiver under the debenture. On 15th January 1971 a further agreement was made between the trustee and Fisher whereby the closing date for the sale contract was extended to 30th April 1971, time would be of the essence and, should completion not take place by that date, all Fisher's rights under the contract would terminate. By letter dated 30th April 1971 the receiver informed the bank that he was satisfied that it would be advantageous both to Fisher and the bank for Fisher to buy the property at the contract price, and he invited the bank to advance the balance of the purchase price to Fisher. The bank consented to make the advance to Fisher. On 30th April, in consideration of the receipt of the balance of the purchase money advanced by the bank and of the delivery of the conveyance and mortgage for registration, the trustee agreed that the conveyance and mortgage between the trustee and Fisher be released from escrow. The conveyance and mortgage were registered under the Registration of Deeds Act on 5th May. Subsequently the trustee and the bank brought separate proceedings in the Supreme Court of the Bahama Islands claiming payment of the moneys due to them from Fisher under the mortgage and the debenture respectively. In those proceedings the trustee claimed that the mortgage had priority over the debenture and the bank claimed the debenture had priority over the mortgage. In a preliminary ruling the court held, inter alia, (i) that the conveyance and mortgage between the trustee and Fisher dated 19th February 1970, being subject to the condition of payment, were simply escrows which did not become absolutely delivered deeds until 30th April 1971, when the condition was fulfilled, and related back for purposes of title to 19th February 1970, i e before the creation of the debenture, and (ii) that the debenture was not entitled to priority under s 10 of the Registration of Records Act by reason of its earlier registration, since at the date of the issue of the debenture the bank's interest in the property was only an equity of redemption subject to the mortgage, and that the charge created by the debenture could only be a charge on that equity which did not compete with the mortgage so as to obtain priority under the Act. The bank appealed. The Court of Appeal accepted that the doctrine of 'relation back' of escrows on fulfilment of condition applied, but held that the property which was the subject of the conveyance and mortgage was 'present freeholds' of Fisher within cl 4(d) of the debenture and, as a fixed first charge, competed with the mortgage and was given priority by virtue of s 10 of the Act. The trustee appealed to the Privy Council.

Held – (i) The effect, if any, of the debenture on the property was to be considered in relation to the circumstances existing at the time when the debenture was created, i e 4th June 1970. On that date Fisher had no interest whatsoever in the property since time was the essence of the contract between the trustee and Fisher and on that

---

a   Section 10 is set out at p 388 g to j, post

date the time for fulfilling the condition of the escrow had elapsed. Accordingly the
a doctrine of relation back had no application and it was not until 15th January 1971,
when the final renewal of the contract once again gave Fisher an interest in the
property, that, by the combined effect of the renewal agreement, the creation of the
debenture and the appointment of the receiver, Fisher's interest under the contract
was assigned to the bank by way of equitable charge (see p 390 *a b* and *e* to p 391 *a*, post);
N W Robbie & Co Ltd v Witney Warehouse Co Ltd [1963] 3 All ER 613 applied.
b   (ii) In those circumstances the mortgage was entitled to priority over the debenture,
and the appeal would therefore be allowed, for the following reasons—
          (a) The debenture amounted to a charge on Fisher's interest under the contract
and could give the bank no greater interest in the property than that which Fisher
possessed. Fisher was unable to obtain a conveyance of the property free from the
obligation to grant back the mortgage to the trustee. Since Fisher had no right to
c obtain an unencumbered fee simple in the property, the debenture could only give
the bank rights which were subject to the prior rights of the trustee (see p 391 *b c* and *g*
and p 392 *c* and *d*, post); *Re Connolly Bros Ltd (No 2)* [1912] 2 Ch 25 applied; *Church of
England Building Society v Piskor* [1954] 2 All ER 85 and *Capital Finance Co Ltd v Stokes*
[1968] 3 All ER 625 distinguished.
          (b) The debenture could not compete with the mortgage for priority under s 10 of
d the Registration of Records Act since on 4th June 1970 Fisher had no interest in the
property which was the subject of the contract entered into on 20th September 1968.
Section 10 was concerned with the creation of two successive dispositions of land which
conflicted with one another so that full effect could not be given to both. Such inconsistency did not exist between the debenture and the mortgage since the combined
effect of the debenture and the agreement of 15th January 1971 was that the charge
e which they jointly operated to create was subject to the prior charge in favour
of the trustee (see p 393 *c* to p 394 *a*, post); *Jones v Barker* [1909] 1 Ch 321 applied.

Notes
For restrictions on the operation of a floating charge created by a company, see
f 7 Halsbury's Laws (4th Edn) para 826, and for cases where a company's interest is
charged, see 10 Digest (Reissue) 840, 4843-4846.
          For the effect of delivery as an escrow, see 12 Halsbury's Laws (4th Edn) para 1234,
and for cases on the subject, see 17 Digest (Reissue) 260, 261, 245-258.

g **Cases referred to in opinions**
Butler and Baker's Case (1591) 3 Co Rep 25a, 1 Ald 348, 3 Leon 271, Moore KB 254,
          Popl 87, 76 ER 684, 17 Digest (Reissue) 253, *171.*
Capital Finance Co Ltd v Stokes, Re Cityfield Properties Ltd [1968] 3 All ER 625, [1969]
          1 Ch 261, [1968] 3 WLR 899, 19 P & CR 791, CA, Digest (Cont Vol C) 111, *5287f.*
Chung Khiaw Bank Ltd v United Overseas Bank Ltd [1970] AC 767, [1970] 2 WLR 858, PC.
h Church of England Building Society v Piskor [1954] 2 All ER 85, [1954] 2 WLR 952, CA,
          35 Digest (Repl) 454, *1458.*
Congresbury Motors Ltd v Anglo-Belge Finance Co Ltd [1970] 3 All ER 385, [1971] Ch 81,
          [1970] 3 WLR 683, 21 P & CR 889, CA, Digest (Cont Vol C) 635, *606a.*
Connolly Bros Ltd (No 2), Re, Wood v Co [1912] 2 Ch 25, 81 LJ 517, 106 LT 738, 19 Mans
          259, CA, 10 Digest (Reissue) 840, *4845.*
j Coptic Ltd v Bailey [1972] 1 All ER 1242, [1972] Ch 446, [1972] 2 WLR 1061, 23 P & CR 231.
Independent Automatic Sales Ltd v Knowles and Foster [1962] 3 All ER 27, [1962] 1 WLR
          974, 10 Digest (Reissue) 863, *4976.*
Jones v Barker [1909] 1 Ch 321, 78 LJCh 167, 100 LT 188, 35 Digest (Repl) *2050.*
Paul & Frank Ltd v Discount Bank (Overseas) Ltd [1966] 2 All ER 922, [1966] 3 WLR 490,
          Digest (Cont Vol B) 108, *5287c.*

Robbie (N W) & Co Ltd v Witney Warehouse Co Ltd [1963] 3 All ER 613, [1963] 1 WLR at
1329, CA, 10 Digest (Reissue) 832, *4795*.

Thompson v McCullough [1947] 1 All ER 265, [1947] KB 447, [1947] LJR 498, 176 LT 493,
CA, 17 Digest (Reissue) 259, *243*.

Wilson v Kelland [1910] 2 Ch 306, 79 LJCh 580, 103 LT 17, 17 Mans 233, 10 Digest
(Reissue) 827, *4763*.

Appeal

This was an appeal by special leave of the Board by Security Trust Co against an order
dated 17th July 1973 of the Court of Appeal (Civil Side) of the Bahama Islands (Bourke
P, Hogan and Archer JJA), setting aside an order of the Supreme Court (Equity Side)
of the Bahama Islands (Bryce CJ), dated 28th December 1972, whereby it was ordered
that a mortgage dated 19th February 1970 executed byCarl G Fisher Co Ltd ('Fisher')
in favour of the appellant should take priority over a debenture dated 4th June 1970
issued by Fisher in favour of the respondent, the Royal Bank of Canada. The facts are
set out in the opinion of the Board.

Michael Albery QC and *Alan Sebestyen* for the appellant.
Paul Baker QC, W J Mowbray QC and *Michael Driscoll* for the respondent.

LORD CROSS OF CHELSEA. This is an appeal by special leave of the Board from
an order dated 17th July 1973 of the Court of Appeal (Civil Side) of the Bahama
Islands (Bourke P, Hogan and Archer JJA) which set aside an order of the Supreme
Court (Equity Side) of the Bahama Islands made by Bryce CJ on 28th December 1972.

The dispute between the appellant and the respondent relates to the respective
priorities of two charges on certain land at Coral Harbour, New Providence. The
appellant contends that a mortgage of this land to it by Carl G Fisher Company Ltd
(hereinafter called 'Fisher') which was dated 19th February 1970 but was not effective
until 30th April 1971 has priority over the charge on such land arising under a debenture issued by Fisher to the respondent on 4th June 1970. The respondent on the
other hand contends that the charge arising under the debenture has priority over
the mortgage. In the court of first instance Bryce CJ held that the mortgage had
priority over the debenture but the Court of Appeal held that his judgment was
wrong and that, subject to certain points which it remitted for consideration by the
lower court, the debenture had priority over the mortgage.

On 20th September 1968 a contract of sale was entered into between the appellant,
as trustee of the will of Leonora Hopkins, and Sara H McKillips and Lindsey Hopkins,
as executors of the will (therein described as 'the sellers'), and Fisher (therein described as 'the purchaser'). By the contract the sellers agreed to sell and the purchaser
to purchase certain real property having an area of 450 acres more or less at Coral
Harbour, New Providence Island, for a purchase price of $2,000 per acre (aggregating
$900,000) of which $200,000 should be paid in cash or good certified cheque at the
closing of the contract and the balance by the purchaser or his assigns executing and
delivering to the sellers a purchase money mortgage on the property in the sum of
$700,000 in the form and containing the provisions therein mentioned. Clause 11
of the contract provided that on receipt of the said payments the deed of purchase
should be delivered on 20th December 1968 at the offices of the purchaser in Nassau
but that the purchaser at its option might defer the closing of the contract for a period
not to exceed 12 months from that date. The purchaser exercised the option to extend
the closing date until 20th December 1969 and by a supplemental agreement made
between the sellers and the purchaser the closing date was extended from 20th
December 1969 to 19th February 1970.

By a further agreement between the parties made on 19th February 1970, after a
recital to the effect that the purchaser had requested an additional period of time

not to exceed 90 days to pay the sellers the initially agreed down payment of $200,000,
a it was agreed (1) that the appellant as trustee should execute as of that date a conveyance to the purchaser of the aforesaid land consisting according to a recent survey
of 461·537 acres, (2) that the purchaser would execute as of that date a purchase
money mortgage covering the unpaid balance of the purchase price, (3) that the
executed deed of conveyance and the executed mortgage would be held in the
possession and custody of the appellant as escrow agent until such time as the purchaser
b should pay and deposit with the appellant the sum of $200,000 and the purchaser
agreed to make such payment and deposit on or before 90 days from 19th February
1970, (4) that the purchaser agreed to pay the appellant as trustee interest at eight per
cent on the $200,000 as from 19th February 1970 until the deposit and payment
of the $200,000, and (5) that time should be of the essence of the contract.

On 19th February 1970 the appellant executed in favour of Fisher the conveyance
c referred to in cl 1 of the contract of that date. It recited, inter alia, that the executors
of the will of the said Leonora Hopkins had assented to a residuary devise in favour
of the appellant as trustee which included the land conveyed and that the appellant
had agreed to sell the land in question to Fisher for an estate in fee simple in possession
free from incumbrances for a sum of $923,074 and by cl 1 of the operative part the
appellant as trustee in consideration of the said sum of $923,074 expressed to have
d been paid to it by Fisher conveyed the land referred to in the said contract to Fisher
in fee simple.

On the same day, 19th February 1970, Fisher executed the mortgage of the land so
conveyed provided for by cl 2 of the contract. It contained a recital to the effect
that the agreement for the sale contained a provision that Fisher should retain
$723,000 part of the purchase price of $923,074 on the payment thereof with interest
e being secured in the manner therein appearing and by the operative part Fisher
covenanted to pay the appellant on 19th August 1970 the said sum of $723,000 with
interest as therein provided and conveyed the lands conveyed to it by the said
conveyance to the appellant by way of mortgage subject to redemption.

The said conveyance and mortgage when executed were retained by the appellant
f as escrows as provided by cl 3 of the contract of 19th February 1970. The 90 days
therein mentioned expired on 20th May 1970 without Fisher having paid the $200,000
the payment of which was the condition of the escrows.

On 4th June 1970 Fisher created in favour of the respondent a debenture whereby
Fisher undertook to pay to the respondent all moneys then due or thereafter to become due by Fisher to it on any account with interest as therein mentioned. Clause 4
g of the said debenture was in the following terms:

'4. The Company as BENEFICIAL OWNER hereby charges with the payment and
discharge of all monies and liabilities intended to be hereby secured (including
any expenses and charges arising out of or in connection with the acts authorised
by 8 hereof) all its undertaking goodwill and other property whatsoever and
wheresoever both present and future including its uncalled capital for the time
h being.
'The charge hereby created shall be:—
'(*a*) A fixed first charge on the goodwill of the Company and uncalled capital
for the time being of the Company; and
'(*b*) A fixed second charge on the real property of the Company described in the
First Schedule hereto and the fixed plant and machinery thereon (subject only to
j an Indenture of Mortgage dated the twelfth day of March A.D. 1969 made between the Company of the one part and Paul Norris Gardner et al of the other
part recorded in the Registry of Records in Volume 1597 at pages 113 to 119)
until such Mortgage shall be discharged whereupon it shall become a fixed first
charge on that real property; and
'(*c*) a fixed second charge on the real property of the Company described in the

Second Schedule hereto and the fixed plant and machinery thereon (subject
only to an Indenture of Mortgage dated the Seventeenth day of April A.D. 1969   *a*
made between the Company of the one part and James Bradley Brown and
Caroline Celeste Brown of the other part recorded in the Registry of Records
in Volume 1417 at pages 318 to 325) until such Mortgage shall be discharged
whereupon it shall become a fixed first charge on that real property; and

'(d) a fixed first charge on all other the present freehold and leasehold property
of the Company and the fixed plant and machinery thereon SAVE AND EXCEPT   *b*
the freehold property brief particulars of which appear on Exhibit "A" hereunto
annexed and purchase moneys payable in respect thereof or any part thereof; and

'(e) a fixed first charge on all future leasehold property of the Company and
the fixed plant and machinery thereon and as to all other premises hereby
charged shall be a floating security but so that the Company is not to be at
liberty to create any mortgage or charge upon and so that no lien shall in any   *c*
case or in any manner arise on or affect any part of the said other premises either
in priority to or pari passu with the charge hereby created it being the intention
that the Company shall have no power without the consent of the Bank (which
will not be unreasonably withheld) to part with or dispose of any part of such
other premises except by way of sale in the ordinary course of its business. Any
debenture mortgages or charges hereafter created by the Company (otherwise   *d*
than in favour of the Bank) shall be expressed to be subject to this debenture.
The Company shall deposit with the Bank and the Bank during the continuance
of this security shall be entitled to hold all deeds and documents of title relating
to the Company's freehold and leasehold property which is the subject of this
security (save that described in the First and Second Schedule hereto so long as
the said Mortgages shall subsist).'   *e*

Clause 8 conferred on the respondent power to appoint a receiver at any time
after it should have demanded payment of any money thereby secured with the
powers thereby specified. Clause 9 was in the following terms:

'The Company hereby covenants with the Bank to execute a First Legal Mort-   *f*
gage in favour of the Bank over all or any of the property hereby subject to a
first fixed charge and to execute a Second Legal Mortgage over all or any of the
property hereby subject to a fixed second charge when called upon by the Bank
to do so to secure all monies for the time being due or to become due to the
Bank on this security with interest thereon as aforementioned.'

g

The first and second schedules contained particulars of certain lands not included
in the said conveyance of 19th February 1970 and exhibit 'A' particulars of certain
other lands not included therein. The debenture was lodged for registration under
the provisions of the Registration of Records Act (c 193) on 30th July 1970 and certified
as recorded therein on 11th August 1970.

By letter dated 19th August 1970 Fisher requested the appellant to extend the time   *h*
for payment of the $200,000 until 19th September 1970 and the appellant acceded to
that request. Time was not expressed to be of the essence of this agreement. Fisher
failed to pay the said sum of $200,000 to the appellant before 19th September 1970.
On 30th November 1970 the respondent appointed a receiver under the said debenture. By a further agreement between the appellant and Fisher made on 15th January
1971, after reciting the various extensions of time hereinbefore mentioned and that   *j*
Fisher had not paid the said $200,000 to the appellant within the times thereby
required and had requested that the contract be further amended to extend the
closing date to 30th April 1971, it was provided that the closing date should be extended to 30th April 1971 unless an earlier date was fixed by mutual agreement
between the parties, that time should be of the essence and that if the closing was not

accomplished on or before 30th April all rights of the purchaser under the contract
a of 20th September 1968 and the various amendments thereto should terminate.

On 30th April 1971 the receiver wrote a letter to C W Minard, the manager of the
respondent in Nassau, in which he stated that the amount of cash required to complete
the purchase from the appellant of the 461 acres which were the subject of the contract of 20th September 1968 and of a further 747 acres over which Fisher had an
option was $465,813·80. The letter continued as follows:
b

'I am satisfied that it will be to the advantage of the Company and its creditors
to buy this land as the contract price is, so I am advised, much less than the
market value.

'As the Company does not have the sum required available, I am proposing to
borrow it under my express and general power, and hereby apply to the Bank
c for a loan. I am not prepared to give my personal undertaking to repay the sum,
but I am advised that I may authorise the Company to give a Mortgage on the
property to be acquired to secure repayment of the sum advanced to purchase
it. The Company will undertake to repay the loan on resale or on six months'
notice, and I undertake to procure the execution of a Mortgage by the Company
to rank immediately after the purchase mortgage. The Mortgage will be exe-
d cuted as soon as possible after the closing in a form to be settled by Higgs &
Johnson. The Mortgage will be in addition to and not in lieu of any charge
which the Bank may have in the debenture.

'If the Bank is willing to advance the purchase price on the terms of this letter,
I would be grateful if the Manager would sign this letter.

                                          'Yours faithfully,
e   '(Sgd.)   R. E. STRANGE
                                          '(*Receiver for Carl G. Fisher Company Limited.*)'

Mr Minard signed this letter as requested. The receiver therupon on the same day
tendered to the appellant the sum of $465,813·80. Of that sum $378,044·97 was
f attributable to the 461·537 acres comprised in the contract of 20th September 1968.
That was made up (1) as to $200,000 odd by the cash payment provided for by the
contract (2) as to about $54,000 of interest and (3) as to $123,000 odd of the price
of some 50 acres (part of the 461 acres) which were to be purchased outright and not
to be comprised in the mortgage back. In consequence of this arrangement the sum
for which the remainder of the 461 acres—some 412 acres—was to be mortgaged
g back to the appellant was reduced from $723,000 to $599,950. After setting out the
relevant figures the receiver's letter making the tender continued as follows:

'Please confirm, by signing this letter, that the above is satisfactory to you
and that you are prepared to close on this basis, and that the said payment is
accepted in full discharge of the amounts required for such closing, and that
h the documents delivered to my attorneys by Mr Leon Potier in escrow, are now
released from such escrow.'

The explanation of the concluding sentence is that the attorney of the appellant
who had retained possession of the conveyance and mortgage dated 19th February
1970 since their execution had handed them to Messrs Higgs & Johnson, the attorneys
j for Fisher, on 27th April 1971 in anticipation of the completion of the contract. The
appellant accepted the tender made by the receiver by signing an endorsement
on his letter in the following terms:

'We, Security Trust Company, acknowledge to have received the sum of
$465,813·80 in the amount needed to complete the sale and purchase of various

tracts at Coral Harbour, and accept the mortgages for the unpaid balances of
the respective purchase prices, on the understanding that the documents relate *a*
back, and shall have effect, from their respective dates, to the intent that the
powers vested in Security Trust Company as legal mortgagee shall be exercisable
on the dates of such respective mortgages, in accordance with the terms of the
documents.

'We understand that you will deliver all of the deeds and mortgages involved
in the transaction to Mr Leon R Potier, our attorney, so that he can record the *b*
deeds and mortgages simultaneously.'

On receiving back the documents from Messrs Higgs & Johnson on 3rd May the
appellant's attorney registered the mortgage to his clients on 5th May 1971. No
second mortgage was granted by Fisher to the respondent to secure the moneys
advanced to complete the contract of 20th September 1968.   *c*

By an originating summons issued on 15th October 1971 and amended on 23rd May
1972 between the appellant as plaintiff and Fisher, the respondent and various persons
and companies who were judgment creditors of Fisher as defendants, the appellant
claimed payment of the moneys due to it under the mortgage dated 19th February
1970 and asked that it be enforced by foreclosure or sale. By another originating summons also issued in 1971 and amended on 28th April 1972 between the respondent as *d*
plaintiff and Fisher, the appellant and the said judgment creditors of Fisher as
defendants, the respondent claimed payment of the moneys due to it from Fisher
under the debenture and asked that it be enforced by foreclosure or sale. It appeared
from the affidavits filed in support of the two summonses that the appellant was
claiming that the mortgage had priority over the debenture and the respondent
was claiming that the debenture had priority over the mortgage. Accordingly both *e*
summonses were heard by Bryce CJ together so that that point might be determined.

On 21st July 1972 Bryce CJ gave a preliminary ruling holding that the conveyance
and mortgage which were delivered on 19th February 1970 subject to a condition
and which until 30th April 1971 were not deeds but simply 'escrows' became absolutely delivered deeds on 30th April 1971 by fulfilment of the condition and related
back for purposes of title to 19th February 1970, i e to a date before the creation of the *f*
debenture.

At a later date Bryce CJ heard further argument on the basis of this preliminary
ruling. Counsel for the respondent then contended that even though by the doctrine
of relation back the mortgage took effect before the debenture the debenture was
entitled to priority by virtue of s 10 of the Registration of Records Act (c 193) which
is in the following terms: *g*

'If any person after having made and executed any conveyance, assignment,
grant, lease, bargain, sale or mortgage of any lands or of any goods or other
effects within the Colony, or of any estate, right or interest therein, shall afterwards make and execute any other conveyance, assignment, grant, release,
bargain, sale or mortgage of the same, or any part thereof, or any estate, right *h*
or interest therein; such of the said conveyances, assignments, grants, releases,
bargains, sales or mortgages, as shall be first lodged and accepted for record in
the Registry shall have priority or preference; and the estate, right, title or
interest of the vendee, grantee or mortgagee claiming under such conveyance,
assignment, grant, release, bargain, sale or mortgage, so first lodged and accepted
for record shall be deemed and taken to be good and valid and shall in no wise *i*
be defeated or affected by reason of priority in time of execution of any other
such documents: Provided that this section shall not apply to any disposition of
property made with intent to defraud.'

Bryce CJ rejected that contention on the ground that at the date of the issue of the *a* debenture the interest of the respondent in the land was only an equity of redemption subject to the mortgage, that the charge created by the debenture could only be a charge on the equity of redemption which did not compete with the mortgage and that the Act did not operate to give it priority. This conclusion was, he thought, in line with the decision of Warrington J in *Jones v Barker*[1]. Accordingly by order dated 28th December 1972 he declared that the mortgage had priority over the debenture.

b The respondent appealed to the Court of Appeal. The arguments there proceeded on the footing—which was accepted as correct by the court—that Bryce CJ had been right in holding that the doctrine of the relation back of escrows on the fulfilment of the condition on which they were delivered applied here and that the legal estate in the lands must be taken to have passed from the appellant to Fisher and from Fisher back to the appellant by way of mortgage on 19th February 1970. In a judgment *c* delivered by Hogan JA in which Bourke P and Archer JA concurred, the court held that the lands the subject of the conveyance and mortgage were present freeholds of Fisher within the meaning of cl 4(d) of the debenture on which the debenture purported to create a fixed first charge which competed with the charge given by the mortgage and was given priority by s 10 of the Registration of Records Act. In this connection the court considered that the Privy Council case of *Chung Khiaw Bank* *d* *Ltd v United Overseas Bank Ltd*[2] afforded a closer analogy to this case than did *Jones v Barker*[1] on which Bryce CJ had relied. Counsel for the appellant submitted that *Wilson v Kelland*[3] and *Re Connolly Bros Ltd (No 2)*[4] showed that Fisher must be taken never to have acquired an unencumbered freehold in the property on which it could create conflicting charges but should be regarded as having acquired only an equity of redemption on which alone the debenture could bite. The Court of Appeal, *e* however, thought that the later cases of *Church of England Building Society v Piskor*[5] and *Capital Finance Co Ltd v Stokes*[6] showed that this was not so, and that if and so far as there was any conflict between the earlier and the later cases—as the court was inclined to think there was—the later cases should be preferred. Accordingly on 17th July 1973 the Court of Appeal made an order setting aside the order of Bryce CJ. But as they thought that the final outcome of the dispute between the appellant *f* and the respondent might be affected one way or the other by the questions of notice and of a vendor's lien, they remitted the case to the court of first instance for further consideration in the light of their decision.

Leave to appeal to the Board from the decision of the Court of Appeal was granted on 20th February 1974.

Their Lordships will deal first with the question of 'relation back' and the construc- *g* tion of the debenture. The appellant delivered the conveyance dated 19th February 1970 on that day as an escrow which was to become a deed on payment by Fisher of $200,000 part of the purchase price and execution by Fisher of a mortgage for the balance on or before 20th May. That condition was not fulfilled, but on 19th August the appellant agreed to the date for the completion of the contract being extended to 19th September and, completion still not having taken place by that date, the *h* appellant agreed on 15th January 1971 to a final extension of the time for completion to 30th April 1971. The contract was completed on that date, though the part of the purchase price which was paid down was greater and the part which was secured by mortgage and the land on which it was secured was less than was originally

j
1 [1909] 1 Ch 321
2 [1970] AC 767
3 [1910] 2 Ch 306
4 [1912] 2 Ch 25
5 [1954] 2 All ER 85, [1954] 2 WLR 952
6 [1968] 3 All ER 625, [1969] 1 Ch 261

intended since Fisher wished to have some of the land free from any mortgage back. The courts below have assumed that the effect of these transactions was that on the con-   *a* veyance dated 19th February 1970 becoming a deed on 30th April 1971, the legal estate must be deemed under the doctrine of relation back of escrows to have passed from the appellant to Fisher on 19th February 1970. Their Lordships are not satisfied that this assumption is justified for, if it is, it must follow that from 20th May to 19th August and again from 19th September to 15th January the 'status' of the conveyance was undetermined. It would seem more in accord with principle to hold that between 20th May and   *b* 19th August the conveyance was not even an 'escrow' and that on the latter day it must be taken to have been delivered afresh as an 'escrow' subject to the condition that the contract be completed on or before 19th September. If that be the right way to view the matter then on the completion of the contract on 30th April 1971 the conveyance—though dated 19th February 1970—only related back to 15th January 1971. It is not, however, necessary for their Lordships to express any concluded   *c* opinion on this point since even if it be assumed that the relation back was to 19th February 1970 the result so far as concerns the construction and effect of the debenture must, as they see it, be the same. On fulfilment of the condition subject to which it was delivered as an escrow a deed is not taken to relate back to the date of its delivery for all purposes but only for such purposes as are necessary to give efficacy to the transaction, ut res magis valeat quam pereat (see *Butler and Baker's Case*[1]). Thus the   *d* fact that the grantor has died before the condition of an escrow is fulfilled does not entail the consequence that the disposition fails. If and when the condition is fulfilled the doctrine of relation back will save it—but not withstanding the relation back for that limited purpose the grantee is not entitled to the rents of the property during the period of suspense or to lease it or to serve notices to quit (see Sheppard's Touchstone[2]; *Thompson v McCullough*[3]). So in considering whether and in what way the   *e* debenture affected the property which was the subject of the contract of 20th September 1968 one must have regard to the surrounding circumstances at the time when the debenture was issued without regard to any operation of the doctrine of 'relation back'. Now on 4th June 1970 Fisher had no interest of any sort in the property which was the subject of the contract. The time for fulfilling the condition had passed and time had been declared to be of the essence of the transaction. It was only if the   *f* appellant was prepared to renew the contract by extending the time for payment that Fisher would get back an interest in the land. In these circumstances it is, their Lordships think, impossible to regard the lands in question as 'present freeholds' of Fisher on which the respondent was given a 'fixed first charge' by cl 4(*d*) of the debenture. The contract lands were property in which Fisher might acquire an interest in the future and which if it did acquire an interest would become subject to a   *g* floating charge. This construction is in line with the concluding words of cl 4 and with cl 9. Fisher was plainly not in a position at the date of the creation of the debenture to deposit the title deeds of the lands with the respondent or to give it a legal mortgage over them. On 19th August 1970 when the contract was renewed Fisher's interest in it became subject to the floating charge created by the debenture. On 30th November when the respondent appointed a receiver the floating charge   *h* 'crystallised'. By that date however the period for which the contract had been extended had expired and though time had not been made of the 'essence' of the agreement for extension made on 19th August it may well be that Fisher did not on 30th November possess any interest in the contract lands on which the 'crystallised' charge could bite. That point is, however, of no importance because there is no doubt that at all events the final renewal of the contract on 15th January 1971 gave Fisher an   *j*

1   (1591) 3 Co Rep 25a
2   7th Edn (1820), p 60
3   [1947] 1 All ER 265, [1947] KB 447

interest in the lands under the contract and that by the joint effect of the renewal
a agreement, the debenture and the appointment of the receiver Fisher's interest under
the contract was on 15th January 1971 assigned to the respondent by way of equitable
charge (see *N W Robbie & Co Ltd v Witney Warehouse Co Ltd*[1]).

Their Lordships turn now to consider what were the relative priorities of this
charge and the appellant's mortgage apart from any question of registration under
the Registration of Records Act. As they see it the mortgage was entitled to priority.
b The respondent's charge was a charge on Fisher's interest under the contract and could
give the respondent no greater interest than Fisher had. Fisher could not obtain a
conveyance of the lands free from the obligation to grant back the mortgage to the
appellant. He had no right to obtain an unincumbered fee simple and the charge
on his interest which he created in favour of the respondent only gave the respondent
rights which were subject to the prior rights of the appellant. The case is exactly
c parallel to *Re Connolly Bros Ltd (No 2)*[2]. There the company borrowed £1,000 from
Mrs O'Reilly for the purpose of buying some property on the terms that she was to
have a charge on it. The same solicitor acted for the three parties. The purchase
price including the £1,000 was paid to the vendor who conveyed the property to the
company and the solicitor retained the deeds on behalf of Mrs O'Reilly in whose
favour the company subsequently executed a memorandum of deposit. The company
d had previously issued debentures creating a floating charge on all its property present
and future which had been duly registered. The charge had not in fact crystallised
but nothing turned on that fact. The solicitor did not know of the debenture and had
not searched the register. Warrington J held that the debenture and the accompanying
trust deed amounted to nothing more so far as concerned after-acquired property
such as the property in question than a contract by the company to give the deben-
e ture holder a security on such interest in it as it might acquire and that it never
acquired any interest at all in the property as against Mrs O'Reilly except subject to
the obligation to give her a charge for the amount of the purchase price which she
advanced. His decision was upheld by the Court of Appeal, Cozens-Hardy MR
saying in his judgment[3]:

f   'Did the company as between themselves and Mrs. O'Reilly ever become
the absolute owners of the property? Or was not the bargain that Mrs. O'Reilly
was to have a first charge, and the company was only to get the property subject
thereto? In my opinion we should be shutting our eyes to the real transaction if
we were to hold that the unincumbered fee simple in the property was ever in
the company so that it became subject to the charge of the debenture-holders.'

g
No doubt whatever was thrown on the correctness of that decision in the two
later cases in the Court of Appeal above referred to and they are clearly distinguishable. In *Church of England Building Society v Piskor*[4] purchasers of property who had
taken possession before completion of their contract granted a tenancy of part of it.
The property was subsequently conveyed to them and on the same day they executed
h a legal charge on it in favour of the plaintiff building society to secure money which it
had advanced to the purchasers to enable them to complete the purchase. When
the plaintiff sought to evict the tenant on the ground that his tenancy was not binding
on it the tenant argued that, though his tenancy was originally merely equitable, his
landlords, the purchasers, were bound by estoppel to clothe it with the legal estate
as soon as they acquired it themselves. Consequently when the legal estate was con-
j veyed to the purchaser by the vendor the estoppel was 'fed' and the tenancy became

---

1 [1963] 3 All ER 613, [1963] 1 WLR 1329
2 [1912] 2 Ch 25
3 [1912] 2 Ch at 31
4 [1954] 2 All ER 85, [1954] 2 WLR 952

a legal one. This it was argued must be taken to have happened in the notional interval of time between the conveyance to the purchasers and the granting of the *a* charge. The Court of Appeal held that this argument was sound and that the tenant had acquired a legal tenancy before the grant of the mortgage which was binding on the mortgagee. But Romer LJ[1], in distinguishing *Re Connolly Bros Ltd (No 2)*[2], was careful to point out that there was no evidence to show that the purchasers had prior to granting the tenancy entered into any binding contract with the plaintiff society to grant them a mortgage on completion in consideration of their advancing some of *b* the purchase price. If there had been such an agreement then the rights of the parties might well have been different—though as the tenancy was undoubtedly subsequently clothed with the legal estate an agreement to grant a mortgage even though made before the grant of the equitable tenancy to him would presumably not have bound the tenant unless he had notice of it. Furthermore the fact that the building society had not inspected the property or enquired as to the rights of any person *c* in occupation might also have been relevant. But the basic difference between the two lines of cases is that in cases such as *Re Connolly Bros Ltd (No 2)*[2] and this case the charge under the debenture only bites on property which is already fettered by the agreement to give the other charge, whereas on the facts of the *Piskor* case[3] the tenancy was created out of an interest which was then unfettered by any such agreement. In *Capital Finance Co Ltd v Stokes*[4] land was sold on the terms that 75 *d* per cent of the purchase money should be secured by a first mortgage. On the same day that the land was conveyed to it the purchasing company mortgaged the property back to the vendor for the appropriate amount. The vendor retained possession of the title deeds but the mortgage was not registered under s 95 of the Companies Act 1948 which provided so far as material as follows:

e

'(1) Subject to the provisions of this Part of this Act, every charge created after the fixed date by a company registered in England and being a charge to which this section applies shall, so far as any security on the company's property or undertaking is conferred thereby, be void against the liquidator and any creditor to the company, unless the prescribed particulars of the charge together with the instrument, if any, by which the charge is created or evidenced, are delivered *f* to or received by the registrar of companies for registration in manner required by this Act within twenty-one days after the date of its creation, but without prejudice to any contract or obligation for repayment of the money thereby secured, and when a charge becomes void under this section the money secured thereby shall immediately become payable.

'(2) This section applies to the following charges . . . (d) a charge on land, *g* wherever situate, or any interest therein . . .'

The purchasing company having been wound up the liquidator contended that the vendor was an unsecured creditor. In answer to that contention the vendor referred to s 97(1) of the 1948 Act which was in the following terms:

h

'Where a company registered in England acquires any property which is subject to a charge of any such kind as would, if it had been created by the company after the acquisition of the property, have been required to be registered under this Part of this Act, the company shall cause the prescribed particulars of the charge, together with a copy (certified in the prescribed manner to be a correct copy) of the instrument, if any, by which the charge was created or is evidenced, to be delivered *j*

---

1 [1954] 2 All ER at 92, [1954] 2 WLR at 961
2 [1912] 2 Ch 25
3 [1954] 2 All ER 85, [1954] 2 WLR 952
4 [1968] 3 All ER 625, [1969] 1 Ch 261

to the registrar of companies for registration in manner required by this Act
within twenty-one days after the date on which the acquisition is completed.'

He argued that it was that section and not s 95 that applied to the case. The court
rejected that argument, holding that s 97 only applied to what could truly be said to
be a purchase of an equity of redemption, i e a purchase of land already subject to a
mortgage created by someone else, and that the fact that the purchaser was contractually bound to mortgage the property back to the vendor as soon as it was
conveyed to him did not mean that the mortgage had not been created by him within
the meaning of s 95. That seems to their Lordships to be, if they may say so, clearly
right—but the conclusion is not in any way inconsistent with *Re Connolly Bros
Ltd (No 2)*[1].

Finally their Lordships turn to consider whether the Registration of Records Act
affects the position. In this connection they would first observe that it is not altogether
clear to them that the charge on which the respondent relies has ever been registered.
No doubt the debenture was a 'mortgage' for the purpose of the Act and its registration in July 1970 was a registration of all the charges—whether fixed or floating—
created by it on the lands in which Fisher had an interest when it was issued on 4th
June 1970. But as their Lordships have already pointed out, Fisher had not at that
date any interest in the lands which were the subject of the contract of 20th September 1968. It only acquired an interest in such lands at a later date. The charge on which
the respondent relies came into existence on 15th January 1971 under the combined
operation of the agreement of that date coupled with the debenture and the appointment of the receiver. It would appear to be arguable that the charge was not 'made
and executed' for the purpose of s 10 of the Act until 15th January 1971. It is not
however necessary for their Lordships to express a concluded opinion on this point,
which would involve the consideration of such cases as *Independent Automatic Sales
Ltd v Knowles & Foster*[2] and *Paul & Frank Ltd v Discount Bank (Overseas) Ltd*[3], because
even if one assumes that the registration of the debenture in July 1970 counts as a
registration of the equitable charge created six months later, s 10 would not operate
to give it 'priority or preference' over the mortgage for the two do not compete
with one another. The situation which s 10 envisages is the creation of two successive
dispositions of land which conflict with one another so that full effect cannot be
given to both; but here there is no inconsistency between the equitable charge
and the mortgage. If one reads the debenture and the agreement of 15th January
1971 together one sees that the charge which they jointly operate to create is
subject to the prior charge in favour of the vendor. Bryce CJ was, their Lordships think, quite right in seeing an analogy here to *Jones v Barker*[4]. Warrington J
there held that the deed of assignment on its true construction only assigned such
property as the debtor then possessed. Accordingly the only interest in the land in
question which passed to the trustee was the equity of redemption subject to the
unregistered equitable mortgage. Section 14 of the Yorkshire Registries Act 1884 did not
operate to confer any priority on the registered assignment over the unregistered
mortgage since they were not in conflict. Their Lordships' Board in the Singapore
case of *Chung Khiaw Bank Ltd v United Overseas Bank Ltd*[5] referred to by the Court of
Appeal did not dissent in any way from the decision in *Jones v Barker*[4] but held that
it did not cover the particular facts of the case before them. Moreover in reaching its
decision the Board was plainly much influenced by the fact that the precise point

1   [1912] 2 Ch 25
2   [1962] 3 All ER 27, [1962] 1 WLR 974
3   [1966] 2 All ER 922, [1966] 3 WLR 490
4   [1909] 1 Ch 321
5   [1970] AC 767

before it had been the subject of a decision in the local courts as long ago as 1897, the
correctness of which had never been doubted and which indeed had been accepted
by the local legislature as correct in 1907. It is *Jones v Barker*[1] rather than the Singapore
case which is in point here.

The respondent argued finally—on this aspect of the case—that even if the mortgage was not postponed to the equitable charge arising on 15th January 1971 because
the two were not in conflict, yet when the legal estate was conveyed to it on 30th
April 1971 Fisher acquired a fresh item of property to which there attached a separate
equitable charge in favour of the respondent under cl 4 of the debenture and that
though an equitable charge in favour of the appellant arose at the same moment
of time by reason of the agreement to grant a legal mortgage—which equitable
charge was a moment later clothed with the legal estate when the mortgage took
effect—the two equitable charges were in conflict with one another and since that in
favour of the respondent was registered first it had priority. Their Lordships while
admiring the ingenuity of this argument cannot accept it. It depends on treating the
charge in favour of the respondent on the legal estate when it was conveyed to Fisher
as in some way different in character from the charge on the benefit of the contract.
As their Lordships have pointed out the effect of the agreement between the parties
was that Fisher was never to acquire the fee simple free from a charge in favour of
the appellant. Therefore the charge in favour of the appellant could never compete
with a charge in favour of the respondent—whether one regards that as a charge on
the benefit of the contract or a charge on the legal estate arising on completion of
the contract. In the result, therefore, their Lordships do not think that the provisions
of the Registration of Records Act assist the respondent here.

The Court of Appeal while setting aside the order of Bryce CJ made no positive
order of its own but remitted the case to the court of first instance to consider whether
the priorities were affected in any way by the doctrine of notice or by the existence
of a vendor's lien. So far as notice is concerned it must have been obvious to the
respondent's manager at Nassau when he read the receiver's letter of 30th April
1971 that the receiver was envisaging and that the vendors would have been envisaging that any security to be given to the respondent for any money which it might
advance to enable the contract to be completed would rank after the mortgage
to the appellant for the balance of the purchase price and that if—as appears to have
happened—the property became worth less than the total of the two charges the
intention was that the loss should fall on the respondent in the first place before
any could fall on the appellant. In the light of this fact it is somewhat surprising to
find the respondent, the Royal Bank of Canada, arguing that its charge has priority.
But as their Lordships think that the points of law taken by the respondent as to the
construction of the debenture and the effect of the registration are misconceived it
is not necessary for them to consider whether if they had taken a different view the
terms of the receiver's letter would have affected the result. Again it is not necessary
for them to consider the point as to a vendor's lien insofar as that point might assist
the appellant since they are in its favour anyway. The Court of Appeal seems however
to have thought that the respondent might have founded some argument on the
point; for after referring to the cases *Congresbury Motors Ltd v Anglo-Belge Finance
Co Ltd*[2] and *Coptic Ltd v Bailey*[3] they continue as follows:

> 'These cases appear to throw up a question whether, if the [respondent's]
> charge does not receive priority over the [appellant's] mortgage for other reasons,
> the [respondent] would nevertheless be entitled, by subrogation, to a lien for that

---

1   [1909] 1 Ch 321
2   [1970] 3 All ER 385, [1971] Ch 81
3   [1972] 1 All ER 1242, [1972] Ch 446

portion of the purchase price provided by it, which would take priority over the
mortgage for the balance of the purchase price.'

Their Lordships cannot follow this suggestion or find anything in the cases cited
which lends support to it. If Fisher had created no charge in favour of the respondent
then no doubt the respondent having provided part of the purchase price would
have been entitled as against Fisher to the benefit 'pro tanto' of the vendor's lien;
but as their Lordships have pointed out it was clearly the intention of the parties
that any moneys advanced by the respondents should rank behind the purchase
mortgage and so any interest in the vendor's lien acquired by the respondent by
subrogation would also rank behind it.

For these reasons their Lordships will humbly advise Her Majesty that the appeal
should be allowed and the order of Bryce CJ restored and that the respondent be
ordered to pay the appellant its costs before the Court of Appeal and the Board,
save the costs of the petition for special leave to appeal which should be borne by the
appellant.

Appeal allowed.

Solicitors: *Simmons & Simmons* (for the appellant); *Clifford-Turner & Co* (for the
respondent).

Gordon H Scott Esq Barrister.

R v Melville

COURT OF APPEAL, CRIMINAL DIVISION
LORD WIDGERY CJ, O'CONNOR AND LAWSON JJ
6th NOVEMBER 1975

*Criminal Law – Appeal – Evidence – Fresh evidence – Evidence on an issue which is the
subject of the appeal – Issue not raised in court below – Whether court obliged to hear fresh
evidence on an issue not raised in court below – Criminal Appeal Act 1968, s 23(2).*

Section 23(2)[a] of the Criminal Appeal Act 1968 does not require the Court of Appeal,
Criminal Division, to receive new evidence at the hearing of an appeal unless that
evidence relates to an issue which was raised in the court below and which is the
subject of the appeal; the court is under no obligation to admit evidence on an issue
which was not litigated at the appellant's trial (see p 399 *f* and *g*, post).

Notes
For the admission of fresh evidence on appeal, see Supplement to 10 Halsbury's Laws
(3rd Edn) para 978, and for cases on the subject, see 14 Digest (Repl) 624-629, 6257-6363.

For the Criminal Appeal Act 1968, s 23, see 8 Halsbury's Statutes (3rd Edn) 706.

Case referred to in judgment
R v Dodd (10th June 1971) unreported, CA.

---

a   Section 23(2) is set out at p 398 *j* to p 399 *b*, post

Case also cited
R v Clark [1962] 1 All ER 428, [1962] 1 WLR 180, CCA.

Appeal and application
This was an appeal by Alan Brian Melville against his conviction, on 4th May 1973 in the Crown Court at Chelmsford before Eveleigh J, for murder. At the hearing the appellant applied for leave to call additional evidence. The facts are set out in the judgment of the court.

Sir Harold Cassel QC and Ronald Trott for the appellant.
Anthony McCowan QC and Timothy Nash for the Crown.

LORD WIDGERY CJ delivered the following judgment of the court: On 4th May 1973 at Chelmsford Crown Court before Eveleigh J the appellant was con-victed of the murder of one Cyril Headley and he was sentenced to life imprisonment. He now appeals against his conviction by leave of Lawson J, and he has applied to call additional evidence which was not available before the court below dealing with his mental condition.

It is not necessary to go into the facts in any detail at all. The appellant killed a homosexual with whom he had been associating. He did not use a weapon, but he used very considerable force, using his boots and his fists, and there is no doubt that he entirely lost control of himself for a period at or near the time of the murder.

At the trial the only substantial defence which was run was the defence of pro-vocation, and the jury did not accept that, so that on 4th May 1973, as I have already said, a conviction of murder was entered against the appellant. At no time was his mental condition put under question, and the reason for that is because the medical reports which were available pretrial both made it clear that in the opinion of the highly qualified psychiatrists making the reports there was no medical issue which could be raised.

For example, Dr Scott, who made a report on 20th March 1973 some months be-fore the trial, refers to certain abnormalities appertaining to the appellant, but says there is no disorder of mood or thinking and nothing to suggest psychotic illness. He concluded by saying:

'He is fit to plead and stand his trial. There is no disability of mind in the McNaughton[1] sense. His mental abnormality does not substantially diminish his responsibility. I cannot suggest any medical defence against the charge.'

Dr Blair, reporting at the same time, also gives a long and very comprehensive report about this man and reaches the same conclusion. He is not suffering from any psychosis or psychoneurosis, nor has he ever suffered from such illnesses in the past. Then the doctor goes on to consider the pros and cons of whether he is a psychopathic personality, and in the end comes to the conclusion similar to that of Dr Scott that when the crime was committed the appellant knew what he was doing. He says: 'He attacked him with tempestuous aggression, in a state of temper which momentarily overwhelmed him.' Dr Blair goes on to say: 'I do not consider it would qualify him for diminished responsibility under the Homicide Act 1957.' Small wonder, one may think, that no mental issue was raised at all at the trial, and the question was provocation or no, and the jury found against the appellant.

After he had been convicted he was sent to Wormwood Scrubs and there he came under the care of Dr Clark and was also seen by Dr Neville. It is, we think, clear

---

1   See M'Naghten's Case (1843) 10 Cl & Fin 200

that the main purpose of those examining the appellant's condition at this time was
to consider what advice they might give to the Home Secretary in regard to an order
being made under s 72 of the Mental Health Act 1959 for his detention in a special
hospital; but be that as it may, further investigations of his mental condition took
place in the months succeeding his trial.

Although such electroencephalograph readings as were available at the trial had
shown nothing of abnormality, the EEG readings obtainable after the trial began
in some instances to show an abnormality. In particular, as a kind of landmark,
on 29th September, three months after the trial, Dr Williams found some abnormalities
in the EEG.

These abnormalities were pursued and considered by other doctors who considered the case. I have already said that a Dr Neville was involved and also a
Dr Williams, who found the initial abnormality on the EEG. The effect of that
abnormality and of others subsequently found is, we find, conveniently summarised
in the report of Dr Blair which is given on 5th April 1975 before the hearing of this
court. He explained how he has now had to reconsider his views in the light of the
EEG evidence which has come before him since the trial. In considering how far
the evidence of abnormality helps the accused to prove a state of diminished responsibility, the doctor says: 'The difficulty in accepting this statement in itself is
that an EEG tracing on Melville before 29th September 1973 was normal and tracings
afterwards showed "slight abnormality and eventually no abnormality".'

Thus, one has what seems to a layman a considerable phenomenon of no abnormality at the time of the trial, abnormality arising and discovered quite soon afterwards and then going away again, and eventually disappearing altogether. That
is the summary or the activities of the appellant's EEG results throughout the time
his case was under consideration.

This is not the first time that this kind of situation has occurred, nor is it the first
time in which an appellant in the position of the present appellant has sought to call
fresh evidence on medical grounds. It is quite obvious, and counsel for the appellant
does not shrink from it, that in order to succeed in this appeal the appellant has got
to show that the introduction of the evidence with regard to his EEG readings is
vital—in other words, that that evidence is enough to get him either a dismissal
of his conviction or at least a new trial. Nothing else will help him. In order that
he may get the evidence of the EEG readings before the court he has to have leave
from this court to call the fresh evidence, because under s 23 of the Criminal Appeal
Act 1968 fresh evidence is not to be called except with the leave of the court.

I have said that this is not in any sense a novel situation, and indeed there is a
very similar case, R v Dodd[1], to which we will make reference now. That case raised
almost exactly the same points but unfortunately was never reported. It is a case
in this court tried on 10th June 1971. The presiding judge was Fenton Atkinson LJ
and he sat with Stephenson LJ and Lawton J. Here again there was a charge of
murder; here again there was a defence of provocation which failed, and here again
after the conviction had been entered and the matter had been completed as far
as the trial court was concerned, evidence came to light which was thought to justify
a conclusion that the appellant had suffered from diminished responsibility at the
material time. This is what Fenton Atkinson LJ said about those issues in that case:

> 'It is now said that fresh evidence is available to show that in truth this appel-
> lant was suffering from such abnormality of mind at the relevant time as sub-
> stantially impaired his mental responsibility, in other words a defence of dimi-
> nished responsibility. That was a defence which the very experienced counsel
> representing this man never attempted to run at the trial from first to last,
> and it is very understandable why they did not because they had a medical

---

1   (10th June 1971) unreported

report from Dr Terry, the senior medical officer at Brixton Prison where the appellant had been for some three months on remand before that report was made, saying in emphatic terms that there was no sign of mental illness and nothing whatever to suggest diminished responsibility.'

This is very much like the present case, as all must admit. He goes on a little later in the judgment:

'That was the material available at the time, and those responsible for the defence decided quite deliberately not to attempt to run any defence of diminished responsibility, but to run the case on provocation, and the case was fought on provocation from first to last.'

He then went on to discuss how a distinguished psychiatrist, Dr Denham, came into the picture some ten months after the trial of the appellant, and Dr Denham had reached conclusions about the mental condition of the appellant which the other witnesses had not reached.

Fenton Atkinson LJ went on to deal with the principle of the matter which is to be applied in those circumstances in these words. He said:

'In the view of this court, cases must be rare indeed when the defence have chosen to run at the trial as their only defence the defence of accident or provocation, or a combination of the two, and when that defence has failed can consult and call a psychiatrist, or a psychiatrist seeing the appellant for the first time many months after the event, with a view to getting a re-trial to run a defence of diminished responsibility. It may well be that if subsequent evidence of diminished responsibility was really overwhelming, the court might well feel moved to substitute a verdict of manslaughter, or to order a new trial. But we have all read and re-read this fresh report from Dr Denham. It is based, of course, on various fresh matters revealed to him for the first time, we have already stated, some months after the event, and it shows certainly that this young man was subject to extreme fits of anger and that at the relevant time he was so enraged by the damage to his face that he was out for revenge. But in our view, if received, that evidence would not afford any ground for allowing the appeal, and that is even assuming in the favour of the defence that there was good reason for not adducing the evidence of a further psychiatrist at the trial.'

We think that we should follow the decision of this court in *R v Dodd*[1] and apply to this case the principles laid down by Fenton Atkinson LJ which I have just referred to; and in so doing the first question which the court has to ask itself is whether it is under any obligation to receive the evidence now tendered before it, which is the evidence of three of the doctors who saw the appellant at one stage or another in the course of these matters.

Counsel for the appellant submits that s 23 of the 1968 Act, properly understood, requires us to hear this evidence, and we must look into this matter first. Section 23(1) in effect provides that this court may in its discretion order the production before it of fresh evidence virtually without limit. It is an extremely wide power, but is it a purely discretionary power. It is a power which the court can exercise however it wants to, but which it is not bound to exercise.

The mandatory provisions in regard to letting in fresh evidence are to be found in s 23(2), and that I should read:

'Without prejudice to subsection (1) above, where evidence is tendered to the

---

1   (10th June 1971) unreported

Court of Appeal thereunder the Court shall, unless they are satisfied that the evidence, if received, would not afford any ground for allowing the appeal exercise their powers of receiving it if—(a) it appears to them that the evidence is likely to be credible and would have been admissible in the proceedings from which the appeal lies on an issue which is the subject of the appeal; and (b) they are satisfied that it was not adduced in those proceedings but there is a reasonable explanation for the failure to adduce it.'

We do not express any opinion in this case on the question whether the evidence of mental disturbance is strong enough so that if received it might afford a ground for allowing the appeal. We leave that matter open, finding it unnecessary to reach a conclusion on it. But we direct our attention to the fact that the duty to admit fresh evidence arises only where the evidence is not only likely to be credible but would have been admissible in the proceedings from which the appeal lies on an issue which is the subject of the appeal.

Argument has centred on the phrase, 'on an issue', in the last sentence, and, as I understand it, counsel for the appellant argues that any contention which can affect the ultimate outcome of the proceedings is an issue for present purposes. That means that all he has to do in order to create an issue to bring before this court is to assert that certain things are or are not the case. Then he says that means the issue has been raised and the jurisdiction of this court to solve the ultimate problem appears.

We find it quite impossible to reach that conclusion on the meaning of s 23(2)(a). We think it inconsistent with the whole of the Criminal Appeal Act 1968 and entirely contrary to any possible intention of Parliament that we should be compelled in this court to receive any quantity of evidence which was put before us merely on the assertion of the party putting the material before us that there was an issue in regard to the point dealt with in the material.

In our judgment the expression 'on an issue' in s 23(2)(a) means on an issue which was raised below and is the subject of the appeal in this court. Giving the words that meaning, we can say with confidence, as might have been said in R v Dodd[1], that there is no issue which was litigated in the court below and which is now to be argued on the basis of the fresh evidence.

In reaching that conclusion we are impressed by the fact, first, that the alternative construction, as I have endeavoured to demonstrate, would be totally unworkable, and, secondly, in the knowledge that the discretionary power in the court to allow fresh evidence under s 23(1) should be available in all cases to avoid any kind of injustice which might occur. We conclude for those reasons that this is not a case in which we are bound to admit the fresh evidence.

The next thing we have to do therefore is to consider whether it ought to be admitted in the exercise of our discretion. In approaching this problem it is also as well to remember that if the evidence is rejected at this stage, then in this case the appeal must fail because counsel for the appellant accepts that he has no other weapons in his armoury if he is refused leave to call fresh evidence. Secondly, we should remember that if we admit the evidence we shall then have to dispose of the appeal finally by one of three orders. The first would be to dismiss the appeal; the second would be to substitute a verdict of manslaughter; and the third would be to order a new trial. So we must mentally go through those stages until we reach the answer in this case.

Should we in our discretion allow this evidence to go in? We turn our minds back to what Fenton Atkinson LJ said in the virtually identical circumstances, in R v Dodd[1], and his words were, it is to be remembered, these: 'It may well be that if subsequent

---

1 (10th June 1971) unreported

evidence of diminished responsibility was really overwhelming, the court might well feel moved to substitute a verdict of manslaughter, or to order a new trial.'   *a*

Thus, if one was faced with evidence which was really overwhelming to show mental deficiency in the appellant at the material time, not only would we admit the evidence, but no doubt we should follow Fenton Atkinson LJ's directions in *R v Dodd*[1] and either order a new trial or substitute a verdict of manslaughter. Like that case, this appellant lacks the overwhelming evidence to which reference was there made.   *b*

Also in deciding whether to exercise the discretion or not regard should be paid, we think, to a proper division of responsibility between this court and the Home Office in matters of this kind. It is to be remembered that the main function of the Court of Appeal is to supervise the operation of the lower courts and to correct their mistakes. It is for that reason that we have power to overrule decisions below and substitute new punishments and the like. But it is not the function of the Court   *c* of Appeal to maintain continuous supervision over prisoners when they have already been committed to prison, and it certainly is no function of the Court of Appeal to be invited two years after a conviction has been entered to make some wholly different sentence merely because of changes of circumstances in the meanwhile. There is of course the kind of twilight area between the functions of the Home Secretary and our functions in which that may be suitable to provide the relief sought,   *d* but in the main, if the functions of the appeal have been completed, if all steps which could be taken according to the Criminal Appeal Rules 1968[2] have either been taken or now cannot be taken owing to lapse of time, then prima facie, if anything happens thereafter which is thought to invalidate the proceedings, the proper person to receive the complaint is the Home Secretary.

This court is concerned with changes in the circumstances occurring whilst the   *e* court is still seised of the case, which would not normally be brought into action on applications for leave being made long out of time merely in respect of developments which have occurred since the hearing and over which it earlier could not have exercised jurisdiction.

However in this case the question is whether, bearing those factors in mind, we ought to allow the evidence in our discretion, and we have come to the conclusion   *f* that we should not. We refuse the application for the calling of fresh evidence, and that, by concession of counsel for the appellant, means that the appeal must be and is dismissed.

Application refused; appeal dismissed.

        g

Solicitors: *R Voss & Son* (for the appellant); *Director of Public Prosecutions.*

N P Metcalfe Esq   Barrister.

---

1   (10th June 1971) unreported
2   SI 1968 No 1262

Derby & Co Ltd v Larsson

COURT OF APPEAL, CIVIL DIVISION
CAIRNS, ROSKILL AND BROWNE LJJ
26th FEBRUARY 1975

HOUSE OF LORDS
VISCOUNT DILHORNE, LORD SIMON OF GLAISDALE, LORD SALMON, LORD FRASER OF
TULLYBELTON AND LORD RUSSELL OF KILLOWEN
15th DECEMBER 1975, 28th JANUARY 1976

Practice – Service – Service out of jurisdiction – Necessary or proper party to action – Action properly brought against a person served within jurisdiction – Person out of jurisdiction a necessary or proper party to action – Counterclaim – Foreign resident bringing action against English defendant – Plaintiff leaving address for service within jurisdiction as required by rules of court – Defendant serving defence and counterclaim on plaintiff – Defendant making another foreign resident second defendant to counterclaim – Whether counterclaim 'properly brought' against plaintiff – Whether court having jurisdiction to give leave to serve defence and counterclaim on second defendant to counterclaim out of the jurisdiction – RSC Ord 11, r 1(1)(j).

The defendants, who were commodity brokers in metal, had dealings with the plaintiffs, a company resident in Sweden. A dispute arose between the defendants and the plaintiffs in which the plaintiffs claimed that in consequence of those dealings the defendants owed them a sum of money. The defendants asserted that the plaintiffs had been a party to certain dealings in zinc through their agent, L, that those dealings had shown a substantial loss and that in consequence the plaintiffs owed the defendants a sum of money. The plaintiffs denied that L had been their agent in the dealings in question and, on the basis of that contention, brought an action in England against the defendants claiming the moneys alleged to be due to them. As required by RSC Ord 6, r 5, the writ was endorsed with the plaintiffs' solicitors' address as the address for service. The defendants defended and counterclaimed moneys due from the plaintiffs on the basis of their contention that L had been the plaintiffs' agent in the zinc dealings. The defendants wished to join L as a defendant to the counterclaim under RSC Ord 15, r 3[a], alleging in the alternative his breach of warranty of authority or personal liability. L was, however, resident outside the jurisdiction. The defendants obtained leave under RSC Ord 11, r 1(1)(j)[b], to serve the counterclaim on L out of the jurisdiction. L appealed and the Court of Appeal allowed the appeal, holding that the court had no jurisdiction to give leave under r 1(1)(j) since the bringing of the action by the plaintiffs was to be regarded as a voluntary submission to the jurisdiction and therefore the counterclaim had not been 'properly brought' against the plaintiffs, within r 1(1)(j), in that it had been brought not merely by virtue of the user of the process of the court but by user of that process with the addition of the voluntary submission of the plaintiffs. The defendants appealed.

Held – Since a person resident outside the jurisdiction who chose to bring an action against a defendant within the jurisdiction laid himself open to the service of a counterclaim within the jurisdiction by the defendant, the defendants' counterclaim against the plaintiffs had been brought in compliance with the rules of court, and furthermore there was no suggestion that the counterclaim was not genuine. It followed therefore

---

a Rule 3, so far as material, is set out at p 406 g to p 407 a, post
b Rule 1(1), so far as material, is set out at p 403 h and j, post

that the counterclaim had been 'properly brought against a person duly served
within the jurisdiction', within r $1(1)(j)$. Accordingly, since there was no question   *a*
that L was a 'proper party' to the counterclaim, within r $1(1)(j)$, it followed that the
court had jurisdiction to give leave for service on L out of the jurisdiction. The appeal
would therefore be allowed (see p 413 *c* and *e*, p 414 *b* to *f*, p 415 *f* to *h* and p 416 *c* to *f*,
post).

John Russell & Co Ltd v Cayzer, Irvine & Co Ltd [1916-17] All ER Rep 630 distinguished.
    b

Notes
For the grounds on which leave may be given for service out of the jurisdiction, see 30
Halsbury's Laws (3rd Edn) 323-326, para 588, and for cases on the subject, see 50 Digest
(Repl) 335-364, 646-852.

    c

Cases referred to in judgments
Allan and Anderson Ltd v A H Basse Rederi A/S, The Piraeus [1974] 2 Lloyd's Rep 266, CA.
Evans v Bartlam [1937] 2 All ER 646, [1937] AC 473, 106 LJKB 568, 157 LT 311, 53 TLR
    689, HL, 50 Digest (Repl) 401, 1113.
Osenton (Charles) & Co v Johnston [1941] 2 All ER 245, [1942] AC 130, 110 LJKB 420,
    165 LT 235, 57 TLR 515, HL, 51 Digest (Repl) 681, 2840.   *d*
Russell (John) & Co Ltd v Cayzer, Irvine & Co Ltd [1916] 2 AC 298, [1916-17] All ER Rep
    630, 85 LJKB 1152, 115 LT 86, HL, 50 Digest (Repl) 364, 846.
Tyne Improvement Comrs v Armement Anversois S/A, The Brabo [1949] 1 All ER 294,
    [1949] AC 326, [1949] LJR 435, 65 TLR 114, HL, 50 Digest (Repl) 364, 842.

Interlocutory appeal   *e*
By a writ issued on 19th April 1974 the plaintiffs, A B Stockholms-Maskiner, a
company incorporated in accordance with the laws of Sweden and having its principal
place of business in Stockholm, brought an action against the defendants, Derby &
Co Ltd, in the Queen's Bench Division (Commercial Court). By their points of defence
and counterclaim the defendants joined Stig Larsson as second defendant to the
counterclaim. On 10th July 1974, on an ex parte application, Ackner J in chambers   *f*
granted leave to the defendants to join Mr Larsson as second defendant to the counterclaim and to serve points of defence and counterclaim on him at Box 10, 541 01
Skorde, Sweden, or elsewhere in the Kingdom of Sweden. On 22nd November 1974
Donaldson J in chambers dismissed an application by Mr Larsson that the order of
Ackner J dated 10th July 1974, the service of the points of defence and counterclaim
pursuant thereto and all subsequent proceedings against Mr Larsson, by counter-   *g*
claim, be set aside. By leave of Donaldson J, Mr Larsson appealed against that order.
The facts are set out in the judgment of Roskill LJ.

Mark Saville for Mr Larsson.
Nicholas Phillips for the defendants.

    h

ROSKILL LJ. This is an appeal by Mr Stig Larsson, the second defendant by
counterclaim, from an interlocutory order of Donaldson J made on the 22nd November 1974 in proceedings brought by the plaintiffs, a Swedish company, against the
defendants, a firm of brokers on the London Metal Exchange, and in further proceedings between the defendants in the original proceedings and the plaintiffs, Mr Larsson   *j*
and another Swedish company called Indusan AB who together were the defendants
by counterclaim.

The appeal raises a point of general interest and some importance on the true
construction and application of RSC Ord 11. The learned judge helpfully gave leave
to appeal in order that his decision might be tested in this court.

a
The matter arises in a rather unusual way. The plaintiffs bring this action against the defendants for a declaration that certain sums deposited by the plaintiffs with the defendants are not to be used by the defendants in part payment of the purchase price of certain contracts which had been listed in a letter passing between the parties. They seek, putting the matter quite shortly, to recover certain sums in the possession of the defendants on the ground that those moneys belong to the plaintiffs and cannot be used by the defendants for purposes of meeting deficiencies on margins caused by
b
large numbers of dealings involving several millions of pounds on the London Metal Exchange.

The defendants have put in a counterclaim as well as a defence against that claim, and they allege in substance that all the dealings in question were dealings carried through by the defendants on behalf of the plaintiffs. But since the plaintiffs claim that a large number of those dealings were not theirs and that those who entered
c
into those dealings had no authority from the plaintiffs so to do, the defendants have sought to join as defendants by counterclaim Mr Larsson and the Swedish company, Indusan AB. Mr Larsson is not resident in England but in Sweden and Indusan, as I have just said, is a Swedish company. Accordingly it was not open to the defendants to bring those two, Mr Larsson and Indusan, before the court unless they could obtain leave to serve their intended counterclaim on each of them out of the jurisdiction
d
under RSC Ord 11. They applied ex parte to Ackner J, who was then in charge of the Commercial Court, on 10th July 1974; and Ackner J gave leave. In passing I would say that the affidavit in support of that application for leave, which was sworn on 5th July 1974 is, with great respect to its draftsman, seriously defective. The absence of detail in it regarding the transactions it was desired to make the subject of the counterclaim is conspicuous. It is of course axiomatic that in all applications for leave
e
under RSC Ord 11 the utmost frankness is required. Counsel for Mr Larsson mentioned this matter in opening this appeal this morning. But very properly he took no independent point on those defects because he rightly said that those defects were put right in a second affidavit. That affidavit supplies detail, and no one can now complain that the fullest information has not been placed before the court.

Ackner J having given leave to serve the counterclaim out of the jurisdiction ex
f
parte, Mr Larsson, but not Indusan, applied to Donaldson J to set that order aside. After hearing argument, Donaldson J refused to make any order. It is against that refusal of Donaldson J that Mr Larsson appeals to this court.

It is necessary in order to consider whether or not Donaldson J reached the right conclusion to have regard to the relevant provisions of RSC Ord 11 because the arguments in favour of the order which Donaldson J made are really twofold. It is said,
g
first, that there was here a contract falling within these provisions and, secondly, that Mr Larsson was a person who could properly be joined as a necessary and proper party to the proceedings, the relevant provision of RSC Ord 11 being r 1(1)(f) and (j). I ought to read them because they are important, and on the second point much turns on the true construction of para (j). Rule 1(1) provides:

h
'Subject to Rule 3 and provided that the writ does not contain any such claim as is mentioned in Order 75, Rule 2(1)(a), service of a writ, or notice of a writ, out of the jurisdiction is permissible with the leave of the Court in the following cases, that is to say . . . (f) if the action begun by the writ is brought against a defendant not domiciled or ordinarily resident in Scotland to enforce, rescind, dissolve, annul or otherwise affect a contract, or to recover damages or obtain
j
other relief in respect of the breach of a contract, being (in either case) a contract which—(i) was made within the jurisdiction, or [I need not read (ii)] . . . (iii) is by its terms, or by implication, governed by English law . . . (j) if the action begun by the writ being properly brought against a person duly served within the jurisdiction, a person out of the jurisdiction is a necessary or proper party thereto . . .'

RSC Ord 11 has a long history, ever since it was first promulgated in 1883. The principles to be applied by the court in exercising its discretion are well summarised *a* in Rule 23 in Dicey & Morris[1]. The learned editors said:

'But under Rule 23 [that is, of course, the rule in Dicey and not the Rules of the Supreme Court], the jurisdiction of the court is essentially discretionary, for the court may, if it sees fit, decline to allow the service or even the issue of the writ, and thus decline to exercise its jurisdiction. Five cardinal points have been *b* emphasised in the decided cases. First, the court ought to be exceedingly careful before it allows a writ to be served on a foreigner out of England. Secondly, if there is any doubt in the construction of any of the sub-heads of Order 11, r. 1(1), that doubt ought to be resolved in favour of the defendant. Thirdly, since applications are made *ex parte*, a full and fair disclosure of all the facts of the case ought to be made. Fourthly, the court will refuse leave if the case is within the letter *c* but outside the spirit of the Rule. Fifthly, if the parties have agreed that the dispute between them shall be referred to the exclusive jurisdiction of a foreign court, leave will probably be refused.'

Those principles are well established, and they have to be borne in mind in every *d* application which is made under this rule for leave to serve out of the jursidiction.

I turn next to the defence and counterclaim. I take it in its original form in order to see how it is that the defendants frame the counterclaim which they seek leave to bring against Mr Larsson. Paragraph 3 of the counterclaim is pleaded thus in its original form:

'At or about the beginning of 1971 an agreement was concluded between the Defendants ("Derby"), Philbro [who were a Swedish company] and Larsson, *e* acting on behalf of and with the authority of the Plaintiffs ("S-M"), whereby it was agreed that Larsson would place orders on behalf of S-M for the purchase and sale of metal futures with Philbro and Philbro would submit the same to Derby for acceptance on the terms of the Standard Contract of the London Metal Exchange. Under the said terms, the metal dealer contracts as principal with the customer, but customarily concludes an identical transaction on the Metal *f* Exchange in order to cover himself and to establish a contract price.'

That, if I read it correctly, clearly asserts that Larsson would be placing orders on behalf of the plaintiffs with Philbro, and Philbro would be placing 'the same' with the defendants in order that the latter might cover themselves on the terms of the Standard Contract of the London Metal Exchange and establish a contract price. *g*

There is no express plea in that paragraph of any representation made direct by Larsson to the defendants of Larsson's authority to contract for the plaintiffs. When one turns to the second affidavit sworn on behalf of the defendants one finds in para 9 exactly how the dealings went:

'In March 1971, pursuant to instructions from Larsson, dealings began as set *h* out in Schedule A to the Points of Defence and Counterclaim. The pattern of dealings was as follows:—(i) Larsson gave a purchase or sale order to Lowenberg [I should explain that the affidavit had earlier said that Mr Lowenberg was a director of Philbro]; (ii) Lowenberg passed the order to Derby, by telephone or telex; (iii) Derby executed the order; (iv) Derby confirmed the transaction to Lowenberg; (v) Lowenberg confirmed the transaction to Larsson by telephone; *j* (vi) Lowenberg (usually but not always) sent a confirmatory letter to Larsson confirming the transaction; communications with Larsson were sent to Indusan;

---

1   Conflict of Laws (9th Edn, 1973), p 173

a (vii) Derby sent a London Metal Exchange contract form recording the transaction concluded with Stockholms-Maskiner to Philbro who then sent this on to Larson . . . confirmation slips were not always returned.'

That sets out very carefully what the course of dealing was.

b I can see no evidence in that affidavit which entitles this court in interlocutory proceedings to take the view that there was any representation or warranty whatever made by Mr Larsson to the defendants of Larsson's authority to commit the plaintiffs by dealings with the defendants. As the pattern of dealings emerges from that affidavit there was a series of transactions: Larsson to Lowenberg of Philbro; Lowenberg of Philbro passing the order to the defendants, and the defendants then executing that order on the instructions of Philbro; and then the reverse procedure for confirmation taking place. Counsel for Mr Larsson stressed forcibly and I think

c rightly that the only authority that Mr Larsson had was the authority to do that which he did between himself and Lowenberg; that, in any event, all that passed between Mr Larsson and Mr Lowenberg took place in Sweden; and that there was nothing to show that there was any conversation with Mr Larsson in this country or any warranty or representation given by Mr Larsson to anybody in this country which would clearly be said to constitute a contract or a warranty of authority, governed by

d English law.

There is a recent decision of this court in an analogous case, *The Piraeus*[1], which was decided on 10th May 1974. There the question was whether there had been a representation made in this country in respect of the issue of certain bills of lading so that it could be said that the alleged representor could properly be served under RSC Ord 11, r 1(1)(*f*). Lord Denning MR[2], after setting out the facts, said:

e
'On that view of the facts, it is plain to me that the warranty of authority was given in Egypt. It was given when the shipping agents took the documents . . . to the Egyptian bank and got payment against those documents . . . The contract (implied warranty of authority) was made out of the jurisdiction. It was broken out of the jurisdiction. Something was said about a claim for negligent misrepre-

f sentation, so as to bring the case within O. 11, r. 1(h). But this fails for a similar reason. The negligent representation was made in Egypt and acted on in Egypt.'

And if I may quote a few words from my own judgment[3]:

g
'It is accepted that the cause of action for breach of warranty of authority is in substance an action for breach of contract. One therefore asks where the relevant alleged breach of contract was committed.'

For my part, I am quite unable to see that in the present case there is any evidence (any more than there was in *The Piraeus*[1]) which would justify our treating any breach of warranty of authority as a breach of a contract made within the jurisdiction, because any such warranty was not given at any time in this country nor was it broken at any

h time in this country. Accordingly, I cannot see how Donaldson J's order,can be justified under RSC Ord 11, r 1(1)(*f*).

Counsel for the defendants, at the end of his admirable argument, submitted that even so it could be said that there was here a contract with Mr Larsson which was governed by English law; and he relied on a passage in Dicey and Morris[4]. I need not read the whole passage. The material part is in a note to Rule 168:

j

1   [1974] 2 Lloyd's Rep 266
2   [1974] 2 Lloyd's Rep at 268
3   [1974] 2 Lloyd's Rep at 268, 269
4   Conflict of Laws (9th Edn, 1973), p 876

'On the same principle it may be assumed that the liabilities and rights of
agents who act for undisclosed or unnamed principals are governed by the *a*
proper law of the contract made between the agent and the third party, and that
the same would be true of the agent's liability for breach of warranty of authority
or as a *falsus procurator.*'

No authority is cited for that proposition; it may or it may not be right. That
is not a matter for decision on an interlocutory appeal. All I can say is that on the *b*
evidence I can see nothing which can fairly be said to be a contract with Mr Larsson
governed by English law even if the passage in Dicey be correct, as to which I express
no opinion.

It is right to add that we were told by counsel for Mr Larsson that the learned judge,
though he did not give reasons for his decision, accepted this part of the argument
for Mr Larsson. Counsel for the defendants by his cross-notice raised this issue, *c*
but in my judgment the judge's order could not be supported on these grounds
and nor did the judge make his order on these grounds.

I now turn to what in my mind is a much more difficult question, namely whether
or not Donaldson J was justified in refusing to set aside Ackner J's order on the ground
that the action was begun by a writ properly brought against a person 'duly served
within the jurisdiction' so that Mr Larsson though out of the jurisdiction was a *d*
necessary party to that action.

As I have already pointed out, the matter arises in rather curious circumstances.
There was originally an action brought by the plaintiffs, a Swedish company, against
the defendants, an English company carrying on business in London.   Therefore,
as has been pointed out in argument, the plaintiffs had to give an address for service
within the jurisdiction. They properly gave as the address for service the name and *e*
address of the solicitors who acted for them. Since the plaintiffs brought this action
in the High Court, counsel for the defendants rightly submitted that this permitted
the defendants to counterclaim against them, which counterclaim could properly
be served on them at the address given in the writ. But the defendants seek not
merely to counterclaim against the plaintiffs, but also to bring in Mr Larsson as a
defendant to that counterclaim. *f*

I therefore turn to RSC Ord 15, r 3, to see what the rules provide in those circumstances. It is necessary to refer to r 3(1), (2) and (5):

'(1) Where a defendant to an action who makes a counterclaim against the
plaintiff alleges that any other person (whether or not a party to the action) is
liable to him along with the plaintiff in respect of the subject-matter of the *g*
counterclaim, or claims against such other person any relief relating to or
connected with the original subject-matter of the action, then, subject to rule
5(2), he may join that other person as a party against whom the counterclaim
is made.
'(2) Where a defendant joins a person as a party against whom he makes a
counterclaim, he must add that person's name to the title of the action and serve *h*
on him a copy of the counterclaim; and a person on whom a copy of a counterclaim is served under this paragraph shall, if he is not already a party to the
action, become a party to it as from the time of service with the same rights in
respect of his defence to the counterclaim and otherwise as if he had been duly
sued in the ordinary way by the party making the counterclaim . . .
'(5) Where by virtue of paragraph (2) a copy of a counterclaim is required to be *j*
served on a person who is not already a party to the action, the following provisions of these rules, namely, Order 10 (except rule 1(4)), Order 11 (except rule
3) [and then there is a reference to RSC Ords 12, 13 and 75, which I need not worry
about] shall, subject to the last foregoing paragraph, apply in relation to the
counterclaim and the proceedings arising from it as if—(*a*) the counterclaim

a   were a writ and the proceedings arising from it an action; and (b) the party
    making the counterclaim were a plaintiff and the party against whom it is made
    a defendant in that action.'

    The note in the White Book[1] sets out how the action should be entitled when this
    procedure under RSC Ord 15, r 3, is adopted. That of course is what the defendants
    sought to do here.

b   It seems to me clear that the effect of para (5) of r 3 of RSC Ord 15, with its reference
    back to RSC Ord 11, is to oblige a defendant who wishes to serve a counterclaim on a
    person who is not a party to an action and who is outside the jurisdiction to satisfy RSC
    Ord 11. I have already explained why in my judgment the present defendants cannot
    bring themselves under r 1(1)(f). The question is whether they can bring themselves
    under r 1(1)(j). I have already read sub-para (j). Counsel for the defendants put his argu-
c   ment in this way: 'Look at the rule and see what as a matter of the ordinary use of
    language it means, all questions of authority apart. The rule says, "if the action
    begun by the writ being properly brought" (and the action was properly begun by
    the writ, and the counterclaim brought against the plaintiffs was equally properly
    begun) "against a person duly served within the jurisdiction, a person out of the
    jurisdiction is a necessary or proper party thereto". There is here a counterclaim
d   against a person who is duly served within the jurisdiction because the plaintiffs have
    given an address for service within the jurisdiction, and the counterclaim was duly
    served on them at that address. Mr Larsson is a necessary and proper party to that
    counterclaim because that counterclaim against him arises out of the same subject-
    matter as the counterclaim against the plaintiffs and only if Mr Larsson is joined will
    the court be able to decide whether the plaintiffs are bound by some or all of these
e   contracts or whether Mr Larsson is responsible to the defendants for some or all of
    them.'

    Looking solely at the language of r 1(1)(j) and interpreting its language as best
    I can, I am bound to say that for myself if I were unfettered by authority I would say
    that there was much to be said in favour of counsel for the defendants' submission.
    But unfortunately the relevant authorities do not permit this court to adopt so simple
f   a course. The most relevant note is in the Supreme Court Practice[2] and will be found
    under the rubric 'Duly served within the jurisdiction'. The note reads:

        'A person out of the jurisdiction, who has appeared and waived objection to
        the jurisdiction, is not "duly served within the jurisdiction", and cannot by his
        consent confer jurisdiction against the other (John Russell & Co. v. Cayzer, Irvine,
g   Ltd.[3]).'

    Counsel for the defendants accepted that if this part of his argument is to succeed
    he must show that the note is wrong, although it has been there for many years and
    has never been challenged.

    Russell & Co Ltd v Cayzer, Irvine & Co Ltd[3] was a curious case. The plaintiffs were the
h   owners of some goods which had been discharged at Madras from a ship which had
    been requisitioned then by the Indian government. Allegedly without the knowledge
    or consent of the plaintiffs, the goods were then loaded on to a ship belonging to the
    Glasgow United Shipping Co Ltd, which at the material time was under charter to
    Clan Line Steamers Ltd, of which company Cayzer, Irvine & Co Ltd were the
    managers. The ship concerned, the Clan Matheson, was then lost with these goods
j   on board. The appellants, John Russell & Co Ltd, sought to sue in respect of that
    loss. Glasgow United Shipping Ltd were outside the jurisdiction of the English

---

1   Supreme Court Practice 1976, p 168, para 15/3/2
2   Ibid, p 84, para 11/1/17
3   [1916] 2 AC 298, [1916-17] All ER Rep 630

courts; they carried on business in Scotland. Cayzer, Irvine & Co Ltd were also outside the jurisdiction of the English courts for the same reason. Accordingly, as a was emphasised in all the judgments in the Court of Appeal and in the House of Lords, proceedings could not be brought in this country either against Glasgow United Shipping Ltd or against Cayzer, Irvine & Co Ltd because each was carrying on business in Scotland. The writ, in accordance with the practice then and now, was properly marked 'Not for service out of the jurisdiction'. Glasgow United Shipping Ltd decided (no doubt for good reason) that they would submit to the juris- b diction, and English solicitors were therefore instructed to accept service and to appear for them. These solicitors duly accepted service and entered an appearance. Thereafter the appellants sought leave to serve a concurrent writ on Cayzer, Irvine & Co Ltd, under the then equivalent of RSC Ord 11, r 1(1)(j), on the ground that they were necessary parties to the action and were therefore within the rule as it then was. The rule as it then was will be found set out in the law reports[1]. It was then RSC Ord XI, c r 1(g): '. . . any person out of the jurisdiction is a necessary or proper party to an action properly brought against some other person duly served within the jurisdiction.'

Both the Court of Appeal and the House of Lords held that such an order could not properly be made. The judgments of the Court of Appeal were not reported. But counsel for Mr Larsson and for the defendants, with their usual industry, have secured us copies of these judgments from the House of Lords' record. It seems plain when one d reads those judgments, and then reads the speeches in the House of Lords, that certainly two of their Lordships decided the case on wider grounds than did the Court of Appeal. It is clear that what obviously impressed Swinfen Eady LJ was that, apart from the voluntary submission of Glasgow United Shipping Ltd, the appellants' action could never have been brought in this country because both the intended defendants were resident in Scotland. He said: e

'. . . it is not an action properly brought within the meaning of this Rule. This Rule is not so wide as, wherever the cause of action may have arisen, and two persons are joined as Defendants, to enable one of them to give a voluntary undertaking to appear so as to enable the Plaintiff compulsorily then to bring the other Defendant within the jurisdiction. In the present case, true it is the f application has reference to Scottish Defendants, but it would be equally true if it applied to Defendants in any other part of the world. It would come to this: it would extend to a case of this sort that whenever two foreigners are sued, no matter what the cause of action, if one of them will consent and give an undertaking to appear, and will appear within the jurisdiction, you can compulsorily bring the other party here. In my opinion, that is too wide a construction to place g upon this Rule. In my judgment an action is not properly brought against some other person within the jurisdiction when it is not a cause of action that could be brought again him in this country and it is only enabled to be maintained because he has voluntarily chosen to appear.'

Later Swinfen Eady LJ said, and counsel for the defendant relied much on this: h 'I should have had difficulty in saying that the Defendant was not duly served within the jurisdiction.' The two Lords Justices, Pickford and Bankes LJJ, dealt with the matter on the basis that the action was one which was not properly brought.

But when the matter reached their Lordships' House, counsel for the respondents was not called on. The whole matter was dealt with in a single day after only counsel for the appellants had been heard. The speeches were extempore. Viscount Haldane j dealt with the matter on the same basis as had Swinfen Eady LJ, namely that this was an action not 'properly brought'. He expressed no opinion on the meaning of

1 [1916] 2 AC at 299, 300, [1916-17] All ER Rep at 630

'duly served'. But Lord Sumner, whilst agreeing with Viscount Haldane on the
a meaning of 'properly brought', said at the end of his speech[1]:

> 'It is unnecessary to express any opinion as to the effect of the words "duly
> served within the jurisdiction", but if I had had a doubt as to the construction
> of the words "properly brought" I should certainly have expected to find that
> the words "duly served" could be so construed as to give the party out of the
> **b** jurisdiction the same protection.'

Although his Lordship said it was unneccessary to express any opinion as to the
effect of the words 'duly served', he was indicating the tentative opinion that Glasgow
United Shipping Ltd was not a party 'duly served' under the rule. Lord Parmoor
agreed with Viscount Haldane and Lord Sumner, but said nothing about 'duly
c served'. But Lord Wrenbury[2] at the end of his speech, after reading the whole
rule including the words 'duly served', said:

> 'My Lords, those words, to my mind, do not mean founded upon a good cause
> of action. . .'' Properly brought" in this rule means, I think, or at any rate includes, ·
> brought with a due observance of the process of the Court against a person who
> **d** could properly be served with the process of the Court, and not because he
> chooses voluntarily to submit himself to the jurisdiction of the Court. That has
> not happened here. The exact question for determination is this: Can one
> defendant by consent by submitting to the jurisdiction confer jurisdiction as against
> another defendant? My Lords, in my opinion he cannot. I think the action
> mentioned in Order XI., r. 1(g), as one "properly brought" means an action
> **e** brought by a plaintiff against a defendant by virtue of the user of the process
> of the Court—not by user of the process with the addition of a voluntary
> submission by the defendant to the jurisdiction of the Court.'

As I have already pointed out, the Supreme Court Practice clearly treats this case
as a decision on the meaning of the phrase 'duly served within the jurisdiction'. It
f was forcibly submitted to us that when one analyses the speeches that is not so and
that it is primarily a decision on 'properly brought'. I see the force of this argument but I do not think it is open to us so to hold, for to do so would be inconsistent
with the long standing note in the Supreme Court Practice and with the speech of
Lord Sumner and certainly with the speech of Lord Wrenbury. It further seems to me
that that conclusion is reinforced when one comes to consider what might for want
g of a better phrase be called the underlying philosophy of the order to which I have
already referred. RSC Ord 11 confers on an intending plaintiff certain rights against
an intended defendant out of the jurisdiction, which that plaintiff would not possess
at common law. The court has always strictly controlled the circumstances in which
it will exercise its discretion to permit the powers accorded by RSC Ord 11 to be
invoked in an individual case. A plaintiff who issues a writ for service within the
h jurisdiction is entitled to issue and serve that writ as of right. But he is not entitled
to serve a concurrent writ or notice of writ outside the jurisdiction as of right because
such service involves or may involve a trespass on the sovereignty of another country.
RSC Ord 11, r 1(1)(j), is primarily concerned with the case of a plaintiff who wishes
to bring an action against two defendants, to whom I will refer for convenience as the
first defendant and the second defendant. The first defendant is within the jurisdiction.
j The action against him can be properly brought and he can be duly served within the
jurisdiction. The second defendant is without the jurisdiction. Paragraph (1)(j) enables
the court to grant the plaintiff leave in appropriate circumstances to join the second

---

1 [1916] 2 AC at 305, [1916-17] All ER Rep at 632, 633
2 [1916] 2 AC at 306, [1916-18] All ER Rep at 633

defendant as a necessary or proper party to an action brought against the first defendant, being a person against whom the action is properly brought and who has been duly served within the jurisdiction. Clearly, if both the defendants are outside the jurisdiction, para (1)(j) has no application. But it is said that if the first defendant, though outside the jurisdiction, nevertheless voluntarily submits to the jurisdiction and voluntarily accepts service as if he were a person within the jurisdiction and liable to be served within the jurisdiction, the first defendant then becomes a person against whom the action is properly brought and who is duly served within the jurisdiction.

This argument involves that the liability of the second defendant to be sued in this country under RSC Ord 11, r 1(1)(f), depends on whether or not the first defendant (ex hypothesi not liable to be served here) voluntarily submits to the jurisdiction. Thus the position of the second defendant would be adversely affected by the action of the first defendant. Or to put the same point the other way—if the plaintiff persuades the first defendant voluntarily to submit to the jurisdiction and to accept service here, he can then seek to exercise a right under RSC Ord 11 against the second defendant which he would not otherwise possess. So to hold is in my judgment contrary to what was stated by at least two of their Lordships in the House of Lords as well as contrary to the underlying philosophy of RSC Ord 11. The plaintiff is fully entitled to persuade the first defendant voluntarily to submit to the jurisdiction if he can do so. But that is something between him and the first defendant. I cannot think that the second defendant can thereby have his position worsened. His immunity from the provisions of RSC Ord 11 remains unaffected. It is still open to him in a case where the first defendant is before the court only because of his own voluntary submission to say: 'I am not a necessary or proper party to this action within the rule because the action which is already before the court is not properly brought against a person duly served within the jurisdiction; that service on the first defendant within the jurisdiction has been effected only because of his own consent and on the true construction of the rule he is not a party duly served within the jurisdiction.' Accordingly, I think that Mr Larsson's position is unaffected by the fact that the defendants are able to bring this counterclaim against the plaintiffs because the plaintiffs by suing the defendants have thus voluntarily submitted to the jurisdiction.

I therefore reach the conclusion, with great respect to Donaldson J, that his order cannot in principle or on the authorities be supported, though I accept that if it could be supported there would be much to be said in favour of letting that stand as a matter of discretion because it is obviously much more convenient to have all the issues decided together. But in my judgment Mr Larsson is entitled to stand on his strict rights under RSC Ord 11; and, he having—as I think successfully—stood on his strict rights, I would allow the appeal, and set aside the order for service out of the jurisdiction made by Ackner J and so make the order Donaldson J declined to make.

CAIRNS LJ. I agree that this appeal must be allowed and the order for service on Mr Larsson must be set aside. So far as concerns RSC Ord 11, r 1(1)(f), I have nothing to add to what Roskill LJ has said in the course of his judgment. With regard to r 1(1)(j), I agree that this court is constrained by the decision of the House of Lords in *Russell & Co Ltd v Cayzer, Irvine & Co Ltd*[1] to reach the conclusion that the words of the paragraph are not such as to authorise service abroad in such a case as this.

Counsel for the defendants sought to distinguish this case from that of *Russell & Co Ltd v Cayzer, Irvine & Co Ltd*[1] on the ground that in that case each of the defendant companies had an office in Scotland, and for that reason it could be said that the action was not properly brought against the original defendant (because of the special

---

1   [1916] 2 AC 298, [1916-17] All ER Rep 630

provision of the rule which was the predecessor of the present r 1(1)(f) of RSC Ord 11)
in a sense in which it is not true of persons resident in other countries or companies
registered in other countries. It is true that in the judgment of Bankes LJ in the Court
of Appeal the matter was firmly based on the particular rule relating to Scotland
and Ireland, but as I read the judgments of Swinfen Eady and Pickford LJJ they did
not do so. I refer again a short passage which has already been read in the judgment
of Swinfen Eady J:

> 'This Rule is not so wide as, wherever the cause of action may have arisen,
> and two persons are joined as Defendants, to enable one of them to give a volun-
> tary undertaking to appear so as to enable the Plaintiff compulsorily then to
> bring the other Defendant within the jurisdiction. In the present case, true it is
> the application has reference to Scottish Defendants, but [and these are the words
> that I emphasise] it would be equally true if it applied to Defendants in any
> other part of the world.'

Pickford LJ said, towards the end of his judgment:

> 'Under those circumstances, I do not think by voluntarily undertaking to appear
> and submitting to the jurisdiction of the English Court they make the action an
> action properly brought so as to enable third parties to be brought in and to
> affect third parties' rights. They may no doubt submit to the jurisdiction, and
> if so they cannot themselves raise any objection, but I do not think they can by
> that procedure affect the rights of third parties.'

When we come to the speeches in the House of Lords, one finds in none of them
specific reference to the special position of Scotland and Ireland, and in all the speeches,
with the possible exception of that of Viscount Haldane, the position is firmly based
on the view that one party by submitting cannot affect the rights of a different party.
I refer to the speech of Lord Sumner[1]:

> 'In the language of Pickford L.J. in the Court below, the persons who are already
> defendants in the action, although they may submit to the jurisdiction and so
> preclude themselves from raising any objection, cannot by that procedure affect
> the rights of third parties.'

Lord Parmoor[2]:

> 'I think that the words "properly brought" clearly enure to the protection
> of the person out of the jurisdiction. In other respects I should like to adopt what
> what was said by Pickford L.J., with whose judgment I entirely agree.'

Lord Wrenbury[3]:

> 'The exact question for determination is this: Can one defendant by consent
> by submitting to the jurisdiction confer jurisdiction as against another
> defendant? My Lords, in my opinion he cannot.'

I think that all those statements, which I regard as the true ratio decidendi in that
case, apply to this one.

Counsel for the defendants says that there was not in the sense in which the expression was used in that case 'voluntary submission to the jurisdiction' on the part

---

1   [1916] 2 AC at 304, [1916-17] All ER Rep at 632
2   [1916] 2 AC at 305, [1916-17] All ER Rep at 633
3   [1916] 2 AC at 306, [1916-17] All ER Rep at 633

of the plaintiffs here because they did not in terms agree to the jurisdiction of the English court in relation to the counterclaim; they brought themselves within the jurisdiction by bringing the action. And, says counsel for the defendants, if by some previous course of conduct a person makes himself subject to the jurisdiction of the court and is properly served here, then it would be impossible for another party sought to be brought in under r 1(1)(j) to say that the first one had not been properly joined and served within the rule. And, says counsel, consider the case of a first defendant being in England on holiday and served with a writ while he was here, or the case of a company registered abroad and setting up a place of business here. Clearly, either of them could be served, and then r 1(1)(j) could be used to bring in another party; and he says the position here is equivalent.

In my view, it is not equivalent. I accept the submission of counsel for Mr Larsson that the true rule is that reliance cannot be placed by the plaintiff, whether the plaintiff in the original writ or plaintiff by counterclaim, on some voluntary act in relation to the proceedings on the part of the first defendant to the action or defendant to the counterclaim; and I can see no difference in principle between a defendant who consents to the jurisdiction by authorising the service on his solicitors on his behalf and a person who brings an action in this country and so voluntarily submits to the jursidiction.

For those reasons, in addition to those given by Roskill LJ with which I entirely agree, I agree the appeal must be allowed.

BROWNE LJ. I agree with regret that, for the reasons given by both Roskill and Cairns LJJ the appeal should be allowed. It seems to me, as it seemed to Roskill LJ, that it would obviously be convenient for the questions between the defendants and Mr Larsson to be considered and decided by the same court at the same time as the questions between the defendants and the plaintiffs and Indusan are considered and decided; but, in my judgment, it is impossible for us to do other than allow the appeal.

So far as RSC Ord 11, r 1(1)(j), is concerned, I think it might be possible by verbal gymnastics to draw distinctions between this case and *Russell & Co Ltd v Cayzer, Irvine & Co Ltd*[1] on the lines suggested by counsel for the defendants, but in my view to hold that this case is distinguishable from that case would be inconsistent with what I agree with Cairns LJ was the true ratio decidendi of the majority of both the Court of Appeal and the House of Lords in that case. In my view, that ratio decidendi was that one defendant who is out of the jurisdiction cannot by voluntary submission to the jurisdiction affect the rights of another defendant who is also out of the jurisdiction. I need not repeat the passages already cited by Cairns LJ from the judgment of Pickford LJ and the speeches of Lord Sumner, Lord Parmoor and Lord Wrenbury. In my view, therefore, we are bound by that decision of the House of Lords to allow this appeal.

So far as counsel for the defendants relied on RSC Ord 11, r 1(1)(f), I do not think I need add anything to what has already been said about that by Roskill LJ. I agree that the appeal should be allowed on the grounds stated by Roskill and Cairns LJJ.

Appeal allowed. Order of 10th July 1974, service of points of defence and counterclaim on Mr Larsson pursuant thereto and all subsequent proceedings set aside. Leave to appeal to the House of Lords refused.

Solicitors: *McKenna & Co* (for Mr Larsson); *Coward Chance* (for the defendants).

---

1 [1916] 2 AC 298, [1917-18] All ER Rep 630

Appeal

With the leave of the House of Lords, the defendants appealed against the order of the Court of Appeal.

Nicholas Philips for the defendants.
Mr Larsson did not appear and was not represented.

Their Lordships took time for consideration.

28th January. The following opinions were delivered.

VISCOUNT DILHORNE. My Lords, I have had the advantage of reading in draft the speech of my noble and learned friend, Lord Russell of Killowen. I agree with it and with his conclusions and I wish only to add a few observations.

When a court is required to consider whether an action begun by a writ or a counter-claim has been 'properly brought', I doubt very much whether the court has to consider whether or not the claim or counterclaim is made bona fide or for some improper purpose. For a court to do that appears to be likely to involve something of the nature of a trial before the trial of the action. I am inclined to think that 'properly brought' in RSC Ord 11, r 1(1)(j), means no more than brought in accordance with the rules of court. But it is not necessary to decide as to that in this appeal for there is no question as to the genuineness of the defendants' counterclaim against the plaintiffs.

LORD SIMON OF GLAISDALE. My Lords, I have had the advantage of reading in draft the speech prepared by my noble and learned friend, Lord Russell of Killowen. I agree with it, and I would therefore allow the appeal.

RSC Ord 11, r 1(1)(j), represents a concern to hold in balance two considerations which are liable to conflict. On the one hand there is the principle of international law that the courts of this country will not as a general rule seek to exercise jurisdiction over persons resident outside the territorial limits of their jurisdiction. On the other hand there is the desirability that, in legal proceedings in this country, all such persons should be before the courts as are required for justice to be done.

RSC Ord 11, r 1(1)(j), holds the balance between these two considerations by certain requirements which must be met for the court at all to have jursidiction under it, and by a residual discretion even if these requirements are met. Two of the requirements which must be met are contained in the rule itself. First, the action (which includes a conterclaim in an action: RSC Ord 15, r 3(1) and (5)) must be properly brought against a party within the jurisdiction, i e it must be brought in accordance with law, in particular the procedural code set out in the Rules of the Supreme Court (*John Russell & Co Ltd v Cayzer, Irvine & Co Ltd*[1]). Secondly, the writ (or, as the case may be, the counterclaim) in the action must be duly served (i e in accordance with law, particularly the Rules of the Supreme Court) on such party within the jurisdiction.

These two requirements generally involve a third limitation; namely that jurisdiction under para (1)(j) cannot be founded on service made by virtue of another paragraph of RSC Ord 15, r 1(1), i e it is independent of the other heads, not cumulative.

But, even when these stipulated limitations (available to a party outside the jurisdiction ex debito justitiae) are satisfied, the judge in chambers still has a discretion

---

1   [1916] 2 AC 298, [1916-17] All ER Rep 630

whether or not to allow service out of the jurisdiction by virtue of sub-para (j). He will exercise this discretion, mindful that RSC Ord 11, r 1, constitutes an invasion of general principles of international law (see Lord Parker in *Tyne Improvement Comrs v Armement Anversois S/A*[1]), in such a way as to conduce to justice and convenience. It is only in exceptional circumstances that the exercise of such a discretion should be displaced by an appellate court (cf *Evans v Bartlam*[2]; *Charles Osenton & Co v Johnson*[3]).

I agree with my noble and learned friend, Lord Russell of Killowen, that the counter-claim here was properly brought against a party (the plaintiffs) who was in the circumstances within the jurisdiction and who was duly served with it within the jurisdiction. So far as that party (the plaintiffs) is concerned there was no need to rely on any other head of RSC Ord 15, r 1(1). The learned judge in chambers exercised his discretion to allow service of that counterclaim against the respondent (Mr Larsson) outside the jurisdiction. The Court of Appeal set the order aside, not because they considered that the discretion had been wrongly exercised, but because they thought that the authority of *Russell & Co Ltd v Cayzer, Irvine & Co Ltd*[4] compelled them to hold that one or other or both of the two inwritten limitations on the operation of the rule had not been satisfied. For the reasons given by my noble and learned friend, Lord Russell of Killowen, I do not think that *Russell & Co Ltd v Cayzer, Irvine & Co Ltd*[4] did have that effect.

LORD SALMON. My Lords, I have had the advantage of reading in draft the speech of my noble and learned friend, Lord Russell of Killowen. I agree with it and I agree that this appeal should be allowed.

LORD FRASER OF TULLYBELTON. My Lords, I have had the benefit of reading in draft the speech prepared by my noble and learned friend, Lord Russell of Killowen. I agree with it, and for the reasons stated in it I would allow the appeal.

LORD RUSSELL OF KILLOWEN. My Lords, the question in this appeal is whether the facts are such as to confer jurisdiction to give leave to serve a counter-claim out of the jurisdiction. Ackner J on an application ex parte by the present appellants gave leave; Donaldson J on an application by the respondents declined to set aside that order; the Court of Appeal (Cairns, Roskill and Browne LJJ) reversed that decision, holding that the authority of *John Russell & Co Ltd v Cayzer Irvine & Co Ltd*[4] in this House forbade such leave in the circumstances of this case.

The question turns on the provisions of RSC Ord 11, r 1(1). So far as now material this provides:

'. . . service of a writ, or notice of a writ, out of the jurisdiction is permissible with the leave of the Court in the following cases, that is to say [there follow a number of sets of circumstances, none of which applies to the instant case, unless it be:] (j) if the action begun by the writ being properly brought against a person duly served within the jurisdiction, a person out of the jurisdiction is a necessary or proper party thereto . . .'

As will be seen we are not here concerned with service of a writ but with service of a counterclaim. However, RSC Ord 15, r 3(1) and (5), provide for the event, such as

---

1 [1949] 1 All ER 294 at 298, [1949] AC 326 at 338
2 [1937] 2 All ER 646 at 654, [1937] AC 473 at 486
3 [1941] 2 All ER 245 at 250, [1942] AC 130 at 138
4 [1916] 2 AC 298, [1916-17] All ER Rep 630

arose in the present case, of a defendant counterclaiming against the plaintiff joining
another person (whether or not a party) as a party against whom the counterclaim
is made; and in that event the provisions of RSC Ord 11 to which reference has been
made apply in relation to the counterclaim as if the counterclaim were a writ. For
present purposes therefore the enquiry under sub-para (j) is whether we have a case of
'a counterclaim being properly brought against a party served within the jurisdiction,
a person out of the jurisdiction is a necessary or proper party thereto.'

The facts may for present purposes be very briefly stated. The defendants, London
commodity brokers, had dealings in metals with the plaintiffs, a Swedish company
resident in Sweden. On one view of the scope of those dealings the defendants owed
a sum to the plaintiffs. On the other view the plaintiffs owed a sum to the defendants.
The difference in view depended on whether the plaintiffs were a party to certain
dealings in zinc which showed substantial loss. The defendants contend that the
plaintiffs were a party through their alleged agent, Mr Larsson; the plaintiffs deny
any such agency. The plaintiffs issued a writ endorsed with a statement of claim claiming against the defendants moneys due, on the basis of their contention that the
zinc dealings were not their concern. The defendants defended and counterclaimed
against the plaintiffs moneys due from the plaintiffs on the basis of their contention
that Mr Larsson was the agent of the plaintiffs for these zinc dealings. The defendants
wish to join Mr Larsson to the counterclaim in the alternative asserting his breach
of warranty of authority or personal liability. Mr Larsson however is also resident in
Sweden, and service of the counterclaim on him out of the jurisdiction is therefore
necessary.

My Lords, it was not doubted by the Court of Appeal that such a counterclaim is
within RSC Ord 15, r 3(1); nor that within sub-para (j) Mr Larsson is a proper party
thereto; and had the Court of Appeal thought that they had jurisdiction it is clear
that they would have supported the exercise of discretion in favour of the defendants. I see no reason to disagree under any of these heads. The question is therefore
whether the counterclaim was 'properly brought against a person duly served
within the jurisdiction'. Leaving aside authority it appears to me that it was plainly so.
Insofar as propriety relates to some lack of genuineness, or by-purpose, there is no
such suggestion here. Insofar as propriety relates to compliance with the rules of
court there was no failure in such compliance. If a person chooses to commence
proceedings in this jurisdiction he lays himself open to the possibility of a counterclaim by the defendant as well as to a defence. The rules of court permit it subject
to compliance with time requirements. Further there can in my opinion be no doubt
that the plaintiffs were duly served with the defence and counterclaim within the
jurisdiction. RSC Ord 6, r 5, requires in a case such this that the writ be endorsed with
the name and address of the solicitor by whom the plaintiff sues and provides that
that is the plaintiff's address for service. This was done, and the defence and counterclaim were duly served at the plaintiffs' solicitor's address in Essex Street, London.

But, my Lords, are those conclusions inconsistent with the decision of your Lordships' House in *Russell & Co Ltd v Cayzer, Irvine & Co Ltd*[1], as the Court of Appeal
thought? In my opinion they are not. In that case a writ was issued claiming damages
against two defendants both resident out of the jurisdiction, as appeared from their
addresses on the writ, which was marked 'not for service out of the jurisdiction'.
One defendant by its London solicitor accepted service on its behalf. The question
was whether under the then equivalent of sub-para (j) there was jurisdiction to give
leave to serve out of the jurisdiction on the other defendant, and it was held that there
was not. It was the unanimous opinion in this House (and also in the Court of Appeal)
that the action was not 'properly brought' because at the time of the issue of the writ,
both defendants being resident out of the jurisdiction, there was no jurisdiction to

---

1   [1916] 2 AC 298, [1916-17] All ER Rep 630

authorise its service on either defendant; and the fact that one defendant subsequently deprived itself of the ability effectively to contend that it was not properly brought by voluntarily entering an appearance, did not deprive the other defendant of that ability. In the concluding words of the speech of Lord Wrenbury[1]:

'. . ."properly brought"means an action brought by a plaintiff against a defendant by virtue of the user of the process of the Court—not by use of the process with the addition of a voluntary submission by the defendant to the jurisdiction of the Court.'

As I understand them each judgment in the Court of Appeal proceeds on this basis: that the bringing of proceedings by writ in this jurisdiction is to be regarded as a voluntary submission by the plaintiffs to the jurisdiction of the court; that that voluntary submission according to the ratio in *Russell & Co Ltd v Cayzer, Irvine & Co Ltd*[2] cannot prejudice Mr Larsson: and therefore the counterclaim is not within the language, properly understood, of sub-para (j). My Lords, in my opinion this approach extracts from the speeches in *Russell & Co Ltd v Cayzer, Irvine & Co Ltd*[2] a general principle which they do not support. There appears to me to be a radical distinction between the circumstances in which in this House reference was made to voluntary submission, i e in the sense of waiver by a person of his right to assert non-compliance with the rules of the court, and the circumstances of the present case, in which the plaintiffs, by setting in motion the rules of court (by bringing an action that perhaps they could not bring elsewhere) subject themselves, in a sense involuntarily, to the risk of a counterclaim.

In this appeal your Lordships were invited if necessary to reconsider the decision in *Russell & Co Ltd v Cayzer, Irvine & Co Ltd*[2]. Had your Lordships thought it necessary on this occasion so to do, the Treasury Solicitor would have been invited to instruct counsel as amicus curiae, Mr Larsson not having appeared at the hearing.

In summary, my Lords, I am of opinion that the facts of this case come squarely within the language of sub-para (j), and that nothing to the contrary is to be found in the speeches or decision in this House in *Russell & Co Ltd v Cayzer Irvine & Co Ltd*[2].

I would accordingly allow the appeal, restore the orders of Ackner J (dated 10th July 1974) and Donaldson J (dated 22nd November 1974), and order Mr Larsson to pay the costs of the defendants both in the Court of Appeal and of this appeal, including in the latter the costs of the petition for leave to appeal.

Appeal allowed; orders of Ackner and Donaldson JJ restored.

Solicitors: *Coward Chance* (for the defendants).

Gordon H Scott Esq Barrister.

---

1 [1916] 2 AC at 306, [1916-17] All ER Rep at 633
2 [1916] 2 AC 298, [1916-17] All ER Rep 630

a

Re F (a minor) (wardship: appeal)

COURT OF APPEAL, CIVIL DIVISION
STAMP, BROWNE AND BRIDGE LJJ
9th, 10th OCTOBER, 14th NOVEMBER 1975

b

Appeal – Discretion – Review of exercise of discretion – Duty of appellate court – Infant – Care and control order – Judge taking all relevant factors into consideration – No error of law – Whether appellate court having power to interfere with exercise of judge's discretion.

Ward of court – Care and control – Factors to be considered – Contest between natural
c *parent and remoter relative – Father and maternal grandmother – Application of grandmother for care and control of deceased daughter's child – Application opposed by father – Child's parents divorced before mother's death – Mother given custody of child – Mother and child living with grandparents before mother's death – Father having illegitimate child by another woman – Father and other woman marrying – Grandmother hostile to father – Whether in circumstances care and control of child should be awarded to grandmother.*

d

The father and mother married in December 1964 when both were aged 19. The child was born in June 1966. The father and mother quarrelled frequently and violently; some of the violence was witnessed by the child. In 1970 the father met a young woman ('the stepmother') who was 18, and who had already had sexual intercourse with five other men. The mother believed that the father was committing
e adultery with the stepmother and in December 1970 insisted that he leave the matrimonial home. He went to live with the stepmother. In January 1971 he was convicted of indecent assault on another woman. In August he returned to the matrimonial home and forced the mother and child to leave. They went to live with the child's maternal grandmother. The stepmother went to live with the father in the matrimonial home. The mother was granted a decree nisi in December 1971
f which was made absolute in December 1972, the mother retaining custody of the child. The father and stepmother had a daughter ('the half-sister'), born in March 1972, and they married in 1973. The mother and the child moved to a flat in 1973. The mother was in poor health, however, and while she was in hospital the child lived with the grandmother. The mother died on 7th March 1974. Shortly afterwards the father took the child to live with himself and the stepmother. The grandmother
g started wardship proceedings seeking an order for care and control of the child. An interim order was made that the child should stay with the father, with regular access to the grandmother, pending hearing of the application. A welfare report was ordered and the welfare officer recommended that the child remain with her father. At the hearing the judge found that the father 'was at all times anxious that that close relationship between [the child] and the [grandmother] should be continued
h and did everything in his power to see that it worked smoothly. On the other hand the [grandmother] has throughout shown a singleminded determination . . . to bring [the child] back under her roof . . . there is a danger, if [the child] spends substantial periods with her, of [the child] being brought up in an atmosphere which shows dislike of her father.' However, the judge concluded that, in view of the parental violence the child had witnessed, the father's conviction and the evidence of the
j stepmother's pre-marital sexual promiscuity, 'the benefits to be derived [from the father] are appreciably outweighed by the substantial risks that are inherent in the characters of the father and [stepmother]' and he awarded care and control to the grandmother. On appeal by the father, the grandmother contended that, in an infant case, the appellate court should not interfere with the judge's decision unless it was shown that he had erred in law or had taken into account some matter which he ought not

Q

to have taken into account or had failed to take into account a matter which he ought
to have taken into account.   a

Held (Stamp LJ dissenting) – The appeal would be allowed for the following reasons—
  (i) The general principle applicable to appeals was applicable in cases concerning
infants; the appellate court was entitled to set aside the decision of a trial judge if
it was satisfied that, although he had taken all relevant factors into consideration,
his decision was wrong in that he had given insufficient weight, or too much weight, b
to certain of those factors. The appellate court would be reluctant to interfere where
the judge had been influenced to a decisive, or even to a substantial, extent by his
impressions based on seeing and hearing the witnesses, but it could not be said that,
in those circumstances, it should never do so (see p 432 g, p 433 c to e and g, p 434 b c
and g h and p 440 a to c, post); *Evans v Bartlam* [1937] 2 All ER 646, dicta of Viscount
Simon LC, Viscount Maugham and Lord Wright in *Charles Osenton & Co v Johnston*   c
[1941] 2 All ER at 250, 251, 253, 256, 257, of Lord Denning MR in *Ward v James* [1965]
1 All ER at 570, of Davies LJ in *Re O (infants)* [1971] 2 All ER at 748, 749, applied;
Re B (an infant) [1962] 1 All ER 872 distinguished.
  (ii) In the instant case the most important factors were: (a) that the choice was
between a father and grandmother, rather than a father and mother, (b) that the
grandmother's household was ageing and childless, whilst the father's was much d
younger and already contained one other child, and (c) that the attitude of the grandmother, in contrast with that of the father, showed that the probability was that the
grandmother would alienate the child from her father. Although the judge had taken
those factors into consideration, he had failed to give enough weight to them, particularly (b) and (c), or to the welfare officer's opinion that it would be better for the child
to be with her father. Those factors were so overwhelmingly in favour of an order e
giving care and control to the father that they should prevail unless the court were
satisfied that the father and stepmother were unfit to have care and control of the
child. That was not established by the evidence, and it was clear that the impression
they had made in the witness box on the judge had not been a decisive factor in his
conclusion. It was therefore in the best interests of the child that care and control
should be given to the father (see p 436 a to e and g h, p 437 d e and g j, p 438 a f
to f, p 439 g to j and p 440 e and f, post).

Notes
For appeals from the exercise of a judge's discretion, see 30 Halsbury's Laws
(3rd Edn) 452, para 856, and for cases on the subject, see 51 Digest (Repl) 790, 791,
3481-3494.   g
  For the father's right to custody of his child, see 21 Halsbury's Laws (3rd Edn) 191,
192, para 425.

Cases referred to in judgments
Allen v Allen [1948] 2 All ER 413, 112 JP 355, 46 LGR 403, CA, 28(2) Digest (Reissue)
  798, 1221.   h
B (an infant), Re [1962] 1 All ER 872, [1962] 1 WLR 550, CA, 28(2) Digest (Reissue)
  811, 1285.
B (B) v B (M) [1969] 1 All ER 891, sub nom *B (B P M) v B (M M)* [1969] P 103, [1969] 2
  WLR 862, sub nom *B v B* 133 JP 245, DC, 27(2) Digest (Reissue) 1006, 8076.
Blunt v Blunt [1943] 2 All ER 76, [1943] AC 517, 112 LJP 58, 169 LT 33, HL, 27(1) Digest
  (Reissue) 565, 4119.   j
*Breen v Amalgamated Engineering Union (now Amalgamated Engineering and Foundry
  Workers Union)* [1971] 1 All ER 1148, [1971] 2 QB 175, [1971] 2 WLR 742, 10 KIR 120,
  CA.
Campbell (Donald) & Co Ltd v Pollak [1927] AC 732, [1927] All ER Rep 1, 96 LJKB 1093,
  137 LT 656, HL, 36 Digest (Repl) 366, 42.

a *Evans v Bartlam* [1937] 2 All ER 646, [1937] AC 473, 106 LJKB 568, 157 LT 311, HL,
   50 Digest (Repl) 401, *1113*.
   Gardner v Jay (1885) 25 Ch D 50, 54 LJCh 762, 52 LT 395, CA, 51 Digest (Repl) 651,
   2588.
   Grimshaw v Dunbar [1953] 1 All ER 350, [1953] 1 QB 408, [1953] 2 WLR 332, CA, 31(2)
   Digest (Reissue) 1116, *8655*.
   H v H and C [1969] 1 All ER 262, [1969] 1 WLR 208, CA, 27(2) Digest (Reissue) 905,
b *7256*.
   Hennell v Ranaboldo [1963] 3 All ER 684, [1963] 1 WLR 1391, CA, 51 Digest (Repl)
   643, *2522*.
   Holland v Holland [1918] P 273, [1918-19] All ER Rep 882, 87 LJP 142, 119 LT 266, 27(2)
   Digest (Reissue) 780, *6244*.
   J v C [1969] 1 All ER 788, [1970] AC 668, [1969] 2 WLR 540, HL, 28(2) Digest (Reissue)
c 800, *1230*.
   Kilpatrick v Dunlop 1916 SC 631, HL.
   O (infants), Re [1971] 2 All ER 744, [1971] Ch 748, [1971] 2 WLR 784, CA.
   Onassis and Calogeropoulos v Vergottis [1968] 2 Lloyd's Rep 403, HL; *rvsg* [1968] 1 Lloyd's
   Rep 294, CA; *rvsg* [1967] 1 Lloyd's Rep 607.
   Osenton (Charles) & Co v Johnston [1941] 2 All ER 245, [1942] AC 130, 110 LJKB 420,
d 165 LT 235, HL, 51 Digest (Repl) 681, *2840*.
   Powell v Streatham Manor Nursing Home [1935] AC 243, [1935] All ER Rep 58, 104 LJKB
   304, 152 LT 563, HL, 51 Digest (Repl) 816, *3720*.
   Thornley v Palmer [1969] 3 All ER 31, sub nom *Re Thornley, Thornley v Palmer* [1969]
   1 WLR 1037, CA, Digest (Cont Vol C) 364, *9799a*.
   Ward v James [1965] 1 All ER 563, [1966] 1 QB 273, [1965] 2 WLR 455, [1965] 1 Lloyd's
e Rep 145, CA, 17 Digest (Reissue) 213, *854*.
   Watt (or Thomas) v Thomas [1947] 1 All ER 582, [1947] AC 484, [1948] LJR 515, 176
   LT 498, 1947 SC (HL) 45, HL; *rvsg* 1946 SC 81, 51 Digest (Repl) 815, *3713*.
   Willoughby v Willoughby [1951] P 184, CA, 28(2) Digest (Reissue) 798, *1222*.

   Case also cited
f *B (T A) (an infant), Re* [1970] 3 All ER 705, [1971] Ch 270.

   Appeal
   This was an appeal by the defendant ('the father') against the order of Bagnall J
   dated 15th May 1975, whereby he ordered, inter alia, that, the father's child ('the
   child') having become a ward of court by virtue of s 9(2) of the Law Reform
g (Miscellaneous Provisions) Act 1949, during her minority or until further order she
   should be committed to the care and control of the plaintiff, her maternal grandmother, and that the grandmother should allow the father reasonable access, including staying access, to the child. The grounds of appeal were (i) that the judge's decision
   was wrong in law in that he had failed to take account of and consider the welfare of
   the child as the first and paramount consideration; (ii) that the judge was wrong in
h exercising his discretion in favour of the grandmother; and (iii) that the judge's
   decision was against the weight of the evidence. The facts are set out in the judgment
   of Stamp LJ.

   William Glossop for the father.
   J J Davis for the grandmother.
j   *Cur adv vult*
   14th November. The following judgments were read.

   STAMP LJ. This is an appeal from an order of Bagnall J made on 15th May 1975
   in wardship proceedings giving the care and control of the child to the plaintiff,
   who is the child's maternal grandmother.

The child's parents were married on 12th December 1964, her mother then being
19 and her father about the same age. She herself was born on 6th June 1966. Her **a**
mother's parents, the plaintiff, whom I will call 'the grandmother', and her husband,
live in the neighbourhood of the child's home.

Five years ago, in the middle of 1970 when the child was about four years of age,
her father met a young woman, who is now the child's stepmother. The stepmother
was then about 18. She had had her first sexual experience when she was 16. The
judge described her as somewhat promiscuous in that regard. She confessed to having **b**
had sexual intercourse with five other men between the age of 16 and 18. The
mother, having formed the opinion that the father was committing adultery with
the stepmother, made it plain to him on 10th December 1970 that she thought he
should leave the home. This he did and went to live with the stepmother in a flat
nearby. The judge remarked in the course of his judgment:

c

> 'Shortly afterwards on 4th January 1971 came the culmination of a dis-
> creditable incident in the father's life. Having been charged with the offences
> of attempted rape and indecent assault, he pleaded guilty to the latter and
> lesser offence; that plea was accepted; the more serious charge was not pursued.
> He was duly convicted by the magistrates and fined £75 with an alternative of six
> months' imprisonment.'

d

The judge remarked in referring to this incident that he was not there to try that
episode, which had already been dealt with.

In August 1971, that is to say not much more than four years ago, the father returned
to the home and in September 1971 he insisted on the mother and the child leaving
the house in what the judge described as 'circumstances which made it impossible
both physically and otherwise for them to return'. They went to live with the **e**
grandmother. The judge in recounting the history of the matter continued thus:

> 'This episode was the start of a dispute between the father and the mother
> as to the rights in and over the matrimonial home which I think was ultimately
> disposed of by the father retaining the home and the mother having substantially
> the whole of the furniture. That was effectively the end of the marriage, and **f**
> apart from the obvious allegation of adultery the mother also alleged, and
> the father has admitted, that from time to time he offered violence to her.
> I am, of course, not trying here the matrimonial dispute and I am conscious
> that it is very seldom if ever that the disruption of a marriage can be attributed
> solely to one of the parties, a state of affairs sometimes summarised in the
> aphorism "happily married men do not go off with other women". I am content **g**
> to assume that in this, as in the majority of marriages, there were faults on
> both sides. I am only concerned with that aspect of the case insofar as it sheds
> light on the character and temperament of those persons with whom I am
> concerned.'

In matrimonial proceedings before the justices in July 1971 the mother obtained **h**
an order committing the custody of the child to her and an order on the father for
him to pay £2 per week for the child's maintenance and £1 per week for the mother.
At that time the father's income was modest and the mother presented a petition
for divorce. It was not contested and on 20th December 1971 a decree nisi was pronounced. It was made absolute on 29th December 1972, the mother retaining custody
of the child.

j

The mother had two married sisters living in the neighbourhood, one of whom
is Mrs H. From the time of the final separation in September 1971, when the child
was just over five, until March 1973, when she was 6½, the child and her mother
lived with the grandmother. During this period it was diagnosed that the mother
was suffering from cancer and for two years she was from time to time in hospital.

a

Nevertheless, as I understand it, the mother in March 1973 obtained a flat quite near the home of Mrs H. During the periods when the mother was in hospital the child was with her grandmother. Tragically for the child, her mother died on 7th March 1974 at her grandmother's home, having been discharged from hospital a week earlier. During that week the child stayed with her mother's sister, Mrs H. She was then a little short of eight years old.

b

About 11 days later, after making preliminary overtures, the father came to Mrs H's house and removed the child to his home. He had by then been married to the step-mother for nearly a year and they had had a daughter, then two years old. During the period from the time he turned mother and child out of the house down to the time of the mother's death, the father had, so the judge found, seen the child, in the sense of spending time with her, comparatively infrequently and the judge went on as follows:

c

'He bought her some clothes and I think other presents. He continued to pay for her maintenance only the £2 a week ordered by the justices, though as will appear his financial situation had significantly improved since the date on which the relevant order was made. I must, however, bear in mind that there were undoubtedly difficulties in the way of the father maintaining contact with [the child] and in particular in visiting her at the home of either the mother or the [grandmother] or Mrs [H]. It perhaps does not need to be stated that he was plainly unwelcome in each of those establishments. I am, however, satisfied that the account he gave in his affidavit of the frequency of his contact with [the child] during that period was exaggerated. Until then [the child] had treated the [grandmother's] home as in all respects the equivalent of her own home. She thereafter started to treat the father's home as her home.'

d

e

Whatever the reason why her father had seen little of her during the three years then last past, to have removed her so soon after the heartbreaking death of her mother to a home presided over by him and a stepmother whom she can hardly have known was, so I would have thought, at least unthoughtful; the judge does not in terms advert to this in his judgment, but it may have been one of the incidents which fortified his opinion regarding the father's suitability to bring up his daughter.

f

With commendable speed the grandmother issued an originating summons on 4th April 1974 asking for the child to be made a ward of court and seeking her care and control. As the result of an ex parte, and then an inter partes, interlocutory application, an order was made, the effect of which was that pending the hearing of the originating summons the child was to stay with her father but to enjoy regular and frequent but not staying access with the grandmother, and a welfare report was ordered. It is a deplorable fact that the originating summons issued on 4th April 1974 did not come on for hearing until May 1975. This delay had an important impact in considering what would be for her benefit in the future.

g

It is at this point that I should, I think, set out verbatim the judge's further findings and the reasons which he gave for coming to the conclusion that he did; a conclusion, if I read those reasons correctly, based primarily on his assessment of the characters of the grandmother, the father and stepmother. The judgment proceeds as follows:

h

'[The child] started to attend, and she still attends, school . . . which is only a few minutes' walk from the father's home, and she has visited the [grandmother] for the day on substantially every Sunday. It is to the father's credit that he was at all times anxious that that close relationship between [the child] and the [grandmother] should be continued and did everything in his power to see that it worked smoothly. On the other hand the [grandmother] has throughout shown a singleminded determination to reverse the status now existing and to bring [the child] back under her roof to be brought up by her. Leaving aside occasions on which she may well have found it to fit in with her other arrangements to

j

move in the vicinity of the father's home to see how things were going, she kept in the form of letters ultimately sent to her solicitor, and from which to some extent *a* when giving her evidence she refreshed her memory, a running account of all the visits paid by [the child] to her in almost inconceivable detail. From her evidence it is plain that those records contained criticisms of matters of detail in the father's upbringing of [the child], but I say at once I am satisfied that there is nothing in those criticisms. Apart from that, the [grandmother], and I think so far as it is relevant Mrs [H] also, have not shrunk from making promises to [the child] of *b* advantages that might accrue to her if indeed in the end she returned to live with the [grandmother]. There is therefore on that aspect of the case a marked contrast between the attitude of the [grandmother] and that of the father to the ultimate outcome of these proceedings. That state of uncertainty continuing, as it has now for some 14 months, necessarily had an important effect on [the child] herself. I think that from the material I have had at my disposal that [the child], *c* though perhaps not mentally outstanding, is of good average intelligence in ordinary matters and a sensitive child. She has throughout the period been conscious of the possibility of a further change in her environment and upbringing and of the rivalry in that respect between the [grandmother] and her family on the one hand, and the father and to some extent [the stepmother] on the other. Inevitably [the child] has found her loyalties divided. She likes spending *d* her days with the [grandmother] and has plainly been sad when the time has come to leave and go home again. This has, I think, produced a quietness and introspection for a short period after her return to her father's house, but I have no doubt that she has quickly readjusted herself to live there and has been assisted in doing so by the presence of her young half-sister and the undoubtedly satisfactory environment which she has found herself in at school. I have been *e* assisted to a very great degree in reaching these conclusions as to [the child's] temperament by the short but extremely helpful report that has been prepared by Mrs Hampton, the welfare officer, and also by the further explanation that she gave orally before me of the matters to which she refers in her written report. I have not seen [the child] herself, though I was pressed to do so by counsel for the [grandmother], but discouraged from doing so by counsel for the father. *f* I am conscious that there is perhaps an increasing tendency on the part of those who have to decide questions such as this to seek assistance from a discussion with even so young a child as [the child]. Nevertheless I decided not to do so because I thought that, having regard to the artificial circumstances that had been caused in the past 12 months by the existence of these proceedings and the attitudes of the several parties to them, anything [the child] told me as to *g* her own wishes would be an unreliable guide to decision. Moreover, the experience would have placed still more strain on her divided loyalties to which I have referred, and in the end if I find that my decision gives effect to her wishes no real advantage would have accrued. If, on the other hand, I find that my duty requires me to reach a conclusion contrary to her wishes, perhaps still further harm might be done. *h*

'Three conclusions I can reach and state without further elaboration: so far as material things are concerned—accommodation, furniture and all the material trappings of a house—there is nothing to choose between that offered by the [grandmother] and that offered by the father. Secondly, I think, and this pays a clear tribute to [the child's] temperament, from the point of view of day to day living, schooling, playing and all the other concomitants of a little girl's life *j* she would be equally happy in either home. Thirdly, though she has now lived, as I have said, for 14 months with the father and [stepmother], such has been the continuity of her relationship with the [grandmother] that no psychological, as it must now be termed, disturbance would be caused to her if in the end she were to go back and live with the [grandmother]. In those circumstances my a decision must, I think, ultimately turn on the characters of the principal parties concerned as I have been able to ascertain them from the written evidence, from the welfare report and from the opportunity that I have had of seeing on the one side the [grandmother] and Mrs [H], and on the other side the father and [stepmother] in the witness box. The [grandmother] is now about 60 and her husband who is still employed, but not underground, in the coal mines . . . is near to that age of 65 at which he will retire. The [grandmother] is, I think,

b the dominant personality in her household and perhaps in her whole family. I have already had occasion to refer to her determination in the context of these proceedings, and I have no doubt that it is a characteristic that plays a large part in the whole of her existence. There is no doubt whatever of her love for [the child] which is not the less because, as I think, it reflects in some measure her love for the mother and her utterly natural grief at the mother's death at

c so young an age. She has, as I have said, criticised the father and unless there is a substantial change, the [grandmother's] character is such that there is a danger, if [the child] spends substantial periods with her, of [the child] being brought up in an atmosphere which shows dislike of her father. As to Mrs [H], there was some criticism of her, as indeed there was of the mother, in the father's Affidavit, but creditably as I think to everyone concerned those criticisms were

d not pursued in cross-examination, and as far as I am concerned no adverse comment is to be made of her. She is, I have no doubt, a competent young mother to the child that she now has and in so far as she was concerned in looking after [the child], she would, as the saying goes, treat [her] as part of the family. I should interpose that I have not seen Mrs [H's] sister, the [grandmother's] other surviving daughter. I understand her to be happily married with, I think, two

e children, and I have no doubt that I should proceed so far as it is relevant on the footing that what I have said about Mrs [H] could equally be said about her sister.

'The father has made his own way in business and is now adequately if not comfortably financially situated. His last tax returns showed a profit from the business of some £3,000 for the year. I have already referred in complimentary

f terms to the fairness that he has shown in preserving the relationship between [the child] and the [grandmother] but he undoubtedly strongly feels that as her father he should now have the joy and the responsibility of bringing up [the child]. However he has undoubtedly shown himself capable of violence and, as he admitted, some of the violence in the matrimonial context was witnessed by [the child]. Though it is inherent in my attitude to the matrimonial

g dispute that some such violence may have been provoked, it remains part of his make-up and its existence is confirmed by his own ultimate oral account of the circumstances leading to his conviction in January 1971. He also confessed that in the same year he had been convicted of a relatively minor stealing offence and had been in some similar trouble leading to a probation order during his youth. Without further elaboration these facts reveal defects of character which

h must cast doubt on his suitability to bring up a young girl. The existence of those defects was to some small extent, I thought, confirmed by the manner in which he gave his evidence, and as I have foreshadowed, I found him in some respects which I need not particularise less than frank both in his written and oral evidence. [The stepmother] is now 23. She had her first experience of sexual intercourse when she was only 16 and was then, as she told me, in some respects

j promiscuous in that regard, a course of conduct which no doubt led to the consummation of her affair with the father. Her attitude to that aspect of morality was, I thought, confirmed by the answers she gave in cross-examination to questions designed to discover what would be her attitude towards the solution of the inevitable problems that would in due course beset [the child]. This behaviour and [the stepmother's] attitude to which I have referred no doubt reflect the relaxed moral standards of the times, standards which had been wholly unacceptable to earlier and more censorious generations, but this very relaxation *a* requires, as it is sometimes said to be justified by, a greater sense of responsibility not only in the young themselves but in those who by virtue of relationship or public duty are responsible for their guidance and upbringing. The character of [the stepmother] leaves me in doubt whether she could be relied upon to give that wise counsel and sure guidance that are so necessary to a young girl growing up and maturing through adolescence into womanhood. *b*

'[Counsel] founds his argument for the father on three principal submissions. First he says a move to live with the [grandmother] would create yet another disturbance and a harmful disturbance in the life of [the child]. That aspect of the matter I have already dealt with and I say no more about it. Secondly, he says that the father is, as is sometimes unnecessarily said, the biological father of [the child] and there are accordingly advantages for her in being brought up *c* by him, not only deriving from that relationship but from his age or perhaps I should say his youth and that of [the stepmother], affected as they would be by the presence of [the half-sister] and possibly other children as half-sisters and brothers. Thirdly, he points to the corresponding disadvantages inherent in the [grandmother's] age and that of her husband and in their household where there would be no other children and where those responsible for [the child's] *d* upbringing would be subject to potential if not actual disabilities inherent in their ages. That disadvantage is, of course, to some extent counteracted by the presence of [the child's] aunts to whom I have referred and existing and possibly future cousins.

'Those arguments are formidable and they are made more formidable by the attitude to the father displayed by the [grandmother] and to a lesser extent *e* by Mrs [H] and indeed the whole family. In treating as I am required to do the welfare of [the child] as the first and paramount consideration, I must look not only to the immediate future but to the whole of [the child's] development through the years of her minority. In doing so I have reached the conclusion that the benefits to be derived if I accede to the father's arguments are appreciably outweighed by the substantial risks that are inherent in the characters of the *f* father and [stepmother] as they have presented themselves to me.

'In my judgment [the child's] welfare will best be served if she returns to live with and be brought up by the [grandmother]. I add only this. The course I have adopted imposes a heavy responsibility on the [grandmother], her surviving daughters and their families. The change of home environment should be accompanied by a change of heart in all of them, particularly in their attitude *g* to the father and to [the stepmother]. The past, regrettable though they may have regarded it, must not be allowed to dominate the future, and [the child] must be taught and encouraged to love and respect her father and to find affection for [the stepmother] and [the half-sister] and any other children the father may have. If that is done she may well have the best of both worlds and access arrangements on which I will hear submissions must be made to that end.' *h*

The law to be applied in determining in whom the care and control of a child should be placed is, in my view, very conveniently and concisely stated in the speech of Lord MacDermott in *J v C*[1]:

'... when all the relevant facts, relationships, claims and wishes of parents, *j* risks, choices and other circumstances are taken into account and weighed, the course to be followed will be that which is most in the interests of the child's welfare as that term has now to be understood.'

---

1 [1969] 1 All ER 788 at 821, [1970] AC 668 at 710, 711

a In the instant case it is not submitted that the judge took into account anything which he should not have taken into account or failed to take into account something which he ought to have taken into account. It is not submitted that he erred in law or departed from principle. What is said is simply that he exercised his discretion wrongly and that his decision was plainly wrong.

What is said, among other things, is that in coming to his conclusion the judge placed too much weight on the factors which he took into account as favouring the *b* grandmother's claim and too little weight on the factors favouring the claim of the father. I am bound to say that in relation to a judgment so careful as that which I have read I find the argument based on weight an elusive one. The judge did not award so many points to the father and so many to the grandmother and then conclude that the grandmother had won more than the father; and it appears to me that the submission based on weight really comes to this. That because the judge *c* has erroneously come down in favour of the grandmother he must have placed too much weight on some factor favouring her or too little weight on some factor favouring the father: a submission which assumes that which falls to be determined. And I think what the submission comes to is that if you take all the circumstances into account the judge exercised his discretion wrongly or was plainly wrong. In other words this court is being asked to substitute its own discretion for that of the judge.

d Of course it is common ground that this court has power to reverse or vary an order made by a judge in the exercise of his discretion. Of that there can be no sort of doubt. It is equally clear that in a proper case it has a duty to do so. But the criticial question is whether this is a proper case to do so. Because we were invited to hold in effect that, if a judge in an appellate court comes to the conclusion or a clear conclusion that he would have exercised his discretion in a way different from that in *e* which the trial judge has done, he ought to reverse the conclusion of the trial judge, I find it necessary to consider not primarily that question but what is a somewhat different one: the question in what circumstances an appellate court ought to do so in an infant case where the trial judge has seen those most concerned and had the advantage of a welfare officer's report and has based his conclusion on his estimate of the characters and personality of those concerned.

f In approaching the question I gratefully borrow the language of Sir Jocelyn Simon P in *B (B) v B (M)*[1] where he said:

> 'The second preliminary matter I must deal with is what is the proper attitude of an appellate court to a court which is exercising a discretionary jurisdiction. Some of the decisions in the Court of Appeal on this question are not entirely *g* easy to reconcile. But, in my view, the matter is stated authoritatively in the speech of Viscount Simon, L.C., in *Blunt* v. *Blunt*[2], with which the other learned Law Lords agreed.'

Having said that, Sir Jocelyn Simon P quoted the well-known passage from Viscount Simon LC's speech[3]. It was in these terms:

h
> 'This brings me to a consideration of the circumstances in which an appeal may be successfully brought against the exercise of the Divorce Court's discretion. If it can be shown that the court acted under a misapprehension of fact in that it either gave weight to irrelevant or unproved matters or omitted to take into account matters that are relevant, there would, in my opinion, be ground for *j* an appeal. In such a case the exercise of discretion might be impeached, because the court's discretion will have been exercised on wrong or inadequate materials.

---

1 [1969] 1 All ER 891 at 901, [1969] 103 at 115
2 [1943] 2 All ER 76, [1943] AC 517
3 [1943] 2 All ER at 79, [1943] AC at 526

But, as was recently pointed out in this House in another connection in *Charles Osenton & Co. v. Johnston*[1]: "The appellate tribunal is not at liberty merely to *a* substitute its own exercise of discretion for the discretion already exercised by the judge. In other words, appellate authorities ought not to reverse the order merely because they would themselves have exercised the original discretion, had it attached to them, in a different way. But if the appellate tribunal reaches the clear conclusion that there has been a wrongful exercise of discretion in that no weight, or no sufficient weight, has been given to relevant considerations . . . *b* then the reversal of the order on appeal may be justified." *Osenton's* case[2] was one in which the discretion being exercised was that of deciding whether an action should be tried by an official referee, and the material for forming a conclusion was entirely documentary and was thus equally available to the appellate court. The reason for not interfering, save in the most extreme cases, with the judge's decision under the Matrimonial Causes Act, 1937, s. 4, is of a *c* far stronger character, for the proper exercise of the discretion in such a matter [and I emphasise these following words] largely depends on the observation of witnesses and on a deduction as to matrimonial relations and future prospects which can best be made at the trial.'

We were referred to a number of authorities in this court, the dicta in which are *d* indeed difficult to reconcile, but as a matter of decision the reconciliation is in my judgment to be found by reference to the remarks of Viscount Simon LC towards the end of the passage I have quoted. There he contrasts one kind of discretion with another, drawing a distinction between interfering with the discretion to decide whether an action should be tried by an official referee where the Court of Appeal is in as good a position as the court below to exercise the discretion, and a discretion *e* the proper exercise of which 'largely depends on the observation of witnesses and on a deduction as to matrimonial relations and future prospects which can best be made at the trial'.

The reason for not interfering is not less strong where the discretion has been exercised in a matter relating to the care of a child where all the relevant facts, relations, claims and wishes of parents, risks, choices and other circumstances can *f* best be considered and weighed by the judge who has tried the case and has had the opportunity of seeing the rival claimants, hearing their views and assessing their character and personality and fitness to have the care of a child. As was said in another context[3]:

'Under these circumstances it is impossible that the Court of Appeal should *g* take upon itself to say, by simply reading printed and written evidence, which is right, when it has not had that decisive test of hearing the verbal evidence and seeing the witnesses, which the judge had who had to determine the question of fact, and to determine which story to believe . . .'

And so, consistently with the views expressed by the House of Lords in *Blunt v* *h* *Blunt*[4], the majority of this court in *Re B (an infant)*[5] (Lord Evershed MR, and Harman LJ) decided that it was wrong to substitute the discretion of the appellate tribunal for that of the justices who had heard the case, even though each of them thought that had he heard the case at first instance he would have decided otherwise. This, I respectfully add, appears to me good sense and the decision is one binding

j

---

1   [1941] 2 All ER 245 at 250, [1942] AC 130 at 138
2   [1941] 2 All ER 245, [1942] AC 130
3   *Kilpatrick v Dunlop* 1916 SC 631 at 632, per Lord Halsbury
4   [1943] 2 All ER 76, [1943] AC 517
5   [1962] 1 All ER 872, [1962] 1 WLR 550

a on this court. Because the personality and character of the parents are often decisive matters this court has insisted on the desirability of the judge who tries the case seeing the parents: see for example *H v H and C*[1]. Are the views of the judge, who complying with that precept has founded his opinion on the character of the parties, to be set at nought by an appellate court which has only the dry words of a transcript and the expressed opinion of the judge to guide it. A judge has not the tongue of an angel to convey his impression of the character of a parent or of that parent's

b suitability to care for and bring up a child, and however carefully his language may be chosen to describe that impression something will be lacking. And, if I may be permitted to speak from experience, a judge giving judgment in an infant case may, for fear of embittering relations which in the interests of the infant ought to be preserved, hesitate to express himself in too downright or offensive terms; for in the exercise of what has been called a difficult and delicate jurisdiction the least that

c is said to justify an adverse conclusion as to the fitness of a parent the better may bitterness be soothed. No doubt he must give his reasons but his duty to the child is not to be submerged in deference to a possible appeal.

Relying on dicta of this court in *Re O (infants)*[2], it was, however, urged on behalf of the father that the proper attitude of an appellate court to a court which has exercised the discretionary jurisdiction in relation to an infant has been radically

d affected by the decision of this court in *Ward v James*[3]; and so by implication it is suggested that the principle stated by Viscount Simon LC is no longer applicable. I must therefore consider the effect of those two cases. That the passages relied on in *Re O*[2] were dicta only is, I think, conceded. There the justices in determining the case against the mother had in the summary of their reasons given as one of them that 'the environment of a public house was not the best place for young children

e although we know that the wife has made successful efforts to find alternative accommodation for them'. There were other unconvincing reasons for depriving the mother of custody but in giving that particular reason the justices had taken something into account against the mother which ought to have been taken into account in her favour, and the appellate court sent the case back for a rehearing. It was, as Davies LJ remarked on appeal to this court[4], 'a curious reason'. But Davies LJ went

f on to say, after referring to *Re B (an infant)*[5], that since *Ward v James*[3] the climate of opinion had changed drastically.

Ward v James[3] had nothing to do with infants. The discretion which came under review by this court was the discretion to order a trial by a judge alone or a trial by jury. The judge had exercised that discretion in a personal injuries case by ordering a trial by jury. It was pointed out in effect that the assessment of damges in per-

g sonal injuries cases is better done by judges who are accustomed to do it than by juries who cannot be made aware of the practice. It followed that in a personal injuries case a judge should only order a trial by jury in special circumstances. Now, as I read that case, it was not one in which this court was laying down any rule governing the principles on which an appellate court will interfere with the exercise of a discretion by the judge in a lower court, but merely laying down a principle in

h accordance with which the court ought to exercise its absolute discretion in a personal injuries case. The judge not having paid regard to that principle had not exercised his discretion correctly. It was a case in which the Court of Appeal was just as well placed as was the judge in the court below to exercise the discretion and where, in the view of the Court of Appeal, the judge in the court below had exercised his discretion wrongly because he had not taken a material consideration into account.

j

1   [1969] 1 All ER 262, [1969] 1 WLR 208
2   [1971] 2 All ER 744, [1971] Ch 748
3   [1965] 1 All ER 563, [1966] 1 QB 273
4   [1971] 2 All ER at 747, [1971] Ch at 753
5   [1962] 1 All ER 872, [1962] 1 WLR 550

With all respect to what was said in *Re O*[1], I cannot regard *Ward v James*[2] as laying down any principle which ought to be applied in relation to an infant case and to hold otherwise would, in my judgment, be to fly in the face of *Blunt v Blunt*[3].

The dicta in *Re O*[4] on which reliance is placed by the appellant are to be found in the judgment of Davies LJ, where he said this:

'In my judgment, however, since the decision in *Ward v James*[2], the climate of opinion with regard to this matter has changed drastically. That can be well illustrated by a decision in this court to which Edmund Davies LJ was a party, *Thornley v Palmer*[5]. That was not a custody case. It concerned an application by a widow under the Inheritance (Family Provision) Act 1938, which had been heard by Buckley J, who had come to the conclusion that the wife was entitled to a small sum of money only, and this court took the view that the sum was indequate. Plainly it was a discretionary matter, in one sense, for the learned judge had to decide how much the widow was entitled to; but that did not stand in the way of this court interfering with the discretion. Harman LJ said[6]: "BUCKLEY, J., does not explain why he thought that £100 rather than any other sum was right, and I do not complain of that because, after all, it is a matter of impression. It is a matter, says counsel for the third defendant, of discretion; the court *may* award such a sum as it thinks 'reasonable'. But, although I quite agree that the court would never interfere if it merely thought there was some slight excess or deficiency, if it comes to the conclusion that the judge was quite wrong in the view that he took and that it ought to have been much more or much less, then I think the court is entitled to interfere; and I think that that is the position here." Then Edmund Davies LJ said[7]: "The opening submission of counsel for the third defendant was that this appeal is against the exercise of a judicial discretion . . . and that, accordingly, the plaintiff must establish that the judge erred in principle if she is to succeed. With respect to counsel, such a submission flies in the face of the House of Lords decision in *Evans* v. *Bartlam*[8], where LORD WRIGHT said: 'It is clear that the Court of Appeal should not interfere with the discretion of a judge acting within his jurisdiction, unless the court is clearly satisfied that he was wrong. But the court is not entitled simply to say that, if the judge had jurisdiction, and had all the facts before him, the Court of Appeal cannot review his order, unless he is shown to have applied a wrong principle. The court must, if necessary, examine anew the relevant facts and circumstances, in order to exercise by way of review a discretion which may reverse or vary the order.' In the light of these observations (which were cited with approval by VISCOUNT SIMON, L.C., in *Charles Osenton & Co.* v. *Johnston*[9]), I approach this appeal on the basis that, if the plaintiff has succeeded in clearly demonstrating that, having decided to make an order, BUCKLEY, J., then proceeded to make one which nevertheless substantially failed to provide reasonable provision for her maintenance, it is not only the right but the *duty* of this court to interfere." I, with respect, entirely agree with those obervations and would follow them. In my considered opinion the law now is that if an appellate court is satisfied that the decision of the court

---

1   [1971] 2 All ER 744, [1971] Ch 748
2   [1965] 1 All ER 563, [1966] 1 QB 273
3   [1943] 2 All ER 76, [1943] AC 517
4   [1971] 2 All ER at 748, [1971] Ch at 754
5   [1969] 3 All ER 31, [1969] 1 WLR 1037
6   [1969] 3 All ER at 33, [1969] 1 WLR at 1040
7   [1969] 3 All ER at 35, [1969] 1 WLR at 1042
8   [1937] 2 All ER 646 at 654, [1937] AC 473 at 486
9   [1941] 2 All ER at 251, [1942] AC at 138

a below is wrong it is its duty to say so and to act accordingly. This applies whether the appeal is an interlocutory or a final appeal, whether it is an appeal from justices to a Chancery judge or from justices to a Divisional Court of the Divorce Division. Every court has a duty to do its best to arrive at a proper and just decision. And if an appellate court is satisfied that the decision of the court below is improper, unjust or wrong, then the decision must be set aside. I am quite unable to subscribe to the view that a decision must be treated as sacro-

b sanct because it was made in the exercise of "discretion": so to do might well perpetuate injustice.'

Now it appears to me clear from those passages in Davies LJ's judgment and those quoted from the judgment of Edmund Davies LJ in *Thornley v Palmer*[1], and the cases cited in the latter judgment, that no distinction was drawn between a situation

c in which the appellate court is in as good a position to exercise the discretion as was the judge at the hearing and the situation described by Viscount Simon LC, where the proper exercise of the discretion 'largely depends on the observations of wit-nesses and on a deduction as to the matrimonial relations and future prospects which can best be made at the trial'. Reliance was placed on *Evans v Bartlam*[2] *Charles Osenton & Co v Johnston*[3], *Ward v James*[4] and *Thornley v Palmer*[1], where

d the appellate court was in as good a position as the judge in the court below to say what ought to be done, and unfortunately the attention of the court was not directed to the judgments in the House of Lords in *Blunt v Blunt*[5], drawing the distinction between that type of case and cases where the proper exercise of the discretion largely depends on the observation of witnesses.

I can find no inconsistency between *Re B (an infant)*[6] and any decision of the House

e of Lords, and *Re B (an infant)*[6], being a decision of this court, is binding on us. And, in my judgment, in infant cases you cannot say that the decision of the judge is wrong, improper or unjust unless he has erred in law or has taken into account some matter which he ought not to have taken into account, or failed to take into account a matter which he ought to have taken into account.

I am fortified in that conclusion by dicta in the House of Lords in *J v C*[7]. It was

f conceded by counsel in that case, which in point of time was subsequent to *Ward v James*[4] and *Re O (infants)*[8], that he could not ask the House to overrule the dis-cretion which had been exercised by the trial judge unless he could show that it had been exercised on some wrong principle. That concession, remarked Lord Guest[9], 'could not have been withheld', adding, 'It is not for this House to retry the case on the facts.' Lord MacDermott, referring to the concession[10], did not

g dissent from it. Lord Upjohn[11] treated the concession as correctly made.

There are, I know, unreported cases not called to our attention, where it has been said that the appellate court will substitute its own discretion for that of a judge who has heard an infant case where it is 'quite plain' that the judge was wrong or as has been said where the judge is 'just plain wrong'. If by that it is meant that the appellate court will interfere where it concludes that the course followed by the judge is one

h that no reasonable judge having taken into account all the relevant circumstances

---

1   [1969] 3 All ER 31, [1969] 1 WLR 1037
2   [1937] 2 All ER 646, [1937] AC 473
3   [1941] 2 All ER 245, [1942] AC 130
4   [1965] 1 All ER 563, [1966] 1 QB 273
j 5   [1943] 2 All ER 76, [1943] AC 517
6   [1962] 1 All ER 872, [1962] 1 WLR 550
7   [1969] 1 All ER 788, [1970] AC 668
8   [1971] 2 All ER 744, [1971] Ch 748
9   [1969] 1 All ER at 804, [1970] AC at 692
10 [1969] 1 All ER at 813, [1970] AC at 702
11 [1969] 1 All ER at 827, [1970] AC at 718

could have adopted, I would not quarrel with it: for he will have gone outside the
ambit of the discretion conferred on him. But that does not mean that because *a*
sitting as the appellate court you yourself, reading the papers and the judgment,
think it quite plain that you would have adopted a different course, you may or
ought to interfere. Different judges of wisdom and experience may in such matters
reasonably come to a different conclusion in identical circumstances. One judge
may think that a particular risk ought to be taken. Another judge may be more
cautious. The law has no yardstick by which to measure, or scales on which to weigh, *b*
'the facts, relationships, claims and wishes of parents, risks, choices and other
circumstances', referred to by Lord MacDermott[1] in the passage I have quoted.

Having read and re-read the judgment of Bagnall J I find it impossible to conclude
that he erred in law or took into account any matter which he ought not to have
taken into account, or failed to take into account any matter to which he ought to
have paid attention. He weighed the factors pointing in each direction and notwith- *c*
standing the submissions which he described as formidable in favour of granting
custody to the father, he came down in favour of the grandmother. That he did
so because of the adverse views he formed of the characters of the father and stepmother is not in doubt. As to the father he thought that violence still remained
part of his make-up, that he was not above stealing and that he was 'less than frank'
in his evidence. That the latter finding was an understatement I think appears from *d*
the father's evidence, and for all I know there may be other understatements in
regard to the judge's finding regarding the characters of the father and stepmother.
It was urged that he had attached undue importance to the sexual promiscuity of
the stepmother when she was only 16 or thereabouts. But he took the view that her
attitude to that aspect of morality was confirmed by what she said in the witness
box, and I know not how she gave her evidence in that regard but only what she said. *e*
He may have got a bad impression regarding her moral standards not only in relation to sexual behaviour but in other respects. I would protest at too analytical
an examination of the language used by the judge in the expression of his views
and impressions regarding the father and stepmother. In the end he had to consider
their capability and suitability to bring up the child not as two separate persons
but as a father with this particular wife living together. The violence of which he *f*
spoke, if directed against his wife, would have important repercussions on the child.
Whether I should have come to the same conclusion as did Bagnall J had I tried the
case, I do not know. I did not have the advantage of seeing the parties concerned
or the opportunity of forming a judgment of their fitness to bring up the child.

There was before us a supplemental report from the welfare officer which I do
not think takes the matter any further. It is right, however, to record that as a result *g*
of a visit or visits to the father and stepmother, the welfare officer stated that the
child had recently shown reluctance to visit her grandmother. On the other hand,
the child herself indicated to the welfare officer that she wished to return to her
grandmother and that her explanation was that she did not want to hurt her
grandmother.

On behalf of the father we are invited to read a report by a psychiatrist who has *h*
seen the father after the date of the judgment of Bagnall J. This we did, but in my
view it again took the matter no further.

Applying *Blunt v Blunt*[2] and *Re B (an infant)*[3], I would dismiss the appeal.

BROWNE LJ. Any judge, and especially a common law judge, must feel great *j*
anxiety about differing from the views of Stamp LJ and Bagnall J in an infant case.

---

1   [1969] 1 All ER at 821, [1970] AC at 711
2   [1943] 2 All ER 76, [1943] AC 517
3   [1962] 1 All ER 872, [1962] 1 WLR 550

But after much anxiety, I have come without hesitation to the conclusion that this
a appeal should be allowed, and that the care and control of this child should be given
to her father.

This case raises the problem of the powers and duties of an appellate court when
it is asked to review a decision made by the court below in the exercise of a discretion,
and in particular its powers and duties when the court below has heard and seen
witnesses.

b The general principle (apart from the complication where the court below has
heard oral evidence) is clear. In *Evans v Bartlam*[1] Lord Wright, after distinguishing
Donald Campbell & Co Ltd v Pollak[2], said[3]:

'But there is in that case no reference to or discussion of the duty or power
of the Court of Appeal to review the general discretion of a judge in interlocutory
c matters, the extent of which has been illustrated by numerous cases before
and since *Pollak's case*[2]. It is clear that the Court of Appeal should not interfere
with the discretion of a judge acting within his jurisdiction unless the court is
clearly satisfied that he was wrong. But the court is not entitled simply to
say that, if the judge had jurisdiction, and had all the facts before him, the Court
of Appeal cannot review his order, unless he is shown to have applied a wrong
d principle. The court must, if necessary, examine anew the relevant facts and
circumstances, in order to exercise by way of review a discretion which may
reverse or vary the order.'

He quoted Bowen LJ[4]: 'That discretion, like other judical discretions, must be
exercised according to common sense and according to justice, and if there is a
e miscarriage in the exercise of it it will be reviewed . . .'

In *Charles Ostenton & Co v Johnston* Viscount Simon LC said[5]:

'The law as to the reversal by a Court of Appeal of an order made by the judge
below in the exercise of his discretion is well-established, and any difficulty that
arises is due only to the application of well-settled principles in an individual
f case. The appellate tribunal is not at liberty merely to substitute its own exercise
of discretion for the discretion already exercised by the judge. In other words,
appellate authorities ought not to reverse the order merely because they would
themselves have exercised the original discretion, had it attached to them, in
a different way. If, however, the appellate tribunal reaches the clear conclusion
that there has been a wrongful exercise of discretion, in that no weight, or no
g sufficient weight, has been given to relevant considerations such as those urged
before us by the appellant, then the reversal of the order on appeal may be
justified.'

He then quoted the statements of Lord Wright and Bowen LJ which I have already
quoted, and concluded[6]: 'In all the circumstances, I reach the conclusion that . . .
the making of [the order] was not a legitimate exercise of discretion, which of course
h would not be disturbed on appeal, but was a wrongful exercise of the discretion
which it is the duty of this House to correct.'

Viscount Maugham said[7] that there were 'sufficient grounds . . . for thinking
that due weight was not given by the learned judge' to one relevant factor, and

j 1 [1937] 2 All ER 646, [1937] AC 473
2 [1927] AC 732, [1927] All ER Rep 1
3 [1937] 2 All ER at 654, [1937] AC at 486
4 *Gardner v Jay* (1885) 25 Ch D 50 at 58
5 [1941] 2 All ER 245 at 250, [1942] AC 130 at 138
6 [1941] 2 All ER at 251, [1942] AC at 139
7 [1941] 2 All ER at 253, [1942] AC at 142

that 'his discretion was exercised without giving sufficient consideration [to this
factor] and that the present order may result in injustice being done'. Lord Wright *a*
also said[1] that he was satisfied that the judge had not given 'due weight' to a relevant
factor, and pointed out[2] that to say that the appellate court must be 'clearly satisfied'
that the discretion had been wrongly exercised really added nothing to saying that
it must be 'satisfied'. In *Ward v James*[3] Lord Denning MR, in a judgment with
which the four other members of this court agreed, said[4]:
b

'REVIEWING DISCRETION. This brings me to the question: in what circumstances
will the Court of Appeal interfere with the discretion of the judge? At one
time it was said that it would interfere only if he had gone wrong in principle;
but since *Evans v Bartlam*[5], that idea has been exploded. The true proposition
was stated by LORD WRIGHT in *Charles Osenton & Co. v. Johnston*[6]. This court can,
and will, interfere if it is satisfied that the judge was wrong. Thus it will interfere *c*
if it can see that the judge has given no weight (or no sufficient weight) to those
considerations which ought to have weighed with him. A good example is
Charles Osenton & Co. v. Johnston[7] itself, where TUCKER, J., in his discretion
ordered trial by an official referee, and the House of Lords reversed the order
because he had not given due weight to the fact that the professional reputation
of surveyors was at stake. Conversely it will interfere if it can see that he has *d*
been influenced by other considerations which ought not to have weighed with
him, or not weighed so much with him, as in *Hennell v. Ranaboldo*[8]. It sometimes
happens that the judge has given reasons which enable this court to know the
considerations which have weighed with him; but even if he has given no reasons,
the court may infer from the way he has decided, that the judge must have
gone wrong in one respect or the other, and will thereupon reverse his decision; *e*
see *Grimshaw v. Dunbar*[9].'

Stamp LJ has said in his judgment: 'In infant cases you cannot say that the decision
of the judge is wrong, improper or unjust unless he has erred in law or has taken
into account some matter which he ought not have taken into account or failed
to take into account a matter which he ought to have taken into account.' In other *f*
words, I understand him to think that in an infant case an appellate court cannot
reverse the court below on the ground that the lower court has gone wrong in the
balancing operation implicit in such phrases as 'due weight', 'no sufficient weight',
or 'too much weight' used in the authorities to which I have referred. I am afraid
I cannot agree. Apart from the effect of seeing and hearing witnesses, I cannot see
why the general principle applicable to the exercise of the discretion in respect of *g*
infants should be any different from the general principle applicable to any other
form of discretion. In *Re O (infants)*[10] (admittedly obiter) this court so held. Stamp LJ
has already quoted from the judgment of Davies LJ in that case[11] (with which the
other two members of the court agreed), and I will not repeat it except to emphasise
this passage[12]:

h

---

1 [1941] 2 All ER at 256, [1942] AC at 147
2 [1941] 2 All ER at 257, [1942] AC at 148
3 [1965] 1 All ER 563, [1966] 1 QB 273
4 [1965] 1 All ER at 570, [1966] 1 QB at 293
5 [1937] 2 All ER 646, [1937] AC 473
6 [1941] 2 All ER at 257, [1942] AC at 148
7 [1941] 2 All ER 245, [1942] AC 130
8 [1963] 3 All ER 684, [1963] 1 WLR 1391
9 [1953] 1 All ER 350, [1953] 1 QB 408
10 [1971] 2 All ER 744, [1971] Ch 748
11 [1971] 2 All ER at 747, [1971] Ch at 754, 755
12 [1971] 2 All ER at 748, 749, [1971] Ch at 755

j

'In my considered opinion the law now is that if an appellate court is satisfied that the decision of the court below is wrong it is its duty to say so and to act accordingly. This applies whether the appeal is an interlocutory or a final appeal, whether it is an appeal from justices to a Chancery judge or from justices to a Divisional Court of the Divorce Division. Every court has a duty to do its best to arrive at a proper and just decision. And if an appellate court is satisfied that the decision of the court below is improper, unjust or wrong, then the decision must be set aside. I am quite unable to subscribe to the view that a decision must be treated as sacrosanct because it was made in the exercise of "discretion": so to do might well perpetuate injustice.'

I agree. I do not think that *Re B (an infant)*[1] is an authority to the contrary. In that case Lord Evershed MR and Harman LJ said that it was their 'strong impression' or their 'impression' that they would have decided the case differently at first instance, but this is well short of being satisfied that the decision of the court below was wrong (or 'clearly', or 'plainly', or 'undoubtedly' wrong, if those words add anything), and this court distinguished *Re B (an infant)*[1] on this ground in *Re O (infants)*[2]: see per Davies LJ[3]. In spite of what is said in the authorities about an appellate court not substituting its discretion for the discretion of the court at first instance, an appellate court, if satisfied that the decision below was wrong, may make its own decision in infant cases: see *Allen v Allen*[4], *Willoughby v Willoughby*[5], and *H v H and C*[6] (in the first two of which the court below seems to have heard oral evidence), though alternatively it may order a new hearing, as in *Re O (infants)*[2]. In the present case neither party suggested that we should order a new hearing, and it would obviously be quite wrong to do so.

In infant cases, however, the court at first instance will almost always have seen and heard the parties and their witnesses: see *H v H and C*[7]; the Matrimonial Causes Rules 1973[8], r 92(4)(a) and (b). Stamp LJ has quoted from the speech of Viscount Simon LC in *Blunt v Blunt*[9]; that was not an infant case, but a case about the exercise of the discretion under s 4 of the Matrimonial Causes Act 1937 to grant a divorce in spite of the petitioner's own adultery. However, Sir Jocelyn Simon P applied it to an infant case in *B (B) v B (M)*[10] in a passage which Stamp LJ has also quoted. Stamp LJ also referred to *J v C*[11] where it was conceded by counsel for the appellant that in that case 'he could not ask the House to overrule the discretion which has been exercised by the trial judge unless he could show that it had been exercised on some wrong principle'. This was a matter of concession, not of decision, though Lord Guest did say that[12] 'this concession could not have been withheld. It is not for this House to retry the case on the facts.' In my judgment, these authorities do not establish that an appellate court can *never* reverse a decision made in the exercise of a discretion when the court below has seen and heard the witnesses (unless the court below has erred in law or gone wrong in principle). In *Blunt*[9] Lord Simon did not say that the appellate court can never interfere, but that in such

1   [1962] 1 All ER 872, [1962] 1 WLR 550
2   [1971] 2 All ER 744, [1971] Ch 748
3   [1971] 2 All ER at 747, [1971] Ch at 754
4   [1948] 2 All ER 413
5   [1951] P 184
6   [1969] 1 All ER 262, [1969] 1 WLR 208
7   [1969] 1 All ER at 263, [1969] 1 WLR at 209, 210
8   SI 1973 No 2016
9   [1943] 2 All ER 76 at 79, [1943] AC 517 at 527
10 [1969] 1 All ER 891 at 901, [1969] P 102 at 115
11 [1969] 1 All ER 788, [1970] AC 668
12 [1969] 1 All ER at 804, [1970] AC at 692

cases 'the reason for not interfering, save in the most extreme cases . . . is of a far
stronger character' than in cases such as *Charles Osenton & Co v Johnston*[1], where *a*
the material was entirely documentary, and thus equally available to the appellate
court; he then quoted with apparent approval what Swinfen Eady MR had said[2]:
'The question for consideration by this court is whether his judgment is erroneous,
and not whether we should have exercised the discretion in the same manner as
the judge below did.' As I have said, *J v C*[3] was a case of concession, not decision.
    Of course an appellate court must be very conscious that it has not had the advan- *b*
tage of seeing and hearing the witnesses. It is obviously more difficult to satisfy
an appellate court in such cases that the court below was wrong. But in my judgment
there is not any different *principle* applicable to the exercise of discretion when the
court below has heard oral evidence; the general principle laid down in the authorities
cited at the beginning of this judgment applies, though there is this special factor
in its application. *c*
    We were referred by way of analogy to some of the authorities about the power
of an appellate court to reverse a finding of fact by a judge who has seen and heard
the witnesses: see for example *Powell v Streatham Manor Nursing Home*[4], *Watt (or
Thomas) v Thomas*[5], *Onassis and Calogeropoulos v Vergottis*[6] in the House of Lords
and *Breen v AEU* per Edmund Davies LJ[7]. In such cases the appellate court must *d*
always bear in mind that it has not had the advantage of seeing and hearing the
witnesses and that the view of the trial judge is entitled to great, and usually conclusive, weight. But even in such cases the trial judge is not to 'be treated as infallible',
and his decision can be disturbed if the appellate court is 'satisfied that it is unsound':
see Lord Simon in *Watt (or Thomas) v Thomas*[8]. I am, however, not satisfied that
the analogy between these cases and discretion cases such as the present is sound.
In my own experience, I have found it difficult enough to decide from seeing and *e*
hearing witnesses whether or not they are telling the truth at that moment. I should
find it even more difficult to form any reliable view of how their characters were
going to develop over, say, the next five years. I am inclined to agree with what
Donovan LJ said in his dissenting judgment in *Re B (an infant)*[9]:

> 'In matters where credibility is an issue, of course that consideration [that *f*
> being seeing and hearing the witnesses] is of great weight. I do not think it is
> of such weight when one is assessing a person's character and ability to look
> after a child. The encounter is too brief for any reliable conclusion.'

In *Blunt*[10] nearly all the matters referred to in Lord Simon LC's speech seem to relate
to the past history of the marriage rather than to the future.
    I accept that where an appellate court can see that the court below in exercising *g*
its discretion in an infant (or any other) case has been influenced in its decision to
a decisive, or probably even to a substantial, extent by its impressions based on seeing
and hearing the witnesses, the appellate court should be very reluctant to interfere.
I am not prepared to go so far as to say that it should never interfere, even in those
circumstances.
    In my view, the most important factors in favour of holding that it would be in *h*

---

1   [1941] 2 All ER 245, [1942] AC 130
2   *Holland v Holland* [1918] P 273 at 280, [1918-19] All ER Rep 882 at 883
3   [1969] 1 All ER 788, [1970] AC 668
4   [1935] AC 243, [1935] All ER Rep 58
5   [1947] 1 All ER 582, [1947] AC 484
6   [1968] 2 Lloyd's Rep 403
7   [1971] 1 All ER 1148 at 1161, 1162, [1971] 2 QB 175 at 199
8   [1947] 1 All ER at 584, [1947] AC at 486
9   [1962] 1 All ER at 875, [1962] 1 WLR at 555
10   [1943] 2 All ER 76, [1943] AC 517

the best interests of this child to give care and control to the father are: (1) He is
the father; this case is not a choice between a father and a mother, but between a
father and a grandmother. (2) The child would be living with a father and stepmother in their twenties and a half-sister aged 3½. The stepmother said in evidence
that she hoped to have more children. The grandmother is about 60, and the grand-
father about 64. One aunt, Mrs H, lives three miles away from the grandmother,
and has one child, a boy aged only 18 months. Although the other aunt has two
daughters about the same age as the child, she lives eight miles away from the grandmother. If the child goes to her grandmother, she will be in an ageing and childless
household; one must look ahead, and this situation will unfortunately become
more unsatisfactory as time goes on—say in five years' time. I doubt whether the
aunts live close enough to have much effect on this situation, and Mrs H's son is
too young to be much of a companion for the child. (3) It is clear from the welfare
officer's report and oral evidence that the attitudes of the father and the grandmother
towards each other are entirely different. The father shows considerable understanding of the grandmother's feelings and does not try to put the child against
her or the aunts. The grandmother is very bitter and prejudiced against the father.
The welfare officer is concerned about the effect of the grandmother's attitude on
the child. She said in evidence: 'I was quite impressed with the different approaches
that I met with in both parties.' In her first report she said:

> 'In discussing the general situation I found that [the father] seemed to show
> considerable insight and understanding of both his daughter's position and that
> of [the grandmother and grandfather]. He was aware of the criticisms and
> hostility that his late wife's family had for him and his care of [the child]. At
> the same time he understood [the child's] real affection and need for her grand-
> parents and while insisting on his rights as [the child's] father avoided any criti-
> cism of them and tried hard to assist [the child] in understanding and accepting
> the situation.'

At the hearing she was asked about this part of her report:

> 'Q. Did you get the impression in the [grandparents'] household that their
> attitude towards the father was in any way the same as his attitude towards
> them? A. No.
> 'Q. Would you just comment on that? A. I felt that during my interview in
> the [grandparents'] house—I feel there is no doubt they are very fond of [the
> child]—but their attitude towards both [the father] and his wife was full of
> criticism . . . certainly the resentments were very much to the fore and I was
> very concerned that this atmosphere must, I feel, affect [the child] to a very great
> degree. My thinking here was that although I am sure [the child] would be
> well cared for here, and access consented to, and all arrangements made could
> well be to the letter rather than the thought. Whereas I thought that [the child]
> in the present environment would be able still to enjoy the affection from
> both her grandparents and her aunts without any real interference.'

In her supplementary report (which was not before the judge) she said:

> 'One must take into account however the long term needs of this child. It
> seems to me that the love and security within her father's home is more likely
> to be conducive to a normal and healthy adolescent than the bitterness and
> prejudice which I feel still continues in her grandmother's home.'

At the end of his judgment the judge said:

> 'The change of home environment should be accompaied by a change of
> heart in [the grandmother and the aunts and their families], particularly in

their attitude to the father and to [the stepmother]. The past ... must not be allowed to dominate the future ...'

Stamp LJ has already quoted that passage in full. Counsel for the grandmother frankly told us that there has not so far been any such change of heart, though he suggested that there would be if the grandmother had her way and got care and control of the child. I can see no reasonable grounds for this suggestion; it seems to me more likely that the result would be the alienation of this child from her father. In my judgment this factor is very important, primarily of course because of its effect on the child, but also because of the very favourable light which it throws on the father's character and which I think must be set against the judge's unfavourable view. I think it also goes a long way to explain his apparent neglect of the child between September 1971 and March 1974.

The judge referred to these factors and described them as 'formidable', but I do not think he gave enough weight to them, especially factors 2 and 3. Nor does he seem to have given any weight to what I think was the welfare officer's opinion that it would be better for the child to be with her father; his tribute to the welfare officer's report and evidence seems to be limited to its help as to the child's temperament. He did not, of course, have the benefit of the further report from the welfare officer which was before us, which seems to me to strengthen the case for giving care and control to the father. But I doubt whether I should be prepared to interfere with the judge's decision on these grounds alone.

His decision was clearly based on his views as to the characters of the parties. He said:

'In those circumstances my decision must, I think, ultimately turn on the characters of the principal parties concerned as I have been able to ascertain them from the written evidence, from the welfare report and from the opportunity that I have had of seeing on the one side the [grandmother] and Mrs [H] and on the other side the father and [stepmother] in the witness box.'

Then, at the end of his judgment, he said:

'In treating as I am required to do the welfare of [the child] as the first and paramount consideration I must look not only to the immediate future but to the whole of [the child's] development through the years of her minority. In doing so I have reached the conclusion that the benefits to be derived if I accede to the father's arguments are appreciably outweighed by the substantial risks that are inherent in the characters of the father and [stepmother] as they have presented themselves to me.'

In my view, the factors to which I have referred, especially factors 2 and 3, are so overwhelmingly in favour of the view that it would be in the child's best intersts to stay with her father that they ought to prevail unless the court is satisfied that the father and stepmother are unfit to have the care and control of the child. Bridge LJ has set out in detail in his judgment the evidence of defects in character on which the judge relied, and I need not repeat it. As to the father, the indecent assault incident in January 1971 is obviously a very serious matter. But it was nearly 4½ years ago; the father was no doubt at that time in a very unsettled condition; since then he has remarried and had another child; and since then he has also built up a substantial business of his own. The evidence of violence by him to his wife (given in re-examination) was very vague. I think that these factors are not enough to displace the factors in favour of giving care and control to the father. As to the stepmother, counsel for the grandmother told us that his impression was that the decisive factor for the judge was the evidence she gave as to the advice she would give to this child in about seven years' time if a boy friend then wanted to have sexual intercourse with her. Her evidence was that she would warn the child of the danger of pregnancy, tell her to consider whether the boy friend was serious and really intending to marry her, and if so, advise her to go to the family planning clinic. From a practical point of view this would, I think, be very sensible advice. I suppose, though I do not know, that the judge thought that she ought to have advised the girl not on any account to have sexual intercourse before marriage. I myself may wish that such advice would be given, but I find it quite impossible to say that a failure to give that advice in 1975—and probably still less in 1982—makes the stepmother unfit to be concerned in the bringing-up of this child. No criticism whatever is made of the characters of the grandmother or of Mrs H, but we have no evidence of what advice they would give to the child in the hypothetical situation assumed in the cross-examination of the stepmother. Counsel for the father quite rightly did not investigate this matter in cross-examination, because he had no idea that counsel for the grandmother was going to cross-examine the stepmother on this line. We were told by counsel that neither of them intended the stepmother to be called as a witness, but that the judge wished to see her. Counsel for the grandmother asked us to infer that the grand-mother has strict moral standards because the psychiatrist, whose report was before us, was told by the father that he had not had sexual intercourse with the mother before their marriage, but this seems to me far too flimsy a foundation. Further, I agree with Bridge LJ that it is unrealistic to suppose that in six or seven years' time this child will ask her grandmother for advice about sexual matters.

In my judgment, the factors on which the judge explicitly relied in deciding that the factors in favour of giving care and control to the father were 'appreciably out-weighed by the substantial risks that are inherent in the characters of the father and [stepmother] as they have presented themselves to me' do not establish that the father is unfit to have care and control of his child, and do not outweigh the factors in favour of the father. But it is said that the judge's conclusion was, or may have been, based not only on the facts and evidence set out in his judgment, but also on the impression which the father and stepmother made on him in the witness box. He only refers twice to such impressions, in a passage I have already quoted, where he puts them third in the materials on which he based his assessment of character (the first and second being the written evidence and the welfare report), and where he said that 'the existence of those defects [of character] was to some small extent, I thought, confirmed by the manner in which he gave his evidence . . .' The judge has set out with (if I may say so) the most admirable fullness and clearness the facts and evidence on which he based his conclusion as to the characters of the father and the stepmother. It is, I think, plain that the impression they made in the witness box on him was not a decisive factor in his conclusion; I am not satisfied that it was even a substantial factor.

I am satisfied that the judge's decision was wrong. In my judgment, there is no reason in law why I should not give effect to my conclusion and it is the right and the duty of this court to allow this appeal.

BRIDGE LJ. It is with diffidence and regret that I have reached a conclusion at variance with that of the trial judge and Stamp LJ. I am only too conscious that I have no experience of the exercise of jurisdiction over children, while they both have much. I take it, however, that the principles governing its exercise are not so esoteric as to be inaccessible to the novice, and having arrived at a clear view in the matter I feel it to be my duty to express it.

The salient features of the alternatives between which a choice falls to be made appear, as far as concerns the child's immediate and short term future, not to be in dispute. If this appeal succeeds she will remain in the home where she has lived now since March 1974 with her young father and stepmother and her half-sister. No one, except the grandmother, has in any way criticised the father's or stepmother's care of the child during this period, and the judge expressly rejected the grand-mother's criticisms. The welfare officer's reports and evidence, on the other hand,

including the latest report prepared since the trial for this court, present a uniformly
favourable picture of the child's situation in her present home and of her relation-   *a*
ships with the other members of the family. If she remains there, she will continue
to attend the school where she is happy and well-settled. Again, if she remains,
it is to be expected that her father and stepmother will continue in the future, as
they have done in the past, to encourage her to maintain a good relationship with
her grandmother, who will of course continue to have access.

If, on the other hand, the learned judge's order stands, the child will spend the   *b*
rest of her childhood as an only child in the home of grandparents now aged about
60 and 65 respectively. True, she will have cousins, but, as we have been told, Mrs H,
who has a son aged 18 months, lives three miles away, and the other maternal aunt,
who has daughters aged 11 and nine, lives eight miles away. It would seem, therefore, that however close-knit the family, the cousins in practice could do little to
mitigate for the child the disadvantage of being an only child. She could, we have   *c*
been told, continue at her present school, but she would have to travel there daily
by bus. More important than this, unless there is on the part of the grandmother
and members of her family that change of heart in their attitude to the father and
stepmother enjoined by the learned judge in the last paragraph of his judgment,
the child will be brought up in an atmosphere of bitterness and hostility towards
her father which might gravely impair her relationship with him. The grandmother's   *d*
feelings of bitterness towards the father are, in the light of the history, understandable. I am not entirely clear whether the learned judge was in any way basing his
conclusion on the expectation that the change of heart he called for would take place;
but, looking at the matter realistically, in such a situation it is unlikely that a lady
of the grandmother's character, as described by the learned judge, will radically
change her attitude because the judge has told her what she ought to do so.   *e*

If I have fairly summarised the factors so far considered, they seem to me to point
so clearly and unequivocally in favour of leaving the child with her father and his
family, as being in the child's best interest, that it must in my judgment require
some other very solid and substantial consideration, pointing in the opposite direction,
to displace this conclusion. Of course, if the father, the stepmother, or both, were
shown, notwithstanding the welfare officer's favourable reports, to be unfit for some
reason to have the upbringing of a girl, that would be such a consideration. I find   *f*
it difficult to see that anything less would suffice.

I take the learned judge's reference to the 'formidable arguments' of counsel for
the father as showing that he was aware of this aspect of the matter. He concluded
that the arguments were outweighed by defects of character in the father and stepmother. He indicated fully and, if I may say so, with admirable precision, the material   *g*
on which he relied in reaching this conclusion.

The defects the judge found in the character of the father were: (1) a capacity for
violence; (2) dishonesty. The basis of (1) was: (a) Evidence given by the father in
the following questions and answers referring to the deceased first wife:

'Q. You and her mother were usually on bad terms? A. Yes.
'Q. There was violence between you—I am not saying whose fault it was,   *h*
but there was violence between you? A. Yes.
'Q. And some of that violence took place in the presence of the little girl?
A. Yes.'

(b) The evidence of the father of the circumstances of the discreditable incident which
led to his conviction in January 1971 of indecent assault on a woman, for which he   *i*
was fined £75. The basis for (2) was that the father had two convictions for minor
offences of dishonesty, one in 1971 and one in his youth. The judge thought that
these defects in the character of the father were 'to some small extent confirmed
by the manner in which he gave his evidence'.

The criticism of the stepmother related exclusively to her sexual morality. She

admitted in evidence that before her affair with the father began she had between
a the ages of 16 and 18 had intercourse with five men. She was asked by counsel for
the grandmother and answered a series of hypothetical questions about the advice
she would give to the stepdaughter if at the age of 16 she sought advice about the
possiblility of having sexual intercourse with a boyfriend. The judge clearly attached
significance to both these aspects of the evidence. The character of the stepmother
left him, he said, 'in doubt whether she could be relied on to give that wise counsel
b and sure guidance that are so necessary to a young girl growing up and maturing
through adolescence into womanhood'.

   This last passage, together with the contrast he points in expressing his final conclusion between 'the immediate future' and 'the whole of the child's development
through the years of her minority', seems to me to indicate that the main, if not
the decisive, consideration which brought the scales down against the father
c and stepmother was that they would not impart to the child when she reached
adolescence proper standards of sexual morality.

   To my mind there was, with all respect, a surprising lack of realism in the judge's
approach to this aspect of the matter. I doubt if teenage girls today ask their parents'
advice whether or not they should have sexual intercourse; so the hypothetical
questions put to the stepmother envisaged a highly artifical situation. But, apart
d from that consideration, the substance of the stepmother's answers, viz that she
would advise the girl of the risks of pregnancy, tell her to seek contraceptive advice
and invite her to consider whether the proposed relationship was to be a serious
and permanent one, probably reflects an attitude to sex which is acceptable to large
sections of society today, including, I would think, a substantial majority of the
stepmother's generation. The view that loss of virginity outside marriage is for a
e girl a fate worse than death is no longer sustainable as a social norm. In any event
it would be quite unreal to expect that the child in her teens would look to a grandmother well on in her sixties for that 'wise counsel and sure guidance' in sexual
matters which the judge thought so necessary and which her stepmother would not
give. The reality of the matter, surely, is that the outlook of the adolescent young
in sexual as in other matters is derived in part from their family background but
f in the greater part from the ethos of the community in which they live, especially
that of their own contemporaries. A degree of tension between parental and contemporary attitudes is no doubt healthy. But if grandparents take the place of parents
and the difference in outlook has to bridge not a single but a double generation gap,
instead of a healthy tension there may well be a breakdown of mutual understanding
and a violent reaction in the adolescent against grandparental standards.

g   The learned judge, in my view, attached a wholly disproportionate weight, as
factors against leaving the child with her father, to the stepmother's past sexual behaviour and present sexual attitudes, as expressed in her evidence. The father's
criminal convictions, particularly the indecent assault, were more serious matters,
but I cannot see in this material or otherwise in the totality of the material on which
the judge explicitly relied sufficient to justify the conclusion that the father and step-
h mother should be condemned as unfit to have the responsibility for the child's
upbringing. As already indicated, nothing less than this would in my judgment
suffice to outweigh the factors summarised at the beginning of this judgment in
favour of the child remaining in her present home. It follows that in my view the
child should remain with her father.

   Can this conclusion prevail or is there some rule of law which bars it? The learned
j judge was exercising a discretion. He saw and heard the witnesses. It is impossible
to say that he considered any irrelevant matter, left out of account any relevant
matter, erred in law, or applied any wrong principle. On the view I take, his error
was in the balancing exercise. He either gave too little weight to the factors favourable, or too much weight to the factors adverse, to the father's claim that he should
retain care and control of the child.

The general principle is clear. If this were a discretion not depending on the judge having seen and heard the witnesses, an error in the balancing exercise, if I may *a* adopt that phrase for short, would entitle the appellate court to reverse his decision: *Evans v Bartlam*[1], *Charles Osenton & Co v Johnston*[2], *Ward v James*[3]. The reason for a practical limitation on the scope of that principle where the discretion exercised depends on seeing and hearing witnesses is obvious. The appellate court cannot interfere if it lacks the essential material on which the balancing exercise depended. But the importance of seeing and hearing witnesses may vary very greatly according *b* to the circumstances of individual cases. If in any discretion case concerning children the appellate court can clearly detect that a conclusion, which is neither dependent on nor justified by the trial judge's advantage in seeing and hearing witnesses, is vitiated by an error in the balancing exercise, I should be very reluctant to hold that it is powerless to interfere.

The full and careful analysis of the authorities in the judgment of Browne LJ *c* demonstates, I think, that the power of the court is not so limited.

Coming back to the instant case, I ask myself, if the trial judge's weighing of the factors which he explicitly considered was, as I think, clearly erroneous, may his conclusion nevertheless be sustainable on grounds which he has left unexpressed, derived from his impression of the witnesses? I fully appreciate that a judge in an infant case may, as Stamp LJ testifies from experience, express less than fully the *d* views he has formed of the parties for fear of embittering relations between them. But I see no hint that the judgment of Bagnall J, which, if I may use the phrase, pulled no punches against the father and stepmother, was subject to any such inhibition. Moreover, if the material on which the judge specifically relied in condemning them did not justify the conclusion that they were not fit persons to have the upbringing of the child, I cannot imagine what other material, derived from an *e* undisclosed impression, could do so.

I have borne in mind throughout that the child's welfare is the first and paramount consideration. I am convinced that it is in the child's interest to stay with her father and stepmother. But I also bear in mind that the child's welfare is not the only consideration. Her father is her only surviving parent. To take her away from him for insufficient reason would not only be wrong from her point of view; it would also, *f* in my judgment, be a grave injustice to the father.

I would allow this appeal.

Appeal allowed to the extent of varying the order by committing the care and control to the father during the minority of the child or until further order. Grandmother to have reasonable access, including staying access.   *g*

Solicitors: *Lucas, Styring & Appleby*, Sheffield (for the father); *Clifford Watts, Compton & Co*, agents for *Dibb & Clegg with Maude & Spark*, Barnsley (for the grandmother).

L I Zysman Esq Barrister.   *h*

---

1   [1937] 2 All ER 646, [1937] AC 473
2   [1941] 2 All ER 245, [1942] AC 130
3   [1965] 1 All ER 563, [1966] 1 QB 273

The Jade
The Eschersheim
Owners of the motor vessel Erkowit v Owners of the motor vessel Salus (formerly Rotesand) and others
Owners of cargo lately laden on board the motor vessel Erkowit v Owners of the motor vessel Eschersheim

COURT OF APPEAL, CIVIL DIVISION
CAIRNS, SCARMAN LJJ AND SIR GORDON WILLMER
9th, 10th, 11th, 12th, 13th JUNE, 22nd JULY 1975

Admiralty – Jurisdiction – Action in rem – Claim arising out of agreement relating to use or hire of a ship – Salvage agreement – Agreement not specifically providing for use of particular salvage vessel – Need to construe agreement in light of surrounding circumstances – Agreement signed on board salvage vessel and providing for ship to be towed to safety – Whether agreement 'relating to . . . the use or hire of a ship' - Administration of Justice Act 1956, s 1(1)(h).

Admiralty – Jurisdiction – Action in rem – Claim for damage done by a ship – Meaning of 'damage done by a ship' – Ship instrument by which damage caused – Salvage vessel – Salvage vessel beaching disabled ship in pursuance of salvage agreement – Disabled vessel becoming total loss following beaching – Owners becoming liable for damage caused by consequent pollution of sea – Allegation that damage caused by beaching – Whether 'damage done by' salvage vessel – Whether claim including consequential loss in respect of liability for pollution – Administration of Justice Act 1956, s 1(1)(d).

Admiralty – Jurisdiction – Action in rem – Claim for damage received by a ship – Claim arising in connection with a ship – Action in rem against 'that ship' – Claim by shipowners against salvage vessel for damage caused to owners' ship in course of salvage operation – Whether a claim 'arising in connection with' salvage vessel or 'in connection with' owners' ship – Whether owners entitled to assert claim for damage received by their ship by action in rem against salvage vessel – Administration of Justice Act 1956, ss 1(1)(e), 3(4).

Admiralty – Jurisdiction – Action in rem – Claim for loss or damage to goods carried in a ship – Claim arising in connection with a ship – Action in rem against 'that ship' – Claim by cargo owners against salvage vessel for loss or damage to cargo in course of salvage operation – Whether a claim 'arising in connection with' salvage vessel or 'in connection with' ship on which cargo being carried – Whether cargo owners entitled to assert claim for loss or damage to cargo by action in rem against salvage vessel – Administration of Justice Act 1956, ss 1(1)(g), 3(4).

Admiralty – Jurisdiction – Action in rem – Claim in the nature of salvage – Claim by owners of salvaged property for negligence in salvage operations – Claim against salvors – Whether a claim 'in the nature of salvage' – Administration of Justice Act 1956, s 1(1)(j).

Arbitration – Stay of court proceedings – Refusal of stay – Multiplicity of proceedings – Collision at sea – Owners of ship damaged in collision entering into salvage agreement – Agreement containing arbitration clause – Loss of ship in course of salvage operations – Actions by owners against other ship and against salvors – Grant of stay resulting in multiplicity of proceedings – Arbitration Act 1950, s 4(1).

Two ships, the Erkowit and the Dortmund, collided some 50 miles off the coast of
Spain. The Erkowit was totally disabled and a salvage tug, the Rotesand, went to her
assistance. A salvage agreement in Lloyd's open form was entered into on board the
Rotesand between the master of the Rotesand on behalf of the salvors and the master
of the Erkowit on behalf of the owners of the Erkowit and the owners of her cargo.
The agreement provided that the salvors would use their best endeavours to salve the
Erkowit and her cargo and take her to a place of safety. The agreement did not
specifically provide that the salvors should use the Rotesand or any other vessel for
the salvage operation. Differences arising under the agreement were to be referred to
arbitration in London. The Rotesand took the Erkowit in tow and beached her off La
Coruna, but the salvors failed in their efforts to save the Erkowit or her cargo and both
became total losses. The cargo, which included a large quantity of insecticide, was
washed into the sea causing pollution and consequent damage to the local fishing interests. The Spanish government brought an action in Spain on behalf of local fishermen against the owners of the Erkowit and against the salvors for damages resulting
from the pollution. While that action was still pending, the owners of the Erkowit
and the cargo owners brought four actions in rem in the Admiralty Court in England.
The first action was by the shipowners against the owners of the Dortmund for
damages in respect of the loss of the Erkowit and the owners' potential liability to the
Spanish government for pollution. The second action was by the owners of the cargo
on the Erkowit against the owners of the Dortmund for damages caused by the collision.
In those actions, which were still pending, the owners of the Dortmund by their defence
contended, inter alia, that the loss of the Erkowit and her cargo and the pollution had
been caused by the negligence of the salvors. The third and fourth actions were
brought by the owners of the Erkowit and the cargo owners against the salvors for
damages for breach of the salvage agreement and for negligence in performance of
the agreement. The damages claimed by the shipowners included an indemnity
against any liability to the Spanish government in respect of the pollution. The salvors
applied (i) to have the writs in the two actions against them set aside on the grounds
that the Admiralty Court had no jurisdiction in rem in respect of the claims in that
they did not come within s 1(1)[a] of the Administration of Justice Act 1956; alternatively
(ii) for an order that those actions, insofar as they had not been set aside or struck out,
be stayed under s 4(1) of the Arbitration Act 1950 on the ground that under the terms
of the salvage agreement they were to be referred to arbitration. Brandon J dismissed
the salvors' applications. The salvors appealed.

Held – The appeals would be dismissed for the following reasons—
    (i) The claims of the owners of the Erkowit and the cargo owners both came within
para (h) of s 1(1) of the 1956 Act as claims arising out of an agreement for the 'use or
hire of a ship' for, even though the agreement contained no express reference to the
use of the ship, the terms of the agreement had to be construed in the light of the
surrounding circumstances and, although the Rotesand was not named as the towing
instrument, in order to give business efficacy to the agreement it was a necessary
implication that she was to be used for the purpose of towage. Accordingly, the
plaintiffs were entitled under ss 1(1)(h) and 3(4)[b] of the 1956 Act to assert a claim in
rem in respect of alleged negligence in the performance of the agreement (see p 448 f
to p 449 a, p 454 d and e and p 459 b to d and h, post).
    (ii) The owners of the Erkowit and the cargo owners were also entitled to assert a
claim in rem under s 1(1)(d) of the 1956 Act as being a claim in respect of 'damage
done by a ship', for if, as was alleged, the actual beaching of the Erkowit by the
Rotesand had caused damage to the Erkowit and its cargo, then the Rotesand was the
instrument whereby the damage had been caused. Furthermore (per Scarman LJ

---

a Section 1(1), so far as material, is set out at p 446 c and d, post
b Section 3(4), so far as material, is set out at p 446 f and g, post

and Sir Gordon Willmer), if the actual beaching of the Erkowit constituted damage done by the Rotesand so as to confer a right in rem under para (d) of s 1(1), the owners of the Erkowit were entitled to include in their claim under that paragraph a claim for consequential loss arising from their potential liability in the Spanish proceedings for pollution, if that pollution had resulted from the actual beaching of the Erkowit by the Rotesand (see p 449 g, p 452 e and f, p 454 c and d, p 458 g and h, p 459 h and p 460 c and d, post); dicta of Lord Halsbury LC and Lord Watson in *Currie v M'Knight* [1897] AC at 101, 106, 107 applied.

(iii) On the assumption that the claims were within the arbitration clause in the salvage agreement, the case was not a proper one for granting a stay under s 4(1) of the 1950 Act and accordingly the judge had not exercised his discretion wrongly in refusing a stay, in particular having regard to the need to avoid an unnecessary multiplicity of proceedings (see p 452 b to e and p 455 c and d, post).

Per Curiam. The claim of the owners of the Erkowit and the cargo owners in respect of damage caused by negligent salvage did not come within the phrase 'any claim in the nature of salvage' in s 1(1)(j) of the 1956 Act for that phrase was restricted to a claim by salvors against the owners of the property salved, and did not extend to claims for damage done in the course of a salvage (see p 446 h and j, p 452 e and f and p 458 a to c, post).

Per Scarman LJ and Sir Gordon Willmer. The shipowners were not entitled to bring an action in rem in respect of their claim, under s 1(1)(e) of the 1956 Act, for 'damage received by a ship', since s 3(4) of the 1956 Act only permitted an action in rem against a ship when the claim was one 'arising in connection with . . . that ship'; the shipowners' claim under s 1(1)(e) arose 'in connection with' the Erkowit, the vessel which had suffered or 'received' the damage, and was not, within s 3(4), 'a claim arising in connection with' the Rotesand which was the wrongdoing vessel. Likewise neither the cargo owners, nor the shipowners as bailees of the cargo, were entitled to bring an action in rem in respect of the claim under s 1(1)(g) of the 1956 Act for 'loss or damage to goods carried in a ship' since that claim was one 'arising in connection with' the Erkowit and not the Rotesand (see p 454 b and c and p 457 g to p 458 a, post).

Decision of Brandon J [1974] 3 All ER 307 affirmed.

Notes

For Admiralty jurisdiction in rem, see 1 Halsbury's Laws (4th Edn), paras 310, 311, and for cases on the subject, see 1 Digest (Repl) 117, 287, 288, *33-35, 1899-1921.*

For the power of the court to stay proceedings, see 1 Halsbury's Laws (4th Edn) para 440, and for a case on the subject, see 1 Digest (Repl) 117, *32.*

For stay of arbitration proceedings where foreign element involved, see 2 Halsbury's Laws (4th Edn) para 556, and for cases on the subject, see 2 Digest (Repl) 486-494, *396-443.*

For the Arbitration Act 1950, s 4, see 2 Halsbury's Statutes (3rd Edn) 437.

For the Administration of Justice Act 1956, ss 1, 3, see 1 Halsbury's Statutes (3rd Edn) 21, 26.

Cases referred to in judgments

Alina, The (1880) 5 ExD 227, 49 LJP 40, 42 LT 517, 4 Asp MLC 257, CA, 1 Digest (Repl) 287, *1899.*

Alnwick, The, Robinson v Owners of Motor Tug Alnwick and Owners of Motor Vessel Braemar [1965] 2 All ER 569, [1965] P 357, [1965] 3 WLR 118, [1965] 1 Lloyd's Rep 320, CA, Digest (Cont Vol B), 655, *7256b.*

Andrea Ursula The, Medway Drydock and Engineering Co v Beneficial Owners of Ship Andrea Ursula [1971] 1 All ER 821, [1973] 1 QB 265, [1971] 2 WLR 681, [1971] 1 Lloyd's Rep 145.

Banco, The, Owners of the motor vessel Monte Ulia v Owners of the ship Banco [1971] 1 All ER 524, [1971] P 137, [1971] 2 WLR 335, [1971] 1 Lloyd's Rep 49, CA.

Beldis, The [1936] P 51, [1935] All ER Rep 760, 106 LJP 22, 154 LT 680, 18 Asp MLC 598, CA, 1 Digest (Repl) 121, *69*.

Bruce (W) Ltd v J Strong [1951] 1 All ER 1021, [1951] 2 KB 447, CA, 2 Digest (Repl) 485, *395*.

Cairnbahn, The [1914] P 25, 83 LJP 11, 110 LT 230, 12 Asp MLC 455, CA, 42 Digest (Repl) 933, *7255*.

Circe, The [1906] P 1, 74 LJP 106, 93 LT 640, 10 Asp MLC 149, 42 Digest (Repl) 920, *7133*.

Conoco Britannia, The, J H Pigott & Son Ltd v Owners of the ships Conoco Britannia, Conoco Espana and Conoco Libya [1972] 2 All ER 238, [1972] 2 QB 543, [1972] 2 WLR 1352, [1972] 1 Lloyd's Rep 342.

Currie v M'Knight [1897] AC 97, 66 LJPC 19, 75 LT 457, 8 Asp MLC 193, HL, 1 Digest (Repl) 117, *33*.

Frankland, The [1901] P 161, 70 LJP 42, 84 LT 395, 9 Asp MLC 196, 42 Digest (Repl) 932, *7247*.

Greaves v Tofield (1880) 14 Ch D 563, 50 LJCh 118, 43 LT 100, CA, 44 Digest (Repl) 259, *833*.

Isca, The (1886) 12 PD 34, 56 LJP 47, 55 LT 779, 6 Asp MLC 63, 42 Digest (Repl) 780, *5507*.

Molière, The [1925] P 27, 94 LJP 28, 132 LT 733, 16 Asp MLC 470, 1 Digest (Repl) 169, *558*.

Pine Hill, The [1958] 2 Lloyd's Rep 146.

Queen of the South, The, Corps (Trading as Corps Bros) v Owners of the Paddle Steamer Queen of the South, Port of London Authority (Interveners) [1968] 1 All ER 1163, [1968] P 449, [1968] 2 WLR 973, [1968] 1 Lloyd's Rep 182, Digest (Cont Vol C) 4, *725b*.

R v City of London Court Judge [1892] 1 QB 273, 61 LJQB 337, 66 LT 135, 7 Asp MLC 140, CA, 1 Digest (Repl) 288, *1912*.

Taunton-Collins v Cromie [1964] 2 All ER 332, [1964] 1 WLR 633, CA, Digest (Cont Vol B) 26, *383a*.

Theta, The [1894] P 280, 63 LJP 160, 71 LT 25, 7 Asp MLC 480, 6 R 712, 1 Digest (Repl) 168, *551*.

Vera Cruz, The (No 2) (1884) 9 PD 96, 53 LJP 33, 51 LT 104, 5 Asp MLC 270, CA; *on appeal sub nom Seward v The Vera Cruz* 10 App Cas 59, [1881-5] All ER Rep 216, 54 LJP 9, 52 LT 474, 49 JP 324, 5 Asp MLC 386, HL, 42 Digest (Repl) 892, *6832*.

Zeus, The (1888) 13 PD 188, 59 LT 344, 6 Asp MLC 312, 1 Digest (Repl) 287, *1902*.

Cases also cited

Argos, Cargo, Ex, Gaudet v Brown, Geipel v Cornforth, The Hewsons (1873) LR 5 PC 134, PC.

Lister v Romford Ice and Cold Storage Co Ltd [1957] 1 All ER 125, [1957] AC 555, HL.

Merak, The [1965] 1 All ER 230, [1965] P 223, CA.

Paterson v Chadwick [1974] 2 All ER 772, [1974] 1 WLR 890.

Pugsley & Co v Popkins & Co Ltd [1892] 2 QB 184, CA.

Sobieski, The [1949] 1 All ER 710, [1949] P 313, CA.

Trustees, Executors and Agency Co Ltd v Reilly [1941] VLR 110.

Interlocutory appeal

This was an appeal by the defendants, the owners of the ship Salus (formerly Rotesand) and her sister ships, the Jade and the Eschersheim, against the judgment of Brandon J[1] given on 10th June 1974 dismissing the defendants' applications to strike out the writs of summons in two actions in rem brought by the plaintiffs, the owners of the Erkowit and the owners of her cargo, against the defendants for damage caused to the Erkowit and her cargo in the course of salvage operations in which the Rotesand was engaged, or alternatively to stay those actions under s 4(1) of the Arbitration Act 1950. The facts are set out in the judgment of Cairns LJ.

J Franklin Willmer QC and *Nicholas Phillips* for the defendants.
Michael Thomas QC and *Anthony Clarke* for the shipowners.
David Steel for the cargo owners.

---

1   [1974] 3 All ER 307, [1975] 1 WLR 83

Cur adv vult

a 22nd July. The following judgments were read.

CAIRNS LJ. This is an appeal from an interlocutory decision of Brandon J in two actions in rem for damage caused to the ship Erkowit and her cargo in the course of salvage operations in which the defendants' tug Rotesand was engaged. The Jade and *b* the Eschersheim were two sister ships of the Rotesand. The owners of the Erkowit proceeded against the Jade and the owners of the cargo against the Eschersheim. (The shipowners also proceeded against the Rotesand, which had been sold and renamed Salus but the action against that ship was discontinued and there is no need to make further reference to it.) In the ship's action the master and crew were joined to claim for loss of their effects. The defendants applied to the judge to strike out the writs or parts thereof, alternatively to stay the actions under s 4(1) of the Arbitration Act 1950. *c* He struck out the claim of the master and crew and from that part of his decision there is no appeal. Otherwise he dismissed the defendants' applications and they appeal. There are respondents' notices supporting the judge's decision on alternative grounds.

The facts are set out with the greatest care and clarity in the judgment of Brandon J[1] and I shall give only a brief summary of them. On 30th October 1970 a collision took place in the Bay of Biscay between the Erkowit and the Dortmund. The Erkowit was *d* holed and the Rotesand went to her assistance. A salvage agreement in Lloyd's open form was signed on behalf of both plaintiffs and of the defendants. The Rotesand towed the Erkowit to La Coruna and beached her. The defendants' servants then carried out operations, which were not effective, to save the Erkowit or her cargo and both (except perhaps for some small part of the cargo) became total losses. The cargo included a quantity of insecticide, partly in drums on deck and partly in holds, which *e* was washed into the sea. The Spanish government alleges on behalf of fishermen that the pollution of the sea caused great damage to their interests and claims heavy damages against the owners of the Erkowit and against the defendants. There is likely to be much delay before those claims are dealt with.

In this country actions in rem have been brought by both the present plaintiffs against the Dortmund and have not yet come to trial. In those actions the owners of *f* the Dortmund by their defence contend, inter alia, that the loss of the Erkowit and her cargo and the pollution were caused by the negligence of the defendant.

Because the plaintiffs apprehended that such allegations would be made on behalf of the Dortmund they started the actions to which this appeal relates, the claims being made in tort or alternatively for the breach of the salvage agreement. The negligence alleged, as appears from an affidavit sworn on behalf of the plaintiffs, is (1) beaching *g* the Erkowit in an exposed place; (2) patching her with wood and canvas instead of with steel; (3) delay in carrying out the operations. The damages claimed in the shipowners' action include an indemnity against any liability to the Spanish government.

In their application to the judge the defendants sought to strike out the shipowners' claim for indemnity on the ground that the court had no jurisdiction in *h* rem in respect of such a claim. In the course of the hearing of the appeal leave was given to the defendants to amend their notice of appeal and to contend that the whole of the writ should be set aside on the ground that the court had no jurisdiction in rem in respect of any part of the claim. Further, leave was given to the defendants to amend their notice of appeal in the cargo owners' case to raise a similar contention.

In both cases the judge refused a stay under the Arbitration Act 1950 because, *j* although he held that the disputes were within the arbitration clause of the salvage agreement, he exercised his discretion by refusing a stay.

In the respondents' notice in the shipowners' case the shipowners sought to found jurisdiction on a basis on which the judge had held against them, as an alternative to

1 [1974] 3 All ER 307, [1975] 1 WLR 83

the bases on which he had held in their favour. As to stay, they contended that the judge was wrong in holding that the dispute was within the arbitration clause and advanced reasons, additional to those on which the judge based his decision, why the discretion should be exercised against a stay. By amendments for which leave was given during the hearing of the appeal, they put forward, in relation to the application to strike out, further alternative bases of jurisdiction.

In the cargo owners' case the original respondents' notice dealt only with the application to stay on broadly similar lines to the shipowners' notice. By supplementary respondents' notice, for which leave was given during the hearing of the appeal, they, like the shipowners, put forward in relation to the application to strike out alternative bases of jurisdiction.

The jurisdiction of the High Court in Admiralty matters is now defined by s 1(1) of the Administration of Justice Act 1956 in terms which, so far as relevant to the present appeal, are as follows:

'The Admiralty jurisdiction of the High Court shall be as follows, that is to say, jurisdiction to hear and determine any of the following questions or claims . . . (d) any claim for damage done by a ship; (e) any claim for damage received by a ship . . . (g) any claim for loss of or damage to goods carried in a ship; (h) any claim arising out of any agreement relating to the carriage of goods in a ship or to the use or hire of a ship; (j) any claim in the nature of salvage (including any claim arising by virtue of the application, by or under section fifty-one of the Civil Aviation Act, 1949, of the law relating to salvage to aircraft and their apparel and cargo . . .'

The mode of exercise of such Admiralty jurisdiction is prescribed by s 3 of the 1956 Act, the relevant provisions of which are as follows:

'(1) Subject to the provisions of the next following section, the Admiralty jurisdiction of the High Court . . . may in all cases be invoked by an action in personam . . .
'(4) In the case of any such claim as is mentioned in paragraphs (d) to (r) of subsection (1) of section one of this Act, being a claim arising in connection with a ship, where the person who would be liable on the claim in an action in personam was, when the cause of action arose, the owner or charterer of, or in possession or in control of, the ship, the Admiralty jurisdiction of the High Court . . . may (whether the claim gives rise to a maritime lien on the ship or not) be invoked by an action in rem against—(a) that ship, if at the time when the action is brought it is beneficially owned as respects all the shares therein by that person; or (b) any other ship which, at the time when the action is brought, is beneficially owned as aforesaid.'

The shipowners contended on the appeal that their claim fell within paras (d), (e), (h) and possibly (g) and (j) of s 1(1). Damage, they claim, was done to the Erkowit by the Rotesand, by beaching the Erkowit in an unsafe place; clearly damage was received by the Erkowit; the claim in contract arises out of the salvage agreement, which was an agreement for the use or hire of the Rotesand. As to (g), the suggestion was that the claim for indemnity in respect of the pollution may in a broad sense be said to be a claim for the loss of goods carried in a ship; and as to (j), it was submitted that a liberal interpretation of the words 'in the nature of salvage' would enable a claim for damage done in the course of salvage to be included. I do not consider that either (g) or (j) is capable of the meaning sought to be attached to it and, if the shipowners are to establish jurisdiction at all, it must in my view be under (d), (e) or (h).

The cargo owners' contentions were similar except that their main reliance was on (d), (g) and (h). Their attempts to apply (e) and (j) to the cargo involved as strained a construction of the paragraphs as that suggested by the shipowners in relation to (g) and (j). So in my opinion the cargo owners must look to (d), (g) or (h) if they are to found jurisdiction. Their case under those paragraphs corresponds exactly with that of the shipowners under (*d*), (*e*) and (*h*).

The defendants' case under (*d*) is that neither the Erkowit nor her cargo was damaged by the Rotesand; that there is no allegation of bad navigation of the salvage tug, the place of beaching may have been chosen by a salvage officer and not by the master or any officer of the Rotesand; and any later negligence, even if any of the crew participated in it, cannot be attributed to the tug.

As to (*e*) and (*g*), there is no doubt that the Erkowit and her cargo received damage and in the court below it was not argued that either plaintiff was unable to found jurisdiction under the relevant one of those paragraphs. What was contended in relation to the shipowners was that their claim to indemnity was not a claim for damage received by a ship. It appeared to us that whatever might be said about jurisdiction under s 1 of the 1956 Act, jurisdiction in rem might not be conferred by s 3(4) in the case of damage received by a ship, or by goods carried in a ship, if not done by a ship. It was for this reason that the defendants were given leave to amend their notice of appeal.

As to (*h*), the defendants contended that the salvage aggreement was not an agreement for the use or hire of a ship. It provided for the defendants to use their best endeavours to salve the Erkowit and her cargo and take them to a place the name of which was left blank. But it made no reference to the use of the Rotesand or any other vessel for this purpose.

The judge did not have to consider whether the cargo claim was within the jurisdiction and, as to the ship, he had only to decide whether the claim to indemnity was within one of the paragraphs relied on. He rejected the plaintiffs' case under (*d*), holding that no damage was done by the Rotesand, but he considered that the salvage agreement was an agreement for the use or hire of a ship, so that the claim was within (*h*) and, as to (*e*), he held that any liability of the owners of the Erkowit towards the Spanish government was covered by the words 'damage received by a ship'.

The Administration of Justice Act 1956 was passed following the adherence of the United Kingdom to the International Convention relating to the Arrest of Sea-going Ships[1] made at Brussels on 10th May 1952. Both sides made some reference to the convention for the purpose of assisting the construction of the Act, as was done by this court in *The Banco*[2]. Admittedly in relation to jurisdiction the Act's provisions are in some ways wider than the convention's provisions (for example the convention has no reference to 'damage received by a ship') and in other ways narrower (for example the convention does not confine the right of proceeding in rem to a ship owned by the person who might be sued in personam). In these circumstances I do not consider that reference to the convention throws such light on the meaning of the relevant provisions of the Act as to afford any assistance to the court.

Reference was also made to Part V of the Act, the only part of it which applies to Scotland, as an aid to the construction of the sections applicable to England. On the one hand it was said that, because the maritime law of Scotland is the same as that of England (*Currie v M'Knight*[3]), the jurisdiction of the English court must be as wide as that of the Scottish court and therefore s 47, which deals with the right of arrest in relation to the Scottish court, can be looked at to assist a liberal interpretation of words in s 1. On the other hand, it was contended that where the words of corresponding provisions differ, Parliament must have intended to differentiate between the two countries. I do not find either argument convincing. The proposition that the maritime law of Scotland is the same as that of England cannot involve that any statutory provision enacted in that field for one country must also apply to the other; while differences in language may be explicable on historical grounds. I therefore do not derive assistance from looking at the provisions for Scotland.

1 (1952) Cmd 8954
2 [1971] 1 All ER 524, [1971] P 137
3 [1897] AC 97

Some help is to be derived from earlier decisions of the courts in sections in earlier Acts corresponding with parts of s 1 of the 1956 Act. We were referred to a considerable number of authorities but I shall confine my citations to those which are most relevant to our problems.

I start with para (h) because it is under that paragraph that in my opinion the plaintiffs' case is strongest. There was a sharp conflict of opinion in the latter part of the 19th century as to the meaning of the words 'any agreement made in relation to the use or hire of a ship', then to be found in s 2 of the County Courts Admiralty Jurisdiction Amendment Act 1869[1]. In The Alina[2] a Court of Appeal presided over by Jessel MR considered that the words clearly covered a charterparty. In R v City of London Court Judge[3], a Court of Appeal presided over by Lord Esher MR, thought that the decision in The Alina[2] was wrong and, while feeling bound to 'obey' it, refused to extend it, to quote the language of Lord Esher MR[4], 'one particle beyond what it actually decides and determines'. There was at that time an understandable reluctance of some judges to give other than the narrowest possible meaning to the words, seeing that they conferred a jurisdiction which was not enjoyed by the High Court. It must, however, be observed that after such jurisdiction was given to the High Court (by s 5 of the Administration of Justice Act 1920) Sir Boyd Merriman P, presiding in the Court of Appeal in The Beldis[5], held that the court was still bound by the decision in R v City of London Court Judge[3]. The actual decision in The Beldis[5] was, however, simply that an action on an award made under an agreement was not an action arising out of the agreement. It is therefore not of direct assistance on the question of what agreements are within the words. In The Isca[6] an agreement for towage by a named vessel was held by a Divisional Court to be an agreement for the use or hire of it. In The Zeus[7] an agreement to load a ship was held by a Divisional Court not to be an agreement for the use or hire of it. Both of these decisions appear to me to be plainly right. In The Queen of the South[8] Brandon J himself held that contracts for mooring services by watermen using motor boats for the purpose were within the words of para (h). Counsel for the defendants invite us to overrule that decision. They submit that only a charterparty or an agreement closely akin to a charterparty is covered.

In my opinion there is no good reason for excluding from the expression 'an agreement for the use or hire of a ship' any agreement which an ordinary businessman would regard as being within it. If A and B make an agreement for A's ship to be used for carrying out any operation for B, I consider that the agreement is one for the use, if not for the hire, of the ship. Thus an agreement for a ship to be employed for dredging, towing, cable-laying or salvage would be an agreement for the use of the ship. But is an agreement for dredging or towage or cable-laying or salvage an agreement for the use of a ship if there is no express reference in the agreement to any such use? If the operations can only be carried out by means of a ship I consider that the agreement must be one for the use or hire of a ship. A towage agreement would therefore always come within the words. Dredging or cable-laying could conceivably be performed by other means, but in the great majority of cases it would be so obvious that the use of a ship must be intended that this would be implied. For salvage, every case must depend on the circumstances but where, as here, the contract is made on board a salvage tug which is in attendance near the casualty and is made between the two

---

1   See now s 56(1)(e) of the County Courts Act 1959, replacing the relevant provision of the Administration of Justice Act 1956, s 1, as to county courts
2   (1880) 5 ExD 227
3   [1892] 1 QB 273
4   [1892] 1 QB at 290
5   [1936] P 51, [1935] All ER Rep 760
6   (1886) 12 PD 34, 6 Asp MLC 63
7   (1888) 13 PD 188
8   [1968] 1 All ER 1163, [1968] P 449

masters and provides for the damaged vessel to be 'taken to a place of safety', it is in
a my opinion an agreement for the use or hire of a ship. I therefore agree with Brandon J
that the actions in rem are properly brought under para (h).

This makes it unnecessary for me to deal at much length with the issues arising
under the other paragraphs but in deference to the arguments of counsel I will state
my views on them.

As to para (d), the expression 'damage done by a ship' was considered in the Court
b of Appeal in The Vera Cruz[1]. Brett MR said[2] that the words applied to a case in
which 'a ship was the active cause, the damage being physically caused by the ship'.
Bowen LJ said[3]: ' "Done by a ship" means done by those in charge of a ship, with the
ship as the noxious instrument.'

In Currie v M'Knight[4] the issue was whether the cutting by the crew of one ship of
the moorings of another was to be regarded as the act or fault of the first ship so as to
c make it liable to a maritime lien. It was held that it was not. In the course of the
speeches Lord Halsbury LC said[5]:

'. . . the phrase that it must be the fault of the ship itself is not a mere figurative
expression, but it imports, in my opinion, that the ship against which a maritime
lien for damages is claimed is the instrument of mischief, and that in order to
d establish the liability of the ship itself to the maritime lien claimed some act of
navigation of the ship itself should either mediately or immediately be the cause
of the damage.'

Lord Watson said[6]:

'I think it is of the essence of the rule that the damage in respect of which a
e maritime lien is admitted must be either the direct result or the natural consequence of a wrongful act or manoeuvre of the ship to which it attaches. Such an
act or manoeuvre is necessarily due to the want of skill or negligence of the
person by whom the vessel is navigated; but it is, in the language of maritime law,
attributed to the ship because the ship in their negligent or unskilful hands is the
instrument which causes the damage.'

f In the present case it was accepted on both sides that the issue in Currie v M'Knight[4]
was in substance the same as the issue whether the damage was 'damage done by a
ship'. On the basis of the dicta I have cited I can see that any damage resulting from
the negligence of the crew of the Rotesand, or of any other servants of the defendants,
after the Erkowit was beached, was probably not to be regarded as done by the
Rotesand. But the plaintiffs claim that damage flowed from the actual beaching and
g that it was negligent to beach in that place. There is no doubt that the Erkowit was
put on the beach by the Rotesand. If that beaching caused damage to the Erkowit and
its cargo then the Rotesand was the 'active cause of the damage', the 'noxious instrument', the 'instrument of mischief'. That is sufficient to enable both the plaintiffs to
rely on para (d) as a foundation for an action in rem.

h Paragraph (e) gives rise to the most difficult questions that were debated before us.
To start with, if damage received by a ship can enable the owner of that ship to proceed in rem, against what ship can he proceed? Counsel on both sides agreed that for
the purpose of para (e) the ship referred to throughout s 3(4) of the 1956 Act, except in
para (b) at the end, is the ship which has received the damage. If that is so then an
action in rem can be brought if the person who is liable in personam was in possession

j
1   (1884) 9 PD 96
2   9 PD at 99
3   9 PD at 101
4   [1897] AC 97
5   [1897] AC at 101
6   [1897] AC at 106, 107   R

or control of the ship which received the damage at the time when the damage was done. Counsel for the plaintiffs contended that that condition was fulfilled here because at the time when the damage was done the Erkowit was so much disabled that the salvors had control, and perhaps possession, of her. Counsel for the defendants contended that 'possession or control' here means something akin to ownership and that the defendants were in no such relation to the ship, whose master could have dispensed with the services of the salvors at any time. though this might have been a breach of contract. Without attempting to define exactly what is meant by 'possession or control' in this context, it is sufficient for me to say that I am not satisfied that on the facts it was established here.

I am, however, by no means convinced that the interpretation of s 3(4) favoured by both counsel is correct. It seems to me that a more natural meaning of it is that the ship referred to throughout the subsection is a ship not belonging to the plaintiffs but having some connection with the damage (not necessarily such as to make that ship the 'instrument of mischief'). Otherwise it is difficult to see why claims under para (e) were included in s 3(1) at all. This would, I think, afford a possible basis of jurisdiction in this case, but as counsel for the plaintiffs did not in the end rely on it I should prefer not to express a concluded opinion on it. Exactly the same considerations apply to para (g) in relation to the cargo owners' claim.

If jurisdiction can be established by the shipowners under para (e), can the 'damage received' include any liability to the Spanish government? Counsel for the defendants relies on the fact that under para (e) only a claim for damage received by a ship is covered, as contrasted with other paragraphs such as para (h) where the wording is 'any claim arising out of any agreement'. It is, however, conceded that 'damage' must include the cost of repairing the damage and any loss caused by detention of the ship during repair. I can see no logical reason why any other consequential loss should be excluded.

Coming then to the defendants' application for a stay under s 4(1) of the Arbitration Act 1950, the first issue is whether the plaintiffs' claims are within the arbitration provisions of the salvage agreement. Those provisions are contained in cl 1 of the agreement which, after specifying the services to be rendered by the salvors, and providing for the amount of their remuneration to be fixed, in certain events, by arbitration 'in the manner hereinafter prescribed' goes on: 'and any other difference arising out of this Agreement or the operations thereunder shall be referred to Arbitration in the same way.' Clauses 4 to 9 of the agreement contain detailed provision as to the manner of arbitration, many of those details being appropriate only to a claim for remuneration. The plaintiffs contended that as the claims here could not be dealt with 'in the manner prescribed', the terms as to arbitration could not apply to such claims, or at least could only apply if the claims were made by way of counterclaim to a claim for remuneration. The judge rejected that argument and on the face of it it seems to me that he was right to do so, because if accepted it would appear to nullify the effect of the provision for arbitration of 'any other difference'. However, we did not hear any argument from counsel for the plaintiffs on this issue so I say no more about it and, on the assumption that the claims are within the arbitration clause, go on to consider whether the judge's decision to refuse a stay is one which this court can and should reverse.

The grounds put forward by the plaintiffs for resisting a stay were first, the avoidance of multiplicity of proceedings, and secondly, that difficult questions of law, or of mixed fact and law, were involved. The judge considered that the avoidance of duplication of proceedings in England was the decisive factor. I do not consider that this court should interfere with his exercise of discretion unless it could be shown either that he was under some misapprehension about such duplication or that he failed to give sufficient weight to countervailing considerations on the other side.

It is said on behalf of the defendants that multiplicity of proceedings is unavoidable because the Spanish government is suing in Spain while the claims of the Erkowit

and her cargo, whether wholly in court or partly by way of arbitration, will of course
be pursued in England. The fact that some multiplicity is inevitable does not mean
that it is not desirable to limit it as much as possible. There are a number of issues
that fall to be tried both as between the plaintiffs and the Dortmund and as between
the plaintiffs and the salvors. If the four English actions continue they can be heard by
the same judge at the same time, costs will be saved and the risk of conflicting decisions will be avoided. The prevention of duplication is not a conclusive ground for
refusing a stay (see *Bruce v Strong*[1]) but it is an important consideration and has often
been the main ground on which a stay has been refused: see, for example, *The Pine
Hill*[2], per McNair J, and *Taunton-Collins v Cromie*[3].

The defendants raise two points in connection with the Spanish proceedings—that
they will wish to counterclaim against the owners of the Erkowit for indemnity or
contribution in respect of any damages that may be found due from them to the
Spanish government, which counterclaim could not be formulated till after the conclusion of the Spanish proceedings; and that if the claims against them in England are
heard in open court before the Spanish action is heard, the publicity (which would be
avoided by arbitration) might be detrimental to them. As to the first of these points,
I think it would be quite wrong that the decision on the plaintiffs' claims, whether
pursued in court or before an arbitrator, should be deferred for what might be a
period of years pending the decision in Spain. As Brandon J said, once the facts have
been decided by the court there would be nothing to prevent the defendants from
raising a claim to contribution or indemnity at a later stage if necessary. As to publicity, the question whether the defendants were negligent is an issue in the collision
actions and the investigation of that issue in the actions against the defendants will not
substantially add to the publicity.

The contention on the defendants' side which most impressed the judge was this.
Section 8 of the Maritime Conventions Act 1911 prescribes a time limit of two years
for, inter alia, proceedings 'in respect of any salvage service'. Under s 27(1) of the
Limitation Act 1939 that time limit applies also to arbitrations. If the actions were stayed
and an arbitration were commenced, the defendants, would be able to rely on the
time bar as a defence. If the actions proceed the defendants are deprived of that defence because the actions were started within the two year period. It is to my mind an
unattractive argument for a party to seek to insist on arbitration so as to enable him to
contend that he can render the arbitration ineffective. The authority relied on in support of the argument is *Bruce v Strong*[1] where it was held that the fact that an arbitration
would be out of time was not a good reason for refusing a stay. That, however, was a
case where the arbitration agreement provided for a special time limit, shorter than
the statutory one, so that if a stay had been granted the plaintiff would have been
able to escape from the obligation to bring his proceedings within the agreed time.
Here no such consideration arises; the plaintiffs have brought their proceedings within
the time which is the same for an arbitration as for an action.

This matter was dealt with in the judgment below on the basis that the only relevant way in which the plaintiffs' claims could be regarded was as claims in respect of
salvage. The judge considered it very doubtful whether they could be so regarded
and I agree with him. If, however, I am right in thinking that the plaintiffs' claims
can be described, at least in part, as claims for damage done by a ship, then such
claims would be subject to the two year time bar. There is, however, the further point
that the proviso to s 8 of the 1911 Act enables any court having jurisdiction (and the
same must apply to an arbitrator) to extend the period to such extent and on such
conditions as it thinks fit. The judge considered it very doubtful whether or not, if the
claims were held to fall within s 8, the time would be extended. It was submitted

---

1   [1951] 1 All ER 1021, [1951] 2 KB 447
2   [1958] 2 Lloyd's Rep 146
3   [1964] 2 All ER 332, [1964] 1 WLR 633

for the defendants that it was clear that the time would not be extended. The only
authority on the proviso to which we were referred was *The Alnwick*[1], where time was **a**
extended by the Court of Appeal, Willmer LJ dissenting. The majority considered
that the time should be extended because the failure to take proceedings in time was
not blameworthy. In the absence of any authority on the question whether time should
be extended where proceedings have been brought within the time limit but the
defendants have succeeded in getting those proceedings stayed so as to compel the
plaintiffs to proceed by arbitration outside the time limit, I do not consider that the **b**
judge was wrong in regarding that as a question to which the answer was very doubtful.

Although I have differed from the judge on one point which he took into account
in exercising his discretion I do not consider that that was of sufficient weight to lead
to the conclusion that his exercise of discretion should be disregarded. I would add,
however, that even if I took the view that the limitation defence if raised would be
bound to succeed, and that for that reason this court should exercise a fresh discretion **c**
in the matter, I should be of opinion that the stay should be refused because I regard
the avoidance of unnecessary multiplicity as a strong ground for letting the actions
proceed and, while *Bruce v Strong*[2] establishes that the expiration of the time for
arbitration is not a ground for refusing a stay, I do not consider that in the circumstances
of this case the deprivation of the defendants of the opportunity of setting up the
defence of limitation is a positive reason in favour of a stay.   **d**

In the result I would dismiss the appeal.

SCARMAN LJ. I have had the advantage of reading the judgments of the other
members of the court. I agree that the appeals should be dismissed. I do not wish to
add to what Cairns LJ has already said on the arbitration clause. I agree with the **e**
construction put by Sir Gordon Willmer on s 1(1) of the Administration of Justice Act
1956, and wish to make only a few general observations as to the approach to the
interpretation of the subsection. But, since I think that the crux of the two appeals is
the construction of s 3(4) of the 1956 Act, I propose to consider that subsection at greater
length.

Part I of the Act deals with the Admiralty jurisdiction of the High Court in England **f**
and Wales, and Part V with the Admiralty jurisdiction of the courts of Scotland. I
would not expect to find any substantial difference between the two jurisdictions,
though there are (and, no doubt, will continue to be) differences attributable to the
need to fit the law of the sea (which is the same in England, Wales and Scotland:
Currie v M'Knight[3]) into the two different legal systems. Subject to that one reservation, I think it right to construe Part I of the Act consistently with Part V, on the basis **g**
that the substance of the maritime law is the same in both jurisdictions; and no doubt
Scots lawyers will construe Part V, subject to the same reservation, in a way consistent
with Part I.

More especially must this approach be correct when interpreting ss 3(4) and 47(1)
which are the subsections that introduce into the law of England and Wales and the
law of Scotland respectively the provisions of the International Convention relating **h**
to the Arrest of Sea-going Ships[4] signed at Brussels in 1952 and ratified by the United
Kingdom in 1959.

Section 1(1) of the 1956 Act specifies the questions and claims which are the subject
of the Admiralty jurisdiction of the High Court. The section is the current statutory
statement of the extent of the jurisdiction. It is, for the time being, the last of a series
of such statements originating with the Admiralty Court Act 1840 which settled **j**
in favour of the Admiralty the ancient strife between the courts of the common law

1   [1965] 2 All ER 569, [1965] P 357
2   [1951] 1 All ER 1021, [1951] 2 KB 447
3   [1897] AC 97
4   (1952) Cmd 8954

and the Admiralty Court as to the jurisdiction of the latter over disputes relating to
a ships within the body of a county, that is to say within internal waters. The price
paid for this victory was that the Admiralty jurisdiction was limited to the questions
and claims specified by the Act—at least so far as internal waters were concerned.

The jurisdiction has been enlarged since 1840 in some respects (for example the
addition of claims arising out of agreements relating to the use or hire of a ship); but
the principle of the list and, subject to some amendment (for instance the 1956 Act has
b dropped specific reference to the body of a county), the descriptions of the claims
have remained intact from statute to statute. It is safe, therefore, to infer, according
to an accepted principle of statutory interpretation (see *Greaves v Tofield*[1]), that
claims specified by the 1956 Act in language the same as that of previous statutes
should be given the same meaning. The extent of the Admiralty jurisdiction is thus
the subject of a considerable case law interpreting statutory provisions that over the
c years have become well known.

But the mode of its exercise was not the subject of comprehensive enactment until,
following the Brussels convention[2], s 3 was enacted. Case law on the section (save as
to its application to 'sister ships') is almost non-existent. The section makes clear that
Admiralty jurisdiction may exist and be exercisable by action in personam without
an action in rem being available. The action in rem may be invoked only in the cases
d mentioned in sub-ss (2) and (5). One of the reasons for thus limiting the availability
of the action in rem is, I have no doubt, that the Brussels convention[2] provides by
art 2 that a ship of a contracting state may not be arrested save in respect of one of the
maritime claims set out in art 1. Put briefly, the convention permits the arrest of ships
(and, therefore, in the Latin language of the English law the institution of an Admiralty
action in rem) in respect of the maritime claims specified in art 1, 'but in respect of no
e other claims': art 2. It further permits the arrest of a 'sister ship' when the ship in
respect of which the claim arises has passed out of the ownership of the defendant:
art 3. While some of the maritime claims in respect of which a ship may be arrested
do not give rise to a maritime lien, each one of them is concerned with either services
rendered to a ship or damage arising from the use of a ship, or with problems concerned
with rights of ownership, possession or mortgage of a ship.

f The convention does not include amongst its maritime claims a claim for 'damage
received by a ship', although it is a claim that under English law gives rise to Admiralty
jurisdiction. In every case covered by the convention there is a clearly defined link
between the claim and the ship sought to be arrested, a link such as makes it just and
reasonable that the claimant should be permitted to look to the ship (or in a proper
case its 'sister ship') as security for the satisfaction of his claim. So far as accidental
g damage is concerned, the convention identifies the claims that justify arrest by
reference not to ships that receive or suffer damage but to ships that cause damage.

Section 3(4) is to be presumed to give effect to the convention and should be construed accordingly. The subsection deals with claims of damage or for services
rendered, i e those mentioned in paras (d) to (r) of s 1(1) of the 1956 Act. It declares
the circumstances in which such a claim, 'being a claim arising in connection with a
h ship', may be pursued by an action in rem against that ship (or its 'sister ship'). No
action in rem is available unless the claim is shown to be a claim against a ship. To
establish, therefore, the availability of an action in rem it is not enough merely to
ascertain whether the claim is one of those mentioned in paras (d) to (r) of s 1(1) of
the 1956 Act. It is also necessary that the claim should relate to a ship which has caused
damage or in respect of which services have been rendered or money disbursed. It
j does not follow that because there is Admiralty jurisdiction to entertain a claim, an
action in rem may be invoked to enforce it. The existence of jurisdiction depends on
s 1 of the 1956 Act; but the availability of an action in rem depends on s 3. When

---

1 (1880) 14 Ch D 563 at 571
2 (1952) Cmd 8954

s 3(4) provides that an action in rem can be invoked only if the claim is 'a claim
arising in connection with a ship', it is referring, in my judgment, to a ship in respect   *a*
of which a maritime claim as specified in the convention arises. Section 47(1) is clearly
so limited, and I would not expect any difference in this matter between English and
Scots law.

If the shipowners' claim is put solely under para (e) of s 1(1), it has to be regarded
as a claim arising in connection with the Erkowit, the ship which suffered or 'received'
the damage. In respect of such a claim the subsection does not permit an action in   *b*
rem; for it is not the Erkowit in respect of which a convention maritime claim arises.
The convention and the subsection contemplate as the 'res' which may be arrested:
(i) in a damage claim, not the victim but the wrongdoing ship; and (ii) in a claim for
services rendered, the ship to which the services were rendered.

The same reasoning would nonsuit the cargo owners if they had to rely on para (g)
alone.   *c*

But in truth neither the shipowners nor the cargo owners are so confined. They can
establish jurisdiction under para (d) by showing, as Sir Gordon Willmer explains,
that their claim is for damage done by a ship, that is to say the defendants' tug Rotesand, in which case they are enabled under the subsection to bring their action in rem
against the Rotesand, or, as they have done, a sister ship of the Rotesand. I think also,
though it is unnecessary to decide the point, that they can show a claim under para (h).   *d*
Both the shipowners and the cargo owners have, in my opinion, a claim arising out
of an agreement relating to the use of the Rotesand, that is to say the salvage agreement, in which case they may also institute actions in rem against the Rotesand or a
sister ship. Taking the view that I do of the scope of s 3(4), I think these appeals
should be dismissed. Each plaintiff may invoke the jurisdiction by action in rem; for
each of them, shipowner and cargo owner, can formulate a claim under para (d) or (h),   *e*
citing the Rotesand as the ship in connection with which the claim arises.

SIR GORDON WILLMER. At the conclusion of his argument against the
adoption of an excessively restrictive approach to the Admiralty jurisdiction of the
court, counsel for the plaintiffs remarked that if there is any case that ought to come   *f*
within the Admiralty jurisdiction in rem, this is it. Counsel for the defendants on
the other hand, advocating a more restricted approach, concluded his final address
by reminding us, quite properly, that this is a jurisdiction which affects foreigners,
and therefore the statute conferring it should be strictly construed. But it is fair to
observe that in the present case not only are the proposed defendants foreign, but so
also are the plaintiffs who invoke the jurisdiction of the court, no doubt in the hope   *g*
that the court's approach to their claims will not be wholly unsympathetic. However
this may be, it is plain to me that the judge whose task it is to navigate in these difficult waters must take care to shape a course which will keep him clear, on the one
hand, of the Scylla of excessive restriction and, on the other hand, of the Charybdis
of too much liberality. For my part I shall do my best to keep in mid-channel.

The relevant facts have already been summarised in the judgment delivered by   *h*
Cairns LJ, and it is unnecessary for me to repeat them. Nor do I need to set out again
the relevant statutory provisions, which have already been quoted. It is sufficient to
say that the plaintiffs in each of the two actions before us seek to bring themselves
within one or more of the following paragraphs of s 1(1) of the Administration of
Justice Act 1956, that is to say:

'. . . (d) any claim for damage done by a ship; (e) any claim for damage received   *j*
by a ship . . . (g) any claim for loss of or damage to goods carried in a ship; (h)
any claim arising out of any agreement relating to the carriage of goods in a ship
or to the use or hire of a ship; (j) any claim in the nature of salvage . . .'

In the case of both actions the claim sought to be enforced in rem is a claim for the

total loss of the plaintiffs' property, that is to say, of the Erkowit herself and the cargo
a laden on board her. In the case of the shipowners' action there is a further claim,
which it is also sought to enforce in rem, for an indemnity against possible claims,
asserted against the owners of the Erkowit by the Spanish government on behalf of
local fishermen, in respect of pollution caused by the escape from the wreck of the
Erkowit of a number of drums containing a noxious chemical. A further question
arises in relation to both actions, namely whether, assuming the assertion of Admiralty
b jurisdiction in rem to be well founded, the respective actions ought to be stayed in
pursuance of s 4(1) of the Arbitration Act 1950 on the ground that the damage and
loss complained of arose in the course of salvage operations being carried on by the
tug Rotesand in pursuance of a salvage agreement on Lloyd's form signed on behalf
of ship and cargo by the master of the Erkowit. As is well known, this form of salvage
agreement makes provision for the reference to arbitration of disputes between sal-
c vors and those interested in the property to be salved. So far as this question is concerned I agree, for the reasons already stated by Cairns LJ, that this is not a proper
case for granting a stay, and I see no reason for saying that the learned judge wrongly
exercised his discretion in refusing it. I do not find it necessary to add any further
observations of my own with regard to this aspect of the case.

I confine myself, therefore, to the two questions relating to the Admiralty jurisdic-
d tion in rem, namely (1) whether there is jurisdiction in rem against the Rotesand or
one of her sister ships in respect of the plaintiffs' claims for the total loss of the Erkowit and her cargo, and (2) whether, if so, the owners of the Erkowit can include in
their claim a declaration that they are entitled to be indemnified, either wholly or
in part, against their possible liability to the Spanish government in respect of the
pollution caused by the escape from the wreck of the drums of noxious chemical.
e The greater part of s 1(1) of the 1956 Act consists of a re-enactment of similar
provisions contained in earlier statutes. I agree with the learned judge in thinking
that where expressions used are the same as those used in earlier statutes, they should
prima facie be construed as having the same meaning as may have been assigned to
them by prior judicial decision. I also agree that, since Part I of the 1956 Act was passed
for the purpose of giving effect to the International Convention relating to the Arrest
f of Sea-going Ships[1], it is permissible to look at the terms of the convention where
phrases used in the Act are thought to be capable of more than one meaning. This
arises particularly in relation to s 3 of the 1956 Act, which governs rights of arrest and
is presumably intended to give effect to art 3 of the convention.

In construing the five paragraphs of s 1(1) of the 1956 Act which have been invoked
in this case, I think it is important to start by considering in relation to each what is
g 'the ship' which is referred to. In the case of para (d), 'damage done by a ship', the
ship referred to can only be the alleged wrongdoer, that is to say the ship whose
faulty navigation is said to be the cause of the damage. In the context of this case that
ship would be the tug Rotesand. As to para (e), 'damage received by a ship', the ship
referred to must clearly be the ship alleged to have been damaged, which in the
context of this case would be the Erkowit. So much appears to be plain beyond
h difficulty.

In the case of para (g), 'loss of or damage to goods carried in a ship', the answer is
perhaps not so immediately obvious. But construing the words used in their natural
and ordinary sense, I conclude that the ship referred to must be the carrying ship.
The paragraph must be designed to cover the claim of a cargo owner against the ship
to which he has entrusted his cargo. The words do not appear to be apt to cover a
j claim against some other ship. If it is alleged that goods carried in ship A were
damaged in consequence of fault on the part of ship B, it seems to me that the plaintiffs would have their remedy under para (d), on the basis that the damage was done
by such other ship, and that they would have no need to invoke para (g), the wording

---

1   (1952) Cmd 8954

of which is at best equivocal. In the context of this case, therefore, I would hold that
the only ship to which para (g) could apply is the Erkowit.   *a*

Paragraph (h), to my mind, also presents some difficulty—for it is directed to two
separate eventualities. Insofar as it is concerned with a claim arising out of an agreement relating to the carriage of goods in a ship, the ship referred to must be the ship
in which the goods are carried (or to be carried) in pursuance of the agreement.
Nothing arises in this case in relation to this part of the paragraph. But the latter
part of the paragraph refers to a claim arising out of an agreement relating to the use   *b*
or hire of a ship. Such a claim does not necessarily have anything to do with the carriage of goods, for a ship can well be hired or used for other purposes. It seems to
me that the ship referred to in relation to any such claim must be the ship alleged to
have been used or hired. In the context of this case that ship is alleged to be the tug
Rotesand.

In relation to para (j), 'any claim in the nature of salvage', it appears to me that the   *c*
only ship in respect of which such a claim could be asserted would be the ship alleged
to have been salved. A claim for damage alleged to have been caused to salved property by fault on the part of the salvors would not be a claim in the nature of salvage.
If the damage is alleged to have been caused by fault on the part of a salving ship,
such a claim could well fall within para (d), but I have difficulty in seeing how it
could possibly be caught by para (j).   *d*

In the present case the learned judge held that neither the shipowners' nor the
cargo owners' claim came within paras (d) or (j). He held that the shipowners' claim
did come within paras (e) and (h), and that the cargo owners' claim came within
paras (g) and (h). It was conceded before him by the defendants that the shipowners'
claim was within para (e) so far as concerned the loss of the Erkowit, and the only
question argued before him in relation to this paragraph was whether the alleged   *e*
consequential damage, that is to say the potential liability for pollution at the suit
of the Spanish government, came within the paragraph. It was also conceded by the
defendants before the learned judge that the cargo owners' claim for the loss of their
cargo came within para (g).

In the course of the argument before us the case underwent a number of kaleido-
scopic changes. Having regard to the manner in which the argument developed we   *f*
thought it right to grant leave to counsel for the defendants to withdraw the concessions which he made in the court below in relation to paras (e) and (g). This necessitated granting leave to amend the notice of appeal in the two actions. We also
thought it right in the circumstances to grant leave to amend the respondents'
notice in the shipowners' action, by adding submissions that the damage alleged fell
within paras (g) and (j), as well as within para (d). In the result we have to consider all   *g*
five of the relevant paragraphs.

In relation to para (e), it is plain that there is Admiralty jurisdiction in respect of
damage received by a ship, and there can be no doubt that such a claim can be enforced by an action in personam: see s 3(1) of the 1956 Act. But the question is whether
any right in rem can be asserted, and if so, against what ship. It is noteworthy that the
Brussels convention[1], which is concerned only with rights of arrest, makes no men-   *h*
tion of the case of 'damage received by a ship'. It is to be implied that those responsible for drafting the convention recognised that in the case of damage received by a
ship there would normally be no question of arrest. If the damage were caused by the
fault of another ship there could be a right to arrest such other ship, because it would
be a case of damage done by that ship and thus within para (d). If the damage received were caused otherwise than by a ship, for instance, by fault on the part of a   *j*
dock or harbour authority, there would be no res capable of being arrested. It was
conceded by counsel for the defendants that there might be one possible case for
asserting a right in rem in respect of damage received by a ship. That might arise in

1   (1952) Cmd 8954

the event of the ship receiving the damage being subject to a demise charter. If the
damage were caused by the fault of the demise charterers then it could be said that
under para (b) of s 3(4) of the 1956 Act it might be possible to arrest a sister ship
beneficially owned by the demise charterers. But that is not this case.

The question must ultimately turn on the true construction of s 3(4) of the 1956
Act. As I read that section, giving the words used their ordinary and natural meaning,
the ship in connection with which the plaintiffs' claim arises is the Erkowit, the ship
which received the damage. The persons who would be liable in an action in personam
would be the salvors, the owners of the Rotesand. I do not see how it is possible to
extract from the subsequent wording of the subsection any right to arrest the Rotesand (or a sister ship of the Rotesand). Only the ship in connection with which the
claim arises (or a sister ship thereof) can be arrested. I think this view receives support
from the terms of art 3(1) of the convention, whereby it is provided that 'a claimant
may arrest either the particular ship in respect of which the maritime claim arose, or
any other ship which is owned by the person who was, at the time when the maritime
claim arose, the owner of the particular ship . . .'

In his argument on behalf of the plaintiffs, counsel put forward two possible alternative ways of construing s 3(4). In the first place he suggested that at the material time
the defendants, the owners of the Rotesand, were in possession and control of the
Erkowit. They were thus virtually in the position of demise charterers, and accordingly it would be possible under para (b) of the subsection to arrest another ship
beneficially owned by them. This is an ingenious suggestion, but in my judgment it
fails on the facts. Those in charge of the Rotesand may have been in physical control of
the Erkowit, in the sense that, in the absence of any crew on board, her movements
were entirely dictated by the action of the Rotesand. But in my view counsel for the
defendants was well founded when he submitted that in the context of s 3(4) of the
1956 Act the words 'possession' and 'control' mean something much more than this,
as was held by Brandon J in The Andrea Ursula¹.

The other alternative suggested was to construe the words 'being a claim arising
in connection with a ship' as meaning a claim arising in connection with the Rotesand.
For my part, I find this suggestion difficult to accept. It strikes me as involving a
strained construction, by no means in accord with the scheme of the Act. It does not
fit very easily with art 3(1) of the convention, which I have already quoted. It over-
looks the fact that what we are dealing with here is damage received by the Erkowit.
Moreover, if all that is contended is that jurisdiction existed to arrest the Rotesand
(or a sister ship thereof) because the Rotesand by her faulty navigation caused the
damage complained of, the plaintiffs could have their remedy in rem under para (d)
of s 1(1), and they do not need to invoke para (e).

In these circumstances I am satisfied that the concession made before the learned
judge below was wrongly made, with the result that the learned judge, through no
fault of his own, arrived at a wrong conclusion in holding that there was jurisdiction
in rem under para (e) against the Rotesand or a sister ship thereof. In my judgment
the defendants are entitled to succeed on this issue.

Much the same applies in relation to the claim of the cargo owners to assert a right
in rem against the Rotesand or her sister ship under para (g). Had the claim been
against the Erkowit as the carrying ship, I entertain no doubt that this would have
given rise to a right in rem against that vessel. The Erkowit, and not the Rotesand, was
the ship in connection with which the claim arose. Here again I think it is helpful to
look at the terms of art 3(1) of the Brussels convention. If the cargo owners make
good their allegation that the loss of their goods was caused by the fault of the Rotesand, it seems to me that they may have their remedy in rem against the Rotesand (or
a sister ship) under para (d), as being damage done by the Rotesand, and that they
have no need to invoke para (g). This also in my judgment applies in relation to the

---

1   [1971] 1 All ER 821, [1973] 1 QB 265

contention in the shipowners' action, first put forward by way of amendment in this
court, that they too are entitled, as bailees of the cargo, to assert a right in rem under   *a*
para (*g*) against the Rotesand or her sister ship. In relation to this paragraph also the
defendants are in my judgment entitled to succeed.

I have already, I think, sufficiently indicated my view as to the claim, put forward
both by the shipowners and by the cargo owners, to invoke para (*j*). To be fair to the
plaintiffs, this point was not very enthusiastically argued on their behalf either before
the learned judge or in this court. Suffice it to say that I am unable to perceive how a   *b*
claim in respect of damage caused by negligent salvage can possibly be brought
within the words 'any claim in the nature of salvage'. A claim in the nature of salvage
could, in my judgment, only arise against the owners of the property salved. On this
issue too my judgment is in favour of the defendants.

That leaves only the claims put forward by both shipowners and cargo owners
under paras (*d*) and (*h*). With regard to para (*d*), the principal authority relied on by   *c*
both sides was the decision of the House of Lords in *Currie v M'Knight*[1]. This was a
Scottish appeal, but it was expressly held that the Admiralty jurisdiction in Scotland
was the same as that in England. It is true that the decision was not directed to the
construction of the words 'damage done by a ship'. The question at issue, however,
was the related question whether in the events which occurred a maritime lien
attached to the alleged wrongdoing ship, so as to entitle the owners of the damaged   *d*
ship to assert a right in rem against her. What happened was that the pursuer's ship
was alleged to have been damaged by the action of members of the crew of the
defender's ship in wrongfully interfering with the moorings of the former. The crew
members of the defender's ship were not on board their ship at the time, and it was
held that accordingly their alleged wrongful action did not give rise to a maritime
lien against the ship. Lord Halsbury LC expressed the view[2] that the ship against   *e*
which a maritime lien for damages is claimed must be 'the instrument of mischief'.
Similarly Lord Watson said[3] that the damage must either be the direct result or the
natural consequence of a wrongful act or manoeuvre of the ship to which it attaches.
This echoes the dictum of Bowen LJ in the earlier case of *The Vera Cruz*[4], where the
question was whether at that date the phrase 'damage done by a ship' was apt to
confer Admiralty jurisdiction in rem in relation to life claims arising from alleged   *f*
negligence on the part of a colliding ship. Bowen LJ said[5] that damage ' "Done by a
ship" means done by those in charge of a ship, with the ship as the noxious instrument'.
See also *The Theta*[6], where this dictum was applied in relation to a claim for personal
injury.

In the present case what is alleged by the plaintiffs in both actions, that is to say
the owners of both ship and cargo, is that the Rotesand, while towing the Erkowit,   *g*
negligently beached her in an exposed position, with the result that with the advent
of adverse weather she broke up, and both ship and cargo were totally lost. Assuming
that the plaintiffs are able to substantiate these allegations, it seems to me that if ever
there was a case where the defendants' vessel was 'the noxious instrument' this was it.
On this point I find myself unable to agree with the decision of the learned judge. I
would hold that the plaintiffs' claim plainly falls within para (*d*), and that they are   *h*
entitled in both actions to assert a right in rem on this ground.

This is sufficient to render it impossible to strike out in limine the plaintiffs' claims
in respect of the loss of the Erkowit and her cargo. It is strictly unnecessary, therefore,
to consider the alternative ground under para (*h*), on which the plaintiffs in both
actions also rely. But as this point was fully argued before us, I think it is only right to

---

1   [1897] AC 97
2   [1897] AC at 101
3   [1897] AC at 106
4   (1884) 9 PD 96
5   9 PD at 101
6   [1894] P 280

express my views on it. The plaintiffs assert, and the defendants deny, the the sal-
a vage agreement entered into by the master of the Rotesand on behalf of the defendants
and by the master of the Erkowit on behalf of the ship and cargo, constituted in effect
an agreement for the use of the Rotesand. It is true that there was no express agreement to this effect. But what was provided was that the contractor, as represented
by the Rotesand (the only salvage instrument on the scene), agreed to use his best
endeavours to salve the Erkowit and her cargo and take them into a place to be
b thereafter agreed with the master. Since the Erkowit was in a totally disabled condition, some 50 miles or so from land in the Bay of Biscay, what the contractor agreed
to do necessarily involved the Rotesand taking the Erkowit in tow for the purpose of
taking her to a place of safety, with or without further assistance. I think it is necessary
to take a realistic view and to construe the terms of the agreement in the light of
these surrounding circumstances. Although the Rotesand was not actually named as
c the towing instrument, in order to give business efficacy to the agreement it must at
least be implied that she was to be used for the purpose of the necessary towage. In
the circumstances I find it impossible to resist the conclusion that the salvage agreement constituted an agreement, inter alia, for the use of the Rotesand. As such it fell
within para (*h*), and in my view would entitle the plaintiffs to assert a claim in rem
in respect of alleged negligence in the performance of the agreement.
d   For my part I do not think that much assistance is to be derived from the numerous
cases cited to us, whereby in the last century the court sought to apply a restrictive
construction to the words of the County Courts Admiralty Jurisdiction Amendment
Act 1869, by which this class of claim was first brought within the Admiralty juridic-
tion, albeit at that time only in the county court. Of the other cases cited, it seems to
me that *The Isca*[1], which was decided as long ago as 1886, is very much in point. It is
e true that that case arose out of an agreement for the use of a specifically named tug,
and on that ground it was sought on behalf of the defendants to distinguish it. But
for reasons already adumbrated I do not think that this is a valid point of distinction.
I have found more difficulty with *The Queen of the South*[2] and *The Conoco Britannia*[3],
both of which were decisions of Brandon J. In the former case the claim was by
watermen, as owners of motor boats, against the ship for whose assistance they were
f used. In the latter case the claim was by the owners of a tug engaged to assist a ship
under a towage contract. In both cases the use alleged was a use of the plaintiffs' own
vessels, that is to say, in both cases these were the vessels 'in connection with which'
the claim arose. I find it difficult to see how under s 3(4) of the 1956 Act jurisdiction
in rem could properly be asserted against the ship which the plaintiffs' vessels were
assisting. In this connection again I bear in mind the provisions of art 3(1) of the
g Brussels convention, to which I have already referred. No point, however, appears
to have been taken in either case that there could be no right of arrest as against the
defendants' ship. It seems to me that it may be necessary, if and when the point
arises again, to reconsider these two decisions. For the purposes of the present case it
does not seem necessary to rely on them in support of the plaintiffs' assertion of
jurisdiction in rem under para (*h*) against the Rotesand or one of her sister ships.
h   For these reasons, so far as concerns the claims for the loss of the Erkowit and her
cargo, I am satisfied that the plaintiffs in both actions are entitled to assert a right in
rem against the Rotesand, whether under para (*d*) or para (*h*), and in aid thereof to
arrest the respective sister ships. Thus I agree with the conclusion at which the learned
judge arrived, albeit for rather different reasons.
       This leaves for consideration the contention of the plaintiffs in the shipowners'
j action that they are entitled to include a claim for indemnity (which would presumably include a claim for contribution) in respect of any sum for which they may

---

1 (1886) 12 PD 34
2 [1968] 1 All ER 1163, [1968] P 449
3 [1972] 2 All ER 238, [1972] 2 QB 543

be found liable in the Spanish proceedings, arising from the alleged pollution caused by the escape of noxious chemical from the wreck of the Erkowit. This is put forward as a claim for consequential loss following on the alleged negligence of those in charge of the Rotesand in beaching the Erkowit in an exposed position. It is further alleged that subsequent to the beaching the defendants, the owners of the Rotesand, were guilty of further acts of negligence in (a) fitting only a wood and canvas patch, instead of a steel patch, over the hole in the side of the Erkowit, and (b) failing to carry out their salvage operations with reasonable expedition. For the defendants it is contended that no part of this claim for consequential loss is capable of forming any ground for asserting a right in rem against the Rotesand. Insofar as it may be found that the pollution was caused by the alleged negligence of the defendants in carrying out their operations subsequent to the beaching of the Erkowit, I am of the opinion that the contention of the defendants is well founded. But insofar as the pollution may have resulted from the earlier alleged negligence of those in charge of the Rotesand in beaching the Erkowit in an exposed position, it seems to me that different considerations apply. If the plaintiffs succeed in proving that the beaching of the Erkowit constituted damage done by the Rotesand, so as to confer a right in rem within para (d) of s 1(1) of the 1956 Act, I do not see why they should not be entitled to include in their damage claim a claim for consequential loss. It is well known that a claim for consequential loss of earnings during the period while a damaged ship is laid up for repair is commonly included as a legitimate head of claim. Not infrequently a claim in respect of liabilities incurred towards third parties is also included. As was said by Lord Sumner in *The Cairnbahn*[1]:

'The word "loss" is wide enough to include that form of pecuniary prejudice which consists in compensating third parties for wrong done to them by the fault of persons for whose misconduct the party prejudiced must answer.'

If in the Spanish proceedings the owners of the Erkowit were held to be answerable for the alleged pollution, this might well give rise to a good claim for indemnity or contribution as against the owners of the Rotesand, whether or not in those proceedings the owners of the Rotesand were also held to be answerable.

The difficulty at the present stage is to know exactly what form the claim of the Spanish government in respect of the pollution may take. If the government's claim is framed in tort, and their action is successful on the basis of fault, whether on the part of the Erkowit or of the Rotesand or both, I do not see any reason why the plaintiffs should not be entitled to include in their claim against the defendants a claim for indemnity or contribution in respect of the damages which they may be adjudged liable to pay: see *The Frankland*[2] and *The Cairnbahn*[3]. But the situation would be different if the Spanish government's claim is based on some provision of Spanish law entitling them to recover compensation in respect of the pollution irrespective of fault. In such case any compensation which the plaintiffs might have to pay could well be held to result solely from the provision of Spanish law, so that it could not properly be included in the plaintiffs' claim against the defendants as part of the damage done by the Rotesand: see *The Circe*[4] and *The Molière*[5]. Since it is impossible at the present stage to foresee whether or not the plaintiffs' claim for an indemnity or contribution in respect of the alleged consequential loss will be sustainable in law, it seems to me that it would be quite wrong to strike it out in limine. In my judgment the present application to do so is premature.

---

1   [1914] P 25 at 33
2   [1901] P 161
3   [1914] P 25
4   [1906] P 1
5   [1925] P 27

a For these reasons I have come to the conclusion, in agreement with Cairns and Scarman LJJ, that the appeals in both actions should be dismissed.

Appeals dismissed. Leave to appeal to the House of Lords refused.

Solicitors: *Richards, Butler & Co* (for the defendants); *Ince & Co* (for the shipowners); *Waltons & Co* (for the cargo owners).

b
Mary Rose Plummer Barrister.

Re St Ann's Church, Kew

c SOUTHWARK CONSISTORY COURT
CHANCELLOR E GARTH MOORE
28th MAY, 15th SEPTEMBER 1975

Burial – Disused burial ground – Erection of building on burial ground – Enlargement of church – Enlargement – Meaning – Physical contiguity – Purpose connected with or ancillary
d *to worship – Extension of church for use as choir vestry and meeting-place for congregation after Sunday services – New building also to be used for Sunday school and as place for mid-week meetings of parishioners – Whether building to be used for purposes connected with worship – Whether material that building also to be used for other purposes – Whether building an enlargement of church – Disused Burial Grounds Act 1884, s 3.*

e The incumbent and churchwardens of a parish church petitioned for a faculty to demolish part of the north side of the church and to erect a new building comprising a church hall, choir vestry, kitchen, lavatories and a 'green room and/or storage room'. The purpose of the proposed alterations was primarily to provide a place where members of the congregation could meet and take refreshments after Sunday services. The extension would also be used by the Sunday school and for mid-week
f meetings of older persons in the parish. Part of the new building was to be erected in the churchyard which was a disused burial ground within the meaning of the Disused Burial Grounds Act 1884, s 2[a], as amended by the Open Spaces Act 1887, s 4[b]. The question arose whether, despite the fact that part of the new building was to be erected on a disused burial ground, the court had jurisdiction to grant the faculty sought on the basis that the new building was 'for the purpose of enlarging' the church, within s 3[c] of the 1884 Act.

g **Held** – In order to consitute an enlargement of a church, within s 3 of the 1884 Act, there had to be a reasonable degree of contiguity between the church and the new building, and the proposed use of the new building had to be closely connected with or ancillary to that of the church itself, i e worship. The proposed use of the new building as a choir vestry and as a place where the congregation could gather after
h a service could properly be described as being ancillary to or connected with worship. The fact that the building might also be used for other purposes not directly connected with the worship of the church did not take it out of the definition of enlargement. Accordingly the court had power to grant the faculty sought (see p 464 c to p 465 b, post).

Re St Mary's, Luton [1966] 3 All ER 638 applied.

j _____

a Section 2, so far as material, is set out at p 463 f, post
b Section 4, so far as material, is set out at p 463 g, post
c Section 3 provides: 'It shall not be lawful to erect any buildings upon any disused burial ground, except for the purpose of enlarging a church, chapel, meeting house, or other places of worship.'

Notes

For the prohibition against building on disused burial grounds, see 10 Halsbury's a
Laws (4th Edn) para 1219, and for cases on the subject, see 7 Digest (Repl) 586-589,
329-353.

For the Disused Burial Grounds Act 1884, ss 2, 3, see 3 Halsbury's Statutes (3rd Edn)
515.

For the Open Spaces Act 1887, s 4, see ibid 517.

b

Cases referred to in judgment

London County Council v Dundas [1904] P 1, 19 TLR 670, 20 Digest (Repl) 588, *351.*
St Mary's, Luton, Re [1966] 3 All ER 638, [1968] P 47; *affg* [1967] P 151.
St Sepulchre, Holborn Viaduct, Re (1903) 19 TLR 723.

Petition for faculty

The vicar and churchwardens of St Ann's Church, Kew, petitioned for a faculty to c
erect a new building attached to the church on a disused burial ground within the
meaning of the Disused Burial Grounds Act 1884 as amended. The petition was
unopposed. The facts are set out in the judgment.

J G Underwood, solicitor, proctor for the petitioners.

Cur adv vult d

15th September. **THE CHANCELLOR** read the following judgment: By this
unopposed petition the incumbent and churchwardens of the parish church of St Ann's,
Kew, seek a faculty to make certain alterations to the church which, if implemented, will
result in the demolition of part of the north side of the church and the erection of a
new building comprising a church hall to seat 90 to 100 persons, divisible by moveable e
screens to provide also a choir-vestry, together with a kitchen, sanitary conveniences
and a further room described in the petition as a 'green room and/or storage room'.
While part of the new building, if erected, will occupy the site of the demolished part,
part, perhaps the larger part, will be in the churchyard which is also a burial ground,
long since disused as such, but, so far as can be ascertained, never formally closed
by order in council or otherwise. If the scheme is implemented, the removal of f
a few old tombstones will be unavoidable, and there is a possibility that some human
remains may be disturbed, and one attractive, though small, tree will have to go.

The object of these fairly extensive proposed alterations (for which planning
permission has been obtained) is, I am told, primarily to provide a meeting-place
where refreshments may be served for the members of the congregation after the
parish communion or after mattins on Sundays, and also to provide a place where g
the Sunday school can meet. It is, too, proposed to use the new room as a meeting-
place for mid-week meetings of older persons in the parish. Despite the fact that
one of the proposed rooms is described as a 'green room and/or storage room', I
am assured that there is no intention to use the extension for theatrical performances.

The church is in every respect an important church, architecturally, historically
and aesthetically, dating from the early 18th century, but with a number of later h
additions, including the part which it is proposed should be demolished, which was
added in 1902. The site, too, is a prominent one on the beautiful Kew Green; the
churchyard is small, but attractive; the Crown is the patron of the living; and, as
one would expect in Kew, the church's connections with royalty are many. It is
clearly a building deserving the utmost care, and any proposal to interfere with it
in any way must be viewed with great circumspection.

That is how I approached the proposal. But, having applied my own cautious j
judgment to the best of my ability, I am myself completely satisfied that the proposals, if implemented, will positively enhance the architectural and aesthetic properties of the site. The architect's designs strike me as excellent, completely in keeping with the main body of the church, and, unlike so many designs today, fully

deserving of the much misused epithet, sensitive. A chancellor, however, must
a always be careful not to rely solely on his own opinion in such matters. But in this
case I am fortified by the knowledge that the Diocesan Advisory Committee, the
Georgian Society, the Victorian Society and the Society for the Protection of Ancient
Buildings are all of one mind with me. Those who are interested in such matters
will know that it is no mean feat for an architect to produce a plan which satisfies
all those bodies. The only dissentient voice (not in fact raised in court) is, I am told,
b that of the Kew Society which thinks that the plan may cause some visible imbalance
architecturally. We should all be grateful to that body for being our watch-dog
in so important a place as Kew; but I do not think that in this case their fears are
justified, the more particularly having regard to the fact that the imbalance is already
there in the shape of the part which it is proposed shall be demolished, erected as
recently as 1902 or thereabouts, and easily the least satisfactory feature of the church.
c   I am also satisfied that the proposed new building and the uses to which it is intended to put it are desirable for enhancing the religious life of the parish. This
applies particularly to the provision of better accommodation for the choir and also
of a place where the congregation may meet socially after the main service on
Sunday. It is clear, too, that, having regard to the comparatively isolated situation
of the church on the Green, there is no other place where such accommodation
d can reasonably be provided.
    I am further satisfied that there can be no valid theological objection to these
proposals.
    For these reasons, if it be open to me in law to do so, this is in my judgment a case
where I ought to grant the prayer in the petition. The only substantial question
which remains is whether the law permits me to do so. The answer to this would
e be immediately clear and in the affirmative by the jus commune and the common
law, were it not for the fact that the new building, if erected at all, must be erected
on a part of a disused burial ground. Apart from statute there would be no impediment. But s 3 of the Disused Burial Grounds Act 1884 prohibits the erection
of any building on a disused burial ground 'except for the purposes of enlarging
a church'. Section 2 of that Act defines a disused burial ground as one 'in respect
f of which an order in council has been made for the discontinuance of burials therein'.
Since there is no evidence that such an order has ever been made in respect of this burial
ground, it would at first sight seem that the 1884 Act has no application. But by s 4 of
the Open Spaces Act 1887, the definition of a disused burial ground in the 1884 Act
is extended to cover 'any burial ground which is no longer used for interments, whether
or not such ground shall have been partially or wholly closed for burials under the
g provision of any statute or Order in Council'.
    It therefore falls to be determined whether the proposed new building will or
will not amount to an enlargement of the existing church. To put the problem
more generally: when is a new building deemed to be an extension of the church?
One might have thought that the answer was obvious, and probably that is what
the legislature thought; but an examination of the decided cases makes it clear
h that in fact the answer can be far from obvious.
    The petitioners have naturally and rightly relied heavily on Re St Mary's, Luton[1].
It has been urged that this case and that case are on all fours. I doubt it. That case
is the latest authority in a long line of cases. I doubt, however, that it is the last
authority, for every case depends on its own facts. But Chancellor Newsom's judgment at first instance, endorsed as it is by the Court of Arches on appeal, is most
j valuable in helping to clarify the principles involved and I respectfully endorse
every word of his jugment and, of course, abide by its endorsement in the Court of
Arches. Over the years the courts have been progressively more liberal in their
interpretation of what amounts to an enlargement of a church, and the Luton case[1]
probably marks the very limit to which the courts can legitimately go.

1 [1966] 3 All ER 638, [1968] P 47

The object of the legislature in imposing a prohibition on the erection of buildings in disused burial grounds is nowhere explicit; but it was probably threefold: first, *a* it was to pay regard to sentiments concerning the resting-place of human remains— sentiments which, whether rational or irrational, are often strongly held and were more universally held in the last century than they are today; secondly, to preserve open spaces; and, thirdly, to achieve the first two objects without restricting the growth of the church itself, the more particularly since sentiment was accustomed to the propriety of human remains being within a church, but was chary of their *b* being under a secular building. The legislature, however, made no attempt to prescribe when a building is to be regarded as secular and when it can be regarded as an enlargement of the church.

Churches are consecrated or dedicated to Almighty God and are intended primarily for His worship. The purpose of an enlargement must, therefore, be closely connected with worship. But that, by itself, is not enough. There must also be a reason- *c* able degree of contiguity with the original building before a new one can fairly be described as an enlargement of the existing church. The extension of the nave or of the choir and the provision of transepts clearly satisfy both these criteria, for they provide more space for worship and are also contiguous to the main body of the existing church. A choir vestry also satisfies the criteria for, although not itself used primarily for worship, its purpose is ancillary to the worship in the body of the *d* church. But a chapel not contiguous to the church would not be permitted for, although it satisfies the criterion of worship, it does not satisfy that of contiguity. Likewise, an isolated bell-tower, though ancillary to worship, would not satisfy the criterion of contiguity: see *London County Council v Dundas*[1]. The provision of a chamber to house the heating-plant or fuel for the church, if connected only by pipes to the main building, would not, I apprehend, satisfy the criterion of contiguity. *e* The building of a church school or of a parsonage house, physically attached to the main building would satisfy the criterion of contiguity, but would not satisfy the criterion of worship. Both schools and parsonage houses are important to the life of the church; but neither is sufficiently associated with the worship of the church to be fairly described as ancillary thereto: see *Re St Sepulchre, Holborn Viaduct*[2].

In the present case, the provision of a choir vestry, together with sanitary facilities, *f* escapes the statutory prohibition, for its sole purpose is to subserve the worship of the church. In my judgment, the provision of a room where the congregation can gather after a service, together with facilities for refreshment, also escapes the prohibition, for, although the social life of the parish is not directly connected with worship, the provision of facilities for a social gathering immediately before or immediately after an act of worship can fairly be described as directly ancillary to *g* that act of worship. The position could well be different were the social gathering to take place divorced from an act of worship in the church. Thus in this case the weekly mid-week gatherings of older persons would not suffice to remove the project from the scope of the prohibition, nor in many cases, and perhaps in this case, would the provision of facilities for a Sunday school, where the building is intended to be in lieu of a gathering in church and not in addition to such a gathering. *h*

The question therefore arises whether in this case these further purposes, the mid-week gathering and the Sunday school, vitiate the ameliorating result of requiring the building for the gatherings on Sundays after divine worship. In my judgment they do not. The main question, apart from contiguity, is whether the proposed new building can fairly be regarded as an enlargement of the church. In order to determine that question one must look at the use to which it is proposed *j* to put the new building. Once one has decided that its use is to be ancillary to the worship in the church, and that such use is not merely a colourable subterfuge,

1 [1964] P 1
2 (1903) 19 TLR 723

a the new building comes within the category of an enlargement of the church. It does not come out of that category simply because it may also be used for other purposes not directly connected with the worship in the church. A vestry, for example, does not cease to be a vestry simply because it is also used for meetings or as an office, as often happens. I am, therefore, of the opinion that the proposed operation, regarded as a whole, may fairly be regarded as one for the enlargement of the existing church and that there is no impediment to my decreeing a faculty

b as prayed. I must, however, point out that petitioners cannot have it both ways. If the new building were not an enlargement of the church, there would be no impediment to its use for secular purposes. In as much as I am prepared to hold that in this case the new building will be an enlargement of the church, it follows that it can with propriety be used only for purposes wholly compatible with the uses to which a church may with propriety be put. I shall not attempt to specify what

c these are. Views on such matters vary from age to age, and what is today considered decorous in a church is more in accord with the views of our mediaeval ancestors than with those of our Victorian forebears. In decreeing that a faculty do pass the seal as prayed, I do not propose, as often happens, to impose any conditions as to the uses to which the extension may be put. I merely remind the parochial authorities that it is an extension to the church and not a secular building. There will be incor-

d porated in the order a note to the effect that, since this is an extension to the church, the incumbent, churchwardens, parochial church council and parishioners (all for the time being) will have the same control and obligations and rights over the extension as they have over the rest of the church with the same duty to preserve decorum.

During the building operations some tombstones will have to be moved. I direct

e that they be resited within the curtilage to the satisfaction of the court, which means that the petitioners should choose the spot for each stone and submit their choice to the court through the registry for final determination.

If any human remains should be disturbed, I direct that they be decorously reinterred in the churchyard, either beneath the extension or elsewhere, under the directions of the incumbent, and, where applicable and convenient, beneath the

f tombstone which refers to them.

A point has arisen as to the material to be used for the roof of the extension. The architect has proposed lead. The Diocesan Advisory Committee were in favour of copper. I advanced the suggestion, which seems to have received some favour, that with no substantial aesthetic loss and a considerable saving of money a carefully chosen substitute might be found. This would have the additional advantage of not

g being so attractive to thieves who might find so isolated a church an easy prey. I intend, therefore, to leave the material for the roof in abeyance for the time being, with liberty to apply.

Subject to these matters, I decree that a faculty do pass the seal as prayed, the work to be completed within 12 months or such further time as the court may allow, with general liberty on all matters to apply.

h

Order accordingly.

Solicitors: *Winckworth & Pemberton.*

Michael Yelton Barrister.

Vandyk v Oliver (Valuation Officer)   *a*

HOUSE OF LORDS

LORD WILBERFORCE, VISCOUNT DILHORNE, LORD SIMON OF GLAISDALE, LORD EDMUND-DAVIES AND LORD FRASER OF TULLYBELTON

27th, 28th, 29th, 30th OCTOBER 1975, 28th JANUARY 1976

b

Rates – Relief – Facilities for disabled persons – Structure supplied for purpose of providing facilities – Structure supplied for use of person in pursuance of arrangements for after-care of persons suffering from illness – Structure of a kind similar to structures which could be provided by local authority or voluntary organisation – Flat acquired by disabled ratepayer – Ratepayer confined to wheelchair – Flat adapted for purpose of after-care – Ratepayer living in flat with wife – Whether flat a structure of a kind similar to one which local authority **c** *could supply for care or after-care of persons suffering from illness – General Rate Act 1967, s 45 – Health Services and Public Health Act 1968, s 12(1).*

The ratepayer was a severely disabled person, confined to a wheelchair. In consequence he needed after-care which was provided by his wife or, in her absence, by professional attendants. After a long search, the ratepayer bought a flat in which he **d** and his wife made their home. The flat was a large one on the second floor of a building, having five rooms, two bathrooms, a dining-hall, kitchen and balconies. He chose the flat because, among other things, the doorways were wide enough to allow easy passage for his chair, and porterage and a lift were available. After moving in he had certain adaptations made to his bedroom and one of the bathrooms suitable, or necessary, for a man suffering from his disability. The ratepayer claimed relief from rates under **e** s 45(d)[a] of the General Rate Act 1967 on the ground that the flat was a structure similar to those referred to in s 45(b), i e one which could have been supplied by a local authority or voluntary organisation formed for the purpose of s 12(1)[b] of the Health Services and Public Health Act 1968 (relating to the prevention of, and to the care and after-care of persons suffering from, illness) for the use of a person in pursuance of arrangements made under s 12(1). *f*

Held (Lord Edmund-Davies dissenting) – The ratepayer was not entitled to the relief claimed for the following reasons—

(i) (per Lord Wilberforce and Lord Fraser of Tullybelton) On the true construction of para (d) of s 45, read in conjunction with para (b), to qualify for relief under s 45 it had to be established that the dominant purpose for which the structure had been **g** supplied was one of those specified in s 12(1) of the 1968 Act, i e the prevention of illness, the care of persons who were ill or the after-care of persons who had been ill. Although the ratepayer had chosen his flat because it would enable him to obtain after-care, his dominant purpose in taking the flat was to provide a home for himself and his wife (see p 470 h to p 471 b, p 479 b to e and h and p 480 a to d, post).

(ii) (per Viscount Dilhorne and Lord Simon of Glaisdale) The purpose of s 45 of the **h** 1967 Act was to secure that the occupier of a hereditament should not have its gross value increased in consequence of it containing a structure put there for the use of someone suffering from a disability or illness. The ratepayer's flat could not be regarded as a structure for the purpose of care, after-care or the prevention of illness, but was an ordinary flat which was the ratepayer's home. Although he received after-care in the flat, it was not a building or structure designed for his after-care **j** (see p 471 f and g, p 472 f and g and p 474 b to f and h, post).

Decision of the Court of Appeal [1975] 2 All ER 264 reversed.

---

a   Section 45 is set out at p 469 *c* to *f*, post

b   Section 12(1), so far as material, is set out at p 478 *c* and *d*, post

Notes

a For structures which should not be taken into account for rating purposes, see 32 Halsbury's Laws (3rd Edn) 53, para 71.

For the General Rate Act 1967, s 45, see 27 Halsbury's Statutes (3rd Edn) 139.

For the Health Services and Public Health Act 1968, s 12, see 23 Halsbury's Statutes (3rd Edn) 174.

b **Cases referred to in opinions**

Almond v Birmingham Royal Institution for the Blind [1967] 2 All ER 317, [1968] AC 37, [1967] 3 WLR 196, 13 RRC 91, [1967] RA 113, HL; *affg* [1966] 1 All ER 602, [1966] 2 QB 395, [1966] 2 WLR 374, 11 RRC 381, [1966] RA 21, CA; *rvsg* (1965) 11 RRC 47, Digest (Cont Vol C) 823, 844bb.

c *Jewish Blind Society Trustees v Henning* [1961] 1 All ER 47, [1961] 1 WLR 24, 7 RRC 113, CA, Digest (Cont Vol A) 1292, 844b.

Minister of Health v Royal Midland Counties Home for Incurables, Leamington Spa, General Committee [1954] 1 All ER 1013, [1954] Ch 530, [1954] 2 WLR 755, CA, 35 Digest (Repl) 824, 127.

Walker (Valuation Officer) v Wood [1962] 3 All ER 188, [1962] 1 WLR 1060, 9 RRC 232, 126 JP 472, CA, Digest (Cont Vol A) 1295, 907a.

d

Appeal

Keith John Oliver ('the valuation officer') appealed against an order of the Court of Appeal[1] (Cairns and Lawton LJJ, MacKenna J dissenting) dated 10th February 1975 dismissing an appeal by the valuation officer against part of a decision of the Lands Tribunal (J Stuart Daniel Esq QC and E C Strathon Esq) dated 28th June 1973, whereby,

e on four consolidated appeals, two by the valuation officer's predecessor and two by the respondent, Neville David Vandyk ('the ratepayer'), against the decision of the Greater London Central Valuation Court dated 30th December 1971, the tribunal dismissed the valuation officer's appeals and allowed the ratepayer's appeals. The facts are set out in the opinion of Lord Wilberforce.

f

Geoffrey Rippon QC and *Alan Fletcher* for the valuation officer.
David Widdicombe QC and *Matthew Horton* for the ratepayer.

Their Lordships took time for consideration.

g 28th January. The following opinions were delivered.

LORD WILBERFORCE. My Lords, the ratepayer is the lessee of a large flat on the second floor in a building in Kensington, London. It has five rooms, two bathrooms, a dining-hall, kitchen and balconies. The present appeal relates to the rateable

h value of this hereditament. The ratepayer in 1968 and again in 1971 made proposals for alteration in the valuation list so as to show the value as nil, as against the previous gross value of £500, rateable value £388. Objection was taken to both proposals and on 30th December 1971 the valuation court ordered that the assessment should be amended to £425 gross, £326 net. Both sides then appealed to the Lands Tribunal which on 28th June 1973 fixed the assessment at site value—making £80 gross, £50

j net. Then a case was stated for the Court of Appeal which, by majority, has dismissed the valuation officer's appeal. The valuation officer seeks to have the original assessment restored. There is an alternative contention on the part of the ratepayer, that in any event the assessment should be reduced as regards two rooms in the flat.

---

1 [1975] 2 All ER 264, [1975] 2 WLR 797

I will now explain the basis for the ratepayer's claim. He is a severely disabled person, as the result of poliomyelitis suffered in 1947, which has left him paralysed *a* in both legs and his left arm. He is confined to a wheelchair. He is—this is not disputed —in need of after-care, both in an ordinary sense and within the statutory meaning of those words. In plain terms he needs constant attention; this is provided by his wife who, of course, lives in the flat and, when she is away, by professional attendants.

He acquired the hereditament in 1968—previously he lived in another flat. Among the reasons why he chose it was that the doorways were wide enough to allow easy *b* passage for his chair, the availability of a lift, porterage and central heating. After moving in, he had certain adaptations made to his bedroom and one bathroom (the two rooms mentioned above), necessary, or suitable, for a man suffering from his disability. In general it is fair to say that the flat is a normal residential flat which suits the circumstances and requirements of the ratepayer.

Should he, in these circumstances, be relieved from the rates in respect of his *c* hereditament except as to the site value? The answer must be found in statute. But before entering the labyrinth, it seems advisable to consider what we are looking for, and to state some general considerations.

Everyone has to live somewhere, but there are alternatives. A man may find his own accommodation, or he may go to a housing authority and ask it to provide a house; or if he is seriously ill—mentally or physically—he may go to a health *d* authority and ask to be put in accommodation where he can be looked after. Health authorities have special powers as to persons requiring care or after-care and these will have to be considered.

If a man provides his own home, but has to spend more on it because he is ill, or because he needs after-care, one might expect to find in the legislation provision for relieving him from having to pay more rates on account of the extra expense. If, *e* for example, he has to provide a garage for an invalid chair, it would be very unfair to charge him rates on it, and the same principle could be applied to adaptations. One might go so far as to expect that if, exercising his choice, a man, on account of a disability, selects a dwelling which is more expensive than one which he would acquire if he were not disabled, he should get some relief on account of this excess. But apart from this type of case, one might question whether a man in need of care or after- *f* care should be relieved from rates on his residence altogether; this seems to introduce a different principle, and if it were to be admitted one would expect to find clear words.

The consequences of giving such relief would be very considerable. It would mean relieving from rates all hereditamants (i e buildings) occupied by persons in need of care or after-care and this whether or not the particular hereditament needed any adaptation. The relief could not be confined to persons like the ratepayer, but would *g* equally have to be available for persons suffering from heart disease, or mental illness, if they could claim to be in need of care and this regardless of whether their condition made adaptation necessary. This was pointed out by MacKenna J[1] in the Court of Appeal, and I see no answer to it. The majority in the Court of Appeal saw the difficulty and tried to meet it. But I do not think that they succeeded. Cairns LJ[3] said: 'I do not consider that the physical characteristics of the structure *h* can be wholly disregarded'. This is a negative formula and I am not clear what positive test it intends to apply. If it is saying that rating relief depends on some physical characteristics, it creates a distinction, for which no justification appears in the legislation, between those who need a specially adapted residence and those who do not. Moreover it cannot be enough to entitle the occupier to relief that the hereditament has *some* physical characteristics; but if these have to be specially relevant to *j* the illness or disability, it is difficult to see how the present residence possesses them. Lawton LJ[2] seems to apply a different test: 'In order to attract rating relief a structure

1   [1975] 2 All ER at 278, [1975] 2 WLR at 813
2   [1975] 2 All ER at 271, [1975] 2 WLR at 806
3   [1975] 2 All ER at 276, [1975] 2 WLR at 811

must be of a size and type reasonably suitable for the ratepayer's need for after-
a care'. These are very general words and it is hard to see how they exclude any residence
the ratepayer may reasonably choose. To say that he may not choose a castle is hardly
a significant restriction. So I do not think that the ratepayer can succeed without carrying with it the consequence that anyone in need of after-care and who
acquires a residence can claim total tax exemption for the building so long as he can
say that it is suitable for the purpose of after-care being provided. Did Parliament
b intend so far-reaching and indiscriminate a bounty at the expense of other ratepayers? Though Parliament could, if it wished, have gone so far as this, one must look
carefully at the provisions relied on.

The relevant provision is s 45 of the General Rate Act 1967. This section was enacted
first in 1955 in an Act called the Rating and Valuation (Miscellaneous Provisions) Act
1955, s 9, but of course it is possible that an Act so styled could introduce a far-reaching
c change. It is necessary to cite the whole section.

'In ascertaining for the purposes of section 19 of this Act the gross value of a
hereditament, no account shall be taken—(*a*) of any structure belonging to the
Minister of Health and supplied by that Minister or, before 31st August 1953,
by the Minister of Pensions for the accommodation of an invalid chair or of any
other vehicle (whether mechanically propelled or not) constructed or adapted for
d use by invalids or disabled persons; or (*b*) of any structure belonging to a local
health authority or to a voluntary organisation formed for any of the purposes
mentioned in section 28(1) of the National Health Service Act 1946 (which relates
to the prevention of, and to the care and after-care of persons suffering from,
illness) and supplied for the use of any person in pursuance of arrangements
made under the said section 28(1); or (*c*) of any structure belonging to a local
e authority within the meaning of section 29 of the National Assistance Act 1948
(which relates to welfare arrangements for blind, deaf, dumb and other handicapped persons) or to such a voluntary organisation as is mentioned in section 30
of that Act and supplied for the use of any person in pursuance of arrangements
made under the said section 29; or (*d*) of any structure which is of a kind similar
f to structures such as are referred to in paragraph (*a*), (*b*) or (*c*) of this section but
does not fall within that paragraph by reason that it is owned or has been supplied
otherwise than as mentioned in that paragraph.'

There are several things that strike one about this.

1. The introductory words do not suggest the total derating of a hereditament.
They suggest that there is a hereditament, but that in valuing it for rates you are not
g to take account of special features related to illness or disability, in other words that
the purpose is to grant the limited relief of the kind I have mentioned, relief for special
features needed on account of the disability.

2. The section throughout refers to 'structure'—no doubt a general enough word—
but the fact that it is used after a reference to the hereditament suggests that the structure is not itself the hereditament but is something added to the hereditament. It is
h this addition which is to be 'disregarded', but you are left with the hereditament to
value. Thus in para (*a*) 'structure' clearly refers to a garage for an invalid chair.

3. This is a more intricate point. In paras (*b*) and (*c*) reference is made to other Acts,
in (*b*) to the National Health Service Act 1946, s 28, in (*c*) to the National Assistance
Act 1948, s 29. Neither of these sections refers to accommodation.

As regards the first Act, it is pointed out that this has now been replaced by the
j Health Services and Public Health Act 1968, whose s 12 (replacing s 28) does now refer to
the provision, equipment and maintenance of residential accommodation for after-
care, and it is said that s 28, through more general language, has the same effect.
But what is relevant is the interpretation of words used in the General Rate Act 1967,
the question being whether, when s 45(*b*) refers to structures, it includes residential
accommodation. Even if the earlier Act covers residential accommodation as well as

'structures' it seems a non sequitur to say that the later Act (that of 1967) when it
refers to structures refers to residential accommodation.

As regards the second Act (of 1948), I regard it as clear that s 29 does not authorise
the provision of residential accommodation. I shall not enlarge on this since I believe
that all your Lordships agree on the point. Section 21 of the same Act does so authorise,
and the reference in para (c) to s 29, not to s 21, seems significantly to suggest that
'structures', at least in para (c), do not include residential accommodation.

One would thus so far be inclined to accept a restrictive interpretation of the word
'structures', and this is what, in the dawn of innocence, all three members of the
Court of Appeal did in *Jewish Blind Society Trustees v Henning*[1]. As the relevant passages
have been superseded, I must deny myself the comfort, and in the case of Harman
LJ's pungent judgment, the pleasure of citing their words. For in *Almond v Birmingham
Royal Institution for the Blind*[2] this House gave its approval to an unrestricted meaning
of 'structure' and we must accept this as the law. But the very fact that 'structure'
now bears a wide meaning may make us more inclined—it certainly permits us—to
find some limitation on the width of the section in other provisions. The considerations
I have stated suggest that it has a limited scope, by way of granting a measure of
rating relief in respect of special features of a hereditament on account of a man's
illness or disability. They do not support the radical argument of the ratepayer
that exemption from rates in respect of a hereditament is to be granted on account
of the circumstances that the ratepayer, for reason of illness or disability, needs
care or after-care.

It is said, however, that this result, far-reaching as it is, follows from the wording of
the section. As to this I would say two things: first, if ever there was a case for preferring a purposive to a literal interpretation, this is such a case. The section is a
labyrinth, a minefield of obscurity. The key paragraph, (d), refers back to (a), (b) or
(c) with a connecting link described as similarity in kind; yet no criterion of similarity
is given; so we are offered criteria based on 'purpose' or 'function', or on these words
in combination. But this introduces yet further difficulties, for there is acute dispute,
if purpose is the test, whose purpose is meant and whether this must be the sole or
dominant purpose, or any purpose: if function is meant whether this is the same
thing as actual use, or whether the word again introduces the conception of purpose.
Then on the incorporated subsections, there is a difference of view whether a National
Health authority had power to provide accommodation for a person in the position
of the ratepayer or whether the power (conferred by the 1968 Act) is an ancillary
power to the provision of care. Similar difficulties arise under para (c). My Lords,
I revolt against a step-by-step approach, from one doubtful expression to another,
where each step is hazardous, through referential legislation, towards a conclusion,
to my mind so far out of accord with any credible policy. The fact that Parliament for
its own purposes chooses to legislate in this obscure manner does not force us to be
the blind led by the blind.

Secondly, it is at least arguable that, even through the literal approach, a result less
far-reaching than that contended for by the ratepayer may follow. The argument
is put very clearly by MacKenna J[3] in his judgment. Put very simply, the argument
is this: para (d) requires one to assume an identical or, I suppose, a similar hereditament supplied by the ratepayer instead of by the local health authority. In accordance
with para (b) and the incorporated legislation, accommodation can only be supplied
if the (dominant) purpose of the supply was to provide after-care or to enable after-
care to be given. But the (dominant) purpose for which this hereditament was supplied
was to provide a residence for the ratepayer. So the case would not come within
para (b), and does not come within para (d). (I will not trace the argument under

1   [1961] 1 All ER 47, [1961] 1 WLR 24
2   [1967] 2 All ER 317, [1968] AC 37
3   [1975] 2 All ER at 276-280, [1975] 2 WLR at 811-816

para (c), since all your Lordships agree that this paragraph cannot be made to apply.)

a I agree with this argument but, whether right or not, it is clearly a maintainable argument, and I rest on the principle that if one possible interpretation of a statute leads to a result contrary to the evident general purpose one should prefer to it an interpretation also reasonably possible which does not lead to such a result. I would therefore hold that the ratepayer does not bring himself within para (d) and that his claim fails. I am also of opinion that the alternative claim for relief in respect of

b the two rooms fails for the reasons given in the opinion of my noble and learned friend, Viscount Dilhorne.

My Lords, whether or not your Lordships are able to agree with this approach to the section, I think that there is a wider issue on which we can all, I hope, agree. We have here legislation; the General Rate Act 1967, s 45, is itself far from clear, containing references, express or implied, to a number of other statutes: the National

c Health Service Act 1946, the Health Services and Public Health Act 1968, the National Assistance Act 1948, the Chronically Sick and Disabled Persons Act 1970, s 2, and now the Local Government Act 1974, s 20. This is apart from other legislation which may have to be consulted: the Disabled Persons (Employment) Act 1944, the Mental Health Act 1959, and the housing legislation. In *Almond's* case[1] Lord Reid found himself quite unable to understand the scope of s 45 of the 1967 Act, and the Lands Tribunal,

d both in the present case and other cases, has forcefully pointed out the very great difficulties for normal minds which this complicated legislation produces. If the scope of s 45 is to be extended far beyond local authorities and charities to many thousands of citizens, many of them ill or handicapped, or if the contrary is the case, Parliament really ought to make its dispositions intelligible. I would hope, too, that it might make them fair and rational.

e I would allow the appeal, and order that the original valuation (£500 gross, £388 net) be restored. As leave to appeal to this House was granted by the Court of Appeal on the onerous, and I think exceptional, terms that the valuation officer should pay the ratepayer his costs in this House on a common fund basis in any event, an order should be made to that effect.

f **VISCOUNT DILHORNE.** My Lords, the object sought to be secured by the enactment of s 9(1) of the Rating and Valuation (Miscellaneous Provisions) Act 1955 (now replaced by s 45 of the General Rate Act 1967) appears to me to have been to secure that the occupier of a hereditament should not have its gross value increased in consequence of it containing a structure put there for the use of someone suffering

g from a disability or illness.

Paragraph (a) of the section tells a valuation officer to ignore a structure belonging to the Minister of Health and supplied by him on or before 31st August 1953 by the Minister of Pensions for the accommodation of an invalid chair or other vehicle constructed or adapted for use by invalids or disabled persons. So, to decide whether a structure comes within this paragraph, a valuation officer must not only ascertain

h to whom the structure belongs and who supplied it but also its function or purpose.

It would have been very unfair if an occupier of a hereditament who supplied such a structure for such a purpose at his own expense, had the gross value of his hereditament increased in consequence when that would not have happened if the structure had belonged to and been supplied by a Ministry; and para (d) when read with para (a) operates to prevent such unfairness.

j Paragraph (b) exempts any structure belonging to a local authority or to certain voluntary organisations supplied for the use of any person in pursuance of arrangements made under s 28(1) of the National Health Service Act 1946, those arrangements being for the prevention of illness, for the care of persons suffering from illness or for the after-care of such persons.

1　[1967] 2 All ER 317, [1968] AC 37

In relation to this paragraph, a valuation officer has again to determine not only
to whom the structure belongs and by whom it was supplied but also that it was   *a*
supplied for use by a person in pursuance of such arrangements. If so supplied, it is to
be inferred that the structure was supplied for use for the prevention of illness or
for care or after-care; and the valuation of the hereditament is not to be increased in
consequence of the presence of a structure which would not be there but for a person's
disability or infirmity.

Again it would be unfair if a structure, which would be ignored if it came within   *b*
para (*b*), led to the valuation being increased if it was provided by an occupier at his
own expense for such a purpose, and in my opinion para (*d*) when read with para (*b*)
operates to prevent this.

Paragraph (*c*) is not well drafted for it begins with the words: 'of any structure
belonging to a local authority within the meaning of section 29 of the National Assistance Act 1948', and s 29 does not state to what local authorities it is to apply and only   *c*
deals with the powers of local authorities. The pattern is nevertheless the same and
the object and purpose of the paragraph is similar to that of paras (*a*) and (*b*). It
requires structures belonging to a local authority or to certain voluntary organisations
and supplied for the use of any person pursuant to arrangements made under s 29
of the 1948 Act for the welfare of blind, deaf and other handicapped persons to be
ignored in ascertaining the gross value of a hereditament.   *d*

Again it would be unfair if a valuation officer increased the valuation of a hereditament on account of the presence of such a structure for the use of such a person when,
if it had been supplied by a local authority or one of the prescribed voluntary organisations in pursuance of such arrangements, he would have had to ignore it and again
para (*d*) operates in relation to para (*c*) to prevent this.

Examination of the section leads me to the conclusion that the first question to be   *e*
considered in relation to the application of the section is whether there is any structure
in or on the hereditament which would not be there but for some person's illness,
disability or infirmity or if it was not required for the prevention of illness. If there
is no such structure, then it is not necessary to consider the extent of a local authority's
powers under s 28(1) of the National Health Service Act 1946 or under s 29 of the
National Assistance Act 1948 or whether para (*d*) applies.   *f*

I agree with my noble and learned friend, Lord Wilberforce, that the introductory
words of s 9(1) do not suggest the total derating of a hereditament. Nor do they in
my view suggest derating to site value. They suggest that the gross value is not to be
increased on account of the presence of structures which would not be there but for
illness, infirmity or disability or for the prevention of illness.

The section does not define 'structure'. It must have been intended to bear the   *g*
same meaning in each paragraph. In *Jewish Blind Society Trustees v Henning*[1] the
question to be decided was whether a home for 64 persons, a three-storeyed house in
10½ acres of grounds, was to be ignored in ascertaining the gross value. Lord Evershed
MR seems to have regarded the house as constituting the hereditament for he said[2]:
'this hereditament [was] in truth not a structure within the meaning of that
subsection . . .' Pearce LJ also thought that the section seemed to anticipate that when   *h*
no account was taken of a structure to which the section applied, there would still
be left a hereditament capable of assessment[3]: '. . . it purports', he said 'to deal
with something that is a part rather than the whole of the hereditament'. Harman LJ
appears to have been of the same opinion. But the case was not decided on this ground.
It was held that if the house was a structure within the meaning of the section, paras (*b*),
(*c*) and (*d*) did not apply as the requirements of those paragraphs had not been met.   *j*

Lord Evershed MR[4] thought that para (*d*) did not apply as in his view the words

1   [1961] 1 All ER 47, [1961] 1 WLR 24
2   [1961] 1 All ER at 49, [1961] 1 WLR at 29
3   [1961] 1 All ER at 53, [1961] 1 WLR at 34
4   [1961] 1 All ER at 52, [1961] 1 WLR at 33

'a structure of a kind similar to' meant a structure 'the purposes or adaptability of which are similar to those previously mentioned', and Pearce LJ[1] thought the words meant 'of a kind similar in the nature of their construction and used for similar purposes'.

In *Almond v Birmingham Royal Institution for the Blind*[2] this House had to consider the meaning of the word 'structure', it being clear that if the buildings in question, a large two storey house, two single storey buildings and various smaller buildings, were structures, para (c) applied. Lord Reid[3] said that the word had a very wide meaning and he rejected the appellants' contention that relief was only intended to be given in respect of buildings of a temporary, prefabricated or removable kind. He did not find it necessary to consider para (d) or to deal with the *Jewish Blind* case[4]. Lord Hodson also rejected the contention that 'structure' should be given a limited meaning and the other members of the House agreed with Lord Reid.

It follows from this decision that a structure however large and however constructed may be regarded as coming within the section. It may be something in or on the hereditament. It may indeed constitute the hereditament but neither para (b) or para (c) will apply unless the other provisions of those paragraphs are satisfied and para (d) will apply despite the fact that the structure is not owned or supplied in accordance with the arrangements to which paras (b) and (c) refer provided that it is a structure supplied for the use of a person for one of the purposes mentioned in s 28(1) of the National Health Act 1946 and in s 29 of the National Assistance Act 1948.

The marginal note to s 9(1) of the Rating and Valuation (Miscellaneous Provisions) Act 1955 is 'Other reliefs from rates'. That was changed in the General Rate Act 1967 to 'Relief in respect of facilities for disabled persons'. While I have not had regard to the marginal notes when seeking to construe the section, I think I should say that in my view the marginal note to the 1967 Act correctly summarises the effect of the section if a wide interpretation is given to the word 'disabled'. For the section to apply, there must in my view be a structure supplied for the use of a person who is or has been ill or for the welfare of a handicapped person or for the use of a person for the prevention of illness.

The ratepayer had occupied a flat in 7B Holland Villas Road, London, W14 until he moved in 1968 to his present flat, 7 Addisland Court, Holland Villas Road. In 1947 he contracted poliomyelitis and as a result is paralysed in both legs and in his left arm. Since 1947 he has been confined to a wheelchair and has had to have after-care. In 1956 he married and his wife gives him constant attention. When she is away, a trained nurse looks after him.

He says that it was after a long search that they moved to their present flat. It is on the second floor of a purpose-built block of flats containing 38 flats broadly similar in layout and construction. It was more convenient for him as the flat has wide doors through which his wheelchair can go and central heating. It has a lift and there are porters who can help him if necessary.

He had a number of alterations made to the flat in order to meet his special needs. A partition wall was removed to enlarge the bathroom. A handle was fixed to the wall by the bath and another by the wc. The seat of the wc was raised above normal height and an electric bell push fitted in the bathroom. The level of the bathroom floor was raised to make it easier for him to get into and out of the bath. In his bedroom the washbasin was altered to enable him to approach it and wash while sitting in his wheelchair. A bracket was fixed with a hanging chain and handle over his bed to enable him to turn over during the night. A bell push was fixed by the bed.

He claims that if his main claim as to the flat as a whole fails, the bathroom and his bedroom as altered should be regarded as a structure to which the section applies.

1   [1961] 1 All ER at 54, [1961] 1 WLR at 35
2   [1967] 2 All ER 317, [1968] AC 37
3   [1967] 2 All ER at 319, [1968] AC at 51
4   [1961] 1 All ER 47, [1961] 1 WLR 24

I regret that I cannot come to the conclusion that by reason of these alterations, his bedroom and bathroom are to be regarded as a structure which would not be there but for his incapacity. Even if they are to be so regarded, I doubt very much if the alterations made would increase the gross value of the flat and it is the increase in gross value due to the presence of a structure to which the section applies which has to be ignored.

In my opinion the ratepayer's claim in relation to these two rooms fails. Although in para 21 of his case the valuation officer contended that it should fail, in the course of opening the appeal his counsel conceded, wrongly in my opinion, that these two rooms qualified for rate relief.

As to his main claim that in ascertaining the gross value of the hereditament, the value of the flat must be ignored as being a structure to which para (b) or (c) or (d) applies, I cannot regard the flat as a structure for the purpose of care or after-care or for the prevention of illness or for the welfare of a handicapped person. It appears to be a perfectly ordinary flat of five rooms, two bathrooms, dining-room and similar to the other 37 flats in the building. The flat is his home. In it he receives after-care but it is not a building or structure designed for his after-care or welfare. It is not a hereditament of which the gross value would, if the section did not apply, be increased due to the presence there of a structure required for his after-care or welfare as a handicapped person.

If it had been the intention of Parliament that persons in the position of the ratepayer and other handicapped and ill persons should be relieved of liability for rates in respect of their homes, I would have expected that to have been clearly stated. I would not have expected the section when originally enacted, if that was its purpose, to have had as the marginal note 'Other reliefs from rates', and I cannot read s 9(1) of the 1955 Act as doing that. All that the section seeks to secure is that an occupier shall not have to pay more in rates than he would otherwise be required to do by reason of the presence of a structure which would not be there if it had not been required for the use of an ill or handicapped person.

For these reasons, in my opinion the ratepayer's main claim fails and the appeal should be allowed. The concession made by counsel creates a difficulty as to the order which should be made. Should the order in view of the concession grant rate relief in respect of the two rooms, or should it not, and an order be made, as asked for in the valuation officer's case, that the hereditament is to be entered in the valuation list for the Rating Area of Kensington and Chelsea at gross value £500, rateable value £388?

In my view that is the order that should be made, and it must be left to the valuation officer to decide whether or not to implement the concession which on the view I take of the law should not have been made, the ratepayer not being in law entitled to relief in respect of the two rooms.

LORD SIMON OF GLAISDALE. My Lords, I have had the advantage of reading in draft the speech prepared by my noble and learned friend, Viscount Dilhorne. I agree with it—all the more wholeheartedly because it credits Parliament with a meaning which seems to me to accord with justice and good sense. It meets the powerful objections raised by the valuation officer and the ratepayer against their respective opponent's interpretations.

I would therefore allow the appeal and concur in the order proposed by my noble and learned friend.

LORD EDMUND-DAVIES. My Lords, in *Almond v Birmingham Royal Institution for the Blind*[1] Lord Reid[2] said of s 9(1)(d) of the Rating and Valuation (Miscellaneous Provisions) Act 1955: 'It raises . . . difficult problems'. That observation is equally

---

1   [1967] 2 All ER 317, [1968] AC 37
2   [1967] 2 All ER at 320, [1968] AC at 51

true of its successor, s 45 of the General Rate Act 1967, as the present appeal amply demonstrates. The facts and the arguments have already been summarised by my Lords, and I propose to do no more than express my conclusions on the issues involved and state shortly the reasons which have led me to form them. I preface my observations by pointing out that my Lords must, of course, now give the important word 'structure' the expansive meaning assigned to it by this House in *Almond's* case[1], namely that it includes 'all kinds of buildings' (per Lord Reid[2]).

I. Before the ratepayer may be derated in respect of his flat under s 45(*d*), it must appear that it is of a kind similar to such structures as are referred to in para (*b*) of that section. The Lands Tribunal and all members of the Court of Appeal rejected the alternative claim to be derated under para (*c*). They were right in so doing, for para (*c*) relates only to a structure belonging to a local authority within the meaning of s 29 of the National Assistance Act 1948, or to such a voluntary organisation as is mentioned in s 30 of that Act. Those two sections are part of the 'welfare services' provisions of the 1948 Act, and confer no power on either body to make arrangements for the provision of private residential accommodation for the handicapped, though s 29(4)(*c*) does confer a power to arrange for *hostels* for persons engaged in workshops set up thereunder. Sections 29 and 30 may be contrasted with ss 21-28, a fasciculus headed 'Provision of Accommodation', which *do* enable a local authority to provide, inter alia, 'residential accommodation for persons who by reason of age, infirmity or any other circumstances are in need of care and attention which is not otherwise available to them' (s 21(1)(*a*)), the premises being required to be managed by the authority (s 21(4)).

II. Subject only to the addition of a reference to s 12(1) of the Health Services and Public Health Act 1968, I adopt the words of MacKenna J[3]:

'Before a structure is exempt under para (*b*), it must appear: (1) that it is owned by an authority or by a voluntary association formed for the prevention of illness or the care or after-care of persons suffering from illness; (2) that it is supplied by an authority in pursuance of an arrangement under s 28(1) of the [National Health Service Act 1946]; (3) that the authority's purpose in supplying it is the prevention of illness or the care or after-care of persons suffering from illness; and (4) that it is used by persons in pursuance of the arrangement.'

III. It is rightly accepted that 'supplied' here means no more than 'provided' (see *Almond's* case[4], per Lord Hodson) and that the structure may be provided by the ratepayer himself (*Walker v Wood*[5] per Lord Denning MR). But what is controversial is the meaning of the words 'of a kind similar to' in s 45(*d*). I respectfully dissent from the view of Pearce LJ in *Jewish Blind Society Trustees v Henning*[6] that they 'mean compendiously "of a kind similar in the nature of their construction . . ."'. It is true that he had said a little earlier that 'Mere physical similarity cannot be enough', but for my part I do not see that physical similarity is even relevant. In my judgment, for the ratepayer's flat to come within para (*d*) it must be found similar in its *function* to a structure coming within para (*b*).

IV. Then what structure does come within para (*b*)? I can find no warrant for the valuation officer's submission that, to get rate relief, the accommodation has to be of an *institutional* character. Furthermore, the proper question is not whether a local health authority or voluntary organisation would be *likely* to provide such private accommodation for private after-care as the flat with which this House is presently

1 [1967] 2 All ER 317, [1968] AC 37
2 [1967] 1 All ER at 320, [1968] AC at 51
3 [1975] 2 All ER 264 at 278, [1975] 2 WLR 797 at 813
4 [1967] 2 All ER at 322, [1968] AC at 55
5 [1962] 3 All ER 188 at 190, [1962] 1 WLR 1060 at 1064
6 [1961] 1 All ER 47 at 54, [1961] 1 WLR 24 at 35

concerned, and still less whether any local authority or voluntary organisation had, in fact, made such provision. The relevant question is whether the authority or organi- a
sation *could* lawfully provide it. The Lands Tribunal and all three members of the Court of Appeal held that they could, and in my judgment that conclusion was correct.

V. I do not think that junior counsel for the valuation officer was correct in saying that a local health authority can do no more than provide *care* (defined by Denning LJ in *Minister of Health v Royal Midland Counties Home for Incurables*[1] as 'the homely art of making people comfortable and providing for their well-being'), or that if this care b
is provided by members of the family of the person being cared for accommodation can never be provided.

VI. Then does the foregoing conclude the enquiry? In other words, if the local health authority *could* have supplied this flat to the ratepayer for the purpose of his after-care by members of his family, does that automatically entitle him to rating relief? Or are (a) his own purpose in taking the flat, and (b) the purpose for which it is being used, c
of relevance? As to (a), Cairns LJ[2] rejected the submission for the valuation officer that the relevant question is whether the ratepayer's 'sole or dominant purpose' was for the purpose of after-care, saying:

> 'Now there is not in the legislation any adjective qualifying the word "purpose".
> This may be contrasted with the Rating and Valuation (Apportionment) Act d
> 1928, s 3(1) proviso, where an industrial hereditament is defined so as not to include
> a factory if it is *primarily* used for non-industrial purposes.'

In similarly rejecting the 'dominant purpose' test which MacKenna J[3] propounded, Lawton LJ[4] said: 'The question which should be asked is this: why did the ratepayer provide himself with this flat, being a structure for the purposes of s 45 of the General Rate Act 1967?' For my part, I think that such enquiry is as relevant as (b) above, e
viz, for the purpose for which the hereditament is at the date of the proposal being used, and that *both* purposes bear on the entitlement to be derated. MacKenna J[3] considered that the ratepayer's dominant purpose 'was to provide a home for himself and his family' and accordingly held against his claim to be derated. As such a purpose is inevitably of considerable importance whenever accommodation is being sought and may indeed have chief prominence and importance, the adoption of the f
'dominant purpose' test would (as counsel for the valuation officer candidly conceded) for all practical purposes mean that no person seeking private accommodation for himself and his family would ever establish entitlement to be derated under s 45, whatever the type of accommodation sought and however specialised his needs. For my part, I cannot accept the 'dominant purpose' test. I think the proper way of looking at this case is that adopted by Lawton LJ[4] in dealing with the question he had posed. g
He said:

> 'On the evidence the answer is clear. He wanted somewhere to live which was
> not an institution; and if he was to live outside an institution his place of abode
> would have to have certain physical characteristics or be capable of being adapted
> to have those characteristics which would enable him to receive after-care, for h
> example the absence of steps, doors wide enough to take a wheelchair, wall or
> ceiling devices to enable him to move in bed, washbasins at a convenient height,
> specially adapted wc seats and reasonable accommodation for his personal
> attendant, without whose help he could do very little.'

Such being the combination of reasons why the ratepayer chose 7 Addisland Court to live in, rather than some other place, and such being the purpose for which it j

1   [1954] 1 All ER 1013 at 1020, [1954] Ch 530 at 547
2   [1975] 2 All ER at 270, [1975] 2 WLR at 804
3   [1975] 2 All ER at 279, [1975] 2 WLR at 815
4   [1975] 2 All ER at 276, [1975] 2 WLR at 811

was used, then, notwithstanding that he was, of course, minded to secure living
a accommodation for himself and his family, in my judgment the Lands Tribunal
and the Court of Appeal were entitled to hold that he had established his right to
rating relief.

VII. It is not presently necessary to determine whether Lawton LJ[1] was correct
in adding: 'I would construe section 45(d) as applying to a structure which had been
adapted physically to enable a ratepayer to receive after-care there', if by those words
b he meant that adaptation is always a sine qua non to rating relief. But the case for
granting it is clearer if the structure already has some special features or if works of
adaptation are carried out, and I therefore agree with Cairns LJ[2] when he said: 'I do not
consider that the physical characteristics of the structure can be wholly disregarded.'
I would also adopt his stressing that:

c   'The conclusions I have reached in this case do not go beyond the facts of this
        case and it is an important part of the facts that the flat was chosen because it had
        special features making it suitable to provide for the needs of a person who re-
        quired after-care and was adapted and equipped to improve its suitability
        for that purpose.'

d VIII. It does not follow that all living accommodation selected by a person needing
after-care is automatically entitled to rating relief. The mere ipse dixit of a man who
had suffered a coronary thrombosis that he had selected a certain dwelling because it
was situated in an area which, being free of hills, enabled him to take exercise without
strain would not necessarily establish his claim to be derated. The facts of the particular
case, and all the facts, would need to be taken into account and, as Lawton LJ[1] said:

e   'In order to attract rating relief a structure must be of a size and type reasonably
        suitable for the ratepayer's need for after-care. A paraplegic living in a castle
        could not be given rating relief for the whole structure but only for those parts
        which had been adapted for his use and the reasonable accommodation of his
        personal attendant.'

f IX. If in some future case it were held after full deliberation that a structure was
entitled to be derated even though it was of a wholly conventional kind and no special
works of adaptation had been carried out, the fears of MacKenna J regarding the difficulty of drawing a line could become very real. But that possibility must not influence
the decision of this House on the different facts of the present case. When in 1968 the
legislature passed the Health Services and Public Health Act, and dealt in s 12(1)(a)
g thereof with 'the provision, equipment and maintenance of residential accommodation
for . . . the care of persons suffering from illness and the after-care of persons who have
been so suffering', it presumably bore in mind the provisions of s 45 of the General
Rate Act 1967 which, passed in the immediately preceding year, had reproduced in its
process of consolidation a provision which had been on the statute book since 1955.
Alternatively, if it did not have the Act in mind, the conclusion that far more people
h may now be able to assert entitlement to rating relief than was ever contemplated
by Parliament is of itself no ground for preventing that unforeseen result by applying
an unwarrantably restrictive interpretation of s 45 to facts such as those of the present
case. The remedy, if any is thought desirable, rests, as always, in the hands of the
legislature.

For these reasons, I would dismiss the appeal.

j **LORD FRASER OF TULLYBELTON.** My Lords, I need not repeat the facts
as they have already been fully stated by others of your Lordships. I proceed at once

---

1 [1975] 2 All ER at 276, [1975] 2 WLR at 811
2 [1975] 2 All ER at 271, [1975] 2 WLR at 806

to consider whether the ratepayer is entitled to have his flat derated under para (d) of s 45 of the General Rate Act 1967, read with either para (b) or para (c) of the same section. The claim for derating under para (d) read with para (c) clearly fails for the reasons already stated by your Lordships, with which I agree.

The claim under para (d) read with para (b) raises a question that I find much more difficult. Paragraph (b) in its original form derated any structure belonging to a local health authority or to a voluntary organisation formed for any of the purposes mentioned in s 28(1) of the National Health Service Act 1946, and supplied for the use of any person in pursuance of arrangements made under s 28(1). It was in effect amended by the Health Services and Public Health Act 1968, Sch 3 to which requires references to s 28(1) of the 1946 Act to be read as references to s 12 of the 1968 Act. The parties are agreed that there is no relevant difference between the provisions of the two sections and I shall refer only to s 12(1) of the 1968 Act. The words in that subsection that are of immediate importance for this appeal are as follows:

'. . . a local health authority may, with the approval of the Minister . . . make arrangements for the purpose of the prevention of illness and for the care of persons suffering from illness and for the after-care of persons who have been so suffering and in particular . . . for—(a) the provision . . . of residential accommodation for the care of persons with a view to preventing them from becoming ill, the care of persons suffering from illness and the after-care of persons who have been so suffering . . .'

The effect of para (b) of s 45 of the 1967 Act, so far as its express terms go, is that in valuing a hereditament for rating no account is to be taken of any structure if it fulfils two conditions, viz (1) if it belongs to a local health authority (or to a voluntary organisation formed for the purposes specified in s 12 of the 1968 Act) and (2) if it is 'supplied for the use of any person in pursuance of arrangements made under' s 12. 'Structure' includes structures and buildings of all kinds: *Almond v Birmingham Royal Institution for the Blind*[1]. Paragraph (d) extends the benefit to any structure 'which is of a kind similar to structures such as are referred to in paragraph . . . (b) . . . but does not fall within that paragraph by reason that it is owned or has been supplied otherwise than as mentioned in that paragraph'. If para (d) were read literally it would refer to para (b) in a form from which almost the whole content had been removed. Ownership of the structure is no longer material, so condition (1) goes. Arrangements made under s 12 have also ceased to be material, so all that is left of condition (2) is that the structure must be 'supplied for the use of any person', which is hardly a significant qualification. A structure 'similar to' that mentioned in what is left of para (b) could include any structure, whoever its owner (except a local health authority or a voluntary organisation of the kind specified in the paragraph) and however it had been supplied, provided only that it was supplied for the use of any person; almost every structure not owned by a local health authority or a specified voluntary organisation would fall within that description and would therefore be entitled to derating. Such an absurd result cannot have been intended by Parliament, and one is therefore forced to abandon the strictly literal construction, but I have pursued it to its reductio ad absurdum because an important part of the argument for the ratepayer was based on a literal reading of s 45.

There must be some limit to the kind of 'structure' that is entitled to derating under para (d). It was suggested that a limit was set by the fact that residential accommodation could only be provided under s 12 of the 1968 Act 'with the approval of the Minister'. No doubt the need for ministerial approval limits the structures belonging to a local health authority or a voluntary organisation which can qualify for derating under para (b), but I do not think it sets any effective limit to the kind of structure that can qualify under para (d). It has to be 'similar' to those qualified under para (b),

1   [1967] 2 All ER 317, [1968] AC 37

that is (on this argument) similar to those that the Minister either has approved or
would be likely to approve. But the difficulties and uncertainties of applying a test
of what a local health authority either had done or would do were pointed out
by Cairns LJ[1] in the Court of Appeal and I agree with him that that test cannot have
been intended by the draftsman of para (d). The same difficulties and uncertainties
would arise if the test were applied to what the Minister had done or would do.
In my opinion the only practicable test is by reference to the powers conferred by s 12,
and the need for ministerial approval does not limit the generality of that test.
   A reasonable construction of s 45 must start from the word 'similar' in para (d).
It has been held to mean not similar in physical construction but similar in purpose
or adaptability (Walker v Wood[2]) and I accept that. That requires one to ascertain
the purposes for which a structure that is referred to in para (b) can be supplied, and
then to see whether the purpose for which the ratepayer's flat has been supplied is
similar to any of them. The purposes which qualify under para (b) are those specified
in s 12 of the Health Services and Public Health Act 1968, the most relevant part of
which I have already quoted. There are three purposes: the prevention of illness,
the care of persons who are ill and the after-care of persons who have been ill. The
provision of residential accommodation must be for one of those purposes if it is to
be intra vires of a local health authority or voluntary organisation acting under s 12,
and in my opinion it is implicit in the section that one of them must be the predominant purpose in the mind of the authority making the provision. I recognise that the
word 'predominant', or any equivalent, does not appear in the section, but in my
opinion it is necessarily implied in order to give effect to the scheme of the section.
Section 12 is dealing, as the sidenote shows, with 'Prophylaxis, care and after-care'
and sub-s (1) begins by conferring on a local health authority a general power to make
arrangements for those three purposes. Then it proceeds, without prejudice to the
generality of the opening provision, to confer some more specific powers, one of which
is the power to make arrangements for the provision of residential accommodation.
I think all the specific powers are intended to be used for one of the three purposes,
and there can be no doubt of that so far as the power of providing residential accommodation is concerned, because it is expressly so stated (s 12(1)(a)). If those were not
intended to be the predominant purposes, the powers of a local health authority
would be extended far beyond the bounds of public health. That appears most clearly
perhaps in relation to the provision of residential accommodation of prophylactic
purposes; if the power conferred on a local health authority by s 12(1)(a) to provide
residential accommodation 'for the care of persons with a view to preventing them
from becoming ill' could be used for that as a merely incidental purpose, it might
extend to rehousing all persons in their area whose existing accommodation was
unhealthy. That might be a very desirable thing to do, but it would normally fall
within the field of the housing authority and not of the health authority, and I do
not believe that any such wide power is conferred by s 12. Further, it is of some
significance that the section authorises the provision of residential accommodation
'for the care' of persons with a view to etc, and 'for the after-care of persons who
have been ill', showing that the reason for providing the accommodation is to
facilitate the giving of care or after-care, and not merely to provide a cheap home.
That may not have to be the sole reason, but in my opinion it must be the main or
dominant one. Accordingly, I agree with MacKenna J[3] in the Court of Appeal that—

   'nothing less than a dominant purpose of the supplier to prevent illness or to
   provide for the care or after-care of persons suffering from illness will in my
   opinion suffice to bring the structure within para (b).'

---

1   [1975] 2 All ER 264 at 270, 271, [1957] 1 WLR 797 at 805
2   [1962] 3 All ER 188, [1962] 1 WLR 1060
3   [1975] 2 All ER at 278, [1975] 1 WLR at 814

If that is the meaning of para (b) then, when para (d) refers to a structure which is of a kind 'similar to' that mentioned in para (b), it must refer to one which is supplied for the predominant purpose of care or after-care. The predominant purpose must in each case be that of the supplier, who in this case is the ratepayer himself. The suggestion that the ratepayer's flat had been 'supplied' for his use by the owner who let it to him seems to me quite untenable. I do not think that the flat was 'supplied' for the use of the ratepayer by the owner any more than it was by the builder. It was supplied for the use of the ratepayer by himself when he took a lease of it. It is therefore the predominant purpose in his mind that is material.

It seems to me that the predominant purpose of the ratepayer in taking this flat was to have somewhere, other than an institution, for himself and his family to live. We know that he chose this particular flat, after a long search, because it suited his requirements by having, among other things, wide doors through which he could pass in a wheelchair, and he has made some alterations in it to make it more convenient. But I do not think it is possible to treat these matters as showing that his main reason for taking it was to obtain after-care. His main reason was to have a home. The result is that, in my opinion, the claim for derating under para (d) read with para (b) must fail. Counsel for the ratepayer argued that, if the view I have just stated was correct, it would mean that no accommodation supplied by a person for himself could ever qualify for derating under para (d). That may be so, and, if it is, it is because of the provisions of the Act. But I doubt whether that result would follow in all cases; for example, a house might qualify for derating if it were in an unattractive area with nothing to commend it to the occupier except that it was suitable for the particular form of care or after-care that he needed, say for tuberculosis in the days before chemotherapy.

If I had felt able to extract from the words of s 45 of the 1967 Act the meaning attributed to them by my noble and learned friend, Viscount Dilhorne, I would gladly have done so, as that would give the section an intelligible scheme which would be in line with what one might expect. Unfortunately, I have not been able to convince myself that it is possible to do so.

I would allow the appeal.

Appeal allowed.

Solicitors: *Solicitor of Inland Revenue*; *N D Vandyk*.

Gordon H Scott Esq Barrister.

a   # Inland Revenue Commissioners v Goodwin

HOUSE OF LORDS
LORD DIPLOCK, LORD MORRIS OF BORTH-Y-GEST, LORD KILBRANDON, LORD SALMON AND
LORD EDMUND-DAVIES
17th, 20th NOVEMBER 1975, 28th JANUARY 1976

b

*Surtax – Tax advantage – Counteracting – Transaction in securities – Transaction carried
out for bona fide commercial reasons – Commercial reasons – Transactions carried out for
purpose of perpetuating family control of business – Family company – Bonus issue of redeemable preference shares – Issue to provide funds for estate duty purposes and thereby
avoid loss of family control of company on death of major shareholders – Redemption of shares*
c   *resulting in tax advantage – Whether issue and redemption of shares 'carried out . . . for
bona fide commercial reasons' – Finance Act 1960, s 28(1).*

In 1935 a private company was incorporated to carry on a long-established family
engineering business. At the time of incorporation the directors were F and J, the
grandsons of the founder of the business. In 1951 the company's shares were held as
d   to 40 per cent by J and the trustees of a family settlement made by J, 30 per cent by F
and the trustees of family settlement made by F, and 30 per cent by the taxpayer, a
great-grandson of the founder. At that time the trust holdings were so constituted
that the shares were aggregable for estate duty together with the estate of the settlors
on their death. Since it might have become necessary to sell shares to pay estate duty,
at the risk of losing family control of the company, the company resolved (a) to
e   increase the company's capital by capitalising £44,525 from its profit and loss account,
(b) to create preference shares redeemable on three months' notice after
12 months, and (c) to issue those shares to existing shareholders as a five to one bonus.
The company considered the possibility of a public issue of shares but decided against
it on the ground that its dividend record was such that adequate support would be
unlikely. In 1958, however, the company decided that its prospects warranted a public
f   issue in order to enable the company to obtain capital for expansion from the money
market and to secure the company further from the danger that family control
would be lost in consequence of estate duty liabilities. Under the scheme adopted
by the company for the public flotation of its shares, the 1951 bonus issue of preference
shares was to be made irredeemable for approximately five years to replace a large
sum which had been used to acquire a subsidiary company, half the ordinary shares
g   in the company were to be converted into deferred ordinary shares, and the offer
to the public was to be made out of the unconverted ordinary shares, while the deferred ordinary shares were to remain as such until after the redemption of the 1951
preference shares. At that point it was discovered that, because of a technical error, the
preference shares created in 1951 were not redeemable. In order to rectify the
situation the company capitalised a sum from its general reserve and applied that
h   sum in part to the paying up of newly created redeemable preference shares, and in
part to paying up newly created ordinary and deferred ordinary shares. The
redeemable preference shares were redeemable at the company's option after 30th
April 1963. The deferred ordinary shares were only to rank pari passu as one class
with the ordinary shares after 12 months had passed following the redemption of
the preference shares. A proportion of the ordinary shares was to be offered to the
j   public. On 18th August 1958 the taxpayer transferred his shareholding to his wife.
On 19th August an offer was made to the public of 540,000 ordinary shares at 2s
each. The offer, which was signed by J, contained particulars relating to the company's
directors and indicated by its general tenor that one of the company's principal
invisible assets was the continuity of family management. On 30th April
1963 the company redeemed the preference shares for cash out of its capitalised

s

reserves and paid the taxpayer's wife the redemption moneys. The Crown issued a
notice to the taxpayer under s 28ª of the Finance Act 1960 in order to counteract the tax   a
advantage which he had received by reason of (i) the resolution of the company in
1958 to capitalise its reserve and apply that sum in the bonus issue of redeemable
preference shares to shareholders, (ii) the issue to the taxpayer of a portion of those
shares, and (iii) the receipt by the taxpayer's wife in 1963 of cash on the redemption of
those shares. The taxpayer appealed against the notice. The commissioners found
(a) that the main object of the 1951 preference share issue by the company was a bona   b
fide commercial one, and that the obtaining of a tax advantage was not a main object;
(b) that the main object of the 1958 preference share issue was to restore the status quo;
(c) that the restoration in itself, and even without regard to the intention at that time
to embark on a public flotation of shares in the company, afforded a bona fide commercial reason for the 1958 issue of redeemable preference shares; (d) that the obtaining of a tax advantage was not a main object of the 1958 transaction; and (e) that   c
accordingly s 28 did not apply to the taxpayer. On appeal the Crown contended,
inter alia, that there were no facts on which the commissioners were entitled to hold
that the transactions of 1958 and 1963 had been carried out for bona fide commercial
reasons.

Held – The transactions of 1958 and 1963 were not to be considered in isolation but in   d
conjunction with the transaction of 1951 since it was in 1951 that the company had
decided on policies which were then considered as being in its best commercial
interests. There was an unchallengeable finding of fact by the commissioners that the
1951 transaction had been carried out for bona fide commercial reasons and, while it
was for the taxpayer to show that the same was true concerning the later transactions,
that burden of proof was not difficult to discharge, provided it was established that   e
the nature of and the reasons for the later transactions were essentially the same as in
the case of the 1951 transaction. The reasons for the transactions of 1951, 1958 and 1963
were essentially questions of fact for the commissioners to determine and there were
no grounds for interfering with the commissioners' findings that the transactions had
been entered into for the purpose of attaining bona fide commercial objects, i e access
to the money market coupled with continuance of family management. It followed   f
that s 28 of the 1960 Act did not apply to the taxpayer since the transactions referred
to in the notice had been carried out for 'bona fide commercial reasons . . . and none
of them had as their main object . . . to enable tax advantages to be obtained', within
s 28(1). Accordingly the appeal would be dismissed (see p 483 g, p 484 a, p 487 f to j,
p 488 b c e h and j and p 489 e and f, post).
Decision of the Court of Appeal [1975] 1 All ER 708 affirmed.   g

Notes
For the cancellation of tax advantages, see Supplement to 20 Halsbury's Laws (3rd Edn)
para 276A, 1, and for cases on the subject, see 28(1) Digest (Reissue) 489-494, 1753-1762.
For the Finance Act 1960, s 28, see 40 Halsbury's Laws (2nd Edn) 447.
For 1970-71 and subsequent years of assessment, s 28 of the 1960 Act has been   h
replaced by the Income and Corporation Taxes Act 1970, ss 460, 461.

Cases referred to in opinions
Edwards (Inspector of Taxes) v Bairstow [1955] 3 All ER 48, [1956] AC 14, [1955] 3 WLR
    410, 36 Tax Cas 207, [1955] TR 209, 34 ATC 198, 48 R & IT 534, HL, 28(1) Digest
    (Reissue) 567, 2089.
Inland Revenue Comrs v Brebner [1967] 1 All ER 779, [1967] 2 AC 18, 43 Tax Cas 705,
    [1967] 2 WLR 1001, 46 ATC 17, [1967] TR 21, 1967 SC (HL) 31, HL, 28(1) Digest
    (Reissue) 490, 1755.

---

a   Section 28, so far as material, is set out at p 487 a to e, post

Inland Revenue Comrs v Hague, Hague v Inland Revenue Comrs [1968] 2 All ER 1252, [1969] 1 Ch 393, 44 Tax Cas 619, [1968] 3 WLR 576, 47 ATC 217, [1968] TR 193, CA, 28(1) Digest (Reissue) 490, *1756*.

Appeal

The Inland Revenue Commissioners served a notice dated 5th May 1969 in accordance with s 28(3) of the Finance Act 1960 on John Goodwin ('the taxpayer'), notifying him of the adjustments which, in the commissioners' opinion, were necessary to counteract the tax advantages obtained or obtainable by the taxpayer as a result of transactions carried out by the taxpayer on or about 18th August 1958 and or about 30th April 1963. The taxpayer appealed to the Commissioners for the Special Purposes of the Income Tax Acts against the notice and, on 10th June 1972, the commissioners allowed the appeal and cancelled the notice, holding that s 28 of the 1960 Act did not apply to the taxpayer since all the transactions referred to in the notice under s 28(3) had been carried out for bona fide commercial reasons and none of them had as their main object, or one of their main objects, to enable tax advantages to be obtained. The Crown, being dissatisfied with the determination of the appeal as being erroneous in point of law, required the commissioners to state a case for the opinion of the High Court. On 9th July 1973 Walton J[1] allowed the Crown's appeal, holding, inter alia, that the transactions referred to in the notice under s 28(3) had not been carried out by the taxpayer for bona fide commercial reasons. Accordingly it was ordered that the notice served on the taxpayer be restored. On appeal by the taxpayer, the Court of Appeal[2] (Russell, Stamp and Scarman LJJ) on 29th January 1975 reversed the decision of Walton J. The Crown appealed to the House of Lords. The facts are set out in the opinion of Lord Kilbrandon.

D C Potter QC and *Brian Davenport* for the Crown.
Michael Nolan QC and *Stephen Oliver* for the taxpayer.

Their Lordships took time for consideration.

28th January. The following opinions were delivered.

LORD DIPLOCK. My Lords, I have had the advantage of reading in advance the speech to be delivered by my noble and learned friend, Lord Kilbrandon.
I agree with him and would dismiss the appeal.

LORD MORRIS OF BORTH-Y-GEST. My Lords, before the commissioners it was for the taxpayer to show that the transactions in question were carried out either for bona fide commercial reasons or in the ordinary course of making or managing investments and further that none of them had as their main object, or one of their main objects, to enable tax advantages to be obtained. As to this latter matter the commissioners found that the obtaining of tax advantage was not a main object of any of the transactions. The point of difficulty in the case concerned the question whether in regard to the 1951 transaction (from which the later transactions stemmed and with which they were linked) the conclusion of the commissioners that its object was a bona fide commercial one was a conclusion which ran counter to and was not warranted by their findings of fact. Was the evidence which was accepted inconsistent with and contradictory of the conclusion? Though a contention to this effect was very forcibly argued and though during our consideration of the appeal I was impressed by the

---

1   [1973] 3 All ER 545, [1974] 1 WLR 380, [1973] STC 456
2   [1975] 1 All ER 708, [1975] 1 WLR 640, [1975] STC 173

reasoning in the careful judgment of Walton J, I came in the end, though after hesitation, to the view that the reasoning of the Court of Appeal was to be preferred, and for the reasons given by my noble and learned friend, Lord Kilbrandon—whose speech I have had the advantage of reading in advance—I agree that the appeal should be dismissed.

LORD KILBRANDON. My Lords, R Goodwin & Sons (Engineers) Ltd ('the company') are incorporated for the purpose of carrying on an engineering business established in the Midlands in 1883. The founders were a Mr Goodwin and his sons. When the incorporation into a private company took place in 1935, two of old Mr Goodwin's grandsons, Frank and John, were directors; in 1954 the board was joined by a great-grandson, who is the taxpayer, and another director. Economic history testifies to the fact that such concerns have been the back bone of English manufacturing prosperity, and this fact may turn out to be important.

The ensuing narrative is derived from the findings in fact made by the commissioners in circumstances which will become apparent. The narrative is given in skeleton form, so as, so far as possible, to include only the facts which are essential to a decision of the appeal, because there is a full statement to be found in the judgment of the Court of Appeal[1], and there is no point in repetition. I may say straight away that I agree with the approach adopted by the Court of Appeal, and the conclusion at which the court arrived.

1. In 1951 consideration was given to the company 'going public', thus obtaining access to fresh capital for expansion purposes. But the time was deemed unpropitious, because, inter alia, the recent dividend record had not been such as to make public support probable.

2. The shares at that time were held as to 40 per cent by John Goodwin senior, then aged 55, and by trustees of family settlements made by him, 30 per cent by Frank Goodwin, then aged 60, and by trustees of family settlements made by him, and 30 per cent by the taxpayer. The trust holdings had been constituted so recently as to make the shares aggregable for estate duty with the estates of the settlors on decease. To meet the duty it would probably have become necessary to sell shares, with the danger of family control being lost. The importance of family control will be adverted to later.

3. It was therefore decided, and the company resolved accordingly, to increase the capital of the company by capitalising £44,525 from profit and loss account, to create six per cent preference shares redeemable by the company at three months' notice after 12 months, and to issue those shares to the existing shareholders as a five to one bonus issue. Thus, on redemption, resources would have become available to meet the threat to the family control. It is important to emphasise that the commissioners[2] found as a matter of fact that the decision referred to under heading 3 above was taken for the reasons given under heading 2, 'that the main object of the 1951 preference share issue was a bona fide commercial one, and that the obtaining of a tax advantage was not a main object'.

4. In 1958 it was decided that the history and prospects of the company were such as to make the time ripe for a public issue. The method by which this was to be effected was described by the Court of Appeal as follows[3]:

'After a good many varying suggestions, the scheme evolved for a public flotation was as follows, accepted by the Goodwin family and trustees of the settlements: (1) acquisition by the company of the outstanding 71 per cent shareholding in a company ("Akron") so as to make it a 100 per cent subsidiary;

---

1   [1975] 1 All ER 708, [1975] 1 WLR 640, [1975] STC 173
2   [1973] 3 All ER at 553, 554, [1973] STC at 464, 465
3   [1975] 1 All ER at 712, [1975] 1 WLR at 644, [1975] STC at 177

(2) the 1951 bonus issue of preference shares to be made irredeemable for a period of some five years to enable expanding trade to replace the substantial sum (some £130,000) of working capital required for the Akron acquisition; (3) half of the ordinary shares in the company to be converted into deferred ordinary shares, the offer to the public to be made out of the unconverted ordinary shares; the deferred ordinary shares to remain as such until after the redemption of the 1951 preference shares.'

5. At this stage a crisis arose; it was discovered that the preference shares had been issued pursuant to an ordinary, not a special, resolution of the company, and that therefore the essential quality of redeemability did not attach to them. The foundation of the scheme was thus insecure.

6. Although the danger of shares having to be sold to meet death duties was now less menacing, owing to the effluxion of time having released the settled shares from liability to duty, it was still real. It was related now in part to the survivorship of the taxpayer. Any action which was to be taken had accordingly still to be effective in the two respects of securing the family control and enabling the issue to the public. The obvious thing to do was, by the most convenient means, so to restructure the capital as to remake the provision which it was thought had been made in 1951. Again to quote the judgment of the Court of Appeal[1]:

'This was done first by converting the 1951 preference shares into deferred ordinary shares. The company then capitalised the sum of £171,095 from its general reserve and applied that sum in paying up at par: (a) 44,525 out of 45,000 newly-created £1 six per cent redeemable preference shares; (b) 81,905 of previously unissued (6,095) and newly-created ordinary shares (75,000); (c) 45,475 previously unissued (475) and newly-created (45,000) deferred ordinary shares: the 475 representing the converted unissued 1951 preference shares.

'The capital structure of the company for the purpose of the public flotation was thus: issued ordinary £90,000, of which a proportion (£54,000) was to be offered to the public; issued deferred ordinary shares, 90,000; issued six per cent redeemable preference shares, 44,525; unissued redeemable preference shares, 475.

'The redeemable preference shares were redeemable at the company's option after 30th April 1963. The deferred ordinary shares were to rank pari passu as one class with the ordinary shares only after 12 months from the redemption of the preference shares.'

7. As regards this scheme the commissioners[2] observed:

'We are satisfied on the evidence that the main object of the 1958 preference share issue was to restore the status quo ante in this respect. We think that the restoration in itself, and even without regard to the then current intention to embark upon a public flotation of shares in the company, affords a bona fide commercial reason for the 1958 issue of redeemable preference shares, and we find that the obtaining of a tax advantage was not a main object of the 1958 transaction.'

Insofar as this passage is a finding of fact, in my opinion the commissioners were well entitled to make it, and so far as it is an inference from facts, I would say that the inference was justifiable if not irresistible.

8. On 19th August 1958 an offer was made to the public of 540,000 ordinary shares of 2s each (that is, £54,000 shares of £1 each sub-divided). The particulars attached to the offer (signed by John Goodwin senior) contained the following paragraph:

---

1   [1975] 1 All ER at 712, 713, [1975] 1 WLR at 645, [1975] STC at 177, 178
2   [1973] 3 All ER at 554, [1973] STC at 465

'MANAGEMENT.—I am 62 years of age and have been actively engaged in the business since the end of the first World War. I have been Chairman of Directors and Managing Director of the Company since its incorporation in 1935.

'Mr Frank Goodwin (my brother) is aged 67 and has spent all his working life with the business. He also has been a Director since the incorporation of the Company in 1935.

'Mr John Goodwin (my son) is 31 years of age and joined the Company in August, 1946 becoming a Director in 1954. He is now Vice-Chairman and Assistant Managing Director.

'Mr Henry Stubbs is aged 47 and has been with the business since June, 1927, becoming a Director in 1954.

'We are all actively engaged in the service of the Company and have no other business commitments. We have each entered into a service agreement with the Company for a minimum period of five years from 1st May 1958 (See Contracts numbered (3) to (6) inclusive below).

'The present management has been responsible for building up the business of the Group and I have every confidence in its ability to maintain continued progress.'

9. On 30th April 1963, that is at the earliest possible date, the company redeemed the preference shares for cash out of capitalised reserves of the company. The taxpayer's holding of 13,355 shares had been transferred by him on 18th August 1958 to his wife, to whom, accordingly, the redemption moneys were paid. The commissioners found[1] that the redemption was 'in order . . . to implement the bargain made with the public in 1958'. This phrase was severely criticised by counsel for the Crown, and for my part I agree that it is not accurate. Such of the public as should subscribe for shares had no interest in the issue or redemption of the preference shares, and no bargain has been made with the public relating to them. In my opinion the Court of Appeal[2] correctly stated the nature of the transaction as 'a fulfilment of the expectation of the trustees and other shareholders on the basis of which the scheme of public flotation went through'. It was a sine qua non of the public issue.

10. On 5th May 1969 the Crown issued a notice to the taxpayer under s 28 of the Finance Act 1960, as amended by s 25(4) of the Finance Act 1962, claiming to make adjustments to his liability to surtax for the year 1963-64 in respect of the following transactions:

'1. the special resolution of R. Goodwin & Sons (Engineers) Ltd. (hereinafter called "the company") on 18th August 1958 to capitalise the sum of £171,095, part of the company's general reserve, and, inter alia, to apply part of that sum to paying up in full 44,525 6 per cent redeemable cumulative preference shares of £1 each, such shares (a) to be distributed amongst the holders of the ordinary shares in the company in the proportions specified in the resolution and (b) to carry rights including the company's right, on giving due notice, to redeem them on or at any time after 30th April 1963;

'2. the issue to you, on or about 18th August 1958, pursuant to the aforesaid special resolution, of 13,355 of the aforesaid redeemable preference shares and the transfer of those shares from you to your wife, Mrs. Patricia H. Goodwin, on or about 1st September 1958;

'3. the receipt by your wife on or about 30th April 1963 of £13,355 by way of redemption of her holding of 13,355 of the aforesaid redeemable preference shares.'

It is necessary at this stage to quote only a portion of s 28, as follows:

---

1 [1973] 3 All ER at 554, [1973] STC at 465
2 [1975] 1 All ER at 715, [1975] 1 WLR at 648, [1975] STC at 180

'(1) Where—(a) in any such circumstances as are mentioned in the next following subsection, and (b) in consequence of a transaction in securities or of the combined effect of two or more such transactions, a person is in a position to obtain, or has obtained, a tax advantage, then unless he shows that the transaction or transactions were carried out either for bona fide commercial reasons or in the ordinary course of making or managing investments, and that none of them had as their main object, or one of their main objects, to enable tax advantages to be obtained, this section shall apply to him in respect of that transaction or those transactions . . .

'(2) The circumstances mentioned in the foregoing subsection are that . . . (c) the person in question receives, in consequence of a transaction whereby any other person—(i) subsequently receives, or has received, an abnormal amount by way of dividend; or (ii) subsequently becomes entitled, or has become entitled, to a deduction as mentioned in paragraph (b) of this subsection, a consideration which either is, or represents the value of, assets which are (or apart from anything done by the company in question would have been) available for distribution by way of dividend, or is received in respect of future receipts of the company or is, or represents the value of, trading stock of the company, and the said person so receives the consideration that he does not pay or bear tax on it as income; or (d) in connection with the distribution of profits of a company to which this paragraph applies, the person in question so receives as is mentioned in paragraph (c) of this subsection such a consideration as is therein mentioned . . .'

The arrangements for counteracting tax advantages and for the consequent procedures follow but need not be quoted.

As affecting the taxpayer personally, there is a special point arising out of the transfer by him to his wife. I will therefore summarise the situation arising on the section in this appeal as it affects the shareholder in general. First, it is conceded that the shareholder is a person who received, within the meaning of s 28(2)(c) and (d), assets of the company which were or would have been available for distribution by way of dividend in such a way that he did not bear tax on them as income, and received them in consequence of a transaction or transactions in securities. He therefore obtained a tax advantage within the meaning of s 28(1). The section will apply to him, that is to say, the Crown will be entitled to make an adjustment to his liability for surtax, unless he can exempt himself in one of the ways set out in the section. It is further conceded that neither of the transactions referred to in the notice had as its main object to enable the tax advantage to be obtained. The questions therefore are, has he shown that the transactions were carried out either (a) for bona fide commercial reasons, or (b) in the ordinary course of making or managing investments? It is with (a) that this appeal is mainly concerned.

Although only the 1958 and 1963 transactions figure in the notice, I believe it is generally agreed that those transactions, although they must be considered independently, cannot be evaluated for the purpose of (a) above, or even intelligibly described, save under colour of the transaction of 1951. The scene was set in 1951, and what followed, in the history of the company over the ensuing 12 years, was the working out of the policies which at that time satisfied the company as being in its best commercial interests. There is an unchallengeable finding in fact by the commissioners that the 1951 transaction was carried out for bona fide commercial reasons. While the onus remains on the taxpayer to show that the same is true of the subsequent transactions, it will, I apprehend, not be difficult to do that if the essentially homogeneous character of the successive transactions, and the 'reasons' for them, can be established. This will be again largely a question of fact; one of the main difficulties I have found in this appeal is to discern a question of law, on which alone your Lordships would be justified in overruling the decision of the commissioners.

An overriding reason for the 1958 transaction—being, besides and apart from the motive of facilitating access to the public money market, as true of 1958 as it was of 1951—was the retention of family control of the company. It was conceded in argu- *a* ment by counsel for the Crown that, if the commissioners had specifically and in so many words found that the loss of family control would have had deleterious commercial consequences to the company, that finding would have amounted to a finding that a transaction entered into for the purpose of protecting that control had been carried out for bona fide commercial reasons. There is no such explicit finding, but the whole tenor of findings is to that effect, and the substance of the matter seems to *b* be clear and indisputable when the management paragraph in the particulars, already quoted, is properly taken into account. The public, whose support was being solicited, were being invited to regard the continuity of family management as part of the invisible commercial assets of the company, and that appears to me to go the whole way to finding a commercial reason for the securing of that management.

As regards the 1963 transaction, it was submitted by the Crown that the only finding *c* in fact justifying its classification as a bona fide commercial transaction, namely, that it was entered into 'in order to implement the bargain made with the public in 1958', having been shown to be erroneous, there were no facts on which the commissioners were entitled to arrive at their conclusion. My Lords, I have already pointed out that, as the Court of Appeal decided, this is a verbal rather than a substantial criticism. What was implemented in 1963 was an agreement between the company and the *d* shareholders, some of whom were under a fiduciary duty to protect rights under settlements, as to the terms on which the issue of ordinary shares was to be made to the public. The transaction, which the commissioners found did not have as a main object the obtaining of a tax advantage, was entered into as the final stage in the attainment of bona fide commercial objects, namely access to the money market coupled with continuance of family management, with the advantages to the company *e* to which I have referred.

It was also submitted for the taxpayer that the transactions escaped the consequences which ensue under s 28 on the grounds that they were carried out 'in the ordinary course of making or managing investments'. It is not necessary to express any opinion on that, and I refrain from doing so.

The special position of the taxpayer is that he had transferred his shares to his wife *f* after allotment and before redemption. On the terms of s 28, accordingly, he could have claimed that not he but his wife, had received the consideration referred to in s 28(2)(c): see *Inland Revenue Comrs v Hague*[1], and that thus he had obtained no tax advantage. The legislature sought to alter this situation by s 25(4) of the Finance Act 1962, which provides that in such circumstances s 28 applies to a husband 'as it would apply if any property, rights or liabilities of the wife were his property, rights or *g* liabilities in relation to which she had acted only as nominee for him'. I am bound to say, my Lords, that it appears to me that that amendment covers the present case, but since it is not necessary to decide the point, I would not do so.

My Lords, since in my opinion the findings in fact of the commissioners amount to this, that the transactions referred to in the notice were carried out for bona fide commercial reasons and that neither of them had as a main object to enable a tax *h* advantage to be obtained, I would dismiss this appeal.

LORD SALMON. My Lords, I have had the advantage of reading the speech prepared by my noble and learned friend, Lord Kilbrandon. For the reasons given by him, I would dismiss this appeal.

LORD EDMUND-DAVIES. My Lords, I cannot help thinking that the commissioners might well have arrived at different findings of fact on the material available

---

1   [1968] 2 All ER 1252, [1969] 1 Ch 193, 44 Tax Cas 619

to them in this case than those they in fact made, and that had they done so those different findings would have been unassailable. I am, nevertheless, in agreement that, for the reasons appearing in the speech of my noble and learned friend, Lord Kilbrandon, this appeal should be dismissed. Why this should be so was explained in *Edwards (Inspector of Taxes) v Bairstow*[1] by Lord Radcliffe, who said[2]:

'. . . the reason why the courts do not interfere with commissioners' findings or determinations when they really do involve nothing but questions of fact is not any supposed advantage in the commissioners of greater experience in matters of business, or any other matters. The reason is simply that, by the system that has been set up, the commissioners are the first tribunal to try an appeal, and in the interests of the efficient administration of justice, their decisions can only be upset on appeal if they have been positively wrong in law. The court is not a second opinion, where there is reasonable ground for the first . . . Their duty is no more than to examine those facts with a decent respect for the tribunal appealed from and if they think that the only reasonable conclusion on the facts found is inconsistent with the determination come to, to say so without more ado.'

Looming over all the details of this case is the crucial question: was the obtaining of a tax advantage the main object, or one of the main objects, of the transactions of 1951, 1958 and 1963, or any of them, to which the taxpayer was a party? As Russell LJ[3] said in the Court of Appeal: 'This is essentially a matter of subjective fact' and the conclusion thereon depended on the evidence, both oral and documentary, which was adduced. There are certain features of that evidence which leave me personally unconvinced that I should have arrived at the same findings of fact, subjective as well as objective, as those formed by the commissioners.

But that is not the test. Accordingly, while I am not prepared to hold that there was here that 'ample evidence' which in, for example, *Inland Revenue Comrs v Brebner*[4] led this House to refuse to interfere with the finding of fact on which the commissioners there arrived, yet since, at the same time, I find it impossible to say that the *only* reasonable conclusion on the facts found is inconsistent with the determination come to in the instant case, I concur in holding that the appeal should be dismissed.

Appeal dismissed.

Solicitors: *Solicitor of Inland Revenue*; *Waltons & Co*, agents for *Pinsent & Co*, Birmingham (for the taxpayer).

Gordon H Scott Esq Barrister.

---

1 [1955] 3 All ER 48, [1956] AC 14, 36 Tax Cas 207
2 [1955] 3 All ER at 59, [1956] AC at 38, 39, 36 Tax Cas at 231
3 [1975] 1 All ER 708 at 715, [1975] 1 WLR 640 at 648, [1975] STC 173 at 180
4 [1967] 1 All ER 779, [1967] 2 AC 18, 43 Tax Cas 705

R v A Justice for Lincoln (Kesteven), ex parte M (a minor)
R v Lincoln (Kesteven) Juvenile Court, ex parte Lincolnshire County Council

QUEEN'S BENCH DIVISION
LORD WIDGERY CJ, PARK AND MAY JJ
11th, 12th NOVEMBER 1975

Children and young persons – Detention – Place of safety order – Application – Abuse of process – Use of statutory provision for purpose not intended – Application following discharge of care order – Child in care of local authority – Juvenile court discharging care order on application of child's father – Court refusing to admit evidence of father's behaviour to other children – Local authority applying immediately for place of safety order – No change in circumstances of child – Justice making order having heard evidence of father's behaviour to other children – Whether application for place of safety order an abuse of process – Children and Young Persons Act 1969, s 28(1).

Children and young persons – Detention – Interim order – Application – Persons who may make application – Parent – Discharge of place of safety order – Power of justices to discharge place of safety order on making of application for interim order – Interim order a care order – Right to apply for care orders limited to local authority, constable or authorised person – Whether parent may apply for an interim order – Children and Young Persons Act 1969, ss 1(1), 20(1), 28(6).

On 2nd May 1972 a care order was made under s 1ᵃ of the Children and Young Persons Act 1969 committing M, a child, to the care of the local authority. On 22nd May 1975 M's father made an application under s 21(2)ᵇ of the 1969 Act to the juvenile court to discharge the care order and to substitute a supervision order. At the hearing of the application on 21st October the local authority wished to tender evidence to the court that M's two sisters, who were living at home with the father, had been the subject of incestuous relations with him. The court refused to admit that evidence, taking the view that it was irrelevant in that the care order was not being supported on the ground specified in s 1(2)(b) of the 1969 Act, i e that another child of the family was being or had been 'neglected or . . . ill-treated'. The justices discharged the care order and allowed M to return to the father's house under a supervision order. On 24th October an officer of the local authority, who was concerned about M, applied to a justice for an order under s 28(1)ᶜ that M be taken to a place of safety for a period not exceeding 28 days. The evidence excluded from the hearing before the juvenile court was given to the justice, who made the order sought. The father applied for an order of certiorari to quash that order on the grounds (i) that it was an abuse of the process of the court to apply for such an order so soon after the hearing at which the care order had been discharged when there had been no material change in M's circumstances, and (ii) that the provision was being abused in that it was being used to exclude M's parents from proper control. The local authority applied for an order prohibiting the juvenile court from hearing any application by the father under

---

a   Section 1, so far as material, is set out at p 492 *d* and *e*, post
b   Section 21(2) is set out at p 492 *g* and *h*, post
c   Section 28(1) is set out at p 493 *f* to *h*, post
d   Section 28(6) is set out at p 495 *g*, post

s 28(6)d fo an interim order releasing M to his care, on the ground that, under s 1(1)
a and 20(1)e of the 1969 Act, such an application could only be made by a 'local authority,
constable or authorised person'.

Held – (i) The father's application for certiorari would be refused since he had failed
to establish that, in making the application under s 28(1), the local authority had
used that subsection for a purpose for which it had not been intended. The purpose
b of an order under s 28(1) was to enable a child in actual danger to be put speedily
and effectively into a place of safety. The application and the order had been properly
made, since the local authority had, rightly or wrongly, believed M to be in danger,
the order had been applied for and granted by the justice bona fide, and there was
no reason to believe it would be abused in order to deprive M's parents of control
on a long-term basis (see p 494 j to p 495 f and p 496 e, post).
c   (ii) The local authority's application for prohibition would also be refused. The
language of s 28(6) was not sufficiently explicit to exclude an application for an
interim order by a parent who might be the person most requiring the benefit of
that provision. Accordingly the application should be allowed to proceed before
the justices and be decided by them (see p 496 a to f, post).

d **Notes**
For the making of a 'place of safety', see Supplement to 21 Halsbury's Laws (3rd Edn)
para 554D, and for the persons who may apply to a juvenile court for a care order,
see ibid para 554A.
     For the Children and Young Persons Act 1969, ss 1, 20, 21, 28, see 40 Halsbury's
e Statutes (3rd Edn) 849, 877, 878, 887.

Case referred to in judgment
R v Paddington and St Marylebone Rent Tribunal, ex parte Bell, London and Provincial
Properties Ltd [1949] 1 All ER 720, [1949] 1 KB 666, DC, 31(2) Digest (Reissue) 1127,
8735.

f **Case also cited**
R v Lewes Justices, ex parte Gaming Board of Great Britain [1971] 2 All ER 1126, [1972]
1 QB 232.

Motions for certiorari and prohibition
By her father and next friend, M, a child, applied for an order of certiorari to bring
g and quash an order made by Dora Emily Willcock, a justice of the peace for the
county of Lincoln (Kesteven), on 24th October 1975 under s 28 of the Children and
Young Persons Act 1969 authorising M's detention in a place of safety.
     The Lincolnshire County Council ('the local authority') applied for an order pro-
hibiting the justices of the Lincoln (Kesteven) Juvenile Court from hearing and
determining an application by M's father for an interim order under s 28(6) of the
h 1969 Act.
     The facts are set out in the judgment of Lord Widgery CJ.

Bernard Livesey for M and the father.
Richard Calder Jose for the local authority.

j _____

e   Section 20(1), so far as material, provides: 'Any provision of this Act authorising the making
    of a care order in respect of any person shall be construed as authorising the making of an
    order committing him to the care of a local authority; and in this Act "care order" shall be
    construed accordingly and "interim order" means a care order containing provision for the
    order to expire with the expiration of twenty-eight days, or of a shorter period specified in
    the order . . .'

LORD WIDGERY CJ. The first matter before the court today is a motion on
behalf of an infant female, whom I will call 'M', for an order of certiorari to bring
up into this court with a view to its being quashed an order made by Dora Emily
Willcock, a justice of the peace for the county of Lincoln (Kesteven), made on
24th October 1975 and authorising the detention of M in a place of safety pursuant
to s 28 of the Children and Young Persons Act 1969. The other matter before the court
is an application by the Lincolnshire County Council for an order of prohibition,
the details of which I will come to when I deal with the second matter.

Confining myself for the moment entirely to the application for certiorari, the
relevant facts are as follows. On 2nd May 1972 a care order was made under s 1 of
the Children and Young Persons Act 1969 in respect of M. A copy of the order is
before us and we find that the grounds on which the order was made were that
it was alleged that 'her proper development is being avoidably prevented or neglected or her health is being avoidably impaired or neglected or she is being ill-
treated; she is exposed to moral danger'. Accordingly, under the powers contained
in s 1 of the 1969 Act a care order was made committing her to the care of the local
authority.

It is necessary at some stage in this case to look at the terms of s 1, and I will look at
them now. Subsection (1) provides:

'Any local authority, constable or authorised person who reasonably believes
that there are grounds for making an order under this section in respect of a
child or young person may . . . bring him before a juvenile court.'

Subsection (2) provides: 'If the court before which a child or young person is brought
under this section is of opinion that any of the following conditions is satisfied with
respect to him', then the court may make a number of orders which are set out
in sub-s (3) and which include '(c) a care order (other than an interim order)'.

What has to be proved in order to authorise the court to make one of those orders
in sub-s (3) is one of the conditions set out in sub-s (2). Thus sub-s (2)(a) as one condition provides that the infant's 'proper development is being avoidably prevented
or neglected or his health is being avoidably impaired or neglected or he is being
ill-treated', and sub-s (2)(c) that 'he is exposed to moral danger'—all matters which,
as we have seen, were referred to in the care order made in respect of M on
2nd May 1972.

Matters rested under that care order with M in the care of the local authority until
1975, but on 22nd May 1975 M's father made an application to a juvenile court to
discharge the care order. He made that application by virtue of s 21(2) of the 1969
Act, which says:

'If it appears to a juvenile court, on the application of a local authority to
whose care a person is committed by a care order or on the application of that
person, that it is appropriate to discharge the order, the court may discharge
it and on discharging it may, unless it was an interim order and unless the person
to whom the discharged order related has attained the age of eighteen, make
a supervision order in respect of him.'

So the father on behalf of M made an application on 22nd May 1975 for the discharge of the care order and the substitution of a supervision order. That would
mean that M would come home but would be visited from time to time by an officer
of the local authority exercising powers of supervision.

That application having been made by the father, it came on for hearing before
the juvenile court on 21st October. We are told, and it is obviously right, that on
that day a long and protracted argument occurred before the juvenile court to try
and determine the destiny of M. At one stage in the proceedings it seems the county
council, who of course were seeking to retain the care order, wished to tender certain

evidence to the juvenile court to the effect that two sisters of M living at home with
a their father had been the subject of incestuous associations with the father. Such
matters, if brought before the notice of the juvenile court when the father was
seeking to have his third daughter brought home, might have a most profound effect;
but objection was taken at the hearing to the admission of this evidence.

We have not had to go into this in detail, and I shall ask for no excuse if I do not
get it entirely accurate in detail, but it seems that objection was taken to the court
b being told about the father's conduct towards the other daughters because it was
not being proposed at the time that the order in regard to M should be supported
under s 1(2)(b) of the 1969 Act. Paragraph (b), which is a separate ground for a care
order in itself, is in these terms:

'. . . it is probable that the condition set out in the preceding paragraph will be
c satisfied in his case, having regard to the fact that the court or another court
has found that that condition is or was satisfied in the case of another child or
young person who is or was a member of the household to which he belongs.'

True, no argument was being put forward to support the care order on that ground,
and it is my understanding that the evidence of the father's conduct was excluded
because the order was not so supported. I do not understand why it was excluded.
d It seems to me that, quite independently of whether para (b) was being relied on,
this was extremely valuable and important evidence. I think it should have been
before the court, but it was not and, after a long argument, the justices eventually
came down in favour of the father and they discharged the care order, thus allowing
M to go back to the father's house under a supervision order.

There is no right of appeal by the local authority from an order of that kind made
e in those circumstances, but it is quite obvious that, rightly or wrongly, the officers
of the local authority who had been concerned with M were extremely upset at
the order made by the juvenile court on 21st October. On 24th October at about
4.00 pm an officer of the local authority went to the justice who is referred to in the
application for certiorari and invited her to make an order commonly called a 'place
of safety' order under s 28(1) of the 1969 Act. Section 28(1) provides:

f
'If, upon an application to a justice by any person for authority to detain a
child or young person and take him to a place of safety, the justice is satisfied
that the applicant has reasonable cause to believe that—(a) any of the conditions
set out in section 1(2)(a) to (e) of this Act is satisfied in respect of the child or
young person [and I pause to remind myself that those are the conditions we
looked at a few minutes ago for the making of a care order] or (b) an appropriate
g court would find the condition set out in section 1(2)(b) of this Act satisfied in
respect of him; or (c) the child or young person is about to leave the United
Kingdom in contravention of section 25 of the [Children and Young Persons
Act] 1933 (which regulates the sending abroad of juvenile entertainers), the
justice may grant the application; and the child or young person in respect
of whom an authorisation is issued under this subsection may be detained in
h in a place of safety by virtue of the authorisation for twenty-eight days beginning
with the date of authorisation, or for such shorter period beginning with that
date as may be specified in the authorisation . . .'

What is in mind there obviously is that one must have a quick-acting emergency
provision to ensure that if a child is in actual danger it can immediately be taken
j and put into a place of safety, and s 28 undoubtedly contemplates cases where children
are already in a situation of danger when immediate action is required. What the
section says is that anybody in those circumstances can go to a justice of the peace,
and the justice, if satisfied of the conditions I have read, may order that the child
be sent to a place of safety for a period not exceeding 28 days—an emergency provision. Rightly or wrongly (I say rightly or wrongly because it is not for us to judge

here today), the officer of the local authority concerned took the view that M, having
been returned to her father's house, was in a place of danger and applied to the justice *a*
under s 28 for a place of safety order.

We are told that the justice was given the whole history of this case. The relationship of the father with his other daughters was told to the justice, although it had
not been told to the juvenile court. Having heard the whole story, the justice made
the order complained of and M was taken away from the father's house again that
night and put into a place of safety controlled by the county council. Now the matter *b*
is challenged by the father, who comes here and contends that the order made by
the justice—the place of safety order—was invalid and should be set aside by this
court. The effect of that of course would be that M would go back to her father's
house again, there being no order to detain her elsewhere.

How is it put? Counsel for M and the father, to whom the court is much indebted
for his argument, has admitted from the outset that, although he says there are *c*
four grounds for upsetting the justice's order, they are really a single ground expressed in four different ways, and that is the kind of frankness which commends
itself to the court when it comes from counsel, because the fact of the matter is that
there is only one ground. That ground is that it was an abuse of the process of the
court for the lady who sought the order from the justice to go around and ask the
justice for such an order at a time when only three days had elapsed since there had *d*
been a full hearing of the matter before the juvenile court, and at a time when there
were no material changes in circumstances as far as one can judge to justify a
different order. It is said by counsel that that conduct was unfair. Insofar as that
means 'not cricket', I do not find it very compulsive, but he says more effectively,
I think, that it was an abuse of the process of the court, and I say he says that more
effectively because if it was an abuse of the process of the court he would bring him- *e*
self in my judgment within the scope of the order of certiorari which is what he
seeks in this case.

His main argument supporting the contention that the action of the social worker
who went along to the justice for an order under s 28 was an abuse of the process
of the court is, unlikely though it may seem, based on *R v Paddington and St Marylebone
Rent Tribunal, ex parte Bell, London and Provincial Properties Ltd*[1], a case well known *f*
to lawyers engaged in disputes on the liability of landlord and tenant. It is a long
and involved case and I am not going to burden this judgment by anything like a
complete reference to it. It suffices to say that in 1949, when that case was decided,
Parliament had recently produced one of the earlier attempts at rent control with
which we are now so familiar. In particular it had invented rent tribunals to whom
a landlord or tenant could refer rents of furnished premises in order to have a reason- *g*
able rent determined. That power of reference was given also to the local authority
as well as to the landlord or the tenant, and in the *Bell* case[1] the local authority, who
may be nameless, had purported to refer to the rent tribunal an entire block of 555
flats. The local authority had made no discernible attempt to see whether these
flats were furnished or unfurnished, whether the rent was fair or unfair, what the
rateable value was and the like; it was just a block reference of 555 flats to the rent *h*
tribunal for determination.

This court, in a judgment which is oft-quoted, as I say, in the sphere to which it is
more closely intended, was to the effect that that was an abuse of the process of the
law, and certiorari was ordered to go to quash the decision reached as a result of
that reference. If counsel for M and the father can bring this case within that sort
of framework he has a prospect of success, but I for my part do not think he does *j*
bring the matter within that framework at the present time.

The basis that one is looking for is that this application to the justice on 29th October
was an abuse of the process of the law. That means it is alleged that it was something

1 [1949] 1 All ER 720, [1949] 1 KB 666

done which was quite inconsistent with the intention of Parliament: that it was using
a section of an Act of Parliament for a purpose which Parliament had never intended
it to be used for and it was deliberately so used with a view to frustrating the true will
of Paliament as expressed in the Act.

I do not think this case, at the moment at all events, comes within those terms
because I think it is apparent, when one examines the situation, that all the requirements to establish an abuse of the process of the law are not satisfied. You ask yourself
first of all: what is s 28 all about? What was the purpose with which Parliament
authorised the making of a place of safety order?

It was, as I have already said, in order that a child in actual danger should be speedily
and effectively put into a place of safety. That is what it was all about—no doubt
about that at all. One asks oneself what was in the mind of the lady who applied
for the order, and the answer is exactly that. She thought, rightly or wrongly, that M
was in a place of danger and she thought, rightly or wrongly, that the thing to do
was to get an order made, and she got it. There is no suggestion that she was doing
other than bona fide applying s 28 to the facts as she believed them to be.

By the same token, one cannot criticise the justice. There is every reason to suppose that she was impressed by the evidence put before her and that she geniunely
and honestly believed that M was in danger, as M may have been for all we can now
say, and she made the order in the bona fide belief that that was the proper way to
exercise the jurisdiction that Parliament had conferred on her.

In my judgment when one looks at this case in that way it becomes quite obvious
that the abuse of process which is relied on is not established in this case. I do emphasise 'in this case' because counsel for M and the father has hinted at the possibility
that the local authority will survive on a diet of orders under s 28 for a long, long time
and thus exclude the parents from ever having an opportunity to control their child's
welfare again. He should not be disturbed on that account, because the purpose of
the s 28 order is to deal with a temporary emergency, and the arm of the court is
quite long enough to stop a local authority from using a provision, intended to deal
with temporary emergencies, on a long-term, unfair basis which would exclude
the parents from proper control. At the moment I am satisfied, speaking for myself,
that certiorari should not go in this case, but whether it might go hereafter will
depend on what happens hereafter.

That is not an end of the matter because, as I said in opening this judgment, there
is a further application, this time made by the local authority for prohibition, and
it arose in this way. Under s 28(6) there are these words:

> 'If while a person is detained in pursuance of this section an application for an
> interim order in respect of him is made to a magistrates' court or a justice, the
> court or justice shall either make or refuse to make the order and, in the case
> of a refusal, may direct that he be released forthwith.'

In this unhappy battle which has been fought over the custody of M, the next
move on the part of the father following the making of the place of safety order was
an application for an interim order under s 28(6). An interim order is a care order
with a limited duration—a care order lasting not more than 28 days—and if the father
can get before the justices and persuade them that an interim care order is appropriate, he may be able to get the place of safety order set aside and get M back in
his house again.

But when this was attempted, the local authority contended, and contend in
this court today, that it was not open to the father to apply for an interim order
under s 28(6) and they say that because an interim order is undoubtedly a care order.
It is a care order of a special kind, and one finds that from s 20(1). A care order, as I
have already indicated, can be applied for only by limited categories of people stated
in s 1(1) of the 1969 Act, namely a local authority, a constable or an authorised person.

The argument is that the father, not being a person who can apply for a care order under s 1, is automatically excluded from applying for an interim order under s 28, because it is said they are both care orders and they are both subject to the restrictions affecting them.

At one time I thought this was a sound point, but I have come to the conclusion, having heard the argument, that it is not. The Act is not explicit and not as plain as it might be as to the circumstances in which an interim order can be made or as to the person who can apply for it. In the state of uncertainty in which I find the language of the Act leaves me, I am not disposed to hold that the father or mother is excluded from making an application under s 28(6). It seems to me that the father or the mother might be the person most requiring the benefit of that provision of that section, and it would be very strange if in those circumstances Parliament had shut him or her out. At all events, in the ambiguous language of the Act, or perhaps the sufficiently ambiguous language of the Act, I am not prepared to hold that the parent has been shut out, and I would therefore refuse the application for prohibition, let the father's application come before the justices and see how the matter develops.

I can only add what must be the feeling of all of us, that the sooner the future of this unfortunate girl can be settled the better. The prospect of her being moved to and fro from local authority home to her father's house and back again at intervals of only a day or two at a time is really too regrettable to bear dwelling on, but that is a matter which this court cannot control.

I would refuse the application for certiorari and I would refuse the application for prohibition.

PARK J. I agree.

MAY J. I also agree.

Applications dismissed.

Solicitors: *Andrew & Co*, Lincoln (for M and the father); *Miss Sarah Gathercole*, Lincoln (for the local authority).

Jacqueline Charles Barrister.

a

Ailion v Spiekermann and another

CHANCERY DIVISION

TEMPLEMAN J

20th, 21st NOVEMBER, 8th DECEMBER 1975

b

Rent restriction – Illegal premium – Specific performance – Agreement to assign tenancy – Protected tenancy – Agreement conditional on payment of illegal premium – Purchasers agreeing to pay vendor substantial sum for chattels – Chattels worth much less to knowledge of parties – Amount of contract sum in excess of value of chattels an illegal premium – Purchasers refusing to pay contract sum – Purchasers offering to pay reasonable sum for chattels – Whether purchasers entitled to specific performance of agreement on payment of reasonable

c

sum – Rent Act 1968, ss 86, 88, 89, 90(1).

The vendor was the tenant of a flat held under a lease for a term expiring on 24th December 1976. The annual rent of the flat was £850 and the vendor was a protected tenant within the Rent Act 1968. By a contract dated 8th April 1974 the vendor agreed to assign the remainder of the lease to the purchasers on payment by them of £3,750 for certain chattels. Neither the vendor nor the purchasers considered that the chattels

d were worth more than a fraction of that sum, and they were aware that the vendor could not lawfully require or receive a premium exceeding the value of the chattels. The purchasers were allowed into possession according to the terms of a letter dated 26th April that they 'should be licensees only and that they will vacate the premises on demand in the event of them failing to complete'. The date fixed for completion

e was 6th May, but the purchasers had trouble in raising the money. On 16th May the vendor served notice to complete and revoked the purchasers' licence. They refused to leave or to pay the contract sum, but offered to complete so far as was lawful by paying a reasonable price on valuation of the chattels. The vendor claimed possession and rescission of the contract and the purchasers counterclaimed for specific performance.

f

Held – The effect of ss 86[a], 88[b] and 89[c] of the 1968 Act was to make neither the contract nor the assignment illegal, but only the receipt by the vendor of a premium. There was a clear and distinct division between the legal and illegal elements of the contract, and they were capable of being severed by the court in a proper case. Although the purchasers had known of the illegality of the premium from the outset, the 1968 Act was designed to protect people in their position, since they could not have

g insisted on the elimination of the premium from the draft contract without losing the flat. Their counterclaim would achieve the same result which they could have obtained under s 90(1)[d] of the 1968 Act. Since specific performance would not put them in a better position than if they had completed the contract on its terms, it would therefore be granted, and the vendor's claim dismissed (see p 500 c to p 501 d

h and p 502 d, post).

Notes

For premiums on the grant, renewal, continuance or assignment of a protected tenancy, see 23 Halsbury's Laws (3rd Edn) 798-801, paras 1576-1577; for excessive

---

j

  a   Section 86, so far as material, is set out at p 499 b, post
  b   Section 88, so far as material, is set out at p 499 c, post
  c   Section 89, so far as material, is set out at p 499 d, post
  d   Section 90(1), so far as material, provides 'Where under any agreement . . . any premium is paid . . . and the whole or any part of that premium could not lawfully be required or received under the preceding provisions of this Part of this Act, the amound of the premium or, as the case may be, so much of it as could not lawfully be requiret or received, shall be recoverable by the person by whom it was paid.'

price for furniture, see ibid 804, para 1584; and for cases on premiums, see 31(2) Digest (Reissue) 1062-1068, 8351-8375.

For the Rent Act 1968, ss 86, 88, 89, 90, see 18 Halsbury's Statutes (3rd Edn) 868, 871, 872.

Cases referred to in judgment

Anderson Ltd v Daniel [1924] 1 KB 138, 93 LJKB 97, 130 LT 418, 88 JP 53, 40 TLR 61, 22 LGR 49, CA, 2 Digest (Repl) 159, *1162*.

Ashmore, Benson, Pease & Co Ltd v A V Dawson Ltd [1973] 2 All ER 856, [1973] 1 WLR 828, [1973] 2 Lloyd's Rep 21, CA.

Grace Rymer Investments Ltd v Waite [1958] 2 All ER 777, [1958] Ch 831, [1958] 3 WLR 337, CA, 31(2) Digest (Reissue) 1066, *8372*.

Gray v Southouse [1949] 2 All ER 1019, 31(2) Digest (Reissue) 1064, *8362*.

Rees v Marquis of Bute [1916] 2 Ch 64, 85 LJ Ch 421, 114 LT 1029, 31(2) Digest (Reissue) 1062, *8351*.

St John Shipping Corpn v Joseph Rank Ltd [1956] 3 All ER 683, [1957] 1 QB 267, [1956] 3 WLR 870, 2 Lloyd's Rep 413, 12 Digest (Reissue) 329, *2372*.

South Western Mineral Water Co Ltd v Ashmore [1967] 2 All ER 953, [1967] 1 WLR 1110, Digest (Cont Vol C) 108, *4330a*.

Case also cited

Brilliant v Michaels [1945] 1 All ER 121, 114 LJCh 5.

Action and counterclaim

By a writ of summons issued on 14th June 1974 and endorsed with a statement of claim, the plaintiff, Jack Albert Ailion ('the vendor'), claimed against the defendants, Erik Spiekermann and Joan Spiekermann ('the purchasers'), (1) possession of a flat, 59 Oakwood Court, London, W14, held under a lease expiring on 24th December 1976 at a yearly rent of £850 of which the purchasers were in possession as licensees in accordance with the terms of a letter dated 26th April 1974, and which, by a contract dated 8th April 1974, he had contracted to assign to the purchasers, (2) a declaration that that contract had been rescinded, or, alternatively, (3) rescission of the contract. The purchasers by their defence and counterclaim served on 19th July 1974 denied that they had failed to complete the contract or that it had been rescinded, or that the vendor was lawfully entitled to determine their licence to occupy the premises, and counterclaimed for specific performance of the agreement. The facts are set out in the judgment.

Robert Pryor for the vendor.
Leonard Hoffmann for the purchasers.

Cur adv vult

8th December. **TEMPLEMAN J** read the following judgment: The question in this case is whether a vendor who contracts to sell a lease for an illegal premium can be compelled to assign the lease to the purchaser without the premium. By a contract dated 8th April 1974 the vendor agreed to assign to the purchasers the flat, 59 Oakwood Court, London, W14, held under a lease for a term expiring on 24th December 1976 at a yearly rent of £850.

The contract provided for the lease to be assigned in consideration of the usual covenants by the purchasers to indemnify the vendor. The contract also provided for the purchasers to pay £3,750 for certain specified chattels. The chattels were subsequently valued at £604·75. Although this valuation has not been proved or accepted, it is common ground that at all material times the chattels were worth much less than £3,750. It is also common ground that at the date of the contract the vendor and

the purchasers were aware that the chattels were not worth £3,750 and that it was not
a lawful for the vendor to require or receive more than the value of the chattels. The
vendor wanted the money and the purchasers needed the flat.

The illegality arises from the admitted fact that possession under the lease of the
flat constituted a protected tenancy within the Rent Act 1968. Section 86 provides:

> '(1) . . . any person who, as a condition of the assignment of a protected tenancy,
b requires the payment of any premium . . . shall be guilty of an offence . . .
> '(2) . . . any person who, in connection with the assignment of a protected ten-
ancy, receives any premium shall be guilty of an offence . . .'

Section 88 provides:

> 'Where the purchase of any furniture has been required as a condition of the
c . . . assignment—(a) of a protected tenancy . . . then, if the price exceeds the
reasonable price of the furniture, the excess shall be treated . . . as if it were a
premium required to be paid as a condition of the . . . assignment of the
protected tenancy . . .'

Section 92(1) defines furniture in a way which includes the chattels the subject of the
d contract dated 8th April 1974. By s 89(1):

> 'Any person who, in connection with the proposed . . . assignment, on terms
which require the purchase of furniture, of a protected tenancy—(a) offers the
furniture at a price which he knows or ought to know is unreasonably high,
or otherwise seeks to obtain such a price for the furniture [is guilty of an offence].'

e The vendor in the present case infringed s 89 when he offered the chattels to the
purchasers for £3,750 and committed an offence under s 86(1) when he required the
purchasers to contract to take the chattels for £3,750. If the contract had been completed according to its terms the vendor would have infringed s 86(2) by receiving
a premium in the form of an excessive price for the chattels.

After the date of the contract the purchasers were allowed into possession of the
f flat as licensees on the terms of a letter dated 26th April, namely that they 'should
be licensees only and that they will vacate the premises on demand in the event of
them failing to complete the purchase in accordance with the contract.'

The date for completion fixed by the contract was 6th May. The purchasers had
trouble in raising the money and on 16th May the vendor served a notice to complete
and thereby committed another offence under s 86(1). The vendor also revoked the
g purchasers' licence to occupy the flat and demanded possession by the following day.
Litigation followed. The vendor claims possession and rescission. The purchasers
claim specific performance of the contract on payment of the reasonable value of the
chattels.

For the present purposes it does not matter whether the vendor committed all the
offences which are alleged. It is admitted and it is sufficient that the contract originated
h in an illegal offer by the vendor under s 89 and cannot be completed without an
illegal receipt by the vendor under s 86(2). The vendor has fallen foul of the statutory
control of rented residential accommodation.

I am not concerned with the merits or demerits of the statutory control of residential accommodation which includes control of rent and security of tenure. But one of
the objects of the 1968 Act is plainly to protect a purchaser requiring accommodation
j from a vendor seeking to exploit the financial value of the controlled rent and
security of tenure established by Parliament.

A purchaser negotiating with a vendor is protected by ss 86, 88 and 89 of the 1968
Act. But Parliament thought it necessary to give further protection to a purchaser
against a vendor who is undeterred by the possibility of punishment for an offence and
pursues a purchaser, desperate for residential accommodation, who dares not invoke

the law until he obtains the accommodation. Thus, s 90 of the 1968 Act provides that where under any agreement any premium is paid which could not lawfully be required *a* or received, the premium shall be recoverable by the person by whom it is paid. In the present case it is common ground that if the purchasers had kept quiet and had paid £3,750 they could have sprung the trap after taking an assignment and sued successfully for the recovery of the amount by which £3,750 exceeds the reasonable value of the chattels.

It is submitted for the purchasers that they are only seeking in these proceedings, *b* without any further breach of the law, the result which s 90 was designed to achieve, namely an assignment without the loss of the premium. It defeats the purpose of the Act and brings the law into disrepute if a purchaser who is offered and contracts to purchase furniture at an unreasonable price as a condition of acquiring a protected tenancy obtains the tenancy and recovers the premium if he enables the vendor to commit the further offence of receiving an illegal premium, but fails to obtain the *c* tenancy if he declines to pay the premium which can only be illegally received. The argument is that the 1968 Act on its true construction requires an illegal premium to be deleted or deducted from a contract for the assignment of a protected tenancy. Such is the logical result of all the provisions and the purpose of the Act.

The argument for the vendor counters logic with logic: the contract is illegal and cannot be performed in accordance with its express terms. Therefore both parties are *d* released from the contract. The parties bargained for the assignment of the lease and for the delivery of the chattels on payment of £3,750. The court has no power to inflict on the parties a different bargain for the assignment of the lease and for the delivery of the chattels on payment of the reasonable value of the chattels.

In my judgment the answer to this conundrum is that Parliament has not made illegal the contract or the assignment which the vendor agreed to execute. Parliament *e* only requires the vendor to decline with thanks any sum of money which constitutes a premium. The court is now asked to compel the vendor to assign the lease which he contracted to assign without the money which Parliament forbids him to accept.

On behalf of the vendor it was argued that severance between the good and bad parts of the contract was not possible or alternatively was unprecedented. In my judgment the effect of the 1968 Act, and in particular the effect of s 88, is to divide *f* the contract into three separate elements. The vendor is contractually and legally bound to assign the lease in return for a covenant of indemnity. The vendor is contractually and legally bound to transfer the chattels in return for the reasonable value of the chattels. The vendor is contractually but illegally entitled to receive a premium which consists of the amount by which £3,750 exceeds the reasonable value of the chattels. Parliament having effected this clear and distinct division between the *g* legal and illegal elements of the contract, the court is not powerless to remove the gilt and leave the gingerbread. The absence of precedent does not worry me so long as there is no lack of principle.

Where there are legal and illegal elements in a contract which are capable of severance, the jurisdiction to enforce the legal elements will only be exercised in a proper case and if the severance is in accordance with the enforcement of the principles *h* which induced Parliament to outlaw the elements which are illegal. The fact that the purchasers knew of the illegality at the outset is a powerful reason why they should not obtain any relief, but the 1968 Act is designed to protect persons in the position of the purchasers. They could not insist on the elimination from the draft contract of the illegal premium without losing the flat. They had no choice if they needed somewhere to live. They committed no offence.

If the purchasers by obtaining specific performance without payment of the illegal premium were able to put themselves in a better position than if they had completed the contract according to its terms, that would be a good reason for the court to decline to assist the purchasers. But in this case s 90 makes all the difference. By that section, whether a purchaser knows of the illegality or not, he can enjoy the fruits of his bargain and recover the illegal payment which he has made, even if he hands over a cheque and a writ in exchange for an assignment.

It does not follow that every purchaser of a protected tenancy at a premium is entitled to specific performance. The remedy of specific performance is discretionary. If the vendor is ignorant of the facts or the law, or if the purchaser tempts the vendor with a chequebook, or if the vendor changes his mind before the purchaser alters his position in reliance on the contract, the court may decline to make a specific performance order. It all depends on the circumstances. In the present case the initiative came wholly from the vendor and he now wants to recoil from the contract because he cannot obtain the illegal payment on which he insisted until the illegality became public. Moreover the purchasers have been allowed to go into occupation of the flat. If they are now evicted by the court, as the vendor requires, it will appear that the purchasers have been turned out because they failed to raise and pay an illegal premium and to keep quiet about the illegality until after the contract had been completed by an assignment. This appearance is not consistent with the purpose of the Act or the administration of justice. If I make no order for possession in favour of the vendor and no order for specific performance in favour of the purchasers, thus following the historical precedent of washing my hands of a contract which contains an illegal element, the vendor will remain liable for the rent and covenants under the lease and the position of both the vendor and the purchasers will be unsatisfactory. In these circumstances I propose to order specific performance of the contract to assign the lease and transfer the chattels in return for the consideration to which the vendor has been confined by Parliament.

I was referred to authority but none of it was directly in point. In Chitty on Contracts[1] authority[2] is cited for the proposition that—

'...."when the policy of the Act ... is to protect the general public or a class of persons by requiring that a contract shall be accompanied by certain formalities or conditions, the contract ... is illegal and cannot be sued upon by the person liable to the penalties". But the other party to the contract is not deprived of his civil remedies because of the criminal default of the guilty party.'

This encourages me as to the right approach to the present case in which only the vendor is a guilty party, but does not assist on the question of severance.

In Gray v Southouse[3] purchasers lending themselves to a scheme for disguising the nature of the payment were allowed to recover the premium. This case assists in showing that knowledge on the part of the payer is not fatal but the case does not assist on specific performance or severance. In Grace Rymer Investments Ltd v Waite[4] illegal payments made by tenants with knowledge that the payments were illegal did not debar them from enforcing rights acquired against the landlords or their mortgagees. Lord Evershed MR[5] said that the payment of the illegal premium did not so taint the payer as to disable the payer from setting up the bargain in any form at all. This is some help, but the court was not dealing with a specific performance action and there was no question of severance. Lord Evershed MR found some support in the transitional provisions of the Landlord and Tenant (Rent Control) Act 1949, but I derive no assistance from those provisions in the present circumstances. In Rees v Marquis of Bute[6] the innocent receipt of an illegal premium entitled the landlord to be discharged from the contract, but in the present case I am not concerned with an innocent vendor.

---

1   23rd Edn (1968), vol 1, para 924
2   Scrutton LJ in Anderson Ltd v Daniel [1924] 1 KB 138 at 147
3   [1949] 2 All ER 1019
4   [1958] 2 All ER 777, [1958] Ch 831
5   [1958] 2 All ER at 780, [1958] Ch at 845
6   [1916] 2 Ch 64

In *South Western Mineral Water Co Ltd v Ashmore*[1] an agreement which infringed s 54 of the Companies Act 1948 was held to be enforceable only by a party who was *a* willing to cure the illegality, but in that case the object of s 54 was not to protect either party but to protect creditors of the company whose assets were depleted by the infringement of s 54. Illegality in the present case can be avoided if the vendor is not paid the illegal premium. Similarly, in *Ashmore, Benson, Pease & Co Ltd v A V Dawson Ltd*[2] the illegality consisted of a breach which could not be remedied of the Motor Vehicles (Construction and Use) Regulations 1966[3] which were intended *b* to protect the public and not one party to the contract. In *St John Shipping Corpn v Joseph Rank Ltd*[4] Devlin J referred to two general principles[5]:

'The first is that a contract which is entered into with the object of committing an illegal act is unenforceable . . . if the intent is mutual the contract is not enforceable at all, and, if unilateral, it is unenforceable at the suit of the party who *c* is proved to have it . . . The second principle is that the court will not enforce a contract which is expressly or impliedly prohibited by statute.'

In the present case the intent to commit an illegal act was not mutual. The purchasers were the unwilling victims. The contract is not illegal, only the receipt by the vendor of a premium.

I propose therefore to order specific performance of a legal contract without pay- *d* ment of the illegal premium. I am obliged to Mr Hoffmann who appeared for the purchasers and Mr Pryor who appeared for the vendor for their clear and succinct arguments; it was a pleasure to listen to them.

Action dismissed. Order for specific performance on counterclaim. *e*

Solicitors: *C M Alfille & Co* (for the vendor); *Davenport, Lyons & Co* (for the purchasers).

Jacqueline Metcalfe Barrister.

---

1   [1967] 2 All ER 953, [1967] 1 WLR 1110
2   [1973] 2 All ER 856, [1973] 1 WLR 828
3   SI 1966 No 1288
4   [1956] 3 All ER 683 [1957] 1 QB 267
5   [1956] 3 All ER at 687, [1957] 1 QB at 283

Europa Oil (NZ) Ltd v Inland Revenue Commissioner

PRIVY COUNCIL
LORD WILBERFORCE, VISCOUNT DILHORNE, LORD DIPLOCK, LORD EDMUND-DAVIES AND
SIR GARFIELD BARWICK
14th, 15th, 16th, 21st, 22nd, 23rd, 24th JULY 1975, 13th JANUARY 1976

New Zealand – Income tax – Assessable income – Deductions in computing income – Expenditure or loss incurred in production of assessable income – Rights obtained in return for expenditure – Expenditure on acquisition of stock-in-trade – Rights under purchase contracts the only legally enforceable rights obtained by taxpayer company – Indirect benefit resulting from expenditure – Taxpayer company not a party to agreements whereby benefit secured on its behalf – Benefit equivalent to a calculated discount on purchase price of stock-in-trade – Benefit obtained by means of dividends paid by third company to subsidiary of taxpayer company – Dividends arising in consequence of agreement between ultimate supplier of stock-in-trade and third company – Whether whole of taxpayer company's expenditure incurred in production of assessable income – Land and Income Tax Act 1954 (New Zealand), s 111 (as amended by the Land and Income Tax Act 1968, s 12).

The taxpayer company, a member of a group of associated companies ('the Todd Group'), marketed petroleum products in New Zealand. It required for the purposes of its trade semi-refined products of crude oil as feedstocks. It purchased the feedstocks from E Ltd in cargo lots under separate contracts as and when they were required. E Ltd was a member of the Todd Group but was not a subsidiary either of the taxpayer company or of the taxpayer company's parent company; each company was wholly owned by a distinct company in the Todd Group, each of which was controlled by the same shareholder. E Ltd purchased the feedstocks required by the taxpayer company from an American company, G Ltd, under a long-term contract at 'posted prices', which included the cost of refining crude oil as well as the refiner's profit. In order to secure an outlet in the New Zealand market, G Ltd was, however, willing to forgo part of the refiner's profit in such a way that that part accrued to the benefit of the taxpayer company. To achieve that end, G Ltd entered into a processing contract with PE Ltd, a company incorporated in the Bahamas, of which one half of the share capital was held by A Ltd, a wholly owned subsidiary of the taxpayer company, and the other half by P Ltd, a wholly owned subsidiary of G Ltd. Under the contract G Ltd undertook to refine crude oil on behalf of PE Ltd for a processing fee and to purchase from PE Ltd the resulting finished products at prices fixed in such a way as to ensure for PE Ltd a profit related to the feedstocks supplied by G Ltd to E Ltd, thereby providing the means by which the taxpayer company could obtain a share of the refiner's profit on the feedstocks sold to E Ltd in the form of dividends on shares in PE Ltd held by A Ltd. In computing its assessable income for the years ended 31st March 1966 to 31st March 1971, the taxpayer company claimed that it was entitled, under s 111[a] of the Land and Income Tax Act 1954, to deduct, as expenditure incurred in the production of its assessable income from its business of marketing petroleum products, the whole of the sums it had paid to E Ltd for the feedstocks. The Inland Revenue Commissioner rejected the claim on the ground that the sums paid by the taxpayer company to E Ltd were for a compound consideration consisting partly of the feedstocks sold and delivered and partly of profits derived by the taxpayer company through PE Ltd and A Ltd. The taxpayer company appealed.

---

a   Section 111, as amended, is set out at p 508 e and f, post

Held (Lord Wilberforce dissenting) – Since the taxpayer company was not a party to
any contract with G Ltd in relation to the supply of feedstocks, the only legally   *a*
enforceable right that the taxpayer company had acquired as consideration for the
expenditure in question was its right under the contracts with E Ltd for the sale and
delivery of the feedstocks. It followed that the true legal nature of the expenditure
was that of the purchase price of the stock-in-trade of the taxpayer company's business.
Accordingly the whole of the expenditure was an allowable deduction in computing
the taxpayer company's assessable income and the appeal would therefore be   *b*
allowed (p 511 *d* to *f*, post).

Inland Revenue Comr v Europa Oil (NZ) Ltd [1971] AC 760 distinguished.

Notes
For deduction of expenditure incurred for the purposes of trade and earning profits,
see 20 Halsbury's Laws (3rd Edn) 158-161, paras 277-279, and for cases on the subject,   *c*
see 28(1) Digest (Reissue) 141-158, 421-505.

Cases referred to in opinions
Ashton v Inland Revenue Comr [1975] 3 All ER 225, [1975] 1 WLR 1615, [1975] STC 471, PC.
Cecil Bros Pty Ltd v Federal Comr of Taxation (1964) 111 CLR 430.
Hallstroms Pty Ltd v Federal Comr of Taxation (1946) 72 CLR 634.   *d*
Inland Revenue Comrs v Duke of Westminster [1936] AC 1, [1935] All ER Rep 259, 19 Tax
    Cas 490, 104 LJKB 383, 153 LT 223, HL, 28(1) Digest (Reissue) 507, *1845*.
Inland Revenue Comr v Europa Oil (NZ) Ltd [1971] AC 760, [1970] 2 WLR 55, sub nom
    New Zealand Inland Revenue Comr v Europa Oil (NZ) Ltd 49 ATC 282, [1970] TR 261,
    PC, 28(1) Digest (Reissue) 203, *670*.
Mangin v Inland Revenue Comr [1971] 1 All ER 179, [1971] AC 739, [1971] 2 WLR 39,   *e*
    sub nom *Mangin v New Zealand Inland Revenue Comr* 49 ATC 272, [1970] TR 249, PC,
    28(1) Digest (Reissue) 543, *1322*.
Newton (Lauri Joseph) v Comr of Taxation of the Commonwealth of Australia [1958] 2 All
    ER 759, [1958] AC 450, [1958] 3 WLR 195, sub nom *Newton v Federal Comr of Taxation*
    (1958) 37 ATC 245; *affg* (1956-57) 96 CLR 578, PC, 28(1) Digest (Reissue) 412, *1142*.
Ronpibon Tin NL and Tongkah Compound NL v Federal Comr of Taxation (1949) 78 CLR 47.   *f*

Appeal
Europa Oil (NZ) Ltd ('the taxpayer company') appealed against the order of the
Court of Appeal of New Zealand (McCarthy P, Richmond and Beattie JJ) dated 19th
November 1974 dismissing an appeal by the taxpayer company against a decision of
McMullin J given in the Supreme Court of New Zealand on 22nd March 1973, whereby   *g*
he confirmed certain assessments made by the Inland Revenue Commissioner against
the taxpayer company in each of the six tax years ended 31st March 1966 to 31st
March 1971. The facts are set out in the majority opinion of the Board.

G P Barton and *R F Pethig* (both of the New Zealand Bar) for the taxpayer company.   *h*
The Solicitor General of New Zealand (*R C Savage QC*), *I L M Richardson* and *G Cain* (both
of the New Zealand Bar) for the commissioner.

LORD DIPLOCK. This is the second time within the last five years that the
Judicial Committee of the Privy Council has been called on to examine the fiscal
consequences of a complex set of contracts connected with the purchase by Europa   *j*
Oil (NZ) Ltd ('the taxpayer company') of its stock-in-trade.

There have been two different sets of contracts. The first set ('the 1956 contracts')
covered the period from 1956 to 1964; the second ('the 1964 contracts') covered the
period from 1964 to 1971. The economic effect of the two sets of contracts and the
business reasons for entering into them are similar and can be stated briefly.

The taxpayer company is one of a group of associated companies which it is con-
a venient to refer to as 'the Todd Group'. The effective management of all the companies
in the group is exercised by Mr Bryan Todd. The principal business of the taxpayer
company is the marketing in New Zealand of petroleum products from the 'light
end' of refining—predominantly motor gasoline but including some gas oil. Its
principal competitors in New Zealand are companies controlled by or associated with
one or other of the major international oil companies which have interests in oilfields
b and refineries in the Middle East or elsewhere east of Suez from which their requirements of light end products can be obtained. In contrast to its competitors the Todd
Group has no interests in any oil field and during the period covered by the first set
of contracts it had no interest in any refinery. It had to purchase its stock-in-trade in
bulk from one or other of the major international oil companies in the fully refined
form in which it was marketed in New Zealand.
c Gulf Oil Corpn ('Gulf'), an American company, is one of the major international
oil companies. By itself or through its subsidiary companies (hereafter referred to
as 'the Gulf Group') it had interests in oilfields in the Middle East and access to refinery capacity there. The Group had ample outlets east of Suez for the heavy end
products of refining crude oil from its oilfields, but an inadequate market for the
light end products, and no outlet for these products in New Zealand. So the petrol-
d eum products of which it had a surplus to dispose of were those of which the Todd
Group needed an assured source of supply. In this respect the business interests of
the two groups were complementary.
The prices at which bulk supplies of crude oil and refined products were bought
and sold on the world market were, at the relevant periods, tightly controlled by the
major international oil companies. Sales were at 'posted prices', the posted price
e for a refined product being greater than the posted price for crude oil by an amount
equivalent to the cost of refining with the addition of a refiner's profit.
In order to secure an assured outlet for the surplus light ends of the crude oil that it
refined in the Middle East, it was in the business interests of the Gulf Group to forgo
some part of the refiner's profit included in the posted prices applicable to those
refined products which it supplied to the Todd Group. The amount to be forgone was
f the subject of hard bargaining between the two Groups in 1956. It was ultimately
fixed at 2·5 cents per gallon of gasoline or gas oil supplied to the taxpayer company.
The Gulf Group, however, was for business reasons unwilling to depart from the
established system of posted prices by making this concession in the form of a reduction in the price at which it sold the refined products to the taxpayer company. So the
benefit of the concession of 2·5 cents per gallon had to be given by the Gulf Group to
g the Todd Group in some other form. For the period from 1956 to 1964 this was done
under the 1956 contracts.
In 1964 a refinery at Whangarei, the first to be constructed in New Zealand, came
on full stream. It was, in effect, a co-operative venture in which the Todd Group and
its principal competitors in the New Zealand market for refined products each had an
interest. Since there is a relatively small demand in New Zealand for the heavy end
h products of refining crude oil, the refinery was designed to deal not only with crude
oil but also, and mainly, with feedstocks in the form of semi-refined products from
which the heavy ends had already been extracted by previous refining. When the
facilities of the Whangarei refinery became available to the taxpayer company there
was no longer any need for it to purchase its stock-in-trade in the form of fully-refined
products; and it was the policy of the New Zealand government to discourage this.
j What was now required by the taxpayer company was feedstocks for the Whangarei
refinery in the form of semi-refined products. The business reasons for which it was
in the mutual interests of the Todd Group and the Gulf Group that the latter should
be the source of supply of the taxpayer company's requirements for fully-refined
light end products applied with equal force to its requirements for semi-refined light
end products as feedstocks for the Whangarei refinery. So the Gulf Group continued

to forgo in favour of the Todd Group part of the refiner's profit included in the posted
prices of those semi-refined products which were supplied to the Todd Group and to *a*
give the benefit of this concession to the Todd Group indirectly and not in the form
of a reduction in the purchase price. This change in the nature of the petroleum
products supplied by the Gulf Group to the Todd Group would in any event have
necessitated some alteration in the contractual relations between the two groups.
This took place in 1964 when the 1964 contracts were substituted for the 1956 contracts.
The economic effect of the two sets of contracts is similar, but there are major *b*
differences in their terms and in the parties to them.

In particular under the 1956 contracts the taxpayer company bought its requirements of fully-refined products directly from the Gulf Group under a long term
contract ('the Products Contract') expiring on 31st December 1966 whereby it undertook to purchase at posted prices the whole of its requirements of motor gasoline
and was granted the option to purchase at posted prices gas oil up to certain limits in *c*
quantity. Under the 1964 contracts the taxpayer company did not itself purchase any
feedstocks directly from the Gulf Group. It purchased them from another company
in the Todd Group, Europa Refining Co Ltd ('Europa Refining') which in turn purchased them from the Gulf Group under a long term contract ('the Supply Contract')
expiring on 31st December 1973 whereby it undertook to purchase at posted prices all
the feedstocks charged by it to the refinery at Whangarei for the purpose of producing *d*
the fully-refined products needed to meet the requirements of Europa Refining or of
the taxpayer company for marketing in New Zealand. Europa Refining is not a subsidiary of the taxpayer company nor are both companies subsidiaries or sub-subsidiaries
of the same parent company in the Todd Group. The taxpayer company was under
no contractual obligation to anyone to purchase any of its own requirements of
feedstocks from Europa Refining. In practice it did so but under separate contracts *e*
entered into with Europa Refining for cargo lots of feedstocks as they were required.

Common to both sets of contracts, however, was the form in which the Todd
Group obtained the benefit of that part of the refiner's profit included in the posted
prices that the Gulf Group was willing to forgo in order to obtain an outlet for its light
end products, as under. For this purpose the two groups in 1956 caused to be incorporated in the Bahamas a company, Pan Eastern Refining Co Ltd ('Pan Eastern'), *f*
of which one half of the share capital was held by a wholly-owned subsidiary of the
taxpayer company, Associated Motorists Petrol Co Ltd ('AMP'), and the other half
by a company in the Gulf Group. The 1956 contracts included a contract between Gulf
and Pan Eastern ('the Processing Contract') under which it was agreed that Pan Eastern
should purchase from Gulf and Gulf should sell to Pan Eastern at posted prices the
quantity of crude oil needed to provide the finished products to be purchased by the *g*
taxpayer company under the Products Contract. Gulf undertook to refine the crude
oil on behalf of Pan Eastern for a processing fee and to purchase from Pan Eastern the
resulting finished products at prices fixed in such a way as to ensure that Pan Eastern
should make a profit out of the Processing Contract equivalent to approximately
5 cents per gallon on the finished products purchased by the taxpayer company from
the Gulf Group under the Products Contract of which AMP's share by way of dividend *h*
would be 2·5 cents per gallon. In 1964 a contract in similar terms ('the New Processing
Contract') was entered into between Gulf and Pan Eastern relating to the feedstocks
to be purchased by Europa Refining under the Supply Contract and the crude oil
needed to provide those feedstocks.

Pan Eastern itself did no refining. Under the Processing Contract and the New
Processing Contract this was done exclusively by the Gulf Group. What the contracts *j*
did was to provide the means by which a share of the refiner's profit on finished
products and feedstocks sold by the Gulf Group to the Todd Group would be obtained
by the Todd Group in the form of dividends on the shares in Pan Eastern held by AMP.

In the instant appeal, as in the previous appeal[1], their Lordships are concerned only
_____
1   *Inland Revenue Comr v Europa Oil (NZ) Ltd* [1971] AC 760

with the liability of the taxpayer company for New Zealand income tax—not with the
a   liability of any other members of the Todd Group of companies. It is common ground
that the dividends receivable by AMP from Pan Eastern or by the taxpayer company
from AMP do not, as such, form part of the assessable income of the taxpayer company. Although he relies also on s 108 of the Land and Income Tax Act 1954, the main
ground on which the commissioner has sought to recover tax on them indirectly
is by attacking the claim of the taxpayer company under s 111 to deduct as expendi-
b   ture incurred in the production of its assessable income from its business of marketing
petroleum products in New Zealand, so much of the price paid by the taxpayer
company for the motor gasoline and gas oil under the 1956 contracts or for the feedstocks under the 1964 contracts as is equivalent to AMP's share of the profits made
by Pan Eastern under the Processing Contract or the New Processing Contract. He
contends that on a true analysis of the legal nature of both sets of contracts the sums
c   which were described in the relevant contracts as being the price of the product sold
to the taxpayer company, were paid for a compound consideration consisting partly
of goods sold and delivered and partly of other advantages to be received, i e profits
to be derived by the taxpayer company through Pan Eastern and AMP.

The previous appeal[1] was in respect of assessments to income tax made on the
taxpayer company for the years ended 31st March 1960 to 31st March 1965 inclusive.
d   In the first five of these years of assessment all the purchases by the taxpayer company
were of motor gasoline and gas oil under the 1956 contracts; but in the last year there
were also some purchases of feedstocks under the 1964 contracts. The evidence at the
hearing in the Supreme Court was directed mainly to the 1956 contracts and the
arguments of the parties there, in the Court of Appeal and before this Board, were
confined to the legal effect of these contracts. No point was taken in relation to the
e   last year of assessment that the 1964 contracts in connection with the purchases of
feedstocks by the taxpayer company might have different legal characteristics.

The consequence of this was that it was the 1956 contracts that were the subject of
detailed examination and analysis in both the majority and the minority judgments of
this Board[1]. That the case under those contracts was a borderline one is apparent from
the conflict of judicial opinion that it caused. The majority of this Board, in agreement
f   with McGregor J[2] in the Supreme Court, upheld the commissioner's contention under
s 111. The minority, in agreement with the Court of Appeal[3], would have rejected it.
The majority, however, while recording[4] that it was not disputed that the 1964
contracts bore the same legal character as the 1956 contracts, did go on to consider the
1964 contracts on such material relating to them as was to be found in the evidence
given at the hearing in the Supreme Court. That evidence did not, in the view of the
g   majority of the Board, disclose any difference in legal character between the taxpayer
company's expenditure on feedstocks under the 1964 contracts and its expenditure on
motor gasoline and gas oil under the 1956 contracts. As stated in the judgment[5] no
point had been taken in the appeal that the purchases of feedstocks under the 1964
Supply Contract were made in the name of Europa Refining instead of that of the
taxpayer company. Consequently no evidence at the hearing in the Supreme Court
h   had been specifically directed to the corporate or, what is more important, the
contractual relationship between Europa Refining and the taxpayer company in
respect of feedstocks purchased by the latter. The Board, in the majority judgment,
dealt with the matter on the footing that the taxpayer company was to be treated as
the undisclosed principal on whose behalf Europa Refining had entered into the 1964
contracts.

j   _____

1   [1971] AC 760
2   (1969) 1 ATR 151
3   1 ATR 453
4   [1971] AC at 775
5   [1971] AC at 776

These lacunae in the evidence relating to the 1964 contracts have now been filled by evidence adduced in the instant appeal which is concerned with the assessments to income tax made on the taxpayer company for the years ended 31st March 1966 to 31st March 1971 inclusive. During each of these years of assessment the expenditure of the taxpayer company which is in dispute was in respect of feedstocks purchased by it from Europa Refining under the 1964 contracts. The taxpayer company contends that the additional evidence now before the Board makes it manifest that the legal character of this expenditure is different from its former expenditure on motor gasoline and gas oil under the 1956 contracts and that the whole of the price paid by it to Europa Refining for feedstocks supplied under the 1964 contracts is deductible under s 111.

During the six years of assessment that were the subject of the previous appeal, s 111 of the Land and Income Tax Act 1954 was in the following terms:

'*Expenditure or loss exclusively incurred in production of assessable income*—(1) In calculating the assessable income of any person deriving assessable income from one source only, any expenditure or loss exclusively incurred in the production of the assessable income for any income year may, except as otherwise provided in this Act, be deducted from the total income derived for that year.

'(2) In calculating the assessable income of any person deriving assessable income from two or more sources, any expenditure or loss exclusively incurred in the production of assessable income for any income year may, except as otherwise provided in this Act, be deducted from the total income derived by the taxpayer for that year from all such sources as aforesaid.'

It remained in the same form for the first two years of assessment that are the subject of the instant appeal; but in 1968 it was amended to read:

'*Expenditure or loss incurred in production of assessable income*—In calculating the assessable income of any taxpayer, any expenditure or loss to the extent to which it—(a) Is incurred in gaining or producing the assessable income for any income year; or (b) Is necessarily incurred in carrying on a business for the purpose of gaining or producing the assessable income for any income year—may, except as otherwise provided in this Act, be deducted from the total income derived by the taxpayer in the income year in which the expenditure or loss is incurred.'

In the last four years of assessment the taxpayer company's claim to the deduction is made under para (a) of the amended section. In their Lordships' view the amendment to the section in 1968 makes no difference for the purposes of the instant appeal.

The actual language of s 111, both before and after the 1968 amendment, is simple enough. It does not, in their Lordships' view, need any detailed exegesis. The general principles of construction of a taxing statute are well-established. Those of particular relevance to s 111 are referred to in the majority judgment of this Board in the previous appeal[1] where there are cited with approval two leading decisions of the High Court of Australia on the corresponding section in the Australian taxing statute (*Ronpibon Tin NL and Tongkah Compound NL v Federal Comr of Taxation*[2] and *Cecil Bros Pty Ltd v Federal Comr of Taxation*[3]). Their Lordships do not find it necessary to repeat them here; they content themselves with emphasising that it is not the economic results sought to be obtained by making the expenditure that is determinative of whether the expenditure is deductible or not; it is the legal rights enforceable by the taxpayer that he acquires in return for making it. The difficulty to which the section gives rise is not one of interpretation of the words it uses, but of the application of those words to particular transactions which may be entered into

1   [1971] AC at 772
2   (1949) 78 CLR 47
3   (1964) 111 CLR 430

in the course of business where those contractual arrangements are complicated and
a involve a multiplicity of parties.

In the majority judgment in the previous appeal, however, one thing was said in
connection with the need to analyse the legal character of the contractual arrangements, that would appear to have given rise to some misunderstanding in the instant
appeal, i e the passage[1] where it is stated:

b   '. . . the Crown is not bound by the taxpayer's statement of account, or by the
          heading under which expenditure is placed. It is entitled to ascertain for what the
          expenditure was in reality incurred.'

Taken in isolation this might be thought to suggest that the court was entitled to
look behind the legal character of a payment made pursuant to the provisions of a
c contract and to take into account economic benefits which would in fact accrue to the
taxpayer otherwise than as a matter of contractual right. Any such suggestion had,
however, already been emphatically repudiated in a preceding paragraph in which
Inland Revenue Comrs v Duke of Westminster[2] had been referred to as authority; and
the repudiation was repeated in the same paragraph as that in which the passage
which their Lordships have just cited appears. Its concluding sentence is[1]: 'Taxation
d by end result, or by economic equivalence, is not what the section achieves.'

Read in this context it becomes clear that the reference to 'reality' was directed only
to the legal character of the payment and not to its economic consequences. All that
was meant was that the court was not bound by the description, such as 'price of
goods', attached to it in the taxpayer's own accounts or in a particular contract, if on
an analysis of the contractual arrangements taken as a whole under which the payment
e was made it appeared that its true legal character did not accord with that description.

In this appeal, as in the previous appeal, the particular expenditure claimed to be
deductible under the section consists of moneys paid by the taxpayer company under
contracts for the sale of goods whereby the property in the goods was transferred by
the seller to the taxpayer company. The moneys so paid were stated in those contracts
to be the price at which the goods were sold; and since the goods were acquired by
f the taxpayer company as stock-in-trade for its business of marketing petroleum
products in New Zealand, there is no question that, if those contracts had stood alone,
the whole of the moneys payable under them would be expenditure by the taxpayer
company that was deductible under s 111. Those contracts, however, did not stand
alone. They formed part of a complex of interrelated contracts entered into by various
companies that were members of the Todd Group or the Gulf Group in connection
g with the same goods. The question in both appeals can accordingly be stated thus: is
the legal effect—as distinct from the economic consequences—of the provisions of the
relevant interrelated contracts such that when the taxpayer company orders goods
under the contract of sale and accepts the obligation to pay the sum stipulated in that
contract as the purchase price, the taxpayer company by the performance of that
obligation acquires a legally enforceable right not only to delivery of the goods but
h also to have some other act performed which confers a benefit in money or in money's
worth on the taxpayer company or some other beneficiary?

If the answer is No, the full amount of the sum stipulated as the purchase price is
deductible under s 111. If the answer is Yes, the sum stipulated as the purchase price
falls to be apportioned as to part to expenditure incurred in purchasing the goods and
as to the remainder to expenditure incurred in obtaining performance of the other
j act, which in the instant case would not be deductible.

In their Lordships' view there is a difference that is crucial to the answer to this
question in the legal character of payments made by the taxpayer company when it

---

1   [1971] AC at 772
2   [1936] AC 1, 19 Tax Cas 490

purchased motor gasoline and gas oil under the 1956 contracts and those made when
it purchased feedstocks under the 1964 contracts.   *a*

The provisions of the 1956 contracts are summarised and analysed in the majority
judgment of this Board in the previous appeal[1]. For present purposes it is only
necessary to draw attention to two respects in which the legally enforceable rights of
the taxpayer company under them differed from its legally enforceable rights under
the 1964 contracts. (1) All purchases by the taxpayer company of motor gasoline and
gas oil were made under a single contract of sale, the Products Contract, providing for   *b*
the delivery by periodic instalments of the taxpayer company's requirements for
those products over a period of ten years. The parties were the taxpayer company
as buyer and Gulf Iran Co ('Gulfiran'), a subsidiary of Gulf. (2) The nature of the
Processing Contract has already been described. It imposed on the parties to it, Gulf
and Pan Eastern, mutual rights and obligations with respect to the purchasing by
Pan Eastern from Gulf of the crude oil necessary to provide the requirements of the   *c*
taxpayer company for motor gasoline and gas oil under the Products Contract, the
processing of the crude oil and the resale of the refined products by Pan Eastern to
Gulf at such prices as would ensure to Pan Eastern a profit of approximately 5 cents
per gallon of motor gasoline or gas oil supplied to the taxpayer company under the
Products Contract. Although the parties to the Processing Contract itself were Gulf
and Pan Eastern, a separate Organisation Contract to which the parties were Gulf and   *d*
the taxpayer company incorporated a covenant by Gulf that it would perform its
obligations to Pan Eastern under the Processing Contract and pay promptly to Pan
Eastern any moneys due to it thereunder.

The majority of the Board in the previous appeal[2] concluded that the combined
effect of these three contracts was that whenever the taxpayer company placed an
order with Gulfiran for delivery of an instalment of goods under the Products Contract   *e*
and accepted an obligation to pay the sum stipulated in that contract as the purchase
price, it acquired by virtue of the placing of that order an enforceable right to have
payments made by Gulf to Pan Eastern under the Processing Contract in such amount
as would ensure Pan Eastern a profit of 5 cents per gallon of goods ordered.

In contrast to the position under the 1956 contracts the taxpayer company was not a
party to any of the 1964 contracts entered into with companies that were members of   *f*
the Gulf Group. All its purchases of feedstocks during the years of assessment with
which the instant appeal is concerned were made from Europa Refining under
contracts of sale for one or more cargo lots of feedstocks entered into from time to
time during the years of assessment. These contracts of sale were not in writing.
Their terms are a matter of inference from the voluminous evidence as to what was
done; and, given the identity of management of the two companies, this has presented   *g*
the courts below with a difficult task. It has not been rendered easier by the fact that
it was apparently the original intention that the sales by Europa Refining to the
taxpayer company should be of refined products into which the feedstocks had been
converted by treatment in the refinery at Whangarei; but government regulations
in New Zealand created obstacles to this; and a careful analysis of the evidence by
both the Supreme Court[3] and the Court of Appeal[4] has resulted in concurrent   *h*
findings that the taxpayer company purchased feedstocks and not refined products
from Europa Refining.

The taxpayer company was under no pre-existing or continuing contractual obligation to purchase its requirements of feedstocks from Europa Refining. Contractually
it was free to buy them wherever it chose. Its liability to pay to Europa Refining the
sums stipulated as the purchase price arose only as and when the individual contracts   *j*
for the sale of particular cargo lots were entered into.

1   [1971] AC 760
2   [1971] AC at 775
3   (1973) 3 ATR 512
4   (1974) 4 ATR 455

a   All the feedstocks sold on by Europa Refining to the taxpayer company had in fact been purchased by Europa Refining from Gulf Exploration Co ('Gulfex'), a member of the Gulf Group, under the 1964 Supply Contract to which the only parties were Europa Refining and Gulfex. As already mentioned, apart from the difference in parties this was in similar terms to the 1956 Products Contract except that the mutual obligations of the parties as to the quantities of feedstocks to be purchased and delivered were so defined as to be limited, as events turned out, to the quantities actually
b   sold on by Europa Refining to the taxpayer company. Any feedstocks that the taxpayer company might buy from other sources were not within the Supply Contract.

The 1964 New Processing Contract relating to feedstocks was also in similar terms to the 1956 Processing Contract relating to motor gasoline and gas oil which it replaced. The parties were the same, Gulf, and Pan Eastern; but whereas in the 1956 Organisation Contract Gulf had covenanted with the taxpayer company that it would
c   perform its obligations to Pan Eastern under the 1956 Processing Contract, it entered into no corresponding covenant with the taxpayer company with respect to its obligations to Pan Eastern under the 1964 New Processing Contract. A covenant by Gulf to perform its obligations to Pan Eastern under the New Processing Contract was contained in a 1964 Re-organisation Contract, but the only parties to this contract were Gulf and Todd Participants Ltd, the parent company of Europa Refining but not of the
d   taxpayer company.

It follows that whenever the taxpayer company entered into a contract with Europa Refining for the sale and delivery of one or more cargo lots of feedstocks and thereby accepted an obligation to pay the sum stipulated in that contract as the purchase price, the only right that it thereby acquired which was legally enforceable against anyone was the right to delivery of the feedstocks by Europa Refining.
e   In their Lordships' view the result on the commissioner's claim under s 111 is that it must fail. The true legal character of the whole of the expenditure claimed to be deductible is that of the purchase price of stock-in-trade for the taxpayer company's business of marketing petroleum products and nothing else. As such it is deductible in full in calculating the taxpayer company's assessable income from that business.

Their Lordships must accordingly now turn to the alternative claim by the com-
f   missioner under s 108 of the Land and Income Tax Act 1954. During the years of assessment that are in issue in the instant appeal it was substantially in the following terms, which, however, incorporate a minor amendment made in 1968 that does not affect the issue in the instant appeal:

> 'Every contract, agreement, or arrangement made or entered into, whether
g   > before or after the commencement of this Act, shall be absolutely void as against
> the Commissioner for income tax purposes in so far as, directly or indirectly, it
> has or purports to have the purpose or effect of in any way altering the incidence
> of income tax, or relieving any person from his liability to pay income tax.'

There are several things to be noted in connection with the application of this section.

First, it is not a charging section; all it does is to entitle the commissioner when
h   assessing the liability of the taxpayer to income tax to treat any contract, agreement or arrangement which falls within the description in the section as if it had never been made. Any liability of the taxpayer to pay income tax must be found elsewhere in the Act. There must be some identifiable income of the taxpayer which would have been liable to be taxed if none of the contracts, agreements or arrangements avoided by the section had been made.

j   Secondly, the description of the contracts, agreements and arrangements which are liable to avoidance presupposes the continued receipt by the taxpayer of income from an existing source in respect of which his liability to pay tax would be altered or relieved if legal effect were given to the contract, agreement or arrangement sought to be avoided as against the commissioner. The section does not strike at new sources of income or restrict the right of the taxpayer to arrange his affairs in relation to income

from a new source in such a way as to attract the least possible liability to tax. Nor
does it prevent the taxpayer from parting with a source of income.   *a*

Thirdly, the references in the section to 'the incidence of income tax' and 'liability
to pay income tax' are references to New Zealand income tax. The section is not concerned with the fiscal consequences of the impugned contracts, agreements or arrangements in any other jurisdiction. In the instant case it would have made no difference if
Pan Eastern, instead of being established in a tax haven, had been established in the
United Kingdom and incurred liability to pay corporation tax there on its profits   *b*
under the New Processing Contract.

Fourthly, the section in any case does not strike down transactions which do not
have as their main purpose or one of their main purposes tax avoidance. It does not
strike down ordinary business or commercial transactions which incidentally result in
some saving of tax. There may be different ways of carrying out such transactions.
They will not be struck down if the method chosen for carrying them out involves   *c*
the payment of less tax than would be payable if another method was followed. In
such cases the avoidance of tax will be incidental to and not the main purpose of the
transaction or transactions which will be the achievement of some business or commercial object (*Newton v Comr of Taxation*[1]; *Mangin v Inland Revenue Comr*[2]; *Ashton v
Inland Revenue Comr*[3]).

Their Lordships' finding that the moneys paid by the taxpayer company to Europa   *d*
Refining are deductible under s 111 as being the actual price paid by the taxpayer
company for its stock-in-trade under contracts for the sale of goods entered into with
Europa Refining, is incompatible with those contracts being liable to avoidance under
s 108. In order to carry on its business of marketing refined petroleum products in
New Zealand the taxpayer company had to purchase feedstocks from someone. In
respect of these contracts the case is on all fours with *Cecil Bros Pty Ltd v Federal*   *e*
Comr of Taxation[4] in which it was said by the High Court of Australia[5]: 'It is not
for the Court or the Commissioner to say how much a taxpayer ought to spend in
obtaining his income'; to which their Lordships would add: it is not for the court or
commissioner to say from whom the taxpayer should purchase the stock-in-trade
acquired by him for the purpose of obtaining his income.

The commissioner must therefore be able to point to some other of the 1964   *f*
contracts the avoidance of which would have the legal effect of making the profits
earned by Pan Eastern under the New Processing Contract, or the dividends payable
out of these profits to AMP, part of the assessable income of the taxpayer company.

He seeks first to avoid the original 1956 Organisation Contract pursuant to which
Pan Eastern was incorporated in the Bahamas. As was held by the Court of Appeal[6]
in the previous appeal, there were good commercial reasons, unconnected with the   *g*
liability of the taxpayer company to New Zealand income tax, for incorporating Pan
Eastern and for selecting the Bahamas as its seat. Furthermore the 1956 Organisation
Contract created a new source of income for the taxpayer company which did not
exist before the 1956 Processing Contract came into force. The taxpayer company was
perfectly entitled to make arrangements whereby the income from that source was
received by it in the form of dividends on the shares of its wholly-owned subsidiary   *h*
AMP paid out of AMP's share of profits earned by Pan Eastern. In their Lordships'
view there is no ground on which the original 1956 Organisation Contract could be
treated as void under s 108.

The commissioner next seeks to avoid the 1964 Supply Contract and the 1964 New

---

1 [1958] 2 All ER 759 at 763, 764, [1958] AC 450 at 465
2 [1971] 1 All ER 179, [1971] AC 739
3 [1975] 3 All ER 225, [1975] STC 471
4 (1964) 111 CLR 430
5 111 CLR at 434
6 (1969) 1 ATR 453

Processing Contract. To neither of these was the taxpayer company a party. Whatever
a effect the avoidance of the Supply Contract might have on the mutual liabilities of
Europa Refining and Gulfex it could not have any effect on the income of the taxpayer
company. The effect of avoidance of the 1964 Processing Contract is easier to discern.
The property in the feedstocks supplied by Gulfex to Europa Refining under the
Supply Contract would never have passed to Pan Eastern but would have remained
vested in the Gulf Group until sold to Europa Refining; and the payments made by
b Gulf to Pan Eastern could accordingly have been treated by the commissioner as
having been made without consideration. But this would have been of no avail to
him. Pan Eastern did in fact receive the payments; it did in fact pay dividends out of
the proceeds; what it paid out to its own shareholders does not lose the legal character
of a dividend because the profits out of which the dividend was paid must be deemed
to have been derived from gratuitous payments. A fortiori this cannot affect the
c legal character of the dividends on its own shares payable by Europa Refining to the
taxpayer company.

So even if s 108 does entitle the commissioner to treat as void for income tax purposes contracts to which the taxpayer himself is not a party and which do not give rise
to any beneficial interest in him (a question which it is not necessary to decide for the
purposes of the instant appeal), there is, in their Lordships' view, no ground on which
d the commissioner's claim can be justified under that section.

Their Lordships will humbly advise Her Majesty that the appeal should be allowed,
the order of the Court of Appeal and the Supreme Court set aside and the matter
remitted to the Supreme Court with a direction that it answer in the affirmative the
question posed in the case stated by the commissioner on 24th October 1972 and amend
the assessments accordingly.

e A cross-appeal by the commissioner concerned questions which do not arise in view
of their Lordships' advice on the appeal and they will humbly advise Her Majesty that
it be dismissed. The commissioner must pay the costs of the appeal and the
cross-appeal to their Lordships' Board.

f *Dissenting judgment by* **LORD WILBERFORCE.** There are three main points for
consideration in this appeal, each of which may involve subsidiary questions. (1)
Whether s 111 of the Land and Income Tax Act 1954, as it stood in 1968, applied so as
to permit the taxpayer company to make certain deductions for the purpose of
calculating its assessable income in the years of assessment 1966, 1967 and 1968; and
correspondingly whether s 111 as amended in 1968 applied so as to permit similar
g deductions to be made as regards the years of assessment 1969, 1970 and 1971. (2)
Whether, if the whole of the claimed expenditure in any year was not deductible, an
apportionment should be made as between deductible and non-deductible expenditure
and if so what the basis of such deduction should be. (3) Whether s 108 of the 1954 Act
applies so as to avoid all or some of the contracts, agreements or arrangements
entered into by the taxpayer company, or otherwise relevant in the case, and if so
h with what consequences as regards the liability of the taxpayer company for income
tax.

The previous appeal to this Board[1], decided in 1971, involved consideration of an
elaborate series of contracts entered into in 1956. The effect of these contracts, very
summarily, was to provide the taxpayer company with a supply of petroleum products by the Gulf Oil Corpn ('Gulf') at Middle East 'posted prices'. At the same time,
j by virtue of the establishment in the Bahamas of Pan Eastern Refining Co Ltd
('Pan Eastern'), a company owned as to 50 per cent by Gulf and as to 50 per cent
by a wholly owned subsidiary of the taxpayer company, a benefit, intended to be the
equivalent of 2·5 cents (US) per gallon supplied to the taxpayer company by Gulf,

---

1   [1971] AC 760

became available to the taxpayer company. It was held by this Board that the consideration paid by the taxpayer company under its supply contract with Gulf was not **a** expenditure exclusively incurred in the production of the assessable income but was in part incurred in order to obtain the benefit through Pan Eastern, and that to that extent it was not deductible.

The 1971 appeal was concerned mainly with the assessments made in years to which the 1956 contracts applied, but there was also a short period covered by fresh contracts of a similar but not identical character made in 1964. These are the contracts **b** involved in the present appeal.

Their Lordships, on the materials then available, made some examination of the 1964 contracts, and concluded that for income tax purposes they had no different effect from the contracts of 1956. In the present proceedings, which are wholly concerned with the 1964 contracts (including in that expression certain documents later than 1964), the taxpayer company has contended, as it has every right to do, that there **c** are important and indeed vital differences between the 1956 contracts and the 1964 contracts, so that a different taxation result should follow. This question, as the learned trial judge and the Court of Appeal found, is not an easy one to answer, so complicated are the arrangements and transactions relevant in the period.

Although the 1956 contracts and the judgment of this Board[1] in 1971 have been fully analysed both in the courts of New Zealand[2] and in the majority judgment in **d** this appeal I think it necessary to explain shortly what, as I understand it, was the basis of the 1971 judgment:

That judgment took as its starting point the terms of s 111 in its pre-1968 form. For convenience, I repeat it:

'*Expenditure or loss exclusively incurred in production of assessable income*—(1) In **e** calculating the assessable income of any person deriving assessable income from one source only, any expenditure or loss exclusively incurred in the production of the assessable income for any income year may, except as otherwise provided in this Act, be deducted from the total income derived for that year . . .'

It is seen that the critical words are 'expenditure . . . exclusively incurred in the production of the assessable income'.

It was in the course of examining these words that the judgment used the words[3] '[the Crown] is entitled to ascertain for what the expenditure was in reality incurred'. As is explained in the majority judgment in this appeal, the context makes plain that this was not an endorsement of taxation by economic equivalence or end result; indeed any suggestion to that effect was repudiated by the Board's judgment[3]. What the passage was saying, and there is nothing new in this, is that it is not sufficient, **g** or decisive, for the taxpayer to call or label his expenditure the purchase price for his trading stock, if in fact the transaction was something different, e g if the money was in part paid as the price of his trading stock, in part paid in order to obtain some other benefit. Concretely in relation to the facts of the case, it was not sufficient for the taxpayer company to point to the products contract under which it agreed to buy gasoline from Gulf at 'posted prices' and to say that the posted price automatically **h** became deductible expenditure. That was the view of the minority in that appeal: they considered that the relevant payments made by the taxpayer company to Gulf under the products contract were simply made as payment for trading stock—as in the Australian case of *Cecil Bros Pty Ltd v Federal Comr of Taxation*[4]—and that the Pan Eastern benefit was something 'collateral' or was simply an inducement to pay posted prices. But that was not the view of the majority, which held that the expenditure

1 [1971] AC 760
2 (1973) 3 ATR 512, (1974) 4 ATR 455
3 [1971] AC at 772
4 (1964) 111 CLR 430

was made in part in order to obtain the Pan Eastern benefit—and for that benefit. The decision of the majority thus involved an interpretation of s 111 and in particular of the words 'incurred in the production of the assessable income' which required the court to examine and analyse the benefit or benefits gained by the expenditure. If what was gained was trading stock and nothing else, the expenditure is wholly deductible. If what is intended to be gained, and what is in fact gained, is some other advantage, the expenditure is not wholly deductible and a problem of apportionment arises. The minority judgment took a narrower view, holding, as I understand it, that it is not legitimate to look beyond the contract between the buyer and the seller, and that if the contract is nothing but a contract of sale, then (following the *Cecil Bros* case[1]) the expenditure is wholly deductible.

In my respectful opinion the present case ought to be decided on the basis of the interpretation adopted by the Board in the 1971 appeal[2], as the courts in New Zealand have considered[3].

This brings me to the question of legal enforceability which perhaps lies at or near the centre of this appeal. The taxpayer company's argument is that if some other benefit (in this case the Pan Eastern benefit) is to be considered as something for which the expenditure was partly incurred, that other benefit must be contractually enforceable by the person making the expenditure. It then continues by pointing out that, whereas in 1956 Gulf was under a direct contractual obligation to the taxpayer company to secure to Pan Eastern the Pan Eastern benefit, there was no such direct obligation in 1966. Therefore, they say, the vital element of contractual obligation is missing. I understand this argument to be accepted by the majority opinion.

Before I attempt to deal with it, I must mention the other important difference between the facts in this appeal and those considered in 1971[2]. This is that the contracting party with 'Gulf' is not the taxpayer company but Europa Refining Co Ltd ('Europa Refining').

The existence of Europa Refining was made known in the 1971 appeal but, as the judgment states[4], no point had been made by the taxpayer company concerning the use of this company instead of itself; it was understood, moreover, that Europa Refining was a wholly owned subsidiary of the taxpayer company.

Evidence in the present case now establishes that the latter understanding was incorrect. Europa Refining is not a subsidiary of the taxpayer company, nor are both companies subsidiaries of the same parent. Each is wholly owned by a distinct company in the Todd group, each of which companies is controlled by the same shareholder. No doubt if one is having regard to economic reality there is no substance in the use of one company or the other. Europa Refining was a paper company with no staff and a minimum organisation: it took no risks and made no profits. The reasons for its creation had mainly to do with requirements of New Zealand law. They are set out fully in the judgment of McCarthy P[5]. But the taxpayer company is perfectly entitled to point to the distinct corporate entities, and in a taxation case to rely on the distinction. It still remains to see what part Europa Refining played.

In the present case it was Europa Refining which on 10th March 1964 entered into the supply contract with Gulf. On the same day Gulf entered into a processing agreement with Pan Eastern, which, as in 1956, would ensure for Pan Eastern a 'profit' related to the gallonage of oil and products supplied by Gulf. The taxpayer company had no supply contract with Gulf, and had no long term contract with Europa Refining. It simply placed a series of individual orders with Europa Refining for its requirements, as needed, these orders being informal, as between closely associated companies. Each order was then automatically followed by a corresponding order by Europa Refining from Gulf. It appears indeed from the terms of the Feed Stock Supply Contract of 10th March 1964 that Europa Refining was under an obligation to Gulf to do this and this was so held by the Court of Appeal[1]. These orders in turn automatically produced, in due course, as the result of contractual obligations, the Pan Eastern benefit. It is right to point out that this benefit was very large; according to a table appearing in the judgment of McMullin J[2] it amounted to about 25 per cent of Europa Refining's (in fact the taxpayer company's) fob payments, or US$ 9·5 million over the six years.

It is difficult to believe that the taxpayer company, which was going to receive this benefit, did not frame its purchasing arrangements, and accept to pay a price, which would enable it to do so. As the Court of Appeal found[3], Europa Refining (and so also the taxpayer company) would not have agreed to pay posted prices for crude oil but for the fact that the processing contract (between Gulf and Pan Eastern) gave Pan Eastern a profit of 15 per cent on the posted prices of crude oil so long as no discounts were arranged under the supply contract. And as and when prices under the supply contract were altered, so automatically were the prices under the processing contract. The taxpayer company's interest in the matter is underlined by letter agreements, contemporaneous with the 1964 contracts, by which Gulf undertook with the taxpayer company not to require the winding-up of Pan Eastern because of the termination of the 1956 processing contract.

There are a number of other differences, real or alleged, between the 1956 situation and that of 1964 which have been painstakingly examined by the Court of Appeal, and which have been covered by unanimous findings. I accept these findings, but since they reinforce rather than weaken the court's ultimate conclusions I need not repeat them.

The question can now be faced whether the differences above mentioned should lead to a different result in this appeal from that reached in 1971[4]. Such difficulty as there is in answering this question arises because it is first necessary to decide which of the elements relied on, or referred to, in 1971 in support of the conclusion then reached were necessary to it. Facts which may be relevant to a given conclusion and which may support it, are not ipso facto necessary for that conclusion. The case relating to the 1956 contracts was, in the view of the 1971 majority[4], a strong one, particularly because of the explicit undertaking by Gulf to the taxpayer company to perform the processing contract and to secure for Pan Eastern the benefit provided for by that contract. But, in my opinion, it would be to take too narrow a view of the majority judgment[4], and s 111, to confine the decision to a case where the benefit obtained by the expenditure is contractually secured in the sense that as part of the purchasing contract, or even as a part of a separate but integrated contract, the seller agreed with the buyer to pay it. The words of the section 'expenditure exclusively incurred in the production of the assessable income' by contrast point to the disallowance of expenditure not so exclusively incurred, and it is this wording which gave rise to the test of 'reality'. What was the expenditure for? What was it intended to gain? What did it gain? What elements entered into the fixing and acceptance of it? These are the questions to be asked. To rephrase this so as to ask, 'What did the other party legally bind himself to pay or do?' is to confine the cases where no deduction is allowed to one special case: to substitute a legalistic test for a commercial test. I think in this context of the often quoted words of Dixon J in *Hallstroms Pty Ltd v Federal Comr of Taxation*[5] where he said in a different but analogous context that what is an outgoing of capital and what

---

1 (1974) 4 ATR at 480
2 (1973) 3 ATR 512 at 528
3 (1974) 4 ATR at 491
4 [1971] AC 760
5 (1946) 72 CLR 634 at 648

is an outgoing on account of revenue depends on 'what the expenditure is calculated to effect from a practical and business point of view, rather than upon the juristic classification of the legal rights, if any, secured . . . in the process'. The words 'in the production of the assessable income' are wide words—wider than 'in order to obtain trading stock', wider than 'in consideration of something which the other party agrees to provide'. This was recognised by the 1971 judgment[1] and reflected in its wording.

If then the test is reality (in the sense described), what was the expenditure really for? how does it fit the facts? The simple approach, for which the taxpayer company contends, is to say that it only entered into one contract, or series of contracts from time to time, with Europa Refining and this was simply to buy products. But I find this far too simple. There was Europa Refining with a supply contract with Gulfex under which (see above) Europa Refining was obliged to buy from Gulfex all products needed to meet the taxpayer company's New Zealand marketing requirements; there was Gulf with a simultaneous contract with Pan Eastern—a contract in which it was recited that Gulf had agreed to guarantee the performance of Gulfex's obligations, and had agreed to enter into a contract with Pan Eastern in order to obtain the benefits of the contract with Europa. Under this contract a substantial benefit was contractually secured for the taxpayer company through its subsidiary AMP.

The taxpayer company knew all about this (in the words of the Court of Appeal it was 'privy' to these arrangements): it knew and contemplated that the moment it placed an order with Europa Refining, Europa Refining would order from Gulfex and that in due course a benefit—very large—would arise for Pan Eastern and so ultimately for itself. If, at the time when the taxpayer company placed orders with Europa Refining, it was not possible to quantify exactly what the amount of this benefit would be because of possible movements in posted prices, the amount could be calculated with reasonable accuracy. I agree with the conclusion of McCarthy P[2] that it is the circumstance, that the taxpayer company was in a position to expect a substantial profit (viz through Pan Eastern) when incurring the obligation to pay, which is of importance, and the fact that the quantum of that profit was not always determinable in advance is relatively unimportant. The taxpayer company would never have agreed to pay 'posted prices' for the products had it not known that, related to these prices, for every gallon ordered, a benefit would arise for Pan Eastern. In my opinion it cannot be said, in these circumstances, that the taxpayer company's payments were for products and nothing else. This was the view of the learned judges in the Court of Appeal.

McCarthy P[3] considered that if he was to follow the route which he believed was directed by the Privy Council, the enquiry should be whether at the time when the stock, whatever it was, was ordered, the taxpayer company knew as a result of the process which it thus put in train that it was to receive, pursuant to the existing machinery, an identifiable advantage. Richmond J[4] summed up his conclusions in the following illuminating passage which I quote in full because I respectfully agree wholly with it:

> 'When [the taxpayer company] in subsequent years, in the closest possible co-operation with Europa Refining, initiated the ordering of feedstocks, it was not just initiating orders by Europa Refining for feedstocks from any source. The orders were for feedstocks from Gulfex under the 1964 supply contract and a portion of the moneys advanced by [the taxpayer company] to Europa Refining was for the specific purpose of meeting payments under invoices rendered under that contract. There was no profit in these transactions from the point of view of

---

1 [1971] AC 760
2 (1974) 4 ATR at 481
3 4 ATR at 482
4 4 ATR at 493

Europa Refining, apart from the opportunity to invest funds held in London and
possibly, the right to retain the alternate freight differential. When one reverts *a*
to the basic question—for what was this expenditure in reality incurred—the
answer can only be that it was to obtain both the feedstocks and the Pan Eastern
benefit. Put in a slightly different way, the consideration for [the taxpayer
company's] expenditure was not just the feedstocks but also the ordering of
those feedstocks from Gulfex. The arrangements between [the taxpayer company]
and Europa Refining under which [the taxpayer company] acquired feedstocks *b*
cannot therefore be isolated from the 1964 series of contracts and were sufficiently
integrated with those contracts to satisfy their Lordships' test.'

Richmond J there refers to the fact that as orders were placed by the taxpayer
company with Europa Refining, the taxpayer company made its money available to
Europa Refining so as to meet invoices when due. He also refers to the fact that *c*
Europa Refining made no profit on orders. These, and other factual details, carefully
found by the court, fully support his argument: the contract between the taxpayer
company and Europa Refining was not a normal contract of purchase and sale at all;
the interested party was the taxpayer company; the benefit to be gained was the taxpayer company's; part of the benefit was the Pan Eastern benefit.   Beattie J[1], after
stating his initial inclination to follow, in effect, the path taken by the majority in this *d*
appeal, continued:

'However, I am now persuaded by what the President has said in his judgment
when discussing their Lordships' expression, "as part of the contractual relationship" that the contractual arrangement here was not simply the agreement
between [the taxpayer company] and Europa Refining. By isolating that agreement and ignoring the inter-relationship of [the taxpayer company] with the *e*
Europa Refining-Gulf-Pan Eastern arrangements, means discarding the "in
reality" approach adopted by the majority of the Judicial Committee. Clearly,
[the taxpayer company] benefited from the arrangement with Pan Eastern when
it made payments or advances to Europa Refining. I say this because, in my
opinion, when the [taxpayer company] arranged its orders with Europa Refining,
that company had no alternative because of the terms of the 1964 feedstock supply
contract, but to pass on those orders to Gulf. At the same time the [taxpayer
company] must have anticipated the benefit that ultimately would accrue to it
through Pan Eastern.'

For these reasons, which the judgments in the Court of Appeal amplify through a
number of factual findings, I would support their conclusions and hold that the de- *f*
duction was not allowable under the former s 111. I agree further with their conclusions—as I think does the majority—that the revision of s 111 in removing
'exclusively' does not lead to a different result.

As regards the new limb (b) of s 111 introduced in 1968, which introduces the words
'necessarily incurred', there was some difference of view expressed in the Court of
Appeal. As this is a comparatively recent section in New Zealand, though the subject *g*
of judicial interpretation in Australia, I prefer to express no opinion on it.

As to the question of apportionment I do not think that there is any doubt that,
if total deduction is prohibited by s 111, some apportionment of expenditure is required. That this may be a difficult matter in individual cases does not, in my respectful opinion, indicate that the case is not one for apportionment at all; the courts must
do their best as on an issue of fact. In the 1971 case[2] it was assumed that if (as was held)
expenditure was to be disallowed, it must be on a pound for pound basis, i e for every
£1 of benefit secured, £1 of expenditure should be disallowed.

1   (1974) 4 ATR at 497, 498
2   [1971] AC 760

a   This assumption has been questioned in the present case, in my opinion with some
force. It may well be that some more scientific attempt should be made to ascertain
how much of the expenditure was incurred in obtaining the benefit, and this has been
attempted by the Courts in New Zealand. Neither side is satisfied with the result and
each side appeals. Since my view as to the necessity for apportionment does not
prevail it would be unhelpful to enter into this difficult matter.

b   As to s 108, on my view of the case this does not arise and I express no view
whether it could be applied to the present facts.

Appeal allowed.

Solicitors: *Macfarlanes* (for the taxpayer company); *Allen & Overy* (for the
commissioner).

c   Rengan Krishnan Esq Barrister.

Director of Public Prosecutions v Luft and another
Duffield v Director of Public Prosecutions

QUEEN'S BENCH DIVISION
LORD WIDGERY CJ, O'CONNOR AND LAWSON JJ
30th OCTOBER 1975

*Elections – Expenses – Expenses incurred with a view to promoting or procuring election
of a candidate at an election – Prohibition on expenses unless incurred by candidate, election
agent or authorised person – Three or more candidates standing at election – Expenses incurred by unauthorised person with a view to preventing election of one of those candidates –
Person not intending to promote or procure election of any particular candidate – Whether
person guilty of corrupt practice – Representation of the People Act 1949, s 63(1)(5).*

*Elections – Publications – Publications printed, published, posted or distributed for the
purpose of promoting election of a candidate – Publication required to bear on face name
and address of printer and publisher – Three or more candidates standing at election –
Publication distributed for the purpose of preventing election of one of those candidates –
Distributor not intending to promote or procure election of any particular candidate – Whether
publication required to bear name and address of printer and publisher – Representation
of the People Act 1949, s 95(1).*

Section 63[a] of the Representation of the People Act 1949 (which prohibits anyone
other than a candidate at an election, his agent or persons authorised by his agent,
from incurring expenses 'with a view to promoting or procuring the election of a
candidate') does not apply to a person who, where there are three or more candidates,
incurs expenses with a view to preventing the election of one of those candidates
(see p 526 a to e, post).

Likewise s 95(1)[b] of the 1949 Act (which prohibits, inter alia, the distribution of
any printed document 'for the purpose of promoting or procuring the election of

---

a   Section 63, so far as material, is set out at p 522 *e* to *j*, post
b   Section 95, so far as material, is set out at p 523 *b* to *d*, post

a candidate' which does not bear on its face the name and address of the printer
and publisher) does not apply to a person who, where there are three or more can- *a*
didates, distributes a printed document for the purpose of preventing the election
of one of those candidates (see p 526 *a* to *e*, post).

R v Tronoh Mines Ltd [1952] 1 All ER 697 and dictum of Lord Migdale in *Grieve
v Douglas-Home* 1965 SLT at 190 applied.

Dicta of Avory J in *R v Hailwood and Ackroyd Ltd* [1928] 2 KB at 281, 282, 283
distinguished.   *b*

Notes

For expenses incurred by persons other than an election agent, see 14 Halsbury's
Laws (3rd Edn) 182, para 323, and for cases on the subject, see 20 Digest (Repl) 98,
795, 796.

For the Representation of the People Act 1949, ss 63, 95, see 11 Halsbury's Statutes *c*
(3rd Edn) 608, 636.

Cases referred to in judgments

Grieve v Douglas-Home 1965 SLT 186.
R v Hailwood and Ackroyd Ltd [1928] 2 KB 277, [1928] All ER Rep 529, 97 LJKB 394, 138
    LT 495, 28 Cox CC 489, 20 Cr App Rep 177, CCA, 20 Digest (Repl) 98, 795.   *d*
R v Tronoh Mines Ltd [1952] 1 All ER 697, 35 Cr App Rep 196, 50 LGR 461, 116 JP 180,
    20 Digest (Repl) 98, 796.

Cases also cited

Cutts, Re [1956] 2 All ER 537, [1956] 1 WLR 728.
Sweet v Parsley [1969] 1 All ER 347, [1970] AC 132.   *e*

Cases stated

Director of Public Prosecutions v Luft and another

This was an appeal by the Director of Public Prosecutions by way of a case stated
by the stipendiary magistrate for the city of Manchester (J Bamber Esq) in respect
of his adjudication as a magistrates' court sitting in Manchester dismissing informations preferred by the Director of Public Prosecutions against the defendants, Michael
Avril Luft and Graeme Atkinson, that they and each of them did (i) on a day unknown
between 1st September and 6th October 1974, in Greater Manchester, not being candidates or election agents and without the authorisation in writing of an election agent,
incur the expense of issuing publications with a view to promoting or procuring
the election of a candidate at the Parliamentary election for the constituency of   *f*
Blackley held on 10th October 1974, contrary to s 63(5) of the Representation of
the People Act 1949; (ii) on 6th October 1974, at Blackley, distribute a printed
document for the purpose of promoting or procuring the election of a candidate
at the Parliamentary election for the constituency of Blackley held on 10th October
1974, not bearing on the face thereof the name and address of the printer and
publisher, contrary to s 95(3) of the 1949 Act.   *g*

Duffield v Director of Public Prosecutions

This was an appeal by the defendant, Neil Duffield, by way of a case stated by justices
for the county of Manchester acting in and for the petty sessional division of Bolton
against his convictions by the justices on informations preferred by William James
Richards on behalf of the Director of Public Prosecutions, against the defendant that
he (i) at Bolton on a day unknown between 1st March and 10th October 1974,
not being a candidate or election agent and without the authorisation in writing
of an election agent, incurred the expense of issuing publications with a view to promoting or procuring the election of a candidate at the Parliamentary election for
the constituency of Bolton East held on 10th October 1974, contrary to s 63(5) of

the 1949 Act; (ii) at Bolton on a day unknown between 1st March and 10th October
a 1974, not being a candidate or election agent and without the authorisation in writing
of an election agent, incurred the expense of issuing publications with a view to promoting or procuring the election of a candidate at the Parliamentary election for
the constituency of Bolton West held on 10th October 1974, contrary to s 63(5) of
the 1949 Act; (iii) at Bolton on a day unknown between 1st and 10th October 1974
caused to be posted a poster having reference to the Parliamentary election for the
b constituency of Bolton East held on 10th October 1974, not bearing on the face thereof
the name and address of the printer and publisher, contrary to s 95(3) of the 1949 Act;
(iv) at Bolton on a day unknown between 1st and 10th October 1974 caused to be
posted a poster having reference to the Parliamentary election for the constituency
of Bolton West held on 10th October 1974, not bearing on the face thereof the name
and address of the printer and publisher, contrary to s 95(3) of the 1949 Act; (v) at
c Bolton on a day unknown between 1st and 10th October 1974 caused to be distributed
a printed document for the purpose of promoting or procuring the election of a
candidate at the Parliamentary election for the constituency of Bolton East held on
10th October 1974, not bearing on the face thereof the name and address of the
printer and publisher, contrary to s 95(3) of the 1949 Act; (vi) at Bolton on a day unknown between 1st and 10th October 1974 caused to be distributed a printed
d document for the purpose of promoting or procuring the election of a candidate
at the Parliamentary election for the constituency of Bolton West held on
10th October 1974, not bearing on the face thereof the name and address of the
printer and publisher, contrary to s 95(3) of the 1949 Act.

John Hugill for the Director of Public Prosecutions.
e *Stephen Sedley* for the defendants.

LAWSON J delivered the first judgment at the invitation of Lord Widgery CJ.
We have before us two appeals by case stated, the first being an appeal by the
Director of Public Prosecutions against the acquittal of the respondents, Mr Luft and
f Mr Atkinson, by the learned stipendiary magistrate for the City of Manchester at
a hearing on 9th April 1975 of offences charged against them under ss 63 and 95 of the
Representation of the People Act 1949. The second appeal is by Mr Neil Duffield
against his conviction by the justices for the county of Manchester sitting at Bolton
in petty sessions on 17th March 1975 of six offences against ss 63 and 95 of the 1949 Act.
We have heard these two appeals together because, in a broad sense, the facts
g of the two cases are the same and can be summarised shortly in this way. The
defendants were members of bodies called 'anti-fascist committees', the one for
the Greater Manchester area and the other for the Bolton area; and those two committees took on themselves, in relation to the Parliamentary elections which were
being held respectively in the Blackley constituency of Manchester on 10th October
and in the Bolton East and Bolton West constituencies on the same day, the dis-
h tribution of leaflets and the publication of posters which were directed against the
members of the electorate voting for the National Front.
It so happened that in the Blackley constituency of Manchester there were four
candidates standing for election, one of whom was a National Front candidate; the
other three were candidates representing the interests of the three well-known
political parties in England; whereas in the Bolton East constituency, there were
j five candidates—a National Front candidate, a candidate described as a More Pros-
perous Britain candidate, and three candidates representing the three major English
political parties; in the Bolton West constituency there were four candidates, the
complexion of which was the same as the four candidates in the Blackley constituency
of Manchester.
These leaflets and posters are in a sense in very similar terms, and broadly the

leaflets conveyed the message: 'Don't vote National Front. Don't vote fascist.' These
leaflets were distributed in the constituency areas referred to, and it was the dis- *a*
tribution of these leaflets and the publication of the posters which are relevant to
the case which led to the prosecutions.

The offences which were charged were in the first place, in the Manchester case,
and I am looking at the case stated by the learned stipendiary magistrate, that on
a day unknown between 1st September and 6th October 1974, not being candidates
or election agents and without the authorisation in writing of an election agent, the *b*
defendants incurred the expense of issuing publications with a view to promoting
or procuring the election of a candidate at the Parliamentary election for the consitu-
ency of Blackley, held on 10th October 1974, contrary to s 63(5) of the 1949 Act. A similar
charge for distributing a printed document for the purpose of promoting or procuring
the election of a candidate for that constituency on that date, not bearing on the face
thereof the name and address of the printer and publisher, contrary to s 95 of the *c*
1949 Act, was also laid.

In the Bolton case, as it is conveniently referred to, there were three pairs of charges,
each pair respectively relating to Bolton East and to Bolton West. The first pair
charged the same offence as in the Manchester case, an offence against s 63(5) of
the 1949 Act. The second pair charged the posting of a poster, contrary to s 95 of the
1949 Act. The third pair charged distributing a printed document (that is a leaflet), *d*
contrary to s 95 of the 1949 Act.

I turn now to the sections concerned. Section 63, which it should be observed is
in very simple and easily understood language, provides by sub-s (1):

> 'No expense shall, with a view to promoting or procuring the election of a
> a candidate at an election, be incurred by any person other than the candidate, *e*
> his election agent and persons authorised in writing by the election agent on
> account—(a) of holding public meetings or organising any public display; or (b) of
> issuing advertisements, circulars or publications [and it was in the terms of sub-s
> (1)(b) that the informations in question were presented] or (c) of otherwise
> presenting to the electors the candidate or his views or the extent or nature of
> his backing or disparaging another candidate . . .' *f*

There are certain provisos which relate to newspaper publications and broadcasts,
and there are certain provisos in relation to the limited expenditure of money in
travelling. Subsection (2) is important in this context because it deals with the procedure which has to be followed when expenditure is incurred with a view to promoting or procuring the election of a candidate within the meaning of sub-s (1).
Subsection (2) provides: *g*

> 'Where a person incurs any expenses required by this section to be authorised
> by the election agent, that person shall within fourteen days after the date of
> publication of the result of the election send to the appropriate officer a return
> of the amount of those expenses, stating the election at which and the candidate
> in whose support they were incurred . . .' *h*

The rest of the subsection is not relevant. Subsection (5) is the subsection which creates
offences, and it provides as follows:

> 'If any person incurs, or aids, abets, counsels or procures any other person
> to incur, any expenses in contravention of this section, or knowingly makes
> the declaration required by subsection (2) thereof falsely, he shall be guilty of a *j*
> corrupt practice . . .'

Subsection (6) deals with the situation where an act or omission which constitutes
a contravention of s 63 is committed by an association or body of persons, corporate
or unincorporated. There is no need in my judgment for the court on this occasion

a   to enter into a discussion of the arguments which counsel for the defendants has
addressed in relation to the status of two of the persons involved in these appeals,
one who was convicted and another of whom was acquitted. This section as a whole—
and it is important to bear this in mind—is about spending money to procure the
election of candidates at Parliamentary elections; that is what it is really about.

Section 95, which is the other section involved in this case, is, as was suggested in
the course of the argument, supportive of s 63. Section 95(1) provides:

b
'A person shall not—(a) print or publish, or cause to be printed or published,
any bill, placard or poster having reference to an election or any printed
document distributed for the purpose of promoting or procuring the election
of a candidate, or (b) post or cause to be posted any such bill, placard or poster
as aforesaid, or (c) distribute or cause to be distributed any printed document
c   for the said purpose, unless the bill, placard, poster or document bears upon
the face thereof the name and address of the printer and publisher.'

The purpose clearly of requiring such literature—I use a broad term—to have the
name and address of the printer and publisher on the face of the document is
obviously connected with the control of expense of which s 63(2) forms an important
d   part. If s 95(1) is contravened, s 95(3) provides:

'A candidate or election agent acting in contravention of this section shall
be guilty of an illegal practice, and any other person so acting shall on summary
conviction be liable to a fine not exceeding one hundred pounds.'

The predecessor of s 63 of the 1949 Act was the Representation of the People Act 1918,
e   s 34. Section 34(1) of the 1918 Act provided:

'A person other than the election agent of a candidate shall not incur any
expenses on account of holding public meetings or issuing advertisements,
circulars or publications for the purpose of promoting or procuring the election
of any candidate at a parliamentary election, unless he is authorised in writing
to do so by such election agent.'

f   That is of course a very short and simple statement of the law as it was when the
1918 Act came into operation.

That section of the 1918 Act was considered by the Court of Appeal in R v Hailwood
and Ackroyd Ltd[1]. That was a case where during an election at which there were
three candidates—Conservative, Liberal and Labour—the appellant, who was a
Conservative in the election but disapproved of the existing Conservative government
g   on special grounds, incurred expenses on account of issuing posters, circulars and
publications which were antagonistic to the Conservative candidate and advised the
constituents not to vote for him, but did not in express terms advise them to vote
for the other candidates or either of them. It was held that the appellant had acted
in contravention of s 34(1) of the 1918 Act and a conviction against him thereunder
h   should stand.

In the course of the judgment of the court, which consisted of Avory, Horridge
and Salter JJ, Avory J, after citing the provisions of s 34 of the 1918 Act, said[2]:

'The object of that section is plain. Prior to the Act of 1918 the statutes dealing
with unlawful practices at parliamentary elections had fixed a maximum amount
which could be lawfully expended by the candidate at an election, and had re-
j   quired that the election agent should make a true return of the candidate's
expenses. It was then found that associations and persons other than the
candidates and their agents might be and were incurring expenses for the purpose

1   [1928] 2 KB 277
2   [1928] 2 KB at 281, 282

of promoting or procuring the election of a candidate, although they were not authorized to do so by the election agent of the candidate, and that expenses *a* so incurred would never be included in the agent's return. It was in order to put a stop to that practice that this section was passed . . . It is now suggested that, in a case like the present, where there are three candidates representing three different political parties, Conservative, Liberal and Labour, if a person who is not authorized by the election agent of a candidate incurs expenses of the kind in question he cannot be convicted under the section, which prohibits *b* the incurring of the expenses for the purpose of promoting or procuring the election of "any candidate," unless it be shown definitely that he had the intention of promoting or procuring the election of one of these three candidates in particular. The answer to that suggestion is that the expression "any candidate" in the section is not limited to one candidate only, since it is provided by the Interpretation Act, 1889 (52 & 53 Vict. c. 63), s. 1, sub-s. 1(*b*), that words in *c* the singular shall include the plural.'

Of course, interposing, that Act also provides 'unless the context otherwise requires'. The second point in the case was dealt with by Avory J[1]:

'As Talbot J. truly said in his summing up: "The motive that is in a gentleman's *d* mind is one thing, the purpose for which he takes his action is another." The section does not say that a person shall not do the acts forbidden with the intention of promoting or procuring the election of a candidate, but that he shall not do these acts for the purpose of promoting or procuring the election of a candidate. What the defendants did would have the effect, and was intended to have the effect and must have had the effect of promoting the election of the candidates *e* other than the Conservative.'

Thus, there are two points which are relevant to the present case which are being made in the judgment of the court in *R v Hailwood and Ackroyd Ltd*[2]. The first point is that the Act, as it then stood, said 'any candidate' and not 'a candidate'. Secondly, the Act, as it then stood, used the formula 'for the purpose of promoting or procuring the election of a candidate', and the distinction was drawn between what might, *f* I think, properly be described as a man's motive and the effect of what he does as being evidence of his intention. The language of the 1949 Act in s 63 is of course different in both those respects because the relevant provision now is 'with a view to promoting or procuring the election of *a* candidate', and it is the election of 'a candidate' and not 'any candidate'.

The second of those two points was touched on in the later case of *R v Tronoh Mines* *g* *Ltd*[3], which is a case on the provisions of the 1949 Act and not the 1918 Act. I read the headnote[4]:

'After writs had been issued in respect of a parliamentary general election a company, through its secretary, caused to be inserted in a newspaper circulating throughout the country an advertisement condemning the financial policy of *h* the Labour Party, and, in particular, that party's proposal to control the dividends of companies. The advertisement continued: "The coming general election will give us all the opportunity of saving the country from being reduced, through the policies of the Socialist government, to a bankrupt 'Welfare State'. We need a new and strong government with Ministers who may be relied upon to encourage business enterprise and initiative . . ." The company, the secretary, *j*

---

1   [1928] 2 KB at 283
2   [1928] 2 KB 277
3   [1952] 1 All ER 697
4   [1952] 1 All ER at 697

and the proprietors of the newspaper, were jointly charged with unlawfully
a incurring expenses with a view to promoting or procuring the election of a candidate other than the Labour candidate at the parliamentary election to be held in
the constituency in which the company had its office and the newspaper was
published [The allegation was, just as some of the allegations in these cases,
that this was an offence under s 63(1)(b) of the 1949 Act.] HELD: section 63(1)(b)
was designed to prohibit expenditure on advertisements supporting a particu-
b lar candidate in a particular constitutency, which, if authorised by the election
agent, would form part of the election expenses for that constituency as distinct
from supporting the interests of a party generally in all constituencies, and,
therefore, there was no case to go to the jury.'

What had happened was that the defendants in that case were indicted for the offence
c under s 63(1)(b). After the evidence for the prosecution was heard, a submission on
the defendants' behalf was that there was no case for them to answer, and NcNair J,
the trial judge, upheld that submission. In the course of his judgment upholding the
submission he made reference to the change from 'any candidate' to the formula
'a candidate' which had been made between the 1918 and the 1949 Acts. What he said
in that respect was[1]:

d
'Furthermore, the Interpretation Act, 1889, s. 1(1), provides that, unless the context otherwise requires, words importing the singular include the plural, and I
think that the context here does necessarily require that references to the election
of a candidate at an election means a candidate at a particular election and not
candidates at elections generally. On the whole, therefore, although I appreciate
that the point is fully arguable, I think that the construction contended for by the
e defence on this point is correct.'

Then he deals with the other aspect of the case, the aspect which is dealt with in
the headnote, and in my judgment the learned judge was incorrect in taking the view
that there was some difference between expenses incurred in a particular constituency in relation to a particular Parliamentary contest and expenses incurred on a
f nationwide basis in relation to Parliamentary contests. But that is a matter which
does not arise for consideration in the present case.
   Section 63 has been further considered in Scotland in a Scottish election petition
case entitled Grieve v Douglas-Home[2]. Their Lordships in that case discussed the provisions of s 63 and dealt with the earlier authorities. I do not personally find it necessary
to cite from their judgments except for one passage, but of course what they do make
g clear is that there is a great deal of difference between the formula which is used in
the 1918 Act 'for the purpose of' and the formula which is used in the 1949 Act 'with
a view to'. Amongst other things, Lord Migdale said[3]:

'I do not think that the maxim that a man must be taken to have intended the
consequences of his acts has application in construing the words "with a view to".
h What has to be considered is the intention or motive in the mind of the person
who arranged the programmes and so occasioned the expense.'

That is a reference to certain broadcast programmes which were the subject of
allegations of corrupt or illegal practices by the petitioner in Grieve v Douglas-Home[2].
   That is an indication, and I find this a very persuasive authority, that the view
j which was taken by Avory J[4] of the difference between 'motive' and 'purpose' is a

---

1 [1952] 1 All ER at 699
2 1965 SLT 186
3 1965 SLT at 190
4 [1928] 2 KB at 283

view which does not necessarily apply when a new and different formula is used, as it was in the 1949 Act, that is to say the formula of 'with a view to promoting or procuring'.

In my judgment the question whether this particular s 63 offence, or the associated offence under s 95, has been committed is always a question of fact, and what one has to do is to apply the language of the section to the facts of the case and ask oneself: did the person who incurred the expense do so with a view to promoting or procuring the election of a candidate at an election? The view or motive of the individuals involved here, as is clear in the present case from the documentation which forms the subject of the charges, was not to procure or promote the election of any candidate or a candidate, but a view to preventing the election of a particular candidate. In my judgment that is not covered by the language of the section, and indeed would require the interpolation into the section of words which are not there, and words which would not fit in with the structure of the section, particularly with the provision of s 63(2).

The other points which are taken on the cases do not in my judgment arise for consideration in the present case. I would dismiss the appeal of the Director of Public Prosecutions in the case of Mr Luft and Mr Atkinson, that is to say against the acquittal by the learned stipendiary magistrate for the city of Manchester of Mr Luft and Mr Atkinson, and I would quash the convictions made by the justices sitting at Bolton of Mr Neil Duffield.

O'CONNOR J. I agree.

LORD WIDGERY CJ. I agree also.

Appeal in first case dismissed; appeal in second case allowed. Leave to appeal to the House of Lords refused but the court certified the following to be a point of law of general public importance: 'Whether on a prosecution under s 63 of the Representation of the People Act 1949 it is necessary to prove that the expense was incurred with a view to promoting or procuring the election of a particular candidate and insufficient to establish that the view or motive of the person incurring the expense was to prevent the election of a particular candidate.'

Solicitors: *Director of Public Prosecutions; Casson & Co*, Salford (for the defendants in the first case); *Brian Thompson*, Manchester (for the defendant in the second case).

Jill Watkins Barrister.

R v Medway

COURT OF APPEAL, CRIMINAL DIVISION

LORD WIDGERY CJ, STEPHENSON LJ, O'CONNOR, LAWSON AND JUPP JJ

23rd, 24th OCTOBER, 6th NOVEMBER 1975

Criminal law – Appeal – Abandonment – Withdrawal – Jurisdiction – Abandonment a nullity – Court functus officio following abandonment – Jurisdiction to allow notice of abandonment to be treated as a nullity – Criminal Appeal Rules 1968 (SI 1968 No 1262), r 10(4).

Criminal law – Appeal – Abandonment – Withdrawal – Circumstances in which court will allow notice of abandonment to be treated as a nullity – Abandonment not the result of a deliberate and informed decision – Deliberate decision taken as result of bad legal advice not in itself capable of vitiating effectiveness of abandonment.

Where an appellant, by notice under r 10(1)[a] of the Criminal Appeal Rules 1968, abandons an appeal or an application for leave to appeal to the Court of Appeal, Criminal Division, the court has no jurisdiction thereafter to entertain an application by the appellant for leave to withdraw the notice of abandonment since, once it has been given, the appeal or application is, under r 10(4) of the 1968 rules, to be 'treated as having been dismissed or refused' and the court is therefore functus officio. The court may, however, allow a notice of abandonment to be treated as a nullity where the court is satisfied that the abandonment was not the result of a deliberate and informed decision, in the sense that the mind of the appellant did not go with his act of abandonment (see p 531 j to p 532 a and p 542 h to p 543 a, post).

A deliberate decision to abandon taken as a result of advice which is founded on a mistaken view of the law is not in itself capable of vitiating the effectiveness of the notice to abandon so as to enable the court to treat it as a nullity (see p 543 h, post).

Where the Court of Appeal is satisfied that the abandonment of an appeal will result in injustice to an appellant, the proper course is to invite the Secretary of State to refer the appellant's case to the court under s 17 of the Criminal Appeal Act 1968 (see p 542 g, post).

Dicta of Lord Reading CJ in *R v Pitman* (1916) 12 Cr App Rep at 14, of Avory J in *R v Van Dyn* (1932) 23 Cr App Rep at 152, of Lord Goddard CJ in *R v Healey* (1956) 40 Cr App Rep at 43, 44 and in *R v Moore* [1957] 2 All ER at 703, of Slade J in *R v Caddy* [1959] 3 All ER at 139, 140, of Lord Parker CJ in *R v Essex Quarter Sessions, ex parte Larkin* [1961] 3 All ER at 931, 932, and of James LJ in *R v Munisamy* [1975] 1 All ER at 912 applied.

R v Noble [1971] 3 All ER 361 explained.

Notes

For the right to withdraw a notice of abandonment of an appeal, see 10 Halsbury's Laws (3rd Edn) 535, para 984, and for cases on the subject, see 14 Digest (Repl) 613, 6088-6095.

Cases referred to in judgment

R v Barnett (16th October 1967) unreported.

R v Bennett [1968] 2 All ER 753, [1968] 1 WLR 988, 52 Cr App Rep 514, CA, Digest (Cont Vol C) 222, 5364fcb.

R v Benson (11th April 1975) unreported.

R v Blackwood (1974) 59 Cr App Rep 170.

R v Bridgeman and Francis [1964] Crim LR 119, CCA.

---

a   Rule 10 is set out at p 513 e to g, post

R v Brown (5th June 1972) unreported.
R v Caddy [1959] 3 All ER 138, [1959] 1 WLR 868, 43 Cr App Rep 198, C-MAC.
R v Clasper (18th October 1971) unreported.
R v Cox (1920) 15 Cr App Rep 36, 14 Digest (Repl) 613, 6090.
R v Downes [1962] Crim LR 541, CCA.
R v Essex Quarter Sessions Appeal Committee, ex parte Larkin [1961] 3 All ER 930, [1962]
    1 QB 712, [1961] 3 WLR 1286, DC, Digest (Cont Vol A) 393, 5967a.
R v French (1975) unreported.
R v Griffin [1967] Crim LR 230, CA.
R v Groves (20th January 1975) unreported.
R v Healey (1956) 40 Cr App Rep 40, CCA, Digest (Cont Vol A) 394, 6093a.
R v Hoare (16th July 1974) unreported.
R v Holland (4th May 1967) unreported.
R v Jones (8th July 1975) unreported.
R v Kempson [1967] Crim LR 230, CA.
R v Laplante (19th May 1972) unreported.
R v Lowbridge [1967] Crim LR 656, CA, Digest (Cont Vol C) 235, 6093a.
R v Mills (13th January 1975) unreported.
R v Moore [1957] 2 All ER 703, [1957] 1 WLR 841, 41 Cr App Rep 179, CCA, Digest
    (Cont Vol A) 394, 6093b.
R v Munisamy [1975] 1 All ER 910, 60 Cr App Rep 289, CA.
R v Najar (21st December 1972) unreported.
R v Noble [1971] 3 All ER 361, [1971] 1 WLR 1772, 55 Cr App Rep 529, CA.
R v Peters (1973) 58 Cr App Rep 328, CA.
R v Pitman (1916) 12 Cr App Rep 14, CCA, 14 Digest (Repl) 613, 6089.
R v Pitt (23rd March 1973) unreported.
R v Siddique (4th November 1974) unreported.
R v Sloan and Waddington (1923) 87 JP 56, 39 TLR 173, CCA, 14 Digest (Repl) 613, 6091.
R v Sutton (Philip) [1969] 1 All ER 928, [1969] 1 WLR 375, 53 Cr App Rep 269, CA,
    Digest (Cont Vol C) 235, 6093d.
R v Van Dyn (1932) 23 Cr App Rep 150, CCA, 14 Digest (Repl) 613, 6093.
R v Waite (19th June 1972) unreported.
R v Ward [1971] 3 All ER 619, [1971] 1 WLR 1450, CA.
R v Wickham [1957] Crim LR 804, CCA.
R v Wilkinson (20th May 1975) unreported.

Cases also cited
R v Barker (1910) 5 Cr App Rep 283.
R v Scott (1924) 18 Cr App Rep 10.
R v Taylor (7th June 1973) unreported.

Application
This was an application by Andrew George Medway for leave to withdraw a notice
of abandonment of his application for leave to appeal against the orders made by
Mais J on 30th July 1973 in the Crown Court at Birmingham under ss 60 and 65 of
the Mental Health Act 1959 whereby it was ordered that the applicant be admitted
to and detained in a hospital subject to restrictions on his discharge. The facts are set
out in the judgment of the court.

Louis Blom-Cooper QC and *Alan Newman* for the applicant.
Frank Blennerhassett QC and *Conrad Seagroatt* as amici curiae.

Cur adv vult

6th November.   **LAWSON J** read the following judgment of the court: This is
an application by Andrew George Medway for leave to withdraw a notice of abandonment of all proceedings in this court in relation to orders made in his case under ss 60

and 65 of the Mental Health Act 1959 (that is to say a special hospital order without
a restriction of time). These orders were made by Mais J at Birmingham Crown Court
on 30th July 1973.

The applicant applied on 22nd August 1973 to the single judge for leave to appeal
against the s 65 order. This application was considered and refused by the single
judge on 22nd March 1974 (the delay at this stage was attributed to requests for time
to be allowed made on behalf of the applicant). The single judge's refusal was
b communicated to the applicant on 2nd April 1974.

On 4th April the applicant renewed his application, in the form that he then sought
leave of the full court to appeal against both the orders made under s 60 of the 1959
Act and as well as that made under s 65.

On 16th May the applicant completed and signed form A, stating that he abandoned
all proceedings in the Court of Appeal. This form was received at the court on 20th
c May. It had been preceded by a letter from the applicant dated 28th April to the
registrar indicating his intention to abandon the proceedings.

This application came before the Court of Appeal, Criminal Division, constituted
by Lord Widgery CJ, O'Connor and Jupp JJ. Having regard to the state of the
authorities on one of the questions arising, the hearing of the application was adjourned
for a full court of five judges as we are now constituted, of Lord Widgery CJ, Stephen-
d son LJ, O'Connor J, Jupp J and myself. The Director of Public Prosecutions was
invited to be and was represented by counsel as amici curiae at the resumed hearing.
This took place on 23rd and 24th October 1975.

The matters which we have to decide are: firstly, it being conceded that this court
has jurisdiction to allow a notice of abandonment of an application for leave to appeal
to be withdrawn, what are the conditions to be satisfied for the exercise of that
e jurisdiction? And, secondly, the conditions for the exercise of this jurisdiction having
been determined, does the present application satisfy them?

Similar questions would in fact arise in a case which involved an abandonment of
an appeal—not the present case which concerns the abandonment of an application.
In this judgment we will therefore refer to the matter as abandonment of an application.

For the purposes of this judgment, the relevant facts apart from those already
f mentioned may be shortly summarised. The applicant, who is now aged 26 years
five months, has a history of mental illness which began in 1971. On 16th March
1973 he pleaded guilty to an offence of arson with intent to endanger life at
Northampton Crown Court when Caulfield J placed him on probation for three
years.

On 3rd May 1973 at Northampton magistrates' court the applicant was convicted
g of dangerous driving and of insulting words and behaviour. Those convictions related to a series of incidents which took place on 20th April 1973. In respect of those
offences the justices committed the applicant in custody for sentence to the Crown
Court under s 56 of the Criminal Justice Act 1967; at the same time he was also
committed to the same court for breaches of the earlier probation order constituted
by the offences of 20th April.

h On the applicant's appearance on these committals, Mais J, on 30th July 1973,
had before him the necessary medical reports and evidence to support the making
of orders under ss 60 and 65 of the Mental Health Act 1959. The applicant's counsel
did not resist the making of the s 60 order, did not challenge the need for the applicant to be in a secure hospital and, with regard to the order under s 65, told Mais J
that the applicant would prefer that such an order should not be made.

j On 21st August 1973, whilst in prison awaiting his removal to Broadmoor special
hospital, the applicant, acting for himself, applied on form N for leave to appeal
against the s 65 order. This application was dealt with by the single judge on 22nd
March 1974. We have already explained the delay but should add that the grounds
considered by the single judge had been drafted by the applicant's solicitors and were
not submitted until 14th March 1974. An independent psychiatrist's report dated

18th December 1973 from Dr Gordon, under whose care the applicant had first come for his mental illness in 1971, was attached to those fresh grounds.

In refusing leave, the single judge gave the following reasons:

'I think this application is misconceived. When the Hospital Order, with restrictions, was made, the evidence for the making of it was unchallenged and apparently sound in opinion upon your mental state. I do not see how the judge could have avoided sending you to Broadmoor in the circumstances made known to him. It may be that you are now in better health and should have your situation reviewed. If so, it is I think the Home Secretary who should be causing a review of your case and possibly refer it to a Mental Health Review Tribunal. I suggest that representations are made on your behalf to him with the opinion of Dr Gordon accompanying them.'

The single judge's refusal was communicated to the applicant, now at Broadmoor, on 2nd April 1974. According to his affidavit sworn on 21st October 1975, the applicant discussed this with Dr Loucas, the medical officer then responsible for him. Dr Loucas told the applicant that there was not much point in pursuing the matter and that in his opinion to do so would be disruptive of his treatment. It is clear that the applicant did not accept this advice because he deposes as follows:

'Nevertheless [that is after receiving this advice] I returned form S. J. indicating that I would renew my Appeal. I wrote to Messrs Wilson & Berry [his then solicitors] informing them of this but as they had been informed of the outcome by my Mother my letter crossed with theirs to me expressing their sympathy at the outcome of my Application and urging me to co-operate fully with the treatment offered by my Doctors so that there might be a happier outcome to a Mental Health Review Tribunal hearing my case.'

As we have already said, the applicant in fact renewed on 4th April 1974. On 28th April he wrote to the registrar indicating intention to withdraw his renewed application and on 16th May he abandoned by completing and signing form A.

As a matter of history a medical review tribunal hearing took place in November 1974, but the result was not favourable to the applicant who, early in 1975, consulted fresh solicitors. Those solicitors, having been informed of the single judge's decision, and the applicant's abandonment, wrote on 24th June 1975 to the registrar intimating that the applicant proposed to apply to withdraw his notice of abandonment. They gave three reasons: firstly, that the single judge had overlooked the provisions of s 11(3) of the Criminal Appeal Act 1968 empowering this court to quash or substitute an appropriate sentence on material available subsequent to the original sentence and thus the applicant would have been misled; secondly, the warning in part 6 of form SJ that dismissal of an application to the full court might result in loss of time—clearly inappropriate to hospital order cases—had not been deleted and may have misled the applicant; and, thirdly, that as a Broadmoor patient he was not in a good position without legal advice to judge the merits of an appeal against sentence.

We shall deal later on with the first point made in this letter. As to the second and third points, we do not think that these are borne out by the applicant's affidavit, but in any case we do not, for reasons which will appear, find that these points would support the grant of leave to withdraw a notice of abandonment. The applicant's affidavit indicates, in our judgment, a deliberate decision on his part to abandon his application.

We turn now to the first question which we have to answer. The jurisdiction of this court and its predecessor, the Court of Criminal Appeal, is and always has been statutory. Until 1966 it stemmed from the Criminal Appeal Act 1907 and since then from the Criminal Appeal Act 1966, now replaced by the consolidated Criminal

Appeal Act 1968. It is not without significance in relation to abandonment by appli-
a cants or appellants to observe that under the earlier Act there was power on the hearing
of an appeal to increase a sentence whereas under the present Act this power no longer
subsists.

Under s 11(3) of the 1968 Act, however, this court can, on an appeal against sentence, substitute one different from that which was imposed by the sentencing court
provided that it is of no greater severity than that which was originally imposed.
b This operates where this court considers, as the Act provides, that the appellant
should be sentenced differently, and it is clear that in exercising this power the court
can, and often does, take into consideration factors which have arisen since the original
sentence was imposed. It is also clear that the court can use this power where the
original sentence (as in this case) was a hospital order: see R v Blackwood[1] where this
court substituted an order of conditional discharge for a hospital order. But the
c exercise of the powers under s 11(3) depends on the court being seised of an appeal.

The abandonment of applications for leave and of appeals is dealt with by rules
made under the powers conferred by s 18 of the 1907 Act and by s 46 of the 1968
Act. The relevant rules were the Criminal Appeal Rules 1908[2]. Rule 23 reads:

d
'An Appellant at any time after he has duly served notice of Appeal, or of
Application for leave to Appeal . . . may abandon his appeal by giving notice of
abandonment thereof in the form (III) in the Schedule to these Rules to the
Registrar, and upon such notice being given the appeal shall be deemed to have
been dismissed by the Court of Appeal.'

The 1908 rules also contained a provision (r 45) empowering the court to waive
any non-compliance with the rules which was not wilful. This is not reproduced
e in the Criminal Appeal Rules 1968[3] (which superseded the 1908 rules). Rule 10, which
is in slightly different language from its predecessor, deals with abandonment:

'(1) An appeal or an application for leave to appeal under Part I of the
[Criminal Appeal Act 1968] may be abandoned before the hearing of the appeal
or application by serving on the Registrar notice thereof in Form 14.
f '(2) The notice shall be signed by, or on behalf of, the appellant.
'(3) The Registrar shall, as soon as practicable after receiving a notice under this
Rule, send a copy of it, endorsed with the date of receipt, to the appellant, to the
Secretary of State and to the proper officer of the court of trial.
'(4) Where an appeal or an application for leave to appeal is abandoned, the
appeal or application shall be treated as having been dismissed or refused by the
g court.'

Rule 12 of the 1968 rules deals with the right of an applicant for leave to have his
application for leave to appeal determined by the full court after refusal by the single
judge. This renewal is exercised by the use of the appropriate forms of notice.
Rule 12(4) says:

h
'If such a notice is not served on the Registrar within . . . 14 days or such longer
period as a judge of the court may fix, the application shall be treated as having
been refused by the court.'

Despite the difference in terminology between r 23 of the 1908 rules and r 10(4)
of the 1968 rules, it is rightly conceded in this case that the effect of the operation of
j both rules is the same.

The situation under the rules, whether of 1908 or of 1968, being that when a notice
of abandonment has been given the application or appeal of which it is the subject

---

1   (1974) 59 Cr App Rep 170
2   SR & O 1908 No 227
3   SI 1968 No 1262

is disposed of—whichever formula be applied, that is (1908) 'deemed to be dismissed', or (1968) 'treated as having been dismissed or refused'—it follows that after abandon- *a* ment the court is functus officio. That being so, there is no longer any proceeding extant before the court in relation to which its jurisdiction can be exercised. But it being clear, as it is agreed, that the court whether under the 1907 Act or the 1966 Act or the 1968 Act could entertain an application for withdrawal of a notice of abandonment—the legislation and the rules being wholly silent on this matter— the basis for the exercise of this jurisdiction must be determined and, in the interests *b* of clarity and certainty, its limits as far as possible defined. It is not surprising that such a jurisdiction should exist because a notice of abandonment does not result in the same factual situation as a dismissal of an appeal on its merits.

The applicant submits that this court and its predecessor have, over the last 65 years, approached the problem of the basis and limits of the jurisdiction in question from two different points of view. The first can, for convenience, be labelled 'the *c* nullity' approach; the second can be called the 'special circumstances' approach. The applicant submits that both these approaches are correct and that, if the 'nullity' test is satisfied, the applicant is entitled as of right to have his notice of abandonment withdrawn. It is submitted, further, that if the 'nullity' test is not satisfied, yet the applicant can show the existence of special circumstances which make it just for the court to hear his appeal on the merits, then in the exercise of the court's *d* inherent jurisdiction the court should exercise a discretion with the same end in view. This is the main contention on which counsel for the applicant bases his case.

We have referred to 'nullity' as a convenient label for the first approach; this is because we do not think that the expression 'nullity', which, as will be seen, has been employed in a number of relevant cases, necessarily indicates the presence of factors which would be required to establish that from the point of view of the civil (as opposed *e* to the criminal) law a transaction was null and void as distinct, for example, from one which was voidable, such as a contract procured by fraudulent representation or undue influence. The cases in fact illustrate that the expression 'nullity' has been used in a very wide sense indeed.

Before we come to review the authorities, we should firstly observe that in many of them where the court has granted or refused leave to withdraw a notice of abandon- *f* ment, the court has been unassisted by argument or the citation of authority. Further, in many of the relevant cases, the court's judgment has been delivered extempore, although it would be wrong to suppose the members of the court to have been unaware of the more important of the decided cases.

The second observation which should be made relates to the practices observed by this court and its predecessor. We have in mind that, until comparatively recently, *g* it was not the general practice of the court when refusing applications (as opposed to dismissing appeals) to give reasons for such refusal and that, at the present time, in the absence of special circumstances, it is not the practice to transcribe reasoned refusals of applications—although by chance this may sometimes happen. Reference to these practices explains why there is somewhat of a dearth of reported or trans- cribed cases relating to refusals of leave to withdraw notices of abandonment. *h*

The history of the reported or transcribed judgments to which we have been referred can conveniently be taken in chronological stages, although it cannot be said that each such stage is a water-tight compartment.

The first stage covers the period 1910 to 1932. This reveals six decisions of which it is only necessary to cite three in any detail. These are: *R v Pitman*[1]. There the appli- cant abandoned under the impression that his friends were unable to finance his *j* appeal, but in the event finance became available. His application to withdraw was refused. Giving the court's judgment, Lord Reading CJ, after referring to r 23 of the 1908 rules, said[2]:

1 (1916) 12 Cr App Rep 14
2 12 Cr App Rep at 14

a
'There is no doubt that this Court has power either to allow the notice of abandonment to be withdrawn or to re-open an appeal which has been dismissed. But that power will only be exercised where there are special circumstances which in the view of the Court justify a departure from the ordinary procedure.'

Lord Reading CJ then referred to the facts on which the application was based
b (which we have summarised). He proceeded[1]: 'In the opinion of the Court these facts do not constitute such circumstances as would justify the re-opening of the appeal.' He concluded the court's judgment by saying: 'There can be no justification for an accused person abandoning his appeal unless he thinks that there is no ground upon which to appeal, and that it would be useless for him so to do.'

In the later case of R v Moore[2], Lord Goddard CJ referred to the first of the passages
c we have cited as a dictum only. We do not find there any claim to an inherent jurisdiction to retain seisin of a dismissed appeal and we find Lord Reading CJ's reasoning helpful since he contrasts the existence of special cirumstances with what can only be regarded as a deliberate decision to abandon and concludes that where there has been such a decision, there is no room for the argument of special circumstances.

The next case we cite is R v Sloan and Waddington[3]. In the course of the argument
d Lord Hewart CJ observed[4]: 'The Court has found it necessary to take a strict view with regard to the effect of notices of abandonment of appeals.' In delivering the court's judgment Salter J said[4]:

'It is not desirable, nor even possible, to enunciate in what circumstances an application for leave to withdraw a notice of abandonment of an appeal will be acceded to. But there must be special circumstances. In this case there are
e none.'

Salter J was, of course, aware of Lord Reading CJ's judgment in R v Pitman[5], since he was a member of the court and he also delivered the judgment in R v Cox[6]. Lord Reading CJ himself was a member of this court and R v Pitman[5] was cited.

The last case we should cite in this period is R v Van Dyn[7]. Avory J presided over
f the court which consisted also of Talbot and Hawke JJ. In delivering the judgment Avory J said[8]: 'The only cases in which the Court has granted an application such as the present were cases in which notice of abandonment was given under some misapprehension or some mistake of fact.' He then cited R v Pitman[5]. He concluded that there was no ground for saying that the notice in that case was given under any misapprehension or mistake of fact.

g Since this stage ends in 1932 and we are not aware of any reported or transcribed judgments for the next 24 years, we can summarise the state of the authorities so far covered by concluding that the Court of Criminal Appeal had adopted the test of special circumstances of which misapprehension or mistake were illustrations (but not exhaustive categories), but that special circumstances could not be found where the applicant had made a deliberate decision to abandon.

h Although the years 1932 to 1956 are barren of reported or transcribed judgments in this jurisdiction, it would be wrong to assume that in this 24 year period there were not quite a number of applications for leave to withdraw notices of abandonment considered by the Court of Criminal Appeal.

j
1 (1916) 12 Cr App Rep at 15
2 [1957] 2 All ER 703, [1951] 1 WLR 841
3 (1923) 39 TLR 173
4 39 TLR at 173
5 12 Cr App Rep 14
6 (1920) 15 Cr App Rep 36
7 (1932) 23 Cr App Rep 150
8 23 Cr App Rep at 152

The next available case is *R v Healey*[1] where Lord Goddard CJ, on refusing leave to withdraw, said[2]:

'There is no doubt that the court has power to allow the withdrawal of a notice of abandonment. It has very seldom allowed it. It is allowed only if there are special circumstances or, as Avory J. put it in *Van Dyn*[3], some misapprehension or mistake of fact. Exactly what the learned judge meant by "misapprehension" as distinct from a mistake of fact is perhaps difficult to understand. He was thinking probably of some misapprehension as to what had happened with regard to the appeal or with regard to the notice of appeal. I am quite certain that misapprehension or mistake of fact does not arise if the prisoner has been weighing up his chances and decides it would be more advantageous to him to abandon his appeal, and he is then advised that that was an unfortunate decision to make.'

Later in the course of the judgment, Lord Goddard CJ referred to 'special circumstances' and posed the question: how can the court say that there are special circumstances which would allow it to reconsider an appeal which has been dismissed? He answered the question by saying[4]: 'The applicant shows that he has weighed up his chances, the advantages and disadvantages, and he has deliberately come to the conclusion that he will abandon his appeal.' It seems to us that this decision is in line with the conclusions we have reached as to the state of the authorities ending in 1932 with *R v Van Dyn*[3].

The second stage in the history of the jurisdiction may be said to begin with *R v Moore*[5] and to end with the case of *R v Clasper*[6]. In *R v Moore*[5] no report indicates on what grounds the application for leave to withdraw was supported. In refusing the application Lord Goddard CJ again delivered the judgment. Byrne and Devlin JJ were the other members of the court. Lord Goddard CJ said[7]:

'There have been from time to time, indeed from quite early days in the history of the court, applications for leave to withdraw a notice of abandonment, and it is exceedingly difficult to understand what power the court have to give leave to withdraw a notice of abandonment, considering that by the Rules of 1908, which have the force of a statute, the appeal has been dismissed. An examination of the cases has shown that, except in one case at any rate, the court have allowed notice of abandonment to be withdrawn only if they are satisfied that there has been some mistake. No doubt if a case could be made out that a prisoner had in some way or another been fraudulently led or induced to abandon his appeal, the court in the exercise of their inherent jurisdiction would say that the notice was to be regarded as a nullity; but where there has been a deliberate abandonment of an appeal, in the opinion of the court there is no power or right to allow the notice of abandonment ᴛo be withdrawn and the appeal reinstated because, the appeal having been dismissed, the court have exercised their powers over the matter and is functus officio. Accordingly, the court will not entertain applications for the withdrawal of notices of abandonment unless something amounting to mistake or fraud is alleged, which, if established, would enable the court to say that the notice of abandonment should be regarded as a nullity.'

Lord Goddard CJ then ref ⸱red to the availability of a petition for the exercise of the prerogative or the power of the Secretary of State to refer a case to the court under

---

1 (1956) 40 Cr App Rep 40
2 40 Cr App Rep at 43
3 (1932) 23 Cr App Rep 150
4 40 Cr App Rep at 44
5 [1957] 2 All ER 703, [1957] 1 WLR 841
6 (18th October 1971) unreported
7 [1957] 2 All ER at 703, [1957] 1 WLR at 842

the 1907 Act (as then amended) as channels which a prisoner in that position might
a pursue.

R v Moore[1] was followed in a whole series of cases during the period 1957 to 1971
during which there appear to be two cases out of line with that decision. We will deal
specifically with these two cases as well as with R v Caddy[2] and R v Essex Quarter
Sessions, ex parte Larkin[3], in both of which there was substantial argument and judgments rather more full than normally found in these cases. The cases following
b R v Moore[1] can be shortly dealt with. We will cite the name of the case, the names of
the members of the court concerned and what seems to us to be the key phrase
used to describe the test of jurisdiction:

R v Wickham[4]. Lord Goddard CJ with Hilbery and Donovan JJ: 'mistake.'

R v Downes[5]. Lord Parker CJ, with Streatfeild and Lawton JJ: 'nullity.'

R v Bridgman[6]. Lord Parker CJ, with Winn and Fenton Atkinson JJ: 'nullity in the
c sense that the prisoner's mind did not go with his pen in other words he may have
thought he was signing a different document, or of course if his signature had been
procured by fraud, which tears up anything.'

R v Kempson[7]. Davies LJ with Fenton Atkinson and Cantley JJ: 'mistake.'

R v Holland[8]. Salmon LJ, Widgery and O'Connor JJ: 'mistake.'

R v Sutton[9]. Winn LJ, Widgery and Lyell JJ: 'mistake or fraud or at any rate bad
d advice'. We observe that the question of legal advice was not, in fact, involved in the
case.

R v Ward[10]. Lord Widgery CJ, Roskill and Caulfield JJ. This was an application for
leave to appeal out of time; but Lord Widgery CJ referred in passing to the jurisdiction in abandonment cases where he said the test was if it were shown to be 'no
real abandonment at all'.

e R v Clasper[11]. Lord Widgery CJ, Edmund Davies LJ and Swanwick J: mistake,
misapprehension or confusion in the applicant's mind 'which meant in effect that his
mind did not go with his pen and his purported abandonment was really no
abandonment at all'.

We note that during this period the Criminal Appeal Act 1907 was replaced first
by the Criminal Appeal Act 1966 and then by the 1968 Act.
f We have referred earlier to R v Caddy[2] which was a court-martial appeal case in
which the court consisted of Byrne, Slade and Salmon JJ. In delivering the court's
judgment Slade J referred to R v Moore[1] and the earlier cases of R v Pitman[12] and
R v Van Dyn[13]. He concluded by saying[14]:

'This court sees no sufficient ground for differentiating the procedure in the
g   Courts-Martial Appeal Court from that prescribed by the Court of Criminal
Appeal. No ground is shown in the present case even approaching the exceptional circumstances in which a similar application would be entertained by the

---

h   1   [1957] 2 All ER 703, [1957] 1 WLR 841
2   [1959] 3 All ER 138, [1959] 1 WLR 868
3   [1961] 3 All ER 930, [1962] 1 QB 712
4   [1957] Crim LR 804
5   [1962] Crim LR 541
6   [1964] Crim LR 119
7   [1967] Crim LR 230
j   8   (4th May 1967) unreported
9   [1969] 1 All ER 928, [1969] 1 WLR 375
10   [1971] 3 All ER 619, [1971] 1 WLR 1450
11   (18th October 1971) unreported
12   (1916) 12 Cr App Rep 14
13   (1932) 23 Cr App Rep 150
14   [1959] 1 WLR at 871, cf [1959] 3 All ER at 139, 140

Court of Criminal Appeal, i.e., "something amounting to mistake or fraud . . . which, if established, would enable the court to say that the notice of abandon-   *a* ment should be regarded as a nullity." Facts which the court might treat as being sufficient to enable the notice of abandonment itself to be treated as a nullity alone will suffice; nothing short of that will do. This application, which the court treats as an application for leave to withdraw a notice of abandonment, is accordingly refused.'

                                                                    b

We also referred to *R v Essex Quarter Sessions*[1] where the Divisional Court consisting of Lord Parker CJ, Ashworth and Veale JJ, were dealing with the question of the abandonment of an appeal to quarter sessions and applied the same test as is relevant here. In delivering the leading judgment, Lord Parker CJ said[2]:

> 'In those circumstances, the learned chairman went on to refer to the practice and the decisions in regard to appeals to the Court of Criminal Appeal and also   *c* in courts-martial appeals. It is really unnecessary to refer to the practice in regard to those appeals in detail. It is fully covered by the judgment of LORD GODDARD, C.J., in *R. v. Moore*[3], in regard to appeals to the Court of Criminal Appeal, and by SLADE, J., in the case of courts-martial appeals in *R. v. Caddy*[4]. It is sufficient to say that, in regard to such appeals, the court has always taken the view that, while there is no jurisdiction in the court to consider an application to withdraw   *d* abandonment, there is, nevertheless, inherent jurisdiction to decide whether a notice of abandonment is, in fact, a complete nullity as having been given under mistake or as the result of fraudulent inducement, in which case they still have seisin of the appeal and there never has been an abandonment.'

Later in the course of his judgment Lord Parker CJ said[5]:   *e*

> '. . . approaching this as a matter of first principles, it seems to me that no court, whether the Court of Criminal Appeal, the Courts-Martial Appeal Court or the appeal committee of quarter sessions, can, in the absence of express statutory power, deal with an appeal once it is abandoned. The jurisdiction of any appellate court is statutory and, in the absence of being seised with an   *f* appeal, they have no discretion at all. In that respect, the position is quite different from that in *R. v. London Quarter Sessions, Ex parte Rossi*[6], where a court having seisin of an appeal has an inherent jurisdiction in regard to setting aside its own orders. All that an appeal court can do in circumstances such as these is to look at the position to see whether there has been an abandonment. Once they find that there is an abandonment, in my judgment they can do nothing further in the matter. If, however, on looking into it they find that there is in fact no   *g* abandonment because the abandonment has been made under mistake or fraudulent inducement, then, of course, it is open to them to say so. It is a nullity and, it being a nullity, they remain seised of the appeal.'

The two cases from this period to which we have referred as out of line with the main stream of authority are, firstly, *R v Lowbridge*[7]. The court consisted of Salmon   *h* LJ, Phillimore and Lyell JJ. The report is too brief to be of much assistance. Leave to withdraw abandonment was given apparently on evidence that the applicant was in a highly disturbed mental state and *might* have signed the notice mistakenly

---

1   [1961] 3 All ER 930, [1962] 1 QB 712
2   [1961] 3 All ER at 931, 932, [1962] 1 QB at 716
3   [1957] 2 All ER 703, [1957] 1 WLR 841
4   [1959] 3 All ER 138, [1959] 1 WLR 868
5   [1961] 3 All ER at 932, [1962] 1 QB at 717
6   [1956] 1 All ER 670, [1956] 1 QB 682
7   [1967] Crim LR 656

                                                                                     i

a
not fully understanding what he was doing. If this decision is correctly reported, we think it was wrong because it is clear that on whatever basis the jurisdiction is to be exercised the court must be satisfied that such basis exists. The second case is R v Barnett[1]. The court consisted of Edmund Davies LJ, Stephenson and James JJ. The application was based on an improvement, since abandonment, in the applicant's mental and physical condition. In giving the court's judgment Stephenson J said:

b
> 'In the very exceptional circumstances of this case this court thinks it would be fair to treat the notice of abandonment as a nullity, it having been given for the medical reasons clearly set out (which this court accepts) in the solicitors' letter, and in the changed circumstances which now prevail the court gives the applicant quite exceptional indulgence, and we grant him leave to withdraw his notice of abandonment.'

c
R v Barnett[1] clearly raises the very question we have to decide.

R v Noble[2] comes towards the end of the second period and the decision has been cited to us to support the view that a proper test for the exercise of the relevant jurisdiction is 'special circumstances' as well as nullity. It seems to us, however, that R v Noble[2] was a clear case of mistake of fact on the applicant's part. He had applied to the single judge for leave to appeal against sentence on 4th December 1970.

d
The single judge gave leave and assigned legal aid on 22nd February 1971, and notification of this was despatched to Noble on 26th February, but owing to a postal strike did not reach him until 8th March. In the meantime, on 1st March, he had abandoned his application in ignorance that it had already been granted. As soon as he became aware of the true position he applied for leave to withdraw. The court hearing the application consisted of Edmund Davies LJ, Lawton and Forbes JJ. In granting leave

e
Edmund Davies LJ said[3]:

> 'We think that perhaps as these applications are rarely granted it might be wise if, in the course of a few observations, we make it clear why we are granting the application, which is for the reinstatement of an abandoned appeal. This court has said repeatedly in R v Moore[4] and recently in 1969 in R v Sutton[5]

f
> that quite extraordinary circumstances must be shown to exist before that course will be allowed by the court.'

After dealing with the facts as we have stated them, he continued[6]:

> 'In R v Sutton[5] certain observations were made by Winn LJ to the effect that this court will not entertain requests for leave to withdraw notices of abandonment unless it is apparent on the face of such a request and application that

g
> some grounds exist for supposing that there may have been either fraud, or at any rate bad advice given by some legal adviser, which has resulted in an unintended, ill-considered decision to abandon the appeal. This court does not regard those observations of Winn LJ as having comprehensively defined and limited the grounds on which this court can in proper circumstances allow an abandonment to be withdrawn. They are to be interpreted as stressing rather that quite

h
> unusual circumstances must be shown to exist. So, applying them, we regard this as a case where, for the reasons I have stated, it would not be just to allow the applicant to be defeated by the fact that he sought to withdraw his application under a complete misapprehension as to the position. It is because of those special factors that in this particular case we accede to the application.'

j

1 (16th October 1967) unreported
2 [1971] 3 All ER 361, [1971] 1 WLR 1772
3 [1971] 3 All ER at 362, [1971] 1 WLR at 1772
4 [1957] 2 All ER 703, [1957] 1 WLR 841
5 [1969] 1 All ER 928, [1959] 1 WLR 375
6 [1971] 3 All ER at 362, [1971] 1 WLR at 1773

In our judgment this is a clear case where it can be said that ignorance of a material fact, namely that he was a successful applicant, at the time of his withdrawal, constituted a mistake or misapprehension sufficient to demonstrate that when he had abandoned, his mind had not gone with his pen. We find this decision in R v Noble[1] wholly in line with the main stream of authority.

The last period, from 1971 to the present date, discloses rather more frequent reports and transcripts relevant to the exercise of the jurisdiction in question. We are satisfied, however, that far more applications for leave to withdraw have been made and disposed of than this available material suggests. For example in 1973, for which year we have one report and two transcripts, we are informed that there were 15 such applications of which three were granted; two of the applications that were granted were reported and one of the applications which was refused was reported. The cases to which we have been referred only constitute therefore a sample. We find that, speaking generally, the mainstream of authority continues to be followed. There are, however, some apparent departures in the direction which the applicant here urges us to follow. These departures we shall discuss later.

We will deal with the mainstream authorities for the period under review as we did with those in the earlier period. Taking them in chronological order, we have:

R v Laplante[2]. Cairns LJ, Nield and Croom-Johnson JJ: inability to read or write; 'genuine mistake'.

R v Waite[3]. Edmund Davies LJ, Stephenson and Browne JJ: 'some sort of mistake or misapprehension.'

R v Najar[4]. Lawton LJ, Melford Stevenson and Brabin JJ: 'misapprehension, mistake, or fraud or bad advice from a legal adviser.' In that case the court held that the abandonment resulted from a deliberate decision.

R v Pett[5]. Edmund Davies LJ, Willis and Bean JJ: 'under a misapprehension.' Edmund Davies LJ cited Winn LJ's observations in R v Sutton[6], namely: 'fraud or at any rate bad advice given by some legal adviser which has resulted in an unintended, ill considered decision.'

R v Peters[7]. Lawton LJ, Thompson and Park JJ: 'something which makes the giving of a notice of abandonment not the applicant's true act.' Lawton LJ then referred to such factors as 'fraud' and 'fundamental mistake' as in R v Noble[1].

R v Siddique[8]. Stephenson LJ, Caulfield and Kilner Brown JJ: abandonment by a foreigner 'under mistaken impression that loss of time was unavoidable.'

R v Groves[9]. James LJ and Boreham J: no such circumstances exist in which the abandonment can be treated as a nullity.

R v Mills[10]. Browne LJ, Swanwick and Griffiths JJ: 'misapprehension that he would be pursuing a purposeless appeal'; 'a complete misapprehension which was in no way his fault'.

R v Munisamy[11]. Scarman, James LJJ and Bristow J. Lord Goddard CJ in R v Moore[12] and Winn LJ in R v Sutton[13] were cited in James LJ's judgment[14]:

---

1 [1971] 3 All ER 361, [1971] 1 WLR 1772
2 (19th May 1972) unreported
3 (19th June 1972) unreported
4 (21st December 1972) unreported
5 (23rd March 1973) unreported
6 [1969] 1 All ER at 929, [1969] 1 WLR at 377
7 (1973) 58 Cr App Rep 328
8 (4th November 1974) unreported
9 (20th January 1975) unreported
10 (13th January 1975) unreported
11 [1975] 1 All ER 910
12 [1957] 2 All ER 703, [1957] 1 WLR 841
13 [1969] 1 All ER 928, [1969] 1 WLR 375
14 [1975] 1 All ER at 912

'fundamental mistake ... so that [the notice of abandonment] can ... be treated
_a_ as a nullity.'

    R v Benson[1].   Orr LJ, Caulfield and Talbot JJ: the applicant's 'mind did not go with
what she did'.

    R v Jones[2].   Stephenson LJ, Nield and Chapman JJ: _R v Munisamy_[3] cited;
'fundamental mistake in relation to the abandonment of the appeal'.

    We now turn to three cases, decided since 1971, which to a greater or lesser extent
_b_ appear to depart from the mainstream of authority.   Taking them in date order,
we find: _R v Brown_[4], Cairns LJ, Stephenson and Willis JJ.   Leave was given to an applicant who had abandoned two days before receiving counsel's opinion that he had
grounds to renew after refusal by the single judge.   Cairns LJ said:

> 'The question for this court is whether, in these very unusual circumstances,
_c_ the applicant can be given leave to withdraw the notice of abandonment. It is
only in very exceptional circumstances that such leave can be given, and there
is no case which this court has knowledge of which corresponds exactly with
the present one.   The nearest reported case is probably the case of _R v Sutton_[5],
where an applicant was allowed to withdraw his notice of abandonment because
he had received bad advice from the adviser.   We express no opinion one way
_d_ or the other whether the advice which he did receive from the legal adviser
was good advice or bad advice.   But the position was, at the time when he gave
notice of abandonment, he had not got the advice at all.   He says, and we see
no reason to disbelieve him, if he had had that advice before giving notice of
abandonment, which he had given with extreme promptitude, he probably
would not have given the notice of abandonment.   We accept that, and in all
_e_ the circumstances we do give him leave to withdraw the notice of abandonment.'

    It will be observed that the effect of _R v Sutton_[5] was misstated.   Nevertheless,
the application to withdraw in _R v Brown_[4] was in fact refused.   The test of 'very
unusual circumstances' unrelated to the factors of mistake or misapprehension was,
in our judgment, misleading.

    The second of these cases is _R v Hoare_[6], Cairns, Stephenson LJJ and Thompson J.
_f_ The applicant had abandoned two days after refusal and before she received her
solicitors' advice that she should renew.   She immediately applied for leave to withdraw.   It might well be that this case was covered by the authorities in relation to
misapprehension, but it is clear that the basis of the decision was different and
precisely the same as that formulated, in our judgment wrongly, in _R v Brown_[4].
Cairns LJ said:
_g_

> 'It is only in very unusual cases that this court will entertain an application
to withdraw the abandonment of an appeal.   There is no provision in the Criminal
Appeal Act or in the rules made under it which authorises at all the withdrawal
of a notice of abandonment.   An abandonment is treated in almost all circumstances as being the end of the matter, and the application for leave to appeal
_h_ is dead.   But there are circumstances in which the court has been prepared to
treat the abandonment as a nullity, and typical cases are where there has been
some misapprehension of the applicant, some mistake of fact, any fraud or any
bad advice from a legal adviser.   It is not possible to say that this case falls strictly
within any of those categories.   But it would appear that the abandonment
notice was given without legal advice, and only very shortly before the advice

_j_
1   (11th April 1975) unreported
2   (8th July 1975) unreported
3   [1975] 1 All ER 910
4   (5th June 1972) unreported
5   [1969] 1 All ER 928, [1969] 1 WLR 375
6   (16th July 1974) unreported

reached her which, had she received it before, would obviously have led to her not giving the notice of abandonment. The application for leave to withdraw   *a* that notice was in fact made within the time available to her for renewing her application to the full court if she had not in the meanwhile given the notice of abandonment. In these very special circumstances this court is prepared to grant leave for the withdrawal of this notice of abandonment.'

The final case for consideration is *R v Wilkinson*[1], Scarman LJ, Cantley and Kerr JJ. *b* The applicant was one of three men sentenced to long terms of imprisonment for a crime of violence. All applied to and were refused by the single judge. The applicant abandoned but the other two renewed to the full court which in due course effected substantial reductions in their sentences. The applicant then applied to withdraw his abandonment. Scarman LJ said:

'He is, however, in considerable difficulties in so doing. It is clear from his *c* notice of application that he abandoned his application to the full court after taking advice from counsel. Counsel clearly advised in the light not only of the sentencing decision of the trial judge, Melford Stevenson J, but also in the light of the refusal of the single judge to grant leave to appeal. It would therefore be going too far on the material available to this court to say that the advice that Wilkinson then received was bad advice. It must be treated as perfectly *d* reasonable advice, given in the circumstances to which I have referred. Wilkinson's application does raise a question as to the power and duty of the court to allow an application for leave to appeal to proceed after a notice of abandonment. The statutory position is as follows. According to s 11(1) of the Criminal Appeal Act 1968, an appeal against sentence lies only with the leave of the Court of Appeal. Rule 10(4) of the Criminal Appeal Rules 1968 provides *e* that where an appeal or an application for leave to appeal is abandoned, the appeal or application shall be treated as having been dismissed or refused by the court. Wilkinson's proceedings got as far as an application for leave to appeal and his notice of abandonment must therefore be treated as though his application had been refused by the court.

'This court has from time to time had to consider the problem with which *f* we are now faced. There have been a number of cases in which this court has made it clear that a notice of abandonment determines, that is to say ends, an appeal or application, unless the court can properly regard the purported abandonment as a nullity. In *R v Peters*[2] Lawton LJ who gave the judgment of the court, put the position in this language: "There must be something which makes the giving of a notice of abandonment not the applicant's true act. If *g* there has been fraud, then clearly what he does is not his true act. If there has been a fundamental mistake . . . then what he does has not been his true act". He concludes the passage as follows: "He", that is the applicant, "was not making a mistake as to his act. He was making a mistake as to his prospect of success in his application, which is another matter altogether". In *R v Munisamy*[3] this court again emphasised the need for "fundamental mistake". *h*

'If the words we have quoted were in fact intended to be laying down a rule of law, Wilkinson's application would be in very great difficulties; he gave notice of abandonment because he had been advised, reasonably at the time but mistakenly as we now know in the event, that his application had no prospect of success. It is significant to observe that Archbold[4], in a passage which was written before *R v Peters*[2] was decided, puts the position as follows. After referring *j*

1 (20th May 1975) unreported
2 (1974) 58 Cr App Rep 328 at 332
3 [1975] 1 All ER 910
4 38th Edn (1973), p 525, para 897

a
to the decided cases, the learned editors comment that the cases are not to be regarded as having comprehensively defined and limited the grounds on which the court can, in proper circumstances, allow a notice of abandonment to be withdrawn, but only as emphasising the clearly established principle that quite unusual circumstances must be shown before leave can be granted.

b
'We think that, insofar as there is any rule of law to be elicited from the rules and the cases on this topic, it is that the circumstances must be wholly exceptional if an application to withdraw a notice of abandonment is to have any success. The particular circumstances with which we are concerned have, so far as we are aware, never before arisen. They certainly were not in the contemplation of the court when it was deciding R v Peters[1] or R v Munisamy[2]: neither do we believe have they been in the contemplation of the court in any of the other decided cases. The circumstances are these. This court, after refusal by the single judge, decided, in the light of authority which itself was decided after the refusal of the single judge, to allow the appeal. It was not really to be expected that counsel advising towards the end of 1974 would necessarily have in mind the pattern of policy and principle subsequently stated in R v French[3], which was decided this year, and in the light of which this court allowed the appeals of O'Brien and Noonan. [The appeals of O'Brien and Noonan were the appeals of the other two persons involved in the crime of violence for which Wilkinson had already been sentenced. Scarman LJ continued:] We think therefore that the problem reduces to the question: What is the just course to take in the wholly exceptional circumstances, even though the circumstances do not fall into the categories specifically mentioned by Lawton LJ in R v Peters[1]?

c

d

e
'It was this court as presently constituted that allowed the appeals of O'Brien and Noonan against sentence. We were careful in our judgment to make it clear that no inference as to Wilkinson's prospects of success should be drawn from the mere fact that we had allowed those appeals. Nevertheless, the three men were concerned in the same offence or series of offences, and it is really quite impossible, as a matter of justice, to deny Wilkinson an opportunity of a review of sentence when his colleagues in crime have had their sentences, each of them, reduced by five years. [Then he dealt with the periods involved in the sentences. He continued:] The decision in those two appeals has therefore radically altered the relationship between the sentences which the sentencing judge thought appropriate. This being so, clearly the demands of justice point to giving Wilkinson an opportunity to apply to this court to review his sentence. We do not believe that there is anything in the statute, in the rules or in the case law that would require so inflexible an interpretation of the words of the rule as to deny a man justice when, through no fault of his own, he has not obtained it and when the court says that it must be just to allow him to have his sentence reviewed. We emphasise, and we think this is the principle that lies behind the case law, that such applications can succeed only in "quite unusual circumstances", as Archbold[4] puts it, or, as we would prefer to put it, in wholly exceptional circumstances.

f

g

h
'We think the history of this case is wholly exceptional. The two successful appellants succeeded largely because of a view as to the relationship between sentences for murder and for other crimes of violence, which has been developed and asserted in this court since the refusal of their applications and Wilkinson's

j

---

1 (1974) 58 Cr App Rep 328
2 [1975] 1 All ER 910
3 (1975) unreported
4 38th Edn (1973), p 525, para 897

application by the single judge. In those circumstances we think we are justified in allowing this application and giving Wilkinson leave to renew his application.' *a*

Scarman LJ referred in the judgment in *R v Wilkinson*[1] to a passage which appears in Archbold[2] in which the learned editors express the view that the decided cases are—

'not to be regarded as having comprehensively defined and limited the grounds *b* upon which the court can, in proper circumstances, allow a notice of abandonment to be withdrawn, but only as emphasising the clearly established principle that quite unusual circumstances must be shown before leave can be granted.'

This should, however, be supplemented by reference to the Eighth Cumulative Supplement to the 38th Edition (published after the decision in *R v Wilkinson*[1]) where it is said: *c*

'The topic was further considered by the Court of Appeal in *R v Munisamy*[3]: an appellant cannot, in the strict sense, withdraw a notice of abandonment . . . He can, however, place before the court sufficient facts to satisfy it that the abandonment was a nullity. Where he has been given bad legal advice the court will only treat his notice of abandonment as a nullity if it is satisfied that, in *d* consequence of the advice, he was acting under a *fundamental mistake* when he purported to give the notice.'

It seems, therefore, that in the light of *R v Munisamy*[3] the learned editors saw fit, and in our judgment rightly, to qualify their earlier view.

It seems to us that the decision in *R v Wilkinson*[1] not only departed from the *e* main stream of authority but unlike *R v Brown*[4] and *R v Hoare*[5] directed it into a new and different course. The point was made that it was necessary to take this new course in order to avoid injustice to the applicant in the circumstances of that case, but we do not believe that the state of the law is such that justice must be denied to a person in Wilkinson's position. This court has recently on occasion in similar cases granted leave to appeal or to renew long out of time to applicants who had *f* not applied or renewed within the prescribed times. That is, of course, a different situation from cases where a notice of appeal has been abandoned, as the appeal is then treated under the 1968 rules as dismissed. Where that position exists, it seems to us that the court being satisfied that injustice would otherwise be done would inevitably resort to the provisions of s 17 of the Criminal Appeal Act 1968 (formerly s 9 of the Criminal Appeal Act 1907 as amended) and invite the Secretary of State *g* to refer the matter to the court, so that the court would then be seised of the case and would do what justice required. Although these provisions are not entirely comprehensive (which is a matter which should be brought to the notice of those concerned), their use would be available in the vast majority of cases. Reference was made, directly or indirectly, to these sections in three cases which we have seen, namely *R v Moore*[6], *R v Griffin*[7] and *R v Groves*[8]. This may not be an ideal solution, *h* but we inhabit an imperfect world.

The answer to the first question which we have to decide depends on whether

---

1 (20th May 1975) unreported
2 38th Edn (1973), p 525, para 897
3 [1975] 1 All ER 910
4 (5th June 1972) unreported
5 (16th July 1974) unreported
6 [1957] 2 All ER 703, [1957] 1 WLR 841
7 [1967] CLR 230
8 (20th January 1975) unreported

j

alongside the jurisdiction which undoubtedly, as all authorities show, exists to give
a leave to withdraw an abandonment where it is shown that circumstances are present
which enable the court to say that that abandonment should be treated as a nullity,
there co-exists an inherent jurisdiction enabling the court, in other special circumstances,
to give such leave.

We are satisfied and hold that there is no such jurisdiction. In our judgment the
kernel of what has been described as the 'nullity test' is that the court is satisfied
b that the abandonment was not the result of a deliberate and informed decision,
in other words that the mind of the applicant did not go with his act of abandonment.
In the nature of things it is impossible to foresee when and how such a state of affairs
may come about; therefore it would be quite wrong to make a list, under such
headings as mistake, fraud, wrong advice, misapprehension and suchlike, which
purports to be exhaustive of the types of case where this jurisdiction can be exercised.
c Such headings can only be regarded as guidelines, the presence of which may justify
its exercise.

As we have said at the outset, the jurisdiction of this court and of its predecessor
is based on statute and we have been referred to and have found no authority to
support the existence of a parallel inherent jurisdiction. Indeed the authorities to
which we have been referred, with the possible exception of Lord Reading CJ's
d observations in R v Pitman[1], support only the proposition that the inherent jurisdiction to regulate proceedings before the court can come into operation where,
in cases of statutory jurisdiction, there is a lis extant before the court on which that
inherent jurisdiction can operate.

It follows that we hold that R v Wilkinson[2] and all such other cases as may be
cited to support the existence of such parallel inherent jurisdiction were wrongly
e decided.

Since we have held that the test of the jurisdiction to allow the withdrawal of a
notice of abandonment is whether or not the abandonment can be treated as a nullity
in the sense we have just employed, we now turn to the second question: on the
facts of the present case, can that jurisdiction be exercised? The answer for the reasons
which follow we find to be no.

f Counsel for the applicant submitted that there were two grounds for saying that
leave to withdraw the notice of abandonment should be given. The first ground
was that the applicant had been induced, at least in part, to abandon by the observation of the single judge on form SJ when he refused leave to appeal on 22nd March
1974. He submitted that the observations on their face showed that at the time they
were written the judge did not have in mind the power of the Court of Appeal,
g Criminal Division, under s 11(3) of the Criminal Appeal Act 1968. He contended
that in the result the judge gave advice which was wrong in law and that insofar
as the applicant acted on that advice he did so because he was under the fundamental
misapprehension that the Court of Appeal had no power to assess the merits of the
sentence as at the date of the hearing of the appeal as opposed to the date at which
it was passed. Even if we accepted the factual basis for this contention, which we do
h not, we do not think that a deliberate decision to abandon taken as a result of advice
which is founded on a mistaken view of the law is in itself capable of vitiating the
effectiveness of the notice to abandon so as to enable the court to treat it as a nullity.
Section 11(3) of the 1968 Act reads as follows:

> 'On an appeal against sentence the Court of Appeal, if they consider that the
j appellant should be sentenced differently for an offence for which he was dealt
> with by the court below may—(a) quash any sentence or order which is the subject
> of the appeal; and (b) in place of it pass such sentence or make such order as

1 (1916) 12 Cr App Rep 14 at 14, 15
2 (20th May 1975) unreported

they think appropriate for the case and as the court below had power to pass
or make when dealing with him for the offence; but the Court shall so exercise   a
their powers under this subsection that, taking the case as a whole, the appellant
is not more severely dealt with on appeal than he was dealt with by the court
below.'

The wording of s 11(3)(b) makes it plain that this court can pass such sentence as
it thinks appropriate at the time of hearing, and the decision of this court in   b
R v Bennett[1], shows that this court may if it thinks fit consider evidence which was
not before the court below.   In R v Bennett[1] the appellant had been sentenced to
three years' imprisonment after the trial judge had tried to get medical reports
without success.   The Home Secretary made an order under s 72 of the Mental Health
Act 1959, and he was transferred to Broadmoor.   This court first received the necessary
medical evidence and then substituted orders under ss 60 and 65 of the 1959 Act.   c
We return to the facts of this case.   On 22nd March 1974 the single judge refused
leave to appeal and made his observations.   The applicant makes it quite clear in
his affidavit that, having discussed the matter with Dr Loucas in whose care he was,
he decided to renew his application to the full court and did this on 4th April.   At
the time he was in receipt of legal advice from his solicitor and did receive legal
advice in the light of the refusal of leave and the observations of the single judge.   d
Thereafter he decided to abandon his application.   There is no element of mistake
in this decision.   We do not think it right to say that it was taken because of the observations of the single judge.   That is enough to dispose of this ground of the
application.

The second ground submitted by counsel for the applicant is that at the time of
taking the decision to abandon the applicant's mental condition was such that we   e
should conclude that he did not really appreciate what he was doing.   The short
answer to this submission is that the applicant himself does not suggest it in his
affidavit; indeed his affidavit, from which we have quoted, demonstrates that the
decision was considered and deliberate.

On our findings therefore this application is refused.

Application refused.

Solicitors: *Brain & Brain* (for the applicant); *Director of Public Prosecutions.*

Jacqueline Charles   Barrister.

1   [1968] 2 All ER 753, [1968] 1 WLR 988

a

Re Tuck's Settlement Trusts
Public Trustee and another v Tuck and others

CHANCERY DIVISION

WHITFORD J

b   22nd, 23rd OCTOBER, 4th NOVEMBER 1975

Settlement – Trust – Uncertainty – Condition precedent – Conditions qualifying beneficiary to receive income – Provision for reference of questions of doubt for determination by specified authority – Marriage to an 'approved wife' – Approved wife defined as wife who is 'of Jewish blood' by both parents and who practises 'the Jewish faith' – Income payable to c *beneficiary so long as he is married to an approved wife – In case of dispute or doubt question whether wife an 'approved wife' to be determined by a chief rabbi – Whether provision for reference to chief rabbi an ouster of the court's jurisdiction – Whether provision rendering qualification sufficiently certain.*

Settlement – Forfeiture – Validity of forfeiture clause – Certainty – Provision for reference d *of questions of doubt for determination by specified authority – Effect – Forfeiture in event of departure 'from the Jewish faith', marriage to a person who is not an 'approved wife' or separation from an 'approved wife' – Approved wife defined as wife who is 'of Jewish blood' by both parents and who practises 'the Jewish faith' – In case of dispute or doubt question to be determined by a chief rabbi – Whether provision for reference to chief rabbi rendering forfeiture clause sufficiently certain.*

e
S created a settlement designed to ensure that his baronetcy would remain in the hands of successors of Jewish faith born of parents of Jewish blood and faith. By cl 3(b) the trustees of the settlement were to pay the income 'to the Baronet for the time being if and when and so long as he shall be of the Jewish faith and shall be married to an approved wife'. An 'approved wife' was defined in cl 1(e) as 'a wife of f Jewish blood by one or both of her parents and who has been brought up in and has never departed from and at the date of her marriage continues to worship according to the Jewish faith as to which facts in case of dispute or doubt the decision of the Chief Rabbi in London of either the Portuguese or Anglo-German community ... shall be conclusive'. Clause 3(c) provided: 'If on the cesser (by death or otherwise) of any marriage of the Baronet for the time being with an approved wife such Baronet g should have lawfully begotten a son or sons in existence born of an approved wife then ... the said income shall continue to be paid to such Baronet during the minority or respective minorities of such son'. Clause 3(e) provided that, if the baronet should, inter alia, either depart 'from the Jewish faith', be married to a person who did not fall within the definition of an 'approved wife', or should judicially or by agreement separate from an approved wife for any cause which either of the chief rabbis referred h to in cl 1(e) should consider to be due to his own fault, £400 per annum should be paid to the baronet out of the trust fund until he should 'be received again formally into the Jewish Faith or until he shall ... marry and live with an approved wife ... and in the meantime ... the residue of the said income shall be held as to one equal half part thereof on trust for the Settlor his executors or adminstrators or assigns and as to the other half part thereof in trust for the Trustees for the time being of a charit-j able institution' appointed by S. B, S's grandson, married an approved wife and had two sons by her. He subsequently married a woman who did not qualify as an approved wife. The trustees applied to the court for the determination, inter alia, of the questions (a) whether the decision of one of the chief rabbis had been made conclusive on all questions, (b) whether, if the opinion of a chief rabbi were conclusive, the trusts were void as purporting to exclude the jurisdiction of the court, (c) whether

U

the qualifying conditions imposed on each beneficiary were void for uncertainty, and (d) whether the provisions in cl 3(c) disqualifying a baronet from receiving the whole income were void for uncertainty.

Held – All the clauses were valid for the following reasons—

(i) S had made specific provision for the resolution of any doubt or difficulty arising with regard to the qualifying conditions in cl 1 and none of the conditions involved any conceptual difficulty. His instruction that all questions should be referred to a chief rabbi was conclusive. It did not amount to an exclusion of the jurisdiction of the court since the conditions were all matters of fact or questions of degree which could properly be submitted to any authority whom the settlor thought appropriate (see p 549 *b* and *c*, p 554 *j* to p 555 *a*, p 558 *c* to *e* and *j*, p 559 *a* to *c* and *f* and p 560 *b*, post); *Clayton v Ramsden* [1943] 1 All ER 16 distinguished.

(ii) A greater degree of certainty was required to support a condition subsequent than a qualifying condition, and the same words could be sufficiently certain for qualification but insufficiently certain for disqualification. However, the conditions of forfeiture specified in cl 3(c) gave rise to no uncertainty since all matters of doubt could be settled conclusively by a chief rabbi (see p 555 *b* to *d* and *g* and p 559 *d e* and *g* to p 560 *a* and *c*, post); *Re Allen* [1953] 1 All ER 308 and *Blathwayt v Lord Cawley* [1975] 3 All ER 625 applied.

Notes
For the requirement of certainty of conditions of defeasance, see 34 Halsbury's Laws (3rd Edn) 504, para 899, and for cases on the subject, see 48 Digest (Repl) 297-304, 2630-2663.

Cases referred to in judgment
Abrahams' Will Trusts, Re, Caplan v Abrahams [1967] 2 All ER 1175, [1969] 1 Ch 463, [1967] 3 WLR 1198, Digest (Cont Vol C), 1063, 2570a.
Allen, Re, Faith v Allen [1953] 1 All ER 308, [1953] Ch 116, [1953] 2 WLR 244; *rvsd* [1953] 2 All ER 898, [1953] Ch 810, [1953] 3 WLR 637, CA; *subsequent proceedings* [1954] 1 All ER 526, [1954] Ch 259, [1954] 2 WLR 333, 48 Digest (Repl) 342, 2931.
Blathwayt v Lord Cawley [1975] 3 All ER 625, [1975] 3 WLR 684, HL.
Clavering v Ellison (1859) 7 HL Cas 707, 29 LJCh 761, 11 ER 282, HL; *affg* (1857) 8 De GM & G 662, LJJ; *affg* (1856) 3 Drew 451, 48 Digest (Repl) 297, 2630.
Clayton v Ramsden [1943] 1 All ER 16, [1943] AC 320, 112 LJCh 22, 168 LT 113, HL; *rvsg sub nom Re Samuel, Jacobs v Ramsden* [1941] 3 All ER 196, [1942] Ch 1, CA, 48 Digest (Repl) 320, 2774.
Coxen, Re, MacCallum v Coxen [1948] 2 All ER 492, [1948] 1 Ch 747, [1948] LJR 1590, 48 Digest (Repl) 618, 5921.
Gulbenkian's Settlement Trusts, Re, Hacobian v Maun [1967] 3 All ER 15, [1968] Ch 126, [1967] 3 WLR 1112, CA; *affd* [1968] 3 All ER 785, [1970] AC 508, [1968] 3 WLR 1127, HL.
Raven, Re, Spencer v National Association for the Prevention of Consumption and other Forms of Tuberculosis [1915] 1 Ch 673, [1914-15] All ER Rep 353, 84 LJCh 489, 113 LT 131, 48 Digest (Repl) 510, 4736.
Selby's Will Trusts, Re, Donn v Selby [1965] 3 All ER 386, [1966] 1 WLR 43, 48 Digest (Repl) 304, 2663.
Sonn, Re (16th October 1958) unreported.
Tarnpolsk, Re, Barclays Bank Ltd v Hyer [1958] 3 All ER 479, [1958] 1 WLR 1157, 48 Digest (Repl) 303, 2661.
Wolffe's Will Trusts, Re, Shapley v Wolffe [1953] 2 All ER 697, [1953] 1 WLR 1211, 48 Digest (Repl) 302, 2658.
Wynn's Will Trusts, Re, Public Trustee v Newborough [1952] 1 All ER 341, [1952] Ch 271, 48 Digest (Repl) 390, 3388.

Cases also cited

a *Dundee General Hospitals Board of Management v Walker* [1952] 1 All ER 896, 1952 SC (HL) 78, HL.

Jones (decd), Re, Midland Bank Executor and Trustee Co Ltd v Jones [1953] 1 All ER 357, [1953] Ch 125.

Kaye (P & M) Ltd v Hosier and Dickinson Ltd [1972] 1 All ER 121, [1972] 1 WLR 146, HL.

b **Adjourned summons**

By a summons dated 13th March 1970 the plaintiffs, the Public Trustee and Desmond Adolf Tuck, sought the determination of, inter alia, the questions whether, on the true construction of a settlement dated 23rd October 1912 and made between Sir Adolf Tuck Bart deceased and the Public Trustee, (1) the decision of one or either *c* of the chief rabbis therein mentioned was by cl 1(e) thereof made conclusive in case of doubt whether the holder of the Tuck baronetcy had married a person falling within the definition in cl 1(e) of 'an approved wife' on (a) all or (b) one or more of the following questions relating to the woman whom the baronet had married, namely (i) whether she was of Jewish blood by one or both of her parents, (ii) whether she had been brought up in the Jewish faith, (iii) whether she had ever departed from the Jewish faith, (iv) whether at the date of her marriage to the baronet she continued to worship *d* according to the Jewish faith; (2) the provisions of cl 1(e) insofar as they purported to make the opinion of a chief rabbi conclusive were valid or void as purporting to exclude the jurisdiction of the court; and (3) cl 3(b), (c), (d) and (e), granting an annuity of £400 per annum to any baronet for the time being who was (i) a pervert from the Jewish faith, (ii) a bachelor, (iii) married to a person who was not an approved wife, (iv) a widower under the age of 55 without male issue born of an approved wife cap-*e* able of inheriting the baronetcy, or (v) judicially or by agreement separated from an approved wife which the chief rabbi shall consider to be a separation due to the baronet's fault, and disposing of the residue of the income, were valid dispositions of income or void for uncertainty. The defendants were (1) Sir Bruce Adolf Reginald Tuck Bart, (2) Lady Pamela Dorothy Tuck, (3) Richard Bruce Tuck, (4) Christopher John Tuck, (5) Muriel Jeanetta Montefiore, (6) Lady Sybil Grace Stern, (7) National *f* Westminster Bank Ltd, (8) John Henry Jacobs, (9) Alan David Nunes Nabarro and (10) the Attorney-General. The facts are set out in the judgment.

Nathaniel Micklem for the Public Trustee.
Gerald Godfrey QC and *T R F Jennings* for the first, second and ninth defendants.
C A Brodie for the third and fourth defendants.
g *Donald Nicholls QC* and *Andrew Goodall* for the fifth to eighth defendants.
Andrew Morritt for the Attorney-General.

Cur adv vult

h 4th November. **WHITFORD J** read the following judgment: The summons before the court raises a number of questions arising under two settlements made on 23rd October 1912 and 12th December 1917 by the late Sir Adolf Tuck Bart, and arising also under his will dated five days after the execution of the first settlement. At the hearing of the summons, I reserved judgment on the first eight questions raised, which all arise on the first settlement. The summons, which was issued in *j* 1970, has taken a long time to come on. I was told the delay had been occasioned by abortive attempts to settle the dispute.

The plaintiffs were originally the Public Trustee and a Mr Desmond Adolph Tuck, whose recent death was apparently in part at least the reason why the negotiations broke down. The defendants are divided into two camps on the first eight questions. On one side stand the fifth, sixth, seventh and eighth defendants, children of the settlor

or their personal representatives. They broadly claim that the whole of this settlement is a nullity. On the other side, we have the personal representative of the eldest
son of the settlor, the late Sir William Tuck, who is the ninth defendant; Sir Bruce,
son of Sir William and grandson of the settlor, the first defendant; and his wife, the
second defendant. There are also Sir Bruce's two sons by his first marriage, the third
and fourth defendants. This group broadly contend that the settlement is valid,
subject to a possible question on certain particular provisions, which it is thought
may be of no effect. The tenth defendant, the Attorney-General, on the issues now to
be considered, was content to adopt the argument put forward by counsel for the fifth,
sixth, seventh and eighth defendants.

The reason for the settlement appears in the recital. When he was made a baronet,
the settlor considered this honour not merely an honour to himself but to the Jewish
race of which he was proud to be a member, and he wanted to try and impose conditions which would ensure that that dignity should remain in the hands of successors
of Jewish faith born of parents of Jewish blood and Jewish faith for as long as the
law might allow. To achieve this aim he set up the trusts of the first settlement,
with the relatively modest sum of £1,000. To this over the years, and there is no need
to go into detail, other moneys have been added, until at the present moment a not
inconsiderable sum is at stake.

The real question is whether the trusts are void for uncertainty, in which case
the fifth, sixth, seventh and eighth defendants will benefit as residuary legatees,
or whether they can be upheld, which is to the advantage of the remaining defendants.
I put the question in this way, because it is my view that it is the first duty of the
court to try to uphold dispositions made by settlement or testament, to do its utmost
to give sensible meaning and effect to the terms of such dispositions as expressed
in the instruments, and to avoid defeating plain intentions by niceties of construction,
by the finding of obscurities which could never have existed in the mind of the
original donor or by applying standards which are unduly exacting.

A settlor makes his dispositions. It is the duty of his trustees to carry them into
effect. If it is quite impossible under the terms of the settlement for the trustees
to reach a conclusion as to the settlor's intentions, it may have to be set aside, but
this, it is to be hoped, is going to be the rare case. If this be the duty of the court
then, setting aside questions of public policy, and no such questions were argued
before me, it seems to me to be of first importance that the court should dismiss
from its mind views which might be formed as to the general desirability or otherwise of the provisions in question. When points of construction arise, it is sometimes
not a bad thing to try to approach the document in question with a mind free from
the doubts which can be induced by skilful advocacy, and undaunted by the hesitations which may be occasioned by views expressed in decisions in other cases on
provisions which may be not dissimilar, but which are never, at least in my experience,
identical.

The first settlement, which starts with a recital of intentions in the form I have
endeavoured to summarise, continues in cl 1 with certain definitions. I can go straight
to cl 1(e), which is central to the issues in this case. It defines an 'approved wife' in
these terms:

> 'An "approved wife" means a wife of Jewish blood by one or both of her parents
> and who has been brought up in and has never departed from and at the date
> of her marriage continues to worship according to the Jewish faith as to which
> facts in case of dispute or doubt the decision of the Chief Rabbi in London of
> either the Portuguese or Anglo-German community (known respectively as
> the Sephardim and the Ashkenazim Communities) shall be conclusive.'

The relevance of para (e) to the intentions of the settlor as recited is immediately
apparent. He can have been in no doubt that he was of Jewish blood and Jewish
faith and, as we shall see, he wanted to encourage a possible successor to the baronetcy

to marry a wife of Jewish blood and Jewish faith. He is apparently prepared to accept
a that one only of the wife's parents may be of Jewish blood, but whether one or both
are of Jewish blood, the wife must have been brought up in, and must never have departed from, and must at the date of her marriage continue to worship according
to, the Jewish faith.

The settlor appears to me to consider quite plainly that the questions whether
a wife is of Jewish blood, and has been brought up in and has never departed from and
b continues to worship according to the Jewish faith, are questions of fact. He recognises
that they are facts about which there may be room for doubt or difficulty. He relieves
his trustees from the duty of reaching a conclusion on any of these matters if doubts
or difficulties should arise by providing that questions of doubt or difficulty may
be decided by either one of the two chief rabbis named. It is convenient to add at
this point that there is unchallenged evidence in this case that given the necessary
c information the chief rabbi, at least of the Ashkenazim community, would be prepared to give a decision on the four tests which an approved wife must pass, and no
one suggested that such information as the chief rabbi might require would not
be forthcoming.

I can turn at once to cl 3, where the trusts are set out. After an accumulation
provision, cl 3(b) is in these terms:
d
> 'From and after the death of the Settlor upon trust (subject to the provisions
> of paragraph (d)) to pay the income of the Tuck Baronetcy Trust Fund to the
> Baronet for the time being if and when and so long as he shall be of the Jewish
> faith and shall be married to an approved wife and shall either continue to live
> with her or if separated (whether judicially or otherwise) he shall be certified
e > by the Chief Rabbi in London of either the Portuguese or Anglo-German Com-
> munity to have in no way caused such separation by any fault of his own and also
> during the period of 18 months after a marriage between him and approved
> wife shall have come to an end by her death or otherwise.'

To those familiar with these arcana, it will be apparent that questions touching what
are referred to in the cases as conditions precedent are going to arise. Just reading
f the paragraph, however, as a trustee must, I should imagine that anyone would
say that the settlor is here providing that anyone holding the baronetcy, if he is to
have the income of the fund, must meet certain qualifying conditions. First he must
be of the Jewish faith. The settlor plainly thought this question would not give
rise to doubt or difficulty. Secondly, he must be married to an approved wife, as
to which in case of doubt the decision of one or other of the chief rabbis was intended,
g I think, by the settlor to be final. Next he must continue to live with her, but if he
is separated from her, it must not be his fault. So far as any question of blame is
concerned, here again the provision is that the certificate of one or other of the chief
rabbis shall be conclusive. If the marriage comes to an end, then the income continues
for 18 months.

Clause 3(b) on the face of it appears to present little difficulty. Questions as to
h faith are commonly asked of all of us on some of the innumerable forms with which
we are faced, where one is frequently asked to make some assertion as to one's faith.
At first sight, it would seem no more difficult to ascertain whether he is of the
Christian or any other faith. The meaning attaching to the words 'approved wife'
is defined. It is true that her Jewish blood has to be established, and it is not enough
that she should be of Jewish faith; she must have been brought up in, and never
j have departed from, and have continued to worship according to the Jewish faith.
Whether this rather more stringent test on the potentially maternal side was inserted
because the settlor had formed the view that subsequent generations were more
likely to be influenced by the mother than by the father we shall never know, and
it is in any event irrelevant. So far as any question of fault is concerned, the settlor
has made a perfectly sensible provision with regard to this, and the trustees need

never be faced with difficulties or doubts because if there should arise any doubts or difficulty touching the status of a wife, the way of resolving them has been provided for.

In the event that death or separation shall have occurred, cl 3(c) provides some further amelioration, and provides as follows:

'If on the cesser (by death or otherwise) of any marriage of the Baronet for the time being with an approved wife such Baronet should have lawfully begotten a son or sons in existence born of an approved wife then after the expiration of the period of 18 months mentioned in paragraph (b) the said income shall continue to be paid to such Baronet during the minority or respective minorities of such son of his born of an approved wife as may for the time being be heir apparent to the said Baronetcy the said Baronet nevertheless maintaining and educating such son thereout in the meantime.'

Under this clause the only possible room for any doubt or difficulty at all would seem to me to be a question touching this point: is this son, or are these sons, the son or sons of an 'approved wife'? This is, of course, exactly the same question as has arisen under the clauses already considered. I need not read cl 3(d). It provides for an income for any heir apparent born of an approved wife, and is subject to a proviso which is no longer of any relevance. Here again the only point which might occasion some possible doubt or difficulty is the question of the 'approved wife'.

Up to now we have been considering qualifying conditions. The questions a trustee has to ask himself have been basically: 'Is this baronet of Jewish faith?', 'Is his wife an "approved wife"?' and so on. Unless all these questions can be answered affirmatively by a trustee, then he cannot start making payment. Clause 3(e) is concerned, at least in part, with disqualifications, although it can be said that it does operate to qualify. It is in these terms:

'But whenever the Baronet for the time being shall be either: (1) A pervert from the Jewish faith (2) A Bachelor or (3) Married to a person who does not fall within the foregoing definition of an approved wife (4) A widower under the age of 55 without male issue born of an approved wife capable of inheriting the said Baronetcy and whose wife has been dead for 18 months (5) Judicially or by agreement separate from an approved wife (who still remains his wife de jure) for any cause which the Chief Rabbi for the time being in London of either the Portuguese or Anglo-German Community shall consider to be due to his own fault then and in such cases the annual sum of £400 and no more shall be paid to him out of the Tuck Baronetcy Trust Fund until he shall be received again formally into the Jewish Faith or until he shall again live with any such separated wife or being a bachelor or widower shall marry and live with an approved wife (as the case may be) but in no case shall the subsequent attainment of 55 years entitle him to the receipt of the income and in the meantime (subject to any payments which may be payable to an heir apparent under paragraph (d) of this clause or under clause 6) the residue of the said income shall be held as to one equal half part thereof on trust for the Settlor his executors or administrators or assigns and as to the other half part thereof in trust for the Trustees for the time being of a charitable institution which the Settlor is about to found or direct the foundation of by his Will or any Codicil thereto in memory of his dear parents to be called the Raphael and Ernestine Tuck Trust Fund for the purpose of augmenting the salaries or stipends of Jewish Ministers and Readers in the United Kingdom and for assisting and training Jewish Ministers and Readers by grants or providing scholarships or exhibitions for Theological students for the Jewish Ministry in the United Kingdom.'

It is of course again at once apparent from this paragraph that the settlor had in mind at all times the idea of ensuring not only adherence by his heirs to the Jewish

faith, but of ensuring that in the event moneys should be forfeited they should be
a paid to assist Jewish causes.

However, so far as is at present material, cl 3(e) appears to be to have this effect.
Assume a baronet, originally qualified, who becomes a pervert from the Jewish
faith, or who, his approved wife having died, makes a second marriage with a wife
who cannot qualify as an approved wife. Assume that his approved wife has died,
and that he, 18 months later, has not married a second approved wife, but is still under
b the age of 55 and has no issue. Assume there has been a separation and no certificate
to the effect that it was not his fault is forthcoming. In all these circumstances, he
is disqualified in the sense that he no longer gets the entire income from the trust
fund. At the same time it can, I suppose, be said that by the same token he qualifies
for £400 a year. Without any question of initial attainment of a qualifying status,
so far as the main income is concerned, he may under this paragraph qualify for
c £400 a year if from the start he is and constantly remains a bachelor.

Once again the questions arising, however, are exactly the same questions as have
to be considered under the earlier clauses, and the same can be said of cll 4 and 6,
the only other clauses which were alleged to be material, and which it is quite
unnecessary for me to read in detail.

It is said that this settlement is bad, because it is tainted with uncertainty. It is
d common ground that cll 3(b)(c)(d), 4 and 6 contain qualifying conditions, conditions
precedent. It is common ground that in fact the conditions which are to be found
in all these clauses are the same conditions repeated with slight variations, according
to the substance of the clause in question.

It was urged on me by counsel for the fifth to eighth defendants that some or at
least one of these qualifying conditions, and it is said one is enough, is so vague as
e to be unenforceable. So far as the disqualifying conditions of cl 3(e) are concerned,
the conditions subsequent, these too are said to be so uncertain as to be unenforceable.
Counsel were really, I think, at least agreed to this extent, that if the conditions in
question are unenforceable in the context of a qualifying provision, they must be
unenforceable in the context of a disqualifying condition. It was perhaps for this
reason that counsel for the first, second and ninth defendants indicated very fairly
f that he was not really concerned to argue the question one way or another for a
rather obvious reason.

The first defendant married first a lady who was accepted by everybody as an
approved wife. It is perhaps interesting to note that at this stage at least it never
occurred to anybody to raise any question concerning any alleged uncertainty attaching
to the qualifying condition that a wife must be an approved wife. She bore him two sons,
g the third and fourth defendants. He has since married a lady who, I was told, it is
accepted, cannot be suggested to be a lady who could be said to qualify as an approved
wife. If, and we shall see that this to me somewhat strange position is undoubtedly
arguable, the provisions as to 'approved wife' are sufficiently certain for the purposes
of qualification, but not sufficiently certain for the purposes of disqualification, then
the first defendant having qualified by marrying an approved wife may perhaps
h be immune from disqualification by his subsequent marriage to a wife who is
admittedly incapable of qualifying.

One thing seems to me quite plain. This result must defeat the clear intention
of the settlor, and counsel for the fifth to eighth defendants relied very strongly,
and to my mind understandably, on the inequity of reaching a conclusion from which
so unjust a result would ensue. It is fair to say that in the course of the hearing counsel
j for the third and fourth defendants indicated that he was not going to argue that
the disqualifying conditions were void, and counsel for the first, second and ninth
defendants made it equally plain that his clients were not pressing this view.

For my own part, as I have already indicated, my mind instinctively rejects the
proposition that in one and the same document the same words can be sufficiently
certain to admit of qualification, but insufficiently certain to admit of disqualification.

No doubt, if no personal interests are involved, it is always nice to be able to say
that a person qualifies for something pleasant, and not so nice to have to say that *a*
he is disqualified. But there are circumstances, such as those arising in the present
case, when one might feel reluctant to be forced to decide that a supplicant is entitled
to have it both ways.

To see how this, on the face of it, strange situation has arisen, it is necessary to turn
to the authorities, and I must start with *Clayton v Ramsden*[1]. This was a case of a
legacy under a will and a share in residue left to an unmarried daughter, who was *b*
subject to a forfeiture of interest if, after the testator's death, she married a person
not of Jewish parentage and of the Jewish faith. It was held that this was a case involving conditions of forfeiture, and that these conditions were void for uncertainty.
Lord Atkin[2], who was presiding, in his speech, with his customary frankness, makes
his position quite plain:

> 'For my own part I view with disfavour the power of testators to control
> from their grave the choice in marriage of their beneficiaries, and should not
> be dismayed if the power were to disappear. But at least the control by for-
> feitures imposed by conditions subsequent must be subject to the rule as to
> certainty described by this House in *Clavering* v. *Ellison*[3] and judged by the
> test there prescribed this forfeiture fails. It is true that, as contended by counsel *d*
> for the respondents, on any possible construction of the clause, Clayton, an
> English Wesleyan, was disqualified. But any possible construction is not the
> question: the actual construction must be certain: and since, it is not, the appeal
> succeeds.'

So Lord Atkin makes the point that if the condition is a disqualification, a disqualifying condition, certainty on any particular set of circumstances is not enough; there *e*
has to be certainty as to the construction of the clause generally.

Lord Russell of Killowen[4] put the matter thus:

> 'The particular matter for our consideration is [the testator's] attempt, by
> means of a forfeiture clause to take effect on the happening of a condition sub-
> sequent, to control his daughter Edna's choice of a husband ... There can be *f*
> be no doubt as to the stringency of this clause if it be effective. Once the terms
> of the condition of defeasance have been fulfilled the daughter, her husband,
> her children by him and their issue, and any aftertaken husband, her children
> by him and their issue are one and all deprived of all the interest previously
> given by the will ... The courts have always insisted that conditions of defea-
> sance, in order to be valid, should be so framed that the persons affected (or *g*
> the court if they seek its guidance) can from the outset know with certainty the
> exact event upon the happening of which their interests are to be divested.
> The principle was enunciated many years ago by LORD CRANWORTH in
> *Clavering* v. *Ellison* ... in the following words[5]: "... where a vested estate is
> to be defeated by a condition on a contingency that is to happen afterwards,
> that condition must be such that the court can see from the beginning, precisely *h*
> and distinctly, on the happening of what event it was that the preceding vested
> estate was to determine." In all such cases that is the test which has to be applied
> to the particular condition which the testator has chosen to impose.'

The Court of Appeal[6], holding that the words 'of Jewish parentage' related to
religion rather than race, had concluded that those words were not too vague. In *j*

1 [1943] 1 All ER 16, [1943] AC 320
2 [1943] 1 All ER at 17, [1943] AC at 325
3 (1859) 7 HL Cas 707
4 [1943] 1 All ER at 17, 18, [1943] AC at 326
5 7 HL Cas at 725
6 [1941] 3 All ER 196, [1942] Ch 1

the House of Lords all their Lordships held that the words were conditions of qualifi-
a cation relating to race, not to religion, and were bad for uncertainty. For present
purposes, in relation to Jewish blood, it is this aspect of the case that is perhaps of
the greatest importance. It must, however, be remembered that in the context of
the forfeiture clause, all their Lordships, save for Lord Wright, also held, contrary
to the view expressed in the Court of Appeal, that the conditions relating to faith
were likewise void for uncertainty, and Lord Russell of Killowen dealt with this aspect
b of the case in these words[1]:

> 'In my opinion, on construction, the words, "of Jewish parentage" refer to race.
> Other elements of doubt surround the words. Must both parents be of the Jewish
> race, or would one alone, and which, suffice? I confess myself unable to find any
> context which provides an answer; but the answer may well be that, in the
c absence of a context to the contrary, the true construction is that both parents
> must be of the Jewish race. But at this point the real difficulty begins, viz., the
> question of degree. The testator has given no information or clue as to what
> percentage or proportion of Jewish blood in the husband will satisfy the require-
> ment that he should be of Jewish parentage. The daughter could never, before
> marrying the man of her choice, be certain that he came up to the requisite
d standard of Jewish parentage, nor could a court enlighten her beforehand.
> The standard is unknown, and incapable of ascertainment. It is this uncertainty
> of degree which prevents the divesting event from being seen precisely and
> distinctly from the beginning, and which makes this condition void for uncer-
> tainty. The uncertainty attaching to the requirement of Jewish parentage avoids
> the whole condition subsequent, with the result that no defeasance takes place.
e In these circumstances it is unnecessary to express an opinion on the certainty
> of the words "of the Jewish faith"; but had it been necessary I should have felt
> a difficulty in holding that their meaning was clear or certain.'

The question of 'one or both' in the case I am at present considering is resolved
by the definition of 'approved wife'. Can it be said that in this case the standard is
both unknown and incapable of ascertainment for, anticipating perhaps the doubts
f and difficulties which troubled Lord Russell, the settlor has told his trustees how
any doubt or difficulty can be resolved and no doubt a prospective beneficiary under
the trust could follow the same route to the resolution of any question of doubt
or difficulty.

I must refer to Lord Wright[2], who said this about the question of Jewish parentage:

> 'It is then necessary to consider each limb of the composite conditions
g separately. In my opinion, the former limb [ie Jewish parentage] fails to pass
> the test of clearness and distinctness. I am prepared to accept that it refers to
> both parents and not merely to one; but I think it refers to race, not to faith.
> These may be regarded as being matters of ambiguity in construction capable
> of being resolved by the court. But it is a different problem to determine what
h is the degree of racial purity in fact required by the condition. In that respect
> the clause falls short of clearness and distinctness. On reading it, the court or
> other party interested is left in complete doubt what degree of racial purity
> will satisfy the condition. Is it to be a 100 per cent., or will 75 per cent. or 50 per
> cent. be sufficient? The words of the clause do not enable any definite answer
> to be given.'

j Lord Wright, of course, was troubled by questions of degree, and he expressed himself as being unable to find any words which would enable an enquirer to ascertain
the answer to the question: is this individual of Jewish parentage?

---

1   [1943] 1 All ER at 19, [1943] AC at 328
2   [1943] 1 All ER at 20, [1943] AC at 330

Lord Romer[1], dealing with the question of Jewish blood, put the matter in this way:

'What then did the testator mean by the stipulation that the daughter's husband was to be of Jewish race or descent? It cannot reasonably be supposed that the husband was to show an unbroken line of descent from the patriarch Jacob. If the daughter were compelled to wait for such a husband, she would remain a spinster all her life and the condition would be void as amounting to a total restraint on marriage. It seems far more probable that the testator meant no more than that her husband should be of Hebraic blood. But what degree of Hebraic blood would a permissible husband have to possess? Would it be sufficient if one only of his parents were of Hebraic blood? If not, would it be sufficient if both were? If not, would it be sufficient if in addition it were shown that one grandparent was of Hebraic blood or must it be shown that this was true of all his grandparents? Or must the husband trace his Hebraic blood still further back? These are questions to which no answer has been furnished by the testator. It is, therefore, impossible for the court to see from the beginning precisely or distinctly upon the happening of what event it was that Mrs. Clayton's vested interests under the will were to determine, and the condition is void for uncertainty.'

He dealt with the question of Jewish faith in these terms[2]:

'For how is it to be ascertained whether a man is of the Jewish faith? . . . the Court of Appeal . . . answered this question by saying that whether a man was or was not of the Jewish faith was a mere question of fact to be determined on evidence and that the assertion by the man that he was of that faith was well nigh conclusive. I should agree entirely with the Court of Appeal as to this if only I knew what was the meaning of the words "of the Jewish faith". Until I know that, I do not know to what the evidence is to be directed. There are, of course, an enormous number of people who accept every tenet of and observe every rule of practice and conduct prescribed by the Jewish religion. As to them there can be no doubt that they are of the Jewish faith. But there must obviously be others who do not accept all those tenets and are lax in the observance of some of those rules of practice and conduct, and the extent to which the tenets are accepted and the rules are observed will vary in different individuals . . . I do not doubt that each of these last mentioned individuals, if questioned, would say, and say in all honesty, that he was of the Jewish faith. On the other hand I do not doubt that one who accepts all the tenets and observed all the rules would assert that some of the individuals I have mentioned were certainly not of the Jewish faith. It would surely depend on the extent to which the particular individual accepted the tenets and observed the rules . . . I cannot avoid the conclusion that the question whether a man is of the Jewish faith is a question of degree. The testator has, however, failed to give any indication what degree of faith in the daughter's husband will avoid and what degree will bring about a forfeiture of her interest in his estate.'

And so he held the condition in regard to faith void, for the same reason. These were both considered by their Lordships to be questions of degree, and the condition failed because the testator in *Clayton v Ramsden*[3] had not taken steps to indicate how any doubt or difficulty in point of degree might be resolved.

This case appears to me to differ so far as faith is concerned from the position in *Clayton v Ramsden*[3]. The settlor has, as I have already pointed out, envisaged the

---

1 [1943] 1 All ER at 22, [1943] AC at 333
2 [1943] 1 All ER at 23, [1943] AC at 334
3 [1943] 1 All ER 16, [1943] AC 320

possibility of doubts and difficulties, and has said that these can be resolved by
reference to rabbinical authority. So, too, with the question of Jewish blood.
I come next to another case, much canvassed in argument, Re Allen[1]. This was
a case of the devise by a testator of freeholds. He devised this interest 'to the eldest
of the sons of [his nephew], who shall be a member of the Church of England, and an
adherent to the doctrine of that church', with a gift over. Vaisey J in this particular
case held that both singly and in conjunction the expressions 'a member of the
Church of England' and 'an adherent to the doctrine of the Church' were void for
uncertainty. But in the Court of Appeal[2] it was held that as it was a case of a condition
precedent or qualification, to satisfy it it was not necessary that its scope should be
capable of exact definition; all that any claimant had to show was that he at least
was within the requirement.

So between these two cases, Clayton v Ramsden[3] and Re Allen[1], we get the difference
of approach so far as the question of certainty is concerned, the division being as
between the approach proper in the case of forfeitures, and the approach proper in
the case of qualification. In certain passages in the judgment of Evershed MR, he
dealt with the matter in this way[4]:

> '. . . the courts . . . will hold a condition subsequent void if its terms are such
> that . . . it cannot be clearly known in advance or from the beginning what
> are the circumstances the happening of which will cause the divesting or
> determination of the gift or estate.'

Dealing with conditions precedent, he said[5]:

> '. . . if the formula constitutes a condition precedent, I will assume that failure
> to satisfy the condition will involve failure to take the benefit of the devise.
> The same result is equally (if not more) clear if the formula is not a condition
> at all but part of a description of the devise . . . All that the claiming devisee
> has to do is at the relevant date to establish, if he can, that he satisfies the con-
> dition or qualification, whatever be the appropriate test. If the formula is such
> as to involve questions of degree (as prima facie is implicit in any requirement
> of "adherence" or "attachment" to a particular faith or creed) the uncertainty
> of the test contemplated may well invalidate the formula as a condition sub-
> sequent, but will not, in my judgment, necessarily do so in the case of a condition
> precedent, for if the claimant be able to satisfy any or at least any reasonable
> test, is he disentitled to the benefit of the gift?'

If you are considering forfeiture provisions, they are void, unless the standards to
be met are known. And it is going to be possible to ascertain in every case whether
they are going to be met. If you are considering questions of qualification, it is enough
if you are going to be able to say in any individual case whether the conditions are,
or are not, met.

Re Allen[1] was followed by Re Selby's Will Trusts[6], a case which came before
Buckley J. Again, it was a case involving a will under which the testator declared
that 'no beneficiary . . . who shall have married, or who before, or on attaining a
vested interest shall marry out of the Jewish faith shall take any interest or benefit'.
This was a case where it was held that the requirement was a condition precedent,
and the reasoning adopted by Buckley J, following the Court of Appeal in Re Allen[1],
was that although there might be difficulty in borderline cases in deciding whether

1   [1953] 1 All ER 308, [1953] 1 Ch 116
2   [1953] 2 All ER 898, [1953] 1 Ch 810
3   [1943] 1 All ER 16, [1943] AC 320
4   [1953] 2 All ER at 900, [1953] 1 Ch at 816
5   [1953] 2 All ER at 901, [1953] 1 Ch at 816, 817
6   [1965] 3 All ER 386, [1966] 1 WLR 43

or not an individual was of the Jewish faith, the phrase was not necessarily meaning-less, and was sufficiently definite and intelligible to be valid as a condition precedent. Of course, for present purposes, the significance of this case is that it was a decision in this division in relation to the words 'Jewish faith', a decision to the effect that these words are not themselves so uncertain as to be incapable of providing a reasonable qualification. Dealing with the observations of the House of Lords in *Clayton v Ramsden*[1], Buckley J said[2]:

'Those are observations which give strong support to the submission that the question whether the particular person is or is not of Jewish faith is a question which the court cannot answer with certainty, but it must be remembered, as I have already indicated, that those are observations which are made in the con-text of conditions subsequent in respect of which it is well settled that the person liable to suffer a forfeiture must be able to understand precisely what act or acts will be liable to work forfeiture. Such cases are to be distinguished from cases of conditions precedent or qualifications to take a benefit. That that is so, is made clear by a decision of the Court of Appeal in *Re Allen*[3]. [And, following the decision of the Court of Appeal, he said in relation to conditions precedent:] ... unless the condition is such that it is clearly impossible for anyone to qualify or unless it is such that it would obviously be impossible for the court in any instance to answer the inquiry whether a particular claimant qualified, I think the condition must pass the test of certainty.'

He next reviewed the circumstances of doubt and difficulty which may arise when the question to be considered is whether a person is or is not of the Jewish faith, and said[4]:

'... I am bound to take the view that this is a sufficiently defined concept to make it clear that in many instances the court would have no difficulty in saying one way or another whether a particular person was or was not of the Jewish faith. The phrase is not, as counsel for the second defendant suggested, a meaningless phrase. It has a sufficiently definite and intelligible meaning.'

He concluded by referring to certain other authorities which had been cited to him, in particular *Re Wolffe's Will Trusts*[5], a case before Harman J, which was cited before me but which I do not think I need separately consider. *Re Selby's Will Trusts*[6] was a case in which of course no express provision had been made to deal with matters of doubt or difficulty, and it was a case dealing with questions of faith rather than race.

I must turn next to *Re Tarnpolsk*[7], a case before Danckwerts J, in which he considered the decision of the Court of Appeal in *Re Allen*[3], but applied the principles enun-ciated by Lord Romer in *Clayton v Ramsden*[8] in these circumstances. He was con-sidering a will in which the testator made a bequest to his grandchildren on their marriage, which he defined as meaning a marriage according to the rites of the Jewish faith with a person of Jewish race and religion, and what Danckwerts J held was that it was impossible to give sufficient meaning to the phrase 'a person of the Jewish race' so as to be able to say in any given case whether the condition had been fulfilled, and that

1   [1943] 1 All ER 16, [1943] AC 320
2   [1965] 3 All ER at 389, 391, [1966] 1 WLR at 47, 49
3   [1953] 2 All ER 898, [1953] Ch 810
4   [1965] 3 All ER at 391, [1966] 1 WLR at 50
5   [1953] 2 All ER 697, [1953] 1 WLR 1211
6   [1965] 3 All ER 386, [1966] 1 WLR 43
7   [1958] 3 All ER 479, [1958] 1 WLR 1157
8   [1943] 1 All ER at 22, [1943] AC at 333

the difficulty was exactly the same if the condition was a condition precedent, as it
a would be if it were a condition subsequent, and that accordingly the bequests were
void for uncertainty.

Commenting on the conclusion of the Court of Appeal that the fact that it may
be difficult to say of some persons whether they are or are not members of the
Church of England does not of necessity make it impossible for some particular
person to establish this fact, Danckwerts J observed[1]:

b

> 'In my view the qualification laid down by the Court of Appeal in *Re Allen*[2]
> is to be considered with regard to the words "of necessity". In the present case
> there seems to me to be a difficulty which renders it impossible for a possible
> candidate to show with reasonable certainty that he satisfies the test which
> the testator has attempted to lay down. It seems to me that "religion" and "faith"
> are interchangeable words, but that the words which cause a difficulty here
c > are "a person of Jewish race". I find great difficulty in seeing what exactly
> "a person of Jewish race" means. The passage in the speech of LORD ROMER in
> *Clayton* v. *Ramsden*[3] shows the difficulties with which anybody is faced in
> trying to decide whether that qualification has been met.'

He then cited the passage from the speech of Lord Romer, which I have already
d cited, and, observing that *Clayton v Ramsden*[4] was a case of a condition subsequent,
he continued[5]:

> '... it seems to me that the same difficulties apply where there is a qualific-
> ation and one cannot say what the qualification is. It was a difficulty to which
> I referred in my decision in *Re Sonn*[6], and it is the difficulty which was apparent
e > to HARMAN, J., in *Re Wolffe's Will Trusts, Shapley* v. *Wolffe*[7]. Since one cannot
> give sufficient meaning to the words used by the testator to say that here is
> a qualification which in any given case has been fulfilled, the result must be,
> in my view, that the qualification is void and that nobody can satisfy the terms
> of the gift ...'

f The result of this dual standard can be seen by referring to *Re Abrahams' Will Trust*[8],
which came before Cross J. He had to consider a case in which by cl 17 of the testator's
will his son might secure a benefit in the event of his becoming engaged to marry
'a person professing the Jewish faith', while by cl 18 marriage to a person not professing the Jewish faith could involve a forfeiture. Cross J held cl 18 was bad for uncertainty, being a condition subsequent, divesting the son of his interest in the
g residuary estate. At the same time, he upheld cl 17, the condition being, as he observed, sufficiently definite to pass the test appropriate to be applied to conditions
precedent. After referring to *Clayton v Ramsden*[4], *Re Wolffe*[7] and *Re Allen*[2],
Cross J observed, and I quote his words[9]: '*Re Tarnpolsk (decd.), Barclays Bank, Ltd.* v.
Hyer[10] turned on the words "a person of the Jewish race", which may perhaps raise
different considerations.' And he concluded by following in relation to the question
h of faith the decision of Buckley J in *Re Selby's Will Trusts*[11].

---

1   [1958] 3 All ER at 481, [1958] 1 WLR at 1159
2   [1953] 2 All ER 898, [1953] Ch 810
3   [1943] 1 All ER at 22, [1943] AC at 333
4   [1943] 1 All ER 16, [1943] AC 320
j 5   [1958] 3 All ER at 481, [1958] 1 WLR at 1160
6   (16th October 1958) unreported
7   [1953] 2 All ER 697, [1953] 1 WLR 1211
8   [1967] 2 All ER 1175, [1969] 1 Ch 463
9   [1967] 2 All ER at 1182, [1969] 1 Ch at 472
10 [1958] 3 All ER 479, [1958] 1 WLR 1157
11 [1965] 3 All ER 386, [1966] 1 WLR 43

The weight of counsel for the fifth to eighth defendants' argument was undoubtedly centred on the uncertainty attaching to the words 'a wife of Jewish blood'. He *a* naturally relied on the speeches in the House of Lords in *Clayton v Ramsden*[1], and on the decision of Danckwerts J in *Re Tarnpolsk*[2]. He argued that in this case, as in those two earlier cases, it was quite impossible to know what the settlor meant when he talked about 'a wife of Jewish blood'. He said that no touchstone had been provided which would resolve the ambiguities inherent in a reference to a wife of Jewish blood by one or both parents. If the question were, as Lord Wright and *b* Lord Romer suggested in *Clayton v Ramsden*[1], how much Jewish blood—the degree of racial purity requisite to the satisfaction of the condition—how could the court or any other interested person resolve their doubts, for the words alone do not enable a definite answer to be given. I would agree with this submission if the words stood alone, even in relation to a condition precedent, and so far as a question of Jewish blood is concerned, it might then have been necessary for me to conclude *c* that this particular condition was so uncertain as to support neither a qualification nor a disqualification. However, the words 'of Jewish blood' do not, to my mind, involve any conceptual difficulty in themselves. What is intended by 'Jewish blood' is to my mind quite plainly this, that one has to look to see the racial descent. When the settlor speaks of a person 'of Jewish blood', he speaks of a person who is a member of that group, now spread throughout the world, who are descended from the *d* ancient Jewish people, and whose religion is Judaism.

But above all, of course, there is the difference, to which I have already referred on more than one occasion, between this condition and the conditions to be found in the earlier cases, that the settlor has made some specific provision for resolution of instances of doubt or difficulty. That in itself raises the question whether in fact the settlor can properly provide for the resolution of questions of doubt or difficulty *e* in this way, or whether it might amount to an ouster of the jurisdiction of the court.

I was referred to a number of cases, and I would turn briefly to *Re Coxen*[3], a case which came before Jenkins J. It was a case of a devise by a testator of a dwelling-house to trustees, and there was a direction that his wife should be permitted to reside there during her life, or for so long as she should desire to reside therein, and there was a declaration that from and after her death, if in the opinion of the trustees she should *f* have ceased permanently to reside therein, the house should fall into the residuary trust. Jenkins J held that this provision for the termination of the wife's interest was sufficiently defined to enable the trustees to come to a proper decision, and that it was a valid limitation on the gift in question. He observed[4]:

> 'If the testator had insufficiently defined the state of affairs on which the trustees
> were to form their opinion, he would not, I think, have saved the condition *g*
> from invalidity on the ground of uncertainty merely by making their opinion the
> criterion, although the declaration by the trustees of this or that opinion would
> be an event about which in itself there could be no uncertainty, but, as I have
> already indicated, I think the relevant double event is sufficiently defined to
> make it perfectly possible for the trustees (as the judges of fact for this purpose)
> to decide whether it has happened or not, and, in my view, the testator, by *h*
> making the trustees' opinion the criterion, has removed the difficulties which
> might otherwise have ensured from a gift over in a double event the happening
> of which, though in itself sufficiently defined, may necessarily be a matter of
> inference involving nice questions of fact and degree.'

In the settlement I have to consider, the question whether a wife is a wife of Jewish *j* blood does not, as I have already said, seem to me to be a meaningless question.

1 [1943] 1 All ER 16, [1943] AC 320
2 [1958] 3 All ER 479, [1958] 1 WLR 1157
3 [1948] 2 All ER 492, [1948] 1 Ch 747
4 [1948] 2 All ER at 502, [1948] 1 Ch at 761

a The settlor himself considered it to be a question of fact on which there might be
differences of opinion. He provided for a reference to resolve doubts and difficulties.
Although it was urged on me that this escape from what might otherwise be a dilemma was not open, because it would amount to an ouster of the jurisdiction of the
court, I am in no sense convinced by this argument.

I was referred to some well-known authorities: Re Raven[1]; and Re Wynn's Will
Trusts[2], which was a case following Re Raven[1] in which Danckwerts J held that a
b clause in a will referring the determination of all questions and matters of doubt
in the execution of certain trusts to the trustees was void on the ground that it ousted
the courts' jurisdiction to construe the will and to control the administration of the
estate. I do not consider that the entrusting by the settlor of any decision on Jewish
blood to rabbinical authority can properly be considered an ouster of the jurisdiction
of the court. The question of construction appears to me to present no difficulty.
c Jewish blood is a question merely of degree. Questions of degree are questions
which have been submitted for determination to an authority which the settlor
thought appropriate, and I see no reason to differ from his view.

Finally, on this aspect of the case, counsel for the fifth to eighth defendants argued
that the decision in Re Allen[3] is inconsistent with a later decision in Re Gulbenkian's
Settlement Trusts[4], which was a case concerned with powers. In the light of
d the observations in the speeches of their Lordships in Re Gulbenkian's Settlement Trusts[4],
it is the submission of counsel for the fifth to eighth defendants that it is no
longer possible to say that the distinction made in Re Allen[3] between uncertainty
for the purposes of qualification as compared with disqualification is valid. That
submission, in my view, cannot stand in the face of the even more recent decision of
the House of Lords in Blathwayt v Lord Cawley[5]. To my mind it has been made
e quite plain by their Lordships that a greater degree of certainty is required to support
a condition subsequent. There is express recognition of this fact.

As I have said, the weight of the case against these conditions, insofar as they constitute conditions precedent, was undoubtedly directed against the question of
'Jewish blood' or 'Jewish race'. No emphasis was really laid on any question of uncertainty attaching to faith, and on the authorities it is quite plain that this kind of
f attack, insofar as it is related to any conditions which are merely qualifying conditions, must fail. As I have already said, I am quite satisfied on the terms of this
settlement that there is no sufficient uncertainty in relation to any of the qualifying
conditions, and I turn accordingly to cl 3(e).

So far as cl 3(e) is concerned, I find no uncertainty attaching to conditions (2), (3) and (4)
of this paragraph, regarding them, as in part they undoubtedly are, as conditions
g of forfeiture. This is because, in my view, and I have already I hope made it plain,
there can never be any doubt or difficulty over the question whether any given wife
is an approved wife; the rabbis decide. Nor can there be any doubt or difficulty
whether on a separation the baronet is at fault. In this latter case, the certificate
is no doubt always essential, probably because in the former case, where the question
is whether or not a wife qualifies as an approved wife, there is frequently likely to
h be no question of doubt or difficulty arising. There appears to have been no such
doubt or difficulty in anybody's mind when the third baronet married for the first
time. Condition (2) provides no difficulty, and is in any event a question of qualification. Condition (1) is possibly at first sight not quite so simple. No separate
argument, however, was directed to this particular condition. A pervert in this
context must mean one who has turned away from the Jewish faith. I cannot see

j

---

1 [1915] 1 Ch 673, [1914-15] All ER Rep 353
2 [1952] 1 All ER 341, [1952] Ch 271
3 [1953] 2 All ER 898, [1953] Ch 810
4 [1968] 3 All ER 785, [1970] AC 508
5 [1975] 3 All ER 625, [1975] 3 WLR 684

that there can be any real uncertainty as to this. The trustees can ask the baronet
in question if they have grounds for so doing, or make such other enquiries as may *a*
be requisite. It may be troublesome, but the fact that it may be difficult to establish
a question of this kind cannot, to my mind, mean that there can be any uncertainty
in relation to any given individual whether or not he is a pervert from his faith.

In my opinion, on the true construction of the settlement, in case of doubt the
opinion of one or other of the chief rabbis mentioned in cl 1(e) is conclusive on all
the issues raised in question 1 of the summons, and the provision under which these *b*
issues are to be submitted to the opinion of a chief rabbi is not invalid as involving
an exclusion of the jurisdiction of the court, but is a valid provision.

So far as the remaining questions relating to cl 3(b), (c), (d) and (e), and cll 4 and 6
are concerned, these are, in my view, all valid. None is void for uncertainty, and I
propose so to declare.

c

Order accordingly.

Solicitors: *Cameron, Kemm, Nordon & Co* (for the Public Trustee and the seventh
defendant); *Nabarro, Nathanson* (for the first, second and ninth defendants); *E P Rugg
& Co* (for the third and fourth defendants); *Waterhouse & Co* (for the fifth defendant);
Coward Chance (for the sixth defendant); *Allen & Overy* (for the eighth defendant);
Treasury Solicitor. *d*

Evelyn M C Budd Barrister.

Anderson and others v Bostock

e

CHANCERY DIVISION AT MANCHESTER
BLACKETT-ORD V-C
4th, 5th, 6th, 7th, 10th, 11th, 12th JUNE 1975

*Profit à prendre – Extent of profit à prendre – Profit appurtenant – Extent of right related
to nature of dominant tenement – Profit unlimited in scope – Express grant – Right of
pasture – Sheep rights – Right to graze unlimited as to number of sheep and period of* *f*
*grazing – Right in severalty appurtenant to dominant tenement created by express grant –
Whether right capable of subsisting as a profit appurtenant.*

The plaintiff was, from 1941, the tenant of a small farm and the agricultural tenant
of an enclosed piece of ground ('the moor') adjoining the farm on which he grazed
his sheep. In 1948 the owner of both the farm and the moor sold them to separate
purchasers. The farm was conveyed to E Ltd with 'the exclusive right of grazing *g*
over' the moor; the conveyance of the moor on the same date was expressed to be
'subject to the exclusive rights of grazing to the owners' of the farm. Subsequent
conveyances of the farm referred to those rights. In 1959 the farm was conveyed
to the plaintiff; although it contained no express reference to the right of grazing,
he continued to pay an annual sum 'as compensation for the grazing'. The defendant
bought the moor subject to the exclusive grazing rights, but refused to recognise *f*
them. The plaintiff brought an action claiming a declaration that the rights had,
by virtue of s 62 of the Law of Property Act 1925, vested in him.

Held – An exclusive right to grazing without limit could not exist as appurtenant
to another property. An appurtenant right had to be related to the needs or use
of the dominant tenement and an exclusive unlimited right was unknown to the
law. That was so whether the right was claimed by express grant or by prescription,
since prescription was based on the fiction of a grant. Accordingly, the plaintiff's
claim would be dismissed (see p 563 *a*, p 564 *d* and p 565 *c* and *g*, post).

Harris v Earl of Chesterfield [1911] AC 623 and *Staffordshire and Worcestershire Canal
Navigation v Bradley* [1912] 1 Ch 91 applied.

Notes

a For limits on profits à prendre appurtenant to another property, see 14 Halsbury's Laws (4th Edn) paras 247, 249, and for cases on the subject, see 19 Digest (Repl) 224, 225, 1650-1659.

For the Law of Property Act 1925, s 62, see 27 Halsbury's Statutes (3rd Edn) 438.

Cases referred to in judgment

b *Bailey v Stephens* (1862) 12 CBNS 91, 31 LJCP 226, 6 LT 356, 8 Jur NS 1063, 142 ER 1077, 19 Digest (Repl) 218, 1604.

Chesterfield (Lord) v Harris [1908] 2 Ch 397, 77 LJCh 688, 99 LT 558, CA; *affd* sub nom *Harris v Earl of Chesterfield* [1911] AC 623, HL, 19 Digest (Repl) 216, 1581.

Staffordshire and Worcestershire Canal Navigation v Bradley [1912] 1 Ch 91, 81 LJCh 147, 106 LT 215, 75 JP 555, 46 Digest (Repl) 386, 286.

c *White v Taylor (No 2)* [1968] 1 All ER 1015, [1969] 1 Ch 160, [1968] 2 WLR 1402, 19 P & CR 412, Digest (Cont Vol C) 128, 527a.

White v Williams [1922] 1 KB 727, [1922] All ER Rep 419, 91 LJKB 721, 127 LT 231, CA, 19 Digest (Repl) 215, 1580.

Action

By writ issued on 19th March 1971 the plaintiffs, (1) Matthew Anderson, (2) John d Samuel Learoyd and (3) Constance Learoyd, claimed a declaration that exclusive grazing rights over Eavestone Moor in the West Riding of Yorkshire, the property of the defendant, Godfrey Stafford Bostock, had been annexed to Smaden Head Farm by a conveyance dated 15th December 1948 and had passed by express transfer to the predecessors in title of the first plaintiff under conveyances dated 11th February 1953, 29th June 1953 and 5th April 1955, or in the alternative that those rights had be-e come vested in the successive owners of Smaden Head Farm by virtue of s 62 of the Law of Property Act 1925 as if they had been expressly conveyed, and had been passed by the first plaintiff to the second and third plaintiffs by an agreement dated 3rd June 1967 for sale of Smaden Head Farm. The facts are set out in the judgment.

Ian McCulloch and *Jonathan Leslie* for the plaintiffs.
George Newsom QC and *Robert Wakefield* for the defendant.
f

BLACKETT-ORD V-C. In this case the first plaintiff was, from 1941, the tenant of Smaden Head Farm, between Pateley Bridge and Ripon on the edge of the Pennines, which seems to be a small farm of about 100 acres, and he was also the agricultural tenant of Eavestone Moor, an enclosed piece of ground of about 500 acres adjoining the farm. He bought the farm as sitting tenant in 1959, and he claims to have acquired g with it the exclusive right of grazing on the moor in perpetuity. In 1967 he sold the farm and the grazing, if he had it, to the second and third plaintiffs, and part of the purchase money has, apparently, been retained pending the decision in this case. The defendant owns the freehold of the moor, and he denies the right which the first and second plaintiffs claim of grazing over it.

There were two conveyances, both dated 15th December 1948, whereby the former h owner of both the farm and the moor sold them off. The farm was conveyed to Eavestone Estate Co Ltd, and, I quote from the citation in the statement of claim, 'The exclusive right of grazing over Eavestone Moor is conveyed with the Smaden Head Farm'. These words were included in a schedule to that conveyance of rights conveyed. It was a conveyance of a large number of farms and was not the most elegant of documents, but clearly the intention was expressed of passing to the pur-j chaser thereunder of the farm the exclusive right of grazing over the moor, and it was conveyed with the farm. And, conversely, in the other conveyance of the same date the moor was conveyed to Studley Estate Co Ltd, and in a schedule to that conveyance it was stated, again I quote from the statement of claim, 'Eavestone Moor is conveyed subject to the exclusive rights of grazing to the owners of Smaden Head Farm'.

Subsequently there were a number of conveyances of the farm, until eventually

it reached the first plaintiff, as I have said, in 1959. The various conveyances began
by containing express references to the rights in the 1948 conveyance, but the actual
conveyance to the first plaintiff does not contain anything which can be construed
as an express reference to the grazing right purported to be granted in 1948, and he
has to rely on s 62 of the Law of Property Act 1925.

The relief which he seeks is stated in the end of the statement of claim as follows.
He (and, of course, the second plaintiff) seek—

'A declaration that the exclusive grazing rights over Eavestone Moor (formerly
part of the Grantley Hall Estate lying between Ripon and Pateley Bridge in
the West Riding of the County of York) and comprising 517.838 acres or thereabouts became, by virtue of the conveyance in paragraph 3 of the Statement of
Claim referred to [i e the conveyance of the farm to Eavestone Estate Co Ltd of
15th December 1948] annexed in perpetuity to the fee simple of Smaden Head
Farm ... and that the said grazing rights are now vested in the Plaintiff
Matthew Anderson or in the alternative in the Plaintiffs John Samuel
Learoyd and Constance Learoyd.'

Now the right claimed is a valuable one. The farm itself is not very large. The
first plaintiff said in evidence that in 1941, owing to its state, he did not think it was
enough to provide him with a living, and he would not take it without the moor.
On the moor he built up a flock of up to 140 ewes, and in addition he used to take
300 or 400 sheep for three months in the winter, and something like 300 ewes for
a month or two in the summer. But nevertheless there is no mention of this right
of grazing in his contract to purchase or in the conveyance to him; and he certainly
did not expect to get it free, because after he bought the farm, he continued to pay
£38 a year, which he called 'compensation for the grazing'. On the other hand,
the defendant's title contains the 1948 conveyance to the Studley Estate Co Ltd,
which expressly excluded the grazing. And so, between the parties, I think the merits
can be said to be equal.

I think it is clear that an appurtenant right of grazing can pass under s 62 of the
Law of Property Act 1925. If authority is required for that, it is provided by *White v
Williams*[1]. But, of course, the right only passes if it is a valid appurtenant right.
The validity of the right was accepted by the Court of Appeal in *White v Williams*[1],
though the contrary seems to have been argued. The facts are not very fully set
out, but the position seems to have been that a farm was sold with rights of
sheepwalk appurtenant to it. Atkin LJ said[2]:

'In my view if the common predecessor in title was the unrestricted owner
in fee simple both of the farm and of the land over which this right of pasture
is claimed, and if there were no common or quasi-common rights over the land,
so that the right which he in fact exercised of depasturing sheep upon the land
was included in his rights as owner in fee simple of both the farm and the land,
the general words in s. 6[3] [of the Conveyancing Act 1881] would still be sufficient
to pass to the purchaser of the farm the right of depasturing sheep upon the
land. Such a right is a right well known to the law and quite capable of being
granted when a hereditament is severed. I think that is enough to dispose of
this case.'

But he did not there go into the question of the limit, if any, on the right, and I do
not regard that case as helping me very much in the present one. Because in the
present case the right claimed as appurtenant to the farm is expressly claimed as
being exclusive, and the case has been put on the footing that it is without limit;
that is to say, it is not a mere customary right of sheepwalk, but a right unlimited

1   [1922] 1 KB 727, [1922] All ER Rep 419
2   [1922] 1 KB at 738, [1922] All ER Rep at 423
3   Now s 62 of the Law of Property Act 1925

as to the type of stock, as to the number of stock and as to the period of grazing. But nevertheless it is said to be appurtenant to the farm and not in gross.

The defendant says that an appurtenant right of this kind is unknown to the law, and I agree with him. The leading case, I think, is *Harris v Chesterfield*[1]. In effect, the House of Lords, by a majority, confirmed and adopted the judgment in the Court of Appeal, but I think the headnote[2] of the case in the House of Lords is perhaps clearer, and I propose to read that. It says:

> 'A prescription in a que estate for a profit à prendre in alieno solo without stint and for commercial purposes is unknown to the law. Freeholders in parishes adjoining the river Wye had been in the habit of fishing a non-tidal portion of the river for centuries, not by stealth or indulgence, but openly, continuously, as of right and without interruption, not merely for sport or pleasure, but commercially, in order to sell the fish and make a living by it. Riparian proprietors claiming to be owners of the bed of the river brought an action of trespass against the freeholders for fishing:—*Held* by the Earl of Halsbury and Lords Macnaghten, Gorell, and Kinnear, that a legal origin for the right claimed by the freeholders could not be presumed, and that the action lay.'

The decision of the Court of Appeal is summarised in a passage from the judgment of Buckley LJ[3]:

> 'I rest my judgment upon the proposition which I think is sound in law, that one cannot prescribe in a que estate for a commercial profit à prendre in alieno solo; it must be for a profit à prendre measured by the nature, size and necessities of the estate. A prescription in a que estate for a profit to be taken without limit, not with reference to the wants of the estate, but commercially for purposes of sale, is unknown to the law. That is the right which the defendants here claim. It is, I think, impossible in law and cannot be maintained.'

Buckley LJ says: '[The right] is, I think, impossible in law and cannot be maintained', and although he is referring initially to prescription, there is at least a hint there that he is not confining himself to that method of creation of the right; and Cozens-Hardy MR put the matter rather more clearly when he said[4]:

> 'Apart from authorities, the very idea of a que estate seems to involve some relation between the needs of the estate or its owner and the extent of the profit à prendre. A right in an indefinite number of people to take a profit à prendre without stint and for sale must tend to the entire destruction of the property.'

He also referred to the earlier case of *Bailey v Stephens*[5], and he said about that[6]:

> 'In *Bailey v. Stephens*[5] a claim of a prescriptive right in the owners of close A to enter close B and to cut down and carry away and convert to their own use all the trees and wood growing and being thereon was held void. The judgments are a mine of learning. Erle C.J. pointed out that it was a claim of a right appurtenant to the land of the defendant to take all the profits of the land of the plaintiff wholly unconnected with the defendant's land, and to take that as passing with the land; and, again, that it was a claim to cut down the trees and to sell and dispose of them at pleasure, wholly irrespective of the land of the defendant. He pointed out the vital distinction between a grant in gross

1 [1911] AC 623, HL; *affg* [1908] 2 Ch 397, CA
2 [1911] AC at 623
3 [1908] 2 Ch at 424
4 [1908] 2 Ch at 410
5 (1862) 12 CBNS 91
6 [1908] 2 Ch at 411, 412

to a man and his heirs and a grant to a man and all who may thereafter own a close. Willes J. was very clear in his language[1]: "With reference to the first plea, which sets up a prescriptive right, it amounts to this, that, before the time of legal memory, some one made a grant to some one else, whereby the occupiers of the defendant's close for the time being, ad infinitum, were to be entitled to cut all the trees growing in the close of which the plaintiff was in possession at the time the trespass was committed. The simple answer to that, is, that it is not an incident which can be annexed by law to the ownership, much less to the occupation of the land." Byles J. points out that a profit à prendre cannot go to assigns unless it is connected with the enjoyment of the dominant tenement or has some natural connection with it, and he adds[2]: "Such a claim of prescription as this is very absurd. That being so, it is unreasonable; and it is laid down that prescriptions must be reasonable. It is not enough to say it is possible to be granted. Even if this could by law be granted, I think it falls within the objection to a prescription, that it is unreasonable, and not only *ought not* to be inferred by a jury, but *cannot* be inferred in point of law, when such a right is claimed." '

And the principle, by which I mean that a prescription for a que estate in a profit à prendre without stint and for commercial purposes is unknown to the law, was applied by Eve J in *Staffordshire and Worcestershire Canal Navigation v Bradley*[3]. The headnote reads as follows[4]:

'Under an Act of 6 Geo. 3, c.xcvii[5], authorizing the construction of a canal there was granted (by s. 74) to each owner of land through which the canal was made the sole, several, and exclusive right of fishing in so much of the canal as was made in, over, or through the land; but the right of fishery thereby granted was to be exercised so that the canal, towing paths, banks and other works should not be prejudiced or obstructed. Under a deed of March 31, 1845, a certain manor and estate through which the canal passed became vested in the Earl of S.; there was no express grant of this particular right of fishery, but there were general words in the deed passing all fisheries, profits, advantages, and appurtenances whatsoever to the manor and estate respectively belonging, or in anywise appertaining. By a lease of July 23, 1910, the Earl of S. granted to an angling club, of which the defendant was a member, the exclusive right to fish for and take away all fish in a specified portion of the canal, at an annual rent, and the lessees covenanted so to exercise their rights as not to prejudice or obstruct the towing paths, banks, and other works of the canal. The plaintiffs having brought an action to test a claim by the defendant to fish in the canal from the towing path, without their consent:—*Held*, (1.) that, having regard to all the circumstances, s. 74 of the Act conferred upon the grantees of the exclusive fishery a right to use the towing paths and banks of the canal for the excercise of that right. But *held*, (2.) that the right, being one to take fish without stint, and without any relation to the needs of the land in respect of which the right was granted, was not a right appurtenant, or capable of being made appurtenant, to the land, but a right in gross, and not capable of passing under the general words of the deed of March 31, 1845. *Earl of Chesterfield* v. *Harris*[6] applied.'

I need not, I think, read any more.

Counsel for the plaintiffs says that this principle does not apply to an express grant of an appurtenant right, such as we have in the relevant 1948 conveyance. He says,

1   (1862) 12 CBNS at 110
2   (1862) 12 CBNS at 115
3   [1912] 1 Ch 91
4   [1912] 1 Ch at 91
5   Staffordshire and Worcestershire Canal Act 1766
6   [1911] AC 623

with justification, that the intention is perfectly clear, that the deed was made between competent parties, and that therefore it does not matter if it is reasonable or not; although I think he also said that it can be controlled by the law of trespass, and if that is so, I am not quite clear how unreasonable it can be before the law of trespass interposes. But, in my judgment, an appurtenant right must be related to the needs or use of the dominant tenement. For this reason an exclusive right to grazing, or taking timber, or fishing, without limit cannot exist as appurtenant to another property. It is a right unknown to the law. As regards prescription, that itself is, of course, based on the fiction of a grant. The matter is well put in a quotation from Comyns' Digest, which was quoted, I see, by counsel for the defendant in his argument in *Bailey v Stephens*[1], where it is said[2]:

'A prescription by immemorial usage can in general only be for things which may be created by grant; for, the law allows prescriptions only to supply the loss of a grant.'

So I hold that for present purposes there is no distinction between prescription and grant, so that the decision in *Harris v Chesterfield*[3] applies to the present case.

Counsel for the plaintiffs, however, says that the principle may apply to preclude a right in common, but it does not apply in the present case where the grant is of a several right to one person for one property only; because in such a case, he says, the servient owner is protected by the law of trespass and can sue if the right is exercised to excess.

I have suggested one objection to that already. Moreover, I do not see why, if the servient owner can be protected by the law of trespass against one owner of grazing rights, he could not also be protected against several owners, as in the case of a common. And if the dominant tenement were to be divided up, then that would in fact be the situation, as I see it, which would be produced: see the observations of Buckley J in *White v Taylor*[4], the case referred to by counsel for the plaintiffs. I only quote one paragraph in it on this subject, where Buckley J said[5]:

'I have been referred to authorities which in my judgment clearly establish that where a right of common of pasture is appurtenant to an hereditament the ownership of which is severed, the right of common is severable so that the right of common may appertain partly to one section of the severed hereditament and partly to another [and he referred to cases].'

That would appear to apply in the present case. I appreciate that the existing right is not one of common unless the dominant tenement were to be severed.

So for these reasons, in my judgment, an exclusive right of grazing without limit appurtenant to the farm—and I am not, of course, concerned with rights in gross— is unknown to the law and cannot have become vested in the plaintiffs. The action is accordingly dismissed with costs.

Action dismissed.

Solicitors: *Eccles, Heddon and Young*, Ripon (for the plaintiffs); *Atkinson, Dacre and Slack*, Otley (for the defendant).

M Denise Chorlton   Barrister.

1   (1862) 12 CBNS at 100
2   Volume 3, title 31, Prescription, ch 1, para 11
3   [1911] AC 623
4   [1968] 1 All ER 1015, [1969] 1 Ch 160
5   [1968] 1 All ER at 1031, [1969] 1 Ch at 189

R v National Insurance Commissioner, ex parte Michael

QUEEN'S BENCH DIVISION
LORD WIDGERY CJ, PARK AND MAY JJ
3rd, 19th DECEMBER 1975

Industrial injury – Disablement benefit – Entitlement – Accident arising out of and in course of employment – Activity out of which accident arose reasonably incidental to employment – Recreational activities – Employee expected to take part in activities but under no duty to do so – Police constable injured in football match – Football match organised by Police Athletic Association – Constable representing his force in match – Match played during constable's off-duty time – Whether injury 'arising out of and in the course of his employment' – National Insurance (Industrial Injuries) Act 1965, s 5(1).

The applicant was a police officer. The Police Athletic Association arranged a cup competition between teams representing different police forces. Although police officers could not be compelled to play in those games, nor be disciplined if they refused to do so, refusal to play was viewed with displeasure. The standing orders of the applicant's local constabulary allowed players time off duty to participate in sport where they were representing their force, on the understanding that they would use their free time when necessary to play in a match. The applicant played in a cup match against another police force, when he was off-duty, and was injured. He claimed industrial injury benefit under s 5(1)[a] of the National Insurance (Industrial Injuries) Act 1965. The case came before the National Insurance Commissioner who found that the applicant's participation in the football match was not something reasonably incidental to his employment as a police officer. In a subsequent passage of his decision he stated: '. . . the playing of football, and indeed any other game, is a recreational activity and is not something done in the course of a police officer's employment and therefore cannot be held to be reasonably incidental to the employment'. The commissioner concluded that the accident was not one which had arisen out of and in the course of the applicant's employment, within s 5(1) of the 1965 Act, and that he was not therefore entitled to benefit. The applicant applied for an order of certiorari to quash the commissioner's decision.

Held – If the commissioner's decision had been based on the proposition that nothing which happened in the course of activities which were recreational and not part of a police officer's duties could be said to arise out of and in the course of his employment, it would have been erroneous in law. Reading the decision as a whole, however, it was clear that it was not based on that erroneous dichotomy. The commissioner had considered all the evidence and applied his mind to the right issue, namely whether the applicant's participation in the football match had been reasonably incidental to his employment as a police officer, and on the facts it was open to him to come to the conclusion that it was not. Accordingly the application would be dismissed (see p 569 d to p 570 d, post).

Dicta of Lord Denning MR in *R v Industrial Injuries Comr, ex parte Amalgamated Engineering Union (No 2)* [1966] 1 All ER at 104 applied.

---

a   Section 5(1), so far as material, provides: 'Subject to the provisions of this Act, where an insured person suffers personal injury caused . . . by accident arising out of and in the course of his employment, being insurable employment, then—(a) industrial injury benefit . . . shall be payable to the insured person if during such period . . . he is, as the result of the injury, incapable of work . . .'

Notes
a For entitlement to benefit, see 27 Halsbury's Laws (3rd Edn) 820-822, paras 1445, 1446.

For the National Insurance (Industrial Injuries) Act 1965, s 5, see 23 Halsbury's Statutes (3rd Edn) 490.

As from 6th April 1975, s 5(1) of the 1965 Act has been replaced by the Social Security Act 1975, s 50(1).
b

Case referred to in judgments
R v Industrial Injuries Comr, ex parte Amalgamated Engineering Union (No 2) [1966] 1 All ER 97, [1966] 2 QB 21, [1966] 2 WLR 97, CA, Digest (Cont Vol B), 216, *3768a*.

Case also cited
c *Fordsham's Case* (4th April 1973 unreported), decision CI 7/73.

Application for certiorari
This was an application by way of motion by Jeffrey Lyn Michael, a police constable in the Gwent Constabulary, for an order of certiorari to bring up and quash a decision of the National Insurance Commissioner (J S Watson Esq MBE QC) dated 18th
d December 1974 whereby he allowed an appeal by an insurance officer against a decision of the local tribunal sitting at Newport, Gwent, that the injury suffered by the applicant on 26th September 1973 had not been caused by an accident arising out of and in the course of his employment within s 5(1) of the National Insurance (Industrial Injuries) Act 1965 and that the applicant, therefore, was not entitled to injury benefit. The facts are set out in the judgment of May J.
e

Brian Neill QC and *David Eady* for the applicant.
Harry Woolf for the insurance officer.

Cur adv vult

19th December. **MAY J** read the first judgment at the invitation of Lord
f Widgery CJ. In this case counsel moves on behalf of the applicant for an order of certiorari to remove into this court in order that it may be quashed a decision of the National Insurance Commissioner of 18th December 1974 that an injury sustained by the applicant on 26th September 1973 was not caused by an accident arising out of and in the course of his employment within the terms of what was then s 5(1) of the National Insurance (Industrial Injuries) Act 1965. The relevant statutory provision
g is now s 50 of the Social Security Act 1975.

Since 1969 the applicant has been a police constable. He joined the Gwent Constabulary in September 1972. He is a player of association football. As I can well understand, members not only of the Gwent Constabulary but also of other police forces who possess athletic skills are expected to take part in sports and games organised by their force. Insofar as association football is concerned, not only are
h games organised within a given force but also, under the auspices of the Police Athletic Association, there is a cup competition and matches take place between teams representing different forces. The evidence before the commissioner was that although police officers could not be compelled to participate, nor would they be disciplined if they refused to play or did not turn out for a match, this conduct would nevertheless be viewed with displeasure. A police officer might decline to participate in police
j sports and games if he preferred not to, but, if he possessed prowess in a particular game or sport, he might not be very popular in police circles.

The material part of the Gwent Constabulary Standing Orders, which were before the commissioner, provides that time off duty for participation in sport will be allowed where an officer is representing his force in a match, up to a limit of eight hours in any month, on the understanding that if he is selected to play in a match which will take place in his off-duty time, then he will for his part play in such match and use so much of his free time as is necessary.

It was against this background that the applicant was selected to play for the Gwent Constabulary in a match against the Dorset and Bournemouth Constabulary which took place on 26th September 1973. It so happened that that was during the applicant's off-duty time. In the course of playing in that match the applicant sustained an injury to his left leg which has proved to be more serious than was at first thought, though the precise details of it are not before this court and indeed are immaterial for present purposes.

In the circumstances I have outlined, the applicant contended that the accident and consequent injury sustained by him on 25th September 1973 arose out of and in the course of his employment and that consequently he was entitled to industrial injury benefit in respect thereof under s 5(1) of the 1965 Act. The local insurance officer decided that the accident was not an industrial one, because in his view it had not arisen out of and in the course of the applicant's employment. The applicant appealed to the local tribunal, which took a different view from the local insurance officer, decided that the accident had been an industrial accident, had arisen out of and in the course of the applicant's employment and consequently that he was entitled to industrial benefit. Finally, the local insurance officer appealed against that decision of the local tribunal to the National Insurance Commissioner who, in his turn, took the same view as the local insurance officer and allowed the latter's appeal. It is this decision of the commissioner that it is now sought to have removed into this court in order that it may be quashed on the basis that the decision on its face shows a clear error of law.

The question for the commissioner was the same as it had been for the local insurance officer and the local tribunal, namely: did the accident to the applicant on 26th September 1973 arise out of and in the course of the applicant's employment? We were told that this is not the first time that this question has had to be decided in connection with a police constable on appeal to one of the commissioners in circumstances very similar to the present case. We were also told that on very similar facts different commissioners have answered the basic question differently. In these circumstances counsel for the applicant suggested it would be of great assistance not only to the Police Federation who have to advise their members on these matters, but also to the commissioners, to receive some guidance from this court about how the basic question should be answered in cases of the present kind.

Nevertheless, whilst I would wish to be as helpful as I could be in such circumstances, it is quite clear on many authorities which need not be specifically cited that a particular act of a servant or a particular accident in which he becomes involved will in law be considered to arise out of and in the course of his employment if that act is done or if the accident is sustained in circumstances which make it reasonably incidental to that servant's employment.

It has also frequently been stressed, however, both in this court and in the Court of Appeal, that whether or not something is or was reasonably incidental to a person's employment is more often than not purely a question of fact and degree which the courts will not investigate either on applications for orders of certiorari as in the present case or when appeals are brought to the High Court under the Tribunals and Inquiries Act 1958.

Faced with this difficulty, counsel for the applicant nevertheless points to two passages in the reasons given by the commissioner in the present case for his decision and contends that these demonstrate not merely that the commissioner reached a wrong decision on the evidence before him, but also that there is an error on the face of his decision which not only entitles but requires this court to interfere.

In para 21 the commissioner said:

'Considerations of morale, esprit de corps, recruiting, physical fitness, a "good

a
image", the encouragement of participation in sport and the provision of sport
facilities are not, in my opinion, sufficient to constitute an activity as necessary
or reasonably incidental to an employment . . . I have reached a clear conclusion
that the playing of football, and indeed any other game, is a recreational activity
and is not something done in the course of a police officer's employment and
therefore cannot be held to be reasonably incidental to that employment. I
imagine that not every police officer participates in sport and, in reality, the
b
playing of games has nothing to do with the duties of a police officer.'

Counsel for the applicant argues that it is clear from these passages, which contain
the essence of the commissioner's decision, that the view he was taking was that
because playing football is a recreational activity and not part of the duties of a police
officer, looked at strictly, it therefore could not be said to arise out of and in the
c course of that police officer's employment. To emphasise the dichotomy, as counsel
for the applicant contends the commissioner has done, between a police officer's
recreational activities on the one hand and other activities more clearly part of his
duties and employment as a police officer on the other, and to say that the one can
never be part of the other, is to err in law. Although the commissioner may have
asked himself the correct question at an earlier stage in his decision, namely: was the
d applicant's participation in the material football match reasonably incidental to his
employment as a police officer? it is apparent, it is suggested, that on a proper
reading of para 21 of his decision he was saying in the end that nothing which was
recreational and not part of a police constable's duties could be said to arise out of
and in the course of his employment.

Counsel for the respondent, however, contends that not only did the commissioner
e pose to himself the correct question earlier in his reasons, but also it is apparent
from a number of passages elsewhere in his decision that he was throughout considering this correct issue. Although, with respect to the commissioner, the passage in
para 21 to which I have referred could, counsel for the respondent accepts, have been
more felicitously expressed, a proper reading of the decision as a whole indicates
that the commissioner was applying his mind to the correct issue and that he did
f not in the end base himself on the erroneous dichotomy to which counsel for the
applicant refers.

For my part, I think that there is considerable force in counsel for the applicant's
submission, particularly when one looks carefully at the second part of the passage
from para 21 of the commissioner's decision which I have quoted. If this stood alone
in para 21, and indeed in the decision as a whole, there could I think be little doubt
g that the commissioner had adopted the wrong approach in law. Further, had I been
hearing this appeal myself I might well have come to a different conclusion from that
of the commissioner. Nevertheless, the legislature has decided that these questions
of fact should not to be brought up to the courts of law for decision, but should be
entrusted to specialised statutory authorities for determination, both in these national
insurance cases and in a number of other fields. Where a real error of law is shown
h then this court will interfere, but it would in my opinion be wrong, by gradual erosion
of the basic principle, to set up this court as in effect a court of appeal on fact from the
decisions of these specialised tribunals: see *R v Industrial Injuries Comr, ex parte
Amalgamated Engineering Union (No 2)*[1] per Lord Denning MR.

Approaching this case on this basis, I think that it is clear that throughout his written
decision, until it reaches the second sentence from para 21 which I have quoted, the
j commissioner was considering the proper question in law, namely: was the football
match in which the applicant was playing at the time that he sustained his accident
reasonably incidental to his employment as a police officer? In the first-quoted
sentence from para 21 he expressed the view that the various matters of fact put
before him to show that such sporting activities were properly to be considered

1   [1966] 1 All ER 97 at 104, [1966] 2 QB 21 at 48, 49

as incidental to the police officer's employment were insufficient to enable him to
reach that conclusion. Having so asked himself the correct question and answered it *a*
there in a way to which no exception can be taken as a matter of law in this court,
I think that it would be wrong to hold that the second-quoted sentence from para 21
demonstrated, contrary to that which had gone before, that his ultimate decision in
the case was reached on a different and legally erroneous basis.

For these reasons, and although I have on the facts of the present case substantial
sympathy with this applicant, I do not think that one can say that an error of law *b*
appears on the face of the commissioner's decision. The question of fact for him,
namely whether taking part in police sport was reasonably incidental to a police
officer's employment, was one on which there was some evidence either way and the
resolution of the question of fact was for the commissioner and not for me. For
these reasons I for my part would dismiss this application.

c

LORD WIDGERY CJ. Park J has authorised me to say that he has read and approves
of the judgment which has been read by May J and I for my part also agree.

I have considerable sympathy with the present applicant and am by no means sure
that I should have reached this conclusion had I been sitting as a commissioner myself.
But for the reasons given by May J I am satisfied that we must keep our interference
with this kind of jurisdiction within bounds in this court and confine ourselves to the *d*
directions in law which is our particular function. Therefore the application is dismissed.

Application dismissed.

Solicitors: *Russell, Jones & Walker* (for the applicant); *Solicitor, Department of Health
and Social Security* (for the insurance officer).

N P Metcalfe Esq Barrister. *e*

R v Lee (Paul Robert)   *f*

COURT OF APPEAL, CRIMINAL DIVISION
ORR LJ, MACKENNA AND FORBES JJ
9th OCTOBER 1975

*Criminal evidence – Character of accused – Evidence of good character tendered – Questions
put to prosecution witnesses with a view to establishing accused's good character – Questions g
seeking to establish bad character of other persons who might have been guilty of offence –
Whether purpose of questions to establish accused's own good character – Whether questions
rendering evidence of accused's bad character admissible – Criminal Evidence Act 1898,
1(f)(ii).*

In October 1974 the accused was living with his brother-in-law, L. One day L found *h*
that a gold ring was missing from his home and also £150 out of a sum of £200 which
he had saved up for the purpose of moving house. The accused, who had been going
out daily with L to work, disappeared and was later seen by a third person in possession
of a large sum of money in notes. The accused was charged with theft and at his
trial alleged that two other people had had access to L's house and therefore had had
an opportunity to commit the theft. Those two men were not witnesses at the trial, *j*
but L was cross-examined by counsel for the accused as to their previous convictions
for dishonesty. The judge took the view that by means of that line of cross-
examination the accused was seeking to establish that the character of the two was
such that they were more likely to have committed the crime than he was and that
he was thus seeking to establish his own good character. Accordingly he allowed

the Crown, under s 1(f)(ii)^a of the Criminal Evidence Act 1898, to cross-examine
a the accused on his previous convictions. The accused was convicted and appealed.

Held – It was not implicit in an accusation of dishonesty that the accuser himself was
honest. Accordingly it could not be held that the questions put to L concerning the
convictions of the other two men were for the purpose of establishing the accused's
own good character. The judge had therefore erred in allowing questions as to the
b accused's previous convictions. Accordingly the appeal would be allowed and the
conviction quashed (see p 572 h and j, post).

Notes
For admissibility of evidence of bad character and cross-examination as to character,
see 10 Halsbury's Laws (3rd Edn) 447, 449-451, paras 823, 828, and for cases on the
c subject, see 14 Digest (Repl) 410-412, 4008-4025.

For the Criminal Evidence Act 1898, s 1, see 12 Halsbury's Statutes (3rd Edn) 865.

Case referred to in judgment
R v Ellis [1910] 2 KB 746, [1908-10] All ER Rep 488, 79 LJKB 841, 102 LT 922, 74 JP 388,
22 Cox CC 330, 5 Cr App Rep 41, CCA, 14 Digest (Repl) 408, *3975*.
d

Case also cited
Stirland v Director of Public Prosecutions [1944] 2 All ER 13, [1944] AC 315, HL.

Appeal
On 12th June 1975 in the Crown Court at Manchester before Mr Recorder Wickham
e the appellant, Paul Robert Lee, was convicted of theft and sentenced to 12 months'
imprisonment. He appealed against conviction following the grant of a certificate by
the trial judge. The facts are set out in the judgment of the court.

Martin Steiger for the appellant.
James Gregory for the Crown.
f

ORR LJ delivered the following judgment of the court: On 12th June 1975 at the
Manchester Crown Court the appellant was convicted of theft and sentenced to 12
months' imprisonment. He now appeals against that conviction with a certificate of
the trial judge on the ground that the judge allowed the prosecution to cross-examine
g him on his previous convictions under the provisions of s 1(f)(ii) of the Criminal
Evidence Act 1898.

The facts of the case were shortly these. In October 1974 the appellant was living
with a man, Robert Ludlain, and his wife, who is a sister of the appellant. Ludlain
had been saving up money which was required for moving his home and for that
purpose had hidden £200 under the carpet of the bedroom. On 19th October Ludlain
h found that a half sovereign ring was missing from the mantelpiece and he then made
a check and discovered that £150 of the £200 he had hidden was also missing.
The appellant, who had been going out daily with him to work, disappeared and
was not seen by him again, but was later seen by a third person in possession of a
large sum of money in notes. There had been an earlier trial on 22nd May 1975 in
the course of which Ludlain had referred to previous convictions of the accused and
j a new trial was ordered on that ground. What happened in the new trial was that before the jury were empanelled counsel for the appellant raised this question with
the judge. He said:

'[The appellant's] case is that there were a large number of people who had

---

a Section 1, so far as material, is set out out p 572 f and g, post access to the house and among those people was a person called Paul Ludlain and a person called Bob Smith. Both of those people have a number of previous *a* convictions for dishonesty. Accordingly, it is a material point, in my submission, that other persons who have convictions for dishonesty had access to the house at the same time as the money disappeared. In my submission it is right the jury should know that.'

The judge then suggested that the accused would be at risk if he proceeded to give *b* evidence. He said:

'If you are letting the jury know that other people who had access to the premises have a bad record you are implying that your client has a good record. You are thereby giving evidence of good character.'

Counsel for the appellant replied:

c

'In my submission asking questions to establish the bad character of one of the brothers of the prosecution witness does not amount by inference to proving my own good character.'

In the end the judge made a ruling on this matter, in which he said:

'What [counsel for the appellant] is seeking to establish is that those people by *d* reason of their 'previous convictions were more likely to have committed the crime. If he is seeking to establish they were more likely to have committed the crime, turn the penny over; what he is seeking to establish is that the defendant was less likely than those other people to have committed the crime.

It was on that basis that he made his ruling. In due course questions were put as to previous convictions of these other persons, who were not called as witnesses, and the *e* judge, on an application by counsel for the Crown to put to the appellant his previous convictions, and after hearing further argument, gave leave for that to be done.

The matter turns in the judgment of this court entirely on the words of s 1(f), proviso (ii), of the Criminal Evidence Act 1898. What that section provides, so far as is material for present purposes, is as follows:

'(f) A person charged and called as a witness in pursuance of this Act shall not *f* be asked, and if asked shall not be required to answer, any question tending to show that he has committed or been convicted of or been charged with any offence other than that wherewith he is then charged, or is of bad character, unless [I then read proviso (ii) which alone is relevant in this case and is as follows:] he has personally or by his advocate asked questions of the witnesses for the *g* prosecution with a view to establish his own good character . . .'

It has been common ground in the argument before us that in order to justify in this case the putting of his previous convictions to the appellant, the matter had to be brought within those words. The words of the section fall to be given their ordinary and natural meaning and this court finds it impossible to hold that the questions which were put to the prosecution witness, Ludlain, as to the convictions of the other *h* men, were with a view to establishing the accused's own good character. The questions were put with a view to establishing the bad character of the two other men and nothing else and the answer Yes to the question, had they previous convictions? had nothing whatever to do with the character of the accused. As MacKenna J put it in argument, and in our view this is entirely right, it is not implicit in an accusation of dishonesty that the accuser himself is an honest man. *j*

For these reasons the court finds it impossible to accept the argument advanced for the Crown and we must allow this appeal. It may be that that proviso (ii) to s 1(f) ought to cover such a case as this but, in our judgment, that can only be a matter for Parliament. We find it impossible to construe the statutory words in the manner contended for by the Crown.

I would add, since we were referred to it, that *R v Ellis*[1] has, in our judgment, no
a bearing on the present question.
The appeal against conviction will accordingly be allowed.

Appeal allowed; conviction quashed.

Solicitors: *Registrar of Criminal Appeals; D S Gandy*, Manchester (for the Crown).

b   Sepala Munasinghe Esq   Barrister.

Carradine Properties Ltd v Aslam

c CHANCERY DIVISION
GOULDING J
6th NOVEMBER 1975

*Landlord and tenant – Notice to quit – Validity – Error or mistake – Meaning of notice clear
to tenant – Erroneous date given for termination of tenancy – Landlord having right to deter-*
d *mine lease on 27th September 1975 by giving 12 months' notice – Notice given in 1974 referring
to termination of lease on 27th September 1973 – Clerical error – Whether a valid notice
to terminate lease on 27th September 1975.*

By a lease made in 1968 premises were let for 21 years less three days from 27th
September 1968. The plaintiff became the assignee of the reversion under the lease
e and the defendant became the assignee of the term. By cl 5 of the lease it was provided
that if either party should determine the lease at the expiration of the first seven or 14
years and should give 12 months' previous notice in writing of such a wish to determine then the lease should cease. On 6th September 1974 or shortly afterwards a
notice was served by the plaintiff's solicitor on the defendant. The notice read: 'In
pursuance of the proviso contained in a Lease dated 27th day of September 1968 . . .
f WE HEREBY GIVE YOU NOTICE that we intend to determine the term created by the
Lease on the 27th day of September 1973 and that we require you to quit and deliver
up possession of the premises comprised in the said Lease on that date.' The plaintiff's
intention had been to determine the lease on 27th September 1975, the date on which
the first seven years expired, but as result of a clerical error 27th September 1973 and
not 27th September 1975 was typed into the notice as the date of determination of
g the lease. The plaintiff sought a declaration that the notice to quit was effective to
determine the defendant's tenancy on 27th September 1975.

Held – In interpreting a notice to quit, the test which was in general to be applied was
to ask whether it would be quite clear what it meant to a reasonable person reading
it. Applying that test, the plaintiff's notice was valid since it would be perfectly
h clear to a tenant who knew the terms of the lease that the reference in the notice given
in 1974 to a date in 1973 was an error and that the reference should have been to the
corresponding date in the year 1975 when the first seven years of the term expired.
Accordingly the declaration would be granted (see p 576 *b* and *c* and p 577 *f* to *h*, post).
Doe d Duke of Bedford v Kightley (1796) 7 Term Rep 63 applied.
Hankey v Clavering [1942] 2 All ER 311 distinguished.

j
Notes
For construction of an incorrect notice to quit, see 23 Halsbury's Laws (3rd Edn)
522-523, *1173*, and for cases on the subject, see 31(2) Digest (Reissue) 775, 776, 6421-6429.

1 [1910] 2 KB 746, [1908-10] All ER Rep 488

Cases referred to in judgment

Cadby v Martinez (1840) 11 Ad & El 720, 3 Per & Dav 386, 9 LJQB 281, 4 JP 105, 113 ER a
587; *previous proceedings* (1838) 2 Jur 543, 31(2) Digest (Reissue) 775, 6428.

Doe d Duke of Bedford v Kightley (1796) 7 Term Rep 63, 101 ER 856, 31(2) Digest (Reissue)
775, 6423.

Doe d Huntingtower (Lord) v Culliford (1824) 4 Dow & Ry KB 248, 31(2) Digest (Reissue)
775, 6424.

Doe d Richmond Corpn v Morphett (1845) 7 QB 577, 14 LJQB 345, 5 LTOS 196, 9 Jur 776, 115 b
ER 606, 31(2) Digest (Reissue) 775, 6421.

Doe d Spicer v Lea (1809) 11 East 312, 103 ER 1024.

Doe d Williams v Smith (1836) 5 Ad & El 350, 2 Har & W 176, 6 Nev & MKB 829, 5
LJKB 216, 111 ER 1198, 31(2) Digest (Reissue) 775, 6425.

Hankey v Clavering [1942] 2 All ER 311, [1942] 2 KB 326, 111 LJKB 711, 167 LT 193, CA,
31(2) Digest (Reissue) 893, 7409.   c

Wride v Dyer [1900] 1 QB 23, 69 LJQB 17, 81 LT 453, 64 JP 118, DC, 31(2) Digest (Reissue)
775, 6427.

Adjourned summons

By an originating summons dated 8th April 1975 the plaintiff company, Carradine
Properties Ltd, sought a declaration that a notice to quit premises on the ground d
floor of 5 Lancelot Parade, Lancelot Road, Wembley, Middlesex, served on the defendant, Miam Mohammed Aslam, by the plaintiff company on 11th September 1974
'operates so as validly to determine the defendant's tenancy of the said premises on
the 27th September 1975 in accordance with the terms of a lease' of 27th September
1968 whereunder the defendant held the premises as tenant and subject to the provisions of Part II of the Landlord and Tenant Act 1954. The facts are set out in the e
judgment.

Richard Moshi for the plaintiff company.
T R F Jennings for the defendant.

GOULDING J. This case concerns a short construction point which is not con-   f
cluded by authority nor entirely easy to decide. By a lease dated 27th September
1968, a company called Hazell & Co (Publicity) Ltd, a predecessor of the plaintiff
company, demised certain small business premises at 5 Lancelot Parade, Wembley,
to Muhammed Shakil, a predecessor of the defendant, at a rent of £1,200 per annum
for a term of 21 years less three days from 27th September 1968. The reversion is
now vested in the plaintiff company and the defendant is the assignee of the lease. g
    Clause 5 of the lease contains a provision in a not unusual form for its earlier deter-
mination at the end of the first seven or 14 years of the term on the giving of
12 months' previous notice by either party. Clause 5 is as follows:

'PROVIDED ALWAYS and IT IS HEREBY AGREED if either party shall desire to determine the present demise at the expiration of the first seven or fourteen years of h
the said term and shall give twelve months previous notice in writing of such
its or his desire and (in the case of determination by the Lessee) if the Lessee shall
up to the time of such determination pay the rent and perform and observe
the covenants on his part hereinbefore contained then immediately on the expiration of such seven or fourteen years as the case may be the present demise and
everything herein contained shall cease without prejudice to the remedies of j
either party against the other in respect of any antecedent claim or breach of
convenant.'

It is common ground that the correct date for termination at the end of the first
seven years would be 27th September 1975, and the case has been argued throughout
on that footing. A notice dated 6th September 1974 was on that day, or very shortly

a thereafter in course of post, served by the plaintiff company's solicitors. It read as follows:

> 'In pursuance of the proviso contained in a Lease dated 27th day of September 1968 and made between HAZELL & COMPANY (PUBLICITY) LIMITED of the one part and MUHAMMAD SHAKIL of the other part WE HEREBY GIVE YOU NOTICE that we intend to determine the term created by the Lease on the 27th day of September
> **b** 1973 and that we require you to quit and deliver up possession of the premises comprised in the said Lease on that date.'

It is clear that a clerical error had occurred and that the year 1973, already passed, was typed instead of 1975, the correct year. The question is whether that invalidates the notice for the purpose of the lease. At the outset, it appeared to me that even were the notice correct, it would have been ineffectual by reason of s 24 of the Land-
c lord and Tenant Act 1954, but I have been assured by both counsel that it does have some effect because it clears the ground, as it were, for a shorter notice under the Act, so I will say no more on that.

Counsel for the plaintiff company cited a number of cases. I will first refer to *Doe d Duke of Bedford v Kightley* which somewhat resembles the present case, and will
d read the essential facts and the judgment[1]:

> 'On the trial of this ejectment at the last assizes before Lord Ch. J. Eyre, the defendant, who was a tenant to the lessor of the plaintiff, objected to the notice to quit, which was served just before *Michaelmas*, 1795 and was to quit "at *Lady-Day, which will be in the year 1795*". . . Lord Kenyon, Ch. J. said the time when the notice was given and the words in it "which will be" manifestly shewed
> **e** that this was a notice to quit at the then next *Lady-Day*; and the conduct of the parties also shewed that they so considered it. Then the year 1795 in the notice may be rejected as an impossible year.'

It does not appear from the report what the conduct of the parties was. All that appears is some indication of a conversation prior to service of the notice.

Counsel for the plaintiff company cited other cases on notices to quit: *Doe d Lord*
f *Huntingtower v Culliford*[2], *Doe d Williams v Smith*[3], *Doe d Richmond Corpn v Morphett*[4] and *Wride v Dyer*[5]. The only relevance of those cases, it seems to me, is that one can see a general principle in them that the court allows common sense to enter into the interpretation of an inaccurate notice to quit. I will cite two passages. In *Doe d Williams v Smith*[6] Patteson J said:

> 'It is not required that a notice should be worded with the accuracy of a plea.
> **g** This is not drawn with strict precision; but I think it is sufficiently clear.'

Then in the latest of the cases, *Wride v Dyer*[7], Ridley J said:

> 'I agree . . . with the rule laid down . . . that we must look at the intention of the landlord, and that when language is used which leaves the effect of the notice open to doubt, the rule of construction is to make it sensible and not insensible.'

h Darling J[8] agreed:

> 'But what is the rule of construction of such documents as this? It is laid down,

---

1 (1796) 7 Term Rep 63 at 64
j 2 (1824) 4 Dow & Ry KB 248
3 (1836) 5 Ad & El 350
4 (1845) 7 QB 577
5 [1900] 1 QB 23
6 (1836) 5 Ad & El at 353
7 [1900] 1 QB at 25
8 [1900] 1 QB at 26

I think, by Bayley J. in *Doe* v. *Culliford*[1], and it was well expressed by Sir John
Jervis in arguing the case of *Doe* v. *Smith*[2]. "The Court," he says, "will give an   *a*
interpretation to the notice consistent with the intention of the party serving it,
if clear." '

I would put the test generally applicable as being this: is the notice quite clear to a
reasonable tenant reading it? is it plain that he cannot be misled by it? Applying that
test, if applicable, to the present case, I think the notice would be saved because the   *b*
tenant receiving that notice and knowing the terms of the lease must have seen there
was a mistake, as it would not say '1973' in the year 1974. Once that is accepted, it
is obvious that the notice is for the year 1975 and not 1973. In no ordinary circumstances would a reasonable tenant knowing the terms of the lease take the notice as
being other than for the year 1975. It therefore seems to me that if one applied the
test I have mentioned, then the notice would be saved.

However, there is a case of a later date and higher authority than those I have referred   *c*
to, which counsel for the defendant says would lead to a different result. It is *Hankey*
v Clavering[3]. The headnote reads as follows:

> 'Under the terms of a lease for twenty-one years from December 25, 1934,
> either party could determine the tenancy at the end of seven years on giving six
> months' notice. The landlord gave to the tenant's solicitors a notice as from   *d*
> June 21, 1941, which purported to determine the lease on December 21, 1941.
> The solicitors subsequently acknowledged the receipt of this notice, saying that
> it had been properly served on them:—*Held*, that the notice, although the
> mistake as to date was obviously due to a slip on the part of the landlord, was
> invalid, and that the acceptance of its service by the solicitors did not cure the
> defect.'   *e*

Lord Greene MR said[4]:

> 'By his letter of January 15, 1940, the plaintiff, on the face of it, was purporting
> to determine the lease by notice on December 21, 1941. The whole thing was
> obviously a slip on his part, and there is a natural temptation to put a strained
> construction on language in aid of people who have been unfortunate enough to   *f*
> make slips. That, however, is a temptation which must be resisted, because
> documents are not to be strained and principles of construction are not to be
> outraged in order to do what may appear to be fair in an individual case . . .
> 'That takes me back to the real point, namely, whether or not the notice was
> good, in the sense that it had the effect of terminating the lease on December 25,
> 1941. Notices of this kind are documents of a technical nature, technical because   *g*
> they are not consensual documents, but, if they are in proper form, they have
> of their own force without any assent by the recipient the effect of bringing
> the demise to an end. They must on their face and on a fair and reasonable
> construction do what the lease provides that they are to do. It is perfectly true
> that in construing such a document, as in construing all documents, the court
> in a case of ambiguity will lean in favour of reading the document in such a way   *h*
> as to give it validity, but I dissent entirely from the proposition that, where a
> document is clear and specific, but inaccurate on some matter, such as that of
> date, it is possible to ignore the inaccuracy and substitute the correct date or
> other particular because it appears that the error was inserted by a slip. By the
> clear wording of this notice the plaintiff purported to bring the lease to an end
> on December 21, 1941. In so doing he was attempting to do something which he   *j*
> had no power to do, and however much the recipient might guess, or however

---

1   (1824) 4 Dow & Ry KB 248
2   (1836) 5 Ad & El 350
3   [1942] 2 KB 326
4   [1942] 2 KB at 328, 329, 330, cf [1942] 2 All ER 311 at 313, 314

a certain he might be, that it was a mere slip, that would not cure the defect because the document was never capable on its face of producing the necessary legal consequences.'

Then Lord Greene MR pointed out that he was following *Cadby v Martinez*[1]. I have been referred to that case also and to *Doe d Spicer v Lea*[2].

b It is to be noted that most of the cases counsel for the plaintiff company has cited to me were referred to by counsel in *Hankey v Clavering*[3], but neither Lord Greene MR nor Lord Clauson commented on them. They did not say they were wrong nor in terms distinguish them. Counsel for the defendant suggests that that was because of a fundamental distinction between an ordinary notice to quit terminating a yearly or periodic tenancy and a break clause in a demise for a fixed term such as that in the present case and in *Hankey v Clavering*[3]. That is not explicitly mentioned by the

c Court of Appeal as a distinction of importance, and I think it must not be pressed too far.

I suppose a break clause can be said to be more in the nature of an option conferring a benefit than a clause providing for a notice to quit in a periodic tenancy, but a notice under a break clause like the notice to quit in a periodic tenancy is a unilateral document which has to be sufficient in form and contents. It acts by its own force to

d release a given party from an obligation otherwise lying on him. Lord Greene MR said[4]: 'Notices of this kind . . . are documents of a technical nature, technical . . . [because] they are not consensual documents.' That description fits a notice to quit under a periodic tenancy as well as one under a break clause so that, while recognising the distinction, I must not take it too far.

Further, I am not persuaded that the distinction is of so much importance for the

e present case as counsel for the defendant submitted. In an option clause the requirement is that a party must strictly comply with the condition for its exercise. If the condition includes the giving of a particular notice, it seems to me that the logical first approach is to interpret the notice, looking at the words and applying legal principles to their construction, and then ask whether it complies with the strict requirements as to exercise of the option. If that is right, I think a benevolent approach

f could be applied in this case, as in the *Duke of Bedford's* case[5], because reasonably read by a reasonable tenant the mistake is obvious on the face of it, and there is no doubt what the mistake was. Therefore one interprets the notice as asserting an intention to determine in the year 1975.

It is true that if whoever made the mistake had typed 1976 instead of 1973, the error would probably have been incurable because although the tenant might suspect

g there was a slip, it might be that the landlord did intend 1976, not knowing or understanding his rights under the lease. In such a case the tenant would be entitled to disregard the notice, but because a past date was given in the notice it is insensible and therefore an authority such as the *Duke of Bedford's* case[5] is in point.

I will make a declaration in favour of the plaintiff company that, on the true construction of the notice to quit, it is a valid notice, subject to the provisions of Part II

h of the Landlord and Tenant Act 1954, to determine the demise at the expiration of the first seven years in accordance with cl 5 of the lease.

Declaration accordingly.

Solicitors: *D J Freeman & Co* (for the plaintiff company); *Child & Child* (for the defendant).

j Evelyn M C Budd   Barrister.

1 (1840) 11 Ad & El 720
2 (1809) 11 East 312
3 [1942] 2 All ER 311, [1942] 2 KB 326
4 [1942] 2 All ER at 313, 314, [1942] 2 KB at 329
5 (1796) 7 Term Rep 63

R v Watkins a

CROWN COURT AT WARWICK
HIS HONOUR JUDGE PAUL CLARKE
20th, 21st, 22nd, 23rd, 24th OCTOBER 1975

Criminal law – Obtaining a pecuniary advantage by deception – Pecuniary advantage – b
Cases in which pecuniary advantage to be regarded as obtained – Being allowed to borrow
by way of overdraft – Whether pecuniary advantage obtained when overdraft facility granted
– Theft Act 1968, s 16(2)(b).

A customer who is allowed to borrow from a bank on overdraft obtains a pecuniary
advantage, within s 16(2)(b)^a of the Theft Act 1968, at the moment when the overdraft c
facility is granted to him without need for proof that he drew on that facility (see
p 579 *b* and *c*, post).

Notes
For obtaining a pecuniary advantage by deception, see Supplement to 10 Halsbury's
Laws (3rd Edn) para 1586A, 2. d
 For the Theft Act 1968, s 16, see 8 Halsbury's Statutes (3rd Edn) 793.

Ruling
The defendant, Wesley Rees Watkins, was arraigned on an indictment containing
five counts, of which three (counts 1, 3 and 4) charged him with obtaining a pecuniary
advantage by deception, contrary to s 16(1) of the Theft Act 1968, and two (counts 2 e
and 5) charged him with obtaining property by deception, contrary to s 15(1) of the
1968 Act. The particulars of offence in count 1 alleged that the defendant—

'on the 3rd day of November 1973, dishonestly obtained for himself a pecuniary
advantage, namely, being allowed to borrow by way of overdraft the sum of
£900 from Messrs. Lombard North Central Limited, by a false representation f
in the proposal form that he, the said Wesley Rees Watkins, had no other regular
monthly commitment except for £78 per month mortgage payment, an account
with Lombard involving a payment of £17·85 per month and £6 per month
television rental, making a total of £101·85 per month.'

 The date on which the offence was alleged to have been committed was that on
which an agreement in writing had been made between the defendant and Lombard g
whereby, in consideration of the defendant making fixed monthly payments to Lombard, he was entitled to draw from Lombard up to £900 but so that the total indebtedness to Lombard should not exceed £900 at any one time. Prior thereto the defendant
had entered into a fixed term loan agreement with Lombard which he was in the
process of discharging by fixed monthly payments. That agreement was discharged
by use of the new facilities granted under the agreement of 3rd November. The h
Crown's case was that, in the proposal form to Lombard, the defendant had falsely
represented that his financial commitments were considerably less than in fact they
were and that Lombard had thereby been deceived into accepting the proposals which
therefore constituted the agreement. At the defendant's trial the Crown alleged
in relation to count 1 that the pecuniary advantage which had been obtained by the
defendant was that defined in s 16(2)(b) of the Theft Act 1968, i e being allowed to j
borrow by way of overdraft, and that the offence had been committed when the
defendant was granted the borrowing facilities by Lombard under the agreement
of 3rd November. The defendant submitted that the offence created by s 16(2)(b)

a Section 16(2), so far as as material, is set out at p 579 c, post

was only committed when the borrowing actually took place and that there was no
evidence that any borrowing had taken place. His Honour Judge Paul Clarke gave the
following ruling on that submission.

D E Roberts for the Crown.
Clive Taylor for the defendant.

JUDGE PAUL CLARKE. Counsel for the defendant makes a submission with regard
to counts 1, 3 and 4 of the indictment, and I will deal with count 1 first. He
submits that such an offence can be committed only if the facility is actually drawn on,
and he said there is no evidence that it was drawn on.

As I understand it, there is no authority on this matter, but I interpret the subsection in question as sufficiently proved if the deception caused only the granting of
facilities for drawing on an overdraft. I reach that conclusion firstly because of the use
of the words 'He is allowed to', the subsection reading as follows: 'The cases in which a
pecuniary advantage within the meaning of this section is to be regarded as obtained
for a person are cases where . . . (b) he is allowed to borrow by way of overdraft . . .' It
seems to me that those words could well be omitted if counsel for the defendant
is correct, and I must seek to give a meaning of the use of those words.

Secondly, I do notice that there is an alternative in the latter part of sub-s (2)(b).
The words are: '. . . or obtains an improvement of the terms on which he is allowed to
do so.' That similarly I think plainly refers to the granting of improved facilities, not
drawing on improved facilities. It seems to me to be a pointer to the fact that it is
granting of facilities that is contemplated in this subsection, not the actual usage of
facilities.

Thirdly, I rely on this, that the drawing on an overdraft, if caused by deception,
would be I think an offence under s 15, i e obtaining property by deception. I accept
that there is some area for doubt here, as counsel for the defendant has submitted,
because there must be an intent permanently to deprive for the purposes of s 15. But
I think that s 15 would ordinarily be an adequate and appropriate provision for the
situation where a deceiver obtains money under an overdraft facility. So, if counsel
for the defendant is correct, there would hardly be any need for this part of s 16(2)(b).
I think that s 16(2)(b) is necessary because when facilities for an overdraft are granted a
customer gets a very real advantage in thereafter being able to go to the counter and
draw on his overdraft. The opportunities for a deception arise when he goes to the
manager and gets the facility, not when he draws on that facility.

So on those grounds I reject the submission on count 1. In any event, I think I
ought to point out that there is some evidence that the accused did draw on his overdraft because of the evidence of Mr Cattermole, who said that the company obtained
judgment in the sum of £953·10, and it seems to me that if one looks at the evidence there is no possibility that that could by made up wholly by interest on the
initial sum of £290 odd that was transferred from the previous account at Lombard,
so I reject the submission on count 1.

Ruling accordingly.

Solicitors: *Director of Public Prosecutions*; *Varley, Hibbs & Co*, Coventry (for the
defendant).

Gwynedd Lewis Barrister.

Ravenseft Properties v London Borough of Newham

COURT OF APPEAL, CIVIL DIVISION
LORD DENNING MR, JAMES AND BRIDGE LJJ
13th, 14th OCTOBER 1975

Rates – Unoccupied property – Newly erected building – Completion – Liability to be rated from date of completion – Meaning of 'completion' – Building not capable of being occupied – Building lacking features necessary for occupation and which when provided would have to be taken into account for valuation purposes – Office block – Main structure completed – No internal partitioning on any of storeys to be occupied as offices – Whether erection of storeys completed – Whether rating authority having power to serve completion notices – General Rate Act 1967, Sch 1, paras 7, 8(1)(5), 10.

Rates – Unoccupied property – Newly erected building – Completion – Completion notice – Appeal – Date of completion – Determination by court – Application – Evidence – Appeal not abandoned or dismissed – Erection of building to be treated as having been completed on 'such date as the court shall determine' – Appeal against completion notice allowed – No application to fix a completion date made until after judgment delivered – No evidence as to likely date of completion – Whether court bound to fix completion date – General Rate Act 1967, Sch 1, para 8(5).

The ratepayers were the owners of a newly erected office block which comprised 14 storeys. By 10th October 1974 the block had been structurally completed, but the floor space on the 13 storeys which were to be used as offices had not been divided up or partitioned into rooms or individual offices and on each of the 13 floors there was nothing except the structural columns. Each floor covered a rectangular space of 8,385 square feet. Furthermore, the electrical wiring system had not as yet been installed and no telephone cables had been connected to the block. In the exercise of their powers under the General Rate Act 1967, Sch 1, paras 1(1)[a] and 7[b], to rate a newly erected building which, on completion, remained unoccupied, the rating authority served on the ratepayers completion notices under para 8(1)[c] in respect of each of the 13 storeys. The completion notices were dated 10th October 1974; they were all in the same terms and, in accordance with para 8(1), stated that the rating authority was of opinion that the building to which the notice related had been completed and that it was 'comprised in a relevant hereditament', and that the erection of the building was therefore to be treated for the purposes of Sch 1 as having been completed on the date of service of the notice. The ratepayers appealed to the county court against the completion notices on the ground that the 13 storeys had not been 'completed' and could not reasonably have been expected to be completed by 10th October 1974. The

---

a Paragraph 1(1) provides: 'Where, in the case of any rating area in which, by virtue of a resolution under section 17 of this Act, this Schedule is in operation, any relevant hereditament in that area is unoccupied for a continuous period exceeding three months, the owner shall, subject to the provisions of this Schedule, be rated in respect of that hereditament for any relevant period of vacancy; and the provisions of this Act shall apply accordingly as if the hereditament were occupied during the relevant period of vacancy by the owner.'

b Paragraph 7 provides: 'For the purposes of paragraph 1 of this Schedule, a newly created building which is not occupied on the date determined under the subsequent provisions of this Schedule as the date on which the erection of the building is completed shall be deemed to become unoccupied on that date.'

c Paragraph 8(1) is set out at p 584 j to p 585 b, post

county court judge allowed the appeals and quashed the notices. The question of determining a fresh date of completion under para 8(5)^d of Sch 1 was not canvassed before the judge until after he had given his judgment and he declined to exercise the power under para 8(5) to specify a fresh completion date. The rating authority appealed against the quashing of the notices. At the hearing of the appeal, no evidence as to the date on which the block should be treated as having been completed was given to the court.

Held – The appeal would be dismissed for the following reasons—
   (i) A newly erected building could not be regarded as having been 'completed', within para 8(1), until it was ready for occupation for the appropriate purposes of the particular hereditament. A building was not ready for occupation so long as it lacked features which would have to be provided before it could be occupied for those purposes, and which, when provided, would have to be taken into account for the purpose of valuation. Having regard to the lack of partitioning, the 13 storeys were not capable of occupation for the purposes of offices and therefore were not completed buildings within the meaning of para 8(1). It followed that the completion notices were invalid (see p 584 e, p 585 c and p 587 b c and j to p 588 a e and f, post); *Watford Borough Council v Parcourt Property Investment Co Ltd* (1971) 17 RRC 19 applied; *Easiwork Homes Ltd v London Borough of Redbridge* [1970] 2 All ER 635 distinguished.
   (ii) The court could not apply para 8(5) of Sch 1 and determine a fresh completion date unless there had been an application to the court to determine that matter and evidence had been given to the court as to when the building could reasonably be expected to be completed. As no such application had been made until after the judge had delivered his judgment, and no evidence had been given as to the date on which the building could be expected to be completed, the judge had been right to decline to specify a fresh completion date (see p 585 d to f, p 587 c e and f and p 589 a to c, post).
   Per Curiam. In para 10^e of Sch 1 to the 1967 Act, which relates to the completion of structural alterations in consequence of which an existing hereditament ceases to exist by becoming part of a different hereditament, the word 'completion' has the same meaning, i e capability of occupation, as in para 8(1) (see p 585 d and h and p 588 e and f, post).

Notes
For rating of unoccupied property, see Supplement to 32 Halsbury's Laws (3rd Edn), para 51A.
   For the General Rate Act 1967, Sch 1, paras 1, 7, 8, see 27 Halsbury's Statutes (3rd Edn) 210, 213.

Cases referred to in judgment
Easiwork Homes Ltd v London Borough of Redbridge [1970] 2 All ER 635, [1970] 2 QB 406, [1970] 2 WLR 1199, 15 RRC 346, 134 JP 520, [1970] RA 227, DC, Digest (Cont Vol C) 817, 9a.
Watford Borough Council v Parcourt Property Investment Co Ltd (1971) 17 RRC 19, [1971] RA 97.

---

d Paragraph 8(5), so far as material, is set out at p 588 j, post
e Paragraph 10 provides: 'Where by reason of the structural alteration of any building a relevant hereditament becomes or becomes part of a different hereditament or different hereditaments, the relevant hereditament shall be deemed for the purposes of this Schedule to have ceased to exist on the date (as determined in pursuance of the foregoing provisions of this Schedule) of the completion of the structural alteration and, in particular, to have been omitted on that date from any valuation list in which it is then included; but nothing in this paragraph shall be construed as affecting any liability for rates under paragraph 1 of this Schedule in respect of the hereditament for any period before that date.'

Cases also cited

Institute of Orthopaedics v Harrow Corpn [1962] 3 All ER 964, [1963] 1 WLR 10.
Walsh (John) Ltd v Sheffield City Council and Tranter (valuation officer) [1957] 3 All ER 353,
[1957] 1 WLR 1074, CA.

Appeal

The appellants, Ravenseft Properties Ltd ('the ratepayers'), were developers and the
building owners of two office blocks, 'block A' and 'block B', at the Stratford Centre,
London, E15; block A comprised 14 storeys and block B comprised six storeys. The
respondents, the London Borough of Newham ('the rating authority'), having resolved
pursuant to s 17 of the General Rate Act 1967 that the provisions of Sch 1 to that Act
relating to the rating of unoccupied property should apply to their rating area, served
on the ratepayers completion notices in respect of block A and block B pursuant to
paras 1(1), 7 and 8(1) of Sch 1. In respect of block A, 14 completion notices were served
covering the office and premises on 13 floors of the block. In respect of block B, one
completion notice was served. All the completion notices were in similar terms.
They stated that the rating authority, being of the opinion that the erection of the
building to which the notice related 'has been completed and that the building is
comprised in a relevant hereditament', gave notice that the erection of the building
was to be treated for the purposes of Sch 1 as completed on the date of service of the
notice. Each notice was dated 10th October 1974. The ratepayers appealed under
para 8(4) of Sch 1 to Bow County Court against all the completion notices. The
ground of each appeal was that the erection of the building to which each notice
related had not been and could not reasonably be expected to be completed by
the date specified in the notice, 10th October 1974. On 18th December 1974 his Honour
Judge Ranking gave judgment allowing the appeals and quashed all the completion
notices on the ground that at the relevant date the lack of any partitioning dividing
up the office areas in each block rendered each block an incomplete building and that
without partitioning each block was not a hereditament. The rating authority
appealed, seeking an order that the ratepayers' appeals against the completion
notices be dismissed; alternatively, that the erection of the building to which each
appeal related should be treated for the purposes of Sch 1 as completed on such date
as the Court of Appeal should determine; or, in the further alternative, that a new
trial be ordered and that in relation to each appeal the county court should be directed
to determine the date on which the erection of the building should be treated as
completed. The grounds of the appeal were that the judge erred in law: (1) in holding
that blocks A and B were not completed buildings for the purpose of Sch 1 on October
10th 1974 notwithstanding the facts as found by him and the evidence before him;
(2) in wrongly taking into account the lack of items which would not be part of the
hereditament, such as telephone cables, partitioning and wiring for a lighting system,
in determining whether a hereditament existed or a building was completed;
(3) in wrongly holding that without partitioning each building was not a hereditament
and was not completed for the purposes of Sch 1; (4) in failing to apply the law in
Easiwork Homes Ltd v London Borough of Redbridge[1], in particular the principle that a unit
of property is a 'hereditament' within the meaning of s 115 of the 1967 Act and for the
purposes of Sch 1 thereto, notwithstanding that it was for the time being incapable of
occupation because of lack of plumbing work, toilet fitting, water supplies, gas
appliances, electrical wiring and flooring; and in seeking to distinguish that decision
on insufficient grounds; (5) in wrongly holding himself bound to follow the decision
of Bridge J in *Watford Borough Council v Parcourt Property Investment Co Ltd*[2] as to the
effect of lack of partitioning on the question whether there were completed buildings
at the relevant date; (6) in rejecting the submission that the test of completion of

---

1 [1970] 2 All ER 635, [1970] 2 QB 406
2 (1971) 17 RRC 19

a building for the purposes of Sch 1 was whether it was completed for the purposes
a of the owner; (7) in applying as the sole test of completion the test whether they had
been completed as offices, without properly regarding the definition of 'relevant
hereditament' in para 15 of Sch 1, and in particular the inclusion therein of the words
'or other building whatsoever', and the meaning of 'office' properly interpreted in the
context thereof; (8) in relation to block A, in failing to consider in relation to each separate hereditament or in relation to each separate notice of completion the question
b whether a building or a part of a building had been completed and considering such
question only in relation to the total block; (9) in holding that he had no power to
determine the date on which the erection of each building or part of a building should
be treated for the purposes of Sch 1 as completed. The facts relating to the condition
of block A on 10th October 1964 are set out in the judgment of Lord Denning MR. In
block B on that date more work was required to be done than was required to be done
c in block A.

Charles Fay for the rating authority.
David Trustram Eve QC and *Michael Fitzgerald* for the ratepayers.

d **LORD DENNING MR.** In the east of London there is a fine new centre called the
Stratford Centre which consists of two blocks (blocks A and B) of new air-conditioned
offices. It has been developed by the London Borough of Newham, the rating authority,
in partnership with a property company called Ravenseft Properties Ltd, the ratepayers. The office blocks are not occupied as yet, but the London Borough of Newham
wish to charge Ravenseft Properties with rates on them. At one time unoccupied
e premises did not bear rates at all. 'Voids' or 'empties', as they were called, were not
liable to pay rates during the time they were unoccupied. But since 1967 there has
been a provision in the General Rate Act 1967, Sch 1, para 1(1), whereby, in the case
of office buildings, they are free of rates for the first three months whilst they are
unoccupied; but after three months, they are liable to pay rates even if they are unoccupied. That is why the London Borough of Newham wish to charge Ravenseft
f with rates. But—and here is the point in the case—the chargeability only arises when
the buildings are 'completed'. The controversy is whether these buildings were
completed or not. The London Borough of Newham say that they are complete as
soon as they are *structurally complete*; whereas Ravenseft Properties say that they are
only complete when they are *ready for occupation*. That is the broad issue between
the parties.
g The London Borough of Newham on 10th October 1974 served notices on Ravenseft
Properties in which they gave notice that they regarded the 14 floors of block A as
'completed'; that the building was comprised in a 'relevant hereditament'; and that
it was to be regarded as completed within para 8 of Sch 1 to the 1967 Act.
Ravenseft Properties took a contrary view. They appealed to the county court,
saying that their offices were not completed and could not reasonably be expected to
h be completed by 10th October 1974.
This dispute depends on the state of the buildings. It has been agreed between the
parties and we have photographs to show it. Block A has 14 storeys of reinforced concrete construction. The whole of the structure, as a structure, is no doubt completed.
There are large floors all the way up 13 storeys. On each of these floors at each end
toilets are installed. Central heating and air-conditioning systems are installed. These
vast floors have not been divided into rooms or offices. There are no partitions in.
j Each of the floors covers a rectangular space of 8,385 square feet with nothing there
except ten structural columns in a line. There is a fuse box on each floor with wiring
for a power circuit. But no points have been installed for any outlets.
There was no wiring for any lighting system. There was no telephone system. No
GPO cables had been installed. No main distribution frame had been installed.

Application had been made for a telephone line in different places. But it was nine
months before the telephone could be installed.   a
   The main contest is as to these floors. As I say, they are enormous floors with
columns down the middle but no divisions whatsoever into rooms or into individual
offices. It seems to me that they could not be occupied or ready for occupation until
they had been divided up by partitions and rooms and so forth.
   So there we have the contest. The London Borough of Newham say they were
complete because they were structurally complete. Ravenseft Properties say No,   b
they are not complete until they are ready for occupation and they are not ready.
The county court judge held that they were not ready. He rejected the claim of the
London Borough of Newham. Now there is an appeal to this court.
   We have been taken through Sch 1 to the 1967 Act dealing with the rating of unoccupied premises. We have been taken to the distinction between a newly erected
building, on the one hand, and, on the other hand, a building which has already been   c
used but has been structurally altered so as to become another hereditament. It does
seem to me that the same test ought to be applied in each. I do not propose to analyse
that schedule in detail. I am only going to take two cases which have come before the
courts. The first is the case where there was a newly erected building, *Watford Borough
Council v Parcourt Property Investment Co Ltd*[1]. That was a case where the Heinz company (the well-known company which make baked beans among their 57 varieties)   d
were building a large office building in Watford. It was a newly erected building.
Much of the building was erected; but Heinz (when they took over the building) did a
lot of work themselves. When they took it over it was devoid of any internal partitioning at all. There were big floors rather like the present case. It was held by
Bridge J that this was not a completed building. Both sides there had agreed that the
appropriate test was whether or not it was ready for occupation. Bridge J held that it   e
an incomplete building and therefore they were not liable to be rated in regard to it
at all. If I may say so, that commends itself to me as being a proper application of the
word 'completed' in this context.
   The other case is on the other branch of the argument—where there is an existing
building which has been structurally altered so as to become a different building.
This was the case in *Easiwork Homes Ltd v London Borough of Redbridge*[2]. The position
there was that there was an old fashioned block of 16 flats in Wanstead. The company
decided to modernise the whole block of flats. The plumbing work had been removed.
Toilet fittings were being replaced. Electric wirings were being renewed and even in
some cases flooring was being relaid. In that case there was an existing building, the
old hereditament. The old valuation list, unless it was altered, continued to apply. It
continued to apply to the building until there was a new hereditament constructed: g
and so constructed as to be complete in that sense, as ready for occupation. In that
case the new modernised flats were not ready for occupation. They were incomplete.
So the old valuation list and the old rating applied. So it was held by the Divisional
Court in that case. The court said that it would be very odd if a person could avoid
paying rates simply by making a few removals of the sanitary fittings, part of the
plumbing, and so forth.   h
   Those two cases were, I think, correctly decided. They illustrate the problem which
arises under this schedule in respect of the two aspects: first, the newly erected
building, and, secondly, the old building which has been structurally altered.
   Now to come to the wording of the schedule, the important paragraph here is
para 8(1) which says:

   'Where a rating authority are of opinion—(*a*) that the erection of a building
   within their area has been completed; or (*b*) that the work remaining to be done

1 (1971) 17 RRC 19
2 [1970] 2 All ER 635, [1970] 2 QB 406

a   on a building within their area is such that the erection of the building can
reasonably be expected to be completed within three months, and that the
building is, or when completed will be, comprised in a relevant hereditament,
the authority may serve on the owner of the building a notice (hereafter in this
paragraph referred to as "a completion notice") stating that the erection of the
building is to be treated for the purposes of this Schedule as completed on the
date of service of the notice or on such later date as may be specified by the
b   notice.'

It seems to me that the schedule uses the word 'completed' there as something different
from 'structural alterations' in paras 10 and 15, and from the words "substantially
completed' in para 9; and I am impressed by the reference to para 6 which we were
referred to. The word 'completed' in para 8(1) seems to me to mean completed in the
c   sense of being ready for occupation.
    The test in this case is that the building should be ready for occupation. Once it is
completely ready for occupation, there is a free period of three months during which
rates are not payable, but after three months rates are payable. That applies not only
to a new building but it applies if there is an alteration to an old building.
    The only remaining point is what is to be done. The judge allowed the appeal.
d   That was all that he had to do, because the notice was not properly given: the building
was not complete. But there is a provision in para 8(5) which says that if the appeal is
in fact allowed 'the erection of the building shall be treated for those purposes as
completed on such date as the court shall determine'. It seems to me plain that the
court cannot apply that provision unless there is evidence on the matter and unless it
is asked to do so; and I should have thought there ought to be evidence to show when
e   it was completed so that the court could determine it. If it had the evidence it could
determine the date on which it was completed. But in the present case, where there
was no evidence given us and no application until after judgment, it seems to me that
that provision does not come into operation.
    We had much discussion as to the telephone cables and the electric wiring,
and how far office buildings could be said to be completed if the electric wiring had not
f   been completed and the telephones were not installed. I think that may give rise to
difficult questions on other matters. I should like to have further evidence as to the
condition of a particular building before giving any ruling on that matter.
    For the reasons I have given I think this appeal should be dismissed.

g   JAMES LJ. I agree with the conclusion of Lord Denning MR that the appeal should
be dismissed and substantially for the reasons that he has given. I will avoid being
repetitious by adding reasons of my own which merely conform to his. It seems to me
that the appeal raises two short points, the first being the meaning to be given to the
words 'completed' and 'completion' where they appear in relation to hereditaments in
Sch 1 to the General Rate Act 1967. It is a schedule that is not free from difficulty in
h   construction; and, if I may say so, not absolutely clear in places. But I see no warrant
whatsoever for importing the word 'structural' into para 8 of that schedule merely
because that word appears in para 10, and there should be the same test for completion in respect of newly erected buildings as for hereditaments which have already
been on the valuation list and are subjected to structural alterations so that they
become different or different parts of hereditaments. It seems to me that to adopt
j   that construction, which is the basis of counsel for the rating authority's argument,
strains the meaning of the statutory words. On the other hand, if one looks at the
following provisions, one finds there strong indications all pointing to the contention
for which the ratepayers contend in this case, namely that the test of completion is
capability of occupation and that is the test to be applied to a newly erected hereditament.
Section 79(1) and (2) of the 1967 Act provide:

'(1) Subject to subsection (2) of this section and to the following provisions of this Act, namely, paragraph 6(4) of Schedule 1, paragraph 5(4) of Schedule 4, paragraph 8(4) of Schedule 5, paragraphs 10(*b*) and 13 of Schedule 6 and paragraphs 14(*b*) and 15 of Schedule 7, where an alteration is made in a valuation list by virtue of sections 71 to 78 of this Act, then, in relation to any rate current at the date when the proposal in pursuance of which the amendment so made was served on the valuation officer, or, where the proposal was made by the valuation officer, current at the date when notice of the proposal was served on the occupier of the hereditament in question, that alteration shall be deemed to have had effect as from the commencement of the period in respect of which the rate was made, and shall, subject to the provisions of this section, have effect for the purposes of any subsequent rate.

'(2) Notwithstanding anything in subsection (1) of this section, where an alteration in the valuation list—(*a*) consists of the inclusion in the valuation list of a newly erected or newly constructed hereditament or an altered hereditament which has been out of occupation on account of structural alterations, or (*b*) is made by reason of any of the events specified in section 68(4)(*b*) to (*h*) of this Act, the alteration shall have effect only as from the date when the new or altered hereditament comes into occupation or as from the happening of the event by reason of which the alteration is made as the case may be.'

Paragraph 5(1) of Sch 1 provides:

'Subject to the provisions of this Schedule, the rateable value of a hereditament for the purposes of paragraph 1 thereof shall be the rateable value ascribed to it in the valuation list in force for the area in which the hereditament is situated or, if the hereditament is not included in that list, the first rateable value subsequently ascribed to the hereditament in a valuation list in force for that area.'

Paragraph 6 provides:

'(1) A rating authority may request the valuation officer to make a proposal for including in the valuation list in force for their area any unoccupied building in their area (together with any garden, yard, court or other land intended for use for the purposes of the building) which in their opinion is, or when completed will be, a newly erected dwelling-house; and if the valuation officer thinks fit to comply with the request he may make a proposal for including the building (together with any such garden, yard, court or other land as aforesaid) as a dwelling-house in that list and for ascribing to it in the list such values as he considers are appropriate or will be appropriate when the building is completed.

'(2) Where such a request is made by a rating authority and the valuation officer serves notice in writing by post or otherwise on the authority stating that he does not propose to comply with the request, the rating authority may, if they think fit, within the period of twenty-eight days beginning with the date of service of the notice, make a proposal for including the building and any other land to which the request relates as a dwelling-house in the list aforesaid and for ascribing to it in the list such values as the authority consider are appropriate or will be appropriate when the building is completed.

'(3) Where a new valuation list is prepared for any area, the valuation officer shall include in the list as transmitted to the rating authority—(*a*) any dwelling-house included in the current list for that area in pursuance of a proposal under sub-paragraph (1) or (2) of this paragraph; and (*b*) any building (with or without other land) in respect of which a proposal for its inclusion in the current list as a dwelling-house has been made by him under the said sub-paragraph (1) and has not been settled, and if any such proposal is made by him after the new list has been so transmitted, shall cause that list to be altered so as to include the building (with or without other land) as a dwelling-house in the new list.

'(4) Where a newly erected dwelling-house is first occupied after its completion and a rateable value has, in pursuance of the foregoing provisions of this
paragraph, previously been ascribed to it in the valuation list currently in force for
the area in which it is situated, any different rateable value subsequently ascribed
to it in that list and which, apart from this sub-paragraph, would have effect from
the date when the dwelling-house is first occupied as aforesaid shall be deemed
to have effect from the date on which the current list came into force or the date
from which the previous rateable value had effect, whichever is the later.'

One looks forward at the time, in considering a newly erected hereditament, to
the type of hereditament which is being required and sees whether at the date of the
notice there is anything lacking which ought to be there in order to satisfy the nature
of that hereditament. If there is something lacking and that which is lacking would,
when done, fall to be part of the hereditament and taken into account for the purposes
of the valuation, then there is no completion in the sense of capability of occupation.

On the other point which arises under the wording of para 8(5) of Sch 1, my view is
this: the trial judge rightly declined to determine a date on which the hereditament
should be regarded as completed. Paragraph 8 provides a number of methods whereby the date can be ascertained. Where the notice has been served under para 8(1)
the date is that specified on the notice or the date of service of the notice. But there may
be circumstances in which that has happened and then the rating authorities and the
ratepayers agree on a different date. Paragraph 8 provides that the agreed date shall
be the relevant one. Having served the notice, the rating authority may, by reason of
ascertaining new facts, withdraw the notice and serve a new one. Then the date of
service of the new one or the date specified in the new one is the relevant date. As I
read para 8(5), that provides, in the event of the notice not being withdrawn and an
appeal being brought, the appeal not being abandoned or dismissed, (which is this
case) then, although the word is 'shall', the court can, if asked, short-circuit the means
of serving a new notice and going through the procedure afresh. That, I think, is the
proper construction to be applied to that sub-paragraph and think the county court
judge rightly declined in this case to specify the date.

BRIDGE LJ. I also agree that this appeal should be dismissed, substantially for
the reasons given in both the judgments which have been delivered, and I too shall
seek to add the few observations that I wish to make in as short a compass as I may and
without setting out in extenso the elaborate and complex provisions of the General
Rate Act 1967 which have led me to the clear conclusion at which I have arrived.
The essential question for decision is what is the appropriate test to be applied under
para 8 of Sch 1 to the 1967 Act as to when a building is properly regarded as completed.
The key phrase in the paragraph, in my judgment, is the phrase 'and that the building
is, or when completed will be, comprised in a relevant hereditament'. 'Relevant
hereditament' is defined in para 15 of the same schedule as meaning—

'any hereditament consisting of, or of part of, a house, shop, office, factory, mill
or other building whatsoever, together with any garden, yard, court or other land
ordinarily used or intended for use for the purposes of the building or part . . .'

Bearing in mind that, under the law as it stood for centuries before unoccupied property became capable of rating, occupation was always the test of liability, if, construing
this provision without having regard to its wider context, I should say without hesitation that what was contemplated was that the building should be completed so as
to be capable of occupation for the appropriate purposes of the particular hereditament, i e as a house, shop, office etc. If the building lacks features which before it
can be occupied will have to be provided and when provided will form part of the
occupied hereditament and form the basis of the valuation of that hereditament, then
I would take the view, unless constrained to the contrary, that that building was not

within the meaning of the relevant provision of a completed building. The two main
arguments of counsel for the rating authority to the contrary are based first on the   *a*
use of the phrase 'the completion of the structural alteration' in para 10 of Sch 1, which
I will not set out, and secondly on the decision of the Divisional Court to which I
was a party in Easiwork Homes Ltd v London Borough of Redbridge[1]. In assessing
the strength of counsel for the rating authority's submissions I take account of other
aspects of the context in which the provisions are construed are found which have
been forcibly drawn to our attention by counsel for the ratepayers. The structural   *b*
test of completion which is suggested to us by counsel for the rating authority seems
to me to be an extraordinarily difficult one to apply in the context of para 9 of Sch 1
which refers to 'substantial completion' and contemplates additional work being
done after substantial completion but before final completion. What on earth could
they be if counsel for the rating authority's test of structural completion is the right
test? Again, without looking at the detail of the provisions, it is clear that by the   *c*
operation of para 5(1) of Sch 1, and ss 69 and 79(2) of the Act, the first valuation which
can reach the valuation list and on which the liability to the unoccupied rate pending
occupation of a new building is retrospectively assessed is a valuation of the new building as it exists when it is occupied. That is in sharp contrast with the valuation possibilities which arise under the provisions of ss 79(2)(b) and 68(4)(b) in relation to an old
hereditament undergoing structural alteration. It is clear that in a situation where an   *d*
old existing hereditament has a valuation based on occupiable value and is undergoing
radical structural alterations, it can be the subject of a proposal for an alteration in the
valuation list for, at all events, any substantial period when by reason of the alteration it is incapable of occupation. That seems to me to provide the answer to the
problem of hardship to an owner which in the Divisional Court we felt could arise in
the Easiwork case[1].   *e*
    In the light of these considerations I come to the conclusion that capability of occupa-
tion is the test of completion which should be applicable both under para 8 to a new
building and under para 10 to a new hereditament which comes into existence by
structural alteration of an old building. To adopt the occupiability test advocated by
counsel for the ratepayers, and not the structural completion test advocated by
counsel for the rating authority, to my mind does no violence to the language of para   *f*
10 where the word 'structural' is used to describe the nature of the operation to which
the paragraph applies and not to indicate a test of completion of that operation.
Similarly the argument based on the decision of the Divisional Court in the Easiwork
case[1] can be rejected for this reason. Counsel for the rating authority submits that the
case establishes that a 'relevant hereditament' can exist notwithstanding that it is not
capable of occupation; and so it does. But in the special situation where an existing   *g*
hereditament is under alteration, then either by direct application of para 10 of Sch 1
or by analogy with it, it is the clear result of express provision that the old hereditament remains in existence and remains (subject to the possibility of a proposal for any
change) at the valuation shown in the valuation list until the moment when the new
hereditament comes into existence. But it does not follow that that would be sensible
or reasonable to apply as the test of completion of a new building under para 8 or of a   *h*
hereditament under para 10 any other test than the completion of that building to the
point where it is capable of occupation as such.
    On the subsidiary point which has been raised as to the power of the county court
judge, it is odd at first blush to find that the only express power given to the court is the
power to determine the date when the building should be deemed to be completed.
Paragraph 8(5) provides: *j*

'. . . if the notice is not withdrawn and such an appeal is brought and is not
abandoned or dismissed, the erection of the building shall be treated for those
purposes as completed on such date as the court shall determine.'

1   [1970] 2 All ER 635, [1970] 2 QB 406

a In a case where the issue is canvassed and fully explored and evidence is put before the court showing that the building has been completed, or, if not, when it can reasonably be expected to be completed and the court has reached a conclusion on those matters and is asked by the local authoriy to substitute a new date for the date in the notice, I have no doubt that that power can and should be exercised. But all that happened here was that the appellants, the ratepayers, established their ground of appeal against the completion notices which had been served, showed that on the proper test the

b notices were incorrect and, at all events until after the county court judge had given judgment, the question of determining a fresh date of completion was never canvassed. In those circumstances I do not see how it was open to the county court judge to exercise in any way his powers under para 8(5). I think he was right not to do so.

Appeal dismissed. Leave to appeal to the House of Lords refused.

c Solicitors: *J J Warren* (for the rating authority); *Nabarro Nathanson & Co* (for the ratepayers).

Wendy Shockett Barrister.

d
R v Annesley

COURT OF APPEAL, CRIMINAL DIVISION
BRIDGE LJ, BRISTOW AND BOREHAM JJ
17th, 21st NOVEMBER 1975

e *Sentence – Postponement – Crown Court – Jurisdiction – Postponement of part of sentence – Postponement for period in excess of 28 days – Road traffic offences – Custodial sentences and periods of disqualification imposed – Defendant's licence not available when sentences imposed – Subsequent research showing that defendant had two previous convictions carrying disqualification –Defendant brought back to court seven weeks later and further period of disqualification imposed under totting-up procedure – Whether court having jurisdiction*
f *to order disqualification after lapse of seven weeks – Courts Act 1971, s 11(2) – Road Traffic Act 1972, s 93(3).*

The appellant was convicted by justices of (1) taking and driving a motor vehicle, (2) driving with a blood-alcohol concentration above the prescribed limit, and (3) driving without insurance. He was committed for sentence to the Crown Court and sentenced for the offences as follows: (1) two years' imprisonment licence en-
g dorsed, (2) three months' imprisonment concurrent and three years' disqualification, licence endorsed, and (3) seven days' imprisonment concurrent, licence endorsed. At the hearing in the Crown Court the appellant's driving licence was missing, and therefore the judge was unable to deal with the appellant's liability to further disqualification under the 'totting-up' provisions of s 93(3) of the Road Traffic Act 1972. Some seven weeks later the appellant was brought back before the court.
h His driving licence was still missing, but his record had been found to include two previous convictions. Accordingly he was sentenced to a further six months' disqualification under s 93(3) of the 1972 Act to run consecutively to the three year period. On appeal, the sentence of two years' imprisonment was reduced to one year and the three year period of disqualification to two years. The appellant also contended that the six month period of disqualification imposed under s 93(3) should be set
j aside on the ground that, since the court had not exercised its powers under s 1(1)[a]

---

a Section 1, so far as material, provides:
    '(1) . . . the Crown Court or a magistrates' court may defer passing sentence on an offender . . .
    '(3) The power conferred by this section shall be exercisable only if the offender consents . . .'

of the Powers of Criminal Courts Act 1973 to defer sentence, the additional disqualification should have been imposed within 28 days of the original sentence, as required *a* by s 11(2)*b* of the Courts Act 1971.

Held – The Crown Court had retained the jurisdiction at common law to postpone passing sentence, or part of a sentence, if the circumstances of a case made it necessary. Although it was bad sentencing practice for different parts of a sentence to be pronounced on separate occasions, in the appellant's case it was justified since it would *b* have been unnecessarily cruel to refuse to disclose to him whether he was to receive a custodial sentence simply because the material for dealing with the totting-up under s 93(3) was not immediately available and would take some time to obtain. Accordingly the appeal against the disqualification order under s 93(3) would be dismissed (see p 592 *c* to *f*, post).

R v Ingle [1974] 3 All ER 811 applied.   *c*

R v Fairhead [1975] 2 All ER 737 and R v Talgarth Justices, ex parte Bithell [1973] 2 All ER 717 distinguished.

Notes

For deferred sentences, see Supplément to 10 Halsbury's Laws (3rd Edn) para 888A.

For the Courts Act 1971, s 11, see 41 Halsbury's Statutes (3rd Edn) 299.   *d*

For the Road Traffic Act 1972, s 93, see 42 Halsbury's Statutes (3rd Edn) 1744.

For the Powers of Criminal Courts Act 1973, s 1, see 43 Halsbury's Statutes (3rd Edn) 290.

Cases referred to in judgment

R v Fairhead [1975] 2 All ER 737, 61 Cr App Rep 102, CA.

R v Ingle [1974] 3 All ER 811, 59 Cr App Rep 306, CA.   *e*

R v Talgarth Justices, ex parte Bithell [1973] 2 All ER 717, [1973] 1 WLR 1327, 137 JP 666, [1973] RTR 546, DC.

Case also cited

R v Northampton Justices, ex parte Nicholson [1974] RTR 97, DC.
                                                                                             f

Appeal

This was an appeal by Kevin Annesley against sentences imposed on him in the Crown Court at Manchester by his Honour Judge Gerrard on 18th April 1975 following his conviction at the Manchester City magistrates' court on 3rd February 1975 of an offence under s 12(1) of the Theft Act 1968 and two offences under the Road Traffic Act 1972. On 1st September 1975 the appeal was allowed in part and the sentences *g* varied. The court adjourned for further consideration so much of the appeal as related to a period of six months' disqualification imposed on the appellant under s 93(3) of the 1972 Act. The facts are set out in the judgment of the court.

Francis Coles for the appellant.
Leslie Portnoy for the Crown.

                                                                       Cur adv vult *h*

21st November. **BRISTOW J** read the following judgment of the court: On 3rd February 1975 this appellant, Kevin Annesley, then aged 23, pleaded guilty at the Manchester City magistrates' court to the following offences: (1) taking away a motor vehicle without the owner's consent; (2) driving with blood-alcohol concen- *j* tration above the prescribed limit; (3) driving without insurance. On 25th March 1975 he was committed for sentence to the Crown Court, and on 18th April was sentenced by Judge Gerrard as follows: (1) two years' imprisonment, licence endorsed;

---

b Section 11(2), so far as material, is set out at p 591 *c*, post

(2) three months' imprisonment concurrent and a three year disqualification, licence
a endorsed; (3) seven days' imprisonment concurrent, licence endorsed.

At the hearing in the Crown Court, the appellant's driving licence was missing,
and the judge was not in a position to deal with the problem of further disqualification under the 'totting-up' provisions of s 93(3) of the Road Traffic Act 1972. Having
delivered the substantive sentences for the three offences, the judge addressed the
appellant in the following terms:

b
'It may be if your driving licence is found and totted up that I will have to
have you brought back in respect of that totting-up. If I have to, you will be
brought back.'

On 6th June 1975, more than 28 days later, the appellant was brought back. His
driving licence was still missing, as indeed it is now, but his previous record
c with the assistance of the computer has been found to contain two previous convictions which caused the totting-up provisions of s 93(3) to bite. Judge Gerrard
accordingly imposed a further period of disqualification of six months.

On 1st September, before another division of this court, the appellant's appeal
against sentence was heard, and the period of two years for the first offence was
reduced to six months. The period of disqualification of three years for driving with
d excess alcohol in the blood was reduced to two years. The court adjourned consideration of the question raised in respect of the further disqualification of six
months under s 93(3), granted the appellant legal aid to cover the adjourned hearing,
and directed that the Crown should be represented on the adjourned hearing. It
is accordingly only this aspect of the matter which has been argued before us.

The appellant's point, vigorously argued by counsel on his behalf, is this. Section 11(2)
e of the Courts Act 1971, which set up the Crown Court in place of courts of assize and
quarter sessions, provides:

'. . . a sentence imposed, or other order made, by the Crown Court when
dealing with an offender may be varied or rescinded by the Crown Court within
the period of 28 days beginning with the day on which the sentence or other
f order was imposed or made . . .'

Counsel for the appellant submits that this express provision involves the consequence that the Crown Court does not enjoy the common law jurisdiction enjoyed by courts of assize and quarter sessions to adjourn sentence. He submits that the
Crown Court can only put off sentence either in pursuance of the power conferred
by s 11(2) of the 1971 Act, or under the power conferred by s 1 of the Powers of Criminal
g Courts Act 1973. It is clear that the judge was not exercising his power under s 1 for
this requires the consent of the offender, and he did not invite the appellant to consent.
Therefore, because more than 28 days elapsed between 18th April and 6th June,
there was no jurisdiction to add the six months' disqualification under s 93 of the 1972
Act, and that part of the sentence, says counsel for the appellant, must be quashed.

Counsel relied on the decision of this court in *R v Fairhead*[1]. In that case the trial
h judge disqualified the offender on the spot but deferred passing sentence under
the statutory powers given by s 1 of the 1973 Act. On appeal this court held that to
'split' the order of the court in this way was not only bad practice, but also contrary
to the statutory power conferred by the section. This court stressed the importance
of care being taken to make clear what course the court was following: see the judgment of James LJ[2]. It is to be noted that in *Fairhead's* case[1] sentence was put off for
j much longer than 28 days. But it was not argued that if the postponement was not
under the powers conferred by s 1 of the 1973 Act, s 11(2) of the 1971 Act would
have deprived the court of jurisdiction to pass sentence after more than 28 days.

---

1   [1975] 2 All ER 737
2   [1975] 2 All ER at 739

Reference was also made to *R v Talgarth Justices, ex parte Bithell*[1]. In that case the Divisional Court held that there was no power under s 14(3) of the Magistrates' Courts *a* Act 1952 for justices to adjourn after conviction and before sentence for more than four weeks or to adjourn part of a sentence. Lord Widgery CJ[2] observed that it is in any event bad sentencing practice to deal on different occasions with different elements in the disposal of a single case. But he also said that the court would not have quashed the justices' decision on certiorari merely because it was not in accordance with good *b* sentencing practice.

Counsel for the Crown submits that the fallacy underlying the argument for the appellant is to suppose that the only powers under which sentence can be put off by the Crown Court are those under s 11 of the Courts Act 1971 or s 1 of the Powers of Criminal Courts Act 1973. He points to s 1(7) of the 1973 Act and s 8 of and Sch 1 to the 1971 Act as showing that the common law power vested in superior courts of putting off sentences or some part of a sentence has not been removed. *R v Ingle*[3] is *c* an authority to this effect; see the judgment of Roskill LJ[4].

In the judgment of this court it is clear from these authorities and statutory provisions that the Crown Court still enjoys the common law jurisdiction vested in its predecessors to put off passing the whole of a sentence, or indeed part of a sentence, if the circumstances make it necessary. While accepting the proposition that to take two bites at the sentencing cherry is bad practice, there may be circumstances in *d* which it may be very desirable, when all the material necessary to complete all elements of a sentencing problem is not immediately available, to deal with the substantive sentence at once and postpone what may have to be done in addition, rather than postpone the whole of the sentence till all the material is to hand.

So here. This court thinks it would have been unnecessarily cruel to keep the appellant in the dark whether, and if so how long, a custodial sentence he was to receive, *e* simply because the material necessary for dealing with 'totting-up' under s 93(3) of the 1972 Act was not immediately available, and must take some time to obtain, up to three weeks in the ordinary way. It took longer than 28 days to obtain it in this case, because the appellant did his motoring under more than one name. We think the judge had jurisdiction to do what he did, and that in the circumstances of this case it was not bad practice for him to do it. *f*

The appeal against the additional six months' disqualification accordingly fails.

Appeal dismissed.

Solicitors: *Pariser & Co*, Manchester (for the appellant); *D S Gandy*, Manchester (for the Crown). *g*

Lea Josse Barrister.

1   [1973] 2 All ER 717, [1973] 1 WLR 1327
2   [1973] 2 All ER at 719, [1973] 1 WLR at 1329
3   [1974] 3 All ER 811
4   [1974] 3 All ER at 815

Re Jones (deceased)
Evans v Harries and others

COURT OF APPEAL, CIVIL DIVISION
BUCKLEY, ROSKILL AND GOFF LJJ
30th, 31st OCTOBER, 3rd NOVEMBER 1975

Will – Revocation – Conditional revocation – Condition unfulfilled – Intention of testator – Revocation with intention of making new will – Mutilation or destruction of existing will – Mutilation or destruction effected with a view to making new will – No new will made – Effectiveness of revocation – Test to be applied – Act of revocation ineffective only if testator's intention that revocation should not be effective until new will made – Inference as to testator's intention to be drawn from surrounding circumstances.

The testatrix made a will dated 12th July 1965. The testatrix had a number of nephews and nieces, one niece being the plaintiff. Under the terms of her will, the testatrix devised a smallholding to the plaintiff and the plaintiff's sister in equal shares and, inter alia, divided the residue of her estate equally among the other nephews and nieces. The testatrix, who had the custody of the original of her will, was on close terms with the plaintiff and the plaintiff's sister and was also on good terms with her other nephews and nieces. In 1970 the testatrix considered making changes in her will and visited her bank manager on a number of occasions in that connection. On 23rd September 1970 the testatrix told her bank manager that she intended to leave the smallholding to the children of her nephew J since she rarely saw the plaintiff or the plaintiff's sister and in any case they had acquired a property of their own. After speaking with the bank manager, the testatrix went to see her solicitor with the intention of making a new will. The solicitor was unable to see the testatrix but it was arranged that he would see her the following week in order to take her instructions for a new will. The testatrix then became seriously ill and sent for another nephew, W. On 27th September the testatrix told W that she was on the point of death and in answer to a question from W stated that she had not made a will. On 5th October the testatrix died before being able to make a new will. Subsequently the testatrix's 1965 will was found in a mutilated condition which suggested that it had been cut by a pair of scissors. The part of the will which had been cut off included clauses relating to the bequest of a rentcharge, the devise of the smallholding to the plaintiff and the plaintiff's sister, part of a clause relating to pecuniary legacies and the signatures of the testatrix and the attesting witnesses. The part which had been cut off was never found. The plaintiff brought an action to propound the will made in 1965. The trial judge found that the testatrix had mutilated the will herself on or about 23rd September. The judge held that, in order to determine whether the testatrix had effectively revoked the will, it was necessary to consider whether she had mutilated the will with the intention of revoking it and dying intestate, or whether she had done so in order to make fresh testamentary dispositions. He concluded that, since the testatrix had mutilated the will with the intention of making a new will and that intention had not been carried out, the 1965 will had not been effectively revoked. The nephews and other nieces of the testatrix appealed.

Held – The appeal would be allowed for the following reasons—
  (i) Where a testator mutilated or destroyed a will with the intention of making a new will but failed to carry out that intention, it did not necessarily follow that the mutilation or destruction was ineffective to revoke the existing will. The revocation was only ineffective where it appeared that, in mutilating or destroying the will, the

x

testator's intention was conditional in the sense that he intended that the revocation
should only take effect when a new will was executed (see p 596 h to p 597 a, p 601 c   a
and d, p 602 d and e, p 603 a to c and e to h, p 605 e and f and p 607 b, post).

(ii) It followed that the judge had applied an incorrect test. The proper inference
to be drawn from the primary facts was that the testatrix did not intend that the
revocation of her existing will should be conditional or dependent on her making a
new one, but that by her mutilation of the will she intended to achieve its absolute
revocation. Such an inference was not necessarily inconsistent with the testatrix's   b
intention to make a new will at the earliest opportunity. It followed that the 1965
will had been effectively revoked and the testatrix had died intestate (see p 599 b to d,
p 604 b and d to g, p 605 a and p 607 c to p 608 d, post).

Re Southerden [1925] P 177 applied.

Re Bromham [1952] 1 All ER 110 explained.

c

Notes

For the doctrine of dependent relative revocation, see 39 Halsbury's Laws (3rd Edn)
899, 900, para 1368, and for cases on the subject, see 48 Digest (Repl) 209-214, 1870-1912.

Cases referred to in judgments

Addison, Re (1964) 108 Sol Jo 504.   d

Botting, Re, Botting v Botting [1951] 2 All ER 997, 48 Digest (Repl) 203, 1802.

Bromham, Re, Wass v Treasury Solicitor [1952] 1 All ER 110, [1951] 2 TLR 1149, 48 Digest
(Repl) 206, 1835.

Dancer v Crabb (1873) LR 3 P & D 98, [1861-73] All ER Rep 692, 42 LJP & M 53, 28 LT
914, 37 JP 663, 48 Digest (Repl) 210, 1877.

Dixon v Treasury Solicitor [1905] P 42, 74 LJP 33, 92 LT 427, 48 Digest (Repl) 211, 1892.   e

Faris, Re, Goddard v Overend (No 2) [1911] 1 IR 469, 48 Digest 165, *637.

Onions v Tyrer (1716) 1 P Wms 343, 2 Vern 741, 24 ER 418, sub nom Onyons v Tryers,
Prec Ch 459, Gilb Ch 130, LC, 48 Digest (Repl) 201, 1774.

Powell v Powell (1866) LR 1 P & D 209, [1861-73] All ER Rep 362, 35 LJP & M 100,
14 LT 800, 48 Digest (Repl) 209, 1870.

Southerden, Re, Adams v Southerden [1925] P 177, 95 LJP 1, 133 LT 505, CA, 48 Digest   f
(Repl) 214, 1910.

Thomas v Howell (1692) 1 Salk 170, 2 Eq Cas Abr 360, Holt KB 225, 4 Mod Rep 66, Skin
301, 91 ER 157, 48 Digest (Repl) 346, 2959.

Cases also cited

Appelbee, Re (1828) 1 Hag Ecc 143, 162 ER 536.   g

Feis, Re, Guilliaume (or Guillaume) v Ritz-Remorf [1963] 3 All ER 303, [1964] Ch D 106.

Green, Re, Ward v Bond (1962) Sol Jo 1034.

Mitcheson, Re (1863) 32 LJPM & A 202, 9 Jur NS 360.

Weston, Re (1869) LRIP & D 633, [1861-73] All ER Rep 364, 38 LJP & M 53, 20 LT
330, 33 JP 312.

h

Appeal

By a writ issued on 6th October 1971 and subsequently amended, the plaintiff, Julia
Ann Evans, suing on her own behalf and as executrix of Elizabeth Ann Evans deceased,
asked the court to pronounce for a will, as contained in a completed draft thereof,
made on 12th July 1965 by Mary Hannah Jones deceased ('the testatrix') of Blaen-
porth, Cardigan, who died on 5th October 1970. The defendants were James Henry   j
Harries, William George Harries, Anne Mary Roberts, Margaret Anne Harries,
Dorothy Ann Codrington, Evelyn Woelfel, Stanley Harries, Norma Jean Hipkins
and David Morris Evans who were persons interested in the estate of the testatrix
in the event of an intestacy. On 31st July 1974 in the Family Division at Swansea
Reeve J pronounced for the force and validity of the will of the testatrix as contained

in a carbon copy thereof. Four of the defendants, James Henry Harries, William
a George Harries, Anne Mary Roberts and Margaret Anne Harries, appealed against
that decision. The facts are set out in the judgment of Buckley LJ.

Peter Millett QC and *Kenneth Thomas* for the defendants.
Roger Gray QC and *Nigel Fricker* for the plaintiff.

b

BUCKLEY LJ. This is an appeal from a judgment of Reeve J at Swansea, on 31st
July 1974 where he was sitting as an additional judge of the Chancery Division. It
was a judgment in a probate action, in which he pronounced in favour of the last
will of the testatrix, Mary Hannah Jones. That will was dated 12th July 1965 and the
c lady died on 5th October 1970 but, as will emerge, the will was found after her death
in a mutilated state. The question for decision is whether the will should be taken
to have been revoked or not.

The testatrix had four brothers and sisters, all of whom had predeceased her. Her
elder brother, David, had four children, who are all resident in the United States of
America. Her second brother, William, had one child, who is the third defendant,
d Anne Mary Roberts. Her third brother, George, had three children: the first, second
and fourth defendants, James Henry Harries, William George Harries and Margaret
Anne Harries. Her sister, Sarah, had three children: the plaintiff, Julia Ann Evans,
another daughter, Elizabeth Anne Evans (who was originally a plaintiff in the proceedings but died after the writ was issued), and the plaintiff now sues on her behalf
as her personal representative, and a brother who is not a party to the proceedings.

e If the testatrix died intestate, the children of David would take one-sixteenth of her
estate each, the third defendant would take one-quarter, the first, second and fourth
defendants would take one-twelfth each, and the plaintiff and her sister's estate and
her brother would take one-twelfth each.

The testatrix had made a will in February 1959 by which she devised a smallholding, of which she was the owner, called 'Dryslwyn', to the two plaintiffs equally.
f She gave various pecuniary legacies to other relations and specifically disposed of a
certain rentcharge, and she left the residue equally between the third and fourth
defendants.

She made her last will on 12th July 1965 and that will was in the following form.
By cl 1 she revoked all previous testamentary dispositions. By cl 2 she appointed
executors and trustees. By cl 3 she made a specific bequest of the rentcharge in
g favour of her nephew, David Evans. By cl 4 she gave 'Dryslwyn' to the plaintiff and
her sister in equal shares. By cl 5, which was divided into five sub-paragraphs, she
gave pecuniary legacies. By cl 6 she gave the residue of her property to her nephews
and nieces, Anne Mary Roberts, Margaret Anne Harries, William George Harries
and James Henry Harries equally.

The will was typed on two sides of a piece of paper. The first side contained every-
h thing down to and including paras (a) and (b) of cl 5, with the exception of the final word
'pounds', and the back side of the paper contained the rest of the will and, of course,
the attestation clause and the signatures of the testatrix and the attesting witnesses.

After her death the will was found mutilated in the following manner. It had been
cut with a pair of scissors at the end of cl 2. The result of that was that cll 3, 4, 5(a) and
(b), with the exception of the word 'pounds' at the end of para (b), and the whole of
j the signatures of the testatrix and the attesting witnesses and the formal part set
opposite to those signatures, with the exception of the words 'signed by the said
Testatrix Mary Hannah', were cut off. The part which was so cut off, that is to say,
cll 3 to 5(b), and the signatures, was never found again. The rest of the will was found
amongst the testatrix's papers.

The learned judge found as a fact that it was the testatrix herself who had mutilated the will and that she had done so certainly before 27th September 1970 and probably on the afternoon of 23rd September 1970. The significance of those dates will emerge *a* presently.

He asked himself this question: did she cut her will with the intention of revoking it and dying intestate, or did she do so because she was determined to make some fresh testamentary dispositions? That question was, I think, not the right question, for reasons which I will explain; or, at any rate, if it was intended to be the right question, it was expressed in unfortunate terms, confusing if not inaccurate, but I *b* think it was really inaccurate.

Where a testator mutilates or destroys a will, the questions which arise, I think, are these: (1) Did he do so with the intention of revoking it? He may have believed that it had been effectively revoked by some other means, but was mistaken. In those circumstances, he may have merely torn it up, thinking that it was no longer worth the paper it was written on. For myself, in those circumstances, I should have *c* thought the right inference to draw was that he did not intend to revoke it at all; he was merely disposing of what he thought was rubbish. He may have destroyed it or mutilated it without realising that the document was in fact his will, or he may have been under some other kind of misapprehension.

However, if the answer is that he did not destroy or mutilate it with the intention of revoking it, he cannot have revoked it, because s 20 of the Wills Act 1837, so far as *d* relevant, provides that a will shall be revoked by burning, tearing or otherwise destroying the same with the intention of revoking it. If there is no intention of revoking it, the act of destruction or mutilation will not effect a revocation.

If, however, the answer to that question is that the testator did have a revocatory intention, the second question arises, which is this: (2) If he had an intention of revoking the will, was his intention absolute or qualified, so as to be contingent or *e* conditional? If it was absolute, that is the end of the investigation, for the act takes effect as a revocation.

If, however, it was qualified, the further question which arises is: (3) What was the nature of the qualification? The testator's intention may have been dependent on an intent to revive an earlier testamentary document, founded on an erroneous belief that the cancellation of the later will would have that effect, as in *Powell v Powell*[1]; *f* or it may have been wholly and solely dependent on an intention to displace it by some new testamentary disposition. An example of this may be taken to be *Dixon v Treasury Solicitor*[2] where there was evidence that the testator thought that the cancellation of an earlier will was a necessary pre-condition of making a new one.

If the testator's intention is found to have been a qualified one, subject to some condition or contingency, the final question arises: (4) Has that condition or contin- *g* gency been satisfied or occurred? If the condition or contingency to which the intention to revoke was subject has not been satisfied or occurred, the revocation is ineffective; if it has been satisfied or occurred, the revocation is effective.

The fact that at the time of the mutilation or destruction the testator intended or contemplated making a new will is not, in my judgment, conclusive of the question whether his intention to revoke was dependent on his subsequently making a new *h* will. A testator who has made a will in favour of A may become disenchanted with A and decide not to benefit him. He may well at the same time decide that in these circumstances he will benefit B instead of A. It does not by any means follow that his intention to disinherit A will be dependent on his benefiting B, or making a will under which B could take.

If he were told that for some reason B could not or would not benefit under his *i* new will, would the testator say, 'In that case, I want my gift to A to stand', or would he say, 'Well, even so, I do not wish A to benefit'? In the former case, his animus

1   (1866) LR 1 P &D 209, [1861-73] All ER Rep 362
2   [1905] P 42

revocandi at the time of the destruction or mutilation of his will could properly
a be regarded as dependent on the execution of a new will, but not in the latter.

It is consequently necessary to pay attention to the circumstances surrounding the
mutilation or destruction of the will to discover whether any intention that the testator then had of revoking the will was absolute or qualified and, if qualified, in what
way it was qualified.

The facts found in the present case are as follows. First of all, the testatrix removed
b her will from her solicitor in February 1967, and there was no evidence that thereafter
it ever left her possession. Secondly, a close relationship existed between the testatrix
and the plaintiff and her sister, and the testatrix was on good terms with the other
members of her family, that is to say, her nephews and other nieces. Thirdly, during
1970 the testatrix was considering making changes in her will, and during that year
she visited her bank manager in this connection on four occasions, the last of which
c was on 23rd September, a Wednesday. Fourthly, on that occasion, on 23rd September,
there was an important conversation between the testatrix and her bank manager,
in the course of which she told him that she had definitely decided to give 'Dryslwyn'
to the children of her nephew, James, the first defendant. She said that under her
existing will she had given that property to the plaintiff and her sister, but that she
hardly ever saw them and it seemed to her as though they did not care whether she
d was alive or dead.

Pausing there, it may be, on the judge's finding that there was a close relationship
between the testatrix and the plaintiff and her sister, that that was an unreasonable
attitude of mind for the testatrix to have adopted, but we are not concerned with
whether her views were reasonable or unreasonable; we are concerned with the
subjective state of her mind at the relevant time.

e The conversation with the bank manager went on in the following way. The testatrix said that in any event her intention to leave 'Dryslwyn' to her nephew's children
was because the plaintiff and her sister had by that time acquired a property of their
own. That was indeed the fact, because they had bought a farm. She went on to say
to the bank manager that her nephew, James, had been very good to her and it was
for that reason that she was leaving the smallholding to his children.

f Following the interview with the bank manager, the testatrix went to her solicitor's
office with the intention of giving him instructions for the making of a new will.
Mr Hugh Evans, the solicitor, was unfortunately otherwise engaged and was not
able to take her instructions on that date, but he told her that, if she would telephone
and make an appointment early during the next week, he would be able to see her
and take her instructions for a new will.

g Unhappily that never took place, because during the weekend the testatrix was
taken ill and eventually, on Tuesday, 29th September, she was admitted to hospital,
where she remained until her death on 5th October. She never gave any instructions
to Mr Evans and she never made any new will.

On 27th September the testatrix had a conversation with her nephew, William.
He visited her in consequence of a telephone conversation he had had with her on the
h previous day, the Saturday. A conversation then took place between them, when the
deceased said that she felt she was at the point of death, and she produced a large
number of business documents to him of one kind and another, dealing so far as he
could see with her financial affairs. He asked her whether she had made a will and
he said in evidence that she replied that she had not. The learned judge accepted
that the testatrix had told her nephew that.

j On the same day, apparently, notwithstanding that the testatrix was feeling very
unwell, she did in fact go for a motor drive with the plaintiff and her brother and
sister, which, of course, is quite consistent with the judge's finding that there was a
close relationship between the testatrix and those relations of hers.

The learned judge found as a fact that the testatrix was a person who would have
been likely to be reticent in the family about her testamentary intentions, but she had

had a conversation at an earlier date than the events which I have been referring to, in July 1970, with a Mr Idwal Thomas, who was a distant relative of hers, in which she had said that she could not leave 'Dryslwyn' to any one person because she had not enough money to leave equal shares to all, by which the learned judge concluded that she was referring to all her nephews and nieces.

There was one other conversation referred to in evidence, which took place about three weeks before the testatrix's death. Mrs James, who was a friend of hers of many years' standing, paid her a visit and she found the testatrix on a ladder decorating some part of the inside of the house. She says that on that occasion the testatrix said to her that she wanted to have the house nicely painted for 'Lizzie and Julia', that is to say for the plaintiff and her sister, indicating, of course, that at the time of that conversation she contemplated that those two nieces of hers would become entitled to the house on her death.

The principal witness at the trial was the plaintiff herself. Her case was that the will had not been defaced by the testatrix, but by someone else after the testatrix's death. The learned judge reached the conclusion that the plaintiff was attempting to throw doubt on the honesty of one or more of the testatrix's nephews and other nieces. The plaintiff gave evidence of a conversation some time in the week commencing 27th September in which she asked the testatrix what was to happen to 'Dryslwyn' at her death and the testatrix had answered, 'It's for Lizzie Anne and you'.

The learned judge took a very adverse view of the plaintiff as a witness. He reached the conclusion that he could not accept any evidence of hers which was not corroborated, and he clearly rejected that part of the plaintiff's evidence.

In the circumstances, the judge considered that the following were reasonable inferences to draw from the primary facts. Firstly, from some time in the year 1970 the deceased was minded to change her 1965 will. Secondly, for some months during the summer of 1970, she was undecided in her mind as to the disposition of 'Dryslwyn'. For some time she may have been minded to treat all her blood relations equally so far as she could, but by the early part of September 1970 she may have vacillated once again to adhering to the disposition in her will, that is the disposition of 'Dryslwyn'.

If, on the evidence, it is reasonable to infer that the mutilation was wholly and solely referable to her intention to make a new will, this was a case of conditional revocation or, as it is sometimes called, dependent relative revocation. If, on the other hand, it was referable wholly to her intention to cut out the plaintiff and her sister, it was not such a case, even if that intention was accompanied by an intention to make a new devise as soon as she could in favour of the children of her nephew, James.

It seems to me, with deference to the learned judge, that his conclusion involves ignoring the evidence of the important conversations with Mr Davies, the bank manager, on 23rd September when the testatrix complained, justly or unjustly, of the attitude of the plaintiff and her sister towards herself, the testatrix, and when she explained that she no longer intended to give the smallholding to them, because they had acquired a property of their own, and that she intended to give it to the children of her nephew, Jim, because he, Jim, had been very good to her.

Moreover, it is inconsistent, in my view, with the conversation with the testatrix's nephew, William, when she said on 27th September that she had not made a will. Of course, taken literally, that was not true, for she had made two wills in the course of her life, one in 1959, and her last will in 1965; but it seems to me much more consistent with that conversation that the testatrix should then have cancelled her last will with an intention to revoke it and should have been of the opinion that she had no will at that moment in force, than that she should have mutilated her will with the intention that that mutilation should not operate as a revocation unless and until she had made a new will.

There was no direct evidence of any belief by the testatrix that the destruction of her will was a necessary pre-condition of making an effective new will. Her last will had contained a revocation clause, by which she had revoked an earlier will, from which it is reasonable to infer in the absence of contrary evidence that she knew that an existing will could be effectively revoked by a revocation clause in a new will without any other form of cancellation.

If, as the judge held, she most probably defaced the will on 23rd September, this was three days before she was taken seriously ill. It was on 27th September that she felt that she was going to die. There is no ground for supposing that on 23rd September she did not fully expect to see Mr Hugh Evans within a week to make a new will. If her intention was merely to displace her existing will by another, what reason could she have had for mutilating the will on 23rd September?

With deference to the learned judge, it seems to me that the inference which most convincingly fits these facts is that the testatrix was not content that the revocation of her existing will should depend on her making a new one, but that she wished and intended to achieve what she could, namely the revocation of her existing will, there and then, and that this was her reason for mutilating it. This is not necessarily inconsistent with her having at the same time an intention to make a new will at the earliest opportunity devising 'Dryslwyn' to the children of her nephew. None of the findings of primary fact is disputed. I accept them without demur, but I differ from the judge in my opinion of the proper inference to draw from them.

I would hold that by defacing her will on or about 23rd September, the testatrix intended there and then to revoke it and that this intention was not conditional or contingent on her making a new will.

We were referred to several authorities. References to other cases on issues of fact are of little assistance, because in this field every case must depend on its own particular facts; but I should, perhaps, refer to the only case in which this subject appears to have been dealt with in the Court of Appeal: Re Southerden[1].

That was not a case in which the testator, who destroyed his will, was intending to make a new one. It was a case in which the testator destroyed his will with the intention of revoking it, but under the misapprehension that by so doing his wife, if she survived him, would become entitled to the whole of his property absolutely under his intestacy. The will in question had been made when the testator and his wife were about to embark on a journey to the United States of America, and on their return the testator said to his wife, referring to his will, 'This is no good now. We have returned safely and it is all yours. We might as well burn it.' He thereupon destroyed the will.

Pollock MR[2] said that the learned judge, from whom the appeal came, had been satisfied that the testator destroyed the will under the impression that all his property would go to his widow under an intestacy, which, of course, was incorrect, and that therefore the revocation was of no use and the original will stood. He referred to the judgment of Lord Meredith, Master of the Rolls in Ireland, in Re Faris (No 2)[3], where the Irish Master of the Rolls adopted a statement from Theobald on Wills[4] in the following passage cited from his judgment[5]:

> ' "The true view may be that a revocation grounded on an assumption of fact which is false takes effect unless, as a matter of construction, the truth of the fact is the condition of the revocation, or, in other words, unless the revocation is contingent upon the fact being true: see Thomas v Howell[6]''. I adopt that statement of the law, merely substituting for the words "may be" the word "is". The true view is, in my opinion, the view so clearly stated by Mr. Theobald.'

1   [1925] P 177
2   [1925] P at 182
3   [1911] 1 IR 469
4   7th Edn (1908), p 750
5   [1911] 1 IR at 472
6   (1692) 1 Salk 170

Pollock MR[1] adopted that statement both of the Master of the Rolls in Ireland and of Mr Theobald. Warrington LJ[2] said: 'The cases also establish that if the truth of a particular fact is a condition of the destruction, and the fact turns out not to be true, there is no revocation'.

Atkin LJ[3] said:

'The question in each case is, had the testator the intention of revoking his will? The intention may be conditional, and if the revocation is subject to a condition which is not fulfilled, the revocation does not take effect.'

Those statements of the principle seem to me to accord precisely with the questions which I have outlined as being the questions which fall to be considered and answered in any case of this kind.

In the course of his judgment in *Re Southerden*[4], Pollock MR referred to *Powell v Powell*[5], to which I have already referred in this judgment, and he cited a statement of Lord Penzance, which is to be found in *Powell v Powell*[6], in the following terms:

'In both cases the act is referable, not to any abstract intention to revoke, but to an intention to validate another paper; and as in neither case is the sole condition upon which revocation was intended fulfilled, in neither is the "animus revocandi" present.'

Lord Penzance was there comparing a case in which a testator destroyed a will in anticipation of making a new one, and a case in which a testator destroyed a will with the mistaken belief that he could thereby revive an earlier one.

Pollock MR[7] also referred to *Dixon v Treasury Solicitor*[8], also mentioned earlier in this judgment, in which Gorell Barnes J[9] had left the following two questions to the jury:

'(1) Whether the testator cut his signature off the will with the intention of revoking the will; or (2) Whether the testator cut his signature off the will with the intention that the will should be revoked conditionally on his executing a fresh will.'

Those cases also appear to me to fit into the pattern I have indicated.

We were referred to Lord Merriman P's decision in *Re Bromham*[10]. What Lord Merriman P[11] said there was criticised as being an inadequate statement of the doctrine, because at the end of his judgment what he said was that he—

'had no doubt that the destruction of the existing will took place with reference to the testator's intention to make a new will. That being so, the act of revocation was conditional and the subsequent lapse of time is immaterial.'

The nature of the criticism is that a finding that a will has been destroyed or defaced with reference to an intention to make a new will is, it is said, insufficient; it must be conditional on the making of a new will. However, when one reads the judgment of Lord Merriman P in its entirety, I think that that is in fact what he was deciding, for at

---

1 [1925] P at 182
2 [1925] P at 184
3 [1925] P at 185
4 [1925] P 177
5 (1866) LR 1 P & D 209
6 LR 1 P & D at 213
7 [1925] P at 183
8 [1905] P 42
9 [1905] P at 46
10 [1952] 1 All ER 110, [1951] 2 TLR 1149
11 [1952] 1 All ER at 111, [1951] 2 TLR at 1155

a the outset of his judgment he states the question thus: '. . . and the sole question in this case is whether that revocation was absolute or conditional.' It is clear that he was holding on the facts of the case that it was conditional and that the condition had not been fulfilled.

There is only one other case that I think I need mention, and that is the decision of Karminski J in Re Addison[1]. In July 1961 the testator there removed his will from the custody of his solicitor and took it away with him, saying that because of the death of
b his wife he wanted to make a new will. He died in April 1962. No will could be found and Karminski J said that the facts showed that the testator took possession of the will for the sole purpose of making a new one. He said that in those circumstances the proper inference for the court to draw was that the testator destroyed the will intending to make a new one and that the doctrine of dependent relative revocation therefore applied to prevent the destruction of the will operating to revoke it.

c I think that that may be a rather misleading statement of the doctrine. The report is a very short one and may well not reflect precisely what the learned judge said. But the fact that the testator destroyed his will and had at the same time the intention of making a new one, is not, in my judgment, something which necessarily leads to the conclusion that the revocation was intended to be conditional on the making of a new will, and if that is what Karminski J was intending to hold, then I think he was
d mistaken. However, I am inclined to think that that was not what he was intending to hold, for he stressed that the testator had taken possession of the will for the sole purpose of making a new one, and he may very well have thought, and indeed he may have held, that the sole purpose of destroying the will had been to make way for a new one which he intended to make. If that had been his sole purpose, then in my judgment the learned judge's decision was perfectly proper.
e For the reasons which I have attempted to make clear, I would allow this appeal.

ROSKILL LJ. The plaintiff in this action seeks to propound, and thus far has successfully propounded, a will of her late aunt, dated 12th July 1965. By that will, the valid execution of which is not in question, the testatrix, inter alia, devised to the
f plaintiff and her sister her smallholding in Cardiganshire. (See cl 4 of the copy will.)

The testatrix died on 5th October 1970. The sister herself died on 1st March 1972. This action is thus brought by the plaintiff for her own benefit and that of her late sister's estate. The defendants are cousins of the plaintiff. They stand to benefit from an intestacy, though it is right to say that they are also beneficiaries for various small sums under the disputed will. The learned judge, Reeve J, on 31st July 1974, gave
g judgment for the plaintiff and pronounced in favour of the will dated 12th July 1965. It would seem from his judgment that he did so with some reluctance, having in certain respects condemned the plaintiff as an untruthful witness; but he felt that on the facts as he found them and in spite of his disbelief of the plaintiff, the doctrine of dependent relative revocation compelled him so to do, for he said that he regarded this as a classic case for the application of that doctrine.
h In Re Southerden[2] Atkin LJ[3] described that doctrine as one which had been brought into existence 'in recent years'. It seems, however, to find its historical origin in a judgment of Cowper LC, in Onions v Tyrer[4]. Atkin LJ preferred to call this doctrine by the less cumbersome name of 'conditional revocation'. I respectfully agree and I shall do the same. He observed in that case[3] that this court was called on for the first time to express an opinion on that doctrine. Today, we in this court have to consider it
j

---

1 (1964) 108 Sol Jo 504
2 [1925] P 177
3 [1925] P at 185
4 (1716) 1 P Wms 343

for the second time, just over half a century later. The reason why we have now to consider this doctrine once again is as follows. About a fortnight before the testatrix *a* died, she mutilated that will dated 12th July 1965. There is no direct evidence when she did that, but the learned judge found, and there is no cross-appeal or cross-notice against this finding, that she did so before Sunday, 27th September 1970, and more probably on 23rd September 1970. She did so by cutting off the bottom part, with the result that on the back she removed her signature, most of the attestation clause and the subscriptions of the two witnesses, whilst on the front she removed *b* cl 3, cl 4 (which contained the devise of the smallholding to the plaintiff and her sister) and part of cl 5.

The learned judge appears to have thought that she effected the mutilation by cutting off her signature and the rest on the back, the excisions on the front being an inevitable consequence of those on the back. The judge may well have been right, although no forensic evidence was called on this topic; but a superficial examination *c* of the surviving part seems to lend some colour to the possibility that she cut from the front rather than the back. However, this is speculation in the absence of evidence, and, this matter not having been investigated at the trial, I shall assume that the judge was right in what he said on this point. What seemed absolutely clear to the judge, and I agree with him, is that the mutilation was effected with the intention of revoking the will. Thus s 20 of the Wills Act 1837 is satisfied. The sole question we have to *d* decide is whether the revocation was conditional or absolute.

By 'conditional' is meant that the efficacy of the revocation was to be dependent on the bringing into existence subsequently of a valid testamentary disposition, or of the existence or future existence of some fact. (See the judgment of Sir J P Wilde, later Lord Penzance, in *Powell v Powell*[1] and of Atkin LJ in *Re Southerden*[2].) By 'absolute' is meant that the revocation was to take effect at once, irrespective of *e* the bringing into existence subsequently of a valid testamentary disposition, or of the existence or future existence of some fact.

There are plenty of examples in the books, which were referred to in argument, of cases falling on one side of the line or on the other. Those cases, with respect, seem to me to be of no help in resolving the present dispute. They lay down no principle; they merely apply or seek to apply the principle, possibly not always consistently, *f* to widely differing facts. Buckley LJ has mentioned the decision of Karminski J in *Re Addison*[3]. I respectfully agree with Buckley LJ's comments on that decision. It is very briefly reported. If the report be accurate, with great respect to any judgment of Karminski J, I have difficulty in agreeing with the conclusion at which he seems to have arrived. On the other hand, if, as Buckley LJ has suggested, the report is unduly abbreviated, it may well be that the decision was right for reasons which do not appear *g* fully from the report. It is, however, important to observe how often the noun 'condition', or the adverb 'conditionally' is used in the cases. Sir J P Wilde used it in the passage quoted from his judgment in *Powell v Powell*[1]. Gorell Barnes J used it in the second question he left to the jury in *Dixon v Treasury Solicitor*[4].

Lord Merriman P said, perfectly correctly, if I may respectfully say so, at the outset of his judgment in *Re Bromham*[5]: '. . . the sole question is whether that revocation *h* was conditional or absolute'. The rather more general language to which Buckley LJ has referred in the last paragraph of the judgment, where Lord Merriman P[6] spoke of 'reference to the testator's intention to make a new will', is but a single phrase at the end of a long extempore judgment, and I think that that latter passage must be

j

---

1   (1866) LR 1 P & D at 213
2   [1925] P at 185
3   (1964) 108 Sol Jo 504
4   [1905] P at 46
5   See [1951] 2 TLR 1149 at 1151
6   [1952] 1 All ER at 111, [1951] 2 TLR at 1155

a read subject to the entirely accurate statement of the law in the opening part of that
judgment.   I respectfully agree with what Buckley LJ has said in his judgment about
that passage.

In short, in a case where the revocation purporting to be effected by mutilation or
some other method of destruction is 'conditional' in the sense that I have described
and the 'condition' is not fulfilled, the act of revocation is itself not fulfilled; it is
ineffective because it was subject to an unfulfilled condition.   But if the revocation
b is 'absolute', in the sense in which I have used that word, then that revocation takes
immediate effect, even if the result may subsequently be to bring about an intestacy,
or some other result which it is difficult to believe the testator can have intended
in his or her lifetime.   But I think counsel for the plaintiff was right when he said in
argument that that consideration is irrelevant, just as the judge's condemnation of the
plaintiff as a liar is for the purpose of determining the present appeal also largely
c irrelevant.   The doctrine is there.   Our duty is to apply it, or to refuse to apply it, to the
facts as we find them.

I have ventured to stress these points, because the learned judge said:

'I then have to ask myself this question, did she cut her will with the intention
of revoking it and dying intestate, or did she do so because she was determined
d   to make some fresh testamentary dispositions?'

With great respect to the learned judge, it seems to me that counsel for the defendants' criticism of this passage is well founded. The judge has not asked himself
the right question or questions.   The first question which he has asked himself is not
the right question, and if one takes the two questions together, they do not, set one
against the other, create a true antithesis.
e   The learned judge appears to have thought that it was enough to decide this case
in the plaintiff's favour, if he were satisfied that the testatrix did not intend to die
intestate, since there was evidence that she intended to make a new will; but a mere
intention to make a new will, however clearly shown, is not enough of itself, as the
authorities show, to make the revocation conditional.

There may well be cases—and we have to decide whether the present case is or is
f not one—where the testator or testatrix says to himself or herself that, however
certain may then be his or her intention of making a new will and however certain or
uncertain he or she may be of the likely content of that new will when made, he or
she is determined to ensure forthwith that the old will shall no longer have any
effect at all, and to that end mutilates or otherwise destroys that old will with that
specific intent. Such a revocation should, in most cases at least, in my judgment, be
g regarded by the courts as absolute and not as conditional on the subsequent execution
of a new will. A mere present intent to make a new will at some future date is not
enough in such a case to prevent such an act or revocation being absolute, thus stopping
some disappointed beneficiary under the old will from seeking to have recourse to the
doctrine of conditional revocation, in the hope of finding relief in that equitable haven.

In this case the learned judge rejected the plaintiff's story that on Monday, 28th
h September, a week before her death, the testatrix said to the plaintiff: 'It [i e
the smallholding] is for Lizzie Ann [i e the sister now dead] and you.'   That leaves
the following important, positive, primary facts as found by the learned judge: (1) the
testatrix had told Mr Davies, the bank manager, in August 1970, that she was thinking
of giving her smallholding to her nephew, Jim, the first defendant; (2) she had
previously told a Mr Thomas, who was a distant relative, in July 1970, that she could
j not leave the smallholding to anyone, because she had not enough money to leave
equal shares to all and was going to make a new will; (3) she had told Mr Davies
on 23rd September that she had definitely decided to give the smallholding to Jim's
children; (4) immediately after the latter conversation, she went to see her solicitor,
clearly intending to take the first step towards making the new will to give effect
to that expressed intention; (5) her solicitor could not then see her, but suggested

an appointment for this purpose the following week; (6) before that appointment
could take place, the testatrix became seriously ill over the ensuing weekend and   *a*
apparently then thought she was dying; and (7) there must be added the judge's
finding, not disputed in this court, that during this period, and probably on 23rd
September, she mutilated the will in the manner I have already described.

These facts taken together suggest to me as a matter of probability that in her mind
the efficacy of the mutilation was not to depend on the subsequent execution of a
new will, but was designed to ensure forthwith that at least the plaintiff and her   *b*
sister should not get the smallholding. I do not find the evidence of Mrs James, any
more than did the learned judge, of sufficient weight to point seriously the other way.

There is the curious story, which the judge accepted as true, that the testatrix
told the second defendant on Sunday, 27th September, that she had not made a will.
The story is told in full in the judgment below, and I shall not repeat it. There are
various possible explanations of this. One is that she had already mutilated the old   *c*
will, thereby intending effectively to revoke it, but had not yet made a new one.
Another is that she was not prepared to discuss her affairs in detail with the second
defendant. But whatever the explanation—and I do not think it necessary to speculate
which, if any, is right—the conversation, accepting the second defendant's account of
it as accurate, is to my mind in no way indicative of the intention underlying the
mutilation being conditional; rather the opposite.   *d*

In a passage immediately following that which I have already ventured to criticise
as asking the wrong question, the learned judge said:

> 'Her frustration can well be imagined and she may well have felt that the least
> that she could do in furtherance of her intention and determination was to
> mutilate her existing will as a preliminary to the making of a fresh will.'   *e*

This seems to me, with respect, an entirely legitimate comment, but to point clearly
to the intention underlying the mutilation being absolute and not conditional on
the execution of the new will. Accordingly, had the learned judge asked himself the
right question in the immediately preceding sentence, I think that this perfectly proper
consideration that I have just read might well have led him to what I consider the right   *f*
answer should have been.

Counsel for the plaintiff urged on us that we should not interfere with the learned
judge's conclusion, because, he argued, it was one of fact. So in a sense it was, as
Atkin LJ pointed out in *Re Southerden*[1]; but it is a question of inference from the
primary facts found by the judge, which I have already tabulated, and we are in as
good a position as he was to draw inferences from those primary facts, having asked
ourselves, in the light of the authorities, the right question which, with great respect,   *g*
the learned judge failed to do. I am afraid, therefore, I find myself unable to agree with
the learned judge's conclusion. I do not think that the doctrine of conditional revocation has any application to this case on the true appraisal of all the facts. Accordingly,
I do not find it necessary to consider possible explanations of two other passages in the
judgment which were discussed at length in argument and which, with respect, I have
some difficulty in following.   *h*

In the result, I find myself in complete agreement with the judgment which
Buckley LJ has delivered, and for the reasons which he has given and which I have
given in this judgment, I would allow the appeal, set aside the order appealed from
and pronounce against the will propounded by the plaintiff. It was not disputed before
us in argument that an intestacy would follow.   *j*

GOFF LJ. I agree that this appeal should be allowed and with the reasons which
Buckley and Roskill LJJ have given for that conclusion. As, however, the doctrine

1   [1925] P at 185, 186

of dependant relative revocation has come before this court once only prior to this
a in its not brief life, I think it would not perhaps be a work of supererogation if I
delivered a judgment expressing briefly in my own words the reasons for agreeing
with the conclusion which has been reached.

It is not necessary for me to state the findings of fact by the learned trial judge, as
they were fully rehearsed by Buckley LJ. I would, however, wish to call attention
to what is quite obviously an error in the transcript of the judgment. The learned
b judge is there reported to have said: 'By the early part of 1970 she may have vacillated
once again to adhering to the disposition in her will . . .'

I think it is clear that he must in fact have said the early part of September 1970,
since the learned judge had previously, under his item 'Secondly', referred to what
had been happening for some months during the summer of 1970. Then, in the
passage I have mentioned, he said: '. . . she may have vacillated once again to adhering
c to the disposition in her will'. Finally, that that reference to the early part of 1970
is an error becomes clear beyond doubt, because the learned judge goes on to say:
'. . . and that would fit in with what Mrs James told me of the time when she saw the
deceased decorating her house'.

On the facts in this case, the question is whether the 1965 will was effectively
revoked, or whether, no subsequent will having been executed, it is saved and stands
d good by virtue of the doctrine of dependent relative revocation.

Very often the applicability of that doctrine comes in question when an act prima
facie revoking a will is done in circumstances where, to use a neutral expression for
the moment, a further will is in contemplation, but it is not confined to such cases.
It arises also, for example, where the testator has made a mistake as to the material
facts, or as to the result in law of an intestacy, or has acted in the erroneous belief
e that by revoking a will he can, without more, thereby revive a previous will which
that will had itself revoked.

In whatsoever way it arises, however, the principle on which it falls to be decided
is, in my judgment, the same and well settled by authority. It is this: was the revocation absolute and unqualified, in which case it takes effect whatever happens, or
conditional, in which case it does not take effect unless the condition be satisfied?
f I agree that each case must turn on its own facts and that reference to the authorities is
of use, therefore, only insofar as they establish, as in my judgment they plainly do,
the principle which I have just stated.

The principal authority for that purpose is, of course, the decision of this court
in *Re Southerden*[1]. I do not think it is necessary for me to take up time reading citations from the judgments in that case, as the passages on which I would rely have
g already been cited by Buckley LJ.

I would, however, wish to refer briefly to *Dancer v Crabb*[2] where Sir James Hannen
said[3]:

> 'Or, to state the proposition in different language, if the testator's act can be
> interpreted thus: "Whatever else I may do, I intend to cancel this as my will
h > from this time forth", the will is revoked; but if his meaning is, "As I have made
> a fresh will my old one may now be destroyed", the old will is not revoked if
> the new one be not in fact made.'

I would further point out that in *Dixon v Treasury Solicitor*[4], which has been cited
by Buckley and Roskill LJJ, Gorell Barnes J made the position very clear indeed,
j

---

1   [1925] P 177
2   (1873) LR 3 P & D 98
3   LR 3 P & D at 104
4   [1905] P 42

because in the course of his judgment, before leaving the question to the jury, he said[1]: 'There is no doubt that the testator did what he did because he was making **a** a new will'. He concluded[2]:

'The questions I leave to you are—(1) Whether the testator cut his signature off the will with the intention of revoking the will; or (2) Whether the testator cut his signature off the will with the intention that the will should be revoked conditionally on his executing a fresh will.' **b**

In *Re Botting*[3] Havers J said:

'It seems to me that in the circumstances of this case I am bound to make that *prima facie* presumption, and then it is open to the plaintiff to bring before me, if he can, evidence to rebut it and to show what the intention of the testator was **c** in destroying the will. If I am satisfied on the whole of the evidence that the destruction was conditional on another will being made, then the doctrine of dependent relative revocation applies . . .'

The only other reference I would make to authority is to the case of *Re Bromham*[4]. I would point out that there was a particular factor in that case tending strongly to **d** support the view that the revocation was indeed conditional, and that was that the testator in that case was illegitimate. Lord Merriman P[5] said:

'Of course if, without any reference to that intention, at some later time after the discussion about the new will, and when he was in a state of complete oblivion of any such intention, or had firmly cast that intention aside, the deceased **e** destroyed his will with the intention of revoking it, one also has to assume that he intended to be intestate, which would mean, on the facts of this particular case, that instead of either Miss Mabel Wass, or Miss Doris Wills, or both, getting anything, he really intended the Chancellor of the Exchequer to get it all.'

There was some discussion in the argument before us whether the doctrine was, **f** or indeed could have been, conceived to give effect to the intention of testators and whether it is necessarily excluded if it does not. In my judgment, however, that is not the right approach. Sometimes, as in *Re Southerden*[6], it clearly does give effect to the testator's intention, which would otherwise have been defeated. In many cases, however, it cannot do so, because the testator wished to make dispositions which could only be effected by a valid new will which he failed to make. **g**

The testator's testamentary intentions, as far as ascertainable, are of course relevant and important considerations in determining on the evidence as a whole whether the revocation is conditional or not, but that is as far as it goes.

There was also some argument about the onus of proof, but I do not think that is really of importance, in all events where both sides have called evidence. It remains a question, what is the proper inference on the evidence as a whole? **h**

It was further argued for the plaintiff that the learned judge's findings of fact should not be disturbed and that in reality he had found that the revocation was conditional. I do not think he had. Certainly he found that this was a classic case of dependent

j

1 [1905] P at 45
2 [1905] P at 46
3 [1951] 2 All ER 997 at 1001
4 [1952] 1 All ER 110, [1951] 2 TLR 1149
5 [1951] 2 TLR at 1153
6 [1925] P 177

relative revocation, but in my judgment that was a conclusion based on a wrong test.
a He said this:

> 'I then have to ask myself this question, did she cut her will with the intention
> of revoking it and dying intestate, or did she do so because she was determined
> to make some fresh testamentary dispositions?'

b
However, in my judgment, the fact that a testatrix revokes her will absolutely
and not conditionally does not necessarily involve her having decided to die intestate;
nor does the fact that she revoked the will because she is determined to make some
fresh testamentary disposition necessarily involve the revocation being conditional.

In any case, although this court ordinarily does accept the trial judge's findings
as to the primary facts, it is free to draw its own inferences from them. We are
c able to do that as well as the trial judge himself. I therefore proceed to consider on
the facts as found by the learned judge whether the revocation was unqualified or
conditional, and I am satisfied that the correct inference is that it was unqualified.

My reasons for this conclusion are as follows. First, there is no evidence that the
testatrix had a belief that it was necessary to revoke an existing will before one could
d make a new one. In the absence of such belief, however, it is difficult to see any
reason why she should have mutilated the 1965 will, save for the purpose of getting
rid of it forthwith and in any event.

Secondly, whether she cut off her signature and that of the witnesses and thereby
also removed cll 3, 4 and part of cl 5 of the will, as the learned judge found and as
I must accept, or whether as has been accepted she cut the paper the other way round,
e the fact remains that she did remove the signatures and a large part of the will
including the all-important cl 4, which devised the smallholding which formed
substantially the whole of her estate. Moreover she apparently destroyed the part,
cut off. Why do this, I ask myself, if she had any idea that the document retained
any capacity for life?

Thirdly, although she vacillated and as late as early September showed a clear in-
f tention to leave the smallholding to the plaintiffs, yet by 23rd September she had
definitely decided to leave it to the children of the first defendant. She gave the bank
manager, Mr Davies, three reasons for this decision. One was that the first defendant's
parents had been very good to her, which is consistent with the revocation being
solely for the purpose of changing the gift of the smallholding, and so tending to the
inference that it was conditional. The other two, however, were personal to the
g plaintiff and her sister: one that they no longer needed the smallholding because
they had bought a place of their own, which they had, and the other that they were
not showing any proper interest in or regard for her, which may well have been
unfair, but which was the view she had formed. In my judgment, these two reasons
strongly support the inference that the revocation was not conditional.

There is another indication also pointing in the same direction, which is that on
h the morning of Sunday, 27th September, she told the second defendant, William
George Harries, that she had not made a will. Too much reliance ought not to be
placed on that, because she may have been merely telling him that, untruthfully,
to stop any further discussion or questioning, but if she was stating the position as she
understood it, then in my judgment it becomes another strong indication that the
revocation was not conditional. With respect, I am unable to agree with the learned
j judge's view that this piece of evidence told the other way. He said: 'I can find no
possible motive for the deceased to have told anyone that she had not made a will at
all, which would have been a completely untrue statement'.

In my view, a person who has revoked her will may really quite accurately say,
'I have not made a will', rather than, 'I did make a will, but I revoked it'. On the other
hand if, in her view, the revocation had not yet taken effect and was conditional on

the completion of her new testamentary dispositions, I cannot see how, if she meant
to speak the truth, she could possibly say, 'I have not made a will'.   *a*

For those reasons, in my judgment, the mutilation of the will was done animo
revocandi, and absolutely not conditionally. I am fortified in this conclusion, because
in my view the learned judge nearly reached the same conclusion himself and might
very probably have done so, had he not made, as for the reasons I have given, with
all respect to him, I consider he did make, an error in the test which he considered
he had to apply. He said: *b*

> 'Her frustration can well be imagined and she may well have felt that the
> least she could do in furtherance of her intention and determination was to
> mutilate her existing will as a preliminary to the making of a fresh will.'

c

I do not readily see how mutilating her will could relieve her frustration, save purely
physically by venting her feelings, and still more I do not see now that could be regarded
as an act preliminary to the making of a fresh will, for which it was not necessary and
which it did not further. His finding, however, that she may well have felt that the
least that she could do in furtherance of her intention and determination was to
mutilate her existing will, really amounts I think to the deceased saying to herself   *d*
in his view: 'I cannot get on with making a new will, but at least I will here and now
get rid of this one, so that at least that shall not take effect'.

For these reasons, which I have expressed in my own words, probably less
felicitously than those of Buckley and Roskill LJJ, I agree that this appeal succeeds
and I agree with the order proposed.

e

Appeal allowed; order pronouncing against the will of July 1965.

Solicitors: *Preston & Kerlys*, agents for *Morgan & Richardson*, Cardigan (for the
defendants); *Monier-Williams & Keeling*, agents for *Morgan & Richardson*, Cardigan
(for the plaintiff).   *f*

Gordon H Scott Esq   Barrister.

a

Re St Luke's, Chelsea

LONDON CONSISTORY COURT

CHANCELLOR G H NEWSOM QC

25th JULY, 1st AUGUST, 4th SEPTEMBER, 27th, 28th NOVEMBER 1974, 15th JANUARY 1975

b *Burial – Disused burial ground – Erection of building on disused burial ground – Building – Meaning – Monument – Petition for faculty to erect monument on burial ground – Monument to be 24 feet high and to cover an area of 400 square feet – Whether monument a 'building' – Whether court having power to grant faculty – Disused Burial Grounds Act 1884, s 3.*

c *Ecclesiastical law – Faculty – Petition – Locus standi – Parties entitled to be joined as petitioners – Petition for faculty to erect monument in churchyard – Memorial committee formed to consider erection of monument – Petition by local authority as freeholder of churchyard for faculty to allow memorial committee to erect monument – Whether members of memorial committee should be joined as petitioners.*

d *Local authority – Open space – Trust to administer open space for enjoyment of public – Disused burial ground – Churchyard converted into open space for benefit of parish – Monument – Proposal to erect monument in open space – Monument unconnected with parish and politically controversial – Monument taking up large part of open space – Whether erection of monument by local authority a breach of trust – Open Spaces Act 1906, s 10.*

e In 1857 the consecrated churchyard of a church built in London about 1800 was closed for burials by order in council. In 1886 the incumbent, churchwardens and clerk to the vestry of the parish petitioned the court for a faculty 'to permit [the burial ground] to be converted into an open space or garden for the benefit of the parish'. A faculty was granted authorising removal of almost all the tombstones and the laying out of gardens, with trees, paths and seats, in an area of approximately 1¼ acres. It was one of the few open spaces in the parish to which the public had access.

f In 1888 the churchyard was vested in the local authority which, by s 5[a] of the Metropolitan Open Spaces Act 1881, was required to administer it 'to allow, and with a view to, the enjoyment by the public of such . . . churchyard . . . in an open condition, free from buildings'. Section 5 of the 1881 Act was superseded by s 11(1)[b] of the Open Spaces Act 1906 which forbade the local authority to 'exercise any of the powers of management . . . with reference to any consecrated burial ground unless . . . authorised

g . . . by . . . faculty'. During the 1939-45 war certain Polish soldiers and citizens were massacred at Katyn in western Russia, by either the Russians or the Germans. After the war, many Poles settled within the district of the local authority, although, being Roman Catholics, they did not worship at the church. Few of them lived in the parish. In 1971 some of those Poles and many English sympathisers, none of whom was a parishioner, formed a committee for the purpose of erecting a monument to

h the victims of the massacre where 'anyone . . . may ponder upon man's inhumanity to man'. The churchyard gardens were proposed as a site and the local authority were in favour of the proposal. The monument was to be 400 square feet in area and nearly 24 feet high and would be inscribed 'Katyn 1940' which effectively charged the Russians with guilt for the massacre. The diocesan advisory committee objected to the proposal on the grounds that there was no connection between the victims and

j the parish, that it would 'materially affect the character of the gardens' and that the gardens 'should not be used to proclaim an injustice perpetrated 30 years ago'. The local authority petitioned for a faculty under s 11(1) of the 1906 Act allowing the

_____

a   Section 5, so far as material, is set out at p 612 c, post

b   Section 11(1) is set out at p 619 f, post   z

memorial to be erected, contrary to s 5 of the 1881 Act and s 3^c of the Disused Burial
Grounds Act 1884. During the hearing some members of the committee were joined a
as petitioners at their request.

Held – (i) Although the members of the committee had no locus standi since they
were not parishioners, in the circumstances, as parties ancillary to the local authority's
petition, they had a sufficient interest to be joined as petitioners (see p 618 b to d, post).
(ii) The faculty would, however, be refused for the following reasons— b
(a) Since the churchyard gardens were consecrated ground no building could be
erected thereon without a faculty. Under s 3 of the 1884 Act, however, the court had
no power to grant the faculty sought, since the gardens were a disused burial ground
and the proposed monument, having regard to its size, was a 'building' within s 3 (see
p 620 e to j, p 622 f to j and p 624 b and c, post); dicta of Buckley J in *Boyce v Paddington
Borough Council* [1903] 1 Ch at 117 and of the Earl of Halsbury LC in *Paddington Corpn v* c
Attorney-General [1904-7] All ER Rep at 363 applied.
(b) Furthermore, the erection of the monument would be a breach of the trusts
set out in s 10 of the 1906 Act under which the local authority held the land, since it
was designed not to increase the public's enjoyment of the gardens as an open space
but to interfere with the facility they offered (see p 625 b to d, post).
(c) Even if the court had had power to grant the petition, it would have refused to do d
so, since the monument with the proposed inscription would be highly controversial
and out of place in a churchyard (see p 626 a to f, p 627 b and p 628 f and g, post).

Notes
For building on disused burial ground, see 10 Halsbury's Laws (4th Edn) paras 1219- e
1221, and for cases on the subject, see 7 Digest (Repl) 586-589, *329-353*.
For faculties relating to churchyards, monuments and disused burial grounds, see
14 Halsbury's Laws (4th Edn) paras 1315-1317.
For the Disused Burial Grounds Act 1884, s 3, see 3 Halsbury's Statutes (3rd Edn)
515, and for the Open Spaces Act 1906, ss 10, 11, see 24 ibid 32, 33.

Cases referred to in judgment f
Bermondsey Borough Council v Mortimer [1926] P 87, 7 Digest (Repl) 586, *331*.
Boyce v Paddington Borough Council [1903] 1 Ch 109, 72 LJCh 28, 87 LT 564; *rvsd* [1903]
2 Ch 556, 72 LJCh 695, 89 LT 383, CA; *rvsd* sub nom *Paddington Corpn v Attorney-
General* [1906] AC 1, [1904-7] All ER Rep 362, 75 LJCh 4, 93 LT 673, 70 JP 41, HL,
7 Digest (Repl) 586, *330*.
Christ Church, Chislehurst, Re [1974] 1 All ER 146, [1973] 1 WLR 1317. g
Fagg v Lee (1873) LR 4 A & E 135, 43 LJ Eccl 1; *affd* sub nom *Lee v Fagg* (1874) LR 6 PC
38, 43 LJ Eccl 17, 30 LT 800, PC, 19 Digest (Repl) 349, *1384*.
Jacobs v London County Council [1950] 1 All ER 737, [1950] AC 361, HL, 26 Digest (Repl)
472, *1604*.
London County Council v Dundas [1904] P 1, 19 TLR 670, 7 Digest (Repl) 588, *351*.
Morley Borough Council v St Mary the Virgin, Woodkirk (Vicar and Churchwardens) h
[1969] 3 All ER 952, [1969] 1 WLR 1867.
St Botolph, Aldersgate Without (Vicar) v St Botolph, Aldersgate Without (Parishioners)
[1900] P 69, 7 Digest (Repl) 586, *329*.
St Dunstan's, Stepney, Re [1937] P 199, 53 TLR 905, 7 Digest (Repl) 588, *352*.
St Mark's Church, Lincoln, Re [1956] 2 All ER 579, [1956] P 336, [1956] 3 WLR 147; *affg*
[1955] 3 All ER 699, [1956] P 166, 7 Digest (Repl) 586, *334*.
St Nicholas Acons (Rector and Churchwardens) v London County Council [1928] AC 469,
[1928] All ER Rep 240, 97 LJPC 113, 139 LT 530, 92 JP 185, PC; *affg* [1928] P 102,
7 Digest (Repl) 587, *345*.

c Section 3, so far as material, is set out at p 618 *j*, post

St Peter the Great, Chichester, Re [1961] 2 All ER 513, [1961] 1 WLR 907, Digest (Cont
a   Vol A) 78, *335a*.

Petition for faculty
By a petition dated 25th February 1974 the council of the Royal Borough of Kensington
and Chelsea sought a faculty authorising the erection, in the churchyard of the parish
church of St Luke's, Chelsea, a disused burial ground set out as gardens, of which
b   they were the freeholders, of a commemorative memorial to Polish soldiers and
citizens massacred at Katyn, western Russia, during the 1939-45 war. Lord Barnby,
Airey Neave, Louis Fitzgibbon, Toby Jessell, Lord St Oswald and Helen Marcinek,
members of the Katyn Memorial Fund Committee, were added as petitioners by
amendment pursuant to leave granted on 28th November 1974. The Archdeacon
of Middlesex intervened in the proceedings at the court's request. The facts are set
c   out in the judgment.

Spencer G Maurice for the petitioners.
Sheila Cameron for the archdeacon.

Cur adv vult
d

15th January. **THE CHANCELLOR** read the following judgment: The petitioners
seek a faculty authorising the introduction into St Luke's churchyard, Chelsea, of a
monument which is to be a memorial to those Polish soldiers and citizens who were
murdered at Katyn. It is to be an obelisk of polished black Nubian granite, with the
top of its needle almost 24 feet above the surface of the ground. It is to have on it the
e   inscription 'Katyn 1940' and some other words recording the event. I shall describe
it in more detail later.
Two questions arise. Can the court lawfully grant such a faculty? If so, ought the
court in the exercise of its judicial discretion to grant it?
The church of St Luke, Chelsea, was built, and the churchyard was laid out, under
two private statutes passed at the end of the reign of King George III. In due course
f   the church was consecrated as a church and the churchyard was consecrated as a
burial ground. In 1857 the churchyard was closed for burials by order in council.
During the following 30 years it became neglected, and in 1886 the incumbent, the
churchwardens and the clerk to the vestry of the parish of Chelsea (a corporate body),
together approached this court for a faculty 'to permit [the burial ground] to be
converted into an open space or garden for the benefit of the parish in accordance
g   with a plan filed in the registry'. The petition was advertised in The Times, on this
footing, and produced a good deal of correspondence. Eventually there was a hearing
before Chancellor Tristram and a faculty was granted on 31st December 1886 in the
terms sought by the petition. The plan filed in the registry shows that what was
authorised was substantially the present arrangement of paths and lawns. Almost all
the tombstones were to be removed from their existing positions to form boundaries
h   round the church and round the outside of the churchyard; most of them still stand
in these positions. There have been various other faculties on specific points, but this
one is still effective in respect of the gardens to the south of the church, with which the
present case is concerned.
The church stands in the middle of the original churchyard dividing it into a
northern and a southern section roughly equal in size. I shall refer to the southern
j   section as St Luke's gardens. The gardens are about 1¼ acres in extent. They are divided
into four parts by paths which are in the positions shown in the plan lodged with the
court in connection with the faculty of 1886, and also in the plan on the 1888 conveyance, to which I shall refer later. The gardens contain many trees, mainly deciduous,
and in summer they are a shady place, except for the part immediately to the south
of the church. This part is in sunshine and people sun themselves, mainly on a row

of seats. They are not allowed to sit on the grass, or to place chairs on the grass. It is immediately to the south of this row of seats that the petitioners now wish to *a* place the proposed monument. Chelsea is very short of open spaces to which the public has access, most of the actual open spaces being square gardens in private ownership. St Luke's gardens are particularly valuable because just to the north there are several blocks of flats, Sutton Dwellings, with many inhabitants.

In 1886 the then local authority for Chelsea, the vestry, was prepared to take over the churchyard and to run it as an open space or garden for the benefit of the parish. *b* On 27th July 1888 the freehold of the whole churchyard was conveyed to the vestry on the trusts of the Metropolitan Open Spaces Act 1881. This conveyance did not, and could not, expunge the sacred uses created by the sentence of consecration of the churchyard as a burial ground for the dead of the parish of St Luke's, Chelsea, but it engrafted on them the statutory trusts of the 1881 Act. The critical provision is in the middle of s 5 of that Act. It is that a churchyard which becomes vested under the *c* provisions of the Act in a local authority—

'shall be held and administered . . . in trust to allow, and with a view to, the enjoyment by the public of such . . . churchyard . . . in an open condition, free from buildings, and under proper control and regulation, and for no other purpose . . .' *d*

Then follows an enumeration of things which the local authority is authorised to do by way of management of the open space as such, and a proviso that if the ground is consecrated those powers are not to be exercised except under a faculty. The legislation has changed from time to time, but the current provisions in ss 10 and 11 of the Open Spaces Act 1906 correspond closely with those of s 5 of the 1881 Act.

The gardens are a valuable advantage to the public, and in particular to the public *e* of the parish for whose benefit the faculty of 1886 was sought and granted and for whose benefit the church authorities in 1888 transferred the freehold to the vestry. The gardens do credit to the various municipal authorities which at one time or another have in fact maintained them. For some reason no faculty authorising any of these authorities to exercise the powers of management has ever been obtained. This *f* omission, now discovered, must of course be put right, and counsel for the petitioners undertook on behalf of the council that a petition would be presented.

At present the council of the Royal Borough of Kensington and Chelsea maintains the churchyard and the fee simple is vested in it. I need not detail the various Acts reforming local government in London under which this vesting has come about. The vesting of the freehold has no effect on the trusts, which are now those of the Open Spaces Act 1906, except insofar as they may have been modified by later legis- *g* lation. The council is a body of recent creation. Its area is extensive. A map shows it as stretching from the River Thames to Harrow Road, and from Sloane Square to Earls Court. Chelsea in general, and St Luke's parish in particular, are but a small part of its area. The council initiated these proceedings as freeholder and was originally the only petitioner.

The individual petitioners were added at their own request at the beginning of the *h* hearing. They are members of a committee ('the memorial committee') which has collected money (detailed in the evidence of the treasurer, Mrs Marcinek) for the purpose of erecting in London a monument to the Polish soldiers and citizens who were massacred at Katyn in western Russia during the 1939-45 war. That the massacre took place is common knowledge, and I propose to take judicial notice of the fact that it occurred, adopting for this purpose the carefully worded reference to the subject in Sir Winston Churchill's The Second World War[1]. Exactly when the massacre took place and who were the persons guilty of it, is not a matter which I propose to discuss. Its victims were Polish soldiers and citizens who had fled eastwards in the

---

1   Volume 4, pp 678-681

autumn of 1939 when their country was invaded from the west by the Germans.
a They fell into the hands of the Russians who were also invading their country from
the east. The Russians then held them captive and the area of the camps was later
occupied by the Germans who invaded Russia in 1941. Many thousands of the Poles
who were at one time in these camps were murdered. The Germans accused the
Russians of this massacre, and the Russians accused the Germans of it. Whoever was
guilty, it is one of those crimes which from time to time stain human history: it is fit
b to be named together with the massacre of St Bartholomew, the Armenian atrocities
and the German gas chambers. No wonder it arouses emotions among Poles, and
especially among those Poles who live here in freedom.

After the war many Poles settled here, often after long and gallant service side by
side with the forces of the Crown against the Germans. Some 70 per cent of the
refugee and exiled population of this country are Poles. They have been welcomed
c here and developed a number of Polish and Anglo-Polish organisations. Several of
these organisations have premises in South Kensington. The concentration in South
Kensington may well have occurred partly because the Polish forces which were in
this country during the war used to worship at Brompton Oratory. There is now a
Polish church at Shepherds Bush. There is a distinguishable Polish colony in Earls
Court, which, I was told, was at least at one time known as 'the Polish corridor': news-
d papers in Polish are sold there and the Polish language is to be heard. All these places
except Shepherds Bush are in the area of the council, but none of them is in Chelsea or
in St Luke's parish. Some Poles reside in the King's Road, Chelsea, but their numbers
are small and the same could no doubt be said of many other streets in London.
On the evidence, I find as facts that neither Chelsea nor St Luke's parish is a centre of
Polish habitation or of Polish institutions or of Anglo-Polish institutions. In South
e Kensington it is different; but South Kensington is not Chelsea.

Among those who sought to help the Poles in this country is Mr Louis FitzGibbon.
In 1968 he was General Secretary of the British Council for Aid to Refugees. In that
year he started to enquire into the circumstances of elderly refugees. As the information came in, he gradually became aware that many elderly ladies here were widows
or other relations of the victims of Katyn. This led to his writing a book on the mas-
f sacre, which was published in April 1971. In August 1971 someone in South Africa
sent him about £30 with the suggestion that a monument be erected to honour
the victims of the Katyn massacre somewhere in the west, until such time as a
monument could be erected in Poland. Mr FitzGibbon mentioned the idea to his
Polish friends, and the memorial committee was formed to consider it. The memorial
committee issued an appeal. The names of the patrons of the committee are stated
g on the appeal as at 1st January 1972. The appeal was for money to 'erect a permanent
and publicly visible monument' to the victims of Katyn—

'In London at some suitably public place [in order to] provide an opportunity
for anyone of any nationality to pay homage to these "martyrs for freedom"
and a place where they may ponder upon man's inhumanity to man.'

h The committee said in the appeal that the monument would be an obelisk. The
committee considered at least four sites, all of which they rejected. One was at
Wormwood Scrubs, one in Battersea Park, another was near the Polish church in
Shepherds Bush. Exactly why that site was rejected does not appear; the answers
of the witnesses about it are not really consistent. The expert witness, Mr Gabrielczyk,
said that he understood that planning permission was refused. But rejected it was.
j Then there was a small site in the angle where two roads meet outside the Victoria and
Albert Museum, which was also thought by the memorial committee to be unsuitable
as being too cramped and being vulnerable to road widening. Counsel for the
petitioners stated, in opening the case, that 'the obvious choice appeared to be Brompton Oratory but the fact is that there is no site, there is nowhere where it can be put up'.
I have been unable to find in the transcript any evidence to support this statement,

unless it be a reference to the evidence of Mr FitzGibbon, about the site outside
the Victoria and Albert Museum. There is indeed no evidence before me that the *a*
committee ever approached the Roman Catholic authorities in charge of Brompton
Oratory. Mr FitzGibbon told me that the committee had also been enquiring about a
site in Thurloe Gardens, and it was after the failure of the site outside the Victoria
and Albert Museum that he met Sir Malby Crofton, the leader of the council, and in
the course of this conversation two sites were mentioned. One was in Redcliffe
Gardens, the other was St Luke's gardens. Having rejected Redcliffe Gardens, Mr *b*
FitzGibbon and other members of the committee inspected St Luke's gardens and
thought it 'ideal' because it is 'a pleasant, almost private-type garden, a quiet place'.
I find, on the evidence of Mr Robinson, at the relevant time chairman of the council's
libraries and amenities committee, that the memorial committee approached the
council, saying that they wanted a site for the monument and asking 'what we could
do about it'. Mr Robinson said that he himself investigated the possibility of St Luke's *c*
gardens. Counsel for the petitioners sought to submit in argument that the initiative
came wholly from the council. The evidence does not justify this submission.
The memorial committee approached people on the council, and Mr Robinson
responded by suggesting St Luke's gardens.

In November 1971 the memorial committee instructed Mr Gabrielczyk, a distinguished civil engineer, to prepare designs for a memorial to commemorate the *d*
Katyn massacre. They had already decided to have an obelisk, as appears from the
appeal issued a few weeks later, and according to Mr Gabrielczyk he was instructed
on the understanding that there was a real prospect that the monument could be
placed in St Luke's gardens. I should like to pay tribute to the quality of Mr
Gabrielczyk as a witness. He was fair and careful, and I am satisfied that a great
deal of conscientious thought, and indeed emotion, has gone into the preparation of *e*
his design for the obelisk.

Mr Gabrielczyk's designs were dated as late as June and July 1973; there is an earlier
layout plan which was prepared in September 1972 by the borough engineer. There
are also some plans, substantially the same but unsigned and undated, which were
attached to the application for planning permission in September 1972. One design
shows a 'new double screen of pine trees supplied by client', 21 in total, to the north *f*
of the monument, and an area of tarmacadam to the south of it. As to the former,
counsel for the petitioners said in opening that there would be 'a symbolic arc of . . . 23
fir trees, symbolic of Katyn Forest' which were to be provided by one of the individual
petitioners. These trees would cut most of the sun off the row of seats along the south
side of the church. On the fourth day of the hearing counsel for the petitioners was
instructed to abandon them. As to the tarmacadam, Mr Gabrielczyk said that it *g*
would be about ten feet by 20 feet and that it was suggested by the borough engineer.
Mr Gabrielczyk said that the monument would be built by the well-known firm of
contractors, Messrs Trollope & Colls, with a specialist firm to prepare the sections of
the obelisk itself. I am sure that Mr Gabrielczyk can be relied on to ensure that the
obelisk and its surroundings will be well and soundly constructed, if its construction
can be, and is, authorised.   *h*

At some stage, perhaps in the spring of 1972 but the evidence is not clear about the
date, Mr Robinson spoke to the rector, Mr Loasby, informally. Mr Robinson told me
that this approach was made 'to get his reactions . . . knowing that they were our
gardens, but he was naturally interested as next door neighbour', and that the matter
was not put by Mr Robinson to his council committee 'until [the rector] had given
his full consent to my putting the proposal forward'. The rector in his evidence *j*
said that this 'go ahead' was a personal view given without seeing plans and that he
was in favour and sympathy with putting up a memorial to 'this historic event'.
I find as a fact that this assent was given by the rector at an early stage, before Mr
Gabrielczyk's plans existed, and that it was a provisional and general expression of
personal sympathy. There were no firm proposals until much later.

The first formal approach to any church authority was in a letter from the borough engineer to the rector, dated 26th June 1972:

'Dear Padre,

St. Luke's Gardens—Katyn Memorial

'An application has been received from the honorary secretary of the Katyn Memorial Fund asking that consideration be given to the erection of a memorial in St Luke's gardens in remembrance of those Polish officers who died in the Katyn massacre. It is envisaged that the memorial will be an obelisk about 20 feet high and rising from steps, the lowest of which would be about 20 feet square.

'I might add that the honorary secretary foresees that the memorial, if erected, would become a place of pilgrimage for Poles and that there would be a yearly remembrance day when hundreds of people would be present.

'I shall be reporting this matter to my committee on 4th July, 1972, but before I do so I would very much appreciate your thoughts and comments.'

The opening sentence of this letter must refer to an application to the council as owner, not to the application for planning permission which was not made until later. It is therefore not consistent with the suggestion made by counsel for the petitioners that the council took the initiative in offering to the committee the site in St Luke's gardens. In reply he sought to disclaim the second paragraph of the letter, which he said was written by the borough engineer without authority. But the borough engineer was quoting Mr FitzGibbon, the honorary secretary. The reply of the rector, dated 6th July 1972, was as follows:

'Thank you for your letter. I have discussed this with my churchwardens. We don't wish to oppose it strenuously, but at the same time, we do not really think St. Luke's gardens are big enough for such a large memorial, nor to receive, without damage, a constant stream and an occasional flood of Polish pilgrims. Nor can we see why it should be placed in Chelsea, where there are no obvious links.'

This reply gave clear notice that the rector and his churchwardens did not like the suggestion. I find that the letter of 26th June 1972 was the first that they had heard of the size of the proposed monument or of the obelisk. The borough engineer replied on 19th July 1972 that there were no firm proposals, but that if the scheme went ahead he presumed that the rector would make representations when a faculty was applied for.

The matter had in the meantime been considered by the libraries and amenities committee on 4th July, and its agenda makes it clear that the application to put the monument in St Luke's gardens had come from the memorial committee. It also notes that there was likely to be no planning objection, but that in the gardens 'the only position which is at all suitable' was the position eventually chosen. The person making the report said that he would report orally on the views of the rector and of the Chelsea Society, which had been consulted 'because St Luke's gardens is a much used amenity in this part of the borough'. The court does not have the advantage of having the views of the Chelsea Society in evidence. This meeting gave approval in principle to the project, and its decision was ratified by the full council on 26th July. The next thing that happened was that on 21st September Mr FitzGibbon applied for planning permission for the monument on behalf of 'the Katyn Memorial Fund'. The application contains at its foot the extraordinary assertion, which I note without further comment, that 'the applicant is applying for a tenancy of every part of the land to which the accompanying application relates'.

The libraries and amenities committee resumed consideration of the subject on 3rd October. It appears that on 4th July the committee had agreed in principle to the monument being put in St Luke's gardens and that in the meantime Mr Fitz-Gibbon had 'submitted a sketch drawing' of the design. This is not before me. He also submitted half a dozen suggested inscriptions among which the committee was invited to choose. The minutes again are not in evidence.

The planning permission was granted on 9th January 1973 and a copy of the permission is before me. Despite my invitation to do so, the petitioners have not put in evidence any of the agenda or minutes of the planning committee. It appears from the evidence of Mr Raven, senior planning officer employed by the council, that the council quite frequently gives notice to neighbours of pending planning applications, but that they did not do so in this case 'because this was being dealt with through the church as a focus for objectors'.

The council next consulted the diocesan advisory committee which was averse to the proposal. That committee considered the case on 27th March 1973 and its views are stated in the formal advice to me in these proceedings. Shortly they were, and are, that there is no connection between the persons to be commemorated and Chelsea, that the memorial would be out of scale with its surroundings, that it would 'materially affect the character of the gardens', that a burial ground is 'principally a place of rest and that the church's ministry of reconciliation requires that it should not be used to proclaim an injustice perpetrated 30 years ago in another land and which is still a subject of controversy'. The diocesan advisory committee reconsidered the matter at the request of the council on 26th June and reaffirmed its view 'that the proposed memorial was unsuitable and inappropriate to this site'.

On 24th October the council resolved to submit this petition. On the same day the borough solicitor wrote to the rector and stated that he believed that the parochial church council had approved the plans. This belief was incorrect. No plans had been supplied. The borough solicitor also asked for a certified copy of the resolution of the parochial church council approving the location and details of the memorial. The rector rejoined by asking on 31st October to see the plans, and on 5th November the borough solicitor sent 'a copy of the drawing of the Katyn Memorial, together with a site plan showing its proposed location in St Luke's gardens'. He also invited the rector and churchwardens to join with the council as petitioners.

On 4th December the parochial church council held a meeting. The relevant parts of the minutes are as follows:

'It was felt that it would be ungracious to say no but as the Poles were Roman Catholics the rector thought that the memorial should be near a Roman Catholic church. After discussion the following resolution, proposed by the rector, seconded by Mr Werner, was agreed by the parochial church council: "This council, sympathising with the Poles in the tragic events recalled by the proposed memorial, does not object to the said memorial being placed in St. Luke's gardens but wishes to record its view that it would be better placed near a Roman Catholic church, such as Brompton Oratory, where Polish people in London worship."'

The effect of this minute was communicated the next day by the rector to the borough solicitor and he added:

'In the matter of my churchwardens and myself being petitioners for the faculty ... we should be obliged to state the view ... that the memorial would be better placed near a Roman Catholic church and I doubt whether this would help in obtaining a faculty.'

There appeared at the first day's hearing of this case to be some confusion exactly what documents had been before the parochial church council on 4th December 1973. I therefore suggested that during the week which elapsed between the first and second days of the hearing a further meeting of the parochial church council should be called so as to express its opinion on the precise proposal which by then was before the court. An emergency meeting was duly called and held on 30th July 1974, and the proposals now before the court were put before it. Sixteen of the 19 members were present.

Fifteen of them voted for the resolution; one member did not vote; and no members
a voted against the resolution which was as follows:

'The parochial church council confirms the resolution passed on 4th December,
1973 but re-iterates its view that the site is ill-chosen. However, since that resolution was passed the parochial church council has been made increasingly aware
of the feelings and concern of parishioners as to the siting of the memorial, the
b unsuitability of its design and its size in proportion to the area of the garden,
and, accordingly, recommends that, if it is considered that the memorial *must*
be in St. Luke's gardens, it should be sited away from the church, of a different
and less aggressive character, and of smaller dimensions than those proposed
so as to avoid provoking hostility. The parochial church council notes that a view
has been expressed that a charitable or educational application of the funds
c contributed would be a positive form of memorial.'

At my instance the two churchwardens, Colonel Large and Mr Edwards, gave
evidence as to the state of opinion in the parish in regard to this petition. It was particularly desirable for me to have this evidence because the borough council, as noticed
above, had not given any local notices or sought local views except those of the Chelsea
Society which were not put in evidence. The churchwardens are the bishop's officers,
d and it is well recognised that the bishop's court is entitled to their assistance in this
manner, notwithstanding the rule of law which usually excludes hearsay evidence.
These witnesses were called as judge's witnesses. But since the Archdeacon of Middlesex was represented by counsel, I asked his counsel to examine them in chief so as to
save my having to do it myself. This is a convenient practice where an appropriate
party is so represented. It saves the judge from appearing to descend into the arena.
e They were extensively cross-examined by counsel for the petitioners. Having heard
their evidence originally, and having twice read through it, I find that it establishes
that there is no general desire among the parishioners that this petition should be
granted. I find that the broad effect of this evidence is that some parishioners who
were consulted are doubtful, some are neutral, some are actually opposed and a few
support the proposal.
f I was informed that on 28th June 1972 a motion was tabled in the House of Commons
condemning the massacre and welcoming the proposal of the memorial committee
'to erect a memorial in London to the victims' and that 194 Members of Parliament
put their names to it. I understand that the motion was never moved or passed, and
it was not suggested that it was with particular reference to the proposal now before
the court to put an obelisk in St Luke's gardens. I take this material only as showing
g that a number of gentlemen who were members of the House of Commons in 1972
favoured the idea of there being a memorial in some form somewhere in London to
the victims of Katyn. My problem, however, is whether the particular memorial now
proposed can and should be put in St Luke's gardens.

I now come to the questions of law. First, there is the issue as to the locus standi of the
individual petitioners. The council obviously has a right to petition the court because
h it is the freeholder. But the other petitioners are not parishioners, nor are they on
the electoral roll of St Luke's parish. Unless they can establish a sufficient and relevant
interest they have no locus standi in this court. Several cases were cited to me, and I
found most helpful the observation of Sir Robert Phillimore, Dean of the Arches,
in *Fagg v Lee*[1], that it would be a great evil if persons having no connection with a
parish should be entitled to interfere in matters relating to the church (or of course
j the churchyard). I do not accept the submission of counsel for the petitioners that these
remarks relate only to proceedings for the removal of articles from churches. To
put things into a church or churchyard, or try to do so, can equally cause trouble,
as has been proved by this very case. In my judgment they apply to any interference

---

1 (1873) LR 4 A & E 135 at 150

with a church or churchyard. It is not the law that anyone can confer on himself a
sufficient interest to be a litigant in the consistory court merely by deciding that he   *a*
wants to do something to a church or a churchyard in the diocese. The concept
of a party interested is in its origin proprietary and is comparatively narrow. It has
had to be extended even to persons on the electoral roll of a parish, or indeed to the
archdeacon himself, by express legislation.

However, I need not examine the authorities exhaustively because in my judgment
the added petitioners do on the special facts of this case have a sufficient interest to   *b*
be petitioners. The council is a qualified petitioner, as freeholder. It has decided to
ask the court to allow it to permit the other petitioners to put up a monument on
its ground at the expense of the other petitioners. That is to say, as freeholder, it
wishes to be allowed to licence the other petitioners to do something on its property.
In those circumstances, although I do not think that the individual petitioners could
have been heard if they had petitioned on their own account, I am of the opinion that,   *c*
as parties ancillary to the petition of the council, they were entitled to be petitioners.
If I were to decide to grant a faculty, it would be convenient to have them before
the court so that they might give personal undertakings as to the due execution
of the work. Such undertakings would probably be necessary, since the council
has made it clear that it is not prepared to spend the money of the ratepayers
on the construction of the monument, and the evidence of Mrs Marcinek, the   *d*
treasurer, shows that the fund is still short of the amount which the construction is
expected to cost. If the work were allowed to start, it would be essential to ensure its
completion. In respect of their locus standi, the submission of counsel for the
petitioners therefore succeeds, and I hold that the individual petitioners were correctly
joined.

The Archdeacon of Middlesex intervened in the proceedings at my request to put   *e*
the petitioners to the proof of their case. Thus the matters of law and fact have been
fully and ably argued before me.

I can now come to the question whether the faculty sought by this petition can lawfully be granted. I start from the proposition that this is a consecrated churchyard. I
respectfully adopt the following words of Owen Stable QC, the deputy auditor
of the Chancery Court of the Province of York, in *Morley Borough Council v St Mary the*   *f*
Virgin, Woodkirk (Vicar and Churchwardens)[1]:

> 'The essential legal act of consecration is the signature by a bishop on what is
> called a sentence of consecration by which, in respect of a churchyard, he separates
> and sets apart the ground from all profane and common uses whatsoever; dedi-
> cates the ground to the service of Almighty God for the interment of the remains   *g*
> of the dead and consecrates the same for such purpose. The sentence further pro-
> nounces, decrees and declares the churchyard to be so separated, dedicated and
> consecrated and that it ought to remain so for ever. The ground by the ordinary
> law of the land then becomes consecrated land, held to sacred uses and subject
> to the jurisdiction of the ecclesiastical courts. In every case the sacred uses are
> perpetual and can never be divested from the consecrated land save by or under   *h*
> the authority of an Act or Measure. Equally, this court's jurisdiction over the
> land cannot be destroyed save by or under the authority of an Act or Measure.'

In 1857 the churchyard was closed for burials by order in council. In 1884 Parliament passed the Disused Burial Grounds Act 1884, s 3 of which provides:

> '. . . it shall not be lawful to erect any buildings upon any disused burial   *j*
> ground, except for the purpose of enlarging a church, chapel, meeting house, or
> other places of worship.'

---

1   [1969] 3 All ER 952 at 955, [1969] 1 WLR 1867 at 1871

So far, then, there were the sacred uses, subject to the jurisdiction of the court,
a and the added prohibition imposed by the 1884 Act.

In 1888 the churchyard was conveyed in fee simple to the vestry, under the authority,
and on the trusts, of the Metropolitan Open Spaces Act 1881. By 1889 the fee simple
was vested in the local authority subject to the express prohibition of the erection
of any buildings by the Disused Burial Grounds Act 1884, subject also to the jurisdiction of the court and to the sacred uses as a burial ground, but those uses had been
b relaxed and modified to the extent indicated by s 5 of the Metropolitan Open Spaces
Act 1881, which authorised and required the user of these premises as an open space.

Counsel for the petitioners submitted that s 42 of the Public Health Acts Amendment Act 1890 had some bearing on the matter. In my judgment that section goes
to the capacity of the local authority to do the act mentioned and has no effect on the
specific enactments as to open spaces and disused burial grounds, still less to the
c sacred uses or the subjection to the jurisdiction of the consistory court.

The next relevant Act is the Open Spaces Act 1906. It repealed the Metropolitan
Open Spaces Act 1881, but not the Disused Burial Grounds Act 1884. Section 10 of
the 1906 Act, in my judgment, supersedes s 5 of the 1881 Act and, therefore, now defines the trusts on which the council holds this open space, except insofar as other trusts
powers and duties may have been created or imposed by subsequent legislation.
d It has, of course, no bearing on the jurisdiction of the court, anymore than s 5 of
the 1881 Act had. So far as relevant, s 10 of the 1906 Act provides that the local
authority is to—

> '. . . (a) hold and administer the open space or burial ground in trust to allow,
> and with a view to, the enjoyment, thereof by the public as an open space within
> *e* the meaning of this Act and under proper control and regulation and for no
> other purpose; and (b) maintain and keep the open space or burial ground in a
> good and decent state . . .'

Then follow certain administrative powers, or powers of management, of a detailed
character. By s 11(1) it is provided:

> *f* 'A local authority shall not exercise any of the powers of management under
> this Act with reference to any consecrated burial ground unless and until they
> are authorised so to do by the licence or faculty of the bishop.'

That provision, in my judgment, extends the jurisdiction of this court so as to require
a faculty for the exercise of those of the powers of management which in an ordinary
g consecrated burial ground would not need a faculty. For example, a faculty would
not normally be needed to turf or plant a burial ground, but turfing and planting
are among the express powers of management in s 10. Section 11(1) does not, in my
judgment, in any way derogate from the general jusrisdiction of the court consequent
on the existence of the sacred uses, but it extends the need for a faculty to these
special cases. Later subsections make certain express provisions as to tombstones.
h The next Act is the London County Council (General Powers) Act 1935[1], a private
statute. Section 42 conferred on a local authority in London power in respect of any
open space in its area to provide a considerable number of recreational facilities,
and buildings in connection therewith, and s 51 provided that these powers might be
exercised notwithstanding the provisions of any other Act. In *Re St Dunstan's, Stepney*[2]
Chancellor Errington held that the effect of s 51 was to negative the prohibition in
j the 1884 Act insofar as the buildings covered by s 42 were concerned, and thus to
give back to the court its power to grant faculties in respect of such buildings. Section
52 provides, so far as material:

---

1 25 & 26 Geo 5 c xxxiii
2 [1937] P 199 at 202, 203

'Section 11 (Special provisions as to management of burial grounds and removal of tombstones) of the Open Spaces Act 1906 shall be incorporated with and *a*
form Part of this Act . . .'

That provision does not, in my judgment, make any addition to or subtraction from
the powers and duties of the court, but is declaratory only. Counsel for the petitioners
conceded in argument that none of the matters authorised by the 1935 Act comes
anywhere near the proposal in the present case.   *b*
    In 1963 all local government arrangements in London were reformed by the London
Government Act 1963, s 87(3) of which provides:

    'For the purpose of securing uniformity in the law applicable with respect to
    any matter in different parts of the relevant area . . . any appropriate Minister
    may [after certain consultations] by provisional order . . . amend, repeal or revoke
    any Greater London statutory provision and extend it, with or without modi- *c*
    fications, to a part of the relevant area to which it did not previously extend; . . .'

That section is expressed to be 'for the purpose of securing uniformity'. A provisional
order was made by the Minister of Housing and Local Government and was confirmed
by a private Act of Parliament, the Ministry of Housing and Local Government
Provisional Order Confirmation (Greater London Parks and Open Spaces) Act 1967[1]. *d*
That Act repealed the relevant part of the London County Council (General Powers)
Act 1935. Article 7 of the provisional order thus confirmed has a sidenote: 'Facilities for
public recreation'. Like s 42 of the 1935 Act, art 7 enables the local authority to provide
a large number of recreational facilities with the necessary buildings for them, in
respect of and on open spaces under their control including disused burial grounds,
and art 11 of the order, like s 51 of the 1935 Act, says that the powers conferred on the *e*
local authority by art 7 may be exercised notwithstanding the provisions of any
enactment. There is nothing in the 1967 Act corresponding to the declaratory s 52 of
the 1935 Act, which incorporated s 11 of the Open Spaces Act 1906. Thus the 1967 Act
is silent about faculties. Counsel for the petitioners submitted that the effect of this
silence is to make it unnecessary to obtain a faculty for the erection on a consecrated
burial ground of any building covered by art 7. I reject that submission. As the deputy *f*
auditor pointed out in *Morley Borough Council v St Mary the Virgin, Woodkirk (Vicar
and Churchwardens)*[2], consecrated ground is 'by the ordinary law of the land' subject
to the faculty jurisdiction, which may be divested only by or under the authority of an
Act or Measure. Section 11 of the 1906 Act was not, in my judgment, substituted for
this ordinary rule of law, but was passed to extend it. By a declaratory section in the
London County Council (General Powers) Act 1935, s 11 was reiterated. The declara- *g*
tory section has now been dropped, so far as things authorised by the 1967 Act are
concerned. That still leaves untouched the jurisdiction imposed by 'the ordinary law
of the land'. I should, perhaps, add in passing, that in an Act confirming a provisional
order made under s 87(3) of the London Government Act 1963, it would be most
surprising to find a provision abolishing a jurisdiction which has existed for centuries.
Such a provision could not be 'for securing uniformity in the law applicable with *h*
respect to any matter in different parts of the relevant area', and I refuse to construe
it in this extended sense in the absence of words compelling me to do so. I hold,
therefore, that although the buildings mentioned in art 7 of the provisional order are
exempted by art 11 from the provisions of the Disused Burial Grounds Act 1884,
they cannot lawfully be erected without a faculty.
    It has been necessary to reach a conclusion on this rather complicated point, al- *j*
though counsel for the petitioners concedes that the proposed memorial is not covered
by art 7, because he relied on the 1967 Act in regard to the exercise of the court's

1   15 & 16 Eliz 2, c cxxix
2   [1969] 3 All ER at 955, [1969] 1 WLR at 1871

discretion, submitting that so much could be done under that Act without a faculty
a that the control of this court over St Luke's gardens is now merely 'vestigial'. I shall
deal with this submission later, when I reach the issue of discretion. But on the question
of whether s 3 of the Disused Burial Grounds Act 1884 forbids the erection of this
proposed monument, I am left simply with that section itself and the cases decided
under it, counsel for the petitioners conceding that nothing in any of the subsequent
legislation (except perhaps the Public Health Acts Amendment Act 1890, the relevance
b of which I have rejected) authorises such a structure as is here proposed.

It is agreed between counsel that in considering s 3 of the 1884 Act I ought to have
regard also to the provision in s 5 of the Metropolitan Open Spaces Act 1881 that land
within that section is to be enjoyed by the public 'in an open condition, free from
buildings'. That agreement was justified by the linking of the two provisions by
Buckley J in *Boyce v Paddington Borough Council*[1] and by the way in which that case was
c dealt with in the House of Lords: see *Paddington Corpn v Attorney-General*[2].

Buckley J said[3] that the word 'buildings' occurs in s 5 of the 1881 Act 'in the connection that the land is to be enjoyed "in an open condition free from buildings".'
He continued:

> 'I think this means such buildings as would preclude or diminish its enjoy-
d > ment in an open condition for exercise and recreation. In section 3 of the Act of
> 1884 the erection of any buildings . . . is forbidden except for the purpose of en-
> larging a church. I think the word "buildings" there means erections which
> would cover some part of the ground, as the enlargement of a church would do.'

In the House of Lords the judgment of Buckley J was approved by all three Lords,
and the Earl of Halsbury LC, dealing further with the question of what was meant
e by the prohibition of 'buildings' in s 3, said[4]:

> 'I am of opinion that it meant what it said—that the space was to remain un-
> built upon. It is to be disused as a burial ground, but it is not to be used as a build-
> ing ground—that is the meaning of it; and it appears to me that anything that
> approaches to the character of a building, whether temporary or permanent, is
> obviously within the prohibition.'

f Having rejected the idea that the cases about the word in other contexts were of much
assistance, the Earl of Halsbury LC said[5]:

> '. . . I have to look at the word "building" here with reference to this subject-
> matter and what the Act of Parliament was doing—It is very obvious, I think,
> that what was intended to be done was to keep this disused burial ground from
g > being used as building ground, to keep it as a place of exercise, ventilation and
> recreation and what not,—to prevent anything being done in the nature of
> building which would interfere with or restrict the free and open use of these
> spaces as constituted under the statute.'

Counsel for the petitioners contended that the Disused Burial Grounds Act 1884
h was to be construed narrowly, as being a penal statute. In my opinion the observations
of the Earl of Halsbury LC are a surer guide. I note particularly the phrases 'anything
that approaches to the character of a building' and 'to prevent anything being done
in the nature of building', both of which were used in connection with ensuring that
the area is not to be used as a building ground, i e that it is not to be built on.

Counsel for the petitioners submitted in effect that a passer-by, seeing the proposed
j monument, would not say to himself 'that is a building', but 'that is a monument',

---

1 [1903] 1 Ch 109
2 [1906] AC 1, [1904-7] All ER Rep 362
3 [1903] 1 Ch at 117
4 [1906] AC at 3, [1904-7] All ER Rep at 363
5 [1906] AC at 4, [1904-7] All ER Rep at 363

and that if it is a monument it cannot be a building. Not surprisingly, counsel for the archdeacon rejoined that in the application for planning permission the individual petitioners, applying to the council, had to answer the request 'State whether the proposal involves (i) new building(s); if yes, state gross floor area of proposed building(s)'; and they filled in 'Yes', adding '400 square feet'. Again Mr Gabrielczyk himself told me that his instructions were to obtain the necessary planning permissions and approvals under the 'building regulations'. But this case cannot be determined either by unguarded remarks of the individual petitioners or of their expert, or by the reactions of a supposed passer-by uninstructed as to the context. The court must first consider exactly what is to be erected, and must then apply the observations of the Earl of Halsbury LC and thus obey the section.

We are not concerned only with the needle of the obelisk, but with the whole structure. To see what that means, I go to the evidence of Mr Gabrielczyk. He said that the base would consist of three layers of Portland stone, each nine inches in height, the first step being 19 feet four inches in plan, the second 15 feet four inches, and the uppermost 11 feet four inches. On this would be a base (also sometimes referred to as a podium or sarcophagus) formed in Nubian granite, seven feet square by five feet ten inches in height. Above that would rise the needle, in Nubian granite, of some 17 feet seven inches above the top of the podium 'three solids interconnected'. The total height above the ground would be 23 feet 8½ inches. He described the foundations, which would be of reinforced concrete and would go three feet below the surface of the ground, and he added that the reinforced concrete would be taken right up to the underside of the needle, through the base and the sarcophagus. The granite of the sarcophagus would only be a four inch cladding. The resultant structure would on any view be massive. There would be 1,200 cubic feet of reinforced concrete in the foundations alone; the sarcophagus, of reinforced concrete and granite, would be about another 300 cubic feet. All this is in addition to the granite needle and the Portland stone steps.

Mr Gabrielczyk said that it would be put up by a contractor of national standing, and that the erection of the memorial could be completed in four weeks, the whole project taking towards three months. To erect this structure is thus a work of considerable time and expense, involving a large quantity of stone, concrete and steel. It is in no way analogous to erecting a simple monument on a grave. In face of this evidence I can only hold that the proposed structure will be something 'which approaches to the character of a building', in the Earl of Halsbury LC's words, and that the construction of it will be something 'in the nature of building', to quote the Earl of Halsbury LC again. Alone, it may perhaps not interfere very much with the 'free and open use' of the open space, though it will undoubtedly take away some space. But if this structure was not a building, another similar one would also not be a building. If even half a dozen of them were put up on St Luke's gardens the loss of open space would be serious. Counsel for the petitioners said, among other things, that a building is something which affords shelter, for people, animals or machinery, and that something at which one merely looks cannot be a building. He conceded that if the sarcophagus had been hollow and had had a door in it, so that it could be used as a potting shed by the gardener, his argument would lose its force. But in the present case we are concerned, as Buckley J said[1], with structures which cover the ground, take up space, and a solid structure takes up just as much space as a hollow one.

Having reached this conclusion on the authority of the *Paddington* case[2], I need not say very much about the other cases on s 3 of the 1884 Act which were cited to me. The case in the Privy Council of *St Nicholas Acons* (Rector and Churchwardens) v *London County Council*[3] is consistent with the view which I have taken. The underground transformer station which was there held to be a building took up space.

1 [1903] 1 Ch at 117
2 [1906] AC 1, [1904-7] All ER Rep 362
3 [1928] AC 469, [1928] All ER Rep 240

a Its dimensions are not given, but it need not have been any larger than the sarcophagus in the present case. What their Lordships decided was that it made no difference that the space was almost entirely below the current level of the ground.

The case much relied on by counsel for the petitioners was *St Botolph, Aldersgate Without (Vicar) v St Bartolph, Aldersgate Without (Parishioners)*[1] where Chancellor Dr Tristram QC held that s 3 of the 1884 Act would not be infringed by constructing a churchyard wall, the inner side of which would be covered with frescos, which in b turn would be protected from the weather by an 'arcade or covered way'. He held that the purpose of the legislation was to leave the parishioners as much space as before in which to walk about, and that this structure would not be a building because they could walk in the colonnade. His decision was not referred to in the *Paddington* case[2], nor in that of *St Nicholas Acons (Rector and Churchwardens) v London County Council*[3]. It was referred to, without any expressions of approval, by Willink, Dean c of the Arches, in *Re St Mark's Church, Lincoln*[4]. In the same case Chancellor Macmorran QC said[5], that *St Botolph's case*[1] was 'the most interesting case', but he gave no further explanation of what he meant. He did not state that he was applying it. I do not see how it bears on the present case where there will be a loss of space to the public, even if a small one.

In *Re St Mark's Church, Lincoln*[6] the Court of Arches held that a portion of a roof, d attached to an undoubted building outside the burial ground, and projecting over the burial ground, infringed s 3 of the Disused Burial Grounds Act 1884. It was part of the building and though it had no contact with the soil of the burial ground it was 'on' it. This part of a building was still a building although it in no way stopped the movements of the public. I find it somewhat difficult to see how *St Botolph's* case[1] can stand with that decision of the appellate court. But that matter does not arise for e my decision.

In *Bermondsey Borough Council v Mortimer*[7] Chancellor Hansell held that the erection of urinals would infringe the 1884 Act, but that a small wooden tool shed would not. The latter decision was based on the fact that a tool shed is a necessity if the ground is to be laid out and improved as an open space.

There remains to be noticed only *Re St Peter the Great, Chichester*[8], which concerned f an electricity sub-station consisting of a rectangular metal cupboard some four feet high, a transformer just over six feet high and some high voltage switchgear in metal boxes. Chancellor Buckle[9] distinguished the *St Nicholas Acons*[3] and *St Mark's, Lincoln*[6] cases, which he said were the only two cases brought to his notice. Thus he did not have the *Paddington* case[2] before him. He said that the question of what is a building is one of first impression, and that it depends on the ordinary meaning of the word. g In this connection counsel had submitted to him that one test of a building is that it should have four walls and a roof. Since Chancellor Buckle did not have the advantage of considering the remarks of the House of Lords or those of Buckley J in the *Paddington* case[10], I cannot accept his decision as laying down any principle relevant to the problem now before me, though I must not be taken as dissenting from what he actually decided.

h On this part of the case counsel for the petitioners submitted that the 1884 Act was an anachronism, and that the court should seek to avoid stretching it. There is no

---

1 [1900] P 69
2 [1906] AC 1, [1904-7] All ER Rep 362
3 [1928] AC 469, [1928] All ER Rep 240
j 4 [1956] 2 All ER 579 at 582, [1956] P 336 at 343
5 [1955] 3 All ER 699 at 702, [1956] P 166 at 172
6 [1956] 2 All ER 579, [1956] P 336
7 [1926] P 87
8 [1961] 2 All ER 513, [1961] 1 WLR 907
9 [1961] 2 All ER at 519, [1961] 1 WLR at 912
10 [1906] AC 1, [1904-7] All ER 362; [1903] 1 Ch 109

question of my doing so. I have sought to construe the Act, and to apply it to this case pursuant to the observations of the Earl of Halsbury LC and Buckley J in the *Paddington* case[1]. A submission that an Act of Parliament is an anachronism is a bold one, especially where, in the course of the same submissions, it was shown that modern legislation, and in particular the 1967 Act, have brought some sorts of building out of the 1884 Act. In my opinion, the presumption is that, in making such alterations, Parliament intended to retain unaltered those parts of the 1884 Act which were not touched, and in consequence they must be construed now as they were construed by the House of Lords in the *Paddington* case[2].

Accordingly, I hold that the proposed structure, the monument as a whole, would be a building within the meaning of that word in s 3 of the 1884 Act. Consequently, I have no power to grant the faculty which the petitioners seek. For this reason, and also for the additional reasons which will appear shortly (see *Jacobs v London County Council*[3]), the petition will be dismissed.

Before coming to the other points in the case, I pause to note one matter which has caused me concern. During the first three days of the hearing of this case I was unaware of the former practice of this court to notify the former London County Council of any applications concerned with a disused burial ground. This practice was mentioned by my predecessor in *St Nicholas Acons (Rector and Churchwardens) v London County Council*[4], and it appears to have originated in 1904: see *London County Council v Dundas*[5]. It has been lost to view in the recent reform of the practice under the Faculty Jurisdiction Measure 1964, which abolished the local rules of particular consistory courts, and in the reorganisation of local government in London. The basis of the former practice was that the Metropolitan Board of Works (Various Powers) Act 1885[6] constituted that board to be 'the authority for preventing the violation of and for enforcing the due observance of the provisions of (the Act of 1884) within the metropolis.' By other legislation those powers (with their concomitant duties) passed at one stage to the former London County Council. Soon after the third day's hearing, I discovered these facts, and I caused enquiries to be made of the Greater London Council. I was informed that the successor authority in respect of these matters is the Greater London Council itself, but that in Inner London the powers and duties have been delegated to the borough councils and to the Common Council of the City of London. Thus the original petitioner, the council, is itself the enforcement authority on which the court is normally entitled to rely to argue against the petition in those cases in which the court needs assistance in deciding whether a proposed structure would or would not involve a breach of the 1884 Act. On the fourth day of the hearing counsel for the petitioners informed me that the council is the enforcement authority, and he sought to pray that fact in aid in support of his submissions, to be noted later, on the issue of discretion. I do not accept the relevance to those submissions of the fact that the council is the enforcement authority, and I shall say no more about that.

But the 1884 Act is not to be treated as an anachronism, and it would be wrong if, now that these matters have been aired, any of the enforcement authorities in this diocese were to be remiss in the exercise of its duties and powers of enforcement. Further, if one of these authorities itself petitions for relief which may be prohibited by the Act, its reasons for submitting that the Act does not apply should be stated in the petition. For my part, I propose to direct the registry to notify the relevant enforcement authority of any petition in which a point under the Act seems likely

1   [1906] AC at 3, 4, [1904-7] All ER Rep at 363; [1903] 1 Ch at 117
2   [1906] AC 1, [1904-7] All ER Rep 362
3   [1950] 1 All ER 737, [1950] AC 361
4   [1928] P 102 at 104
5   [1904] P 1 at 16
6   48 & 49 Vict c clxvii

to arise. I make no criticism of what has happened here. The council no doubt over-
a looked the point, as I did myself, and the court has not been put to inconvenience,
since the case against the petition has been fully argued by counsel on behalf of the
archdeacon.

It must almost necessarily follow from the conclusion which I have reached on
the 1884 Act that the erection of this monument would be a breach of the trusts of
the 1906 Act on which the borough council holds this land. Anything that a person
b having the freehold does with reference to the open space must be calculated to
further its enjoyment by the public as an open space. Thus the erection of a gardener's
tool shed would obviously be legitimate. But none of the witnesses in this case
suggested that this open space would be improved as an open space by the erection
of this monument, or that the council ever thought that it would. Mr Robinson said
that the monument was being erected 'as a token of our regard for the Poles and for
c their war effort' and that 'we were very near to their national headquarters and very
anxious to pay our tribute in this way'. On the other hand, the churchwarden, Mr
Edwards, said that the monument was completely out of scale to the gardens 'unless
the gardens are to be considered only as a setting for the memorial' and that this
was one of the few public open spaces in the area, that people frequented it, 'and I
cannot think that this would in fact add to their comfort or pleasure when they go
d there'. This observation appears to me to be amply justified. The gardens are there
to be enjoyed as gardens and not to be a receptable for objects signifying that the
council wishes to pay tribute to any person or section of the community. I hold
therefore that to put up such a monument would be a breach of trust.

As the third ground for my decision, I now come to the issue of discretion. I must
first deal with the submission of counsel for the petitioners that the powers and duties
e of the court are now 'vestigial' and that a petition presented by the council ought
to be granted 'almost as of course'. The basis of this submission is the contention,
which I have already held to be misconceived, that there is so much which the council
can do under the 1967 Act without the authority of the court that it would be idle for
the court to apply ordinary considerations to the few cases, of which this is one,
where counsel for the petitioners concedes that a faculty is still needed. Even if I had
f upheld the contention about the 1967 Act, I should still not have acceded to the consequential submission. For the legislature, in depriving the court of some powers
and duties, decided to leave the court still invested with others. So those others
should be exercised on established principles, unless and until the legislature provides otherwise. Accordingly, I reject the submission that this court's powers and
duties are vestigial and anything which is said to follow from that proposition. In
g this connection I recall the observations of Chancellor Errington in Re St Dunstan's,
Stepney[1]:

> 'Our country churchyards are, I think, the most beautiful in Europe, and our
> town churchyards, often thanks to the local authority, now the best maintained.
> It is owing to their sacred character that they remained so long intact. . . The
h consistory courts have long been recognized as the proper guardians of these
> sacred spaces . . .'

That the court's protection does serve a useful purpose, and that it would be unsafe
to leave matters purely to the judgment of the local authority, is well shown by what
occurred in this very case about the proposal to plant 23 pine trees. This proposal
was included in the petition, but had to be withdrawn on the fourth day of the hearing
j as being indefensible, and indeed probably impracticable.

I approach the exercise of the discretion keeping clearly in view the question which
the deputy auditor put to himself in Morley Borough Council v St Mary the Virgin,
Woodkirk (Vicar and Churchwardens)[2]: 'What is the duty of the church in this situation?'

---

1 [1937] P 199 at 203, 204
2 [1969] 3 All ER 952 at 958, [1969] 1 WLR 1867 at 1876

Here we have a garden, described by Mr FitzGibbon as 'a pleasant, almost private type garden, a quiet place' and by Mr Edwards as 'a sort of oasis of quiet'. It is clearly much enjoyed and appreciated by those who live round about, many of them in blocks of flats closely packed. It was for this purpose that the church authorities made over the gardens to the vestry in 1888. In my judgment, the gardens as they now are serve a purpose very useful to the community and the duty of the church is to protect that useful purpose. I ought not to allow anything which would interfere, or tend to create interference, with the substantial facility to the public which the gardens in their present condition afford.

The proposed monument is massive and I cannot recall ever having been asked for a faculty to authorise the introduction into a churchyard of anything like so large. Thus, even in an open churchyard, or in a closed churchyard which has not been cleared, there would be little chance of a petition of this kind succeeding. But in this case St Luke's gardens, as they now exist, are what they have become because the court, in 1886, allowed most of the existing tombstones to be cleared away and arranged round the edges so as to produce a clear area to be laid out with lawns and paths. An overwhelming case would have to be made for reversing this regime, and there is no such case because the witnesses all agree that the gardens look very well as they are, that they are much used and appreciated by the public as they are, and that they serve a valuable public purpose. If this monument was now let in, there would be no reliable ground for excluding the next one which was proposed, especially if it were to a Chelsea worthy (or, if counsel for the petitioners is right about the result of Kensington and Chelsea being joined for certain local government purposes, a Kensington worthy). Having allowed one monument, the court would be driven to invidious distinctions to prevent the erection of others, and before long there could easily be enough to alter the gardens radically, even if the present monument would not make a radical alteration in itself, which in my opinion it would.

The victims of Katyn had no connection with Chelsea or with St Luke's parish. Counsel for the petitioners says that that does not matter because the Polish community has centres of organisations in South Kensington and a population there and in Earls Court, and that all these places are now grouped with Chelsea in an area throughout which the council exercises certain of the powers of local government. This recent association seems to me to have nothing to do with the present case. The trusts on which the council holds this land are the same as those on which the former municipal authority held the land, save insofar as the trusts themselves have been altered by express enactment or by the necessary implication of some enactments. To change a trustee does not change a trust.

This is a burial ground, a cemetery, a place of rest and peace. It has been appropriated to the public for use as a garden. The symbolism of an obelisk may be a matter of personal taste, but I cannot ignore the view of the diocesan advisory committee, echoed in his evidence by the Archdeacon of Middlesex, that the significance of this obelisk is not restful, nor consistent with the Church's ministry of reconciliation. However that may be, and I do not found my decision on the symbolism of the obelisk as such, it is, in my judgment, plain that this monument is intended to be political and to be politically controversial. It is true that, under the guidance of counsel for the petitioners, the text of one part of the proposed inscription has been toned down from what was originally sought in the petition, and that that version was in its turn less abrasive than several of the forms of words proposed to the council by Mr FitzGibbon. Counsel for the petitioners refused the invitation of counsel for the archdeacon to substitute for the date '1940' (which in effect charges the Russians with the massacre), the words 'during the Second World War' (which leaves it open who committed the massacre and makes no direct accusation). Counsel for the petitioners said in the speech in reply '1940 is essential'. I make no finding of the truth or otherwise of the date 1940; I intimated at the outset of the hearing that it would only be necessary to hear evidence on that matter if I decided to grant the petition.

a I should perhaps say that it would be difficult, according to English ideas of justice, to make a finding of guilt of this sort without giving those who were accused an opportunity to defend themselves. But in view of my decision that does not arise. For the present purpose the critical point is that the petitioners say '1940 is essential': that is the monument is intended to make and to perpetuate in stone a specific accusation. In my judgment, it is no part of the duty of the courts of the Church of England

b to allow land under their jurisdiction to be used to advertise accusations of crime. I do not recall ever having been asked to sanction an inscription naming the murderer on the tombstone of a murdered person, and I should be most unwilling to allow any such thing in an ordinary churchyard. I do not think that the scale of the massacre makes any difference.

The declared purposes of the memorial committee in their appeal for funds include

c 'to mark an event in history which so many have for so long conspired to erase' and to provide 'a place where [people] may ponder upon man's inhumanity to man'. Counsel for the petitioners said that the monument would comfort his clients and their supporters and this is in line with the appeal which says 'to bring some solace to the widows of these victims, their surviving relatives, brother officers and men'. This last is an object which will endure only for a short time: the massacre was at least

d 30 years ago and those who are to be solaced must by now be of advancing age. The monument itself will be enduring, and if it is erected it will be there for many years to come, probably far into the next century. I do not think that it is part of the functions of the Church of England, acting through its courts, to help to perpetuate bitter feelings in the years ahead. I do not think that it has ever been the Church's practice to do so. At least I am not aware of any churchyard monuments to any of the well-known

e massacres or atrocities, of which there have been all too many. We are enjoined to forgive our enemies.

The honorary secretary of the memorial committee apparently told the council that the monument would become a place of pilgrimage. His remarks, or some similar ones on another occasion, were quoted by the borough engineer in his letter of 26th June 1972. During his speech in reply, counsel for the petitioners said that

f that sentence was written by the borough engineer without authority and that the council repudiated it. This seems to me to be hard on the borough engineer, who in the letter expressly said that he was quoting the honorary secretary, and the honorary secretary had in fact said precisely this. I propose to deal with the case on the footing that the monument will become a place of pilgrimage if it is allowed to be erected and that substantial numbers of people, who would not otherwise come to

g St Luke's gardens at all, would in fact come to them. The gardens now serve the public as a place of 'exercise, ventilation, recreation and whatnot' in an area short of public open spaces and near some areas of dense population. To encourage the arrival of substantial numbers of people from outside Chelsea, who would not otherwise come at all, would at least not assist in the present useful purposes which the gardens serve, even if the incumbent was wrong in the opinion which he expressed that the result

h of putting up the monument would be to convert St Luke's gardens into a Katyn memorial garden. By this observation I understood him to mean not that the name would be changed, but that in fact the monument would so dominate the gardens that people would come to think of it as the significant thing about this area of land rather than to think of the gardens as gardens associated with St Luke's Church.

As to the matter of local public opinion, counsel for the petitioners made much of

j the motion which was tabled in the House of Commons in June 1972 and to which nearly 200 signatures were appended. But that motion does not relate to St Luke's gardens at all. A monument anywhere in London would satisfy it. He also urged that the council in full council had decided unanimously in favour of the monument being in St Luke's gardens. Mr Thom told me that he was present when the relevant committee report came up for ratification and said that he was pleased that the council was unanimous in approving it. But he said in cross-examination that he had voted 'without close detailed knowledge. That is the custom . . . it is customary for the   *a* council, if it has confidence in the committees, to support their reports'. I have no reason to suppose that Mr Thom was exceptional in this attitude; that being so, little can be made of the unanimity of the council. Mr Thom said that none of his constituents had spoken to him against the proposal but that he had heard 'many encouraging and supporting remarks from people I know'. There is no evidence when those remarks were made or what those who made them knew of the specific proposal which   *b* is now before me. If they knew as little as the parochial church council knew in 1972 and knew throughout most of 1973, this piece of evidence is of no value. On the other side there is the resolution of the parochial church council passed during the hearing and after the precise nature of the proposal in the petition was known. It can be said that the petition was later amended and that the removal of the pine trees could make some difference, but the pine trees are not referred to in this resolution. It can   *c* also be said that the feelings of the parochial church council would have been more impressive if they had felt strongly enough to enter appearance in opposition. Perhaps this consideration detracts from the weight of their resolution; but not very much.

Finally there were the enquiries made by the churchwardens, the bishop's officers, at my instance and particularly those of Mr Edwards. The evidence of Colonel Large pointed in the same direction, but it has less weight because his enquiries were not   *d* so systematic as those of Mr Edwards. I found the latter a convincing and reliable witness who had taken a lot of care to find out the state of opinion in an admittedly small area, namely St Luke's Street. I reject utterly the submission of counsel for the petitioners that the evidence of Mr Edwards is in pari materia with the 'memorials' and 'petitions' with which consistory courts are often troubled and which were criticised recently by Chancellor Goodman in *Re Christ Church, Chislehurst*[1], following a decision   *e* of the Court of Arches much earlier[2]. In the present case the evidence of Mr Edwards shows that he made enquiries as a bishop's officer: he is not in the least in the position of a person, on his own initiative, collecting signatures on a memorial. The enquiries of Mr Edwards were made pursuant to his duty and to my request, and all I need say is that I accept his evidence as far as it goes.

The result is that the council wants the monument, the parochial church council   *f* does not, and there is no evidence remotely suggesting a local consensus in favour of having it. In a highly controversial matter, this is not sufficient to redress the strong balance against the proposal on the other grounds which I have endeavoured to state. For these reasons, if I had held that I had power to grant the petition, I should in the exercise of my discretion have refused it. The petition is therefore dismissed.

g

Petition dismissed. Leave to appeal granted.

Solicitors: *A Ellery*, Royal Borough of Kensington and Chelsea (for the petitioners); *Lee, Bolton & Lee* (for the archdeacon).

Mary Rose Plummer   Barrister.   *h*

1   [1974] 1 All ER 146 at 151, [1973] 1 WLR 1317 at 1321
2   See *Capel St Mary, Suffolk (Rector and Churchwardens) v Packard* [1927] P 289

R v Michael

INNER LONDON CROWN COURT
HIS HONOUR JUDGE RUBIN
25th APRIL, 16th JUNE 1975

Criminal law – Costs – Award out of central funds – Defendant acquitted – Order made for payment of defence costs out of central funds – Scope of order – Whether order including costs of committal proceedings – Costs in Criminal Cases Act 1973, s 3(1)(b)(9).

Crown Court – Order – Amendment – Jurisdiction – Order not giving effect to court's intention – Costs – Defendant acquitted – Order that defence costs be paid out of central funds – Intention that order should include costs of committal proceedings – Order entered on record containing no reference to costs of committal proceedings – Whether court having jurisdiction to order that record be amended – Courts Act 1971, s 11(2).

The defendant was tried in the Crown Court on an indictment containing 24 counts and acquitted. At the conclusion of the trial his counsel applied for an order that the defence costs should be paid out of central funds. The application was granted. It was the intention of the court that the order should include the costs of the committal proceedings, but no specific reference was made to those costs in the order. The order was entered on the record as an order for costs out of central funds under s 3(1)(b)^a of the Costs in Criminal Cases Act 1973. On taxation the taxing office refused to allow the costs of the committal proceedings on the ground that they had not been included in the order. The defendant applied to have the record of the order amended so as to give effect to the court's intention.

Held – (i) An order for payment of defence costs out of central funds made under s 3(1)(b) of the 1973 Act did not automatically carry with it the costs of the committal proceedings. The word 'may' in s 3(9) indicated that the court had a discretion whether or not to include such costs when making the order, and therefore if those costs were to be included it was necessary that there should be an express reference to them in the order. It followed that the taxing office was right in taking the view that the order entered did not include the costs of the committal proceedings (see p 631 c to f, post).

(ii) The court had an inherent jurisdiction to amend or rectify the order recorded in its record in such a way as to carry out the intention of the court. Section 11(2)^b of the Courts Act 1971 was not to be construed as having by implication limited the power to alter or recall an order to the circumstances mentioned in that subsection. Accordingly, in exercise of the court's inherent jurisdiction, the record would be amended to

---

a Section 3, so far as material, provides:
'(1) Subject to the provisions of this section, where a person is prosecuted or tried on indictment before the Crown Court, the court may—(a) order the payment out of central funds of the costs of the prosecution: (b) if the accused is acquitted, order the payment out of central funds of the costs of the defence . . .
'(9) The costs of carrying on the defence that may be awarded to any person under this section may include the costs of carrying on the defence before the examining justices who committed him for trial, or as the case may be before the magistrates' court who convicted him.'
b Section 11(2) provides: 'Subject to the following provisions of this section, a sentence imposed, or other order made, by the Crown Court when dealing with an offender may be varied or rescinded by the Crown Court within the period of 28 days beginning with the day on which the sentence or other order was imposed or made, or where subsection (3) below applies, within the time allowed by that subsection.'

give effect to the court's intention by showing that the costs to be recovered by the
defendant included the costs of the committal proceedings (see p 631 *j* to p 632 *b* and   *a*
p 633 *c d* and *f*, post).

Dictum of Lord Penzance in *Lawrie v Lees* (1881) 7 App Cas at 34, *Re Swire* (1885)
30 Ch D 239, *Milson v Carter* [1893] AC 638 and *Re Inchcape* [1942] 2 All ER 157 applied.

Notes

For the amendment of a judgment or order after it has been drawn up, see 22 Halsbury's   *b*
Laws (3rd Edn) 785, para 1665, and for cases on the subject, see 50 Digest (Repl) 530-536,
1970-2035.

For the Courts Act 1971, s 11, see 41 Halsbury's Statutes (3rd Edn) 299.

For the Costs in Criminal Cases Act 1973, s 3, see 43 Halsbury's Statutes (3rd Edn) 269.

Cases referred to in judgment   *c*

Hatton v Harris [1892] AC 547, 62 LJPC 24, 67 LT 722, HL, 50 Digest (Repl) 531, *1977.*
Inchcape, Re, Craigmyle v Inchcape [1942] 2 All ER 157, [1942] Ch 394, 111 LJCh 273,
  167 LT 333, 50 Digest (Repl) 533, *1998.*
Lawrie v Lees (1881) 7 App Cas 19, 51 LJCh 209, 46 LT 210, HL, 50 Digest (Repl) 536, *2029.*
Milson v Carter [1893] AC 638, 62 LJPC 126, 69 LT 735, PC, 50 Digest (Repl) 536, *2032.*
R v Smith (Martin) [1974] 1 All ER 651, [1975] QB 531, [1974] 2 WLR 495, CA.   *d*
Swire, Re, Mellor v Swire (1885) 30 Ch D 239, 53 LT 205, CA, 50 Digest (Repl) 530, *1974.*

Application

In November 1974 the defendant, Phillip Michael, and a co-defendant were tried
before his Honour Judge Rubin in the Crown Court sitting at Sessions House,
Newington Causeway, SE1, on an indictment containing 24 counts. The defendant
was acquitted on all the counts against him. He applied for an order that the defence   *e*
costs be paid out of central funds under s 3(1)(*b*) of the Costs in Criminal Cases Act
1973. His application was granted and an order entered for costs to be paid out of
central funds. The defendant applied to the judge for an order that the record of the
costs order be amended to include the costs of the committal proceedings. The facts
are set out in the judgment.   *f*

Michael Lewis QC for the defendant.
Michael Gale for the Crown.

Cur adv vult

16th June 1975.   **JUDGE RUBIN** read the following judgment: This application
raises an important question on the jurisdiction of the Crown Court over its own   *g*
record. The matter arises in the following way. In November 1974 the defendant was
tried before me with another defendant on an indictment containing 24 counts. The
trial extended over a number of days and at its conclusion the defendant was acquitted
on all the counts with which he was concerned. At the conclusion of the trial counsel
for the defendant made an application for an order for the payment of the costs of
his client's defence out of central funds. I acceded to that application and my order   *h*
was entered in the record as an order for costs out of central funds, under s 3(1)(*b*)
of the Costs in Criminal Cases Act 1973. The taxing office of this court has taken the
point that such an order does not include the costs of the committal proceedings
unless the judge specifically orders they should be paid out of central funds.

Counsel for the defendant tells me, and this accords with my own memory, that
no specific reference was made in court to the costs of the committal proceedings. I   *j*
have a fairly clear memory of this case and I am sure that if the officious bystander had
asked: 'Does your order include the costs of the committal proceedings?' he would
have been met with a curt, 'Of course'.

The solicitors instructing counsel for the defendant, when they presented their
bill for taxation, discovered that the taxing office was not prepared to allow the

costs of the committal proceedings on the order which was entered in the record.

a Counsel for the defendant tells me, and of course I accept, that immediate steps were taken to bring the matter before me by way of application to rectify the record of my order. I was away from this court for a period in the spring. Counsel applied ex parte soon after my return. I then thought that the application raised a difficult question over the jurisdiction of this court over its orders, and accordingly I directed that the application be listed for argument and, moreover, as a decision might affect the pub-

b lic purse, the Crown should be given an opportunity to be represented. Counsel has appeared for the Crown. I am grateful to him and counsel for the defendant for their clear arguments in this case. Having heard those arguments I reserved my judgment, primarily because it would appear from *R v Smith (Martin)*[1] that my decision might not be open to review in any appellate court and also because the decision might affect other cases.

c   Where an order for costs was made under s 1(1)(b) of the Costs in Criminal Cases Act 1952 that order, by virtue of the definition contained in s 17(b) of that Act, carried with it the costs of the committal proceedings. In my judgment the position altered under the Costs in Criminal Cases Act 1973. By s 3(1)(b) of that Act, the court has power, on an acquittal, to order payment out of central funds of the costs of the defence. I can find no equivalent definition section in that Act, but in s 3(9) there is a provision

d that the costs of the defence may include the costs of carrying on the defence before the examining justices. It seems to me under this section that the court has two powers. The first is to deal with the costs in this court and if the court is minded to exercise that power then it has a further power, if so minded, to include the costs of the committal proceedings. I am unable to accept counsel for the defendant's argument that an order in exercise of the first power carries with it the costs of committal pro-

e ceedings unless the court expressly excludes these costs. In my judgment the word 'may' used in s 3(9), on its natural meaning, is apt to describe a power to include but not an obligation to include. In my judgment, therefore, the taxing office was right when it took the view that the order entered did not include the costs of the committal proceedings.

  I turn to the question whether there is any power to alter or amend the record and,

f if so, whether it should be exercised in this case. The Crown Court was created by the Courts Act 1971. Section 1(1) of that Act provides: 'The Supreme Court shall consist of the Court of Appeal and the High Court together with the Crown Court established by this Act'. Section 4(1) provides that the Crown Court shall be a superior court of record. Section 11(2) contains an express though limited power to vary or rescind certain orders made by the Crown Court within a period of 28 days. It is

g clear the subsection cannot apply in the present case, if only for the reason that the period of 28 days has long since expired. Counsel for the defendant has advanced a further reason: the subsection uses the words 'when dealing with an offender' and he argues that, his client having been acquitted, the court was not dealing with 'an offender' when dealing with costs. I see the force of that argument but do not find it necessary to decide that on this application. If he is right it would mean that even

h within the 28 days no successful defendant could apply to the Crown Court under that section to remedy a mistake in the court office in recording an order pronounced by the judge. I can find no other express power in the Act which would enable the court to alter any order which it has made or to rectify an incorrect record of any order pronounced by the court.

  I now consider whether the courts have an inherent power over orders and if so

j whether and to what extent those powers apply to the Crown Court. In my judgment it has long been recognised that a court may have power to alter or recall an order which it has made before that order has been perfected by entry in the court's records. This is a power which is well recognised in the civil courts. It would appear to have

---

1   [1974] 1 All ER 651, [1975] QB 531

been a power exercised both by courts of assize and quarter sessions, aided by the
fiction that the order was not entered or perfected until the last day of the assizes   *a*
or sessions. It seems to me that this power is reflected in s 11(2) of the 1971 Act and
accordingly there is considerable force in the argument that s 11(2) has by necessary
implication limited the power to alter or recall an order in the Crown Court to the
circumstances mentioned in that subsection. Quite apart from the power to alter or
recall an order before it has been perfected by entry, in my judgment the cases show
that the court can have an inherent jurisdiction to amend or rectify the order recorded   *b*
in its record to make such record accord with the order intended by the court. In
Lawrie v Lees[1] Lord Penzance said:

> 'I cannot doubt that under the original powers of the Court, quite independent
> of any order that is made under the Judicature Act, every Court has the power to
> vary its own orders which are drawn up mechanically in the registry or in the   *c*
> office of the court—to vary them in such a way as to carry out its own meaning
> and where language has been used which is doubtful, to make it plain. I think
> that power is inherent in every court.'

In *Re Swire*[2] the Court of Appeal recognised that it had such an inherent jurisdiction
over its own orders. The Court of Appeal, like the Crown Court, was created by   *d*
statute and accordingly this decision establishes that the statutory creation of a court
is no bar to that court having that inherent jurisdiction. Cotton LJ said[3]:

> '. . . in my opinion the Court has jurisdiction over its own records, and if it
> finds that the order as passed and entered contains an adjudication upon which
> the Court in fact has never adjudicated upon, then, in my opinion, it has juris-
> diction, which it will in a proper case exercise, to correct its record, that it may be   *e*
> in accordance with the order really pronounced.'

Lindley LJ protested against the notion that once an order had been entered it could
not be put right. Bowen LJ said[4]:

> 'I think the true view is . . . that every Court has inherent power over its own   *f*
> records as long as those records are within its power, and that it can set right any
> mistake in them. It seems to me that it would be perfectly shocking if the Court
> could not rectify an error which is really the error of its own minister.'

The decision in *Re Swire*[2] received the approval of Lord Watson in *Hatton v Harris*[5].
In my judgment these cases establish that this court, as a court of record, has an
inherent jurisdiction to remedy mistakes in its record. There are two other cases   *g*
to which I must refer which show, in my judgment, that an omission from an
order should be rectified if it is of such a character that if it had been mentioned before
the order had been entered the omission would have been supplied as a matter of
course without further argument.

The first is *Milson v Carter*[6]. In that case the Supreme Court of New South Wales
in granting leave to appeal to the Privy Council had omitted, when dealing with the   *h*
costs of the appeal, any provision for those costs if the appeal should be struck out for
want of prosecution, as in fact happened. Lord Hobhouse, in delivering the opinion
of their Lordships, seemed to have no doubt that the Supreme Court could correct
that accidental omission.

---

1 (1881) 7 App Cas 19 at 34
2 (1885) 30 Ch D 239
3 30 Ch D at 243
4 30 Ch D at 247
5 [1892] AC 547 at 560
6 [1893] AC 638

The other case was the decision of Morton J in *Re Inchcape*[1]. In that case counsel
a had failed to ask for certain costs incurred before the issue of the originating summons
to be included in the order for costs. Morton J made his order to provide a provision
for those costs under the slip rule as it then existed in RSC Ord XXVIII, r 11, but in my
judgment that rule was no wider in that regard than the inherent jurisdiction of
the court. Morton J said[2]:

b   'It is true that, when the case was before me, I made the order which I in-
       tended to make in regard to the costs for which I was asked to make provision.
       There was, however, an accidental omission on the part of counsel, and I did not
       make the order which I would have made if that accidental omission had not
       occurred.'

I am satisfied that I have jurisdiction to direct an amendment of the record of the
c order which I made so that the record shall show that the costs to be recovered by
the defendant include the costs of the committal proceedings. The jurisdiction is a
discretionary jurisdiction and should not be exercised if it is not equitable. Delay of
itself, it appears from the cases, is not a bar to the remedy, but an adverse consequence
to a third party might well be a ground for refusing to exercise the jurisdiction.
       It is said on behalf of the Crown that there must be an end to matters of taxation in
d a case and it causes grave inconvenience if, after completion of taxation, the taxing
office cannot put aside its papers. I can see the force in that argument and in a case
where a party has elected to conduct a taxation on the order with knowledge of the
mistake he should not be allowed to apply to rectify the recorded order after the
conclusion of the taxation. That is not the present case as the defendant's advisers
tried to apply to me but could not because of my absence from this court. I can also
e see force in the argument that the Crown has a duty to protect the public purse but
not against a claim which would have been met without question but for the defect
as it now appears in the record of the court.
       I can find no reason in the present case why I should not exercise the inherent
jurisdiction of the court and accordingly I direct that the record of the order I made
at the conclusion of the trial so far as it concerns the defendant's costs be amended to
f include in those costs the costs of the committal proceedings. I am glad that I am able
to reach this conclusion as otherwise the defendant would have been deprived of any
remedy in respect of the loss he has suffered from the slip made at the conclusion of
his trial.
       As far as the costs of this application are concerned, I direct that the taxed costs of
the prosecution be paid out of central funds. Counsel for the defendant has told me
g that in the best traditions of the profession the burden of the defendant's application
is being borne by his advisers and accordingly I say nothing about the defendant's
costs of the present application.

Application granted.

h Solicitors: *Devonshire & Co* (for the defendant); *Solicitor, Metropolitan Police.*

                                                        Mary Rose Plummer Barrister.

---

1   [1942] 2 All ER 157, [1942] Ch 394
2   [1942] 2 All ER at 160, [1942] Ch at 399

Freer v Unwins Ltd

CHANCERY DIVISION
WALTON J
18th DECEMBER 1975

Land registration – Rectification of register – Date from which rectification effective – Effect on dispositions before date of rectification – Restrictive covenant – Title of servient tenement unregistered – Covenant registered against servient tenement – Title of servient tenement subsequently registered – Notice of restrictive covenant omitted from register – Lease of servient tenement subsequently granted – Lease assigned to defendants – Defendants having no knowledge of covenant – Plaintiff owner of dominant tenement – Plaintiff obtaining rectification of register – Notice of restrictive covenant entered – Whether covenant binding on defendants – Land Registration Act 1925, s 82.

Certain land was laid out as a parade of shops. In 1953 the owners of the land conveyed one of the shops to the plaintiff with the benefit of a restrictive covenant that the rest of the land would not be used or suffered to be used for the sale by retail of tobacco, cigarettes etc. The benefit of the restrictive covenant was registered against the land under the Land Charges Act 1925. Subsequently the titles to the land were registered. The registered title of the owner of one of the other shops ('the second shop') did not, however, show the restrictive covenant of which the plaintiff had the benefit. On 8th December 1969 the owners granted a lease of the second shop for a term of 21 years and on 16th December 1974 the lease was assigned to the defendants, who were vintners and who wished to sell tobacco, cigarettes etc from the second shop. Before taking the assignment the defendants took particular care to ensure that there was nothing on the freehold title that would affect the carrying on of their business from the second shop. Having satisfied themselves in that respect, they moved in and started to carry on their business. The plaintiff thereupon took steps to enforce the restrictive covenant. Having discovered that the restrictive covenant was not registered against the freehold title of the second shop, the plaintiff applied for rectification of the register under s 82 of the Land Registration Act 1925. The land registrar granted the application and there was no appeal against his decision. A new edition of the register was opened on 28th April 1975 and the charges register contained an entry, '1. 28th April, 1975', followed by a reference to the restrictive covenant imposed by the 1953 conveyance. The plaintiff then claimed an injunction restraining the defendants from selling tobacco, cigarettes etc from the second shop, contending that, following rectification, the covenant was binding on the defendants.

Held – The general scheme of the Land Registration Act 1925 was that a person obtained priority according to the date on which the interest was registered and a disposition of land took effect subject only to those interests which had been registered at the date when the disposition was registered or, in the case of a lease which was not itself registrable, when the lease was granted. Accordingly, since the lease was dated 8th December 1969 and the date on which notice of the restrictive covenant had been entered was 28th April 1975, it followed that the defendants, as assignees of the lease, took free from the restrictive covenant. The plaintiff's claim therefore failed (see p 638 g, p 639 d and h and p 640 a and b, post).

Notes

For rectification of the register, see 23 Halsbury's Laws (3rd Edn) 203-206, paras 425-431, and for cases on the subject, see 38 Digest (Repl) 899-900, 944-950.

For the Land Registration Act 1925, s 82, see 27 Halsbury's Statutes (3rd Edn)
a 856.

Motion
By a writ issued on 12th February 1975, the plaintiff, Ronald Arthur Frederick Freer,
brought an action against the defendants, Unwins Ltd, claiming an injunction
to restrain the defendants by their servants, agents or otherwise howsoever from
b carrying on or permitting to be carried on on the property known as 11 The Parade,
Valley Drive, Gravesend, Kent, the sale by retail of tobacco, cigarettes, smokers'
sundries, sweets or chocolates, and damages for breach of contract. By their defence
served on 21st March 1975 the defendants, inter alia, admitted that they were selling,
and, unless restrained by the court, intended to continue selling, those goods on the
property, but alleged that by a lease dated 8th December 1969 the then proprietor
c of the property had demised it to Shaws Laundries Ltd for a term of 21 years from
29th September 1969, and that by an assignment dated 16th December 1974 Shaws
Laundries Ltd had assigned the property to them for the residue of the term created
by the lease, and that, neither at the date of the lease, nor at the date of the assignment, nor at any other material time, had the restrictive covenant been protected
by any entry on the title of the property at the Land Registry and that, accordingly,
d the restrictive covenant was not binding on the defendants by virtue of the provisions
of the Land Registration Act 1925. By notice of motion dated 9th December 1975,
the plaintiff applied for an injunction in similar terms to that claimed in the writ.
At the hearing of the motion it was agreed that the motion was misconceived since
the cause of action was not subsisting at the date of the issue of the writ. The court
however gave leave to the plaintiff to issue a fresh writ and pro forma notice of motion
e in the same terms as the existing writ and notice of motion. The facts are set out
in the judgment.

Dirik Jackson for the plaintiff.
W R Stewart Smith for the defendants.

f

WALTON J. The motion before me in this action arises out of very curious chain
of events. Some time ago, a property known as The Parade, Valley Drive, Gravesend,
in Kent, appears to have been laid out as a parade of shops, with the fairly obvious
intention, so far as one can tell from the documents connected with the conveyancing that are now before the court, that each shop in the parade should be used for
g a particular trade or business and should have no competitors among the other
shops in that parade. And to that effect, certain restrictive covenants were imposed.
Counsel for the plaintiff has frankly conceded that there is no hope of getting a
building or letting scheme out of those covenants, but they were properly imposed
as valid restrictive covenants for the benefit of the appropriate land; and, in particular,
by a conveyance of 12th May 1953, made between the Gravesend Land Co Ltd, who
h were the proprietors then and who apparently laid the parade out, and the plaintiff.
One of those shops was conveyed to him with the intention that he should use it
as a tobacconist's, for the sale of tobacco, cigarettes and smokers' sundries, sweets
and chocolates, and on the remainder of the parade, because this appears to have
been the first shop sold, there was a restrictive covenant imposed for the benefit
of the shop that he took, that the land would not be used or suffered to be used for
j the sale by retail of tobacco, cigarettes, snuff, pipes, smokers' sundries, sweets or
chocolates.
The benefit of that restrictive covenant appears to have been registered against
the land, which was then unregistered, under the provisions of the Land Charges
Act 1925. I do not think I am concerned with the details of that registration, save
to say that the designation of the land affected thereby, the servient land, was in

such vague terms that I am by no means surprised that errors arose in relation to
the registration later.   *a*
At some stage, the titles to the land were registered, and the title of the then owner
of the servient tenement was duly registered and it did not show the relevant restrictive covenant of which the plaintiff had the benefit. It was in that state of affairs
that on 8th December 1969 a lease was made between the Land and House Property
Corpn Ltd, who were then the registered proprietors of the land, and Shaws Laundries
Ltd, the term being for a term of 21 years from 29th September 1969. That lease *b*
was assigned to the defendants on 16th December 1974 with a licence to change
the user given by the landlord, the then registered proprietor, Daejan Properties
Ltd.
The defendants are in fact a chain of vintners. They sell all kinds of drink and,
as ancillary thereto, they also sell tobacco, cigarettes and indeed boxes of chocolates
and things of that nature. Before the defendants took the assignment and effected *c*
the change of user, they particularly made certain that there was nothing on the
freehold title, as registered, which would affect them or prevent them in any way
from carrying on the business that they wished to carry on there. So they duly
moved into the premises and commenced to carry their ordinary trade on from those
premises. But, of course, this was quite contrary to the restrictive covenant of which
the plaintiff had the benefit and so, on 12th February 1975, he issued the writ in this *d*
action, claiming an injunction restraining the defendants from carrying on on their
premises, 11 The Parade, Valley Drive, Gravesend, Kent, the sale by retail of tobacco,
cigarettes, smokers' sundries, sweets or chocolates.
That was answered by a defence served on 21st March 1975 which, after the formal
parts, said simply:

                                                                     e

'Neither at the date of the said Lease nor at the date of the said Assignment
nor at any other material time was the restriction mentioned in the Statement
of Claim protected by any entry on the title of the said property at H.M. Land
Registry. The said restriction is accordingly not binding on the Defendant by
virtue of the provisions of the Land Registration Act 1925 including in particular
section 20(1) and 59(6) ... In the premises the Plaintiff is not entitled to the *f*
relief claimed or any relief.'

And that undoubtedly was the situation at the date when the defence was delivered.
In fact, it follows that the later motion in this action which is now before me is
completely misconceived, in that, in order to have a cause of action, that cause of
action must be subsisting at the date of the issue of the writ, and in the present case
it certainly was not, because of the state of the register. However, both counsel *g*
in front of me have been extremely sensible about the whole procedural muddle
that creates, and besides agreeing to treat the motion as the trial of the action, it has
been agreed, of course subject to all questions of costs, that if I decide in favour of
of the plaintiff, that will mean the issuing by the plaintiff of another pro forma writ
and notice of motion. I only mention that in order to get it out of the way, because
neither counsel for the plaintiff nor counsel for the defendants are people who in- *h*
dulge in shadow-boxing for the sake of shadow-boxing, and we have been dealing
with the meat of the matter and not with technical points, however valid they may be.
On discovering that there was this complete defence to the action as matters stood,
the plaintiff's solicitors got in touch with the Land Registry, with a view to obtaining
a rectification of the register. Now, I find it very difficult indeed to see how that
could ever have been expected to get off the ground, because the provisions of the *i*
Land Registration Act 1925 dealing with rectification provide in s 82(3):

'The register shall not be rectified, except for the purpose of giving effect to
an overriding interest [which does not apply here] so as to affect the title of
the proprietor who is in possession [and, pausing there, the freehold owners

a were in possession by receipt of the rents and profits through their tenant] (*a*) unless [first of all] such proprietor is a party or privy or has caused or substantially contributed, by his act, neglect or default, to the fraud, mistake or omission in consequence of which such rectification is sought [and that has not been suggested]; or (*b*) unless the immediate disposition to him was void, or the disposition to any person through whom he claims otherwise than for valuable consideration was void [and that has not been suggested, leaving only]; or (*c*) unless for any

b other reason, in any particular case, it is considered that it would be unjust not to rectify the register against him.'

I cannot see that there was any ground whatsoever for rectifying the register against the freehold proprietor, who wrote and told the land registrar—and nobody has suggested that this was not perfectly accurate—that he did not have constructive notice of the covenant in question. The land registrar appears to have replied to that

c objection by saying that that was not a valid objection. There was no appeal from the land registrar's decision to rectify the register and therefore I will say no more about it, save that the decision is a very great surprise to the court, especially in a case where the erroneous form of the original registration under the Land Charges Act 1925 may very well have contributed to the mistake which has occurred. But however that may be, the register has been rectified. It is somewhat of a puzzle to

d discover the precise date on which it was rectified, because it appears fairly obvious, from the correspondence, that it had not been rectified by 29th July 1975, but was probably rectified by September. However that may be, the register was rectified and a new edition of the register was opened on 28th April 1975, and hence one finds on the charges register, '1. 28th April, 1975', and then it refers to the restrictive covenant on the land created by the conveyance of 12th May 1953 to which I have

e already referred.

The register having been rectified in that way, the question arises whether that rectification is binding on the defendants in the sense that they are now bound by the restrictive covenant, and it has been agreed, I think, by both counsel that either way round there is something of an anomaly, because if the defendants are not bound, then there does not appear to be any way in which, since the register has

f now been rectified, the plaintiff can obtain any benefit, compensation, or has any other remedy against any other person, notwithstanding that until the expiry of the lease the defendants will be able to act in breach of that restrictive covenant. On the other hand, so far as the defendants are concerned, they have done everything that they possibly could in order to ensure that they were entitled to use the property for the purposes for which they wished to use it, and it is hard to see what

g else they could have done; and further, they were not given any notice of the proposal to rectify, so that they were unable to make any submissions to the Chief Land Registrar about it. So that if the plaintiff wins, the defendants will then feel that they have been stabbed in the back, without any opportunity to turn round and face their attacker, although, of course, there would be no doubt that under the wide words of s 83(1) of the Land Registration Act 1925 they would be within the category of

h 'any person suffering loss by reason of any rectification of the register', and therefore entitled to an indemnity.

That has led counsel for the plaintiff to submit to me that rectification and indemnity are complementary, the one being the mirror of the other, and that it must follow, since the plaintiff cannot get any indemnity against the defendants if they take free of the restrictive covenant for the duration of the lease, that that cannot

j be the right solution; whereas the fact that the defendants will be entitled to indemnity points to the fact that they are subject to the restrictive covenant. I see the force of that as an argument, but I think one is bound to take the Act as one finds it, and one of the odd things about rectification is that there is no provision in s 82, which is the section which deals with rectification, which states in terms or by implication what date is to be inserted against any entry which is inserted pursuant

to rectification. One would perhaps have expected to have found some guidance
as to the date, but no guidance whatsoever is given at all. It merely says, 'The register   **a**
may be rectified', and then, apart from setting out the provision, the circumstances
under which it may be rectified and making certain qualifications as to when it may
be and when it shall not be rectified, it does not, I think, tell one anything more
about the date as from which the restriction takes effect.

Of course, if one were dealing with the ordinary sort of rectification with which
courts of equity are accustomed to deal in relation to documents, that always relates   **b**
back to the date when the document was itself executed; but, of course, correspondingly, the rights of all parties, who have in the meantime gained interests on the faith
of the unrectified document for value without notice, are strenuously protected.
So that I do not think that one can, having regard to the rather different provisions
of the Land Registration Act 1925, really equate a rectification in equity with
rectification under the Act.   **c**

So I turn to the effect of registration of dispositions of freeholds, bearing in mind
for the moment of course that the lease which was granted and which the defendants
now hold was not a lease which was registered or indeed could be registered. But
s 19(2) says:

> 'All interests transferred or created by dispositions by the proprietor, other   **d**
> than a transfer of the registered estate in the land, or part thereof, shall, subject
> to the provisions relating to mortgages, be completed by registration in the
> same manner and with the same effect as provided by this Act with respect
> to transfers of registered estates and notice thereof shall also be noted on the
> register: Provided that nothing in this subsection—(a) shall authorise the regis-
> tration of a lease granted for a term not exceeding twenty-one years [and then   **e**
> it goes on to say:] Every such disposition shall, when registered, take effect as a
> registered disposition, and a lease made by the registered proprietor ... which
> is not required to be registered ... shall nevertheless take effect as if it were
> a registered disposition immediately on being granted.'

Therefore, one must take it that for the purposes of the general scheme of the 1925   **f**
Act the lease of 8th December 1969 must be taken to have taken effect as if it were a
registered disposition immediately on being granted. That being so, it is subject
to the incumbrances and other entries appearing on the register and to overriding
interests, if any, affecting it, but free from all other estates and interests whatsoever,
and that is the language of s 20(1).

So, prima facie, one must look at what the position was on 8th December 1969,
when the lease was granted, and see what it was that was on the register then, and,   **g**
of course, it is common ground that on that date there was nothing on the register
in relation to the restrictive covenant. Now, what should have been on the register
in relation to the restrictive covenant which the plaintiff now relies on? That is stated
in s 50 of the 1925 Act, and sub-s (1) provides: 'Any person entitled to the benefit
of a restrictive covenant [I leave out a few words] may apply to the registrar to enter
notice thereof on the register.' Subsection (2), to which I shall have to return in a   **h**
moment, provides:

> 'When such a notice is entered the proprietor of the land and the persons
> deriving title under him (except incumbrancers or other persons who at the time
> when the notice is entered may not be bound by the covenant or agreement)
> shall be deemed to be affected with notice of the covenant or agreement as   **j**
> being an incumbrance on the land.'

Then, s 52(1):

> 'A disposition by the proprietor shall take effect subject to all estates, rights
> and claims which are protected by way of notice on the register at the date of

a

the registration or entry of notice of the disposition [and then there is a proviso with which I am not concerned].'

It seems to me that the scheme of that requires one to look in every case at the date of the notice of the restrictive covenant on the register. Section 50(2) provides:

b

'When such a notice is entered [and that must mean when the notice is entered and not from any earlier date] the proprietor of the land and the persons deriving title under him [and then there is the exception which I will come back to in a moment] shall be deemed to be affected with notice of the covenant or agreement as being an incumbrance on the land.'

But there is excepted in clear language, 'except incumbrancers or other persons who at the time when the notice is entered may not be bound by the covenant or

c agreement'.

What counsel for the plaintiff has submitted to me, in relation to those words, is that those words are inconsistent with the general scheme of the 1925 Act and should therefore be given a very narrow ambit. I am not myself persuaded in any way that those words are inconsistent with the general scheme of the Act. It appears to me that the general scheme of the Act is that one obtains priority according to

d the date of registration, and one is subject or not subject to matters appearing on the register according to whether they were there before one took one's interest, whatever that interest may be, or one took one's interest after. That seems to me to be the only sensible way in which the provisions of the Act can all be made to mesh together. For example, supposing now, for the first time, the defendants' landlords, the registered proprietors, were to impose a restrictive covenant on the land, which

e they are fully entitled to do, that restrictive covenant would then have to be protected by notice on the register, and it would have the effect stated in s 50(2): 'When such a notice is entered the proprietor of the land and the persons deriving title under him (except incumbrancers or other persons, who at the time when the notice is entered may not be bound by the covenant or agreement) . . .' and that exception surely must include a lessee who was not a party to the covenant or agreement and

f who has taken his lease prior to the date when the notice was entered.

So it seems to me that so far from being an exception to the scheme of the Act, those words are fully consistent with it, especially in view of the extremely simple example that I have given, which all must concede, I think, could not possibly result in the lessee being bound by the subsequent restrictive covenant. The words 'other persons' in the exception in s 50(2) must surely include lessees. Indeed, I think

g there are many places in the Act in which leases are referred to as incumbrances, so that possibly even without that, one might be driven to including lessees in the first exception, 'incumbrancers', but certainly they are 'other persons who at the time when the notice is entered may not be bound by the covenant or agreement'. Of course, if it is contemplated that they may be bound, for example if the defendants joined with their landlords in granting a restrictive covenant, then they would be

h bound and of course the exception caters for that, but in general they would not be.

So, in my view, at the end of the day the matter comes down to the fact that, for better or for worse, the date which is given in the charges register for the entry of this notice of the restrictive covenant is 28th April 1975. Counsel for the defendants was quite content to take that date for the purposes of the present case, although of course, so far as he was concerned, it might be that date or any later date, so long

j as it was not any earlier date, and, of course, just to complete this, because this is a matter which puzzled me at the beginning, the charges register notes that the date at the beginning of each entry is the date on which the entry was made on this edition of the register. That of course results that a large number of things are dated as of 28th April 1975, but all such matters appeared on the first edition of the register to which one could refer, in order to discover whether they were on the first edition at the date of any particular disposition. It is not disputed that in the present case there was no such entry on the charges register on the first edition prior to 28th April **a** 1975, and that is therefore the earliest date to which one can back-date the entry of this notice. The entry of the notice being subsequent to the date of the lease of 8th December 1969, in my judgment Shaws Laundries Ltd took free from that notice, therefore free from the restrictive covenant to which it related, and their assignees, the defendants, are in exactly a similar position. Therefore, it appears to me that the plaintiff, for whom I have the greatest possible sympathy, is not entitled to en- **b** force this covenant quoad the defendants. I realise that this is a very curious result, in that it appears that the plaintiff would have no claim to any indemnity against anybody because of the fact that he cannot enforce this restrictive covenant against the defendants, but it seems to me that if that is the position, that is a defect in the Act, and the Act is clear in its general outlines and specific provision under which it is only matters which are actually registered at the time that the disposition is made **c** which affect the person who derives title under the registered proprietor. Of course, I should like to make it clear that in other cases that may not be the end of the story. In the present case one is dealing with a lease which is not registrable and therefore has not been registered and therefore there is no proprietorship register in relation to it because it is not a separately registered parcel of leasehold land with a title of its own. But if there were to be a lease of that nature, then it might very well be that **d** rectification would be available against that title, as well as the title of the freehold; but, of course, equally in that case the provisions of s 82(3)(c) would apply, and I cannot, as at present advised, think that a lessee who has taken every precaution to see that he is entitled to use the land for the purpose for which he wishes to use it, so far as he can see, would have the title rectified against him because so far from it being unjust not to rectify the register against him (at any rate, in the usual case **e** which is likely to happen), it seems to me that it would be most unjust to rectify the register against him. Vigilantibus non dormientibus servit aequitas—equity aids the vigilant and not the indolent—and here the defendants have been very vigilant, although I am not ascribing any sleeping on his rights to the plaintiff. But the defendants having been vigilant, even if they had a separate registered title, I do not think there would be any prospect of rectification as against them. **f**

Finally, I cannot part with this case which raises a novel, and may be an important, point, but certainly a novel one, without expressing my great indebtedness to both counsel, who have on behalf of their respective clients argued this matter fully and exhaustively and persuasively, and, I may add, without wasting a single word. I am much indebted to both of them.

g

Motion by consent treated as the trial of the action. Action dismissed.

Solicitors: *Trower, Still & Keeling* (for the plaintiff); *Field, Fisher & Martineau* (for the defendants).

Jacqueline Metcalfe Barrister.

Lord Chetwode v Inland Revenue Commissioners

COURT OF APPEAL

BUCKLEY, JAMES LJJ AND SIR JOHN PENNYCUICK

5th, 8th, 9th, 10th, 11th DECEMBER 1975

Income tax – Avoidance – Transfer of assets abroad – Prevention of avoidance of liability to tax – Income of transferee deemed to be income of transferor – Meaning of 'income' – Revenue or profit – Computation of income – Taxpayer resident in United Kingdom – Taxpayer transferring assets to investment company resident outside United Kingdom – Investment company incurring expenses in collecting dividends and managing portfolio – Whether management expenses deductible in computing income of company – Income Tax Act 1952, s 412(1).

Income tax – Avoidance – Transfer of assets abroad – Prevention of avoidance of liability to tax – Income of transferee deemed to be income of transferor – Gains accruing from acquisition and disposal of chargeable assets – Short-term capital gains tax – Taxpayer transferring assets to investment company resident outside United Kingdom – Company selling certain assets and making gain – Abolition of short-term capital gains tax on companies – Whether company's gain deemed to be income of taxpayer – Whether gain to be computed in the same way as profits – Income Tax Act 1952, s 412(1) – Finance Act 1962, s 16(8), Sch 10 – Finance Act 1968, s 82(2).

In 1967 the taxpayer, who was ordinarily resident in the United Kingdom, transferred to TCB Ltd, a foreign trust company, a certain sum on trust to pay the income to himself for life with remainder, subject to a power of appointment in favour of a surviving widow, to his issue. Soon after the settlement was constituted TCB Ltd acquired the entire share capital in A Ltd, an investment company incorporated in the Bahamas, and transferred to it all the assets of the trust fund, part in consideration of the issue of the shares and part on interest-free loans. A Ltd used those assets to acquire land in the Bahamas and securities in the United States. In 1967 and 1968 A Ltd sold some of those securities making a gain on the sales. At no time did A Ltd carry on a trade. The taxpayer was assessed to income tax for the years 1967-68 and 1968-69 in respect of the income payable to A Ltd by virtue of the transfer of assets, on the basis that, under s 412[a] of the Income Tax Act 1952, that income was deemed to be his income. In arriving at the income of A Ltd for the purpose of the assessments, the commissioners refused to allow any deduction in respect of A Ltd's management expenses (which consisted of an investment advisory fee, management fees, safekeeping charges, security handling fees and bank charges, and registered and executive office fees), on the ground that the expression 'income' in s 412(1) had the same meaning as the phrase in the preamble to s 412 'income payable to' and, in relation to an investment company, should be construed as referring to dividends and interest immediately payable as they arose. The taxpayer appealed, contending (i) that for the purposes of s 412(1), A Ltd's income was to be ascertained by deducting its management expenses from its receipts; (ii) that the taxpayer could not be charged in respect of A Ltd's short-term gains since s 82(2)[b] of the Finance Act 1965 had removed A Ltd's liability to tax on such gains, which by virtue of s 16(8)[c] of, and Sch 10[d] to, the Finance Act 1962 had thitherto been included in the references to income in s 412(1) of the 1952 Act; and (iii) that in any event, even if A Ltd's short-term gains were deemed to be the

---

a Section 412, so far as material, is set out at p 643 h to 644 b, post
b Section 82(2) is set out at p 652 e, post
c Section 16(8), so far as material, is set out at p 652 b, post
d Schedule 10, so far as material, is set out at p 652 c and d, post

AA

income of the taxpayer, those gains were, by virtue of Sch 10, to be treated as though
they were the notional profits of a trade and therefore the tax had to be computed *a*
by reference to the difference between the sale price and the open market value of
the asset disposed of at the time of the disposal.

Held – (i) On the true construction of s 412(1) and the preamble to s 412, the word
'income' in the expressions 'income of' and 'income becomes payable to' was to be
treated as denoting profit, i e the excess of receipts properly attributable to revenue *b*
account over outgoings similarly attributable, as ascertained from year to year. It
followed that, in determining the amount of A Ltd's income which was to be treated
as income of the taxpayer under s 412(1), it was proper to deduct A Ltd's management
expenses and the taxpayer's appeal on that point would therefore be allowed (see
p 647 *f* to *h*, p 649 *h* to p 650 *c*, p 655 *e*, p 657 *f* to *j* and p 658 *f*, post); *Lord Howard de
Walden v Inland Revenue Comrs* [1942] 1 All ER 287 distinguished.
                                                                                         c
(ii) The taxpayer's appeal on the other points would, however, be dismissed for
the following reasons—

(a) The abolition of tax on a company's short-term gains by s 82(2) of the 1965 Act
had no relevance to A Ltd for, being a foreign company, it had never been within
the charge to short-term capital gains tax under the 1962 Act. Accordingly, by virtue
of s 16(8) of and Sch 10 to the 1962 Act, the taxpayer was liable to tax on the gains *d*
which fell to be treated as the income of A Ltd (see p 653 *e* to *g*, p 654 *b c* and *j* and p 658
g, post).

(b) The effect of Sch 10 to the 1962 Act was not that a foreign company was, for the
purposes of s 412(1), to be deemed to be carrying on a trade, but that the gains were
to be ascertained as if it were carrying on a trade. Accordingly, there were no grounds
for introducing the concept of notional trading in computing the gains. The actual *e*
gains were to be computed in accordance with the 1962 Act and, having been so computed, were then to be treated for the purpose of s 412(1) as though they were the
profits from a trade (see p 653 *h* to p 654 *d* and *j* and p 658 *g*, post); *Sharkey (Inspector of
Taxes) v Wernher* [1955] 3 All ER 493 distinguished.

Decision of Megarry J [1974] 3 All ER 625 reversed in part, affirmed in part.

Notes   *f*
For avoidance of tax by means of the transfer of assets abroad, see 20 Halsbury's Laws
(3rd Edn) 588-592, paras 1154-1161, and for cases on the subject, see 28(1) Digest
(Reissue) 439-445, *1579-1592*.

For the Income Tax Act 1952, s 412, see 31 Halsbury's Statutes (2nd Edn) 390. For the
Finance Act 1962, s 16, Sch 10, see 42 ibid 354, 388. For the Finance Act 1965, s 82,
see 45 ibid 626.   *g*

For 1970-71 and subsequent years of assessment, s 412(1) of the 1952 Act has been
replaced by s 478(1) of the Income and Corporation Taxes Act 1970. Section 16(8) of
and Sch 10 to the 1962 Act were replaced by s 478(8) of the 1970 Act, and s 82(2)
of the 1965 Act was replaced by ss 160(1) and 250(6) of the 1970 Act. Section 160, and the
relevant parts of ss 250(6) and 478(8), of the 1970 Act were repealed with effect from
6th April 1971 by the Finance Act 1971, s 56 and Sch 14, Part IV.   *h*

Cases referred to in judgments
Congreve v Inland Revenue Comrs [1948] 1 All ER 948, 30 Tax Cas 163, 27 ATC 102, 41
R & IT 319, HL; *affg* [1947] 1 All ER 168, CA; *rvsg* [1946] 2 All ER 170, 28(1) Digest
(Reissue) 443, *1590*.
Howard de Walden (Lord) v Inland Revenue Comrs [1942] 1 All ER 287, [1942] 1 KB 389,
25 Tax Cas 121, 111 LJKB 273, CA, 28(1) Digest (Reissue) 442, *1586*.
Latilla v Inland Revenue Comrs [1943] 1 All ER 265, [1943] AC 377, 25 Tax Cas 107, 22
ATC 23, 112 LJKB 158, 168 LT 411, 59 TLR 163, HL, 28(1) Digest (Reissue) 442, *1587*.
Mangin v Inland Revenue Comr [1971] 1 All ER 179, [1971] AC 739, [1971] 2 WLR 39,
sub nom *Mangin v New Zealand Inland Revenue Comr* 49 ATC 272, [1970] TR 249,
PC, 28(1) Digest (Reissue) 543, *1322*.

a

Mapp (Inspector of Taxes) v Oram [1969] 3 All ER 215, [1970] AC 362, [1969] 3 WLR 557, 45 Tax Cas 651, sub nom *Oram v Mapp* 48 ATC 270, [1969] TR 269, HL, 28(1) Digest (Reissue) 448, 1606.
Philippi v Inland Revenue Comrs [1971] 3 All ER 61, [1971] 1 WLR 1272, 47 Tax Cas 75, 50 ATC 37, [1971] TR 167, CA.
Sharkey (Inspector of Taxes) v Wernher [1955] 3 All ER 493, [1956] AC 58, [1955] 3 WLR 671, 36 Tax Cas 275, 34 ATC 263, [1955] TR 277, 48 R & IT 739, HL, 28(1) Digest

b   (Reissue) 123, 363.
Simpson v Grange Trust Ltd [1935] AC 422, [1935] All ER Rep 671, 19 Tax Cas 231, 14 ATC 16, 104 LJKB 276, 152, LT 517, 51 TLR 320, HL, 28(1) Digest (Reissue) 222, 667.

Cases also cited
Cape Brandy Syndicate v Inland Revenue Comrs [1921] 2 KB 403, 12 Tax Cas 358, CA.
c   *Fattorini (Thomas) (Lancashire) Ltd v Inland Revenue Comrs* [1942] 1 All ER 619, [1942] AC 643, 24 Tax Cas 328, HL.
Inland Revenue Comrs v Wood Bros (Birkenhead) Ltd (in liquidation) [1959] 1 All ER 53, [1959] AC 487, 38 Tax Cas 275, HL.
Odeon Associated Theatres v Jones (Inspector of Taxes) [1972] 1 All ER 681, [1973] Ch 288, 48 Tax Cas 257, CA.
d   *Taylor v Good (Inspector of Taxes)* [1974] 1 All ER 1137, [1974] 1 WLR 556, [1974] STC 148, 49 Tax Cas 237, CA.
Union Trustee Co of Australia Ltd v Bartlam [1948] AC 495, PC.

Appeal
The taxpayer, Lord Chetwode, appealed against an order of Megarry J[1] made on
e   18th July 1974, whereby, on a case stated by the Commissioners for the Special Purposes of the Income Tax Acts, he dismissed an appeal by the taxpayer against the decision of the Special Commissioners confirming the assessments to income tax made on him for the years 1967-68 and 1968-69 by the respondents, the Inland Revenue Commissioners ('the commissioners'). The facts are set out in the judgment of Sir John Pennycuick.

f

Desmond Miller QC, Peter Whiteman and *Ian Richards* for the taxpayer.
Leonard Bromley QC and *Brian Davenport* for the commissioners.

SIR JOHN PENNYCUICK delivered the first judgment at the invitation of
g   Buckley LJ. This is an appeal from an order of Megarry J[1] made on 18th July 1974. The appellant ('the taxpayer') is Lord Chetwode; the respondents are the Inland Revenue Commissioners ('the commissioners'). Summarily, the principal question is whether, in computing the income of a foreign company for the purpose of s 412 of the Income Tax Act 1952, it is proper to take expenses of management into account. There is a secondary question relating to capital gains tax, which I will deal with
h   altogether separately after the first question.
Dealing then with the first question I will, in order to make it intelligible, read the preamble to and the first sub-section of s 412:

'For the purpose of preventing the avoiding by individuals ordinarily resident in the United Kingdom of liability to income tax by means of transfers of assets by virtue or in consequence whereof, either alone or in conjunction with associ-
j   ated operations, income becomes payable to persons resident or domiciled out of the United Kingdom, it is hereby enacted as follows:—(1) Where such an individual has by means of any such transfer, either alone or in conjunction with associated operations, acquired any rights by virtue of which he has, within the meaning

1   [1974] 3 All ER 625, [1975] 1 WLR 34, [1974] STC 474

of this section, power to enjoy, whether forthwith or in the future, any income
of a person resident or domiciled out of the United Kingdom which, if it were *a*
income of that individual received by him in the United Kingdom, would be
chargeable to income tax by deduction or otherwise, that income shall, whether
it would or would not have been chargeable to income tax apart from the provisions of this section, be deemed to be income of that individual for all the
purposes of this Act.'

b

The only other relevant subsection in s 412 is sub-s (5), which defines and expands
the scope of the expression 'deemed to have power to enjoy income'. I will come
back to that subsection at a later stage.

The facts of the case are relatively simple. I will take them from the case stated by
the Special Commissioners.

'5(a) On the 9th May, 1967, the [taxpayer] who at all material times was ordin- *c*
arily resident in the United Kingdom executed a Deed of Settlement . . . By the
Settlement the Trust Corporation of Bahamas Limited, a Company incorporated
and existing under the Law of the Bahama Islands, was appointed the first
Trustee thereof. By the terms of the Settlement the Trustees were to pay the
income of the Trust Fund to the [taxpayer] during his life and subject to a power
of appointment in favour of a surviving widow the capital and income of the *d*
Trust Fund was to be held for the benefit of the [taxpayer's] issue.'

I interpose that the settlement contained a proviso that, notwithstanding anything
to the contrary, the settlor should have power to revest in himself title to all or any
part of the capital and unpaid income. To return to the case stated, the amount of the
fund transferred by the taxpayer to the trustee was some £167,000. *e*

'(b) Immediately after the establishment of the Settlement the Trust Corporation of Bahamas Limited as trustee thereof acquired the entire share capital
of Attleborough. Attleborough was a Company incorporated on the 21st March
1967 under the Laws of the Bahama Islands. All the assets of the Trust Fund
were transferred by the Trustee to Attleborough (part in payment for the said *f*
share capital and the remainder upon interest-free loans) and were used by
Attleborough to acquire land and securities. Attleborough was at all material
times an investment company and did not at any such time carry on a trade.
(c) It was common ground that the [taxpayer] had power to enjoy the income
of Attleborough within the meaning of section 412(1) of the Income Tax Act
1952. (d) Attleborough invested the sums transferred to it by the Trustee in the
purchase of United States stocks and land in the Bahamas. [Then a schedule of *g*
the stocks was exhibited.] (e) In connection with the acquisition and management
of its portfolio and purchases and sales of stocks, Attleborough incurred the
following expenses and charges.'

There are then set out, under the two respective years with which the appeal is concerned, namely 1967 and 1968, the expenses and charges incurred by Attleborough. *h*
Those consist of an investment advisory fee, management fees, safekeeping charges,
security handling fees and bank charges, registered office and executive office fees.
The largest items were, in each year, the investment advisory fee and the management fees. The total sterling equivalent of the expenses and charges is £878 for 1967 and
£1,243 for 1968. I mention in passing that certain other expenses were included in the
accounts of Attleborough, but those items have (I think by agreement between the *i*
parties) been omitted from the expenses in respect of which deduction is sought.
The case stated then set out a trifling sum in each year representing collection costs.

The case stated then referred to evidence of accountancy practice given by Mr Hobson
on behalf of the taxpayer, Mr Hobson being a partner in the firm of Messrs Cooper &
Lybrand, chartered accountants, and by Mr Lawson on behalf of the commissioners.

The Special Commissioners said: 'We took the view that the questions we had to
a decide were questions of law and not of accountancy practice. We accordingly made
no findings with regard to their evidence.' They did, however, set out the evidence in
an appendix. I agree that this appeal turns wholly on questions of law, and that
accountancy evidence takes the matter no further, except possibly on a matter of detail
to which I will refer right at the end of this judgment.

They then referred to a considerable number of cases which were cited before them,
b and proceeded to set out the contentions of the parties:

'It was contended on behalf of the [taxpayer]: (a) The accounts of Attleborough
were prepared in accordance with the normal principles of commercial accountancy. (b) Attleborough's income was the balance shown by the receipts and
expenditure account. (c) Section 412 did not authorise any attribution to the
c [taxpayer] of sums in excess of the said balance . . . It was contended on behalf
of the [commissioners]: (a) The income of Attleborough which by Section 412
was deemed to be the [taxpayer's] was the investment income which he would
have received if the investment income actually received by Attleborough had
instead been received by him. (b) The "income of a person resident out of the
United Kingdom" referred to in Section 412(1) was, in these appeals, the dividends
and interest received by Attleborough undiminished by any of the "expenses
d and charges" itemised in paragraph 5(e) above, and diminished only by the conceded costs of collection mentioned in paragraph 5(g). (c) Attleborough did not
carry on a trade and accordingly for tax purposes it had no profit consisting of
the balance of receipts over expenditure. If it had been a United Kingdom
investment company Attleborough would have been taxable by deduction on its
e receipts. Any claim for relief in respect of "expenses of management"—as which
some or all of the expenses itemised in paragraph 5(e) above might qualify—
would require a computation for the purposes only of section 57(1) Finance
Act 1965: but for the purposes of Section 412 they were irrelevant. (d) The
[taxpayer] was therefore in exactly the same position, vis-a-vis expenses, as if
Attleborough's role had been played by an individual instead of a company.'

f They gave their decision as follows:

'It is common ground that Section 412 of the Income Tax Act, 1952 applies
to the transactions in question and accordingly that income of [Attleborough]
is deemed to be income of the [taxpayer]. Dealing first with the submission on
behalf of the [taxpayer] that the income deemed to be his is the "net" income of
g Attleborough (i.e. receipts less expenses), we think that a distinction is to be made
between the income of an investment company and the profits of a trading company. The receipts of the latter are normally not "pure" income, whereas the
receipts of the former usually are. Section 412(1) deems income "which would
be chargeable to income tax by deduction or otherwise" to be income of the
individual concerned. Section 413(2) gives him the same reliefs as if the income
h deemed to be his had actually been received by him. Read in conjunction with
the preamble to Section 412, and taking Chapter IV of Part 18 as a whole, the
language appears to us to be apt to treat the "pure" income of the non-resident
person as income of the individual. We are fortified in this conclusion by a
similar view expressed by our colleagues in *Philippi v Inland Revenue Comrs*[1].
Accordingly we reject the submission.'

j The taxpayer appealed to the High Court. The case was heard by Megarry J[2], who
gave a full judgment upholding the decision of the commissioners. I will cite a few

---

1 [1971] 3 All ER 61, [1971] 1 WLR 1272, 47 Tax Cas 75
2 [1974] 3 All ER 625, [1975] 1 WLR 34, [197˙ ˙ STC 474

passages from this judgment, confining myself to those which seem to me to set out the reasoning on which the judge came to his conclusion. He said[1]:

'At the centre of the dispute are the words "income" that appear in s 412(1), and in particular, "any income of a person resident or domiciled out of the United Kingdom", here, Attleborough: for it is that income which under the subsection is to be deemed the taxpayer's income. Counsel for the taxpayer contends that since Attleborough is admittedly an investment company, it is impossible to ascertain what is the "income of" Attleborough until one has set Attleborough's management expenses against Attleborough's receipts, and struck a balance: and Attleborough's income is that balance. On the other hand, counsel for the Crown contends that although this would be appropriate if Attleborough were carrying on a trade, it would be quite wrong to do so in the present case, where Attleborough has been found not to be trading. "Income", he said, meant "income arising", or "income as it arises". In the case of dividends from investments the income arising consisted of the whole of the dividends with no deductions save for the cost of collection. Apart from the cost of collection, Attleborough's income consisted of the dividends as they arrived on Attleborough's threshold. If Attleborough had been trading, its income as it arose would have been the profits emerging on taking the proper accounts. I propose to refer to counsel for the taxpayer's construction of "income" as "net income" and that of counsel for the Crown as "gross income", for although neither expression is particularly explicit or accurate, each is sufficiently indicative of the meaning and has the great merit of brevity.'

He then referred to the authorities put before him by counsel for the taxpayer, and read the preamble to s 412. He said[2]:

'The preamble is of assistance here because it states the purpose of the section as being to prevent individuals resident in the United Kingdom from avoiding liability to income tax by transferring assets whereby "income becomes payable to" persons resident or domiciled outside the United Kingdom. That is a phrase which seems to me to be compatible with "income" meaning "gross income" rather than with "income" meaning "net income". I shall discuss this further in due course ... The initial phrase "income becomes payable to" a person is not, of course, verbally identical with the expressions "income of" a person, or "income" simpliciter, which occur later in the subsection. The question then arises whether the verbal contrast indicates a difference in meaning. I do not think that it does. For one thing, I find it difficult to imagine that a draftsman who had any intention that the meanings of the expressions should differ would entrust his intention to so frail a craft as this. For another thing, when the subsection is stripped down to its essentials, it sufficiently appears that there is at least identity of nature between the various mentions of "income" in the subsection.'

He then illustrated this by a simplified example, and continued[3]:

'The question, of course, is whether the words "income of" a foreigner under (c) [in the example] can mean net income while the phrase the "income becomes payable to" foreigners in (b) is referring to gross income. It would, I think, be very remarkable if it could, for both are linked to the self-same transfer by A: it is by virtue or in consequence of that transfer that income becomes payable to foreigners under (b), and it is by means of that transfer that A has acquired rights by virtue of which he has power to enjoy any income of a foreigner under (c).

1 [1974] 3 All ER at 631, 632, [1975] 1 WLR at 37, 38, [1974] STC at 480, 481
2 [1974] 3 All ER at 632, 633, [1975] 1 WLR at 38, 39, [1974] STC at 481, 482
3 [1974] 3 All ER at 633, [1975] 1 WLR at 39, [1974] STC at 482

That is not all. I accept to the full that great care must be exercised in relying on
statements made by judges, however great, in cases in which a point did not
arise and so the judges' minds may well have not been directed to that point.
But I cannot regard it as wholly irrelevant that in the *Congreve* case[1] Lord Simonds
(with whose speech the other law lords simply concurred) set out the section
and then referred repeatedly[2] to "income payable to" certain companies resident outside the United Kingdom, rather than, in the statutory phrase, the
"income of" those companies. In my judgment, therefore, the various references
in s 412(1) to "income" are all to be construed as referring to gross income and
not net income, in the sense in which I am using these expressions in this judgment; and I do not think that this construction is affected by any of the authorities cited by counsel for the taxpayer on the meaning of "income" in the taxing
statutes generally.'

He then dealt with an argument by counsel for the taxpayer that s 412 was fiscally
'restorative' in its effect, restoring the fiscal state by making the taxpayer liable in the
same way as if he had not made the transfer. I do not think I need refer separately
to that argument, because the question turns on the construction of the section read
in its context. Then Megarry J said[3]: 'A further question that arose was that of
accountancy practice . . . I think that the Special Commissioners were right in their
view.' Then he referred to *Latilla v Inland Revenue Comrs*[4] and to one or two other cases,
and at greater length to *Lord Howard de Walden v Inland Revenue Comrs*[5], and quoted
the words of Lord Greene MR[6]: 'It scarcely lies in the mouth of the taxpayer who
plays with fire to complain of burnt fingers.' He concluded[7]: 'In the result, therefore,
I think that the Special Commissioners were right on this branch of the case, and that
the appeal on this accordingly fails.'

The grounds of appeal perhaps slightly mask the true issue in this case. The relevant
ground is: 'That in the absence of any statutory rules governing its computation,
that income must necessarily be ascertained in accordance with the normal principles of commercial accounting.' The question, as is not in dispute, is whether
'income' in s 412 denotes profit in the sense of the balance of receipts over outgoings,
or simply dividends and interest.

I have reached a different conclusion on this question from that of the Special
Commissioners and Megarry J. It seems to me that on the natural construction of
s 412(1), read in conjuction with the preamble, the word 'income' should be treated
as denoting profit, i e the excess of receipts over outgoings. That means, of course,
receipts and outgoings properly attributable to revenue account.

I observe first, for what it is worth, that the subject-matter of the charge to income
tax under the Income Tax Act 1952 is profits or gains: see s 1 and ss 122 and 123,
which latter sections impose the charge under Sch D. The income of an investment
company, in the true sense, consists of profit; that is to say, the excess of receipts over
outgoings. That is nonetheless so because in the case of a United Kingdom company
dividends and interest are charged separately as such normally by deduction, the
expenses being set off by way of allowance against the tax chargeable in respect of
the dividends and interest: see on this point the Income Tax Act 1952, s 425, which I
need not read, and *Simpson v Grange Trust Ltd*[8]. But, as a matter of reality and substance, it seems to me really clear that the income of an investment company is
profit in the sense of excess of receipts over outgoings.

1   [1948] 1 All ER 948, 30 Tax Cas 163
2   [1948] 1 All ER at 951, 954, 30 Tax Cas at 202, 203, 207
3   [1974] 3 All ER at 634, [1975] 1 WLR at 40, 41, [1974] STC at 483
4   [1943] 1 All ER 265, [1943] AC 377, 25 Tax Cas 107
5   [1942] 1 All ER 287, [1942] 1 KB 389, 25 Tax Cas 121
6   [1942] 1 All ER at 289, [1942] 1 KB at 397, 25 Tax Cas at 134
7   [1974] 3 All ER at 635, [1975] 1 WLR at 42, [1974] STC at 484
8   [1935] AC 422, 19 Tax Cas 231

The conclusion expressed above is supported by a number of considerations.

(i) The income attributed to an individual under s 412 indisputably includes trading income as well as investment income: see the *Latilla* case[1]. Trading income is admittedly ascertained by reference to profit over a period of account. One might expect investment income to be treated in the same way. I doubt whether there is much weight in this point by itself, but it leads up to what I think is a very important point, to which I will refer below.

(ii) Where the foreign company concerned is subject to foreign tax, or where it has liabilities of a revenue character—for instance, mortgage interest—it is quite impossible to determine its income for any period without taking these into account. Counsel for the commissioners sought to meet this point by referring to s 413(2) of the 1952 Act, which runs as follows:

'In computing the liability to income tax of an individual chargeable by virtue of the provisions of the last preceding section, the same deductions and reliefs shall be allowed as would have been allowed if the income deemed to be his by virtue of that section had actually been received by him.'

That section, however, does not fit the position; for if indeed the income deemed to be his by virtue of the section, i e the income of Attleborough, had actually been received by the taxpayer, he would not have been entitled to any relief by reference to the liabilities of Attleborough in respect of foreign tax or mortgage interest. We were told that, by way of concession, that subsection is treated as permitting an allowance from the tax payable under s 412 of these liabilities of the foreign company. That concession is not relevant on the construction of the section.

(iii) Those considerations to which I have been referring lead up to this consideration, which seems to me to be of very great importance. Section 412 applies to persons resident or domiciled anywhere in the world other than in the United Kingdom. I mention in passing that the word 'persons' of course includes individuals or partnerships as well as companies; but it is convenient to refer to foreign companies. Now if, as must be the fact, the tax structure of many foreign countries is different from that of the United Kingdom, it is extremely difficult to see how, in computing the income of a company in such a country, one could apply the United Kingdom tax structure. If, for instance, one takes an investment company in any foreign country—say Ruritania —the tax law of which is entirely different from that of this country, then it seems to me that there is no justification for treating the income of that company as what it would be if (contrary to the fact) the English tax structure were applicable. It seems to me that one can only compute the income of the Ruritanian company by reference to the law of Ruritania.

(iv) Finally, the result seems to me to be fair. I cannot myself see any reason why it should be just to charge an individual resident in this country with a notional income greater than the income which in fact arises in favour of the foreign resident to whom he has transferred his assets. I appreciate that this section has been described as a penal section; but I do not think that is any reason, as far as fairness is concerned, for attributing to the English resident income which he never in any sense of the word had power to enjoy.

I should at this stage refer to s 412(5). That subsection runs as follows:

'An individual shall, for the purposes of this section, be deemed to have power to enjoy income of a person resident or domiciled out of the United Kingdom if—(a) the income is in fact so dealt with by any person as to be calculated, at some point of time, and whether in the form of income or not, to enure for the benefit of the individual; or (b) the receipt or accrual of the income operates to increase the value to the individual of any assets held by him or for his benefit;

---

1   [1943] 1 All ER 265, [1943] AC 377, 25 Tax Cas 107

or (c) the individual receives or is entitled to receive, at any time, any benefit provided or to be provided out of that income or out of moneys which are or will be available for the purpose by reason of the effect or successive effects of the associated operations on that income and on any assets which directly or indirectly represent that income; or (d) the individual has power, by means of the exercise of any power of appointment or power of revocation or otherwise, to obtain for himself, whether with or without the consent of any other person, the beneficial enjoyment of the income, or may, in the event of the exercise of any power vested in any other person, become entitled to the beneficial enjoyment of the income; or (e) the individual is able in any manner whatsoever, and whether directly or indirectly, to control the application of the income.'

That subsection defines by way of enlargement the meaning of the expression 'power to enjoy income'. The subsection is in a form familiar in deeming provisions in taxing Acts, the effect being that the words 'power to enjoy income' have a much wider scope than would be covered by the words in their unexpanded sense. I do not think, however, that sub-s (5) has any bearing on what is meant by the expression 'income' in the preamble and sub-s (1). Subsection (5) is concerned only with the circumstances in which someone is deemed to have power to enjoy income when that income has been ascertained.

Counsel for the commissioners stressed the purpose of s 412 as set out in the preamble. He contended that one should construe the operative provision, sub-s (1), so as to give effect to the purpose set out in the preamble. I agree with that contention so far as the terms of the operative provision permit. But it is not, I think, legitimate to distort the natural meaning of the operative provision in order to achieve this result.

We were referred to a statement of principle on construction by Lord Donovan in *Mangin v Inland Revenue Comr*[1], which appears to me to be exactly in point here. Lord Donovan said this:

'These contentions pose the question of the true construction of [a certain section]. It may be useful to recall at the outset some of the rules of interpretation which fall to be applied. First, the words are to be given their ordinary meaning. They are not to be given some other meaning simply because their object is to frustrate legitimate tax avoidance devices . . . Secondly, ". . . one has to look merely at what is clearly said. There is no room for any intendment. There is no equity about a tax. There is no presumption as to tax. Nothing is to be read in, nothing is to be implied. One can only look fairly at the language used". . . . Thirdly, the object of the construction of a statute being to ascertain the will of the legislature it may be presumed that neither injustice nor absurdity was intended. If therefore a literal interpretation would produce such a result, and the language admits of an interpretation which would avoid it, then such an interpretation may be adopted. Fourthly, the history of an enactment and the reasons which led to its being passed may be used as an aid to its construction.'

So here one must certainly, insofar as it is possible to do so, construe the operative provision in sub-s (1) so as to give effect to the intention declared by the preamble; but one cannot go outside the natural meaning of the words contained in sub-s (1).

On the question of construction, counsel for the commissioners contended that the expression 'income becomes payable' in the preamble, and the expression 'income of' in sub-s (1), bear the same meaning. I agree with that contention, as I have already indicated. He then contended that the expression 'income becomes payable' in the preamble indicates immediate payability of dividends and interest as they arise, and that the expression 'income of' in sub-s(1) must bear the same meaning. It seems

---

1   [1971] 1 All ER 179 at 182, [1971] AC 739 at 746

to me, however, that it is impossible to put that construction on the expression
'income becomes payable to' in the preamble without more ado, because the words *a*
so construed are wholly inapplicable to the income of a trade, which is likewise
covered by the preamble and sub-s (1). One is left then with these two expressions
differently worded but bearing the same meaning, namely 'income becomes payable
to' and 'any income of'. The problem is to determine their scope in their context.
For the reasons I have given, I think that in both expressions the word 'income'
should be construed as meaning 'profit'.   *b*

Counsel for the commissioners summarised his contentions under ten heads. It will
be convenient to deal with his contentions under those heads, which, if I may say so,
clearly and admirably express the purport of his argument. (1) The time to ascertain
income from investments is the time when the income arises. That is to say, on his
contention, the relevant time is from day to day as the dividend or interest is payable.
I agree that the relevant time is when the income arises, in the sense that one must *c*
ascertain the income from year to year in the same way as one ascertains the income
from a trade. I do not agree that the proper time is from day to day. (2) 'Income of,
in sub-s (1) bears the same sense as 'income becomes payable to' in the preamble. I
agree with this point; but, as I have already said, it seems to me that in both expressions
the word 'income' means 'profit' and it is not possible to construe the expression
'income' in relation to an investment company as income arising from day to day. *d*
(3) The purpose of s 412 is to prevent the avoidance by an individual resident in the
United Kingdom of liability to income tax by means of transfers abroad. With that
I agree. (4) This purpose fails if deductions are permitted which would not be available
to the individual. I do not know whether it can be truly said that, by allowing deductions to a foreign company which would not be available to a United Kingdom individual, the purpose of the section can be said to fail. However that may be, the purpose *e*
of the section is effectuated, so far as it is effectuated, by the operative provision and
if that provision fails in any respect to effectuate the purpose, then I think it must be
accepted that to that extent the section has misfired, and one must not distort the
operative provision. (5) The Income Tax Act 1952 requires the balancing of receipts
and expenditure in relation to a trade but not in relation to the holding of investments. (6) Section 425 recognises a limited balancing in the case of an investment *f*
company. Generally speaking on these two points, it is true that the scheme of the
Income Tax Acts is to charge investment income as such, leaving expenses in the case
of a company to be repaid by way of allowance. But here one is concerned with the
meaning of 'income' in relation to a foreign resident. It seems to me, as I have already
indicated, that different considerations must apply. (7) Section 412 does not affect
the foreign recipient. Indeed, it does not do so; but one has to measure the income *g*
of the foreign recipient. (8) Dividends are 'income' for the purpose of the Income
Tax Act 1952. That, I think, is the same point as under (5) above. (9) On the taxpayer's
construction, 'power to enjoy' under sub-s (5) has a limited operation defeating the
purpose of the preamble. It seems to me that the construction of 'income' as meaning
'profit' does not of itself in any way limit the operation of sub-s (5). That sub-section
is concerned only with the circumstances in which the income is deemed to be enjoyed, *h*
and not with the ascertainment of the income. (10) Section 413(1) does not apply to
earned surplus, but does apply to dividends.   I have not read s 413(1), which is in
these terms:

> 'Tax at the standard rate shall not be charged by virtue of the last preceding
> section in respect of income which has borne tax at the standard rate by deduction
> or otherwise but, save as aforesaid, tax chargeable at the standard rate by virtue of *j*
> that section shall be charged under Case VI of Schedule D and all assessments in
> respect thereof shall be made by the Special Commissioners.'

With great respect, I do not follow the bearing of this point. So far as I can see,
s 413(1) saves from double taxation United Kingdom income received by the foreign

resident which has already borne English tax, e g a dividend, and goes on to provide
a that with this exception the income chargeable on the United Kingdom taxpayer by
reference to the income of the foreign resident shall be chargeable under Case VI.

We were referred to a number of cases of high authority, including *Latilla v Inland
Revenue Comrs*[1] in the House of Lords; *Lord Howard de Walden v Inland Revenue Comrs*[2]
in the Court of Appeal; *Congreve v Inland Revenue Comrs*[3] in the House of Lords;
and *Mapp (Inspector of Taxes) v Oram*[4] in the House of Lords. In none of these cases
b did the present point arise for decision, and I think it unlikely that it was in the mind
of any of those who gave the judgments in those cases. I have not myself found any help
from reference to occasional words or phrases used in those cases in connection with
some quite different issue. That comment applies in particular to the words or
expressions used by Lord Simonds in the *Congreve* case[3]. I do not think it would be
useful to go through the judgments or speeches in those cases in order to show that
c they do not throw any light on the issue in the present case. I observe in passing that
the decision of this court in the *Howard de Walden* case[2] seems to me a strikingly
harsh one; and, although we are bound, of course, to apply it in proper circumstances,
I do not find it a very easy decision.

I should perhaps mention *Philippi v Inland Revenue Comrs*[5]. In that case, the present
point did arise before the Special Commissioners, and they gave a decision to the same
d effect as the Special Commissioners and Megarry J[6] did in the present case. The case
went to the High Court and the Court of Appeal; but, for some good reason, this
particular point was not pursued, and the judgments in the High Court[5] and the
Court of Appeal[7] throw no light on the point.

I conclude that on this first question the appeal should be allowed.

I turn to the second question, which can be much more shortly dealt with. There,
e summarily, the question is whether the taxpayer is liable in respect of short-term
capital gains made by Attleborough. Turning back to the case stated, the facts are
set out as follows: 'In the years 1967 and 1968 Attleborough sold the following
securities'. There follow particulars showing in respect of two securities a gain and
in respect of the other a loss.

I will next read, in order that the point may be intelligible, the relevant statutory
f provision dealing with this point. The Finance Act 1962 imposed a charge in respect
of gains from acquisition and disposal of assets. Section 10 provides:

'(1) Without prejudice to any other provision of the Income Tax Acts directing
income tax to be charged under Schedule D, tax under that Schedule for the
year 1962-63 or any subsequent year of assessment shall be charged, subject to
g and in accordance with the rules contained in this Chapter, in respect of all gains
accruing to any person resident and ordinarily resident for the year in the United
Kingdom from his acquisition and disposal of any chargeable assets, not being
gains which accrue as profits of a trade . . .

'(3) Tax charged under Schedule D by virtue of this section shall be charged
under a new Case VII of that Schedule . . .'

h
Section 13(1) provides:

'Subject to the provisions of this Chapter the gain accruing to a person from his
acquisition and dispoal of any asset shall be computed for purposes of Case VII

---

j 1 [1943] 1 All ER 265, [1943] AC 377, 25 Tax Cas 107
    2 [1942] 1 All ER 287, [1942] 1 KB 389, 25 Tax Cas 121
    3 [1948] 1 All ER 948, 30 Tax Cas 163
    4 [1969] 3 All ER 215, [1970] AC 362, 45 Tax Cas 651
    5 [1971] 3 All ER 61, [1971] 1 WLR 684, 47 Tax Cas 75
    6 [1974] 3 All ER 625, [1975] 1 WLR 34, [1974] STC 474
    7 [1971] 3 All ER 61, [1971] 1 WLR 1272, 47 Tax Cas 75

in the like manner as it would fall to be computed for purposes of Case I of
Schedule D if the acquisition and disposal (together with anything done by him *a*
to or in relation to the asset in connection with the acquisition and disposal or
with a view to the disposal) had been an adventure in the nature of trade . . .'

Section 16(8) provides:

'. . . the enactments mentioned in the first column in the Tenth Schedule to
this Act shall, for the purpose of adapting or applying them in relation to the *b*
provisions of this Chapter, have effect subject to and in accordance with the provision made in respect thereto in the second column in that Schedule.'

Then, turning to Sch 10, one finds it is headed 'MODIFICATION OF ENACTMENTS FOR
CASE VII OF SCHEDULE D'. Then, in the left-hand column: '*Enactment and subject-
matter* . . . Chapter IV of Part XVIII (Avoidance of tax by transfers of income to persons
abroad)'. (That is s 412.) Then, in the right-hand column: *c*

'*Adaptation* . . . References to income shall apply in the case of gains accruing
from the acquisition and disposal of chargeable assets as they would apply if the
gains were profits from a trade of dealing in the assets, and any such gains shall
be treated as payable in the first instance to the person to whom they accrue.'

d

Pausing there, the effect of the Schedule is that where the foreign company makes a
gain accruing from the acquisition or disposal of chargeable assets, that gain is treated
as payable in the first instance to the foreign company, and then by virtue of s 412 it is
to be treated as an element in computing the income which is deemed to be the income
of the United Kingdom resident.

Then the Finance Act 1965, s 82(2), provides: 'Income Tax shall not be charged by *e*
virtue of section 10 or section 14 of the Finance Act 1962 (short-term gains) in respect
of an acquisition and disposal of any chargeable assets by a company.' That provision
is part of a code of new provisions relating to the charge of income tax on companies. There is no repeal by the Finance Act 1965 of Sch 10 to the Finance Act 1962.

In that state of affairs and on the facts of the present case, the following contentions
were advanced on behalf of the taxpayer: *f*

'By reason of the partial recall of short-term gains by section 82 of the Finance Act
1965, Attleborough was not liable to tax under Case VII on its short-term gains.
The 10th Schedule, Finance Act 1962, provided that short-term gains should be
treated as payable in the first instance to the person to whom they accrued. In
the present case, that person was Attleborough, which was never liable to tax on
short-term gains. Accordingly the [taxpayer] was not taxable in respect of *g*
Attleborough's short-term gains.'

Then there is an alternative contention:

'Tax on short-term gains should be computed by reference to the difference
between the sale price and the open market value of the asset disposed of at the
time of disposal on the principle of *Sharkey (Inspector of Taxes) v Wernher*[1].' *h*

The contention on this point of the commissioners was as follows:

'By section 16(8) and the 10th Schedule, Finance Act 1962, references to income
in section 412 include short-term gains. The abolition of tax on a company's
short-term gains by section 82(2) Finance Act 1965 did not affect Attleborough
which being a foreign company had never, whether before or after the enactment *j*
of Finance Act 1965, been liable to United Kingdom tax on short-term gains.
The principle in *Sharkey v Wernher*[1] did not apply to the deeming provisions
mentioned in the last sub-paragraph.'

---

1 [1955] 3 All ER 493, [1956] AC 58, 36 Tax Cas 275

The commissioners dealt with this as follows:

'The next question is whether the short-term gains of Attleborough are deemed to be the [taxpayer's] income, and, if so, the amount thereof. In our view the answer turns on the effect of the 10th Schedule to the Finance Act 1962 whereby references to income in the said Chapter IV apply to short-term gains as if the gains were trading profits. We do not think that the impact of this provision is affected by Section 82 of the Finance Act 1965 (or the subsequent amendments thereof), which abolished a company's liability to short-term gains [tax]. Those gains were never chargeable in the hands of Attleborough, and, as we have indicated above, it is the trading and investment income of Attleborough, as the case may be, which is deemed to be the [taxpayer's] income. The [taxpayer] sought to apply the principle in *Sharkey v Wernher*[1] to the computation of the gains. The gains to which the 10th Schedule refers are the gains accruing from an acquisition and disposal of an asset and, in our view, such acquisition and disposal fall to be taken together and there is no room for the substitution of the market value for the price.'

The learned judge came to the same conclusion, his reasoning being expressed as follows[2]:

'Now the contention of counsel for the taxpayer is, putting it shortly, that s 82 removed the foundation on which rested any liability of the taxpayer to short-term capital gains tax. Since under s 82(2) the charge of tax under Case VII of Sch D ceased to apply to any company, there could thereafter be no avoidance of such tax, and so no basis for applying s 412 to chargeable gains. Alternatively, he said, as the expressed object of s 16(8) of the Finance Act 1962 was to apply s 412 for the purposes of Case VII of Sch D, the repeal of that tax as respect any company involved that application ceasing to have effect in the case of any company. If these contentions failed, counsel for the taxpayer had an alternative contention based on *Sharkey v Wernher*[1], to which I shall turn in due course . . . The short answer to these contentions seems to me to be that, as counsel for the Crown pointed out, the charge to short-term capital gains tax is imposed by s 10(1) of the Finance Act 1962 only on those resident and ordinarily resident in the United Kingdom. Others, such as Attleborough, were never within the charge. There was thus never any question of s 82 of the Finance Act 1965 taking Attleborough out of the charge, for Attleborough was never within it, and so the section did nothing that is relevant to this case . . . The *Sharkey (Inspector of Taxes) v Wernher*[1] point is this. On the footing that Case VII of Sch D is still applied, counsel for the taxpayer said that its application involved a deemed or notional trade of dealing with the assets from which the gain or surplus arose. As the transactions consisted of dealings in shares, the value to be attributed to them, and to be set against the sale price, was the open market value at the date when the relevant decision to deal in them was taken and implemented. In effect that, I think, meant that the open market value would be taken at the time of disposal, and so there would be no profit on the transaction. Counsel for the Crown, on the other hand, said that there was nothing to support any concept of deemed or notional trading, and that the gain was to be computed in accordance with the general provisions of the Finance Act 1962, s 13. For the purposes of s 412 of the Income Tax Act 1952, references to income, by virtue of the Finance Act 1962, Sch 10, apply in the case of gains "as they would apply if the gains were profits from a trade of dealing in the assets": but that does not seem to me to introduce any concept of notional trading in computing the gains. What s 412 says about income is to

1 [1955] 3 All ER 493, [1956] AC 58, 36 Tax Cas 275
2 [1974] 3 All ER 625 at 636, 637, [1975] 1 WLR 34 at 43, 44, [1974] STC 474 at 485, 486

apply to gains, computed in accordance with the general provisions of the Act, in the same way as it would apply to profits from a trade: but that is very far *a* from saying that the gains are to be computed in the same way as profits, or that there is to be any deemed trading. I can therefore see no basis for any application of the *Sharkey (Inspector of Taxes) v Wernher*[1] principle.'

On this question I am in complete agreement with what was said by the Special Commissioners and by Megarry J[2], and really there is nothing which can usefully *b* be added. So far as the first part of the question is concerned, Attleborough is a foreign company to which the charge under the 1962 Act has never applied. One is concerned only with the ascertainment of its income for the purpose of making a charge on the United Kingdom resident. That was dealt with by Sch 10 to the 1962 Act. The position of Attleborough itself is in no way affected by the 1965 Act. The provision in the Sch 10 to the 1962 Act stands unaffected, and there is no reason why *c* by implication one should treat that provision as having been in some way superseded by the 1965 Act.

So far as the *Sharkey v Wernher*[1] point is concerned, it is quite clear that the effect of the 1962 Act is not that the person concerned (including, as regards Sch 10, the foreign company) is deemed to be carrying on a trade, but that the gains are to be ascertained as if it were carrying on a trade. The principle of *Sharkey v Wernher*[1] has *d* no application in such a case. I would only add that if this argument were well founded, it would, as far as I can see, knock the bottom out of the whole of the capital gains provisions except possibly in respect of somebody who was in truth carrying on a trade. So, on this question, I would dismiss the appeal.

There is only one further matter which I should mention. I referred to it earlier in this judgment and said I would come back to it. The expenses shown by the accounts *e* of Attleborough include an investment advisory fee and management fee as the two largest expenses. There is a finding by the Special Commissioners that Attleborough incurred those expenses. There is no finding that the expenses were properly attributable to revenue account. This matter is left in the air. Evidence was given by the accountants concerning these items on either side. Mr Hobson, the accountant called on behalf of the taxpayer, said he did not know to whom and for what purpose the *f* investment advisory fee had been paid, and he had not seen a breakdown of the expenses in the accounts. Mr Lawson, for the commissioners, said he would require an explanation of the item 'Investment Advisory Fee' before approving it; he would also require to know what services the management fee covered, and for what purpose the 'Registered Office and Executive Office Fees' were included.

As I have said, the Special Commissioners made no finding on this point. So it *g* remains open to the commissioners, if they are so minded, to challenge these two times of expenditure in the account, not on the ground that they were not incurred, because we have the Special Commissioners' finding on that, but on the ground that they are not properly chargeable to revenue. We can perhaps come back to this point after the judgments. So far as I can see, the case must, if necessary, be remitted to the Special Commissioners on this particular point.

JAMES LJ. I do not wish to add anything to what has been said in the judgment just delivered on the short-term gains point, save to say I find myself in agreement with the learned judge and with the Special Commissioners, whose conclusions are set out in the case stated[3].

The question whether the amount of income deemed by s 412 of the Income Tax *j* Act 1952 to be the taxpayer's income is the investment income of Attleborough

---

1　[1955] 3 All ER 493, [1956] AC 58, 36 Tax Cas 275
2　[1974] 3 All ER 625 at 636, 637, [1975] 1 WLR 34 at 43, 44, [1974] STC 474 at 485, 486
3　[1974] 3 All ER at 629, 630, [1974] STC at 478, 479

a without deduction save for minor expense of collection, or that investment income less deductions of management and other expenses incurred by Attleborough, is one which, to one coming from a less sophisticated field in the common law, can I think be answered on a narrow basis. The answer surely must depend in the end on the construction of the word 'income' in the expression 'that income shall . . . be deemed to be income of that individual' in s 412(1). I apply, I hope correctly, the principles of construction stated by Lord Donovan in *Mangin v Inland Revenue Comr*[1]. There is no

b definition of 'income' in the 1952 Act itself. There is a presumption that where the section of a statute uses the same word in different places, then, unless the context clearly indicates that contrary, the word shall be given the same meaning in each place it is used. The preamble to s 412 includes the words 'income becomes payable to persons'. In the operative part of the section there are some 24 references to 'income', and I find nothing in the context in which the word is used in those places

c to indicate that it should not be given the same meaning wherever it is used. Contrast the position in s 413, a section dealing with double taxation, where the words appear 'income which has borne tax at the standard rate by deduction or otherwise', where a particular type of income is by the context defined, namely that income which has so borne that tax. The words 'payable to' in the preamble to s 412, and the words 'income arising from any such assets' in s 412(4), on which some reliance has been

d placed in the course of the argument, do not in my judgment help to define the word 'income'. They merely describe respectively for the purposes of the preamble and sub-s (4) the destination of and the source of the income that is there referred to. In the absence of any definition of 'income', I think it is right (as we have been invited to do) to have regard to the charging provisions of the 1952 Act, and there in s 1 and again in s 123 one finds the reference to profits or gains as the basis for the liability to

e tax. In the absence of any authority compelling a different construction to be placed on the word 'income' in s 412, in my judgment that word should be given the meaning of 'profit' in accordance with the meaning, as I see it, to be derived by way of assistance from the charging provisions.

I find some support for this construction of the word 'income' in the association of that word with the expression 'power to enjoy'. I agree with what has already been

f said, that s 412(5) provides for the circumstances in which a person shall be deemed to have the power to enjoy, and does not in any way define the word 'income' in s 412(1). Nevertheless, the argument addressed to us by junior counsel for the taxpayer on the wording of sub-s (5), stressing the aspect of income in the sense of something capable of enjoyment, was a powerful one. If the construction for which the commissioners contend is adopted, it follows in my judgment that a taxpayer may be

g taxed on something which could never be his to enjoy. To adopt that construction would be to use the section for a purpose beyond the undoubted purpose of the section, of preventing the avoidance of liability to pay tax.

I have so far dealt with the question—I will not say untrammelled by authority—but without such assistance as can be derived from authority. In the numerous cases which have been cited in the course of argument, I find no principle which leads me to

h a different conclusion. It is difficult, and often dangerous I think, to seek to derive help from isolated passages in the speeches or judgments in other cases in which the present point was not in issue. But I do find some support for the views I have formed, in particular, in *Mapp v Oram*[2], in the opening words of the judgment of Salmon LJ[3], and in the passage in the speech of Lord Upjohn[4] in the House of Lords. Lord Upjohn was considering a different section, s 212, but his words[4]: 'It [i e the income]

j cannot mean gross receipts, for every person earning an income has expenses' are telling words, and I think they are relevant to a consideration of s 412.

---

1 [1971] 1 All ER 179 at 182, [1971] AC 739 at 746
2 [1968] 3 All ER 1, [1969] 1 Ch 293, 45 Tax Cas 651
3 [1968] 3 All ER at 6, [1969] 1 Ch at 312, 45 Tax Cas at 665
4 [1969] 3 All ER 215 at 222, [1970] AC 362 at 376, 45 Tax Cas at 681

I agree with the reasoning and the conclusion expressed in the judgment delivered; and, for those reasons, I would allow the appeal on that one point.   *a*

Before parting with it, may I add my feeling of unease at the decision in *Lord Howard de Walden v Inland Revenue Comrs*[1], which decision is of course binding on us and to which one must loyally adhere, though it makes no difference to my reasoning in the present case.

b

BUCKLEY LJ. I agree with both the judgments which have been delivered, and I do not propose to cover the general ground again. But I would say something about *Lord Howard de Walden v Inland Revenue Comrs*[1], which was relied on strenuously by counsel for the commissioners in support of his contention that the relevant income here was the income of Attleborough consisting of the dividends and interest received by Attleborough from the investments held by that company without deduction for   *c*
expenses incurred in the management of the company. Lord Howard de Walden had transferred assets of very considerable value to four Canadian companies. The Canadian companies had no other assets. At the relevant time the only relevant interests of Lord Howard de Walden in the Canadian companies consisted of a life interest in certain promissory notes of the companies, a share of certain sums of money on deposit with the companies payable on demand, a very small number of   *d*
shares in the Canadian companies, and certain annuities payable by one or other of those companies. He had divested himself of all other interests in the companies. The transfers in question were admittedly within the terms of the preamble to the Finance Act 1936, s 18, which was the precursor of s 412 of the Income Tax Act 1952. Lord Howard de Walden was assessed on the basis that the whole income of the Canadian companies would be chargeable to income tax as if it were his income received by him in the United   *e*
Kingdom. The argument presented on behalf of Lord Howard de Walden was to the effect that he could only be taxed under s 18 on so much of the income of the Canadian companies as he had power to enjoy or should be deemed to have power to enjoy. Accordingly, it was contended[2], only so much of the Canadian companies' income as should remain after giving effect to all other rights in those companies should be taxed. Lord Greene MR[3], delivering the judgment of this court, said that the only   *f*
question was whether the assessment should be based on that part only of the Canadian companies' income which Lord Howard de Walden was actually in a position to enjoy —a very small part of the companies' income—or on the whole income. The grounds relied on in that case for saying that Lord Howard de Walden had power to enjoy income for the purposes of the section were paras (*b*) and (*c*) of s 18(3), now replaced by paras (*b*) and (*c*) of s 412(5). Because the receipt by each company of its income was   *g*
regarded as operating to increase the value of the notes in which Lord Howard de Walden had a life interest and to enhance the value of the debts due to him on account of the deposits, and because the payments made in respect of these obligations and the annuities out of the companies' income were benefits received by Lord Howard de Walden out of that income, all of that income was held to be deemed to be Lord Howard de Walden's income for the purposes of the charge under the section. Lord Greene   *h*
MR[4] said that an examination of the language of s 18(3), in conjunction with s 18(1), made it clear that the power to enjoy income with which sub-s (1) was dealing need not by any means necessarily extend to the whole of the income of the non-resident person, but that the court was unable to accept the argument that the income which was caught by sub-s (1) was limited to the income which the taxpayer was in fact entitled or able to receive. Lord Howard de Walden had in that case no reserve   *j*

1   [1942] 1 All ER 287, [1942] 1 KB 389, 25 Tax Cas 121
2   See [1942] 1 KB at 393
3   [1942] 1 All ER at 288, [1942] 1 KB at 394, 25 Tax Cas at 132
4   [1942] 1 All ER at 288, [1942] 1 KB at 395, 25 Tax Cas at 133

a powers enabling him to undo the transactions and to recover the Canadian companies' assets into his own possession as the taxpayer has in the present case. His interest in the Canadian companies was irrevocably confined to the limits I have stated. The rival arguments were that, on the true construction of the section, (a) the extent to which he should be treated as having a power to enjoy income of the Canadian companies should be ascertained by reference to the limited extent of his actual interest in the companies, and (b) that the extent to which he should be treated as

b having such a power should be treated as extending to the whole of the income of the companies. No question appears to have been raised or debated as to what constituted the whole income of the companies for this purpose. No one could, I think, deny that the consequence of the decision of this court in that case was extremely harsh. The court justified this on the ground that the section is a penal section. To tax a taxpayer on income he does not in fact receive may perhaps properly be

c described as penal; but I am sure that none of the distinguished members of that court would have considered that the fact that a statutory provision was of a penal character could justify adopting a harsher construction than the language required. One cannot tell from the report how far and in what way the question of construction was developed, but I can see no sign in either the report of the argument[1] or in the judgment[2] that certain considerations which seem to me to arise on the language of

d the section were taken into account. In any case, however, I do not think that that decision can be treated as authority for the proposition that where the non-resident recipient of income is a non-trading company the gross receipts of that company must be treated as the income of a United Kingdom resident who has or is to be treated as having power to enjoy the income of that company.

   Section 412, stated shortly, provides that where a United Kingdom resident has, by

e means of a transfer of assets whereby income becomes payable to a non-resident, acquired any rights by virtue of which he has power to enjoy any income of a non-resident which, if it were his income received in the United Kingdom, would be chargeable to income tax, *that* income—and I italicise the word 'that'—shall be deemed to be his income. The relevant income is, in my judgment, any income of the non-resident which the United Kingdom resident had, within the meaning of the section,

f power to enjoy. One must then turn to sub-s (5) to discover what amounts to a power to enjoy within the meaning of the section. I will not read the subsection again. The paragraph directly applicable here is para (*d*). Of what income of Attleborough had the taxpayer at the relevant date (which I will discuss in a moment) power to obtain for himself the beneficial enjoyment? Clearly he could not obtain the beneficial enjoyment of any income which before the relevant date had been properly spent

g by Attleborough; nor, in my opinion, could he be properly regarded as having power to obtain the beneficial enjoyment of any income which on proper accounting principles Attleborough ought to set aside to provide for any expenditure properly chargeable against revenue already incurred before the relevant date but not then yet discharged.

   What, then, is the relevant date for this purpose? I apprehend that, as a practical

h matter at any rate, the earliest date would be the end of the fiscal year or other period in respect of which the assessment is made. Until that date, the total income of the company for that period could not be known and no assessment could be raised. By that date the company's expenditure for that period would all have been incurred, if not actually paid.

   Counsel for the commissioners has submitted that the date at which it must be

j determined whether the section applied is the date when the income becomes payable to the non-resident party. He relies on *Congreve v Inland Revenue Comrs*[3], and in

---

1   [1942] 1 KB at 392, 393
2   [1942] 1 All ER 288, [1942] 1 KB 389, 25 Tax Cas 132
3   [1947] 1 All ER 168, 30 Tax Cas 163

particular on what was said by Cohen LJ[1], delivering the judgment of the court. Cohen LJ was there considering the date at which it must be shown that the person *a* to whom income becomes payable in consequence of a transfer of assets and associated operations is a non-resident. The answer to that question must be the date when the income becomes payable, for if the recipient is not then a non-resident, the transfer is not, so far as that income is concerned, a transfer such as is described in the preamble to the section. The question when it must be determined whether a United Kingdom resident has 'power to enjoy' is a different question. In the case of a *b* trading company, this obviously could not be the date at which each trade receipt occurs, for such a receipt is not income and the company's income for the period cannot be ascertained until the end of the accounting period, when there might turn out to have been no profit and so no income. I can see no good reason why in this respect a non-trading company should be treated differently from a trading company. It might, I think, be suggested that the date for determining the existence *c* or want of a 'power to enjoy' is the date of assessment; but whether this rate or the end of the relevant accounting period be selected the consequence is, I think, the same. The United Kingdom resident could not, by the exercise of any such powers as are referred to in sub-s (5)(*d*), obtain for himself the beneficial enjoyment of any income of the non-resident company which had then been expended or incurred for any such purpose that it is proper to be charged against the company's revenue account. *d*

Counsel for the commissioners has suggested that paras (*a*) and (*b*) of s 412(5), might also apply in this case. But, on the construction which I, in common with Sir John Pennycuick and James LJ, think should be put on the word 'income', expenditure on the management of the company's affairs would not be an application of income; and therefore it seems to me that those paragraphs cannot apply. In any case, for my part, I think that I should feel great difficulty in agreeing to the proposition that income *e* spent by Attleborough on ordinary management expenses, or it may be in paying foreign taxes relative to the dividends or interest received by the company, could properly be described as being so dealt with as to be calculated to enure to the taxpayer's benefit within the meaning of para (*a*), or that the receipt or accrual of income which is so spent could be properly said to operate to increase the value of any asset held by the taxpayer or for his benefit within the meaning of para (*b*). *f*

These considerations reinforce me in the view that Attleborough's income for any year for the purpose of the section consists of its receipts of an income character less the amount of any expenditure properly chargeable against its revenue account.

For these reasons, and for those which have been developed in the judgments delivered by Sir John Pennycuick and James LJ, I agree that this appeal should be allowed on the first and perhaps major point, but should be dismissed as regards that *g* part of it which relates to short-term capital gains.

Appeal allowed in part. Case remitted to the Special Commissioners to determine the amount of Attleborough's income. Leave to appeal to the House of Lords granted to the Crown on terms as to costs.

h

Solicitors: *Withers* (for the taxpayer); *Solicitor of Inland Revenue.*

Rengan Krishnan Esq   Barrister.

1   [1947] 1 All ER at 173, 30 Tax Cas at 197

a

R v Charles

COURT OF APPEAL, CRIMINAL DIVISION
BRIDGE LJ, BRISTOW AND BOREHAM JJ
18th NOVEMBER 1975

b Criminal law – Obtaining pecuniary advantage by deception – Deception – Implied representation – Cheque – Representation by drawer – Cheque card – Card containing undertaking
by bank to honour cheque – Payee not having any interest in question whether drawer having
authority from bank to draw cheque for amount in question – Defendant drawing cheque
for amount in excess of permitted overdraft – Cheque backed by cheque card – Whether
implied representation to payee that defendant had authority of bank to draw cheque –
c Whether defendant having deceived payee – Theft Act 1968, s 16(1).

The appellant opened a current account at the branch of a bank. The branch manager
agreed to give the appellant authority to overdraw his account up to £100. The manager also issued him with a cheque card. The card was in common form and contained
an undertaking by the bank that any cheque not exceeding £30 would be honoured
d subject to certain conditions relating to the manner in which the cheque was to be
drawn. In the course of one evening, at a gambling club, the appellant drew 25
cheques for a total of £750. Each of those cheques was backed by the cheque card.
At no time did the appellant have funds in his account to meet that sum or the amount
by which it exceeded the overdraft limit. The appellant was charged with obtaining
a pecuniary advantage by deception, contrary to s 16(1)ᵃ of the Theft Act 1968. The
e charge alleged that he had obtained a pecuniary advantage for himself, i e increased
borrowing by way of overdraft from the bank, by deception, i e by deliberately or
recklessly representing that he was entitled and authorised to use his cheque card
when issuing the cheque which was the subject of the charge. The appellant was
convicted and appealed, contending that when a cheque was drawn which was backed
by a cheque card such as the appellant's, there were no grounds for implying a repre-
f sentation to the payee that the drawer had authority from the bank to draw such a
cheque, since, in view of the bank's undertaking contained in the card, the payee had
no interest in the question whether the drawer had authority to draw the cheque.

Held – Where the holder of a cheque card drew a cheque for a certain amount backed
by the card, the inference to be drawn from the transaction was that the drawer was
g representing to the payee that, as between himself and the bank, he had authority
to draw a cheque for the amount in question. Since the appellant did not in fact have
his bank's authority to draw the cheque, it followed that in the circumstances he had
obtained a pecuniary advantage by deception. The appeal would therefore be
dismissed (see p 668 c and d, post).
R v Kovacs [1974] 1 All ER 1236 followed.

h
Notes
For obtaining a pecuniary advantage by deception, see Supplement to 10 Halsbury's
Laws (3rd Edn) para 1586A, 2.
For the Theft Act 1968, s 16, see 8 Halsbury's Statutes (3rd Edn) 793.

j **Cases referred to in judgment**
R v Ettridge [1909] 2 KB 24, [1908-10] All ER Rep 848, 78 LJKB 479, 100 LT 624, 73 JP 253,
22 Cox CC 101, 2 Cr App Rep 62, CCA, 14 Digest (Repl) 606, 6009.

---

a   Section 16(1) provides: 'A person who by any deception dishonestly obtains for himself or
another any pecuniary advantage shall on conviction on indictment be liable to imprisonment for a term not exceeding five years.'

R v Gould [1968] 1 All ER 849, [1968] 2 QB 65, [1968] 2 WLR 643, 132 JP 209, 52 Cr App
Rep 152, CA, Digest (Cont Vol C) 249, 8591a.   *a*
R v Kovacs [1974] 1 All ER 1236, [1974] 1 WLR 370, 138 JP 425, 58 Cr App Rep 412, CA.
R v Newsome, R v Browne [1970] 3 All ER 455, [1970] 2 QB 711, [1970] 3 WLR 586, 134
JP 684, CA, Digest (Cont Vol C) 226, 5364r.
R v Norman [1924] 2 KB 315, 93 LJKB 883, 131 LT 29, 88 JP 125, 27 Cox CC 621, 18 Cr
App Rep 81, CCA, 14 Digest (Repl) 581, 5805.
R v Page [1971] 2 All ER 870, [1971] 2 QB 330, [1971] 2 WLR 1308, 135 JP 376, 55   *b*
Cr App Rep 184, CA.

Cases also cited
Bell v Lever Bros Ltd [1932] AC 161, [1931] All ER Rep 1, HL.
Director of Public Prosecutions v Ray [1973] 3 All ER 131, [1974] AC 370, HL.
Greenwood v Martins Bank Ltd [1933] AC 51, [1932] All ER Rep 318, HL.   *c*
R v Laverty [1970] 3 All ER 432, 134 JP 699, CA.

Appeal
This was an appeal by Derek Michael Charles against his conviction on 6th December
1974 in the Crown Court sitting at Newington Causeway, London, SE1, before his
Honour Judge Finestein QC of one offence of obtaining property by deception and *d*
two offences of obtaining a pecuniary advantage by deception. Sentence was deferred
until 6th June 1975 when a fine of £150 was imposed. The facts are set out in the
judgment of the court.

Eldred Tabachnik for the appellant.
Michael Worsley and *Colin Hart* for the Crown.   *e*

BRIDGE LJ delivered the following judgment of the court: On the 6th December
1974, at the Inner London Crown Court, after a retrial lasting six days, the appellant
was convicted of one offence of obtaining property by deception and two offences
of obtaining a pecuniary advantage by deception. Sentence was deferred until 6th   *f*
June 1975 when a fine of £150 was imposed. The appellant appeals against his
convictions by leave of the single judge.
    The history of the transactions out of which this prosecution arose was as follows.
On 31st October 1972 the appellant opened a current bank account at the Peckham
Rye branch of the National Westminster Bank. On 23rd November he went to see
the manager, Mr Mason, asked for, and was granted, authority to overdraw on his
account for a period of one month up to a limit of £100. He went to see Mr Mason   *g*
again shortly before Christmas and asked that the overdraft up to a limit of £100
should be extended for a further month. That request was granted. He further
indicated to Mr Mason that he was having certain difficulties, having regard to where
his business activities took him, in cashing cheques when he wished to do so. It was at
Mr Mason's suggestion that he was issued with a cheque card. The cheque card was
in what is now, no doubt, a common and very familiar form, but since important   *h*
questions arise in the case as to the implications of a transaction in which a cheque is
presented, backed by a cheque card, it is appropriate to set out in full the terms of
the card which was issued to the appellant in this case. It bore on its front the legend:
'National Westminster Bank £30 for conditions see over'. On the back is written
the following:

    'The issuing Banks undertake that any cheque *not exceeding* £30 will be   *j*
honoured subject to the following conditions: a. The cheque must be signed
in the presence of the payee. b. The signature on the cheque must correspond
with the specimen signature on this card. c. The cheque must be drawn on a
bank cheque form bearing the code number shown on this card. [I interpose to

observe that the code number on the card was of course the code number of
the appellant's account with the bank.]   d. The cheque must be drawn before
the expiry date of this card.   e. The card number must be written on the reverse
of the cheque.'

Between 28th and 31st December 1972 the appellant issued a total of 18 cheques
backed by this cheque card, each for £30, amounting, therefore, in total to £540.
The issue of those cheques for that aggregate amount was going to have the consequence, in the events which happened and which, as the jury must be taken to have
found, must have been foreseeable, by the appellant, of putting his account with
the bank into debit to an amount substantially in excess of the £100 authorised overdraft. Some of the 18 cheques issued in the period before the end of the year had, we
understand, been presented at banks for encashment. The bulk of them, however,
had been paid for the purchase of gambling chips to a gambling club resorted to by
the appellant known as the Golden Nugget Club.

On 2nd January 1973 the first four of those 18 cheques including, it would seem,
at least two which had been cashed on the same day at different banks, reached the
Peckham Rye branch of the National Westminster Bank. They immediately caused
Mr Mason concern, partly because of the two cheques that had been cashed on the
same day at different banks and partly because the immediate state of the appellant's
account was then such that the four cheques for £30 each would, themselves, put
the account in debit to an amount of £120.

There had, however, been paid into another branch of another bank on that same
day a cheque for £500 to the appellant's credit of which Mr Mason was aware; but
that cheque had not at that time been cleared and therefore had not been credited
to the appellant's account.

It was in those circumstances that Mr Mason got in touch with the appellant and
asked him to call at the bank, which the appellant did later on 2nd January. There
was a discussion between the appellant and Mr Mason to which further reference will
have to be made hereafter. At the end of the interview the appellant asked for a
new cheque book and was supplied with one containing 25 cheques. That evening
the appellant went to the Golden Nugget Club again. Perhaps it is not an unreasonable inference that he was hoping to redeem his fortunes at the gaming tables but,
as so often happens in such a situation, instead of saving the day he plunged still
further into disaster and in the course of the night's gambling he used all 25 cheques
from his new cheque book, paying them out to the manager of the Golden Nugget
Club, £30 at a time, each cheque backed by the cheque card and duly completed in
accordance with the conditions on the cheque card. The 25 cheques amounted, in
the aggregate, to £750 and on their presentation to the appellant's bank, put his
account into debit far beyond the limit of his authorised overdraft.

The three counts, in an indictment originally containing ten counts, of which the
appellant was eventually convicted, were as follows. Count 3 charged him with dishonestly obtaining the cheque book which had been issued to him following his
interview with Mr Mason, on 2nd January, by deception, namely by falsely representing the true state of his bank account. Counts 9 and 10 of the indictment related to
two of the cheques he had issued on the night of 2nd/3rd January, the last one
dated 2nd January and the first one dated 3rd January, each for £30. The charge in
each count was dishonestly obtaining a pecuniary advantage for himself, namely
increased borrowing by way of overdraft from the National Westminster Bank by
deception, namely by deliberately or recklessly representing that he was entitled and
authorised to use his cheque card when issuing the cheque in question.

It is important to observe at the outset that since these counts were laid under ss 15
and 16 of the Theft Act 1968, it was an essential ingredient in each of the offences charged
which the Crown had to establish, that the appellant had, by words or conduct, been
guilty of a deception and that in each case that deception had operated on the mind

of the party deceived to induce thim to do that which enabled the appellant to obtain, in the case of count 3, goods, the chequebook, and, in the case of counts 9 and 10, a pecuniary advantage, the illegitimate increase of his overdraft with the bank.

The central point which arises in the appeal, albeit it arises in a different form in relation to count 3 on the one hand and counts 9 and 10 on the other, is whether on the evidence led by the Crown there was prima facie evidence proper to be left to the jury of the relevant deception alleged to have been practised by the appellant and that that deception operated to induce the party deceived to act as he did.

It is necessary to go back now to examine in more detail the substance of the interview between Mr Mason and the appellant on the afternoon of 2nd January which had the result, as one of its consequences, of the issue to the appellant of the new chequebook he requested.

First Mr Mason pointed out to the appellant that of the four cheques, which by that time had arrived back at the Peckham Rye branch, more than one had been cashed at a bank on the same day and, although this had not been explained to the appellant by Mr Mason when the cheque card had originally been issued to him before Christmas, Mr Mason now told the appellant that it was one of the bank's rules, which customers holding cheque cards should observe, that they were not available for cashing more than one cheque for £30 at any bank or banks on any one day. These transactions, it should be pointed out, occurred before it became the common practice of the banks to stamp on the back of the drawer's cheque book a record of his cashing a cheque backed by his cheque card on any day.

Mr Mason further said to the appellant that apart from cashing cheques at banks the cheque card should not be used to issue any cheques for more than £30 in relation to any one transaction. He further pointed out to the appellant that as the £500 cheque paid in that day had not yet been cleared, the four cheques received would create an overdraft in the appellant's account in excess of the permitted limit of £100. The appellant's reply to this was, first, that he had drawn the four cheques in question innocently, not knowing the bank's restriction on the number of cheques to be drawn on the strength of the card on any single day; secondly, he said that he was surprised that the £500 cheque had not been paid in earlier and he said further that he had paid the four cheques on two days, 28th and 29th December, because he had been moving house and had extra expenses.

There was undoubtedly a general discussion between Mr Mason and the appellant regarding the state of the appellant's account. At the end of the interview, Mr Mason said, he was quite happy. He also said that had he known that in addition to the four cheques, which had reached the Peckham Rye branch on 2nd January, the appellant, between 28th and 31st December, had issued another 14 cheques each for £30 he certainly would not have issued him with a further chequebook; but at no time did Mr Mason ask the appellant whether any other cheques were outstanding. Mr Mason, at one point in his evidence, did say that his impression was that the appellant was indicating he would not require an overdraft any further. If that impression was directly given by something said by the appellant and was unqualified, it would certainly have been a half truth involving a deception in not revealing that the further 14 cheques were outstanding.

At the end of the day, after he had been cross-examined about this, Mr Mason's evidence was vague in the extreme as to precisely what had been said regarding the future of the overdraft. The crux of the whole matter really turns on a passage in the course of Mr Mason's cross-examination by counsel for the appellant:

'Q. Now going back to this interview on 2nd January, did the [appellant] say to you explicitly that he no longer required an overdraft? Or was that your general impression? A. I cannot recall. Certainly by the end of the time he went out I had made up my mind he would not want any. Whether it was specifically raised or not I would not like to say. But certainly this was the impression, a because to the best of my recollection the conversation went along the lines that he'd got £500 in now and everything was looking all right for him.

'Q. Yes. So certainly the question of the cancellation of an overdraft was something that had not really been specifically discussed between you? A. Not to my recollection.

'Q. Because you see [the appellant] was under the impression that his overdraft was still continuing until the 19th January: might that be reasonable in your

b view? A. The overdraft limit of £100?

'Q. Yes? A. I think that is a reasonable supposition, yes.'

Really the high water mark of the argument on behalf of the Crown that there was here sufficient evidence of half truths being represented by the appellant to Mr Mason, such as to make the non-disclosure of the outstanding cheques a suggestio

c falsi, has to be extracted, if anywhere, from the last part of his answer in the passage just quoted: 'But certainly this was the impression, because to the best of my recollection the conversation went along the lines that he'd got £500 in now and everything was looking all right for him.' That has to be considered in the context that Mr Mason also said in terms, with reference to the cheques that had come in: 'It was my impression that these were the only four. My impression was not based on any-

d thing that the [appellant] said to the best of my recollection. My impression was not based on anything that the [appellant] did.'

Having given this aspect of the matter careful consideration all three members of this court have reached the conclusion that there was here insufficient evidence of any representation by words or conduct by the appellant of such a half truth as would enable the Crown properly to invite the jury to say that the non-

e disclosure to Mr Mason by the appellant of the fact that a further 14 cheques, each for £30, were outstanding was a false representation as to the true state of his bank account. We think that the evidence was too tenuous for that. In essence we think that this was a simple failure to disclose something which, so far as the criminal law is concerned at all events, the appellant was under no duty to disclose. Accordingly we take the view that this count should not have been left to the jury and that the

f conviction on count 3 must be quashed.

Turning now to counts 9 and 10, the point in the appeal in respect of these counts is one of very much wider, indeed of considerable, general importance. It is a point which raises the whole issue what are the implications of the common form of transaction, so familiar in everyday life since the practice of banks to issue cheque cards became common, represented by the presentation of a cheque backed by a cheque

g card and completed in accordance with the conditions of the cheque card in payment for goods or services or in exchange for cash.

Before turning to the general point which the arguments have raised, it is again convenient to examine in a little more detail the relevant evidence given by the payee of the cheques which were given by the appellant, in payment for gambling chips, on the night of 2nd/3rd January 1973, who was Mr Cersell, the manager of the

h Golden Nugget Club. What he said, as recorded in the summing-up, was: '. . . if the club was aware that someone was using his cheque card without authority, and without being entitled . . . they would not accept his cheque or the use of the cheque card.' But then he went on:

'We accept the cheque card on the basis that we do not know of any reason why not. There was no reason why the club should not accept, or should not have

j accepted the 25 cheques within a few hours. The club suffered no loss. The only reason we cashed the cheques, was that the cheque card was produced. That is our policy regarding any customer. What we need is the bank's guarantee of payment to us. So long as the conditions on the back of the card are met, the bank will honour the cheque in relation to which the card is presented, whatever the state of the customer's bank.'

He added later:

'If a cheque is backed by a cheque card, it is the bank who takes the risk. So
if there is the cheque card, we make no enquiries as to his credit-worthiness,
or as to the state of his account with the bank. All this is irrelevant unless the
club has knowledge that he has no funds, or the club has knowledge that he has
no authority to draw.'

Pausing there, that was the specific evidence of the person who received the cheques
and treated them as valid in this case, but it also seems to us to be an eminently
common sense view, which we think most people would take, of the situation arising
when a cheque is presented in accordance with conditions on the back of a cheque
card.

The essential question which we have to determine is: what are the implied representations, if any, which the drawer of the cheque, who completes it in accordance
with the cheque card and backs it with the authority of the cheque card, makes to
the payee?

The convenient starting point is to consider the comparable representations which
are implied by the presentation of a cheque which is not backed by a cheque card.
In R v Page[1] this court considered that matter and in the judgment of the court,
delivered by Phillimore LJ, this passage appears[2]:

'What is the law in regard to a cheque? It is set out very conveniently and very
clearly in Kenny on the Outlines of Criminal Law[3], and I am indebted to Geoffrey
Lane J for its assistance. It is put like this: "Similarly the familiar act of drawing
a cheque (a document which on the face of it is only a command of a future act)
has been held to imply at least three statements about the present: (1) that the
drawer has an account with that bank; (2) that he has authority to draw on it
for that amount; (3) that the cheque, as drawn, is a valid order for the payment
of that amount (i.e. that the present state of affairs is such that, in the ordinary
course of events, the cheque will on its future presentment be duly honoured).
It may be well to point out, however, that it does not imply any representation
that the drawer now has money in this bank to the amount drawn for, inasmuch
as he may well have authority to overdraw, or may intend to pay in (before the
cheque can be presented) sufficient money to meet it." '

Is it to be implied that the same representations are made by the conduct of one who
presents a cheque completed in accordance with the conditions on such a cheque card
as that with which we are here concerned?

Counsel for the appellant, in a cogent submission for which we are most grateful,
concedes that the first implied representation of what have been referred to in the
argument as the three 'Page' representations is made, namely that the drawer has an
account with the bank. Closely linked to that, no doubt, there is an implied representation in the situation under consideration that the drawer of the cheque is the
authorised holder of the cheque card in question. It is immaterial whether there is
an implied representation on the lines of the third 'Page' representation because
if there is, given that the cheque has been completed in accordance with the cheque
card, the representation is true because the cheque will necessarily be a valid order
for payment of the amount for which it has been made out.

The whole argument turns on the question whether the second 'Page' representation should be implied in this situation: namely a representation that the drawer
has authority to draw that cheque for that amount, in the sense that he is drawing a
cheque for an amount which he has no reason to expect, according to his contractual

1   [1971] 2 All ER 870, [1971] 2 QB 330
2   [1971] 2 All ER at 874, [1971] 2 QB at 333
3   19th Edn (1966), p 359, para 346

arrangements with the bank, that the bank would not meet when presented,
a independently of their pledge to meet it by virtue of the cheque card.

Counsel for the appellant's submission is that when a cheque card is presented no
such representation is to be implied for the simple reason that the payee is not,
in the slightest degree, concerned with the question of the drawer's credit-
worthiness. The state of the drawer's account at the bank, the state of the contractual relationship between the bank and the drawer is, so the submission runs,
b a matter of complete indifference to the payee of the cheque; it is a matter to which
he never needs to apply his mind.

The necessity for the three 'Page' representations to be implied in the different
circumstances where a cheque is presented in payment for goods or services or in
exchange for cash to a stranger without being backed with a cheque card is obvious,
says counsel for the appellant. Without such representations to rely on, a person who
c takes a cheque has nothing to assure him that he can expect payment when the cheque
is presented. Accordingly the implication of the three 'Page' representations, including in particular the second, is, in these circumstances, necessary to give the
transaction business efficacy.

In the different case where the recipient of the cheque has the bank's express undertaking held out in the form of a cheque card to rely on, there is no necessity, in order
d to give business efficacy to the transaction, that there should be any collateral representation implied on the part of the drawer of the cheque as to the state of his account
with the bank or the state of his authority to draw on that account. Still less is there
any basis for an inference that any such representation operates on the mind of the
recipient of the cheque as an inducement persuading him to accept it. He relies, so
runs the submission, and relies exclusively, on the bank's undertaking embodied in
e the cheque card.

The argument the other way is canvassed in an interesting commentary to be found
in the Criminal Law Review for 1974[1] on *R v Kovacs*[2]. The commentator points out,
as indeed the evidence of Mr Cersell in this case affirms, that when someone is asked
to accept a cheque backed by a cheque card he cannot properly do so and, plainly, if he
is honest will not do so, if he has actual knowledge that the cheque is in fact being
f issued outside the ambit of the drawer's authority to draw on his account. The reason
for that is plain. If the recipient of the cheque is aware that the drawer is already
beyond his overdraft limit or is otherwise exceeding his authority as between himself
and the bank, and nevertheless accepts the cheque intending to rely on the bank's
undertaking embodied in the cheque card that the cheque will be met, he is, in effect,
making himself party to a conspiracy to defraud the bank. The argument accordingly
g is that, at least in a negative sense, the recipient of the cheque backed by the cheque
card is concerned to some degree with the question whether or not the drawer is
issuing the cheque within or without the ambit of his authority vis-à-vis the bank.

From that premise the inference, it is said, follows that notwithstanding the availability of the cheque card and the bank's undertaking which it embodies, there should
also be implied from the transaction a representation by the drawer that he is draw-
h ing that cheque within his authority as between himself and the bank, and at least a
partial reliance on that representation by the recipient of the cheque.

The point is a difficult one. If it were free of authority, which it is not, all members
of the court would be inclined to give effect to counsel for the appellant's arguments.
That is not to say that the court has reached a concluded view on the matter, but our
provisional view is that common sense is on the side of counsel's argument and that
j the contrary argument based on the premise of the recipient's negative interest, so
to speak, in the state of affairs as between the bank and the bank's customer is a
somewhat tortuous and legalistic one.

1 [1974] Crim LR 183
2 [1974] 1 All ER 1236, [1974] 1 WLR 370

Again it is right, we think, to shun the temptation, which sometimes presses on the mind of the judiciary, to suppose that because a particular course of conduct, as *a* was this course of conduct, was anti-social and undesirable, it can necessarily be fitted into some convenient criminal pigeon-hole. Before the repeal of s 13 of the Debtors Act 1869 by the Theft Act 1968, we have no doubt that the present circumstances would have led, and led without difficulty, to a charge of obtaining credit by fraud other than by false pretences. It does not follow from that that there is necessarily a convenient alternative criminal pigeon-hole provided which fits the facts under the *b* provisions of the 1968 Act.

However, the point is not res integra. It arose in this court in *R v Kovacs*[1]. In that case the appellant, a lady, had been convicted of two counts of obtaining a pecuniary advantage by deception when she had presented cheques backed by and in accordance with the conditions of a cheque card, in one instance to a railway booking clerk for purchase of a railway ticket and in another instance to a pet shop owner in purchase *c* of a Pekinese dog. The counts against her in respect of her offences alleged as the relevant deception a representation on the part of the appellant that she was in valid possession of, and entitled to use, the cheque card in question. The judgment of the court given by Lawton LJ[2] indicates as follows:

'The prosecution's evidence was that by the end of November 1972 the appel- *d* lant's account at the Tring branch of the National Westminster Bank was overdrawn in the sum of £572. By letter dated 30th November 1972 the bank told her the extent of her indebtedness and said that no more cheques drawn by her would be met. Shortly afterwards a bank official named Hedges called on her and asked her for her cheque book and the cheque card referred to in the indictment which had been issued to her. She said they were not in her possession.' *e*

The principal argument in the case appears to have been that the conviction for the s 16 offence could not be sustained because the deception had been practised on one party, on the railway clerk and the owner of the pet shop, whereas the pecuniary advantage had been obtained from another party, namely the bank. That appears from the following passage[3]: *f*

'The appellant's counsel accepted that as a result of his client's conduct she had increased her overdraft by the amounts of the two cheques without the consent and contrary to the intentions of the bank, but he submitted that those results had been brought about by the deception of the railway booking clerk and the pet shop owner, not of the bank. [The judgment goes on, still, as we read it, summarising the arguments of counsel:] The railway booking clerk and the pet *g* shop owner had been deceived because the appellant in presenting the cheque card with her cheque had represented that she was entitled to be in possession of it and to *use it*.'

The court then goes on to reject that argument as not in any way invalidating the convictions on the footing that it is of no moment that the party deceived is a different *h* person from the party from whom the pecuniary advantage is obtained. But the crucial passage with regard to the point with which we are concerned is[3]:

'The next question is—how did she obtain this pecuniary advantage? On the facts the answer is clear, namely by inducing the railway booking clerk and the pet shop owner to believe that she was entitled to use the cheque card when she *i* was not.'

We have heard much argument on the question whether that is a decision of this

---

1 [1974] 1 All ER 1236, [1974] 1 WLR 370
2 [1974] 1 All ER at 1238, [1974] 1 WLR at 372
3 [1974] 1 All ER at 1238, [1974] 1 WLR at 373

court on the very point with which we are concerned this morning and if so whether
a it is binding on us. Rather half-heartedly, if he will not be offended by our saying so,
yesterday counsel for the appellant suggested that there might be a ground on which
the decision could be distinguished. It does appear on the facts that when the bank
official had called on Mrs Kovacs and demanded the return of the cheque book and
the cheque card but had not obtained them, because she falsely stated that she had not
got them, her authority as holder of the cheque card had been withdrawn and of
b course part of the deception alleged against her was her representation that she was
in valid possession of the card.

In the view we take that is not a solid or sufficient ground on which we can say that
the case can be distinguished because equally the case proceeded on the footing that
she was making a false representation which deceived the railway booking clerk
and the pet shop owner as to her entitlement to use the cheque card.
c Counsel for the appellant realistically does not argue that we can properly treat
R v Kovacs[1] as a decision which, in relation to this point, was per incuriam, but what
he does say is that it was a decision which was reached without argument on the point
which we are called on to decide. Certainly the passage quoted[2], where counsel for
the appellant is recorded as submitting that the results were brought about by the
deception of the booking clerk and the pet shop owner, would seem to indicate that
d no argument on the lines addressed to us had been addressed to the court at all.

Our attention has been drawn to the well-known authorities of R v Gould[3] and
R v Newsome[4] which certainly indicate that there is a less rigorous adherence to the
doctrine of stare decisis in the criminal division of this court than in the civil division.
We do not think it helpful to examine those authorities in detail, nor that they go to
the central point which we have to determine. More important, counsel for the
e appellant read us a passage from Professor Cross's book on Precedent[5] dealing
with the question of the binding authority of cases which appear to have decided a
point sub silentio and he specifically drew our attention to cases where the Court
of Criminal Appeal assumed jurisdiction to overrule a previous decision of its own
basically on the ground that the previous decision on the point at issue had not been
argued.
f The first of these authorities is R v Ettridge[6]. The point at issue is of no materiality
but it does appear there that the court in which Darling, Walton and Pickford JJ
were sitting together overruled a previous decision of their own, that is to say of the
same court similarly constituted the previous week, in which the point in question
had not been argued. Another instance of the same process is to be found in the decision
of the Court of Criminal Appeal in R v Norman[7] where, confronted with a previous
g decision where a point not argued had been decided in a certain way, Lord Hewart CJ
constituted a court of no less than 13 judges to consider the matter and by a majority
of nine to four they decided that the earlier decision should not be followed.

We think there is force in the three submissions made to us on this issue by counsel
for the Crown. He submits first that the practice in relation to the question whether
it is appropriate for one division of this court to take a different view on a point which
h has been, even if without argument, apparently decided by another division has
changed substantially since the change in the accessibility of the House of Lords
as an appellate tribunal in criminal matters. He says secondly that it is, to some
extent, a matter of expediency in the circumstances whether this court should, even
assuming it has power to do so, depart from a previous decision. He says thirdly,

j 1 [1974] 1 All ER 1236, [1974] 1 WLR 370
2 [1974] 1 All ER at 1238, [1974] 1 WLR at 373
3 [1968] 1 All ER 849, [1968] 2 QB 65
4 [1970] 3 All ER 455, [1970] 2 QB 711
5 Precedent in English Law (2nd Edn, 1968), pp 142, 143
6 [1909] 2 KB 24, [1908-10] All ER Rep 848
7 [1924] 2 KB 315, 93 LJKB 883

and with great force, that there is a distinction to be made between a point which has been decided sub silentio in circumstances in which the proper inference must be that *a* the point was never in the mind of the court at all, and a point which has been decided without argument, even perhaps following a tacit concession by counsel, where, nevertheless, it is apparent from the judgment that the court must have applied its mind to the point and at least seen no obstacle in the way of the conclusion which it has expressed.

We think that the decision in *R v Kovacs*[1] on the point we are concerned with clearly *b* falls into the second category. Lawton LJ could not have said[2]: '. . . how did she obtain the pecuniary advantage? On the facts the answer is clear, namely by inducing the booking clerk and the pet shop owner to believe that she was entitled to use the cheque card', unless the court had thought that it was to be implied from the presentation of a cheque backed by a cheque card that the drawer was representing that she had authority to draw that cheque at that time for that amount.   *c*

In one sense, of course, the question of the implications arising from any particular transaction is a question of fact but the presentation of a cheque backed by a cheque card is such a common form everyday transaction that it must be a question of law for the court to decide what inferences can properly be drawn from such a transaction. We take the expression of opinion in the passage to which reference has been made in *R v Kovacs*[2] as indicating the court's view that it could and probably should properly *d* be inferred from such a transaction that the drawer was representing that she had authority as between herself and the bank to draw that cheque for that amount.

However, even if we had felt more strongly than we do in relation to the argument of principle we think it would be undesirable that two divisions of this court should speak with conflicting voices on such an important issue. Counsel for the appellant's powerful arguments deserve the fullest consideration but if they are to be given *e* effect then, in present circumstances, the proper tribunal to give effect to them is not this court but the House of Lords.

Accordingly the appeal against conviction on counts nine and ten will be dismissed. £50 of the £150 fine will be remitted. The order will stand on the footing that there is a £50 fine on each of counts nine and ten on which the convictions still stand. There will be a sentence of three months' imprisonment in default and six months *f* to pay.

Appeal dismissed. The court granted leave to appeal to the House of Lords having certified the following point of law of general public importance: 'When the holder of a cheque card presents a cheque in accordance with the conditions of the card which is accepted in exchange for goods, services or cash, does this transaction provide evidence of itself from which it can *g* *or should be inferred (a) that the drawer represented that he then had authority, as between himself and the bank, to draw a cheque for that amount and (b) that the recipient of the cheque was induced by that representation to accept the cheque.'*

Solicitors: *B M Birnberg & Co* (for the appellant); *Director of Public Prosecutions.*

h

Lea Josse Barrister.

1   [1974] 1 All ER 1236, [1974] 1 WLR 370
2   [1974] 1 All ER at 1238, [1974] 1 WLR at 373

Practice Direction

Judgment – Payment of sum of money – Foreign currency – Claims in foreign currency – Applications for transfer of claims to county court – Payment of foreign currency into court – Interest – Enforcement of judgment debt in foreign currency – Forms.

1. Subject to any order or directions which the court may make or give in any particular case, the following practice shall be followed in relation to the making of claims and the enforcement of judgments expressed in a foreign currency.

2. *Claims for debts or liquidated demands in foreign currency*

For the purpose of ascertaining the proper amount of the costs to be indorsed on the writ pursuant to RSC Ord 6, r 2(1)(b), before a writ of summons is issued in which the plaintiff makes a claim for a debt or liquidated demand expressed in a foreign currency, the   writ   must be indorsed with the following certificate, which must be signed by or on behalf of the solicitor of the plaintiff or by the plaintiff if he is acting in person:

'*Sterling equivalent of amount claimed*
  'I/We certify that the rate current in London for the purchase of [*state the unit of the foreign currency claimed*] at the close of business on the   day of   19 [*being the date next or most nearly preceding the date of the issue of the writ*] was to the £ sterling and at this rate the debt or liquidated demand claimed herein, namely [*state the sum of the foreign currency claimed*] amounts to £   or exceeds £650 [*as the case may be*].
  'Dated the   day of   19
                          Signed
                                  (Solicitor for the plaintiff).'

3. *Pleading claims for debts or liquidated demands in foreign currency*

The writ or statement of claim in which a claim is made for payment of a debt or liquidated demand in foreign currency must contain the following statements, namely: (i) that the contract under which the debt is claimed in the foreign currency is governed by the law of some country outside the United Kingdom; and (ii) that under *that* contract the money of account in which the debt was payable was the currency of that country or of some other foreign country.

4. *Default judgment for debts or liquidated demands in foreign currency*

A judgment in default of appearance or in default of defence may be entered in foreign currency by adapting RSC Appendix A, Form 39, as follows:

  'It is this day adjudged that the Defendant do pay the Plaintiff [*state the sum in which foreign currency is claimed*] or the Sterling equivalent at the time of payment.'

5. *Judgment under RSC Ord 14*

Wherever appropriate, a judgment under RSC Ord 14, r 3, may be entered for a debt or liquidated demand in foreign currency by adapting RSC Appendix A, Form 44, as follows:

  'It is this day adjudged that the Defendant do pay the Plaintiff [*state the sum in foreign currency for which the court has ordered judgment to be entered*] or the Sterling equivalent at the time of payment and £   costs) [*or costs to be taxed*]'.

The amount of the fixed costs will be calculated on the sterling equivalent of the

amount of the foreign currency claimed as indorsed and certified on the writ, unless
the court otherwise orders.

6. *Transfer to the county court*

On the hearing of an application for an order under the County Courts Act 1959,
s 45, for the transfer to a county court of an action for a debt or liquidated demand
expressed in foreign currency, on the ground that the amount claimed or remaining
in dispute does not exceed £1,000, the court will have regard to the sterling equivalent
of the foreign currency claimed as indorsed and certified on the writ, unless at the time
of the application it is shown to the court that the said sterling equivalent does exceed
the sum of £1,000.

7. *Payment of foreign currency into court in satisfaction*

In an action for the recovery of a debt or liquidated demand, whether in sterling
or in foreign currency, the defendant may, subject to the requirements of the Exchange Control Act 1947, pay into court in satisfaction of the claim, under RSC Ord 22,
r 1, a sum of money in foreign currency by adapting Form 2 of the Supreme Court
Funds Rules 1975[1]. If it is desired that the money should be placed on deposit after
the expiry of 21 days, the necessary directions must be given on a Part II order.

8. *Orders for conditional payment of foreign currency into court*

Where the court makes a conditional order for payment of money into court,
e g when granting conditional leave to defend on an application for summary judgment under RSC Ord 14, or when setting aside a default judgment or granting an
adjournment of the hearing of a summons or the trial or hearing of an action or making
any other order conditional on payment of money into court, the court may order
that such money be paid into court in a foreign currency, and the court may further
order that such money should be placed in a foreign currency account and if
practicable should be placed in such an account which is an interest-bearing account.

9. *Entry of judgment in foreign currency*

A judgment may be entered in foreign currency by adapting the relevant forms
in RSC Appendix A as follows:

> 'It is this day adjudged that the Defendant do pay the Plaintiff [*state the sum in
> foreign currency in which judgment has been ordered to be entered*] or the sterling
> equivalent at the time of payment.'

10. *Interest on judgment debt in foreign currency*

A judgment entered in foreign currency will carry the statutory rate of interest
on the amount of the judgment in foreign currency and such interest will be added
to the amount of the judgment itself for the purposes of enforcement of the judgment.

11. *Enforcement of judgment debt in foreign currency by writ of fi fa*

(a) Where the plaintiff desires to proceed to enforce a judgment expressed in foreign
currency by the issue of a writ of fieri facias, the praecipe for the issue of the writ
must first be indorsed and signed by or on behalf of the solicitor of the plaintiff or by
the plaintiff if he is acting in person with the following certificate:

> '*Sterling equivalent of judgment*
> 'I/We certify that the rate current in London for the purpose of [*state the unit of
> the foreign currency in which the judgment is expressed*] at the close of business on
> the   day of   19   [*being the date nearest or most nearly preceding the*

date of the issue of the writ of fi fa] was   to the £ sterling and at this rate the
sum of *[state the amount of the judgment debt in foreign currency]* amounts to £
'Dated the   day of   19

Signed

(Solicitor for the Plaintiff)'.

(b) The amount so certified will then be entered in the writ of fi fa by adapting RSC
Appendix A, Form 53, to meet the circumstances of the case, but substituting the
following recital:

'Whereas in the above named action it was on the   day of 19   adjudged
[*or* ordered] that the Defendant C D do pay the Plaintiff A B [*state the sum of the
foreign currency for which judgment was entered*] or the sterling equivalent at the
time of payment, and whereas the sterling equivalent at the date of issue of this
writ is £   as appears by the certificate indorsed and signed by or on behalf of
the Plaintiff on the praecipe for the issue of this writ.'

12. *Enforcement of judgment debt in foreign currency by garnishee proceedings*
(a) Where the plaintiff desires to proceed to enforce a judgment expressed in
foreign currency by garnishee proceedings, the affidavit made in support of
an application for an order under RSC Ord 49, r 1, must contain words to the following
effect:

'The rate current in London for the purchase of [*state the amount of the judgment
in foreign currency*] at the close of business on the   day of   19   was
to the £ sterling, and at this rate the said sum of amounts to £ sterling.
I have ascertained the above information [*state the source of the information*] and
verily believe the same to be true.'

The master will then make an order nisi for the sterling equivalent of the judgment
debt as so verified.

(b) Where the plaintiff desires to attach a debt due or accruing due to the defendant
within the jurisdiction in the same unit of foreign currency as the judgment debt
is itself expressed, the affidavit made in support of an application for an order under
RSC Ord 49, r 1, must state all the relevant facts relied on and in such event the
master may make the order to attach such debt due or accruing due in *that* foreign
currency.

13. *Enforcement of judgment debt in foreign currency by other modes of enforcement*
Where the plaintiff desires to proceed to enforce a judgment expressed in a foreign
currency by other means of enforcement, e g by obtaining an order imposing a
charge on land or interest in land under RSC Ord 50, r 1, or by obtaining an order
imposing a charge on securities under RSC Ord 50, r 2, or some other similar order,
or by obtaining an order for the appointment of a receiver by way of equitable
execution, under RSC Ord 51, r 1, the affidavit made in respect of any such application
shall contain words similar to those set out in para 1(a) above. The master will then
make an order for the sterling equivalent of the judgment expressed in foreign
currency as so verified by such affidavit.

14. These directions are issued with the concurrence of the Chief Chancery Master
acting on the authority of the Vice-Chancellor so far as they apply to the practice in
the Chancery Division, and of the Senior Registrar of the Family Division so far as
they apply to the practice in that division.

I H JACOB

18th December 1975   Senior Master of the Supreme Court.

Practice Direction

CHANCERY DIVISION

Originating summons – Date of hearing – Requirement of fixed date for hearing – Adjournment – Hearing 'on a day to be fixed' – New business tenancy – Application to determine interim rent – Procedure to bring summons on for hearing – Landlord and Tenant Act 1954, s 24A– RSC *Appendix A, Forms 10, 12.*

1. Much time is wasted by first appointments for the hearing of originating summonses for new business tenancies under the Landlord and Tenant Act 1954 because both landlord and tenant wish to negotiate a new tenancy and merely ask the master, by letter or otherwise, to adjourn. This results from the prescribed form of originating summons requiring a date for the first hearing to be inserted in the summons itself, which has to be issued within a strict time limit.

2. In future, where the parties are in negotiation and neither side wishes to press on with the proceedings, the tenant may, in issuing his originating summons in RSC Appendix A, Form 10, delete the words 'on   day, the   day of 19   , at   o'clock' and insert in their place the words 'on a day to be fixed'. Either party may at any time thereafter issue a notice of appointment to hear the originating summons in Form 12 in Appendix A.

3. It is of the greatest importance that the landlord should be informed promptly of the issue of the originating summons, which must be served strictly within one calendar month from the date of its issue. It is not be assumed that the time will necessarily be extended if this requirement is not complied with.

4. If the landlord wishes the court to determine an interim rent under s 24A of the Landlord and Tenant Act 1954, but is content that the determination should await the determination of the application for a new lease and, in reliance on the procedure specified above, the originating summons has not been brought on for hearing, he may likewise issue a general summons for the determination of the interim rent which states the hearing as being for a day to be fixed instead of for a fixed date and time. Such a summons must be served promptly, and it may be bought on for hearing by either party on a date to be fixed by the court on not less than two days' notice to the opposing party.

5. The practice direction of 15th May 1974[1] is to be read subject to the above; it is still not permissible to issue an originating summons with the provision for a date of hearing left blank and not replaced in accordance with para 2 above.
   By direction of the Vice-Chancellor.

R E BALL
30th January 1976   Chief Master.

---

1 [1974] 2 All ER ER 566, [1975] 1 WLR 708

a

Re Manly's Will Trusts (No 2)
Tickle and others v Manly and others

CHANCERY DIVISION

WALTON J

b 14th NOVEMBER 1975

Res judicata – Issue estoppel – Construction of document – Settlement – Shares in settled fund – Destination of shares governed by same clause – Construction summons to determine meaning of clause in relation to one share – Subsequent proceedings in relation to other share – Proceedings raising same point of construction as earlier proceedings – Whether parties estopped by determination of court in earlier proceedings.

c *Settlement – Issue – Substitutional gift – Meaning of 'issue' – Gift over to children of settlor – In event of any child being then dead leaving issue who attain 21, such issue to take deceased parent's share – Whether 'issue' meaning children of deceased child or issue of all degrees.*

Settlement – Distribution – Per stirpes or per capita – Class gift – Substitutional gift – Gift over to children of settlor – In event of any child being dead leaving issue who attain 21 such
d *issue to take deceased parent's share – Whether distribution to issue per stirpes or per capita.*

T, who died in 1913, left half his residuary estate on trust for his three daughters for life. He then provided: 'And I declare that in the case of the death of any daughter . . . and on failure of her issue then the others of my sons and daughters shall take such deceased daughter's share equally, but in the event of any of them being dead, leaving issue who shall live to attain the age of 21 years, such issue shall
e take their deceased parent's share.' In 1922 the first daughter died, without issue, and her share was divided, on the order of the court, between her surviving brothers and sisters subject, in the case of the sisters, to the settlement provisions of the will. The testator's son, J, the only child who had had any issue, died in 1963; a second daughter, M, died in 1964, without issue. In 1969, in proceedings[a] to determine the destination of M's share, the court held that the word 'issue' meant issue of all
f degrees, and that distribution should be per stirpes. After the death of M none of J's issue died, but five more of his great-grandchildren were born. In 1972 the third daughter, E, died, also without issue. The trustees of T's will applied to the court to determine the destination of E's share. Three of J's grandchildren contended that the previous proceedings raised an issue estoppel which prevented the question being argued again. One of J's great-grandchildren contended that, on a true construction of
g the phrase 'their deceased parent's share', distribution should be per capita, while two of J's children claimed that the true construction was that the only persons entitled to a share were children of people who would have taken if they had not died, i e T's grandchildren.

Held – (i) The doctrine of estoppel could apply only if the question in issue in proceed-
h ings was precisely the same as the question in prior proceedings and between precisely the same parties as were parties to the original suit or their privies. In the instant case, the question in issue in the prior proceedings was the destination of the share taken by M, whereas the issue in the instant proceedings was the destination of E's share. Although the same points of construction were raised in the two matters, the issues were different, as were the parties, some of whom had not been in existence
j at the time of the earlier proceedings. The doctrine did not therefore operate (see p 676 a c and d, p 676 h to p 677 a and p 677 c, post); dictum of Lord Maugham LC in *New Brunswick Railway Co v British & French Trust Corpn* [1938] 4 All ER at 754, 755 applied.

(ii) Reading the will as a whole, the word 'issue' was to be construed as meaning

---

a   *Re Manly's Will Trusts* [1969] 3 All ER 1011   BB

issue of all degrees and the words 'their deceased parent's share' were not sufficient to
negative that conclusion. Furthermore, since one could only have a deceased parent's   *a*
share to the exclusion of that parent, that was a sufficient indication that distribution
was to be per stirpes; if distribution were per capita the situation could arise where
children would take more than their deceased parent's share. The will would therefore be construed accordingly (see p 678 *c* to *e* and p 678 *h* to p 679 *a*, post); *Sibley v Perry*
(1802) 7 Ves 523 distinguished.

b

Notes
For issue estoppel, see 15 Halsbury's Laws (3rd Edn) 185, 186, paras 358-360, and for cases
on the subject, see 21 Digest (Repl) 230-235, 242-277.
  For the meaning of issue, see 39 Halsbury's Laws 1059-1062, paras 1584-1586, and for
cases on the subject, see 49 Digest (Repl) 695-703, 6556-6609.
  For distribution per capita or per stirpes, see 39 Halsbury's Laws 1105-1108, paras   *c*
1637-1639, and for cases on the subject, see 49 Digest (Repl) 917-927, 8636-8719.

Cases referred to in judgment
Manly's Will Trusts, Re, Burton v Williams [1969] 3 All ER 1011, [1969] 1 WLR 1818.
New Brunswick Railway Co v British & French Trust Corpn Ltd [1938] 4 All ER 747,
    [1939] AC 1, 108 LJKB 115, 160 LT 137, 44 Com Cas 82, HL, 21 Digest (Repl) 231, 247.   *d*
Sibley v Perry (1802) 7 Ves 523, 32 ER 211, 49 Digest (Repl) 768, 7200.

Cases also cited
Badar Bee v Habib Merican Noordin [1909] AC 615, PC.
Birkett (deceased) Re, Holland v Duncan [1950] 1 All ER 316, [1950] Ch 330.
Earle's Settlement Trusts, Re, Reiss v Norrie [1971] 2 All ER 1188, [1971] 1 WLR 1118.
Peareth v Marriott (1882) 22 Ch D, CA.   *e*

Adjourned summons
By an originating summons dated 22nd August 1974 the plaintiffs, Henry Alfred
Tickle, Ruth Burton and Patrick Arthur Hartley Burton, trustees of a will dated
19th April 1912 and codicil of John Biddle Manly deceased, sought the following
relief: (1) that it might be determined on the true construction of the will whether   *f*
the moiety of the share of the testator's estate of his deceased daughter, Edith Mabel
Williams, which in the events which had happened was to be held for issue of the
testator's deceased son, John Herbert Manly, ought to be held on trust (i) for those of
his children who attained the age of 21 years and were living at the death of Edith
Mabel Williams in equal shares, or, alternatively, as joint tenants; (ii) for such of his
issue through all degrees as were living at the death of Edith Mabel Williams and had   *g*
attained or thereafter attained the age of 21 years in equal shares per stirpes; (iii) for
such of his issue through all degrees as were born in his lifetime, or alternatively at any
time whether before or after his death, and were in either case living at the death of
Edith Mabel Williams and had attained or thereafter attained the age of 21 years in
equal shares per capita, or, alternatively, as joint tenants; or (iv) for some other and
what class of his issue in some other and what shares or manner   The defendants   *f*
were (1) John Manly (known as John Docker Hayward Manly), (2) Eugenie Mary
Williamson (both of whom were children of John Herbert Manly), (3) Rosemary
Joan Sinclair Ashley, (4) Brian Meredith Moore, (5) James David Moore and (6) Joyce
Ann Hobby (grandchildren of John Herbert Manly) and (7) Julia Susan Manly (a
great-grandchild of John Herbert Manly). The facts are set out in the judgment.

R J S Thompson for the plaintiffs.
J O Taylor for the first and second defendants.
Ian McCulloch for the third, fourth and fifth defendants.
Colin Braham for the sixth defendant.
R A G White for the seventh defendant.

WALTON J. The present proceedings are an originating summons in the matter
a of the trusts of the will and codicil of John Biddle Manly deceased, and the first
question which arises is:

> 'That it may be determined upon the true construction of the Testator's said
> Will whether the moiety of the share of the Testator's estate of his deceased
> daughter Edith Mabel Williams which in the events which have happened is to
b > be held for the issue of the Testator's deceased son, John Herbert Manly ought
> to be held upon trust, (1) for those of his children who attained the age of 21 years
> and who were living at the death of the said Edith Mabel Williams in equal
> shares or alternatively as joint tenants [and then there are other various possible
> alternatives adumbrated].'

The first question is the one which has been argued in front of me so far, but, in
c arguing it, another and really totally different question has been raised on the question
of issue estoppel. The matter arises in this way, that the testator left—simplifying the
matter slightly but perfectly accurately for present purposes—a moiety of his
residuary estate on trust for each of his daughters, of whom he had three, and he
went on to settle those shares, and to provide that each daughter should take a life
interest with certain powers, in some cases, to appoint the income to a widower for
d his life or any less period. The testator then went on:

> 'And I declare that in the case of the death of any daughter (and her husband if
> an interest has been given to him by Will as aforesaid) and on failure of her issue
> then the others of my sons and daughters shall take such deceased daughter's
> share equally but in the event of any of them being then dead leaving issue who
e > shall live to attain the age of twenty-one years such issue shall take their deceased
> parent's share.'

The testator had three daughters and on the death of the first to die, in 1922, the
question of the distribution of her share (there were other questions, but that was the
main question for present purposes) was referred to the court. Eve J decided that it
f went in certain shares as follows: that the share ought to be divided between her
surviving brothers and sisters, of whom at that stage there were in fact four, subject
in the case of sisters to the settlement provisions of the will. There could not be any
particular difficulty about that, because all the remaining children of the testator
were then alive.

However, on the death of Mary Amphlett Parry Manly, the second daughter to die,
in 1964, that was not the case at all. The only child who had in fact any issue, John
g Herbert Manly, was by then already dead, and so it became a question what was
meant by 'issue', and whether the people who were designated took per capita or
per stirpes, or howsoever otherwise. That matter came before this court and the
judgment of the court was given by Ungoed-Thomas J: see *Re Manly's Will Trusts*[1].

What has happened is that the third daughter, Edith Mabel Williams, has in her
h turn died on 21st October 1972 and like her two sisters she has died without issue. All
the descendants of the testator who were living at the date when Ungoed-Thomas J[1]
decided how Mary Amphlett Parry Manly's share of the estate should go are, in
fact, in existence, but there are in addition various great-great-grandchildren who were
not in being then and who were therefore not then in front of the court; at any rate
we have one such in the seventh defendant.

The point which has been raised, and raised very forcibly, by counsel for the third,
j fourth and fifth defendants, who succeeded in their argument in front of Ungoed-
Thomas J[1], is that there is an issue estoppel here which prevents all the parties, save
possibly—but counsel would not even concede this—the seventh defendant, from

---

1 [1969] 3 All ER 1011, [1969] 1 WLR 1818

arguing the point; he said they were all estopped. Certainly the doctrine of estoppel is a sensible and useful doctrine; it prevents the court being troubled by having to decide *a* the same matter again that has already been decided, otherwise than by way of appeal. But all the statements in the cases to which I have been referred make it perfectly plain, in my judgment, that in order to get an estoppel on its feet in any way, the question must be between precisely the same parties as were parties to the original suit, or, of course, their privies. But, anticipating a little, what counsel for the seventh defendant and those in the same interest are proposing to argue here, is that *b* the distribution of the estate should be per capita and not, as Ungoed-Thomas J held, per stirpes, and that therefore there can be no question of the seventh defendant claiming through her own parents. Perfectly true it is that if such parents had not been her parents counsel would not be here to be arguing the matter at all, but he would not be claiming as a privy to her parents; indeed, he would be claiming in competition with them, and therefore, for the purposes of the doctrine of estoppel she is certainly *c* not a privy.

But before the doctrine of estoppel can operate at all, in my judgment, the question in issue in the subsequent proceedings must be precisely the question at issue in the prior proceedings. That is made very plain by a decision of the House of Lords in *New Brunswick Railway Co v British & French Trust Corpn Ltd*[1], in which it was held that a judgment delivered, as a matter of fact in default of defence or appearance, on one *d* bond, would not operate as an estoppel to prevent the appellants raising as a defence to a subsequent action questions as to the construction of the bonds, though the two bonds were couched in identical terms. That case demonstrates that one has to be very, very careful indeed to define the precise issue. This is what Lord Maugham LC said[2]:

    e

'If an issue has been distinctly raised and decided in an action in which both parties are represented, it is unjust and unreasonable to permit the same issue to be litigated afresh between the same parties, or persons claiming under them. In my view, however, the doctrine cannot be made to extend to presumptions or probabilities as to issues in a second action which may be, and yet cannot be, asserted beyond all possible doubt to be identical with those raised in the previous *f* action. In the earlier action here, the only relevant issue was as to the true construction of the only bond then sued upon, and an allegation that other bonds of the same issue were in precisely the same form would have been irrelevant and improper. In fact, however, the statement of claim contained no such allegation.'

And so, Lord Maugham LC said that the issue of construction in the second action *g* could indeed be proved in the second action to be similar to that decided in the first, but it related to a different cause of action based on other bonds and could not be asserted to be the same issue.

In my judgment, that case applies directly here. What was in issue in the prior proceedings in front of Ungoed-Thomas J[3] was the true destination of the share of the estate taken by Mary Amphlett Parry Manly. What is in issue in the proceedings *h* presently in front of me is the destination of that share of the estate taken by Mrs Edith Mabel Williams, and, of course, doubtless the same points of construction are raised in the two matters, but the issues are different, and I think that the fact that the issues are different is made perfectly plain when one considers whether the parties who are now parties to the present action, could, since they were not then in existence, have been parties to the proceedings dealing with the share of Miss Mary *i* Amphlett Parry Manly. The answer, quite clearly, is that they could not have been,

1   [1938] 4 All ER 747, [1939] AC 1
2   [1938] 4 All ER at 754, 755, [1939] AC at 20
3   [1969] 3 All ER 1011, [1969] 1 WLR 1818

a and, indeed, a representation order even would not have been proper because they could not under any circumstances have been interested in the matter as it then stood. If that were not right, then one would have the extraordinary position that parties, such as the seventh defendant, having come into existence since the date of the earlier case, would be able quite freely to argue for any construction of the will that they chose on the present occasion—because by no stretch of the imagination could any estoppel conceivably extend to them—while other parties would be bound,

b and bound by the estoppel presumably, to do just what?—to repeat, I suppose, exactly what the judge said and nothing else, when, of course, what is under attack is whether the judge came to a correct decision or not. It seems to me that it is quite impossible to imagine an argument on construction in which some of the parties thereto are bound and others are not bound by a previous estoppel. It would make absolute nonsense of any sensible and rational argument on the question of the

c true construction of the will. For those reasons therefore I reject the submission of counsel for the third, fourth and fifth defendants that there is here an issue estoppel, and I think that the true subject-matter of the decision on the originating summons today is: how should the share of Mrs Edith Mabel Williams in the estate, in the events which have happened, now be distributed?

That leads me then to a consideration, having disposed of the question of issue

d estoppel, of the first point, which is really that raised by counsel for the first and second defendants, John Manly and Eugenie Mary Williamson, who are in fact the two surviving children of the testator's son, John Herbert Manly, and the argument which he puts up is that the gift over which I have already read should be construed in what, for the sake of shorthand, I will call the *Sibley v Perry*[1] sense. I will read the clause again:

e
> 'And on failure of her issue, then the others of my sons and daughters shall take such deceased daughter's share equally but in the event of any of them being then dead, leaving issue who shall live to attain the age of twenty-one years such issue shall take their deceased parent's share.'

f Counsel for the first and second defendants says that the phrase 'their deceased parent's share' shows quite clearly that what the testator had in mind was that the people to take should be the persons who would be the children of people who would have taken if they had not been deceased. That is to say, he says that here John Herbert Manly, who is deceased, comes within the words 'but in the event of any of them being then dead', that is John Herbert Manly, he is then dead, 'leaving issue'—and he has left issue, whatever meaning you give to issue—'who shall live to attain the age

g of twenty-one years'—and that has happened—'such issue shall take their deceased parent's share'. He says, reading the phrase, 'such issue shall take their deceased parent's share', it is quite clear that the only issue to which that phrase can properly relate are children, and they will take their deceased parent's share, that is John Herbert Manly's share, and that is the way that the will must be read.

Whether or not the rule in *Sibley v Perry*[1] is a dying rule, or whether Ungoed-

h Thomas J did not in fact in *Re Manly's Will Trusts*[2] preside over its obsequies, I do not think it falls on me to decide. But, however one takes that rule, I do not think that anybody has ever really seriously considered that it prevented one from looking at the will as a whole and deciding what, on the will as a whole, the language used by the testator was intended to provide. Now, looking at the language used by the testator's draftsman in the present case, there are occasions where the words 'son' and 'daughter'

j are used, so that where the testator wanted to use 'son' or 'daughter', he was in a position to do so. There are also in a number of cases the word 'issue' used, where the only sensible way in which one can construe that word is by giving it the ordinary

1 (1802) 7 Ves 523
2 [1969] 3 All ER 1011, [1969] 1 WLR 1818

meaning of 'issue' through all degrees. Therefore, when one comes to the words 'but in the event of any of them being then dead leaving issue who shall live to attain the age of twenty-one years, such issue shall take their deceased parent's share', I think that one carries forward the meaning of 'issue' which has already been established in other parts of the will, and says that, prima facie, that means issue of all degrees, and one is not driven to a *Sibley v Perry*[1] construction.

Counsel for the first and second defendants says that that is the wrong way of looking at the will. One should not, as Ungoed-Thomas J[2] suggested, commence at the beginning of the will picking up one's definitions as one goes, and go to the end of the will, and carry the first definitions that one has found established to the end of the will. I think he would have me start at the back of the will, read it backwards to the front, and carry to the front any definitions which I found at the back of the will.

Well, I decline to adopt either of those positions. I read the will as a whole to see what in general the testator means throughout it by 'issue', and I have no doubt, looking at the will as a whole, that, just as Ungoed-Thomas J[2] found, 'issue' means issue of all degrees; and I cannot regard the few words 'their deceased parent's share' as a sufficient context to negative that conclusion. It depends, of course, very much on the terms of the will, the other provisions of the will, and I can well imagine that in other wills those precise words would be quite sufficient to carry the matter into the *Sibley v Perry*[1] camp. But looking at this will, it seems to me that there is no reason for construing the will in that way at all, and that it makes perfectly good sense, perfectly straightforward, nothing to be said against it, either as producing an unexpected result or as something which is contrary to the express language. I think one can read this perfectly sensibly by giving 'issue' the ordinary meaning of issue through all degrees, and therefore, I shall answer question (1) of the summons by saying that it is not in that sense.

[Argument then followed on questions (2) and (3).]

I now have to decide the second and third questions, that is to say whether the share of the deceased's daughter, Edith Mabel Williams, is held for such of the testator's issue through all degrees as were living at the death of Edith Mabel Williams and had attained, or thereafter attained, the age of 21 years in equal shares per stirpes, or for such of his issue through all degrees as were born in his lifetime, or alternatively at any time, whether before or after his death, were in either case living at the death of Edith Mabel Williams and had attained, or thereafter attained, the age of 21 years in equal shares per capita, or alternatively as joint tenants.

It seems to me in spite of extraordinarily valiant efforts by counsel for the sixth and seventh defendants that this is virtually unarguable.

The gift that I am considering is one which says:

'In the event of any of them [that is the others of the deceased's sons and daughters other than the one dying] being then dead, leaving issue who shall live to attain the age of 21 years, such issue shall take their deceased parent's share.'

You can only take a deceased parent's share to the exclusion of that parent, and therefore it seems to me that immediately you have words of that nature you are in a stirpital construction, because that is the only way in which the whole thing works. It is intended to go down stirpitally, and where you have people taking their deceased parent's share, that is the only way in which it works. If you try and work it out per capita you can easily get to a situation where the children will be taking more than their deceased parent's share, using, of course, 'parent' here in the sense of being on a sliding scale, which is the only way in which you can give any sense to the meaning of the word 'parent' once you have determined, as I already have determined, following, with respect, the lead set by Ungoed-Thomas J[2], that 'issue' means issue of all degrees.

1   (1802) 7 Ves 523
2   [1969] 3 All ER 1011, [1969] 1 WLR 1818

a It seems to me, really, that once that point has been decided the rest follows, because 'parent' means the parent at any particular step in the scale, and if the parents are dead their children take the share that the deceased parent would have got equally between them and not per capita, so the whole thing, I think, must be, once you can see that 'issue' means issue, on the sliding scale which leads to stirpital distribution.

b *Declaration accordingly.*

Solicitors: *Gregory, Rowcliffe & Co*, agents for *Shakespeare & Vernon*, Birmingham (for the plaintiffs); *Gamlens*, agents for *Cottrell Son & Wm Kentish*, Birmingham (for the first and second defendants); *Light & Fulton* (for the third, fourth and fifth defendants); *Bower Cotton & Bower*, agents for *Heppenstalls*, Lymington, Hants (for the sixth and seventh defendants).

c Jacqueline Metcalfe   Barrister.

R v Urbanowski

d COURT OF APPEAL, CRIMINAL DIVISION
SCARMAN LJ, WILLIS AND MAIS JJ
20th JANUARY 1976

Criminal law – Trial – Commencement of trial – Time limit – Trial to begin within prescribed
e *period beginning with date of committal – Extension of time – Whether provision as to time limit mandatory or directory – Whether court having power to extend period where application made after expiration of period – Courts Act 1971, s 7 (4).*

The provision in s 7(4)[a] of the Courts Act 1971 that the trial of a person committed to the Crown Court by a magistrates' court is to begin not later than the expiration of the prescribed period, is directory and not mandatory. It is therefore open to the Crown
f Court to grant an application for an extension of the time in which the trial is to begin if it thinks fit, even though the application is made after the prescribed period has expired (see p 681 g, post).

Notes
g For the time limit within which a trial should begin, see Supplement to 10 Halsbury's Laws (3rd Edn) para 685A.
For the Courts Act 1971, s 7, see 41 Halsbury's Statutes (3rd Edn) 295.

Cases referred to in judgment
Caldow v Pixell (1877) 2 CPD 562, 46 LJQB 541, 36 LT 469, 41 JP 647, DC, 19 Digest (Repl)
h 545, 3830.
Hughes v Wavertree Local Board (1894) 58 JP 654, 10 TLR 357, DC, 33 Digest (Repl) 319, 1426.
Moore v Hewitt [1947] 2 All ER 270, [1947] KB 831, [1947] LJR 1276, 177 LT 576, 111 JP 483, 63 TLR 476, 45 LGR 558, DC, 33 Digest (Repl) 319, 1427.
R v Edwards (18th April 1975) unreported.

j **Appeal**
This was an appeal by Peter John Urbanowski against his conviction in the Crown Court at Chester on 1st October 1975 before his Honour Judge David on two counts of

---

a   Section 7(4), so far as material, is set out at p 680 *b* and *c*, post

unlawful wounding, contrary to s 20 of the Offences Against the Person Act 1861. The
facts are set out in the judgment of the court.   a

R H Montgomery for the appellant.
R Waterhouse QC and E Edwards for the Crown.

SCARMAN LJ delivered the following judgment of the court: This appeal raises   b
a short point of construction of s 7(4) of the Courts Act 1971. The subsection provides,
so far as material:

> 'The trial of a person committed by a magistrates' court . . . (b) shall, unless the
> Crown Court has otherwise ordered, begin not later than the expiration of the
> prescribed period beginning with the date of his committal . . .'   c

The Crown Court Rules 1971[1], r 19, have prescribed a period of 56 days or, otherwise expressed, eight weeks. In the present case by an administrative oversight, and I
shall have to give the details later, the trial of this appellant did not begin until 117 days
after the expiration of the prescribed period.
   He was arraigned on two counts of unlawful wounding, to one of which he pleaded
not guilty, and to the other of which he pleaded guilty. He was convicted and   d
sentenced to a total of two years' imprisonment.
   The point is now taken that the trial was a nullity because the language of s 7(4)
of the 1971 Act is mandatory and not directory, and the provision in the subsection
that the Crown Court may order an extension of the time is a provision that has to be
activated before the expiration of the prescribed period, and not after. The submission for the Crown is a simple one, that in all the circumstances and in the context   e
the subsection is directory only.
   Before I come to consider the question of construction and to give the judgment
of the court on it, I will outline the course of the proceedings. The appellant was
committed for trial by the Runcorn magistrates' court on 7th April 1975 on the two
charges of wounding. The prescribed time (that is to say the period prescribed under
r 19 of the Crown Court Rules 1971) expired on 2nd June. The case was listed for   f
hearing on 9th May before Mars-Jones J but was taken out of the list at the request
of the defence, counsel being in difficulties. The case was released to Judge David on
20th May. Thereafter there occurred some administrative confusion in the office
of the Crown Court. As a result of this confusion the case was not listed within the
prescribed period and the failure to list was not noticed until shortly before an
application was made on 11th August for an extension of time. This application was   g
heard by Judge David in chambers. He granted an extension of 28 days, saying that
no further extension would be granted.
   After that the case was listed for hearing on 11th September. Again the office
must have overlooked the fact that that was more than 28 days after the date on which
the extension of time had been granted. Even so, it was then taken out of the list
because a long trial of some other case was occupying the time of the court. Ulti-   h
mately it was relisted for hearing on 22nd September, no further application having
been made for an extension of time and no order having been made by the Crown
Court judge extending the time.
   When on 22nd September the case came before the Crown Court judge, counsel for
the appellant pleaded to the jurisdiction of the court and moved to quash the indictment on the ground that s 7(4) of the 1971 Act had not been complied with. The   i
response (if I may say so in passing, the very sensible response) of Judge David was not
only to reject the submission but to make there and then a further extension order.

---

1   SI 1971 No 1292

It is now, as I have already indicated in the introductory passage of the judgment,
the case for the appellant that the judge had no power to make that extension order
and that the proceedings which then ensued were a nullity. It is to be observed that
the failure to bring on this case within the time prescribed by the rules, or within any
extension of that time ordered by the Crown Court, arose from the administrative
error or errors of a public official.

Counsel for the Crown accordingly submits that it would be in accordance with
principle to construe the subsection as directory only. He has referred us to the analogous law dealing with the time limit for stating cases to the Divisional Court, and he
has referred us to authority which offers guidance as to when the court should hold
statutory words to be directory, and when mandatory.

We find considerable assistance in the interpretation of this subsection from a consideration of the law relating to the time limit for stating cases and I will indicate very
shortly why. Rule 67 of the Magistrates' Courts Rules 1968[1] provides that the time
within which justices shall state a case shall be three months after the application
for the case to be stated. The rule contains no provision expressly authorising
extension of that period.

This rule has been in the law for a very long time, and the leading authority as to
its construction is *Hughes v Wavertree Local Board*[2]. In that case a Divisional Court
of the Queen's Bench Division considered the rules then in force under the Summary
Jurisdiction Act 1879 as to time limits. Cave J said[3]:

> 'The rule in question provides that on an application to the Court of Summary
> Jurisdiction under that Act at any time within seven clear days a case shall be
> stated in three months after the date of the application and after the recognizances
> are entered into. It is contended that the whole of the rule is a condition prece-
> dent, and that it is not merely directory. It may be so as far as relates to acts to be
> done by the appellant, but not so far as it relates to the magistrates; as to their
> act it is only directory.'

The judgment elaborates that point.

In *Moore v Hewitt*[4] the Divisional Court attached importance to the decision in
Hughes v Wavertree Local Board[2], and in giving the judgment of the court Lord
Goddard CJ emphasised that it was important to observe whether the Act was deal-
ing with what was required of a public official or of a party. See also *Caldow v Pixell*[5].

It seems to us plain that s 7(4) of the 1971 Act is primarily addressed to the Crown
Court, and obliges the court to take steps to ensure that cases are begun within the
prescribed period. Accordingly in our view this provision, being addressed to the court
and its officials, is directory and not mandatory; and it follows from that view of
the subsection that it is open to the Crown Court to grant an extension of time if it
thinks fit after the expiration of the prescribed period.

Counsel for the appellant has urged that such a construction puts altogether too
much power in the hands of the Crown Court judge and that the Act must be construed
as mandatory and as conferring no more power on the Crown Court judge than a
power to grant an extension of time before the expiration of the prescribed period.

We see absolutely no reason why the Crown Court should not have the more extended power, and we see nothing in the Act, once granted that it is directory in
character, abridging the power of the Crown Court. It is as well to remember that
the Crown Court, established by the 1971 Act, is part of the Supreme Court of Justice
in England, and its judges will of course act judicially. One need have no fear, I

1   SI 1968 No 1920
2   (1894) 10 TLR 357
3   10 TLR at 358
4   [1947] KB 831
5   (1877) 2 CPD 562 at 566

should have thought, that there is any risk of abuse of the power conferred to grant an extension of time.   *a*

We are reinforced in our view of the subsection by an unreported decision of this court, *R v Edwards*[1]. That was an application dealt with by two judges, and the same point was taken on that application, though it had not been taken in the court below, and in the course of giving the judgment of this court Talbot J said, shortly but plainly, that in the view of the court the subsection was directory only. In our view therefore the appeal must fail on the short point of construction.   *b*

We have been urged by counsel to give some directions or some guidance as to the appropriate way in which to administer this provision. This of course is very much a matter for the Crown Court judges, but it would appear to us as a convenient course for the court or the court office to notify parties, both the Crown and the defence, when it is necessary to make an application for an extension to time. If the parties are perfectly happy for the extension of time to be granted, there is no need   *c* for either of them to go to the expense of attending the court on the hearing of the application. If either party wishes to object or to make submissions, then they must have their opportunity at the hearing of the application.

We have been told that in some circuits these applications are dealt with in chambers whereas in other circuits—and we believe the Central Criminal Court—they are dealt with by the judge in open court. There is no need to give any direction as to   *d* which is the better course. Plainly if a point of importance falls to be argued the court would be wise to adjourn the matter into court so that there may be a public hearing and a public decision.

We have also been urged to consider the time limit dealing with the date for the preferment of a bill of indictment under r 5 of the Indictment (Procedure) Rules 1971[2]. That period is one of 28 days from the date of committal and, though the   *e* language is different, there is also a provision for extension of time.

Nothing that we have said on the true construction of the 1971 Act can be directly binding when considering the construction, if the point ever arises, of the 1971 rules. Nevertheless it may be of some assistance if we say that we would expect this time limit to be construed in a directory way—just as the court has now construed the 1971 Act, and as in the past the courts have construed the rules relating to the time   *f* limit for a case stated. There are differences between the preferring of a bill of indictment and the listing of a case for hearing, but we do not think that the differences are such as to require the courts to construe the relevant indictment rule as mandatory; we think it is directory only.

For those reasons the appeal is dismissed.

          g

Appeal dismissed.

Solicitors: *Nyland & Beattie*, Widnes (for the appellant); *E C Woodcock*, Cheshire Police Authority, Chester (for the Crown).

Jacqueline Charles Barrister.

---

1   (18th April 1975) unreported
2   SI 1971 No 2084

a   Ogilvy and others v Hope-Davies

CHANCERY DIVISION
GRAHAM J
5th, 6th, 13th NOVEMBER 1975

b

Sale of land – Requisitions on title – Time limit – Abstract of title imperfect – Effect – Duty of purchaser – Abstract deficient only in unimportant aspects – Duty to raise requisitions so far as possible on information supplied within prescribed time limit – Right to raise further requisitions when new material received – Purchaser not entitled to delay making any requisitions until abstract complete – Law Society's General Conditions of Sale (1973
c Revision), condition 10(1)(3).

By a contract of sale dated 2nd August 1973 the vendors as trustees agreed to sell a house. The contract incorporated the Law Society's General Conditions of Sale (1973 Revision) and stated that completion should be on 30th August. On 6th August an abstract of title was delivered to the purchaser's solicitor who, under condition 10(1)[a],
d had 14 days within which to make his requisitions. The abstract, however, was incomplete since it omitted, inter alia, the deed appointing the vendors as trustees, although the deed was referred to in the abstract. On 14th August the purchaser's solicitor wrote to the vendors' solicitors stating that the abstract was not complete and that he would be unable to complete by the due date as he was going on holiday. On 15th August the vendors' solicitors sent some of the missing documents, but not the
e deed of appointment, together with a letter stating that the title was complete and insisting on due completion. Their letter added: 'We would prefer that all your requisitions on title are raised at the same time.' The purchaser's solicitor wrote again on 16th August requesting a copy of the deed, which was sent on 20th August. The purchaser's requisitions were delivered by letter dated 30th August and completion eventually took place, after the vendors' solicitor had returned from holiday, on 15th
f October. The vendors claimed interest on the unpaid balance of the purchase money for the period 30th August to 15th October on the ground that the delay in completion had been caused by the failure of the purchaser's solicitor to make his requisitions within 14 days, in accordance with condition 10(1). The purchaser contended that he was relieved from complying with condition 10(1) since the vendors had delivered an incomplete abstract of title and the abstract was not to be deemed to be perfect
g under condition 10(3), since condition 10(3) only applied to an abstract which, although imperfect, was perfect on its face.

Held – (i) Where an abstract of title was only deficient in respects that were unimportant in that a solicitor investigating the title would, or ought to, assume that
h the gaps could be and would be likely to be filled in a way in which he would expect from the information supplied in the abstract, the purchaser should raise the requisitions possible on the abstract submitted and call for any further information necessary. He would still be entitled to make further requisitions on the new material. In the instant case the abstract was nearly complete and there was no real difficulty in guessing the position. The purchaser's solicitor was therefore responsible for some
j delay in making his requisitions and that delay had contributed to the delay in completion (see p 686 *g h* and p 686 *j* to p 687 *a b*, post).
     (ii) However, the vendors' solicitors' letter of 15th August, coupled with their failure

---

a Condition 10 is set out at p 685 *e* to *h*, post

to deliver the deed of appointment until 20th August, amounted to a waiver of the time limit on requisitions, until a reasonable time after delivery of the deed. Accordingly, in the circumstances, it would be inequitable to allow the vendors to insist on their strict rights and their claim would therefore be dismissed (see p 687 c and j and p 689 b, post); dictum of Lord Denning MR in W J Alan & Co v El Nasr Export & Import Co [1972] 2 All ER at 139, 140 applied. a

Note

For procedure after signing a contract for the sale of land, see 34 Halsbury's Laws (3rd Edn) 193-194, para 323. b

Cases referred to in judgment

Alan (W J) & Co Ltd v El Nasr Export & Import Co [1972] 2 All ER 127, [1972] 2 QB 189, [1972] 2 WLR 800, CA. c

Bruner v Moore [1904] 1 Ch 305, 73 LJCh 377, 89 LT 738, 21 Digest (Repl) 455, 1567.

Central London Property Trust Ltd v High Trees House Ltd [1956] 1 All ER 256, [1947] KB 130, [1947] LJR 77, 175 LT 332, 21 Digest (Repl) 376, 1133.

D & C Builders Ltd v Rees [1965] 3 All ER 837, [1966] 2 QB 617, [1966] 2 WLR 288, Digest (Cont Vol B) 142, 3744a. d

Furst (Enrico) & Co v W E Fischer Ltd [1960] 2 Lloyd's Rep 340.

Hughes v Metropolitan Railway Co (1877) 2 AC 439, [1874-80] All ER Rep 187, 46 LJQB 583, 36 LT 332, 21 Digest (Repl) 392, 1221.

Panoutsos v Raymond Hadley Corpn of New York [1917] 2 KB 47, [1916-17] All ER Rep 448, 86 L JKB 1325, 117 LT 330, 22 Com Cas 308, CA; affg [1917] 1 KB 767, 22 Com Cas 207, 39 Digest (Repl) 576, 1009.

Plasticmoda Societa Per Azioni v Davidsons (Manchester) Ltd [1952] 1 Lloyd's Rep 527. e

Rickards (Charles) Ltd v Oppenheim [1950] 1 All ER 420, [1950] 1 KB 616, Digest (Cont Vol A) 287, 2708a.

Tool Metal Manufacturing Co Ltd v Tungsten Electric Co Ltd [1955] 2 All ER 657, [1955] 1 WLR 761, Digest (Cont Vol A) 1250, 1872a.

f

Case also cited

Re Ossemsley Estates Ltd [1937] 3 All ER 774, CA.

Adjourned summons

By an originating summons dated 16th September 1974 the plaintiffs, the Hon James Donald Diarmid Ogilvy, Mabel Edith, Dowager Viscountess Wimborne, Samos g Investments Ltd and Mysia Investments Ltd, the trustees of the Salisbury Trust ('the vendors'), claimed against the defendant, James Hubert Hope-Davies ('the purchaser'), inter alia, (1) a declaration that the purchaser was indebted to the vendors in the sum of £503·60 being interest at 12 per cent per annum on the unpaid balance of purchase money, payable under a contract of sale dated 2nd August made between the trustees of the Salisbury Trust and the purchaser, between 30th August and h 15th October 1973, or (2) alternatively, a declaration as to what interest was payable, and (3) an order that the purchaser pay interest on the sum declared to be due from him. The facts are set out in the judgment.

C P F Rimer for the vendors.
S L Newcombe for the purchaser. j

Cur adv vult

13th November. **GRAHAM J** read the following judgment: This is a vendor and purchaser summons and the vendors claim, inter alia:

'3. A declaration that the [vendors] are entitled to give a good receipt to Messrs. Frere Cholmeley & Co. and to Mr J. M. B. Law (being respectively the [vendors'] and the [purchaser's] solicitors and who hold the said sum of £503.60 on a deposit account in joint names to abide the outcome of these proceedings) for the said sum of £503.60, or for such amount thereof as they are declared to be entitled to; 4. An order that the [purchaser] do pay interest pursuant to Section 3 of the Law Reform (Miscellaneous Provisions) Act 1934 to the [vendors] on such sum as aforesaid as is payable to the [vendors] by the [purchaser].'

It is, it seems to me, a case which might well not have come before this court if the instructing solicitors on both sides had not, as the correspondence shows, become irritated with each other shortly after the end of the summer term in 1973. As it is, the small amount at stake, £503·60, is bound to be swallowed up in fighting the case to no one's advantage. In the absence of a settlement, however, which would clearly have been sensible, I must decide the matter on what I conceive to be the proper legal basis.

The contract in question relates to a sale on 2nd August 1973 of a house on the Dorset/Hampshire border known as Creech Hill Farmhouse, Cranborne. The plaintiffs are the vendors and the defendant is the purchaser, the price agreed being £37,000. The contract stated that completion should be on 30th August and incorporated the Law Society's General Conditions of Sale (1973 Revision). The case raises, inter alia, for the first time, I am told, the question of the scope and effect of condition 10(3) and (5) which makes time the essence of such condition. Condition 10 relates to requisitions and reads as follows:

'Requisitions. 10(1) Within fourteen days after the day of delivery of the abstract or of the documents, particulars and information specified in Condition 7 (whether or not the same are respectively delivered at the time prescribed) or within fourteen days after the date of the contract if later, the purchaser shall send to the vendor's solicitors a statement in writing of all objections and requisitions, if any, to or on—(a) the title or evidence of title, (b) the abstract or the said documents, particulars and information and (c) the contract as regards matters not thereby specifically provided for, and subject thereto, the title shall be deemed to be accepted.

'(2) All objections and requisitions not included in any statement sent within the time aforesaid and not going to the root of the title shall be deemed to have been waived.

'(3) The abstract or the said documents, particulars and information though in fact imperfect, shall be deemed to be perfect, except for the purpose of any objections or requisitions which could not have been taken or made on the information therein contained.

'(4) The replies to any objections or requisitions shall be answered in writing within seven days after the day of delivery thereof, and if not so answered shall be considered satisfactory.

'(5) In all respects, time shall be deemed of the essence of this Condition.'

The two affidavits filed and the correspondence set out the material facts and the history of the matter. The abstract of title was admittedly deficient as sent, but the vendors say that they are relieved from the effects of the general obligation as to title in respect of unregistered land, namely to deliver a perfect abstract of title, by the effect of condition 10(3). They say they delivered an abstract on 6th August and, although this was admittedly deficient in three respects, nevertheless the purchaser was bound to make his requisitions by the time limited, namely 14 days from that date as far as he was able. The abstract actually delivered, they say, must be deemed, as condition 10(3) says, to be perfect and this means, so far as it goes, when delivered. Though the purchaser might have to make further requisitions when it was in fact completed, he could not wait to make his requisitions on that part of the abstract which was first delivered until the second part, making the whole perfect, was received. This second part, which included the deed of appointment dated 6th September *a* 1972, was delivered on 20th August 1973 and the purchaser's solicitor made and delivered all his requisitions on the whole abstract ten days later on 30th August, which was in fact the date of completion specified in the contract.

Counsel for the vendors says that the purchaser's solicitor was at fault in doing as he did and that he was responsible for the delay by holding up his requisitions as long as he did, so that completion did not in fact take place until 15th October. On *b* the other hand, he admits that if the purchaser's solicitor was not at fault up to 20th August, when the abstract was completed by the vendors' solicitors, then he could not complain that the lapse of time which in fact took place after that date until 15th October was unreasonable or due to any fault on the part of the purchaser's solicitor.

Counsel for the purchaser, on the other hand, takes his stand firmly on the general *c* requirement in respect of unregistered land that a vendor must deliver a perfect abstract and says that condition 10(3) does not apply in the circumstances of this case. Condition 10(3) only relates, he says, to cases where the abstract is on its face apparently perfect, even if ultimately it turns out not to be so, and does not relate to a case such as the present, where the abstract as delivered was admittedly not perfect and has some essential link in the chain of title missing. In such a case, it is said, the purchaser *d* is entitled to wait, unless this deficiency is made good. This is primarily a matter of construction.

At this point I feel bound to say that I think the Law Society might well consider looking at condition 10(3) with a view to revision when the next opportunity arises. Though apparently hallowed by time, it is, to my mind, in its context avoidably obscure and uncertain in scope and, indeed, it seems that such an authority as *e* Williams on Vendor and Purchaser[1] also takes the same view that the scope of the condition is uncertain, though his criticism is perhaps not so harsh as mine. What then does it mean and what is its proper construction? I do not think the condition should be construed so as to make it necessary to deem 'perfect' any so-called abstract, however deficient. This would lead to loose conveyancing with deplorable results. Neither do I think that the argument and construction of counsel for the purchaser *f* can be right. The logical conclusion of his argument is that any deficiency, however small or unimportant, entitles the purchaser to sit back and do nothing until the deficiency is made good.

Giving the matter the best consideration I can, I think that the proper construction (which, incidentally, produces a common sense result) is that the matter must be looked at as one of substance. An abstract does not cease to be an abstract on which a pur- *g* chaser must make his requisitions within the time specified if it is only deficient in respects which are unimportant in that a solicitor investigating the title would, or ought to, assume that the gaps could be and would be likely to be filled in a way which he would expect from the information supplied in the abstract. In such a case, he ought to get on with it, raise what requisitions he can on the abstract submitted, and at the same time call for the obvious gaps to be filled. Of course, when these *h* are filled, he will be entitled to make further requisitions if such turn out to be necessary in respect of the new material. This is what I think the draftsman of the conditions must have had in mind and, without attempting to lay down any all-embracing rules, I think the words 'except for the purpose of any objections or requisitions which could not have been taken or made on the information therein contained' are included, inter alia, to protect a purchaser who, as a matter of sub- *i* stance, is baffled by some part of the abstract and really cannot guess what the true position is, or where there is some wholly unexpected defect in the title, the existence of which there is no reason a purchaser should suspect, or where the proper conclusion

1   4th Edn (1936), p 71

is that the abstract has so many deficiencies in it that it cannot really properly be
a considered to be an adequate abstract at all.

On the above construction, I consider that I must reject counsel for the purchaser's
argument in the present case. The abstract here was nearly complete and there was
no real difficulty in guessing what the position was. Indeed, the most important
missing link, namely the deed appointing the vendors as trustees of the Salisbury
Trust, was in fact referred to, albeit at the end of the schedule, in the legal charge
b to the Agricultural Mortgage Corpn dated 10th October 1972.

If, therefore, the matter ended there, I think the proper view would be that the
purchaser here ought to be held responsible for some delay in making his requisitions
and that this delay was a real contribution to completion being eventually some 46
days late. In this event, it would be necessary to decide what was the proper length of
the period of delay for which the purchaser might be held responsible, and this
c would probably involve a substantial discount of 46 days by reason of the delays
caused by the vendors such as their failure to deliver the abstract until 6th August.
As it is, in the view I take of the matter, it would be wrong in all the circumstances
to lay the blame for the delay which in fact took place as due wholly to the fault of
the purchaser.

The correspondence shows that on 14th August the purchaser's solicitor wrote
d asking for the indulgence of the vendor's solicitors, since he was going on holiday
'next week' and would not be in a position to complete by the due date. He makes
it clear, however, that the abstract was not complete, and that other solicitors besides
himself were involved on behalf of his client's bankers.

On 15th August the vendors' solicitors replied, enclosing death certificates of two
former trustees, and stated that the title was now complete. They did not apparently
e appreciate, or had forgotten, at that time that the deed of appointment of the vendors
as trustees was also missing. Then, after saying that they appreciated the purchaser's
difficulties, they reminded the purchaser's solicitor that the purchaser was under
obligation to complete by 30th August. If the matter had rested there, then there
would, I think, have been a good deal to say for the vendors' contention that the delay
to date was, as a matter of substance, the fault of the purchaser. But it does not rest
f there, and they go on to say in the last paragraph:

> 'Finally, we observe that you have sent us some enquiries but, with respect
> we feel enquiries should have been made before contract so that if the selfsame
> questions are to be asked now they should be raised as Requisitions on Title.
> However, we would prefer that all your requisitions on title are raised at the
> same time since if we have to refer any matters to the Mortgagees they can all
g > be dealt with at the same time. We await hearing from you further.'

By this last paragraph, despite their earlier reference to the completion date, it
seems to me the vendors' solicitors are accepting the position that in the circumstances
the purchaser should hold up making his requisitions until he could do so comprehensively, and their reference 'to the Mortgagees' was referable no doubt to the
h Agricultural Mortgage Corpn who held the charge already referred to over the
property. At this time, although the vendors' solicitors seem to have thought otherwise, the abstract still lacked the deed of appointment of 6th September 1972. This
was specifically referred to by the purchaser's solicitor in his letter of 16th August
and a photostat of it was in fact sent with the letter dated 20th August. This letter was,
I assume, delivered on 21st August, the next day. In all the circumstances, it seems to
j me the proper view is that by reason of their letter of 15th August, in spite of their
references to the necessity for completion on the due date, the vendor's solicitors
must be deemed to have waived the date for the requisitions until a reasonable time
after the delivery of the deed of appointment, and that the strict provisions of
condition 10(3) and (5) ought not to be applied. In fact, the purchaser's solicitor did
deliver his requisitions by letter dated 30th August, and thereafter the matter

proceeded with normal despatch on both sides, except that if the matter has to be
treated strictly, I think it might well be that the vendors were guilty of some un-   **a**
necessary delay in the resulting period, possibly no doubt because their representative
dealing with the matter in his turn went on holiday.

Legally, I consider the position is governed by the principles of waiver or promissory estoppel, however it may be classified, which are set out, for example, in the
judgment of Lord Denning MR in *W J Alan & Co Ltd v El Nasr Export & Import Co*[1].
There, after referring to *Panoutsos v Raymond Hadley Corpn of New York*[2] and *Enrico*   **b**
Furst & Co v W E Fischer Ltd[3], he said[4]:

> 'What is the true basis of those decisions? Is it a variation of the original contract
> or a waiver of the strict rights thereunder or a promissory estoppel precluding
> the seller from insisting on his strict rights or what else? In *Enrico Furst*[3] Diplock J
> said it was a "classic case of waiver". I agree with him. It is an instance of the general   **c**
> principle which was first enunciated by Lord Cairns LC in *Hughes v Metro-*
> *politan Railway Co*[5], and rescued from oblivion by *Central London Property Trust Ltd*
> *v High Trees House Ltd*[6]. The principle is much wider than waiver itself; but waiver
> is a good instance of its application. The principle of waiver is simply this: if
> one party, by his conduct, leads another to believe that the strict rights arising under
> the contract will not be insisted on, intending that the other should act on that   **d**
> belief, and he does act on it, then the first party will not afterwards be allowed to
> insist on the strict legal rights when it would be inequitable for him to do so:
> see *Plasticmoda Societa Per Azioni v Davidsons (Manchester) Ltd*[7]. There may be no
> consideration moving from him who benefits by the waiver. There may be no
> detriment to him by acting on it. There may be nothing in writing. Nevertheless,
> the one who waives his strict rights cannot afterwards insist on them. His strict   **e**
> rights are at any rate suspended so long as the waiver lasts. He may on occasion
> be able to revert to his strict legal rights for the future by giving reasonable
> notice in that behalf, or otherwise making it plain by his conduct that he will
> thereafter insist on them: see *Tool Metal Manufacturing Co Ltd v Tungsten Electric Co*
> *Ltd*[8]. But there are cases where no withdrawal is possible. It may be too late to
> withdraw; or it cannot be done without injustice to the other party. In that   **f**
> event he is bound by his waiver. He will not be allowed to revert to his strict
> legal rights. He can only enforce them subject to the waiver he has made.
> Instances of these principles are ready to hand in contracts for the sale of goods.
> A seller may, by his conduct, lead the buyer to believe that he is not insisting on
> the stipulated time for exercising an option: see *Bruner v Moore*[9]. A buyer may,
> by requesting delivery, lead the seller to believe that he is not insisting on the
> contractual time for delivery: see *Charles Rickards Ltd v Oppenheim*[10]. A seller   **g**
> may, by his conduct, lead the buyer to believe that he will not insist on a con-
> firmed letter of credit: see *Plasticmoda*[7], but will accept an unconfirmed one
> instead: see *Panoutsos v Raymond Hadley Corpn of New York*[2]; and *Enrico Furst &*
> *Co v Fischer*[3]. A seller may accept a less sum for his goods than the contracted
> price, thus inducing him to believe that he will not enforce payment of the
> balance: see *Central London Property Trust Ltd v High Trees House Ltd*[6] and *D & C*   **h**
> *Builders Ltd v Rees*[11]. In none of these cases does the party who acts on the belief

1   [1972] 2 All ER 127, [1972] 2 QB 189
2   [1917] 2 KB 47, [1916-17] All ER Rep 448
3   [1960] 2 Lloyd's Rep 340
4   [1972] 2 All ER at 139, 140, [1972] 2 QB at 212
5   (1877) 2 AC 439   **j**
6   [1956] 1 All ER 256, [1947] KB 130
7   [1952] 1 Lloyd's Rep 527 at 539
8   [1955] 2 All ER 657, [1955] 1 WLR 761
9   [1904] 1 Ch 305
10 [1950] 1 All ER 420, [1950] 1 KB 616
11 [1965] 3 All ER 837, [1966] 2 QB 617

suffer any detriment.   It is not a detriment, but a benefit to him, to have an
a   extension of time or to pay less, or as the case may be.   Nevertheless, he had
conducted his affairs on the basis that he has that benefit and it would not be
equitable now to deprive him of it.'

So here it would, in my judgment, in all the circumstances, be inequitable to allow
the vendors to insist on the strict rights to which they would have been entitled if
b   they had not led the purchaser to believe that they were not insisting on them.   The
time was in fact getting very short when they wrote the letter of 15th August and this,
coupled with the failure to deliver the deed of appointment until 20th August,
entitled the purchaser to assume that completion by 30th August would not in fact
be possible.   Any question of withdrawal of the waiver was impossible before 30th
August because the time was far too short.
c   The vendors therefore fail and the purchaser is entitled to judgment.

Action dismissed.

Solicitors: *Frere Cholmeley & Co* (for the vendors); *J M B Law* (for the purchaser).

Evelyn M C Budd Barrister.

d

Roberton v Secretary of State for the Environment and another

e   QUEEN'S BENCH DIVISION
PHILLIPS J
9th DECEMBER 1975

*Highways – Diversion – Footpaths and bridleways – Efficient use of land – Diversion for
securing efficient use of land crossed by footpath or bridleway or of other land held therewith
f   – Other land – Dwelling-house – Use to best advantage as a dwelling-house – Attributes
of dwelling-house – Safety – Peace and quiet – House occupied by Prime Minister – Footpath
crossing land held with house – Proximity of path to house causing danger to occupier from
terrorist activities – Diversion of path to safer distance–Whether house 'other land' – Whether
purpose of diversion to secure the 'efficient use' of the house – Highways Act 1959, s 111(1).*

*g   Highways – Diversion – Footpaths and bridleways – Land crossed by footpath or bridleway –
Land – Meaning – Whether restricted to soil over which footpath or bridleway runs or including
all the relevant holding of land – Highways Act 1959, s 111(1).*

Under a deed of settlement, subsequently confirmed in the Chequers Estate Act
1917, the owner of the Chequers Estate gave the estate, consisting of a mansion house
h   and surrounding land, for the purpose of it being used by successive Prime Ministers.
The object of the gift was to make the house available as the official country residence
of the Prime Minister of the day and to tempt him to live there, whatever his means
might be, so that he would enjoy the quiet of the countryside.   The estate was thereafter used by successive Prime Ministers for that purpose and to entertain visiting
statesmen and other persons of distinction in public life.   A public footpath ran
j   across the land at a distance of about 450 yards from the house.   In consequence of the
increase in assassinations, terrorism and violence in the early 1970s, the police who
were responsible for the safety of the occupants of the estate took the view that the
close proximity of the house to the path, from which the terrace of the house could be
seen, created a danger to the Prime Minister or other occupants from possible terrorist
activities.   Accordingly the trustee of the estate applied to the local authority for an

order under s 111(1)[a] of the Highways Act 1959 that the path should be diverted to a different route at a safer distance from the house. The order was made and, following a a public inquiry, confirmed by the Secretary of State on the ground that it had been 'made for the purpose of securing the efficient use of land held with that crossed by the existing path, such land being occupied by the house, Chequers Court'. The applicant applied for an order quashing the diversion order on the ground that it was not within the powers conferred by s 111(1) of the 1959 Act, in that the words, 'the efficient use of ... other land held' with the land crossed by the path, referred to the use of land as b land, e g for husbandry.

Held – The word 'land', in the expression 'the efficient use of ... other land' in s 111(1) of the 1959 Act, included buildings and therefore regard could be had to the efficient use of the house in determining whether it was expedient to make a diversion order under s 111. The question to be determined was whether the diversion was necessary c in order to enable the land, i e the house, to be used to its best advantage according to the purpose for which it was occupied. One of the attributes of a house which was used as a dwelling-house was peace and quiet. Accordingly, if the diversion of the footpath would reduce to any sensible degree the risk to the occupiers of the house from terrorist activities, then it could properly be said that the diversion of the path would help to secure the 'efficient', in the sense of the best possible and most advan- d tageous, use of the house within s 111(1). The application would therefore be dismissed (see p 695 b to d and j and p 696 h, post).

Per Phillips J. The expression 'land crossed by a footpath or bridleway' in s 111(1) of the 1959 Act is not restricted to the soil over which the footpath or bridleway runs, but refers to the area of land which constitutes the relevant holding and which for rating purposes would be described as the hereditament (see p 694 c to e, post).   e

Notes
For the diversion of public paths and the procedure for making orders, see 19 Halsbury's Laws (3rd Edn) 188-198, paras 298-306, 312-319.
For the Highways Act 1959, s 111, see 15 Halsbury's Statutes (3rd Edn) 254.
                                                                                                  f
Motion
This was an application by Kenneth Bantock Roberton for an order quashing the Wycombe District Council (Footpath No 28 Chequers Estate, Ellesborough) Public Path Diversion Order 1974 made, on the application of the Public Trustee on behalf of the Chequers Trust, by the second respondent, Wycombe District Council, and confirmed by the first respondent, the Secretary of State for the Environment, by a g letter dated 13th August 1975. The facts are set out in the judgment.

Mr Roberton appeared in person.
Harry Woolf for the Secretary of State.
The second respondent was not represented.
                                                                                                  h

PHILLIPS J. This case concerns the Chequers Estate. Across the front of the mansion house at a distance of between 400 and 500 yards there runs a public footpath. It has been used by the public for very many years, upwards of 100 or more. That user has continued since the mansion house became a residence available to the Prime Minister. As far as I can tell from the evidence, after that date the footpath continued to be so j used with satisfaction both to members of the public who liked to use it, partly in order to think that they were still going across the grounds of a mansion that was used by the Prime Minister, and also to successive Prime Ministers because it was felt that

---

a Section 111(1), so far as material, is set out at p 693 g and h, post

a such user could continue without undue interference with their occupation, and that it was a fine thing that members of the public used it as well as they. But we live in changing times and we have to adapt to them. The particular thing that has happened in this connection is the sad increase in assassination, terrorism and violence, and this has led to a fear on the part of the police, who are responsible for the safety of the occupants of Chequers, that the ready availability of the footpath at such a distance from the mansion house, from which the terrace, and the persons on the terrace, can

b be seen, will end unfortunately unless the user is restricted in future. This has led to the making of the Wycombe District Council (Footpath No 28 Chequers Estate, Ellesborough) Public Path Diversion Order 1974 made under the Highways Act 1959, s 111. It was made on 23rd October 1974. There was a public inquiry (because the Order had to be confirmed by the Secretary of State) on 6th May 1975, and it was confirmed on 13th August.

c The grounds on which it is made are thus described in the Secretary of State's letter confirming the Order, in para 2:

'The Order was made for the purpose of securing the efficient use of land held with th'at crossed by the existing path, such land being occupied by the house, Chequers Court. The present route of the path was thought to constitute a
d security risk to the occupants of the house, being within easy range of possible terrorist activities.'

In this motion, Mr Roberton, who has appeared in person and argued with great skill and moderation, seeks to quash the Order, and he has approached his task, and the decision whether to take these proceedings, very carefully and without undue haste. He told me that before starting he asked himself three questions. First of all,
e should a public right be reduced except by express statutory provisions? And to that he gave me the answer, No. Secondly, is it wise to make permanent changes in long-established practices on account of what one may hope are merely transient dangers? In effect, he says that this path has been there for 150 years and has seen many troubles in the past, and will no doubt see many troubles in the future, and that it is not right or wise to abolish it merely because of the difficulties that we are, as he hopes, tem-
f porarily enduring. So he would say, No, it is not wise. Thirdly, he asks himself, will the proposed diversion achieve its intended object? And to that again he gives a negative answer. So in effect, although as anxious as anybody for the safety of the occupants of Chequers, whoever from time to time they may be, he feels that other considerations outweigh that, and that he is right to make this application. And so it is with a full sense of responsibility that he has done so. In his affidavit in para 1
g he says:

'In moving this application . . . my sole desire is to draw attention to its possible serious effect on the protection of public rights. It is no part of my purpose to minimise the dangers which have been said to exist although I consider that these must be judged in the balance of public rights and private amenity and safety
h common in all such situations.'

So he recognises the need for protection, but is full of apprehension as to the precedents that the Order in this case may have set in other cases where the risk is even less great than he thinks it is in this case. For my part I fully accept the genuiness of his approach and the sincerity of his motives.

Before getting down to the substance of the grounds on which he makes the appli-
j cation, it is right to mention one other matter. In order to make the application he has to be a party aggrieved, and it may be that some argument could have been advanced by counsel for the Secretary of State to the effect that technically he is not a party aggrieved. Counsel does not take that point, and I only mention it because it is not desired that his failure to take it should be regarded as a concession in other cases. The first thing which I ought to say—I think it is generally understood but perhaps

not always as thoroughly as it might be—is that the powers of the court in a case of
this kind are strictly limited. Some people think, not knowing very much about it, *a*
and perhaps it is rather a flattering thought, that the court is a law unto itself and can
do what it likes, in other words exercise a discretion which has been entrusted to it
by the people. That is not the case, and the power of the court in this case is to be
found in Sch 2 to the Highways Act 1959, which is the Act under which this Order
purports to have been made. Paragraph 2 of Sch 2 provides:

> 'If a person aggrieved by a scheme or order to which this Schedule applies *b*
> desires to question the validity thereof . . . on the ground that it is not within the
> powers of this Act or on the ground that any requirement of this Act . . . has not
> been complied with . . . he may . . . make an application for the purpose to the
> High Court.'

Paragraph 3(*b*) provides: *c*

> '[the court] if satisfied that the . . . order . . . is not within the powers of this
> Act or that the interests of the applicant have been substantially prejudiced by
> failure to comply with any such requirement . . . may quash . . . the order . . .'

So the powers are limited, and to be able to quash the Order I have to be satisfied
that it is not within the powers of the 1959 Act, or that the making of the Order or *d*
the Order itself fails to comply with the requirements laid down by the Act. To all
intents and purposes, as the argument has developed here, it is a question of powers.
That is the main point. On a fair construction of the Act and on a reasonable view of
this Act, was there power to make this Order? I repeat, there is no appeal on what is
called the merits. Indeed, Mr Roberton, I think, recognises that fact and has tried to
channel his argument into submissions which would fall within Sch 2.   *e*

The first point which he takes is that this land and this mansion house are all subject
to the provisions of the Chequers Estate Act 1917, as amended. It is not necessary for
the purposes of this case to go through it in detail, but the Act is entitled: 'An Act to
confirm and give effect to a deed of settlement relating to the Chequers Estate and
other property and for purposes connected therewith.' There is annexed to the Act
a schedule which is the settlement by Sir Arthur Hamilton Lee of Chequers, who *f*
gave his house and land for the purpose of it being used for occupation by successive
Prime Ministers, or, in the event that they declined to occupy it, by other named
persons.

It was necessary for there to be an Act of Parliament for a number of reasons, one of
which at least is that the settlement would have offended the rule against perpetuities
because it is intended to endure forever. The schedule in its beginning sets out the *g*
objects of the gift, and I will return to that later.

Mr Roberton's first point is this. Under s 111 of the 1959 Act the application is to be
made by the owner, lessee or occupier of land crossed by a footpath. In this case the
application was made by the Public Trustee, and by virtue of the Chequers Estate
Act 1917 and the amending Act of 1958 the Public Trustee is what is described as the
'Custodian Trustee of the Chequers Estate'. There is no doubt that the land and all *h*
of it is vested in him; to put it in ordinary language, he is the owner of it.

So all other things being equal he would be a proper person to make the application, as indeed he did, but Mr Roberton draws attention to s 1 of the 1917 Act
which provides:

> 'The said deed of settlement is hereby confirmed, and shall have effect as if *j*
> enacted in this Act, but nothing in this Act shall prejudice or affect the right, title,
> or interest, if any, of any person in or to the Chequers Estate other than the right,
> title, or interest of the parties to the said deed of the first, second, and third parts.'

What he says about this is that the ownership as custodian trusteee is of an unusual
kind, being an encumbered ownership, the land being held in trust for the nation in

that by virtue of s 1 the Public Trustee is restrained from taking action disturbing
a the rights of the public in and to the estate.
  I do not think there is anything in this point. Ordinarily where there is a conveyance
of property or a settlement it can only affect immediately the parties to it, though of
course other persons may acquire rights under it, but it cannot affect other persons'
rights except to the extent that the settlor or the transferor enjoyed those rights. Because
it was necessary for the reason I have given, and I think other reasons, that the settlement
b should be given effect to by Act of Parliament, it was also necessary in the Act of
Parliament to insert a section preserving the rights of third parties. That I think is
the effect of s 1. So, whereas before the passing of the 1917 Act or the execution of the
settlement, members of the public had rights as members of the public over the rights
of way and on the public footpaths over the estate, nothing in the settlement or the
Act interfered with those rights in the public. They continued unabated, so far as this
c footpath is concerned, until the making of the Order in 1974. There is nothing in s 1,
as I read it, to prevent the Public Trustee as owner, if he thought fit and he did here,
albeit reluctantly, from making an application. If it were not so it would indeed be
impossible to manage the estate at all, because it is a fairly extensive estate, and if
on some part of it it were necessary in the interests, say, of husbandry, to have a footpath
diverted there would be no power in him to make an application to that end. So
d I find nothing in this first point.
  The second point is a combination of two points and is that interference of this kind
in public rights ought only to be allowed where it is expressly authorised by a particular Act of Parliament. Allied to that point, it is said that there was an earlier unsucess-
ful application to divert this footpath on different grounds which properly failed,
and that it must have been known by those responsible for that application at the
e time they made it that it was possible to apply under s 111 of the 1959 Act. The
reason they did not do so, it is said, was because they thought at that time that it was
inappropriate to the case. In my judgment these arguments take the matter no
further. Either there is power to do what has been done under s 111 or there is not.
If there is not, then the argument is superfluous; but if there is, then it is of no assistance. The fact that some earlier application was made, I do not think can help. The
f fact that there is no particular Act of Parliament dealing with this particular footpath
is really nothing to the point if s 111 in fact confers the power which purports to have
been used in this particular case.
  The third point, which in my judgment has more substance in it, relates to s 111(1)
of the 1959 Act, which provides:

g   'Where an owner, lessee, or occupier of land crossed by a footpath or bridleway
      (not being a trunk road or a special road) satisfies the local authority in whose
      area the land is situated that for securing the efficient use of the land or of other
      land held therewith or providing a shorter or more commodious path or way
      it is expedient that the line of the path or way across his land, or part of that line,
      should be diverted . . . the authority may by order . . . made by them and sub-
      mitted to and confirmed by the Minister of Housing and Local Government [do
h   various things]'

—and do what they have done in this case, which, if one looks at the schedule to the
Order, which has a plan attached to it, is to extinguish the brown footpath running
near to the mansion house and to create a new right of way which is shown purple
which runs further away starting and ending at the points between which the old
j footpath is extinguished. So the footpath will run in a loop with the effect of taking
pedestrians further away from the mansion house. Section 111(5) of the 1959 Act
provides that the Secretary of State shall not confirm an Order unless he is satisfied that
it is expedient and that the path or way will not be substantially less convenient to the
public, and there are various other matters mentioned which I need not take time
over. So going back to s 111(1), first of all there must be land crossed by a footpath

which there is in this case. Then the applicant, here the Public Trustee, must satisfy
the local authority that it is expedient—and these are the important words—'for   *a*
securing the efficient use of the land or of other land held therewith . . . that the line
of the path . . . should be diverted . . .'

It is desirable to get out of the way certain preliminary points. The application here
was made and granted on the ground that for securing the efficient use of other land
held with the land it was expedient, and so on; the other land being the land which
the mansion house constituted. It is not wholly clear on a construction of this section   *b*
what is meant by 'the land'. I read the words again: 'Where an owner . . . of land
crossed by a footpath . . . satisfies the local authority . . . that for securing the efficient
use of the land . . .' I do not think that 'the land' can be restricted merely to the
soil over which the footpath itself runs. It can obviously be open to argument in
different cases what is the extent of the land which has to be taken into consideration
in determining whether the proposal is necessary for securing the efficient use of it.   *c*
For example, suppose a house and a garden of one acre with a footpath across it, and
an application by the owner of the house and garden, is the land, the efficient use of
which is being secured, the whole of the house and garden or only part of it? While
it must be a matter of argument in every case, I see no reason why the words 'the
land' should not extend to the holding in question or what in rating parlance would
be called the hereditament. There are well-understood rules there for determining   *d*
what is a single hereditament. So it seems to me that it might well have been arguable
here that the mansion house itself was part of the land and that really it was not necessary to make use of the words 'other land held therewith'. I only say this in passing
because the case has been argued and decided on the footing that the mansion house
was 'other land held therewith', and it is right, I think, for me to deal with it on that
footing too. I did not wish to leave the point unnoticed in case the judgment in this   *e*
case should come up for consideration in other cases.

What is submitted by Mr Roberton about this is expressed in para 5 of his affidavit:

> 'The interpretation of the words "the efficient use of . . . other land held there-
> with" to mean in this context the private enjoyment of a house raises fundamental
> questions about the nature of nuisance which can be said to reduce the efficiency   *f*
> of use and the extent of other land held therewith. It is admitted that a footpath
> across a domestic lawn might properly be the subject of a diversion application,
> but this need not be true of a footpath separated from the lawn by a hedge or,
> as the present case may imply, of any footpath on the estate of a mansion house
> however distant from the house.'

g

He goes on to say that there is nothing in the 1959 Act or this section of the Act about
security provisions or fear of assassination or terrorism or anything of that kind,
and that no one at the date of the passing of this Act—though I think he would say
even today—could say that the prevention of terrorism has got anything to do with
securing the efficient use of the land.

There are, I think, two separate points involved here. One is that he is very much   *h*
afraid that this application will be the thin end of the wedge for all sorts of other
applications in all sorts of different circumstances and will spell disaster for those who
have at heart the preservation of public rights of way in the countryside. Of course
I can only deal with the case before me, but I would certainly deprecate this case
being used as any kind of charter in other dissimilar cases. Indeed it has to be noted,
I think, that an Order cannot be made under this section unless it secures the approval   *j*
of the local authority who have to be satisfied not merely that the facts are made out
but that it is expedient. It then has to be confirmed by the Secretary of State who will
usually hold an open inquiry and test local opinion, and is not to confirm it unless the
matters as set out in s 111(5) for the protection of the public are satisfied. But that
aspect of the matter has nothing to do with me. I am concerned with the second point

which arises in this connection, and that is: is it a legitimate exercise of the powers
a granted by s 111, and, in particular, can it be said to secure the efficient use of the land
when the purpose has nothing whatever to do with husbandry or the use of the land as
land, but is really designed to secure the safety from assassination of the occupants of a
dwelling-house? That is an important point which merits and has received serious
arguments on both sides. It is clear in the first place that the word 'land' here includes
land and buildings. There is therefore no doubt that the mansion house, whether
considered as part of the land or whether considered as being held with the land, is
b itself land. It seems to me that in applying those words, by which I mean 'securing
the efficient use of the land', one has to take account of circumstances as they exist
at the date of the application or of the inquiry if there is one. Thus, whereas it may well
be that when the Act was passed as recently as 1959, so quickly have things changed,
no one would have thought then of the dangers of terrorism or assassination, that does
not mean that they must necessarily be excluded from consideration in deciding
c whether it has or has not been made out to the satisfaction of the local authority
that the diversion is necessary to secure the efficient use of the land. What the words
seem to me to mean is this: that one has to look to see whether the diversion is necessary in order to enable the land to be used to its best advantage according to the
purpose for which it is occupied. Land, of course, can be occupied for all sorts of pur-
d poses. In the case of houses it can be used for private occupation. In the case of land
thought of as land it can be used for husbandry and agriculture, and so on. Buildings
themselves can be used for different purposes, not only as private residences but as
old people's homes, offices, shops and so on. It seems to me that what is necessary
to secure the efficient use of land will differ in different cases at different times and in
different ages according to the circumstances as they obtain from time to time.
e   This mansion house, although of an unusual character, is used as a dwelling-house,
and the only differences between it and any other dwelling-house are its size and its
splendour, its situation and the importance of the persons to whose use it is devoted.
It is quite clear, I think, from the objects of the gift referred to in the schedule to the
Chequers Estate Act 1917 that the whole intention is that Prime Ministers from time
to time, particularly if they are what is described as 'city-bred men', should have a
f periodic contact with this most typical rural life which will enable them to preserve
a just sense of proportion between the claims of town and country. It goes on:

> 'To the revolutionary statesman the antiquity and calm tenacity of Chequers
> and its annals might suggest some saving virtues in the continuity of English
> history and exercise a check upon too hasty upheavals, whilst even the most
> reactionary could scarcely be insensible to the spirit of human freedom which
g > permeates the countryside of Hampden Burke and Milton.'

And it ends up:

> 'The main features of this scheme are therefore designed not merely to make
> Chequers available as the official country residence of the Prime Minister of the
> day, but to tempt him to visit it regularly and to make it possible for him to
h > live there, even though his income should be limited to his salary.'

One of the attributes that one looks for in any dwelling-house, particularly one of
this kind, I suppose, is that there should be peace and quiet, and I would have thought
that if there is any real risk of disturbance by terrorists or any likelihood of assassination that would be inclined to make the occupation of the dwelling-house disadvan-
j tageous. If the diversion of the footpath will reduce that risk to a sensible degree,
then in my judgment it will help to secure that the dwelling-house is put to the best
possible and most advantageous use. I think that giving fair weight to the words of
the section it could then be said that what is being done is to secure the efficient
use of the dwelling-house, which is within the word 'land' in the section. So I reach
the conclusion that on a fair reading of the words of the section the object which was

in mind in this application and in the making of the Order was one within the contemplation of the Act. I am unable to find that what was done here was beyond the powers *a* conferred by s 111 of the Highways Act 1959.

There are certain other matters raised in argument. It was said that there was no evidence that the use by the public of the path in the past had resulted in a diminution in the use of the estate by the Prime Minister. That may be so, but of course if there is a real apprehended risk that the continued use of the footpath by the public in the future may lead to assassination, then what has happened in the past, although *b* not irrelevant, is by no means conclusive. As the state of terrorism and violence mounts no doubt there would come a time, or might come a time, when those whose duty it is to advise Prime Ministers might advise them that they could no longer safely stay at Chequers, or if they could that they ought not to go on those parts of the ground visible from that footpath. Another matter is this. It was said that there is no evidence here, beyond evidence of opinion, on which it was possible to conclude either that *c* there was a danger, or, if there was a danger, that the diversion of the footpath was going to reduce it. That is a question of evidence. I only have jurisdiction to interfere if something has gone wrong in point of law, and I can only really look at the facts if it can be said that there is no evidence to justify the conclusions of fact come to by the inspector. I agree that the conclusions here are based substantially on the opinion of the police authorities. I accept readily that that opinion ought not to be *d* accepted conclusively just because they say so, but I do not think that is what the inspector did. Everybody's opinion was given; he listened to everybody's opinion and he recorded it. He reached this conclusion in para 11(1) of his report where he said: 'On the question of security the Police evidence is quite clear and positive and I conclude that their expert view must be accepted'. I do not read that as accepting it just because that is what they said. It is quite clear, I think, that he looked into it and *e* heard what everybody else said, and he was satisfied that their evidence was evidence which ought to be accepted. It is noteworthy here that part of the police evidence was to this effect. In particular, they said in para 3(13) that just to the west of the drive there was a clear view of the terrace from the old path at a range of not more than 475 yards. 'Any skilled marksman using modern, easily portable firearms would have no difficulty in hitting a person or group of persons on the terrace at that range.' *f* So there was evidence on which the view that the inspector and the Secretary of State reached could be based, and it is not for me or within my jurisdiction to say that it is wrong. So this point, I think, is not really something that I can go into beyond the extent that I have. Lastly it is said that there is no real evidence that the new footpath would be any safer than the old footpath. Again, that is a matter of opinion. It is perfectly true that the police would have preferred quite a different solution, and this *g* solution is a compromise. Nonetheless, it was their view that half a loaf is better than no bread, and that it would be safer but not the ideal solution which they would have preferred. Again that is a matter of fact, and it is not something that I can interfere with.

So none of the grounds that have been carefully and persuasively argued by Mr Roberton in my judgment justifies an interference by the court. Accordingly the *h* application must be refused.

Application dismissed.

Solicitor: *Treasury Solicitor.*

Janet Harding   Barrister.

a

Congreve v Home Office

QUEEN'S BENCH DIVISION
PHILLIPS J
25th, 26th NOVEMBER 1975

b COURT OF APPEAL, CIVIL DIVISION
LORD DENNING MR, ROSKILL AND GEOFFREY LANE LJJ
28th NOVEMBER, 4th DECEMBER 1975

Public authority – Statutory powers – Misuse of power – Exercise of power for unlawful
purpose – Validity – Licence – Power to revoke licence – Threat to exercise power for unlawful
c *purpose – Wireless telegraphy – Broadcast receiving licence – Colour television – Licence*
holder obtaining new licence before expiry of current licence – Purpose to avoid payment
of increased statutory fee coming into force on date of expiry of existing licence – Home
Office threatening to revoke new licence unless licence holder pay additional sum representing
difference between increased fee and former fee – Home Office having no lawful authority to
demand payment of additional sum – Whether threatened revocation of licence valid –
d *Wireless Telegraphy Act 1949, s 1(4).*

The plaintiff was the owner of a colour television set. He held the appropriate broadcast receiving licence issued to him under the Wireless Telegraphy (Broadcast
Licence Charges & Exemption) Regulations 1970[a]. The licence was due to expire on
31st March 1975. In January 1975 it was announced that the fee prescribed for the
issue of a colour television licence was to be increased from £12 to £18. On 20th
e February the Home Secretary made the Wireless Telegraphy (Broadcast Licence
Charges & Exemption) (Amendment) Regulations 1975[b] which gave effect to that
increase. Those regulations were expressed to come into operation on 1st April 1975.
In order to avoid payment of the increased fee, the plaintiff decided to obtain a
new licence before the expiry of his existing licence. Accordingly, on 26th March,
f he obtained a new licence from a post office and paid the prescribed fee of £12
which, under s 2(1)[c] of the Wireless Telegraphy Act 1949, was payable 'on the issue
of the licence'. The licence was dated 26th March and was expressed on its face to
expire on 29th February 1976. It came to the attention of the Home Office that a
considerable number of licence holders were taking the same course as the plaintiff
and that in consequence a substantial part of the anticipated revenue from the issue
g of licences was being lost to the Crown. Accordingly, the Licence Records Office,
as agent for the Home Secretary, wrote to the plaintiff, in common with other
licence holders who had taken the same action, demanding payment of an additional
sum of £6 for the licence issued to him on 26th March and threatening that, if that
additional sum were not paid, the Home Secretary, in exercise of his power under
s 1(4)[d] of the 1949 Act, would revoke the plaintiff's licence. By a subsequent letter
h dated 11th November, the Records Office told the plaintiff that, if he did not pay
the additional £6, his licence would be allowed to run for eight months from 31st
March and thereafter the licence would be revoked as from 1st December. None
of the letters offered, on revocation of the licence, to refund the £12, or any part
thereof, paid by the plaintiff for the issue of the licence. The plaintiff refused to pay
the £6, and brought an action against the Home Office claiming a declaration that
j revocation of the licence would be unlawful, invalid and of no effect.

---

a SI 1970 No 548
b SI 1975 No 212
c Section 2(1), so far as material, is set out at p 700 *h*, post
d Section 1(4), so far as material, is set out at p 700 *f*, post

Held – The licence issued to the plaintiff on 26th March had been obtained lawfully
and was a valid licence for the period expressed on its face. At the date when it was   *a*
issued the Home Office had no lawful authority to require, as a condition of its
issue, a sum greater than the prescribed fee which was then current, i e £12. It followed
that the subsequent demand made on the plaintiff for the payment of an additional
sum of £6 was an unlawful demand and it would be an unlawful exercise of the Home
Secretary's power of revocation to revoke, or to threaten to revoke, the licence as a
means of enforcing that demand. Accordingly the plaintiff was entitled to the   *b*
declaration sought (see p 709 *d*, p 710 *f* to *j* and p 711 *a*, p 715 *b d* and *e* to *f*, p 716 *a b d*
and *h* and p 718 *h* to p 719 *b*, post).

Attorney-General v Wilts United Dairies (1922) 91 LJKB 897 and Padfield v Minister
of Agriculture, Fisheries and Food [1968] 1 All ER 694 applied.

Per Lord Denning MR. The power conferred on the Home Secretary to revoke
licences is one which must be exercised in accordance with the law, taking all relevant   *c*
considerations into account, omitting irrelevant ones, and not being influenced by any
ulterior motives. Where a licensee has done nothing wrong, the Home Secretary
cannot lawfully revoke the licence without offering to refund the licence fee and not
even then except for good cause (see p 708 *f* and p 709 *f* and *g*, post).

Notes   *d*
For judicial control over the exercise of discretionary powers, see 30 Halsbury's Laws
(3rd Edn) 687-689, paras 1326, 1327.

For the Wireless Telegraphy Act 1949, ss 1, 2, see 35 Halsbury's Statutes (3rd Edn)
94, 95.

Cases referred to in judgments   *e*
Associated Provincial Picture Houses Ltd v Wednesbury Corpn [1947] 2 All ER 680, [1948]
    1 KB 223, [1948] LJR 190, 177 LT 641, 112 JP 55, CA, 45 Digest (Repl) 215, *189*.
Attorney-General v Wilts United Dairies (1922) 91 LJKB 897, 127 LT 822, 38 TLR 781,
    HL; affg 37 TLR 884, CA, 25 Digest (Repl) 153, *638*.
Brocklebank Ltd v R [1925] 1 KB 52, 94 LJKB 26, 132 LT 166, 16 Asp MLC 415, CA, 17   *f*
    Digest (Reissue) 522, *251*.
Liverpool Corpn v Arthur Maiden Ltd [1938] 4 All ER 200, 45 Digest (Repl) 362, *139*.
Marshall Shipping Co (in liquidation) v R (1925) 41 TLR 285, 17 Digest (Reissue) 522, *252*.
Padfield v Minister of Agriculture, Fisheries and Food [1968] 1 All ER 694, [1968] AC 997,
    [1968] 2 WLR 924, HL, Digest (Cont Vol C) 280, *1237a*.

Cases also cited   *g*
Fawcett Properties Ltd v Buckingham County Council [1960] 3 All ER 503, [1961] AC 636,
    HL.
Thorne v Motor Trade Association [1937] 3 All ER 157, [1937] AC 797, HL.

Action   *h*
By a specially indorsed writ issued on 14th November 1975, the plaintiff, Andrew
Christopher Congreve, brought an action against the Home Office. By his statement
of claim the plaintiff alleged (i) that in March 1975 he had been issued with a wireless
telegraphy licence, being a television broadcast receiving licence, and had paid therefor
the sum of £12 being the sum prescribed by the Wireless Telegraphy (Broadcast
Licence Charges & Exemption) (Amendment) (No 2) Regulations 1971 made pursuant   *j*
to s 2 of the Wireless Telegraphy Act 1949; (ii) that the licence continued in force until
29th February 1976; (iii) that by letter dated 11th November 1975 written for and on
behalf of the Home Office by one L T Byford, the Home Office had threatened to
revoke the licence as from 1st December 1975 unless the plaintiff paid the Home
Office the sum of £6, and (iv) that the plaintiff contended and the Home Office denied

that such revocation by the Home Office would be illegal, invalid and of no effect. The
a plaintiff claimed a declaration that revocation of the licence by the Home Office
by their servants or agents or howsoever, would be unlawful, invalid and of no effect.

Gerald Levy for the plaintiff.
Roger Parker QC and *Harry Woolf* for the Home Office.

b
PHILLIPS J. The Wireless Telegraphy (Broadcast Licence Charges & Exemption)
Regulations 1970 were amended by the Wireless Telegraphy (Broadcast Licence
Charges & Exemption) Amendment Regulations 1975. The 1975 regulations came into
operation on 1st April 1975. They were made on 20th February 1975 and laid before
Parliament on 3rd March 1975. The effect of those amendment regulations is to amend
c the 1970 regulations, the principal regulations, and the effect of the amendments
broadly is this: to increase the fee payable for a licence for colour television from £12
to £18 with effect from 1st April 1975. That intention had been made public even
before the regulations were made on 20th February 1975. It is necessary to give notice
so that people may know in advance of the increase, which will enable them to put
the money by to pay the fee when the time comes.

d On 26th March 1975 the plaintiff obtained a colour television licence expiring on 29th
February 1976 for which he paid £12, the fee then in force. He did not tell the post
office clerk that he already had a licence expiring on 31st March. If he had done
so, and this clerk had observed the instructions then in force in the post office, she
would not have issued another licence to him before 1st April 1975. At all times
material to this case, the responsible Minister has been the Secretary of State for the
Home Department, and the management of the television licensing system has been
e in the hands of the National TV Licence Records Office. On 30th April the manager
of that office wrote to the plaintiff a letter, part of which I shall read. In the first
paragraph he drew attention to what had happened and then continued:

'By renewing the licence before the existing licence expired the increased fee
has been avoided and we have been instructed by the Home Office, for whom we
f act as agent in operating the television licensing system, not to allow this. I am,
therefore, required to ask you to remit the additional fee of £6 together with the
enclosed receipt form within 14 days of receipt of this letter, using the enclosed
prepaid envelope. [Then there were some instructions which I need not read, and
the last paragraph read:] In the event of failure to pay the additional fee, we
have been instructed by the Home Office to revoke the licence taken out in ad-
g vance. It will then no longer be valid and you will have to renew your licence
which expired at the end of March 1975 at the new rate.'

This seems to me to have been a very tactless letter, especially the first three lines
of the last paragraph, which I would have thought were calculated to raise the
hackles of someone preening himself at having scored a neat point over the authori-
h ties by obtaining in advance a licence at what would after 1st April 1975 be a cheap
price.
Seeing that at the date the licence was issued the fee had not been increased, the use
of the word 'avoided' is inept, and that of the words 'not to allow this' was bound to
infuriate by its superior tone. But as is so often the case there is another side to the
matter, and that is explained in paras 13 and 14 of the affidavit of Mr Johnson, an
j assistant secretary in the Home Office. He deposed as follows in para 13:

'The vast majority of licence holders have not sought to avoid the impact of
the higher fees and the Home Office believes that these people would have a
legitimate grievance if a minority, who whether by not disclosing the full facts
or deliberately or intentionally or through departmental or Post Office administrative failures were allowed to escape the clear intention that they should,

following the expiry of their existing licences, pay the announced higher fees. Persons such as the Plaintiff who held overlapping licences are not under the *a* proposed revocation being put in any worse position by the Home Office than the majority who did not take the course of renewing their licences early as was done by the Plaintiff. 14. About 500,000 colour television licences expired with March 1975 [that means the end of March 1975]. Of these about 17,000 were renewed early, that is to say, at a fee of £12 instead of £18. Of these 17,000 licence holders, all but 5,000 have now paid out the balance of £6.' *b*

The letter of 30th April 1975 was followed by others to a similar effect to which I shall refer later, namely those of 27th August, 11th November and the letter intended to be sent today, 26th November. Neither party has moved from his original position, and on 14th November the plaintiff issued a writ claiming the following relief:

'A Declaration that the revocation of the Plaintiff's said television broadcast *c* receiving licence by the Defendant, by his servants or agents or howsoever, would be unlawful invalid and of no effect.'

The first thing which it is necessary to do is to consider the powers which the Home Secretary has. I do not propose to take time for the purpose of this judgment to explain the devolution by which the Home Secretary has become the responsible *d* Minister. The relevant Act is the Wireless Telegraphy Act 1949, s 1 of which provides, under the heading 'Licensing of wireless telegraphy':

'(1) No person shall establish or use any apparatus for wireless telegraphy except under the authority of a licence in that behalf granted by the Postmaster General, and any person who establishes or uses any station for wireless telegraphy or instals or uses any apparatus for wireless telegraphy except under and in *e* accordance with such a licence shall be guilty of an offence under this Act. [Then there is a proviso.]
'(3) A wireless telegraphy licence shall, unless previously revoked by the Postmaster General, continue in force for such period as may be specified in the licence.
'(4) A wireless telegraphy licence may be revoked, or the terms, provisions or *f* limitations thereof varied, by a notice in writing of the Postmaster General served on the holder of the licence',

and there follow other words which I need not read.

Subsection (5) contains provisions dealing with the duty of the holder of the revoked or expired licence to return it. Section 2 deals with charges for wireless telegraphy *g* licences and provides in sub-s (1):

'On the issue or renewal of a wireless telegraphy licence, and, where the regulations under this section so provide, at such times thereafter as may be prescribed by the regulations, there shall be paid to the Postmaster General by the person to whom the licence is issued such sums as may be prescribed by regulations to be made by the Postmaster General with the consent of the *h* Treasury, and different provision may be made in relation to different licences, according to the nature, terms, provisions, limitations and duration thereof . . .'

The proviso I do not think is relevant. Section 3 is a section giving futher powers to make regulations, but it is not under that section that the regulations in question here have been made. The 1970 regulations were made in the exercise of the powers *j* granted by ss 1 and 2 of the 1949 Act. Regulation 4 provides:

'(1) On the issue of a broadcast receiving licence of the type and description specified in Schedule 1 the licensee shall pay an issue fee of the amount specified in relation to that type and description of the licence in Schedule 1, whatever may be the duration of the licence . . .

a
'(3) On and after 1st April 1971 [that was subsequently amended to 1st July 1971] on the issue of a broadcast receiving licence of a type and description specified in Schedule 3 the licensee shall pay an issue fee of the amount specified in relation to that type and description of licence in Schedule 3 whatever may be the duration of the licence.'

b
The schedule sets out the appropriate fee, that relevant for the present purposes being up to and including 31st March 1975, £12; 1st April 1975 and thereafter, £18.

I turn now to make certain findings. First of all, licences are not renewed. There is plainly here a departure between what the statute and the rules say and what the administrative practice has been. Even in the letters exhibited to the affidavits the words 'renewal' and 'renew' are used. Indeed it is difficult to avoid them, because anybody getting a new television licence still thinks that he is renewing his old one.
c
In fact that is not the case. The licences issued are licences for a fixed term of 12 months and every time somebody goes to the post office on the expiry of his old licence he gets a new licence. That fact very much conditions the way in which the administration of these duties is carried out in practice. Secondly, the power to charge, which of course is confined to that conferred by the statute and the order, is in the order limited to charging on the issue of a new licence. Thirdly, the power to revoke or
d
waive contained in the Act is used administratively to correct errors which arise. For example: (1) errors made by the post office itself; (2) errors made by the subject, for example when a licence is taken out prematurely perhaps by forgetting the date of expiry of the old one, or the husband or wife perhaps forgetting that the wife or husband has already got one; or the licence is taken out late, for example after an interval after the expiry of the old one during which time the set has continued to be
e
used. That also requires adjustment because if there has been a gap then the period of the new licence has got to be abridged, for otherwise the subject has been using a television set for a period in respect of which it is not licensed and for which he has paid nothing. Fourthly, all licences expire on the last day of the month, so that were a licence, for example, first issued on, say, 4th March it would expire at the end of Febrary the following year. The subsequent year the new licence would be issued
f
to expire at the end of February the next year. Fifthly, after an announcement of the proposed increases in the licence fees, instructions were issued to post offices to the clerks not to issue new licences before 1st April 1975 except to (1) those people who had not had a licence before, or (2) those who had a licence before but whose licence expired on 28th February or earlier. The person whose licence expired on 31st March 1975 was meant to go to the post office on 1st April or thereafter and acquire a new
g
licence expiring on 31st March 1976. No doubt the habits of different people differ about the purchase of a second and subsequent television licence. Some people never buy one at all and just go on using their set. Some people get it before their licences expire, and some people, perhaps the majority, go a little while after their licences have expired. In that event their new licence would expire at the same date as the expiry date of the existing licence, in the next year. To give an example, suppose
h
a licence expires on 31st March, and the subject goes along to the post office to get a new one on 5th April, having listened to his set on 1st, 2nd, 3rd and 4th April. What the position was between those dates, when he used his set without a licence, may be open to debate. Technically, at all events, it looks like the commission of an offence under s 1 of the 1949 Act; though it may be that the new licence (which would expire on 31st March of the following year) would operate retrospectively.
j
I do not find it necessary to decide that question.

That I think is a sufficient statement of the background to make the arguments, which have been most helpfully presented to me, intelligible. The plaintiff's case is constructed along these lines. It is said that it is a fundamental principle of English law that no Minister of the Crown has power to demand the payment of money from any subject for any purpose unless authorised to make that demand by express

plain words of the statute or other legislative enactment. Secondly, it is submitted
that where such a question is in issue the onus is on the Minister to establish that what *a*
he has done has lawful authority. Reliance is placed on *Attorney-General v Wilts United
Dairies Ltd*[1] and the same case in the House of Lords[2]. It is said that here the Home
Secretary has threatened to exercise a power of revocation to enforce an unlawful
demand of a sum of money. Reliance is placed on the letters of 30th April, 27th
August, 11th November and 26th November. In effect, and these are my words,
not counsel for the plaintiff's, what is being said is that the effect of what was done *b*
is to antedate or to seek to antedate the coming into operation of the 1975 regulations.
It is said that the power of revocation is a discretionary power, and one which can
only lawfully be exercised for the purpose for which it was conferred, and cannot be
exercised for an unlawful purpose. It is said that the exercise here, or the threatened
exercise, of the power is not a lawful exercise of the discretion, because it is a disguised
and, indeed, according to counsel for the plaintiff, not a very well disguised, threat, as *c*
an indirect method of levying money the recovery of which is unlawful. Reliance
is also placed on *Brocklebank Ltd v R*[3], *Marshal Shipping Co v R*[4] and *Liverpool Corpn v
Arthur Maiden Ltd*[5].

In a sentence, it is being said that the demand of a payment, as the price for not
revoking, if the payment is not authorised, is plainly unlawful. So, therefore, is the
threatened revocation. Reliance is placed, of course, on *Associated Provincial Picture d*
Houses Ltd v Wednesbury Corpn*[6], especially the judgment of Lord Greene MR. That
does not exhaust the very helpful submissions that have been made, but it sufficiently
summarises, I think, the general way in which they were put.

It is said by counsel for the Home Office that all the Minister is doing is to give
effect to the obvious intention of Parliament that those whose need for a new licence
did not arise until 1st April or later should pay £18 and no less; and he further submits *e*
that the licence granted on 26th March to the plaintiff which was in the nature of a
concurrent licence—because of course he already had a licence not due to expire until
31st March—was a nullity, and not a licence at all, with the consequence that the
plaintiff's position has to be considered not on 26th March but on 1st April. That
second submission is, I think, in the nature of an alternative one.

At this point I can make certain preliminary findings. First of all I accept counsel *f*
for the plaintiff's broad propositions of law as propositions of law. They are well
founded, I think, on the authorities cited and in accordance with the principles as
generally understood. Secondly, I accept counsel for the Home Office's summary
of the matter, the factual matter that is, looked at from an administrative point of
view. Thirdly, I do not accept the submission that the licence of 26th March was a
nullity. I think it was a true licence, and I see no reason why one cannot have concurrent *g*
licences any less than one can have a person detained in pursuance of concurrent
sentences of imprisonment. It seems to me that if one licence was found to be defective for some reason, there would be no impediment to reliance on the other licence.

Turning then to the main question, which I think is a difficult one, the answer must
hang less on a statement of the legal position and an examination of the authorities
and more on an anlysis of the statute, the order made under it, and especially, I think, *h*
precisely what it is that the parties, and in particular the Home Secretary, have done.
I think the most helpful way in which I can express my conclusions in case they are of
any assistance to the Court of Appeal, which I gather is shortly to be troubled with
this matter, would be to make a series of findings. First of all, I am satisfied that the

---

1   (1921) 37 TLR 884
2   (1922) 91 LJKB 897
3   [1925] 1 KB 52
4   (1925) 41 TLR 285
5   [1938] 4 All ER 200
6   [1947] 2 All ER 680, [1948] 1 KB 223

power to charge is limited by s 2 of the 1949 Act and reg 4(1) and (3) of the 1970 regu-
a lations to the occasion of the issue of a licence. Secondly, the document of 26th March
1975 was a true licence issued on that date operating concurrently with the plaintiff's
other licence. Thirdly, in my judgment, the Home Secretary was entitled in the exercise of his discretion to refuse to issue a licence in March except to those who had not
had a licence previously, or to those whose old licence expired before March. In my
judgment that is a legitimate exercise of his discretion. I do not accept the submission
b made by counsel for the plaintiff that it is tainted by the underlying desire to charge
persons applying before 1st April a fee higher than that authorised by the amended
1975 regulations. I think there is a difference, and I think it is a difference which is more
than a quibble. I think what the Home Secretary was doing was seeking to prevent
people before 1st April who did not need a licence geting one at the cheaper rate
then in force. Fourthly, in my judgment, a great deal turns here on the nature of the
c power to revoke. I have already read s 1(4) of the 1949 Act:

> 'A wireless telegraphy licence may be revoked, or the terms, provisions or
> limitations thereof varied, by a notice in writing of the Postmaster General served
> on the holder of the licence or by a general notice applicable to licences of the
> class to which the licence in question belongs published in such manner as may
d be specified in the licence.'

It is clear that that power is a wide one. It is not unfettered, because no power is unfettered, and there is no power which the courts cannot review; but the grounds of
review are now well settled, and include cases where the powers are exercised in
bad faith, or capriciously or arbitrarily or whimsically as it is sometimes put, or for
e some ulterior purpose, and, of course in the circumstances summarised in the judgment of Lord Greene MR in the *Associated Provincial Picture Houses* case[1]. It is now
well understood, I think, that very often those descriptions overlap. They are merely
ways of saying that the court is satisfied that there has been an abuse of power. I
think that it is cardinal to the consideration of this case, forgetting for the moment
what the Home Secretary in fact did, for me to decide whether in a case like this he
f could have used the power to revoke simpliciter, without any request or demand for
money. In my judgment, the Home Secretary was entitled so to use that power to
revoke the plaintiff's licence at a date appropriate to the fee which he had paid,
calculated at the new rate from 1st April, which would be 1st December 1975. It
seems to me it would have been quite unobjectionable if the Home Secretary had
said: you have paid £12; your previous licence did not expire until 31st March;
g you did not need a new licence before the 1st April; I propose to exercise my power
of revocation to revoke your concurrent licence so that it will buy you as much
listening time as a licence issued on 1st April would have done. I conclude that that
would have been a lawful exercise of the Home Secretary's discretion. I think it
could reasonably be claimed that such a revocation served an apparent purpose of
the legislation, namely that licences required for a period commencing on or after
h 1st April 1975 should be paid for at the new rate. I do not accept what counsel for the
plaintiff has said about that, that that is a covert way of charging before 1st April
licence fees which came into operation on 1st April. The question is whether a revocation in those circumstances would have been *unlawful*, not whether it would have
been administratively prudent.
    Assuming that that is right, it seems to me that the final question in this case is:
j what precisely has the Home Secretary done? Like most things one can look at it in
different ways. Was it an attempt at what the plaintiff claims, to exact an additional
fee, that is to say £6, for which in my judgment there was no lawful authority, or was
it rather a notice by the Home Secretary of an intention to revoke (which I have

---

1   [1947] 2 All ER 680, [1948] 1 KB 223

found would have been lawful) coupled with an opportunity to the plaintiff to pay
the additional fee if he thought fit? This matter turns on the letters, some of which **a**
I have already mentioned but not read. The letter of 30th April I have already read
and it is certainly in strong terms:

'By renewing the licence before the existing licence expired the increased fee
has been avoided and we have been instructed by the Home Office, for whom we
act as agent in operating the television licensing system, not to allow this. I am, there- **b**
fore, required to ask you to remit the additional fee of £6 together with the enclosed receipt form within 14 days of receipt of this letter, using the enclosed
prepaid envelope. [And the last paragraph:] In the event of failure to pay the
additional fee, we have been instructed by the Home Office to revoke the licence
taken out in advance. It will then no longer be valid and you will have to renew
your licence which expired at the end of March 1975 at the new rate.'   **c**

That letter is a little ambiguous because it does not specify the date at which it is
intended to revoke the licence in the event of the failure to pay the £6, but the later
letters become more specific. The letter of 8th August was in these terms. The first
two paragraphs summarised the previous correspondence, and the letter continued:

'Currently the additional fees due from [the plaintiff] and Mr Hart are still **d**
outstanding [so again here it is true to say as counsel for the plaintiff says that
they are demanding an extra £6], and in view of the Home Secretary's statement
we will shortly be writing to each of them asking for the sum of £6·00. [This
letter I should have said is written to the plaintiff's solicitors.] On receipt of the
remittance we will allow each licence to run for a period of twelve months from
the expiry date of the previous licence [interpolating there that would have **e**
involved in the case of the plaintiff an extension of one month from 29th March
1975 to 31st March 1976] and your clients will then be notified to this effect.
However if [the plaintiff] and Mr Hart choose not to make the additional payment
their licences will only be allowed to run for eight months [and I interpolate
there eight months at 30 shillings a month is £12 which of course had been paid]
from the expiry date of the previous licence [namely 31st March] and will then **f**
be revoked. Letters of revocation will be sent to both of them after eight months
have elapsed and if they use television sets after that date another licence will
have to be purchased at the current rate.'

On 27th August, after further intermediate correspondence, the National TV Licence
Records Office wrote to the plaintiff a letter which in a way sounds as though the
writer was slightly unaware of some of the previous correspondence: **g**

'According to our records [he writes almost as though it has come as a great
surprise to him], earlier this year you obtained a television licence at a time when
you already had a licence which was not due to expire before 31 March. Licences
issued after that date were chargeable at the new rates of licence fees announced
by the Home Secretary on 29 January 1975 [I think I have done him an injustice **h**
because he goes on], and we therefore wrote to you, at the request of the Home
Office on behalf of whom we operate the licensing system as an agency service,
to ask you to send an additional amount of £6·00 so that we could arrange for
the licence that you obtained recently to run for twelve months from the expiry
date of your previous licence. We told you that your most recent licence was
liable to be revoked if the additional amount was not paid. We do not appear to **j**
have received the additional payment from you. If you will now send a remittance
for £6 together with our receipt form (I enclose a pre-paid envelope for this
purpose), we will then arrange accordingly for the licence to run for a period of
twelve months from the date of expiry of your previous licence. If you do not
make this additional payment now, your licence will be allowed to run for eight

a months from the date of your previous licence and will then be revoked, in accordance with arrangements announced in a reply (a copy of which I enclose) given by the Home Secretary on 16 June to a question in the House of Commons.'

The answer is attached. It was written on 11th November, and is the letter particularised in the statement of claim. The first paragraph refers to the previous correspondence, to the activities of the Parliamentary Commissioner for Administra-

b tion, and the paragraph ends:

'The Home Secretary has accordingly informed the House of Commons today that these arrangements still stand and has given the House a note, a copy of which I enclose, setting out how individual categories of licence holders are affected. If you would now send me a remittance of £6, together with the enclosed receipt forms, I will arrange for the validity of your licence to be extended

c to 31 March 1976. I am sorry to have to remind you that, unless you do so, your television licence will be revoked as from 1 December 1975. If thereafter you use a television set without holding a valid current licence, I am afraid that you will render yourself liable to prosecution under section 1 of the Wireless Telegraphy Act 1949.'

d Finally there is a letter dated 26th November 1975, which has not yet been sent, waiting in the wings so to speak, which reads in part:

'We have written to you previously to explain that by means of a new licence having been obtained before the expiry date of the old one you avoided payment of the increased fee which came into force on 1 April 1975 and would have been due if you had taken out a new licence on expiry of the old one. On the instruc-

e tions of the Home Office, for whom we operate the television licensing system, we ask you for remittance of the £6 increase so that this matter might be dealt with as if this licence had been obtained at the proper time and at the appropriate fee. We should have then been able to extend the validity of your licence until 31 March 1976. We explained that if the £6 was not paid your licence would be allowed to run for 8 months from the expiry of the previous licence covering

f use of television at your address. We sent you a reminder of these arrangements on 11 November 1975. The sum of £6 has not been received. Accordingly I am directed by the Secretary of State to give you NOTICE that the LICENCE obtained by you in March 1975 is hereby REVOKED with effect from 1 December 1975. This notice is issued under section 1(4) of the Wireless Telegraphy Act 1949 [as amended, and so on]. If you are to continue using a colour television set you

g should take out a fresh licence promptly at the current fee of £18. Provided that the new licence is taken out as from the date on which the existing licence is revoked, the licence will of course run for a full year.'

And they enclose a form of application.

As I have indicated, it seems to me that at the end of the day a great deal turns on

h how one approaches those letters, in particular the letter of 11th November because that is the one specified in the statement of claim. Counsel for the plaintiff invites me to an attractive way of putting it, that is to say that this is a demand with menaces. He is not suggesting it is a criminal offence, because he is not suggesting that those who made it did not believe in the honesty and propriety of what they are doing. In other words he interprets it as meaning: 'Pay £6 or your licence will be revoked.' I must

j say that although that is an attractive way of looking at it, I do not think it is the right way of looking at it. I think it may be the fault of those who wrote the letters if that is the way in which people have come to look at it, and I think that the letters could have been better phrased. It seems to me that if one bears in mind the facts which I have set out, somebody in the position of the plaintiff was, as a result of what the Home Secretary was doing, being put in this position: he was being left with a number

cc

of open choices, and there were a number of possibilities open to him; there were at
least three. It is quite plain from the correspondence that his licence would be re- *a*
voked on 1st December, after his £12 had bought eight months' viewing time at
rates current on 1st April. Then he had two alternatives. He could give up watching
television altogether, or he could get himself a new licence. If he got himself a new
licence it would be a licence for a period of 12 months at the then current rate, and he
would be in the same position as others who took out a licence on or after 1st April;
or alternatively, if he preferred and obviously in many ways it would be more con- *b*
venient, he could pay £6, in which case the licence issued to him would be extended
from 29th Februay 1976 to 31st March 1976. To some extent it is almost impossible
to avoid playing with words, because it depends how you look at it. I think the proper
way of looking at it is this. What the Home Secretary is doing is preventing people
whose licences did not expire until 31st March 1975 from getting a new licence at the
old rate. Counsel for the plaintiff says the way it ought to be looked at is that what *c*
was being done was to demand the payment of £6 (for which there was no justification) as the price of not revoking the licence. One can so describe it if one wishes;
but it does not really seem to me that that is the reality of the situation at all. The
truth as it seems to me, and all that is being said in those letters, is that there are a
number of choices open to him. On its true interpretation I do not read it as being a
demand for £6 in the sense in which that is interpreted by counsel.   *d*
    At the end of the day I think that everything turns—subject of course to my crucial
finding about the exercise of the power to revoke simpliciter—everything turns on
the view that one takes of those letters, in particular that of 11th November. Taking
the view which I do, it follows that the substratum of counsel for the plaintiff's case
goes, because that is founded, and all its elaboration is founded, on the one foundation
that what is being made here is an unlawful demand for the payment of money.   *e*
Taking the view I do of those letters, it of necessity follows that in my judgment that
case is not made out, and that the plaintiff is not entitled to the declaration which he
seeks. I give judgment accordingly.

Action dismissed.

                                                                                f
Solicitors: *Herbert Smith & Co* (for the plaintiff); *Treasury Solicitor.*

Appeal
The plaintiff appealed against the judgment of Phillips J.

Gerald Levy for the plaintiff.   *g*
Roger Parker QC and *Harry Woolf* for the Home Office.

                                                                 Cur adv vult

4th December. The following judgments were read.

                                                                                h

LORD DENNING MR. Every person who has a colour television set must get a
licence for it. It is issued for 12 months, more or less. The fee up to 31st March 1975
was £12. As from 1st April 1975 it was increased to £18. This increase was announced
beforehand by the Minister, but it did not become law until the very day itself,
1st April 1975. Up till that date the department could only charge £12 for a licence. *i*
On and after that date it was bound to charge £18. This gave many people, who
already held a licence, a bright idea. Towards the end of March 1975 they took out new
licences at the then existing fee of £12. These would overlap their old licences by a
few days, but the new licences would last them for nearly the next 12 months. So
they would save the extra £6 which they would have had to pay if they had waited

after 1st April 1975. To my mind there was nothing unlawful whatever in their trying
a to save money in this way. But the Home Office were furious. They wrote letters to
every one of the overlappers. They said, in effect: 'We are not going to let you get
away with it in this way. You must pay up the extra £6 or we will revoke your new
licence'. I will quote the very words:

b
'By renewing the licence before the existing licence expired the increased fee
has been avoided and we have been instructed by the Home Office, for whom
we act as agent in operating the television licensing sytem, not to allow this.
I am, therefore, required to ask you to remit the additional fee of £6 together with
the enclosed receipt form within 14 days . . . In the event of failure to pay the
additional fee, we have been instructed by the Home Office to revoke the licence
taken out in advance. It will then no longer be valid and you will have to renew
c your licence which expired at the end of March 1975 at the new rate.'

So the overlappers would forfeit the £12 which they paid and would have to pay
£18 for another licence.
A lot of timid ones succumbed to that threat. They paid up the £6. But the strong-
minded ones did not. They went on using their television sets under their £12
d licences. Two months later, as a sop, the Home Office modified their threat. They
said to the recalcitrants: 'Pay up the £6 or we will revoke your new licences after
eight months. By that means we will make you pay at the increased rate.' I will
again set out their very words of the letter of 27th August 1975:

'If you do not make this additional payment now, your licence will be allowed
to run for eight months from the date of your previous licence and will then be
e revoked . . .'

After getting that letter, again the ranks of the overlappers broke. Some paid up.
But others stood firm. Their £12 licences were still in force. They went on using
their television sets. On 11th November 1975 the Home Office gave another warning:

f
'If you would now send me a remittance for £6 . . . I will arrange for the
validity of your licence to be extended to 31st March 1976. I am sorry to have to
remind you that, unless you do so, your television licence will be revoked as
from 1 December 1975. If thereafter you use a television set without holding a
valid current licence, I am afraid that you will render yourself liable to
prosecution . . .'

g A few days later the Home Office carried out their threat. On Wednesday 26th
November 1975—even whilst an appeal to this court was known to be pending—
they sent out notices revoking the £12 licences with effect from 1st December 1975.
I set out the words of the letter of revocation:

'This sum of £6 has not been received. Accordingly, I am directed by the
h Secretary of State to give you NOTICE that the LICENCE obtained by you in March
1975 is hereby REVOKED with effect from 1 December 1975 . . . If you are to
continue using a colour television set, you should take out a fresh licence
promptly at the current fee of £18.'

If those notices are valid, every one of the overlappers must stop using his television
j set or be guilty of a criminal offence. They appeal to this court to help them.
Mr Congreve is their leader. His case is brought to test all of them. Counsel on
his behalf submitted that the demand of the Home Office for £6 was an unlawful
demand; that the licence was revoked as a means of enforcing that unlawful demand;
and that, therefore, the revocation was unlawful.
Counsel for the Minister submitted that, by taking out an overlapping licence,

Mr Congreve was thwarting the intention of Parliament; that the Minister was
justified in using his powers so as to prevent Mr Congreve from doing it.   *a*
    Now for the statutory provisions. The granting of television licences is governed by
the Wireless Telegraphy Act 1949, and the regulations made under it. The 1949 Act
said (so far as material):

> '1.—(1) No person shall . . . instal or use any apparatus for wireless telegraphy
> except under the authority of a licence in that behalf granted by the [Minister].   *b*
> '(2) A licence . . . may be issued subject to such terms, provisions and limitations
> as the [Minister] may think fit . . .
> '(3) A licence shall, unless previously revoked by the [Minister], continue in
> force for such period as may be specified in the licence.
> '(4) A . . . licence may be revoked, or the terms, provisions or limitations thereof
> varied, by a notice in writing of the [Minister].   *c*
> '2.—(1) On the issue or renewal of a . . . licence, and . . . at such times thereafter
> as may be prescribed by the regulations, there shall be paid to the [Minister] by
> the person to whom the licence is issued such sums as may be prescribed by
> regulations . . .'

The 1970 and 1971 regulations provided:

> 'On and after 1st July 1971 on the issue of a broadcast receiving licence . . . the   *d*
> licensee shall pay an issue fee of the amount specified . . . in Schedule 3, whatever
> may be the duration of the licence.'

The amount specified in Sch 3 for colour television was £12.
    The 1975 regulations came into operation on 1st April 1975 and said: 'These
Regulations . . . shall come into operation on 1st April 1975 . . . The principal   *e*
Regulations shall be amended by substituting . . . (b) for "£12" . . . "£18".'
    Now for the carrying out of the statutory provisions. Undoubtedly those statutory
provisions give the Minister a discretion as to the issue and revocation of licences.
But it is a discretion which must be exercised in accordance with the law, taking all
relevant considerations into account, omitting irrelevant ones, and not being influenced
by any ulterior motives. One thing which the Minister must bear in mind is that the   *f*
owner of a television set has a right of property in it; and, as incident to it, has a right
to use it for viewing pictures in his own home, save insofar as that right is prohibited
or limited by law. Her Majesty's subjects are not to be delayed or hindered in the
exercise of that right except under the authority of Parliament. The statute has conferred a licensing power on the Minister; but it is a very special kind of power. It
invades a man in the privacy of his home, and it does so solely for financial reasons so   *g*
as to enable the Minister to collect money for the Revenue. It is a ministerial power
which is exercised automatically by clerks in the Post Office. They cannot be expected
to exercise a discretion. They must go by the rules. The simple rule—as known to
the public—is that, if a man fills in the form honestly and correctly and pays his
money, he is to be issued with a licence.
    Now for a first licence. Test it by taking a first licence. Suppose a man buys on   *h*
26th March 1975 a television set for the first time for use in his own home. He goes
to the Post Office and asks for a licence and tenders the £12 fee. He would be entitled to have the licence issued to him at once; and it would be a licence to run from
the 26th March 1975 until 29th February 1976. I say 'entitled', and I mean it. The
Home Secretary could not possibly refuse him. Nor could he deliberately delay the
issue for a few days—until after 1st April 1975—so as to get a fee of £18 instead of £12.   *j*
That would not be a legitimate ground on which he could exercise his discretion to
refuse. The Minister recognises this. He allows newcomers who apply for a licence
before 1st April 1975 to get their licence for the next 12 months for the £12 fee.
    Now for a second licence. But the Minister says that it is different with a man who
already has a licence for a television set expiring on 31st March 1975. The Minister

says that he is entitled to refuse to issue such a man with a new licence until after the
a old licence has expired. See what this means. The man must wait until some time
in April to get his new licence. It may be two or three days—or even weeks—before
he can get to the Post Office. Meanwhile, he will be guilty of a criminal offence
every time he turns on the television. The Minister says that does not matter. He
will make it right afterwards. This seems to me a very cynical approach to the law.
I think the man is entitled to protect himself—and keep within the law—by taking
b out a new licence before the end of March 1975. Take a simple case. Suppose on the
26th March 1975 a man is going away for a month and wants to get his new licence
at once so that his family can use the television whilst he is away. He goes to the Post
Office and tenders the £12 fee. The Minister could not lawfully refuse to issue it.
He would have to issue the then current licence, that is from the 26th March 1975
onwards for 12 months, more or less. There would be no legitimate ground on which
c he could refuse. Not until 1st April 1975 could the Minister have demanded the £18;
and then he must demand the £18, and no less. That is a simple illustration of an
overlapping licence which is perfectly lawful. So with many others. To my mind
any man is entitled, if he pleases, to take out an overlapping licence; and the Minister
has no discretion to stop him. It would be a misuse of his power for him to do so.
In the present case, however, there is no difficulty. On 26th March 1975 Mr Congreve
d went to the Post Office. The Minister did not refuse to issue him with a licence. The
lady clerk did not even ask him whether he had an existing licence. Mr Congreve
filled in the form. He paid his money, £12. She issued him with a licence from 26th
March 1975 to last until 29th February 1976. That licence was obtained perfectly
lawfully. The Minister cannot dispute it. Nor does he now; though he did before the
judge.

e   Now for the power of revocation. But now the question comes: can the Minister
revoke the overlapping licence which was issued so lawfully? He claims that he can
revoke it by virtue of the discretion given him by s 1(4) of the 1949 Act. But I think not.
The licensee has paid £12 for the 12 months. If the licence is to be revoked—and his
money forfeited—the Minister would have to give good reasons to justify it. Of course,
if the licensee had done anything wrong—if he had given a cheque for £12 which
f was dishonoured, or if he had broken the conditions of the licence—the Minister
could revoke it. But, when the licensee has done nothing wrong at all, I do not think
the Minister can lawfully revoke the licence, at any rate, not without offering him
his money back, and not even then except for good cause. If he should revoke it
without giving reasons, or for no good reason, the courts can set aside this revocation
and restore the licence. It would be a misuse of the power conferred on him by
g Parliament: and these courts have the authority—and I would add, the duty—to
correct a misuse of power by a Minister or his department, no matter how much he
may resent it or warn us of the consequences if we do. *Padfield v Minister of Agriculture, Fisheries & Food*[1] is proof of what I say. It shows that when a Minister is
given a discretion—and exercises it for reasons which are bad in law—the courts can
interfere so as to get him back on to the right road. Lord Upjohn[2] put it well when
h he said:

      '. . . [the Minister] is a public officer charged . . . with the discharge of a public
      discretion affecting Her Majesty's subjects; if he does not give any reason for his
      decision it may be, if circumstances warrant it, that a court may be at liberty to
      come to the conclusion that he had no good reason for reaching that conclusion
j   and order a prerogative writ to issue accordingly.'

      Now for the reasons here. What then are the reasons put forward by the Minister
in this case? He says that the increased fee of £18 was fixed so as to produce enough

1 [1968] 1 All ER 694, [1968] AC 997
2 [1968] 1 All ER at 719, [1968] AC at 1061, 1062

revenue for future requirements. It was calculated on previous experience that no
one would take out an overlapping licence before the 1st April 1975—or, at any rate, *a*
that no appreciable number of people would do so. When he found out that many
more were doing so, he tried to prevent it so far as he could. He gave instructions to
the clerks that anyone who applied towards the end of March 1975 for an overlapping
£12 licence should be told to come back on or after the 1st April 1975, and thus made
to pay the increased fee of £18. His policy would be thwarted, he said, and the
revenue rendered insufficient, if large numbers of people were allowed to take out *b*
overlapping licences. He said, too, that other licence holders (being the vast majority)
would have a legitimate grievance. So he considered it proper to revoke the overlapping
licences of those who had acted contrary to his policy.

Are those good reasons? I cannot accept those reasons for one moment. The
Minister relies on the intention of Parliament. But it was not the policy of Parliament
that he was seeking to enforce. It was his own policy. And he did it in a way which *c*
was unfair and unjust. The story is told in the report of the Parliamentary Commissioner[1]. Ever since 1st February 1975 the newspapers had given prominence to
the bright idea. They had suggested to readers that money could be saved by taking
out a new colour licence in March 1975 instead of waiting till after the 1st April 1975.

The Minister did nothing to contradict it. His officials read the articles and drew
them to his attention. They raised the query: should a letter be written to The Times, *d*
or should an inspired question be put in Parliament, so as to put a stop to the bright
idea? But the Minister decided to do nothing. He allowed the bright idea to circulate without doing anything to contradict it. And all the time he kept up his sleeve
his trump card—to revoke all overlapping licences. Thousands of people acted on the
bright idea; only to be met afterwards by the demand, 'Pay another £6'.

The conduct of the Minister, or the conduct of his department, has been found by *e*
the Parliamentary Commissioner to be maladministration. I go further. I say it was
unlawful. His trump card was a snare and a delusion. He had no right whatever to
refuse to issue an overlapping licence or, if issued, to revoke it. His original demand,
'Pay £6 or your licence will be revoked', was clearly unlawful—in the sense that it
was a misuse of power—especially as there was no offer to refund the £12, or any
part of it. His later demand, 'Pay £6 or your licence will be revoked after eight *f*
months', was also unlawful. Suppose that, owing to mistaken calculation, the original
£12 had been found inadequate. Would it be legitimate for the Minister to say after
eight months: 'I am going to revoke your licence now and you must take out a new
licence'? I should think not. The licence is granted for 12 months and cannot be
revoked simply to enable the Minister to raise more money. Want of money is no
reason for revoking a licence. The real reason, of course, in this case was that the *g*
department did not like people taking out overlapping licences so as to save money.
But there was nothing in the regulations to stop it. It was perfectly lawful; and the
department's dislike of it cannot afford a good reason for revoking them. So far as
other people are concerned (who did not have the foresight to take out overlapping
licences) I doubt whether they would feel aggrieved if these licences remained valid.
They might only say: 'Good luck to them. We wish we had done the same.' *h*

There is yet another reason for holding that the demands for £6 to be unlawful.
They were made contrary to the Bill of Rights[2]. They were an attempt to levy money
for the use of the Crown without the authority of Parliament; and that is quite enough
to damn them: see *Attorney-General v Wilts United Dairies*[3].

My conclusion is that the demands made by the Minister were unlawful. So were
the attempted revocations. The licences which were issued lawfully before the 1st *j*
April 1975 for £12 cannot be revoked except for good cause; and no good cause has

___

1 Seventh Report of the Parliamentary Commissioner for Administration, Session 1974-75,
   680
2 1688 (1 Will & Mar Sess 2 c 2)
3 (1921) 37 TLR 884, (1922) 38 TLR 781

been shown to exist. They are, therefore, still in force and the licensees can rely on
a them until they expire at the date stated on them.

I would add only this. In the course of his submissions, Mr Parker QC said at one
point—and I made a note of it at the time—that if the court interfered in this case, 'it
would not be long before the powers of the court would be called in question'. We
trust that this was not said seriously, but only as a piece of advocate's licence.

b **ROSKILL LJ.** The plaintiff is a partner in a very well-known firm of solicitors in
the City of London. He has taken on himself the burden of challenging the action of
the Post Office acting on behalf of the Home Office, the defendants in this action, in
threatening to revoke a colour television licence issued to him at the Throgmorton
Avenue Post Office, 57 London Wall in the City of London on 26th March 1975. The
counter clerk at that office did not ask whether the plaintiff already possessed such a
c licence in force at the date of his application. She issued him without demur with the
licence for which he asked, date stamping it for 26th March 1975, completing the form
with the plaintiff's name and private address and giving the expiry date of the licence
which she issued as the last day in February 1976, that is to say 29th February 1976,
since 1976 is a leap year. This last mentioned date was almost one calendar month
short of the period of twelve calendar months from the date of issue but her action
d conformed with what we were told was the normal post office practice in the case of a
television licence such as the plaintiff received.

In return for that licence the plaintiff paid the sum of £12 in cash. That sum, and I
regard this fact as of crucial importance, was at that date the maximum sum lawfully
exigible on behalf of the Crown in respect of the issue of any colour television licence
on that date.

e In fact, unknown to the counter clerk, the plaintiff was at that date in possession of a
previous colour television licence which had been issued to him on 28th March 1974,
and expired on 31st March 1975. Therefore, at the date of the application, the plaintiff
had in force a valid colour television licence and if his new licence acquired validity
on its issue on 26th March, it follows that for the period from 26th March to 31st March
1975 (both dates inclusive) the plaintiff possessed two valid licences in respect of the
f same television installation at the same address and had unnecessarily paid a
relatively small extra sum to the Crown by way of duty in respect of these six overlapping days.

This apparent waste of money by the plaintiff and apparent resulting benefit to
the Crown has not caused distress to the plaintiff nor has the extra duty been received with gratitude by the appropriate servants of the Crown. The reason in each
g case is not hard to seek. On 29th February 1975, that is just over one month before the
plaintiff made the application, the present Home Secretary had with the consent of
the Treasury made the Wireless Telegraphy (Broadcast Licence Charges and Exemption) (Amendment) Regulations 1975[1]. I shall call that 'the 1975 order'. That order
was laid before Parliament on 3rd March 1975 and, not having been the subject of
timeous or any Parliamentary disapproval, came into operation on 1st April 1975
h but not one moment before that date. The relevant provision in the 1975 order will
be found in reg 3. That regulation provided that the £12 fee to which I have referred
should be increased on and from that date to £18.

The plaintiff was on 26th March 1975 aware of the pending change. One did not
need to be a distinguished city solicitor to be so aware. It is common knowledge
that possible ways whereby the incidence of this additional burden might be avoided
j or, if one prefers to use the language of counsel for the Home Office in argument, the
alleged intention of Parliament thwarted, had already been widely discussed in certain
national newspapers. It is obvious from paras 10 and 11 of the report[2] of the

---

1   SI 1975 No 212
2   Ordered by the House of Commons to be printed 15th November 1975

Parliamentary Commissioner into this matter published last month that this discussion
had been extremely unwelcome in the Home Office. That department had intended   **a**
to put into action the same procedure that had been used on previous occasions when
there had been a change of duty to a higher rate in order to forestall—or again to
borrow the words of counsel for the Home Office to thwart—the action of those
who like the plaintiff might be minded to act as he ultimately did for the purpose,
neither wholly unusual nor usually regarded as illegal, of saving themselves money
if they lawfully could do so, albeit at the expense of others perhaps less fortunately   **b**
placed or less well advised. The proposed action, to which no publicity had previously
been given or was apparently intended to be given on this occasion, was simple enough.
Post Office counter staff—apparently known as 'countery' (see the letter of 9th May;
in the short time available I have not been able to trace that word in any dictionary
of repute or in Sir Ernest Gowers's book for the Civil Service on 'Plain Words')—
were to be instructed to refuse any application for a licence (I avoid the word 'renewal'   **c**
for a reason which will appear in a moment) where in any case the applicant's current
licence did not expire until after the date on which the higher duty became payable,
such an applicant being invited to re-apply after that date. This instruction was not to
apply to those applying for a television licence for the first time, i e those who had not
got a current licence in force at the time of their application: see paras 8 and 9 of the
report.   **d**
　　I have avoided the use of the word 'renewal' because, although that is exactly what
most people would call an application for a fresh licence to run consecutively with an
existing licence, when one looks at s 2 of the Wireless Telegraphy Act 1949 it seems that
the granting of every licence, whether a first licence or a subsequent consecutive
licence, is an 'issue' of a licence within that section and not a 'renewal'. That was
accepted in argument.   **e**
　　The supposed justification for this intended action was, it seems, that the Home Office
took the view that 'the Secretary of State is not obliged to issue licences if he does not
want to': see para 11 of the report and also the letter to the plaintiff's solicitors
of 4th November 1975. I will consider this point later.
　　For some reason this so-called administrative action, whether legally justifiable   **f**
or not, did not serve to prevent the plaintiff's application on 26th March succeeding.
It is not necessary to detail the controversial correspondence which followed. No
criticism of a government department could be more devastating than that contained
in the Parliamentary Commissioner's report. It is no part of our duty in this court to
condemn the conduct of the Home Office. If their various actions vis-à-vis the
plaintiff after 26th March were lawful, they do not become unlawful because the
Home Office conducted the whole matter both before and after that date with   **g**
lamentable incompetence. If their actions were at any time unlawful, they cannot be
made lawful merely because the Home Office had acted, if they had, with extreme
administrative efficiency and the most laudable of motives in serving what they believed to be the true public interest. No doubt in 1919 the Food Controller thought
that the levy which he sought to impose on distributors of milk was a levy to be imposed
in the public interest, as it may well have been. But that did not prevent this court   **h**
and the House of Lords unhesitatingly and unanimously holding the levy to be
unlawful as an unauthorised charge on the subject made without clear Parliamentary
sanction: see *Attorney-General v Wilts United Dairies*[1].
　　I of course accept that the courts must not exercise their undoubted powers of control over the executive merely to penalise administrative incompetence or to extend
those powers beyond well-established limits merely as a means of showing judicial   **j**
disapproval of a particular course of action otherwise lawful. But that said, it is or at
least used to be a commonplace in matters of public administration that sound

1　(1922) 91 LJKB 897, 38 TLR 781

administration must rest on a sound legal basis. Much of the controversy that has

a arisen in this case arises because so much has been done or has been sought to be done as a matter of so-called executive or administrative discretion claimed to have been conferred by the 1949 Act and the various orders made under it. For good reason or bad, the 1975 order was only brought into operation on 1st April 1975. It was of no effect whatever before that date. Yet the Home Office sought to anticipate its effect by executive or administrative action in the way I have described. As at present ad-

b vised, I can see no reason why the 1975 order should not have been drafted so as to attain the result which the defendants now contend that they were entitled to seek, to attain in this case first by their intended refusal of 'renewal' before 1st April 1975 and then when that failed by their declared intention to revoke the licence issued to the plaintiff on 26th March 1975 unless the plaintiff paid an extra £6 as the price of avoiding that revocation. Call it what you will—a demand, a threat or

c administrative action designed to avoid the thwarting of the intention of Parliament that all holders of licences whose validity began on and after 1st April 1975 should pay a duty of £18 and not £12—the intention of the Home Office as declared in their letter of 11th November is obvious if the words used in that letter are to be given ordinary plain meaning in the English language. It was that letter which led to the issue of the present writ. See Messrs Herbert Smith & Co's letter of 14th November

d 1975. I am content to accept that part of the submission of counsel for the Home Office in which he invited us to look only at that letter and to ignore all the ante-cedent correspondence save insofar as it led up to that letter.

I have I am afraid repeated much of what Lord Denning MR has already said about the facts but it is impossible closely to analyse the rival contentions of the parties without so doing. It is however a remarkable fact, unusual in litigation in my experi-

e ence, that the two extremely able arguments to which we had the advantage of listening last Friday seemed to me to have no point of contact at all. They appeared to proceed like parallel lines far apart. The plaintiff's case was simplicity itself. He received the licence in return for the payment of the only sum then lawfully exigible, namely £12. He is threatened with revocation during its currency unless he pays a further £6. That he claims is a demand for a payment unauthorised by

f Parliament and contrary to the Bill of Rights and a long line of famous judicial authorities to which it is not necessary to refer.

The Home Office's case is equally simple. The demand, if such it was, was not an unathorised demand. The licence ought never to have been issued to the plaintiff on 26th March as in fact it was. The plaintiff's licence, to use a colloquialism, escaped through the net owing to an administrative error. If the full facts had been known to

g the counter clerk that licence would not have been issued. The plaintiff ought not to have had two concurrent licences in force at the same time—it was suggested with more apparent enthusiasm before Phillips J than this court that the licence issued on 26th March was a nullity at any rate when first issued, a contention which the learned judge rejected. But it was argued that, assuming the licence became effective at any point of time after its issue, the threatened revocation if the extra £6

h were not paid was the lawful exercise of the Secretary of State's discretion to revoke that licence entrusted to him under s 1 of the 1949 Act in order thereby to enable the intention and policy of Parliament to be fulfilled and not thwarted. To decline to revoke that licence in those circumstances would be for the Secretary of State to join with the plaintiff in attaining the plaintiff's objective instead of carrying out his constitutional duty of fulfilling the intention of Parliament and the policy declared

j by Parliament and of correcting the untoward consequences of previous administrative error.

I agree with counsel for the Home Office that it is necessary closely to examine the background to this dispute in order to see whether what was written in the letter of 11th November 1975 was lawful or not. It is not enough simply to assert that this was a threat to revoke unless payment of money was forthcoming and thus an unlawful demand. Nor, with great respect to the learned judge, do I think the problem is answered by calling the letter and its predecessors a giving to the plaintiff of a **a** number of 'perfectly open choices' for in truth every option offered (if 'option' be the right word) was and was intended only to be one of the several ways laid down by the Home Office in which the plaintiff could avoid the threatened revocation of the licence. None of these so-called options accorded him the right which he was claiming to retain his licence unrevoked without further payment until its validity expired on 29th February 1976. **b**

I therefore retrace my steps to the beginning. To my mind, as I have already said, the most important single fact in this case is that the plaintiff secured the issue of, as I think, a valid colour television licence on 26th March 1975 in return for the payment by him of the only fee then lawfully exigible, namely £12, for the period stated on the face of the licence. It is no doubt true that according to the administrative practice by which the Home Office were then seeking to work he should not then have **c** got that licence. But I can see no reason whatever why, if he were not asked, he should have revealed that he still held a television licence valid for a few days more. An application for a television licence is not a proposal for a contract uberimma fides whereunder there is a duty to disclose all material facts. If those who levy tax wish to impose on the subject a duty of disclosure of any particular kind, such as exists in certain fields of income tax law, they should take statutory power lawfully to require such disclosure. **d** I can see nothing wrong in what the plaintiff did on 26th March for he was well entitled if he wished so to arrange his affairs as to minimise his liability to tax of any kind.

I confess I have been greatly troubled by the Home Office claim that the Secretary of State has an unfettered discretion to grant or withold a licence unless, as counsel for the Home Office conceded, the refusal was wholly arbitrary. I am well aware of what has been said in *Associated Provincial Picture Houses Ltd v Wednesbury Corpn*[1] and **e** *Padfield v Minister of Agriculture, Fisheries and Food*[2] regarding judicial control over the exercise of executive powers. Nothing I am about to say goes in any way outside or beyond what was authoritively laid down in those cases. But the law does not stand still and those cases, while stating the relevant principles, leave open their application to the particular facts of particular cases which from time to time come before the courts. **f**

I ventured to put to counsel for the Home Office in argument what the position would have been on his argument on the facts of this case if the counter clerk on instructions had in fact refused the plaintiff a licence on 26th March and the 1st April had been a Sunday or Bank Holiday on which no licence could have been obtained. Was it not inevitable that on 1st April the plaintiff if he used his set would have committed a criminal offence? If it was, was it a proper exercise of discretion to refuse **g** a licence if it must or even in all probability would, if the plaintiff, being a busy man, was unable to find time to buy a licence on a 1st April which was not a Sunday or Bank Holiday, lead to the commission of a criminal offence? On those assumed facts might not the plaintiff, if he were swift to move as he has been in this case, have obtained an order of mandamus on some day between 27th and 31st March directed to the Secretary of State to issue such a licence so as to avoid the plaintiff committing **h** a criminal offence on 1st April?

I was surprised by the reply of counsel for the Home Office that this was legal fantasy because these were not the facts of the present case. It was, he suggested, fanciful to suppose that there could or would be a prosecution on those facts which I have posed. With great respect, the commission of a criminal offence depends on whether one is committed and not on whether there is an executive decision not to **j** prosecute for fear of some outraged judicial comment that would, as counsel for the Home Office conceded, be likely to follow a prosecution based on facts such as I have

---

1 [1947] 2 All ER 680, [1948] 1 KB 228
2 [1968] 1 All ER 694, [1968] AC 997

posed. So to exercise an executive discretion as inevitably to cause or to be likely
a to cause a breach of the criminal law seems to me hardly likely to encourage respect
for the law or indeed for those who would then in those circumstances be directly
responsible for its breach.

I do not find it necessary to decide this point since a licence, as I think a valid licence,
was issued to the plaintiff on 26th March. But I wish to make it clear that for my part
I am not without further argument accepting that the Secretary of State in such a
b case has such an unfettered discretion or that the courts could not in such a case
interfere with that discretion without going one centimetre outside the principles
laid down in the *Wednesbury Corpn*[1] and *Padfield* cases[2]. If the Secretary of State
wishes to put his position in this respect beyond all argument, he should seek the
necessary Parliamentary powers—if he can obtain them.

I have already said that I think the licence issued on 26th March was a valid
c licence. Counsel for the Home Office suggested that there could not be two valid
licences in force at the same time. Whether or not there can be two precisely concurrent licences validly in force at the same time for the same installation does not
arise for decision in this case, as for example where two applicants, perhaps a husband
and wife, have each applied for a licence for the same installation on the same day
neither knowing of the application by the other. But I can see no reason why over-
d lapping licences should not be valid. Either this licence was valid when issued until
it either expired or was revoked, or it was not. If it was not, I find it difficult to see
on what principle it acquired sudden validity on 1st April. If it were originally invalid, it would seem to me always invalid. This last contention was not advanced,
rightly I think, because it would involve that the plaintiff has held no valid licence
since 1st April. Therefore like the learned judge I hold that this was a valid licence
e when issued. No more than £12 could then have been lawfully exacted for the issue
of that licence.

Is it then a lawful exercise of the undoubted power of revocation possessed by the
Secretary of State for him subsequently to seek to revoke that licence in order to exact
from the plaintiff in relation to a part of the licence period arising on and after 1st
April 1975 a sum of money which could not lawfully have been exacted from him in
f relation to that same or indeed any other period of time when the licence was first
issued?

That I think is the real question which has to be answered on this appeal. I hope
I do no injustice to the argument of counsel for the Home Office if I say that it
really rested on the submission that only in this way could effect be given to what he
claimed to have been the plain intention of Parliament that on and after 1st April
g the licence fee should be £18 and that that plain intention could not and should not be
allowed to be thwarted by persons such as the plaintiff who before 1st April 1975 had
successfully procured the issue of television licences extending beyond that date when
there was no need for them to do so since they possessed a licence which was valid at
least up to that date.

It was noticeable how much counsel for the Home Office relied on the report of the
h Parliamentary Commissioner in order to support this argument. That the intention
of the Home Office emerges from that report is clear. But that intention and the
intention of Parliament are two different things. The latter, at any rate in the majority
of cases, is to be ascertained only from the relevant legislation be it statute or delegated
legislation. How the Home Office interpreted or sought to administer that legislation
is irrelevant. I therefore turn back to the relevant legislation. Reading the 1975
j order with the 1970 and 1971 orders[3], which it amends, I read these as enacting no

---

1   [1947] 2 All ER 680, [1948] 1 KB 223
2   [1947] 2 All ER at 683, [1948] 1 KB at 231
3   See the Wireless Telegraphy (Broadcast Licence Charges & Exemption) Regulations 1970
    (SI 1970 No 548) and the Wireless Telegraphy (Broadcast Licence Charges & Exemption)
    (Amendment No 2) Regulations 1971 (SI 1971 No 3295)

more and no less than that on and after 1st April 1975 every licensee shall on the issue
of the relevant type and description of broadcast receiving licence pay an issue fee of *a*
(so far as relevant) £18. I am quite unable to read this legislation as having any application at all to anyone who has lawfully taken out a licence before 1st April 1975,
whether or not in law he required such a licence before that date. I can see nothing
in these orders which would justify me in imputing to Parliament an intention to
prevent the early issue of television licences. Assuming—as already stated, it is only
an assumption—that the Secretary of State could lawfully have refused to issue the *b*
plaintiff with a licence before 1st April, he did not so refuse. Can he then properly
exercise his power of revocation so as to force the plaintiff for all practical purposes
into the same position as if there had been such an initial refusal before 1st April
1975? As I have already said, it would not have been difficult to frame the 1975 order
so as to achieve the result for which the Home Office now contend though it would
probably have involved altering the structure of the various orders issued between *c*
1970 and 1975—a simple amendment such as the 1975 order made would not have
sufficed. But that is neither here nor there. If the Home Office want to attain the result
they have sought to attain, they must obtain the necessary legislative powers. In my
view they have not got them and did not possess them at the material time and they
cannot be allowed to act as if they had possessed them through what I regard as a
misuse of the power of revocation.   *d*
   I have arrived at this result without regard to the fact at no time in the correspondence was it ever suggested that, if the plaintiff's licence were revoked, there would
be any refund of any part of the £12 which he paid on 26th March. Paragraph 16 of
the Parliamentary Commissioner's report shows that such a refund was considered
as a possible alternative if revocation took place. But reg 8 of the 1970 order prohibited any refund on revocation save with ministerial and Treasury consent. In *e*
the absence of any public communication of the fact that such a refund was under
consideration, the recipient of the various letters (and the plaintiff was not the only
recipient of such letters) might have been forgiven if he had thought that a further
consequence of the threatened revocation would have been the loss of the benefit
of so much of the £12 as related to the period between the dates of revocation and
the expiry of the original licence plus an obligation to pay a fresh fee of £18, a part of *f*
which would be referable to that same period thus, in the absence of a refund, enabling
the Crown to receive duty twice in respect of the same period. There is no evidence
that the Treasury was ever prepared to authorise such a refund. But I regard this
as irrelevant to the issue we have to decide. Nonetheless this would appear to be a
logical consequence if the main argument of counsel for the Home Office be accepted.
   I have also ignored as equally irrelevant the unchallenged evidence that in the past *g*
the only times when licences have been revoked were when cheques given for
licences have been dishonoured, an obviously proper use of the power given by the
1949 Act. In the result therefore, with very great respect to the able and experienced
judge who decided this case at first instance, I think he decided the case against the
plaintiff on too narrow a ground. I would allow the appeal and grant the plaintiff
the declaration which he seeks in the prayer in his statement of claim.   *h*

GEOFFREY LANE LJ. The plaintiff held a colour television licence due to
expire on the last day of March 1975. On 26th March 1975 he went to a branch
of the Post Office and applied for another colour television licence which was issued
to him on payment of the then correct fee of £12. That new licence (for reasons *j*
which are not material) was expressed to expire on the last day of February 1976. He
was not asked to nor did he state whether or not he had a current licence.
   There is no regulation which prohibits the holding of two licences which cover
as to part of their currency the same period. Indeed, anyone applying in the ordinary
way for a new licence before the expiry of the old will be given a licence which will

a be concurrent with the old from the date of issue of the new until the date of expiry of the old.

By virtue of the Wireless Telegraphy (Broadcast Licence Charges and Exemption) (Amendment) Regulations 1975 the fee was due to be increased on 1st April 1975 from £12 to £18. Thus, by taking out a fresh licence when he did, the plaintiff made a net saving of some £4·50, making allowance for the period of overlap and the fact that the new licence expires on the last day of February rather than the last day of b March 1976. The fact that he was issued with the new licence at all was due to an error by the counter clerk. She had been instructed to refuse to issue before 1st April a fresh licence to any holder of a current licence to the end of March. From those simple facts has arisen a dispute which is said to have far-reaching constitutional implications.

It is said that some 24,500 colour television licence holders, some of them stimulated c by newspaper articles, adopted the same tactics as the plaintiff. Of this number, by September, all save about 8,000 had paid the extra money.

The Post Office is the agent of the Home Office for collecting the licence fees. After deducting the cost of collection the Post Office hands the balance to the Home Office and it then becomes part of the general fund in the hands of the Exchequer.

When the finance and licensing division of the Home Office became aware that the d plaintiff and others had effected an economy at the expense, as they saw it, of the Revenue, they took steps to remedy the loss by threatening to revoke the new licence. They contend that these steps were no more than a legitimate use of their powers under Act and regulations to implement the intentions of Parliament. The plaintiff on the other hand maintains that the actions were an abuse of their powers, were illegal and therefore of no effect. He claims a declaration accordingly.

e This is what happened. On 30th April 1975 the National Television Licence Records Office acting as agent for the Home Office wrote a letter to the plaintiff, the material parts of which read as follows:

'By renewing the licence before the existing licence expired the increased fee has been avoided and we have been instructed . . . not to allow this. I am, there-
f fore, required to ask you to remit the additional fee of £6 . . . within 14 days . . . We will then amend our records to show your address as being covered by a licence expiring at the end of March 1976 . . . In the event of failure to pay the additional fee, we have been instructed by the Home Office to revoke the licence taken out in advance. It will then no longer be valid and you will have to renew your licence which expired at the end of March 1975 at the new rate.'

g
The plaintiff's solicitors replied setting out their arguments in objection to the proposed action, but the Records Office staff were clearly out of their depth, and on 29th May an attempt was made to get an answer from the Home Office themselves. In the meantime the whole matter had been placed before the Parliamentary Commissioner for consideration.

h On 10th July the Home Office replied, simply enclosing a copy of Hansard of 16th June 1975 in which the Home Secretary was reported to have given the following answer to a Parliamentary question:

'In the case of a licence holder who chooses not to make the additional payment now I propose to allow his new licence to run for eight months . . . from the expiry date of his old licence and then to revoke it. This will give him his money's
j worth from his new licence, but at the new rate not the old rate.'

On 8th and 27th August 1975 the Records Office again wrote requesting payment of £6, in default of which, they said, the new licence would be revoked after eight months of its currency.

On 11th November 1975 came another demand for £6, again coupled with the threat or intimation that failing payment the licence would be revoked on 1st December and that thereafter use of the television set would render the plaintiff liable to a prosecution in the event of no new licence being taken out.

The plaintiff took the view that he had acted in accordance with the law; that the Home Office had not; that he should not be put in peril of prosecution. He therefore issued a writ on 14th November seeking his declaration. The hearing was expedited. On 26th November Phillips J gave judgment for the Home Office and on 29th November the plaintiff appealed to this court.

Counsel for the Home Office put his case in this way. The court can only interfere with actions of the executive if it is shown that the executive have acted in excess of the powers which Parliament has conferred on them.

It is not for the court to decide whether or not the executive have acted reasonably, save in the sense that, if the action is shown to be such that no reasonable authority could have taken it, then and then only should the court interfere. In the words of c Lord Greene MR in *Associated Provincial Picture Houses v Wednesbury Corpn*[1]: '. . . provided they act . . . within the four corners of their jurisdiction, this court, in my opinion, cannot interfere.'

The Secretary of State is by s 1 of the Wireless Telegraphy Act 1949 given a discretion: (1) whether to grant a licence or not; (2) on what terms or for what period to grant it if he does; (3) to revoke it or vary it. That discretion must be exercised, d it is conceded, to further the policy of the Act, including the charging policy. But the Secretary of State is entitled to use his discretionary powers to hold the balance fairly between the various licence holders. Accordingly, it is said, he is entitled to use his discretionary powers to thwart a bona fide but undesirable attempt by the plaintiff to evade the provisions of the Act to the possible detriment of less enterprising licence holders.

Counsel for the Home Office contends that the matter should be viewed in the following way. The Secretary of State undoubtedly has powers to revoke. If he had done so, he would have refunded the £12 paid for the licence. The plaintiff would have had to buy another licence. The fee would then have been £18. By requesting the payment of £6, therefore, all that the Secretary of State was doing was to condense the sequence of events and to produce the same result as if each step had been duly f and separately taken. Unhappily this was not the way it was put in any of the letters to the plaintiff. Nor was the plaintiff ever told by the Secretary of State that his £12 would be refunded on revocation. It is interesting to note that reg 8 of the 1970 regulations provides as follows: 'On the revocation . . . of a licence no part of any fee already paid . . . shall be refunded . . . unless the Minister . . . with the consent of the Treasury so determines.'

Counsel for the Home Office concedes and the Parliamentary Commissioner has found that there was maladministration by the Home Office and their agents; that distress and confusion were caused because insufficient attention had been paid to make policy officially and openly clear to the public.

No court would declare the actions of a government department void and illegal merely because it had acted ineptly or without tact. But is that the limit of the h proper criticism which can be made here, or did the Home Office exceed the powers which were conferred on them by statute and regulation? In my judgment they did.

Viewed objectively, the effect of the various letters written to the plaintiff was to demand the sum of £6 as the price of not exercising the powers to revoke the licence. The licence was a valid one at the time of its issue. At that time the new regulation increasing the fee to £18 had not come into operation and therefore did not in law j exist. There was no power to demand the extra £6 nor to receive it. The fact that the demand came after 1st April did not make it any more lawful.

---

1   [1947] 2 All ER 680 at 683, [1948] 1 KB 223 at 231

It is, however, the legality of the proposed revocation which is the crucial question.
a In my judgment it is illegal for two reasons. First, it is coupled with an illegal demand
which taints the revocation and makes that illegal too. Secondly, or possibly putting
the same matter in a different way, it is an improper exercise of a discretionary
power to use a threat to exercise that power as a means of extracting money which
Parliament has given the executive no mandate to demand: see *Attorney-General v
Wilts United Dairies*[1].

b The plaintiff is entitled to his declaration, and I would allow the appeal
accordingly.

Appeal allowed. Leave to appeal to the House of Lords refused.

Solicitors: *Herbert Smith & Co* (for the plaintiff); *Treasury Solicitor.*

c
Wendy Shockett Barrister.

Chaterjee v Chaterjee
d

COURT OF APPEAL, CIVIL DIVISION
STAMP, ORMROD LJJ AND SIR JOHN PENNYCUICK
6th, 7th NOVEMBER, 2nd DECEMBER 1975

e *Divorce – Financial provision – Lump sum payment – Property adjustment order – Statutory
powers – Retrospective operation – Decree granted before provision conferring power
enacted – Power to order payment of lump sum or make property adjustment order 'on granting a decree of divorce . . . or at any time thereafter' – Whether court having power to make
orders when decree granted before enactment of statutory powers – Matrimonial Proceedings
and Property Act 1970, ss 2, 4 – Matrimonial Causes Act 1973, ss 23, 24.*

f *Divorce – Financial provision – Application – Leave – Application which should have been
included in petition or answer – Principles on which leave should be granted – Protection
of parties from unjust harassment or claims long after divorce – Leave to be granted in cases
where applicant appears to have reasonable chance of success – Matrimonial Causes Rules
1973 (SI 1973 No 2016), r 68 (2).*

g The husband and wife were married in March 1952 and divorced in December 1955.
They lived together again as man and wife from 1961 to 1966 and from 1966 to 1974
separately but under the same roof. During much of that time they ran the business
of an old people's home in the house in which they lived. The house was owned by
the husband who also owned another freehold property. After their separation
in 1974 the wife, who was in her fifties, went to live in a house belonging to her mother
h and sister. She was dependent on social security. The husband was aged 70 and in
poor health. He had a state retirement pension and a small pension from his former
employers. They had an illegitimate daughter, aged 12, who lived with the wife.
The wife was granted leave under r 68(2)[a] of the Matrimonial Causes Rules 1973 to

_____

1 (1922) 91 LJKB 897
j a Rule 68, so far as material, provides:
     '(1) Any application by a petitioner or by a respondent who files an answer claiming
     relief, for . . . (b) a financial provision order, (c) a property adjustment order, shall be
     made in the petition or answer, as the case may be.
     '(2) Notwithstanding anything in paragraph (1), an application for ancillary relief which
     should have made in the petition or answer may be made subsequently—(a) by leave of
     the court . . .'

apply, inter alia, for a lump sum and/or property adjustment order under ss 23 and 24 of the Matrimonial Causes Act 1973. The husband appealed, contending (i) that *a* the court had no power to grant such relief in a case where the decree of divorce had been granted before the enactment of ss 2 and 4 of the Matrimonial Proceedings and Property Act 1970 which introduced the powers subsequently re-enacted in ss 23 and 24 of the 1973 Act, and (ii) that in any event the court ought to refuse leave in the exercise of its discretion.

Held – The appeal would be dismissed for the following reasons—

(i) The provisions enacted by ss 2 and 4 of the 1970 Act, empowering the court to make orders for the payment of a lump sum or the transfer of property 'On granting a decree of divorce . . . or at any time thereafter', were retrospective in effect and so empowered the court to make an order in cases where the decree had been granted before the commencement of the 1970 Act and at a time before the court had power *c* to make such orders (see p 723 *d* and *e*, p 725 *j* to p 726 *a*, p 726 *c e* and *f*, post); *Williams v Williams* [1971] 2 All ER 764 and *Powys v Powys* [1971] 3 All ER 116 approved.

(ii) The object of requiring a party to obtain leave to apply for ancillary relief under r 68(2) of the 1973 rules where such an application had not been made in the petition, was to protect respondents from being unjustly harassed or put to expense *d* in resisting claims for financial or other provision put forward long after the divorce and the consequent financial arrangements had apparently been settled, and the discretion under r 68(2) should not be exercised to give new forms of relief except when it was asked for by justice. However, the court ought not to refuse leave to apply in a case in which, on the evidence, the applicant appeared to have reasonable prospects of obtaining the relief claimed. Since, in the circumstances of the case, *e* the parties might as well have been a married couple until 1974, there had been no delay in any relevant sense and it could not be said that their financial affairs had in any sense been settled after the divorce. The wife had reasonable prospects of obtaining a property adjustment order giving her an interest in the house or a lump sum. Accordingly it was a proper case in which to grant leave (see p 724 *f* and *g* and p 725 *a* and *f* to *j* and p 726 *e* and *f*, post); *L v L* [1961] 3 All ER 834 and dictum of Lord *f* Simon P in *Williams v Williams* [1971] 2 All ER at 772 applied; dictum of Brandon J in *Powys v Powys* [1971] 3 All ER at 128 disapproved.

Notes

For the retrospective effect of statutes, see 36 Halsbury's Laws (3rd Edn) 423-428, paras 643-648, and for cases on the subject, see 44 Digest (Repl) 284-289, 1136-1188.

For the powers of the court to make financial provision for parties after divorce *g* and the kinds of order which may be made, see Supplement to 12 Halsbury's Laws (3rd Edn) para 987A, 1, 2, and for the powers of the court to order the transfer of property after divorce, see ibid para 992A, 1.

For the Matrimonial Proceedings and Property Act 1970, ss 2, 4, see 40 Halsbury's Statutes (3rd Edn) 800, 802.

For the Matrimonial Causes Act 1973, ss 23, 24, see 43 Halsbury's Statutes (3rd Edn) *h* 564, 566.

Cases referred to in judgments

H v H [1966] 3 All ER 560, 27(2) Digest (Reissue) 843, 6710.

Jones v Jones [1971] 3 All ER 1201, CA, 27(2) Digest (Reissue) 844, 6720.

L v L [1961] 3 All ER 834, [1962] P 101, [1961] 3 WLR 1182, CA, 27(2) Digest (Reissue) *j* 830, 6630.

Powys v Powys [1971] 3 All ER 116, [1971] P 340, [1971] 3 WLR 154, 27(2) Digest (Reissue) 844, 6712.

Robertson v Robertson and Favagrossa (1883) 8 PD 94, 48 LT 590, CA, 27(2) Digest (Reissue) 828, 6619.

Scott v Scott [1921] P 107, [1920] All ER Rep 285, 90 LJP 171, 124 LT 619, CA, 45 Digest
a   (Repl) 266, 333.
Williams v Williams [1971] 2 All ER 764, [1971] P 271, [1971] 3 WLR 92, 27(2) Digest
(Reissue) 821, 6587.

Cases also cited
Madden v Madden [1974] 1 All ER 673, [1974] 1 WLR 247.
b   *Porter v Porter* [1971] 2 All ER 1037, [1971] P 282.
Wachtel v Wachtel [1973] 1 All ER 829, [1973] Fam 72, CA.
Wilson v Wilson [1975] 3 All ER 464, [1975] 3 WLR 537, CA.

Appeal
This was an appeal by the husband, Marcel Kamala Prosad Chaterjee, against an
c   order of Arnold J on 22nd July 1975 dismissing the husband's appeal against an order
of Mrs Registrar Butler-Sloss made on 24th June 1974 giving the wife, Heidy Chaterjee,
leave under r 68(2) of the Matrimonial Causes Rules 1973 to apply for a lump sum
order and/or a transfer of property order in respect of the former matrimonial
home. 24 Baldslow Road, Hastings, Sussex. The facts are set out in the judgment
of Ormrod LJ.
d
John Samuels for the husband.
Arnold Russell Vick for the wife.

Cur adv vult

e   2nd December.   **ORMROD LJ** read the first judgment at the invitation of
Stamp LJ: This is an appeal from an order made by Arnold J on 22nd July 1975
dismissing an appeal from an order of Mrs Registrar Butler-Sloss dated 24th June 1974
by which she gave leave to the wife, under r 68(2) of the Matrimonial Causes Rules
1973 to apply inter alia for a lump sum order and/or a transfer of property order
in respect of a property known as 24 Baldslow Road, Hastings, Sussex, owned by
f   the husband.
The grounds of appeal as set out in the notice of appeal in substance are that in
dismissing the appeal from the registrar the learned judge had misdirected himself
in various respects in holding that the registrar had properly exercised her discretion
under r 68(2). At an early stage in counsel for the husband's argument it appeared
to this court that, in the existing state of the authorities, it was necessary before con-
g   sidering whether or not the discretion had been properly exercised in the courts
below to determine whether or not, on the facts of this case, there was jurisdiction
to entertain the application for leave at all. The facts, which are wholly exceptional,
will be referred to later in this judgment. At this stage it is only necessary to say
that the parties were married on 20th March 1952, divorced in December 1955, but
lived together again from 1961 to 1974, for five years as husband and wife and, from
h   1966, separately but under the same roof. Therefore, to succeed on the application,
the wife has to show that the relevant sections of the Matrimonial Proceedings and
Property Act 1970 were retroactive.
Counsel for the husband gallantly shouldered the burden of arguing a point which
he had not intended to argue and, as he later explained, he personally did not think
a good one. This court is extremely grateful to him for his able and lucid guidance
j   through the undergrowth which surrounds this question. It might have been resolved
very simply by including in the Act an express provision whether or to what extent
each of its provisions was intended to have retroactive effect. In the result, the
question can only be answered by detailed examination of the Act and some of its
predecessors. The power of the court to award a lump sum after a decree of divorce
was first introduced by the Matrimonial Causes Act 1963, s 5, and there are conflicting

decisions at first instance whether this section had retroactive effect. In *H v H*[1].
Sir Jocelyn Simon P held that it was not retroactive; in *Powys v Powys*[2], on the other *a*
hand, Brandon J found himself unable to agree with Sir Jocelyn Simon P and came
to the conclusion that this section was retroactive for reasons which he gave in some
detail. I agree with the reasoning of Brandon J on this point which depends primarily
on the opening words of s 5(1) which read:

> 'In any case in which the Court has power to make an order (other than an *b*
> interim order) under section 19 or section 20 of the Matrimonial Causes Act
> 1950 (maintenance and alimony) the Court may . . . make an order for payment
> of a lump sum.'

Sections 19 and 20 of the 1950 Act were the sections which at that time contained
the power to grant ancillary relief in the forms then available. The relevant sub- *c*
sections all begin with the words 'On any decree . . .' This phrase was first used in
this connection in the Matrimonial Causes Act 1857 and has been reproduced in each
successive Act, up to and including the Matrimonial Causes Act 1950. It has been
the source of a considerable body of case law. It could not be construed in its narrow
sense of 'at the time of making the decree', for the practical reason that such ancillary
matters were, as a matter of practice, dealt with in separate proceedings after those *d*
in which the decree was pronounced. So it had to be construed as meaning 'within
a reasonable time after the decree': *Scott v Scott*[3]. What was a reasonable time in all
the circumstances of the case gave rise to a considerable number of reported cases
in which the period underwent a progressive extension from a year in the view of
Jessel MR in *Robertson v Robertson*[4], to periods of the order of ten years or more in
later cases. Parliament ultimately intervened and by the Matrimonial Causes *e*
(Property and Maintenance) Act 1958, s 1, provided that '(1) Any power of the court,
under [ss 19 and 20 of the 1950 Act and other sections] shall . . . be exercisable either
on pronouncing such a decree or at any time thereafter.'
By 1963, therefore, the court could exercise its powers to order ancillary relief
on pronouncing a decree or at any time thereafter. The class of case referred to in
s 5 of the 1963 Act was therefore any case in which a decree of divorce or nullity or *f*
judicial separation had been pronounced. Consequently an application for a lump
sum could be made in any such case, subject only to the provisions of the following
subsection under which leave of the court was required if a prayer for ancillary
relief had not been included in the petition or answer. Like Brandon J[2] I find it impossible to construe s 5(1) as limited to decrees pronounced after the coming into
force of the 1963 Act, and so conclude that this section was retroactive in its effect. *g*
The question whether the relevant sections of the 1970 Act were intended to have
retroactive effect is more difficult. This Act was an integral part of the fundamental
revision of our divorce law which was begun by the Divorce Reform Act 1969, and
completed by the 1970 Act. New and far-reaching powers were given to the court
to make property adjustment orders of a kind which had not previously been contemplated. Moreover the courts were instructed to approach the exercise of these *h*
and the older powers to award ancillary relief along markedly different lines, some
of which were described in detail in s 5 (now s 25 of the Matrimonial Causes Act 1973);
others flow from the change in the basis of divorce from matrimonial offence
to irretrievable breakdown. It would not have been surprising if Parliament had
restricted the exercise of these new powers, in the new ways, to spouses whose marriages were dissolved on the new basis of breakdown, leaving the financial affairs *j*

---

1   [1966] 3 All ER 560
2   [1971] 3 All ER 116, [1971] P 340
3   [1921] P 107, [1920] All ER Rep 285
4   (1883) 8 PD 94

of those who had been divorced under the old law to be governed by it. But there
a is no such provision in the 1970 Act. Moreover, the 1970 Act repealed the relevant
provisions of the 1965 Act altogether except insofar as the transitional provisions
preserved them for certain limited purposes. In *Williams v Williams*[1] Lord Simon P,
in a careful analysis of these transitional provisions, demonstrated that if the 1970
legislation was not retroactive in its effect the court would be unable to deal with
many cases arising under the old law because its powers under the old law had gone
b with the repeal of the 1965 Act. I agree also with Brandon J's observations in *Powys v
Powys*[2]. In enacting the new provisions relating to ancillary relief (ss 2 and 4),
Parliament chose to use the same words 'on granting a decree . . . or at any time
thereafter' without any qualification or restriction (except the reference in s 24 to
the necessity to obtain the leave of the court in certain circumstances). It is difficult
to think of wider language, or of a situation which called more clearly for the use of
c limiting words, if limitation were intended. Moreover, in one case where this Act
was certainly not intended to have retroactive effect, specific words to that effect
were included in the section: see s 21 (which relates to the effect of remarriage) in
which the words 'after the commencement of this Act' occur. For these reasons,
even if it involves the risk that some people may be exposed to retrospective interference with their rights and obligations, I do not think that it is possible to come
d to any other conclusion but that these provisions of the 1970 Act are fully retroactive
in their effect. This conclusion is in accordance with the view expressed by this court
in *Jones v Jones*[3], which would have been binding on us but for the fact that counsel
for the husband in that case (Mr Wood QC) conceded the point in advance. In my
opinion this issue should now be regarded as settled in favour of the practice which
has been adopted since the decision in *Powys v Powys*[2].
e The next question is how this jurisdiction to grant or refuse leave to apply for
ancillary relief should be exercised. It is probably wise to draw a distinction between
cases which involve the retroactive use of these sections of the 1970 Act and those
in which the decree was granted after the new legislation came into force, not so
much because there is a difference in principle between the two classes but because
the factors to be taken into account may have to be weighted differently if justice
f is to be done to both parties.
Not much assistance is to be found in the authorities. There are numerous decisions
prior to the 1958 Act but these are of limited value because the approach was
different. The applicant had to get over the hurdle presented by the words 'On a
decree', which placed the onus heavily on the party seeking leave. The formula
originally introduced by the 1958 Act, 'or at any time thereafter', must be given
g effect to, more particularly because this phrase was introduced in substitution for
the former rule which was 'or within a reasonable time thereafter', thereby indicating
a significant change of policy in favour of applicants who require the leave of the court.
Since the 1958 Act there have been four reported cases in which this question has
been discussed, *L v L*[4], *Williams v Williams*[1], *Powys v Powys*[2] and *Jones v Jones*[3].
In *L v L*[5] Willmer LJ stressed the importance of bearing in mind that the husband
h had ordered his financial affairs in the belief that he was quit of his financial obligations
to the wife. In *Williams v Williams*[1] Lord Simon P said:

'Applications to reopen old orders (other than by way of variation, which has
always been available and is dealt with expressly by para 3 of Sch 1 to the 1970
Act) are unlikely to be allowed to go forward unless justice clearly so indicates.

j
---
1 [1971] 2 All ER 764 at 772, [1971] P 271 at 281
2 [1971] 3 All ER 116, [1971] P 340
3 [1971] 3 All ER 1201
4 [1961] 3 All ER 834, [1962] P 101
5 [1961] 3 All ER at 841, [1962] P at 120

Secondly, these ancillary reliefs are in any event the subject of judicial discretion; and the discretion will not be exercised to give new forms of relief except where *a* this is called for by justice. The courts are, in particular, unlikely to look with favour on attempts to reopen cases long concluded.'

I respectfully agree with this general approach to these applications.

In *Powys v Powys*[1] Brandon J, however, felt constrained to refuse leave to the applicant because he was greatly influenced by the provisions of s 9(5) of the 1970 *b* Act (s 31 of the 1973 Act) which expressly precludes the court from making a lump sum or property adjustment order on an application to vary an order for periodical payments. He took the view that if leave were given to present a fresh application for a lump sum this provision would be 'outflanked' and the intention of Parliament, as expressed in this subsection, defeated. In support of this view he referred expressly to certain paragraphs in the Law Commission's Report on Financial Provision in *c* Matrimonial Proceedings[2], paras 85-90, but with respect to Brandon J, I do not think that the discretion of the court should be circumscribed in this way, not only because the subsection is limited to applications to vary when it could very easily have been made to refer to fresh applications if that was the intention, but also because the Law Commission itself envisaged that original and fresh applications for lump sums might be made: see the concluding words of para 90. *d*

In *Jones v Jones*[3] Davies LJ said that the question before the court 'is simply what, in all the circumstances of the case and in the light of the financial position of the parties, is a fair and proper order to be made'. He mentioned the point taken by Brandon J in *Powys v Powys*[1] but without expressing approval or disapproval. I do not think that the headnote to the report accurately reflects the substance of this judgment. In my judgment, the purpose of s 9(5) was to reverse the ruling which *e* had been made by Sir Jocelyn Simon P in *H v H*[4] and so to ensure that such applications did not evade the requirement that leave of the court was required in cases caught by s 24(2) of the 1970 Act and the rules made pursuant to it, now r 68 of the Matrimonial Causes Rules 1973.

The real problem is how to reconcile the principle which is implicit in the words 'or at any time thereafter', that applicants should have free access to the court, with *f* the constraint implied by the necessity of obtaining leave to make an application. The broad intention is clear, namely that respondents should be protected from being unjustly harassed or put to expense in resisting claims for financial or other provision put forward long after the divorce and the consequent financial arrangements have been apparently settled, and so to enable the court to hold the balance of justice between the parties. Unfortunately, the rule in its present form is a very *g* inadequate protection to respondents and produces unjustifiable anomalies between applicants of different classes. It is purely procedural and formalistic; to secure the right to apply for ancillary relief of all kinds, at any time, it is only necessary to include appropriate words in the pleadings, if any. No time limits are prescribed, so a party, whose pleading was in order, is free to activate an application at any time, whereas a party whose pleading is defective requires leave to apply or to amend at *h* all times. Moreover, a party who allows the suit to go through undefended is free of constraint at all times.

Furthermore, in its present form r 68 of the 1973 rules provides even less protection than its predecessors. Now it is unnecessary to specify a lump sum in the prayer; all that is required is a reference to financial provision and/or a property adjustment

j

---

1 [1971] 3 All ER 116 at 128, [1971] P 340 at 355
2 Law Com 25
3 [1971] 3 All ER at 1207
4 [1966] 3 All ER 560

order. Such arbitrary distinctions between those who are and those who are not
caught by the rule may cause hardship to both applicants and respondents.

In my judgment, the court ought not to refuse leave to apply in any case in which
on the evidence the applicant has or appears to have reasonable prospects of obtaining
the relief claimed, or, to put it in another way, has a seriously arguable case. It will not
be enough merely to demonstrate that on the one-third yardstick the applicant
can make a case on the figures (as certain passages in Arnold J's judgment in the
present case seem to suggest). To assess the prospects of success (as indicated by
Davies LJ in *Jones v Jones*[1]) all the facts referred to in s 25 of the 1973 Act, including,
in particular, practicability and conduct, in the sense of the way in which the parties
have conducted themselves and their affairs up to the time of the application, must
be considered. Delay, if it really is delay in the sense of prejudicing the other party,
may have an important influence on the justice of the case. So may conduct which
can be described as 'lulling' the other party into the belief that all claims have already
been dealt with. Similarly it may be unjust to interfere with property rights after
a lapse of time during which the other party has ordered his or her affairs in a reasonable and proper manner in the belief that the financial consequences of the divorce
have been settled (as was said in *L v L*[2]). On the other hand, the purpose of r 68 will
be frustrated if the hearing of the application for leave is made the occasion for a
detailed investigation with consequent expense.

In cases in which the respondent to such an application decides to contest it and
to introduce detailed evidence of his financial position, it may save expense and time
if the application for leave is treated as the substantive application. If this is not
done a procedure designed to protect respondents will be turned into one which
doubles the expense for them, as I fear will be the fate of the husband.

Turning briefly to the facts of this case and approaching the application on the
lines I have indicated, it is enough to say that, extraordinary as it may seem, these
parties lived together before the divorce for three years and after it, for 12 or 13 years,
for much of that time running together the business of an old people's home in
the house at Baldslow Road, Hastings. Both now have very little to live on; the wife
who is in her fifties lives on social security in a house which is said to belong to her
mother and sister; the husband, who is 70 and in poor health, has the state retirement
pension and a small pension from his former employers, but he owns two freehold
properties. They have an illegitimate daughter aged 12, who lives with the wife.
On the evidence before us the wife would seem to have a reasonably good claim on
the husband's bounty. In my judgment, she has reasonable prospects of obtaining
a property adjustment order, giving her an interest in Baldslow Road, subject,
perhaps, to further investigation of her interest, if any, in the house in which she
lives, or a lump sum, if the husband prefers to sell the property in the near future.
As to conduct, they might as well have been a married couple up to 1974; all that
was lacking was an appointment at the registry office. There is no delay in any
relevant sense, nor can it be said that their financial affairs after the divorce were
in any meaningful sense settled or concluded. In these circumstances I have no hesitation in holding that this is a proper case for granting leave to apply for a lump sum
or a property adjustment order. I would dismiss the appeal.

SIR JOHN PENNYCUICK. I agree on all points with the judgment of Ormrod LJ.
If one could approach the formula contained in s 2 of the Matrimonial Proceedings
and Property Act 1970, and now reproduced in s 23 of the Matrimonial Causes Act
1973, in isolation from its statutory and judicial background, I should, in common
with Stamp LJ, be disposed to construe it as not having retroactive effect. But when

---

1   [1971] 3 All ER 1201
2   [1961] 3 All ER 834, [1962] P 101

one reads the provision in the context of its statutory and judicial background I
find the conclusion inescapable that it is retroactive. I, too, agree with the analysis   *a*
contained in the judgment of Brandon J in *Powys v Powys*[1] and I would dismiss
the appeal.

STAMP LJ. On the question whether the relevant sections of the Matrimonial
Proceedings and Property Act 1970 were retroactive I confess, as no doubt had   *b*
appeared from my interlocutory observations, that at the conclusion of counsel for
the husband's opening speech I thought that in the phrase 'On granting a decree . . .
or at any time thereafter', the words 'On granting a decree' point to a decree made
after the coming into force of the Act and that the superadded words 'or at any time
thereafter' accordingly referred to a period subsequent to a decree so made. But
as Ormrod LJ and Sir John Pennycuick were clearly of the contrary opinion we did   *c*
not call on counsel for the wife on that part of the case and I will say no more about
it and proceed on the footing that it is competent for the court to grant ancillary
relief in the form of a lump sum payment notwithstanding that the marriage was
dissolved at a time when no such ancillary relief could have been granted or sought
in the petition.
   The parties were divorced as long ago as December 1955 at a time when the court   *d*
had no power to order a lump sum payment, or a transfer of property, and the application for leave to apply, inter alia, for a lump sum payment was not made until 1974.
If matters had rested there I would have thought it wrong to give the required leave.
As Ormrod LJ has pointed out, the broad intention of requiring a would-be applicant
to obtain leave is to protect the other party from harassing tactics. And where that
other party has over so long a period been led to believe that no such application   *e*
would be made, leave should in my view, unless there are exceptional circumstances,
be refused. And this must I think be so despite the anomalies to which Ormrod LJ
has called attention, and which it is to be hoped will be corrected. But as Ormrod LJ
has also pointed out, the facts of this case are of a most exceptional nature and I think
it should be left to the judge on the hearing of the substantive application to determine whether in all the circumstances, including the facts regarding the delay,   *f*
the relief sought should be granted to any and if so to what extent.
   I too would dismiss the appeal.

Appeal dismissed.

Solicitors: *Percy Walker & Co*, Hastings (for the husband); *Perring & Co*, Hastings   *g*
(for the wife).

                                                L I Zysman Esq Barrister.

---

1 [1971] 3 All ER 116, [1971] P 340

McCall v Abelesz and another

COURT OF APPEAL
LORD DENNING MR, ORMROD AND SHAW LJJ
4th, 5th, 19th DECEMBER 1975

Statutory duty – Breach – Civil liability – Landlord and tenant – Harassment – Residential occupier – Acts calculated to interfere with peace or comfort of occupier – Acts done with intent to cause occupier to give up occupation – Criminal offence – Whether commission of offence giving rise to civil liability at suit of occupier – Rent Act 1965, s 30(2)(4).

In March 1968 the plaintiff became the tenant of a furnished room in a house. In May 1973 the defendants purchased the house. A few months later the defendants received a large bill for gas which had been supplied to the house before they bought it. They failed to pay the bill and so, in October 1973, the gas board cut off the supply to the house which was not restored until June 1974. For a time, the electricity and water supplies were also cut off. The defendants offered the plaintiff alternative accommodation but he refused to accept it since it was at a higher rent and in a different area. The plaintiff brought an action in the county court claiming damages against the defendants for breach of their statutory duty under s 30(2)[a] of the Rent Act 1965 not to harass him with intent to cause him to give up occupation. The judge upheld the plaintiff's claim, having found that the defendants had withheld services reasonably required by the plaintiff, and awarded damages of £75. The plaintiff appealed against the award and the defendants cross-appealed.

Held – Section 30(4) of the 1965 Act was to be construed as meaning that nothing in s 30 was to prejudice any liability or remedy in civil proceedings to which a person was subject apart from the section, but did not create any new liability or remedy in civil proceedings. Section 30(2) did not, therefore, give rise to a civil remedy for damages for harassment in addition to imposing a criminal sanction. The appeal would therefore be dismissed and the cross-appeal allowed (see p 730 g and h, p 733 f and g and p 735 e to g, post).

Notes

For unlawful harassment of residential occupiers, see Supplement to 10 Halsbury's Laws (3rd Edn) para 1106A.

For the construction of a statute to ascertain whether a civil action lies, see 36 Halsbury's Laws (3rd Edn) 451-455, paras 687-692, and for cases on the subject, see 44 Digest (Repl) 354-357, 1912-1938.

For the Rent Act 1965, s 30, see 18 Halsbury's Statutes (3rd Edn) 620.

Cases referred to in judgments

Cutler v Wandsworth Stadium Ltd [1949] 1 All ER 544, [1949] AC 398, [1949] LJR 824, HL, 25 Digest (Repl) 504, 582.

Groves v Lord Wimborne [1898] 2 QB 402, [1895-9] All ER Rep 147, 67 LJQB 862, 79 LT 284, CA, 44 Digest (Repl) 357, 1938.

Jackson v Horizon Holidays Ltd [1975] 3 All ER 92, [1975] 1 WLR 1468, CA.

Jarvis v Swan's Tours Ltd [1973] 1 All ER 71, [1973] QB 233, [1972] 3 WLR 954, CA, 17 Digest (Reissue) 111, 166.

Kenny v Preen [1962] 3 All ER 814, [1963] 1 QB 499, [1962] 3 WLR 1233, CA, 31(1) Digest (Reissue) 363, 2892.

Ministry of Housing and Local Government v Sharp [1969] 3 All ER 225, [1970] 2 QB 223, [1969] 3 WLR 1020, 133 JP 595, 20 P & CR 1101; *rvsd* [1970] 1 All ER 1009, [1970] 2 WLR 802, 134 JP 358, 68 LGR 187, 12 P & CR 166, CA, Digest (Cont Vol C) 830, 926f.

---

a   Section 30, so far as material, is set out at p 729 j to p 730 a, post

Monk v Warbey [1935] 1 KB 75, [1934] All ER Rep 373, 104 LJKB 153, 152 LT 194, 50 Ll L
Rep 33, CA, 29 Digest (Repl) 537, 3686.   *a*
Perera v Vandiyar [1953] 1 All ER 1109, [1953] 1 WLR 672, CA, 31(1) Digest (Reissue)
366, 2920.
Phillips v Britannia Hygienic Laundry Co Ltd [1923] 2 KB 832, [1923] All ER Rep 127, 93
LJKB 5, 129 LT 777, 21 LGR 709, CA, 45 Digest (Repl) 144, *553.*
Solomons v R Gertzenstein Ltd [1954] 2 All ER 625, [1954] 2 QB 243, [1954] 3 WLR 317,
52 LGR 433, CA, 44 Digest (Repl) 354, *1917.*   *b*

Cases also cited
Asinobi v Chuke [1971] CLY 6561, CA.
Bollinger (J) v Costa Brava Wine Co Ltd [1959] 3 All ER 800, [1960] Ch 262.
Cassell & Co Ltd v Broome [1972] 1 All ER 801, [1972] AC 1027, HL.
Coote v Stone [1971] 1 All ER 657, [1971] 1 WLR 279, CA.   *c*
Luganda v Service Hotels Ltd [1969] 2 All ER 692, [1969] 2 Ch 209, CA.
Mafo v Adams [1969] 3 All ER 1404, [1970] 1 QB 548, CA.
Norton v Knowles [1967] 3 All ER 1061, [1969] 1 QB 572, DC.
R v Abrol (1972) 116 Sol Jo 177, CA.
Rookes v Barnard [1964] 1 All ER 367, [1964] AC 1129, HL.
Warden v Cooper [1970] 1 All ER 1112, [1970] 1 Ch 495.   *d*
Waterer (John) Sons & Crisp Ltd v Huggins (1931) 47 TLR 305, DC.

Appeal and cross-appeal
This was an appeal by the plaintiff, Leonard McCall ('the tenant'), against the judgment of his Honour Judge Counsell sitting at Willesden County Court on 18th
December 1974 whereby he awarded the tenant £75 damages against the defendants, *e*
Erno Abelesz and Jacob Ostreicher (trading as Riverside Property Services) ('the
landlords'), for harassment under s 30(2) of the Rent Act 1965. The tenant claimed
that the award was too low having regard to the judge's finding that the landlords
had wrongfully and persistently withheld gas, electricity and water services from him.
The landlords cross-appealed on the ground that the judge had been wrong in law in
holding that s 30 of the 1965 Act gave rise to a civil remedy in addition to imposing a *f*
criminal sanction for harassment. The facts are set out in the judgment of Lord
Denning MR.

Peter Singer and *Patrick Clarke* for the tenant.
The first defendant appeared in person.
Hugh Carlisle as amicus curiae.   *g*
The second defendant did not appear and was not represented.

Cur adv vult

19th December 1975. The following judgments were read.

LORD DENNING MR. The tenant, Mr McCall, comes from Dominica in the *h*
West Indies. He has been here for 17 years. In March 1968 he became the tenant of a
room on the ground floor of 3 Claremont Road NW2. There were other tenants in the
house. They shared a lavatory and bathroom with Mr McCall.
    It was a furnished room. There was a gas cooker for which he had to put coins in the
gas meter. There was also electricity for light for which he had to put coins in the
electricity meter. These coins were for the use of the landlord. The gas board and the *j*
electricity company supplied the landlord and he supplied the tenants. They charged
the landlord for all the gas and electricity supplied to the whole house. The landlord
recouped himself by taking the coins from the meters. There was also a water supply
to the premises, which was paid for by the landlord.
    In May 1973 the landlords, Mr Abelesz and Mr Ostreicher, bought the premises.

They bought it 'blind' at an auction sale without even going to see it. They made no
a enquiries about the gas and electricity but assumed that the tenants had meters
operated by coins. They left everything to their manager, Mr Arran. Mr McCall
paid his rent of £3·50 a week by post to the landlords. He paid quite regularly.

A few months later the new landlords found themselves faced with a large bill for
gas supplied to the house. It was for £435·40. Most of it had accrued before they
bought the house. The landlords were aggrieved about this bill. The gas board
b threatened to cut off the gas unless this big bill was paid. The landlords did not pay it.
So in October 1973 the gas board cut off the gas from the house.

In December 1973 the public health authorities drew the attention of the landlords
to the condition of the house. Mr Arran, the landlords' manager, went to see it then
for the first time. He found three tenants in the house. He saw the meters in the
rooms, but in the rooms of the other tenants the locks on the meters had been broken.
c The coins had been taken. But in Mr McCall's room the locks were intact and the
money there. Mr Arran suggested to the tenants that they should ask the gas board to
give them a direct supply of gas, but the gas board declined to do so. They preferred
to look to the landlord.

Things went from bad to worse. In March 1974 the other two tenants left, owing
about £200 in rent, which they never paid. So Mr McCall was left there alone. About
d this time the electricity was cut off too, as well as the gas. The water supply was cut
off as well. The landlords offered Mr McCall alternative accommodation in Randolph
Avenue, but he did not take it because it was at a higher rent and in a different area.

At length, however, the landlords did pay £100 deposit to the gas board and got the
gas restored. They also got the electricity and water restored. But Mr McCall got
legal assistance and took proceedings in the county court. He alleged that the landlords
e had harassed him, contrary to s 30(2) of the Rent Act 1965, and claimed damages. At
the first hearing it was suggested that his claim might be put in breach of contract.
But, after consideration, his counsel decided to confine it to damages for breach of
s 30(2). The judge awarded damages. He said that from March 1974 the landlords
considered 'it no longer an economic proposition to let to Mr McCall so that . . . they
sought to persuade [Mr McCall] to leave in such a manner as to constitute harassment
f on their part', and it was their intention to see whether it was possible to persuade
him 'to leave the property by inactivity on their part'. 'I therefore find', he said, 'that
the landlords were withholding services that were reasonably required by the tenant,
and I make that finding with regard to all three utilities and the bath', but he felt that
a measure of blame attached to Mr McCall for failing to deal with his problems. He
said that it was not a case for aggravated damages. He awarded £75 damages.

g Mr McCall appealed to this court. He wanted to get more damages. The landlords
put in a cross-appeal. They submitted that s 30(2) of the 1965 Act only created a
criminal offence and did not give a civil remedy in damages. The landlords did not
instruct counsel but, as the point raised was one of public importance, this court
sought the help of an amicus curiae, and we are grateful to him for his assistance.

Counsel for Mr McCall brought to our attention one or two textbooks in which it
h is suggested that there is a civil remedy for damages for harassment under s 30(2) of
the 1965 Act; and he told us that he had had several cases in which judges of county courts
had awarded damages for harassment under s 30(2), but in most of them the point
had been assumed without argument. This case is brought to test the position.

With regard to s 30 itself, sub-s (2) says:

j   '. . . If any person with intent to cause the residential occupier of any premises—
(a) to give up the occupation of the premises or any part thereof . . . does acts
calculated to interfere with the peace or comfort of the residential occupier or
members of his household, or persistently withdraws or witholds services
reasonably required for the occupation of the premises as a residence, he shall be
guilty of an offence.'

Subsection (3) contains provisions for fine or imprisonment. Subsection (4) says:

'Nothing in this section shall be taken to prejudice any liability or remedy to which a person guilty of an offence thereunder may be subject in civil proceedings.'

First, I would consider the section as if sub-s (4) were not there. It creates a criminal offence punishable by fine or imprisonment. It does not give a civil remedy in damages. Nevertheless it would be possible for the courts to hold that there was a civil remedy, but they would only do so if they saw on examination of the whole Act that Parliament had so intended. The classis example where a criminal offence was held to give a remedy in damages is *Groves v Lord Wimborne*[1]: and where it was held not to give a remedy is *Cutler v Wandsworth Stadium Ltd*[2]. So difficult is the question that Lord du Parcq[3] made a plea that Parliament should state explicitly whether it intended that there should be a civil remedy or not.

Secondly, I turn to consider sub-s (4). It is intended to comply with the plea made by Lord du Parcq. In some statutes Parliament has *expressly* stated that the breach of a particular statutory obligation shall give rise to a civil remedy in damages. There are three instances: s 43(8) of the Copyright Act 1956; s 3(1) of the Consumer Protection 1961 and s 4(2) of the Resale Prices Act 1964.

But I have found no Act in which it has been expressly stated that a criminal offence shall *not* give rise to a civil remedy in damages. The draftsmen have used a different technique. It is illustrated by the Protection from Eviction Act 1964. It says in s 1(3):

'. . . if any person contravenes the provisions of this subsection he shall, without prejudice to any liability or remedy to which he may be subject in civil proceedings, be liable on summary conviction to a fine . . . or to imprisonment . . .'

Similarly in the Caravan Sites Act 1968, s 3(3) says:

'A person guilty of an offence under this section shall, *without prejudice* to any liability or remedy to which he may be subject in civil proceedings, be liable on summary conviction . . . to a fine . . .'

In those sections the words 'without prejudice' etc preserve any liability or remedy which exists *apart* from the subsection. The Shorter Oxford English Dictionary gives the meaning of 'without prejudice' as 'without detriment to any existing right or claim'. So it preserves existing rights, but excludes any new rights. By putting in the clause 'without prejudice' the draftsman shows that that section itself only gives rise to a criminal offence, and not to civil proceedings.

Turning now to sub-s (4), it is to be construed in the same way as those sections. It means that nothing in s 30 is to prejudice any liability or remedy in civil proceedings to which a person is subject *apart* from the section. It thus preserves any liability or remedy which already exists in civil proceedings, but does not create any new liability or remedy in civil proceedings.

Furthermore, I see no need to give any new civil remedy for harassment. As I understand it, the law already gives a perfectly good civil action for damages. In the present case, where the gas and electricity were cut off, the tenant could sue the landlord for breach of the implied term that he would supply the gas and electricity through the meters so long as the tenancy continued. I should have thought, too, that it would be a breach of the covenant for quiet enjoyment. This covenant is not confined to direct physical interference by the landlord. It extends to any conduct of the landlord or his agents which interferes with the tenant's freedom of action in

1 [1898] 2 QB 402, [1895-9] All ER Rep 147
2 [1949] 1 All ER 544, [1949] AC 398
3 [1949] 1 All ER at 549, [1949] AC at 410

exercising his rights as tenant: see *Kenny v Preen*, per Pearson LJ[1]. It covers, therefore,
a any acts calculated to interfere with the peace or comfort of the tenant, or his family.

I think, too, that *Perera v Vandiyar*[2] would be decided differently today. It is now
settled that the court can give damages for the mental upset and distress caused by the
defendant's conduct in breach of contract. That was done in the cases on holiday tours:
see *Jarvis v Swan's Tours Ltd*[3]; and not only to the plaintiff, but also his family: see
Jackson v Horizon Holidays Ltd[4].

b So, if the facts in *Perera v Vandiyar*[2] were to occur again today, the plaintiff would
recover not only the £25 for his own inconvenience, but also the additional £25 for the
injury and inconvenience which his wife and child suffered, and the mental distress
which he and they suffered. Not as damages for tort, but as damages for breach of
contract. Likewise in *Kenny v Preen*[1] the damages of £100 would stand.

It seems to me, too, that the courts could grant an injunction to restrain any
c breaches; and this could be brought in the county court as ancillary to a claim for
damages. Those civil remedies are sufficient to deal with most cases of harassment.
So it is unnecessary to give a civil remedy for breach of s 30(2) of the 1965 Act.

In conclusion, in this present case, I doubt whether on the evidence it was right to
find the landlords guilty of harassment under s 30(2). Ormrod LJ has analysed
the judge's findings and I agree with all that he is about to say. But this does not arise
d for decision. Suffice it that s 30(2) does not give rise to a civil action for damages. I
would therefore allow the cross-appeal and give judgment for the landlords on the
claim. The landlords are entitled on their counterclaim to the rent outstanding which,
we are told, Mr McCall put aside pending the result of the case.

e **ORMROD LJ.** I agree. The tenants' appeal in this case is confined to the issue
of damages. He complains that the judge's award of £75 was much too low and
should be substantially increased. The landlords have served a notice of cross-appeal
in which they say that the tenant is not entitled to any damages at all, on the ground
that the tenant has no cause of action in law, or alternatively, if he has a cause of action,
he has failed to prove his case on the facts.

f The first question, therefore, is whether there was a cause of action in law. The
tenant relied solely on s 30 of the Rent Act 1965. The landlords contend that this is a
penal section which does not give rise to a civil remedy in damages or otherwise.
This is always a difficult question. In *Cutler v Wandsworth Stadium Ltd*[5] Lord Simonds
declined to attempt the formulation of any rules except in the most general terms.
He said:

g 'The only rule which in all circumstances is valid is that the answer must
depend on a consideration of the whole Act and the circumstances, including the
pre-existing law, in which it was enacted.'

The reference to pre-existing law is particularly relevant in the present case. Some
observations by Atkin LJ in *Phillips v Britannia Hygienic Laundry Co Ltd*[6] indicate
h how the court should approach this problem. He said:

'In my opinion, when an Act imposes a duty of commission or omission, the
question whether a person aggrieved by a breach of the duty has a right of action
depends on the intention of the Act. Was it intended to make the duty one which
was owed to the party aggrieved as well as to the State, or was it a public duty

---

j
1   [1962] 3 All ER 814 at 820, [1963] 1 QB 499 at 513
2   [1953] 1 All ER 1109, [1953] 1 WLR 672
3   [1973] 1 All ER 71, [1973] QB 233
4   [1975] 3 All ER 92, [1975] 1 WLR 1468
5   [1949] 1 All ER 544 at 548, [1949] AC 398 at 407
6   [1923] 2 KB 832 at 840, 841, [1923] All ER Rep 127 at 132

only? That depends on the construction of the Act and the circumstances in which it was made and to which it relates. One question to be considered is, Does the Act contain reference to a remedy for breach of it? Prima facie if it does that is the only remedy. But that is not conclusive. The intention as disclosed by its scope and wording must still be regarded, and it may still be that, though the statute creates the duty and provides a penalty, the duty is nevertheless owed to individuals.'

In *Ministry of Housing and Local Government v Sharp*[1] Fisher J referred with approval to a formula which had been suggested by counsel in that case for resolving the question whether breach of a statutory provision gives rise to a civil remedy. In my judgment, this formula, though useful, must be cautiously applied, for it purports to do just what Lord Simonds declined to do in *Cutler's* case[2], namely to formulate a set of rules. Moreover, it depends largely on the distinction between provisions designed for the benefit of the public at large and provisions intended to protect or benefit a particular category of persons, the validity of which was challenged by Atkin LJ in *Phillips's* case[3], by Greer and Maugham LJJ in *Monk v Warbey*[4] and Somervell LJ[5] in his dissenting judgment in *Solomons v R Gertzenstein Ltd*.

So the question which we must ask ourselves remains: was it the intention of the 1965 Act to provide, by s 30, a new civil remedy for aggrieved tenants? For this purpose attention must be concentrated on Part III of the 1965 Act into which s 30 falls, for Part III deals with a separate subject-matter. It is headed 'Protection against Harassment and Eviction without due process of Law', and has little direct connection with the rest of the Act. It deals separately with unlawful eviction and harassment (s 30), restriction on re-entry without due process of law (s 31), and prohibition of eviction without due process of law (s 32). Similar provisions were first introduced by s 1 of the Protection from Eviction Act 1964, which was repealed and re-enacted, but with extensive and for present purposes significant changes, by the 1965 Act.

It will be convenient to begin by considering the provisions as they originally appeared in the 1964 Act. They are to be found in s 1(3) which reads as follows:

'It shall not be lawful for the owner of any premises—(a) to enforce against the occupier, otherwise than by proceedings in the court, his right to recover possession of the premises; or (b) to withhold or withdraw from the occupier any services or furniture which are for the time being provided for him, except to the extent authorised in the proceedings or for reasonable cause; and if any person contravenes the provisions of this subsection he shall, without prejudice to any liability or remedy to which he may be subject in civil proceedings, be liable on summary conviction to a fine not exceeding one hundred pounds or to imprisonment for a term not exceeding six months, or to both.'

Subsection (4) provided a limited defence for the owner based on reasonable belief that the occupier had ceased to reside on the premises.

It would not have been easy to derive a new civil remedy from a statutory provision in that form. Paragraph (a) does not impose a duty on anyone; its effect is to deprive the owner of the premises of his common law right to recover possession without obtaining a court order, so he is now exposed to an action for trespass to which formerly he would have had a good defence. Paragraph (b) might be said to create a duty not to withold or to withdraw, but the owner is already under a contractual obligation not to act in such a way; so it was unnecessary to provide an additional

1   [1969] 3 All ER 225 at 234, 235, [1970] 2 QB 223 at 237
2   [1949] 1 All ER 544, [1949] AC 398
3   [1923] 2 KB 832, [1923] All ER Rep 127
4   [1935] 1 KB 75, [1934] All ER Rep 373
5   [1954] 2 All ER 625 at 631, [1954] 2 QB 243 at 255

cause of action. It could hardly be contended that an owner who withholds or with-
a draws something which he has been providing voluntarily is caught by this provision
which imposes comparatively severe penalties for breach. Then the subsection
expressly provides that any person contravening its provisions shall be liable to a
fine or imprisonment 'without prejudice to any liability or remedy to which he may
be subject in civil proceedings'. The penalty therefore is to be additional to any civil
liability. Counsel for the tenant submitted that this was a positive indication that
b Parliament intended to provide a civil remedy as well as a criminal sanction. It would
be difficult in the present state of the law to think of a more devious way of
communicating to the public such a simple intention.

   But when we come to the 1965 Act the position, in my view, is even clearer. Subsection (3) of the 1964 Act has been split up into three separate sections, apparently
with the object of segregating the criminal and the civil remedies. The restrictions on
c the owner's common law and contractual rights to re-enter or to recover possession
have been put into ss 31 and 32 respectively. Neither of these sections provides a
specific remedy for breach of its terms but the effect of them, as before, is to deprive
the owner of his defence to an action for trespass. Section 30, however, is in an entirely
new form. Now it is, in form, a purely penal section. Subsection (1) creates the
criminal offence of unlawful eviction. It applies to anyone who unlawfully deprives
d or attempts to deprive a residential occupier of his occupation of the premises. The
existing law already provides the occupier with a remedy in the form of an action for
trespass against any person other than the owner, so acting, and ss 31 and 32 render
the owner or lessor equally liable in trespass. No additional remedy is therefore
required. Subsection (2) is even more clearly a penal provision. First, a specific intent
or mens rea must be proved before the offence is complete: that is the intent to
e cause the residential occupier either to give up the premises or to refrain from
exercising some right in respect of the premises. Secondly, the actus reus of the
subsection is the doing of acts calculated to interfere with the peace or comfort of the
occupier or the persistent witholding or withdrawal of services reasonably required
for the occupation of the premises. All such acts must in the existing state of the law
give rise either to a remedy in trespass or for breach of contract or for breach of the
f covenant of quiet enjoyment. Again it is unnecessary to imply into the subsection an
intention to create a new civil remedy for breach of statutory duty. Finally, sub-s (4)
again preserves all the existing liabilities or remedies in civil proceedings. Following
Lord Simonds's precept in Cutler's case[1], and considering the relevant sections of the
Act and the surrounding circumstances, including the pre-existing law, my conclusion
is that this section does not create a new statutory cause of action.

g   I do not reach this conclusion with any satisfaction because I have considerable
sympathy with counsel for the tenant's submission that, in practice, it is much easier
for a tenant and his advisers to obtain an injunction in the county court for breach of
statutory duty than for breach of contract or trespass, because the latter may give rise
to legal argument. It ought not to be so but may well happen in fact. It is very
unfortunate that Parliament still seems reluctant to act on Lord du Parcq's suggestion
h in Cutler's case[2] that it should state explicitly whether or not such a statutory provision
as s 30 is intended to create both criminal and civil liability or criminal liability only.
The civil remedy of injunction is particularly valuable in situations which require the
rapid intervention of the court to stop some unwarranted conduct or to restore the
status quo within a matter of hours or days. Such situations frequently arise in a
domestic context or between landlords and tenants and cannot be satisfactorily dealt
j with in the criminal courts. But Parliament seems curiously reluctant to take advantage of so convenient a remedy. Damages, on the other hand, are a clumsy and slow
way of remedying such situations and may be used as a means of putting undue
pressure on defendants.

1 [1949] 1 All ER at 548, [1949] AC at 407
2 [1949] 1 All ER at 549, [1949] AC at 410

I must now consider the facts, in case I am wrong on my view of the law. It is quite clear on the evidence in this case that the landlords were utterly indifferent to, and *a* unconcerned for, this tenant. They did not make contact with him for some months after acquiring the house, merely receiving his rent through the post and being unaware for a long time of his plight, living in this very poor house without a supply of gas, and later of electricity. They are open to criticism and were undoubtedly in breach of contract, but whether they could have been convicted of an offence under s 30(2) of the 1965 Act is quite another matter. It is significant that Mr Ward, the local *b* authority's harassment officer, was involved in the case throughout and yet no prosecution under this section was ever launched.

The landlords bought this house in May 1973 at or after an auction. No one on their behalf visited the premises until December 1973. In October 1973 the gas supply was cut off by the gas board, not by the defendants. They then found that £435 was owing to the gas board by the previous owners. It is clear from the evidence that the land- *c* lords had some considerable difficulty with the gas board over re-connecting the supply. The precise details do not appear clearly from the evidence. It may be that the landlords did not bother very much about it. The judge found that they were 'completely indifferent' about it. They did not arrange for the supply to be restored until June 1974 after the present proceedings had been started. The judge held that there had been a withholding of gas from October 1973. I doubt whether the evidence *d* justified that finding in view of the large arrears which were not the responsibility of the landlords, and the attitude of the gas board. Then the judge asked himself the question: 'Was it [the cutting off of the gas] because of the landlords' calculated act, was it a deliberate withholding?' He did not immediately answer his own question although he did at a slightly later stage, saying that in October 1973 the landlords 'were not deliberately acting with a view to causing the tenants to leave'. But he had *e* already said that he was satisfied that he could find harassment under the 1965 Act. Later in his judgment he found as a fact that from March 1974 the landlords sought to persuade the tenant to leave the premises in such a manner as to constitute harass-ment on their part. He thought it was 'their intention to see whether it was possible to persuade the [tenant] to leave the property by inactivity on their part'. He added: '. . . they were content to let it drift along purporting to be doing things that they *f* were not. They were dilatory.'

In my judgment, these findings are insufficient to support the tenant's case. He must prove that the landlords withheld the gas supply with intent to cause him to give up the premises. I do not think that the necessary intention was proved. The other two complaints, relating to electricity and water, were dealt with in less detail by the judge and stand or fall with the alleged withholding of the gas supply. *g*

The result is that the appeal must be dismissed and the cross-appeal allowed. The consequence will be that the tenant will lose his £75 damages altogether, because it is conceded that, having been given the opportunity in the county court to amend his particulars of claim to allege breaches of contract to which the landlords have no obvious defence, he declined on legal advice to do so, and it is now too late. This, I am afraid, is the price that has to be paid for rejecting the obvious remedy in an attempt *h* to establish another one.

I too would like to express my gratitude to counsel as amicus curiae for his careful and thorough review of all the relevant authorities. Without his assistance the case would have been extremely difficult. I am conscious that I have not referred to many of the authorities which were cited to us, not out of disrespect for the arguments on both sides but to avoid unduly lengthening this judgment. *j*

I would dismiss the appeal and allow the cross-appeal.

SHAW LJ. I agree with the judgments which have been given for the reasons which have been stated. Section 30 of the Rent Act 1965 is concerned only to impose penal sanctions on the conduct described respectively in sub-ss (1) and (2). The

object of its provisions is to discourage such conduct. It does not purport to give a
a special cause of action to the victims of it, who might include all the members of a
numerous household and who might suffer in varying degrees. The proliferation
of relatively small claims if the contrary view were right presents an alarming
prospect, and the courts would be required to perform an impossible task in measuring the individual damage to several persons resulting from the same course of
harassment.

b   The argument that, although the provisions of sub-ss (1) and (2) are in themselves
penal, a concomitant civil remedy is also created, is partly founded on the language
of sub-s (4), which enacts: 'Nothing in this section shall be taken to prejudice any
liability or remedy to which a person guilty of an offence thereunder may be
subject to civil proceedings.' It is said that this points to the genesis of a civil remedy
under the section. In my view it points in the opposite direction. The negative
c introductory sentence, 'Nothing in this section shall be taken to prejudice', is hardly
indicative of a procreative statutory intention; and the phrase 'any liability or remedy'
which follows refers to liabilities or remedies which have an independent origin such
as a breach of a contract of tenancy or the commission of a trespass or a nuisance.
That this is so, is demonstrated by what is defined as the intent giving rise to an
offence under sub-s (2)(*b*), namely to cause a residential occupier 'to refrain from
d exercising any right or pursuing any remedy in respect of the premises'. The right or
the remedy referred to must clearly be one that already exists at the time of the
commission of the acts which constitute the offence under sub-s (2)(*b*).

Something is added in support of this view by the heading to Part III of the Act.
It reads: 'Protection against Harassment and Eviction without due process of Law'.
No reference is made to redress or compensation; and s 30 is the first provision of
e Part III which follows this heading.

As has been indicated in the judgment of Ormrod LJ, the formulation of general
rules as to when a penal statute may give rise by implication to a civil remedy for the
benefit of a person harmed by an offence created by it is a dubious exercise. The
numerous authorities which have been cited in this regard do, however, suggest that
the following conditions must be satisfied before such a remedy will be held to be so
f conferred: (1) the offence created must consist of a failure to perform a defined duty
which the statute imposes on the potential offender; (2) the duty must be imposed for
the benefit of a class of persons which includes the person harmed; and (3) the
contemplated beneficiaries of the performance of the duty would, unless a correlative
remedy is implied by the statute, be without any, or any effective, remedy for the
harm they may suffer from the failure to perform that duty, that is to say from the
g commission of the offence created by the statute.

The offence created by s 30(2) of the Rent Act 1965 plainly does not satisfy the first
of these conditions and probably not the third. Accordingly I would allow the
landlords' cross-appeal and set aside the order of the judge. The tenant's appeal on
quantum must necessarily fail.

h *Appeal dismissed; cross-appeal allowed.*

Solicitors: *Alexander & Partners* (for the tenant); *Treasury Solicitor.*

Gavin Gore-Andrews Barrister.

Practice Note

QUEEN'S BENCH DIVISION
LORD WIDGERY CJ, KILNER BROWN AND WATKINS JJ
13th FEBRUARY 1976

Practice – Chambers – Queen's Bench Division – Chambers applications – Hearing before judge in chambers – Sittings in chambers outside London wherever High Court sittings held – Issue of notice of appeal or summons in district registry – Applications for bail.

Notes

For the jurisdiction of a single judge of the Queen's Bench Division, see 10 Halsbury's Laws (4th Edn) para 853.

For applications to a judge in chambers, see 30 Halsbury's Laws (3rd Edn) 341, 342, para 622.

LORD WIDGERY CJ, at the sitting of the court, gave the following practice direction on the subject of the sittings of a Queen's Bench judge in chambers out of London on civil business.

1. To the extent that the business of the courts permits, and subject to the provisions of this direction, judges of the Queen's Bench Division will sit in chambers at any place where sittings of the High Court are held, as well as in London, to deal with any business which may be dealt with by a judge of the Queen's Bench Division in chambers except any business which may from time to time be notified.

2. Where a party desires that a matter be heard before a judge in chambers outside London, the notice of an appeal or summons shall bear the title of the district registry in which the action is proceeding but shall be issued in the district registry at the place at which it is to be heard.

3. Before a party issues a judge's summons or a notice of appeal in a district registry, he should enquire at the registry whether the state of business will permit the matter to be heard there and it is proper to be so heard.

4. A judge's summons or notice of appeal issued in a district registry may be transferred for hearing to a judge in chambers sitting in London or at another place outside London on the application of a party made to the judge or by the court of its own motion, and such a summons or notice issued in the Central Office may similarly be transferred for hearing to a place outside London. Before a transfer to a place outside London is ordered, the court will require to be informed, from enquiries made by the parties or the court officers, whether the matter can conveniently be taken there.

5. In cases not specifically provided for, the practice of the Central Office as to district registry appeals shall be followed as nearly as circumstances permit.

6. Applications for bail under RSC Ord 79 to a judge in chambers may, and should wherever possible, be made to a judge of the Queen's Bench Division at any place where sittings of the High Court or of the Crown Court are held, being the place nearest to the court where the applicant has appeared; provided that such applications made through the Official Solicitor may in any case be made in London. Outside London the summons should be issued in the district registry at the place where the application can be heard, and the order drawn up and perfected in that registry.

Lea Josse Barrister.

Horrocks and another v Forray

COURT OF APPEAL, CIVIL DIVISION
MEGAW, SCARMAN AND BRIDGE LJJ
6th, 7th NOVEMBER 1975

*Licence – Licence to occupy premises – Contractual licence – Unmarried couple – Circumstances
in which contract will be inferred – Circumstances indicating meeting of minds with intention
to affect legal relationship – Contractual terms reasonably clearly made out – House acquired
by man to provide accommodation for mistress and children – House owned by man – Relationship of man and mistress continuing over period of 17 years until death of man – Mistress
generously supported by man – Whether contractual licence for mistress to remain in house to
be inferred.*

S married in 1951 and a son of that marriage was born in 1952. In 1957, unknown to
his wife, S began to keep a mistress, the defendant, and that relationship continued up
to the time of his death. A daughter was born of the association in July 1961. S was at
that time a wealthy man and he treated the defendant generously. Following the
birth of his daughter he wholly supported the defendant to the extent of some
£4,000-£5,000 a year in addition to the provision of accommodation. In September
1966 the defendant married another man and had a child by him, but that marriage
effectively lasted only six weeks and ended in divorce. While it continued the defendant continued to be S's mistress. In May 1973 S bought a house in Kensington for
£36,500 for the defendant and her children to live in. The house was conveyed into
his own name. S contemplated transferring the house to the defendant, but decided
against it when he discovered the amount of stamp duty and capital gains tax for
which he would be liable if that step were taken. As an alternative, he considered
creating a trust for the benefit of his daughter but, again for tax reasons, he decided to
take the matter no further. In April 1974 S was killed in a motor accident. His wife
had never known of S's relationship with the defendant and it was not until after his
death that she and S's executors learnt of the existence of the Kensington house.
Although S had at one time been a wealthy man, he had lived extravagantly for many
years and by the time of his death he had dissipated most of his resources. If the
executors were unable to sell the Kensington house with vacant possession it was
probable that S's estate would be insolvent. The executors wrote to the defendant
requiring her to give up possession of the house and, on her failure to do so, brought
proceedings for possession. The defendant contended that, from the circumstances of
her relationship with S, a contract was to be inferred whereby she had, at the request
and instance of S, subordinated her mode of life and choice of residence to S in return
for an undertaking by S to maintain her and her family and to provide her with a
permanent home; and that, by virtue of that contract, she had an irrevocable licence
to remain in the Kensington house, either (a) for her life, (b) so long as the daughter
was receiving full-time education, or (c) so long as she and the daughter reasonably
required the accommodation.

Held – In order to establish a contract, whether it was an express contract or a contract
implied by law, it had to be shown that there had been a meeting of the minds of the
parties, with a definition of the contractual terms reasonably clearly made out, with
an intention to affect their legal relationship. In the circumstances no contract such as
that alleged by the defendant could be inferred from the conduct of the parties and
accordingly there was no contractual licence. Accordingly, since the executors had
terminated the defendant's licence, they were entitled to possession (see p 742 *d* to *g*,
p 744 *g* and *h*, p 745 *b* and p 746 *e* to *g*, post).

DD

Ward v Byham [1956] 2 All ER 318 and *Tanner v Tanner* [1975] 3 All ER 776
distinguished.

Notes
For the nature of a licence to occupy property, see 23 Halsbury's Laws (3rd Edn)
430-432, para 1026, and for cases on the subject, see 31(1) Digest (Reissue) 201-223,
1678-1821.

Cases referred to in judgments
Seaborne v Maddy (1840) 9 C & P 497, 3 Digest (Repl) 439, 316.
T B, Re [1966] 3 All ER 509, [1967] Ch 247, [1967] 2 WLR 15, Digest (Cont Vol B) 525,
710b.
Tanner v Tanner [1975] 3 All ER 776, [1975] 1 WLR 1346, CA.
Ward v Byham [1956] 2 All ER 318, [1956] 1 WLR 496, CA, 3 Digest (Repl) 439, 327.

Case also cited
Binions v Evans [1972] 2 All ER 70, [1972] Ch 359, CA.

Appeal
This was an appeal by the defendant, Maxine Forray, against the order made by his
Honour Judge McDonnell in the West London County Court on 18th July 1975,
whereby he ordered that the plaintiffs, Arthur Edward Leslie Horrocks and John
Stephen Lloyd, the executors of the will of William Charles Ayshford Sanford
deceased, should recover possession against the defendant of premises known as and
situate at 7 Farm Place, London, W8. The facts are set out in the judgment of Megaw LJ.

Simon Goldblatt QC and *J G McK Laws* for the defendant.
Walter Blum for the plaintiffs.

MEGAW LJ. On 6th April 1974 Mr William Charles Ayshford Sanford was killed
in a motor accident. He was 68. He had been married twice. His second marriage was
in 1951. There was one child of that marriage, a son, born in 1952. By his will, Mr
Sanford appointed Mr Arthur Edward Leslie Horrocks and Mr John Stephen Lloyd as
his executors. They, in their capacity as executors, are the plaintiffs in the action out
of which this appeal arises. The defendant in the action is Mrs Maxine Forray. She
had been Mr Sanford's mistress for, it is said, some 17 years, and had so continued up
to the time of his death. It would seem that he first met her when she was 15 years
old. Though there was evidence, given by the defendant herself, as to the circumstances in which she met Mr Sanford and became his mistress, I do not think that that
evidence—or indeed a good deal of the rest of the evidence relating to her subsequent
life and activities—is of relevance to the issue which this court has to decide. The
evidence has been carefully reviewed by the learned judge, Judge McDonnell, who
heard the action out of which this appeal arises in the West London County Court
on 7th July 1975. He delivered his judgment on 18th July. There has been no substantial criticism of the learned judge's findings of fact, based on the evidence of the
witnesses whom he saw and heard giving evidence. I shall refer hereafter, I hope not
at any great length, to such of the facts, found by him as appear to me to be relevant
to the issues now before this court: issues which are substantially more limited in
scope than those which the learned judge in the county court had to consider on the
basis of the much more wide-ranging arguments which were presented before him
on behalf of the defendant.
    The claim by the plaintiffs is a claim for possession of a house 7 Farm Place,
Kensington, W8. That house is, and has since about May 1973 been, occupied by the
defendant and, as I understand it, two children of hers. One of those children, a girl,

born in July 1961, is the child of the late Mr Sanford. The other, a boy born in July
a 1968, is the son of another man, a Mr Forray, whom the defendant married in September 1966. As I understand it, that marriage ended in divorce. But during its
continuance, the defendant continued to be the late Mr Sanford's mistress. She has
also had not infrequent sexual intercourse with another man, apparently a great
friend of the late Mr Sanford, and apparently with his knowledge. She has sometimes
been known by the name of that other man.

b   Mrs Sanford, the widow of the late Mr Sanford, had no knowledge or inkling of
her husband's relationship with the defendant, whom she never met. Mrs Sanford,
as the judge records, throughout her marriage regarded her husband as a 'marvellous
husband'. It was only after his death that his widow came to know of the defendant
and of this relationship which had in fact existed, concealed from her by her husband,
for many years. It was only after his death that she, or his executors, the plaintiffs,
c became aware of his ownership of 7 Farm Place, which the late Mr Sanford had in
fact bought, and which had been conveyed to him in his own name, in May 1973, and
which since then had been the residence of the defendant and her children. He had
paid £36,500 for it in May 1973.

Mr Sanford had at one time been a wealthy man. But he had lived extravagantly
for many years. At the time of his death he was, as the judge said, 'coming to the end
d of his financial tether'. If the plaintiffs, the late Mr Sanford's executors, are unable to
sell 7 Farm Place with vacant possession, it is probable that the estate will be insolvent.
The widow, to whom the late Mr Sanford by his will left all his estate for life, with a
gift over on her death to their son, would in those circumstances receive nothing from
the estate. She, like the defendant's daughter, the late Mr Sanford's illegitimate child,
may recover compensation under the Fatal Accidents Acts as being dependants of the
e late Mr Sanford, if negligence resulting in the death of Mr Sanford is proved as
against the driver of the car, who was understood to be his brother. But so far as
anything from the late Mr Sanford's own estate is concerned, the widow, if the
defendant is permitted by the law to remain in possession of 7 Farm Place, is likely
to be left with nothing.

If, on the other hand, 7 Farm Place can be sold with vacant possession—that is if
f the claim in this action against the defendant for possession succeeds—the estate is
likely to be, at least, solvent. The widow will get something. So far as concerns the
defendant's daughter, who is also the late Mr Sanford's daughter, she, as I have said,
may be entitled to damages under the Fatal Accidents Acts as being a dependant of
the late Mr Sanford. She would also be entitled to claim against the estate—should
the estate have anything to make such a claim fruitful—under the Inheritance
g (Family Provision) Act 1938, as amended. In the county court proceedings it was
thought that there might be a conflict of interest between the defendant and her
daughter; so the Official Solicitor became guardian ad litem of the daughter. We
are given to understand that he does not think that there is a conflict which requires
any intervention on his part.

It is in those circumstances that the plaintiffs, as executors, started the proceedings
h which have led to this appeal. By their particulars of claim, which are dated 21st
March 1975, they set out the late Mr Sanford's ownership of 7 Farm Place. That is not
challenged. They aver that the defendant, since about May 1973, has occupied the
house pursuant to licence of the plaintiffs. That is not challenged: indeed, it is asserted
on behalf of the defendant. The plaintiffs, in their particulars of claim, assert that the
licence terminated with the death of Mr Sanford or was determined by a letter
j dated 2nd August 1974. By that letter the plaintiffs' solicitors wrote to the solicitor
who was then acting for the defendant, in these terms:

'With reference to 7 Farm Place, London W8 this property clearly falls into the
estate and we shall be obliged if you will let us have the Deeds of the property
as soon as possible. The Executors require vacant possession of the house but

think it reasonable that Mrs. Forray and her daughter should be given a reasonable period in which to make arrangements for alternative accommodation. We   *a*
would therefore suggest that Mrs. Forray make arrangements to vacate the
premises by 30th November 1974.'

The defence and counterclaim, which was originally delivered on 28th April 1975,
has been amended and re-amended, the re-amendment being by leave of the court
at the trial in the county court. It is a formidable document, but as events have   *b*
turned out a substantial part of it is not now relevant. The defence 'admits and avers'
that the defendant and her daughter had a licence from the late Mr Sanford to occupy
7 Farm Place. There was then an allegation, which is no longer pursued in this court,
that the property was held in trust for the defendant, or her daughter, or for both.
There was also a defence that the defendant had acquired a beneficial interest in the
property as a result of contribution made by her to expenditure. It was also said   *c*
that the plaintiffs were estopped from disputing the beneficial ownership of the
house by the defendant or her daughter or both; and various particulars were given
which are said to give rise to that estoppel. We in this court need not trouble about
those defences because they are no longer pursued. It is not now, in this court, contended for the defendant that she has any proprietary right to—any right of ownership
in—7 Farm Place. Her claim is solely that she is entitled to remain in occupation by   *d*
reason of a licence—in ordinary language, by reason of permission to occupy—given to
her by the late Mr Sanford.
So the defence which, having been pleaded by amendment, still remains is, in
substance and effect, that the licence for the occupation of the premises—and both
parties agree that there was a licence—was and is a contractual licence, the contractual terms of which were binding on Mr Sanford and remain binding on his   *e*
executors after his death. Those terms were pleaded, or at least are now put forward
on behalf of the defendant perhaps not in precisely the form in which they were
pleaded, as involving three possible alternatives. Those alternatives are: (a) that
the licence was to be for the lifetime of the defendant, so that no one could turn
her out as long as she lived; or (b) that the licence was to continue so long as the
daughter should be undergoing full-time education; or (c) that it was to continue   *f*
so long as either or both of them—the defendant and her daughter—reasonably
needed the accommodation. In amplification of those terms, which are put forward
as alternatives, I think it became clear from the argument presented by counsel for
the defendant in this court that so far as each of them was concerned he would say
that it was an implied term that, although the defendant was entitled to continue to
live in the house for one or other of those periods, she was not obliged to live there for   *g*
one moment longer than she herself wished so to do.
Then the pleading sets out, by reference forwards and backwards to later and
earlier parts of the pleading, various matters on which the defendant would rely in
support of this assertion in the amended pleading of a contractual licence. Thus, by
reference to earlier particulars in the pleading, there was included reliance on the
assertion that the defendant and Mr Sanford had, as it is put, 'cohabited' for some   *h*
17 years prior to the testator's death, and from and since the birth of the daughter he
wholly maintained and supported the defendant and the daughter and provided
living accommodation for them, as well as clothes and holidays and all their day-to-
day living expenses.
I shall not refer to the other points that were indicated in the pleadings because
they seem to me to be appropriate to the now abandoned allegations of trust or   *j*
acquisition of a beneficial interest in the property, rather than to the only point now
maintained—that is a contractual licence. It is perhaps desirable, however, to refer to
the pleading which appears in sub-para (iii) of the particulars given under para 3 of
the defence as to the consideration which is alleged to exist as giving legal force to the
alleged contractual licence. What is said on that is this:

'Further, so far as necessary the Defendant will say that she had offered and given consideration for the licence (a) by relinquishing her possession or occupation of her previous dwellinghouse, and (b) by reason of the facts and matters pleaded in Paragraph 5 of this Defence [those are matters pleaded in relation to estoppel] and further (c) [and this was added by re-amendment at the trial] by her agreement and acceptance that the Testator [i e Mr Sanford] should fulfil his legal obligation to support [the daughter] principally by the provision of accommodation and accordingly by her withholding any action or process to enforce such obligation, by seeking an affiliation order or otherwise. In the premises the said licence is not determinable at the behest of the Plaintiffs in these proceedings.'

So much for the pleadings. The way in which this defence to the claim for possession is now presented on behalf of the defendant is this. There is authority of the court, particularly the decision in *Tanner v Tanner*[1], which was decided on 30th April 1975, that a woman who had been the mistress of a man was entitled to remain in occupation of a house which had been provided for her and her child by the man whose mistress she had been. The facts of the case are, as I think, accurately, though briefly, summarised in the headnote. What the headnote says is this[2]:

'In November 1969 the defendant, a spinster, gave birth to twin daughters of whom the plaintiff was the father. In early 1970 the plaintiff and the defendant decided that a house should be purchased to provide a home for the defendant and her baby daughters. In July 1970 the plaintiff bought a house on mortgage, and the defendant left her rent-controlled flat and moved with the babies into the house. Three years later the plaintiff offered the defendant £4,000 to move out of the house. The defendant refused on the ground that the house was hers and the children's until the latter left school. The plaintiff's solicitor wrote to the defendant purporting to terminate her licence to live in the house and asking her to leave. When she did not do so the plaintiff brought possession proceedings in the county court. The defendant counterclaimed for a declaration that she was entitled to a beneficial interest in the house. The county court judge rejected the defendant's contentions and made an order for possession, in pursuance of which the defendant and her children were rehoused by the local authority.'

The defendant, the lady, appealed; and this court allowed the appeal. There was a complication there which does not arise in the present case—that as, by order of the county court, the defendant had gone out of possession, there was not any order by the court restoring her to possession of the house; but she was in lieu of that given damages because what had been done at the instance of the plaintiff had been inconsistent with her contractual rights. Continuing with the headnote:

'*Held*, allowing the appeal, that the inference to be drawn from all the circumstances was that the defendant had a contractual licence to have accommodation in the house for herself and the children so long as the children were of school age and reasonably required the accommodation; and that, accordingly, the order for possession ought not to have been made.'

That is a decision of this court, and it is a decision which any other division of the court would, of course, follow. We have got to ascertain, as that is the case which is and was principally relied on here and below in support of the defendant's contention, what it was that was decided in *Tanner v Tanner*[1] and, having seen what it was that was there decided, to apply that to the facts of this case.

What was decided in *Tanner v Tanner*[1] was really very simple. It was decided that on the evidence that had been adduced in that case there was a fair inference to be

1 [1975] 3 All ER 776, [1975] 1 WLR 1346
2 [1975] 1 WLR 1346

drawn that the man and his mistress had entered into a contract by which the man
had agreed, for consideration, that the house which was being bought by him for the   *a*
occupation of the woman and her children should remain available to her, with a
continuing licence for her to occupy it so long, at any rate, as the children were of
school age, or unless some other circumstances arose meanwhile which would make
it reasonable for the possession to cease. It was, therefore, a decision on the facts of
that case that there was a contract. There was not an express contract: that is to say,
there was no evidence that one had said to the other 'I promise that I will do so-and-so'.   *b*
But of course this court is entitled to infer a contract, even though it is clear that
words have not been spoken expressly stating a contractual promise or an offer and
acceptance in express words. The court is entitled to infer the existence of a contract.
In the circumstances of that case, this court inferred that there was a contract such as
I have mentioned.

There is really no doubt about what was the basis of the decision there. It may be   *c*
that the bringing in of the conception of contract into situations of this sort does give
rise to difficulties. It may be that some other approach to situations of this sort would
be preferable. But that is not a matter for us. We have got to take the law as it is and
to apply it as it stands. The law as it stands does involve that the defendant can only
succeed in this case, on the submission now made on her behalf, if she shows that it is
proper to infer the existence of a contract which permitted her to remain in this house   *d*
for one or other of the three alternative periods which have been put forward and
which I have already mentioned. And, of course, she has to establish that that is a
contract which, properly viewed and in accordance with the terms which have to be
applied, was one which continued to exist as a matter of law after the death of the
late Mr Sanford.

In order to establish a contract, whether it be an express contract or a contract   *e*
implied by law, there has to be shown a meeting of the minds of the parties,
with a definition of the contractual terms reasonably clearly made out, with an
intention to affect the legal relationship: that is that the agreement that is made is
one which is properly to be regarded as being enforceable by the court if one or the
other fails to comply with it; and it still remains a part of the law of this country,
though many people think that it is time that it was changed to some other criterion,   *f*
that there must be consideration moving in order to establish a contract. All those
elements, on the facts in *Tanner v Tanner*[1], on the evidence accepted by the court,
were present. Are they present in this case? The learned judge in the county court
thought not, and therefore he held that there was here no contract and, therefore, no
contractual licence, and the question did not fall to be considered whether, if there
was a contract, its terms were alternative (a) or alternative (b) or alternative (c), as to   *g*
the length of the period for which the defendant was to be entitled to remain in this
house.

The basis of the assertion that there existed here a contractual licence is really this:
that there was evidence that over a period of a good many years, beginning at any
rate soon after the birth of the daughter, the late Mr Sanford had continuously
provided accommodation for the defendant and her daughter. That accommodation   *h*
had, I think we were told, involved about nine different addresses at one time or
another. In addition to continuing to provide accommodation for the defendant, the
late Mr Sanford had expended a very great deal of money, either by way of buying
things for the defendant and her child or children, or by way of providing her with
money with which she could herself provide things; and it is apparent that she was
provided with what one I think could fairly describe as a reasonably luxurious   *j*
existence. Her own evidence, as summarised by the learned judge in his judgment,
was that the deceased had expended on her and her children something of the order of
£4,000 or £5,000 a year. That was, as I understand it, in addition to the provision of
accommodation.

1   [1975] 3 All ER 776, [1975] 1 WLR 1346

There was also evidence that the late Mr Sanford had at some time indicated to a
a solicitor a desire to make some provision for the defendant. But the principal matter
which is put forward here as supporting the existence of a contract is what happened in
relation to the purchase of 7 Farm Place itself. That is summarised, and as I think
quite fairly and lucidly summarised, by the learned judge in the passage in his
judgment where he said:

b   'In 1973 the deceased [i e Mr Sanford] decided to buy the house at 7 Farm
     Place, the subject matter of this action. He did not instruct the first-named
     plaintiff, who was his family solicitor, but a Mr Signy to whom the defendant had
     introduced him. He told Mr Signy that he was buying it for the defendant and her
     child so that they should have some security if anything happened to him but
     he did not ask for the house to be conveyed to the defendant. Completion of the
c   purchase took place on the 10th May 1973 and the deceased was registered as
     the owner of the freehold on the 24th May 1973. After completion the deceased
     consulted Mr Signy about transferring the property to the defendant. When he
     was told that there might be a liability to capital gains tax and that ad valorem
     stamp duty would be payable he decided against doing so. On a later occasion he
     suggested to Mr Signy that a trust should be created for the benefit of his child . . .
d   and was advised that ad valorem stamp duty would still be payable and so he took
     the matter no further. He later asked Mr Signy to draft a codicil to his will
     leaving the house in trust for the child; Mr Signy said he would like to see the
     will itself before doing so and the matter proceeded no further.'

Pausing at that point in the learned judge's judgment, it may well be said that those
facts, which were not really in dispute, at any rate indicated that the late Mr Sanford,
e however anxious he was to make provision for the defendant, balked at the financial
responsibility that he was told would be involved by way of tax and stamp duty if this
step were to be taken to transfer this house to the defendant. That he was not prepared to do. Nor, apparently, having thought about the completely different idea of
leaving the house by his will in trust for the child, had he done anything about that
at the time of his death. Of course, all those things do not make it impossible that he
f also had agreed with the defendant, or was minded to agree thereafter with the
defendant, that she should, without obtaining any ownership of the property, nevertheless have a right to continue to live there under one or other of the three alternatives which have been put forward.
The judge then went on:

g   'The defendant said in evidence that for 16 years the deceased had said that he
     would eventually get her a house and I accept that he may well have expressed
     such an intention in general terms from time to time. When 7 Farm Place was
     purchased she may well have believed that it would become her property but I
     do not believe that the deceased ever expressly told her so.'

Then the learned judge, having reviewed the evidence and having dealt with various
h other issues, which no longer arise in this court because they have been decided
against the defendant and are not the subject of appeal, went on to deal with *Tanner v
Tanner*[1]. He analysed that decision, as I think entirely correctly, and went on to say:

     'In the present case I can find no circumstances whatsoever from which to
     infer an agreement that the defendant was entitled to live in the house for her
j   life or whilst [the daughter] was of school age. There is a strong moral obligation
     on a man to provide and care for his illegitimate child and an additional obliga-
     tion for the deep wrong he has done to that child by inflicting illegitimacy on her:
     Re T B[2]. At common law there was no obligation on the father to provide for his

---

1   [1975] 3 All ER 776, [1975] 1 WLR 1346
2   [1966] 3 All ER 509, [1967] Ch 247

illegitimate child: *Seaborne v Maddy*[1], but he may be ordered to provide weekly
payments unlimited in amount under an affiliation order at the suit of the   *a*
mother, the Supplementary Benefits Commission or a local authority under the
Affiliation Proceedings Act 1957, as amended. It is also well settled that a putative
father may make a binding contract with the mother to contribute to the child's
maintenance for which her undertaking to care for the child affords the consideration: *Ward v Byham*[2]. In the present case there was no such contract because
the deceased provided handsomely for the maintenance of the child during his   *b*
lifetime. Where an affiliation order has been made the death of the putative
father puts an end to the order and arrears are not recoverable from his estate . . .
I therefore hold that the right of the child or its mother to maintenance from the
putative father continues only during the latter's lifetime.'

Then he referred to the provisions of the Inheritance (Family Provision) Act 1938, to
which I have referred, which would enable this daughter to present a claim against the   *c*
estate, if there was anything in the estate from which a claim could be met.

The judge, in substance, as I see it, was saying that on the facts of this case, as
contrasted with the facts that emerged in *Tanner v Tanner*[3], he was unable to hold that
there were shown any events or facts from which the inference could fairly be drawn,
on the balance of probability, that there was here a contract such as is suggested giving
this defendant a legal right to remain in possession of the house for any of the periods   *d*
suggested.

In this court counsel for the defendant summarised his submission to the contrary
in this way. He submitted that, on the facts, over a period of years the defendant was,
at the request and the instance of the late Mr Sanford, subordinating her mode of
life, or her 'life-style', and her choice of residence to the directions of the late Mr
Sanford, on the 'understanding' that he, Mr Sanford, would generously maintain the   *e*
defendant and her family in the meanwhile and would, when circumstances permitted, provide her with a permanent home. Then counsel for the defendant, as I
understand it, submitted that that contract was made long before the purchase of
7 Farm Place, but soon after the birth of the daughter. But, said counsel for the
defendant, that contract, made earlier and being in existence earlier, was varied when   *f*
7 Farm Place was bought, and was varied so that the home that was to be given to the
defendant on these terms was now no longer left uncertain, but was now defined as
being 7 Farm Place. The 'understanding' which is referred to in that summary of the
position was amplified by counsel for the defendant as involving that a promise—a
contractually binding promise—had been given by the late Mr Sanford, and that it
related to the occupation of 7 Farm Place.

With great respect to counsel for the defendant's argument, I am quite unable to   *g*
see, on the facts and circumstances of this case, that there was here any conceivable
basis for an implication that any such binding promise had been made by Mr Sanford
as is suggested. The fact that he had it in mind to seek to provide some security for
the defendant in the event of his death certainly does not go anything like far enough
to bring into existence what is necessary to show a binding contract of this nature.
There was here, in my judgment, simply nothing on the evidence that would have   *h*
entitled the learned judge to come to the conclusion that there was any such contractual licence. I say that without going on to consider what I think might well be an
extremely difficult further barrier in the way of the defendant. Supposing that she
had established something which otherwise could be regarded as being a contract,
where is the consideration for that contract to be found? In *Tanner v Tanner*[3] the
consideration was perfectly clear: the lady had given up her rent-controlled flat as a   *j*

---

1   (1840) 9 C & P 497
2   [1956] 2 All.ER 318, [1956] 1 WLR 496
3   [1975] 3 All ER 776, [1975] 1 WLR 1346

part of the bargain that she would move into the other accommodation. There is no
a such consideration here. However, I do not wish to decide this case, as far as I am
concerned, on any question relating to absence of consideration. But I am satisfied
that the learned judge was completely right in his view that the defendant had wholly
failed to show the existence of a contractual licence. I would accordingly dismiss the
appeal.

b **SCARMAN LJ.** So fully do I agree with the judgment of Megaw LJ that I wish to
add only a few comments.
   When an illegitimate child has been born, there is certainly nothing contrary to
public policy in the parents coming to an agreement, which they intend to be binding
in law, for the maintenance of the child and the mother. Parents of an illegitimate
child have obligations towards the child. So far from its being contrary to public policy
c that those obligations should be regulated by contract, I would have thought it was in
the public interest that they should be so. Certainly it seems to me far better that
parents in such a situation should seek to regulate their position by contract than that
they should have to resort to the court under the Affiliation Proceedings Act 1957.
   But it does not follow that, because there exists a relationship which can be regulated
by contract, the proper inference is that the parties in their particular circumstances
d have so regulated their relationship. In the present case there is no express contract.
   Counsel for the defendant has sought to persuade the court that a contract is to be
inferred from a course of conduct, from the development of the relationship between
the parties and its course over a period of years. This submission is, as a matter of
law, open to him. That has been clearly decided, as I understand it, in two cases in the
Court of Appeal to which he has referred us: *Ward v Byham*[1] and *Tanner v Tanner*[2].
e In each of those cases, however, the relationship of man and mistress was either broken
or on the point of collapse. The parties to the relationship, the man and the woman,
had to consider what best should be done for the innocent product of their relationship, the illegitimate children. In a very real sense, both in *Ward v Byham*[1] and in
Tanner v Tanner[2], the man and the woman were making arrangements for the
future at arm's length. The woman was concerned for herself and her children: the
f man was concerned to limit and define his financial responsibilities towards the
woman and the children. Here is a fertile area for the growth of an inference of a
legally binding contract; and for myself I do not find it surprising, when I look at the
facts in *Ward v Byham*[1] or *Tanner v Tanner*[2], that the court came to the conclusion
that a contract was to be inferred from the conduct of the parties. But how different
is this case. Right up to the death of the man there was a continuing, warm relation-
g ship of man and mistress. He was maintaining his mistress in luxurious, even, so the
judge thought, extravagant, style, and, we now know, in a style beyond his means;
his estate is now at risk of being insolvent.
   Counsel for the defendant has tried to tempt us to draw an inference of contract by
dangling in front of our eyes various contracts that might be inferred. If one looks at
that sort of fishing exercise with a dispassionate lawyer's eye, one begins to wonder
h whether he is not in difficulty in finding in the relationship any one, certain, contract.
Since he is saying that three or four possibilities arise (Megaw LJ has analysed them),
one wonders whether these parties, in fact, entered into a legally binding agreement
or intended to create legal relations on the basis of terms sufficiently formulated to
be clear and certain. But his real difficulty is that, whatever relationship did exist
between these two, it could as well be referable to the continuance of natural love
j and affection as to an intention to enter into an agreement which they intended to
have legal effect. In the other two cases, that relationship had ended, and it was
necessary to tie up the bits. In the present case the relationship was continuing until

---

1 [1956] 2 All ER 318, [1956] 1 WLR 496
2 [1975] 3 All ER 776, [1975] 1 WLR 1346

the unhappy and unexpected death of the man. Therefore counsel for the defendant is in difficulty with the facts of the case.

Fortunately for this court, the facts have been subjected to a most careful and detailed analysis by the trial judge, who, as Megaw LJ has already commented, directed himself absolutely correctly on the question of law, that is to say the effect and scope of *Tanner v Tanner*[1].

In the course of his analysis of the facts, the judge commented that the deceased had said, according to the defendant in evidence, that he would eventually get her a house, and the judge accepted that the deceased may well have expressed such an intention in general terms from time to time. But then the judge went on to find as follows: 'When 7 Farm Place was purchased she may well have believed that it would become her property but I do not believe that the deceased ever expressly told her so.' The judge later commented on the luxurious provision that this man chose to make for his mistress and their child (the relevance of that I have already mentioned); and then at the very end of his judgment, when he came to consider the effect of his findings, he said—rightly, in my judgment: 'It is well settled that a putative father may make a binding contract with the mother to contribute to the child's maintenance for which her undertaking to care for the child affords the consideration.' Then he said: 'In the present case there was no such contract because the deceased provided handsomely for the maintenance of the child during his lifetime.'

When I first read those words I was puzzled. But now that I have had the benefit of considering the judgment as a whole, and the benefit of counsel's argument on behalf of the defendant, I see exactly what the judge was saying. Here was a generous provision made for a woman who was still the mistress and for the child of that relationship. It was generous beyond what one would reasonably expect the man to accept a legally binding obligation to provide. It was generous, not because he was bound, or was binding himself, to be generous, but because he chose to be generous to the woman for whom there was a big place in his heart. Once one reaches that situation, one can see how the judge inferred that this was a case where there was no contract and where really it was unreasonable to infer a contract.

For those reasons, as well as for the reasons developed by Megaw LJ, I think this appeal should be dismissed.

BRIDGE LJ. I agree with both the judgments in this court, and indeed with the careful, reserved judgment of the learned judge who tried the case in the county court. I have nothing of my own to add.

Appeal dismissed. Vacant possession of premises in question to be given in 28 days.

Solicitors: *Rendall & Co* (for the defendant); *Frere Cholmeley & Co* (for the plaintiffs).

Mary Rose Plummer Barrister.

---

1   [1975] 3 All ER 776, [1975] 1 WLR 1346

a   # Vehicle and General Insurance Co Ltd (in liquidation) v H & W Christie Ltd

QUEEN'S BENCH DIVISION
HIS HONOUR JUDGE FAY QC
b   27th OCTOBER 1975

Costs – County court scale – High Court action – Recovery of less than prescribed amount – Reasonable ground for supposing amount recoverable exceeded prescribed amount – Action for an account – Insurance company – Renewal premiums collected by brokers on behalf of company – Brokers denying that they owed anything to company – List of old policies indicating
c   *that over £1,000 might have been payable in ordinary course of events on renewal – Company issuing writ in High Court – Subsequent examination of accounts disclosing that sum less than prescribed amount in fact owed – Company obtaining judgment for that sum – Whether company entitled to costs on High Court scale – County Courts Act 1959, s 47(1) (as amended by the Administration of Justice Act 1969, s 4).*

d   *Practice – Payment into court – Costs – Sum recovered no greater than sum paid in – Discretion as to costs after date of payment in – Award of costs to plaintiffs – Action for debt – Parties coming to agreement on amount of debt after issue of High Court writ – Defendants refusing to pay interest or costs on High Court scale – Defendants paying amount of debt into court – Plaintiffs subsequently obtaining judgment for interest and costs on High Court scale – Plaintiffs awarded costs after date of payment in.*

e   The defendants, a firm of insurance brokers, transacted business and collected premiums on behalf of the plaintiffs, an insurance company. The plaintiffs went into liquidation and negotiations took place between the liquidators and the defendants with a view to settling how much of the plaintiffs' money the defendants had in their possession. The defendants paid a sum to the plaintiffs and thereafter asserted that
f   they owed the plaintiffs nothing further and, in particular, that there had been no renewals of a number of policies which, in the ordinary course, would have been renewed. The plaintiffs doubted the accuracy of that assertion. The sums due on renewal which might have been paid in the ordinary course of events totalled over £1,000. In those circumstances the plaintiffs decided to issue a writ in the High Court claiming £1,535 and interest. Shortly before the trial of the action, a closer examina-
g   tion of the accounts established that a sum of £314·30 was in fact owed by the defendants to the plaintiffs, some renewal items having lapsed. The defendants agreed to pay that sum to the plaintiffs but they refused to pay interest, and they disputed their liability to pay costs. The plaintiffs declined to accept a cheque for £314·30 in full settlement of the account and so the defendants paid that sum into court. The plaintiffs pursued the action for the purpose of obtaining interest and
h   costs. In due course judgment was given for the plaintiffs in the same amount as the sum paid into court, with interest. The defendants claimed (i) that under s 47(1)[a] of the County Courts Act 1959 the plaintiffs were only entitled to costs on the county court scale since the amount recovered by the plaintiffs was less than £500 and (ii) that, since the plaintiffs had recovered the precise amount paid into court, the defendants were entitled to costs as from the date of payment in.

j   **Held** – (i) Since the premiums payable under the policies which in the ordinary course might have been renewed exceeded £1,000, the plaintiffs had reasonable ground for supposing that the amount recoverable in respect of their claim would be in

---

a   Section 47(1), as amended and so far as material, is set out at p 749 *b* to *d*, post

excess of the amount recoverable in the county court and therefore they were entitled
under s 47(1) of the 1959 Act to costs on the High Court scale (see p 750 *d* to *f*, post). *a*
    (ii) Although the plaintiffs had recovered the exact sum paid into court there had
in reality been no dispute about that sum. The issues to be decided by the court
related solely to the questions of interest and costs. Since the plaintiffs had been
forced to come to court to obtain the payment of interest and costs on the High Court
scale, an order would be made that the defendants should pay the plaintiffs the whole
costs of the action both before and after the date of payment in (see p 752 *e* to *h*, post). *b*

Notes
For costs where the action could have been commenced in the county court, see
30 Halsbury's Laws (3rd Edn) 424, 425, para 803, and for costs after payment into
court, see ibid 424, para 802.
    For the County Courts Act 1959, s 47, see 7 Halsbury's Statutes (3rd Edn) 334. *c*
    As from 1st October 1974, s 47 of the 1959 Act has been further amended by the
County Courts Jurisdiction Order 1974 (SI 1974 No 1273).

Cases referred to in judgment
Jefford v Gee [1970] 1 All ER 1202, [1970] 2 QB 130, [1970] 2 WLR 702, CA, Digest (Cont
    Vol C) 709, *182a*. *d*
Wagman v Vare Motors Ltd [1959] 3 All ER 326, [1959] 1 WLR 853, CA, 51 Digest (Repl)
    903, *4530*.

Cases also cited
Brown v New Empress Saloons Ltd [1937] 2 All ER 133, CA.
Findlay v Railway Executive [1950] 2 All ER 969, CA. *e*
Newall v Tunstall [1970] 3 All ER 465, [1971] 1 WLR 105.

Action
The plaintiffs, Vehicle and General Insurance Co Ltd (in liquidation), brought an
action against the defendants, H & W Christie Ltd, a firm of insurance brokers,
claiming the sum of £1,535·37 and interest. The defendants paid into court the sum of *f*
£314·30. At the hearing the plaintiffs did not ask for more than the amount paid in
and the defendants submitted to judgment for that amount. The judge also made an
award of interest under the Law Reform (Miscellaneous Provisions) Act 1934 on the
amount of the judgment from 1st April 1971 to date of judgment. The parties then
made their submissions on the question of costs. The facts are set out in the judgment.
                                                                          g
Paul Miller for the plaintiffs.
Allen Labor for the defendants.

JUDGE FAY. This is my judgment on costs in this action in which the plaintiffs
are the liquidators of the Vehicle and General Insurance Co Ltd and the defendants *h*
are a firm of insurance brokers, H and W Christie Ltd.
    By their writ issued in May 1973 the plaintiffs claimed the sum of £1,535·37 and by
their writ they also claimed interest. The action duly proceeded and on 23rd April
1975 the defendants paid into court the sum of £314·30. Today the case has been in
the list for hearing and has been heard.
    The plaintiffs have not asked today for more than the amount in court, and the *j*
defendants have submitted to judgment for that amount. Accordingly there was
judgment given by me earlier today for that precise sum which had been paid into
court, for £314·30. I also earlier today heard argument on a matter contested between
the parties, namely whether there should be any interest awarded under the powers
conferred on me by the Law Reform (Miscellaneous Provisions) Act 1934, and I

decided that point in favour of the plaintiffs and made an award of interest on the
a amount of the judgment as from 1st April 1971 down to today.

There remains costs and on costs two quite different questions arise. The first one
arises from the amount of the judgment and from the provisions of s 47 of the County
Courts Act 1959. Section 47(1) as amended reads as follows:

b 'Where an action founded on contract or tort is commenced in the High Court
which could have been commenced in the county court then, subject to subsections (3) ... of this section, the plaintiff—(a) if he recovers a sum less than
£500 [since the issue of the writ varied to £650], shall not be entitled to any more
costs of the action than those to which he would have been entitled if the action
had been brought in the county court ...'

Pausing there, the defendants say that the amount for which judgment has been given
c being clearly far below that sum referred to in para (a), para (a) applies and the costs
to which the plaintiffs are entitled are county court costs on whatever scale is appropriate. But there is a proviso to this subsection which reads as follows:

'... so, however, that this section shall not affect any question as to costs if it
appears to the High Court or a judge thereof (or where the matter is tried before
d a referee or officer of the Supreme Court, to that referee or officer) that there was
reasonable ground for supposing the amount recoverable in respect of the
plaintiff's claim to be in excess of the amount recoverable in an action commenced
in the county court.'

The note on that part of the section in the Supreme Court Practice[1] summarises the
e cases on that proviso in the following way:

'The test to be applied is whether it would have been clear to a reasonable man
in the position of the plaintiff at the time of the issue of the writ that no judge
would award more than £750 damages; if that were not clear, then High Court
costs are recoverable by the plaintiff, although less than £500 has been awarded
or recovered ... This has to be considered as at the time of the commencement
f of the proceedings and on the basis of the evidence which was then or at least
could then reasonably have been available to the plaintiff and the question is
whether there was reasonable ground for supposing that more than £750 could
or might be recovered, not that it was likely to be recovered ...'

Counsel for the plaintiffs asks me to look at the surrounding circumstances particu-
g larly as referred to in contemporary correspondence preceding the issue of the writ.

The defendants, as insurance brokers, conducted insurance business on behalf of
the plaintiffs in the way that brokers do and had in their hands and in their offices the
arranging of affairs and the transaction of business, and what business they transacted
on behalf of the plaintiffs was unknown to the plaintiffs until the defendants apprised
them of it. The defendants are clearly accounting parties. The practice of the plaintiffs
h was to send the defendants a monthly statement produced in tabular form by a
computer which, however unintelligible it is to the layman, ought to be intelligible
to those in the insurance world who deal with such documents month by month.
There had been, prior to the issue of this writ, negotiations between the parties with a
view to settling how much of the plaintiffs' money the defendants had in their possession, and it is clear that the defendants had in fact paid a cheque for a sum which they
said they owed to the plaintiffs. But the plaintiffs' accountants looked further into the
j matter and in particular they looked at renewals of old policies which had been listed
by their computer and they found that the defendants were saying that none of these
policies had in fact been renewed. They had reason to doubt that statement and I will
read part of a letter which was written by the joint liquidators to the defendants

---

1 Supreme Court Practice 1976, vol 2, p 1121, para 3919

on 16th April 1973. Referring to the account which had been the subject of the
discussion, the letter says: *a*

'Page 2 of the account contained only renewal entries and you will note that in
respect of A. Bonson we have established that this item was not paid in the
October, 1970 account as suggested and doubtless you will let us have a remittance. In respect of the remaining entries on page 2 you have, on your earlier
reconciliations, commented that these cases were not renewed, but we must   *b*
inform you that we have substantive evidence from a number of the policy
holders indicating that the cases were in fact renewed and renewal premiums
were paid to you.'

So there is the position that the liquidators have some evidence that when the
defendants assert, as the plaintiffs' agents, that they owe them nothing, and that there
were no renewals, that that statement cannot be accepted as accurate. In those   *c*
circumstances, bearing in mind the duties of a liquidator to the creditors of the
company it is clear that steps had to be taken to pursue the matter.

Page 2 of the account to which that letter refers has been produced and shown to
me. It contains a list of renewal premiums which after making all due adjustments
totals well over £1,000. That is a list of renewals and sums due on renewal which
should have been paid, not ones which the plaintiffs and the liquidators of the   *d*
plaintiffs knew had been renewed, but ones which in the ordinary course might have
been renewed. They had reason to think that a net sum of nil as put forward by the
defendants was wrong. They had no means of telling what sum was right. The
closer examination of the accounts which this case has produced at a late hour before
trial established that there was a sum owing in fact of £314·30. So there was clearly
justification for the liquidators' suspicions that some sum was owing. With a list of   *e*
renewals totalling well over £1,000, in my view it was eminently reasonable for them
to issue their writ in the High Court. They were not to know that the ultimate result
would be to produce a sum below £500. They were in a position where it might well
have been over the county court jurisdiction and where, if they had abandoned the
excess and gone to the county court, they would have been abandoning some of the
rights of those creditors for whom they were collecting the money. In my view they   *f*
were in fact acting reasonably and accordingly on this part of the case I hold that the
High Court scale of costs applies.

I now turn to the other point, which is a quite separate one. Counsel for the
defendants points out that the plaintiffs have recovered the exact amount paid into
court, and he says, and says with some force, that the rule—it is virtually a rule—is
that where a plaintiff recovers no more than the amount paid into court then the   *g*
defendant is entitled to his costs as from the date of payment in. That is a well-
known rule of course, and indeed is the foundation of the payment into court system,
and is the sanction which induces people to take out money which is paid in. Attempts
to alter the rule for other than good reason, in particular reasons of sympathy or
sentiment, have been sternly discouraged by the courts: see for example *Wagman v
Vare Motors Ltd*[1]. But counsel for the plaintiffs asks me to look at the correspondence   *h*
which preceded the payment in in order that I may apprehend just why the payment
in was made and what were the circumstances which led to the contest and lack of
contest of today. The facts are that in March 1975 the parties' representatives met and
they looked at the documents and agreed this sum of £314·30 as being the true
amount which was in fact due by way of collected premiums net from the defendants
to the plaintiffs. Accordingly and on being instructed about those matters the   *j*
plaintiffs' solicitors wrote on 19th March a letter which I will read in full. It is addressed
to the defendants' solicitors.

'Further to our letter of the 28th February as your clients have most probably

---
1   [1959] 3 All ER 326, [1959] 1 WLR 853

a informed you our client Mr. Woodhouse attended your clients' office on the 11th March and was given the opportunity to prove the brokers' records. As a result items were agreed and those agreed items are shown on the attached list totalling a nett amount of £314·30. From the records disclosed by your clients our clients were able to establish that the renewal items were lapsed and therefore our claim can now be restricted solely to the agreed items on the list. You will no doubt be good enough to bespeak your clients' cheque for £314·30 and there will

b thereafter only be outstanding the question of interest as claimed in the writ on all sums recovered since action brought plus costs. We are arranging to draw our bill of costs and the same will be submitted to you with a view to agreement. In the interim period we look forward to receiving your clients' cheque for the agreed sum plus interest.'

c That was a reasonable letter to write in the circumstances as it seems to me, but it did not commend itself to the defendants' solicitors, and they regarded the agreement about the £314·30 as being the be-all and end-all of the matter. They pointed out that interest could not be claimed unless there was a judgment and they disputed liability to pay costs. On 24th March they sent their cheque for that amount saying: 'We will now be glad to hear that the enclosed cheque settles the matter in toto.'

d That was not satisfactory, not surprisingly, to the plaintiffs, who returned the cheque, and that is how the defendants came to pay the sum of money into court.

Since the accountants or representatives met and agreed the sum of £314·30 on 11th March there has been no dispute about that sum whatever. What has been in dispute and all that has been in dispute is the question of interest which I have decided today and the question of costs, part of which I have already decided and the other part

e which I am now deciding. This puts flesh and blood on counsel for the plaintiffs' submission that this is not the ordinary case of payment into court and judgment for the amount or less with the consequence that the plaintiff is penalised in costs. The parties came to court today solely to dispute matters other than that amount or that liability and, so far, the plaintiffs have succeeded in the matter which has been litigated today. The difficulty about costs arises from the fact that one cannot pay

f into court in respect of interest. This matter was touched on in the well-known decision of the Court of Appeal in *Jefford v Gee*[1], where Lord Denning MR, it will be remembered, laid down guidelines following the provisions about interest on judgments for damages for personal injury. Lord Denning MR[2], under the sub-heading '*Payment into court*', stated:

g 'Seeing that a claim for interest under the 1934 Act need not be pleaded ... it is plain that it is not itself a cause of action. It is no part of the debt or damages claimed, but something apart on its own. It is more like the award of costs than anything else. It is an added benefit awarded to the plaintiff when he wins the case. Such being the character of interest, we do not think a defendant can, or should, make any payment into court in respect of it. If it is not claimed by a plaintiff in the pleadings, a defendant cannot be expected to make a payment

h into court in respect of it. Even if it is claimed, it is no part of the cause of action. A defendant is only allowed to make a payment into court "in satisfaction of the cause of action", see RSC Ord 22, r 1(1). Interest being no part of the cause of action, he cannot make a payment in respect of it. A defendant should, therefore, in future make any payment into court in the same way as he always has done,

j namely, an amount which he says is sufficient to satisfy the cause of action apart from interest. If a plaintiff recovers more (apart from interest) he gets his costs. If he recovers no more (apart from interest) he does not get his costs from the date of the payment in and he will have to pay the defendant's costs. A plaintiff

---

1 [1970] 1 All ER 1202, [1970] 2 QB 130
2 [1970] 1 All ER at 1211, [1970] 2 QB at 149, 150

will, of course, in either case, get the appropriate award of interest irrespective
of the payment into court. If a plaintiff takes the money out of court in satisfaction *a*
of the claim, that is the end of the case. He gets no interest because there is no
judgment. The 1934 Act only entitles a plaintiff to interest when he gets a
judgment. As a matter of practice, however, if a plaintiff is disposed to think that
the payment into court will cover his claim, he will tell the defendant that he is
disposed to go to trial in order to collect the interest but that such a course would
be to their mutual disadvantage because the Revenue would extract tax on it: so *b*
it would be better for them to split the interest and settle for a sum somewhat
higher than the sum in court.'

   That pious fraud which the Court of Appeal suggested is not open in a commercial
case because a case such as the present is one where there is no doubt as to which is
capital and which is interest, and it is not open to the parties to follow that line. What *c*
I find of interest in that passage from Lord Denning MR's judgment is not what he
said but what he did not say. He did say that if the plaintiff is disposed to think that
the payment into court will cover his claim he would tell the defendant that he is
disposed to go to trial in order to collect the interest. What he did not say is that it
would be stupid and disadvantageous for him to do so because when he got to court
he would find that he had to pay the other side's costs even though he had won. It *d*
seems to me likely that Lord Denning MR did not say that because he did not think
that. He would have thought that, if counsel for the defendants' argument were
correct, and if one had had one's eyes so fixed on the payment in and the amount of
the judgment that there was no other factor to be taken into account in deciding
where the costs shall lie. It is clear that I have a discretion as regards the costs after the
date of payment in. It is equally clear that it is a discretion which I cannot exercise *e*
capriciously, I must do so judicially, which means I must do so on adequate grounds
and in order to do what is just.
   I find that the reality of what we have been doing today in this court is that the parties
came here by counsel to argue three matters. Firstly, whether any interest should be
paid; secondly, whether costs should be on the county court scale or the High Court
scale; and thirdly, the present issue which I am now deciding. Apart from those *f*
matters there is no dispute. The question of the amount in court, the question of the
sum to be paid in satisfaction of the plaintiffs' claim was decided and settled between
the parties months ago. And the reality is that the payment into court has nothing to
do with what we have decided or with the justice of where costs should lie. I have
come to the conclusion that justice requires me to exercise my discretion on this part
of the matter in the plaintiffs' favour, despite the fact that counsel cannot point to any *g*
previous case in which on such facts such a decision has been taken. It is somewhat
singular that there is this dearth of authority but there it is. The plaintiffs were
forced to come to court, forced in the sense that their alternatives were to come here
today and spend the money which had to be spent in coming here today, or to forgo
interest and to forgo costs on the High Court scale. They have succeeded on the issues
on which they came here today and I think they should get their costs. That means *h*
that in the exercise of my discretion I order that the defendants pay the plaintiffs the
whole costs of this action after as well as before the date of payment in.

   *Judgment for the sum of £314·30 together with the interest from 1st April 1971 to 27th
October 1975 at eight per cent; plaintiffs to have their costs throughout on the High Court scale,
to be taxed or agreed; payment out of the sum in court to the plaintiffs' solicitors without* *j*
further order in part satisfaction.

Solicitors: *D J Freeman & Co* (for the plaintiffs); *Simpson, Silvertown & Co* (for the
defendants).

                                                      Mary Rose Plummer   Barrister.

Munby v Furlong (Inspector of Taxes)

CHANCERY DIVISION
FOX J
10th, 11th, 12th NOVEMBER, 19th DECEMBER 1975

Income tax – Capital allowances – Plant – Books – Books purchased by barrister – Necessary for barrister to consult books for purpose of carrying on his profession – Whether 'plant' limited to things used simply as physical objects – Whether expenditure on books expenditure on 'plant' – Finance Act 1971, s 41(1).

The taxpayer was a practising barrister. During the relevant period it was necessary for him to purchase certain books which he needed to consult for the purposes of his practice. The books in question were not purchased as replacements of earlier editions. Most of them were books which were likely to be replaced by new editions in the future. The taxpayer claimed that he was entitled to an allowance under ss 41(1)[a] and 47(1)[b] of the Finance Act 1971 on the ground that the expenditure which he had incurred in acquiring the books was capital expenditure on the provision of 'plant'.

Held – The books were not 'plant' within s 41(1) of the 1971 Act, since they were not simply physical objects used by the taxpayer as implements for the purpose of carrying on his profession (see p 762 *e* to *h* and p 763 *a* and *b*, post).

Daphne v Shaw (Inspector of Taxes) (1926) 11 Tax Cas 256 followed.
Dictum of Cross J in *McVeigh (Inspector of Taxes) v Arthur Sanderson & Sons Ltd* [1969] 2 All ER at 775 applied.

Notes

For the allowances available in respect of machinery and plant, see 20 Halsbury's Laws (3rd Edn) 493, 494, paras 941-946, and for cases on the meaning of 'plant', see 28(1) Digest (Reissue) 214-216, 637-643.

For the Finance Act 1971, ss 41, 47, see 41 Halsbury's Statutes (3rd Edn) 1459, 1469.

Cases referred to in judgment

Daphne v Shaw (Inspector of Taxes) (1926) 11 Tax Cas 256, 6 ATC 21, 43 TLR 45, [1926] WN 327, 28(1) Digest (Reissue) 215, 639.

Hinton (Inspector of Taxes) v Maden & Ireland Ltd [1959] 3 All ER 356, [1959] 1 WLR 875, 38 Tax Cas 381, 38 ATC 231, [1959] TR 233, 52 R & IT 688, HL, 28(1) Digest (Reissue) 193, 598.

Inland Revenue Comrs v Barclay Curle & Co Ltd [1969] 1 All ER 732, [1969] 1 WLR 675, 45 Tax Cas 221, 48 ATC 17, [1969] TR 21, 1969 SLT 122, [1969] 1 Lloyd's Rep 169, [1969] RVR 102, HL, 28(1) Digest (Reissue) 466, 1676.

Jarrold (Inspector of Taxes) v John Good & Sons Ltd [1963] 1 All ER 141, [1963] 1 WLR 214, 40 Tax Cas 681, 41 ATC 335, [1962] TR 371, [1963] RVR 653, CA, 28(1) Digest (Reissue) 215, 642.

Lyons (J) & Co Ltd v Attorney-General [1944] 1 All ER 477, [1944] Ch 281, 113 LJ Ch 196, 170 LT 348, 60 TLR 313, 17 Digest (Reissue) 542, 324.

---

a Section 41(1), so far as material, provides: '. . . where—(a) a person carrying on a trade incurs capital expenditure on the provision of machinery or plant for the purposes of the trade, and (b) in consequence of his incurring the expenditure, the machinery or plant belongs to him at some time during the chargeable period related to the incurring of the expenditure, there shall be made to him for that period an allowance (. . . referred to as "a first year allowance") . . .'

b Section 47(1), so far as material, provides: 'Except as otherwise provided, the provisions of this Chapter shall, with any necessary adaptations, apply in relation to—(a) professions . . .'

EE

McVeigh (Inspector of Taxes) v Arthur Sanderson & Sons Ltd [1969] 2 All ER 771, [1969]
1 WLR 1143, 45 Tax Cas 273, 47 ATC 478, [1968] TR 451, 28(1) Digest (Reissue) *a*
215, *643*.
Rose & Co (Wallpaper & Paints) Ltd v Campbell (Inspector of Taxes) [1968] 1 All ER 405,
[1968] 1 WLR 346, 44 Tax Cas 500, 46 ATC 281, [1967] TR 259, 28(1) Digest (Reissue)
465, *1675*.
Yarmouth v France (1887) 19 QBD 647, 57 LJQB 7, 4 TLR 1, 34 Digest (Repl) 299, *2159*.
b

Cases also cited
Campbell College, Belfast (Governors) v Valuation Comr for Northern Ireland [1964] 2 All
ER 705, [1964] 1 WLR 912, HL.
Cooke (Inspector of Taxes) v Beach Station Caravans Ltd [1974] 3 All ER 159, [1974] 1 WLR
1398, [1974] STC 402, 49 Tax Cas 514.
Derby (Earl) v Aylmer (Surveyor of Taxes) [1915] 3 KB 374, 9 Tax Cas 665.   *c*
Dixon (Inspector of Taxes) v Fitch's Garage Ltd [1975] 3 All ER 455, [1975] STC 480.
St John's School (Mountford and Knibbs) v Ward (Inspector of Taxes) [1975] STC 7, 49
Tax Cas 524, CA; *affg* [1974] STC 69.
Schofield (Inspector of Taxes) v R & H Hall Ltd [1975] STC 353, 49 Tax Cas 538, CA (NI).

Case stated   *d*
1. At a meeting of the Commissioners for the General Purposes of the Income
Tax Acts for the division of Lincoln's Inn held on 9th December 1974 the taxpayer,
James Lawrence Munby, appealed against assessments under Sch D, Case II, of £407
(less capital allowances £80) and £762 made on him for the income tax years 1972-73
and 1973-74 respectively.
2. For the purposes of s 5(1) of the Taxes Management Act 1970, both the inspector of *e*
taxes and the taxpayer expressly consented to the commissioners' hearing the appeal
notwithstanding such personal interest (if any) as they in their capacity as practising
barristers might have had in relation to the subject-matter of the appeal.
3. The following facts were agreed: (1) The taxpayer was a barrister in practice at
the Chancery Bar with chambers in Lincoln's Inn. He started practice on 1st September 1972, having previously been in pupillage since 1st October 1971. (2) The taxpayer's *f*
professional accounts were prepared to 31st August each year. The accounts for the
first year of his practice were prepared in two parts: (i) 1st September 1972 to 5th April
1973; (ii) 6th April 1973 to 31st August 1973. (3) The relevant professional accounts for
the income tax year 1972-73 were those for the period 1st September 1972 to 5th April
1973 (opening year basis); for the income tax year 1973-74 the combined accounts
for the period 1st September 1972 to 31st August 1973 (second year basis). (4) During *g*
the period 1st September 1972 to 31st August 1973, it was necessary for the taxpayer
to purchase certain law reports and books for the purpose of his practice as a barrister.
Some of those were purchased as replacements of earlier (out of date) editions; some
of the law reports consisted of the current weekly and monthly issues which were
paid for by means of an annual subscription. The inspector allowed the appropriate
deductions in respect of those two categories in making the assessments and accord- *h*
ingly the appeals were not concerned with them. At the hearing before the commissioners he also agreed to allow as a deduction the cost of the County Court Practice which was an annual publication. (5) The majority of the books were likely to be
replaced by new editions in the future. The frequency of new editions varied with the
different books. However, it appeared that none of those books would normally be
replaced by a new edition in less than four years and in many cases an average period *j*
of about six to nine years seemed to be normal. (6) The inspector in making the
assessements had refused to allow any deduction in respect of the expenditure on the
books whether as a deduction in computing profits or as qualifying for a capital allowance. Consequently the taxpayer gave notice of appeal in writing so that the matter
might be considered by the commissioners.

a 4. The questions originally raised for determination by the commissioners were whether any or all of the expenditure incurred in the purchase by the taxpayer of law reports and books for the purpose of his practice as a barrister qualified for deduction or allowance under Sch D, Case II, either (a) as revenue expenditure to be deducted when computing the profits of that practice; or (b) as capital expenditure qualifying for a capital allowance under Chapter I of Part III of the Finance Act 1971. The taxpayer did not, however, pursue question (a).

b [Paragraph 5 listed the agreed documents admitted before the commissioners and para 6 listed the cases[1] referred to.]

7. It was contended by the taxpayer that (a) if the books in question were both 'capital' and 'plant' they qualified for capital allowances under Chapter I of Part III of the 1971 Act; (b) the Crown admitted that the books were 'capital' and accordingly the only question was whether they were 'plant'; (c) in the course of his judgment *c* in *Yarmouth v France*[2] Lindley LJ defined 'plant' as including—

'whatever apparatus is used by a business man for carrying on his business— not his stock-in-trade which he buys or makes for sale; but all goods and chattels fixed or movable, live or dead, which he keeps for permanent employment in his business.'

d That passage had been subsequently approved by the House of Lords and cited with approval in the Court of Appeal (see *Hinton (Inspector of Taxes) v Maden and Ireland Ltd*[3] and *Jarrold (Inspector of Taxes) v John Good & Sons Ltd*[4]); (d) it was sufficient for the taxpayer to show that (i) the books were 'plant' within Lindley LJ's definition and (ii) they were not within any relevant exception; (e) the books were clearly 'plant' within Lindley LJ's definition and they were not excepted (see *Hinton v Maden & Ireland* *e* *Ltd*[5] and *McVeigh (Inspector of Taxes) v Arthur Sanderson & Sons Ltd*[6]); (f) the Crown relied on *Daphne v Shaw (Inspector of Taxes)*[7] but that case should not be followed because it was inconsistent with the subsequent decision of the House of Lords in *Hinton v Maden & Ireland Ltd*[3] and had been impliedly overruled; (g) *Rose & Co (Wallpaper & Paints) Ltd v Campbell (Inspector of Taxes)*[8] was to be distinguished because it was decided on the ground of the duration of the life of the property alleged to be 'plant' and not by *f* reference to the character of such property; and (h) there was no relevant distinction in law between plant used for physical purposes and plant used for intellectual purposes.

8. It was contended by the Crown that (a) the books were not plant, so that expenditure incurred on their purchase did not qualify for capital allowances under Chapter I of Part III of the 1971 Act; (b) the books contained information to which *g* the taxpayer might have recourse when he saw fit but they did not fall within the

---

1   *Cooke (Inspector of Taxes) v Beach Station Caravans Ltd* [1974] 3 All ER 159, [1974] 1 WLR 1398, [1974] STC 402; *Daphne v Shaw (Inspector of Taxes)* (1926) 11 Tax Cas 256; *Hinton (Inspector of Taxes) v Maden & Ireland Ltd* [1959] 3 All ER 356, [1959] 1 WLR 875, 38 Tax Cas 391, HL; *Inland Revenue Comrs v Barclay Curle & Co Ltd* [1969] 1 All ER 732, [1969] 1 WLR 675, 45 Tax *h* Cas 221, HL; *Jarrold (Inspector of Taxes) v John Good & Sons Ltd* [1963] 1 All ER 141, [1963] 1 WLR 214, 40 Tax Cas 681, CA; *J Lyons & Co Ltd v Attorney-General* [1944] 1 All ER 447, [1944] Ch 281; *McVeigh (Inspector of Taxes) v Arthur Sanderson & Sons Ltd* [1969] 2 All ER 771, [1969] 1 WLR 1143, 45 Tax Cas 273; *Rose & Co (Wallpaper & Paints) Ltd v Campbell (Inspector of Taxes)* [1968] 1 All ER 405, [1968] 1 WLR 346, 44 Tax Cas 500; *Yarmouth v France* (1887) 19 QBD 647.
2   (1887) 19 QBD 647 at 658
j 3   [1959] 3 All ER 356, [1959] 1 WLR 875, 38 Tax Cas 391
4   [1963] 1 All ER 141 at 144, 148, [1963] 1 WLR 214 at 219, 224, 40 Tax Cas 681 at 691, 695
5   [1959] 3 All ER 356 at 362, 363, 369, [1959] 1 WLR 875 at 889, 890, 898, 38 Tax Cas 391 at 417, 424
6   [1969] 2 All ER 771, [1969] 1 WLR 1143, 45 Tax Cas 273
7   (1926) 11 Tax Cas 256
8   [1968] 1 All ER 405, [1968] 1 WLR 346, 44 Tax Cas 500

common or ordinary meaning of the phrase 'machinery or plant', which was
necessarily limited to some physical, movable or immovable, apparatus or imple- **a**
ment which had some physical or mechanical function in an industrial or business
process; (c) *Daphne v Shaw*[1], which had been decided after *Yarmouth v France*[2] and
followed in *McVeigh v Arthur Sanderson & Sons Ltd*[3] had not been overruled and
concluded the question against the taxpayer; and (d) the appeal should be dismissed.
  9. The commissioners gave their decision as follows:

b

'We . . . considered that the limitation placed by the Inspector on the meaning
of machinery or plant referred to in paragraph 8(b) above was unjustified; it
would, for instance, be difficult to apply to a computer. Like Cross J in *McVeigh
v Arthur Sanderson and Sons Ltd*.[4] we also felt unable to see as a matter of principle why, "if a barrister has to buy a new edition of a textbook in order to help
him write his Opinions . . . the book should not be regarded as a tool of his trade **c**
just as much as the typewriter on which his Opinions are typed". Except, therefore, for the decison in *Daphne v Shaw*[1] we would have held that the books were
"plant". Nevertheless we, like Cross J, came to the conclusion that, having
regard to that decision, if any extension of the meaning of the word "plant"
beyond a purely physical object is to be made, it ought to be made by a higher
Court. Accordingly we dismissed the Appeal.'   **d**

  10. Figures having been agreed between the parties on the basis of their decision,
the commissioners determined the assessments for the years under appeal at £400
and £755 respectively less any capital allowances which fell to be made on account
of expenditure other than the expenditure referred to above.
  11. The question of law for the opinion of the court was whether the commissioners'
decision set out in para 9 above was correct.   **e**

The taxpayer appeared in person.
Brian Davenport for the Crown.

Cur adv vult

19th December. **FOX J** delivered the following judgment: This is an appeal from the **f**
General Commissioners for Lincoln's Inn. The taxpayer is a barrister in practice at
the Chancery Bar. He started practice on 1st September 1972. During the period
from 1st September 1972 to 31st August 1973, the taxpayer purchased certain
textbooks and law reports (none of them renewals) for the purpose of setting up
practice. The majority of the books are likely to be replaced by new editions in the
future. The frequency of the new editions varies with different books, but none of **g**
the books would normally be replaced by a new edition in less than four years and
in many cases an average period of six to nine years would be normal.
  The issue is whether the purchase by the taxpayer of these books was capital
expenditure qualifying for a capital allowance under Chapter I of Part III of the
Finance Act 1971. The taxpayer is entitled to this allowance if the expenditure was
'capital expenditure on the provision of machinery or plant' for the purposes of the **h**
profession (see ss 41(a) and s 47(1) of the 1971 Act). The Crown concedes that
the expenditure was 'capital expenditure'. The sole question is whether the books
and reports are 'plant' (which is not defined in the Act).
  The commissioners, following with reluctance the decision of Rowlatt J in *Daphne v
Shaw (Inspector of Taxes)*[1], held that they were not plant. In *Daphne v Shaw*[1] it was held
that a solicitor's law library was not 'plant' for the purposes of the Income Tax Act **j**

---

1 (1926) 11 Tax Cas 256
2 (1887) 19 QBD 647
3 [1969] 2 All ER 771, [1969] 1 WLR 1143, 45 Tax Cas 273
4 [1969] 2 All ER at 775, [1969] 1 WLR at 1154, 45 Tax Cas at 285

a 1918, Sch D, Cases I and II, rr 6 and 7, which gave allowances in respect of wear and
   tear of machinery or plant and expenses incurred on replacing obsolete machinery
   or plant. Rowlatt J said[1]:

      'I cannot bring myself to say that such books . . . are "plant". It is impossible
      to define what is meant by "plant and machinery". It conjures up before the
      mind something clear in the outline, at any rate; it means apparatus, alive or
b   dead, stationary or movable, to achieve the operations which a person wants to
      achieve in his vocation. But the books which he consults, on his shelves, and which
      he does not use as "implements", really, in the direct sense of the word, at all, I
      cannot believe are included in it . . . The extension of the allowance to professions,
      employments, vocations or offices, that is to say, to all the Schedules and all parts
      of them, I do not think involves an extension to the ordinary, common sense
c   meaning of the word "plant", because . . . undoubtedly there are many pro-
      fessions and vocations where machinery and plant is used, but still machinery
      and plant of the sort that was understood before.'

   Daphne v Shaw[2] is therefore a direct decision on the point before me. The taxpayer
   contends, however, that it is wrong in law, and, in particular, is inconsistent with later
d decisions of higher courts and should not be followed. The basis of the taxpayer's
   case is that the correct meaning of 'plant' is that stated by Lindley LJ in *Yarmouth v
   France*[3], and that this meaning is now firmly established by decisions of the House
   of Lords.
      Yarmouth v France[3] was an action to recover compensation under the Employers'
   Liability Act 1880. The plaintiff was in the employment of the defendant, who was a
e wharfinger. The plaintiff drove carts for the defendant, and loaded and unloaded the
   goods that were carried in them. The plaintiff was injured by one of the cart-horses,
   and the question was whether the horse was 'plant' within s 1(1) of the 1880 Act.
   Lindley LJ said[3]:

      'There is no definition of plant in the Act; but, in its ordinary sense, it includes
f   whatever apparatus is used by a business man for carrying on his business,—not
      his stock-in-trade which he buys or makes for sale; but all goods and chattels,
      fixed or moveable, live or dead, which he keeps for permanent employment
      in his business.'

   The taxpayer says that the books in the present case (by which I mean both the textbooks and the reports) fall squarely within the definition.
g   I turn now to the later authorities. In *J Lyons & Co Ltd v Attorney-General*[4], a
   Lyons teashop was damaged by enemy action in 1941. Lyons claimed a cost-of-works
   payment under the War Damage Act 1943, which included the cost of replacing
   electric lamps used for lighting the premises, and fittings annexed to the lamps, as
   being 'plant or machinery' on the hereditament within s 103(5) of the 1943 Act. Uthwatt
   J[5] said that he did not think that the use of the word 'plant' as part of the phrase
h 'plant or machinery' had the effect of confining the word to such plant as is used for
   mechanical operations or processes. Also, after saying that he did not think it necessary
   to attempt a general definition of the word 'plant', he continued[5]:

      'No definitions of "plant" would include the lamps and fitments here under

j ───

   1 (1926) 11 Tax Cas at 258, 259
   2 11 Tax Cas 256
   3 (1887) 19 QBD 647 at 658
   4 [1944] 1 All ER 477, [1944] Ch 281
   5 [1944] 1 All ER at 479, [1944] Ch at 286

consideration, if they were found in a private house supplied with electricity by
public suppliers. If these articles are plant, it can only be by reason that they are *a*
found on premises exclusively devoted to trade purposes. Trade plant alone
need be considered. Confining my attention to trade plant, I am content to
accept the general description in *Yarmouth* v. *France*[1], that "plant" includes
whatever apparatus or instruments are used by a business man in carrying on his
business. The term does not include stock-in-trade, nor does it include the place
in which the business is carried on. Whether any particular article more properly *b*
falls within "plant" as thus understood, or in some other category, depends
on all the circumstances of the case.'

The next case is a decision of the House of Lords, *Hinton (Inspector of Taxes) v Maden
& Ireland Ltd*[2]. In that case the taxpayer company carried on the business of shoe and
slipper manufacturers. It used machines which could only function when furnished *c*
with knives or lasts. The question was whether expenditure on new knives and
lasts was expenditure on 'plant or machinery' for the purposes of s 16(3) of the Finance
Act 1954 (dealing with investment allowances). It was held that it was. Lord Reid
said[3]:

'It is not disputed that "plant" is also used in the Act as an ordinary English *d*
word. It is not altogether an easy word to construe; it may have a more or less
extensive meaning according to its context. As a general statement of its meaning
I would adopt the words of LINDLEY, L.J., in *Yarmouth* v. *France*[1]. . .'

Lord Reid then cited the passage which I have set out above. He also referred (as I
read it, with approval) to the passage which I have set out above from the judgment *e*
of Uthwatt J in *J Lyons & Co Ltd v Attorney-General*[4].
Lord Tucker[5] agreed with Lord Reid as to the meaning of 'plant'. Lord Keith and
Lord Denning did not deal in any detail with the meaning of the word. Lord Jenkins
said[6]:

'I have no doubt that the knives and lasts were "plant". On this point I am for
the present purpose, content to accept as a sufficient statement of the ordinary *f*
meaning of the expression "plant" the words of LINDLEY, L.J., in *Yarmouth* v.
France[1].'

Jarrold (Inspector of Taxes) v John Good & Sons Ltd[7] was a decision of the Court of
Appeal. A company's office accommodation consisted of a large open floor space in
which partitions could be erected so as to subdivide the floor space into any number *g*
of rooms of any size. The partitions were screwed to the floor and ceiling only, and
could easily be moved if it was desired to alter the size or number of the rooms. The
question was whether the partitions were 'plant' within the meaning of s 279 of the
Income Tax Act 1952, which gave certain allowances in respect of expenditure on
'machinery or plant'. It was held that the partitions were plant.
The case is of significance in a number of respects. First, the Crown contended that *h*
as the partitions played a purely 'passive' role they were not plant. Donovan LJ[8]
rejected this. He said:

1   (1887) 19 QBD 647 at 658
2   [1959] 3 All ER 356, [1959] 1 WLR 875, 38 Tax Cas 391   *j*
3   [1959] 3 All ER at 362, [1959] 1 WLR at 889, 38 Tax Cas at 417
4   [1944] 1 All ER at 479, [1944] Ch at 286
5   [1959] 3 All ER at 364, [1959] 1 WLR at 891, 38 Tax Cas at 418
6   [1959] 3 All ER at 369, [1959] 1 WLR at 898, 38 Tax Cas at 423, 424
7   [1963] 1 All ER 141, [1963] 1 WLR 214, 40 Tax Cas 681
8   [1963] 1 All ER at 147, [1963] 1 WLR at 223, 40 Tax Cas at 694

'I do not understand this division of assets into passive and active vis-à-vis the
accomplishment of the trading purpose, followed by the argument that there
can be no "plant" among the passive assets. The heating installation of a building
may be passive in the sense that it involves no moving machinery, but few would
deny it the name of "plant".'

Ormerod LJ said[1]:

'But it may well be going much too far to say that [plant] cannot refer to such
part of the building, or to such part of the equipment of the building, as performs
anything other than a merely passive role . . .'

Secondly, the case contains a consideration by Donovan LJ[2] of what is not plant
(at any rate for the tax purposes with which I am concerned in this case). Thus, there
are excluded (a) buildings; (b) machinery (since in the statute with which the court
was concerned there, and here, the word is used in contra-distinction to machinery);
(c) utensils (the cost of which is allowable by other provisions of the Income Tax Acts);
and (d) stock-in-trade. Donovan LJ added[2]:

'When all these things have been excluded from the scope of the word "plant",
there will still be some chattels left, the character of which may be debatable.
In the present case we have these partitions. The definition given of "plant" by
LINDLEY, L.J., in *Yarmouth* v. *France*[3] clearly embraces them . . . These partitions
are required by the nature of the taxpayers' trade, as the lamps in *J. Lyons &
Co., Ltd.* v. *A.-G.*[4] were not. I can therefore discover no good reason for excluding
these partitions from LINDLEY, L.J.'s definition of "plant" . . .'

Thirdly, Donovan LJ[2], expressed some surprise at coming to the conclusion that
such things as the partitions could be plant, but, he added '. . . no more than, I
expect, some people were surprised by finding that a horse is also "plant" '. It may
be, therefore, that one must be cautious of any approach to this problem based on
what a layman would normally understand by 'plant'.

Fourthly, the case contains Pearson LJ's aphorism[5]: '. . . the short question in this
case is whether the partitioning is part of the premises *in* which the business is carried
on or part of the plant *with* which the business is carried on'.

In *Rose & Co (Wallpaper & Paints)* v *Campbell (Inspector of Taxes)*[6], the company
was a retailer of wallpapers. It purchased samples of wall paper from a manufacturer
and had them printed and bound as pattern-books, which were either distributed
free of charge to decorating contractors (while remaining the property of the company)
or kept for use at the company's branches. The books had a minimum useful life of
about two years. The company claimed to be entitled to investment allowances
under s 16(3) of the Finance Act 1954 in respect of expenditure on the pattern books
on the ground that the expenditure was capital expenditure on 'plant'. The commissioners held that the expenditure was not capital expenditure and the books
were not plant. Pennycuick J[6], on appeal, concluded that the expenditure was not
capital expenditure. The question whether the books were 'plant' did not therefore
arise, but he expressed the view[7] that the commissioners' decision that the books
were not plant was reasonable. As I read it, however, the judgment on this point

---

1   [1963] 1 All ER at 146, [1963] 1 WLR at 221, 40 Tax Cas at 691
2   [1963] 1 All ER at 148, [1963] 1 WLR at 223, 224, 40 Tax Cas at 695
3   (1887) 19 QBD at 658
4   [1944] 1 All ER 477, [1944] 1 Ch 281
5   [1963] 1 All ER at 149, [1963] 1 WLR at 225, 40 Tax Cas at 696
6   [1968] 1 All ER 405, [1968] 1 WLR 346, 44 Tax Cas 500
7   [1968] 1 All ER at 408, 409, [1968] 1 WLR at 351, 352, 44 Tax Cas at 505, 506

proceeds primarily on the question whether the books possessed sufficient durability to fall within the word 'permanent' in the *Yarmouth v France*[1] definition.. No **a** similar question arises in the present case. It is not suggested that the books in the present case lack whatever degree of permanence may be necessary to constitute plant.

The taxpayer referred me to the statement by Pennycuick J[2] that if expenditure on a chattel is capital expenditure the chattel is 'well on its way to being plant'. That may well be so. But Pennycuick J was there indicating only a broad approach to the **b** matter. In the borderline cases and the grey areas such a test would in most cases be insufficiently precise to determine the matter, more particularly in cases such as the present, where the expenditure must be capital expenditure before it can qualify at all for the allowance.

The next case, *Inland Revenue Comrs v Barclay Curle & Co Ltd*[3], is a decision of the House of Lords. It again raised the question whether expenditure qualified for an **c** allowance under s 279(1) of the Income Tax Act 1952, as being expenditure for the provision of machinery or plant. The case concerned a dry dock which the company built for use in its trade as shipbuilders and repairers. The expenditure in issue was the cost of excavating a new basin and lining the excavation with concrete. The House of Lords, by a majority of three to two, decided that the dock was 'plant'. Although Lord Hodson and Lord Upjohn dissented, I do not think there was much difference **d** in the basic approach.

Lord Hodson said[4]:

'The word "plant" though difficult of precise definition is an ordinary English word which has received judicial consideration on a number of occasions. What was said by LINDLEY, L.J.[1], in construing the word as it appears in the Employers' **e** Liability Act 1880, has been long accepted as good guidance.'

Lord Hodson[5] also referred to the *Yarmouth v France* definition[1] as having been adopted as 'a general test' in *Hinton v Maden & Ireland Ltd*[6]. Lord Guest[7] described the *Yarmouth v France* test[1] as the 'locus classicus'.

Lord Upjohn[8] also referred to *Yarmouth v France*[1] as the locus classicus, but said that Lindley LJ was dealing with plant of such a different nature—a horse—that his **f** words could not safely be bent to the circumstances of the *Barclay Curle* case[3]. Lord Upjohn[9] again emphasised that 'plant' is an ordinary English word.

Lord Donovan, after saying that there was no statutory definition of 'plant' and that the courts had been left to formulate the test, said[10]:

'LINDLEY L.J., did it in *Yarmouth v. France*[1] in language which despite the great **g** technological advances since his day is still of great help. UTHWATT J., said in *J. Lyons & Co., Ltd.* v. *A.-G.*[11] that plant did not include the place where the business was carried on: and ... PEARSON, L.J., when sitting in the Court of Appeal in *Jarrold (Inspector of Taxes)* v. *John Good & Sons, Ltd.*[12] spoke of plant being that

h

1   (1887) 19 QBD at 658
2   [1968] 1 All ER at 408, [1968] 1 WLR at 351, 44 Tax Cas at 505
3   [1969] 1 All ER 732, [1969] 1 WLR 675, 45 Tax Cas 221
4   [1969] 1 All ER at 742, [1969] 1 WLR at 681, 45 Tax Cas at 240, 241
5   [1969] 1 All ER at 743, [1969] 1 WLR at 681, 45 Tax Cas at 241
6   [1959] 3 All ER 356, [1959] 1 WLR 875, 38 Tax Cas 392
7   [1969] 1 All ER at 746, [1969] 1 WLR at 685, 45 Tax Cas at 244
8   [1969] 1 All ER at 749, [1969] 1 WLR at 688, 45 Tax Cas at 247
9   [1969] 1 All ER at 749, [1969] 1 WLR at 689, 45 Tax Cas at 248
10 [1969] 1 All ER at 751, [1969] 1 WLR at 691, 45 Tax Cas at 249
11 [1944] 1 All ER at 479, [1944] Ch at 286, 287
12 [1963] 1 All ER at 149, [1963] 1 WLR at 225, 40 Tax Cas at 696

j

with which the trade is carried on, as opposed to the place where it was carried

a on. All these definitions are helpful, but in the nature of things they cannot be exact, and so provide an answer incapable of reasonable dispute in every case.'

Later Lord Donovan said[1]:

'At the end of the day I find the functional test propounded by LINDLEY, L.J.[2]
b and by PEARSON, L.J.[3] to be as good as any, though, as was said in *Jarrold* v. *John Good & Sons*[4], some plant may perform its function passively and not actively.'

From these authorities I think that the following propositions emerge. (1) 'Plant' is an ordinary English word which is not very easy to construe. Lindley LJ's definition in *Yarmouth v France*[2] is a good general definition. (2) Lindley LJ's definition is not to be treated as exact. (3) For present purposes, buildings, utensils and stock-in-trade
c are not plant (though they, or some of them, might come within the Lindley LJ definition). But it is not correct to say that, after excluding these items, anything left within Lindley LJ's definition is plant. As Donovan LJ said in *Jarrold v John Good & Sons Ltd*[5], when all these things have been excluded from the scope of the word 'plant', there will still be some chattels left the character of which may be debatable. (4) 'Plant' is not limited to (a) chattels involving mechanical operations
d or processes or (probably) (b) active as opposed to passive articles (though as to (b) Lord Guest took the contrary view in the *Barclay Curle* case[6]). (5) The test of what the ordinary person would understand by 'plant' may not be reliable. Whilst, however, it may be surprising that a horse should be described as 'plant' a wharfinger's horse in 1887 represented motive power.

It seems to me that one thing which is clear from all the cases is that the meaning of
e 'plant' is purely a matter of construction to be determined according to ordinary principles of construction and taking into account all the circumstances of the individual case. The modern cases clearly establish Lindley LJ's definition[2] as a valuable general guide, and they clarify various other matters. But they do not attempt to lay down a hard and fast meaning or to delineate boundaries with precision. The matter is, as it always was, one of construction.

f If I were free to determine that question of construction in the present case, I would take the view that the taxpayer is right and that these books are plant. It seems to me, in the first place, that they do fall within Lindley LJ's definition[2]. Put more generally, they are part of the apparatus used by a professional man for carrying on his profession. They do not fall within any of the exceptions so far classified. And, as a matter of principle, I do not see good ground for excluding them if as a matter of
g construction they could properly be included in plant.

But if I depart from *Daphne v Shaw*[7] I am merely substituting my view of a question of construction for that of Rowlatt J in an uncertain and difficult area of the law. It does not seem to me that Rowlatt J in *Daphne v Shaw*[8] seriously misdirected himself. He said that plant 'means apparatus, alive or dead, stationary or movable, to achieve the operations which a person wants to achieve in his vocation.' That, for
h practical purposes, is the same as the Lindley LJ's definition[2]. Rowlatt J uses 'stationary' instead of 'fixed'; he omits the word 'permanent', and he does not exclude stock-in-trade. But as a working definition it seems to be substantially the same as Lindley LJ's; it is no less wide.

1   [1969] 1 All ER 751, 752, [1969] 1 WLR at 691, 45 Tax Cas at 250
j 2   (1887) 19 QBD at 658
3   [1963] 1 All ER at 149, [1963] 1 WLR at 225, 40 Tax Cas at 696
4   [1963] 1 All ER 141, [1963] 1 WLR 214, 40 Tax Cas 681
5   [1963] 1 All ER at 148, [1963] 1 WLR at 224, 40 Tax Cas at 695
6   [1969] 1 All ER 732, [1969] 1 WLR 675, 45 Tax Cas 221
7   (1926) 11 Tax Cas 256
8   11 Tax Cas at 258, 259

Rowlatt J said[1] that the extension of the allowance to professions (which was effected by the Finance Act 1925, s 16) did not extend the meaning of the word 'plant'. That *a* is, I think, correct; the word merely has to be applied to different circumstances. Rowlatt J[1] may have gone too far in applying the test of what 99 people out of 100 would understand by 'plant'. But 'plant' is, as the authorities emphasise, an ordinary English word, and I think it must be admitted that to describe books as 'plant' is going well beyond the everday usage of the term.

Rowlatt J's interpretation is, at the least, a perfectly possible one, and although the *b* modern cases make it easier to come to the opposite conclusion I do not think that, recognising as they do that the matter is one of construction on the facts of the individual case, they are necessarily inconsistent with *Daphne v Shaw*[2]. In these circumstances, the decision having stood for nearly 50 years, I would, in any event, have felt some hesitation at departing from it. But the matter does not end there. In *McVeigh (Inspector of Taxes) v Arthur Sanderson & Sons Ltd*[3], the question of the correctness of *c* *Daphne v Shaw*[2] was raised before Cross J. In that case the taxpayer company was the well-known manufacturer of wallpaper and fabrics. The designs which it used were in part acquired by the company from freelance artists and in part produced in its own studios. In order to have a wide field of choice, the company acquired far more designs than it needed. All the designs were filed and kept for at least six years so that a design not used immediately might be used later. The company maintained, *d* therefore, a library of designs. The question was whether the expenditure on the designs was expenditure on 'new machinery or plant' within s 16(3) of the Finance Act 1954.

Cross J[4], after quoting Lindley LJ's definition[5] of plant, said that the Crown had submitted that to fall within the definition the chattel in question must be nothing more than a material object. The designs in question, according to that submission, *e* were no doubt in one sense pieces of paper filed in the company's library, but the paper was only the material vehicle through which the concept of the artist was conveyed to the eye and lacked, said the Crown, the gross materiality necessary to qualify it as plant. The Crown relied on *Daphne v Shaw*[2].

Cross J[6], after quoting from the judgment in *Daphne v Shaw*[2], said:

'If I thought that I was free to do so, I am not sure that I would accept the limitation which the Crown's argument imposes on the meaning of "plant". If a barrister has to buy a new edition of a textbook in order to help him to write his opinions, I cannot see as a matter of principle why the book should not be regarded as a tool of his trade just as much as the typewriter on which his opinions are typed. Similarly, the designs, which are the tools of the trade of the styling *g* committee and many of which are scrapped after a few years, might, I should have thought, qualify as "plant" just as fully as the hand blocks, silk screens and rollers, many of which are periodically scrapped. But, having regard to the decision in *Daphne v Shaw*[2], I think that if any extension of the meaning of the word "plant" beyond a purely physical object is to be made, it ought to be made by a higher court. So I will proceed on the footing that these designs are not "plant".' *h*

The *Barclay Curle* case[7] had not been decided at the time of this decision, but both

---

1 (1926) 11 Tax Cas at 259
2 11 Tax Cas 256
3 [1969] 2 All ER 771, [1969] 1 WLR 1143, 45 Tax Cas 273
4 [1969] 2 All ER at 774, [1969] 1 WLR at 1153, 45 Tax Cas at 285
5 (1887) 19 QBD at 658
6 [1969] 2 All ER at 775, [1969] 1 WLR at 1154, 45 Tax Cas at 285
7 [1969] 1 All ER 732, [1969] 1 WLR 675, 45 Tax Cas 221

a *Hinton v Maden & Ireland Ltd*[1] and *Jarrold v John Good & Sons Ltd*[2] were cited to Cross J.

The position therefore is this, that *Daphne v Shaw*[3] has now stood for nearly 50 years, and as recently as 1968 Cross J[4] came to the conclusion that he could not depart from it. In the circumstances, I think I must follow *Daphne v Shaw*[3] and hold that the books are not plant. I therefore dismiss the appeal.

b *Appeal dismissed.*

Solicitors: *Solicitor of Inland Revenue.*

Rengan Krishnan Esq Barrister.

c

Mood Music Publishing Co Ltd v De Wolfe Ltd

COURT OF APPEAL, CIVIL DIVISION
LORD DENNING MR, ORR AND BROWNE LJJ
d 27th, 28th OCTOBER 1975

Evidence – Admissibility – Similar facts – Circumstances in which similar fact evidence admissible – Probative weight – Prejudice to defendant – Rebuttal of defence – Action for infringement of copyright – Issue whether similarity of plaintiffs' and defendants' works result of copying by defendants or mere coincidence – Evidence that on three other occasions
e *defendants had reproduced copyright works – Whether evidence admissible.*

The plaintiffs owned the copyright of a musical work. The defendants supplied a musical work for use in a television play. The plaintiffs complained that that work infringed the plaintiffs' copyright in their work. The defendants conceded that the works were very similar and that their work had been composed after the plaintiffs', *f* but asserted that the similarity was coincidental. The plaintiffs brought an action for infringement of copyright and procured evidence which indicated that in three other cases the defendants had reproduced musical works which were subject to copyright. The plaintiffs, having given the defendants notice of their intention, sought to adduce that evidence at the trial of the action.

g **Held** – In civil cases the courts would admit evidence of similar facts if it was logically probative and it was not oppressive or unfair to the other side to admit the evidence. Since the issue in the action was whether the resemblance between the two works was mere coincidence or the result of copying by the defendants, the evidence procured by the plaintiffs concerning the other three cases was of sufficient probative weight to render it admissible (see p 766 *d* to *j*, post).
h *Boardman v Director of Public Prosecutions* [1974] 3 All ER 88 and dictum of Lord Goddard CJ in *R v Sims* [1946] 1 All ER at 701 applied.

Notes
For the admissibility of evidence as to similar facts, see 15 Halsbury's Laws (3rd Edn) 291-293, paras 527-529, and for cases on the subject, see 22 Digest (Reissue)
j 73-76, 450-470.

1 [1959] 3 All ER 356, [1959] 1 WLR 875, 38 Tax Cas 391
2 [1963] 1 All ER 141, [1963] 1 WLR 214, 40 Tax Cas 681
3 (1926) 11 Tax Cas 256
4 [1969] 2 All ER 771, [1969] 1 WLR 1143, 45 Tax Cas 273

Cases referred to in judgments

Boardman v Director of Public Prosecutions [1974] 3 All ER 887, [1975] AC 421, [1974] 3   *a*
WLR 673, 139 JP 52, HL.

Brown v Eastern & Midlands Railway Co (1889) 22 QBD 391, 58 LJQB 212, 60 LT 266, 53
JP 342, CA, 22 Digest (Reissue) 61, 369.

Hales v Kerr [1908] 2 KB 601, 77 LJKB 870, 99 LT 364, DC, 22 Digest (Reissue) 76, 469.

Moore v Ransome's Dock Committee (1898) 14 TLR 539, CA.

R v Sims [1946] 1 All ER 697, [1946] KB 531, [1947] LJR 160, 175 LT 72, 31 Cr App Rep   *b*
158, CCA, 14 Digest (Repl) 260, 2279.

Cases also cited

Austin v Columbia Gramophone Co (1923) 67 Sol Jo 790.

Blake v Albion Life Insurance Society (1878) 4 CPD 94.

D'Almaine v Boosey (1835) 1 Y & C Ex 288, 160 ER 117.   *c*

Day (Francis) & Hunter Ltd v Bron (trading as Delmar Publishing Co) [1963] 2 All ER 16,
[1963] Ch 587, [1963] 2 WLR 868, CA.

R v Robinson [1953] 2 All ER 334, [1953] 1 WLR 872, CCA.

Sifam Electrical Instrument Co Ltd v Sangamo Weston Ltd [1971] 2 All ER 1074.

Interlocutory appeal   *d*

The plaintiffs, Mood Music Publishing Co Ltd, brought an action against the defendants, De Wolfe Ltd, claiming that a musical work published by the defendants called
'Girl in the Dark' had infringed the plaintiffs' copyright in a work published by them
called 'Sogno Nostalgico'. The defendants denied infringement of the plaintiffs' copyright and alleged prior composition of the work published by the defendants. At
the trial of the action the plaintiffs sought to adduce evidence to show that in other   *e*
cases the defendants had reproduced musical works which were subject to copyright.
The defendants contended that that evidence was inadmissible. On 27th October
1975 Fox J ruled that some of the evidence which the plaintiffs were seeking to adduce
was admissible but gave the defendants leave to appeal against that ruling. The
defendants appealed. The facts are set out in the judgment of Lord Denning MR.

Andrew Bateson QC and *John Mummery* for the defendants.   *f*
John Wilmers QC and *E P Skone James* for the plaintiffs.

LORD DENNING MR. The plaintiffs, Mood Music Publishing Co Ltd, keep a
library consisting of records of musical works. They own the copyright in the works
and supply them to television producers, who use them for background music for their
productions. One of the works in the plaintiff's library is a musical work called   *g*
'Sogno Nostalgico'. It was composed by an Italian, Mr Sciascia, in 1963. The copyright of
it was assigned to the plaintiffs in 1964. A record was made of it in Italy. One of the
records was brought to England and kept in the plaintiffs' library here. After 1967
copies were made here and were available in the library.

Mr de Wolfe is in the same line of business. In 1967 he had in his library a musical
work called 'Girl in the Dark'. He supplied it to television producers for use in a play   *h*
called 'Magnum for Schneider'. Someone in the plaintiffs' employment saw that play
and heard the music. He thought that 'Girl in the Dark' was very like 'Sogno Nostalgico'
and might have been copied from it. So on 10th March 1967 the plaintiffs wrote to
Mr de Wolfe complaining that 'Girl in the Dark' was an infringement of 'Sogno
Nostalgico'.

On 23rd March 1967 the solicitors for Mr de Wolfe replied in these terms: *j*

'Girl in The Dark'
'It appears from your letter that you have in your library a musical work entitled 'Sogno Nostalgico' which apparently bears some resemblance to the above
work which is included in our Clients' Music Library and in which they own the

a
copyright. Our Clients' work was composed by J. Trombey who resides in Holland and from whom they took an assignment of copyright in 1966. The fact that your work [i e Sogno Nostalgico] was composed prior to our Clients' work is not really relevant in the circumstances, as, of course, mere similarity between two musical works does not constitute any infringement. Infringement only occurs where there has been an actual copying of a copyright work by another person without the owner's consent. It would appear therefore that the similarity between the
b
works is coincidental, in which event neither work infringes the other.'

That letter shows that Mr de Wolfe recognised that the two works were very similar. Also, that the plaintiffs' work was produced prior to his own. But that his answer to the claim was that the similarity had arisen by sheer coincidence without any copying from the plaintiffs' work. The plaintiffs did not take the matter further until 1970.
c
They then raised the matter again. Mr de Wolfe's solicitors replied in the same terms as in their letter of 26th March 1967 which I have read.

On 11th December 1970 the plaintiffs issued a writ against Mr de Wolfe's company, the defendants. In the statement of claim they said they were the owners of the copyright in the musical work 'Sogno Nostalgico' and that the defendants had infringed it by their work, 'Girl in the Dark'. The defendants denied that there was any
d
infringement; and, by an amendment in 1973, they alleged that their work 'Girl in the Dark' was composed by a Dutchman called Stoeckart, known as J Trombey, in or about the first half of 1960, and that they had acquired title from him. On discovery, they disclosed a book of music said to have been composed by the Dutchman in 1960 including this work.

Last week the trial started before Fox J. Some days were spent in taking evidence.
e
Some of the evidecne was as to 'similar facts'. Part of it was taken de bene esse. But then counsel for the defendants asked the judge for a definite ruling whether or not evidence of 'similar facts' was admissible. The judge yesterday morning ruled that some of it was admissible. Counsel for the defendants challenges his ruling; and, with the leave of the judge, appeals to this court for a decision now. The hearing has been adjourned pending our decision.
f
In order to appreciate the point, I must state the nature of the evidence which is sought to be admitted. One matter relates to a 'trap order' which was given by or on behalf of the plaintiffs. It was arranged in this way. The plaintiffs made a record of a distinctive piece of music called 'Fixed Idea'. The copyright undoubtedly belonged to the plaintiffs. They wrote on the record 'Taken off air U.S.A.' That was not true It was not taken from a piece which had been broadcast in the United States. It had
g
been made by the plaintiffs from their own copyright. Those words 'Taken off air U.S.A.' would lead anyone to believe that it was copyright, though not in the plaintiffs. The plaintiffs then got Mr Shillingford, an agent provocateur, to take it to the defendants and ask them to make a new record from the piece of music. Mr Shillingford saw a Mr Chambers and arranged that, in return for a sum altogether of £250, the defendants would make a new record from that piece of music. Now this is where the
h
defendants fell into the trap They made the new record, but they called it a de Wolfe work. In a letter of 12th November 1970 they sent to Mr Shillingford two versions of their recording. They called it 'Visions'. They said the composer was Mr Reg Tilsley, the defendants were the publishers and £250 had been paid for it.

The plaintiffs say that the work 'Visions' is a copy of their own 'Fixed Idea', which was their copyright. No doubt they invited it, they asked for it, they paid for it;
j
but here were the defendants copying their music and putting it out to the world as if it was their own publication of a work by a different composer altogether.

The plaintiffs gave notice to the defendants some time ago of their intention to put those matters in evidence relating to the 'trap order'.

There are two other matters which the plaintiffs desire to give in evidence. They have only been discovered in the last week or so. It appears that records have been

made by other publishers of music by Sibelius and Elgar. Both of them are the
subject of copyright. We have had them played before us. The plaintiffs say that Mr **a**
de Wolfe has recorded music which bears a close resemblance to those copyright
airs. They also were played before us. There is indeed a very close resemblance so
that one may well think that the defendants may well have copied them from the
copyright works.

The plaintiffs wish to give those matters in evidence. They say that they go to
show that, in other cases, Mr de Wolfe has been reproducing musical works which **b**
are subject to copyright; and so he may have done the same in regard to the work
'Sogno Nostalgico'. Counsel for the defendants says that those matters are not
admissible.

The admissibility of evidence as to 'similar facts' has been much considered in the
criminal law. Some of them have reached the highest tribunal, the latest of them
being *Boardman v Director of Public Prosecutions*[1]. The criminal courts have been very **c**
careful not to admit such evidence unless its probative value is so strong that it
should be received in the interests of justice: and its admission will not operate
unfairly to the accused. In civil cases the courts have followed a similar line but have
not been so chary of admiting it. In civil cases the courts will admit evidence of
similar facts if it is logically probative, that is if it is logically relevant in determining
the matter which is in issue; provided that it is not oppressive or unfair to the other **d**
side; and also that the other side has fair notice of it and is able to deal with it. Instances are: *Brown v Eastern & Midlands Railway Co*[2], *Moore v Ransome's Dock Committee*[3],
Hales v Kerr[4].

The matter in issue in the present case is whether the resemblances which 'Girl in
the Dark' bears to 'Sogno Nostalgico' are mere coincidences or are due to copying.
On that issue it is very relevant to know that there are these other cases of musical **e**
works which are undoubtedly the subject of copyright, but yet the defendants have produced musical works bearing close resemblance to them. Whereas it might be due to
mere coincidence in one case, it is very unlikely that there would be coincidences in
four cases. It is rather like *R v Sims*[5] where it was said: 'The probative force of all the
acts together is much greater than one alone.' So the probative force of four
resemblances together is much better than one alone. **f**

Counsel for the defendants urges that this is virtually a charge of fraud; and fraud
is not pleaded. But in infringement of copyright fraud is not an essential ingredient.
Reproduction without the owner's consent is enough. Even subconscious copying is
an infringement. And even if there were a charge of fraud, it would not mean that
evidence of similar fraud should be excluded. It might be very relevant to prove
the fraud. **g**

It seems to me the judge was right. He said the evidence of these three matters is of
sufficient probative weight to be relevant to this issue and should be admitted.
Incidentally, he rejected evidence of other matters which was not of sufficient
probative value. I would dismiss the appeal.

ORR LJ. I agree. **h**

JAMES LJ. I also agree.

Appeal dismissed.

Solicitors: *White & Webb* (for the defendants); *Davenport Lyons & Co* (for the plaintiffs).

Wendy Shockett Barrister. **i**

---

1   [1974] 3 All ER 887, [1975] AC 421
2   (1889) 22 QBD 391
3   (1898) 14 TLR 539
4   [1908] 2 KB 601
5   [1946] 1 All ER 698 at 701, [1946] KB 531 at 540

a   # R v Guildhall Justices, ex parte Marshall

QUEEN'S BENCH DIVISION
LORD WIDGERY CJ, KILNER BROWN AND WATKINS JJ
28th JANUARY 1976

b   *Legal aid – Criminal cases – Representation by counsel – Indictable offence – Legal aid not including representation by counsel except in the case of an indictable offence – Meaning of 'indictable offence' – Whether including offence triable either summarily or on indictment – Legal Aid Act 1974, s 30(2)(a).*

The expression 'an indictable offence' in s 30(2)(a)^a of the Legal Aid Act 1974 means an
c   offence for which an indictment lies and therefore includes 'hybrid offences' which may be tried either summarily or on indictment. Accordingly, where a person is tried before justices for a hybrid offence the justices may, under s 30(2)(a), grant him legal aid which includes representation by counsel, where, because of circumstances which make the case unusually grave or difficult, representation by both solicitor and counsel is desirable (see p 769 *h* and p 770 *a* and *b*, post).
d   *Hastings and Folkestone Glassworks Ltd v Kalson* [1948] 2 All ER 1013 applied.

Notes
For the extent of legal aid in criminal cases, see Supplement to 10 Halsbury's Laws (3rd Edn) para 1019A, 2.
For indictable offences triable summarily, see 25 Halsbury's Laws (3rd Edn) 176-179,
e   paras 325-328, and for cases on the subject, see 33 Digest (Repl) 186-188, *347-364*.
For the Legal Aid Act 1974, s 30, see 44 Halsbury's Statutes (3rd Edn) 130.

Case referred to in judgments
Hastings and Folkestone Glassworks Ltd v Kalson [1948] 2 All ER 1013, [1949] 1 KB 214, [1949] LJR 627, 113 JP 31, 47 LGR 155, CA, 9 Digest (Reissue) 564, *3379*.
f
Motion for certiorari
This was an application by way of motion by William Marshall, who had been summoned under five informations laid by the Director of Public Prosecutions under para 1(1) of Part II of Sch 5 to the Exchange Control Act 1947 alleging that he had conspired with others to contravene certain provisions of the 1947 Act, for an order of
g   certiorari to quash the refusal by the Guildhall justices to extend legal aid to cover representation by counsel on 18th December 1975. The facts are set out in the judgment of Lord Widgery CJ.

W Glossop for the applicant.
G Cheyne for the justices.
h   *David Jeffreys* for the Director of Public Prosecutions.

LORD WIDGERY CJ. In these proceedings counsel moves on behalf of the applicant for an order of certiorari to bring up and quash a refusal by the Guildhall justices of an extension of legal aid to cover representation of the applicant by counsel on 18th December 1975 in respect of certain proceedings to which I must return in a
j   moment. It seems to me just possible that mandamus would have been a more effective approach, but the point has not been raised in argument, and no doubt certiorari will serve if the substance of the applicant's case is a good one.
The applicant is at present being tried by the machinery of summary trial under

---
a   Section 30(2), so far as material, is set out at p 768 *g* and *h*, post

five informations, all of which allege that he conspired with others to contravene *a*
ss 17, 9, 2, 7 and 24 of the Exchange Control Act 1947. The matters are extremely
complex and unusually difficult. The pile of documents stands 12 inches high. The
Crown is represented by leading and junior counsel and has a number of experts in
support, and some 20 working days have been allotted in the future for a continuation
of this complicated summary trial.

The applicant was granted legal aid under an order of the court dated 11th December
1975, but for representation by a solicitor only. An application was made to the *b*
justices by counsel on behalf of the applicant asking for legal aid to be extended to
cover representation by counsel, and the justices indicated that they were sympathetic
towards the application but believed that they were unable to do so because the
circumstances of the case deprived them in their view of making a legal aid order
which included representation by counsel.

The matter is accordingly brought into this court so that we may determine the *c*
legal question, which is: are the justices in this case prohibited as a matter of law from
extending legal aid to counsel on behalf of the applicant?

The offences under the Exchange Control Act 1974 are governed so far as penalty is
concerned by Sch 5, Part II, para 1(3), to the 1947 Act, and that shows that these
offences are what are commonly called 'hybrid offences', that is to say they can be
proceeded against either summarily or by trial on indictment. In para 1(3) of Part II of *d*
the Schedule it is provided:

> 'Any person who commits an offence punishable under this Part of this
> Schedule shall be liable—(*a*) on summary conviction, to imprisonment for not
> more than three months or to a fine or both; (*b*) on conviction on indictment, to
> imprisonment for not more than two years or to a fine or both . . .'
e

This is a classic example of the so-called hybrid offence, where provision is specifically
made for it to be tried by a magistrates' court or on indictment.

The difficulty arises in this way. The Legal Aid Act 1974, s 30, first requires that there
shall generally be representation under Legal Aid in the form of solicitor and counsel.
I read sub-s (1):

> 'For the purposes of this Part of this Act legal aid, in relation to any proceedings *f*
> to which a person is a party, shall be taken, subject to the following provisions of
> this section, as consisting of representation by a solicitor and counsel assigned by
> the court, including advice on the preparation of that person's case for those
> proceedings.'

So we start with the proposition that legal aid normally means solicitor and counsel. *g*
Section 30(2) provides:

> 'Notwithstanding anything in subsection (1) above, legal aid ordered to be
> given for the purposes of any proceedings before a magistrates' court shall not
> include representation by counsel except—(*a*) in the case of any indictable offence,
> where the court is of the opinion that, because of circumstances which make the *h*
> the case unusually grave or difficult, representation by both solicitor and counsel
> would be desirable . . .'

The justices in the present case, as I understand it, have taken the view that these
offences are not indictable offences within s 30(2)(*a*), and they have taken that view
because of the method of trial being employed in connection with these offences,
which is summary trial, as I have already described. We have to decide whether *j*
that restricted view is right, or whether the terms permitting representation by
counsel in a magistrates' court are not in fact much wider in their application.

The critical word is 'indictable'. The legal aid order may extend to counsel in the
case of an indictable offence subject to the conditions stated in the section. The word
'indictable' has appeared in innumerable Acts. Very often—probably more often

than not—the Act has contained a definition section which makes clear what an
a indictable offence means in that Act, but it is of course of very little value to look at
such statutes unless closely related to the present one for assistance, and I think the
proper approach to this problem is to go straight to the word 'indictable' and ask
oneself what it means in ordinary common use. I think the answer to that is that
you speak of an offence as being 'an indictable offence' when it is an offence for which
an indictment lies. In other words, it includes offences like murder, which must be
b tried on indictment, and also hybrid offences.

That is my view of the ordinary straightforward meaning of the word and, if that
is so, the present offences were indictable offences because they were capable of being
tried on indictment, even though not so tried.

I am supported in the view I have expressed by the only authority which we have
been invited to look at: *Hastings and Folkestone Glassworks Ltd v Kalson*[1]. The question
c arose in this way. The company's articles provided that a director convicted of an
indictable offence should vacate his office. A director of a company pleaded guilty
before a court of summary jurisdiction to a charge under the defence regulations
and was convicted and fined. The offence was a hybrid offence like the present offence.
It could have been tried on indictment or summarily. In fact it was tried summarily.
The Court of Appeal[1] held that whether or not an offence was 'indictable' within the
d meaning of the company's articles depended on the nature and quality of the offence
when committed, irrespective of the procedural manner in which it might subsequently be dealt with, and, therefore, as the offence of which the defendant was
convicted was one which could be dealt with on indictment, he was 'convicted of an
indictable offence' within the meaning of the articles, and the company was entitled
to the declaration asked for.

e I am further reinforced in my view as to what is the correct approach to this problem
by a word or two of Harman J, who was the junior member of the Court of Appeal
in question. He said[2]:

> 'Articles in this form, though not favoured in the best models, have been a
> familiar feature for many years, and I cannot bring myself to think that dis-
f > qualification can depend on whether the offence in question is to be found in the
> schedule to an Act of 1925 or on the method by which the authorities choose
> to bring it home to the offender. In my judgment, the argument of counsel for
> the defendant lays too much stress on the word "convicted". Of course, it is a
> condition precedent to disqualification that there should have been a conviction.
> Mere accusation may be wholly unjustified, but, once a conviction has been
> recorded, the test is the nature of the offence. Not every offence brings the sanction
g > into effect. It must have been "indictable", and that in plain English means "for
> which an indictment lies". This offence satisfies that test, and the defendant's
> disqualification, in my judgment, follows.'

I would follow Harman J by saying that the word 'indictable' in plain English means
'for which an indictment lies', and consequently the hybrid offences to which I have
h referred, amongst others, are indictable offences for present purposes. This no doubt
means that it will be open to the justices to extend the legal aid order in the instant
case, and maybe to grant extended legal aid orders in a number of cases which are to
follow. Those who are concerned with the possible burden on the taxpayer may
perhaps take some comfort from a reminder that in order to employ counsel under
legal aid in the magistrates' court it is not just enough to show that the offence is an
j indictable offence. It has to be an indictable offence and to be considered unusually
grave or difficult. I would stress the importance when extended applications for legal
aid are made in the future, as they will be made, of the court considering both points
before granting the order, namely considering whether the offence is an indictable

1   [1948] 2 All ER 1013, [1949] 1 KB 214
2   [1948] 2 All ER at 1017, [1949] 1 KB at 222

offence as defined here this afternoon, and, if it is, whether the case is so unusually grave or difficult as to make representation by counsel desirable. *a*

In the event, in my judgment, the order should go quashing the refusal of the justices to grant the extended order for legal aid, and thus leaving them in a position to make that order if they are so minded, having regard to the other features to which I have referred.

KILNER BROWN J. I agree. *b*

WATKINS J. I agree.

Certiorari granted. *c*

Solicitors: *Herbert & Gowers & Co* (for the applicant); *The Comptroller, City Solicitor* (for the justices); *Director of Public Prosecutions*.

N P Metcalfe Esq Barrister.

d

Re W J King & Sons Ltd's Application

COURT OF APPEAL, CIVIL DIVISION
BUCKLEY, ORR LJJ AND SIR JOHN PENNYCUICK
20th, 21st, 22nd, 23rd JANUARY, 13th FEBRUARY 1976 *e*

Mines – Grant of working facilities – Application – Interim order pending determination of status quo – Jurisdiction – Implied or inherent jurisdiction to make interim order – Company working hardstone under lease of quarry – Company applying for right to continue working on expiry of lease – Lessor opposing application – Lease expiring before application heard – Company applying for interim order to continue working pending hearing – Whether court ***f*** *having jurisdiction to make interim order – Mines (Working Facilities and Support) Act 1966, s 1 (as amended by the Mines (Working Facilities and Support) Act 1974, s 1).*

The appellant's father was the owner of a quarry and certain land adjoining it. By a lease dated 1st February 1947 the appellant's father demised approximately 12 acres of land forming part of the quarry to a company which carried on the business of *g* quarrying hardstone. The lease was due to expire on 25th December 1974. In 1971, following the death of his parents, the appellant became entitled to the freehold reversion under the terms of a family settlement. Following the enactment of s 1[a] of the Mines (Working Facilities and Support) Act 1974, amending s 1 of the Mines (Working Facilities and Support) Act 1966, the company became entitled to apply to the Secretary of State for the Environment ('the Minister') under s 4(1)[b] of the 1966 Act for *h* the grant of rights to search for and work hardstone in the land which was the subject of the lease and in the adjoining land. By a letter dated 18th November the company applied for such rights. After the expiry of the lease on 25th December,

---

a Section 1, as amended and so far as material, provides: 'The court may, subject to and in *j* accordance with this Act, confer any rights described in the table below ... Paragraph 1 of Table. (1) This paragraph applies to any minerals other than coal and peat cut for purposes other than sale. (2) A right to search for or work any minerals to which this paragraph applies may be conferred on any person (exercisable either by himself or through a lessee) ...'

b Section 4, so far as material, is set out at p 773 *c* to *f*, post

a the company continued to extract hardstone from the appellant's quarry. The Minister referred the application to the court under s 4(3) of the 1966 Act. The appellant opposed the company's application. The company issued an originating summons for the grant of the statutory rights and subsequently made an interlocutory application for the right to search for and work hardstone on part of the appellant's land during the interim period before the determination of the originating summons.

b On the company's application the judge held, inter alia, that, despite the absence of any relevant provisions in the Supreme Court of Judicature (Consolidation) Act 1925 or in the Rules of the Supreme Court, the court by reason of its previous practice had jurisdiction on an interim application to make an order preserving the status quo, thus guarding the rights, if any, of the applicant. Accordingly he granted the company the right to search for and work hardstone at the appellant's quarry until the trial of the company's application. The appellant appealed.

c

Held – The 1966 Act did not confer on the court any jurisdiction to grant working facilities either retrospectively or by way of interim order, nor was there anything in the court's previous practice to indicate such a jurisdiction. Moreover, since the lease granted to the company had already expired, the company were acting unlawfully by

d continuing to work the stone and the continuation of the working would not preserve the status quo as regards the stone which was the property of the appellant. It followed that the court had no inherent power by way of interim order to override the private rights of the appellant or to anticipate rights which might or might not be granted in the future and which, even if granted, could have no retrospective effect. Accordingly the appeal would be allowed (see p 778 d to p 779 d, post).

e *Manchester Corpn v Connolly* [1970] 1 All ER 961 and *F Hoffman-La Roche & Co AG v Inter-Continental Pharmaceuticals Ltd* [1965] 2 All ER 15 applied.

Re an Application of the National Coal Board [1958] 2 All ER 351 doubted.

Per Curiam. The fact that there has been a reference to the court by the Minister under s 4(3) of the 1966 Act does not of itself lend support to an application for the grant of rights under s 1 of the 1966 Act (see p 777 f to p 778 a, post).

f

Notes

For interlocutory injunctions, see 21 Halsbury's Laws (3rd Edn) 364-370, paras 763-776, and for cases on the subject, see 28(2) Digest (Reissue) 966-987, 60-209.

For the Mines (Working Facilities and Support) Act 1966, ss 1, 4, see 22 Halsbury's Statutes (3rd Edn) 601, 607, and for the Mines (Working Facilities and Support Act)

g 1974, s 1, see 44 ibid 730.

Cases referred to in judgment

Archibald Russell Ltd v Nether Pollock Ltd 1938 SC 1, 33 Digest (Repl) 764, *214.

Heathstar Properties Ltd, Re [1966] 1 All ER 628, [1966] 1 WLR 993, Digest (Cont Vol B) 109, 5303a.

h *Hoffmann-La Roche (F) & Co AG v Inter-Continental Pharmaceuticals Ltd, Geigy (JR) SA v Inter-Continental Pharmaceuticals Ltd* [1965] 2 All ER 15, [1965] Ch 795, [1965] 2 WLR 1045, [1965] RPC 226, CA, Digest (Cont Vol B) 587, 1923b.

Manchester Corpn v Connolly [1970] 1 All ER 961, [1970] Ch 420, [1970] 2 WLR 746, 21 P & CR 154, CA, Digest (Cont Vol C) 342, 1729a.

National Coal Board, Re an Application of the [1958] 2 All ER 351, [1958] 1 WLR 599, 33

j Digest (Repl) 762, 354.

Cases also cited

Glassbrook Bros Ltd v Leyson [1933] 2 KB 91, [1932] All ER Rep 698, CA.

Henry Lawson Ltd, Re Application of (1930) 144 LT 128.

Townend v Askern Coal & Iron Co [1934] 1 Ch 463.

Interlocutory appeal
This was an appeal by William Geoffrey King and Edward Rowland Siddle against an   *a*
order of Whitford J made on 3rd October 1975 whereby it was ordered that the right
to search for and work hardstone at Triscombe Quarry, near Triscombe, Somerset
should be granted to the respondents, W J King & Sons Ltd, until trial or further order.
The facts are set out in the judgment of the court.

Richard Scott QC and Timothy Lloyd for the appellants.   *b*
Jeremiah Harman QC and Elizabeth Appleby for the respondents.

Cur adv vult

13th February. **ORR LJ** delivered the following judgment of the court: Mr W G King,
the effective appellant in this case (and whom we shall call 'the appellant') is the son of
the late Mr W J King, who by a lease dated 1st February 1947 demised to the respon-   *c*
dents for the purposes of their business of quarrying hardstone, some 12 acres of land,
part of an area known as the Triscombe quarry at West Bagborough in Somerset,
for a term of 28 years from 25th December 1946, but subject to an express provision
that the respondents should be at liberty during the six months following the expiry
of the lease on 25th December 1974 to make merchantable on the demised land any
material gotten by them during the term and also to remove their plant. By the   *d*
combined effect of the Mines (Working Facilities and Support) Acts 1966 and 1974,
the respondents became entitled as from 31st July 1974 (the date of the enactment of
the 1974 Act) to apply to the appropriate Minister (now the Secretary of State
for the Environment) for the grant to them of rights to search for and work
hardstone in the demised land and also in adjoining land, and by a letter dated 18th
November 1974, they made application to the Minister for such rights within an area   *e*
of some 34 acres comprising the demised land, a three acre site known as the Parish
Quarry to which we shall later refer, and certain land adjoining the demised land
in respect of which planning permission had been obtained for stone quarrying.
By a subsequent letter of 16th December 1974 they extended the application to
comprise a further area of adjoining land comprising some 32 acres which was the
subject of a pending planning application for such development, giving as their   *f*
reason for this amendment that, whereas they had previously estimated that there
were four to five years' supply of stone in the 34 acres, they now had reason to believe that
the supply might be as little as two years. The Minister having referred the application to the court under s 4 of the 1966 Act, the respondents on 16th May 1975 issued
an originating summons in the Chancery Division for the grant of such rights, and
thereafter on 4th June 1975 made an interlocutory application for the right to search   *g*
for and work hardstone during the interim period before the hearing of the originating summons, but only, as the application was presented to the court, over the
smaller area of 34 acres. This interlocutory application came before Whitford J on
3rd October 1975 who granted the relief sought and it is in respect of this order that
the appellant now appeals and the respondents by a cross-notice seek to support the
the judge's decision on grounds other than those relied on by him.   *h*
   The relevant provisions of the 1966 and 1974 Acts, so far as material for the present
purposes, may be summarised as follows. Section 1 of the 1966 Act provides that the
court may, subject to and in accordance with the Act, confer any rights described in
the table thereto. Paragraph 1(1) of the table, as originally enacted, specified certain
minerals not including hardstone, but by the 1974 Act a new para 1(1) was substituted
which includes hardstone. Paragraph 1(2) of the table provided: *j*

'A right to search for or work any mineral to which this paragraph applies
(but not including coal) may be conferred on any person (exercisable either by
himself or through a lessee).'

Paragraph 5 of the table empowered the court to confer ancillary rights as defined

in s 2 of the 1966 Act on a person on whom the right to work minerals is conferred
under the Act and the remaining sections of the Act provided, so far as material, as
follows:

'3.—(1) No right shall be granted under section 1 of this Act unless the court is
satisfied that the grant is expedient in the national interest.

'(2) No right shall be granted under section 1 of this Act unless it is shown that
it is not reasonably practicable to obtain the right by private arrangement for any
of the following reasons—(a) that the persons with power to grant the right are
numerous or have conflicting interests; (b) that the persons with power to grant
the right, or any of them, cannot be ascertained or cannot be found; (c) that the
persons from whom the right must be obtained, or any of them, have not the
necessary powers of disposition, whether by reason of defect in title, legal disability or otherwise; (d) that the person with power to grant the right unreasonably refuses to grant it or demands terms which, having regard to the
circumstances, are unreasonable.

'4.—(1) An application for the grant of a right under section 1 of this Act shall
be sent to the Minister, and the applicant for an ancillary right for the purpose of
or in connection with working any minerals may be a person either having or
applying for the right to work those minerals.

'(2) The application shall set out the circumstances alleged to justify the grant
of the right, and shall be in such form and accompanied by such information
verified in such manner as the Minister may direct.

'(3) The Minister shall consider the application, and shall, unless after communication with such other parties interested (if any) as he may think fit, he is of
the opinion that a *prima facie* case is not made out, refer the matter to the court:

'Provided that, where it is alleged that the right in question cannot be obtained
by reason of any person not having the necessary powers of disposition, or having
unreasonably refused to grant it, or having demanded terms which are unreasonable, the Minister shall not refer the application to the court without first having
communicated with that person . . .

'5.—(1) Where a matter is referred to the court under the last foregoing section,
the court, if satisfied that the requirements of this Act are complied with in the
the case of the applicant, may, by order, grant the right on such terms and subject
to such conditions, and for such period, as the court may think fit, and upon such
an order being made, the right specified in the order shall, subject to the following
provisions of this Act, vest in the applicant.

'(2) Where a right is granted, such compensation or consideration as in default
of agreement may be determined by the court shall be paid or given by the
applicant in respect of the acquisition of the right to such persons as the court may
determine to be entitled thereto . . .

'10. A right granted under this Act shall not confer on the person to whom it is
granted any greater or other power than if the right had been granted by a
person legally entitled to grant the right, or relieve the grantee from any obligation or liability to which he would have been subject had the right been granted
by such a person.'

Section 15 of the 1966 Act repealed certain provisions as to the grant of working
facilities contained in, inter alia, the Mines (Working Facilities and Support) Acts 1923
and 1925, and the Mines (Working Facilities) Act 1938.

At the hearing the following matters were not in dispute. In February 1936 the
appellant's father incorporated the respondent company for the purpose, inter alia, of
acquiring the business of a quarry proprietor previously carried on by him, and he and
the appellant became at that time directors of the company, and the latter in December of the same year managing director, which office he held until July 1970. In May
1945 the appellant's father bought the Bagborough House estate which embraces the

Triscombe quarry and the land adjoining it, and in January 1947 he granted to the
respondents the lease in question. Surrounded, save on one side, by the demised land *a*
is an area called the Parish Quarry from which the parishioners claim the right to
take stone, and in respect of this area the appellant's father held a licence to quarry
stone, granted to him in 1932 by the West Bagborough Parish Council, the benefit of
which, and of other quarrying licences held by him, he undertook by an agreement
dated 15th February 1936 to hold on behalf of the respondents. In 1952 the
appellant's father died, leaving the income of the Triscombe quarry to his wife, who *b*
died in 1971, for her life, and the freehold reversion on the lease to the appellant,
with the result that it is now held in trust for the appellant absolutely and will be
vested in him as soon as certain estate duty questions have been resolved.

In April 1948 the respondents became a wholly-owned subsidiary of Anglo-American
Asphalt Co Ltd (which we will call 'Anglo-American') and have since been under
common management with that company and others in the same group. On *c*
8th July 1970 following differences of opinion which had arisen between him and the
directors of Anglo-American, the appellant ceased to be managing director of the respondents, and thereafter in an action brought in the Queen's Bench Division made
claims for compensation against Anglo-American, who in their defence pleaded
serious allegations against him, but that action has now been settled by a payment
of money made by Anglo-American to the appellant. On 1st April 1974 the Bag- *d*
borough Parish Council granted a 28 year lease, the validity of which is disputed by
the appellant, of the Parish Quarry to Anglo-American, but it is common ground that
there is no workable stone left in that area and the respondents use it, because it is
conveniently level, as a site for most of their plant and also for stocking of processed
stone. During the period of the 1947 lease the respondents have extended their
quarrying operations beyond the boundary of the demise up to an approximate line *e*
coloured red on the exhibited sketch plan, and in an action for trespass brought by
the appellant in the Chancery Division have alleged that on various alternative
grounds they had a right to do so, but the appellant has challenged these claims.
The respondents have also recently obtained in the county court new leases of two
areas of land of which they previously held tenancies from the Bagborough estate
and which they use as a washing plant and a transport yard. Finally, it is not in dispute *f*
that since the expiry of the 1947 lease on 25th December 1974 the respondents,
contrary to legal advice given to them, have continued to extract stone from the
quarry.

On the hearing of the interlocutory applications no witnesses were called and the
evidence before the judge consisted of three affidavits sworn by Mr Lawrence,
general manager of the relevant division of Anglo-American, and one sworn by the *g*
appellant, and the exhibits thereto; Mr Lawrence's evidence being directed to
establishing that the two conditions imposed by s 3 of the 1966 Act on the grant of
rights are satisfied in that (i) the grant is expedient in the national interest, and (ii) it
is not reasonably practicable for the respondents to obtain the rights by private
arrangement because the appellant has unreasonably refused to grant them or has
demanded unreasonable terms; and the appellant's affidavit being directed to showing *h*
that no detriment to the national interest is involved if the rights are refused, since
he can himself undertake the quarrying of the stone within a comparatively short
time, and that he has not unreasonably refused to grant the rights or demanded
unreasonable terms. On the national interest issue, the evidence in Mr Lawrence's
first two affidavits may be summarised as follows.

(i) As to the quality of stone, it is known in the trade as 'premium stone' and in the *j*
1974 report of the Transport and Road Research Laboratory, which refers to tests
carried out since 1962 on premium stone, it is described as 'one of the best stones in the
country for road surfaces, particularly in respect of its non-skid and abrasive qualities',
and it is further stated that on these tests the Triscombe aggregate gave the best
overall performance.

(ii) As to demand for the stone, in 1973 the total (including by-products) produced
a and sold was 198,800 tons of the value of some £373,000, of which some 69,000 tons
(excluding by-product gravel and scalpings) went to the Somerset County Council
and various tonnages up to 5,000 tons to other county councils as far afield as Kent,
Sussex and Surrey. For 1974 the tonnage produced was substantially lower but was
affected by the three day week, and the demand for the stone is continuing.

(iii) As to the provision of employment as a factor of the national interest, the
b respondents employ 25 men on working and treating the stone and a further 24 on
transport, apart from haulage contractors.

(iv) As to the practicability of the appellant taking over the working of the stone,
that in order to do so he would, because of the respondents' lease of the Parish
Quarry, have to find another level site of sufficient size to accommodate his fixed
plant, which it was claimed that he would be unable to do, and also provide a new
c entrance to the site and find sites for a washing plant and transport yard, and in
addition acquire the requisite plant; and it was claimed that even if these difficulties
could be overcome, it was unlikely that the appellant would be able to begin operations until after the hearing of the substantive application, with the result that
Triscombe stone would not be available during that period.

In answer to this evidence the appellant claimed in his affidavit that there is an area
d within the demised land of sufficient size, and level enough, to accommodate the plant;
that he could construct a new entrance and find on his own land sites for a washing plant
and transport yard; and could himself provide some of the necessary plant and acquire
without any serious delay such major items of plant as he would have to buy.

In an affidavit in reply, Mr Lawrence estimated that the cost, if they are bought
new, of the major items of plant which the appellant himself cannot provide would be
e £250,000 and that there would be a delay of six to 12 months before delivery
could be obtained; and in an affidavit sworn on 13th January 1976, which we admitted
by way of fresh evidence in the appeal, Mr Gaymer, secretary and a director of
Anglo-American, disputes the availability of any level area of sufficient size, other
than the Parish Quarry, to accommodate the plant and estimates that the major items
of plant required could not be obtained new in less than six months to 12 or second-
f hand in less than nine months.

As to the issue of unreasonable refusal, the respondents relied on a bundle of correspondence between the respective solicitors extending from July 1970 to May 1975,
as to which it is, for the present purposes, sufficient to say that on 24th January 1975,
by which time the interim position was under discussion, the appellant's solicitors
accepted that their client had impliedly, if not expressly, refused to grant any rights
g after the expiry of the lease, and that the final letter in May 1975 conveys an outright
refusal by the appellant of any licence for the interim period and requires the respondents to make an immediate application to the court which it is said will be strongly
contested. The appellant's case on this issue, as outlined in his affidavit, is that the land
and the stone are his, that he has been concerned in stone-quarrying all his working
life, and wishes to quarry the stone in question; and that in these circumstances his
h refusal is not unreasonable.

These being in summary the facts of the case, and before turning to the issues which
arose at the hearing and to the judgment of Whitford J, it should be recorded that
before this court, and as we understand before the learned judge, counsel on both
sides were agreed that, having regard to the present state of the lists in the Chancery
Division, the parties to this case would be fortunate if the substantive application on
j the originating summons is heard before the end of 1976. Since we reserved judgment,
an announcement has been made that additional judges are to be allocated to the
Chancery Division, but it can only be a matter of speculation whether a substantially
earlier hearing can in fact be obtained.

Before the learned judge the first issue in the case was whether he had any power
to grant the interim rights sought by the respondents, and the second issue was

whether, if he had such power, it should be exercised in all the circumstances of the case. As to the first issue, it was accepted by counsel on both sides that in the absence of *a* oral evidence, tested by cross-examination, and on the material before him, it was not open to the judge to come to a conclusion whether, for the purposes of the substantive application, the requirements of s 3 of the 1966 Act as to the national interest and as to unreasonable refusal had on a balance of probabilities been satisfied, but it was argued by counsel for the applicants (although this fact does not clearly emerge from the judgment) that it was open to the judge to decide that such require- *b* ments had been satisfied as respects the interim period before the substantive application would be heard.

On the first issue, the judge made no finding that the conditions imposed by s 3 had been satisfied either in the long-term or as respects the interim period, and as to the law accepted that s 3, like s 101 of the Companies Act 1948 with which Buckley J was concerned in *Re Heathstar Properties Ltd*[1], confers jurisdiction on the court only *c* when satisfied that the specified conditions have been fulfilled; and he also accepted on the authority of the judgment of Lord Diplock (with whom the other members of the court agreed) in *Manchester Corpn v Connolly*[2] that jurisdiction to make the order sought must, in the absence of any provision conferring jurisdiction contained in the 1966 Act itself, be found 'either in the Supreme Court of Judicature (Consolidation) Act of 1925, or in the rules made thereunder, or in the previous practice *d* of the court'. In these circumstances, it being common ground that there was no relevant provision either in the Judicature Act 1925 or in the Rules of the Supreme Court, he considered that the matter must turn on the previous practice of the court, as to which he came to the conclusion that there is both a principle whereby the court on an interim application may make such an order as will ensure that if the applicant ultimately succeeds his victory will not be a hollow one, and also a principle *e* whereby the court may make such an order as will preserve the status quo as it existed at the commencement of the proceedings, and he found some support for this conclusion in the provisions of RSC Ord 29 with reference to the detention and preservation of the subject-matter of a cause or matter pending trial and also in the judgment of Roxburgh J in *Re an Application of the National Coal Board*[3].

Early in his judgment the judge referred to the requirement contained in s 4(3) of *f* the 1966 Act that 'The Minister shall consider the application, and shall, unless after communication with such other parties (if any) as he may think fit, he is of the opinion that a prima facia case is not made out, refer the matter to the court', and said that he must proceed on the assumption that the Secretary of State had come to a conclusion that a prima facie case had been made out, for otherwise he would not under the Act have directed the reference to the court, and at the end of his judgment he referred to *g* the fact of the reference having been made as a matter to which he had had regard.

The appellant's grounds of appeal against the judge's decision are that he had no jurisdiction to make the order he did and was wrong in thinking that *Re an Application of the National Coal Board*[3] supported his conclusion that he had inherent jurisdiction, and that he also misdirected himself in placing reliance on the fact that the Minister had referred the matter to the court. By a respondents' notice it is claimed that *h* the judge should have held on the evidence that the conditions specified in s 3 of the 1966 Act had been satisfied as respects the interim period, and on the hearing of the appeal counsel for the respondents offered undertakings that they would confine any interim quarrying to an area of 2½ acres and would also, if they should ultimately fail on the substantive application, render a full account of their interim operations and pay to the appellant compensation to the extent that their net profit from *j* such operations exceeded the royalties already paid in respect of the stone.

---

1   [1966] 1 All ER 628, [1966] 1 WLR 993
2   [1970] Ch 420 at 428, [1970] 1 All ER 961 at 965
3   [1958] 2 All ER 351, [1958] 1 WLR 599

It will be convenient to deal first with the ground of appeal contained in the res-
a pondents' notice, which turns on the evidence in the case; thereafter with the appellant's second ground of appeal; and finally with the issue of law as to jurisdiction.
On the first of these issues, counsel for the respondents' submission was that the judge
ought to have been satisfied, on the evidence contained in Mr Lawrence's affidavit as
to the qualities of the Triscombe stone and its value for road-making, particularly
from the aspect of road safety, that there would be a detriment to the public interest
b if the stone were not quarried during the interim period, and that taking this detriment into account the appellant's refusal to grant rights was unreasonable; but, with
great respect to this submission, we are unable to accept it. The evidence as to the
quality of the stone amounted to no more than that it is one of the best stones for
road surfacing, particularly in respect of its non-skid and abrasive qualities, and that
Triscombe aggregate had on certain tests given the best overall performance; and as
c to the demand for the stone that a very substantial tonnage of it had been supplied to
the Somerset County Council and smaller quantities to other county councils. It is,
however, in our judgment, an important feature of the case that if Triscombe stone
were not worked for a period of months it would not be denied altogether to the
councils concerned but would merely be delivered later and there was no evidence
that this would involve any detriment to the public interest. In particular there was
d no evidence as to the requirements of, or stocks held by, the councils, or as to any
difficulty in obtaining, during the period in question, other comparable stone of
which the Road Research Laboratory report admitted the existence in the words 'one
of the best stones', or as to the degree of inferiority of other stone outside that
category. Equally, in the absence of any evidence as to local employment conditions,
there was no evidence of any detriment to the public interest which might arise from
e the respondents having to dismiss their employees. For these reasons, in our judgment, the evidence fell far short of establishing even a prima facie case of detriment
to the public interest even if the interim rights are refused, and in the absence of proof
of detriment to the public interest we do not see any ground on which the refusal
of the rights, which has to be considered in relation to any detriment to the public
interest (see *Archibald Russell Ltd v Nether Pollock Ltd*[1]) could be held unreasonable.
f As to the appellant's second ground of appeal, it is clear that the judge did not
treat the fact of the reference having been made by the Minister as itself establishing
the existence of a prima facie case on the interim application, but it appears from his
second reference to this matter that he took it into consideration as a matter lending
some support to the respondents' case. In this, with great respect, we think that he
was wrong. It is to be noted, in the first place, that the Minister is not required as a
g condition of referring the matter to the court to make a positive finding that a prima
facie case has been made out, but if he is of opinion that a prima facie case has not
been made out the reference is not to be made, and there is, it seems to us, an important difference between a negative finding that no prima facie case has been made
out, which may amount to no more than that the claim is frivolous, and a positive
finding that a prima facie case has been established. But in any event the inquiry
h which s 4(3) requires the Minister to make is not in any sense a judicial inquiry embracing examination and cross-examination of witnesses. It consists merely of considering written representations the contents of which have not been disclosed to
other persons interested, and it is left entirely to the Minister's discretion with what
other persons he will communicate. For these reasons, we think that the judge was
wrong in treating the fact of the reference having been made as a matter which could
j lend support to the respondents' case. It was no more than a step in the proceedings
which had resulted in the matter coming before the court and could not, in our
judgment, be treated as reinforcing the respondents' case. What weight the judge
gave to it can only be a matter of speculation. He may well have given it very little

1   1938 SC 1

weight, and having regard to the conclusion we have reached on the issue of jurisdiction, we do not find it necessary to decide whether, if this matter stood alone, it would **a** be sufficient ground for allowing the appeal.

The remaining and very important issue is that of jurisdiction. There is no doubt that in certain respects it would be convenient that the court should have power to make an interim order in such a case as this, for it is obvious that if the respondents have to discontinue their operations it may not be economically possible to resume them in the event of rights being granted on the substantive hearing. Counsel for the respond- **b** ents also argued that, if there is no power to grant interim relief, applicants under the 1966 Act may be put in great difficulty because a lessor who is asked to grant rights may refuse to give a definite answer, with the result that the application under the Act is postponed and cannot be heard until after the expiry of the lease. In the present case, however, the special difficulty which arose was that the respondents were not in law entitled to apply for rights until the enactment of the 1974 Act, some **c** five months before the expiry of the lease. In future cases, if the lessor persistently refuses to give a definite answer, the lessee's remedy, in our judgment, is to make his substantive application in sufficient time for it to be heard before the lease expires. The present issue is, however, one of law.

It was argued by counsel for the respondents that on the true construction of the 1966 Act the rights to which it refers may be granted retrospectively and may also **d** be granted by way of interim order; but we are unable to accept either part of this argument. In our judgment, if it was intended to confer such powers they would have been conferred by clear and specific language, and we derive some support for that conclusion in the view adopted by this court in *Hoffmann-La Roche & Co v Inter-Continental Pharmaceuticals Ltd*[1], which concerned s 41 of the Patents Act 1949.

It follows, in our judgment, on the authority of Lord Diplock's judgment in *Man-* **e** *chester Corpn v Connolly*[2] and in the absence of any relevant provision either in the Judicature Act 1925 or in the Rules of the Supreme Court, that the jurisdiction claimed must be found, if at all, in the previous practice of the court, as to which the judge based his conclusion in part on the provisions of RSC Ord 29, which he thought indicated the existence of a wider principle, in part on a basis of preserving the status quo, and in part on the judgment of Roxburgh J in *Re an Application of the National* **f** *Coal Board*[3]; but, with respect, we are unable to accept any of these grounds for his conclusion. RSC Ord 29 contains rules for the preservation or disposal of property with the object, inter alia, of transferring a plaintiff's title from goods themselves to the proceeds of their sale, but we do not consider that it is possible to infer from these very limited provisions the existence of some much wider principle not to be found in the rules. **g**

As to preservation of the status quo, the courts frequently make an interim order which will secure that object, and counsel for the respondents claimed that the order under appeal has that effect, in that it enables the respondents to continue working the stone as they had been doing before the order. But another aspect of the matter is that after the expiry of the lease they were working without any right to do so, and unlawfully, and that the continuation of the working will not preserve the status quo **h** as regards the stone, which belongs to the appellant and will be progressively reduced by the operations. In these circumstances it was argued for the appellant that the court has no inherent power, by way of interim order, to override private rights or to anticipate rights that may or may not be granted in the future and, when granted, would have no retrospective effect. In our judgment, this argument is well founded and we consider that it derives some support from the judgment in the *Hoffmann-La Roche* **j** case[1] which seems to us closely analogous.

---

1   [1965] 2 All ER 15, [1965] Ch 795
2   [1970] 1 All ER 961, [1970] Ch 420
3   [1958] 2 All ER 351, [1958] 1 WLR 599

There remains the judgment of Roxburgh J in *Re an Application of the National Coal*
Board[1] where the applicants, whose workings were approaching areas in which they
were doubtful whether they had any rights to work, had made a substantive application under the Mines (Working Facilities and Support) Act 1923 to work such areas,
and, because that application could not be heard for some time, made an interim
application for leave to continue their operations. On the substantive application
there were a large number of objectors, but only as to method of working and compensation, who were given until 9th May 1958 to file evidence. The master ordered
service of the interim application on seven persons who it was thought might be
affected by the interim workings, and on the hearing of that application on 6th May
1958 six of these had replied that they did not object and the seventh had not
replied. Roxburgh J[2], in granting the relief sought, took the view that the seventh had
acquiesced, but added that even if that view was wrong he would have granted the
application. His judgment does not clearly indicate whether he considered that he
had jurisdiction under the Act to make the order or relied on an inherent jurisdiction.
It is possible that he had jurisdiction under the Act; but if he based the order on
inherent jurisdiction, we consider, with respect, that the decision was wrong for the
reasons already indicated.

For these reasons, we allow the appeal and quash the order of Whitford J.

Appeal allowed. Leave to appeal to the House of Lords refused.

Solicitors: *Kenneth Brown, Baker, Baker* (for the appellants); *Edwards Son & Noice* (for
the respondents).

Gordon H Scott Esq   Barrister.

Anton Piller KG v Manufacturing Processes Ltd and others

COURT OF APPEAL, CIVIL DIVISION
LORD DENNING MR, ORMROD AND SHAW LJJ
2nd, 8th DECEMBER 1975

Practice – Preservation of subject-matter of cause of action – Inspection – Interlocutory motion –
Ex parte application – Documents on premises controlled by respondents – Orders requiring
respondents to permit applicants to enter premises for purpose of inspection etc – Circumstances
in which order will be made ex parte – Nature of order – Danger that in default of order
applicants might be deprived of a remedy in the action – Danger that if notice of motion given
documents might be destroyed or taken out of the jurisdiction – Action for infringement of
copyright – Order requiring respondents to permit applicants to enter respondents' premises
for purposes of inspection and removal of documents.

The plaintiffs were foreign manufacturers who owned the copyright in the design of a
high frequency converter used to supply computers. They learnt that the defendants,
their English agents, were planning to supply rival manufacturers with information
belonging to the plaintiffs which would enable their rivals to produce a similar product. The plaintiffs wished to restrain the defendants from infringing the copyright,
using confidential information or making copies of their machines, but they were
afraid that the defendants, if notified, would take steps to destroy the documents or
would send them out of the jurisdiction so that there would be none in existence by

---

1 [1958] 2 All ER 351, [1958] 1 WLR 599
2 [1958] 2 All ER at 352, [1958] 1 WLR at 602

the time the action reached the stage of discovery of documents. The plaintiffs accordingly made an ex parte application for an order requiring the defendants to permit the   *a*
plaintiffs to enter the defendants' premises in order to inspect, remove or make copies
of documents belonging to the plaintiffs.

Held – The court had an inherent jurisdiction to make such an order ex parte, but
should exercise it only in an extreme case where there was grave danger of property
being smuggled away or of vital evidence being destroyed. The plaintiff had to show   *b*
that it was essential so that justice could be done between the parties and when
it would do no real harm to the defendant or his case. The order was not, however,
a search warrant authorising a plaintiff to enter a defendant's premises against
his will, but an order on the defendant in personam to permit the plaintiff's entry
or be in peril of proceedings for contempt of court. In the instant case, there was
sufficient justification for making the order on an undertaking by the plaintiffs   *c*
in damages (see p 782 *j* to p 783 *a* and *e* to p 784 *h*, post).
    United Company of Merchants of England, trading to the East Indies v Kynaston (1821)
3 Bli 153 applied.
    EMI Ltd v Pandit [1975] 1 All ER 418 approved.

Notes   *d*
For inspection and preservation of property, see 21 Halsbury's Laws (3rd Edn) 419,
para 879, and for cases on the subject, see 28(2) Digest (Reissue) 1125, *1234-1242*.

Cases referred to in judgments
EMI Ltd v Pandit [1975] 1 All ER 418, [1975] 1 WLR 302.
Entick v Carrington (1765) 2 Wils 275, [1558-1774] All ER Rep 41, 19 State Tr 1029,   *e*
    95 ER 807, 11 Digest (Reissue) 675, *115*.
Hennessey v Rohmann, Osborne & Co (1877) 36 LT 51, sub nom *Hennessey v Bohmann
    Osborne & Co* [1877] WN 14, 28(2) Digest (Reissue) 1125, *1238*.
Morris v Howell (1888) 22 LR Ir 77, 28(2) Digest (Reissue) 1125, *694*.
United Company of Merchants of England, trading to the East Indies v Kynaston (1821) 3
    Bli 153, 4 ER 561, HL.   *f*

Cases also cited
Anwyl v Owens (1853) 22 LJCh 995, 1 WR 205.
Bowler v Lewy (1875) 1 Char Cham Cas 14, sub nom Anon, Bitt Prac Cas 39.
Nippon Yusen Kaisha v Karageorgis [1975] 3 All ER 282, [1975] 1 WLR 1093, [1975] 2
    Lloyd's Rep 137, CA.   *g*

Interlocutory appeal
This was an appeal by the plaintiffs, Anton Piller KG, against the order of Brightman J
dated 26th November 1975 whereby he refused to grant an ex parte application by
the plaintiffs for an order that the defendants, Manufacturing Processes Ltd, Bernard
Preston Wallace and Alfred Henry Stephen Baker, and each of them, whether acting   *h*
by their servants, agents or any of them or otherwise howsoever, permit such persons
not exceeding two as might be duly authorised by the plaintiffs and members or
employees not exceeding two of the plaintiffs' solicitors, to enter forthwith the premises known as Belvedere Works, Bilton Way Lane, Industrial Estate, Hayes, Middlesex
or such parts thereof as should be occupied or used by the defendants at any hour
between 8 am and 9 pm for the purpose of (i) inspection of all documents, files   *j*
or things relating to the design, manufacture, sale or supply of copies of the plaintiffs' equipment or parts thereof; (ii) removal into the plaintiffs' solicitors' custody
of (a) all original documents relating to the manufacture, operation or maintenance
or the plaintiffs' equipment, which had been supplied by the plaintiffs to the defendants, together with copies of all such documents; (b) all documents, files or things

a relating to the design, manufacture, sale or supply of the plaintiffs' equipment or parts thereof. The facts are set out in the judgment of Lord Denning MR.

Hugh Laddie for the plaintiffs.

Cur adv vult

b 8th December.   The following judgments were read.

LORD DENNING MR.   During the last 18 months the judges of the Chancery Division have been making orders of a kind not known before. They have some resemblance to search warrants. Under these orders the plaintiff and his solicitors are authorised to enter the defendant's premises so as to inspect papers, provided the
c defendant gives permission.
Now this is the important point: the court orders the defendant to give them permission.   The judges have been making these orders on ex parte applications without prior notice to the defendant. None of the cases has been reported except *EMI Ltd v Pandit*[1] before Templeman J on 5th December 1974. But in the present case Brightman J refused to make such an order.
d On appeal to us, Mr Laddie appears for the plaintiffs. He has appeared in most of these cases, and can claim the credit—or the responsibility—for them. He represented to us that in this case it was in the interests of justice that the application should not be made public at the time it was made. So we heard it in camera. It was last Tuesday, 2nd December. After hearing his submissions, we made the order. We now come to give our reasons in public. But at the outset I must state the facts, for it is obvious that
e such an order can only be justified in the most exceptional circumstances.
The plaintiffs are German manufacturers of high repute. They make electric motors and generators. They play an important part in the big new computer industry. They supply equipment for it. They have recently designed a frequency converter specially for supplying the computers of International Business Machines.
Since 1972 the plaintiffs have had, as their agents in the United Kingdom, a company
f here called Manufacturing Processes Ltd, which is run by Mr A H S Baker and Mr B P Wallace. These agents are dealers who get machines from the plaintiffs in Germany and sell them to customers in England. The plaintiffs supply the English company with much confidential information about the machines, including a manual showing how they work, and drawings which are the subject of copyright.
Very recently the plaintiffs have found out—so they say—that these English agents
g have been in secret communication with other German companies called Ferrostaal and Lechmotoren. The object of these communications is that the English company should supply these other German companies with drawings and materials and other confidential information so that they can manufacture power units like the plaintiffs. The plaintiffs got to know of these communications through two 'defectors', if I may call them so. One was the commercial manager of the English company,
h Mr Brian Firth; the other was the sales manager, Mr William Raymond Knight. These two were so upset by what was going on in the English company that on their own initiative, without any approach by the plaintiffs whatever, on 2nd October 1975 one or both flew to Germany. They told the plaintiffs what they knew about the arrangements with Ferrostaal and Lechmotoren. They disclosed also that the English company were negotiating with Canadian and United States firms. In making these
j disclosures, both Mr Firth and Mr Knight were putting themselves in a perilous position, but the plaintiffs assured them that they would safeguard their future employment.
The disclosures—coming from defectors—might have been considered untrustworthy. But they were supported by documents which emanated from both Ferrostaal

---

1 [1975] 1 All ER 418, [1975] 1 WLR 302

and Lechmotoren. They showed that the English company were in regular communication with those German companies. They were sending them drawings and arranging for inspection of the plaintiffs' machine, for the express purpose that the Lechmotoren company might manufacture a prototype machine copied from the plaintiffs. One of the most telling communications was a telex from Lechmotoren to Mr Wallace saying:

> 'It is the opinion of Mr S (of Lechmotoren) that the best way to find a final solution for the . . . prototype is to send Mr Beck to you as soon as the . . . latest design of [the plaintiffs] has arrived in your factory. In this case it is guaranteed that the Lech prototype will have exactly the same features as the [the plaintiffs'] type. We hope you will agree to this proposal and we ask you to let us have your telex in order to arrange Mr Beck's visit accordingly.'

On getting this information, the plaintiffs were extremely worried. They were about to produce a fine new frequency converter called 'the silent block'. They feared that the English company, in co-operation with the German manufacturers, would make a copy of their 'silent block' and ruin their market. They determined to apply to the court for an injunction to restrain the English company from infringing their copyright or using confidential information or making copies of their machines. But they were fearful that if the English company were given notice of this application, they would take steps to destroy the documents or send them to Germany or elsewhere, so that there would be none in existence by the time that discovery was had in the action.

So, on Wednesday, 26th November 1975 the plaintiffs' solicitor prepared a draft writ of summons and, with an affidavit, they went before Brightman J and asked, first, for an interim injunction to restrain infringement etc, and, secondly, for an order that they might be permitted to enter the premises of the English company so as to inspect the documents of the plaintiffs and remove them, or copies of them. Brightman J granted an interim injunction, but refused to order inspection or removal of documents. He said:

> 'There is strong prima facie evidence that the defendant company is now engaged in seeking to copy the plaintiffs' components for its own financial profit to the great detriment of the plaintiffs and in breach of the plaintiffs' rights.'

He realised that the defendants might suppress evidence or misuse documentary material, but he thought that that was a risk which must be accepted in civil matters save in extreme cases. 'Otherwise', he said—

> 'it seems to me that an order on the lines sought might become on instrument of oppression, particularly in a case where a plaintiff of big standing and deep pocket is ranged against a small man who is alleged on the evidence of one side only to have infringed the plaintiff's rights.'

Let me say at once that no court in this land has any power to issue a search warrant to enter a man's house so as to see if there are papers or documents there which are of an incriminating nature, whether libels or infringements of copyright or anything else of the kind. No constable or bailiff can knock at the door and demand entry so as to inspect papers or documents. The householder can shut the door in his face and say, 'Get out'. That was established in the leading case of *Entick v Carrington*[1]. None of us would wish to whittle down that principle in the slightest. But the order sought in this case is not a search warrant. It does not authorise the plaintiffs' solicitors or anyone else to enter the defendants' premises against their will. It does not authorise the breaking down of any doors, nor the slipping in by a back door, nor getting in by an open door or window. It only authorises entry and inspection by the permission of the

1   (1765) 2 Wils 275, [1558-1774] All ER Rep 41

defendants. The plaintiffs must get the defendants' permission. But it does do this:
a it brings pressure on the defendants to give permission. It does more. It actually orders them to give permission—with, I suppose, the result that if they do not give permission, they are guilty of contempt of court.

This may seem to be a search warrant in disguise. But it was fully considered in the House of Lords 150 years ago in *East India Co v Kynaston* and held to be legitimate. Lord Redesdale said[1]:

b
> 'The arguments urged for the Appellants at the Bar are founded upon the supposition, that the Court has directed a forcible inspection. This is an erroneous view of the case. The order is to permit; and if the East India Company should refuse to permit inspection, they will be guilty of a contempt of the Court . . . It is an order operating on the person requiring the defendants to permit inspection, not giving authority of force, or to break open the doors of their ware-
c
> house.'

That case was not, however, concerned with papers or things. It was only as to the value of a warehouse; and that could not be obtained without an inspection. But the distinction drawn by Lord Redesdale affords ground for thinking that there is jurisdiction to make an order that the defendants 'do permit' when it is neccessary
d in the interests of justice.

Accepting such to be the case, the question is in what circumstances ought such on order be made. If the defendant is given notice beforehand and is able to argue the pros and cons, it is warranted by that case in the House of Lords and by RSC Ord 29, r 2(1) and (5). But it is a far stronger thing to make such an order ex parte without giving him notice. This is not covered by the rules of court and must be based on the
e inherent jurisdiction of the court. There are one or two old precedents which give some colour for it, *Hennessey v Bohmann Osborne & Co*[2], and *Morris v Howell*[3], an Irish case. But they do not go very far. So it falls to us to consider it on principle. It seems to me that such an order can be made by a judge ex parte, but it should only be made where it is essential that the plaintiff should have inspection so that justice can be done between the parties; and when, if the defendant were forewarned, there
f is a grave danger that vital evidence will be destroyed, that papers will be burnt or lost or hidden, or taken beyond the jurisdiction, and so the ends of justice be defeated; and when the inspection would do no real harm to the defendant or his case.

Nevertheless, in the enforcement of this order, the plaintiffs must act with due circumspection. On the service of it, the plaintiffs should be attended by their solicitor, who is an officer of the court. They should give the defendants an opportunity of
g considering it and of consulting their own solicitor. If the defendants wish to apply to discharge the order as having been improperly obtained, they must be allowed to do so. If the defendants refused permission to enter or to inspect, the plaintiffs must not force their way in. They must accept that refusal, and bring it to the notice of the court afterwards, if need be on application to commit.

One might think that with all these safeguards against abuse, it would be of little
h use to make such an order. But it can be effective in this way: it serves to tell the defendant that, on the evidence put before it, the court is of opinion that he ought to permit inspection—nay, it orders him to permit—and that he refuses at his peril. It puts him in peril not only of proceedings for contempt, but also of adverse inferences being drawn against him; so much so that his own solicitor may often advise him to comply. We are told that in two at least of the cases such an order has been effective. We are
j prepared, therefore, to sanction its continuance, but only in an extreme case where there is grave danger of property being smuggled away or of vital evidence being destroyed.

---

1   (1821) 3 Bli 153 at 163
2   [1877] WN 14
3   (1888) 22 LR Ir 77

On the evidence in this case, we decided on 2nd December that there was sufficient justification to make an order. We did it on the precedent framed by Templeman J[1]. It contains an undertaking in damages which is to be supported (as the plaintiffs are overseas) by a bond for £10,000. It gives an interim injunction to restrain the infringement of copyright and breach of confidential information etc. It orders that the defendants do permit one or two of the plaintiffs and one or two of their solicitors to enter the defendants' premises for the purpose of inspecting documents, files or things, and removing those which belong to the plaintiffs. This was, of course, only an interim order pending the return of the summons. It is to be heard, we believe, tomorrow by the judge.

ORMROD LJ. I agree with all that Lord Denning MR has said. The proposed order is at the extremity of this court's powers. Such orders, therefore, will rarely be made, and only when there is no alternative way of ensuring that justice is done to the plaintiff.

There are three essential pre-conditions for the making of such an order, in my judgment. First, there must be an extremely strong prima facie case. Secondly, the damage, potential or actual, must be very serious for the plaintiff. Thirdly, there must be clear evidence that the defendants have in their possession incriminating documents or things, and that there is a real possibility that they may destroy such material before any application inter partes can be made.

The form of the order makes it plain that the court is not ordering or granting anything equivalent to a search warrant. The order is an order on the defendant in personam to permit inspection. It is therefore open to him to refuse to comply with such an order, but at his peril either of further proceedings for contempt of court—in which case, of course, the court will have the widest discretion as to how to deal with it, and if it turns out that the order was made improperly in the first place, the contempt will be dealt with accordingly—but more important, of course, the refusal to comply may be the most damning evidence against the defendant at the subsequent trial. Great responsibility clearly rests on the solicitors for the plaintiff to ensure that the carrying out of such an order is meticulously carefully done with the fullest respect for the defendant's rights, as Lord Denning MR has said, of applying to the court, should he feel it necessary to do so, before permitting the inspection.

In the circumstances of the present case, all those conditions to my mind are satisfied, and this order is essential in the interests of justice. I agree, therefore, that the appeal should be allowed.

SHAW LJ. I agree with both judgments. The overriding consideration in the exercise of this salutary jurisdiction is that it is to be resorted to only in circumstances where the normal processes of the law would be rendered nugatory if some immediate and effective measure was not available. And, when such an order is made, the party who has procured the court to make it must act with prudence and caution in pursuance of it.

Appeal allowed.

Solicitors: *Collyer-Bristow & Co* (for the plaintiffs).

Gavin Gore-Andrews Esq　Barrister.

1　See *EMI Ltd v Pandit* [1975] 1 All ER 418 at 424, [1975] 1 WLR 302 at 308

a

Campbell v Edwards

COURT OF APPEAL, CIVIL DIVISION
LORD DENNING MR AND GEOFFREY LANE LJ
27th NOVEMBER 1975

b   *Valuer – Valuation – Mistake – Validity – Contractual purchase price – Valuation to determine price under contract – Determination giving no reasons for figure determined – Evidence that figure determined by valuer excessive – No fraud or collusion – Whether open to purchaser to obtain order setting aside valuer's determination on ground of mistake.*

The landlord let a flat under a lease which provided that if the tenant desired to assign
c the lease she must first offer to surrender it to the landlord at a price to be fixed by
a chartered surveyor, the surveyor to be agreed on by the landlord and the tenant.
The lease also provided that in assessing the surrender price the surveyor should
assume certain matters. The tenant wished to assign the lease and by letter dated 17th
January 1974 offered to surrender it to the landlord 'at a price to be fixed in the manner
provided by the lease'. The landlord accepted the offer to surrender and he and the
d tenant agreed to instruct an eminent firm of chartered surveyors ('the surveyors')
to assess the proper price for the surrender. The parties' solicitors jointly signed and
sent a letter to the surveyors instructing them to assess the price. The surveyors
inspected the flat and by a letter dated 21st March 1974, addressed to the parties'
solicitors, stated that they had read the lease and had taken into account in assessing
the price the matters set out in the lease, and that after careful consideration they
e were of the opinion that the proper price for the landlord to pay to the tenant for the
surrender of the lease, as at 25th March 1974, was £10,000. The surveyors gave
no reason for their valuation or any calculations. Following that assessment the tenant
surrendered the lease and went out of possession of the flat. The landlord then got
two other firms of chartered surveyors to assess the surrender value of the lease.
Those firms assessed the surrender value as at 25th March 1974, respectively, at
f £3,500 and £1,250. The landlord brought an action against the tenant claiming a
declaration that he was not bound by the surveyors' valuation and an order that the
tenant should concur with him in obtaining a new valuation. The statement of claim
alleged that the surveyors' valuation was incorrect in that the true surrender value
of the lease as at 25th March 1974 was under £4,000 and that the surveyors must be
presumed to have assessed the value in an incorrect manner so as to vitiate their
g valuation. Both the master and the judge held that the statement of claim disclosed
no reasonable cause of action and ordered that it be struck out. The landlord appealed.

Held – Where two parties had agreed that the price of property was to be fixed by a
valuer on whom they should agree and the valuer gave his valuation honestly and in
good faith in a non-speaking report, i e one that did not give reasons or calculations,
h the valuation could not be set aside by either party on the ground that the valuer had
made a mistake, for, in the absence of fraud or collusion, the valuation was binding
on the parties by contract. Accordingly, as the surveyors' valuation was not a speaking
valuation and had been given honestly, and (per Geoffrey Lane LJ) there was nothing
to suggest that the surveyors had failed to take into consideration all the matters
which they should have taken into consideration, the landlord was bound by the
j valuation and could not allege that it was incorrect. Accordingly the appeal would be
dismissed (see p 788 *d e* and *j* and p 789 *a* to *e*, post).

Dictum of Lord Denning MR in *Arenson v Arenson* [1973] 2 All ER at 241 applied.
Dean v Prince [1954] 1 All ER 749 doubted.
Per Lord Denning MR. The position of a valuer differs from that of an arbitrator.
If a valuer is negligent in making a valuation he may be sued by the party, vendor or

purchaser, who has been injured by his wrong valuation. But an arbitrator cannot be
sued by either party to the dispute even if he has been negligent. The only remedy *a*
is to set aside the award if there are grounds for doing so (see p 788 *g* and *h*, post);
Arenson Casson Beckman Rutley & Co [1975] 3 All ER 901 applied.

Notes

For the finality of valuations to fix a contractual purchase price, see 39 Halsbury's
Laws (3rd Edn) 6, para 7, and for cases on the subject, see 47 Digest (Repl) 560-562, *5-12*. *b*
For the distinction between valuations and arbitrations, see 39 Halsbury's Laws
(3rd Edn) 4-6, paras 5-7.

Cases referred to in judgments

Arenson v Casson Beckman Rutley & Co [1975] 3 All ER 901, [1975] 3 WLR 815, HL;
　rvsg sub nom *Arenson v Arenson* [1973] 2 All ER 235, [1973] 1 Ch 346, CA. *c*
Dean v Prince [1954] 1 All ER 749, [1954] Ch 409, [1954] 2 WLR 538, CA, 47 Digest
　(Repl) 561, *12*.
Sutcliffe v Thackrah [1974] 1 All ER 859, [1974] AC 727, [1974] 2 WLR 295, [1974] 1
　Lloyd's Rep 319, HL; *rvsg* [1973] 2 All ER 1047, [1973] 1 WLR 888, CA.

Cases also cited

Collier v Mason (1858) 25 Beav 200. *d*
Emery v Wase (1803) 8 Ves 505.
Jones (M) v Jones (R R) [1971] 2 All ER 676, [1971] 1 WLR 840.
Parken v Whitby (1823) Turn & R 366.
Weekes v Gallard (1869) 21 LT 655.
Wright (Frank H) (Constructions) Ltd v Frodoor Ltd [1967] 1 All ER 433, [1967] 1 WLR 506.
e

Interlocutory appeal

This was an appeal by the plaintiff, John Colin Campbell ('the landlord'), with leave
of May J, against the order of May J dated 26th March 1975 dismissing the landlord's
appeal against the order of Master Warren dated 19th November 1974 whereby it
was ordered that the landlord's statement of claim should be struck out and his
action be dismissed and that judgment be entered for the defendant, Irene Donalda *f*
Edwards ('the tenant'), on her counterclaim for £10,000 and interest. The facts are set
out in the judgment of Lord Denning MR.

Andrew Bateson QC and *S Silber* for the landlord.
J M Chadwick for the tenant.
g

LORD DENNING MR. We are concerned here with a house in Trebeck Street
in the very centre of Mayfair. It was built about 200 years ago as a private house.
But it is now converted to other uses. On the ground floor there is a restaurant. On
the first floor there are offices. On the second floor there is a residential flat. It has
its own entrance from the street; and has three rooms, kitchen and bathroom.
On 28th June 1973 the landlord let this second floor flat to the tenant for seven years *h*
and two months free of rent. The tenant was liable to do repairs and there was a
prohibition against underletting.
The lease contained a special provision that if the tenant desired to assign the
premises she had first to offer to surrender them to the landlord, and the price was to
be fixed by a surveyor to be agreed on by the parties. It is cl 3(11)(b), which says *j*
in the material part:

'... If the Tenant desires to assign the whole of the Premises as aforesaid she
shall first by notice in writing to the Landlord offer to surrender this lease ... at a
price fixed by a chartered surveyor to be agreed by the Landlord and the Tenant
or failing agreement to be nominated by the President for the time being of

a the Royal Institution of Chartered Surveyors and the Landlord may within twenty-one days of the service of such notice upon him accept such offer the acceptance to be in writing.'

Six months after the lease was made the tenant desired to assign the lease. Under that clause she had to offer to surrender it to the landlord. By a letter dated 17th January 1974 her solicitors offered to surrender it 'at a price to be fixed in the manner

b provided by the Lease'. By a letter of 24th January the landlord accepted the offer. Some names of surveyors were suggested but these were not agreed. Eventually however both sides did agree on a very eminent firm of surveyors, Chestertons, a firm who were recognised by both to be quite unimpeachable.

On 6th March the solicitors for each side signed jointly and sent a letter to Messrs Chesterton. It referred to the lease and said:

c 'It has been agreed between the parties to instruct yourselves to assess the proper price for the surrender in accordance with the provisions of the Lease.'

Chestertons duly inspected the premises. On 21st March they wrote this important letter, assessing the price at £10,000:

d 'We confirm with thanks, receipt of your letter of the 6th March 1974 giving your two firms' instructions to us to inspect the above premises in order to assess the proper price to be paid by the Landlord to the tenant for the surrender of the residue of the term of the lease dated 27th June 1973 . . . We have read the lease carefully and have taken into account in assessing the price to be paid, those matters set out in clause 3(11)(c). After carefully considering the matter, we are of the opinion that the proper price for the Landlord to pay to the tenant for

e the surrender of the lease as at the 25th March 1974, is the sum of £10,000 (ten thousand pounds).'

Following that assessment, the tenant went out of possession and the landlord went into possession of the flat. There was some dispute about fixtures and fittings but undoubtedly there was a surrender by operation of law. The landlord then

f turned round and disputed the assessment of the price. He got new valuations for the value of the remainder of the lease. He got them from two other surveyors. Mann Winkworth made a valuation dated 18th April 1974 putting the value as £3,500 Hinton & Co on the 18th June 1974 put it at £1,250. I must say that, even to a layman that seems a remarkably low assessment, especially when you remember that there were over six years to run of this lease and that no rent was payable under it.

g Having got those two new valuations the landlord challenged Chestertons' valuation of £10,000. On 17th June 1974 he issued a writ claiming that he was not bound by it. In the statement of claim he said:

'The valuation was incorrect in that the true surrender value of the lease at the specified date was under £4,000. In the circumstances, Messrs. Chesterton must be presumed to have assessed the price in an incorrect manner and their valuation

h is therefore vitiated.'

He claimed '(a) a declaration that he is not bound by the valuation' and '(b) an order that the [tenant] concurs with the [landlord] in obtaining a new valuation . . .'

The tenant, by her solicitors, put in a defence and counterclaim, relying on Chestertons' price, and counterclaiming £10,000. She sought judgment for the £10,000,

j and she applied to strike out the statement of claim of the landlord as disclosing no cause of action. The summons came before the master and before the judge. Both held that the claim by the landlord disclosed no reasonable cause of action. They struck it out and gave the tenant judgment for £10,000. The landlord appeals to this court.

The appeal was stood over pending the decision of the House of Lords in *Arenson v*

Casson Beckman Rutley & Co[1]. It was decided only two weeks ago. The law on this subject has been transformed by two cases in the House of Lords, *Sutcliffe v Thackrah*[2]   **a** about architects, and *Arenson v Casson Beckman Rutley & Co*[1] about vaiuers. Previously, for over 100 years, it was thought that when vendor and purchaser agreed that the price was to be fixed by a valuer, then the valuer was in the position of a quasi-arbitrator and could not be sued for negligence. It is now clear that he owes a duty to both parties to act with reasonable care and skill in making his valuation. If he makes a mistake owing to want of care and skill he may be liable in damages. If he negli-   **b** gently gives a figure which is too high, he may be sued by the purchaser. If it is too low, he may be sued by the vendor. If he wants to avoid such a responsibility he must put in a special clause exempting him when he accepts the appointment. Unless he stipulates for exemption, he is liable for negligence.

In former times (when it was thought that the valuer was not liable for negligence) the courts used to look for some way of upsetting a valuation which was shown to be   **c** wholly erroneous. They used to say that it could be upset, not only for fraud or collusion, but also on the ground of mistake. See for instance what I said in *Dean v Prince*[3]. But those cases have to be reconsidered now. I did reconsider them in the *Arenson* case[4]. I stand by what I there said. It is simply the law of contract. If two persons agree that the price of property should be fixed by a valuer on whom they agree, and he gives that valuation honestly and in good faith, they are bound by it. Even if he has   **d** made a mistake they are still bound by it. The reason is because they have agreed to be bound by it. If there were fraud or collusion, of course, it would be different. Fraud or collusion unravels everything.

It may be that, if a valuer gives a speaking valuation—if he gives his reasons or his calculations—and you can show on the face of them that they are wrong, it might be upset. But this not such a case. Messrs Chesterton simply gave the figure. Having   **e** given it honestly, it is binding on the parties. It is no good for either party to say that it is incorrect. But even if the valuation could be upset for mistake, there is no room for it in this case. The premises have been surrendered to the landlord. He has entered into occupation of them. Months have passed. There cannot be restitutio in integrum.

I may add that counsel for the tenant put forward an additional argument. He said: **f** 'If this valuation is set aside, what is to take its place?' The answer is, 'nothing'. The only surveyors on whom the parties have agreed are Messrs Chesterton. The parties are unlikely to agree on any other surveyors. And Messrs Chesterton cannot reasonably be asked to make another valuation. So there would be nothing to take the place of this valuation.

In my opinion therefore the landlord is bound by this valuation of £10,000. I would   **g** just like to add this. The position of a valuer is very different from an arbitrator. If a valuer is negligent in making a valuation, he may be sued by the party—vendor or purchaser—who is injured by his wrong valuation. But an arbitrator is different. In my opinion he cannot be sued by either party to the dispute, even if he is negligent. The only remedy of the party is to set aside the award; and then only if it comes within the accepted grounds for setting it aside. If an arbitrator is guilty of misconduct,   **h** his award can be set aside. If he has gone wrong on a point of law, which appears on the face of it, it can be corrected by the court. But the arbitrator himself is not liable to be sued. I say this because I should be sorry if any doubt should be felt about it.

This case is just a postcript to *Arenson v Casson Beckman Rutley & Co*[1]. The valuation is binding on the parties. The master and the judge were right and we dismiss the appeal.   **j**

1   [1975] 3 All ER 901, [1975] 3 WLR 815
2   [1974] 1 All ER 859, [1974] AC 727
3   [1954] 1 All ER 749 at 758, 759, [1954] Ch 409 at 427
4   [1973] 2 All ER 235, [1973] 1 Ch 346

GEOFFREY LANE LJ. I agree. The parties here had agreed on a valuer. They had agreed as to the terms on which the valuer was to value the property and on which he was to be instructed. The valuation took place, it was acted on, and the tenant surrendered the lease. It is a common law situation in which there is no room for an equitable remedy. The most up-to-date and accurate statement of the law in the circumstances is in a passage of Lord Denning MR's judgment in *Arenson v Arenson*[1] in this court which states as follows:

'At common law—as distinct from equity—the parties are undoubtedly bound by the figure fixed by the valuer. Just as the parties to a building contract are bound by the architect's certificate, so the parties are bound by the valuer's valuation. Even if he makes a mistake in his calculations, or makes the valuation on what one or other considers to be a wrong basis, still they are bound by their agreement to accept it.'

In this case counsel for the landlord has argued that there is sufficient discrepancy between the valuer's report and the subsequent valuations obtained by his client to indicate that the valuers, Chestertons, must have acted on a wrong principle. He says that, despite the fact that this is not a speaking report, that wide discrepancy is sufficient to cast doubt on the valuation. I disagree. There is nothing to suggest that the valuer here did not take into consideration all the matters which he should have taken into consideration, and where the only basis of criticism is that another valuer has subsequently produced a valuation a third of the original one it does not afford, in my view, any ground for saying that Chestertons' valuation must have been or may have been wrong.

The other matter which perhaps I should mention is this. Counsel for the landlord asked for leave to amend the statement of claim in order to join the valuer as a defendant as well as the tenant, alleging that the valuer had acted negligently in his work. This would have had the effect, desirable from the landlord's point of view, of permitting him to obtain discovery, no doubt, of the valuer's (Chestertons') papers relating to their inspection of the premises, and so on, and then to use that information by way of attack against the tenant so that the valuation could be set aside vis-à-vis the tenant.

It seems to me that it is undesirable that valuers undertaking this type of duty should be subject to this additional peril. It is not only technically undesirable; it produces, as I see it, an anomalous situation, for this reason. If the discovery shows that there was no negligence on the part of the valuer, then the action against the valuer will of course fail. If on the other hand the discovery shows that there was negligence on the part of the valuer, then that means it would be possible, on the argument of counsel for the landlord, to set aside the valuation vis-à-vis the tenant, in which case no damage would have been suffered by the landlord, and likewise the valuers would not be liable in negligence.

When that sort of anomalous situation is produced, it cannot be right that this sort of amendment should be allowed. For the reasons I have already indicated and those adumbrated by Lord Denning MR I agree that there is no fault in the reasoning or conclusion of the learned judge and that this appeal accordingly should be dismissed.

Appeal dismissed; stay of execution refused.

Solicitors: *Roney Vincent & Co* (for the landlord); *Jaques & Co* (for the tenant).

Wendy Shockett   Barrister.

---

1   [1973] 2 All ER 235 at 241, [1973] 1 Ch 346 at 363

Ross v Pearson a

FAMILY DIVISION
SIR GEORGE BAKER P AND LATEY J
3rd NOVEMBER 1975

Magistrates – Husband and wife – Maintenance – Order – Arrears – Remission – Power to b
remit arrears – Discretion – Exercise of discretion – Practice – Time limit – Retrospective time
limit of one year – Usual practice to remit earlier years – Magistrates' Courts Act 1952, s 76.

In 1964 justices made an order under the Matrimonal Proceedings (Magistrates'
Courts) Act 1960 that the husband pay £5 a week to the wife and £1 a week for each
of the four children of the family. Arrears were allowed to accrue. The wife was c
granted a decree of divorce and remarried in 1969. In September 1969 the justices
discharged the order relating to the wife, remitted the arrears which had accumulated
since her remarriage and, since the eldest child had by then reached 16 years of age,
discharged the order in respect of him. The order in respect of the other three children
remained unaltered, and 50p per week arrears was added, making a total of £3·50. In
1970 an attachment of earnings order was made to enforce payment of the mainten- d
ance The youngest child reached 16 years of age in September 1973. By July 1974 the
arrears stood at £770·54 and the wife complained to the justices. They refused the
husband's application to remit the arrears under s 76ᵃ of the Magistrates' Courts Act
1952 and ordered payment by instalments of £2 per week. The husband appealed.

Held – In exercising their discretion under s 76 of the 1952 Act, justices should usually e
follow the practice of the Family Division and enforce only arrears which had accrued
within the year before the date of complaint. Since the justices, when hearing the
wife's complaint, had not had regard to that practice and since between 1970 and July
1974 the wife had taken no steps to enforce payment of the arrears, it could not be
said that the justices had exercised their discretion properly. Accordingly the appeal
would be allowed and the husband ordered to pay £50 of the arrears, the balance f
being remitted (see p 794 f to p 795 d, post).
Pilcher v Pilcher (No 2) [1956] 1 All ER 463 applied.

Notes
For enforcement of orders and remission of arrears, see 13 Halsbury's Laws (4th Edn)
paras 1213, 1214, 1337, 1338, and for cases on the subject, see 27(2) Digest (Reissue) g
923, 924, 7416-7439.
For the Magistrates' Courts Act 1952, s 76, see 21 Halsbury's Statutes (3rd Edn) 249.

Cases referred to in judgments
Freeman-Thomas v Freeman-Thomas [1963] 1 All ER 17, [1963] P 157, [1963] 2 WLR 107,
27(2) Digest (Reissue) 917, 7337. h
Luscombe v Luscombe [1962] 1 All ER 668, [1962] 1 WLR 313, CA, 27(2) Digest (Reissue)
933, 7527.
Pilcher v Pilcher (No 2) [1956] 1 All ER 463, [1956] 1 WLR 298, DC, 27(2) Digest (Reissue)
1003, 8055.

Case also cited j
Grimshaw v Dunbar [1953] 1 All ER 350, [1953] 1 QB 408, CA.

---

a Section 76 provides: 'On the hearing of a complaint for the enforcement, revocation, revival,
variation or discharge of an affiliation order or an order enforceable as an affiliation order,
the court may remit the whole or any part of the sum due under the order.'

Case stated

a On 24th July 1974 a complaint was preferred in accordance with s 74 of the Magistrates' Courts Act 1952, as amended, against John Gibson Ross, the husband, in respect of arrears of £770·54 due under a maintenance order. The husband sought to have all the arrears remitted in accordance with s 76 of the 1952 Act.

The justices found the following facts. An order was made under the authority of the Matrimonial Proceedings (Magistrates' Courts) Act 1960 by the West

b Hartlepool justices on 12th August 1964. The husband was ordered to pay to the wife, Olga Pearson, through the office of the clerk to the justices, the total weekly sum of £9, namely £5 in respect of the wife and £1 in respect of each of the four children while under the age of 16 years. Complaint was made in respect of arrears under the order, amounting to £839, on 3rd September 1969 to the Hartlepool magistrates' court. The wife had obtained a decree of divorce and remarried on 29th April 1969 and

c the court varied the order in respect of the wife and also discharged the arrears under the order in respect of her which had accrued since the date of remarriage. The court also ordered that the balance of the arrears be paid at the rate of 10s per week and reduced the total order to £3 per week. On 18th May 1970 the Fylde magistrates' court made an attachment of earnings order with a normal deduction rate of £3 per week. The youngest child attained the age of 16 years on 11th September 1973 thus

d terminating the obligation to make weekly payments and leaving only arrears. The arrears on that date were £274·54 and it was impossible to record what amounts were owed respectively for the wife and for the children of the family. The wife went to South Africa in July 1972 for a three month holiday. The clerk to the justices was not informed. Due to the prolonged illness of the wife's new husband, who became ill in October 1972, she remained in South Africa until returning to England in July 1973.

e The youngest child went to join the wife in South Africa in November 1972. Maintenance payments paid by the husband were received by the wife's mother and paid into the joint bank account in England of the wife and her mother.

On 6th March 1973 the clerk to the justices wrote to the husband informing him that the wife was in South Africa but that no settled address was available, and that maintenance payments were being paid into a joint bank account in England of the

f wife and her mother. The husband was advised to seek legal advice. The husband was unemployed for about ten months in 1966 after well-paid employment came to an end and he had the following periods of unemployment in 1972 and 1973: from 21st August to 23rd September 1972; from 20th October to 7th November 1972; from 15th November 1972 to 13th January 1973 and from 2nd April to 2nd June 1973. The justices were unable on the evidence before them to reach any finding as to unemployment or

g periods of sickness which the husband may have suffered between 1967 and 1971. The husband had remarried and there were two children of that marriage. After absence of work through illness he was in regular employment. His weekly net wage varied between £18 and £25. His second wife was an unstable diabetic and unable to work.

It was contended by the wife that the husband had always been in arrears under the

h order and had availed himself of any excuse not to pay; that although she had taken the youngest child out of the country without the husband's permission. it had to be kept in mind that he had not seen any of the children for 12 years and the maintenance payment for the child was only £1 per week; that there was nothing wrong with having the maintenance paid into the joint bank account with her mother; that the money was properly used for the benefit of the child; that the greater part of the

j arrears were in respect of herself and the other children and she had been deprived of that income when bringing them up; that the husband should not be allowed to discard his responsibilities and payment of the arrears should be made in full.

It was contended by the husband that the wife should not have taken the youngest child out of the country without his permission, thus denying him access, and by doing so she has forfeited her right to maintenance; that the payment of maintenance into a

joint bank account by the wife's mother was open to suspicion as there was no evidence
that the money was being used for the proper purpose; that the periods of unemploy-   *a*
ment and sickness were such that he had been unable to fulfil his obligations to the
full and the serious accumulation of arrears had occurred for that reason; and that
having regard to the circumstances it would be a proper course if the justices remitted
all or a substantial part of the arrears.

The justices gave their opinion as follows:
                                                                                        b

'. . . the [husband] was now well able to pay the arrears in full as he was in good
employment. The [wife] had no doubt gone short of many things because of the
[husband's] failure to pay in the past. She had not slept on her rights and suddenly
decided to claim arrears. On the contrary her whole conduct over the years had
been such that the [husband] must have been, at all times, fully aware that she
would expect him to pay every penny of the arrears. We considered this attitude   *c*
to be understandable as a substantial part of the arrears must have accrued during
the [husband's] earlier days of well paid employment. Having regard to the fact
that the wife had doubtless often had to go on short commons prior to her
remarriage we felt unable to remit the whole of the arrears and having regard
to the fact that he had quite clearly not paid when he could we felt unable, for
the present at least, to remit part. We therefore ordered the [husband] to pay   *d*
the arrears at £2·00 per week. We did not see fit to enforce that order by way of
Attachment of Earnings Order or any suspended committal to prison in default
of payment.'

The husband appealed. The question for the opinion of the High Court was whether
the refusal of the court to remit all or any substantial part of the £770·54 arrears owed   *e*
by the husband was a conclusion which any reasonable bench of justices could reach on
a proper consideration of the facts as found and whether the refusal constituted a
proper exercise of judicial discretion.

J J Hodgson for the husband.
The wife did not appear and was not represented.   *f*

SIR GEORGE BAKER P. This is an appeal by way of case stated from what was
in effect the refusal of the Hartlepool justices, on 13th August 1974, to remit all or any
of the sum of £770·54 arrears owed by the husband on a maintenance order.

The relevant background facts are that on 12th August 1964 the West Hartlepool   *g*
justices made an order under the Matrimonial Proceedings (Magistrates' Court) Act
1960 that the husband should pay through the office of the clerk to the justices the
total weekly sum of £9, being £5 for his wife and £1 in respect of each of the four
children of the marriage under the age of 16 years.

The matter again came before the court on 3rd September 1969 (that is over five
years later) when the arrears amounted to £839. By that time the wife had obtained a   *h*
divorce and had remarried on 29th April 1969. Presumably nothing had been done in
the divorce about the children's order; so the court varied the 1964 order by discharging the payment in respect of the wife, discharging arrears under the order in
respect of the wife which had accrued since her remarriage on 29th April, and ordered
that the balance of the arrears should be paid at 10s a week. One of the boys had
reached the age of 16 so the court reduced the total order to £3 a week, that is £1 in   *j*
respect of each of the relevant children, and of course to that was added the 10s a week
arrears.

Then on 18th May 1970 the Fylde justices made an attachment of earnings order,
with a normal deduction rate of £3 a week. Whether any application was then made
in respect of the arrears, or whether it was only in respect of the £3 a week order, we

a do not know. The matter has not been argued, but it seems to me, without going into detail, that by reason of the definition of 'maintenance order' in s 2(a) of the Attachment of Earnings Act 1971 the arrears could have been the subject of an attachment of earnings order, if that had been requested, and if the man's earnings had justified the making of an order of £3·50 instead of £3.

The next action that was taken, so far as we know, was a complaint on 24th June 1974 by Mr Shaw, the clerk to the justices, on behalf of the wife, who is now Mrs *b* Pearson, in respect of the arrears which then amounted to £770·54, that is to say the arrears in respect of the children had actually increased since September 1969, whereas they should have decreased by 10s a week. Obviously, some sum was in arrears in respect of the existing order, as well as the pre-existing arrears.

The mathematics of the matter have been analysed by counsel for the husband and, if I may say so, very helpfully. He concludes that £16 must be the amount which has *c* accumulated by reason of non-payment of the orders, as distinct from non-payment of arrears. By September 1973 the children had all attained the age of 16 and, therefore, from that date, only the question of arrears remained. The calculations are based on that fact.

In July 1972 the wife went to South Africa. She took the younger boy with her. Neither of these matters seem to me to have any bearing on this particular case, nor is *d* it material that the maintenance payments were made into a joint bank account in England held in the name of the wife and her mother. The husband seems to have had periods of unemployment between 1972 and 1973 amounting to six months out of ten. He is now remarried, and we are told that he has a gross wage of between £23 and £30 a week. His new wife is unable to work because of ill health.

The wife, the respondent to this appeal, does not appear and is not represented. *e* Consequently we have not had the advantage of argument in respect of what could be difficult points. The essence of the case put by the husband, the appellant, is that it was the practice in the Probate Divorce and Admiralty Division, carried through to the Family Division, not to enforce arrears for more than a year backwards. In *Pilcher v Pilcher (No 2)*[1] Lord Merriman said:

f   'Moreover, as a matter of practice but not of law, courts which are asked to enforce orders of this sort, usually consider that there should be a time limit retrospectively. The custom in this Division is not to enforce arrears for more than a year backwards.'

Note the word 'usually'. In *Freeman-Thomas v Freeman-Thomas*[2] Scarman J referred to *Pilcher v Pilcher (No 2)*[3] in these words:
g
'It is pertinent to observe that, had these fees [the school fees] been the subject of a maintenance order made by this court, it is extremely unlikely that in 1962, some three years after the last of them and eight years since the first of them, the court would have tolerated enforcement of the order: see *Pilcher v. Pilcher (No. 2)*[3].'

h Finally, in *Luscombe v Luscombe*[4], Ormerod LJ referred, with approval, to *Pilcher v Pilcher (No 2)*[3] in these terms:

'It is true that LORD MERRIMAN was there referring to the form of enforcement which may result in a committal to prison, and that in a later paragraph he gave as one of the reasons, if not the reason, for the existence of this rule that it was pointless to make an order committing a man to prison for so large a sum that the *j* man would go to prison rather than pay. That does not apply in this case, of

1 [1956] 1 All ER 463 at 465, [1956] 1 WLR 298 at 302
2 [1963] 1 All ER 17 at 18, [1963] P 157 at 159
3 [1956] 1 All ER 463, [1956] 1 WLR 298
4 [1962] 1 All ER 668 at 670, [1962] 1 WLR 313 at 315

course, because here clearly there is no question of committal of the husband to prison; it is an application for a garnishee order in respect of funds which are in the *a* possession of the bank as garnishee, but at the disposal of the husband, and therefore the considerations may be different. But there would appear to be no doubt that that practice of enforcing arrears in the Divorce Division for one year only is commonly adopted in that Division; and it may well be that the learned registrar, in considering this order, had in mind that such was the practice.'

Note that he uses the words 'for one year only'. This has raised the question whether in a case like the present, where several years have passed since the substantial part of the arrears came into being, the court should enforce only one year of the outstanding arrears, or should remit all the arrears as having been incurred more than one year ago, or more than one year, at any rate, before the complaint. Some guidance on that may be derived from the provision of s 13(5) of the 1960 Act, which was added to that *c* Act by s 32 of the Matrimonial Proceedings and Property Act 1970. It is in the following terms:

'A person shall not be entitled to enforce through the High Court or any county court the payment of any arrears due under an order made by virtue of this Act without the leave of that court if those arrears became due more than twelve *d* months before proceedings to enforce the payment of them are begun.'

It seems to me that Lord Merriman P in the words that he used, namely not to enforce arrears for more than a year backwards, was in fact saying once the year has passed from the time when the arrears accumulated then there should be no enforcement. But that, unfortunately, does not quite deal with the present case, because *e* it is almost impossible to see when the arrears accumulated; one can only approach the problem in a very rough and ready way, and remember that at 10s a week, the order still being current, payment of the arrears will be £26 in the last year. There is also £16 attributable to non-payment of the children's order, although the last child, as I say, became 16 almost a year before the complaint, in September 1973, the complaint being on 24th June 1974.

This is not a matter for which there is a rule of law; it is a rule of practice which is *f* 'usually' followed. The court can consider whether in the circumstances of any given case it is right to follow the practice either in whole or in part. One question which has been discussed, although we have not had an argument the other way, is whether, this being a matter of discretion for the justices, and there being no rule of law, it can be said that they have failed to exercise their discretion properly when they have *g* disregarded the practice. I think the answer is twofold. First of all, neither *Pilcher v Pilcher (No 2)*[1] nor either of the other cases that I have referred to were mentioned to the justices; they do not seem to have had them in mind. Secondly, in *Pilcher v Pilcher*[1] this court came to the conclusion that action should be taken to remit arrears, and, of course, could not have done that unless it was considered that the metropolitan magistrate came to a wrong decision in the exercise of his discretion, that he was *h* wrongly exercising his discretion, that he proceeded on a wrong principle, or that he did not have information before him which he should have had, and which would have been relevant to the exercise of his discretion. It seems to me, therefore, that the justices, if they had exercised their discretion with all the matters before them including the decision in *Pilcher v Pilcher*[1], must have come to a different decision.

They referred to the fact that the wife had not slept on her rights and suddenly *j* decided to claim arrears, but the fact is, as I have indicated, that nothing, so far as we know, had been done between 1970 and 24th July 1974. I, for my part, would therefore answer the question which they have asked, namely whether the refusal of the court

1　[1956] 1 All ER 463, [1965] 1 WLR 298

to remit all or a substantial part of the arrears was a conclusion which any reasonable
a bench of justices could reach on a proper consideration of the facts as found and whether
such refusal constituted a proper exercise of the judicial discretion, in the negative.
In saying that, I do not wish to criticise the justices, because, I think, if *Pilcher v Pilcher*
(No 2)[1] or the other cases had been brought to their attention with s 13(5) of the 1960
Act, they would probably have come to a very different conclusion.

What can we do? I think that the only course we can take is a practical one. I
b would remit all the arrears except for £50. The £50 is made up by taking the
nearest round figure of £26 (arrears at 10s a week) plus the arrears of £16. That is
£42 so £50 is, I think, near enough. That will be substituted for the justices' order
We are told that he has already paid £50. We were told that after we had already
reached this solution; so he will not have to pay any more if he has, in fact, paid.
Therefore, having answered the question as above I would substitute the order I have
c indicated, as we are entitled to do under the provisions of the Summary Jurisdiction
Act 1857, as amended: see Stone's Justices' Manual[2].

LATEY J. I agree, and I wish only to say for myself what Sir George Baker P has
already said on three points. One, it is unfortunate that the justices did not have their
d attention drawn to the decision in *Pilcher v Pilcher (No 2)*[1] that being, together with the
other cases cited, the lynch-pin of the argument which has been addressed to us by
counsel on behalf of the husband on the hearing of this case stated. The second is
that, as Sir George Baker P has said, more than one point of substantial difficulty and
possible importance has been raised during the argument. We have not had the
advantage of argument the other way, which is not, of course, in any way to suggest
e that counsel for the husband has not done his best to refer us to any authorities or
statutory enactments which apply. The third point is that, as Sir George Baker P has
pointed out, in *Pilcher v Pilcher (No 2)*[1] Lord Merriman P, in his judgment, uses the
word 'usually'. Again, in the enactment which applies to the High Court and to the
county court there is power for leave to be given for more arrears than one year's to
be enforced. So that, speaking for myself, I would not want this decision to be taken
f by magistrates' courts as an indication that there is a universal absolute rule that
justices should never go back further than the last year's arrears. In that respect also,
I would wish very much to echo what Sir George Baker P has himself said. I agree with
the order proposed.

Order accordingly.

g
Solicitors: *Houghton, Craven, Dicksons & Co*, Preston (for the husband).

Phua Kai-Swan Esq Barrister.

---

1   [1956] 1 All ER 463, [1956] 1 WLR 298
2   (1975) vol 1, p 154

Wright v Wright   a

FAMILY DIVISION
REES J
16th, 17th OCTOBER, 10th NOVEMBER 1975

Divorce – Decree absolute – Financial protection for respondent – Separation cases – Court **b**
to be satisfied as to financial provision before making decree absolute – Failure to comply with
provision – Effect – Decree made absolute before court having been satisfied as to financial
provision for respondent – Whether decree absolute void or voidable – Divorce Reform Act
1969, s 6(2).

In 1971 the husband instituted proceedings for divorce under s 2(1)(e) of the Divorce   **c**
Reform Act 1969 and the wife, in her acknowledgment of service, gave notice of her
intention to apply under s 6ᵃ of the 1969 Act for the court to consider her financial
position after the decree nisi had been granted. In November 1972 a decree nisi
was granted to the husband. Hearing of proceedings to determine the financial provision for the wife was adjourned. Solicitors for both parties then negotiated by letter.
In February 1973, on the husband's application, the decree was made absolute notwith- **d**
standing that the requirement of s 6(2) of the 1969 Act, that before the decree was
made absolute the court should be satisfied that proper financial provision had been
made for the wife, had not been complied with. Agreement was reached on the
financial arrangements but the wife subsequently became concerned about her
financial position in the event of the husband's death, should he have remarried. In
June 1975 the husband applied for an order that the decree absolute should be declared **e**
valid.

Held – A failure to comply with the provisions of s 6(2) rendered the decree absolute
voidable and not void. Accordingly the court retained a discretion to decide whether
to declare that a decree so made should be void or valid. That discretion would only
be exercised after all the relevant circumstances had been considered, including the   **f**
financial provision for the wife which the court had power to order or which was
offered. In the circumstances of the case the husband was entitled to the declaration
sought (see p 804 e to j, post).

F v F [1970] 1 All ER 200 and P v P and J [1971] 1 All ER 616 applied.
Dictum of Sir George Baker P in *Dryden v Dryden* [1973] 3 All ER at 537 considered.
Woolfenden v Woolfenden [1947] 2 All ER 653 distinguished.   **g**
B v B [1961] 2 All ER 396 not followed.

Notes
For financial protection for the respondent in separation cases, see 13 Halsbury's
Laws (4th Edn) para 644.
For the Divorce Reform Act 1969, s 6, see 40 Halsbury's Statutes (3rd Edn) 774.   **h**
As from 1st January 1974, s 6(2) of the 1969 Act has been replaced by the Matrimonial
Causes Act 1973, s 10(3).

Cases referred to in judgment
B v B [1961] 2 All ER 396, [1961] 1 WLR 856, 27(2) Digest (Reissue) 945, 7642.
Dryden v Dryden [1973] 3 All ER 526, [1973] Fam 217, [1973] 3 WLR 524.   **j**
F v F [1970] 1 All ER 200, [1971] P 1, [1970] 2 WLR 346, 27(2) Digest (Reissue) 945, 7649.
Meier v Meier [1948] 1 All ER 161, [1948] P 89, [1948] LJR 436, CA, 27(2) Digest (Reissue)
    788, 6342.

---

a Section 6, so far as material, is set out at p 801 b to d, post

N v N (1964) 108 Sol Jo 99, 27(2) Digest (Reissue) 724, 5635.

a   *P v P and J* [1971] 1 All ER 616, [1971] P 217, [1971] 2 WLR 510, CA, 27(2) Digest (Reissue) 945, 7648.

Woolfenden v Woolfenden [1947] 2 All ER 653, [1948] P 27 [1948] LJR 622, 27(2) Digest (Reissue) 941, 7604.

Cases also cited

b   *Colquitt v Colquitt* [1947] 2 All ER 50, [1948] P 19, DC.

Lloyd-Davies v Lloyd-Davies [1947] 1 All ER 161, [1947] P 53, CA.

McPherson v McPherson [1936] AC 177, PC.

Marsh v Marsh [1945] AC 271, PC.

Roberts v Roberts [1968] 3 All ER 479, [1970] P 1, DC.

c   **Summons**

By a summons dated 9th May 1975 the husband, Bruce Wright applied for an order that the order made on 14th February 1973 making absolute the decree of divorce granted to the husband against the wife, Maria Samut Wright, on 23rd November 1972 was valid. The hearing was in chambers and judgment was given in open court. The facts are set out in the judgment.

d

Henry Summerfield for the husband.

Stella Hydleman for the wife.

Cur adv vult

e   10th November.   **REES J** read the following judgment: I have decided to deliver this judgment in open court as it involves a point of law of some public importance. This is an application by a husband for an order that a decree nisi granted in a divorce suit on the sole ground of irretrievable breakdown evidenced by five years' separation be made absolute. Alternatively, the husband seeks a declaration that the decree absolute already granted is valid.

f   The case raises a point of law on which there appears to be no direct authority. The husband instituted proceedings for divorce under s 2(1)(e) of the Divorce Reform Act 1969, and the wife served notice of application under s 6 of that Act for the court to consider her financial position. I have been told at the bar that when the decree nisi was granted consideration of the wife's claims for financial provision was adjourned. Thereafter, on the application of the husband, the decree nisi of divorce was made g   absolute notwithstanding that the court had neither considered nor been satisfied as to the financial provision for the wife. The decree absolute was accordingly granted without compliance with the strict and important requirements of s 6(2) of the 1969 Act.

The point of law for decision in this case is whether, as the husband contends, the decree absolute is merely voidable or whether, as the wife contends, it is void so as to h   be a nullity. Counsel for the husband argued that I am bound by the ratio decidendi of the Court of Appeal decision in *P v P and J*[1] to hold that the decree absolute granted in the instant case, contrary to the provision of s 6(2) of the 1969 Act, is voidable for the same reasons that a decree absolute granted contrary to the provisions of s 33 of the Matrimonial Causes Act 1965 relating to arrangements for children is voidable. Counsel for the wife argued that not only am I not so bound but that there are cogent reasons j   for holding that a decree absolute granted without compliance with s 6(2) of the 1969 Act is void and a nullity. Both counsel, to whom I am indebted for their helpful arguments, agreed that I should deliver judgment on the issue of law whether the decree absolute is void or voidable. Thereafter they will have an opportunity of

---

1   [1971] 1 All ER 616, [1971] P 217

adducing evidence and addressing the court as may be appropriate in the light of my
decision.   a
    I start with a brief review of the basic facts. The parties were married on 18th
November 1944, when the husband was 24 years of age and the wife 22, and they are now
respectively about 55 and 53. They had five children, of whom only the youngest,
a daughter, is under 18 years of age. The wife has custody of that child by order of the
court. The parties separated in February 1965 when the husband left the matrimonial
home and they have lived apart ever since. On 29th June 1976 the High Court pro-   b
nounced a decree of judicial separation on a petition by the wife on the ground of
the husband's adultery. Pursuant to that decree a registrar ordered that so long as the
wife continued to reside at the former matrimonial home at an address in Twickenham, Middlesex, the husband should pay to her by way of permanent alimony the
sum of £680 per annum less tax. The order also made financial provision for two of
the children then under the age of 18 years. The husband was and is a civil servant   c
employed on a wage structure which affords substantial pension rights for him on
retirement and also on his death to any widow who survives him. Proceedings for
divorce were instituted by the wife on 31st March 1971 on the grounds of irretrievable breakdown as evidenced by adultery committed by the husband and also by
five years' separation. The husband also instituted proceedings for divorce by a
petition dated 3rd February 1971 alleging irretrievable breakdown and five years'   d
separation. In the form of acknowledgement of service of this latter petition the
wife indicated that she did not intend to defend the case nor to oppose the grant of the
decree but stated that she did intend to apply to the court to consider her financial
position as it would be after the divorce. By a notice of application dated 17th February
1972, the wife's solicitors gave notice that she applied to the court under s 6 of the
1969 Act, for the court to consider her financial position immediately on the decree   e
nisi being granted. These two suits were subsequently consolidated and came on for
hearing together before a deputy circuit judge on 23rd November 1972. The deputy
circuit judge granted a decree nisi on the prayer in the husband's suit on the sole
ground of irretrievable breakdown and five years' separation. Custody of the two
youngest children was awarded to the wife. He dismissed the prayers for dissolution
and costs in the wife's petition. As I have stated earlier, the claims for financial   f
relief were not dealt with and I was informed at the bar that consideration of her
financial provision after divorce was adjourned.
    In these circumstances, as from the granting of the decree nisi on 23rd November
1972, the wife was entitled to the protection of s 6(2) of the 1969 Act, which provided:
'. . . the court shall not make absolute the decree of divorce unless it is satisfied' as to
the financial provision for the wife. As will appear, this statutory provision was not   g
complied with.
    The solicitors for the parties entered into the negotiations by correspondence
between November 1972 and December 1973 in order to try to reach agreement as to
the financial provisions to be made for the wife. Copies of the principal letters passing
between the parties' legal advisers are available in an agreed bundle and have been
read to and by me. During the course of this commendable process a crucial event   h
occurred apparently without its significance being appreciated by any of those concerned, whether they were the Divorce Registry officials, the lawyers or, understandably, the lay parties themselves. On 14th February 1973 the husband's solicitors made
application by notice in due form for the decree nisi pronounced on 23rd November
1972 to be made absolute. A copy of this notice of application was received by the
wife on the following day, and by her solicitors on a date which is not precisely fixed   j
but which is conceded to have been before the end of February 1973. Notwithstanding
that the provisions of s 6(2) of the 1969 Act and those of r 65(2)(g) of the Matrimonial
Causes Rules 1973[1] had not been complied with, the decree was made absolute on

─────────────────────────────
1   SI 1973 No 2016

14th February 1973, pursuant to the husband's application. The decree nisi was
a endorsed accordingly and, on 15th February 1973, the appropriate certificates were
sent to the husband and the wife in accordance with r 67 of the 1973 rules. Despite
this decisive event the negotiations between the parties' legal advisers continued
until agreement was finally concluded by the exchange of letters of which the last is
dated 5th December 1973. Thereafter discussions continued as to the terms of a
summons seeking to embody the agreed terms as to the financial provision for the
b wife and the then one remaining relevant child in a consent order. Agreement as to
the terms of the summons was eventually achieved and an appropriate consent order
was make by a registrar of the Family Division on 23rd May 1974. Stated in summary
form that order provided that the husband having agreed to pay and the wife to
accept periodical payments at the rate of 25 per cent of the husband's salary or pension
after certain specified deductions and on the husband undertaking to inform the wife
c of any change in his salary and to supply her with an annual statement of earnings it
was ordered that the husband should pay to the wife £1,889·75 per annum less tax
during joint lives or until earlier remarriage or further order. Provision was also made
in the order for the support of the youngest child. The agreement reached between
the legal advisers on behalf of the parties included a term that the husband would
transfer to the wife the former matrimonial home in Twickenham absolutely and free
d of mortgage. The order directed by consent that this transfer should take place within
four weeks of the date of the order. This last mentioned term was not implemented in
accordance with the order apparently owing to doubts in the minds of the legal
advisers as to what method of transfer should be adopted so as to avoid attracting
capital gains tax.

On 12th September 1974 a representative of the wife's solicitors attended at the
e Divorce Registry in London and invited the attention of the assistant principal clerk
to the fact that the decree of divorce had been made absolute notwithstanding that
the wife's application under s 6 of the 1969 Act had not been considered by the court.
It appears from a letter dated 7th October 1974 that this intervention on the part of
the wife's solicitors was prompted by an enquiry made by the wife herself. It is however conceded by counsel for both parties that all the facts relevant to the making of
f the decree absolute had been known to the parties and their legal advisers by the end
of February 1973. It seems that what was lacking prior to September 1974 was an
appreciation that what had been done was contrary to the Act and rules and as to
the consequences.

By a letter addressed to the husband's solicitors and dated 12th September 1974 the
assistant principal clerk concerned informed them that a registrar was of opinion
g that the decree had been made contrary to the provisions of r 65(2)(g) of the 1973
rules and s 6(2) of the 1969 Act, and suggested that they should consider making an
appropriate application to a registrar or a judge.

Although the husband has for many years desired to marry the lady with whom he
has been living, he accepted the advice of counsel that he should not do so until the
validity or otherwise of the decree absolute had been decided. By November 1974 it
h appeared that the wife was disturbed because the agreement reached between the
parties for the transfer of the matrimonial home to her and for periodical payments
did not make any financial provision for her future in the event of the husband's
death. This has remained the main, if not the only, issue between the parties.
Negotiations have continued in an effort to reach a compromise on it, but without
success.

j On 9th May 1975 the husband made his application, inter alia, for a declaration as to
the validity of the decree absolute. Despite the unresolved disputes between the parties
as to the validity of the decree absolute and as to the wife's claim for financial provision in the event of the husband's death, the husband completed his agreement by
transferring absolutely to the wife the matrimonial home in Twickenham free of
mortgage on 27th May 1975. On 16th June 1975 the husband's application came before

a registrar in the Family Division who directed that the cause should no longer be
treated as pending in a divorce county court and that the summons should be   **a**
adjourned to a judge.

It is in these circumstances that the matter came before me. No submission has
been made to me by either counsel in regard to my jurisdiction to make the order
sought in the instant case. The application was originally made to a registrar seeking
an order making the decree absolute or alternatively for a declaration that the decree
absolute already granted is valid. The present proceedings are distinguishable from   **b**
those in *Dryden v Dryden*[1], in which Sir George Baker P considered applications to
determine the validity of the decree absolute in a case in which a judge, having
granted a decree nisi in an undefended suit based on s 2(1)(*e*) of the 1969 Act on a Friday,
directed that the decree be made absolute on the Monday following. Since neither
the respondent wife nor her solicitors knew that the decree nisi was to be expedited no
application for consideration of the wife's financial provision had been made under s 6   **c**
of that Act.   Accordingly, the applications made to Sir George Baker P were in the
nature of applications for a rehearing of a cause tried by a judge alone under r 54(1) of
the Matrimonial Causes Rules 1971[2] (see now r 54(1) of the 1973 rules). Sir George
Baker P held that he had jurisdiction and set out his reasons for so holding in *Dryden v
Dryden*[3].

In the well-known children's cases of *F v F*[4] and *P v P and J*[5] the court was concerned   **d**
with summonses to determine whether a decree absolute was valid, notwithstanding
that the judge who granted the decree nisi and expressed satisfaction with the arrangements for the children did so, in *F v F*[4] without being told that another child had been
born to the wife between the filing of the petition and the hearing of the suit, and in
P v P and J[5] without being told that the wife was pregnant with a child who was born
before the decree was made absolute. In neither of these cases does it appear that any   **e**
issue was raised as to the jurisdiction of a single judge to make a declaration as to the
validity of the decree absolute notwithstanding in *P v P and J*[5] that there was an appeal
to the Court of Appeal. In the much earlier case of *Woolfenden v Woolfenden*[6] a motion
came before Barnard J to show cause why a decree absolute should not be treated as a
nullity because the respondent had obtained a certificate under seal that a decree of
divorce had been made absolute notwithstanding that the period of three months pre-   **f**
scribed by s 9 of the Matrimonial Causes Act 1937 had not expired. No question seems
to have been raised as to the jurisdiction of a judge to make the order sought, and
Barnard J made an order setting aside the decree absolute.

In these circumstances, I am satisfied that there is ample authority to justify me in
accepting jurisdiction to deal with the matter and accordingly I shall now deal with the
issue as to the validity of the decree absolute in the instant case.   **g**

It is plain from the material placed before me that there is no question of bad faith
on the part of anyone concerned in the making of the decree absolute in this case.
Unhappily, the solicitors acting for the husband knew when they applied to make
absolute the decree nisi that an application under s 6(2) of the 1969 Act had been made
by the wife and had not been decided, and accordingly they should have realised, but
did not, that the decree absolute ought not to be granted. The solicitors for the wife   **h**
also knew the position by the end of February 1973, but took no steps to protect their
client until 12th September 1974. Assuming, as I do, that the wife's application under
s 6 of the 1969 Act, which is dated 17th February 1974, duly reached the court file, then
it appears clear that there was a failure of the court official or officials concerned to

j

1   [1973] 3 All ER 526, [1973] Fam 217
2   SI 1971 No 953
3   [1973] 3 All ER at 544, [1973] Fam at 241, 242
4   [1970] 1 All ER 200, [1971] P 1
5   [1971] 1 All ER 616, [1971] P 217
6   [1947] 2 All ER 653, [1948] P 27

comply with r 65 of the 1973 rules in that either the court minutes did not properly
a record the application or the search was inadequate. This series of mistakes all made
in good faith have combined to give rise to the delay and stress and to the problem
with which I must now deal.

The relevant parts of s 6 of the 1969 Act are as follows:

'(1) The following provisions of this section shall have effect where—(a) the
b respondent to a petition for divorce . . . has applied to the court under this section
for it to consider for the purposes of subsection (2) hereof the financial position
of the respondent after the divorce.

'(2) The court hearing an application by the respondent under this section shall
consider all the circumstances . . . and notwithstanding anything in the foregoing
provisions of this Act but subject to subsection (3) of this section, the court
c shall not make absolute the decree of divorce unless it is satisfied—(a) that the
petitioner should not be required to make any financial provision for the respondent, or (b) that the financial provision made by the petitioner for the respondent
is reasonable and fair or the best that can be made in the circumstances.

'(3) The court may if it thinks fit proceed without observing the requirements
of subsection (2) of this section if—(a) it appears that there are circumstances
d making it desirable that the decree should be made absolute without delay, and
(b) the court has obtained a satisfactory undertaking from the petitioner that
he will make such financial provision for the respondent as the court may
approve.'

It follows that in the instant case, unlike the situation in Dryden v Dryden[1], there
e has been a breach of s 6 itself because the wife had applied to the court under the
section for the court to consider her financial position, yet nevertheless the court did
make absolute the decree of divorce without complying with requirements of the
section. It also seems likely that there was a breach of r 65(2) of the 1973 rules. The
case in which the point I have to decide was most nearly considered is that of Woolfenden v Woolfenden[2] to which I have referred earlier. In that case a respondent against
f whom a decree nisi had been pronounced successfully applied to the Divorce Registry
for the decree to be made absolute. This application was made notwithstanding that
the period of three months from the earliest date when the petitioner could have
made such an application had not elapsed. Accordingly, the respondent's application
was made and was granted without complying with the time limit imposed by s 9 of
the Matrimonial Causes Act 1937 then in force. Furthermore, no notice of the applica-
g tion by the respondent was given to the petitioner or her solicitors. So there was also a
failure to comply with r 40(3) of the Matrimonial Causes Rules 1947. Barnard J said[3]:

'Until the passing of the Matrimonial Causes Act, 1937, a party against whom
a decree nisi had been pronounced could not in any circumstances apply to
have the decree made absolute, and it was only s. 9 of that Act which made such
h a step possible . . . This provision merely regulates the procedure by which the
guilty party is enabled to apply for the decree to be made absolute under the statute.
It is obvious from the date of the certificate of the decree absolute in the case
before me that the time required by the statute had not elapsed to enable the
guilty party to apply under r. 40(3) to the court for the decree to be made
absolute.'

j The learned judge expressed his decision in these words[4]:

1   [1973] 3 All ER 526, [1973] Fam 217
2   [1947] 2 All ER 653, [1948] P 27
3   [1947] 2 All ER at 655, [1948] P at 31
4   [1948] P at 32, cf [1947] 2 All ER at 655

'In view of the fact that the husband has not complied with the statute, I have
come to the conclusion that I cannot treat the making of this decree absolute   *a*
as a mere irregularity, and I must treat it as a nullity. I regret having to come
to this conclusion, because I am informed that on July 10, 1947, the husband
went through a ceremony of marriage with another woman. The certificate,
dated June 24, 1947, to the effect that the decree was on that date made final
and absolute must therefore be set aside.'

I have been referred to a number of cases in which judges have had to consider the   *b*
failure of the court to comply with the provisions of s 2 of the Matrimonial Proceedings (Children) Act 1958, and its successor, s 33 of the Matrimonial Causes Act 1965.
There is no difference in the terms of these two sections which is material for the
present purpose. The essential words of those sections are identical with the words of
s 6 of the 1969 Act in that it provides that 'the court shall not make absolute the decree   *c*
of divorce unless it is satisfied that . . .' But those sections of the 1958 and the 1965 Acts
related to the courts being satisfied as to the arrangements for the relevant children
of the family and not to financial provision for the wife. Scarman J decided in two
cases that failure to comply with the provisions of s 2 of the 1958 Act rendered the
decree absolute void. The cases of *B v B*[1] and *N v N*[2]. He stated his reasons thus in
B v B[3]:   *d*

'I find that the decree absolute was a nullity because, looking at the statute, I
take the view that the disobedience here to the requirement of s. 2 of the Act (a
strong word perhaps to describe the non-compliance with the section) was so
fundamental that it does render the decree absolute void. I cannot regard the
provision for the care and upbringing of the children in s. 2 of the Act of 1958 as
being a matter which the court could call either subsidiary or collateral. It seems   *e*
to me a matter of such grave importance that I must give effect to it by declaring
that the decree absolute is void.'

I confess to a considerable respect for the logic of those impressive words. I have
been pressed by counsel for the wife to give weight to the well-known presumption
arising from the circumstances that when Parliament passed s 33 of the 1965 Act in the   *f*
same terms as those of s 2 of the 1958 Act, that it intended that the subsequent statute
should be given the same meaning as had already been given its predecessor by a
judicial decision. So it is argued that the decision of Scarman J that a failure to comply
with s 2 of the 1958 Act renders the decree absolute void should be presumed to
represent the intention of Parliament in respect of s 33 of the 1965 Act. I am unable
to take the view that I should give any weight to this argument or to the argument   *g*
that Parliament enacted s 17(3) of the Matrimonial Proceedings and Property Act 1970
on 29th May 1970, expressly providing that if a court made a decree absolute without
having declared that it is satisfied of certain specified matters, the decree shall be
void. I respectfully adopt, in support of my view, without repeating them, the reasons
given by Sir George Baker P in *Dryden v Dryden*[4].

I now turn to consider the formidable argument presented by counsel for the   *h*
husband that I am bound by the decision of the Court of Appeal in *P v P and J*[5] to
hold that the decree absolute in the instant case is voidable. That decision was that
a failure to comply with the requirements of s 33 of the Matrimonial Causes Act 1965
rendered the decree absolute voidable and not void. This decision overruled the two
earlier decisions of Scarman J to which I have referred, as well as the decision of the

j

1   [1961] 2 All ER 396, [1961] 1 WLR 856
2   (1964) 108 Sol Jo 99
3   [1961] 2 All ER at 398, [1961] 1 WLR at 857
4   [1973] 3 All ER at 537, [1973] Fam at 233
5   [1971] 1 All ER 616, [1971] P 217

trial judge in *P v P and J*[1] who was Cairns J and approved a decision of Sir Jocelyn Simon
a P in *F v F*[2] which did not adopt the views of Scarman J. As I have already indicated,
all these cases dealt with arrangements relating to children and not with financial
provisions for a wife although the relevant statutory words are identical. All the members of the Court of Appeal approved the reasoning and the decision of Sir Jocelyn
Simon P in *F v F*[2]. That being so, I cite the passage in his judgment which summarises
the considerations which moved him to differ from the view of Scarman J that Parlia-
b ment must have intended that a failure to comply with the provisions of the section
rendered void any decree absolute purported to have been made thereafter. The
passage reads[3]:

'In the first place, if that had been the intention of Parliament, nothing would
have been simpler than so to have stipulated; compare, for example, the Marriage
c   Act 1949, s 25. Secondly, as Cairns J pointed out, to treat the decree absolute as
void will rarely promote the interest of the children of the family in question; and
in some cases (eg where a parent has "remarried" in reliance on an ostensibly valid
decree absolute) it will actually do no harm. Thirdly, there are indications elsewhere of the importance that Parliament attaches to the certainty of the change
of status arising out of a decree absolute: see s 8 of this very Act (remarriage of
d   divorced persons); Supreme Court of Judicature (Consolidation) Act, 1925, s 31
(1)(e) (restrictions on appeals against decrees absolute). The general approach of
the law in this respect was evidenced by Scott LJ in *Meier v Meier*[4]. "The policy of
Parliament requires that a decree absolute should be protected unless there is
some ground on which the court could reasonably exercise its inherent jurisdiction
to vary the order in the interests of justice." Fourthly, to hold that non-compliance
e   with s 33 renders the decree absolute void would sometimes cause hardship to
innocent third parties: eg a husband petitioner might without any fault be ignorant of the relevant child's birth; and if he has remarried on the faith of an apparently valid decree absolute his after-taken "wife" and their children might suffer.
In my view, Parliament is to be presumed not to have intended such injustice,
unless it is the consequence of the only reasonable meaning which suits the scope
f   and object of the statute.'

It will be sufficient to cite only two short passages from the judgments delivered in the
Court of Appeal to illustrate the views of that court on the point. I start with the
view of Davies LJ[5]:

g   'I have taken a little time in relating the history of this case. I have not to any
extent referred to the authorities, for the reason, which I think I have already
indicated, that in my view the issues in this case are completely covered and
governed by the judgment that Sir Jocelyn Simon P gave in *F v F*[2], resulting in a
decision at which, if he thought he had been free to do so in the present case,
Cairns J would undoubtedly have arrived.'

h
Phillimore LJ said[6]:

'However, the real basis of the issue here is this, that, as counsel for the Queen's
Proctor rightly says, a court ought not lightly to treat a decree absolute as void.

j   1   [1971] 1 All ER 616, [1971] P 217
2   [1970] 1 All ER 200, [1971] P 1
3   [1970] 1 All ER at 205, [1971] P at 13
4   [1948] 1 All ER 161 at 162, [1948] P 89 at 93
5   [1971] 1 All ER at 621, [1971] P at 224
6   [1971] 1 All ER at 622, [1971] P at 225

Parliament has not said, in either the 1958 Act or the 1965 Act, that it should be
void in the sort of circumstances which have occurred here. In contrast, where *a*
Parliament desires to say that it is to be treated as void, there are the provisions of
s 25 of the Marriage Act 1949, and of s 17(3) of the Act of 1970.'

On the basis of these two decisions, one at first instance but expressly approved
by the Court of Appeal, and the other a decision of the Court of Appeal itself, counsel
for the husband argues that I am bound to decide in the instant case that the decree *b*
absolute is voidable only and not void. This argument was also presented to Sir
George Baker P in *Dryden v Dryden*[1], although in that case there was no failure to
comply with the terms of the Act. His approach to the point appears in these terms[2]:

> 'I would therefore be content to consider myself bound by the Court of Appeal's
> decision in *P v P and J*[3] but for the second and much more formidable argu- *c*
> ment, which is that whereas a void decree will rarely help children—it is enough
> if it is voidable—the protection of wives is very different and can be achieved only
> by a void decree which will take no account of remarriage and of rights and
> interest, acquired in pursuance of its ostensible validity by innocent third parties
> having an equal equity with the wife . . .'

Accordingly there is no decision by Sir George Baker P that he was bound by the *d*
ratio decidendi of *P v P and J*[3]. His judgment does, however, invite attention to a vital
distinction between the provisions of s 33 of the 1965 Act and those of s 6 of the 1969
Act. The former relates to arrangements for children whose interests are rarely
served by holding that a decree absolute is void. The latter relates to the financial
provision for a wife, some at least of whose rights may well be jeopardised if a decree *e*
absolute is not held to be void when it is obtained without complying with the
requirements of s 6.

Having carefully considered all the arguments presented on both sides, I have
reached the conclusion, not without a good deal of hesitation, that the decree absolute
in the instant case is voidable and not void. My reasons stated in summary form are
these. Because of the possibly severely damaging effects on the adults and the *f*
children who may be involved, I am of opinion that a court should only hold a decree
absolute to be void if driven by the terms of the relevant statute so to hold. I do not
find the terms of s 6 of the 1969 Act do drive me to that conclusion. While the
decision of the Court of Appeal in *P v P and J*[3] is a compelling authority, I am of opinion
that it does not bind me to reach that conclusion. I am impressed, as was Sir George
Baker P in *Dryden v Dryden*[1], by the argument that a wife's interests may be adversely *g*
affected in some cases if the decree absolute is not held to be void. Nevertheless,
this possible disadvantage to the wife must be balanced against the far graver disadvantages which may flow from holding that in every case a decree absolute shall be
void automatically if obtained without compliance with the provisions of s 6 of the
1969 Act or its modern successor, s 10(3) of the 1973 Act. Furthermore, if the decree
absolute be held voidable and not void, the court retains a discretion to decide whether *h*
to declare that the decree absolute shall be void or valid. This discretion will only be
exercised after all the relevant circumstances have been considered, including
the financial provision for the wife which the court has power to order or which
is offered. In my opinion, the possibility of doing justice to all concerned, whether
they be the wife, husband, the children of the family, or the third parties, is enhanced
if the decree absolute is held to be voidable but diminished if it is held to be void in *j*
every case irrespective of the circumstances.

1   [1973] 3 All ER 526, [1973] Fam 217
2   [1973] 3 All ER at 537, [1973] Fam at 233
3   [1971] 1 All ER 616, [1971] P 217

For all these reasons I hold that the decree absolute in the instant case is voidable and
a I invite counsel to address me as to the consequential directions which I should now
give.

[After considering the submissions of counsel His Lordship declared the decree
absolute valid.]

b *Declaration accordingly.*

Solicitors: *Philip Ross, Elliston & Beiber* (for the husband); *Crawley & de Reya* (for the wife).

Phua Kai-Swan Esq Barrister.

c

Note
Chaudhry v Chaudhry

COURT OF APPEAL, CIVIL DIVISION
d STAMP, ORR LJJ AND SIR JOHN PENNYCUICK
12th, 13th NOVEMBER 1975

*Husband and wife – Property – Summary proceedings – Jurisdiction – Polygamous marriage –
Application by party to polygamous marriage – Marriage valid according to law of parties'
domicile – Application for declaration of parties' interests in matrimonial home – Whether*
e *court having jurisdiction to entertain application – Whether parties 'husband and wife' –
Married Women's Property Act 1882, s 17.*

Notes
For the recognition of and jurisdiction over polygamous marriages, see 8 Halsbury's
f Laws (4th Edn) paras 478, 479, 481.
For the Married Women's Property Act 1882, s 17, see 17 Halsbury's Statutes (3rd
Edn) 120.

Interlocutory appeal
This was an appeal by the husband, Abdur Rehman Chaudhry, against the decision
g of Dunn J[1] given on the 12th June 1975 whereby on a preliminary issue it was determined that the wife, Kishwar Sultana Chaudhry, was entitled under s 17 of the
Married Women's Property Act 1882 to proceed with her application by summons
issued on 22nd February 1974 for (i) a declaration that the property of 9 Protheroe
Road, London, SW6, was owned by the wife in equal shares with the husband, and
(ii) an order for sale of the property.

h
A M Abbas and *A M Azhar* for the husband.
Jonathan Sofer for the wife.

ORR LJ gave the first judgment at the invitation of Stamp LJ. The parties to this
j appeal are Moslems who were born in Pakistan and were married there in 1959 under
Islamic rites with the consequence that the marriage was potentially polygamous.
Some years later, two children having been born to them, they came to England and
made their home here. In 1972 the husband pronounced in the Pakistan Embassy in
London a talaq of divorce which became final on 2nd October 1972 and, under

---

1 [1975] 3 All ER 687, [1975] 3 WLR 559

English law as it stood at that time, validly dissolved the marriage. In consequence
divorce proceedings which the wife had previously begun in England were stayed or   *a*
dismissed and thereafter, in February 1974, she issued a summons entitled 'In the
Divorce Registry', and also, 'In the matter of the Married Women's Property Act,
1882', for a declaration that the last matrimonial home, a house in Fulham, was owned
by the parties in equal shares, and for sale of that property. On 11th July 1974 this
application was transferred by order of a registrar of the Family Division to the High
Court for determination of a preliminary point of law, namely whether the wife,   *b*
having been party to a potentially polygamous marriage, was entitled in the circumstances to apply to the court under s 17 of the 1882 Act. On 12th June 1975 Dunn J[1]
gave judgment holding that she was so entitled, and also expressing obiter certain
conclusions as to the effect of s 47 of the Matrimonal Causes Act 1973 in such a case.
From that judgment the husband has now appealed, with leave of the judge, to this
court.   *c*
    So far as the matter has proceeded I for my part have formed no view as to its likely
outcome, but it is an unfortunate feature of the case that if the appeal were to be
allowed it would be necessary for the wife to commence fresh proceedings for such
relief as may be due to her otherwise than in her capacity as a wife for the purpose of
s 17, whereas if the summons had not been entitled 'In the Divorce Registry' and 'In
the matter of the Married Women's Property Act, 1882', it would have been open to   *d*
the court to grant her whatever relief in respect of the house is due to her, whether in
the capacity of a wife under s 17 or otherwise. This matter was raised by Stamp LJ at
the beginning of the hearing yesterday afternoon.
    An alternative course with regard to the form of the summons would be that the
headings to which I have referred should be left, but that a note be added at the foot of
the summons that the relief sought is sought under s 17 of the Married Women's   *e*
Property Act 1882 and also under the inherent jurisdiction of the court. In my judgment
the proper course for this court to take is to order that the summons be amended by
the addition of such a note, that amendment being permissible under RSC Ord 2, r 3.
To proceed with the present appeal would in my judgment be potentially wasteful
in costs and could delay the final ascertainment of the wife's rights, and in any event I
cannot consider it right that we should be required to decide as a preliminary question   *f*
one which may well never arise.
    For these reasons I would make the order which I have indicated and dismiss the
appeal.

SIR JOHN PENNYCUICK. I suppose it may conceivably be necessary on the   *g*
hearing of this summons under the inherent jurisdiction for the court to decide
whether for some relevant purpose the applicant is or is not the wife of the respondent.
If so, the court on hearing the summons will then decide that question. But it seems
to me that it would be altogether inappropriate for this court to decide as a preliminary
point a question which in all probability will never arise.

                                                                                    h
STAMP LJ. I agree.

Appeal dismissed. Summons to be amended to read that the relief sought is sought under s 17
of the Married Women's Property Act 1882 and also under the inherent jurisdiction of the
court. Leave to appeal to the House of Lords refused.
                                                                                    j
Solicitors: *A S Cohen & Co* (for the husband); *Myers, Ebner & Deaner* (for the wife).

                                                        L I Zysman Esq   Barrister.

---

1   [1975] 3 All ER 687, [1975] 3 WLR 559

Re Whitfield's Estate

Inland Revenue Commissioners v Whitfield and another

COURT OF APPEAL, CIVIL DIVISION

STAMP, ORR AND GOFF LJJ

1st, 2nd, 3rd DECEMBER 1975, 30th JANUARY 1976

Estate duty – Valuation – Allowances – Debts incurred by deceased – Debts incurred bona fide for full consideration in money or money's worth wholly for deceased's own use and benefit – Consideration for deceased's own use and benefit – Deceased having borrowed substantial sum from bank – Borrowing in order to purchase policies of assurance on her life for benefit of residuary legatees – Borrowing by way of a bona fide commercial transaction involving no element of bounty or gift to bank – Whether debt incurred for full consideration wholly for deceased's own use and benefit – Whether debt deductible in determining value of deceased's estate – Finance Act 1894, s 7(1)(a).

Shortly before her death, the deceased decided to effect four policies of assurance on her life. As the deceased did not have the necessary sum immediately available, arrangements were made with her bank to obtain a loan of £80,000 on the security of certain stocks and shares which she owned. The deceased executed a power of attorney in favour of her son empowering him to effect the policies and to borrow from the bank the sums required to pay the premiums. The bank did not open a loan account and credit the deceased's current account with £80,000 but opened a 'no 2 account' on which she was entitled to a temporary overdraft up to the required amount. On the day the transactions were to be completed, a representative of her bank, a representative of an assurance society, the deceased's solicitor and her attorney met at the deceased's bank. The attorney drew a cheque on the no 2 account for £80,000 in favour of of the assurance society. The representative of the society thereupon presented the cheque which was credited to the bank's 'draft account' and received in turn a banker's draft for £80,000. Thereupon he issued receipts and the policies commenced. The deceased died on the following day. Her executors claimed that the sum of £80,000 owing by her estate in respect of the debit balance in the no 2 account was deductible from her estate for estate duty purposes by virtue of s 7(1)(a)[a] of the Finance Act 1894 on the ground that it had been incurred for 'full consideration in money or money's worth wholly for the deceased's own use and benefit'. Walton J[b] rejected the executors' claim, holding that the requirements of s 7(1)(a) had not been satisfied since the deceased had obtained, in exchange for her liability to repay the bank, a consideration in the shape of policies of assurance, which were not for her own use and benefit, but only for the use and benefit of the beneficiaries. The executors appealed.

Held – In determining whether the debt to the bank had been incurred wholly for the deceased's own use and benefit, the only relevant transaction was that which had taken place between the deceased and the bank whereby the debt had been incurred. That transaction was a bona fide commercial transaction involving no element of bounty or gift to the bank. Accordingly the debt had been incurred for full consideration and, since the bank was not concerned with how the deceased

a   Section 7(1), so far as material, provides: 'In determining the value of an estate for the purpose of Estate duty . . . an allowance shall not be made—(a) for debts incurred by the deceased, or incumbrances created by a disposition made by the deceased, unless such debts or incumbrances were incurred or created bona fide for full consideration in money or money's worth for the deceased's own use and benefit . . .'

b   [1974] 3 All ER 802, [1974] 1 STC 511

disposed of the money lent, the debt had, so far as the bank was concerned, been incurred wholly for the deceased's own use and benefit. The bank was not *a* concerned with the transaction between the deceased and the assurance society, except to see that the money lent to its customer was not dealt with otherwise than in accordance with her authority. Furthermore, it was immaterial that the deceased had chosen to dispose of the money lent by directing the bank to pay it direct to the assurance society rather than receiving it herself before paying it to the society. Accordingly, the consideration obtained by the deceased in return for the *b* debt had been obtained 'wholly for [her] own use and benefit', within s 7(1)(*a*), and the appeal would therefore be allowed (see p 810 *d e* and *f* to *h*, p 811 *d* and *e*, p 812 *e f* and *j*, p 813 *e* and *f*, p 814 *j* to p 815 *a* to *c* and *h*, p 816 *a* to *c* and p 817 *a*, post).

Dicta of Lord Macnaghten and of Lord Atkinson in *Attorney-General v Duke of Richmond and Gordon* [1909] AC at 472, 473, 479 applied.

Decision of Walton J [1974] 3 All ER 802 reversed.	*c*

Notes

For the deduction for estate duty purposes of debts incurred for full consideration in money or money's worth, see 15 Halsbury's Laws (3rd Edn) 81, 82, para 170, and for cases on deductions for estate duty purposes, see 21 Digest (Repl) 59-62, 228-242.

For the Finance Act 1894, s 7, see 12 Halsbury's Statutes (3rd Edn) 467.	*d*

Cases referred to in judgment

Attorney-General v Duke of Richmond and Gordon [1909] AC 466, 78 LJKB 998, 101 LT 241, HL, 21 Digest (Repl) 60, 236.

London Chartered Bank of Australia v McMillan [1892] AC 292, 61 LJPC 44, 66 LT 801, PC, 3 Digest (Repl) 293, 899.	*e*

Cases also cited

Attorney-General v Duke of Richmond, Gordon and Lennox (No 1) [1907] 2 KB 923; *on appeal* [1908] 2 KB 729, CA.

HM Advocate v Gunning's Trustees (1902) 39 SLR 534.

Inland Revenue Comr v New Zealand Insurance Co [1958] NZLR 1077, CA (NZ).

Inland Revenue Comrs v Alexander's Trustees (1905) 7 F 367.	*f*

Law v Coburn (Inspector of Taxes) [1972] 3 All ER 1115, [1972] 1 WLR 1238.

Lord Advocate v Warrender's Trustees (1906) 8 F 371.

Whitfield's Estate, Re, Inland Revenue Comrs v Whitfield [1974] 3 All ER 802, [1975] Ch 290, [1974] STC 511.

### Appeal	*g*

In November 1963 Rebecca Augusta Whitfield ('the deceased') made arrangements with William Spencer Whitfield, her son, and David Charles Humphrey Townsend, her solicitor, ('the executors') in order to save estate duty. Under the scheme, the deceased was to purchase four policies of assurance, in the sum of £20,000 each, on her life in favour of four beneficiaries who were the residuary legatees under her will dated 5th June 1962. On 16th November the deceased executed a power of attorney *h* in favour of her son, conferring on him powers: '1. To take and effect a new policy or policies of assurance . . . on my life' in favour of the four beneficiaries, and '2. To borrow from any Banker . . . either by way of overdraft or by way of advances or otherwise any sums of money which he may think fit to borrow for the purpose of paying the premiums on the said policy or policies and on such terms and either with or without security as he shall think fit.' The deceased's solicitor took the special *j* power to the local branch of her bank, which had agreed to lend £80,000 under the special power against deposit of certain securities belonging to the deceased. The bank opened a no 2 account in favour of the deceased with agreed overdraft facilities up to £100,000. The special power was inspected by the branch manager and the deceased's son drew a cheque for £80,000 in favour of the Sun Life Assurance Society *a* Ltd. The cheque was handed to a representative of the assurance society who was present. Receipts were given and under each policy a sum of £19,501·35 became payable on the deceased's death. On 17th November the deceased died. By her will, her son and her solicitor were appointed executors and probate was granted to them out of the Durham District Registry on 8th May 1964. The Inland Revenue affidavit of the deceased's estate sworn by the executors deducted the loan of £80,000 in determining the value of the estate for the purpose of estate duty, on the ground *b* that each policy had been effected in such a manner that the deceased had never had an interest in it and that the proceeds of the policies were accordingly not aggregable with other property passing on her death for the purpose of determining the rate of estate duty on her estate. The Inland Revenue Commissioners were not, however, satisfied that the debt of £80,000 to the bank had been incurred 'for full consideration in money or money's worth wholly for the deceased's own use and *c* benefit' within s 7(1)(a) of the Finance Act 1894 and claimed that no allowance should have been made for it in determining the value of the deceased's estate. Accordingly, by an originating summons dated 24th January 1973, the commissioners sought an order under ss 1, 6 and 8 of the 1894 Act for the payment by the executors of £46,282·50 in respect of additional estate duty and under s 18 of the Finance Act 1896, s 27 of the Finance Act 1943 and s 30 of the Finance Act 1970 for interest on that sum. On *d* 18th July 1974 Walton J[1] granted the order sought. The executors appealed.

Peter Oliver QC and *L L Ware* for executors.
John Balcombe QC and *Peter Gibson* for the Crown.

Cur adv vult

e
30th January. **STAMP LJ** read the following judgment of the court: The facts of this case are fully stated in the judgment of Walton J[2] and we will not repeat them except to summarise the vital transactions which took place on 16th November 1963 at the Weybridge branch of Barclays Bank Ltd. There were present, so far as is material, a representative of the bank, a representative of the Sun Life Assurance *f* Society Ltd, the deceased's solicitor, Mr Townsend, and the deceased's son, Mr Whitfield. Mr Whitfield was armed with a power of attorney conferring on him an authority to carry out on behalf of the deceased the transactions which then took place. We shall make a further reference to that authority hereafter because it was a very limited power and that fact explains one feature of the transactions on which reliance was placed on behalf of the Crown.
g At the moment when the four parties gathered together at the bank and before anyone became bound in law to carry either of them into effect, two transactions were in contemplation. Pursuant to discussions which had taken place, it was contemplated that in consideration of four several sums of £20,000 to be paid to the assurance society by the deceased, the assurance society should issue to her four policies of life assurance each securing the payment of a principal sum on her death. It was to be *h* a term of each contract of assurance that the deceased should have no benefit thereunder but should from the outset hold the policy and all its benefits on trust for the beneficiary therein named. By this means it was thought that the sums which became payable on the death of the deceased, though liable to estate duty, would not be aggregable one with the other or with the rest of the deceased's estate in ascertaining the rate of duty payable on her death. We have referred to these contracts of assurance *j* as a single transaction—and it is convenient so to do—but there were in truth four transactions in contemplation between the deceased, always acting by her attorney, and the assurance society.

---

1   [1974] 3 All ER 802, [1975] Ch 290, [1974] STC 511
2   [1974] 3 All ER at 804, [1975] Ch at 293, [1974] STC at 513

To carry out the transaction with the assurance society the deceased required the sum of £80,000; and the second transaction which was in contemplation was a borrow- *a* ing from the bank by the deceased of £80,000 on the security of scrip which had been deposited with the bank as security for the contemplated loan. It is at this point that the terms of the power of attorney held by Mr Whitfield become relevant. That power was, as we have said, a limited power. It empowered Mr Whitfield to effect such policies of assurance as were in fact effected and although it was open to Mr Whitfield to effect them with some assurance society other than the Sun, it did *b* not extend to allow the attorney to effect policies other than policies of the character there specified for the benefit of the specified beneficiaries. It of necessity empowered the attorney to borrow 'for the purpose of paying the premiums on the said . . . policies and on such terms and either with or without security as he shall think fit'. If the bank was to act on the authority so conferred by its customer on Mr Whitfield and lend £80,000, it was essential for the bank to see that 'the sums of money which *c* he might think fit to borrow' were applied 'for the purpose of paying the premiums' on the policies which the attorney was empowered to effect. Had the bank failed to do so it would have been in breach of its duty to the deceased, its customer: see, for example, *London Chartered Bank of Australia v McMillan*[1]. The bank accordingly required that the money to be lent should be paid to the assurance society. We would add at this point that had the deceased herself been present it is probable *d* that the transactions would have taken place in precisely the way in which they did take place. A customer who has overdraft facilities with his bank naturally draws a cheque in favour of the payee to whom he wishes to make a payment and does not not first obtain mastery or dominion over the amount which he is permitted to overdraw.

A cheque was drawn by the attorney on a new no 2 account opened with the bank's *e* customer in favour of the assurance society. In order that the contemplated contract of assurance should thereupon become a binding contract, the representative of the assurance society thereupon presented the cheque which was credited to the bank's 'draft account' and received in return a banker's draft for £80,000. We accept that as from that moment, and not before, the debt to the bank was 'incurred'.

As between the bank and the deceased it appears to us that the transaction was a *f* normal banking transaction. The deceased incurred a liability to the bank to pay £80,000 in return for the bank paying to the assurance society by her order the sum of £80,000. Nothing whatsoever in the way of bounty passed from the bank to the payee of the deceased's cheque and we are unable to accept that the debt was incurred or that the consideration was otherwise than 'wholly for' the customer's 'own use and benefit'. A bank which complies with its customer's order to pay does not in *g* any ordinary sense do so 'for the use' or 'benefit' of the payee, although the payee will no doubt normally use and benefit from the payment. As between the bank and the customer nothing is withheld by the bank from the consideration which supports the debt. The argument to the contrary fails in our judgment to distinguish between the two transactions: the transaction by which the deceased borrowed the money and the transaction by which she paid it to the assurance society in return *h* for the promises contained in the policy of assurance. The assurance society was no party to the former transaction and the bank was no party to the contract of assurance. Nor was the bank in the least concerned with the latter contract except to see that the money lent to its customer was not dealt with otherwise than in accordance with her authority.

Finding nothing in s 7(1)(*a*) of the Finance Act 1894, which in terms introduces the *j* requirement that the consideration should have been received by the deceased or that he should have it under his personal control, we would decide this case on the short grounds which we have given. We must, however, deal with the submission

---

1   [1892] AC 292

to the contrary. It is based on the view that, in order to satisfy the condition of s 7(1)(a),
a the consideration for the debt which was incurred must at some point of time have
been received by the deceased in the sense that he had dominion over or was master
of it. Only if at some moment was the deceased master of the consideration, so the
argument on behalf of the Crown runs, can it be said to have been 'wholly for the
deceased's own use and benefit'.

Section 7(1) of the 1894 Act cannot be read out of context but falls to be construed
b by reference to the scheme and other sections of the Act. The Act introduced a new
tax or duty on the principal value of the property of a deceased passing on his death.
There was deemed to be included in the property so passing property 'taken under a
disposition made by the deceased not more than twelve months before the death of
the deceased': see the joint effect of s 38(2)(a) of the Customs and Inland Revenue
Act 1881, as amended by s 11 of the Customs and Inland Revenue Act 1889. We
c remark in parenthesis that it is not in question that the policies effected by the
deceased in the instant case were property 'taken under a disposition made by' the
deceased; and apart altogether from the fact that the contention of the Crown regarding the construction of para (a) of s 7(1) of the 1894 Act would, if well founded, involve in effect a double charge for duty, we find a difficulty in seeing how the disposition can have been 'made by' the deceased unless the consideration for the debt
d incurred by the deceased was 'wholly for the deceased's own use and benefit': for
you cannot make a disposition by way of gift of something of value if you are not
the beneficial owner. We say 'by way of gift' because s 3 of the 1894 Act exempted
from the duty property passing 'by reason only of a bona fide purchase from' the
deceased 'where such purchase was made . . . for full consideration in money or
money's worth paid to the vendor . . . for his own use or benefit . . .'

e Section 7(10) of the 1894 Act is also, we think, relevant to the construction of s 7(1)(a),
for it provided in terms that property passing on the death should not be aggregated
more than once, nor should estate duty in respect thereof be 'more than once levied
on the same death'. A construction of sub-s (1) of that section, which would disallow
a debt incurred for a consideration which became the subject of a disposition falling
within s 2(1)(c), would operate to impose duty on the deceased's investments as
f well as on the policies purchased out of the money raised on the security of those
investments and would in effect impose a double charge for duty. And so it would be
in the simple case of a gift made by the deceased in favour of a relative by cheque
drawn on overdraft, duty being payable on the amount of the gift and there being no
allowance of the debt to the bank thereby incurred. If s 7(1)(a) is fairly open to a
construction which will not have that result, that construction ought in our judg-
g ment to be adopted. We do not forget that the Crown in the instant case disclaimed
duty on the policies themselves preferring the higher rate of duty exigible on the
footing that the debt incurred in paying for them is not allowable.

Having provided by s 1 of the 1894 Act that estate duty should be payable on the
principal value of property passing or deemed to pass on the death of a deceased, it
was necessary to provide how that principal value was to be ascertained. In particular,
h in order to prevent absurdity, it was necessary to provide that the principal value
should be taken to be the net value after deduction of debts and incumbrances. Where
the deceased has incurred a debt for full consideration in money or money's worth,
the value of the deceased's property is increased by the amount of that money or
money's worth and unless the debt be allowed in computing the value of the estate
for the purposes of the duty, the borrowing will have operated to increase the amount
j of the duty. And so s 7(1) of the 1894 Act provided that in determining the value
of an estate 'allowance shall be made for . . . debts and incumbrances'.

If s 7(1) had stopped there, it would have provided a ready means of avoiding the
charge for duty by in effect making a gift to the creditor, e g by a covenant in a deed
to pay £100,000 to the creditor unsupported by any valuable consideration. In such
a case the dutiable value of the estate passing on the death will not have been increased

by the amount of the debt which has been incurred and para (*a*) of s 7(1) comes into
play to prevent the allowance of a debt unless it was incurred 'bona fide for full　*a*
consideration in money or money's worth wholly for the deceased's own use and
benefit'. Just as s 2(1)(*c*) brought into charge the value of property disposed of by way
of gift by the deceased within one year of his death, so s 7(1)(*a*) operates to disallow
in valuing the property passing on the death the deduction of a debt where there
was an element of gift in the incurring of the debt, or where the consideration or
part thereof is withheld by the creditor. That this is the purpose of s 7(1)(*a*) is shown　*b*
by the speech of Lord Atkinson in *Attorney-General v Duke of Richmond and Gordon*[1].
Calling attention to s 3 of the 1894 Act, providing that in order that the property
alienated or the interest created by the deceased may escape taxation when it passes
on his death full consideration in money or money's worth must have been paid
to him 'for his own use or benefit', and to the provisions of s 7(1), Lord Atkinson[2]
remarked.　　　　　　　　　　　　　　　　　　　　　　　　　　　　　　　　　*c*

　　'The aim and object of both provisions is apparently the same—first, to prevent
　evasion by fictitious sales or the creation of fictitious interests or incumbrances,
　or the acknowledgement of fictitious debts, and, second, to prevent the tax
　being in effect levied twice over on the same property.'

Lord Macnaghten in a passage in his speech in the *Duke of Richmond and Gordon* case[1],　*d*
to which we will refer later in this judgment, rejected a too literal approach to the
words 'wholly for the deceased's use and benefit', and in our judgment it is wrong
to subject them to a close and separate analysis without regard to the fact that they
appear in a much longer phrase and in the context of the other provisions of the
Act to which we have referred. The condition to be satisfied under para (*a*) of s 7(1)
is that the debt or incumbrance should have been incurred or created 'bona fide for　*e*
full consideration in money or money's worth wholly for the deceased's own use
and benefit . . .'; and in our judgment, reading those words in the context of the Act,
the condition is satisfied if the transaction whereunder the debt is incurred or the
incumbrance is created is a bona fide commercial transaction in which there is no
element of gift to or bounty in favour of the creditor. Putting it in another way, the
condition excludes from allowance a debt incurred or an incumbrance created by　*f*
the deceased operating by way of bounty to the creditor and for which the creditor
gave less than full consideration in money or money's worth. Gifts made otherwise
than by the creation of a debt or incumbrance for less than full consideration are
dealt with by s 2(1)(*c*) and, so construed, s 7(1)(*a*) becomes complementary to and
not a duplication of s 2(1)(*c*) and also, we must add, s 2(1)(*d*).
　If para (*a*) be so construed, the anomalies and difficulties which were discussed by　*g*
the judge in the court below and in argument before this court are, we think, avoided.
A 'guarantee debt' would not be of necessity excluded from allowance by the effect
of the paragraph.
　Whether the words 'wholly for the deceased's own use and benefit' in para (*a*)
refer back to the word 'incurred' or to the 'consideration', the use of the words
'debts incurred by the deceased, or incumbrances created by a disposition made by　*h*
the deceased' at the beginning of the paragraph shows in our judgment that in determining whether that paragraph is applicable in any particular case you must focus
attention on the relationship between the deceased and the creditor in whose favour
the debt was incurred; and we can see no necessity for introducing as a condition that
the deceased should have become master of or have had dominion over the consideration. No doubt, as Lord Macnaghten indicated in *Attorney-General v Duke of*　*j*
Richmond and Gordon[1], if you find that the deceased *did* become 'master' of the whole

1　[1909] AC 466 at 472, 473
2　[1909] AC at 479

consideration it would be conclusive that it was as between the deceased and the
a creditor 'wholly for the deceased's own use and benefit'; but it does not in our judgment follow that, because the deceased was not master of or did not handle the
consideration but directed its application, it was not for his use and benefit.
It is a commonplace of a commercial transaction operating to create a debt that the
debtor does not handle or become master of or have dominion over the consideration.
Whenever A at the request of B pays money to C on the terms that A will be reim-
b bursed by B, the debt and the consideration come into being simultaneously and B
never becomes master of the sum paid to C, the payment of which is the consideration
for the debt incurred.

Faced with the difficulty that a customer drawing a cheque in favour of a third
party on an overdrawn account never becomes master of the consideration for the
debt to the bank incurred when the cheque is honoured, counsel on behalf of the
c Crown sought to draw a distinction between the honouring of a cheque drawn in
favour of a volunteer and one drawn in favour of a creditor of the deceased. You
must, so the argument runs, examine the relationship between the deceased and
the payee of the cheque, and if you find that the customer obtained no benefit from
the payment because it operated neither to relieve him of an obligation nor to confer
a corresponding advantage on the customer—e g by a payment for goods to be
d delivered to the customer—the condition of para (a) will not be satisfied.

It is, however, conceded by the Crown that if for example the payment being a
payment of £x operates to discharge a liability of the customer to the payee for
that amount the debt thereby incurred to the bank will be allowable. We do not
see how this concession could be withheld without making nonsense of s 7(1)(a);
for unless it be made, no part of a debt to a bank on overdraft account would be
e allowable unless it be represented by a cash payment to the customer himself. But
the concession that on the true construction of para (a) a debt to a bank on overdraft
account incurred on the honouring of a cheque drawn in favour of the deceased's
creditor is allowable is in our judgment destructive of the Crown's contention that
the deceased must have been master of the consideration for the debt in order to
satisfy the requirements of the paragraph. We would accordingly for that reason
f alone reject the submission, which was accepted by the learned judge in the court
below, that in order to satisfy the words 'wholly for the deceased's own use and benefit' the deceased must have become master of or had dominion over or had in his
hands the consideration for the debt.

It is to be emphasised that if the submissions of the Crown on the construction of
s 7(1)(a) were well founded, the effect would be, as we have already indicated, to
g deny the allowance in just those cases where the amount borrowed was paid directly
to a donee and where s 2(1)(c) comes into play to tax the payment itself and so to
introduce the double claim for duty which s 7(10) forbids. Such a construction
ought in our judgment to be rejected if the words used are fairly open to another
construction. It is to be observed in this connection that the Crown is in the instant
case having resort to para (a) in order to defeat the relief from aggregation of the
h policies accorded by s 4 of the 1894 Act to 'property in which the deceased never
had an interest'.

In the court below attention was called to one particular anomaly which would
arise if the Crown's submissions were accepted. If in the instant case the deceased
had authorised the attorney to draw the required £80,000 in cash and to carry out
the transaction by handing it to the assurance society, and the attorney, or she her-
j self for that matter, had for a period, however short, had dominion over the cash, it
would not have mattered that the purpose for which the money was borrowed was
to make a gift. The deceased would have had the money 'wholly for her own use
and benefit'. Or let it be supposed that a loan account had been opened for £80,000
and the deceased's current account credited with that sum. She would have been
mistress of the £80,000 and so would have incurred the debt on the current account

for full consideration in money or money's worth 'wholly for her own use and benefit'. Walton J[1], facing these anomalies, dealt with them by pointing out, in effect, that *a* the machinery by which a transaction is carried out may, and indeed often does, affect the liability to taxation. That of course is so. But if nevertheless startling anomalies do arise on one construction of a section of an Act of Parliament, then if that section is fairly open to another construction it is in our judgment a strong reason for preferring that other construction. In the instant case a further anomaly arises in that had the attorney entered into a binding contract with the assurance *b* society to effect the insurances and to pay the £80,000 forthwith, and had he done so at any time prior to the honouring of the cheque, the payment, because it would have operated to relieve the deceased of the liability to pay £80,000, would, if we understand the submissions and concession of the Crown, have created an allowable debt.

If in relation to a debt due to a bank on overdraft the Crown had during the years *c* following 1894 adopted the construction of s 7(1)(a) now contended for, the practice would, as we see it, have been attended with great administrative inconvenience and would have introduced difficult questions of law. So construed, the provisions of the paragraph become an indirect means of imposing duty on gifts whenever made and of an amount however small made by cheque drawn on an overdraft account. It would, accordingly, as we see it, have been the duty of the commissioners *d* to consider each debit in the account and prima facie to disallow at least so much of the debts as at the date of the death represented cheques honoured by the bank from the payment of which the deceased did not receive the proceeds or the equivalent of the proceeds. The implications of this in relation to other provisions of the Act were not, we think, explored in argument. It is, however, to be observed, for example, that there is nothing in s 7(1)(a) to exclude from its operation debts incurred *e* in purchasing small annuities (cf s 15(1)) or pictures, etc of national or scientific or historical interest given or bequeathed for national purposes, or to any university (cf s 15(2)). So if it was found that a small annuity purchased from an insurance company which would otherwise be exempt from duty under s 15(1) had been paid for by a cheque drawn on the overdraft account, the cost of the annuity would in effect be subjected to the duty by a sidewind. And so it would be if a cheque had *f* been drawn in favour of a university on the terms that the money should be applied in aquiring an article of scientific interest for the university. These situations and those which would arise when there had been payments into and out of the overdraft account between the date of the payment in question and the date of the death were, as we have said, not explored in the course of the debate.

The construction favoured by the Crown would produce a further and, as we *g* think, a preposterous result. Walton J[1] remarked that if a receiver borrowed for the purposes of his receivership—and this would apply equally to a borrowing by a trustee for the purposes of his trust—it could not be said that the money so raised was in any sense for his own use and benefit. If the approach of the Crown to the construction of s 7(1) was a correct approach, we would accept that on the death of the receiver or trustee the debt, so far as irrecoverable from the trust estate, would *h* nevertheless not be allowable. We would also accept that although such a case might be a hard case it would not be open to the court to bend the construction of the section to fit it. But we are not prepared to impute to the legislature an intention to produce so prepostereous a situation, and if the section is fairly open to another construction we would adopt it.

We said earlier in this judgment that we find nothing in para (a) of s 7(1) of the 1894 *j* Act which in terms introduces the requirement that the consideration in money or money's worth should have been received by the deceased or that he should for some instant have been master of it. And for all the reasons we have indicated we

---

1   [1974] 3 All ER at 809, [1975] Ch at 299, [1974] STC at 518

would not imply such a requirement. The paragraph is in our judgment concerned
a with the relationship between the creditor and the deceased at the time the debt
sought to be allowed was incurred; and determining whether the debt was incurred
for 'full consideration . . . wholly for the deceased's own use and benefit' you are
not concerned with what the deceased did with the consideration or how he directed
the creditor to deal with it. Finding that the debt was incurred for full consideration
in money paid by the creditor, the consideration was in our judgment as much for
b the deceased's own use and benefit whether it was paid to him and then passed on
to a third person, or as here passed to that third person by his order or by his direction.
The paragraph is not in our judgment concerned with the relationship between
the deceased who borrowed and some third person to whom the money borrowed
was paid but with the relationship between the deceased and the creditor.

We are fortified in our conclusions that it matters not that the beneficiaries of
c the policies derived a benefit from the payment of £80,000 which the deceased
directed her bank to make, by the speech of Lord Macnaghten in *Attorney-General v
Duke of Richmond and Gordon*[1]. In answer to the question, were the debts and incumbrances incurred and created 'wholly for the deceased's own use and benefit'?
Lord Macnaghten[1] remarked to the effect that it was perfectly true in the result
that they were mainly if not wholly for the benefit of the deceased's successors:
d

'If you give the expression its strict meaning, adhering slavishly to the letter,
no allowance can be made for any debt incurred by the deceased or any incumbrance created by him which in the slightest degree operates for the benefit of any
other human being. The argument must go this length. The word "wholly"
forbids anything short of it. The condition that a debt or incumbrance or the
e consideration for such debt or incumbrance (if that be the true reading) must
be wholly for the benefit of a particular individual excludes every case where
anybody else participates in the benefit. If the construction for which the appellant contended be right, a man who burdens his property to portion his daughter,
to educate or advance his son, to save a friend from ruin, to effect some lasting
improvements on his estate which cannot give an immediate return, or to pro-
f mote some benevolent object or some object of real or supposed public utility,
to endow a hospital, for instance, or save a famous picture for his country, cannot
hope for an allowance from the Commissioners of Inland Revenue. That concession is reserved for the man who spends on himself alone, for the prodigal,
the gambler, and such like. I cannot bring myself to think that the Legislature
deliberately intended to put a premium on extravagance purely selfish, and
g to penalize expenditure on objects generally considered more worthy.'

Applying those last words to the situation where the money is borrowed from a
bank, we cannot bring ourselves to think that the legislature deliberately intended
to differentiate between a borrowing of cash from a bank and immediately using
the cash in making a gift and a borrowing from the bank made in the more usual
h way by directing payment to the intending donee.

To escape the absurdity to which he had drawn attention, Lord Macnaghten[1]
found that the words of the expression were satisfied—

'If the direct and immediate purpose of the person incurring the debt, or
creating the incumbrance, is to make himself master of a sum of money over
j which he, and he alone, has power of disposition; and that it was not intended
that there should be any inquiry into the ulterior and more remote purposes
of the transaction or any investigation into motives.'

---

1 [1909] AC at 472, 473

Read in the context of what had gone before, we take Lord Macnaghten to have been
saying there that what you are concerned to ascertain is whether *as between the creditor* **a**
and the deceased the debt was incurred or the incumbrance created 'or the consideration
for such debt or incumbrance (if that be the true reading)' was wholly for the benefit
of the deceased and that you are not concerned with the destination of the money
borrowed or the relationship between the deceased borrower and a third party
for whom he may hold the consideration as a trustee.

The learned judge[1] in the court below fastened we think on the words 'master **b**
of a sum of money' in the passage in Lord Macnaghten's speech which we have
quoted and concluded that the conditions of s 7(1)(a) are not satisfied unless the deceased 'received [the consideration] in such a way that, however temporarily, he or
she was full master thereof'. But Lord Macnaghten was not redrafting s 7(1)(a) and
we find nothing in the speech to indicate that Lord Macnaghten, when he spoke of
the deceased making himself master of a sum of money over which he alone had **c**
power of disposition, was laying down a test for determining whether the condition
was satisfied or insisting that the deceased should have received the money. If a
man draws a cheque on overdraft in favour of an insurance company in payment
of the premium on a policy of insurance, he is neither more nor less the master of
the money according to whether the policy is effected for his own benefit or for the
benefit of another; and whatever his purpose be in paying the money to the insurance **d**
company, he and not the bank is in our judgment disposing of it in the sense in which
Lord Macnaghten spoke.

We turn to consider the point which was accepted by the learned judge in the court
below as an additional reason for holding that the contention of the Crown was
well founded. What is said is that as between the deceased and the bank it was a
condition of the lending that the money should be applied in effecting the policies **e**
in which the deceased was to have no beneficial interest. And it is said that this
being so the advance cannot be said to have been made wholly, if at all, for the
deceased's own use and benefit. We think this confuses the purpose of the borrowing
with the consideration. Nor can we accept that as between the deceased and the
bank it was a condition of the loan that the money should be applied in effecting
the policies. The cheque was not drawn by the deceased but by her attorney and **f**
of course the bank could not honour the cheque unless satisfied that the attorney
had the deceased's authority to draw it. The authority on which the attorney relied
and which was of necessity produced to the bank was a limited authority. And,
in fact, the bank, in their letter of 15th November 1963, imposed four conditions,
namely: (1) that the power of attorney should appear to be in order, (2) that the
certificates of the stock exchange investments be brought in and instructions given **g**
for sale through the bank, (3) that there be a good report on Mr Townsend, which
'we now have', and (4) that the cheques in question be payable to the Sun Life
Assurance. As we read these conditions, they were administrative requirements
for the protection of the bank and were not introduced in order to confer some benefit
on the beneficiaries of the policies which the bank wished to confer. We would accept
the statement in the affidavit of Miss Tomlinson, the bank inspector, that the use of **h**
the word 'condition' was perhaps an unfortunate one as it merely recorded the
arrangement which had been made at the request of the borrower. We would add in
relation to the 'condition' relied on that in the affidavit filed in support of the originating summons it was said that it was 'not an essential part of the plaintiff's case that
such a condition should have been imposed' and we did not understand the argument
before us as being dependent on it. **j**

But whatever 'conditions' were imposed one must in our judgment look at what
was in fact done. As between the creditor bank and the deceased the transaction was
a common place and bona fide commercial transaction involving no element of

---

1 [1974] 3 All ER at 810, [1975] Ch at 301, [1974] STC at 519

a   bounty or gift to the creditor and so did not in our judgment fall within para (*a*) of s 7(1). The deceased had the use of the money just as much as if she had withdrawn it and paid it to the assurance society.

We find nothing in any of the cases cited which constrains us to hold that a commercial transaction such as is here in question does not satisfy the requirements of para (*a*) of s 7(1) of the 1894 Act.

The appeal is allowed.

b

Appeal allowed. Leave to appeal to the House of Lords refused.

Solicitors: *Archer, Parker & Townsend*, Stockton-on-Tees (for the executors); *Solicitor of Inland Revenue.*

c   L I Zysman Esq   Barrister.

Wilson, Smithett & Cope Ltd v Terruzzi

d

COURT OF APPEAL, CIVIL DIVISION

LORD DENNING MR, ORMROD AND SHAW LJJ

1st, 2nd, 3rd, 4th DECEMBER 1975, 20th JANUARY 1976

e   *Currency – Control – Foreign exchange control – Bretton Woods Agreements – Exchange contracts – Enforceability – Exchange contracts involving currency of member of International Monetary Fund and contrary to exchange control regulations of that member – Meaning of 'exchange contracts' – Contract for sale of goods – Plaintiffs English brokers dealing in metals – Defendant resident in Italy – Defendant buying and selling metals through agency of plaintiffs – Contracts involving currency of Italy and contrary to Italian exchange control regulations – Whether 'exchange contracts' and therefore unenforceable in England – Bretton*

f   *Woods Agreements Order in Council 1946 (SR & O 1946 No 36), Sch, Part I, art VIII, s 2(b).*

The plaintiffs were members of the London Metal Exchange ('the LME') carrying on business as dealers and brokers in metals. The defendant, who was resident in Italy, was a dealer in a large way of business in Milan. In 1972 the plaintiffs appointed G as their agent in Milan with a view to introducing customers from Italy who also wished to deal on the LME through the plaintiffs. In January 1973 G introduced the defendant

g   to the plaintiffs and they began to deal for him on his instructions. During 1975 the defendant speculated through the plaintiffs on the LME in zinc and copper. The transactions were, however, carried out by the defendant in breach of the Italian exchange control regulations. In October 1973 the forward price of zinc (i e for three months' delivery) was about £470 per ton. Between 18th October and 7th November

h   the defendant went 'short' by giving instructions to sell a total of 1,200 tons of zinc when the price had risen to £520 per ton. He expected the price to fall back to normal levels but it did not. By the middle of November the defendant's balance of account with the plaintiffs had reached a debit of about £195,000. On 12th November the plaintiffs requested the defendant to provide a 'margin' of £50,000 as, under their contract with the defendant, they were entitled to do. The defendant refused to pay

j   any money by way of margin or otherwise. On 14th November the plaintiffs proceeded to close out the defendant's open contracts as they were entitled to do in the event of his failing to comply with his undertakings under the contract, and subsequently brought an action against him claiming the debit balance of £195,022. The defendant contended that the open contracts, having been concluded without the necessary permission of the Italian exchange control authorities, were unenforceable

GG

in English law by virtue of art VIII, s 2(b)^a, of the Bretton Woods Fund Agreement
for the establishment of the International Monetary Fund, as incorporated in the   **a**
Bretton Woods Agreements Order in Council 1946, since they were 'Exchange
contracts which involve the currency of [a] Member [of the International Monetary
Fund] and are contrary to the exchange control regulations of that member'.

Held–The words 'exchange contracts' in art VIII, s 2(b), meant contracts to exchange the
currency of one country for the currency of another and could not be construed as   **b**
including all contracts which in any way affected a country's exchange resources. The
contracts between the plaintiffs and the defendant were legitimate contracts for the
sale and purchase of metals and were not monetary transactions in disguise. It
followed that they were not 'exchange contracts' and therefore were enforceable
against the defendant in England (see p 822 j to p 823 c, p 826 g to j, p 829 f to h and
p 832 e and f, post).   **c**
    Dictum of Lord Radcliffe in *Re United Railways of the Havana and Regla Warehouses
Ltd* [1960] 2 All ER at 350 applied.
    Dictum of Lord Denning MR in *Sharif v Azad* [1966] 3 All ER at 787 disapproved.
    Decision of Kerr J [1975] 2 All ER 649 affirmed.

Note   **d**
For the Bretton Woods Agreements, see 27 Halsbury's Laws (3rd Edn) 105, 106,
para 178.

Cases referred to in judgments
Banco do Brasil SA v AC Israel Commodity Co Inc (1963) 12 NY 2d 371.
Bassett v Sanker (1925) 41 TLR 660.   **e**
Clearing Dollars Case (1955) 22 ILR 730.
de Boer (Anna), Re [1961] Journal du Droit International 721.
Emek v Bossers & Mouthaan (1955) 22 ILR 722.
Garnac Grain Co Inc v HMF Faure & Fairclough Ltd and Bunge Corpn [1965] 3 All ER 273,
    [1966] 1 QB 650, [1965] 3 WLR 934, [1965] 2 Lloyd's Rep 229, CA, Digest (Cont Vol
    B) 12, 2725a.   **f**
Ironmonger & Co v Dyne (1928) 44 TLR 497, CA, 25 Digest (Repl) 418, 19.
Lessinger v Mirau (1955) 22 ILR 725.
Sharif v Azad [1966] 3 All ER 785, [1967] 1 QB 605, [1966] 3 WLR 1285, CA, 17 Digest
    (Reissue) 512, 213.
United Railways of the Havana and Regla Warehouses Ltd, Re [1960] 2 All ER 332, sub nom
    Tomkinson v First Pennsylvania Banking and Trust Co [1961] AC 1007, [1960] 2 WLR 969,   **g**
    HL, 11 Digest (Reissue) 489, 919.
Weddle, Beck & Co v Hackett [1929] 1 KB 321, [1928] All ER Rep 539, 98 LJKB 243, 140
    LT 303, 44 Digest (Repl) 325, 103.
Woodward v Wolfe [1936] 3 All ER 529, 155 LT 619, 1 Digest (Repl) 325, 116.

Case also cited   **h**
Harris v Knight (1890) 15 PD 170, CA.

Appeal
This was an appeal by the defendant, Angelo Guido Terruzzi (trading as Terruzzi
Metalli), against the judgment of Kerr J[1] given on 31st January 1975 whereby he
held that contracts made during October and November 1973 between the plaintiffs,   **j**
Wilson, Smithett & Cope Ltd, dealers on the London Metal Exchange, and the
defendant, a dealer in metal in Milan, Italy, were not 'exchange contracts' within the

---

a   Section 2, so far as is material, is set out at p 820 j to p 821 a, post
1   [1975] 2 All ER 649, [1975] 2 WLR 1009

a   meaning of art VIII, s 2(b), of the Bretton Woods Fund Agreement for the establishment of the International Monetary Fund incorporated in the Bretton Woods Agreements Order in Council 1946 and therefore were enforceable against the defendant and
that accordingly the plaintiffs were entitled to recover against the defendant the sum
of £195,022·01 due from the defendant to the plaintiffs under the contracts. By a
respondent's notice the plaintiffs gave notice that on the hearing of the appeal they
would seek to support the order of Kerr J on the following additional grounds: (i) that
b   the judge should have held that the exchange control regulations contained in
Italian Decree-Law No 476 of 6th June 1956 had not been 'imposed and maintained
consistently' with the Bretton Woods Agreement, within the meaning of art VIII,
s 2(b), and (ii) that the judge should have found that the contracts did not 'involve'
Italian currency within the meaning of art VIII, s 2(b), and that for those further
reasons the Bretton Woods Agreements Act 1945 did not apply to the contracts
c   between the plaintiffs and the defendant. The facts are set out in the judgment of
Lord Denning MR.

Andrew J Bateson QC and *Michael Tugendhat* for the defendant.
Robert Alexander QC and *Peregrine Simon* for the plaintiffs.

d   *Cur adv vult*

20th January. The following judgments were read.

LORD DENNING MR. Signor Terruzzi lives in Milan. He is a dealer in metals,
trading under the name Terruzzi Metalli. But he is also, it seems, a gambler in dif-
e   ferences. He speculates on the rise or fall in the price of zinc, copper and so forth. He
speculated in 1973 on the London Metal Exchange. He did so in plain breach of the
Italian laws of exchange control. These provide that residents in Italy are not to come
under obligations to non-residents save with ministerial authority. Signor Terruzzi
never obtained permission.
    In making his speculations, Signor Terruzzi established an account with London
f   dealers, Wilson, Smithett & Cope Ltd. He was introduced to them by their Milan
agent, Signor Giuliani, and made his deals through him. All the transactions were in
sterling and reduced into writing on the standard contract forms of the London Metal
Exchange. Sometimes Signor Terruzzi was a 'bull'. That is, he thought that the price
was likely to rise in the near future. So he bought metal from the London dealers at a
low price for delivery three months ahead, not meaning ever to take delivery of it,
g   but intending to sell it back to the London dealers at a higher price before the delivery
date, thus showing him a profit in his account with the London dealers. At other
times he was a 'bear'. That is, he thought that the price was likely to fall in the near
future. So he sold metal 'short' (which he had not got) to the London dealers at a high
price for delivery three months ahead, not meaning ever to deliver it, but intending to
buy back from the London dealers a like quantity at a lower price before the delivery
h   date, thus showing him a profit in his account with the London dealers. Such transactions would have been gaming contracts if *both* parties had never intended to make
or accept delivery, and they would not have been enforced by the English courts.
But the London dealers were not parties to any such intention. They always intended
to make or accept delivery according to the contracts they made. So far as the London
dealers were concerned, they were genuine commercial transactions. They were
j   enforceable accordingly by the English courts: see *Bassett v Sanker*[1] (London Metal
Exchange), *Weddle, Beck & Co v Hackett*[2] (London Stock Exchange), *Woodward v Wolfe*[3]

---

1   (1925) 41 TLR 660
2   [1929] 1 KB 321, [1928] All ER Rep 539
3   [1936] 3 All ER 529

(Liverpool Cotton Exchange), *Garnac Grain Co Inc v HMF Faure & Fairclough Ltd and Bunge Corpn*[1] (contracts for lard). But they were not enforceable in the Italian *a* courts because they infringed the exchange control.
The critical months here were October and November 1973. The price of zinc was very high. The price for 'forward' delivery (that is for delivery three months ahead) had been steadily rising from £465 on 18th October 1973 to £520 on 7th November. Signor Terruzzi thought that the price was much too high and that it was likely to fall soon. So he made a series of contracts with the London dealers whereby he sold to *b* them 1,200 tons of zinc for delivery in the next three months. He sold 'short', that is he had then no zinc to meet his obligations. Unfortunately for Signor Terruzzi, his forecast was wrong. Even after 7th November the price did not fall. It rose steeply. So much so that within a week it had risen to £650 a ton. By 12th November 1973 the London dealers were anxious as to the ability of Signor Terruzzi to meet his commitments. They asked him to provide a deposit or 'margin' of £50,000, as they *c* were entitled to do under the contracts. On the evening of Tuesday, 13th November, Signor Giuliani, on behalf of the London dealers, met Signor Terruzzi at the Café Ricci in Milan. He told him the state of the account. Signor Terruzzi flamed with anger. He said that he was not going to pay anything to the London dealers by way of margin, or otherwise, and they could take him to court. Signor Giuliani telephoned the London dealers. They were fearful that the price might go still higher. There were *d* frantic telexes. In the result the London dealers 'closed' the contracts with him, as they were entitled to do under the written terms thereof. They sold back to him 1,200 tons of zinc at the ruling price. They telexed him with details. The result showed a balance due to the London dealers amounting to £220,440·38; and credit due to him on previous profits of £25,418·37. So on balance the sum of £195,022·01 was due from him to them. On 10th January 1974 they issued a writ against him for *e* that amount in the High Court in England. He got leave to defend by swearing, quite untruly, that the transactions had been carried out without his knowledge or authority. Afterwards he took a different line. He said that the London dealers had failed to advise him properly about the transactions. The trial opened on 9th October 1974. He came to London for the first day. He went back to Italy for the weekend. He had a heart attack there. He never returned to the trial. All his defences crumbled. *f* So did his counterclaim. The only point which remained was that the contracts were 'exchange contracts' and were unenforceable against him by reason of the Bretton Woods Agreements. Kerr J decided this against him[2]. Signor Terruzzi appeals to this court.
Now for the Bretton Woods Agreements. Bretton Woods is a small town in New Hampshire, USA, but it has a place in history. During the Second World War, even in *g* the midst of raging hostilities, there was a conference there attended by the members of the United Nations. The object was to organise their monetary systems so as to meet the post-war problems. At this conference the United Kingdom was represented by the distinguished economist, Lord Keynes, and by the legal adviser to the Foreign Office, Sir Eric Beckett. In July 1944 articles of agreement were drawn up and signed. By the agreement the International Monetary Fund was established and provisions *h* were made (amongst other things) 'to promote international monetary co-operation' and 'to promote exchange stability'.
In 1945 Parliament passed an Act[3] to give effect to the agreement. In January 1946 an order in council, the Bretton Woods Agreements Order in Council 1946, was made giving the force of law to this provision, among others:

> '*Article VIII, Section 2(b)*. Exchange contracts which involve the currency of any *j*
> Member and which are contrary to the exchange control regulations of that

---

1   [1965] 3 All ER 273, [1966] 1 QB 650
2   [1975] 2 All ER 649, [1975] 2 WLR 1009
3   Bretton Woods Agreements Act 1945

member maintained or imposed consistently with this Agreement shall be unenforceable in the territories of any member . . .'

That provision is part of the law of England, but it has given rise to much controversy, particularly as to the meaning of the words 'exchange contracts'. There are two rival views. First, the view of Professor Nussbaum set out in 1949 in the Yale Law Journal[1]. He said that 'an exchange contract' is exclusively concerned with the handling of international media of payment as such. Therefore, contracts involving securities or merchandise cannot be considered as exchange contracts except when they are monetary transactions in disguise. This view is in accord with the meaning given by Lord Radcliffe in Re United Railways of the Havana and Regla Warehouses Ltd[2]:

'. . . a true exchange contract . . . is a contract to exchange the currency of one country for the currency of another . . .'

Second, the view of Dr F A Mann set out in 1949 in the British Year Book of International Law[3] and in his book, The Legal Aspect of Money[4]. He said that 'exchange contracts' are contracts which in any way affect a country's exchange resources—a phrase which I accepted without question in Sharif v Azad[5], in the belief that, coming from such a source, it must be right. Dr Mann recognises that his view makes the word 'exchange' redundant and thus seems counter to established methods of interpretation. But he contends that it is in better harmony with the purpose of the agreements.

Dr Mann suggests that the lawyers did not take much part in drafting the Bretton Woods Agreements. In this he is mistaken. I trust that I may be forgiven a digression if I borrow from the argument of counsel for the plaintiffs and recite part of the speech which Lord Keynes made at the Final Act[6] of the conference (as recorded by Sir Roy Harrod in his biography[7] of Keynes):

'And, for my own part, I should like to pay a particular tribute to our lawyers. All the more so because I have to confess that, generally speaking, I do not like lawyers. I have been known to complain that, to judge from results in this lawyer-ridden land, the *Mayflower*, when she sailed from Plymouth, must have been entirely filled with lawyers. When I first visited Mr. Morgenthau in Washington some three years ago accompanied only by my secretary, the boys in your Treasury curiously enquired of him—where is your lawyer? When it was explained that I had none,—"Who then does your thinking for you?" was the rejoinder . . . only too often [our lawyers] have had to do our thinking for us. We owe a great deal of gratitude to Dean Acheson, Oscar Cox, Luxford, Brenner, Collado, Arnold, Chang, Broches and our own Beckett of the British Delegation.'

So the lawyers did play a large part. I have no doubt that they had in mind an evil which was very much in evidence in the years after the First World War. It is strikingly illustrated by the notorious case of *Ironmonger & Co v Dyne*[8] in which a lady, Mrs Bradley Dyne, speculated in foreign currency. She did it at the instance of prominent officials in the Foreign Office. She dealt with bankers in Throgmorton Street. She used to buy from the bankers French francs and Italian lire for delivery three months

1   59 YLJ 421 at 426, 427
2   [1960] 2 All ER 332 at 350, [1961] AC 1007 at 1059
3   29 BYBIL 259 at 279
4   3rd Edn (1971), p 441
5   [1966] 3 All ER 785 at 787, [1967] 1 QB 605 at 613
6   Final Act of the United Nations Monetary and Financial Conference, Annex A, (1944) Cmd 6546
7   R F Harrod, Life of John Maynard Keynes (1951), p 583
8   (1928) 44 TLR 497

in the future; but, before the time for delivery arrived, she sold them again. If the price went up, she took the difference as a 'profit'. If the price went down, she was *a* liable to pay the difference as a 'loss'. In no single case was any currency delivered. She operated on an enormous scale. In three years the turnover amounted to 421 million francs and 17 million lire, and large sums in other currencies as well. At the end she was much in debt to the bankers for her 'losses'. They sued her for it. She pleaded the Gaming Act. Her plea failed because, so far as the bankers were concerned, they were genuine transactions which created obligations to fulfil the contracts *b* according to their tenor if circumstances required it. She was held liable. The British government declared that the transactions were a disgrace to the Civil Service and punished the Foreign Office officials who had engaged in them. But the case is important for present purposes because it shows the great mischief which can be done by such speculations. Scrutton LJ[1] described it in these words:

c

'The transactions in question were not of a pleasant nature. After the War, while Europe was recovering from the various upheavals which were the result of it, the value of currency fluctuated extremely. Contracts for the purchase or sale of currency, which, before the War had been a comparatively sober business, became very speculative in their making and their result. It was possible to make very large profits and equally possible to make very great losses, and, as was to be *d* expected when great profits might be made, the birds of prey gathered together. Reckless speculators, absolutely indifferent to the damage that they were doing to the country in the currency of which they were dealing, began operations. People bought and sold currency to a very large extent, with the most disastrous results to the countries concerned. That was particularly the case with regard to the sales and purchases of French currency, which went near to bringing that *e* country to ruin. People who indulged in those speculations were beneath contempt and ought to be condemned. They were utterly selfish, and had no regard at all to the enormous injury which they were inflicting on the legitimate trade of the country in whose exchange they were speculating.'

The mischief being thus exposed, it seems to me that the participants at Bretton *f* Woods inserted art VIII, s 2(b), in the agreement so as to stop it. They determined to make exchange contracts of that kind—for the exchange of currencies—unenforceable in the territories of any member. I do not know of any similar mischief in regard to other contracts, that is contracts for the sale or purchase of merchandise or commodities. Businessmen have to encounter fluctuations in the price of goods, but this is altogether different from the fluctuations in exchange rates. So far from there *g* being any mischief, it seems to me that it is in the interest of international trade that there should be no restriction on contracts for the sale and purchase of merchandise and commodities; and that they should be enforceable in the territories of the members.

The Bretton Woods Agreements make provision to that end. Thus art 1(ii) says that one of the purposes of the International Monetary Fund is to 'facilitate the *h* expansion and balanced growth of international trade . . .' Article VI, s 3, and art VIII, s 2(a), coupled with art XIX (i), say that no member is to impose restrictions on payments due 'in connection with foreign trade, other current business, including services, and normal short-term banking and credit facilities'.

In conformity with those provisions, I would hold that the Bretton Woods Agreements should not do anything to hinder legitimate contracts for the sale or purchase *i* of merchandise or commodities. The words 'exchange contracts' in art VIII, s 2(b), refer only to contracts to exchange the currency of one country for the currency of another. The words 'which involve the currency of any member' fit in well with this

1 (1928) 44 TLR at 498

meaning, but it is difficult to give them any sensible meaning in regard to other contracts. They show that the section is only dealing with the currencies of members of the fund, and not with the currencies of non-members. The reference to regulations 'maintained or enforced consistently with this agreement', covers such regulations as those of Italy here.

It is no doubt possible for men of business to seek to avoid art VIII, s 2(*b*), by various artifices. But I hope that the courts will be able to look at the substance of the contracts and not at the form. If the contracts are not legitimate contracts for the sale or purchase of merchandise or commodities, but are instead what Professor Nussbaum[1] calls 'monetary transactions in disguise', as a means of manipulating currencies, they would be caught by s 2(*b*).

I will not say more save to express my appreciation of the judgment of Kerr J[2]. He has covered the whole subject most satisfactorily. In my opinion the contracts here were legitimate contracts for the sale and purchase of metals. They were not 'exchange contracts'. The London dealers are entitled to enforce them in this country. I would dismiss the appeal accordingly.

ORMROD LJ. It is common ground that the contracts sued on by the plaintiffs in this case are to be treated as ordinary contracts for the sale and purchase of goods; in this case of quantities of metallic zinc and copper. The question to be asked, therefore, is, 'Is the seller who has sold and delivered the contract quantities to the buyer prevented from recovering the price thereof by reason of the provision of art VIII, s 2(*b*), of the Bretton Woods Agreements which has been incorporated into English law by the Bretton Woods Agreements Order 1946?' Delivery must be assumed because, on 14th November 1973, the plaintiffs, who are brokers on the London Metal Exchange, 'closed out' the defendant's 'open position', as they were entitled to do under the terms of their contracts with the defendant. As I understand it, that means that the plaintiffs, in effect, sold to the defendant on 14th November 1973 sufficient quantities of zinc to enable him to meet his forward commitments in zinc as and when they fell due in January or February 1974, that is to enable him to sell and deliver on the due dates the requisite amounts of zinc to his buyers.

By the Bretton Woods Agreements Order in Council 1946 the following verbatim extract from art VIII, s 2(*b*), of the International Monetary Fund Agreement 1945 has the force of law in England:

'Exchange contracts which involve the currency of any Member and which are contrary to the exchange control regulations of that member maintained or imposed consistently with this Agreement shall be unenforceable in the territories of any member...'

Three questions arise for decision. (i) Were the contracts in question 'exchange contracts' within the meaning of the order? (ii) Did these contracts 'involve the currency of any member state'? (iii) It being admitted that these contracts were contrary to the Italian exchange control regulations and that the defendant, under Italian law, was subject to these regulations, were these regulations maintained or imposed 'consistently with' the IMF Agreement?

The answer to the first question depends on the construction of the two words 'exchange contracts' in the order in council. Strictly speaking, it is for this court to construe these words as they appear in the order. The order itself, however, is so brief that it affords no assistance, and it is common ground that we must look to the terms of the IMF agreement itself for such help as can be extracted from it, and to any authority which bears on the matter.

1 (1949) 59 YLJ at 427
2 [1975] 2 All ER 649, [1975] 2 WLR 1009

The phrase 'exchange contracts' has no recognised or established usage in English law or practice—at least we have been referred to none. Nor, apparently, has the corresponding phrase in other languages any generally accepted meaning, judging by the various decisions of foreign courts, which counsel for the defendant has helpfully put before us, and the views of experienced commentators, all of whom regard the meaning of the phrase as obscure.

Its primary meaning must be contracts concerned with exchange, that is, of currency. It was used in this sense by Lord Radcliffe in his speech in Re United Railways of the Havana and Regla Warehouses Ltd[1]. In a wholly different context, he used it to mean 'a contract to exchange the currency of one country for the currency of another'.

In the only other reported English case, Sharif v Azad[2], Lord Denning MR[3] said that it meant 'any contracts which in any way affect the country's exchange resources', and Diplock LJ[4] said that the phrase 'should be liberally construed having regard to the objects of the Bretton Woods Agreement to protect the currencies of the states who are parties thereto . . .' In that case, this court was concerned with contracts which, quite clearly, were 'exchange contracts' in the sense in which the phrase was used by Lord Radcliffe[1], and it was unnecessary to consider whether or not the phrase might have a wider meaning.

The next question, therefore, is whether there is any indication in the IMF agreement itself that the phrase was not used in its primary sense. In my judgment, as a pure matter of construction the indications are all the other way. The word 'exchange' appears frequently in other articles of the agreement, in all of which it is plainly used in its ordinary meaning, that is, an exchange of one currency for another currency. This appears, perhaps most clearly, in art IV, s 3, where the phrase is 'exchange transactions between the currencies of members'.

Is there then any reason to be found in art VIII itself which indicates that in that article the word 'exchange' is used in a special sense or that the phrase 'exchange contracts' is not used in its primary sense? Again, the answer appears to me to be to the contrary. Article VIII is headed 'General Obligations of Members' and contains a number of quite separate obligations, each section dealing with a different subject matter. Section 2, which is the material part of the article for present purposes, consists of two sub-paragraphs under the common heading 'Avoidance of restrictions on current payments'. It is to be contrasted with art VI, s 3, which deals with the control of capital transfers. By the latter provision, members are free to exercise such controls over capital movements as may be necessary so long as these controls do not restrict payments for current transactions or unduly delay transfers of funds in settlement of commitments, except in the emergency situations dealt with in arts VII and XIV. Under art VIII, s 2(a), no member without the approval of the Fund is to impose restrictions on making payments and transfers for current international transactions. Article XIX (i) makes clear that this phrase includes 'All payments due in connection with foreign trade, and other current business [etc]', and again emphasises the contrast with capital transfers. This is a clear indication to my mind that the policy underlying the IMF Agreement is to control capital transfers on the one hand and to keep restrictions on current international transactions to a minimum in the interests of expanding world trade. The contracts under consideration in this case are plainly within this class. If, however, they are also within the class described as 'exchange contracts' in the second part of this section, they are to be subjected to the full restrictions of exchange control regulations, not only in the country whose law is applicable

---

1   [1960] 2 All ER 332 at 350, [1961] AC 1007 at 1059
2   [1966] 3 All ER 785, [1967] 1 QB 605
3   [1966] 3 All ER at 787, [1967] 1 QB at 613
4   [1966] 3 All ER at 789, [1967] 1 QB at 618

to them, but also in the courts of every member state. It is an odd thing to find such
a a restrictive provision in a section of an article dealing expressly with the avoidance
of such restrictions. This, in my judgment, is a strong indication that 'exchange contracts' are to be distinguished from current international transactions such as contracts
for the sale of goods. Finally, it is impossible to find a meaning for the word 'exchange'
if art VIII, s 2(*b*), is intended to apply to such current international transactions.

Counsel for the defendant suggested that a distinction was to be made between the
b making of payments and the enforceability of contracts, but I do not find it in the
least convincing.

All these considerations point to the conclusion that the phrase 'exchange contracts'
is used in its primary sense. There are, however, two considerations which, using
the ordinary technique of construction, might suggest that this conclusion was not
correct. The first is the fact that the draftsman differentiated between 'exchange
c transactions' in art IV, s 3, and 'exchange contracts' in art VIII, s 2(*b*), presumably for
some reason. It appears that in the original draft the same phrase was used in both
articles. This is historically interesting as an indication of what was originally intended
by art VIII, s 2(*b*), but on the question of construction of the final draft it is not relevant
since it remains a matter of speculation why the change was made. For my part,
however, I am unable to conclude that this is sufficient to displace what I have called
d the primary meaning of 'exchange contracts'. The second consideration is the inclusion of the words 'which involve the currency of any member' in article VIII, s 2(*b*),
which, it is said, are unnecessary if 'exchange contracts' is used in its primary sense.
It may be that the omission of these words would not affect the sense but they are not
otiose because they may have been included, ex abundanti cautela, to exclude non-
members. Applying the ordinary principles of construction, therefore, contracts for
e the sale of goods are not affected by art VIII, s 2(*b*).

However, counsel for the defendant in a strenuous and eloquent argument has
urged the court not to proceed on these lines—he called it the 'dissecting table approach'
—but to look at s 2(*b*) as a whole, in its setting in an international treaty, which represents one of the greatest achievements of inter-state co-operation, and give it the
widest possible interpretation in order to promote the objects of the IMF agreement.
f He also submitted that it would be wrong to apply to the construction of a treaty
the methods evolved by the courts in this country to ascertain the meaning of
domestic statutes and other documents. He went on to stress the importance of conformity in the interpretation of a provision which is now part of the domestic laws of
all member states. The force of the latter submission is weakened by the divergence of
views which has developed on the continent between the French and West German
g courts on the one hand, and the Belgian court on the other: *Re Anna de Boer*[1], *Clearing
Dollars Case*[2], *Emek v Bossers & Mouthaan*[3].

I accept the second point to the extent that this court should adopt as liberal a
construction as possible of provisions contained in international agreements in accordance with Diplock LJ's views in *Sharif v Azad*[4]. But it is one thing to speak of liberal
construction in the confined space of that case which was concerned with an exchange
h contract in the most literal sense; it is quite another in the wide open spaces of international commercial contracts like those with which we are concerned. The fallacy
of extrapolation on such a scale is obvious.

The defendant's case, therefore, stands or falls on his counsel's main argument
which can be stated in a sentence. He says that this court should adopt the suggestion
j first put forward by Dr F A Mann in his article in the British Year Book on International

---

1 [1961] Journal du Droit International 721
2 (1955) 22 ILR 730
3 (1955) 22 ILR 722
4 [1966] 3 All ER at 789, [1967] 1 QB at 618

Law[1], and subsequently in his well-known book, The Legal Aspect of Money[2], and in other places. His suggestion is that the phrase 'exchange contracts' should be *a* read as meaning 'any contracts which in any way affect the country's exchange resources', the phrase quoted by Lord Denning MR in his judgment in *Sharif v Azad*[3]. It is clear from the cases which have been cited to us, that Dr Mann's suggested reading of art VIII, s 2(b), has had a wide influence, especially on the French and West German court's, but notably less on the courts of the United States where, at best, it has had a sceptical reception. Burke J[4] in giving the judgment of the majority of the New York *b* Court of Appeals in *Banco do Brasil SA v AC Israel Commodity* observed:

> 'We are inclined to view an interpretation of sub-division (b) of section 2 that sweeps in all contracts affecting any members' exchange resources as doing considerable violence to the text of the section.'

That might reasonably be regarded as a judicious understatement. In my *c* view, Dr Mann's suggested reading goes well beyond the bounds of the most liberal construction, and amounts to an amendment of an important provision in the treaty, which, from internal evidence in the treaty, might not have been acceptable to its signatories at the time when the treaty was concluded. It is extremely difficult to accept that the statesmen, economists and lawyers present at Bretton Woods so signally failed to express their true meaning. *d*

The basis for Dr Mann's[2] suggested interpretation is his view that 'the paramount purpose of the International Monetary Fund is to promote international monetary co-operation' and that his interpretation 'would appear to be in better harmony with the purpose of the Agreement and the true intentions of its authors to be gathered from it'. He concedes that on this view the word 'exchange' must be regarded as redundant. With great respect I find it impossible to treat as redundant a word which *e* is clearly intended to define a particular class of contracts as distinguished from contracts between persons resident in member states in general. Moreover, the justification for doing such 'considerable violence to the text', is open to question at several points. The purposes of the IMF agreement are set out in art I. The first is 'To promote international monetary co-operation', but the second is 'To facilitate the expansion and balanced growth of international trade'. There is nothing to *f* indicate that the former is paramount over the latter. Moreover, there are many indications in the agreement itself that one of the intentions of its authors was to ensure that ordinary international commercial dealings, as opposed to capital transfers, were subjected to as little interference as possible.

For these reasons, notwithstanding Dr Mann's experience, knowledge and authority in this field, I am unable to adopt his proposed interpretation of art VIII, s 2(b). I *g* much prefer Dr Nussbaum's view as expressed in his article in the Yale Law Journal[5]:

> 'Exchange transactions are generally understood to mean transactions which have as their immediate object "exchange", that is, international media of payment. The meaning of "exchange contracts" cannot be broader.' *h*

I would also adopt his conclusion that[6] 'contracts involving securities or merchandise cannot be considered as exchange contracts except where they are monetary transactions in disguise'. This construction gives to the phrase the widest construction which in my judgment it can bear.

j

1   (1949) 26 BYBIL 259
2   3rd Edn (1971), p 441
3   [1966] 3 All ER at 787, [1967] 1 QB at 613
4   (1963) 12 NY 2d 371 at 375, 376
5   (1949) 59 YLJ 421 at 426
6   Ibid at 427

a   In these circumstances it is unnecessary to deal in detail with the second and third questions formulated at the beginning of this judgment. So far as the second of these is concerned, I do not think that the word 'involve' has any special significance. The phrase 'which involve the currency of any member' is not very precise; it should, in my view, be given a sufficiently wide construction to include the kind of transaction described by Dr Nussbaum's phrase 'monetary transactions in disguise'. In the present case the contracts provided for payment in sterling and did not involve the

b   currency of Italy. Had these transactions proved profitable to the defendant he would have received payment in sterling and the lire would not have come into the picture at all; had he made a loss, as he did, he might or he might not have had to sell lire to acquire the necessary sterling, depending on whether or not he had funds available in sterling, dollars, or some other currency. It would be absurd to hold that a contract was enforceable if one party made a profit on it but unenforceable if he made a

c   loss on it or that the question of enforceability should depend on whether the defendant had available resources in currencies other than lire, presumably at the date when the contract was made.

The third question raises difficult problems of proof and I would prefer to reserve it until it becomes necessary to decide it. Having listened with interest to the discussion on it, it seems to me that the court could only resolve it either by evidence

d   that the IMF had approved the regulations in question, or by applying the presumption, omnia praesumuntur rite esse acta, or by expert evidence as to the effect of the regulations. Without such assistance I would find myself in great difficulty in evaluating the true effect of the regulations and their impact on the IMF agreement.

Finally, I would like to express my gratitude to Kerr J[1] for the assistance which I have had from his most lucid analysis of the issues raised in this case and my

e   agreement with his decision. I would dismiss this appeal.

SHAW LJ. At the trial of this action the defence to the plaintiffs' claim was founded not on any merits but on what was said to be the effect of the operation of the Bretton Woods Agreements Order in Council 1946 on the enforceability in this

f   country of the plaintiffs' contracts with the defendant. His counsel described the Bretton Woods Agreement as an expression of high idealism in international affairs. If, as is generally accepted, the description is justified, the provisions of the agreements could hardly be invoked for reasons shoddier than those which obtain in the present case. The defendant, whose sole concern is to save his pocket from depletion through having to pay his debts to the plaintiffs, piously declares that for him to be

g   made to pay those debts would violate the high purposes of the Bretton Woods Agreement; and, what is more, that the courts ought to extricate him from his predicament by declaring that the contracts under which he would otherwise be obliged to pay are made unenforceable in the United Kingdom by art VIII, s 2(*b*), of the agreement.

Kerr J[1] rejected the main argument advanced before him and gave judgment

h   for the plaintiffs. The question before this court, with two subsidiary questions, is a matter of law and so, as counsel for the defendant has said, merits are irrelevant. In that he was of course right. But whether the rule relied on by the defendant be inspired by idealism or founded in expediency, a law which would produce so bizarre and seemingly unjust an outcome as that contended for on his behalf demands the most careful scrutiny and consideration. This may reveal that the law in question is

j   not, after all, perverse in its operation but that it has been misunderstood because the language in which it is enacted has been given a tortuous and erroneous construction.

The history of the matter has already been recounted and I need refer to it only incidentally.

---

1   [1975] 2 All ER 649, [1975] 2 WLR 1009

It is common ground that by the law of Italy, to which the defendant as a resident
in that country is subject, he was required to obtain Ministerial authorisation there *a*
before he entered into his contracts with the plaintiffs. He did not procure that
authorisation and accordingly those contracts were unlawful under the exchange
control regulations of Italy. The contracts could not therefore be sued on in that
country.

Both Italy and the United Kingdom were parties to the Bretton Woods Agreement (to which I shall refer as 'the agreement') and both countries are accordingly *b*
members of the International Monetary Fund which was established by it.

The question to be decided is whether in the circumstances indicated, the contracts made in England between the plaintiffs and the defendant are rendered
unenforceable here by the operation of art VIII, s 2 (*b*), of the agreement as adopted
by the order in council of 1946. Section 2 of that article must be looked at as a whole
but in reading it I omit what is immaterial for present purposes. Paragraph (*a*) *c*
states that 'no member shall, without the approval of the Fund, impose restrictions
on the making of payments and transfers for current international transactions.'
Paragraph (*b*) provides:

'Exchange contracts which involve the currency of any Member and which are
contrary to the exchange control regulations of that member maintained *d*
or imposed consistently with this Agreement shall be unenforceable in the
territories of any member . . .'

Before attempting an analysis of these provisions it is necessary to look also at art
XIX which gives guidance in the interpretation of certain provisions of the agree-
ment. In relation to art VIII, s 2(*a*), such guidance is to be found in para (*i*) of art
XIX which states: *e*

'Payments for current transactions means payments which are not for the
purpose of transferring capital, and includes, without limitation: (1) All payments due in connection with foreign trade, other current business, including
services, and normal short-term banking and credit facilities; (2) Payments due
as interest on loans and as net income from other investments; (3) Payments of *f*
moderate amount for amortization of loans or for depreciation of direct investments; (4) Moderate remittances for family living expenses.'

The paragraph ends by stating that the Fund may after consultation with the
members concerned determine whether certain specific transactions are to be
considered current transactions or capital transactions.

This last provision is important in that it enables the Fund to take certain transac- *g*
tions which might be regarded as current transactions out of the principle of freedom from restriction generally envisaged by art VIII, s 2(*a*), by determining (after
due consultation) that they are to be regarded as capital transactions.

It is apparent that para (*i*) of art XIX is defining or describing the subject-matter
of art VIII, s 2(*a*). It omits all reference to exchange contracts which are the subject
of art VIII, s 2(*b*), and which are not defined in art XIX or elsewhere. The omission *h*
is not without significance for it suggests that the draftsman (and the contracting
parties) considered that the expression 'exchange contracts' spoke for itself and did
not require elucidation.

It may be observed also that art VIII, s 2(*a*), reflects in particular the purposes of
the International Monetary Fund specified in art I (ii) and (iv). Shortly stated, they
are the facilitation of the expansion and balanced growth of world trade in correla- *j*
tion with the establishment of a multilateral system of payments for current transactions and the elimination of foreign exchange restrictions which hamper the growth
of world trade.

Before leaving art XIX, it is to be noted that the payment by the defendant of the
sums claimed by the plaintiffs in the action would come within the scope of 'pay-

ments and transfers for current international transactions'. Accordingly that payment
a could be enforced by legal process in the United Kingdom unless elsewhere than in
art VIII, s 2 (*a*), which declares there shall be no restriction on payment, there can be
found in the agreement some provision which declares the contrary.

Counsel for the defendant asserts that there is such provision in the same section
of the same article, namely in s 2(*b*). He contends that the term 'exchange contracts'
there used is to be understood in a sense wide enough to include contracts of the
b kind entered into between the defendant and the plaintiffs. It would follow that
since those contracts were contrary to the Italian Exchange Control Regulations
(which may for present purposes be assumed to be maintained consistently with the
agreement) they are unenforceable in the territories of any member state including
the United Kingdom.

This was a surprising proposition, in that it seemed at first sight to make nonsense
c of art VIII, s 2(*a*). Reflection has not served to abate the surprise, still less to alter
my view. A fundamental distinction exists between the two types of transaction
with which paras (*a*) and (*b*) of s 2 of art VIII respectively deal.

Paragraph (*a*) is concerned principally with mercantile transactions involving the
payment of money for goods supplied or services rendered. These are the ordinary
incidents of trade and commerce. Their subject-matter is relatively easy to scru-
d tinise and to supervise. Trading activity so long as it is honest and bona fide poses no
direct or obvious threat to the economy of the countries involved.

Paragraph (*b*) is not concerned with trading and commerce but simply with currency. Transactions in this sphere may easily be inimical to the economic interests
of a country whose currency is involved in those transactions. There is need for the
power to render such transactions ineffectual in the general interests of all members
e of the Fund.

Counsel for the defendant was driven to concede that on his argument exchange
contracts must be regarded as a species of current international transactions; but he
offered no criterion for distinguishing the species. I doubt whether for all his forensic
resourcefulness he would have advanced the proposition that his client's dealings
with the plaintiffs were exchange contracts but for the fact that support for it is to be
f found in sundry quarters.

It seems clear enough to me that a person of ordinary intelligence who read para
(*b*) in the context of the whole agreement with an understanding of its declared
objectives, would construe the phrase 'exchange contracts' as meaning contracts for
the exchange of the currency of one country for that of another. Contracts of this
nature are not of themselves productive of benefit in goods or services. If they are
g made in contravention of exchange control regulations so as to threaten some prejudice to the exchange resources of a member state, there is justification for rendering
those contracts ineffectual by preventing their enforcement. This concept reflects
the purposes set out in art I (i) and (iii) of the agreement. These may be summarised
as the promotion of international monetary co-operation and of exchange stability.

Thus far there would appear to be no difficulty that arises from attributing to the
h term 'exchange contracts' what is called its narrow but what I think is better described
as its ordinary meaning, namely contracts by which the currency of one country is
exchanged for that of another. That this is the intended as well as the apparently
obvious sense in which the word 'exchange' is used in the term 'exchange contracts'
is supported by the fact that the wider phrase 'exchange transactions' occurs several
times in the agreement, before one reaches art VIII, in contexts where it can only refer
j to an exchange of currency for currency (see for example art IV, ss 3 and 4). To adopt
a wider construction would have the result of bringing paras (*a*) and (*b*) of s 2 of art
VIII into conflict with each other with no possibility of reconciliation. The simple
construction was one which commended itself to Lord Radcliffe: see *Re United
Railways of the Havana and Regla Warehouses Ltd*[1]. In 1949 Dr Nussbaum had in a

1   [1960] 2 All ER 332 at 350, [1961] AC 1007 at 1059

closely reasoned article which appeared in the Yale Law Journal[1] arrived at a similar conclusion.

It is perhaps worth recalling that if some special or extended or unusual meaning was intended to be given to 'exchange contracts' for the purposes of art VIII, s 2(b), the term would have been given by express provision whatever was the appropriate definition required. As it is, one can only have recourse to the dictionary where one of the meanings of 'exchange' is defined as giving currency for currency. The absence of any legal definition from art XIX reinforces the view that the narrow or ordinary or natural meaning is the right one to adopt and that its validity does not become suspect merely because it is also elementary. It may give rise to some anomalies but this is hardly a surprising outcome of an attempt to rationalise an international system of immense complexity. The anomalies which would result from a wider interpretation, whatever it was, would be of a far higher order of magnitude; and to broaden the scope of art VIII, s 2 (b), would threaten and not foster the totality of the purposes set out in art I. Counsel for the defendant in the course of his submissions in support of a wider interpretation of exchange contracts appeared to assign a descending measure of importance to those purposes corresponding to the order in which they appear in that article. This seems to me an extraordinary proposition, but it calls for no other comment than that those various purposes are all aspects of the same grand design. They are interdependent and must be considered in combination. They are not to be isolated one from another.

I turn now to the wider meaning of the term 'exchange contracts' for which counsel for the defendant contends. It had its genesis in the publications of Dr F A Mann. It is unnecessary but proper to state that on the subject of money and exchange control Dr Mann's views must command respect even if it is not always possible to agree with them. He first applied himself to the question of the meaning of exchange contracts as long ago as 1947. In the Modern Law Review he wrote[2]:

'The interpretation of [art VIII] gives rise to many problems. The term "exchange contracts" is by no means free from ambiguity, but probably means a contract by which one of the parties promises to give consideration in the form of funds denominated in the currency of the country, the regulations of which prohibit the transaction . . .'

This was already wider than the basic or narrow interpretation which has been adverted to. It proved to be merely Dr Mann's first tentative flirtation with the meaning of 'exchange contracts' which he later delineated and embraced in more ample proportions in an article which appeared in 1949 in the British Year Book of International Law[3]. After describing the term 'exchange contracts' as 'unusual', he went on to say:

'This probably refers to contracts which in any way affect a country's exchange resources; the term would seem to include, therefore, not only contracts for the exchange of one currency (e.g. francs) against another currency (e.g. sterling) but also contracts creating a debt in favour of a non-resident or providing for the transfer of securities from a resident to a non-resident and so forth.'

It is probable that Dr Mann has in mind contracts the operation or effect of which will be to deplete or diminish the exchange resources of a member without any equivalent accretion of goods or services. Indeed, in his book The Legal Aspect of Money[4] where he repeats this idea, he explains 'affect' as meaning 'affect prejudicially'. If this is what Dr Mann has in mind he appears to include in exchange contracts what are transfers of capital or of securities in whatever form they may be

1   59 YLJ 421
2   10 MLR at 418
3   29 BYBIL 279
4   3rd Edn (1971), p 441

dressed up. Such an extension of the meaning is not, however, necessary in order to
a serve the objects and purposes of the agreement. Member states are not inhibited
by art VIII, s 2(*a*), from imposing restrictions on such transfers. The application of
art VIII, s 2(*b*), to such cases would therefore be superfluous and uncalled for. Dr
Mann having sowed the seed and germinated it, the interpretation suggested by his
formula became self-propagating here and there. It was adopted and applied
by a court in Schleswig-Holstein[1] and possibly in Paris[2]; but it failed to find favour
b in Hamburg[3] or New York[4].

Dr Mann developed the theme in The Legal Aspect of Money[5]. After expressing
regret that the term exchange contracts is 'wholly obscure' the author considers
three suggested interpretations of it. The first is the narrow one, but this is dismissed as 'unlikely' on the ground that the draftsman—

c   'would not have been prepared to limit the scope of the provision so as to
make it applicable only to a relatively small group of transactions and to exclude
dealings in gold or securities, capital transfers or current transactions.'

The answer to this objection to adopting the narrow meaning is that there is no
need, as I have earlier pointed out, to extend its scope to include such transactions
as he mentions, for they can be regulated so far as is consistent with the purposes
d of the agreement by other of its provisions. Dealings in gold or in securities can be
effectively controlled at source without making contracts relating to such dealings
unenforceable in the courts of any member state; while capital transfers are outside
the protective aegis of art VIII, s 2(*a*). As for current transactions they are the important beneficiaries of that protection. Not only is it unnecessary to give the term
'exchange contracts' a meaning which would encompass those transactions, but it
e would run counter to the declared purposes of the agreement if that meaning were
adopted and applied.

The second suggestion is that which had been advanced by Dr Mann himself in
1947 in the Modern Law Review[6], and which I have already mentioned. By 1949[7]
he had concluded that it was not wide enough. So he propounded a third meaning,
namely that exchange contracts are contracts which in any way affect (that is pre-
f judice) a country's exchange resources. He goes on to justify this panoramic concept
by the assertion that[8]: 'This would appear to be in better harmony with the purpose
of the Agreement and the true intentions of its authors to be gathered from it . . .'
However he is compelled to concede that this interpretation—

g   'admittedly makes the word "exchange" redundant: in order to express the
idea, the provision could have referred simply to "contracts which involve the
currency of any member". So to disregard an important word may run counter
to established principles of interpretation. Yet it is submitted that this objection,
grave though it may be, is outweighed by the fact that no other interpretation
would achieve the overriding purposes of the Agreement.'

h With due respect to Dr Mann's learning, this is all obfuscation. Whatever may be the
'overriding' purposes of the agreement, those set out in art I are effectively served
by ascribing to the expression 'exchange contracts' the narrow but ordinary meaning
the two words bear in this conjunction. No doubt the proper interpretation of a

1   *Lessinger v Mirau* (1955) 22 ILR 725
j 2   *Re Anna de Boer* [1961] Journal du Droit International 721
3   (7th July 1959) 2 U 191/58
4   *Banco do Brasil SA v AC Israel Commodity Co Inc* (1963) 12 NY 2d 371
5   3rd Edn (1971), p 381
6   10 MLR 418
7   29 BYBIL 259
8   The Legal Aspect of Money (3rd Edn, 1971), p 441

treaty demands that the intentions of the parties to it and the objectives of the accord
it represents must be borne in mind; but to delete from the text of the agreement   *a*
a qualifying adjective with an important connotation is not interpretation but mutilation. To deform the text in this way *can* only thwart the asserted purposes of the
agreement. The theory that 'no other interpretation would achieve the overriding
purposes of the agreement' involves the assumption that its exponent understands
better what the parties wished to achieve than they did themselves. This is intem-
perate logic and I reject both the process and the conclusion it purports to establish.   *b*

There remains to be considered in this regard the decision of the Court of Appeal in
Sharif v Azad[1]. It is unnecessary to recapitulate the facts. In the course of his judgment Lord Denning MR[2] said: 'The words "exchange contracts" are not defined
but I think they mean any contracts which in any way affect the country's exchange
resources.' This view thus tentatively expressed was based on a citation of the passage
in Dr Mann's book. On the facts of that case the contracts under consideration   *c*
amounted to exchange contracts in the narrow sense of the expression; therefore
they *did* affect the country's exchange resources. The converse proposition was not
necessary to support the decision and Lord Denning MR's view was not only tentative
but obiter.

Diplock LJ[3] considered that the expression exchange contract 'should be liberally
construed having regard to the objects of the Bretton Woods Agreement to protect   *d*
the currencies of the states who are parties thereto'. It is, however, clear from the
illustrations which he gives that what was contemplated by that statement were
contracts which, though ostensibly made for other purposes, had the object and
ultimate outcome of bringing about an exchange of currencies. It is in this specific
and restricted sense that Dr Mann's phrase 'contracts which in any way affect a
country's exchange resources' may be validly employed.   *e*

I therefore agree with Kerr J[4] that the defendant's contracts with the plaintiffs
were not exchange contracts within art VIII, s2(*b*), of the Bretton Woods Agreements.
It follows that those contracts are not rendered unenforceable in this country by
the article. Accordingly the action brought by the plaintiffs was maintainable, and
the judgment in their favour was right.

This is sufficient to dispose of the appeal and it is unnecessary to decide the matters   *f*
raised by the respondent's notice. I content myself with saying that here also I find
myself in agreement with the views expressed by the learned judge to whose clear
and comprehensive judgment I would wish to add my respectful tribute.

I too would dismiss the appeal.

Appeal dismissed. Leave to appeal to the House of Lords refused.   *g*

Solicitors: *Crawley & de Reya* (for the defendant); *Coward Chance* (for the plaintiffs).

Gavin Gore-Andrews Esq Barrister.

h
1   [1966] 3 All ER 785, [1967] 1 QB 605
2   [1966] 3 All ER at 787, [1967] 1 QB at 613
3   [1966] 3 All ER at 789, [1967] 1 QB at 618
4   [1975] 2 All ER 649, [1975] 2 WLR 1009

a

Lap Shun Textiles Industrial Co Ltd v Collector of Stamp Revenue

b PRIVY COUNCIL
LORD WILBERFORCE, VISCOUNT DILHORNE AND LORD FRASER OF TULLYBELTON
13th, 14th JANUARY, 2nd MARCH 1976

Stamp duty – Voluntary disposition – Inadequate consideration – Conveyance or transfer
c *operating as voluntary disposition – Intention of transferor – Relevance – Conveyance by*
reason of inadequacy of consideration conferring substantial benefit on transferee – Bargain
at arm's length – No intention on part of transferor to confer any benefit on transferee –
Whether open to collector to charge stamp duty on value of property conveyed rather than
amount of consideration – Stamp Ordinance (Hong Kong) (c 117), s 27(1)(4).

d By a conveyance dated 8th February 1973 certain land in Hong Kong was conveyed to
the taxpayer company for a stated consideration of $16,465·68. The conveyance was
presented for stamping and on 21st February was stamped with $330, i e $2 per
$100 on the stated consideration, that being the appropriate rate for a 'conveyance
on sale'. Subsequently the district officer valued the land sold at $76,800 and on
that basis the Collector of Stamp Revenue considered that the stated consideration
e of $16,465·68 was inadequate. The collector accordingly applied s 27(4)*a* of the Stamp
Ordinance (c 117) under which the document became liable to be charged as a conveyance operating as a voluntary disposition inter vivos. On that basis the collector
claimed duty at two per cent on the assessed value, i e $1,536. Subsequently the
district officer re-assessed the value of the land at $37,500. The taxpayer company
did not challenge the re-assessment. The re-assessment was also accepted by the
f collector who claimed $750 stamp duty from the taxpayer company, although he
conceded (a) that the stated consideration of $16,465·68 was the whole consideration,
(b) that that sum had been reached by way of an arm's length bargain, based on a price
of 15 cents per square foot, and (c) that the taxpayer company had acted in good
faith. On appeal, the taxpayer company contended that the conveyance was not
chargeable with stamp duty under s 27(4) since the expressions 'the inadequacy of
g the sum paid as consideration' and 'a conveyance or transfer [which] confers a substantial benefit on the person to whom the property is conveyed or transferred'
contained therein applied only to cases where the transferor intended to confer a
substantial benefit on the transferee.

Held – On its true construction, s 27(4) indicated that the collector was to be guided
h by an objective and not a subjective test. The references in the subsection to the
inadequacy of consideration and to the conveyance conferring, in the opinion of
the collector, a benefit, clearly stated factual elements whose existence or non-existence appeared on the face of the transaction. Section 27(4) did not require the
collector to investigate whether an evident inadequacy or an evident benefit was
deliberate or intended. The liability to stamp duty depended on the nature and effect
j of documents and was not to be determined with reference to the parties' intentions.
It followed that the collector had properly applied the provisions of s 27(4) and the
taxpayer company's appeal would be dismissed (see p 837 *f* to *h* and p 838 *b* to *h*, post).

---

a Section 27, so far as material, is set out at p 836 *e* to *h*, post.

Notes
For stamp duty on conveyances or transfers operating as voluntary dispositions, see
33 Halsbury's Laws (3rd Edn) 351-353, paras 611-614, and for cases on the subject, see
39 Digest (Repl) 331-333, 714-723.

The Stamp Ordinance (Hong Kong), s 27, corresponds with the Finance (1909-10)
Act 1910, s 74. For s 74 of the 1910 Act, see 32 Halsbury's Statutes (3rd Edn) 217.

Cases referred to in judgment
Baker v Inland Revenue Comrs [1924] AC 270, [1923] All ER Rep 566, 93 LJKB 211, 130
LT 513, HL, 39 Digest (Repl) 332, 718.
Indo-China Steam Navigation Co, Re [1917] 2 Ch 100, 86 LJCh 723, 117 LT 212, 9 Digest
(Reissue) 213, 1271.
Wigan Coal & Iron Co Ltd v Inland Revenue Comrs [1945] 1 All ER 392, 173 LT 79, 39
Digest (Repl) 333, 722.

Appeal
On 26th March 1974, at the request of the appellants, Lap Shun Textiles Industrial
Co Ltd ('the taxpayer company'), the following case was stated by the Collector of
Stamp Revenue for Hong Kong.

1. On 10th February 1973 a conveyance on sale ('the assignment') was presented
on behalf of the taxpayer company to the Kowloon branch office of the collector for
stamping.

2. The assignment was dated 8th February 1973 and made between the Chartered
Bank of one part and the taxpayer company of the other part.

3. The assignment was stamped with $330, being stamp duty at the rate of $2 per
$100 or part thereof of the stated consideration of $16,465·68 in accordance with head
19(2) of the Schedule to the Stamp Ordinance.

4. On 14th June 1973 and on 30th July 1973 the collector informed Messrs Deacons,
solicitors for the taxpayer company ('the solicitors'), that the district officer, Yuen
Long, had valued the property comprising the assignment at $76,800·00. The collector
pointed out to the solicitors that it would therefore appear that the consideration
of $16,465·68 stated in the assignment was inadequate for the purposes of s 27(4) of
the Ordinance. They were invited to comment before an assessment calling for
additional duty to be assessed under s 27(1) of the Ordinance was issued.

5. The solicitors replied on 23rd July 1973 requesting the collector to set aside the
matter for 28 days while they sought instructions from the taxpayer company.

6. No further communication had since been received from the solicitors. The
collector therefore issued an assessment under s 27(1) of the Ordinance to the appellants on 2nd October 1973, calling for additional duty of $1,206·00 calculated as follows:

	$
Under head 53(2) in the Schedule to the Ordinance:—	
two per cent of $76,800·00	1,536·00
Less already paid	330·00
Balance payable	1,206·00

7. On 17th October 1973 the solicitors remitted a cheque for $1,206 in satisfaction
of the additional duty. On 19th October they required the collector to state and sign
a case in accordance with the provisions of s 18(1) of the Ordinance with reference
to the assessment of the duty on the assignment.

8. The solicitors informed the collector that the purpose of the appeal was to test
whether s 27(4) of the Ordinance had any application to a transaction between a
vendor and a purchaser in good faith and for valuable consideration. The taxpayer
company contended that in such a purchase the collector had no power to raise any

additional assessment over and above an assessment on the amount or value of the
a consideration actual paid as shown in the assignment.

9. The collector did not intend to challenge the taxpayer company's contention
that (i) that the consideration of $16,465·68 was the whole consideration paid by the
taxpayer company to the vendor; (ii) that that sum had been reached by way of an
arm's length bargain and was based on a price of 15 cents per square foot; and (iii)
that the taxpayer company had acted in good faith.

b 10. The collector contended: (a) that the assignment conferred a substantial benefit
on the taxpayer company by reason of the inadequacy of the sum paid as consideration; (b) that the consideration of $16,465·68 stated in the assignment was correctly
deemed not to be valuable consideration for the purposes of s 27(4) of the Ordinance
and accordingly the assignment was correctly deemed to operate as a voluntary
disposition inter vivos within the meaning of s 27(4).

c 11. The district officer later reviewed the valuation of the property comprised
in the assignment. He revised the valuation to $37,500·00. The solicitors were advised of
the revised valuation on 12th February 1974. On the basis of the revised valuation
the assignment attracted the following duty assessed in accordance with s 17(3) of
the Ordinance:

d

	$
Under Head 53(2) in the schedule to the Ordinance:—	
two per cent of $37,500	750·00
Less total duty already paid	1,536·00
Excess duty refundable	786·00

e 12. The questions submitted for the opinion of the court were: (1) whether in the
circumstances as aforesaid, the $16,465·68 referred to above should or should not be
deemed to be valuable consideration for the purposes of s 27 of the Ordinance;
(2) whether or not the assignment conferred a substantial benefit on the taxpayer
company within s 27 of the Ordinance; (3) whether the assignment was chargeable
with duty as assessed by the collector; (4) if not, with what duty it was chargeable.

f 13. The taxpayer company expressed its dissatisfaction with the collector's decision
as being erroneous in point of law and required the collector to state and sign a case
for the opinion of the court.

On 31st July 1974, in the District Court of Hong Kong, Garcia DJ held: (a) that the
consideration shown in the conveyance on sale as $16,465·68 was not deemed to be
valuable consideration for the purpose of s 27(4) of the Ordinance; (b) that a sub-
g stantial benefit had been conferred on the taxpayer company by the conveyance on
sale; and (c) that the conveyance on sale was chargeable with duty of $750 as assessed
by the collector. On 24th January 1975 the Supreme Court of Hong Kong (Huggins
and McMullin JJ) affirmed the decision of Garcia DJ. The taxpayer company appealed
to the Privy Council.

h *Andrew Park* for the taxpayer company.
Michael Wheeler QC and *William P K Lee* (of the Hong Kong Bar) for the collector.

LORD WILBERFORCE. This is an appeal from the Supreme Court of Hong
Kong (Appellate Jurisdiction) which has upheld a judgment of Garcia DJ in the
District Court. It concerns the amount of stamp duty to be charged on a conveyance
j on sale dated 8th February 1973 by which certain land in the New Territories was
conveyed by the Chartered Bank to the taxpayer company for a stated consideration
of $16,465·68.

This conveyance was presented for stamping in the normal way and on 21st
February 1973 was stamped with $330·00, being $2·00 per $100 on the stated consider-
ation, the appropriate rate for a 'conveyance on sale'.

Several months later, however, the district officer assessed the value of the property at $76,800 and, on the basis of this, the Collector of Stamp Revenue ('the collector'), whose statutory duty it is to collect the stamp duties, took the view that the stated consideration ($16,465·68) was inadequate. He accordingly applied s 27(4) of the Stamp Ordinance (c 117), under which the document became liable to be charged as a conveyance operating as a voluntary disposition inter vivos. On this basis on 2nd October 1973 he claimed duty at two per cent on the assessed value, namely $1,536·00.

On 19th October 1973 the taxpayer company appealed against the assessment and requested the collector to state a case. Later the district officer revised his valuation to a figure of $37,500, which the collector accepted. This would give rise to a liability of $750.00.

In the case which was signed on 26th March 1974, the collector expressly stated that he did not intend to challenge the taxpayer company's contentions that the stated consideration of $16,465·68 was the whole consideration, that such sum was reached by way of an arm's length bargain, based on a price of 15 cents per square foot, and that the taxpayer company had acted in good faith. On its side, the taxpayer company, for the purpose of this case, does not dispute the value of $37,500·00 put on the property by the district officer. Thus the appeal raised the question whether, when a sale has been made between parties at arm's length, in good faith, for an agreed consideration, it is open to the collector to charge the conveyance as one operating as a voluntary disposition inter vivos, with duty based on what he considers to be the true value of the property.

It is now appropriate to set out the relevant statutory enactment. This is contained in s 27(1)(1A)(2) and (4) of the Stamp Ordinance:

'(1) Subject to subsection (1A), any voluntary disposition inter vivos, and any conveyance or transfer operating as a voluntary disposition inter vivos, shall be chargeable with stamp duty under head 53 in the Schedule.

'(1A) Any transfer, including a letter of renunciation, operating as a voluntary disposition inter vivos or shares of marketable securities shall be chargeable with duty under head 48(1) in the Schedule.

'(2) Notwithstanding anything in section 17, the Collector may be required to express his opinion under that section on any conveyance or transfer operating as a voluntary disposition inter vivos, and no such conveyance or transfer shall be deemed to be duly stamped unless the Collector has expressed his opinion thereon in accordance with that section . . .

'(4) Any conveyance or transfer (not being a disposition made in favour of a purchaser or incumbrancer or other person in good faith and for valuable consideration) shall for the purposes of this section be deemed to be a conveyance or transfer operating as a voluntary disposition inter vivos, and (except where a marriage is the consideration) the consideration for any conveyance or transfer shall not for this purpose be deemed to be valuable consideration where the Collector is of opinion that by reason of the inadequacy of the sum paid as consideration or other circumstances the conveyance or transfer confers a substantial benefit on the person to whom the property is conveyed or transferred.'

Under head 53(2) a voluntary disposition inter vivos of land or other property, and a conveyance or transfer of land or other property operating as a voluntary disposition inter vivos, is chargeable with duty at the rate of $2 per $100 of the value of the land or other property.

It is reasonably clear what s 27 was intended to achieve. In the first place it charges voluntary conveyances, i e conveyances for which no valuable consideration is given, with ad valorem duty based on the value of the property conveyed. In the second place it prevents evasion of this duty by presenting what may in substance be a voluntary disposition as a conveyance for valuable consideration through the insertion of

a nominal consideration, or an inadequate consideration. The question is whether
a in addition to these objectives it achieves another, namely the charging on a value
basis of conveyances on sale where the consideration is inadequate. The question
whether this was intended cannot be answered a priori; it can only be answered
on a consideration of what s 27(4), fairly construed as a whole, can be found to
achieve.

As to this, their Lordships are in no doubt: the subsection is clear and lacking in
b ambiguity. Having, in the initial parenthesis, excepted from its grasp dispositions in
good faith and for valuable consideration, it continues in the second limb to remove
from this exception certain particular cases. One such case is composed of the following elements: (i) inadequacy of consideration (ii) the opinion of the collector that by
reason of this inadequacy a substantial benefit is, by the conveyance or transfer,
conferred on the transferee. Another such case, not directly relevant to the present
c case, depends on the existence of 'other circumstances' instead of inadequacy of
consideration.

If this is the correct analysis, there can be no doubt that the conveyance of 8th
February 1973 comes squarely within the charge, as both courts in Hong Kong have
held.

The consideration is inadequate because it is less than 50 per cent of the real value.
d The collector, by reason of this inadequacy, has formed—and has material on which
to form—the opinion that the conveyance confers a substantial benefit on the
transferee.

The taxpayer company seeks to answer this argument by suggesting another reading of the subsection. This it endeavours to reinforce by an enumeration of the consequences, described as alarming, which would follow if the collector's view is right.
e The reading of the subsection which the taxpayer company suggests is not easy
to state in textual terms. It is described as giving to the second limb a subjective
rather than an objective meaning, so as to confine it to cases where the transferor
intends to confer a substantial benefit on the transferee. Thus there would be
excluded from the subsection all cases where the intention, assuming that this was
in good faith, was to enter into a sale; the subsection would only deal with cases of
f intended gifts including those for which some nominal or inadequate consideration
was given.

Their Lordships cannot accept this submission. It runs counter, in their opinion,
to the plain wording of the subsection which, contrary to the argument, indicates
that the tests by which the collector is to be guided are objective. When the section
refers to inadequacy of consideration, and when it refers to the conveyances con-
g ferring, in the opinion of the collector, a benefit, it is clearly stating factual elements
whose existence, or non-existence, appears on the face of the transaction. It cannot
require the collector to investigate whether an evident inadequacy, or an evident
benefit, is deliberate or intended; such a requirement, if it were to be imposed,
would have to be stated in clear words. The stamp duty legislation generally proceeds
by way of stamping documents according to their nature and effect, and not by
h references to parties' intentions, and any departure from this principle would require
clear indication.

Their Lordships would add, in this part of the argument, that the English authorities
cited by the taxpayer company on the identical s 74 of the Finance (1909-10) Act 1910
(*Baker v Inland Revenue Comrs*[1], *Wigan Coal & Iron Co Ltd v Inland Revenue Comrs*[2]),
dealing as they were with quite different situations from the present, do not provide
j any support for its argument. Indeed, the opinions expressed in the House of Lords
in the former case clearly support what has been called the 'objective' approach to
the second part of the subsection rather than the subjective. And, as was said by
Lord Sumner, the construction of the section is very plain and decisive.

1 [1924] AC 270, [1923] All ER Rep 566
2 [1945] 1 All ER 392

In view of the clarity and lack of ambiguity of the statutory language, as their
Lordships understand it, it is not perhaps strictly necessary to examine the supposed   *a*
difficulties, in practice, to which, if the collector's contentions are right, it is said to
give rise. The statutory language must in any event prevail. But there are some
observations which may be necessary in order that the implications of the present
decision may be understood.

First, it does not in the least follow that, if the collector succeeds in the present
case, every conveyance or transfer on sale will require an official valuation of the   *b*
property or an adjudication of the stamp duty. Any stamp authority has to start
from the point that valuation of much, if not most, property is a matter of judgment
and is only possible within fairly broad limits, and that sound, if not the best, evidence
of value is to be found in bona fide, arm's length dealings. It is for this reason that,
when s 27(4) authorises the substitution for the agreed consideration of the 'real'
value, it requires that a substantial benefit for the transferee should be found to   *c*
exist. In the great majority of cases the normal procedure of presentation for stamping and routine stamping according to the stated consideration will continue to be
followed; such cases as the present will continue to be exceptional. Thus their Lordships on this account do not envisage any dislocation of the normal process of
stamping.

On the other hand there is another type of difficulty, which may well arise and   *d*
which gives their Lordships some concern. Under the Ordinance (s 5(4) and heads
19 and 53) all executing parties to a conveyance are civilly liable for the duty, and
moreover (s 5 (5)), if the instrument is not duly stamped, each is deemed to commit
an offence. The schedule further requires instruments to be stamped within a specified period (30 days after execution). These consequences, which do not arise in the
United Kingdom, seem to have been imposed in Hong Kong by legislation posterior   *e*
to the enactment of s 27.

It appears that their effect may be to impose a civil and criminal liability on parties
such as those concerned in the instant transaction, who have entered into a genuine
commercial transaction and bona fide presented a document for stamping and had
it stamped, if, as the result of investigation, the collector is able to invoke the provisions of s 27. Their Lordships accept of course that the collector, a public official,   *f*
would desire to act reasonably, but he can only do so within the limits of his statutory
duty and the parties may remain uncomfortably at risk. It may well be that the
interaction of these legislative provisions requires examination.

A third head of possible difficulty was said to relate to matters of title. But their
Lordships were not satisfied of the reality of this difficulty under the system prevailing
in Hong Kong. The dictum of Eve J in *Re Indo-China Steam Navigation Co*[1] suggesting   *g*
that registration of a transfer while inadequately stamped would not bring about
a legal transfer does not appear to their Lordships to be correct. On the other hand
some difficulty may arise in applying s 7(2) of the Ordinance to instruments such as
the present if the duty is liable to be increased through the application of s 27.

Such difficulties as these—to which their Lordships hope that some consideration
may be given—cannot however lead to a different interpretation of the section such   *h*
as the taxpayer company contends for. Their Lordships will humbly advise Her
Majesty that the appeal be dismissed. The taxpayer company must pay the costs
of the appeal.

Appeal dismissed.

j

Solicitors: *Lovell, White & King* (for the taxpayer company); *Charles Russell & Co*
(for the collector).

Gordon H Scott Esq   Barrister.

---

1   [1917] 2 Ch 100 at 106

a   # R v Newham Justices, ex parte Hunt
       # R v Oxted Justices, ex parte Franklin

QUEEN'S BENCH DIVISION
LORD WIDGERY CJ, KILNER BROWN AND WATKINS JJ
b   29th JANUARY 1976

Nuisance – Statutory nuisance – Abatement   notice – Failure   to   comply – Complaint   to justices – Procedure – Initiation of proceedings – Complaint by individual – Information laid by person aggrieved by nuisance – Jurisdiction of justices – Whether person entitled to lay information against local authority – Public Health Act 1936, ss 94, 99.

c

The words 'the like proceedings' in s 99*ᵃ* of the Public Health Act 1936 are not limited to civil proceedings for the abatement of a statutory nuisance, but give any person aggrieved the right to apply by way of information for the penal orders available under s 94*ᵇ* of the 1936 Act.   Accordingly, a person who wishes to complain of a statutory nuisance is not required to issue an abatement notice before laying an

d   information (see p 841 *j*, p 842 *d* to *h* and p 843 *j* to p 844 *b*, post).

Notes
For statutory nuisances outside London, see 31 Halsbury's Laws (3rd Edn) 367-369, para 546, and for cases on the subject, see 36(1) Digest (Reissue) 434, 435, 259-272.

e   For the power to abate statutory nuisances, see 31 Halsbury's Laws (3rd Edn) 363, 364, para 540, and for summary abatement outside London, see ibid 374-376, paras 551, 552, and for cases on the subject, see 36(1) Digest (Reissue) 439, 294-297.
       For the Public Health Act 1936, ss 94, 99, see 26 Halsbury's Statutes (3rd Edn) 272, 275.

f   **Cases referred to in judgments**
Cocker v Cardwell (1869) LR 5 QB 15, 10 B & S 797, 39 LJMC 28, 21 LT 457, 34 JP 516, 36(1) Digest (Reissue) 508, *801*.
Northern Ireland Trailers Ltd v County Borough of Preston [1972] 1 All ER 260, [1972] 1 WLR 203, 136 JP 149, DC, 36(1) Digest (Reissue) 513, *826*.
Nottingham Corpn v Newton, Nottingham Friendship Housing Association Ltd v Newton
g   [1974] 2 All ER 760, [1974] 1 WLR 923, 72 LGR 535, DC, 36(1) Digest (Reissue) 436, 276.
R v Hughes (1879) 4 QBD 614, 48 LJMC 151, 40 LT 685, 43 JP 556, 14 Cox CC 284, CCR. 14 Digest (Repl) 185, *1512*.
Salford City Council v McNally [1975] 1 All ER 597, [1975] 1 WLR 365, 139 JP 254, 73 LGR 15: *affd* [1975] 2 All ER 860, [1975] 3 WLR 87, 139 JP 783, 73 LGR 408, HL, 36(1)
h   Digest (Reissue) 436, *277*.

Motions for mandamus and certiorari

R v Newham East Justices, ex parte Hunt
This was an application by way of motion by David Leslie Hunt for an order of
j   mandamus directing the Newham East justices to hear and determine the summons issued under s 99 of the Public Health Act 1936 by the applicant on 27th October 1975 against the Greater London Council requiring them to abate a nuisance at 22

---

a   Section 99 is set out at p 842 *c* and *d*, post
b   Section 94, so far as material, is set out at p 841 *c* to *f*, post

Queensland House, Rymill Street, London E16, which was dismissed by the justices
on 27th November 1975.   *a*

R v Oxted Justices, ex parte Franklin
This was an application by way of motion by Bertram Frederick Franklin for an order
of certiorari to remove into the High Court and quash a decision made by the Oxted
magistrates' court on 11th December 1975 dismissing a complaint made by the
applicant on 14th November 1975 against the Tandridge District Council requiring   *b*
them to abate a nuisance at 'Jenners', The Old Vicarage. Vicarage Road, Lingfield,
Surrey, and for an order of mandamus requiring the justices to continue the hearing
of the complaint.
      By consent the two applications were heard together. At the hearing of the applic-
ation in respect of the Oxted justices counsel abandoned his application for certiorari.
The facts are set out in the judgment of Kilner Brown J.   *c*

Stephen Sedley for the applicants.
J R T Rylance for the Greater London Council.
Anthony Thompson for the Tandridge District Council.

                                                                                                                                   d
KILNER BROWN J delivered the first judgment at the invitation of Lord Widgery
CJ: In the first matter counsel moves on behalf of David Leslie Hunt for an order of
mandamus directing the Newham East magistrates' court to hear and determine
a summons brought under s 99 of the Public Health Act 1936.
      In the second matter counsel moves on behalf of Bertram Frederick Franklin for
orders of certiorari to remove a decision of the Oxted justices and of mandamus to   *e*
continue the hearing of proceedings (as in the first matter) brought under s 99 of the
Public Health Act 1936.
      By common consent, the two matters have been taken together because both
involve the interpretation and effect of s 99 of the 1936 Act. This section has recently
been considered in two cases which have become generally known as the *Nottingham*
case[1] and the *Salford* case[2]. The *Nottingham* case[1] was a decision of this court under the   *f*
name of *Nottingham Corpn v Newton*[1]. The *Salford* case[2] is reported under the name of
Salford City Council v McNally[2]. It was a decision of this court which was affirmed in
the House of Lords.
      By way of preamble it is appropriate to observe that ss 42, 43 and 44 of the Magistrates'
Courts Act 1952 make it plain that questions of civil jurisdiction should be initiated
by complaint and questions of criminal jurisdiction should be initiated by information   *g*
and summons. It is also clear, on the authority of *Northern Ireland Trailers Ltd v
County Borough of Preston*[3], that the effect of s 94(2) of the 1936 Act is to involve the
possibility of a fine and therefore has to be considered as a penal section of the Act.
If this subsection is called into being, it should therefore be initiated by information
and summons. So much therefore for questions which are beyond argument.
      In the first of these two cases the justices were dealing with an information laid under   *h*
s 99 of the 1936 Act alleging that the Greater London Council as landlords of premises
at 22 Queensland House, Rymill Street, were in default by reason of nuisance at those
premises as defined by s 92 of the 1936 Act. Section 92, which is headed with the title
'Statutory nuisances', provides in sub-s (1):

      'Without prejudice to the exercise by a local authority of any other powers
      vested in them by or under this Act, the following matters may, subject to the   *j*
      provisions of this Part of this Act, be dealt with summarily, and are in this

---

1   [1974] 2 All ER 760, [1974] 1 WLR 923
2   [1975] 2 All ER 860, [1975] 3 WLR 87
3   [1972] 1 All ER 260, [1972] 1 WLR 203

Part of this Act referred to as "statutory nuisances", that is to say:—(*a*) any
premises in such a state as to be prejudicial to health or a nuisance . . .'

That is all that is necessary to read from s 92.   Section 93 deals with the service of an
abatement notice.   It provides:

'Where a local authority are satisfied of the existence of a statutory nuisance,
they shall serve a notice (hereafter in this Act referred to as "an abatement notice")
on the person by whose act, default or sufferance the nuisance arises or continues
. . .'

Turning then to s 94, that deals with the power of the court to make a nuisance
order if an abatement notice is disregarded.   It provides:

'(1) If the person on whom an abatement notice has been served makes default
in complying with any of the requirements of the notice, or if the nuisance,
although abated since the service of the notice, is, in the opinion of the local
authority, likely to recur on the same premises, the authority shall cause a complaint to be made to a justice of the peace, and the justice shall thereupon issue a
summons requiring the person on whom the notice was served to appear before a
court of summary jurisdiction.
'(2) If on the hearing of the complaint it is proved that the alleged nuisance exists,
or that although abated it is likely to recur on the same premises, then, subject
to the provisions of subsections (4) and (5) of this section the court shall make an
order (hereafter in this Act referred to as "a nuisance order") for either, or both,
of the following purposes—(*a*) requiring the defendant to comply with all or any
of the requirements of the abatement notice, or otherwise to abate the nuisance,
within a time specified in the order, and to execute any works necessary for that
purpose; (*b*) prohibiting a recurrence of the nuisance, and requiring the defendant, within a time specified in the order, to execute any works necessary to prevent a recurrence [It goes on in these words:] and may also impose on the
defendant a fine not exceeding five pounds . . .'

That sum is now increased to £200[1].

It is clear from the reading of those sections that where a local authority wish to
abate a nuisance caused by the owner or occupier of premises there are two stages of
process. There has first to be a service of an abatement notice. If that is not effective,
the authority may then bring the defaulter before the court under s 94. They may
then obtain an order requiring abatement and an order prohibiting recurrence and
if appropriate also request the imposition of a fine. The short point in this case, and
(as will appear) in the other case also, is whether s 99 gives to the individual the right
to invoke s 94 in all its powers without the prior service of a notice of abatement and
is so whether process under s 99 has to be initiated by complaint or by way of
information.

The Newham East justices heard a summons by the applicant on 27th November 1975.
They went to a great deal of trouble, as their most admirably clear affidavit reveals.
They found it a difficult matter. This is not surprising in view of the extent of argument deployed before this court with a wealth of forensic talent, and I intend no
discourtesy to counsel if I deal with the arguments shortly.

Counsel for the applicant submits that s 99 is comprehensive and gives to the individual the right to apply for the orders available under s 94. As this is a penal
section process should be initiated by way of information. That is what the applicant
did, and it is submitted that the justices were wrong in deciding that he should have
applied by way of complaint and were wrong in holding that s 99 invoked civil and
not criminal jurisdiction.

---

1   See the Control of Pollution Act 1974, s 99, Sch 2, para 11

Counsel for the Greater London Council sought to uphold the justices' decision. He argued that the words of s 99 should not be extended to the criminal aspect of s 94(2). *a* It is said that the legislature could not have contemplated giving to the individual the privilege of short-circuiting a prior warning by means of notice. Section 99 does not lead directly to the power to fine set out in s 94(2). It refers to the making of orders but not to the imposition of a fine. There ought to be a severance of s 94(2) and the penal consequences should be excluded. Once the power to fine is excluded, s 99 ceases to cover the criminal process envisaged by s 94(2). The process, it is said, remains *b* civil. If so, proceedings may be by way of complaint and the justices were right in dismissing the information. The court was invited to consider by analogy reference to the history of the various Public Health Acts and to matters in similarity such as Acts dealing with pollution. Section 99 provides:

> 'Complaint of the existence of a statutory nuisance under this Act may be made *c* to a justice of the peace by any person aggrieved by the nuisance, and thereupon the like proceedings shall be had, with the like incidents and consequences as to the making of orders, penalties for disobedience of orders and otherwise, as in the case of a complaint by the local authority, but any order made in such proceedings may, if the court after giving the local authority an opportunity of being heard thinks fit, direct the authority to abate the nuisance.'
>
> *d*

It seems to me that the words, 'the like proceedings shall be had, with the like incidents and consequences as to the making of orders, penalties for disobedience of orders and otherwise, as in the case of a complaint by the local authority', can be construed, and should be construed, to give to the individual the right to go to the justices by way of information and summons and to take the justices straight to s 94. It is to be observed that the word 'procedure' is not used in this section. It refers to 'proceedings'. *e* It refers in terms to the making of orders, penalties for disobedience of orders and otherwise.

In my opinion, the mere fact that there is no mention of the word 'fine' in s 99 does not mean that s 94 cannot be invoked. Starting with s 92, the Act deals with the position of a local authority. It sets out preliminary steps. It moves on in s 94 to deal with powers of enforcement and punishment. Then in s 99 it sets out in general and *f* comprehensive terms that an individual may resort to the court so that like proceedings shall be had with like incidents and consequences as to the making of orders, penalties for disobedience of orders and so forth. It is to be observed that the precise point in this instant case was not before this court in the *Nottingham* case[1], nor in the *Salford* case[2]; nor when it reached the House of Lords was it also a question which their Lordships had to consider.

g

In my judgment, the proper interpretation of this section leads to the conclusion that the individual can by information invoke s 94. Whereas in the past it has, as it was in both the *Nottingham* case[1] and the *Salford* case[2], been done by complaint, once the question calls for decision, as it does now, by this court, it seems to me that the justices were wrong to hold that this was a civil process.

The court has been informed that local authorities fear all sorts of untoward con- *h* sequences if this be the case. I would have thought that these fears are more imagined than real. To begin with, as the Newham East justices in the affidavit of one of their number properly recognised, there is a heavier burden of proof when recourse is made to process by way of information and summons. Secondly, I am confident that the justices will bear in mind the words used by Lord Wilberforce in his speech in the *Salford* case[3] where he said:

j

> 'This aspect of the matter was well explained by the Divisional Court in

---

1 [1974] 2 All ER 760, [1974] 1 WLR 923
2 [1975] 1 All ER 597, [1975] 1 WLR 365
3 [1975] 2 All ER 860 at 864, [1975] 3 WLR 87 at 92

a
Nottingham Corpn v Newton[1] the keynote of which is the need, in making abatement notices, to use discretion and common sense'.

The words of Lord Widgery CJ in *Nottingham Corpn v Newton*[1], which were cited with approval by Lord Edmund-Davies in the *Salford* case[2], were:

b
'This court made it perfectly clear that justices faced with this situation, although bound to make an order under the Act, can use their common sense and are entitled to take into account all the circumstances, and thus avoid the expenditure of public money unnecessarily in a case where the house is likely to be pulled down shortly in any event . . .'

True, both those cases were dealing with a somewhat different situation where the individual was complaining in respect of houses which were subject to demolition c orders. In my view, the words are equally applicable in circumstances such as this. For the reasons I have given, I am of the opinion that the justices came to a wrong decision and the applicant has made out his case for the order which he seeks.

I turn now to the case involving the decision of the Oxted justices. In this case the applicant, Mr Franklin, purported to serve a notice on the Tandridge District Council calling on them to abate a nuisance, namely defects in a report made on inspection of d property known as 'Jenners', The Old Vicarage, Vicarage Road, Lingfield, Surrey. On 14th November 1975 he issued a complaint pursuant to s 99 of the Public Health Act 1936. It was heard on 11th December 1975, when the justices dismissed the complaint, holding that there was no case to answer for the reason that the abatement notice had not been properly served. It is common ground that the notice was not served on the proper officer and therefore did not comply with the provisions of e s 285(d) of the 1936 Act. That of course deals only with the situation in which it is necessary and incumbent on any person to serve a notice.

The applicant now seeks to have the matter heard to its conclusion on the relevant issue in accordance with the provisions of s 94 of the 1936 Act. It is said that their decision implied that no process was open to the applicant under ss 94 and 99 unless an abatement notice had been served under s 93.

f
Counsel submitted that the applicant did not need to serve a notice. He repeated his arguments in general as to the effect of s 99. He referred to two authorities, *Cocker v Cardwell*[3] in which it was held under the old Act[4] in the mid-Victorian period (the predecessor of the present Act) that notice was not a prerequisite. He referred also to *R v Hughes*[5] which is authority for saying that the presence of the party in court, that is to say the magistrates' court, gives jurisdiction to try the issue.

g
Counsel for the Tandridge District Council relied on and adopted the general argument used by counsel for the Greater London Council as to the effect of s 99, and he went on to take the further point, which was this. The applicant based his case on an abatement notice and the justices were right because they held on the facts that the applicant had not made out his case, which was that there was a failure to comply with a notice. But the real substance of his complaint was that there was a nuisance in h existence in fact.

In my judgment, it would have been wrong to refuse relief on that narrow ground. Everybody in this case, and both sides, initially proceeded on the wrong basis. In my opinion there was no need for a notice and the whole thing, as it was developed before the magistrates' court, turned on an irrelevancy.

For the reasons given in the previous case, the applicant in my view was entitled to j rely on s 99 and call on the justices to invoke s 94 if he made out his case. He has

---

1   [1974] 2 All ER 760, [1974] 1 WLR 923
2   [1975] 2 All ER at 869, [1975] 3 WLR at 98
3   (1896) LR 5 QB 15
4   Public Health Act 1875
5   (1879) 4 QBD 614

of course to shoulder the burden imposed by invoking a penal section. In all such
cases in future the initiation process should be by way of information. I would say   *a*
that this applicant succeeds on this motion and the justices should hear the case on the
merits as if it were brought by way of information.

WATKINS J. I agree.

LORD WIDGERY CJ. I also agree.   *b*

Motions for mandamus granted.

Solicitors: *Hilary Fassnidge* (for Mr Hunt); *Hilary Fassnidge*, agent for *Turner, Garrett &
Co*, Weybridge (for Mr Franklin); *A G Gardner* (for the Greater London Council);   *c*
Robert C Wilson, Caterham (for the Tandridge District Council).

N P Metcalfe Esq Barrister.

d

Sullivan v Earl of Caithness

QUEEN'S BENCH DIVISION
LORD WIDGERY CJ, PARK AND MAY JJ
12th, 13th NOVEMBER 1975
                                                                                        e

*Firearms – Possession – Possession of firearm without a certificate – Meaning of 'possession' –
Firearm not in physical custody of accused – Firearm kept in house of accused's mother –
Firearm under accused's control – Whether firearm 'in his possession' – Firearms Act 1968,
s 1(1).*

f

In March 1971 D was issued, by the chief officer of police for Gloucestershire where he
lived, with a firearms certificate in respect of firearms which were stored for safety at
his mother's flat in Surrey. D moved to Oxfordshire, but the firearms remained in
Surrey. The firearms certificate expired in March 1974 and was not renewed. In
August 1974 D was charged with having in his possession at Swalcliffe, Oxfordshire,
firearms without holding a firearms certificate, contrary to s 1(1)[a] of the Firearms Act
1968. The justices dismissed the information on the ground that D was not in   *g*
possession of the firearms in Oxfordshire. On appeal by the prosecutor.

Held – Since D was at all material times the owner of the firearms, and could obtain
them from his mother's flat at any time he wanted them, the firearms were 'in his
possession' in Oxfordshire for the purposes of s 1(1) of the 1968 Act, even though he did   *h*
not have physical custody of them. Moreover, he could properly be convicted of the
offence of unlawful possession by justices in either Oxfordshire or Surrey. Accordingly,
the justices had come to a wrong decision and the case would be remitted to them with
a direction to convict (see p 847 *b c* and *f* to *j* and p 848 *e* to *h*, post).
    Dicta of Earl Jowitt in *United States of America v Dollfus Mieg et Cie SA* [1952] 1 All ER
at 581 and of Lord Parker CJ in *Towers & Co Ltd v Gray* [1961] 2 All ER at 71 applied.   *j*

Notes
For restrictions on the possession of firearms and exemptions from holding a firearms

---

a   Section 1, so far as material, is set out at p 846 *b*, post

certificate, see 10 Halsbury's Laws (3rd Edn) 593-596, paras 1107, 1108, and for cases on
a firearms, see 15 Digest (Repl) 804, 7645-7648.
   For the Firearms Act 1968, s 1, see 8 Halsbury's Statutes (3rd Edn) 729.

Cases referred to in judgments
   Director of Public Prosecutions v Brooks [1974] 2 All ER 840, [1974] AC 862, [1974] 2 WLR
   899, 59 Cr App Rep 185, PC.
b *Towers & Co Ltd v Gray* [1961] 2 All ER 68, [1961] 2 QB 351, [1961] 2 WLR 553, 125 JP
   391, DC, 46 Digest (Repl) 167, 1115.
   United States of America v Dollfus Mieg et Cie SA [1952] 1 All ER 572, [1952] AC 582, HL,
   1 Digest (Repl) 58, 433.
   Woodage v Moss [1974] 1 All ER 584, [1974] 1 WLR 411, 138 JP 253, DC.

c **Case stated**
   This was a case stated by justices for the petty sessional division of North Oxfordshire
   in respect of their adjudication as a magistrates' court sitting at Banbury on 13th
   February 1975.
   1. On 14th November 1974 an information was preferred by the appellant, Brian
   Sullivan, against the respondent, Malcolm Ian, Earl of Caithness, that he on a day
d between 19th March and 22nd August 1974 at Swalcliffe in the county of Oxford had
   in his possession certain firearms, namely a .22 pistol No 2762, a .22 Winchester rifle
   and a .38 Smith & Wesson revolver, to which s 1 of the Firearms Act 1968 applied,
   without holding a firearms certificate in force at that time contrary to s 1(1) of the
   Firearms Act 1968.
   2. The justices found the following facts. (i) On 19th March 1971 the respondent
e was issued with a firearm certificate No 2052A by the chief officer of police for the
   Gloucestershire constabulary for the firearms specified in the information; that the
   certificate expired on 18th March 1974. (ii) At all material times the respondent
   was the owner of the firearms, and no later certificate had been applied for prior to
   22nd August 1974. (iii) On 22nd August 1974 Pc Powell spoke to the respondent at his
   home at Barn Court Cottage, Swalcliffe in the county of Oxford and the respondent then
f admitted possessing the certificate and that the firearms were stored at Hampton
   Court Palace, East Molesey, Surrey. (iv) Barn Court Cottage, Swalcliffe was the respondent's permanent address at all material times (he having moved there from the
   Gloucestershire constabulary area) but the firearms had never been brought there,
   having being kept at all material times at the respondent's mother's flat in Hampton
   Court Palace since it was a more secure place than Barn Court Cottage.
g 3. Apart from the admission of the respondent, no other evidence was adduced by
   the appellant as to the existence or whereabouts of the firearms between the material
   times.
   4. It was contended by the respondent that he had never had possession of the
   firearms at Swalcliffe.
   5. The justices were of the opinion that the respondent was never in possession of
h the firearms at Swalcliffe and accordingly they dismissed the information.
   6. The question for the opinion of the High Court was whether they were right in
   that decision, namely that a person could not be in possession of a firearm at a place
   other than that at which the firearm physically was.

   Anthony Hidden (who did not appear in the court below) for the appellant.
j *T Scott Baker* (who did not appear in the court below) for the respondent.

   MAY J delivered the first judgment at the invitation of Lord Widgery CJ. This is a
   prosecutor's appeal by way of case stated from a decision of the North Oxfordshire
   justices sitting at Banbury on 13th February 1975 dismissing an information preferred
   by the appellant against the respondent alleging that on a day between 19th March and

22nd August 1974 at Swalcliffe in the county of Oxford he had in his possession certain firearms to which the Firearms Act 1968 applied without holding a firearm certificate *a* in force at that time, contrary to s 1(1) of that Act. The section itself is in just these terms and provides, insofar as is relevant:

'Subject to any exemption under this Act, it is an offence for a person—(*a*) to have in his possession, or to purchase or acquire, a firearm to which this section applies without holding a firearm certificate in force at the time . . .' *b*

The facts found by the justices on the respondent's own admissions are simple. First, he has at all material times been the owner of the firearms specified in the information and to which it is not disputed that s 1(1) of the 1968 Act applied. On 19th March 1971 he was issued with a firearm certificate under the Act for those firearms by the chief officer of police for Gloucestershire; at that time he lived in that county. That *c* certificate expired on 18th March 1974. The respondent omitted to apply for a fresh certificate to take its place. At all material times his permanent address was Barn Court Cottage, Swalcliffe in Oxfordshire, to which he had moved from Gloucestershire. However, the firearms themselves were never there. They were kept throughout at his mother's flat in Hampton Court, because that was considered to be a more secure place for their retention than his home at Barn Court Cottage in Swalcliffe. *d*

Before the justices the respondent contended that on these facts he had never had possession of the firearms at Swalcliffe and that thus the information as preferred should be dismissed. This was a contention which went more than just to form. The suggested defect could not effectively be cured under s 100 of the Magistrates' Courts Act 1952 because if the information had been amended to aver the unlawful possession of the firearms at Hampton Court in Surrey then, as these were proceedings *e* which were being dealt with by the Oxford justices summarily, they would have had no jurisdiction to try the amended alleged offence and would thus similarly have had to dismiss the amended information.

In the event the justices decided that on the facts before them that the respondent had never had possession of the firearms at Swalcliffe and they dismissed the information on that ground. The question they pose for the opinion of this court is whether *f* they were right in that decision, namely that a person cannot be in possession of a firearm at a place other than that at which the firearm physically is.

For my part I have considerable sympathy with the justices in this case. They appear to have had very little assistance by way of argument on what is by no means an easy point, but at the end of the day, and with all respect to them, I think that they came to a wrong conclusion. In my opinion, and for the purposes of s 1 of the *g* 1968 Act, a person who is at a given time in Oxford can there have possession of firearms which are themselves at that time physically in Surrey.

The Act itself contains no definition of the word 'possession'. This is not unusual in statutes creating this type of criminal offence. As a result, as Lord Parker CJ said in *Towers & Co Ltd v Gray*[1]: 'The term "possession" is always giving rise to trouble.' He then went on to quote briefly from a speech of Earl Jowitt in the earlier case of *h* *United States of America v Dollfus Mieg et Cie SA*[2]:

'The person having the right to immediate possession is, however, frequently referred to in English law as being the "possessor"—in truth, the English law has never worked out a completely logical and exhaustive definition of "possession".'

A little later in Lord Parker CJ's judgment[1] appears the passage quoted by Ashworth *j* J in *Woodage v Moss*[3], a decision of this court to which we have also been referred:

1   [1961] 2 All ER 68 at 71, [1961] 2 QB 351 at 361, 362
2   [1952] 1 All ER 572 at 581, [1952] AC 582 at 605
3   [1974] 1 All ER 584, [1974] 1 WLR 411

a   'For my part I approach this case on the basis that the meaning of "possession"
depends on the context in which it is used . . . In some contexts, no doubt, a bailment for reward subject to a lien, where, perhaps, some period of notice has to be
given before the goods can be removed, could be of such a nature that the only
possession that there could be said to be, would be possession in the bailee.
In other cases it may well be that the nature of the bailment is such that the
owner of the goods who has parted with the physical possession of them can
b   truly be said still to be in possession.'

Looking at the context of the word 'possession' in s 1 of the 1968 Act in the present
case, I have no doubt that one can be in possession of a firearm even though one is at a
place other than that at which the firearm physically is. To agree with the justices'
decision in the present case would in my view effectively be to equate the word
c   'possession' in s 1 with custody, and this I am satisfied would be wrong.

Counsel for the appellant pointed out that under s 26 of the Act an application for
the grant of a firearm certificate has to be made in the prescribed form to the chief
officer of police for the area in which the applicant resides. The prescribed form is by
virtue of r 12 of the Firearms Rules 1969[1] that set out in Sch 4 to those rules. This form
requires the applicant to state not only his residence but also where the firearm
d   will be kept, which clearly may be a different place from that where he resides.
Further, s 27(2) of the Act provides that the firearm certificate itself shall also be in the
prescribed form and shall specify conditions subject to which it is held. By virtue of
r 11 of the 1969 rules, every certificate must be subject to the four conditions there set
out, of which the second and the fourth read as follows:

e   '(ii) the firearms and ammunition to which the certificate relates must at all
times when not in actual use be kept in a secure place with a view to preventing
access to them by unauthorised persons . . .
'(iv) the holder must, without undue delay, inform the chief officer of police
by whom the certificate was granted of any change in his permanent address.'

In my opinion the purpose of s 1 of the 1968 Act and its ancillary provisions is to
f   regulate and license not merely those who have physical custody of firearms, or who
keep them in the place in which they live, but also those who have firearms under
their control at their behest, even though for one reason or another they may be kept
at their country cottage, at the local shooting range or indeed at Bisley.

As a matter of construction, therefore, which must to some extent also be a matter
of first impression, and looking at the context and what I believe to have been the
g   intent of s 1 of the 1968 Act, it may well be, I think, that the owner of a firearm who
does not at the relevant time have physical possession of it can nevertheless truly be
said still to be in possession of it.

In the present case, the respondent was at all material times the owner of the
firearms. He could no doubt obtain them from his mother's flat at any time when
he wanted them. She had the barest custody of them, not because she had any
h   interest in them, but because her flat was safer than the respondent's home in Oxford.

In these circumstances and on the admitted facts, in my judgment the respondent
was at material times in Swalcliffe in possession of those firearms for the purposes of
the 1968 Act, and consequently I think the justices were wrong and should on the
facts as they found them have convicted the respondent.

In deference to the arguments on this first point which were addressed to this court,
j   I add, first, that I have not obtained assistance in the present case from the short
passage from the judgment of Lord Diplock in the Privy Council in *Director of Public
Prosecutions v Brooks*[2]. True, one can say that there is some similarity in the regulatory

1   SI 1969 No 1219
2   [1974] 2 All ER 840, [1974] AC 862

purpose between the Firearms Act 1968 and the Dangerous Drugs Law of Jamaica with
which that case was concerned, but as I read the judgment, the real point there   *a*
was not whether the word 'possession' in the Jamaican statute meant more than
physical custody, but the extent to which it was necessary to show that the defendant
knew that that of which he in fact had physical custody comprised dangerous drugs.

Secondly, counsel for both the appellant and the respondent in the present case
drew attention to the difficulties which could arise, given different sets of facts, if the
court were to adopt the construction of s 1 contended for by their opponent. For   *b*
my part, I think that one can exaggerate the value of such arguments. Where the
point in issue in the case is a question of construction it is usually possible for experienced counsel on each side to postulate quite reasonable sets of facts which would give
rise to difficulty, if not absurdity, if the construction of the Act or argument against
which they contend were to be upheld by the court.

The opinion I have already expressed in this judgment is sufficient in itself to dispose   *c*
of this appeal. However, I think that I should also deal briefly with a further and
wider contention of counsel for the appellant. The concept of the possession by a
person or thing, he submitted, is that of a mutual relationship between that person
and that thing, and thus when each is in a place different from the other it can co-exist
at both places. On the facts of the present case, as found by the justices, therefore,
the argument proceeded, this respondent could properly have been convicted of an   *d*
offence under s 1 of the 1968 Act both before the Oxfordshire justices on the information the subject of this appeal and also before the Surrey justices on an information
alleging possession without the necessary licence of the firearms at his mother's flat
in Hampton Court.

I have had my doubts about this contention and was at first impressed by counsel
for the respondent's answer to it, namely that if it were correct it meant that one   *e*
offence was being committed by the same person in two places at one and the same
time. In the end, however, I have come to the conclusion that in relation to offences
which I can generally describe as those comprising some form of unlawful possession
this may well be so, and that it would in truth be unreal so as to construe a statute
creating such an offence that the latter is not committed where the goods in fact are,
wherever else the offence may be being committed by the possessor at the same time.   *f*

For the earlier reasons which I have given, however, I think that the justices came
to an incorrect decision in this case and consequently for my part I would allow the
appeal and send the case back to them with a direction to convict.

PARK J. I agree.
                                                                                       g

LORD WIDGERY CJ. I also agree and would add a word of sympathy with the
justices in the difficult problem which they faced in this case.

Appeal allowed. Case remitted to justices with direction to convict.
                                                                                       h

Solicitors: *Sharpe Pritchard & Co*, agents for *J Malcolm Simons*, Kidlington, Oxford (for
the appellant); *Johnson & Gaunt*, Banbury (for the respondent).

N P Metcalfe Esq Barrister.

a # R v Rent Officer for the London Borough of Brent, ex parte Ganatra

QUEEN'S BENCH DIVISION
LORD WIDGERY CJ, PARK AND MAY JJ
b 10th, 11th NOVEMBER, 3rd DECEMBER 1975

Rent restriction – Rent – Determination of fair rent – Jurisdiction – Preliminary issue – County court – Reference to county court – Status of applicant – Landlord contending applicant not tenant of house – Jurisdiction of rent officer or rent assessment committee to consider and determine issue – Whether proper course to leave parties to refer issue to county court –
c *Rent Act 1968, s 105(1).*

C applied for the registration of a fair rent of a dwelling-house pursuant to s 44 of the Rent Act 1968. The applicant, acting as agent for his brother, the owner of the house, wrote to the rent officer stating that C was not the tenant and therefore had no locus standi to make the application. In the alternative, and on the basis that C was the tenant, the letter went on to describe the accommodation and to suggest
d that the economic rent ought to be in excess of £50 per week. Subsequently the rent officer made an appointment but neither the applicant nor anyone on his behalf appeared. The rent officer invited the parties to discuss C's application with him at his office. C kept the appointment but the applicant did not. As a result of the information given to him, and bearing in mind the contents of the applicant's letter,
e the rent officer decided that C was the tenant and determined the rent at £11 per week. Following an objection by the applicant, the rent officer referred the matter to the rent assessment committee. Before the committee the applicant contended that they had no jurisdiction as C was only one of four joint tenants of the house. The committee heard evidence on that preliminary point and decided that C was not a tenant with the result that the original application was invalid and that in consequence
f they had no jurisdiction to hear the objection referred to them. On being notified of the decision, the rent officer made an entry in the register in the panel recording the rent determined by the committee which read: 'No jurisdiction', but he refused to expunge the fair rent entered by himself. The applicant applied for orders of mandamus or certiorari with a view to securing the cancellation or removal from the register of the entry relating to the house.

g **Held** – (i) Where a question was raised as to the jurisdiction of the rent officer, the proper course was for the rent officer to refuse to consider the application and to leave the disputed issue to be decided by the county court under s 105(1)*ᵃ* of the 1968 Act on an application by either the tenant or the landlord. Similarly, where the rent officer's determination was referred to a rent assessment committee and new evidence
h came to light which cast doubt on the jurisdiction of the rent officer or the committee, the committee should refuse to consider the case and leave the question to be determined by the county court (see p 853 *c d* and *g* to p 854 *b* and p 856 *a*, post).

(ii) There were no grounds for impugning the decision of the rent officer since the applicant had in effect abandoned his contention before him that someone other than C was the tenant. The circumstances in which a rent assessment committee would
j be justified in embarking on an enquiry into the question of jurisdiction following a reference would be very rare and, in the circumstances of the instant case, the decision of the committee to do so was wrong. In the light of that decision, however, there was nothing which the rent officer could be required to do other than what he had in

---

a Section 105(1), so far as material, is set out at p 853 *b*, post

fact done. Accordingly the applications would be refused (see p 853 *d* to *f* and *j*, p 854 *b* to *d*, p 855 *f* and *h* and p 856 *a*, post).   *a*

Notes

For the jurisdiction of the county courts in relation to proceedings arising out of the Rent Acts, see 23 Halsbury's Laws (3rd Edn) 831-833, para 1618.

For the power of the rent officer to register a fair rent and who may apply for such registration, see Supplement to 23 Halsbury's Laws (3rd Edn) para 1571B.   *b*

For the Rent Act 1968, ss 44, 105, see 18 Halsbury's Statutes (3rd Edn) 832, 884.

Cases referred to in judgments

Briscoe v Stephens (1824) 2 Bing 213, 9 Moore CP 413, 3 LJOSCP 257, 130 ER 288, 21 Digest (Repl) 309, *692*.

London Corpn v Cox (1867) LR 2 HL 239, 36 LJEx 225, 16 Digest (Repl) 416, *2184*.   *c*

R v City of London Rent Tribunal, ex parte Honig [1951] 1 All ER 195, [1951] 1 KB 641, 49 LGR 252, DC, 31(2) Digest (Reissue) 1130, *8751*.

R v Fulham, Hammersmith and Kensington Rent Tribunal, ex parte Zerek [1951] 1 All ER 482, [1951] 2 KB 1, 49 LGR 275, DC, 31(2) Digest (Reissue) 1044, *8238*.

R v Judge Pugh, ex parte Graham [1951] 2 All ER 307, [1951] 2 KB 623, 49 LGR 659, DC, 31(2) Digest (Reissue) 1058, *8328*.   *d*

R v Westminster (City) London Borough Rent Officer, ex parte Rendall [1973] 3 All ER 119, [1973] QB 959, [1973] 3 WLR 118.

Case also cited

R v London Rent Assessment Panel, ex parte Braq Investments Ltd [1969] 2 All ER 1012, [1969] 1 WLR 970, DC.   *e*

Motions for mandamus and certiorari

This was an application by Ramesh Gordhandas Ganatra for an order of mandamus directed to the respondent, the rent officer for the London Borough of Brent, requiring him to remove or cancel the entry in the rent register relating to a dwelling-house known as 7 Whitby Gardens, London, NW9, or alternatively for an order of *f* certiorari to quash the determination of the rent officer relating to that dwelling-house. The facts are set out in the judgment of Park J.

Roger Bartlett for the applicant.
Harry Woolf for the respondent.

                                                                                         g
                                                  Cur adv vult

3rd December 1975. **PARK J** read the first judgment at the invitation of Lord Widgery CJ. In these proceedings counsel moves on behalf of the applicant for an order of mandamus directed to the rent officer for the London Borough of Brent requiring him to remove or cancel the entry in the rent register for the borough re-   *h* lating to 7 Whitby Gardens, NW9, or alternatively for an order of certiorari to remove into this division of the High Court of Justice and quash the determination of the rent officer relating to that dwelling-house.

The facts are these. In October 1974 Mr Chandrakant Radia made an application for the registration of a fair rent for this dwelling-house to the rent officer pursuant to s 44 of the Rent Act 1968. The rent officer followed the procedure on such an application laid down in Sch 6 to the 1968 Act. In due course, the applicant, acting as agent for *j* his brother (the owner of the house), wrote a letter dated 21st October 1974 in which he stated, inter alia:

'... Mr. Chandrakant P. Radia is not the tenant of my brother. The tenant is Mr. Virendra P. Radia. The house is let furnished to Mr. V. P. Radia, and therefore, a the applicant herein has no locus standi to make any application. This application must therefore be dismissed with costs. ALTERNATIVELY, and only if satisfactory evidence is produced to prove that Chandrakant is the tenant, but not otherwise, I would say as under . . .'

The letter then goes on to describe at great length the accommodation in the house: the fixtures and fittings and their cost; the furniture and furnishings and the out-
b goings, and concludes with the submission that the economic rent ought to be in excess of £50 per week.

In November 1974 the rent officer wrote to the parties requesting them both to be present on the occasion of a visit he proposed to make to the dwelling-house on 28th November. Mr Chandrakant Radia turned up, but neither the applicant nor anyone on his behalf kept the appointment. Thereafter, by further letters to the parties, the
c rent officer invited them to discuss the application with him at his office on 12th December. Once again, Mr Chandrakant Radia kept the appointment, but the applicant did not.

As a result of the information given to him on 28th November and 12th December by Mr Radia and bearing in mind the contents of the applicant's letter dated 21st October, the rent officer decided that Mr Chandrakant Radia was the tenant and
d determined the rent of the premises at £11 per week. That rent was duly registered, along with all the other particulars required to be entered in the register kept pursuant to s 43 of the Rent Act 1968.

On receiving the rent officer's notice of his determination, the applicant wrote him a letter dated 16th December 1974 in which he stated: 'I hereby give you notice that I am not satisfied with the *rent* [my italics] as confirmed by you on the 12th December
e 1974 and would like to appeal from the said decision.' The rent officer then referred the matter to the appropriate rent assessment committee.

When the matter eventually came before the committee, counsel for the applicant submitted, as a preliminary point, that the tribunal had no jurisdiction to hear the application as Mr Chandrakant Radia was only one of four joint tenants. The committee was told that the letter dated 21st October 1974 to the rent officer had been
f written in haste and that Mr Dhirendra P Radia, who was therein described as the tenant, had done no more than conduct the negotiations for a tenancy on behalf of four brothers Radia, who included himself and Chandrakant.

The rent assessment committee decided to hear the evidence on the preliminary point. Having done so, they came to the conclusion that they were not satisfied that there was a joint letting to the four Radia brothers; that Chandrakant Radia was not
g a tenant and that, in consequence, the original application made by Chandrakant Radia was invalid, so that the committee had no jurisdiction to hear the objection referred to them by the rent officer.

On being notified of the rent assessment committee's decision, the rent officer wrote an entry on the reverse side of the page of his register dealing with this application. In the panel for recording the rent determined by the rent assessment
h committee, he wrote: 'No jurisdiction.'

Thereafter the applicant's solicitors wrote to the rent officer requesting him to expunge the entry in the register relating to this dwelling-house. The rent officer has refused to do so, contending that in law no power has been conferred on him to expunge the entry, which must remain until this court has made an order quashing his determination and directing that the entry be removed or cancelled.

i It was argued in this court on behalf of the applicant that the rent assessment committee were compelled to enquire into the facts in order to decide whether or not they had jurisdiction to determine the matter which had been referred to them; that, having made that enquiry and having decided that there was no competent applicant, the whole proceedings were a nullity from the start; that their decision was binding on the rent officer who had to give effect to it; that, while the committee was not given any power to cause an entry to be made in the register, the rent officer, who is required by s 43 to prepare and keep the register up to date, had a duty imposed on him to keep it according to law and that that duty involved more than merely recording the words 'No jurisdiction' in the appropriate panel; it included the removal or cancellation of the entry.

I think that it is necessary to consider first the scope of the rent officer's jurisdiction after an application has been made under s 44 for the registration of a rent. That matter was considered by the Court of Appeal in *R v Westminster (City) London Borough Rent Officer, ex parte Rendall*[1]. In that case the tenant of a flat in a six-floored house made as application under s 44. The rateable value of the whole house was £1,597 but it had not been apportioned between the six floors. Section 1(1)(a) of the 1968 Act provides that a tenancy of such a dwelling-house is a protected tenancy unless it had on the appropriate day a rateable value exceeding £400. As there was no separate rateable value for the flat, the rent officer made his own assessment of it. He came to the conclusion that it was less than £400 and therefore within his jurisdiction.

Section 6 of the 1968 Act provides:

'(1) Except where this Act otherwise provides, the rateable value on any day of a dwelling-house shall be ascertained for the purposes of this Act as follows:— (a) if the dwelling-house is a hereditament for which a rateable value is then shown in the valuation list, it shall be that rateable value; (b) if the dwelling-house forms part only of such a hereditament or consists of or forms part of more than one such hereditament, its rateable value shall be taken to be such value as is found by a proper apportionment or aggregation of the rateable value or values so shown.

'(2) Any question arising under this section as to the proper apportionment or aggregation of any value or values shall be determined by the county court, and the decision of the county court shall be final ...'

On an application for an order of certiorari by the landlord, the Divisional Court held that the rent officer had no jurisdiction to apportion the rateable value of the whole house as that could be done only by the county court and quashed the registration. The Court of Appeal allowed an appeal from that decision. In the course of his judgment, with which Orr and Lawton LJJ agreed, Lord Denning MR said[2]:

'Section 6(2) only applies where there is a "question arising". If the rent officer makes his own estimate of the rateable value of the part (by doing his own apportionment, rough and ready though it be) and it comes under £400, and there is no challenge to his jurisdiction, then there is no "question arising". There is nothing to refer to the county court. But if he has doubt whether it is over or under £400, so that a question arises in his own mind about it, then he should refer it to the county court. Again, if the landlord takes objection or if there is a challenge to the jurisdiction, then, of course, a question arises and it must go to the county court. Except in those cases, it seems to me the rent officer is entitled to say: "On the face of it, this part appears to me to be within the rateable limits. I am entitled to rely on s 1(3) which says that the rateable value is deemed to be within the limits unless the contrary is shown. It is not shown here. So I have jurisdiction." In doing so, the rent officer is acting within the principle of such cases as *R v City of London etc Rent Tribunal, ex parte Honig*[3], where it has been held that a tribunal has jurisdiction to decide on the facts necessary to found its own jurisdiction.'

---

1   [1973] 3 All ER 119, [1973] QB 959
2   [1973] 3 All ER at 122, [1973] QB at 975
3   [1951] 1 All ER 195, [1951] 1 KB 641

I think that Lord Denning MR's words can apply with equal force to the situation of
a rent officer who finds that his jurisdiction to consider an application for the registration of a rent is disputed by a landlord on the ground that the applicant is not the
tenant of the premises in question.

Section 6(2), of course, is concerned only with ascertaining rateable value and could
not apply to such a dispute. On the other hand, I think that s 105(1) would apply.
This subsection provides:

> 'A county court shall have jurisdiction, either in the course of any proceedings
> relating to a dwelling or on an application made for the purpose by the landlord
> or the tenant, to determine any question—(a) as to whether a tenancy is a pro-
> tected tenancy or whether any person is a statutory tenant of a dwelling-house . . .
> or as to any matter which is or may become material for determining any such
> question.'

Accordingly, I think that if a rent officer finds that his jurisdiction if challenged in
this manner by a landlord and if in consequence there is a doubt in his mind about his
jurisdiction, then a question falls to be determined by the county court under s 105.
In such circumstances the rent officer must refuse to consider the application and must
leave the disputed issue to be decided by the county court on an application by either
tenant or landlord.

In the present case, in his original objection to the registration, the applicant did not
raise the issue of the rent officer's jurisdiction otherwise than in general terms and he
went on to leave the question to be decided by the rent officer 'on satisfactory
evidence'. Thereafter, the applicant twice had the opportunity of putting his case on
this point to the rent officer, but, on each occasion, he failed to keep the appointment.
In these circumstances I think that the rent officer was fully justified in coming to the
conclusion, on the material before him, that this application was not one which he
should refuse to consider and that, on the contrary, Mr Chandrakant Radia was the
tenant of the premises.

I turn now to consider the jurisdiction of the rent assessment committee. When a
landlord or a tenant lodges an objection in writing to the rent officer's determination
and registration of a fair rent, 'the matter' has to be referred to the rent assessment
committee (Sch 6, para 5, to the 1968 Act). Thereafter, the rent assessment committee
conduct an enquiry and, if requested to do so, hear representations from the landlord
and tenant; at the conclusion of the enquiry, the rent assessment committee confirm the
rent registered by the rent officer or, if that rent does not appear to them to be fair,
determine a fair rent, which in due course is registered by the rent officer in the
register.

Thus, in the first instance, the jurisdiction of the rent assessment committee is
confined to making a decision on the matter referred to them by the rent officer. The
rent officer has no power under the 1968 Act to refer to the rent assessment committee
any matter other than his determination of the rent. He certainly cannot refer to
them any disputed question relating to jurisdiction to determine the rent, because any
such question would and should have been referred, as I have already said, to the
county court.

In the present case the rent officer properly determined the jurisdiction issue.
The applicant in effect abandoned his contention that someone other than Mr
Chandrakant Radia was the tenant, so that, at the time of the rent officer's reference, there was no issue as to the jurisdiction of the rent assessment committee to
entertain the reference. But, as counsel for the respondent said in the course of his
submissions to this court, it would be possible, after a reference by the rent officer, for
a situation to arise in which the rent officer's jurisdiction to consider the application in
the first place could be disputed, for example, by the discovery of a tenancy agreement which showed that the applicant was not the tenant. In such a situation the

parties might agree that in the light of the new evidence neither the rent officer nor the rent assessment committee had any jurisdiction to deal with the application.

On the other hand, the new evidence might be in dispute so that in consequence any enquiry into the rent assessment committee's jurisdiction to consider the reference would also be in dispute. In such circumstances I think that the rent assessment committee should refuse to proceed with the case, and, like the rent officer in a similar situation, should leave the question to be determined by the county court on an application made for the purpose by the landlord or the tenant under s 105.

In the present case the applicant was not in a position to say that he had discovered new evidence. All he did was to alter slightly the basis of his original objection to the jurisdiction of the rent officer. He contended before the rent assessment committee that Mr Dhirendra Radia, whom he had previously alleged was the tenant, had in fact negotiated a joint tenancy consisting of himself, Chandrakant Radia and two other Radia brothers as tenants. I doubt if this new case constituted a sufficient basis for the rent assessment committee's decision to enquire into a matter falling outside the rent officer's reference. But even if it did, I think that the rent assessment committee's decision to enquire into it was wrong. The procedure outlined above should have been followed. The consequences of their enquiry vividly illustrate the difficulties that can arise when the correct procedure is not followed. The rent officer has decided that Chandrakant Radia is the tenant. On the other hand, the rent assessment committee have decided that he is not and that, contrary to the applicant's contention, the four Radia brothers are not tenants either. The rent assessment committee, because it was not necessary for them to do so, failed to indicate who in their opinion is the tenant. Finally, since they made their decision, solicitors acting for the applicant have written letters to the four Radia brothers, threatening to sue them all for arrears of rent. Thus, the rent assessment committee's decision has contributed nothing towards the determination of a fair rent for the premises; it is not binding on the parties (see *R v Judge Pugh, ex parte Graham*[1]) and it has merely succeeded in throwing into confusion that which before the reference was made to them had become reasonably clear.

In the submission made on behalf of the applicant that the rent assessment committee had to enquire into the facts in order to decide whether or not they had jurisdiction, reliance was placed on *R v Fulham, Hammersmith and Kensington Rent Tribunal, ex parte Zerek*[2]. In that case, a landlord let two rooms in his house to a tenant at a weekly rent of 35s. The tenant referred the letting to a rent tribunal under the Landlord and Tenant (Rent Control) Act 1949. At the hearing, the landlord produced to the tribunal a document signed by the tenant and referring to the letting as a furnished one. He relied on the document as proving that the rooms were let furnished, so that the reference was out of order because not made under the Furnished Houses (Rent Control) Act 1946. The tenant had an explanation for the document. The tribunal decided that the rooms had been let unfurnished, so that they had jurisdiction and reduced the rent. On the application of the landlord for an order of certiorari to quash the tribunal's determination, the Divisional Court held that the tribunal were entitled to satisfy themselves whether the letting was, for the purposes of the Rent Restriction Acts, of furnished or unfurnished rooms. In the course of his judgment Devlin J said[3]:

'In my opinion, the argument on behalf of the applicant is based on a misconception of what it is that a tribunal in cases such as this is doing. When, at the inception of an inquiry by a tribunal of limited jurisdiction, a challenge is made to its jurisdiction, the tribunal has to make up its mind whether it will act or not,

1 [1951] 2 All ER 307, [1951] 2 KB 623
2 [1951] 1 All ER 482, [1951] 2 KB 1
3 [1951] 1 All ER at 488, [1951] 2 KB at 10

and for that purpose to arrive at some decision on whether it has jurisdiction or not. If its jurisdiction depends on the existence of a state of facts, it must inform itself about them, and, if the facts are in dispute, reach some conclusion on the merits of the dispute. If it reaches a wrong conclusion, the rights of parties against each other are not affected. For, if the tribunal wrongly assumes jurisdiction, the party who apparently obtains an order from it in reality takes nothing. The whole proceeding is, in the phrase used in the old reports, *coram non judice*. If, for example, the applicant in the present case wishes . . . he can sue for his 35*s*. rent. He will be met with the defence that by the order of the tribunal it has been reduced to 15*s*. He can reply that that order is bad for want of jurisdiction, and the defendant will have to justify the order on which he relies and so prove the facts which give the tribunal jurisdiction. This seems to me to be what is laid down by the decision in *Briscoe* v. *Stephens*[1], and to be in accordance with the opinion of WILLES, J., in *London Corpn.* v. *Cox*[2]. In such an action, I apprehend, the findings of the tribunal would be irrelevant and in-admissible. They are findings in a preliminary inquiry whose only object is to enable the tribunal to decide for itself how to act. They are findings, therefore, that cannot ultimately prejudice either party. In these circumstances, I am unable to see why the tribunal should, in making its preliminary inquiry, be restricted to any particular class of case or how it can be restrained from investigating for its own purposes any point which it thinks it necessary to determine so that it can decide on its course of action.'

It is to be observed, however, that the Landlord and Tenant (Rent Control) Act 1949, taken in conjunction with the principal Acts, contained no section comparable with s 105, so that a rent tribunal, faced with the situation which confronted the tribunal in *Zerek's* case[3], was compelled to decide for itself whether it had jurisdiction to hear and determine the reference.

By virtue of s 105, however, rent assessment committees are not compelled to determine whether or not the applicant is competent, though no doubt they may do so if they wish, provided the matter casting doubt on his competence has come to light since the rent officer's reference. But the circumstances in which a rent assessment committee would be justified in ignoring the existence of s 105 and in embarking on an enquiry into such a matter or indeed into any matter not referred to them by the rent officer must be very rare.

In the present case, no reason has been put forward for the rent assessment committee's decision to enquire into the jurisdiction question. The rent assessment committee do not appear to have directed their minds to the question of refusing to proceed with the case and thereby allowing the parties to apply to the county court. I have already mentioned some of the consequences of their decision. Another is that, not having the power to order discovery, as would the judge in the county court if the question had been decided there, they apparently never saw a copy of the applicant's letter dated 16th December 1974 in which by implication he accepted the rent officer's decision that Chandrakant Radia was the tenant.

For these reasons I think that the rent assessment committee's decision themselves to decide the question of jurisdiction was in the circumstances a wrong decision. That being so, I can see no reason why the rent officer should be required to do any more than he has done already, namely to enter in the appropriate place in the register, the words: 'No jurisdiction'.

I would therefore refuse these applications.

---

1   (1824) 2 Bing 213
2   (1867) LR 2 HL 239
3   [1951] 1 All ER 482, [1951] 2 KB 1

MAY J. I agree.

LORD WIDGERY CJ. I also agree.

Applications refused.

Solicitors: *Bernard Elliston, Sandler & Co* (for the applicant); *Treasury Solicitor.*

Jacqueline Charles Barrister.

The Halcyon Skies
Powell v Owners of the proceeds of sale of the ship Halcyon Skies and another

QUEEN'S BENCH DIVISION (ADMIRALTY COURT)
BRANDON J
15th, 20th, 22nd OCTOBER, 1st DECEMBER 1975

*Master and servant – Contract of service – Breach – Damages – Pension fund contributions –
Employer's contributions – Contract providing for payment of contributions by employer to
pension fund for employee – Failure of employer to pay contributions – Employee's loss of
entitlement to pension rights – Amount of damages – Amount necessary to restore employee
to position in which he would have been if contributions had been paid – Whether employee
entitled to claim damages equal to sum of unpaid contributions.*

*Admiralty – Jurisdiction – Action in rem – Claim for wages – Pension fund contributions –
Seaman employed on ship – Contract providing for payment of contributions to pension fund
by employer and seaman – Employer deducting seaman's contributions from wages – Employer
not paying contributions to fund – Action by seaman for amount of contributions – Whether
a 'claim for wages' – Administration of Justice Act 1956, s 1(1)(o).*

*Shipping – Maritime lien – Wages – Seaman – Special contract – Wages payable under a
special contract – Pension fund contributions – Employer's and employee's contributions –
Failure of employer to pay contributions to fund – Lien on ship – Whether seaman entitled to
maritime lien in respect of unpaid contributions – Administration of Justice Act 1956, ss 1(1)(o),
3(3).*

The plaintiff was employed by CL Ltd as a deck officer on board a tanker from 1st
June 1974. His contract of employment provided that he should be a member of an
occupational pension scheme, that CL Ltd should pay employer's contributions in
respect of him to the fund, and that CL Ltd should, with his authority, deduct
employee's contributions from his wages and pay them to the fund. On 16th August
a petition was presented for the winding-up of CL Ltd and a liquidator was appointed.
The tanker on which the plaintiff was employed was appraised and sold by order of
the court on 14th October in an action brought by the second mortgagees, and the
proceeds of sale were paid into court. The plaintiff ceased to work for CL Ltd on
16th November 1974. The amount of employer's contributions which CL Ltd
should have paid to the fund in respect of the plaintiff's employment was £97·46 and
the amount of employee's contributions which they had deducted from the plaintiff's

a wages, and which should have been paid to the fund, was £52·97. Neither of those sums had been paid to the fund. The plaintiff brought an action in rem against the proceeds of sale of the ship to recover the two sums of £97·46 and £52·97, contending (i) that he could claim either in debt or for damages for breach of contract; (ii) that his claim was a claim 'by a . . . member of the crew of a ship for wages' within s 1(1)(o)[a] of the Administration of Justice Act 1956, enabling him to invoke the Admiralty jurisdiction of the court; and (iii) that he had a maritime lien for the claim, so that

b (a) he could proceed in rem against the proceeds of sale of the ship under s 3(3)[b] of the 1956 Act, and (b) he was entitled to priority over the competing claim of the second mortgagees.

Held – (i) The plaintiff had a good claim in debt for the amount of the employee's contributions. Under his contract of employment he had given CL Ltd authority

c to deduct contributions from his wages and to pay them to the fund; CL Ltd had acted on the first part of that authority, but not on the second. In those circumstances, the plaintiff was entitled to revoke the second part of the authority, and to require CL Ltd to pay those sums to him instead. There was no doubt that those sums, having been deducted from the plaintiff's pay in the first place, were part of his wages for the purpose of s 1(1)(o) of the 1956 Act (see p 860 c and d, post).

d (ii) The plaintiff was also entitled to judgment for the sum of £97·46 in respect of the unpaid employer's contributions for the following reasons—

(a) The failure of CL Ltd to pay employer's contributions to the fund was a breach of contract for which the plaintiff was entitled to damages in a sum which, so far as an award of money could do, would put him in the same position as if CL Ltd had performed their obligation to pay employer's contributions to the fund, thereby

e conferring on the plaintiff an entitlement to certain future pension benefits. Accordingly, the proper measure of damages for CL Ltd's failure was the sum of £97·46 which the plaintiff could pay to the pension fund himself, thereby restoring his entitlement to those benefits (see p 862 g and h and p 863 b to f, post).

(b) Employer's contributions to a pension fund were, in principle, part of the employee's total earnings. It was irrelevant that the plaintiff was not claiming the

f contributions themselves, since the Admiralty jurisdiction in wages had long extended to claims founded in damages as well as debt. The plaintiff's claim was, therefore, a claim for 'wages' within s 1(1)(o) of the 1956 Act (see p 864 a to f and p 869 b, post); dictum of Lord Reid in Parry v Cleaver [1969] 1 All ER at 559, 560 applied.

(iii) The plaintiff was entitled to a maritime lien in respect of both employee's and employer's contributions. Although the contract under which the plaintiff had

g been employed was a special contract rather than an ordinary mariner's contract, the statutory provisions which had extended Admiralty jurisdiction to claims for wages under a special contract, and which had subsequently been re-enacted in s 1(1)(o) of the 1956 Act, had had the effect of extending maritime liens to such claims (see p 864 g, p 867 e to p 868 a and c to f and p 869 b, post); The British Trade [1924] P 104 not followed.

h **Notes**

For Admiralty jurisdiction in respect of wages, see 1 Halsbury's Laws (4th Edn) paras 338-343, and for cases on the subject, see 1 Digest (Repl) 153-162, 395-501.

For maritime liens in respect of wages, see 35 Halsbury's Laws (3rd Edn) 782, 783, 785, 786, paras 1204, 1208, and for cases on the subject, see 1 Digest (Repl) 151, 371-378, 42 Digest (Repl) 1083-1084, 1089-1093, 8956-8965, 9018-9057.

j For the Administration of Justice Act 1956, ss 1, 3, see 1 Halsbury's Statutes (3rd Edn) 21, 26.

---

a   Section 1(1), so far as material, is set out at p 860 j, post
b   Section 3(3), so far as material, provides: 'In any case where there is a maritime lien or other charge on any ship . . . for the amount claimed, the Admiralty jurisdiction of the High Court . . . may be invoked by an action in rem against that ship . . .'

Cases referred to in judgment

Arosa Kulm (No 2), The [1960] 1 Lloyd's Rep 97.

Arosa Star, The [1959] 2 Lloyd's Rep 396.

Beswick v Beswick [1967] 2 All ER 1197, [1968] AC 58, [1967] 2 WLR 932, HL, Digest (Cont Vol C) 903, *181a*.

Blessing, The (1878) 3 PD 35, 38 LT 259, 3 Asp MLC 561, 1 Digest (Repl) 289, *1937*.

British Trade, The [1924] P 104, [1924] All ER Rep 519, 93 LJP 33, 130 LT 827, 16 Asp MLC 296, 18 Lloyd LR 65, 1 Digest (Repl) 153, *401*.

Elmville (No 2), The [1904] P 422, 74 LJP 69, 91 LT 330, 10 Asp MLC 23, 42 Digest (Repl) 1095, *9098*.

Fairport, The [1965] 1 Lloyd's Rep 183.

Fairport (No 3), The [1966] 2 Lloyd's Rep 253, Digest (Cont Vol C) *3451a*.

Gee-Whiz, The, Sheldon v MV Gee-Whiz (Owner) [1951] 1 All ER 876, [1951] 1 Lloyd's Rep 145, 42 Digest (Repl) 1090, *9033*.

Great Eastern, The (1867) LR 1 A & E 384, 36 LJ Adm 15, 17 LT 228, 2 Mar LC 553, 1 Digest (Repl) 157, *448*.

Hamilton v Baker, The Sara (1889) 14 App Cas 209, 58 LJP 57, 61 LT 26, 6 Asp MLC 416, HL, 1 Digest (Repl) 151, *375*.

Hartland v Diggines [1926] AC 289, [1926] All ER Rep 573, 95 LJKB 392, 134 LT 492, 10 Tax Cas 261, HL, 28(1) Digest (Reissue) 334, *1206*.

Justitia, The (1887) 12 PD 145, 56 LJP 111, 57 LT 816, 6 Asp MLC 198, 42 Digest (Repl) 724, *4752*.

Liverpool (No 2), The, Steamship Enterprises of Panama Inc, SS Liverpool (Owners) v SS Ousel (Owners) [1960] 3 All ER 307, [1963] P 64, [1960] 3 WLR 597, [1960] 2 Lloyd's Rep 66, CA, 42 Digest (Repl) 1080, *8928*.

Northcote v Henrich Bjorn (Owners), The Henrich Bjorn (1886) 11 App Cas 270, 55 LJP 80, 55 LT 66, 6 Asp MLC 1, HL, 1 Digest (Repl) 151, *371*.

Parry v Cleaver [1969] 1 All ER 555, [1970] AC 1, [1969] 2 WLR 821, [1969] 1 Lloyd's Rep 183, HL, Digest (Cont Vol C) 750, *1061e*.

Phillips v Highland Rail Co, The Ferret (1883) 8 App Cas 329, 52 LJPC 51, 48 LT 915, 5 Asp MLC 96, PC, 1 Digest (Repl) 293, *1984*.

Tergeste, The [1903] P 26, 72 LJP 18, 87 LT 567, 9 Asp MLC 356, 42 Digest (Repl) 1105, *9216*.

Veritas, The [1901] P 304, 70 LJP 75, 85 LT 136, 9 Asp MLC 237, 1 Digest (Repl) 165, *526*.

Westport (No 4), The [1968] 2 Lloyd's Rep 559.

Cases also cited

Alberzero, The, Albacruz (Owners) v Alberzero (Owners) [1975] 3 All ER 21, [1975] 3 WLR 491, CA.

Beaver, The (1800) 3 C & Rob 92.

Bold v Brough, Nicholson & Hall [1963] 3 All ER 849, [1964] 1 WLR 201.

Brown v Bullock [1961] 3 All ER 129, [1961] 1 WLR 1095, CA.

Elizabeth, The (1819) 2 Dodson 403.

Exeter, The (1799) 2 C & Rob 201.

Hewlett v Samuel Allen (trading as F Allen & Sons) [1894] AC 393, HL.

Hill v CA Parsons & Co Ltd [1971] 3 All ER 1345, [1972] 1 Ch 305, CA.

Household Finance Corpn of Canada v Hill CNR Co (1970) 13 DLR (3d) 737.

London County Council v Boot (Henry) & Sons [1959] 3 All ER 636, [1959] 1 WLR 1069, HL.

Action

By a writ issued on 18th June 1975 and subsequently amended, the plaintiff, Anthony Powell, a Merchant Navy officer, brought an Admiralty action in rem against the first defendants, the owners of the proceeds of the sale of the ship Halycon Skies, and the second defendants, Bankers Trust International Ltd. The plaintiff's claim was

a

(i) against the first defendants, for £150·43 (namely £97·46 employer's contributions and £52·97 employee's contributions to the Merchant Navy Officers' Pension Fund), being part of the wages earned by the plaintiff in the course of his employment as an officer and crew member on board the ship Halycon Skies during the period 1st June to 16th November 1974 pursuant to the plaintiff's contract of employment with the owners of the Halcyon Skies during that period; alternatively, for damages of £97·46 for breach of contract; alternatively, for an order for specific performance of the term

b

of the contract requiring payment of £97·46 to the Merchant Navy Officers' Pension Fund; (ii) against both defendants, for a declaration that the plaintiff had a maritime lien for wages against the proceeds of sale of the ship Halcyon Skies in respect of the sum of £150·43. The facts are set out in the judgment of Brandon J.

Geoffrey Brice for the plaintiff.

c

David Steel for the defendants.

Cur adv vult

1st December. **BRANDON J** read the following judgment: This is another action arising out of the collapse of Court Line Ltd, last year. It raises the question whether

d

a seaman can recover, in an Admiralty action for wages, and with the priority accorded by a maritime lien, the amount of pension contributions which the shipowners employing him should have paid to a pension fund on his behalf but have failed so to pay. It is, I was informed by counsel, a test case, on the result of which a considerable number of other cases depend.

The material facts are not in dispute. The plaintiff is an officer in the British

e

Merchant Navy. He was employed by Court Line as a deck officer on board their tanker Halcyon Skies from 1st June to 16th November 1974. His contract of employment provided, firstly, that he should be a member of the Merchant Navy Officers' Pension Fund, which is an occupational pension scheme approved by the Board of Inland Revenue; secondly, that Court Line should pay employer's contributions in respect of him to the fund; and, thirdly, that Court Line should, with his authority,

f

deduct employee's contributions from his pay and pay them also to the fund.

On 16th August 1974, while the plaintiff was still serving in the Halcyon Skies, a petition was presented in the Companies Court for the winding-up of Court Line, and a provisional liquidator was appointed. On 7th October an order for winding-up was made and the provisional liquidator was appointed liquidator. Early in November 1974 joint liquidators were appointed in place of the previous single liquidator.

g

The amount of the employer's contributions which Court Line should have paid to the fund in respect of the plaintiff's employment on board the Halcyon Skies was £97·46. The amount of the employee's contributions, which Court Line properly deducted from the plaintiff's pay and should thereafter have paid to the fund, was £52·97. In the events which occurred, however, neither of these sums was ever paid to the fund by Court Line.

h

On 14th October 1974 this court, in an action brought against the Halcyon Skies by the second defendants as second mortgagees, ordered her to be appraised and sold. The ship was sold pursuant to that order and the proceeds of sale were paid into court. The plaintiff has brought the present action, with the leave of the Companies Court, against those proceeds of sale, in order to recover the two amounts of £97·46 for employer's contributions and £52·97 for employee's contributions referred to

j

above. The action is defended by Court Line in liquidation, and during the hearing I made an order by consent that the second mortgagees, who have a competing claim on the proceeds of sale, should be joined as defendants to the action, so that they should be bound by its result. They have not, however, been separately represented before me, being content that counsel instructed on behalf of the joint liquidators should protect their interests also.

The case for the plaintiff, in relation to each of the sums claimed, is (1) that he has a good cause of action, either in debt or in damages, against the first defendants in respect of it; (2) that his claim, whether it be in debt or damages, is a claim for wages within s 1(1)(*o*) of the Administration of Justice Act 1956, so that he can invoke the Admiralty jurisdiction of the court in respect of it; and (3) that he has a maritime lien for the claim, so that (a) he can proceed in rem against the proceeds of sale of the ship under s 3(3) of the 1956 Act, and (b) he is entitled to priority over the competing claim of the second defendants as second mortgagees against the same fund.

The first defendants at one time disputed the plaintiff's case in relation to both sums. At the hearing, however, his case in relation to the sum of £52·97 for employee's contributions was conceded. This concession with regard to employee's contributions was, in my view, rightly made. So far as cause of action is concerned, the plaintiff has, in my opinion, a good claim in debt. He had under his contract of employment given Court Line authority to deduct such contributions from his pay and pay them to the fund. Court Line had acted on the first part of that authority but not on the second. In these circumstances the plaintiff was entitled to revoke the second part of the authority, namely for payment of the sums deducted to the fund, and to require the first defendants to pay such sums to him instead. This he did by issuing his writ in the present action. So far as the nature of the claim is concerned there can, I think, be no doubt that the sums concerned, having been deducted from the plaintiff's pay in the first place, were part of his wages for the purpose of s 1(1)(*o*) of the 1956 Act. I also think, for reasons which will appear later, that he had a maritime lien in respect of the claim.

I turn therefore to the matter which remains in dispute, namely the claim in respect of employer's contributions. Claims by seamen (including officers) for wages in Admiralty have a long history. Before 1861 the High Court of Admiralty had jurisdiction over such claims, but only in cases where the seaman had been employed under an ordinary mariner's contract, as distinct from a special contract. In the latter case the common law courts had exclusive jurisdiction.

Since 1861 the jurisdiction has been defined by statute. Section 10 of the Admiralty Court Act 1861 provided:

'The High Court of Admiralty shall have jurisdiction over any Claim by a Seaman of any Ship for Wages earned by him on board the Ship, whether the same be due under a special Contract or otherwise, and also over any Claim by the Master of any Ship for Wages earned by him on board the ship, and for Disbursements made by him on account of the Ship . . .'

This provision was repealed by s 226(1) of and Sch 6 to the Supreme Court of Judicature (Consolidation) Act 1925, and replaced by s 22(1)(*a*)(viii) of that Act, which was in substantially similar terms. The jurisdiction so conferred was in either case exercisable either in rem or in personam: see s 25 of the 1861 Act and s 33(2) of the 1925 Act. Sections 22 and 33 of the 1925 Act were in turn repealed by s 57(2) of and Sch 2 to the Administration of Justice Act 1956 and replaced, as regards s 22(1)(*a*)(viii), by s 1(1)(*o*), and as regards s 33(2), by s 3 of the latter Act.

Section 1(1)(*o*) of the 1956 Act provides:

'The Admiralty jurisdiction of the High Court shall be as follows, that is to say, jurisdiction to hear and determine any of the following questions or claims . . . (*o*) any claim by a master or member of the crew of a ship for wages . . .'

Section 3 of the 1956 Act provides that the jurisdiction so conferred could be exercised both in personam (sub-s (1)) and in rem (sub-ss (3) and (4)). These provisions remain applicable today.

Although both according to the law administered by the High Court of Admiralty *a* before 1861 and by the express terms of s 10 of the 1861 Act and s 22(1)(*a*)(viii) of the 1925 Act, the Admiralty jurisdiction over claims for wages was limited to wages earned on board the ship, this concept was very broadly interpreted. In particular the jurisdiction was regularly exercised, both before and after 1861, not only in respect of claims in debt for unpaid wages in the strict sense, but also in respect of claims in damages for wrongful dismissal, including claims for wages lost and for the cost of repatriation (viaticum). As to this, see, as regards the period before 1861, the cases

b set out in Williams and Bruce[1]; and, as regards the period after 1861, *The Great Eastern*[2], *The Blessing*[3] and *The Ferret*[4].

There were other extensions of the wages concept. The claims covered by it were held to include emoluments other than wages in the strict sense, which were payable direct to the seaman, such as victualling allowances and bonuses: *The Tergeste*[5], *The Elmville (No 2)*[6]. This approach was in accordance with s 742 of the Merchant Shipping

c Act 1894, which defined 'wages' as including 'emoluments'.

It was further held in one case that the jurisdiction in wages extended to claims for damages for breach of a seaman's contract of employment during its subsistence: *The Justitia*[7]. That was a strange case, in which seamen recovered, in an Admiralty action in personam for wages, general damages for hardship suffered and risks run when they were obliged to remain on board a ship while she was being used, contrary

d to the articles on which they had been engaged, as an armed cruiser in support of insurgents.

It is to be observed that, when the Admiralty jurisdiction over claims for wages was redefined by Parliament in 1956, the requirement that wages should have been 'earned on board the ship' was removed. This was in accordance with the description of the corresponding 'maritime claim' in para 1(m) of art 1 of the Brussels Ship Arrest

e Convention 1952, which refers simply to claims arising out of 'wages of Masters, Officers, or crew'.

Since 1950 there have been a number of further cases bearing on the scope of Admiralty claims for wages. In *The Gee-Whiz*[8] Willmer J held that an English master was entitled to recover, in an Admiralty action in rem for wages, the amount of both the employer's and the employee's national insurance contributions which the

f shipowner had agreed to pay. In *The Arosa Star*[9] the Supreme Court of Bermuda (Worley CJ) held that a foreign seaman could recover, in an Admiralty action in rem for wages and with the priority accorded by a maritime lien, full pay during sick leave and employer's contributions for social insurance, as being emoluments in the nature of wages to which he was entitled under his contract of employment. In *The Arosa Kulm (No 2)*[10] Hewson J held that a foreign master and crew could recover, in an

g Admiralty action in rem for wages, social benefit contributions said to be similar to national insurance contributions, which were payable by the shipowners under their contracts of employment. In *The Fairport*[11] Hewson J held that a foreign master could recover, in an Admiralty action in rem for disbursements, notional deductions from unpaid seamen's wages in respect of insurance and pension contributions payable under their contracts of employment. He further expressed the opinion that the

h

---

1 Jurisdiction and Practice of the English Courts in Admiralty Actions and Appeals (3rd Edn, 1902), p 202, notes (*y*) and (*z*)
2 (1867) LR 1 A & E 384
3 (1878) 3 PD 35
4 (1883) 8 App Cas 329
j 5 [1903] P 26
6 [1904] P 422
7 (1887) 12 PD 145
8 [1951] 1 Lloyd's Rep 145
9 [1959] 2 Lloyd's Rep 396
10 [1960] 1 Lloyd's Rep 97
11 [1965] 2 Lloyd's Rep 183

seamen themselves, who had already recovered their wages net of such contributions
in an earlier action, would have been entitled to include the amounts of such con- *a*
tributions in their own wages claim. In *The Fairport (No 3)*[1] the question arose whether
the master's maritime lien for disbursements extended to the amounts recovered by
him in respect of insurance and pension contributions under the judgment in the
preceding case. Karminski J held that his lien did so extend, on the ground that such
contributions formed part of the seamen's wages. In *The Westport (No 4)*[2] Karminski *b*
J held that a foreign master could recover, in an Admiralty action in rem for disbursements, firstly, sums which he was bound to pay in respect of deductions from
seamen's wages for insurance, pension, provident and union contributions; and,
secondly, sums which he was bound to pay jointly with the owners in respect of
owners' own insurance and other contributions. The ground of the decision seems
to have been that all the contributions concerned were emoluments of the seamen
under their contracts of employment or according to their national law. *c*

Insofar as these more recent cases between 1951 and 1968 decide that, where a
seaman is employed by a shipowner on board a ship, employer's as well as employee's
contributions payable in respect of him to pension or other similar funds are, if
unpaid, recoverable by him as wages, they are clearly favourable to the plaintiff's
claim in the present case. I feel bound to say, however, that I do not find in any of
those cases a clear analysis of the basis on which such contributions are so recoverable. *d*
In particular I do not find any analysis of the primary question whether the cause
of action in respect of such claims is in debt or damages, or of the further question
whether, if the cause of action is in damages, they can nevertheless still be regarded
as wages claims in Admiralty. In these circumstances, while paying due regard to the
cases concerned and due respect to the judges who decided them, I think that it will be
helpful to approach the matter afresh in the light of the principles applicable. In *e*
doing so I shall divide the problem up into four parts. First, is the plaintiff's cause of
action in debt or in damages? Second, if his cause of action is in damages, what is the
measure of damages recoverable? Third, is the claim one for wages within the meaning of s 1(1)(o) of the 1956 Act? Fourth, does the plaintiff have a maritime lien in
respect of it?
  f

1. *Is the plaintiff's cause of action in debt or in damages?*
It was argued for the first defendants that the plaintiff's only cause of action was in
damages for breach of contract. It was argued for the plaintiff, on the other hand, that
he had a cause of action in debt, on the basis that it was an implied term of his contract
of employment that, if the first defendants did not pay the employer's contributions
to the fund, they would pay them to him instead. In my opinion, it is not necessary *g*
to imply the term contended for in order to give business efficacy to the contract and
it would not therefore be right to do so. The true view, I think, is that the failure of
Court Line to pay the employer's contributions was a breach of contract for which
the plaintiff is entitled to recover damages at law. It follows that his cause of
action in respect of such contributions is in damages and not in debt. It seems that, if
damages were not an adequate remedy, the plaintiff could seek the alternative *h*
equitable remedy of specific performance: *Beswick v Beswick*[3]. For reasons which
will appear, however, I am of opinion that an adequate remedy in damages is
available.

2. *On the footing that the plaintiff's cause of action is in damages, what is the measure of
damages recoverable?*
For the plaintiff it was argued that the measure of damages was the amount of the *j*
unpaid contributions, on the ground that it was only by paying such contributions to

---

1   [1966] 2 Lloyd's Rep 253
2   [1968] 2 Lloyd's Rep 559
3   [1967] 2 All ER 1197, [1968] AC 58

a the fund himself that he could obtain the same legal rights to pension benefits as he would have had if Court Line had fulfilled their obligations. For the first defendants it was argued that the measure of damages was the value of future pension benefits which the plaintiff had lost; that the trustees of the fund had a discretion to pay him ex gratia, even though the contributions had not been paid, the same future pension benefits as he would have been entitled to as of right if they had been paid; that the evidence showed that, if the contributions proved irrecoverable, the trustees

b would be likely, if not certain, to exercise their discretion to produce this result; and that, in these circumstances, the plaintiff would not suffer any loss of future pension benefits at all.

I do not accept the argument for the first defendants on this matter. The plaintiff is entitled, so far as an award of money can do it, to be put in the same position as if Court Line had performed their obligations. If they had performed their obliga-

c tions of paying the employer's contributions to the fund, the plaintiff would have been entitled as of right to certain future pension benefits. Because they have not performed their obligations, his legal entitlement to such benefits has been reduced. It is no answer to say that the trustees of the fund are likely to make up the difference on an ex gratia basis. The plaintiff is entitled to be put back in a position where he has a legal entitlement to the benefits concerned, and the way in which that can most

d readily be done is by awarding him money so that he can pay to the fund himself the contributions which Court Line should have paid in respect of him. If he had already made such payments out of his own resources, it could not, I think, be successfully argued that he had acted otherwise than reasonably in mitigating his damage. It cannot make any difference that he has not in fact done so. As to the principle that payments made voluntarily or out of benevolence do not reduce a person's entitlement

e to damages, see *Parry v Cleaver*[1] per Lord Reid.

For the reasons which I have given I hold that the proper measure of damages for the first defendants' admitted breach of contract in failing to pay the employer's contributions is the amount of those contributions, namely £97·46.

f 3. *Is the claim one for wages within the meaning of s 1(1)(o) of the 1956 Act?*

The nature of contributions to pension funds was discussed, in another context, in *Parry v Cleaver*[2]. Lord Reid said with regard to them:

'What, then, is the nature of a contributory pension? Is it in reality a form of insurance or is it something quite different? Take a simple case where a man and his employer agree that he shall have a wage of £20 per week to take home

g (leaving out of account P.A.Y.E., insurance stamps and other modern forms of taxation) and that between them they will put aside £4 per week. It cannot matter whether an insurance policy is taken out for the man and the £4 per week is paid in premiums, or whether the £4 is paid into the employer's pension fund. And it cannot matter whether the man's nominal wage is £21 per week so that, of the £4, £1 comes from his "wage" and £3 comes from the employer, or the

h man's nominal wage is £23 per week so that, of the £4, £3 comes from his "wage" and £1 comes from the employer. It is generally recognised that pensionable employment is more valuable to a man than the mere amount of his weekly wage. It is more valuable because by reason of the terms of his employment money is regularly being set aside to swell his ultimate pension rights whether on retirement or on disablement. His earnings are greater

j than his weekly wage. His employer is willing to pay £24 per week to obtain his services, and it seems to me that he ought to be regarded as having earned that sum per week. The products of the sums paid into the pension fund are

---

1 [1969] 1 All ER 555 at 558, [1970] AC 1 at 13, 14
2 [1969] 1 All ER at 559, 560, [1970] AC at 16

in fact delayed remuneration for his current work. That is why pensions are regarded as earned income.'

This authoritative explanation of the nature of contributions to a pension fund seems to me to justify the view that employer's contributions to such a fund, as well as employee's contributions, can properly be regarded as part of an employee's total wages in the broad sense of that word.

That view gains further support from the consideration that employer's contributions to pension funds are, unless specially exempted, treated as part of an employee's income from his employment for income tax purposes: see s 220(1) of the Income and Corporation Taxes Act 1970 and compare *Hartland v Diggines*[1]. It is true that, since the particular pension scheme here concerned was one approved by the Board of Inland Revenue, the contributions payable by Court Line were exempted from the operation of s 220(1) by the provisions of s 221. This does not, however, alter the basic concept that such contributions are, in principle, part of the employee's total earnings or remuneration. This concept appears to me to accord with the reality of the matter.

Does it make any difference that the plaintiff's claim is not, if I am right in my answer to question 1 above, a claim in debt for the contributions themselves, but a claim in damages for breach of contract in failing to pay them? In my judgment, it does not, because the Admiralty jurisdiction in wages has long extended, as I explained earlier, to claims founded in damages as well as debt. Further, that extended jurisdiction has not only been exercised regularly in respect of claims for damages after termination of the contract of employment by wrongful dismissal, but also at least once prior to 1951 in respect of a claim for damages for breach of such contract during its subsistence. Indeed, it may well be that the reason why the judges, who decided the group of further cases from 1951 to 1968 referred to above, did not pause to analyse the precise cause of action on which the claims in respect of employer's contributions succeeded was that they did not think it mattered, so far as the seaman's right to recover was concerned, whether such cause of action was in debt or in damages.

For the reasons which I have given, I hold that the plaintiff's claim relating to employer's contributions is a claim for wages within the meaning of s 1(1)(o) of the 1956 Act, so that the plaintiff is entitled to invoke the Admiralty jurisdiction of the court in respect of it.

4. Does the plaintiff have a maritime lien in respect of his claim?

It appears to me that the contract under which the plaintiff was employed in this case was a special contract rather than an ordinary mariner's contract. It is, therefore, necessary to consider what is the law with regard to the existence of a maritime lien in respect of wages claims founded on a special contract.

For the plaintiff it was contended that, provided a claim was a wages claim within s 1(1)(o) of the 1956 Act at all, then, whether the claim arose out of an ordinary mariner's contract or a special contract, there was a maritime lien in respect of it. Counsel for the first defendants, while arguing strenuously that the plaintiff's claim was not within s 1(1)(o) at all, did not contend that, if it was, the circumstance that it arose out of a special contract rather than an ordinary mariner's contract prevented there being a maritime lien in respect of it.

The difficulty, however, is that there is an earlier decision of this court that, in certain cases at any rate, a seaman, who would have a maritime lien if his claim arose out of an ordinary mariner's contract, does not have such a lien when it arises out of a special contract. Doubts on the existence of a maritime lien in respect of claims under a special contract have also been expressed in more than one textbook in which the topic is discussed. In these circumstances, even though counsel for the defendants

---

1 [1926] AC 289, [1926] All ER Rep 573

a disclaimed any reliance, in this connection, on the fact that the claim was founded on a special contract, I feel bound to examine the law on the matter and to express an opinion on it. Two questions with regard to that law have arisen in the past, and this action, if I am right in holding that the plaintiff's claim is a wages claim within s 1(1)(o) of the 1956 Act, raises a third such question.

The first question is whether, in a special contract case, there is a maritime lien in respect of claims in debt for unpaid wages, by which I mean wages in the strict sense *b* together with emoluments in the nature of wages payable to the seaman direct. This question was expressly left open in *The British Trade*[1]; it was treated as still open in the only modern English textbook on the subject, the Law of Maritime Liens by Price[2], and it has not, so far as I know, at any time since 1924 been the subject-matter of an express decision in a contested case. According to my experience, however, the existence of a lien in respect of such a claim has been generally assumed in uncontested *c* cases over many years.

The second question is whether, in a special contract case, assuming that there is a maritime lien at least in respect of a claim in debt for unpaid wages, there is also such a lien in respect of a claim in damages for wrongful dismissal. This question was raised and answered in the negative in *The British Trade*[1], and has not, again so far as I am aware, been reconsidered in a contested case at any time since.

d The third question raised, as I have said, by the present action is whether, in a special contract case and on the same assumption as I mentioned in relation to the second question, there is also a lien in respect of a claim in damages for breach, during the subsistence of the contract, of a term of it providing for the payment by the shipowners of employer's contributions to a fund for the benefit of the seaman.

These questions arise and present difficulty because of the history of Admiralty *e* jurisdiction. I have already had to refer earlier to some aspects of that history, and it is necessary that I should now deal with other aspects of it. The jurisdiction of the High Court of Admiralty over maritime claims, as it existed before 1840, was confirmed and extended by two statutes, the Admiralty Court Act 1840 and the Admiralty Court Act 1861. Some of the extensions involved giving the court jurisdiction in respect of new subject-matters, for instance necessaries and masters' disbursements; *f* others involved giving the court enlarged jurisdiction in respect of subject-matters over which it already had some jurisdiction, for instance damage, salvage and wages. In the case of damage and salvage, the existing jurisdiction related to matters arising on the high seas and the extension was to similar matters arising within the body of a county. In the case of wages, the existing jurisdiction related to wages due under an ordinary mariner's contract and the extension was to wages due under a special *g* contract.

It was supposed for a considerable period of time after the passing of the 1840 and 1861 Acts that their effect was, in cases where they gave the court jurisdiction over new subject-matters, to create new maritime liens in respect of claims relating to them. This supposition was subsequently held to have been erroneous by the House of Lords, which decided that the statutory provisions concerned did not create new *h* maritime liens, but only gave statutory rights of action in rem, in respect of such claims. This was decided, as regards the jurisdiction in respect of necessaries conferred by s 6 of the 1840 Act, in *The Henrich Bjorn*[3]; and, as regards the jurisdiction in respect of masters' disbursements conferred by s 10 of the 1861 Act, in *The Sara*[4]. Following the latter decision, Parliament intervened promptly to give to a master the lien which the House of Lords had held that he did not have: see s 1 of the Merchant *j* Shipping Act 1889, replaced subsequently by s 167(2) of the Merchant Shipping Act

---

1 [1924] P 104, [1924] All ER Rep 519
2 (1940), pp 58, 59
3 (1886) 11 App Cas 270
4 (1889) 14 App Cas 209

1894. That intervention, however, left the authority of *The Sara*[1], as a decision on the effect of the 1861 Act, unimpaired.   **a**

A further question arose, following the passing of the 1840 and 1861 Acts, whether in cases where those Acts had enlarged the existing jurisdiction of the court as distinct from conferring new jurisdiction, it was intended that maritime liens recognised in respect of claims under the existing jurisdiction should extend also to claims of a similar kind under the enlarged jurisdiction. This further question did not fall to be decided in *The Henrich Bjorn*[2] or *The Sara*[1]. Significant observations with regard to it,   **b** however, were made by Lord Bramwell in the former case[3] and by Lord Halsbury LC in the latter case[4] These observations appear to indicate that, if it had been necessary to decide the point, both Lord Bramwell and Lord Halsbury LC would have held that, in such cases, the relevant maritime lien should be regarded as extending to claims under the enlarged jurisdiction.

The correctness of this last view, so far as damage and salvage cases are concerned,   **c** appears to have been accepted early on, and I do not consider that it is any longer open to challenge today. An example of a salvage case relating to services rendered within the body of a county, in which it was assumed that a maritime lien existed, can be found in *The Veritas*[5].

So far as wages cases are concerned, however, the situation has been different, as appears from *The British Trade*[6] to which I referred earlier. In that case there were   **d** claims by a master and a chief officer, who had been employed under special contracts, first in debt for unpaid wages, expenses and disbursements, and secondly in damages for wrongful dismissal. The claims were not resisted by the shipowning company itself, but two other persons, a receiver for a debenture holder and a mortgagee, intervened in the action and put in a defence in which they disputed that the court had jurisdiction in rem over the claims at all. At the hearing the interveners   **e** indicated their willingness to pay off the claims for wages, expenses and disbursements, on the court allowing them to be subrogated to the plaintiff's rights in respect of such claims. They denied, however, that the plaintiffs, even assuming that there was jurisdiction in rem over their claims for wrongful dismissal, had a maritime lien in respect of such claims.

In view of the attitude taken by the interveners at the hearing, it was not necessary   **f** for the court to decide either whether the plaintiffs had a maritime lien in respect of their claims for wages, expenses and disbursements, or whether there was jurisdiction in rem in respect of their claims for wrongful dismissal. The first question went by default as a result of the interveners' concession, and the second question was left to be decided later on a reference if necessary. The court (Sir Henry Duke P) did, however, decide that the plaintiffs did not, in any case, have a maritime lien in respect of their   **g** claims for wrongful dismissal.

The argument put forward for the interveners is set out in the judgment[7]. It was that there could only be a maritime lien in respect of wages which had, in the words of s 10 of the 1861 Act, been 'earned . . . on board the ship'. In so arguing, the interveners appear to have been conceding that s 10 gave a lien in respect of wages due under a special contract, provided that such wages had been earned on board, but disputing   **h** that it gave a lien in respect of damages for wrongful dismissal which, according to the argument, had not been so earned. That argument, if correct, would, as I see it, lead to the conclusion not merely that there was no maritime lien in respect of claims in

---

1 (1889) 14 App Cas 209
2 (1886) 11 App Cas 270
3 11 App Cas at 282, 283
4 14 App Cas at 216
5 [1901] P 304
6 [1924] P 104, [1924] All ER Rep 519
7 [1924] P at 107, [1924] All ER Rep at 522

j

a damages for wrongful dismissal arising out of a special contract, but that there was no Admiralty jurisdiction in respect of such claims under s 10 at all.

While this was the argument put forward for the interveners, the judgment of the court[1] was based on other and wider grounds, which can be summarised as follows. First, that the claims of the plaintiffs in damages were founded on special contracts. Second, that the court had jurisdiction to entertain such claims only, if at all, by virtue of the extended jurisdiction conferred on it by the Admiralty Court Act 1861. Third,
b that the 1861 Act was not, on the authority of the House of Lords in The Sara[2], to be construed as having created any new maritime liens in respect of the extended jurisdiction conferred by it. Fourth, that, having regard to these matters and assuming, without deciding, that the court had jurisdiction under the 1861 Act to entertain the claims at all, there was no maritime lien in respect of them.

c It seems to me that this reasoning, if carried to its logical conclusion, would produce the result, in a special contract case, not merely that a claim in damages for wrongful dismissal carried no maritime lien, but that a claim in debt for unpaid wages did not do so either. The existence of a lien in respect of the latter kind of claim was, however, conceded by the interveners in The British Trade[3], and has, as I indicated earlier, been generally assumed in uncontested cases over many years.

d The claim in the present case differs from the claims in The British Trade[3] in that it is a claim for damages for breach of a term of the plaintiff's contract during its subsistence, rather than for damages for repudiation of such contract by wrongful dismissal. If, therefore, The British Trade[3] had been decided on the narrow ground relied on by the interveners, it might have been possible to distinguish the present case from The British Trade[3] on the basis of that difference. In support of such distinc-
e tion it could have been said that, even if lost wages recovered as damages for wrongful dismissal did not qualify as wages earned on board the ship for the purposes of s 10 of the 1861 Act, unpaid employer's pension contributions, assuming them to be wages at all, did so qualify. Since, however, The British Trade[3] was decided on the wider ground that there could be no maritime lien in respect of a claim which the court had power to entertain only by virtue of the extended jurisdiction conferred on it by the 1861
f Act, I think that it is not open to the court to distinguish the present case on the basis which I have mentioned. The court must rather consider whether The British Trade[3], having been decided on that wider ground, should be followed or not.

I shall say at once that I have reached the conclusion, after the most careful consideration, that The British Trade[3] was incorrectly decided and ought not to be followed. With great respect to Sir Henry Duke P, I think that both the decision itself
g and the reasoning on which it was based were wrong.

As I explained earlier, the decision in The Henrich Bjorn[4] and The Sara[2] that no maritime liens had been created in respect of claims covered by the extended jurisdiction conferred on the court by the 1840 and 1861 Acts were given in relation, and only in relation, to claims covered by new, as distinct from enlarged, jurisdiction. Further, as I also said earlier, there are observations in the speeches of Lord Bramwell[5]
h in the former case and Lord Halsbury LC[6] in the latter case, which indicate that, if it had been necessary to decide the point, they would have held that, where existing jurisdiction had been enlarged, maritime liens recognised in respect of claims under the existing jurisdiction should be regarded as extending also to claims of a similar kind under the enlarged jurisdiction. There is, in my view, both in principle and on

j

1 [1924] P at 111, 112, [1924] All ER Rep at 523, 524
2 (1889) 14 App Cas 209
3 [1924] P 104, [1924] All ER Rep 519
4 (1886) 11 App Cas 270
5 11 App Cas at 281-286
6 (1889) 14 App Cas at 214-216

authority, a vital distinction between the two kinds of case, and I think that the reasoning in *The British Trade*[1], since it takes no account of this distinction, cannot be　*a* supported.

I have considered whether the decision in *The British Trade*[1], on the footing that it cannot be supported on the wider ground given in the judgment, could nevertheless be supported on the narrower ground, based on the words in s 10 of the 1861 Act 'earned . . . on board the ship', which was relied on in the argument for the interveners. In my opinion, however, the decision cannot be supported on this narrower ground　*b* either.

As I said earlier, the requirement that wages, in order to be recoverable in Admiralty, should have been earned on board the ship existed, in theory at least, under the law as administered by the High Court of Admiralty before 1861. In practice, however, such limitation was never interpreted strictly and did not prevent that court, as was recognised in *The British Trade*[2], from exercising jurisdiction, under　*c* the head of wages, over claims for wrongful dismissal arising out of ordinary mariners' contracts, or from according to seamen the same maritime lien in respect of such claims as they had in respect of claims for wages in the strict sense. In these circumstances, it seems to me reasonable to infer that when the legislature, by s 10 of the 1861 Act, enlarged the existing jurisdiction over claims for wages due under ordinary mariners' contracts so as to cover similar claims due under special contracts, it intended,　*d* despite the use of the hallowed phrase 'earned . . . on board the ship', that the enlarged jurisdiction should, so far as concerned the kinds of claims covered, be co-extensive with the existing jurisdiction.

For the reasons which I have given, I would hold that the effect of s 10 of the 1861 Act was, first, to give the court all the same jurisdiction over wages claims arising out of special contracts as it had previously had over wages claims arising out of ordinary　*e* mariners' contracts, including claims in damages for wrongful dismissal; and, secondly, to extend the maritime lien which had been recognised as existing in respect of the latter claims to the former claims.

If I am wrong in thinking that s 10 of the 1861 Act achieved this result because of the inclusion in it of the words 'earned . . . on board the ship', then I would hold that such result has nevertheless been achieved since by s 1(1)(*o*) of the 1956 Act, which does not　*f* include those or any similar words.

I would add that I am glad to have been able to reach a conclusion which means that, so far as a seaman's rights and remedies in Admiralty are concerned, the old distinction between a special contract and an ordinary mariner's contract is no longer significant. As pointed out in effect by Worley CJ in *The Arosa Star*[3], special contracts are today the rule and what were formerly called ordinary mariners'　*g* contracts are the exception. That being so, it would, in my view, be a reproach to the law if seamen did not have the same rights and remedies in respect of claims under the former as under the latter.

There is one other argument put forward on behalf of the first defendants with which I must deal. This was that the fund was entitled, under a separate contract between it and Court Line, to claim the unpaid contributions from Court Line　*h* in debt; that such a claim would have to be made in the liquidation without any special priority based on a maritime lien; and that it was in these circumstances unjust to allow the plaintiff, by pursuing a parallel claim for the same amounts as wages in Admiralty, to gain such special priority.

I must confess that I do not understand the legal basis of this argument. There is no reason, as a matter of law, why two different persons should not have concurrent　*j* rights of recovery, based on different causes of action, in respect of what is in substance

1　[1924] P 104, [1924] All ER Rep 519
2　[1924] P at 108-110, [1924] All ER Rep at 522, 523
3　[1959] 2 Lloyd's Rep 396 at 402, 403

the same debt. The court will not allow double recovery or, in a case of insolvency,
a double proof against the insolvent estate: *The Liverpool (No 2)*[1]. Subject to this,
however, either of the two persons is entitled to enforce his right independently of the
other. I therefore reject this further argument against the plaintiff's claim.

The result is that the plaintiff is entitled to judgment against the first defendants,
not only for the sum of £52·97 for employee's contributions, liability for which was
admitted, but also for the further sum of £97·46 for employer's contributions, liability
b for which was denied. He is also entitled, as against both defendants, to a declaration
that he has a maritime lien in respect of both these sums.

Judgment for the plaintiff.

Solicitors: *Hill, Dickinson & Co* (for the plaintiff); *Norton, Rose, Botterell & Roche* (for the
defendants).
c
                                                        N P Metcalfe Esq Barrister.

R v Johnson

d COURT OF APPEAL, CRIMINAL DIVISION
LAWTON LJ, CROOM-JOHNSON AND PAIN JJ
8th DECEMBER 1975, 16th JANUARY 1976

*Sentence – Extended term of imprisonment – Conditions to be satisfied – Three year period
from previous conviction – Offence committed before expiration of three years from previous
e conviction or from release from prison – Offence committed before release from prison –
Defendant absconding shortly before end of five year term of imprisonment and committing
further offence – Whether jurisdiction to impose extended term of imprisonment on conviction of further offence – Criminal Justice Act 1967, s 37(4)(a).*

Whilst he was serving the last few weeks of a five year prison sentence the defendant
f absconded and committed a robbery. At the time of the offence he had not been
finally released from prison within s 37[a] of the Criminal Justice Act 1967. On conviction he was sentenced to an extended term of imprisonment under s 37 of the
1967 Act. The defendant appealed against sentence contending that, under s 37(4)(a)
of the 1967 Act, the court had no jurisdiction to impose an extended sentence since
the robbery had not been committed before the expiration of three years from a
g previous conviction nor within three years from his final release from prison.

Held – On the true construction of s 37(4)(a), the court, in considering whether an
offender qualified for an extended term of imprisonment, had to determine what had
happened during the three years preceding the commission of the offence for which

---

h 1 [1960] 3 All ER 307, [1963] P 64
a Section 37, so far as material, provides:
   '... (2) Where an offender is convicted on an indictment of an offence punishable with
   imprisonment for a term of two years or more and the conditions specified in subsection (4)
   of this section are satisfied, then, if the court is satisfied, by reason of his previous conduct
   and of the likelihood of his committing further offences, that it is expedient to protect the
   public from him for a substantial time, the court may impose an extended term of imprison-
j ment under this section ...
   '(4) The conditions referred to in subsection (2) of this section are:—(a) the offence was
   committed before the expiration of three years from a previous conviction of an offence
   punishable on indictment with imprisonment for a term of two years or more or from his
   final release from prison after serving a sentence of imprisonment, corrective training or
   preventive detention passed on such a conviction ...'

he had just been convicted. If during that period he had been in prison for an offence, punishable on indictment with imprisonment for two or more years, he was liable to an extended sentence. It followed that the extended term had been properly imposed on the defendant and the appeal would be dismissed (see p 872 *b* to *h*, post).

Notes
For extended terms of imprisonment, see Supplement to 10 Halsbury's Laws (3rd Edn) para 932A.

For the Criminal Justice Act 1967, s 37, see 8 Halsbury's Statutes (3rd Edn) 600.

As from 1st July 1974, s 37 of the 1967 Act has been replaced by the Powers of Criminal Courts Act 1973, s 28.

Cases referred to in judgment
R v Clark (3rd July 1970) unreported.
R v Ettridge [1909] 2 KB 24, [1908-10] All ER Rep 848, 78 LJKB 479, 100 LT 624, 73 JP 253, 22 Cox CC 101, 2 Cr App Rep 62, CCA, 14 Digest (Repl) 606, 6009.
R v Gillingham (24th November 1970) unreported.
R v Norman [1924] 2 KB 315, 93 LJKB 883, 131 LT 29, 88 JP 125, 27 Cox CC 621, 18 Cr App Rep 81, CCA.

Cases also cited
Director of Public Prosecutions v Merriman [1972] 3 All ER 42, [1973] AC 584, HL.
Director of Public Prosecutions v Ottewell [1968] 3 All ER 153, [1970] AC 642, HL.
Kennedy v Spratt [1971] 1 All ER 805, [1972] AC 83, HL.

Appeal
This was an appeal by Harry Johnson, on a reference by the Home Secretary under s 17(1)(*a*) of the Criminal Justice Act 1968, against an extended term of 12 years' imprisonment imposed on him by Talbot J at Derby Assizes on 6th May 1969 following the appellant's conviction of robbery. The sentence was consecutive to a term of five years' imprisonment passed on the appellant in July 1964. The facts are set out in the judgment of the court.

Alistair Troup for the appellant.
F Maurice Drake QC and *Douglas Hogg* for the crown.

Cur adv vult

16th January.   **LAWTON LJ** read the following judgment of the court: On 6th May 1969 at Derby Assizes the appellant was convicted of robbery and was sentenced to 12 years' imprisonment. This sentence was certified to be an extended one under the provisions of s 37 of the Criminal Justice Act 1967. These provisions have been re-enacted as ss 28 and 29 of the Powers of Criminal Courts Act 1973. On 21st July 1969 the appellant applied for an extension of time in which to appeal against sentence. After his application had been refused by a single judge he renewed it to the full court which dismissed it on 24th November 1969. His case comes back to this court as a reference by the Secretary of State pursuant to s 17 of the Criminal Appeal Act 1968.

In 1974, whilst serving his sentence, he attacked another prisoner and on 26th June 1974 he was sentenced to three years' imprisonment to run consecutively to the extended sentence imposed in 1969. By 1974 there had been two cases in this court, *R v Clark*[1] and *R v Gillingham*[2], which seemed to support a submission made by the appellant's solicitor to the Secretary of State that the extended sentence had been made without jurisdiction. The reference has been made to determine this submission. The doubt about the validity of the extended sentence arises because the offence in respect of which it was imposed was committed whilst the appellant was

1   (3rd July 1970) unreported
2   (24th November 1970) unreported

still serving the last few weeks of a five year sentence. He had been living in a prison
a hostel from which he had absconded. He had not been finally released from prison
within the meaning of ss 37 and 38 of the Criminal Justice Act 1967.

Section 37 provides for the punishment of persistent offenders. Subsection (1) abolished the forms of punishment for such offenders which had been established by the
Criminal Justice Act 1948. The difference between the conditions precedent for the
new form of punishment and the old is important for the purposes of this appeal.
b Subsection (2) enacted that, subject to conditions specified in sub-s (4), the courts may
impose extended terms of imprisonment if satisfied that by reason of the offender's
previous conduct and of the likelihood of his committing further offences, it is expedient to protect the public from him for a substantial time. The appellant is such an
offender. Subsection (4) sets out the conditions in three paragraphs lettered (*a*), (*b*)
and (*c*). The conditions in paras (*b*) and (*c*) were complied with. The query arises
c about para (*a*) which is in these terms:

> 'the offence was committed before the expiration of three years from a pre-
> vious conviction of an offence punishable on indictment with imprisonment for a
> term of two years or more or from his final release from prison after serving a
> sentence of imprisonment, corrective training or preventive detention passed on
> *d*   such a conviction . . .'

How is this condition to be construed? There are two possibilities. The first would
envisage two qualifying periods of three years, the second of them having as a starting
point for the running of time final release from prison. The other construction requires the court to look back for three years and to find out what the offender had
been doing during that period.

e If the first construction be right, the appellant would not have been liable for an
extended sentence because the robbery for which he was sentenced in 1969 was
committed after the expiration of three years from 31st July 1964, the date of his conviction for the offence which had put him into prison for five years. A second
qualifying period would not have started because he had not been finally released
from prison when he committed the robbery. In both *R v Clark*[1] and *R v Gillingham*[2]
f this court followed this construction. In both these cases, being appeals against
sentence only, the Crown had not been represented. No alternative construction was
considered.

In this appeal the Crown has been represented. Counsel for the Crown submitted
that on its true construction, condition (*a*), when read in its context in the 1967 Act
and against the background of its legislative history, provides an offender, with con-
g victions qualifying him for an extended sentence, with an opportunity of avoiding one
if he has kept away from crime for the specified period.

Penal legislation has often had to provide additional punishments for persistent
offenders. Section 21(2) of the Criminal Justice Act 1948 introduced the concept of
preventive detention for persistent offenders about whom the court was satisfied that
it was expedient for the protection of the public that they should be detained in custody
h for a substantial time. A person qualified for preventive detention who was not less
than 30 years of age and had been convicted at least four times on indictment for
offences punishable with imprisonment for a term of two years or more. Once a
person had become liable to be sentenced to preventive detention he remained liable for
the rest of his life, no matter what efforts he had made to rehabilitate himself, between
the conviction for which he was being sentenced and the conviction immediately
j preceding it.

Section 37(1) of the 1967 Act abolished preventive detention and substituted the
concept of extended sentences. Subsection (2) sets out what the court has to be satisfied about before imposing an extended sentence, namely his previous conduct and the

---

1 (3rd July 1970) unreported
2 (24th November 1970) unreported

likelihood of his committing further offences. This was in addition to being satisfied about the conditions specified in sub-s (4). Counsel for the Crown submitted that s 37(2) of the 1967 Act envisaged a more flexible approach to the circumstances   *a* in which an extended sentence could be imposed than s 21(1) of the 1948 Act had done in relation to preventive detention. Condition (a) introduced another flexible factor. No longer was a persistent offender always to be such. Extended sentences could only be imposed for offences committed within a specified period of three years. This period, said counsel for the Crown, was defined by condition (a). A court which was considering imposing an extended sentence, he submitted, had to decide what had   *b* happened in the three years before the present offence was committed. If the offender had been in prison during that period, he continued to be liable for an extended sentence; but if he had not been and he had been free of convictions for that period he was not liable. The key words in condition (a) were 'before' and 'after serving a sentence of imprisonment'. If one wrote out the two conditions set out in sub-s (4)(a) in their entirety, the subsection would read as follows: *c*

'the offence was committed before the expiration of three years from a previous conviction of an offence punishable on indictment with imprisonment for a term of 2 years or more

'or   *d*

'the offence was committed before the expiration of three years from his final release from prison after serving a sentence of imprisonment . . . passed on a conviction of an offence punishable on indictment with imprisonment for a term of 2 years or more'.

If it was the intention of the 1967 Act to free an offender from liability to an extended   *e* sentence in specified circumstances (as we find it was), counsel for the Crown's suggested construction fits in with both the grammar and the intention of the Act. It makes more sense than the construction followed in *R v Clark*[1] and *R v Gillingham*[2]. It gets rid of the absurdity which this reference has revealed. The appellant is a dangerous criminal from whom the public should be protected. Had he been serving a three year sentence instead of one of five years when he committed the robbery   *f* after absconding from the prison hostel, or had he committed it the day after his final release from prison after completing his sentence, he could have been given an extended sentence. But as he committed it in between times, if the *R v Clark*[1] and *R v Gillingham*[2] construction is right, the public must be deprived of the protection against him which Parliament envisaged.

We are satisfied that counsel for the Crown's suggested construction is the right one.   *g* As the Court in *R v Clark*[1] and *R v Gillingham*[2] did not have the benefit of full argument we need not follow those decisions: see *R v Ettridge*[3] and *R v Norman*[4].

The Secretary of State having referred the whole of the case to this court for determination in respect of sentence, pursuant to s 17 (1)(a) of the Criminal Appeal Act 1968, we treat the reference as an appeal against sentence and dismiss it.   *h*

Appeal dismissed.

Solicitors: *Registrar of Criminal Appeals; Director of Public Prosecutions.*

Lea Josse Barrister.   *j*

1   (3rd July 1970) unreported
2   (24th November 1970) unreported
3   [1909] 2 KB 24, [1908-10] All ER Rep 848
4   [1924] 2 KB 315

Kapur v Shields

QUEEN'S BENCH DIVISION
PHILLIPS J
31st JULY 1975

Unfair dismissal – Excluded classes of employment – Employment in undertaking where less than four employees employed for prescribed period – Employed – Identity of employer – Relevance – Employees in undertaking employed by different employers – Whether identity of employer relevant – Industrial Relations Act 1971, s 27(1)(a).

Unfair dismissal – Excluded classes of employment – Employment in undertaking where less than four employees employed for prescribed period – Onus of proof – Onus on employer to establish that employment within excluded class – Evidence that separate activities of employer constitute single 'undertaking' – Onus on employer to show that activity in which employee employed a separate undertaking – Industrial Relations Act 1971, s 27(1)(a).

The respondent was employed by the appellant as a housekeeper at a flatlet house. The appellant owned the house. A number of other properties were owned by companies controlled by the appellant and his wife. The respondent left the appellant's employment and subsequently claimed compensation from him on the ground that she had been unfairly dismissed within s 22 of the Industrial Relations Act 1971. At the hearing before the tribunal the appellant contended, inter alia, that by virtue of s 27(1)(a)[a] of the 1971 Act the respondent was not entitled to the protection afforded against unfair dismissal by s 22 since there were less than four people employed by the appellant in the relevant undertaking. The tribunal rejected that contention, holding that the activities carried out by the appellant as a property owner or through the medium of the companies which he controlled constituted an 'undertaking' within s 27(1)(a) and that they were not 'concerned with whether the employee, or the other employees we have to count, were employees of different places; we have to find out whether they were employees in different places of an "undertaking"'. They held that the respondent had been unfairly dismissed and awarded her compensation. On appeal,

Held – (i) For the purposes of s 27(1)(a) the identity of the employer was irrelevant in determining the question whether less than four employees had been employed in an undertaking during the relevant period. Accordingly, if four persons were employed in an undertaking, s 22 was not excluded even though they were not all employed by the same employer (see p 879 d, post).

(ii) It was open to a tribunal to find that the distinct but somewhat similar activities of a number of persons, such as the appellant, his wife and the various companies, constituted a single 'undertaking' for the purposes of s 27(1)(a) provided there was evidence on which such a finding could be based (see p 879 g, post).

(iii) Once the fact of employment had been proved, the burden was on the employer to establish that the employment was excluded from s 22. Accordingly, the burden was on the appellant to establish that the respondent's employment fell within s 27(1)(a) and in the circumstances the tribunal were justified in finding that he had failed to discharge that burden. The appeal would therefore be dismissed (see p 880 g to p 881 c, post).

Notes

For unfair dismissal and excluded classes of employment, see Supplement to 38 Halsbury's Laws (3rd Edn) para 677c, 3, 7.

---

a   Section 27(1) is set out at p 875 j to p 876 c, post

For the Industrial Relations Act 1971, ss 22, 27, see 41 Halsbury's Statutes (3rd
Edn) 2088, 2093.

As from 16th September 1974, ss 22 and 27 of the 1971 Act have been replaced by
the Trade Union and Labour Relations Act 1974, Sch 1, paras 4, 9.

Cases referred to in judgment

Boston v Chilton (5th February 1974) unreported, NIRC.
Haque v Stitchen & Co (1937) Ltd [1973] ICR 474.
Harold Baim Motion Pictures Theatres (Coleford) Ltd v Nunn (30th October 1973)
unreported, NIRC.
Holdsworth (Harold) & Co (Wakefield) Ltd v Caddies [1955] 1 All ER 725, [1955] 1 WLR
352, HL, 9 Digest (Reissue) 570, 3411.
Mayhew v Richard Alexander & Son [1973] 3 All ER 39, [1973] ICR 441, NIRC.
R v Edwards [1974] 2 All ER 1085, [1975] QB 27, [1974] 3 WLR 285, 138 JP 621, CA.
Salomon v Salomon & Co Ltd [1897] AC 22, [1895-9] All ER Rep 33, 66 LJCh 35, 75 LT
426, 4 Mans 89, HL, 9 Digest (Reissue) 19, 10.

Appeal

This was an appeal by Sagar Kapur against a decision of an industrial tribunal sitting
in London on 16th January 1975 whereby it was decided that the respondent,
Margaret Shields, had been unfairly dismissed by the appellant and was entitled to
compensation in the sum of £706. The facts are set out in the judgment.

Norman Primost for the appellant.
Roger Toulson for the respondent.

PHILLIPS J. This is an appeal by Mr S Kapur from a decision of an industrial
tribunal, sitting in London, dated 16th February 1975, finding that he had unfairly
dismissed the respondent, his employee, and ordering him to pay compensation to
her in the sum of £706. The appeal raises two points, one of which, concerning the
jurisdiction of industrial tribunals, is of general importance.

The respondent was employed at a flatlet house owned by the appellant at 48 and
49 Evelyn Gardens, London, SW7. as a housekeeper. The tribunal found that she had
been unfairly dismissed on 24th June 1974. By his appearance, dated 1st August 1974,
to the respondent's claim, the appellant stated the grounds on which he intended
to resist it, as follows: '(1) The applicant requested me to give her notice. (2) The
applicant is not redundant as she has been replaced by another housekeeper.'
Accordingly, apart from certain questions as to jurisdiction, to which I shall return,
the issue in the case was whether the respondent was dismissed, or whether, as the
appellant contended, she had asked for notice to be given in order to make it easier
for her to obtain a council flat. The case was presented accordingly. During the
cross-examination of the respondent, counsel for the appellant sought to question
her about her alleged inefficiency and neglect of duty. The relevance of this line of
cross-examination being doubted, he applied for leave to amend. The course which
the case then took is summarised in the notes of evidence as follows:

'The respondent applies to amend, by adding the allegation: "Alternatively
if the applicant was dismissed the reason was inefficiency and misconduct in
neglecting to supervise the cleaning of the staircases and the entrances in both
houses from January to June 1974 and not being available at times when the
respondent gave notice and called to collect the money in the period from
January to June 1974." [Counsel] on behalf of the [respondent] strongly opposed
the application. It was too late in the day to make the amendment. There had
been proceedings for possession, etc etc. [Counsel for the appellant] had nothing
further to say. He added that he was instructed that solicitors were instructed

a   in regard to this in August or September. The ruling was given that the
     amendment be not allowed.'

     The first point taken in support of the appellant's appeal is that the tribunal was
     wrong in law in refusing to allow him to amend his notice of appearance to allege
     that the respondent had been inefficient and had misconducted herself between
     January and June 1974, which would, it was alleged, have justified the dismissal.
b   Proceedings before industrial tribunals are intended to be as simple and informal
     as possible. The parties are often unrepresented and need assistance from the tribunal
     in presenting their case. There is no system of formal pleadings. In many cases, the
     applicant and the respondent will fill up the application and the appearance without
     the benefit of legal advice. In fact, the appellant, though represented at the hearing
     and having the assistance of a solicitor in August and September 1974, filled up the
c   appearance in this case by himself. Ordinarily, no doubt, tribunals will strive to
     allow a party to bring before it all the questions and matters which that party feels to
     be important, insofar as this can be done with justice to the other party, and will as far
     as possible not shut out matters of complaint or defence on technical grounds. The
     guiding principle must be to allow the parties to have their say. But the circum-
     stances of every case are different. There is an appeal to this court only on a point of
d   law. It is impossible to say that in this case the tribunal erred in law in exercising
     its discretion in the way in which it did, having regard particularly to the fact that
     the question of the respondent's alleged inefficiency and neglect of duty was raised
     for the first time in the course of cross-examination of her by counsel for the appellant.
     The second point taken in support of the appellant's appeal concerns the juris-
     diction of industrial tribunals in complaints of unfair dismissal and is, as I have said,
e   of general importance. It is not every employee who is entitled to make such a
     complaint. In particular, as is well known, there is an exclusion in the case of 'small
     organisations'. It is impossible to summarise the effect of the exclusion satisfac-
     torily. Complete accuracy requires a reference to the statute, but it is normally
     put in some such words as[1]:

f   '. . . before an applicant can come within the unfair dismissal protection
         there must have been no less than four employees (including the claimant)
         who, immediately before the effective date of termination, had been continu-
         ously employed for 13 weeks or longer.'

     At the material time the relevant statutory provisions were contained in the
     Industrial Relations Act 1971. That Act has now been repealed, but these provisions
g   have, with one exception, been re-enacted in the Trade Union and Labour Relations
     Act 1974, Sch 1, Part II. Section 22 of the 1971 Act provided:

         '(1) In every employment to which this section applies every employee shall
         have the right not to be unfairly dismissed by his employer; and accordingly, in
         any such employment, it shall be an unfair industrial practice for an employer
h   to dismiss an employee unfairly.
         '(2) This section applies to every employment in so far as its application is
         excluded by or under any of sections 27 to 31 of this Act.
         '(3) In the following provisions of this Part of this Act "the claimant" means
         the employee who claims that he has been unfairly dismissed by his
         employer.'

j   Section 27(1), under the general heading 'Excluded cases', provided:

         'Section 22 of this Act does not apply to any of the following, that is to say,—
         (a) any employment in an undertaking in which immediately before the

---

1   Harvey on Industrial Relations, Division IX, para 61.00

effective date of termination there were in the aggregate (including the claimant)
less than four employees, who had been continuously employed for a period of   a
not less than thirteen weeks, whether they are, or had been, all employed at
the same place or are, or had been, employed at different places; (b) any employment where the employer is the husband or wife or a close relative of the
employee; (c) any employment as a registered dock worker, as defined by any
scheme for the time being in force under the Dock Workers (Regulation of
Employment) Act 1946, not being employment by virtue of which the employee   b
is wholly or mainly engaged in work which is not dock work as defined by the
scheme; (d) any employment as master or as a member of the crew of a fishing
vessel, where the employee is not remunerated otherwise than by a share in the
profits or gross earnings of the vessel; (e) any employment as a teacher to whom
section 85 of the Education (Scotland) Act 1962 (dismissal of teachers) applies;
(f) any employment under a contract which normally involves employment   c
for less than twenty-one hours weekly.'

Section 167, which was the interpretation section, read:

'(1) In this Act, except in so far as the context otherwise requires, the following
expressions have the meanings hereby assigned to them respectively, that is to
say . . . "employee" (subject to subsection (4) of this section) means an   d
individual who has entered into or works under (or, where the employment
has ceased, worked under) a contract of employment; "employer" (subject to
subsection (2) of this section)—(a) where the reference is to an employer in relation
to an employee, means the person by whom the employee is (or, in a case where
the employment has ceased, was) employed, and (b) in any other case, means a
person regarded in that person's capacity as one for whom one or more workers   e
work or have worked or normally work or seek to work . . . "undertaking"
includes a business and, in relation to any body of persons (whether corporate
or unincorporate) whose activities would not, apart from this provision, be
regarded as constituting an undertaking, includes the aggregate of those
activities . . .'

The part of s 167 relating to 'employer' and 'undertaking' has not been re-enacted   f
in the 1974 Act, and that relating to 'employee' has been re-enacted in somewhat
different terms.

The respondent was the only person employed at 48 and 49 Evelyn Gardens, and
so it was contended on behalf of the appellant that, though employed by him, her
employment was excluded by virtue of the provisions of s 27(1)(a). The tribunal found
in favour of the respondent on this preliminary question of jurisdiction and its reasons   g
are set out in paras 4 and 5 of the decision, as follows:

'4. The next matter which goes to the jurisdiction is section 22(1)(a). It may
be mentioned that none of these matters were raised initially in regard to the
application of [the respondent] for unfair dismissal; the number of employees,
the matter now to be raised, and the hours of duty were raised when in Septem-   h
ber she brought the other application under the Contracts of Employment Act.
Section 27(1)(a) provides that the section giving a right to unfair dismissal does
not apply to: "any employment in an undertaking in which immediately before
the effective date of termination there were in the aggregate (including the
claimant) less than four employees who had been continuously employed for a
period of less than thirteen weeks, whether they are, or had been, all employed   j
at the same place or are, or had been, employed at different places;" [The
appellant] in his evidence said: "I am a company director and property owner.
I own 48 and 49 Evelyn Gardens personally. The Kiwi Court Hotel, SW5, is
owned by Arlovale Ltd. I own shares. It is a family concern. My wife and I each
have one share. 3 Beaufort Gardens is owned by Southra Developments Ltd.

My wife and I each have one share. 33 Cranleigh Gardens [which was sold after
the respondent was dismissed] was owned by the Golden Slipper Caterers
Ltd, one share belonging to me and one to my wife." 64 Elm Park Road was
owned by the same company and it was held until 1 July. An hotel in Dublin
is owned by the Great Northern Hotel Group Ltd with three shares, one held
by the [appellant], one by his wife, and one by Mr Khanna. There is no evidence
at all as to the number of employees in employment at any one time or for
any period in these other places. So that if the other places can be regarded as
part of the undertaking in which the [respondent] was employed this objection
to jurisdiction also would not be valid.

  '5. In deciding whether she was employed in any undertaking in which there
were more than four employees we have to have regard to the definition of
"undertaking" in section 167(1): "includes a business and, in relation to any body
of persons (whether corporate or unincorporate) whose activities would not,
apart from this provision, be regarded as constituting an undertaking, includes
the aggregate of those activities;" Leaving aside for the moment the definition,
we think that if a person sets up business as a property owner, and decides to
conduct that business by operating through a number of companies in which he
and his wife are the sole shareholders, or in one case the majority shareholders,
then it can be said that he is carrying on the business of a property owner through
the agencies of these various companies. No doubt the companies are brought
into the matter for reasons of taxation and ease of disposal of the properties
because it is easier to dispose of the shares in a company than to dispose of the
property itself as far as transfer is concerned. It seems to us that if a person
does set up to operate, to make money, in this way, then the undertaking in
which he is engaged includes those operations which he carries out through the
means of using companies as agents to do them. Of course companies are separate
persons to the person who may control them; we are not here concerned with
whether the employee, or the other employees we have to count, were
employees of different persons; we have to find out whether they were
employees in different places of an "undertaking". We think that here it must
be said that the undertaking of [appellant] was, through these various companies, to carry on the business of being a property owner, with the ability to
sell those properties he wished to dispose of. Even if that were wrong there is
much to be said, we do not propose to deal further with it, for the submission
on behalf of the [respondent] that this may well fall under the second part of
the definition of "undertaking". The tribunal therefore has jurisdiction to deal
with this application. We have to consider whether it was an unfair dismissal.'

  It is not wholly clear to me what is the precise basis of the decision. But the use
of the words 'we are not concerned with whether the employee, or the other employees we have to count, were employees of different persons: we have to find
out whether they were employees in different places of an undertaking' seems to
suggest that the tribunal assumed, without argument, that, in applying s 27(1)(a) of
the 1971 Act, the identity of the employer is irrelevant, so that it is not necessary
that the essential four employees should be employed by the same employer.
Counsel for the appellant's first contention to this court has been (and no doubt was
to the tribunal) that the employment must be in an undertaking in which not less
than four persons are employed by the same employer; and he submits that the
paraphrase used by the tribunal, 'we have to find out whether they were employees
in different places of an undertaking', is inaccurate and misleading. It seems to me
that this is the main question in the case; i e must the four employees be employed
by the same employer?

  However, before turning to the construction of s 27(1)(a), it is useful to consider
the second limb of the definition of 'undertaking" in s 167(1):

'. . . and, in relation to any body of persons (whether corporate or unincorporate) whose activities would not apart from this provision, be regarded as *a* constituting an undertaking, includes the aggregate of those activities.'

Even with the assistance of counsel, which in this case has been considerable, I have been unable to think of good examples of the kind of case to which the words are aimed. I do not think they can be of direct assistance here for they concern the aggregation of activities (in order to constitute an undertaking) rather than of *b* employments. But a proper understanding of the words could throw light on the construction of s 27(1)(a). It may be that they are aimed at cases such as co-operatives, or clubs, or partnerships, where individual activities considered alone do not, but considered together do, constitute an undertaking. If it be that in most such cases the employees are employed by individual employers, rather than the group, it would follow that, since the intention must have been that such cases were not to *c* be excluded under s 27 (for otherwise it would not have been necessary to extend the definition of 'undertaking' to include them), s 27(1)(a) would be construed accordingly, so as not to require identity of employer. But, being unable to think of convincing examples, I have thought it better not to take this possibility into account. Counsel for the respondent founded a subsidiary argument in support of the decision on this limb of the definition. According to this, the appellant and his wife and the *d* various companies together constitute a body of persons whose activities, when aggregated, constitute an undertaking, the respondent and the employees of the companies, being employed in that undertaking. I cannot accept this, because it seems to me that the activities of the appellant and the companies, considered singly and apart from this provision, would in each case constitute an undertaking. The tribunal, which seems to have found a similar difficulty over this part of the *e* definition, though inclined to think that it could assist the respondent, eventually shied away and put it on one side, too.

In support of his main contention that s 27(1)(a) is dealing with the employees of a single employer, counsel for the appellant relies strongly on the fact that the whole 1971 Act is concerned with the relationship between employer and employee. He draws attention to the definition of 'employer' and 'employee', and points out that *f* in paras (b), (c), (d), (e) and (f) of s 27(1) the attention is directed to the nature of the particular employment. By way of illustration he cited *Mayhew v Richard Alexander & Son*[1] and *Haque v Stitchen & Co (1937) Ltd*[2] as showing the importance of the particular relationship of employer-employee involved. Reference was also made to the unreported decision of the National Industrial Relations Court in *Harold Baim Motion Pictures Theatres (Coleford) Ltd v Nunn*[3] in which this section was considered. But, *g* except inferentially, it does not deal with the question immediately under consideration, but turns more on the circumstances in which two widely separated businesses can be said to constitute a single undertaking. The purpose of s 27(1)(a), counsel for the appellant submits, is to exclude from the ambit of the unfair dismissal provisions of the 1971 Act small businesses, i e small employers, on whom the burden of compliance would lie too heavily. If the intention is to protect the employer of small *h* means, it is not easy to see why s 27(1)(a) did not do so simply by reference to the number of persons employed by the respondent employer, or why it was necessary to introduce the test of the number of persons employed in an undertaking. Whichever way the section is construed there are difficulties. Construed as counsel for the appellant would have it, it would follow that even though an employer employs a thousand employees, two or three may be excluded from the Act if they are all *j* employed in a separate undertaking employing less than four employees; or persons

1   [1973] 3 All ER 39
2   [1973] ICR 474
3   30th October 1973

employed in the same undertaking may find that some are, and some are not,
a excluded; cf a partnership of architects employing 15 employees, who vest their
premises in a service company which employs a liftman and a boilerman. Construed
the other way, single employees may be protected provided that they work in an
undertaking with at least three others, each of whom may be a single employee.
The difficulties only disappear if it can be said that it is impossible to have an undertaking in which there are employed the employees of different employers. I think
b it is possible. The firm which runs its office administration through the medium of a
separate service company is a familiar example.

In these circumstances, I approach the language of the Act without any particular
preference or assumption one way or the other. Section 22 applies to every employment except insofar as its application is excluded. The construction of s 27(1)(a) for
which counsel for the appellant contends requires certain words to be read into para
c (a). There can be no justification for doing this, unless it can be seen to be clearly
necessary in order to make sense of the provision, and clearly seen what addition is
necessary. It is difficult to know what the addition should be. For example, is the
requirement to be that all employees in an undertaking should be employed by the
same person, or is it sufficient if at least four are employed by one employer? I prefer
to take the language as it is, with the result that an employment is excluded under
d para (a) where there are less than four employees employed in the undertaking,
irrespective of the identity of the employer. In short, for the purpose of counting
the number of employees one is concerned only with whether they are employed
in the undertaking and not with who employs them.

On this construction of the section, the remaining question in the appeal concerns
the finding by the tribunal that there was here a single undertaking comprising the
e activities of the appellant and his wife and the various companies. In this connection,
it is convenient to consider a submission made by counsel for the respondent. The
circumstances, he said, justified the tribunal in disregarding the principle in *Salomon
v Salomon & Co Ltd*[1] and lifting the corporate veil in order to see that the activities
of the companies were the activities of the appellant. In support of this submission
he cited *Harold Holdsworth & Co (Wakefield) Ltd v Caddies*[2] and passages in Gower's
f Modern Company Law*[3]. Unless the arrangements made by the appellant constituted a sham (of which there is no evidence), I do not think that the facts found by
the tribunal would justify the conclusion that the acts or activities of the companies were those of the appellant, or that the employees of the company were, in
truth, his employees. But it is not necessary to go so far. The situation was the perfectly ordinary one of a man conducting affairs, partly personally, and partly through
g the medium of companies of which he and his wife were the only shareholders. It
seems to me that what the tribunal had to ask itself on this question was whether
the distinct but somewhat similar activities of a number of persons, i e the appellant
and his wife and the various companies, could, and did, for the purposes of s 27(1)(a),
constitute a single undertaking. I see no reason why they could not. The tribunal
found that they did.

h The question, then, is whether there was evidence on which the tribunal could
so find. Counsel for the appellant submits that there was not. He criticises the
description of the appellant's business as that of a property owner. He points out
that one of the hotels was in Dublin, seeks support from *Harold Baim Motion Pictures
Theatres (Coleford) Ltd v Nunn*[4] and says that hotels are very different from flatlet
houses. Nor, he says, was there any evidence how many persons were employed
j in each place. There is a good deal with which I would agree in these criticisms.

1 [1875] AC 22, [1895-9] All ER Rep 33
2 [1955] 1 All ER 725, [1955] 1 WLR 352
3 3rd Edn (1969), pp 189, 201
4 (30th October 1973) unreported

Furthermore, there is an absence of evidence of a kind which might be expected. Where it is sought to show that the activities of separate persons together constitute *a* an undertaking, it is not necessarily enough to show that the persons are connected and that the separate activities are similar. One would expect some evidence of organisational unity, eg common accounting, management, purchasing arrangements, insurance and so on. There was none of this, Accordingly, it is of importance to see where was the burden of proof. The respondent has established that she came within s 22 of the 1971 Act. Did she have to prove that her employment was not *b* excluded under s 27, or did the appellant have to prove that it was? The burden, submits counsel for the respondent, lay on the appellant, and he cited the decision of the National Industrial Relations Court in *Boston v Chilton*[1] where it was said that the burden of proving that an employment was excluded by s 27(1)(*a*) lay on the employer. The following is an extract from the judgment of that court, delivered by Sir Hugh Griffiths, in that case: *c*

'The first point taken on the appeal concerns an application to adduce further evidence to establish that because the employer allegedly employed less than four employees at the time of the dismissal, his case fell within one of the excluded categories set out in s 27(1) of the Industrial Relations Act 1971. The employer was legally represented before the tribunal and called no evidence *d* to establish that he fell within the excluded categories. Accordingly there was no material upon the face of the tribunal's decision to suggest that they did not have jurisdiction to deal with the application. It is not accepted by the respondent that this was a case in which the employer would be able to establish that he fell within the excluded categories. This court has already said in a number of its judgments that it will not permit a point of law to be raised in this court *e* which could and properly should have been taken before a tribunal. The employer, having had the advantage of legal representation, was in a position if he wished to raise this matter in evidence before the tribunal [to do so]. The burden was upon him to seek to establish the exclusion. He did not do so. There is no reason why he should not have done so, if so minded, and it is not open to him now to raise it before this court. Accordingly this first ground of appeal is *f* rejected.'

It is true that the primary matter under consideration in that case was the propriety or otherwise of raising, for the first time on an appeal, a matter in respect of which no evidence had been given before the tribunal. Nonetheless there is a clear statement by that court on a matter which it had necessarily to take into consideration *g* in reaching its decision, to this effect (I quote): 'The burden was upon him to seek to establish the exclusion.' That case appears to me to offer helpful guidance, and I shall follow it.

While the formal burden must be on the claimant to establish that the tribunal has jurisdiction, the framework of the Act by which all employments qualify, unless excluded by ss 27-31, supports the view that once employment is proved it is for *h* the employer to prove that it is excluded. In a different field, *R v Edwards*[2] provides a useful analogy. It has to be remembered that the typical case of exclusion under s 27(1)(*a*) is that of the small shop or business where less than four people are employed by one employer. There, no difficulty arises. It is only in unusual cases that difficulties can arise. Where the respondent to a claim for unfair dismissal is (with others, or through the medium of companies) apparently employing four or more persons *j* in a single undertaking, it is reasonable that the burden of proving that an employment is excluded under s 27(1)(*a*) should fall on him, for he alone can know the

---

1 (5th February 1974) unreported
2 [1974] 2 All ER 1085, [1975] QB 27

facts and raise the point. This being so, though I accept some of the criticisms of the
a reasoning of the tribunal on this point, I find that it was justified in overruling this
objection to the jurisdiction raised on behalf of the appellant. It follows therefore
that the decision must stand and the appeal be dismissed.

Appeal dismissed.

b Solicitors: *Loxdales* (for the appellant); *Knapp Fishers* (for the respondent).

Janet Harding Barrister.

c # Capital and Suburban Properties Ltd v Swycher and others

COURT OF APPEAL, CIVIL DIVISION
BUCKLEY, ORR LJJ AND SIR JOHN PENNYCUICK
d 19th, 20th JANUARY, 13th FEBRUARY 1976

*Sale of land – Contract – Breach – Remedy – Damages or specific performance – Election –
Contract providing that vendor permitted to resell land if purchaser failed to complete –
Provision that if vendor resold at a loss purchaser to pay difference as liquidated damages –
Vendors seeking specific performance of contract – Purchaser not complying with decree of
e specific performance – Vendors seeking to repudiate contract and resell land – Whether
vendors entitled to claim damages for any loss on resale.*

By a contract in writing dated 25th March 1974 the vendors agreed to sell a piece of land·
The contract was subject to the Law Society's General Conditions of Sale (1973 Revision)
and the date fixed for completion was 25th July 1974. The contract provided that if the
f sale were not completed within 28 days of service of a notice making time of the
essence, the vendors could forfeit the deposit and resell the property and that if the
resale took place within one year of the completion date and was at a loss, the vendors
were entitled to repayment by the purchaser of the loss as liquidated damages. The
purchaser failed to comply with a completion notice served by the vendors on 16th
August. On 3rd December the vendors obtained an order for the specific perform-
g ance of the contract by the purchaser, but that order was not complied with. On
18th November 1975, on a motion by the vendors, the judge declared that the purchaser's deposit had been forfeited and ordered that the vendors were at liberty to
resell the land and that the purchaser should pay the vendors any loss incurred on a
resale. The purchaser appealed.

h **Held** – Where a vendor obtained a decree for specific performance of a contract for
the sale of land and the purchaser failed to complete, the original breach of contract,
i e the purchaser's failure to complete when time had been made of the essence, was
neither waived by the claim for specific performance nor superseded by the decree
made on that claim. That breach continued to subsist so long as the purchase price
remained unpaid, and it could not be said that a new breach was committed by the
j purchaser failing to comply with the decree. A vendor was obliged to elect at the
trial whether to repudiate the contract and claim damages, or to affirm the contract
and recover any moneys due; he did not acquire concurrent remedies on the purchaser's default. There was accordingly no ground on which the claim for damages
at common law, having been abandoned in favour of specific performance, could
later be revived. The appeal would therefore be allowed and so much of the order

as related to the contingency of a resale at less than the contract price would be
deleted (see p 885 *d* to *j*, p 886 *f* to p 887 *a*, p 888 *c* to *j* and p 889 *c* to *g*, post).   *a*

Dicta of Jessel MR in *Henty v Schröder* (1879) 12 Ch D at 667 and of Romer J in
Barber v Wolfe [1945] 1 All ER at 400 applied.

Sweet v Meredith (1863) 4 Giff 207 and *Watson v Cox* (1873) LR 15 Eq 219 disapproved.

Per Curiam. Except on some kinds of interlocutory application a judge should
always give reasons for the order he makes. It is of importance to the legal profession,
and both litigants and the Court of Appeal are entitled to know on what grounds   *b*
cases are decided, particularly when questions of law are involved (see p 884 *f* to *h*, post).

Notes
For a vendor's remedies under an uncompleted contract, see 34 Halsbury's Laws
(3rd Edn) 320-324, paras 543-549, and for cases on the subject, see 40 Digest (Repl)
239, 240, 1989-2016.   *c*

Cases referred to in judgments
Austins of East Ham Ltd v Macey [1941] Ch 338, 110 LJ Ch 159, 165 LT 47, CA, 40 Digest
(Repl) 240, 2014.
Barber v Wolfe [1945] 1 All ER 399, [1945] Ch 187, 114 LJ Ch 149, 172 LT 384, 40 Digest
(Repl) 240, 2016.   *d*
Griffiths v Vezey [1906] 1 Ch 796, 75 LJ Ch 462, 94 LT 574, 40 Digest (Repl) 141, *1084*.
Hall v Burnell [1911] 2 Ch 551, [1911-13] All ER Rep 631, 81 LJ Ch 46, 105 LT 409, 40
Digest (Repl) 245, *2057*.
Henty v Schröder (1879) 12 Ch D 666, 48 LJ Ch 792, 40 Digest (Repl) 239, *1994*.
Sweet v Meredith (1863) 4 Giff 207, 32 LJ Ch 147, 7 LT 664, 9 Jur NS 569, 66 ER 680,
40 Digest (Repl) 239, *1990*.   *e*
Watson v Cox (1873) LR 15 Eq 219, 42 LJ Ch 279, 27 LT 814, 40 Digest (Repl) 239, *1992*.

Cases also cited
Broadstairs Picture House Ltd v Littman [1940] 3 All ER 419, [1940] Ch 860.
Clark v Wallis (1866) 35 Beav 460.
Foligno v Martin (1853) 16 Beav 586.   *f*
Harold Wood Brick Co Ltd v Ferris [1935] 2 KB 198, [1935] All ER Rep 603.
Hirji Mulji v Cheong Yue SS Co Ltd [1926] AC 497, [1926] All ER Rep 51.
Horsler v Zorro [1975] 1 All ER 584, [1975] 2 WLR 183.
Hutchings v Humphreys (1885) 54 LJ Ch 650.
Jackson v De Kadich [1904] WN 168.
Jeffery v Stewart (1899) 80 LT 17.   *g*
Lowe v Hope [1969] 3 All ER 605, [1970] Ch 94.
Mussen v Van Diemen's Land Co [1938] 1 All ER 210, [1938] Ch 253.
Shuttleworth v Clews [1910] 1 Ch 176.
Simpson v Terry (1865) 34 Beav 423.

Appeal   *h*
By a writ issued on 12th September 1974 Capital and Suburban Properties Ltd ('the
purchaser') claimed specific performance with an abatement of £27,000 of the purchase price, further or alternatively damages, in respect of a contract dated 25th
March 1974 for the sale of land at Savile House, 74/90 Savile Street, Sheffield, against
Sonia Swycher, Dennis David Swycher, Frank Joseph Kershaw, Adrienne Shaw Kershaw ('the vendors') and Kershaw Tudor & Co, a firm. By a defence and counter-   *j*
claim dated 29th October 1974 the vendors counterclaimed, inter alia, for (i) specific
performance of the contract of sale, (ii) damages for breach of contract in lieu of or
in addition to specific performance, (iii) a declaration that the vendors were entitled
to a lien on the property for the unpaid balance of the purchase price payable under
the contract, alternatively, (iv) rescission of the contract and (v) a declaration (a) that

a   the deposit of £5,000 paid by the purchaser under the contract had been forfeited
    to the vendors and (b) that the vendors were entitled to damages for breach of
    contract and all other remedies provided by condition 19 of the Law Society's Con-
    ditions of Sale (1973 Revision). On 3rd December 1974, on an application for summary
    judgment by the vendors, it was ordered that the contract of sale be specifically
    performed by the purchaser. The order directed, inter alia, that there be an enquiry
    whether there should be any and if so what abatement of the purchase price on any
b   of the grounds alleged in the purchaser's writ. On 5th November 1975, on a sum-
    mons by the vendors, Foster J ordered that, notwithstanding the order of 3rd Decem-
    ber 1974, and with the vendors' consent, the vendors should convey the property
    to the purchaser on 12th November 1975 on payment by the purchaser to the vendors
    of £126,000. No payment was made by the purchaser pursuant to the order of
    5th November. On 18th November 1975, on a notice of motion by the vendors,
c   Foster J declared that the deposit of £5,000 paid by the purchaser to the vendors
    under the contract had been forfeited and ordered (i) that the vendors be
    at liberty to resell the property, (ii) that should the property be resold by the
    vendors before 12th November 1976 for less than the contract price of £150,000,
    the purchaser should pay to the vendors the difference, being credited with the
    deposit. The purchaser appealed against, inter alia, that part of the order which
d   related to the contingency of a resale by the vendors. The facts are set out in the
    judgment of Buckley LJ.

    Michael Miller QC and *Martin Reynolds* for the purchaser.
    Donald Nicholls QC and *Michael Hart* for the vendors.

                                                                    Cur adv vult

e   13th February. The following judgments were read.

    BUCKLEY LJ. This is an appeal from an order dated 18th November 1975 of
    Foster J in a vendors' specific performance action (by counterclaim) whereby he
    declared the deposit paid by the purchaser to have been forfeited, ordered that the
f   vendors be at liberty to resell the property and ordered that, should the property
    be sold on or before 12th November 1976 for less than the contract price, the pur-
    chaser should pay the vendors the difference, after giving credit for the deposit,
    and the expenses of the resale. The order also vacated the registration as an estate
    contract of the sale agreement.
        By an agreement in writing dated 25th March 1974 the vendors agreed to sell to
    the purchaser a piece of land fronting to Savile Street, Sheffield, with the building
g   on it for £150,000, with certain additional sums as and when the property should be
    substantially let. The property was expressed to be sold subject to the Law Society's
    General Conditions of Sale[1] with certain modifications which are presently irrelevant.
    The date fixed for completion was 25th July 1974. The property was at the date of
    the agreement partly let and partly in hand.
        On 16th August 1974 the vendors gave notice to the purchaser under general
h   condition 19 to complete in accordance with that condition, that is to say within
    28 days of the service of the notice, time being made of the essence of the contract in
    this respect. This notice expired on 17th September 1974. On 6th March 1974, not
    long before the date of the sale agreement, the council of the Sheffield Metropolitan
    District, being the relevant local authority, passed a resolution under the General
    Rate Act 1967, s 17, as amended, taking power to impose a general rate on unoccupied
j   property. The vendors did not know of this at the date of the agreement. The
    resolution was not gazetted until 1st April 1974.
        The purchaser did not complete the purchase by 17th September 1974. On 12th
    September 1974 the purchaser issued the writ in the action, alleging that the vendors

    _____
    1 (1973 Revision)

by an agent had falsely represented that the local authority had not passed any such
resolution as aforesaid, and that the purchaser had entered into the agreement in   a
reliance on that representation. They claimed specific performance with an abatement of the purchase price by £27,000. They also sued the vendors' solicitors, the
last defendants, for damages for negligence.

The defendants denied the alleged representation and alleged that they knew
nothing about the resolution until notice of it was served on the vendors on 29th
April 1974. The vendors counterclaimed for specific performance of the agreement   b
without abatement of the price, damages in lieu of or in addition to specific performance, a declaration of lien, and alternatively rescission, forfeiture of the deposit and
a declaration that they were entitled to damages for breach of contract and all the
remedies provided by general condition 19.

The defendants applied for summary judgment under RSC Ord 86, and on 3rd
December 1974 the master made an order for specific performance. The order   c
directed, among other accounts and enquiries, an enquiry whether there should be
any and if so what abatement of the purchase price on any of the grounds alleged
in the statement of claim.

On 5th November 1975 the defendants' summons to proceed under that order
came before Foster J, when, the defendants consenting, the learned judge ordered
that notwithstanding the order of 3rd December 1974 the vendors should convey the   d
property to the purchaser on 12th November 1975 on payment by the purchaser to
the vendors of £126,000 and on payment by the purchaser into a joint account in
the names of the parties of a further sum of £27,000 pending the determination of
the accounts and enquiries ordered on 3rd December 1974 and two further enquiries
then ordered by the judge. The purchaser did not make any payment in accordance
with the last-mentioned order and, except for a deposit of £5,000 paid under the   e
agreement, no part of the purchase price has been paid.

By notice of motion dated 13th November 1975 the vendors sought a declaration of
forfeiture of the deposit, a declaration that they were at liberty to resell and an
order that in case the property should be sold for less than the amounts payable to
the vendors under the agreement, the purchaser should pay to the vendors the
difference (after giving credit for the deposit) together with the expenses of the sale.   f

On that motion Foster J on 18th November 1975 made the order now under
appeal. The learned judge unfortunately gave no reasons for his decision. This I
consider a most unsatisfactory practice. There are some sorts of interlocutory applications, mainly of a purely procedural kind, on which a judge exercising his discretion on some such question as whether a matter should be expedited or adjourned
or extra time should be allowed for a party to take some procedural step, or pos-   g
sibly whether relief by way of injunction should have been granted or refused, can
properly make an order without giving reasons. This, being an application involving
questions of law, is in my opinion clearly not such a case. Litigants are entitled to
know on what grounds their cases are decided. It is of importance that the legal
profession should know on what grounds cases are decided, particularly when questions of law are involved. And this court is entitled to the assistance of the judge of   h
first instance by an explicit statement of his reasons for deciding as he did. In the
present case we happen to know from a transcript of the argument what submissions
were made to the judge. We may infer, but we cannot know, that the judge preferred
those presented by counsel for the vendors to those presented by counsel for the
purchaser. The judge ought not to have spared himself the trouble of expressing his
reasons for deciding as he did. The purchaser, with the leave of this court, appeals   j
against so much of the learned judge's order as dealt with the contingency of a resale
of the property on or before 12th November 1976 for less than the contract price.
This evidently treats general condition 19(4) as applicable to the circumstances of
this case as if the 'date fixed for completion' for the purposes of that condition were 12th
November 1975, the date fixed for completion under the order of 5th November 1975.

General condition 19, so far as relvant in this respect, reads as follows: paras
a (1), (2) and (3) relate to the giving of a notice to complete and the effect of giving such
a notice, and para (4) is in the following terms:

'If the purchaser does not comply with the terms of an effective notice served
by the vendor under this condition, then—(a) the purchaser shall forthwith on
the expiry of that notice, or within such further period as the vendor may allow,
b return all abstracts and other papers in his possession belonging to the vendor
and at his own expense procure the cancellation of any entry relating to the
contract in any register and (b) without prejudice to any other rights or remedies
available to him at law or in equity, the vendor may—(i) forfeit and retain for
his own benefit the deposit paid by the purchaser and (ii) resell the property
whether by auction or by private treaty without previously tendering a convey-
c ance to the purchaser (c) if on any such re-sale contracted within one year from
the date fixed for completion the vendor incurs a loss, the purchaser shall pay
to the vendor as liquidated damages the amount of such loss, which shall include
all costs and expenses reasonably incurred in any such re-sale or any attempted
re-sale, subject to the vendor giving credit for any deposit and any money paid
on account of the purchase price, but any surplus money shall be retained by
d the vendor.'

I do not think I need read sub-paras (5) or (6).
Before writing this judgment I have had the advantage of reading the judgment
which Sir John Pennycuick will presently deliver. With that judgment I entirely
agree. I wish to add nothing to his judgment on the first point with which he deals;
but as the questions raised by the vendors' new contention on this appeal, that an
e enquiry should be included in the order what damages they have suffered by reason
of the purchaser's failure to complete the agreement, are not without importance
and are not dealt with altogether explicitly in reported cases, it may perhaps be
useful if I state in my own words and as succinctly as I can the principles which seem
to me to be involved.
If, time having been made of the essence of a contract for a sale of land, the pur-
f chaser does not complete within due time, the vendor may (a) treat the purchaser as
having repudiated the contract and pursue his remedy at law in damages for breach
of contract, or (b) he may pursue his equitable remedy of specific performance. He
may seek both these remedies in one writ, but at the trial he must elect which road
he wishes to travel. If he pursues his common law remedy, he does so on the basis
that he is no longer obliged to perform the contract, and he recovers damages on the
g footing that he will not do so and will retain the property agreed to be sold. If, on
the other hand, he elects to pursue his equitable remedy, he affirms the contract.
By affirming the contract, he does not waive the purchaser's breach of contract by
failing to complete in due time; but, if the sale is eventually carried through under
a decree of specific performance, he suffers no damage except to any extent to which
he is unable to recover from the purchaser additional expense to which he has been
h put. He may in addition be entitled to a monetary remedy under the express terms
of the contract of the nature of liquidated damages, but we are not concerned with
this for present purposes. These two remedies are mutually exclusive. The vendor
cannot both retain the property in the land and enforce payment of the purchase
price: he cannot both recover damages for a fundamental breach of the contract
and at the same time compel the purchaser to remedy the breach by performing the
j contract. At trial, therefore, the vendor plaintiff must elect which remedy he will
seek.
If a purchaser fails to comply with a decree of specific performance, the vendor
can forfeit the deposit and claim any monetary relief which may be available to him
under the terms of the contract. What further relief is open to him?
It is not in dispute that a vendor can, if he so chooses, seek an order of the court

rescinding the contract at this stage. In this context the word 'rescind' does not import treating the contract as though it had never been made: it means that the vendor will *a* be permitted to retain the land on the basis that he is no longer bound to perform his part of the contract in consequence of the purchaser's repudiation of it. I use the word in that sense in this judgment. The vendor may wish to follow this course because the value of the property has risen, so that the land is worth more to him than the purchase price. The first question for our consideration is whether it is right that, if the vendor chooses to ask for rescission at this stage, he cannot also have *b* damages for breach of contract. Can he retain the land and have damages?

If the vendor does not seek rescission, his alternative remedy is enforcement of the specific performance decree and recovery of any moneys which may become due to him under any judgment or order resulting from working out the decree. Thus he may recover the balance of the purchase price due from the purchaser and his costs by way of execution. If he cannot recover all that is due to him in this way, he *c* can have recourse to his vendor's lien on the land. When in these ways or either of them he has received every amount awarded to him under the decree, the vendor must convey to the purchaser any of the land which has not been disposed of under the lien and account to the purchaser for any surplus proceeds of disposing of the land. The vendor could not, it seems to me, be any better off by retaining the land and claiming damages for repudiation of the contract than by working out the *d* specific performance decree in this way with the aid of his vendor's lien. The value of the land (assuming it not to have appreciated since the contract) plus damages at common law could not, I think, exceed the amount recoverable by working out the decree in this way. If the vendor could not recover the full amount awarded to him under the decree by way of execution and his vendor's lien, he could be no better off by retaining the land and enforcing payment of any common law damages. *e* Rescission may be valuable to a vendor if the land has risen in value, but cannot benefit him otherwise. So what virtue would there be in this court allowing a vendor both to rescind and claim damages? The vendor already has at his disposal an equally valuable remedy under the decree for specific performance.

Accordingly, it seems to me to be justified in principle to hold that if a purchaser fails to complete in accordance with a specific performance decree and the vendor *f* then seeks to rescind the contract, he cannot at the same time recover damages at common law for repudiation of the contract. But in the present case the vendors say that they do not ask to rescind the contract. They say that, the purchaser having failed to complete in accordance with the order of the court, they are entitled to common law damages for repudiation of the contract which they have affirmed, while at the same time retaining the property agreed to be sold: in other words, *g* as I understand the argument, they can go back to exercising the option which they rejected when they chose to pursue their equitable remedy in preference to their common law one. This, in my judgment, they should not be permitted to do, first, because they have already opted against this remedy; secondly, because it will not enable them to recover any greater relief than they can obtain if they pursue the course they elected to follow to its conclusion. *h*

I have purposely avoided citing authorities because, as Sir John Pennycuick will point out in his judgment, it is desirable that we should consider the position in principle. My analysis, however, leads me to the conclusion that the orders made in *Sweet v Meredith*[1] and *Watson v Cox*[2] were wrong so far as after a failure by a purchaser to comply with an order for specific performance, they associated an enquiry as to damages with an order permitting a vendor to treat a sale contract as no longer *j* binding him.

I would allow this appeal and delete from Foster J's order the declaration relating

1   (1863) 4 Giff 207
2   (1873) LR 15 Eq 219

to the contingency of the resale of the property on or before 12th November 1976
a for less than the contract price.

SIR JOHN PENNYCUICK. I agree with the judgment delivered by Buckley LJ.
I will consider first the issue on which the case was argued before Foster J on 18th
November 1975. As I understand the transcript of what took place, the learned
b judge based his decision on the view that the consent order dated 5th November 1975
providing for completion on 12th November had the effect of making condition 19 of
the Law Society's General Conditions of Sale operate as if 12th November were 'the
date fixed for completion' for the purpose of condition 19(4)(*c*). I put it that way because the judge did not give any reason for his decision. I do not think this view can
be supported. Condition 2 of the special conditions provides that the date fixed for
c completion is 25th July 1974. It seems to me that the expression 'the date fixed for
completion' wherever it occurs in the general conditions must bear the same meaning.
Admittedly it does so in conditions 15 and 16, and I do not see how it can bear different
meaning in condition 19(4)(*c*). Insofar as the judge was treating the consent order
dated 5th November as by implication varying the meaning of the expression in
condition 19(4)(*c*). I think such an implication was unwarranted. Insofar as the judge
d was purporting to vary the meaning of the expression by his own order, I think he
had no power to do so.
On the appeal to this court, the vendors gave notice of a new contention, namely
that there should be included in the order an enquiry what damages the vendors
have suffered by reason of the purchaser's breach of contract in failing to complete
the sale agreement. The argument in support of this contention, as developed by
e counsel for the vendors, was, in summary terms, to the effect that, where the purchaser fails to complete and the vendor elects to take a decree of specific performance
rather than order for damages, but the purchaser fails to comply with the decree,
the vendor thereupon acquires anew the right to claim damages at common law.
The new contention is contrary to a line of authorities dating back to the decision of
Jessel MR in *Henty v Schröder*[1], almost exactly a century ago. In that case, as in several
f others, the defaulting purchaser did not appear and no doubt for that reason the
judgment is very short. But it is quite explicit. Jessel MR said[2]:

'The Plaintiffs could not at the same time obtain an order to have the agreement rescinded and claim damages against the Defendant for the breach of the
agreement'.

g The decision has been repeatedly followed, and in *Barber v Wolfe*[3] Romer J, after
hearing full argument, restated the rule, by which he rightly regarded himself as
bound. He said[4]:

'So it comes down, really, as I see it, to a question whether [the purchaser] is
bound to pay something in the nature of occupation rent, either under some
general principle or equity, or as forming part of damages properly awardable to
h the [vendor]? In a vendor's action for specific performance, if the vendor elects
to take a decree for specific performance, and that decree is worked out, and the
certificate is made and the purchaser fails to complete, undoubtedly the [vendor]
is entitled to come back to the court and ask for the rescinding of the contract.
But, if the [vendor] elects to take that course I thought it was abundantly established
that he could not, at the same time, obtain damages for the breach of the con-
j tract which he was asking the court to rescind, and I still believe that to be the

---

1 (1879) 12 Ch D 666
2 12 Ch D at 667
3 [1945] 1 All ER 399, [1945] Ch 187
4 [1945] 1 All ER at 400, [1945] Ch at 189, 190

practice. The relevant cases are summarised in 3 SETON, JUDGMENTS AND ORDERS[1], and they range over a considerable period of time, the latest being a decision of Eve, J., in *Hall v. Burnell*[2]. Whatever the foundation of the rule is I am not sure that it is necessary to inquire into it at the present moment. If that is established, as I think it is, it seems to me that only a decision of a higher court can introduce some new rule.'

This line of authorities is not binding on the Court of Appeal and we are invited by counsel for the vendors to hold that the rule is not good law. We must of course consider the position, but we should, I think, only entertain counsel for the vendors' invitation if we reach the clear conclusion that the rule is not in accordance with sound principle. I turn, then, to consider the position as it would stand, apart from the line of authorities commencing with *Henty v Schröder*[3].

Where the purchaser under an enforceable contract for sale makes default in completion after the expiry of a notice making time of the essence, the vendor may elect between two remedies: (i) he may accept the purchaser's default as a repudiation of the contract and claim damages at common law or (where available) under an express provision for liquidated damages contained in the contract; or (ii) he may refuse to accept the default as a repudiation and claim a decree of specific performance. If he elects to claim damages, he cannot thereafter claim specific performance. If he elects to claim specific performance, he cannot thereafter claim damages, at any rate in respect of the original breach: see Williams on Vendor and Purchaser[4].

I leave out of account in this connection a claim for recission in the proper sense of that word, which is only marginally relevant in the present connection. As was pointed out in argument, the loose use or the word 'recission' to denote either recission in the proper sense of the word or acceptance of default as a repudiation sometimes causes confusion.

Should the vendor elect in favour of specific performance, then, if the purchaser complies with the decree, no further question arises. But what is the position if the purchaser fails to comply with the decree? It is not in dispute that in these circumstances the vendor may forfeit the deposit: *Hall v Burnell*[5]; he may claim liquidated damages under an express provision in the contract (where available): *Griffiths v Vezey*[6]; and he may levy execution in respect of the money payable by the purchaser under the decree: Fry on Specific Performance[7]; Williams on Vendor and Purchaser[8]; Halsbury's Laws of England[9]. I need not pause to consider how far these remedies interlock or the precise manner in which they work out. Finally, the vendor can admittedly claim recission in the sense indicated by Buckley LJ and thereby extricate himself from the contract at this stage. This last remedy is alternative to those mentioned above, except that he may still forfeit the deposit.

There remains the question which is raised on the present appeal, namely whether the vendor, assuming that he does not claim rescission, is entitled at this stage to claim damages at common law.

Counsel for the vendor's contentions on this question may, I think, be summarised under the following three propositions, namely: (i) where a vendor elects for specific performance, the contract remains in existence at the time when the purchaser is

---

1 7th Edn (1912), vol 3, p 2220
2 [1911] 2 Ch 551, [1911-13] All ER Rep 631
3 (1879) 12 Ch D 666
4 4th Edn (1936), p 1025
5 [1911] 2 Ch 551, [1911-13] All ER Rep 631
6 [1906] 1 Ch 796
7 6th Edn (1921), p 547
8 4th Edn (1936), p 1064
9 36 Halsbury's Laws (3rd Edn) 352

bound to complete under the decree; (ii) if the purchaser then fails to complete, **a** he then commits a new breach of the contract; (iii) this new breach gives rise to a new claim for damages at common law.

As regards these propositions, (i) is not in dispute: cf *Austins of East Ham Ltd v Macey*[1]; (ii) was conceded by counsel for the purchaser: I feel great difficulty over this concession and will return to the point in a moment; (iii) here counsel for the purchaser joined issue; he contended that the vendor, acquiring as he does a right of **b** execution on the purchaser's default under the remedy for which the vendor has elected, namely specific performance, cannot at the same time obtain a concurrent right by way of damages at common law.

I return to proposition (ii). The true position, as I see it, is that the original breach of contract, ie failure to complete when time has been made of the essence, is neither waived by the claim for specific performance nor superseded by the decree made on **c** that claim. The original breach continues to subsist so long as the purchase price remains unpaid. Where the purchaser fails to comply with the decree, he certainly commits a breach of the decree. But I do not see how he can be said to commit a new breach of the contract. The position is simply that the original breach continues unremedied.

If there is no new breach, I see no ground on which the claim for damages at common **d** law, against which the vendor has elected in favour of specific performance, could be revived at this stage.

I feel great hesitation in declining to accept a concession made by experienced counsel, and no doubt it would not as a rule be proper to do so. But we are here concerned to review on principle a long-standing rule, and I think we are bound to analyse the true legal position as best we can.

e (iii) Should I be wrong on the last point, one has to consider whether on the purchaser's default the vendor acquires two concurrent remedies. I do not myself think a question really arises in this form. If it does so, I would adopt the reasoning of Buckley LJ on it. I too am not at all clear what advantage the vendor would derive from the acquisition of this second concurrent remedy.

I conclude that the rule in *Henty v Schröder*[2] is founded on correct principle. We **f** are not therefore faced with the problem whether this court should interfere with an illogical rule which has stood for a century.

I would allow the appeal.

BUCKLEY LJ. Orr LJ has authorised me to say that he agrees with both the **g** judgments delivered.

Appeal allowed. Leave to appeal to the House of Lords refused.

Solicitors: *Stowe & Co* (for the purchaser); *Bower, Cotton & Bower*, agents for *Kershaw, Tudor & Co*, Sheffield (for the vendors).

h

Gordon H Scott Esq Barrister.

1 [1941] Ch 338
2 (1879) 12 Ch D 666

Mount Charlotte Investments Ltd v Leek and Westbourne Building Society

CHANCERY DIVISION

TEMPLEMAN J

19th, 20th JUNE 1975

Landlord and tenant – Rent – Review – Failure to comply with time limit – Option to require review – Right conferred on landlord in nature of option – Right conferred on landlord to require arbitration in event of failure to agree on revised rent – Right to be exercised within specified time limit – Whether time limit mandatory – Whether landlord capable of making valid application for arbitration after expiry of time limit.

The landlords' predecessors in title granted a lease of certain premises to the tenants for a term of 21 years from 25th March 1967. Clause 1(a) provided that the rent, defined as 'the basic rent', was to be £2,750 per annum for the first eight years. Clause 1(b) provided that 'during the next six years of the said term' i e from 25th March 1975 to 25th March 1981, the rent was to be 'whichever of the two following yearly rents is the greater that is to say: (i) The basic rent or (ii) Such amount as may be agreed between [the landlords] and [the tenants] before the expiration of six calendar months before the end of the eighth year of the said term or (in the absence of such agreement by such last mentioned date) such amount as may be determined by an Arbitrator to be nominated by the President for the time being of the Royal Institution of Chartered Surveyors on the application of [the landlords] to be made within fourteen days after the date six calender months before the end of the eighth year of the said term . . .' Clause 1(c) contained a similar provision for a review of the rent for the last seven years of the term. In September 1974 the landlords opened negotiations with the tenants for the purpose of fixing a revised rent under cl 1(b). The negotiations continued without agreement being reached. The date for making an application to the President of the RICS passed; negotiations still continued until, on 27th February 1975, the tenants took the point that the landlords were out of time with the result that the rent could not be increased. On 5th March the landlords applied to the President of the RICS to appoint an arbitrator. The landlords commenced proceedings for a declaration that they were entitled to apply, and had validly applied, for the appointment of an arbitrator.

Held – Since cl 1(b) empowered the landlords alone to go to arbitration, the right conferred on the landlords was in substance in the nature of an option and accordingly the condition as to time which was attached to the exercise of that right was to be treated as mandatory. It followed that, since the landlords had failed to comply with the time limit imposed by cl 1(b), their application for the appointment of an arbitrator was invalid (see p 896 f to h, post).

Samuel Properties (Developments) Ltd v Hayek [1972] 2 All ER 881 applied.

C H Bailey Ltd v Memorial Enterprises Ltd [1974] 1 All ER 1003 and *Kenilworth Industrial Sites Ltd v E C Little & Co Ltd* [1975] 1 All ER 53 distinguished.

Notes

This case should be contrasted with *Accuba Ltd v Allied Shoe Repairs Ltd* [1975] 3 All ER 782, a decision of Goff J on 23rd May 1975.

For agreements to review rents subject to a time limit for giving notice, see Supplement to 23 Halsbury's Laws (3rd Edn) para 1197, and for cases on the subject, see 31(1) Digest (Reissue) 481, 482, 3952, 3953.

Cases referred to in judgment

a   *Bailey (C H) Ltd v Memorial Enterprises Ltd* [1974] 1 All ER 1003, [1974] 1 WLR 728, CA.
  Hare v Nicoll [1966] 1 All ER 285, [1966] 2 QB 130, [1966] 2 WLR 441, CA, Digest (Cont
    Vol B) 665, 300a.
  Kenilworth Industrial Sites Ltd v E C Little & Co Ltd [1974] 2 All ER 815, [1974] 1 WLR
    1069; *affd* [1975] 1 All ER 53, [1975] 1 WLR 143, CA.
  Richards (C) & Son Ltd v Karenita Ltd (1972) 221 Estates Gazette 25.

b   *Samuel Properties (Developments) Ltd v Hayek* [1972] 2 All ER 881, [1972] 1 WLR 1064,
    24 P & CR 9; *affd* [1972] 3 All ER 473, [1972] 1 WLR 1296, 24 P & CR 223, CA, 31(1)
    Digest (Reissue) 481, 3952.
  Stylo Shoes Ltd v Wetherall Bond St W1 Ltd (14th October 1974) unreported, [1974] Bar
    Library transcript 318A.
  United Scientific Holdings Ltd v Burnley Corpn (1974) 231 Estates Gazette 1543.

c

Adjourned summons

By an originating summons dated 10th April 1975, the plaintiffs, Mount Charlotte
Investments Ltd ('the landlords'), sought a declaration (i) that on the true construction
of a lease dated 8th April 1968 and made between the landlords' predecessors in
title, The Park Hall and Hotel Co Ltd, and the defendants, Leek and Westbourne
d Building Society Ltd ('the tenants'), and in the events which had happened, the
landlords were entitled to apply, and had validly applied, to the President of the
Royal Institution of Chartered Surveyors for the appointment of an arbitrator to
determine the fair yearly rent under the lease for the period of six years commencing on 25th March 1975 and ending on 25th March 1981, in accordance with cl 1(b)(ii) of
the lease; and (ii) that the rent payable under the lease with effect from 25th March
e 1975 and for the period of six years commencing thereon and ending on 25th March
1981 was the greater of (i) the basic rent as defined in the lease and (ii) such amount
as should be determined by the arbitrator under cl 1(b)(ii) of the lease. The facts are
set out in the judgment.

f   *John Stuart Colyer* for the landlords.
  Christopher Slade QC and *J A Moncaster* for the tenants.

TEMPLEMAN J. This is the latest (but I fear not the last) dispute over a rent review
clause in a lease. The landlords failed to refer the rent to arbitration within the time
g provided by the lease and the tenants claim that the landlords have lost their chance
to increase the rent. The lease is dated 8th April 1968. It was made between the landlords' predecessors in title and the tenants. It was a lease of a shop and premises, 89
Queen Street, Cardiff, for a term of 21 years from 25th March 1967, and for use
as offices of a building society or any trade or business which the landlords might
permit.
h   The lease provided that the tenants should hold the premises—

    'YIELDING AND PAYING therefor during the said term and so in proportion
    for any less time than a year the respective rents following:—(a) During the
    first eight years of the term [£2,750 per annum, which was defined as "the basic
    rent"; then:] (b) During the next six years of the said term from [25th March
j   1975 to 25th March 1981] whichever of the two following yearly rents is the greater
    that is to say (i) The basic rent or (ii) Such amount as may be agreed between the
    Lessors and the Lessees before the expiration of six calendar months before the
    end of the eighth year of the said term or (in the absence of such agreement by
    such last mentioned date) such amount as may be determined by an Arbitrator
    to be nominated by the President for the time being of the Royal Institution of

Chartered Surveyors on the application of the Lessors to be made within fourteen
days after six calendar months before the end of the eighth year of the said term
and so that in case of such arbitration the amount to be determined by the
arbitrator shall be such as in his opinion shall represent the fair yearly rent for
the demised premises at the end of the eighth year of the said term having
regard to rental values of property then current [and then:] (c) During the last
Seven years of the said term . . . whichever of the two following rents is the
greater that is to say:—(i) The rent reserved for the previous six years or (ii)
The rent equivalent to a fair yearly rent as at the end of the fourteenth year of
the said term to be agreed or calculated on the same basis mutatis mutandis as
set out above in respect of the eighth year.'

There followed a provision that the rent should be paid on the usual quarter days, in
arrears.

The lease thus provided for negotiations between the landlords and the tenants
before 25th September 1974 and, if those negotiations failed to reach an agreement,
then a reference to arbitration by the landlords before 9th October 1974, with the
obvious objective of seeing that the new rent should be determined before 24th June
1975 if possible, before the new rent became payable for the first time.

The landlords opened negotiations with the tenants with a letter dated 20th
September 1974 and negotiations proceeded through surveyors. The date for an application to the President of the Royal Institution of Chartered Surveyors passed;
negotiations still continued until, on 27th February 1975, the tenants took the point
that the landlords were out of time, and, therefore, that the rent could not be
increased. The landlords, in a letter dated 5th March 1975, applied to the President
of the Royal Institution of Chartered Surveyors to appoint an arbitrator, and the
question is whether that application is valid or whether, as the tenants say, the
landlords have lost their opportunity.

The authorities disclose that there are at least two kinds of rent revision clauses.
The first kind has been analysed as 'an option to the landlord to obtain a higher
rent' and in that case if the landlord does not comply with any time limits provided
for the exercise of the option then he wholly fails. The time limits are said to be
mandatory. The second kind of clause has been analysed as 'creating an obligation on
the landlords'—or sometimes the tenants as well—'to take the steps necessary to
determine what the rent is going to be'. If in the obligation cases the time limits
prescribed by the document are not complied with, then the court construes those
time limits as being purely directory, and, provided that the tenant has not been
prejudiced by any delay, then the rent is fixed after the time limits have expired. The
analysis of the option rent review clause is a triumph for theory over realism. In
practice landlords insist on a rent review clause. They are only prepared to grant a 21
year lease if the rent is increased to keep pace with inflation every seven years or so.
The concept of the tenant granting the landlord an option and conferring benefits on
the landlord does not accord with reality. The courts could have come to the
conclusion that all times imposed by rent revision clauses are directory and not
mandatory because an increase in rent is a condition imposed by the landlord for the
favour of a long term. Certainly in the obligation clauses the courts have no difficulty
in ignoring the express words of the clause and treating the time limits as directory;
but they have refused to do the same in the case of the clauses which they have
designated option clauses. The authorities begin in 1972. When the landlord before
1972 went to his draftsman to draft a rent revision clause the draftsman might, in all
innocence, produce an option type of clause or an obligation type of clause or something which is neatly halfway between the two. Since 1972 the drafting cannot be
done wholly in innocence but can quite often be done in ignorance. The draftsman
may lay a trap and the landlord may fall into the trap by forgetting the time limit.
But that is the effect of the authorities.

In *C Richards & Son Ltd v Karenita Ltd* [1] the rent revision clause provided:

a

> '. . . if the landlords shall by giving notice in writing to the tenants at any time during the first three months of the seventh year of the term hereby created require a review of the rent payable hereunder, such rent shall be revised with effect from the expiration of the seventh year . . .'

Goulding J rejected the argument that time was not of the essence, an argument
b adopted from the relationship of vendor and purchaser.

In *Samuel Properties (Developments) Ltd v Hayek* [2] if the landlords desired to have the rent reviewed by reference to the open market rental value, and served a notice in writing to that effect not later than two quarters before the expiry of the seventh and 14th years, then by agreement or abitration the rent was to be increased. Whitford J said[3]:

c

> '. . . clauses of the character which I am considering run very closely with the type of option clauses . . . I think it right that a review to bring about an increase in rent at the end of seven and 14 years can reasonably be described as a benefit to one party alone. It might not be unreasonable for it to be described as a privilege . . . I do think that in a case of this character it is important that the party seeking to secure the benefit should comply strictly with the provisions stipulated just as in the case of option for renewal of leases, or for example options for the repurchase of shares.'

d

And after referring to *Hare v Nicoll* [4], the classic case which reiterated that in the exercise of an option the terms must be strictly complied with if the option is properly to be exercised, the learned judge then held that in the *Samuel Properties* case[2] the
e rent revision clause was an option type of clause and, not being complied with, the landlord had lost his opportunity.

That decision was affirmed by the Court of Appeal[5], and Russell LJ referred to the arguments that a rent review clause should come within a general approach that time provisions should not be construed as inflexible and mandatory unless there be special reasons for so doing; and that there were no special reasons for importing in-
f flexibility into provisions that were basically mere machinery for achieving what the parties must have regarded as an equitable alteration in rent to safeguard the lessor against the consequences of possible, or indeed probable, continuing depreciation of the value of money in relation to housing accommodation. Russell LJ said[6]:

> 'I am not myself impressed by these arguments. The right or privilege of exacting an additional rent was conferred by the bargain between the parties
g as an express option which would be effective if a condition precedent was com- plied with; it could be equated with an offer by the lessee to pay an increased rent only in certain circumstances which it lay in the power of the lessor unilaterally to bring about, which offer was not accepted in those terms. It was argued that there was a distinction (as to time limits) between options to determine, or to renew, or to acquire the reversion, and a right such as the present. I do not see
h why this should be so. Accordingly in my judgment the time requirement . . . is to be treated as inflexible and mandatory.'

That is binding on me.

In *C H Bailey Ltd v Memorial Enterprises Ltd* [7] a rent review clause provided:

j 1 (1972) 221 Estates Gazette 25
   2 [1972] 2 All ER 881, [1972] 1 WLR 1064
   3 [1972] 2 All ER at 886, [1972] 1 WLR at 1070
   4 [1966] 1 All ER 285, [1966] 2 QB 130
   5 [1972] 3 All ER 473, [1972] 1 WLR 1296
   6 [1972] 3 All ER at 478 [1972] 1 WLR at 1302
   7 [1974] 1 All ER 1003, [1974] 1 WLR 728

'If on [21st September 1969] the Market Rental Value . . . shall be found to exceed the rent of [£2,375] hereby reserved there shall be substituted from such *a* date for the yearly rent hereby reserved an increased yearly rent equal to the market rental value so ascertained.'

There were provisions for the market rental value to be agreed or to be determined by arbitration. That rent review clause was to operate at the end of the first five years of the term and, unless it did so operate, there would be no rent at all fixed by *b* the lease or capable of being fixed. Eveleigh J held that the market rental value on 21st September 1969 could be ascertained after that date but that the increased rent only became payable on the quarter day following its ascertainment. The Court of Appeal held that, since the rent review clause provided for the increased rent when ascertained to be substituted from 21st September 1969, it was payable retrospectively from that date. In coming to that decision the Court of Appeal rejected the tenants' *c* argument that the landlords had lost their right to increase the rent at all because it was not in fact ascertained on 21st September 1969. This was not an option which the landlord had power to excercise but an obligation on both parties to determine what the rent should be as from 21st September 1969.

In *Kenilworth Industrial Sites Ltd v E C Little & Co Ltd*[1], before Megarry J, in a 21 year lease the annual rent for the first five years was £2,980. A rent revision clause provided: *d*

'NOT more than twelve months nor less than six months before the expiration of the fifth, tenth and fifteenth years of the term the Landlord shall serve upon the tenant a notice to agree the rent of the said property for the ensuing five years and thereupon the parties hereto shall agree a new rent.'

There was an express proviso that 'Any failure to give or receive such notice shall not *e* render void the right of the landlord hereunder to require the agreement or determination as aforesaid of a new rent.' Megarry J decided that the failure of the landlord to give the notice did not render void his right to an increased rent and the Court of Appeal[2] agreed.

Between the judgment of Megarry J in the *Kenilworth* case[1] at first instance and the decision of the Court of Appeal there occurred *United Scientific Holdings Ltd v Burnley* *f* *Corpn*[3]. A 99 year lease provided that during that year immediately preceding the first 10 year period of the term:

'the [landlord] and the [tenant] shall agree or failing agreement shall determine by arbitration the . . . rack rent . . . and one quarter of the sum total so ascertained or [£2,000] whichever is the greater shall be the rate of rent reserved by this *g* lease in respect of the . . . next . . . period.'

And then it provided for a reference to arbitration to be agreed by the parties or to be nominated by the President of the Royal Institution of Chartered Surveyors. That was a rent review clause where at first blush the language appeared to be language of obligation and not of option. In the event the parties failed to reach agreement during the year immediately preceding the end of the period and failed to go to arbitration. *h* Pennycuick V-C assumed in favour of the landlords that the requirement that the arbitration should be during the relevant year was satisfied if a reference to arbitration were made during the specified period. It had been argued for the landlords that time was not of the essence, that 'all one was concerned to do was to quantify the amount of rent under the existing obligation to pay rent', and there was no reason why that should not be done outside the year. Pennycuick V-C continued[4]: *j*

1 [1974] 2 All ER 815, [1974] 1 WLR 1069
2 [1975] 1 All ER 53, [1975] 1 WLR 143
3 (1974) 231 Estates Gazette 1543
4 231 Estates Gazette at 1545

a   ... although the rent review provision was expressed merely as a provision for the quantification of additional rent, it was in substance a unilateral right or privilege vested in [the landlords] alone, the nature of the right being to increase the rent payable by the tenants. The tenants were entitled under the lease to possession of the property for the whole 99 years at [the original rent] unless [the landlords] elected to require a rent review'.

b   Similarly, says counsel for the tenants in the present case, although there may be some indications in the instant lease which appear at first blush to be language of obligation, on analysis it will be found that the lease created an option for the landlords to increase the rent above the original rent if they took the proper steps to do so.

The last authority is a decision of the Court of Appeal, decided on 14th October 1974, *Stylo Shoes Ltd v Wetherall Bond Street W1 Ltd*[1]. A review clause provided :

c   'The landlords shall be entitled to require the rent to be revised from the commencement of the eighth year of the said term being the 29th day of September, 1972, and, if the landlords shall so require then the yearly rent payable during the residue of the said term shall be either the said sum of £2,750 or such amount as may be agreed in writing between the landlords and the tenants before commencement of the eighth year of the said term as represents the full

d   rack rental value as hereinafter defined of the demised premises or (in the absence of agreement as aforesaid) as shall be determined by arbitration, whichever amount shall be the greater. The Arbitrator shall in default of agreement between the parties be nominated by the President for the time being of the Royal Institution of Chartered Surveyors on the application of the landlords made not more than twelve months nor less than three months before the 29th

e   September 1972 and the decision of the Arbitrator shall be final and binding upon the parties.'

In the event there was no reference to arbitration before the time limit required by the clause expired. The approach of the Court of Appeal was that the lease was in a form put forward by the landlords; it plainly provided that the landlords could not apply for the appointment of an arbitrator less than three months before 29th

f   September 1972. It showed, said Lord Salmon, that—

'if the landlord wants to ensure he will obtain a revised rent otherwise than by written agreement he has to initiate an arbitration not less than three months before the beginning of the eighth year.'

Counsel for the tenants submits that the similarities between that case and the
g   present are too plain to be ignored; in both cases the landlord and the tenant could agree a higher rent during a particular period; if there was no agreement the landlord had the right to set in motion arbitration machinery by applying to the President of the Royal Institution of Chartered Surveyors. This right was exercisable by the landlord; it was for the benefit of the landlord alone because the rent could not be decreased, it could be increased, and the right to apply to the president was given a
h   time limit, and mutatis mutandis counsel says that in the same way as the landlord was caught by his own defective drafting in *Stylo Shoes*[1], so in the present instance.

I come back to the present lease to determine whether it is in truth an option rent review clause or an obligation rent review clause. The first indication supports counsel for the landlords; there is not one rent of £2,750 for the whole term, there are the respective rents for three separate periods. During the first period there is the
j   basic rent. Then the rent for the second period must be determined. I agree with him this is some indication of an obligation. It is necessary to determine the rent for the second six years of the term. The rent is to be 'whichever of the two following

1   [1974] Bar Library Transcript 318A

yearly rents is the greater that is to say' the basic rent, £2,750, or the amount which is agreed or determined by arbitration. Counsel for the landlords submits that in order to   *a* determine which of the rents is the greater there must be two rents which can be compared; that would seem the language of obligation. A rent must be calculated in order to make a comparison. But then the clause which deals with the ascertainment of the rack rent, the amount to be compared with the basic rent, provides that the rack rent is to be such an amount as *may* be agreed—and that is permissive—between the landlord and the tenant before 25th September 1974, and if there is no agreement   *b* such amount as *may* be determined, not *shall* be determined. If there is a determination by an arbitrator he is to be nominated. The application of the landlords for his nomination is to be made within a certain time limit and *in case* of such arbitration the amount to be determined by the arbitrator shall be the rack rent as assessed by him at the ending of the eighth year.

In my judgment, in the same way as in *Stylo*[1] and in the *United Scientific* case[2],   *c* the indications of an obligation are overruled by contra-indications of option. The clause merely empowers the landlord and the landlord alone to go to arbitration if there is no agreement, and imposes on him the right to go to arbitration only if he applies to the President of the Royal Institution of Chartered Surveyors within the 14 days, that is to say before 9th October 1974. Dealing with the last period, the rent is said to be the rent 'agreed or calculated on the same basis mutatis mutandis as set out   *d* above in respect of the eighth year'. That reads in the whole of the language of the rent revision clause attributable to the second period, and the argument for the landlords is not advanced.

Counsel for the landlords submitted that this was a case where, if there is no arbitration because the time limit is exceeded, then there can be no rent for the second period, but I do not take that view. There is a basic rent and a provision whereby the   *e* landlords can, if they like, obtain an arbitration with regard to a higher rent. If they fail to exercise their right then the basic rent remains; that basic rent compares with such amount as may be agreed or may be determined. In the events which have happened, nothing has been agreed, nothing has been determined and therefore the basic rent is greater.

This is a clause in which there are some indications that could have led to the view   *f* that this was a rent revision clause of obligation rather than option, but, construing the clause and paying attention as I must to the decisions to which I have referred, it seems to me that I am bound to come to the conclusion that this is an option type clause, and that it would only make the law more confused than it is if I were able on the wording of this clause to find some subtle distinction between it and the earlier authorities.   *g*

In my judgment, in substance this is an option type form of rent review clause, and the time limit was mandatory. It is common ground that the landlords failed to comply with the time limit, and it follows that the application for the appointment of an arbitrator was out of time, and out of order.

Declaration accordingly.   *h*

Solicitors: *Baileys, Shaw & Gillett* (for the landlords); *Gouldens*, agents for *Knight & Sons*, Newcastle-under-Lyme (for the tenants).

Jacqueline Metcalfe   Barrister.

  j

---

1   [1974] Bar Library Transcript 318A
2   (1974) 231 Estates Gazette 1543

a

R v Bloomsbury and Marylebone County Court, ex parte Villerwest Ltd

COURT OF APPEAL, CIVIL DIVISION

LORD DENNING MR, ROSKILL AND GEOFFREY LANE LJJ

b 21st NOVEMBER 1975

County court – Jurisdiction – Inherent jurisdiction – Jurisdiction to amend order – Extension of time – Order for payment into court of sum of money before specified time – Application to extend time – Application made after expiry of time – Whether court having jurisdiction to extend time – Whether jurisdiction exercisable after expiry of time – CCR Ord 13, r 5(1).

c

County court – Practice – Application of High Court practice – Case not expressly provided for – High Court practice applicable to matters of principle not expressly provided for in county court rules – Judgment or order – Finality – Judge setting aside order on terms to be complied with within specified time limit – Failure to comply within time limit – Judge having no power under county court rules to extend time limit afer expiry – Whether provisions of
d *Supreme Court rules applicable so as to give jurisdiction to extend time – County Courts Act 1959, ss 98, 103 – RSC Ord 3, r 5(1) – CCR Ord 13, r 5(1).*

The landlords of certain premises brought an action for possession in the county court against the tenant and sub-tenant of those premises. The matter came before Judge A on 30th April 1974 and he made an order for possession in favour of the landlords together with judgment for £864 and costs. That order was, however, made in the
e absence of the tenant, and an application was made to the county court, under CCR Ord 37, to set it aside. The application came before Judge A on 8th July and he made an order that the judgment of 30th April be set aside conditional on the tenant paying certain sums into court before 22nd July; the order went on to state that failing compliance with those conditions the original order of 30th April was to stand.
f The condition was not complied with by 22nd July and, on 27th July, the tenant and sub-tenant applied to the county court to vary the order by extending until 14th August the time within which the sums of money were to be paid into court. The application came before Judge B on 31st July and he made the order sought. The landlords moved for an order of certiorari quashing the order of Judge B. The Divisional Court[a] granted the motion on the grounds that, under s 98[b] of the County
g Courts Act 1959, the order of Judge A was final and conclusive between the parties and the county court rules contained no provision whereby the time limit specified in the order could be extended. The tenant and sub-tenant appealed, contending (i) that CCR Ord 13, r 5(1)[c], permitted the extension of any time limit, whether fixed by the rules or by the court; (ii) that, in any event, s 103[d] of the 1959 Act imported into the county court rules the wider provisions of the Supreme Court rules relating
h to extension of time, and (iii) that Judge B had an inherent jurisdiction to extend time by varying Judge A's order.

Held – The county court had a wide inherent jurisdiction to control its own procedure. That included the power to enlarge or extend any time limits attaching to an order granted at an earlier hearing by a different judge. The court's powers were not
j limited to what was expressly stated in the rules of practice and applied even where

---

a [1975] 2 All ER 562

b Section 98 provides: 'Every judgment and order of a county court shall, except as provided by this or any other Act or county court rules, be final and conclusive between the parties'.

c Rule 5(1) is set out at p 899 *e*, post

d Section 103 is set out at p 899 *g*, post

the application for an extension of time was made after the relevant period had
elapsed. Judge B had therefore had jurisdiction to extend time. Accordingly, the *a*
appeal would be allowed (see p 900 *b d* and *g* and p 901 *c* to *h*, post).

Dictum of Farwell LJ in *Keymer v Reddy* [1912] 1 KB at 221 applied.

Manley Estates Ltd v Benedek [1941] 1 All ER 248 approved.

Per Lord Denning MR. RSC Ord 3, r 5, contains a general principle of High Court
practice which should be imported into the county court practice by virtue of s 103
of the 1959 Act (see p 900 *a*, post).   *b*

Decision of the Divisional Court of the Queen's Bench Division [1975] 2 All ER 562
reversed.

Notes

For the power of the county court to grant an extension of time, see 10 Hasbury's Laws
(4th Edn) para 423, and for the application of High Court practice in the county court, *c*
see ibid para 2.

For the County Courts Act, ss 98, 103, see 7 Halsbury's Statutes (3rd Edn) 362, 367.

Cases referred to in judgment

Keymer v Reddy [1912] 1 KB 215, 81 LJKB 266, 105 LT 841, CA, 50 Digest (Repl) 258, *104*.
Manley Estates Ltd v Benedek [1941] 1 All ER 248, CA, 50 Digest (Repl) 257, *96*.   *d*
Whistler v Hancock (1878) 3 QBD 83, 47 LJQB 152, 37 LT 639, 50 Digest (Repl) 139, *1223*.

Case also cited

R v His Honour Judge Sir Shirley Worthington-Evans, Clerkenwell County Court, ex parte
   Madan [1959] 2 All ER 457, [1959] 2 QB 145, DC.

                                                                                    e
Appeal

The plaintiffs, Villerwest Ltd, brought an action for possession and arrears of rent of
premises at 22 Clifton Gardens, London W9, of which they were landlords, against the
defendants, (1) Maxine McGregor, the tenant, and (2) Joel Gumede, the sub-tenant.
On 30th April 1974 at the Bloomsbury and Marylebone County Court his Honour
Judge Llewellyn ordered that the defendants give possession by 28th May 1974 and   *f*
that the first defendant should pay the plaintiffs £890 rent and mesne profits together
with costs. The defendants appealed against that order and on 8th July Judge Llewellyn
ordered that it be set aside conditional on the first defendant paying £890 into court
on or before 22nd July. On 24th July the defendants applied to vary the order by
extending time for payment until 14th August. On 31st July his Honour Judge Figgis
granted the defendants' application. The plaintiffs applied for an order of certiorari
to remove the order of Judge Figgis into the High Court for that purpose of its being *g*
quashed and for an order of prohibition prohibiting the Bloomsbury and Marylebone
County Court from further hearing the case. On 19th February 1975 the Divisional
Court[1] of the Queen's Bench Division (Lord Widgery CJ, Ashworth and Bridge JJ)
granted the orders sought. The defendants appealed.

Richard Perkoff for the defendants.   *h*
Peter Ralls for the plaintiffs.

LORD DENNING MR. The plaintiffs let a flat at 22 Clifton Gardens, W9, to a
tenant (the first defendant). They served notice to quit and issued proceedings in the
county court against the tenant and sub-tenant (the second defendant). They sued for *j*
possession and arrears of rent. On 30th April 1974 the first defendant did not appear
but the second defendant did. The judge ordered both defendants to give possession
on 28th May 1974. He ordered that the plaintiffs should recover against the first

---

1   [1975] 2 All ER 562, [1975] 1 WLR 1175

a defendant £864·50 for rent and for mesne profits, and £25·50 for costs, making £890. Both defendants applied to set aside that judgment. On 8th July 1974 the county court judge ordered that it be set aside conditional on the first defendant paying into court on or before 22nd July 1974 the judgment debt and costs of £890. The order contains this special direction: 'Failing compliance with payment of all such money payments as have been ordered to be paid on or before 22nd July, 1974, judgment of 30th April, 1974, to stand.'

b The first defendant did not pay in that sum by 22nd July 1974. She had gone to South Africa and there was difficulty in getting hold of her. Two days later, namely on 24th July, the defendants gave notice that they intended to apply to the court to vary the order so as to extend the time for the payment until 14th August 1974. That application came before Judge Figgis on 31st July 1974. Counsel then appeared for the plaintiffs and submitted that the judge had no jurisdiction to extend the time. We

c are told that the judge was amused to hear this suggestion. He rejected it courteously. He had done it so often that he could not doubt that he had jurisdiction. So he granted an extension of time. He made an order that provided £325 was paid forthwith into court and the remaining balance by 14th August 1974, the order setting aside would stand. The defendants duly complied with these conditions by 14th August 1974. So under the order the judgment was set aside.

d The plaintiffs went to the Divisional Court and applied to quash the judge's order. The Divisional Court[1] held that the county court had no jurisdiction to extend the time as it did. The result was that, although the defendants had paid all the money into court, they were not allowed to defend the case. The defendants appeal to this court.

In the county court rules there is only one rule which deals with extension of time.

e It is CCR Ord 13, r 5(1). It says:

> 'Subject to the provisions of these Rules, any of the times fixed by these Rules for—(a) taking any steps in any proceedings; or (b) filing any document; or (c) giving any notice; may be enlarged or abridged by consent of all parties or by the court on the application of any party.'

f The Divisional Court held[1] that the rule did not apply because the time for paying this money was not 'fixed by these rules'. It was a time fixed by the order of the judge which he made on 8th July 1974.

The defendants next sought to rely on the High Court rules which they said were imported into the county court powers by s 103 of the County Courts Act 1959.

g It says:

> 'In any case not expressly provided for by or in pursuance of this Act, the general principles of practice in the High Court may be adopted and applied to proceedings in a county court.'

The defendants submitted that that section imports the rules of the High Court so

h as to make them applicable in the county court, in particular RSC Ord 3, r 5:

> '(1) The Court may, on such terms as it thinks just, by order extend or abridge the period within which a person is required or authorised by these rules, or by any judgment, order or direction, to do any act in any proceedings.
> '(2) The Court may extend any such period as referred to in paragraph (1)

j although the application for extension is not made until after the expiration of that period.'

The Divisional Court held[1] that that rule was not brought into the county court practice. They thought it was not a 'general principle of practice in the High Court'

---

1   [1975] 2 All ER 562, [1975] 1 WLR 1175

within s 103; and that s 103 only brought in matters which were not dealt with in the county court rules.

I am afraid that I cannot agree with the Divisional Court. I think that RSC Ord 3, r 5, is a general principle of practice which comes well within s 103. In dozens of cases in this court we have applied s 103. Wherever we find a situation for which the county court rules do not make provision, we turn to the High Court rules and apply them without any hesitation.

If this be wrong, nevertheless there is a very wide inherent jurisdiction, both in the High Court and in the county court, to enlarge any time which a judge has ordered. In *Keymer v Reddy*[1], Farwell LJ said—and his words seem very appropriate here:

'It is said on behalf of the respondent that, because the Master is acting without statutory authority the Court has no power to enlarge the time. The argument is that the court cannot enlarge the time because the rule as to enlarging time applies only to a case where the time is fixed under the rules of the Court. That seems to me to be a fatal argument. It is inconceivable that the Court should allow itself to be hampered in that way.'

Equally I say that it is inconceivable that the county court should be hampered in the way that is suggested here. The court obviously has power to enlarge the time when the application is made within the time originally fixed. So also when it is made after the time has elapsed. Instances were suggested in argument. Suppose a man is on his way to the court in time with the money in his pocket. Then he is run down in an accident, or he is robbed of it. Or suppose that his cheque has been held up at the bank for a short time. Has the court no power to enlarge the time in such a case? Every court has inherent power to control its own procedure, even though there is nothing in the rules about it.

There is a decision which supports this view. It is *Manley Estates Ltd v Benedek*[2]. In that case the plaintiff signed judgment in default of appearance. The master set it aside provided that the defendant paid the money into court within seven days. He failed to pay the money within the time and, after the seventh day elapsed, applied for an extension. This court held that there was jurisdiction to extend the time. The Divisional Court seem to have thought that that decision was erroneous. I think that it was a perfectly correct decision.

I have one further observation to make. It is about *Whistler v Hancock*[3]. It seems there to be suggested that if a condition is not fulfilled the action ceases to exist, as though no extension of a time can be granted. I do not agree with that line of reasoning. Even though the action may be said to cease to exist, the court always has power to bring it to life again by extending the time.

In my opinion the county court judge had ample jurisdiction to make the order he did.

I would allow the appeal accordingly.

ROSKILL LJ. I confess I have found this a more difficult case than I think Lord Denning MR has done, because in certain respects there is much to be said, if I may say so, for the view which the Divisional Court took, particularly on the interaction of the Rules of the Supreme Court and the County Court Rules by reason of s 103 of the County Courts Act 1959.

I ventured to ask counsel for the plaintiffs in the course of his admirable argument what he would say if the application which was made for an extension of time after the time originally limited for making the payment into court had expired had been made

---

1 [1912] 1 KB 215 at 221
2 [1941] 1 All ER 248
3 (1878) 3 QBD 83

a between the date of the original order and its expiry. Consistently as I think with the rest of his argument, he said that the learned county court judge would even at that time have had no jurisdiction to extend the order. But is it right? It seems to me that it would be the most astonishing limitation on the powers of county court judges, with the multitude of Rent Acts, landlord and tenant and other possession cases which come before them, if we held that when a county court judge says there shall be no order for possession provided that certain conditions for payment of arrears of rent

b are complied with within a limited time, and an application is then made to him within the time so limited for the purpose of extending that time, he had automatically to send the applicant away from his court. So to hold would, in my judgment, upset the practice which has led to the making of the many thousands of such orders which county court judges must have made.

If one rejects that submission of counsel for the plaintiffs, it is difficult to see in

c logic why the position should be different according to whether the application is made before the time runs out or after the time has run out, unless a different answer is compelled by the language of the relevant rules. There seems no doubt that the relevant language of CCR Ord 13, r 5, is more limited than the language of the comparable RSC Ord 3, r 5. But the powers of the court are by no means always limited to what is expressly stated in the rules of practice applicable to that court.

d The High Court, and indeed the Supreme Court, has an inherent jurisdiction, and so, in my judgment, has the county court. A good illustration of the inherent jurisdiction of the court is afforded by what Farwell LJ said in *Keymer v Reddy*[1] in the passage to which Lord Denning MR has already referred. I do not doubt that a county court judge has an inherent jurisdiction, for it is necessary for him to possess it in order to do justice between the parties, to extend the time, whether before or after

e it has expired, for complying with such an order as paying into court arrears of rent or the like, within the time originally limited.

As I have already indicated, I feel much more difficulty, with great respect to Lord Denning MR, in saying that we can, as it were, write RSC Ord 3, r 5, into the county court rules. I venture to think there is much to be said in favour of the view which Lord Widgery CJ expressed[2]. But however that may be, and whether the view that

f the Divisional Court took on that point is correct or not, or whether the view which Lord Denning MR prefers is correct, I agree that there is for the reasons I have already given inherent jurisdiction in a county court judge to make the order which the tenants sought in this case.

Accordingly for that reason I would allow the appeal and say that the orders of certiorari and prohibition which the Divisional Court ordered to issue should not

g issue.

GEOFFREY LANE LJ. I also agree. Judge Figgis had an inherent jurisdiction to make the order which he did regardless of the provisions of s 103 of the County Courts Act 1959 and regardless of whether under that provision or not the relevant

h provisions of the Rules of the Supreme Court could be imported into the County Court Rules.

For those reasons this appeal should be allowed.

Appeal allowed.

j Solicitors: *Ian Sheratte & Co* (for the defendants); *Kaufman, Krammer & Shebson* (for the plaintiffs).

Gavin Gore-Andrews Barrister.

1 [1912] 1 KB 215 at 221
2 [1975] 2 All ER 562 at 567, [1975] 1 WLR 1175 at 1180

Ismail v Polish Ocean Lines

COURT OF APPEAL, CIVIL DIVISION
LORD DENNING MR, ORMROD AND SHAW LJJ
17th, 18th, 19th DECEMBER 1975, 4th FEBRUARY 1976

Arbitration – Special case – Conclusiveness of arbitrators' findings – Appeal – Questions of law – Whether court having jurisdiction to amend questions of law in special case – Whether jurisdiction limited to arbitrators' findings.

Shipping – Charterparty – Construction – Loading – Loading and stowage of cargo –Supervision of master – Master responsible for proper stowage and dunnaging of cargo – Stowage and dunnage instructions given by charterer – Damage to cargo – Improper stowage – Master having followed charterer's stowage instructions – Whether master liable for damage to cargo resulting from improper stowage.

Estoppel – Estoppel in pais – Estoppel by representation – Loading and stowage of cargo – Liability of shipowners – Master responsible for stowage of cargo – Charterer's agent representing that cargo safe if stowed in certain manner – Master stowing cargo in accordance with agent's instructions – Damage to cargo resulting from improper stowage – Whether master exempted from liability by agent's representations – Whether charterer estopped from relying on rights under charterparty.

A vessel was chartered to carry potatoes to England for a fixed price irrespective of the size of the cargo. The vessel could carry cargo up to 1,400 tons in weight, but the chief officer calculated that only 1,000 tons of potatoes could be loaded since potatoes had to be properly ventilated and would require 20 cubic metres of dunnage. Under the terms of the charterparty the obligation to load and stow the cargo lay on the charterer. Clause 18(c) provided: 'The Charterers shall load and stow the cargo free of any expense whatsoever to the Owners ...'; cl 19(b): 'The Charterers shall provide and pay for all dunnage material as required by the Master for the proper stowage and protection of the cargo, the Owners allowing the use of all dunnage available on board. The dunnage shall be laid under the Master's supervision'; cl 49: 'Dunnaging and stowage instructions given by the Charterers to be carefully followed, *but to be executed under the supervision of the Master and he is to remain responsible for proper stowage and dunnaging'*. The vessel was due to load at Alexandria. The charterer was not present, but his brother was there and was authorised to give instructions on behalf of the charterer for the loading of the vessel. The brother insisted on loading 1,400 tons of potatoes, contrary to the master's advice, and claimed that the potatoes were paccked in a new type of bag which made dunnage unnecessary. On arrival, most of the bagged potatoes were found to be rotten. The charterer claimed damages and arbitrators appointed in accordance with the charterparty found that two-thirds of the damage was due to improper stowage and one-third to inherent vice in the potatoes. The arbitrators held that the owners were liable for the improper stowage and awarded the charterer two-thirds of the damage. The arbitrators stated a special case and the owners appealed on the grounds that they were not liable under cl 49 and that in any event the charterer was estopped by the brother's conduct from claiming damages. The charterer contended that the appeal could not be heard, since the questions in the special case did not support those grounds of appeal and there was no jurisdiction to alter the special case.

Held–(i) Where there was an appeal by way of a special case stated by arbitrators,
a the court had jurisdiction to amend or reformulate the questions of law before it, on
the application of one or both of the parties, so that the real issues between them
could be decided, provided that the facts had been sufficiently found for the purpose.
In the instant case, all the necessary facts raised by the owner's appeal had been
found and, furthermore, one of the questions had been framed sufficiently broadly
to cover those issues (see p 906 *f* and *g*, p 907 *b*, p 910 *a b* and *f* and p 912 *b* to *f* and *h* to
b p 913 *a*, post); dictum of McNair J in *Minister of Food v Reardon Smith Line* [1951] 2
Lloyd's Rep 265, *Government of Ceylon v Chandris* [1963] 2 All ER 1 and dictum of
Mocatta J in *Iles aux Moines* [1974] 1 Lloyd's Rep at 265 disapproved.

    (ii) The appeal would be allowed for the following reasons—

    (a) On a true construction of the charterparty, the obligation to load and stow the
cargo and to give dunnage instructions was firmly placed on the charterer. Under
c cl 49, the master had an overriding power to supervise the stowage to ensure the
safety of the ship and the cargo, but he was entitled to assume that the goods to be
stowed were fit to withstand the ordinary incidents of the voyage. Since he had been
assured by the brother that the cargo was packed so that no dunnage was necessary
and a full 1,400 tons could be loaded, he had been relieved pro tanto of his responsibility for dunnage and cl 49 did not therefore apply (see p 907 *c* to *g*, p 911 *e* to *h* and
d p 914 *h* to p 915 *a*, post); *Gould v South Eastern and Chatham Railway* [1920] 2 KB 186 and
Canadian Transport v Court Line Ltd [1940] 3 All ER 112 applied.

    (b) Furthermore, even if the master had been responsible for proper stowage,
the charterer would have been estopped from relying on his strict legal rights. If a
shipper or his representative was present when goods were loaded and supervised
their stowage or insisted on their being stowed in a particular manner, he could not
e complain if they were damaged by having been stowed in a bad manner. The
charterer had entrusted the brother with the task of giving instructions for the loading
of the vessel and the master could not have refused to load the cargo in accordance
with those instructions. The owners, therefore, were not liable for the damage to the
cargo (see p 907 *h* to p 909 *a*, p 910 *j* to p 911 *b* and *h j* and p 914 *b* to *d*, post); *Ohrloff v
Briscall, The Helene* (1866) LR 1 PC 231, *Upper Egypt Produce Exports v Santamana* (1923)
f 14 Ll L Rep 159 and *Panchaud Frères SA v Etablissements General Grain Co* [1970] 1 Lloyd's
Rep 53 applied.

Notes

For appeal by way of special case stated by arbitrators, see 2 Halsbury's Laws (4th
Edn) paras 599-601, and for cases on the subject, see 2 Digest (Repl) 579-587, *1114-1117*.
g   For liability for stowage, see 35 Halsbury's Laws (3rd Edn) 392-395, paras 563-567,
and for cases on the subject, see 41 Digest (Repl) 354-361, *1475-1542*.
    For estoppel by representation, see 16 Halsbury's Laws (4th Edn) paras 1591-1603,
and for cases on the subject, see 21 Digest (Repl) 369-396, *1103-1250*.

Cases referred to in judgments

h *Canadian Transport Co Ltd v Court Line Ltd* [1940] 3 All ER 112, [1940] AC 934, 110
    LJKB 14, 163 LT 317, 19 Asp MLC 374, 45 Com Cas 276, HL, 41 Digest (Repl) 358,
    1516.
Crabb v Arun District Council [1975] 3 All ER 865, [1975] 3 WLR 847, CA.
Freeman & Lockyer v Buckhurst Park Properties (Mangal) Ltd [1964] 1 All ER 630, [1964]
    2 QB 480, [1964] 2 WLR 618, CA, Digest (Cont Vol B) 101, *3701a*.
j *Gould v South Eastern and Chatham Railway Co* [1920] 2 KB 186, [1920] All ER Rep 654,
    89 LJKB 700, 123 LT 256, DC, 8(1) Digest (Reissue) 25, *138*.
Government of Ceylon v Chandris [1963] 2 All ER 1, [1963] 2 QB 327, [1963] 2 WLR 1097,
    [1963] 1 Lloyd's Rep 214, Digest (Cont Vol A) 38, *818a*.
Heatons Transport (St Helens) Ltd v Transport and General Workers Union [1972] 3 All
    ER 101, [1973] AC 15, [1972] 3 WLR 431, [1972] ICR 308.

Minister of Food v Reardon Smith Line Ltd [1951] 2 Lloyd's Rep 265, 41 Digest (Repl) 308, 1163.

Moorgate Mercantile Co Ltd v Twitchings [1975] 3 All ER 314, [1975] 3 WLR 286, [1975] RTR 528, CA.

Ohrloff v Briscall, The Helene (1866) LR 1 PC 231, 4 Moo PCCNS 70, 14 LT 873, 16 ER 242, PC, 41 Digest (Repl) 356, 1495.

Panchaud Frères SA v Etablissements General Grain Co [1970] 1 Lloyd's Rep 53, CA, Digest (Cont Vol C) 856, 1046a.

Pyrene Co v Scindia Steam Navigation Co Ltd [1954] 2 All ER 158, [1954] 2 QB 402, [1954] 2 WLR 1005, [1954] 1 Lloyd's Rep 321, 41 Digest (Repl) 237, 593.

Renton (G H) & Co Ltd v Palmyra Trading Corpn of Panama [1956] 3 All ER 957, [1957] AC 149, [1957] 2 WLR 45, [1956] 2 Lloyd's Rep 379, HL, 41 Digest (Repl) 419, 2045.

Upper Egypt Produce Exports v Santamana (1923) 14 Ll L Rep 159.

Vanda Compania Limitada di Costa Rica v Société Maritime Nationale of Paris (The Iles aux Moines) [1974] 1 Lloyd's Rep 263.

White Rose, The, AB Helsingfors SS Co Ltd v Rederiaktiebolaget Rex [1969] 3 All ER 374, [1969] 1 WLR 1098, [1969] 2 Lloyd's Rep 52, Digest (Cont Vol C) 28, 1151b.

Cases also cited

London Dock Co v Shadwell Parish (1862) 1 New Rep 91, 32 LJQB 30.

Sack v Ford (1862) 13 CBNS 90, 1 New Rep 96.

Union Castle Mail Steamship Co Ltd v Bordendale Shipping Co Ltd [1919] 1 KB 612, [1918-19] All ER Rep 927.

Appeal

This was an appeal by Polish Ocean Lines, owners of the vessel Ciechocinek ('the owners'), against the order of Kerr J[1] on 11th April 1975 whereby, on a special case stated by John Selwyn and Cedric Barclay, arbitrators appointed under the terms of a charterparty made between the owners and Fawzi A Ismail ('the charterer') on 2nd April 1970, he affirmed an award dated 29th April 1974 by the arbitrators of damages to the charterer. The facts are set out in the judgment of Lord Denning MR.

Christopher Staughton QC and *Anthony D Colman* for the owners.
Anthony Lloyd QC and *Jonathan Mance* for the charterer.

Cur adv vult

4th February. The following judgments were read.

LORD DENNING MR. The people of Egypt grow new potatoes in the Nile Valley and ship them to England. In April 1970 Dr Ismail shipped a cargo at Alexandria on the vessel Ciechocinek. She was owned by the Polish Ocean Lines, a state corporation. He had chartered her for a voyage to England. She was a brand-new ship, built at Constanza in Romania, and this was to be her first commercial voyage. She could carry cargo up to 1,400 tons in weight, if there was space in the holds for it. But potatoes were a bulky cargo needing good ventilation. So on her way from Constanza to Alexandria the chief officer made a plan to see what quantity of potatoes she could carry. He calculated that the vessel could carry 1,000 tons of potatoes properly ventilated. To do this they would require 20 cubic metres of 'dunnage', that is lengths of wood placed in position so as to make space between the bags. But they only had 7 cubic metres of dunnage aboard, so they would need another 13 cubic metres to be supplied at Alexandria.

When they got to Alexandria, there were lorries full of potatoes waiting on the quay ready for them to be loaded on to the vessel. Dr Ismail was not himself there. But he

---

1   [1975] 2 Lloyd's Rep 170

a had his brother Mr Ismail there and he had authorised Mr Ismail to give instructions on his behalf as regards the loading. Now, Mr Ismail was not willing to restrict the cargo to 1,000 tons, as the master and chief officer wished. Dr Ismail was paying a lump sum freight of £9,250 for the voyage, irrespective of the quantity. No matter whether it was 1,400 tons or 1,000 tons, Dr Ismail would still have to pay only £9,250. At any rate, Mr Ismail insisted on the vessel loading 1,400 tons. He said that the 1,400 tons must be loaded at once, and as quickly as possible. He said that no dunnage was

b available at Alexandria and that the potatoes were packed in a new kind of bags which made dunnage unnecessary. The master demurred. He was dubious about it. Mr Ismail said that he would get a surveyor's certificate to say that dunnage was unnecessary and that he would give the master a guarantee in writing against the consequences of stowing the cargo in this way. In addition Mr Ismail appeared to have an expert knowledge of potato shipments—far more than the master or the chief

c officer. So the master felt that he must accept Mr Ismail's word. He agreed to the 1,400 tons being loaded and they were loaded.

The master made several requests for the promised certificate and guarantee. But they were not forthcoming. The master delayed sailing for a short time in the hope that they would come. But they did not come. In the end he decided that he could wait no longer. He set sail from Alexandria on 14th April 1970 and arrived at

d Boston in Lincolnshire on 27th April 1970. On discharging the cargo, a large number of the bagged potatoes were found to be rotten. Dr Ismail claimed damages. The total of rotten potatoes was £63,000. And the total freight was only £9,250. Even under the Merchant Shipping Acts, the liability of the ship would be limited to £40,000. But Dr Ismail wanted £63,000.

The matter was referred to arbitration in London. It was heard for ten days.

e There was much dispute as to the cause of the damage. The arbitrators found that two-thirds was due to improper stowage (because there was no dunnage etc); and one-third due to inherent vice (because the potatoes were too hot when shipped and the bags were not suitable etc). The arbitrators held that the ship was liable for the improper stowage and awarded Dr Ismail two-thirds of the damage. But they stated a special case. The judge[1] affirmed the award. The owners appeal to this court.

f
The material clauses of the charterparty

The obligation to load and stow the cargo was put on the charterer—not on the owners—by these printed clauses:

'18 . . . (c) *Free in and stowed*—The Charterers shall load and stow the cargo free of any expense whatsoever to the Owners . . .'

g '19 . . . The Charterers shall provide and pay for all dunnage material as required by the Master for the proper stowage and protection of the cargo, the Owners allowing the use of all dunnage available on board. The dunnage shall be laid under Master's supervision . . .'

There was this typewritten cl 49 which is of special importance:

h '49. Dunnaging and stowage instructions given by the Charterers to be carefully followed, *but to be executed under the supervision of the Master and he is to remain responsible for proper stowage and dunnaging.*'

There were these incorporated clauses of the Hague Rules. Article III, r 2, provides: 'Subject to the provisions of Article IV the carrier shall properly and carefully load,

j handle, stow, carry, keep, care for and discharge the goods carried.'

In one or two places, the judge[1] seemed to think that that rule applied here. But I do not think it did. Article III, r 2, does not mean that the shipowner is to do all the loading, stowing etc himself. It only means that, in respect of any loading or stowing which he is obliged under the contract to do, he must do it properly and carefully: see *Pyrene Co Ltd v Scindia Navigation Co Ltd*[1] per Devlin J approved in *G H Renton & Co Ltd v Palmyra Trading Corpn of Panama*[2]. In the present case the owners were under no obligation to do any of the loading or stowing. So art III, r 2, did not apply. Article IV, r 2, provides:

> 'Neither the carrier nor the ship shall be responsible for loss or damage arising or resulting from . . . (i) Act or omission of the shipper or owner of the goods his agent or representative . . .'

The questions for the court

A serious question arises on the award because of the way in which the questions for the court are stated. This was not the fault of the arbitrators, but of the procedure that was adopted, and often is adopted, in these cases. The arbitrators heard for ten days much evidence on many disputed questions of fact. Counsel had to make their submissions briefly because it was the end of term. But they made them plainly enough, as indeed it was their duty to do: see *The White Rose*[3] per Donaldson J. In particular, the owners contended that they were exempt from liability by reason of cl 49 or, alternatively, by reason of an estoppel. And the arbitrators found every single fact necessary to the decision of those contentions. But the questions which were afterwards drafted did not reflect the contentions so simply. Some were drafted by counsel on one side, the others by counsel on the other. They were sent to the arbitrators who took them as they stood and set them out in their award. As it turned out, these questions were too complex and gave rise to much discussion before the judge. And he was faced with cases which appear to say that on the hearing of a special case a judge is not entitled to alter the question of law stated for the decision of the court: see *Minister of Food v Reardon Smith Line* by McNair J[4]; *Government of Ceylon v Chandris*[5]; and *Iles aux Moines* by Mocatta J[6]; with the result that, if the question is not correctly stated, the only course is to remit the matters referred to, or some of them, to the arbitrators under s 22(1) of the Arbitration Act 1950.

Now, I must say that I do not think the parties should be tied hand and foot to the precise way in which those questions are formulated for decision—especially when they are formulated by the parties in advance of the findings of fact. If the findings of fact, when made, give rise to a question of law which ought to be decided in order to do justice between the parties, then that question is a 'question of law arising in the course of the reference'. And I see no reason why the court should not itself amend the question or formulate it afresh—at the request of one or both of the parties—so that the real issues between them can be decided, provided, of course, that the facts are sufficiently found for the purpose. It would be a work of supererogation to send it back to the arbitrators for them to reformulate the question when that would be an automatic exercise—merely endorsing the formula submitted by the parties.

The judge said here[7]:

> '. . . the present case, like others in the past, is one in which time has been spent in argument, and some difficulty has arisen as to whether or not a crucial and obvious question of law is open on the questions as framed. [In the end he held that all the questions] could have been covered by one question in an agreed

1 [1954] 2 All ER 158 at 163, [1954] 2 QB 402 at 417, 418
2 [1956] 3 All ER 957 at 966, 968, [1957] AC 149 at 169, 170, 174
3 [1969] 3 All ER 374 at 378, [1969] 1 WLR 1098 at 1103
4 [1951] 2 Lloyd's Rep 265
5 [1963] 2 All ER 1, [1963] 2 QB 327
6 [1974] 1 Lloyd's Rep 263 at 265
7 [1975] 2 Lloyd's Rep at 183, 184

general form, e.g. whether on the facts found and the true construction of the
charter-party (together with the incorporated Hague Rule provisions) the owners
are under any liability to the charterer.'

I trust that in future, time will be saved and difficulties avoided, by a simple amendment of the questions—at any rate in those cases where the facts are fully and sufficiently found so as to raise the question of law which the party desires to be stated.

In the present case I would, therefore, if need be reformulate the questions for the
court so as to ask specifically whether cl 49 affords any defence to the shipowners; or,
alternatively, whether the charterer is estopped from claims for improper stowage.
But I do not think it is necessary. I agree with the judge who held that, on close
analysis, the questions as at present framed do permit the real questions to be decided.
So I proceed to consider them.

Clause 49

In this charterparty the obligation to load and stow the cargo and to provide and lay
dunnage is firmly placed on the charterer. It is to be done by the charterer and at his
expense. The charterer is also entitled to give dunnage and stowage instructions to the
master, which he is carefully to follow.

Notwithstanding those provisions, the master has an overriding power to supervise
the stowage. He must have this as a matter of course: see *Canadian Transport Co Ltd
v Court Lines Ltd*[1]. The master is responsible for the stowage of the cargo so as to
ensure the safety of the ship: and also of the cargo so as to see that it is stowed so as to
be able to withstand the ordinary incidents of the voyage. That is the meaning of the
last words of cl 49: 'He is to remain responsible for proper stowage and dunnaging.'

But there is this qualification to be made to the master's responsibility: he is
entitled to assume that the goods are fit to withstand the ordinary incidents of the
voyage. That is to say, that they are properly packed and ventilated, and so forth.
If the owner or shipper voluntarily leaves them in a condition in which they will not
withstand the ordinary incidents of the voyage, he takes the responsibility on himself
and the master is excused from responsibility for any damages which occur to them in
consequence: see *Gould v South Eastern and Chatham Railway Co*[2].

Similarly here. The master was assured by Mr Ismail (who appeared to be an
expert) that the potatoes were packed in suitable bags so that no dunnage was
needed and 1,400 tons could be loaded. It seems to me that, on that assurance, the
shipper or owner assumed responsibility and the master was relieved pro tanto of his
responsibility for dunnage, and so forth. So that the concluding words of cl 49 do not
apply to this case.

Alternatively, it seems to me that the master and the ship can rely on art IV, r 2(i), of
the Hague Rules; because the damage resulted from an act or omission of Mr Ismail,
who was the representative of the owner of the goods.

Estoppel

Assuming, however, that, according to the strict legal rights under cl 49, the master
did remain responsible for proper stowage and dunnaging, nevertheless it seems to
me that Dr Ismail is disentitled from relying on those strict legal rights. It is a case
of estoppel by conduct. If a man has led another to believe that a particular state of
affairs is settled and correct, he will not be allowed to depart therefrom and assert
they were erroneous and incorrect when it would be unjust and inequitable for him
to do so: see *Panchaud Frères SA v Etablissements General Grain Co*[3]. Applied to the
stowage of goods aboard a ship, it may be stated thus. If a shipper or his representative

---

1   [1940] 3 All ER 112, [1940] AC 934
2   [1920] 2 KB 186, [1920] All ER Rep 654
3   [1970] 1 Lloyd's Rep 53

is present when the goods are loaded—and superintends the stowage—or if he insists
on their being stowed in a particular manner, he cannot afterwards complain if they *a*
are afterwards damaged by being stowed in a bad manner: see *The Helene*[1] and the
Santamana[2] per Hill J and the cases there cited. The present case is a classic one of its
kind. Here Mr Ismail instructed the master to carry 1,400 tons of potatoes. He told
him that no dunnage was necessary, and that the bags were of a new kind, such that
the potatoes would not suffer on the voyage. On those representations, I do not see
that the master could possibly have refused to load the cargo. If he had refused, he *b*
would expose the owners to a claim for damages which they would be quite unable
to refute—because they had no evidence that the representations were untrue.
Again, Mr Ismail allayed the master's misgivings by promising to get a surveyor's
certificate and a guarantee and on the faith of that promise the master loaded the
1,400 tons. In this situation it would be quite contrary to all fairness and to all justice
that the shipper or owner should be able to hold the master liable for improper *c*
stowage. Counsel for the charterer did not seriously dispute this, but he suggested
that Mr Ismail had no authority, actual or ostensible, to make representations of this
kind on behalf of his brother, Dr Ismail, and he relied on the findings in the special
case. But I cannot accept this suggestion for a moment. Dr Ismail entrusted his
brother, Mr Ismail, with the task of giving instructions as regards the loading of the
vessel and Dr Ismail must be answerable for the conduct of his brother in the course *d*
of it.

In these cases of estoppel by the conduct of an agent, it is not a question of 'holding
out' or 'ostensible authority' as it would be in considering whether a principal is
bound by a contract: see *Freeman & Lockyer v Buckhurst Park Properties*[3]. It is a question
of whether the agent is acting on behalf of, and within the scope of, the authority
conferred by the principal; as it would be in considering whether the principal is liable *e*
for his agent's torts, including his misrepresentations: see *Heatons Transport v Transport
and General Workers Union*[4]. In the present case, Dr Ismail clearly put his brother, Mr
Ismail, in his place to see to the loading of the cargo and he must be answerable for the
manner in which he conducted himself therein, and in particular for the representations which he made to the master about the stowage: see *Moorgate Mercantile Co Ltd v
Twitchings*[5]; *Crabb v Arun District Council*[6]. *f*

Conclusion

The arbitrators performed a most valuable service in finding the facts so fully
and completely that there is no need for the case to be remitted to them at all. But
the decisive point in the case—estoppel—was only just mentioned before them.
Similarly before the judge[7]. If it had been stressed before them, as it was before us, I *g*
fell sure that they would have come to a different conclusion.

I would answer questions 4 and 5 in the special case as follows:

(4) There was sufficient evidence to show that Mr Ismail had authority to act on
behalf of Dr Ismail in regard to the loading of the vessel.

(5) The owners are entitled to rely on the conversations and conduct by Dr Ismail's
brother, Mr Ismail, at Alexandria in support of the allegation that the charterer is *h*
estopped from asserting that the stowage was defective and of the allegation that the
damage was caused by the act or omission of the representative of the shipper or
owner of the goods.

---

1 (1866) LR 1 PC 231
2 (1923) 14 Ll L Rep 159
3 [1964] 1 All ER 630, [1964] 2 QB 480
4 [1972] 3 All ER 101, [1973] AC 78
5 [1975] 3 All ER 314, [1975] 3 WLR 286
6 [1975] 3 All ER 865, [1975] 3 WLR 847
7 [1975] 2 Lloyd's Rep 170

j

a   These answers are different from those contained in the award. I would, therefore, remit the award to the arbitrators for further consideration in accordance with the judgment of the court.

ORMROD LJ. The first point to be decided on this appeal arises on the respondent's notice which raises, in effect, an issue as to jurisdiction. The contention is that

b   the owners cannot be heard on any of the points of law which they seek to argue, either in this court or in the court below, because none of them arises out of the questions asked in the special case. The premise of counsel for the charterer's argument is that under this procedure the court is restricted to answering the questions formulated by the arbitrator in his award and may not consider any other points of law arising out of the award, however obvious the error in law. He then contends that

c   none of counsel for the owners' submissions is covered by the questions asked in this case. Counsel for the owners was content to accept the premise but maintained that —admittedly fortuitously—the fifth question covered all the submissions he wished to make.

Counsel for the charterer's first point, however, is clearly of considerable general interest and, particularly in the light of the observations made by Kerr J[1], in the

d   course of his judgment in this case, it would not be right to leave the matter there.

The jurisdiction of the court now depends on s 21(1) of the Arbitration Act 1950, which is in these terms:

> 'An arbitrator or umpire may, and shall if so directed by the High Court state . . . (b) An award . . . in the form of a special case for decision of the High Court.'

e

The initiative for making an award in the form of a special case under this section can, therefore, come from one of two sources, the court or the arbitrator. If an arbitrator decides to make his award in this form and to invite the court to rule on certain questions of law, it seems self-evident that the court should confine itself to providing the appropriate answers. However, the practice has developed in a different

f   direction. The parties themselves, through counsel, ask for the award to be made in this form and themselves propose the questions of law to be included in the special case. These may or may not be agreed between counsel. In some cases this may be a convenient and satisfactory way of dealing with the matter, but in others, as the instant case vividly demonstrates, it is quite the reverse. This practice suffers from one grave defect which is inherent in it. If the questions of law are to be formulated by

g   counsel, this must, of necessity be done after the conclusion of the hearing before the arbitrator and before his findings of fact are known. This is like aiming at a moving object in the dark. The questions have to be based on guess-work with the result that some of them are likely to be irrelevant when the arbitrator's findings of fact appear in the special case, others may prove to be inappropriately phrased, while some may, with luck, hit the target of relevance. This is obviously an unsatisfactory way of

h   determining the rights of the parties in a complicated dispute.

In the present case, questions 1, 2, 4 and 5 were formulated by counsel for the charterer. Counsel for the owners put forward one question only, namely question 3, which, like question 2, is admittedly now irrelevant. We were told by counsel that question 5 was originally formulated by counsel for the charterer with a view to raising the point that parol evidence was inadmissible to vary the terms of the written

j   contract contained in the charterparty. This has also become irrelevant. But counsel for the owners has argued that, as framed, it goes far beyond this and opens up all the issues originally raised by the re-amended points of defence and counterclaim. He says that the owners can take advantage of the charterer's question to argue any

---

1   [1975] 2 Lloyd's Rep 170

point of law arising from that paragraph which is open to them on the facts as found
by the arbitrators. In my judgment, this apparently bizarre argument is well-   *a*
founded. Question 5, as framed, is clearly wide enough to cover all three of the
points raised in the owners' notice of appeal. This seems to be the reductio ad absurdum
of the argument that the form of the question determines the limits of the court's
jurisdiction.

The learned judge below[1], whose experience of this procedure is great, has drawn
attention to the increasing difficulties which are arising from the tendency of counsel   *b*
in these cases to put forward numerous questions raising or purporting to raise
'narrow and excessively elaborate' points of law. He said that it would be 'far better
to have left the legal issues for argument in one or more general questions, preferably
to be agreed between the parties'. He went on to suggest that while arbitrators
should always leave to the court questions of law for which the parties had asked, it
was always open to them to add one or more questions on their own initiative. It is   *c*
sometimes said that the onlooker sees more of the game than the players. It seems to
me, very much an onlooker in this field, that we are witnessing the evolution of a
general form of appeal on law from arbitrators to the court. At present, it has reached
a clumsy and obviously unsatisfactory stage. Counsel for the charterer's argument
for excluding counsel for the owners' submissions at times sounded as formalistic as
those which are only to be found in the old reports. It would make the outcome of the   *d*
litigation dependent on the precise words chosen by counsel in framing the question
or questions to be included in the special case, just as, in the past, cases turned on pure
pleading points. This is an entirely obsolete way of settling a commercial or any
other kind of dispute and is to be avoided as far as possible. Given that these questions
are formulated by counsel, there is no justification in my view for allowing them to
have any more conclusive or exclusive effect than an ordinary pleading. In my   *e*
judgment, Kerr J's suggestion is entitled to the fullest respect but if questions are to be
formulated in a limited or restrictive manner, then with the greatest respect to the
decisions of Mocatta J, in *Government of Ceylon v Chandris*[2] and *Iles aux Moines*[3], the
court should decline to allow itself to be rigidly confined to such questions and should
itself adopt a broad and realistic approach to the legal problems arising from the
findings of fact in the special case.   *f*

For these reasons, in my judgment, the owners would have been entitled to have
their submissions considered on their merits even if they had not been able to take
advantage of question 5 in the special case. The interests of justice in this case demand it.

Turning then to the merits of the appeal, it will be convenient to deal first with the
estoppel point since this is, in my opinion, the strongest. The arbitrators rejected the
evidence called by the charterer on the issue of the instructions as to stowage and   *g*
dunnage. They have found as a fact that Mr Ismail did instruct the master that
dunnaging was unnecessary owing to the method used for packing the potatoes, and
did insist on 1,400 tons of potatoes being loaded, although the master thought that
1,000 tons was the limit which could be stowed safely. They have also found that Mr
Ismail had actual authority from the charterer to give instructions on these matters.
It is true that they have found that Mr Ismail had no authority, actual or ostensible,   *h*
to vary the terms of the charter or to 'make representations regarding the [charterer's]
exercise of his rights under the charterparty'. Counsel for the charterer contends that
there can be no estoppel in view of this latter finding of fact.

It is quite clear that a charterer may in proper circumstances be estopped from
complaining about damage to cargo arising out of his interference with the stowage
arrangements: the *Santamana*[4]. I think that I understood counsel for the charterer to   *j*

1   [1975] 2 Lloyd's Rep at 183
2   [1963] 2 All ER 1, [1963] 2 QB 327
3   [1974] 1 Lloyd's Rep 263
4   (1923) 14 Ll L Rep 159

concede that if the instructions in question had been given by the charterer personally,
a   he could not recover damages from the owners for damage to the cargo arising from
following his instructions as to stowage or dunnaging. It would be difficult to conceive
of any other result. Can it make any difference if such instructions are given by an
agent expressly authorised to give such instructions? In my judgment the result must
be the same. If an agent has authority to give instructions the principal must, as a
matter of law, be bound by the consequences of complying with such instructions, as
b   if he personally had given them. In my judgment, therefore, the owners are entitled
to succeed on this point, unless there is some provision in the charterparty which
overrides the estoppel.
    The only relevant provision in the charterparty is cl 49, a typewritten clause, which
reads as follows:

c   'Dunnaging and stowage instructions given by the Charterers to be carefully
        followed, but to be executed under the supervision of the Master and he is to
        remain responsible for proper stowage and dunnaging.'

It would be hard to find a form of words better adapted to promoting disputes
between owners and charterers than this. On the face of it, it places the master in the
impossible position of being under obligations which are, at least potentially, mutually
d   inconsistent. The first part of the clause requires him to comply with the charterer's
instructions as to stowage and dunnaging; the second leaves the responsibility for
proper stowaging and dunnaging on him. So, if he declines to comply with his instructions, he may be in breach and, if he does comply with them, he may also be in breach
if damage occurs due to improper stowage. On the facts as found in this case the
master was placed in an impossible position and it really is no answer to say that he
e   should have got an indemnity from the charterer or refused to load more than 1,000
tons of potatoes or to have gone out and bought sufficient dunnaging (which was not
available in Alexandria anyway) or to have consulted his P and I club by telex. On any
view of cl 49, some words must be read into it to make it workable. Either, words
such as 'reasonable or proper' must be implied in the first part, limiting the instructions with which the master is obliged to comply, or some corresponding words must
f   be read into the latter part of the clause, limiting the master's responsibility for
improper stowage where damage occurs through complying with the charterer's
instructions. If I had to choose I would prefer the latter solution. The former leaves
the master still in doubt whether he is justified in refusing to accept certain instructions
or not. In this case the master's position was made more difficult by the fact that Mr
Ismail had or appeared to have much more experience and knowledge about the
g   properties of these potatoes than he had, so his choice between complying or refusing
to comply was as hazardous as it could be. I am satisfied that this clause does not
prevent an estoppel from arising out of Mr Ismail's instructions to the master. If the
estoppel point had not succeeded, I would arrive at the same result on the construction
of cl 49. In those circumstances it is unnecessary to consider the owners' third point
that the charterer was in breach of cl 19 of the charterparty in failing to supply proper
h   dunnage.
    I would therefore allow the appeal and hold that the charterer is not entitled to rely
on any damage to this cargo which is properly attributable either to inadequate
dunnaging or to loading an extra 400 tons of potatoes over and above the 1,000 tons
which the master was prepared to accept.
    I respectfully agree with the order proposed by Lord Denning MR.
j

SHAW LJ. I agree. In the light of the submissions addressed to this court, it is
necessary to consider how far the substantive issues raised on this appeal are competent
questions for decision at this stage. Counsel has contended on behalf of the charterer
that the court has no jurisdiction to decide any question of law, however relevant or

material to the matters in difference between the parties, unless the question is posed
by the special case. Authority for this proposition is to be found in cases which have   *a*
been mentioned in the preceding judgments of Lord Denning MR and Ormrod LJ.
They were cited by Kerr J[1] in the course of his judgment when dealing with this
aspect of the case.

There is a plausible argument to support the proposition. The reference to the
arbitrator results from the agreement of the parties. His jurisdiction is derived from
that agreement and, save as to questions of law, once the arbitrator has duly exercised   *b*
his jurisdiction and made his award, the matter is at an end.

But if some question or questions of law arise in the course of the reference on
which the opinion of the High Court is thought desirable, the arbitrator may, and
must if so directed by the court on the application of a party, state his award in the
form of a special case for the decision of the High Court. The questions of law on
which an arbitrator may feel in need of guidance or in regard to which a party may   *c*
consider that the arbitrator's views need correction, can only originate from the
arbitrator or from one or other of the parties. Unless any of them wishes for clarifica-
tion or correction of the arbitrator's view or any question of law, why should the court
meddle in the matter? So the argument would run. If a question, though pertinent,
is not asked by the arbitrator and is not required by the parties to be raised in a stated
case, it must be assumed that all concerned are content with the answer the arbitrator   *d*
proposes. It would be officious for the court to assume jurisdiction to deal with that
question.

This is not only a plausible but also a cogent argument, for one object of arbitration
(not always achieved in practice) is to confine the proceedings within bounds set by
the parties. However, once the matter is brought before the court the position is
different. If a case is stated for decision by the court its supervisory jurisdiction is   *e*
thereby invoked. Once that jurisdiction is so invoked, it cannot be right or proper that
the parties should presume to set limits to its exercise. It is the function of the court
to ensure that justice is done between the parties and the discharge of that function
cannot be circumscribed by the way in which the questions on which the court is
approached have been formulated.

Kerr J[2], in dealing with this matter, attributed the difficulties which arise from   *f*
time to time to the practice of posing specific questions on a number of narrow
points of law, instead of compounding them in a single question which is general in
its scope. Each of the respective parties will wish to preserve a decision on a question
of law which seems in his favour; and may wish for a review of the abritrator's
answers to questions of law which tell against that party. So a plethora of specific
questions may be required by one side or both to be raised. As they generally have to   *g*
be formulated before the arbitrator's findings of fact are known to the parties there
is a tendency to ask too many rather than too few questions.

The practice is not a good one as Kerr J pointed out in his judgment[2]. He went on
to say: 'It would have been far better to have left the legal issues for argument in one
or more general questions, preferably to be agreed between the parties.'

I would reject counsel for the charterer's proposition that the court's jurisdiction is   *h*
limited to the decision of such questions as are in terms posed by the special case.
That proposition was advanced in an effort to exclude from consideration by this
court the defence of estoppel which the owners sought to set up. Counsel for the
charterer contended that no question in that regard was raised by the case. As I have
said, in agreement with the other members of this court, I do not consider that even
if this were so the owners would be precluded from raising it here since it was argued   *j*
before the arbitrator and the question of estoppel therefore arose on the reference
to him. Nor would the court be precluded from considering and ruling on it.

1   [1975] 2 Lloyd's Rep 170
2   [1975] 2 Lloyds Rep at 183

a   Even if counsel for the charterer's contention were right, it would not in the circumstances of this case avail him. The terms of question 5 of the special case are wide enough to embrace the issue of estoppel for they refer to 'any other of the allegations made in . . . the further re-amended points of defence and counterclaim'. There follows a statement that 'for the avoidance of doubt a copy of the [relevant paragraph] is annexed hereto.' In that paragraph there is the plea that 'by virtue of the facts pleaded . . . the [charterer] is estopped from asserting that the stowage was defective'.

b   The terms of question 5 were drafted on behalf of the charterer; but counsel for the charterer argued that those terms were not intended to introduce into the question any issue other than the admissibility of the evidence as to the matters referred to in the first part of the question and that it should be regarded as limited to that issue.

The text of the question cannot, however, be gainsaid. It speaks for itself albeit its author may not have intended it to ask as much as it clearly does. So the question of estoppel would be competent for consideration by the court even if the restrictive principle exemplified in *Government of Ceylon v Chandris*[1] is well founded.

c

Related to the question of estoppel was a further question whether the terms of the charterparty had been varied so as to relieve the owners from responsibility for inadequate dunnage or bad stowage. This was posed in question 4 of the case. It seems to me that these two separate questions of variation of the terms and of estoppel were to some extent confused one with the other.

d

The arbitrators' answer to the two questions is bracketed together. The answer reads thus: 'In the affirmative to the extent necessary to support our findings in paragraph 14.6 above.' That paragraph says:

e   'In so far as it is a question of fact we find and in so far as it is a question of law we hold, subject to the opinion of the court:—

'(1) Mr Ismail had actual authority to give instructions on behalf of the Claimant as regards the loading of the vessel.

'(2) Mr. Ismail had actual or alternatively ostensible authority to give instructions on behalf of the [charterer] under clause 49 of the charterparty.

f   '(3) Mr. Ismail had no authority, actual or ostensible, to vary the charterparty or to make representations regarding the [charterer's] exercise of his rights under the charterparty.

'(4) Mr. Ismail's promise to provide a surveyor's certificate and a letter of guarantee and the Master's agreement to allow loading to proceed did not constitute a variation of the charterparty.

g   '(5) The [charterer] is not estopped by reason of the said promise from recovering damages for improper stowage if otherwise due under the charterparty.'

The last sub-paragraph indicates, I think, that the arbitrators misconceived the nature of the estoppel to which their findings of fact could give rise. The estoppel was not a consequence of Mr Ismail's promise to provide a surveyor's certificate and a *h* letter of guarantee; still less did it depend on a variation of the charterparty.

Kerr J dealt with question 4 in this way[2]. He said:

'There is now no challenge on the part of the charterer that his brother, Mr. Ismail, had the authority, which it was found he had in paragraph 14.6(1) and (2) of the special case. On the other side, the owners did not challenge the conclusion in the remainder of para 14.6 that there was no variation of the charter-party as *j* the result of the events in Alexandria. They contended that there was an estoppel

---

1   [1963] 2 All ER 1, [1963] 2 QB 327
2   [1975] 2 Lloyds Rep at 185

as the result of Mr. Ismail's words or conduct so as to preclude the charterer from relying on his rights under the charter-party. While not abandoning this contention, it was not strongly pressed before me by [counsel for the owners]. I agree with the arbitrators that there was no estoppel in this case. I therefore answer question (4) in agreement with both parties: "Yes" to the extent found in para. 14.6(1) and (2). It therefore follows that Mr. Ismail had authority from the charterer inter alia to give instructions under cl. 49 of the charter-party.'

With all respect to the learned judge, I demur to the implicit suggestion that what the owners had to establish was 'an estoppel as the result of Mr. Ismail's words or conduct so as to preclude the charterer from relying on his rights under the charter-party'. If there be an estoppel as the result of Mr Ismail's words or conduct it would operate to preclude the charterer from asserting the very facts which formed the basis of his claim, namely insufficient dunnage and bad stowage. One does not get to the stage of considering whether or not the charterer is entitled to rely on his rights under the charterparty, for he is denied the opportunity of relying on the facts which could make those rights effective. On the findings of the arbitrators as to Mr Ismail's authority and instructions and statements, I have no hesitation in concluding that the charterer is estopped from asserting that the dunnage was insufficient or the stowage bad. Mr Ismail's demands and assertions to the master were in a diametrically opposed sense and the owners changed their position to their detriment in reliance on those assertions.

I fear I was unable to follow counsel for the charterer's argument that Mr Ismail had no authority to create an estoppel against the charterer. The arbitrators' findings as to the nature and extent of his authority show that he was empowered to give the instructions and to make the statements that he did in relation to the cargo to be carried (albeit not in regard to any variation of the charterparty). Those instructions and statements are to be attributed to his principal so that an estoppel is raised against the charterer.

It follows that the charterer's claim founders on the reef of estoppel before it can begin to get under way.

This is sufficient to dispose of the matter, but there is the further question as to the construction of cl 49 of the charterparty. The clause must be given a meaning notwithstanding that it appears to be self-contradictory, at least at first sight. It is I think necessary to relate the language of the clause to the context in which it was introduced. This was a charterparty for the carriage of a single cargo consisting entirely of potatoes. The charterer had available to him the expert knowledge of persons experienced in the shipment of potatoes from Egypt. It is understandable that he would think it expedient in his interests to reserve to himself as large a measure of control as he could over the shipment which would include loading and stowage. As a necessary corollary, this would involve that the charterer would assume a co-extensive responsibility. Nonetheless, the master would necessarily remain responsible for the safety of the vessel in all circumstances; and while the charterer would wish to direct the mode of stowage, he would properly require the master to supervise the carrying out of that process in accordance with the instructions given.

Thus the master would remain responsible insofar as he either (a) endangered the seaworthiness of the vessel and thereby imperilled the cargo or (b) failed to ensure by due supervision of the stowage that the charterer's instructions were properly carried out.

This is the best that I can make of language as opaque as that in which cl 49 is expressed. As it is an added typed clause, it must be read as intending to modify the printed provisions of the charterparty in regard to the owner's responsibility for proper stowage and so on. It is this consideration that persuades me to a conclusion different from that arrived at by Kerr J in dealing with this conundrum of construction.

a If this be the true effect of cl 49 the charterer's claim would fail quite apart from any question of estoppel.

I would allow the appeal and make the order proposed in the judgment of Lord Denning MR.

Appeal allowed. Leave to appeal to the House of Lords refused.

b Solicitors: *Holman, Fenwick and Willan* (for the owners); *Ince & Co* (for the charterer).

Gavin Gore-Andrews Esq   Barrister.

c
R v Immigration Appeal Tribunal, ex parte Subramaniam

QUEEN'S BENCH DIVISION
LORD WIDGERY CJ, KILNER BROWN AND WATKINS JJ
d 25th FEBRUARY 1976

Immigration – Deportation – Expiration of leave to remain in United Kingdom – Variation of leave – Refusal of application to vary leave – Appeal pending – Applicant not to be deported so long as appeal pending – Applicant who has a limited leave to enter or remain in the United Kingdom – Applicant's leave having expired before application made for further period of
e *leave – Whether applicant immune from deportation until application determined and appeal procedure exhausted – Immigration Act 1971, ss 3(5)(a), 14 (1).*

The applicant, a non-patrial, obtained leave to remain in the United Kingdom until 24th September 1973. He remained, however, after his entry permit had expired. He was thereupon ordered to leave the United Kingdom by the Home Secretary by
f 30th June 1974. On 19th June his employers applied for a work permit to be issued to him, but that application was refused. In July 1974 an appeal was lodged by them against that refusal, but was withdrawn on 26th November. Meanwhile, on 19th November the applicant applied for an extension of leave to remain in the United Kingdom and repeated the application in December 1974. In January 1975 the Home Secretary, pursuant to his powers under s 3(5)(a)[a] of the Immigration Act 1971,
g notified the applicant that he would be deported and, on appeal, the Immigration Appeal Tribunal upheld that decision. The applicant applied for an order of certiorari to quash the tribunal's decision, contending that under s 14(1)[b] of the 1971 Act, as a person who had had a limited leave to remain in the United Kingdom, he could not be required to leave the United Kingdom by reason of the expiration of his leave until, in the event of a refusal of his pending application, the appeal procedure had been
h exhausted.

Held – The words 'a person who has a limited leave under this Act' in s 14(1) did not include a person who had had a limited leave but whose leave had expired before he made a further application for leave. Accordingly, since the Home Secretary had commenced deportation proceedings at a time when the applicant had had no right
j to remain in the United Kingdom, the Home Secretary could not be prevented from pursuing those proceedings on the ground that the applicant had made an application for leave to remain in the United Kingdom. The application would therefore be dismissed (see p 918 j to p 919 b and d to f, post).

---

a Section 3(5), so far as material, is set out at p 917 j, post
b Section 14(1), so far as material, is set out at p 918 f and g, post

Notes

For appeals by immigrants against conditions of entry or stay, see 4 Halsbury's Laws   *a*
(4th Edn) para 1018.

For the Immigration Act 1971, ss 3, 14, see 41 Halsbury's Statutes (3rd Edn) 20, 35.

Motions for certiorari and mandamus

This was an application by way of motion by Kunaseelan Subramaniam for (a) an order
of certiorari to bring up and quash the determination of the Immigration Appeal   *b*
Tribunal dated 17th October 1974 dismissing the applicant's appeal against the
determination of an adjudicator; and (b) an order of mandamus directed to the
tribunal to hear the appeal in accordance with the immigration law applicable to the
applicant's case. The grounds of the applications were: (a) that the Secretary of State
had not considered the applicant's applications dated 19th November and 11th
December 1974 under the powers conferred on him under s 4(1) of the Immigration   *c*
Act 1971 and reg 3(3) of the Immigration Appeals (Notices) Regulations 1972[1]; (b) that
under s 14(1) of the 1971 Act the applicant had a statutory right of appeal in the event
of the refusal of the application referred to in (a) above, and that the decision taken to
deport the applicant under s 3(5)(a) of the 1971 Act was therefore premature and of
no legal effect and contrary to para 39 of the Immigration Rules[2]; and (c) that at the
time of the withdrawal of the appeal dated 26th November 1974 the applicant's   *d*
application dated 19th November was pending in the Home Office; that the applicant
had sent a further application and had received confirmation dated 12th December
1974 that his application was receiving attention; and that the tribunal had erred in
law in coming to the conclusion that the applicant did not have authority to remain in
the United Kingdom after he withdrew his appeal in November 1974. The Secretary
of State for the Home Department appeared as respondent to the motions. At the   *e*
hearing the applicant did not pursue the application for mandamus. The facts are set
out in the judgment of Lord Widgery CJ.

K S Nathan for the applicant.
Harry Woolf for the Secretary of State.

f

LORD WIDGERY CJ. This comes before the court as an application made by
counsel on behalf of one Kunaseelan Subramaniam for an order of certiorari to bring
up into this court with a view to its being quashed a decision of the Immigration
Appeal Tribunal which was given on 17th October 1975, and the effect of which
decision was to dismiss an appeal brought by the applicant from a decision of an   *g*
adjudicator, who in turn had dismissed an appeal brought by the same applicant from
a notice given by the Secretary of State on 8th January 1975 that he was going to make
a deportation order in respect of the applicant.

The brief history of the matter is that the applicant arrived from Sri Lanka on 18th
January 1970 and was originally given leave to remain in the United Kingdom for
12 months. He wanted to pursue a course of study in this country and it was not very   *h*
long before he was asking the Secretary of State for an extension of time. Indeed in
January 1971 he wrote to the Secretary of State asking for an extension of his stay and
the Secretary of State refused the application. The applicant appealed to the adjudicator, as he was entitled to do, and the adjudicator allowed the appeal and directed that
the applicant could stay in this country so as to obtain three years' experience with
Electric Power Storage Ltd, Manchester, who were in the line of business that the   *j*
applicant wished to study. That meant that the applicant had permission to remain

---

1   SI 1972 No 1683
2   Statement of Immigration Rules for Control on Entry: Commonwealth Citizens (HC 79),
     laid before Parliament on 25th January 1973 under s 3(2) of the Immigration Act 1971

a in this country until 24th September 1973, that being three years from the basic date fixed by the adjudicator.

All went well for the next three years. At least the applicant did not always pass his examinations, but apart from that, all went well. He remained in this country and he was concerned to learn the practical side of the electric power business and the making of batteries. He was well received by his employers as one can say to his credit, and they obviously wanted to keep him. So in due course his employers, *b* Chloride Industrial Batteries Ltd, managing agents for Electric Power Storage Ltd, applied to the Secretary of State asking for permission for him to remain in their employment and to re-sit the examination in June 1974.

The Secretary of State again refused this application, and the date fixed at that time for the applicant to leave this country was 30th June 1974. That is rather an important date because it was from that date that the period began during which he had no *c* authority to remain in this country at all.

The date 30th June 1974 passed by without any extension of time. There had meanwhile, as I understand it, been an application by the employers for the grant of a work permit for the applicant. That means that they wanted the prohibition on taking work in this country to be removed so that he could be employed. The case has been a somewhat puzzling one for us because considerations affecting the work *d* permit tend to get mixed up with considerations affecting the leave to remain in this country. However, the employers made an application for a work permit, and on refusal by the Secretary of State an appeal was lodged again with a view to overriding his decision.

Then the applicant appears to take a slight change of course because on 19th November 1974 we find his employers writing, saying that he is now asking to become *e* a full-time student and does not want a work permit. This was to be the subject of a further appeal, but when the appeal was being heard, or at about the time when it was heard, an application was made to withdraw it, and we find therefore that on 26th November 1974 the appeal is withdrawn and, as I understand it, we are now back in the position which had been achieved in the previous June that the applicant has no right to remain in this country and has no pending proceedings still available which *f* might confer a right on him.

It is at this time that he made two applications to the Secretary of State asking for permission to stay still further. No doubt he appreciated that his position was somewhat insecure and he made these two applications, and I should now refer to them because they received much attention in the course of the argument.

One is dated 11th December 1974. It is in manuscript written by the applicant *g* himself. It is addressed to the Home Office and it says, amongst other things: 'Please be kind enough to extend my visa so as to enable me to complete this course of studies. Also please note the change of address.' It is fully accepted that that was an application for the granting to the applicant of a further period in which he might stay in this country, and that was backed up by his employers, in the letter dated 19th November 1974 already referred to.

h However, the Secretary of State, if he considered these applications at all, was not moved by them, because on 8th January 1975 he decided to make a deportation order. He could on the face of it make a deportation order by virtue of s 3(5) of the Immigration Act 1971 which provides:

j 'A person who is not patrial shall be liable to deportation from the United Kingdom—(a) if, having only a limited leave to enter or remain, he does not observe a condition attached to the leave or remains beyond the time limited by the leave . . .'

In other words, exactly the situation presented by the applicant at the end of 1974 and beginning of 1975.

This notice was duly given. The applicant then appealed against the notice. This again is something for which the appeal machinery is available, and on 15th January 1975 he entered an appeal against the notice. The matter in due course came before an adjudicator who dismissed the appeal.

An application was made to the Immigration Appeal Tribunal to hear an appeal from the adjudicator. That application was accepted in the sense that the appeal was heard, but the tribunal dismissed the appeal. Therefore, on the face of it, the notice of intention to deport could stand and there is no doubt that, believing that to be true in law, the Secretary of State on 8th December 1975 made an order of deportation based on the notice of intention to deport which had been given on 8th January 1975.

The point raised here can be put quite shortly. This is an application for certiorari on the footing that there is an error of law on the face of the record. The record for this purpose includes obviously the formal decision of the tribunal, and we are allowed on an application for certiorari to look at the reasons given in the speaking order which the tribunal has made and see whether those reasons are good in law. The tribunal refers to the two applications which I read a few moments ago, and the tribunal refers to the fact that the applicant says that those two documents are in truth applications by him for further leave to remain in this country. The tribunal accepts that that is the case, and accepts that those two documents are valid applications.

This allows counsel for the applicant to contend that the applications were never refused, and indeed there is no record of their having been considered favourably or unfavourably; certainly they have never been refused. Counsel says that on their being refused, if they were refused, he would have yet another right of appeal under the 1971 Act. He says further that had he had that right of appeal he could not have been ejected from the country until after the appeal proceedings had been determined.

As authority for that part of his submission counsel refers us to s 14(1) of the 1971 Act which provides:

'Subject to the provisions of this Part of this Act, a person who has a limited leave under this Act to enter or remain in the United Kingdom may appeal to an adjudicator against any variation of the leave . . . or against any refusal to vary it; and a variation shall not take effect so long as an appeal is pending under this subsection against the variation, nor shall an appellant be required to leave the United Kingdom by reason of the expiration of his leave so long as his appeal is pending under this subsection against a refusal to enlarge or remove the limit on the duration of the leave.'

So s 14(1), counsel for the applicant submits, not only gives a right of appeal but also gives interim security to the appellant whilst the appeal proceedings are pending. Accordingly he says the Secretary of State was wrong in law to try and deport him, and the tribunal was wrong in law in supporting the Secretary of State.

The answer which is put before us by counsel for the Secretary of State, if I state it correctly, is this. First of all he draws attention to the fact that the two applications to which I have referred were anterior in date to the Secretary of State deciding to make the deportation order. He says that there is nothing in s 14 to render this impracticable or impossible in law because he says that s 14 only gives a right of appeal with its associated security of tenure to someone who has a limited leave under this Act at the time. In other words, counsel distinguishes between the present applicant, who did have permission to stay in this country but whose permission has long since lapsed, with someone who has permission to remain in this country and who as yet has not run out his time. It is conceded that the second of those, by virtue of s 14, could make an application for an extension of time and he would have a right of appeal as of right and the interim security of tenure as of right. But as a matter of a construction counsel for the respondent contends that the phrase 'a person who has a limited leave under this Act' is not wide enough to include someone who did have a limited leave under this Act but no longer has.

I think that is right. I think that is a proper construction of the section, and I think that giving that construction to the first half of the subsection assists in construing the later half which again is relied on by the applicant. The second half reads thus:

b   '... a variation shall not take effect so long as an appeal is pending under this subsection against the variation, nor shall an appellant be required to leave the United Kingdom by reason of the expiration of his leave so long as his appeal is pending'.

Counsel for the Secretary of State says that section does not prevent the Secretary of State, who has once had a right to begin deportation proceedings, pursuing those proceedings merely because the immigrant has made a new application for leave to stay in this country.

As I ventured to point out in argument, if that were not so an immigrant could apparently remain here almost indefinitely by continually making new applications for leave to remain and claiming a right of appeal and interim security every time.
d The answer to that absurdity is I believe, as counsel for the Secretary of State has submitted, that the privileges of s 14(1) are really confined to an applicant who currently has a limited leave under the Act to remain in this country.

As the applicant at the material time did not have that right, it seems to me that the Secretary of State was perfectly entitled to give the notice of intended deportation and make the deportation order. The tribunal was right in law in upholding the Secretary
e of State's decision. I would therefore refuse the application.

KILNER BROWN J. I agree.

f **WATKINS J.** I also agree.

Certiorari refused.

Solicitors: *Mrs M Paranahetty* (for the applicant); *Treasury Solicitor.*

N P Metcalfe Esq   Barrister.

The Jade
The Eschersheim
Owners of the motor vessel Erkowit v Owners of the ship Jade
Owners of cargo lately laden on board the motor vessel Erkowit v Owners of the ship Eschersheim

a

b

c

HOUSE OF LORDS

LORD DIPLOCK, LORD SIMON OF GLAISDALE, LORD KILBRANDON, LORD SALMON AND LORD EDMUND-DAVIES

28th, 29th JANUARY, 2nd FEBRUARY, 31st MARCH 1976

Admiralty – Jurisdiction – Claim arising out of agreement relating to use or hire of a ship – Salvage agreement – Agreement not specifically providing for use of a particular salvage vessel – Use of salvage vessel only possible means of carrying out agreement – Agreement signed on board salvage vessel at sea – Agreement providing for disabled ship to be towed to place of safety – Whether an agreement 'relating to . . . the use or hire of a ship' – Administration of Justice Act 1956, s 1(1)(h).

d

e

Admiralty – Jurisdiction – Claim for damage done by a ship – Damage done by a ship – Causation – Indirect damage – Ship instrument by which damage caused – Salvage vessel beaching disabled vessel for temporary repairs in pursuance of salvage agreement – Beaching not itself causing damage to disabled vessel – Vessel subsequently becoming total loss in consequence of action of weather – Action against salvors for negligence and breach of contract – Whether a claim for 'damage done by a ship' – Administration of Justice Act 1956, s 1(1)(g).

f

Admiralty – Jurisdiction – Action in rem – Claim for damage received by a ship – Claim arising in connection with a ship – Action in rem against 'that ship' – Claim by shipowners against salvage vessel for damage caused to owners' ship in course of salvage operation – Whether a claim 'arising in connection with' salvage vessel or 'in connection with' owners' ship – Whether owners entitled to pursue claim for damage received by their ship by action in rem against salvage vessel – Administration of Justice Act 1956, ss 1(1)(e), 3(4).

g

Admiralty – Jurisdiction – Action in rem – Claim for loss or damage to goods carried in a ship – Claim arising in connection with a ship – Action in rem against 'that ship' – Claim by cargo owners against salvage vessel for loss or damage to cargo in course of salvage operation – Whether a claim 'arising in connection with' salvage vessel or 'in connection with' ship on which cargo being carried – Whether cargo owners entitled to pursue claim for loss or damage to cargo by action in rem against salvage vessel – Administration of Justice Act 1956, ss 1(1)(g), 3(4).

h

Two ships, the Erkowit and a German vessel, collided in the Bay of Biscay. The Erkowit was badly holed and a salvage tug, the Rotesand, went to her assistance. A salvage agreement was entered into by the master of the Erkowit, on behalf of the shipowners and the owners of the cargo on board the Erkowit, and by the tugmaster, on behalf of the salvors. Pursuant to the agreement the Rotesand took the Erkowit in tow. The tugmaster decided to beach the Erkowit and patch the hole in her before proceeding to port. The Erkowit was therefore beached by the Rotesand.

j

a   While she remained on the beach exposed to the weather the salvors attempted to
    patch her with canvas and wood. The patches proved ineffective; the vessel was
    broken up by the waves and in consequence both she and her cargo became a total
    loss. The shipowners and the cargo owners brought actions in rem against sister ships
    of the Rotesand claiming against the salvors for breach of the salvage agreement and
    negligence in the performance of the agreement. The negligence alleged was (i)
    beaching the Erkowit in a place exposed to wind and waves; (ii) patching her with
b   wood and canvas instead of steel; and (iii) delay in carrying out the operation. The
    salvors contended that the High Court had no jurisdiction to entertain the actions
    under s 3(4)^a of the Administration of Justice Act 1956 since none of the claims of the
    shipowners or the cargo owners was a claim in connection with the Rotesand which
    fell within ss 1(1)^b and 3(4) of the 1956 Act.

c   **Held** – The High Court had jurisdiction to entertain the actions for the following
    reasons—
        (i) There were no grounds for giving a restricted meaning to the words, 'agreement
    relating to the use or hire of a ship', in s 1(1)(h) of the 1956 Act. Since the only possible
    way in which the salvors could perform their primary contractual obligation to take
    the Erkowit to a place of safety was by taking her in tow and using the Rotesand for
d   that purpose, the salvage agreement was 'an agreement relating to the use or hire of
    a ship', i e the Rotesand, within s 1(1)(h). Accordingly, the shipowners and the cargo
    owners were entitled to pursue a claim in rem under ss 1(1)(h) and 3(4) of the 1956 Act
    against the Rotesand or any of her sister ships (see p 925 h to p 926 a and f g and
    p 928 c to f, post).
        (ii) Furthermore, they were also entitled to pursue a claim in rem, under ss 1(1)(d)
e   and 3(4) of the 1956 Act, for 'damage done by a ship', i e the Rotesand. Although it
    was not alleged that the actual beaching had caused any physical damage to the ship
    or her cargo, the failure of the salvors to take steps to avert the risk of damage did not
    prevent the Rotesand from remaining the actual instrument by which the damage
    subsequent to the actual beaching had been done (see p 926 h to p 927 d and p 928 c to
    f, post).

f   Per Curiam. Section 3(4) of the 1956 Act did not permit the shipowners or the cargo
    owners to pursue by means of an action in rem against the Rotesand or a sister ship
    their respective claims under s 1(1)(e) for 'damage received by a ship' and under
    s 1(1)(g) for 'loss or damage to goods carried in a ship', for those were claims 'arising in
    connection with' the ship which had received the damage or carried the goods, i e the
    Erkowit and not the Rotesand, and s 3(4) only permitted an action in rem against a
g   ship (or a sister ship) where the claim was one 'arising in connection with . . . that
    ship', i e the ship which had received the damage or carried the goods (see p 925 d and
    e, p 927 e to h and p 928 a to f, post).
        Decision of the Court of Appeal, p 441, ante, affirmed.

Notes
    For Admiralty jurisdiction in rem, see 1 Halsbury's Laws (4th Edn) paras 310, 311, and
h   for cases on the subject, see 1 Digest (Repl) 117, 287, 288, *33-35, 1899-1921.*
        For the Administration of Justice Act 1956, ss 1, 3, see 1 Halsbury's Statutes (3rd
    Edn) 21, 26.

Cases referred to in opinions
Alina, The (1880) 5 ExD 227, 49 LJP 40, 42 LT 517, 4 Asp MLC 257, CA, 1 Digest (Repl)
j   287, 1899.

---

a   Section 3(4), so far as material, is set out at p 925 b and c, post
b   Section 1(1), so far as material, provides: 'The Admiralty jurisdiction of the High Court shall
    be as follows, that is to say, jurisdiction to hear and determine any of the following questions
    or claims . . . (d) any claim for damage done by a ship; (e) any claim for damage received by
    a ship . . . (g) any claim for loss of or damage to goods carried in a ship; (h) any claim arising
    out of any agreement relating to the . . . use or hire of a ship . . .'

Bilbao, The (1860) Lush 149, 3 LT 338, 1 Mar LC 5, 1 Digest (Repl) 163, *510.*
Currie v M'Knight [1897] AC 97, 66 LJPC 19, 75 LT 457, 8 Asp MLC 193, HL, 1 Digest *a* (Repl) 117, *33.*
Post Office v Estuary Radio Ltd [1967] 3 All ER 633, [1968] 2 QB 740, [1967] 1 WLR 1396, [1967] 2 Lloyd's Rep 299, CA; *affg* [1967] 1 WLR 847, [1967] 2 Lloyd's Rep 34, Digest (Cont Vol C) 188, *1174b.*
R v Judge of City of London Court [1892] 1 QB 273, CA, 1 Digest (Repl) 120, *66.*
Salomon v Customs and Excise Comrs [1966] 3 All ER 871, [1967] 2 QB 116, [1966] 3 WLR *b* 1223, CA; *rvsg* [1966] 2 All ER 340, [1967] 2 QB 116, [1966] 3 WLR 36, Digest (Cont Vol B) 621, *77a.*
Vera Cruz, The (No 2) (1884) 9 PD 96, 53 LJP 33, 51 LT 104, 5 Asp MLC 270, CA; *on appeal* sub nom *Seward v The Vera Cruz* 10 App Cas 59, [1881-5] All ER Rep 216, 54 LJP 9, 52 LT 474, 49 JP 324, 5 Asp MLC 386, HL, 42 Digest (Repl) 892, *6832.*

c

Appeal
These were consolidated appeals by the owners of the ships Jade and Eschersheim ('the salvors') against the judgment of the Court of Appeal[1] (Cairns, Scarman LJJ and Sir Gordon Willmer) dated 22nd July 1975, dismissing appeals by the salvors against the judgment of Brandon J[2] given on 10th July 1974 whereby he dismissed the salvors' applications to strike out the writs of summons in two actions in rem brought by the *d* plaintiffs, the owners of the motor vessel Erkowit ('the shipowners') and the owners of the cargo lately laden on board the Erkowit ('the cargo owners'), in which they claimed against the salvors for damage caused to the Erkowit and her cargo in the course of salvage operations in which the salvors' vessel, the Rotesand, had been engaged. The facts are set out in the opinion of Lord Diplock.

e

J Franklin Willmer QC and *Nicholas Philips* for the salvors.
Michael Thomas QC and *Anthony Clarke* for the shipowners.
David Steel for the cargo owners.

Their Lordships took time for consideration.   *f*

31st March. The following opinions were delivered.

LORD DIPLOCK. My Lords, in these conjoined appeals the owners of the ship Jade seek to set aside writs issued in actions in rem against that vessel, on the ground *g* that by reason of their subject-matter the claims in the actions lie outside that part of the jurisdiction of the High Court that may be invoked by an action in rem.
There are two actions: in one of them, the owners of the ship Erkowit ('the shipowners') are the plaintiffs; in the other, the owners of the cargo on the Erkowit ('the cargo owners'). The facts that are relevant to the question of jurisdiction are set out in the judgment of Brandon J[2] and call for no more than a brief summary here. *h*
On 30th October 1970 the Erkowit, a vessel on the Sudanese registry, was involved in a collision with a German vessel and was badly holed. This happened in the Bay of Biscay some 50 miles from La Coruna. Some three hours later in response to a summons a salvage tug the Rotesand arrived on the scene from La Coruna and a salvage agreement in Lloyd's open form ('the salvage agreement') was entered into by the master of the Erkowit on behalf of the shipowners and the cargo owners and by the *j* tugmaster on behalf of the appellants in these appeals ('the salvors') who are professional salvors. The salvage agreement was signed on the Rotesand, the master and

---

1 Page 441 ante, [1976] 1 WLR 339
2 [1974] 3 All ER 307, [1975] 1 WLR 83

crew of the Erkowit having by this time abandoned ship. Pursuant to the salvage
a agreement the Rotesand took the Erkowit in tow and made for the port of La Coruna.
The tugmaster decided to beach the Erkowit on an open beach before reaching the
entrance to the harbour and to patch the hole in her before proceeding further. The
Erkowit was accordingly beached by the tug. Subsequently, while she remained on
the beach exposed to the weather, the salvors attempted to patch her with canvas and
wood. The patches proved ineffective; the vessel was broken up by the waves and her
b cargo swept away. Both the vessel and her cargo became a total loss. Some of the
cargo consisted of drums of insecticide which is alleged to have caused pollution of the
coastal fisheries in the area. In respect of this alleged pollution a suit claiming very
substantial damages has been brought in Spain by the Spanish government against the
shipowners.

The claims of the shipowners and the cargo owners against the salvors are for
c negligent performance of the salvage agreement. The negligence alleged is (1)
beaching the Erkowit in a place exposed to wind and waves; (2) patching her with wood
and canvas instead of with steel; and (3) delay in carrying out the operation, sc after
the beaching. The damages claimed by the shipowners include an indemnity against
any liability to the Spanish government.

The salvors have no place of business in England where they could be served with a
d writ in an action in personam. The Jade is a vessel belonging to the salvors; while
within the jurisdiction she was arrested in actions in rem commenced by writs issued
in purported pursuance of s 3(4) of the Administration of Justice Act 1956. The
question in these appeals is whether any of the claims of the shipowners and the cargo
owners respectively against the salvors are claims in connection with the Rotesand
which fall within that subsection. If any of them does the High Court has jurisdiction
e to entertain an action in rem against the Jade and this appeal must accordingly fail.

The Admiralty jurisdiction of the High Court and the mode in which it can be
exercised, i e in actions in rem and actions in personam, is regulated by Part I of the
1956 Act. Like Part V, which deals with 'Admiralty Jurisdiction and Arrestment of
Ships in Scotland', and Sch I, which contains similar provisions for Northern Ireland,
Part I of the Act was passed for the purpose, among others, of enabling the United
f Kingdom to ratify and to comply with the international obligations accepted by states
which become parties to the International Convention Relating to the Arrest of
Seagoing Ships which had been signed on behalf of the United Kingdom in 1952.

The purpose of that convention was to provide uniform rules as to the right to
arrest seagoing ships by judicial process to secure a maritime claim against the owner
of the ship. Article I defined by reference to their subject-matter various classes of
g maritime claim in respect of which alone a right of arrest was to be exercisable; while
arts 2 and 3 granted and confined the right of arrest to either (a) the particular ship in
respect of which a maritime claim falling within one or more of those classes arose, or
(b) any other ship owned by the person who was, at the time when the maritime
claim arose, the owner of the particular ship.

The provisions of art 3 represented a compromise between the wide powers of
h arrest available in some of the civil law countries (including for this purpose Scotland)
in which jurisdiction to entertain claims against a defendant could be based on the
presence within the territorial jurisdiction of any property belonging to him, and the
limited powers of arrest available in England and other common law jurisdictions,
where the power to arrest was exercisable only in respect of claims falling within the
Admiralty jurisdiction of the court and based on a supposed maritime lien over the
j particular ship in respect of which the claim arose.

The Admiralty jurisdiction of the High Court of England has always been statutory.
In 1875 the newly created High Court of Justice had inherited the jurisdiction previously vested in the High Court of Admiralty. Its Admiralty jurisdiction was
subsequently added to piecemeal by statute. Immediately before the passing of
Part I of the 1956 Act the claims and questions which fell within Admiralty jurisdiction

of the High Court were listed by reference to their subject-matter in s 22 of the
Supreme Court of Judicature (Consolidation) Act 1925, and by s 33(2) this jurisdiction   *a*
was stated to be exercisable 'either in proceedings in rem or in proceedings in
personam'. What distinguished the Admiralty jurisdiction from the other civil
jurisdiction of the High Court was that it was exercisable in proceedings in rem.

The claims listed as falling within the Admiralty jurisdiction of the High Court
under s 22 of the 1925 Act were substantially the same as the maritime claims listed
in art 1 of the 1952 convention, though with some variation in language which is   *b*
readily accounted for by the fact that the convention was drawn up in the English and
French languages, both texts being equally authentic.

The way in which the draftsman of Part I of the 1956 Act set about his task of
bringing the right of arrest of a ship in an action in rem in the English courts into
conformity with art 3 of the convention was (a) by s 1, to substitute a fresh list of
claims falling within the Admiralty jurisdiction of the High Court, and (b) by s 3, to   *c*
regulate the right to bring an action in rem against a ship by reference to the claims so
listed.

Sections 22 and 33 of the 1925 Act were repealed. Apart from the addition of
claims in respect of salvage, towage and pilotage of aircraft (which in any event
are not subject to the convention), there is again no significant difference between
what is contained in the new list and what was contained in the 1925 list, except that   *d*
the language is rather more succinct and a little closer to the language of art 1 of the
convention. In contrast to what the English draftsman did, the draftsman of Part V
of the 1956 Act, which deals with the Scots courts, was content merely to list in s 47(2)
the claims in respect of which a warrant might be issued for the arrest of a ship; and in
doing so he followed much more closely than his English counterpart the language
and order of art 1 of the convention.   *e*

One is thus confronted with three lists of claims by reference to which a right of
arrest of a ship in an action in rem may be regulated: (1) the English list in s 1 of the
1956 Act; (2) the Scottish list in s 47; and (3) the international list in art 1 of the convention. Except that both English and Scottish lists refer to claims for 'damage
received by a ship' as well as for damage done by one, and the English list includes
some services rendered to aircraft, whereas the international list does not, all three   *f*
lists cover the same ground, though with some variations in language and in order.

As the Act was passed to enable Her Majesty's government to give effect to the
obligations in international law which it would assume on ratifying the convention to
which it was a signatory, the rule of statutory construction laid down in *Salomon v
Customs and Excise Commissioners*[1] and *Post Office v Estuary Radio Ltd*[2] is applicable. If
there be any difference between the language of the statutory provision and that of the   *g*
corresponding provision of the convention, the statutory language should be construed in the same sense as that of the convention if the words of the statute are
reasonably capable of bearing that meaning.

In the instant case the obligation assumed by HM government under the convention was to give effect to it in all three jurisdictions of the United Kingdom. So there is
also a presumption that the Act was intended to have the same consequences as   *h*
respects the right of arrest of ships in Scotland as it has in England. Accordingly if the
language used in the English list is capable of more than one meaning that meaning
is to be preferred that is consistent with the language used to describe the corresponding claim in the Scottish list.

Similar considerations apply to the provisions of the Act and the convention which
provide for the right of arrest of a ship. By art 1(2) of the convention 'arrest' is defined   *j*
as 'the detention of a ship by judicial process to secure a maritime claim', and by art 2
of the convention the right is confined to securing those maritime claims only that

---

1   [1966] 3 All ER 871, [1967] 2 QB 116
2   [1967] 3 All ER 633, [1968] 2 QB 740

a   are listed in art 1. By art 3 the subject of the arrest is 'the particular ship in respect of which the maritime claim arose' or one of its sister ships. The corresponding reference in s 47(1) of the 1956 Act to the subject of the arrest in Scotland is 'the ship with which the action is concerned'.

In England the matter is governed by s 3(4) of the 1956 Act which reads as follows:

b   'In the case of any such claim as is mentioned in paragraphs (d) to (r) of sub-
        section (1) of section one of this Act, being a claim arising in connection with a
        ship, where the person who would be liable on the claim in an action in personam
        was, when the cause of action arose, the owner or charterer of, or in possession
        or in control of, the ship, the Admiralty jurisdiction of the High Court . . . may
        (whether the claim gives rise to a maritime lien on the ship or not) be invoked by
c   an action in rem against (a) that ship, if at the time when the action is brought
        it is beneficially owned as respects all the shares therein by that person; or
        (b) any other ship which, at the time when the action is brought, is beneficially
        owned as aforesaid.'

It is clear that to be liable to arrest, a ship must not only be the property of the defendant to the action but must also be identifiable as the ship in connection with
d   which the claim made in the action arose (or a sister ship of that ship). The nature of the 'connection' between the ship and the claim must have been intended to be the same as is expressed in the corresponding phrase in the convention 'the particular ship in respect of which the maritime claim arose'. One must therefore look at the description of each of the maritime claims included in the list in order to identify the particular ship in respect of which a claim of that description could arise.

e   The claims described in the separate paragraphs in the lists in s 1(1) and s 47(2) of the 1956 Act and art 1(1) of the convention are not mutually exclusive. As art 1(1) of the convention explicitly recognises, a claim may well fall under two or more of them. The shipowners have sought to classify their claim under paras (d), (e) and (h) of s 1(1) of the 1956 Act; the cargo owners have relied on (d), (g) and (h).

f   As it is sufficient to dispose of this appeal that the claims should fall within any of these paragraphs, I propose first to deal with para (h). In the English list in s 1(1) of the 1956 Act this reads: 'any claim arising out of any agreement relating to the carriage of goods in a ship or to the use or hire of a ship . . .' The corresponding provision in art 1(1) of the convention is split into two paragraphs:

g   '. . . a claim arising out of . . . (d) agreement relating to the use or hire of any
        ship whether by charterparty or otherwise; (e) agreement relating to the carriage
        of goods in any ship whether by charterparty or otherwise . . .'

The Scottish list in s 47(2) of the 1956 Act follows the same wording as the convention.

My Lords, neither Brandon J[1] nor any of the members of the Court of Appeal[2] had any doubt that both the shipowners' and the cargo owners' claims fell within
h   para (h) as being a claim arising out of an agreement relating the use of a ship, the Rotesand.

The salvage agreement was entered into by the master of the Erkowit on behalf of the cargo owners as well as the shipowners. The primary contractual obligation of the salvor under the agreement in Lloyd's open form is to use his best endeavours to bring the vessel and her cargo to a place of safety, providing at his own risk, in the time-honoured phrase, 'all proper steam and other assistance and labour'. The
j   only possible way in which the salvors could perform their contract was by taking the Erkowit in tow and using the tug that had been sent to the scene of the casualty for that very purpose—the Rotesand.

1   [1974] 3 All ER 307, [1975] 1 WLR 83
2   Page 441, ante

I agree that in any ordinary meaning of those words the salvage agreement was 'an agreement relating to the use of a ship', the Rotesand, for the purpose of salving the Erkowit and her cargo and bringing them to a place of safety, which it was contemplated by the parties would be La Coruna. The shipowners' and cargo owners' claims are claims for damages for negligent performance of that agreement and, so far as the negligence alleged includes an averment that the Erkowit was towed by the Rotesand on a course which beached her on a dangerous shore, the claim arises out of the negligent performance of that part of the agreement for which a ship was to be used.

On behalf of the salvors it has been submitted that the words 'agreement relating to the use or hire of any ship' should be understood in a very restricted meaning. The ground of this submission is that very similar words 'any claim arising out of any agreement made in relation to the use or hire of any ship' appeared in s 2 of the County Courts Admiralty Jurisdiction Amendment Act 1869, as one of three subject-matters in respect of which that Act conferred on county courts jurisdiction exercisable in an action in rem. No similar jurisdiction was exercisable in rem at that date by the High Court of Admiralty or after 1875 until 1920 by the High Court of Justice. In *R v Judge of City of London Court*[1] Lord Esher in the Court of Appeal expressed the view that Parliament should be presumed not to have intended to confer on a county court a jurisdiction exercisable in rem which was wider than the corresponding jurisdiction in rem of the High Court and that though the court was bound by a previous decision (*The Alina*[2]) to accept that a claim arising out of a charterparty was within the section although it did not give rise to an action in rem in the High Court, the words should so far as possible be construed so as to confine the jurisdiction of the county court to subject-matters in respect of which jurisdiction in an action in rem was exercisable by the High Court.

My Lords, this was not a decision which ascribed a specific and precise meaning to the words 'an agreement relating to the use or hire of a ship'. The reasons given in the judgment for giving a restricted meaning to words conferring admiralty jurisdiction on county courts, in the context in which they appeared in the 1869 Act, have no application in the context of Part I of the Administration of Justice Act 1956, which is dealing with the jurisdiction of the High Court itself. I see no reason in that context for not giving to them their ordinary wide meaning. That would include the salvage agreement in the instant case. I would therefore hold that the claims of both shipowners and cargo owners fall within para (*h*) of s 1(1); that they are claims in connection with the Rotesand; and that they are enforceable under s 3(4) by an action in rem against the Rotesand or any of her sister ships.

Strictly speaking this makes it unnecessary to decide whether the shipowners' and cargo owners' claims also came within para (*d*), viz 'damage done by a ship' or, as it is phrased in art 1 of the convention, 'damage caused by any ship either in collision or otherwise'; but as this was a matter on which the Court of Appeal differed from Brandon J, I will express my views on it briefly. The figurative phrase 'damage done by a ship' is a term of art in maritime law whose meaning is well settled by authority (*The Vera Cruz*[3]; *Currie v M'Knight*[4]). To fall within the phrase not only must the damage be the direct result or natural consequence of something done by those engaged in the navigation of the ship, but the ship itself must be the actual instrument by which the damage was done. The commonest case is that of collision, which is specifically mentioned in the convention; but physical contact between the ship and whatever object sustains the damage is not essential—a ship may negligently cause a wash by which some other vessel or some property on shore is damaged.

1   [1892] 1 QB 273
2   (1880) 5 ExD 227
3   (1884) 9 PD 96
4   [1897] AC 97

In the instant case the act of casting off the Erkowit in such a way as to beach her on an exposed shore was something done by those engaged in the navigation of the Rotesand, as a result of which the Erkowit and her cargo were left exposed to the risk of being damaged by wind and wave if the weather worsened before she could be removed to a more sheltered position.

I do not understand it to be claimed that the actual beaching caused any physical damage to ship or cargo, but for the purposes of this appeal it must be assumed that the chain of causation is unbroken between the beaching of the Erkowit and her subsequent breaking up by wind and wave. Had the damage been caused by the beaching, there could in my view have been no question but that the Rotesand could properly be regarded as the actual instrument by which that damage was done. Although for my part I find this a borderline case, I do not think that the intervening failure of the salvors to take steps to avert the risk of damage, which forms the subject of the alternative grounds of negligence, prevents the Rotesand from remaining the actual instrument by which the damage subsequent to the beaching was done. I accordingly agree with the Court of Appeal that the shipowners' and cargo owners' claims also fall under para (d) of s 1(1) of the 1956 Act.

Before concluding I should deal with the suggestions (i) that the cargo owners' claims fell also under para (g) of s 1(1) as being a 'claim for loss or damage to goods carried in a ship', and (ii) that the shipowners' claim fell also under para (e) as being a claim for 'damage received by a ship'. These were both matters of concession by the salvors before Brandon J where the argument was confined to the exclusion from para (e) of so much of the shipowners' claim as related to an indemnity in respect of any liability of the shipowners to the Spanish Government for pollution of the fisheries. The concessions were, however, withdrawn when the case reached the Court of Appeal.

The cargo owners' claim clearly falls within the description in para (g) which reproduces in terms that are practically identical para (f) of art 1(1) of the convention; but, as I have already pointed out, the right of arrest conferred by s 3(4) is confined to the ship in connection with which the claim arose (or a sister ship). The claims to which the right of arrest is confined are those mentioned in paras (d) to (r) of s 1(1). With three exceptions, each of those paragraphs contains an express reference to 'a ship'. The ship referred to in each of these paragraphs is the ship in connection with which a claim under that paragraph arises. The three exceptions relate to claims in respect of salvage, general average and bottomry where there can be no doubt as to the ship in connection with which claims of that nature arise. Paragraph (g) therefore permits the arrest of the ship in which the goods which have been lost or damaged were carried, in an action in rem by cargo owners against the owner of the carrying vessel. It does not authorise the arrest of any other ship; authority for that must be found under some other paragraph. So the arrest of the Rotesand as security for the cargo owners' claim was not authorised under para (g) of s 1(1).

Paragraph (e) has no counterpart in art 1(1) of the convention. 'Damage received by a ship' if it gives rise to any claim against a ship at all gives rise to a claim against the ship that caused the damage and not the ship that received it. So any right of arrest under the convention could not arise in respect of a claim of this description. Insofar as s 1(1) of the 1956 Act defines the Admiralty jurisdiction of the High Court, by reference to which a similar jurisdiction is by s 2 conferred on the Liverpool Court of Passage and county courts, the inclusion of para (e) is not inappropriate. 'Damage received by a ship' is a time-honoured phrase that was first used in s 6 of the Admiralty Court Act 1840 to extend the jurisdiction of the High Court of Admiralty to claims for damage received by a ship when within the body of a country. Such jurisdiction had been previously confined to damage received by a ship while on the high seas. This section was narrowly construed by Dr Lushington in The Bilbao[1] so as to exclude

---

1   (1860) Lush 149

damage done *by* a ship—a lacuna that was promptly filled by s 7 of the Admiralty
Court Act 1861. These two sections regulated the Admiralty jurisdiction of the High   *a*
Court until 1925, when the expressions 'damage received by a ship' and 'damage
done by a ship' were reproduced in s 22 of the Supreme Court of Judicature (Consolidation) Act 1925 to describe a part of its Admiralty jurisdiction.

The description 'any claim for any damage received by a ship' describes a claim
arising 'in connection with' the ship that receives the damage. In such a claim the
owners of the ship that receives the damage would be plaintiffs. They cannot invoke   *b*
the Admiralty jurisdiction by an action in rem against their own ship; and any claim
to arrest some other ship must be founded on some paragraph other than (*e*). Had
the draftsman of s 3(4) been meticulous he would have omitted any reference to
para (*e*) of s 1(1); but the other requirements of the subsection prevent any right of
arrest arising under that paragraph.

I would dismiss this appeal.   *c*

LORD SIMON OF GLAISDALE. My Lords, I have had the advantage of
reading in draft the speech prepared by my noble and learned friend, Lord Diplock.
I agree with it, and I would therefore dismiss the appeal.

d

LORD KILBRANDON. My Lords, I have had the advantage of reading the
speech prepared by my noble and learned friend, Lord Diplock. I agree with it and
I too would dismiss this appeal.

LORD SALMON. My Lords, I have had the advantage of reading the speech   *e*
prepared by my noble and learned friend, Lord Diplock. For the reasons given by
him, I would dismiss this appeal.

LORD EDMUND-DAVIES. My Lords, for the reasons appearing in the printed
speech of my noble and learned friend, Lord Diplock, I concur in holding that the   *f*
appeal should be dismissed.

Appeal dismissed.

Solicitors: *Richards, Butler & Co* (for the salvors); *Ince & Co* (for the shipowners and
the cargo owners).

Gordon H Scott Esq   Barrister.   *g*

End of Volume One